THE HOUSE OF ROTHSCHILD

The House of Rothschild

THE WORLD'S BANKER

1849–1999

Niall Ferguson

∼ Viking ∼

VIKING
Published by the Penguin Group
Penguin Putnam Inc., 375 Hudson Street,
New York, New York 10014, U.S.A.
Penguin Books Ltd, 27 Wrights Lane,
London W8 5TZ, England
Penguin Books Australia Ltd, Ringwood,
Victoria, Australia
Penguin Books Canada Ltd, 10 Alcorn Avenue,
Toronto, Ontario, Canada M4V 3B2
Penguin Books (N.Z.) Ltd, 182-190 Wairau Road,
Auckland 10, New Zealand
Penguin India, 210 Chiranjiv Tower, 43 Nehru Place,
New Delhi, 11009, England

Penguin Books Ltd, Registered Offices:
Harmondsworth, Middlesex, England

First American edition
Published in 1999 by Viking Penguin,
a member of Penguin Putnam Inc.

1 3 5 7 9 10 8 6 4 2

This is the second of two volumes of *The House of Rothschild*. In Great Britain *The House of Rothschild* was published as one volume by Weidenfeld & Nicolson as *The World's Banker*.

LIBRARY OF CONGRESS CATALOGING-IN-PUBLICATION DATA
Ferguson, Niall.
The house of Rothschild / Niall Ferguson.
p.   cm.
Includes bibliographical references and index.
Contents:—v. 2. The world's banker, 1849–1999.
ISBN 0-670-88794-3
1. Rothschild family.   2. Bankers—Europe biography.   3. Businesspeople—
Europe biography.   4. Europe—Politics and government.   I. Title.
HG1552.R8F47   1999   99-41868
332.1'092'2—dc21

This book is printed on acid-free paper.

Printed in the United States of America
Set in AGaramond
Designed by Jaye Zimet

FOR LACHLAN

CONTENTS

ILLUSTRATIONS IN THE TEXT

1.i: Anon., *Der 99ste Geburtstag der Gro[ss]mutter, Fliegende Blätter* (*c.* 1848). Source: Fuchs, *Juden in der Karikatur*, p. 146.

1.ii: Anon., *ONE OF THE BENEFITS OF THE JEWISH EMANCIPATION*. Source: Fuchs, *Juden in der Karikatur*, p. 55.

2.i: The weekly closing price of French 3 per cent and 5 per cent rentes, 1835–1857. Source: *Spectator*.

3.i: The profits of the Naples house, 1849–1862 (ducats). Sources: AN, 132 AQ 13 and 14; Gille, *Maison Rothschild*, vol. II, pp. 573f.

3.ii: Profits as a percentage of capital at N. M. Rothschild & Sons, Barings and Schröders, 1850–1880. Sources: RAL, RFamFD/13F; Ziegler, *Sixth great power*, pp. 373–8; Roberts, pp. 527–35.

3.iii: *Das goldene Kalb* (1862). Source: Cowles, *Rothschilds*, p. 136.

3.iv: *Ferrières: Auf der großen Jagd beim Rothschild* (1862). Source: Wilson, *Rothschild*, 19th plate.

4.i: The Prussian–Austrian yield gap (Austrian minus Prussian bond yields), 1851–1875. Source: Heyn, "Private banking and industrialisation," pp. 358–72.

4.ii: M. E. Schleich, *Rothschild's Kriegsbereitschaft, Ein humoristisches Originalblatt, Münchener Punsch*, 19, Nr. 20 (May 20, 1866). Source: Herding, "Rothschilds in der Karikatur," illustration 16. (Marburg Universitätsbibliothek.)

5.i: *Baron Lionel de Rothschild (The Modern Croesus), The Period* (July 5, 1870). Source: Rubens, "Rothschilds in caricature," plate XVII.

6.i: The weekly closing price of French 3 per cent rentes, 1860–1877. Source: *Economist*.

7.i: Max Beerbohm, *A quiet evening in Seymour Place. Doctors consulting whether Mr Alfred may, or may not, take a second praline before bedtime.* Source: Cowles, *Rothschilds*, p. 172.

8.i: C. Léandre, *Dieu protège Israel, Le Rêve* (April 1898). Source: Herding, "Rothschilds in der Karikatur," p. 55, illustration 28. (Stadt- und Universitätsbibliothek, Frankfurt am Main.)

8.ii: Lepneveu, *Nathan Mayer ou l'origine des milliards*, cover of *Musée des Horreurs*, no. 42 (*c.* 1900). Source: Herding, "Rothschilds in der Karikatur," illustration 30. (Museum für Kunst und Gewerbe, Hamburg.)

TABLES

ACKNOWLEDGEMENTS

A full list of acknowledgements appeared in the first volume of *The House of Rothschild*. I would nevertheless like to take this opportunity to thank Barbara Grossman, Molly Stern and everyone else at Penguin Putnam for their work in preparing both halves of the American edition.

Family tree of the Rothschild family.

Jeanette (1771–1859)
m. 1795*
Benedikt Moses Worms
(1772–1824)

Mayer Anselm Léon
(1827–28)

Georg (1877–1934)

Albert (1922–38)

Hannah (b.1962)
m. 1994
William Brookfield

Julie (1830–1907)
m. 1850
Adolph (1823–1900)

Alphonse (1878–1942)
m. 1911
Clarice Sebag-Montefiore
(1894–1967)

Bettina (b.1924)
m. 1943*
Matthew Looram (b.1921)

Beth (b.1964)
m. 1991
Antonio Tomassini
(b.1959)

Hannah Mathilde
(1832–1924)
m. 1849
Wilhelm Carl
(1828–1901)

Gwendoline Looram (1927–72)

Emily (b.1967)
m. 1998
Julian Freeman-Attwood

Amschel (1773–1855)
m. 1796
Eva Hanau (1779–1848)

Sara Louise (1834–1924)
m. 1858*
Baron Raimondo
Franchetti (1829–1905)

Louis (1882–1955)
m. 1946
Countess Hildegard
Auersperg (1895–1981)

Sarah (b.1934)*
m. 1948*
Roland Hoguet
(1920–85)

Nat (b.1971)
m. 1995
Annabel Neilson (b.1969)

Nathaniel (1836–1905)

Jacob (b.1936)
m. 1961
Serena Dunn (b.1935)

Eugène (1884–1976)
m. 1925
Countess Kitty
Schönborn-Bucheim (née
Wolff) (1885–1946)

Miriam (b.1908)
m. 1943*
George Lane (b.1915)

Miranda (b.1940)
m. 1962*
Boudjemâa Boumaza
(1930–64)
m. 2nd 1967
Iain Watson (b.1942)

Ferdinand (1839–98)
m. 1865
Evelina (1839–66)

m. 2nd 1952
Jeanne Stuart (b.1908)

Elizabeth (1909–88)

Salomon (1774–1855)
m. 1800
Caroline Stern
(1782–1854)

Anselm (1803–74)
m. 1826
Charlotte (1807–59)

Salomon Albert
(1844–1911)
m. 1876
Bettina (1858–92)

Valentine (1886–1969)
m. 1911*
Sigismund, Baron
Springer (1875–1928)

Charlotte Esther
(b.&d.1885)

Victor (1910–90)
m. 1933
Barbara Hutchinson
(1911–89)
m. 2nd 1946
Teresa Mayor
(1915–96)

Emma (b.1948)
m. 1991
Amartya Sen (b.1933)

Benjamin (b. &d.1952)

Betty (1805–86)
m. 1824
James (1792–1868)

Alice (1847–1922)

Oscar (1888–1909)

Kathleen (1913–88)
m. 1935*
Jules de Kœnigswarter
(1904–95)

Victoria (1953)
m. 1997
Simon Gray (b.1936)

Kate (b.1982)

Alice (b.1983)

Amschel (1955–96)
m. 1981
Anita Guinness (b.1957)

James (b.1985)

Leonora (1837–1911)
m. 1857
Alphonse (1827–1905)

Walter (1868–1937)

Rosemary (b.1913)
m. 1934*
Denis Gomer Berry
(1911–83)
m. 2nd 1942*
John Antony Seys
(1914–89)

Katherine (b.1949)
m. 1971*
Marcus Agius (b.1946)

Charlotte (1807–59)
m. 1826
Anselm (1803–74)

Evelina (1839–66)

Evelina (1873–1947)
m. 1899*
Clive Behrens
(1871–1935)

Nicholas (b.1951)
m. 1985
Caroline Darvall (b.1955)

Chloë (b. 1990)

Nathan (1777–1836)
m. 1806
Hannah Barent Cohen
(1783–1850)

Lionel (1808–79)
m. 1836
Charlotte (1819–84)

Ferdinand (1839–98)

Charles (1877–1923)
m. 1907
Rozsika von Wertheimstein
(1870–1940)

Edmund (b.1916)
m. 1948
Elizabeth Lentner
(1923–80)
m. 2nd 1982
Anne Harrison (b.1921)

Charlotte (b.1955)
m. 1990
Nigel Brown (b.1936)

Nathaniel (Natty)
(1840–1915)
m. 1867
Emma (1834–1935)

Lionel (1882–1942)
m. 1912
Marie-Louise Beer
(1892–1975)

Naomi (b.1920)
m. 1941*
Jean Pierre Reinach
(1915–42) m. 2nd 1947*
Bertrand Goldschmidt
(b.1912)

Elizabeth (b.1992)

Leopold (b.1994)

Alfred (1842–1918)

Leopold (1845–1917)
m. 1881
Marie Perugia
(1862–1937)

Evelyn Achille
(1886–1917)

Lionel (b.1955)
m. 1991
Louise Williams (b.1955)

Amschel (b.1995)

Anthony (1810–76)
m. 1840
Louisa Montefiore
(1821–1910)

Constance (1843–1931)
m. 1877
Cyril Flower (1st Lord
Battersea) (1843–1907)

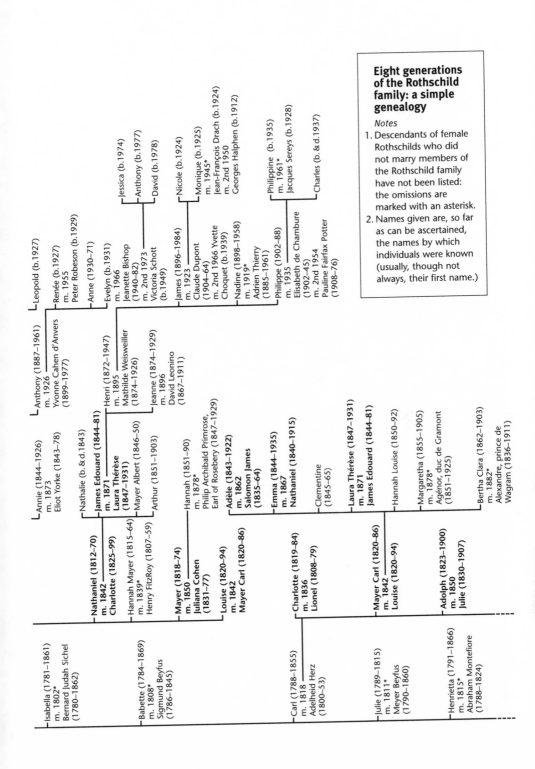

Eight generations of the Rothschild family: a simple genealogy

Notes

1. Descendants of female Rothschilds who did not marry members of the Rothschild family have not been listed: the omissions are marked with an asterisk.

2. Names given are, so far as can be ascertained, the names by which individuals were known (usually, though not always, their first name.)

Leopold (b.1927)

Annie (1844–1926)
m. 1873
Eliot Yorke (1843–78)

Anthony (1887–1961)
m. 1926
Yvonne Cahen d'Anvers
(1899–1977)

Renée (b.1927)
m. 1955
Peter Robeson (b.1929)

Anne (1930–71)

Nathaniel (1812–70)
m. 1842
Charlotte (1825–99)

Nathalie (b. & d.1843)

James Edouard (1844–81)
m. 1871
Laura Thérèse
(1847–1931)

Henri (1872–1947)
m. 1895
Mathilde Weissweiler
(1874–1926)

Evelyn (b.1931)
m. 1966
Jeanette Bishop
(1940–82)
m. 2nd 1973
Victoria Schott
(b.1949)

Jessica (b.1974)

Anthony (b.1977)

David (b.1978)

Babette (1784–1869)
m. 1808*
Sigmund Beyfus
(1786–1845)

Hannah Mayer (1815–64)
m. 1839*
Henry FitzRoy (1807–59)

Mayer Albert (1846–50)

Arthur (1851–1903)

Jeanne (1874–1929)
m. 1896
David Leonino
(1867–1911)

Nicole (b.1924)

Mayer (1818–74)
m. 1850
Juliana Cohen
(1831–77)

Hannah (1851–90)
m. 1878*
Philip Archibald Primrose,
Earl of Rosebery (1847–1929)

James (1896–1984)
m. 1923
Claude Dupont
(1904–64)
m. 2nd 1966 Yvette
Choquet (b.1939)

Monique (b.1925)
m. 1945*
Jean-François Drach (b.1924)
m. 2nd 1950
Georges Halphen (b.1912)

Louise (1820–94)
m. 1842
Mayer Carl (1820–86)

Adèle (1843–1922)
m. 1862
Salomon James
(1835–64)

Nadine (1898–1958)
m. 1919*
Adrien Thierry
(1885–1961)

Charlotte (1819–84)
m. 1836
Lionel (1808–79)

Emma (1844–1935)
m. 1867
Nathaniel (1840–1915)

Philippe (1902–88)
m. 1935
Elisabeth de Chambure
(1902–45)
m. 2nd 1954
Pauline Fairfax Potter
(1908–76)

Philippine (b.1935)
m. 1961*
Jacques Sereys (b.1928)

Carl (1788–1855)
m. 1818
Adelheid Herz
(1800–53)

Clementine
(1845–65)

Charles (b. & d.1937)

Julie (1789–1815)
m. 1811*
Meyer Beyfus
(1790–1860)

Mayer Carl (1820–86)
m. 1842
Louise (1820–94)

Laura Thérèse (1847–1931)
m. 1871
James Edouard (1844–81)

Hannah Louise (1850–92)

Adolph (1823–1900)
m. 1850
Julie (1830–1907)

Margaretha (1855–1905)
m. 1878*
Agénor, duc de Gramont
(1851–1925)

Henrietta (1791–1866)
m. 1815*
Abraham Montefiore
(1788–1824)

Bertha Clara (1862–1903)
m. 1882*
Alexandre, prince de
Wagram (1836–1911)

Isabella (1781–1861)
m. 1802*
Bernard Judah Sichel
(1780–1862)

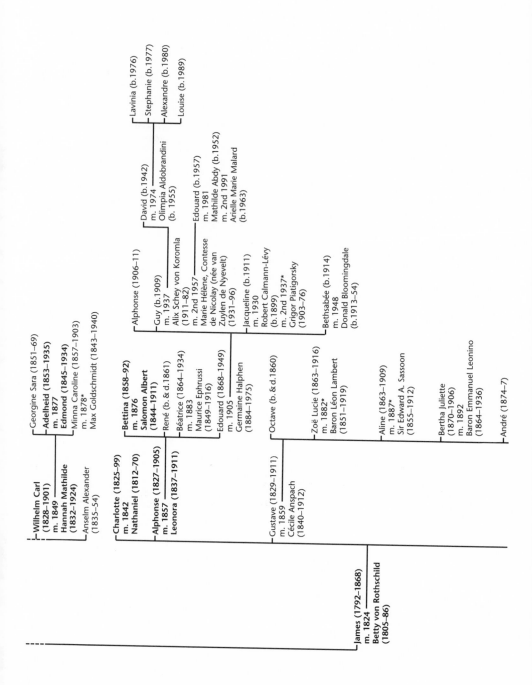

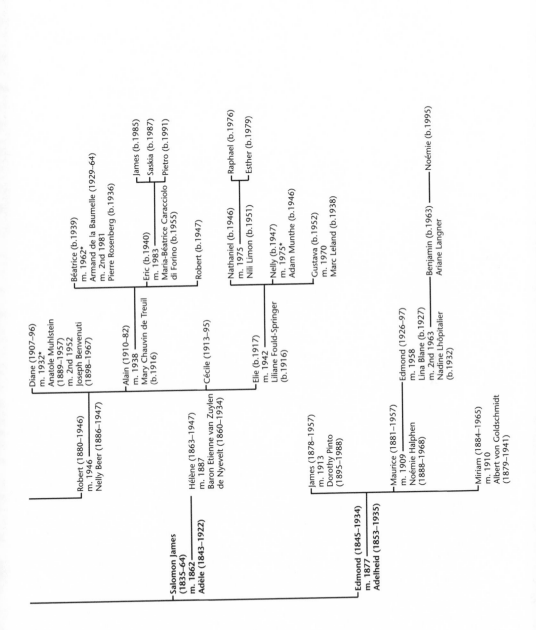

Salomon James
(1835–64)
m. 1862
Adèle (1843–1922)

Robert (1880–1946)
m. 1946
Nelly Beer (1886–1947)

Diane (1907–96)
m. 1932*
Anatole Muhlstein
(1889–1957)
m. 2nd 1952
Joseph Benvenuti
(1898–1967)

Béatrice (b.1939)
m. 1962*
Armand de la Baumelle (1929–64)
m. 2nd 1981
Pierre Rosenberg (b.1936)

Alain (1910–82)
m. 1938
Mary Chauvin de Treuil
(b.1916)

Eric (b.1940)
m. 1983
Maria-Béatrice Caracciolo
di Forino (b.1955)

James (b.1985)
Saskia (b.1987)
Pietro (b.1991)

Robert (b.1947)

Hélène (1863–1947)
m. 1887
Baron Etienne van Zuylen
de Nyevelt (1860–1934)

Cécile (1913–95)

Elie (b.1917)
m. 1942
Liliane Fould-Springer
(b.1916)

Nathaniel (b.1946)
m. 1975
Nili Limon (b.1951)

Raphael (b.1976)
Esther (b.1979)

Nelly (b.1947)
m. 1975*
Adam Munthe (b.1946)

Gustava (b.1952)
m. 1970
Marc Leland (b.1938)

Edmond (1845–1934)
m. 1877
Adelheid (1853–1935)

James (1878–1957)
m. 1913
Dorothy Pinto
(1895–1988)

Maurice (1881–1957)
m. 1909
Noémie Halphen
(1888–1968)

Edmond (1926–97)
m. 1958
Lina Blane (b.1927)
m. 2nd 1963
Nadine Lhôpitalier
(b.1932)

Benjamin (b.1963) ——— Noémie (b.1995)
Ariane Langner

Miriam (1884–1965)
m. 1910
Albert von Goldschmidt
(1879–1941)

If we consider the period between 1789 and 1848 as the "age of revolution," then the Rothschilds were surely its supreme beneficiaries. To be sure, the political upheavals of 1848–49 had cost them dear. As in 1830, though on a far larger scale, revolutions caused the bonds of the governments affected to plummet in value. For the Rothschilds, who held a large proportion of their immense wealth in the form of bonds, that meant heavy losses of capital. Worse, it brought their "houses" in Vienna and Paris to the brink of insolvency, obliging the others—in London, Frankfurt and Naples—to bail them out. Yet the Rothschilds survived even this, the greatest of all the financial crises between 1815 and 1914, as well as the greatest revolution. Indeed, it would have been a strange irony if they had not: without revolution, they would have had little to lose in the first place.

For it had been the original French Revolution that, in 1796, had literally demolished the walls of the Frankfurt ghetto and enabled the Rothschilds to begin their phenomenal, unprecedented and since unmatched economic ascent. Before 1789, Mayer Amschel Rothschild and his family's lives had been circumscribed by discriminatory legislation. Jews were prohibited from farming, or from dealing in weapons, spices, wine and grain. They were forbidden to live outside the ghetto and were confined there at night, on Sundays and during Christian festivals. They were subject to discriminatory taxation. No matter how hard Mayer Amschel worked, first as a rare coin dealer then as a bill broker and merchant banker, there were strict and low limits to what he could achieve. All that changed when the French exported their revolution to south Germany. Not only was the Judengasse opened; the legal restrictions on the Frankfurt Jews were also largely removed—thanks not least to Mayer Amschel's financial influence over Napoleon's henchman in the Rhineland, Karl von Dalberg. Despite the best efforts of the Frankfurt Gentiles after the French and their collaborators had been ousted, the old apartheidlike system of residential and social restriction could never wholly be restored.

Moreover, the Rothschilds were presented with undreamed-of business opportunities by the revolutionary wars. As the scale and cost of the conflict between France and the rest of Europe rose, so too did the borrowing needs of the combatant states. At the same time, the disruption of established patterns of trade and banking created room for ambitious risk takers. Thus it was Napoleon's decision to drive the Elector of Hesse-Kassel into exile, which allowed Mayer Amschel (one of the Elector's "court agents" since 1769) to become his principal fund manager, collecting the interest on those assets that eluded the French and reinvesting the money. This was dangerous business: the French police were suspicious enough about Mayer Amschel's activities to interrogate him and his family, though no prosecution resulted. But the profits were in proportion to the hazard; and the Rothschilds quickly mastered the art of secrecy.

Likewise, revolution and war made possible the ascent of Mayer Amschel's domineering son Nathan from exporting British textiles in Manchester to financing the British war effort in the City of London. In normal times, Nathan would doubtless have prospered as a cloth merchant: his strategy of cutting prices and increasing volumes was right; his energy, ambition and capacity for work were all prodigious. ("I do not read books," he told his brothers in 1816. "I do not play cards, I do not go to the theatre, my only pleasure is my business.") But Britain's wars with France created conditions especially favorable to the bold and innovative newcomer. By prohibiting British exports to the Continent in 1806, Napoleon inflated the risks but also the potential returns for those, like Nathan, willing to beat the blockade. The naive willingess of the French authorities to allow British bullion to cross the Channel gave Nathan a still more lucrative line of business. In 1808 he was able to leave Manchester for London, now unrivaled as the world's biggest financial center since the Napoleonic occupation of Amsterdam.

The "masterstroke" which enabled Nathan to leap into the first league of merchant bankers was his use of the Elector of Hesse-Kassel's English investments to bolster his own resources. In 1809 Nathan secured authorization to make new purchases of British bonds with the interest the Elector's existing portfolio was earning; over the next four years he bought securities worth more than £600,000. In peacetime this would have made him a major fund manager; in the turmoil of war, however, Nathan was able to treat the Elector's bonds like his own capital. Unwittingly, the exiled Elector became a sleeping partner in a new banking house: N. M. Rothschild. (His minister Buderus was a more willing investor in the Frankfurt house.) In 1813 Nathan was therefore able credibly to offer his services to the British government as it struggled to finance Wellington's penultimate campaign against Napoleon. This was what Carl meant when he said later that "the Old Man"— meaning William—had "made our fortune."

In truth, they probably owed more to the industry and acumen of their own "old man." It was Mayer Amschel who in 1810 designed the partnership structure that was to endure, modified but essentially the same, for very nearly a century, binding together the male line over four generations, rigorously excluding female Rothschilds and their spouses. And it was Mayer Amschel who taught his sons such hard-nosed business rules as: "It is better to deal with a government in difficulties than with one that has luck on its side"; "If you can't make yourself loved, make yourself feared"; and "If a high-placed person enters into a [financial] partnership with a Jew, he belongs to the Jew" ("*gehört er dem Juden*"). This last piece of advice lay behind the brothers' practice of plying politically powerful individuals with gifts, loans, investment tips and outright bribes. Above all, Mayer Amschel taught his sons to value unity: "Amschel," he told his eldest son on his deathbed in 1812, "keep your brothers together and you will become the richest people in Germany." His sons were still repeating these precepts to the next generation thirty years later, by which time they were the richest people in the world; indeed, the richest family in all history.

The operations of 1814 and 1815, in which Nathan and his brothers raised immense quantities of bullion not only for Wellington but also for Britain's continental allies, ushered in a new era in financial as well as political history. The Rothschilds stretched their credit to breaking point, sometimes losing sight altogether of their assets and liabilities, gambling everything they owned for the sake of governmental commissions, interest payments and speculative gains from exchange rate and bond yield fluctuations. In 1815 alone, Nathan's account with the British government totalled close to £10 million, a huge sum at that time. Lord Liverpool employed heroic English understatement when he called Nathan "a very useful friend." It was, as other contemporaries acknowledged, Napoleonic finance, without which Napoleonic generalship could not have been defeated. Ludwig Börne justly called the brothers "*Finanzbonaparten*"; Nathan, as Salomon acknowledged, was their "commanding general." Though they came perilously close to ruin when the French were defeated at Waterloo—a much quicker end to the war than Nathan had foreseen—the Rothschilds emerged in 1815 as sterling millionaires. Almost at once, Nathan embarked on perhaps the most successful transaction of his career: a huge investment in British government bonds (consols) whereby he rode the upswing caused by the government's postwar financial stabilization, taking his profits just before the market peaked. This was Nathan's supreme *Meistergeschäft,* realizing profits of more than £250,000 at a stroke.

The 1820s were a time of political as well as fiscal restoration. Throughout the Continent, the deposed were (mostly) put back on their thrones. Under the leadership of Prince Metternich, the great continental powers combined to resist new revolutionary impulses wherever they might occur. The Rothschilds bankrolled this restoration, no doubt. They enabled Austria, Prussia and Russia—the members of the Holy Alliance—as well as the restored Bourbons in France, to issue bonds at rates of interest only Britain and Holland had previously been able to enjoy. In that this made it easier for Prince Metternich to "police" Europe—notably when Austria and France intervened to restore the Bourbon regimes in Naples and Spain—there was truth in the jibe that the Rothschilds were the "chief ally of the Holy Alliance." Rothschild loans also bolstered the private finances of many of the "high-placed persons" of the period, including Metternich himself, King George IV and his son-in-law Leopold of Saxe-Coburg, later King of the Belgians. As Ludwig Börne complained, "Rothschild" was "someone who gives nobles the power to spite freedom and deprives peoples of the courage to resist violence . . . the high priest of fear . . . on whose altar liberty, patriotism, honour and all civil virtues are sacrificed."

Yet there was always an ambivalence about the Rothschilds' view of the restoration. They could hardly relish the return to power of conservative elites which—most obviously in Germany—sought to reimpose second-class citizenship on the Jews. Nor was Nathan the kind of man to turn down good business on ideological grounds. Interventions by the Holy Alliance against revolutionary movements in Spain or Italy were not necessarily good for business: war unsettled the bond markets, not least because of its deleterious effect on state budgets. The new regimes that emerged in countries like Spain, Brazil and Greece were also potential new customers; and experience seemed to suggest that parliamentary monarchies were better creditors than absolutist regimes. Significantly, the Rothschilds were tempted to lend to the Spanish liberals, but refused to bankroll Ferdinand VII after he had been restored to absolute power. As Byron put it in *Don Juan,* the Rothschilds held sway over "royalist and liberal" alike. Heinrich Heine went further in calling Rothschild a revolutionary on a par with Robespierre, because

> Rothschild . . . destroyed the predominance of land, by raising the system of state bonds to supreme power, thereby mobilising property and income and at the same time endowing money with the previous privileges of the land.

It was also Heine who memorably declared: "[M]oney is the god of our time and Rothschild is his prophet." Without doubt, the Rothschilds' most important contribution to economic history was the creation of a truly international bond market. There had, of course, been cross-border capital flows before: the Dutch had invested in British government bonds in the eighteenth century while the Rothschilds' rivals in Frankfurt, the Bethmanns, had marketed large issues of Austrian bonds in the same period. But never before had a country's bonds been simultaneously issued in multiple markets with (as in the case of Prussia in 1818) such alluring conditions as denomination in sterling, payment of interest at the place of issue and a sinking fund.

Bond issuance was not the Rothschilds' sole business. They also discounted commercial bills, acted as bullion brokers, dealt in foreign exchange, engaged directly in commodity trade, dabbled in insurance and even offered private banking services to an elite of indivual clients. Their role in the gold and silver markets was important: it was the Rothschilds' role as "lender of last resort to the lender of last resort" that prevented a suspension of convertibility by the Bank of England in 1825. But it was the bond market which came first. Moreover, buying and selling in the various secondary markets for bonds was almost as important a source of profit as issuance: this was the principal form of speculation in which the brothers engaged.

It was partly the multinational character of their operations that distinguished the Rothschilds from their competitors. While Nathan's eldest brother Amschel continued the original family business in Frankfurt, his youngest brother James established himself in Paris. Later in the 1820s, Salomon and Carl established subsidiaries of the Frankfurt house in Vienna and Naples. The five houses formed a unique partnership, acting jointly in big transactions, pooling profits and sharing costs. Regular and detailed correspondence overcame the obstacle of geographical separation. The partners met together only every few years, when changing circumstances necessitated modification of their contractual agreement.

This multinational structure gave the Rothschilds several important advantages. First, it enabled them to engage in arbitrage, exploiting price differences between, say, the London and Paris markets. Secondly, they could bail one another out in the event of liquidity or solvency squeezes. Never—not even in 1848—did financial crises strike everywhere in Europe simultaneously and with equal severity. When Britain suffered in 1825, James could bail out Nathan. When Paris collapsed in 1830, Nathan could reciprocate. There is no doubt that the Vienna house would have gone bankrupt in 1848 if it had been an independent entity. Only the willingness of the other houses to write off substantial sums allowed Salomon's son Anselm to restore it.

By rapidly accumulating capital—the Rothschilds did not distribute profits, contenting themselves with a low interest on their individual partnership shares—they were soon able to conduct such operations on an unparalleled scale. They were certainly the biggest bank in the world; by 1825 ten times the size of their nearest rivals, Baring Brothers. This in turn allowed them to modify their business strategy. After the early years of high risk and high returns, they were now able to content themselves with lower profitability without compromising their position of market dominance. Indeed, this shift away from profit maximization helps to explain the Rothschild partnership's longevity as a firm. Time and again they would encounter competitors—Jacques Laffitte was the classic example of the restoration period—who gained on them during market upswings by taking bigger risks, only to come unstuck when the cycle dipped.

With riches came status. In the eyes of contemporaries, the Rothschilds personified new money: they were Jews, they were ill educated, they were coarse—yet within a few years they had accumulated net paper wealth worth far more than most aristocratic estates. Outwardly, the arrivistes seemed to crave acceptance by the old elites. As if to expunge the memory of the days when (as Carl recalled) "we all slept in one little attic room," they bought the smartest of town houses in streets like Piccadilly and the rue Laffitte and, later, their first country houses at Gunnersbury, Ferrières and Schillersdorf. They filled them with seventeenth-century Dutch paintings and eighteenth-century French furniture. They hosted lavish dinners and glittering balls. They sought titles and other honors: plain Jacob Rothschild became Monsieur le Baron James de Rothschild, Austrian consul general in Paris, chevalier of the Legion of Honour. They brought up their sons as gentlemen, giving them tastes for pleasures that had been unknown in the ghetto: horses, hunting and fine art. Their daughters had their piano lessons from Chopin. Men of letters—notably Disraeli, Heine, Balzac—sought patronage from these new Medicis, only to caricature them in their work.

Yet the Rothschilds privately viewed their own social ascent with cynicism. Titles and honors were "part of the racket," helpful in giving the brothers access to the corridors of power. Playing host was an uncomfortable duty, to the same end: much of it was corporate hospitality, as we would now say. Even the gentrification of the next generation was superficial: their sons' real education was still in the "counting house."

The Rothschilds' most important reservation about social assimilation was religious. Unlike many other wealthy European Jews, who opted to convert to Christianity in the 1820s, the Rothschilds remained firmly attached to the religion of their forefathers. Though the extent of their individual religiosity varied—while Amschel was strict in his observance, James was very lax—the brothers shared the view that their worldly success was intimately bound up with their Judaism. As James put it, religion meant "everything. Our good fortune and our blessings depend upon it." When Nathan's daughter Hannah Mayer converted to Christianity in order to marry Henry Fitzroy in 1839, she was ostracized by nearly all her relatives, including her own mother.

The corollary of the Rothschilds' belief that fidelity to Judaism was integral to their worldly success was the interest they took in the fate of their "poorer co-religionists." This commitment to the wider Jewish community extended beyond traditional charitable donations to embrace systematic political lobbying for Jewish emancipation. The practice that Mayer Amschel had established in the Napoleonic period, of using Rothschild money to secure or defend the civil and political rights of Jews, continued more or less uninterruptedly throughout the century. When the Jews of Damascus were falsely accused of "ritual murder" in 1840, the Rothschilds orchestrated a successful campaign to end their persecution. This was only the most celebrated of many cases. Rothschild loans to the pope were also used as a lever to improve the lot of the Jews in the papal states. Ironically, the English Rothschilds' efforts closer to home were less successful. Nathan and his wife Hannah had first become involved in the campaign to end Jewish exclusion from Parliament as early as 1829. By the time of Nathan's death seven years later, nothing had been achieved. It was left to his son Lionel to lead the campaign for Anglo-Jewish emancipation: the subject of this volume's opening chapter.

Nevertheless, the Rothschilds' sense of identification with the wider Jewish community was not unqualified. Not only their wealth but their genealogy set them apart from the rest of European Jewry. For the Rothschilds pursued a strategy of endogamy—marrying not just within their own faith but within their own immediate kinship group. Only a Rothschild would do for a Rothschild, it seemed: of twenty-one marriages involving descendants of Mayer Amschel between 1824 and 1877, no fewer than fifteen were between his direct descendants. Typical was the marriage of Nathan's son Lionel to Carl's daughter Charlotte in 1836, an arranged and not very happy match. The main rationale behind this strategy was to fortify the cohesion of the financial partnership. It certainly did this, though to modern eyes the family tree of the period looks fraught with genetic risk. Cousin marriages ensured that the family's capital was not dispersed. Like the strict rule that excluded daughters and sons-in-law from the partnership's hallowed books, and the repetition of Mayer Amschel's imprecations to maintain fraternal unity, it was one of the devices that prevented the Rothschilds from going the way of Thomas Mann's decadent Buddenbrooks. Of course, other dynasties behaved in similar ways. Cousin marriage was relatively common in Jewish business families. Nor was it confined to Jews: British Quakers practiced it too. Indeed, even Europe's royal families used cousin marriage to cement their political relationships. Yet the Rothschilds practiced endogamy to a degree not even the Saxe-Coburgs could match. It was this that prompted Heinrich Heine to call them "the exceptional family." Indeed, other Jews came to regard the Rothschilds as a kind of Hebrew royal family: the "Kings of the Jews" as well as the "Jews of the Kings."

The revolution of 1830 revealed two important things. First, the Rothschilds were not tied to the Holy Alliance but were perfectly willing to offer their financial services to liberal and even revolutionary regimes. If anything—once he had got over the initially severe shock of the revolution—James found it easier to do business with the "bourgeois monarchy" of Louis Philippe. Equally congenial was the new Belgian state, especially when it (like Greece) accepted a "tame" German prince as its monarch—one who was already a Rothschild client—and subordinated itself to collective international regulation by the great powers. The second point was that the Rothschilds had a strong interest in seeing the great powers reach such arrangements and believed that here too financial leverage could be exerted.

The outbreak of revolution had caused a major slump in the price of French rentes (the perpetual bonds that were to France what consols were to Britain). The slump had taken James almost wholly by surprise, plunging his balance sheet into the red. But what made the European financial markets so volatile in the early 1830s—and delayed the recovery of the rente even after a more or less stable parliamentary monarchy had been established—was the fear that, as in the 1790s, a French revolution would engender a European war. It was this fear as much as anything else which caused the financial contagion of the period, pushing up bond yields even in countries unaffected by revolution.

At various times in the early 1830s war threatened to break out over Belgium, Poland or Italy. The Rothschilds were now well enough connected to act as peace brokers on each occasion. Their uniquely fast communications network—which relied principally on private couriers to-ing and fro-ing with copies of letters—was by now also being used by the leading statesmen of the continent as an express postal service. This gave the family one form of power: knowledge. James saw Louis Philippe, heard his views, wrote them down in his letter to Salomon, who went to see Metternich, and passed them on. The process then repeated itself in reverse, with Metternich's reply reaching Louis Philippe via at least two Rothschilds. Needless to say, the messengers could subtly alter the messages along the way; or the news could be acted upon in the stock exchanges before being passed on.

At the same time, the Rothschilds' dominance of the international bond market gave them a second form of power. Because any state that seriously contemplated going to war would have to borrow money to do so, the Rothschilds discerned the possibility that they could exercise a veto: no peace, no cash. Or as the Austrian diplomat Count Prokesch von Osten said in December 1830: "It is all a question of ways and means and what Rothschild says is decisive, and he won't give any money for war."

It did not quite work so neatly. Though contemporaries were enchanted by the idea that the Rothschilds could keep the European peace merely by threatening to ration credit, in reality there were other reasons why war did not break out in the 1830s. Still, at certain times the Rothschilds were able to wield political power by financial means. Metternich's bellicosity was, if not thwarted, at least dampened by Salomon's explicit refusal to support a new loan in 1832. And the creation of Greece and Belgium as new states was literally underwritten by Rothschild finance in the form of loans guaranteed by the great powers and floated by the Rothschilds.

By the time of Nathan's untimely and painful death in 1836, the Rothschilds had therefore established a formidable business with unrivaled resources and geographical reach. They were able to extend that reach even further by using agents and affiliated banks not only in other European markets but also all over the world, from Weisweiller in Madrid to Gasser in St. Petersburg to Belmont in New York. Their power fascinated contemporaries, not least because of their so recent lowly origins. An American observer portrayed the five brothers "peering above kings, rising higher than emperors, and holding a whole continent in the hollow of their hands": "the Rothschilds govern a Christian world . . . Not a cabinet moves without their advice . . . Baron Rothschild . . . holds the keys of peace or war." This was exaggeration, but not fantasy. Yet this huge and powerful organization remained at its core a family firm. It was run as a private—indeed, strictly secret—partnership, with its main business the management of the family's own capital.

There was no loss of entrepreneurial momentum as the third generation joined the partnership, though the relations between the five houses did become slightly more confederal. To some degree, James carried on where Nathan left off, as *primus inter pares*. He too was a masterful man, indefatigably devoted to business, as addicted to the bread and butter of bill broking and arbitrage as to the big bond issues that delivered the fattest profits. His longevity kept the ethos of the Frankfurt ghetto alive in the firm well into the 1860s. Yet James was never able to dominate the other houses as Nathan had done. Though one of Nathan's own sons—Nat—became his chafing adlatus in Paris, the others were never under his thumb. Lionel in particular proved as successful a businessman as his father, though his manner was *sotto voce* where Nathan had been explosive. Salomon's son Anselm also proved a man of strong will. Nor could James really control his older brothers: Salomon in particular tended to pay more heed to the interests of the Austrian government and the other Vienna banks than his partners liked.

In some ways, this shift from monarchy to oligarchy within the family was advantageous: it allowed the Rothschilds to respond to the new financial opportunities of the mid-century more flexibly than Nathan might have allowed. For example, Salomon, James and Amschel were able to play leading roles in railway finance in Austria, France and Germany, which their brother had conspicuously omitted to do in England.

Nathan had been inclined to extend the practices of the 1820s into the 1830s. As the finances of the major European states stabilized, he looked for new clients farther afield: in Spain, Portugal and the United States. But to become "master of the finances" of Belgium was one thing; to repeat the process in Iberia or America quite another. Political instability in both Spain and Portugal led to embarrassing defaults on Rothschild-issued bonds. In the United States the problem was the decentralization of fiscal and monetary institutions. The Rothschilds hoped the federal government would prove a good source of business, but it tended to leave the business of foreign borrowing to the states. Likewise, they expected the Bank of the United States to evolve into an American Bank of England. Instead, politically undermined and financially mismanaged, it went bust in 1839. The Rothschilds' failure to establish a strong foothold in the United States—they had little confidence in their self-appointed agent on Wall Street—proved to be the single biggest strategic mistake in their history.

Such reverses in the familiar field of government finance made diversification logical. Thus the decision to acquire control over the European mercury market was partly a response to the risks of governmental default. By controlling a tangible asset like the Almadén mines, then the world's biggest, the Rothschilds could finance the Spanish government with minimal risk, advancing money against consignments of mercury. The involvement in mercury mining made sense doubly because of the use of mercury in silver refining. Already experienced bullion brokers before 1815, the Rothschilds branched into minting too.

Railway finance was the most exciting new line, however. In most European countries, the state played some role in railway building, either directly financing construction (as in Russia or Belgium) or subsidising it (as in France and some German states). This meant that issuing shares or bonds for railway companies was not so very different from issuing government bonds—except that the volatility of railway shares was much greater. To begin with, the Rothschilds sought to play a purely financial role. But they were drawn inevitably into closer involvement by the long lags between a rail company's flotation and the actual opening of its lines, not to mention the payment of dividends on its shares. By the 1840s, Lionel's brothers Anthony and Nat were spending a substantial proportion of their time supervising their uncle James's French railway interests. It was a sign of the third generation's greater aversion to risk that Nat strongly criticized James's "love" of lines like the Nord and the Lombard and, when accidents happened (as at Fampoux in 1846), Nat saw his fears fulfilled. James was nevertheless right: capital gains on continental railway shares in the course of the nineteenth century were the principal reason the French house subsequently outgrew the English. By the middle of the century, the Rothschilds were already well on the way to building a highly profitable pan-European railway network.

In one respect, however, Nat's fears were justified. Unlike the management of government debts, the management of railways directly and tangibly affected the lives of ordinary people. The Rothschilds' involvement in railways therefore exposed them to unprecedented public criticism. Radical and (for the first time) socialist writers began to portray them in a new and lurid light: as exploiters of "the people," pursuing capital gains and profits at the expense of taxpayers and ordinary travelers. There had been press attacks on the Rothschilds before; but in the 1820s and 1830s they had mainly stood accused of financing political reaction, or (by business rivals) of sharp commercial practice. In the 1840s, hostility to wealth fused with hostility to Jews: anticapitalism and anti-Semitism complemented one another. The Rothschilds provided the perfect target.

Along with inflammatory polemics, the depressed economic conditions of the mid-1840s were intimations of political instability. Unlike 1830, the revolution of 1848 could be seen coming from afar. The Rothschilds were not blind to its approach, yet underestimated the magnitude of the crisis. The problem was that economic stagnation increased government deficits by reducing tax revenues; in the short term, that meant new business for the Rothschilds, which they could not resist. Both Salomon and James undertook major loans on the very eve of the insurrections. With the spread of revolution eastward from Paris, Salomon's industrial and railway bonds and shares simply became impossible to sell, and his contractual obligations to the Austrian state equally impossible to fulfill. James was only able to ride out the storm by negotiating major changes to his most recent loan contract with the new and financially naive government.

By dint of their multinational structure, immense resources and superb political contacts, the Rothschilds were able to survive the upheaval of 1848–49. In conditions of near-universal loss, their relative position may even have been slightly enhanced. However, the recovery of the European economies and the (not-coincidental) return of political stability brought new challenges.

First, one of the unspectacular achievements of the revolution was to weaken the resistance of state bureaucracies to the ideas of joint-stock company formation and limited liability. Once company formation became easier, the number of new entrants into finance began to rise. The Pereire brothers had started life as railway enthusiasts, with technical visions but without much money to realize them—hence their subordinate relationship with the Rothschilds in the 1830s. In the 1850s they were able to break free, mobilizing the resources of numerous smaller investors in raising the capital of the Crédit Mobilier.

Related to the challenge symbolized by the Pereires was a change in the relationship between state finance and the bond market. The 1850s saw the first serious attempts by states to sell bonds by public subscription, without the mediation of bankers, or with bankers acting as underwriters rather than buying new bonds outright. If nothing else, states began to exploit the growing competition between private and joint-stock banks in order to whittle down commissions. Though still dominant in the bond market, the Rothschilds' position became less monopolistic. The spread of the telegraph further weakened their grip, bringing to an end the period when their couriers had been able to deliver market-sensitive news ahead of the competition.

But perhaps the most important threat to the Rothschilds' financial hegemony was political. The triumph of Louis Napoleon Bonaparte in France introduced a new uncertainty into European diplomacy. The possibility that he might seek to emulate his uncle never wholly disappeared until 1870. At the same time, the rules of the international game were subtly altered by the tendency of politicians elsewhere—notably Palmerston, Cavour and Bismarck—to elevate national self-interest above international "balance," and to place as much trust in cannons as in conferences. Compared with the relatively peaceful thirty-three years from 1815 until 1848, the next thirty-three years would be marked by a succession of wars in Europe (not to mention America): wars that the Rothschilds found themselves unable, despite their best efforts, to prevent.

In May 1848 Charlotte de Rothschild affirmed her belief "in a bright, European and Rothschildian future." Her confidence in the waning of the French revolutionary era was well founded. In the second half of the nineteenth century, the threats to monarchical politics and bourgeois economics did indeed recede. But the brightness of the Rothschildian future would depend on the family's ability to meet new challenges. Of these, nationalism and then socialism would prove the greatest—especially when combined.

I

Uncles and Nephews

ONE

Charlotte's Dream
(1849–1858)

I went to sleep at 5 and woke against 6; I had dreamt that a huge vampire was greedily sucking my blood . . . Apparently, when the result of the vote was declared, a loud, enthusiastic roar of approval resounded . . . throughout the House [of Lords]. Surely we do not deserve so much hatred.

CHARLOTTE DE ROTHSCHILD, MAY 1849[1]

Though they had managed to weather its storms financially, 1848 might still have proved a fatal turning point for the Rothschilds—but for reasons unrelated to economics and politics. For in the years immediately after the revolution the very structure of the family and the firm was called into question. It is easy to forget as one reads their letters that the four remaining sons of Mayer Amschel were by now old men. Amschel was seventy-seven in 1850, Salomon seventy-six and Carl an ailing sixty-two. Only James was still indefatigable at fifty-six.

Longevity, on the other hand, was a family trait: though their father had died aged sixty-eight, their mother, born in 1753, lasted long enough to see the crown of a united Germany offered to a Prussian king by a national assembly gathered in her own home town. Indeed, Gutle Rothschild had become something of a by-word by the 1840s, as *The Times* reported:

> The venerable Madame Rothschild, of Frankfort, now fast approaching to her hundredth year, being a little indisposed last week, remonstrated in a friendly way with her physician on the inefficiency of his prescriptions. "Que voulez-vous Madame?" said he, "unfortunately we cannot make you younger." "You mistake, doctor," replied the witty lady, "I do not ask you to make me younger. It is older I desire to become."[2]

Cartoons were published on the subject: one, entitled *Grandmother's 99th Birthday*, depicted James, with Gutle in the background, telling a group of well-wishers: "When she reaches par, gentlemen, I will donate to the state a little capital of

Der 99ste Geburtstag der Großmutter.

1.i: Anon., *Der 99ste Geburtstag der Gro{ss}mutter, Fliegende Blätter* **(c. 1848).**

100,000 gulden" (see illustration 1.i). A different version of the same joke has a doctor assuring her she will "live to be a hundred." "What are you talking about?" snaps Gutle. "If God can get me for 81, He won't take me at a hundred!"[3]

Her dogged refusal to quit the old house "zum grünen Schild" in the former Judengasse appealed to contemporaries, suggesting as it did that the Rothschilds' phenomenal economic success was rooted in a kind of Jewish asceticism. Ludwig Börne had sung her praises on this score as early as 1827: "Look, there she lives, in that little house . . . and has no wish, despite the world-wide sovereignty exercised by her royal sons, to leave her hereditary little castle in the Jewish quarter."[4] When he visited Frankfurt sixteen years later, Charles Greville was amazed to behold "the old mother of the Rothschilds" emerging from her "same dark and decayed mansion . . . not a bit better than any of the others" in the "Jews' street":

> In this narrow gloomy street, and before this wretched tenement, a
> smart *calèche* was standing, fitted with blue silk, and a footman in blue
> livery was at the door. Presently the door opened, and the old woman
> was seen descending a dark, narrow staircase, supported by her grand-
> daughter, the Baroness Charles Rothschild, whose carriage was also in
> waiting at the end of the street. Two footmen and some maids were in
> attendance to help the old lady into the carriage, and a number of
> inhabitants collected opposite to see her get in. A more curious and
> striking contrast I never saw than the dress of the ladies, both the old
> and the young one, and their equipages and liveries, with the dilapi-
> dated locality in which the old woman persists in remaining.[5]

But on May 7, 1849, in her ninety-sixth year and with her surviving sons at her bedside, Gutle finally died.

It was one of a spate of deaths in the family. The year before, Amschel's wife Eva had died. In 1850, so did Nathan's widow Hannah[6] as well as—to the great distress of the Paris Rothschilds—her youngest grandson, Nat's second son Mayer Albert. Carl's wife Adelheid died in 1853, followed a year later by Salomon's wife, Caroline. The effect of these events on the older members of the second generation may easily be imagined. Mayer Carl noticed how "deeply affected" Amschel had been by the death of his mother. "It is a great loss to [him] . . . & I cannot tell you how many wretched hours we have spent lately . . . Uncle A. is confined to his room but feels rather better after the first shock which was really fearful."[7] He was only slightly "calmer" when the family gathered in Frankfurt for Gutle's funeral.[8] Indeed, he and his brother Salomon cut rather forlorn figures in their twilight years, spending less and less time in the counting house and more and more time in Amschel's garden.[9]

To the new Prussian delegate to the Diet of the restored German Confederation—a mercurial and ultra-conservative Junker named Otto von Bismarck— Amschel seemed a pathetic old man. "[I]n monetary terms," Rothschild was of course the "most distinguished" man in Frankfurt society, Bismarck reported to his wife shortly after arriving in the town. But "take their money and salaries away from the *lot* of them, and you would see how undistinguished" he and the other citizens of Frankfurt really were. The newcomer was characteristically rebarbative when Amschel invited him to dinner ten days in advance (to be sure of an acceptance), replying that he would come "if he was still alive." This answer "alarmed him so much that he repeated it to everybody: 'What, why shouldn't he live, why should he die, the man is young and strong!' "[10] With his limited private means and meagre stipend, the Junker diplomat was bound to be impressed as much as he was repelled by the "hundredweight of silverware, golden forks and spoons, fresh peaches and grapes, and excellent wines" which were laid before him on Amschel's dinner table. But he could not conceal his disdain when the old man proudly showed off his beloved garden after their meal:

> I like him because he's a real old wheeling and dealing Jew, and does not pretend to be anything else; he is strictly Orthodox with it, and refuses to touch anything but kosher food at his dinners. "Johann, take some pread vit you for the deer," he said to his servant, as he went out to show me his garden, in which he keeps tame deer. "Herr Paron, this plant cost me two tousand gulden, honestly, two tousand gulden cesh. You can hef it for a tousand; or if you'd like it es a present, he'll pring it to your house. Gott knows I regard you highly, Paron, you're a hendsome man, a fine man." He is a short, thin, little man, and quite grey. The eldest of his line, but a poor man in his palace, a childless widower, cheated by his servants and despised by smart Frenchified and Anglicised nephews and nieces who will inherit his wealth without any love or gratitude.[11]

As Bismarck shrewdly divined, it was this last question—who should inherit their wealth—which most preoccupied the old Rothschilds, who accordingly spent long hours tinkering with their wills. Years before—in 1814—Amschel had joked that the difference between a rich German Jew and a rich Polish Jew was that the latter would "die just when he was losing, whilst the rich German Jew only dies when he has a great deal of money."[12] Forty years later, Amschel was living up to his own stereotype, with a share in the family firm worth nearly £2 million. But who should inherit this fortune? Denied the son he had so long prayed for, Amschel brooded on the merits of his twelve nephews, particularly those (principally Carl's sons Mayer

Carl and Wilhelm Carl) who had settled in Frankfurt. In the end, his share of the business was divided in such a way that James got a quarter, Anselm a quarter, Nathan's four sons a quarter between them and Carl's three sons the last quarter.[13]

Salomon had an heir, of course, and a daughter well provided-for in Paris; but—perhaps because of the harsh words they had exchanged in Vienna at the height of the revolutionary crisis—he sought to avoid making Anselm his sole heir. Instead, he devised complicated provisions designed to transmit most of his personal wealth directly to his grandchildren. At first he seems to have considered leaving almost all of it (£1.75 million) to his daughter Betty's children (£425,000 apiece for the boys and just £50,000 for Charlotte, whom he had already given £50,000 on the occasion of her marriage to Nat), leaving only his three houses to Anselm and his sons, and just £8,000 for their married sister Hannah Mathilde. Even his Paris hôtel, he told Anselm, would go to "you and your sons . . . I repeat it is for you *and your sons.* I have thought about it and put in a clause [to ensure it remains their property for] over a hundred years. No sons-in-law or daughters can have any claim on it." This was partly a self-conscious strategy to exert the maximum posthumous influence, rather as Mayer Amschel had done in 1812; indeed, the exclusion of the female line was an idea he had inherited from his father. But, unlike his father, Salomon decided that only one of his grandsons would ultimately inherit his share of the family business from Anselm—a new development in a family which had hitherto treated all male heirs more or less equally. In a final codicil to his will dated 1853, he scrapped the clause which left the choice of successor to Anselm, specifying (unsuccessfully, as it turned out) his eldest grandson Nathaniel.[14] Ultimately, all Salomon's schemes came to naught; in practice, it was Anselm who inherited his fortune and who decided which of his sons should succeed him. Bismarck was right too that the younger Rothschilds ridiculed their old uncles. Visits to the invariably "sad and morose" Uncle Carl were especially dreaded.[15] If there was great grief in 1855 when Salomon, Carl and Amschel one after another expired in the space of just nine months, no record of it has come to light.[16]

This wave of mortality came in the wake of a dramatic upheaval in the Rothschilds' financial affairs. As we have seen, the huge sums which had to be written off in the wake of the Vienna house's effective collapse were not easily forgotten, especially by the London partners, whose worst fears about their uncles' reckless business methods appeared to have been confirmed. Unfortunately, the structure of the firm meant that losses of the sort sustained by Salomon had to be borne collectively; his *personal* share of the firm's total capital was not proportionately reduced. This explains why, in the period immediately after the revolution, unprecedented centrifugal forces threatened to break the links which Mayer Amschel had forged nearly forty years before to bind his sons and grandsons together. In particular, the London partners sought to "liberate" themselves from the commitments to the four continental houses which had cost them so dear in the wake of the revolution. As Nat put it in July 1848, he and his brothers wished to "come to some sort of an arrangement so that each house may be in an independent position."[17] Small wonder the prospect of a "commercial and financial congress" had filled Charlotte with such dread when it was first proposed in August 1848: "Uncle A. is weakened and depressed by the loss of his wife, Uncle Salomon by the loss of his money, Uncle James by the uncertain situation in France, my father [Carl] is nervous, my husband, though splendid, is stubborn when he is in the right."[18]

When James set off to see his brothers and nephews in Frankfurt in January 1849, Betty fully expected the congress to "alter the bases of our Houses, and following the London house, [to] grant mutual freedom from a solidarity which is incompatible with the movements in politics . . ."[19] Characteristic of the strained relations between Paris and London was the row later that year when James heard that Mayer had "ordered" one of the Davidson brothers "*not* to send any gold to France"—an assertion of English paramountcy he found intolerable.[20] In Paris itself, there was constant friction between Nat and James. The former had always been a good deal more cautious than his uncle, but the revolution, as we have seen, all but broke his nerve as a businessman. "I advise you to be doubly cautious in business generally," he exhorted his brothers in a typical letter at the height of the crisis:

> As for me I have taken such a disgust to business that I should particularly like to have no more of any sort or description to transact . . . What with the state of things all over the world, the revolutions that spring up in a minute & when least expected I think it downright madness to go & plunge oneself up to one's neck into hot water for the chance of making a little money. Our good Uncles are so ridiculously fond of business for business' sake and because they cannot bear the idea of anybody else doing anything that they can't let anything go if they fancy another person wishes for it. For my part I am quite sure there is no risk of Baring advancing much [on Spanish mercury] & if he chooses so to do let him do it, be satisfied and take things *easy*.[21]

Betty saw the force of this. As she commented, "Our good Uncle [Amschel] can't tolerate a lessening of our fortune, and in his desire to restore it along previous lines, he wouldn't think twice about throwing us back into the disturbance of hazardous affairs."[22] But James was increasingly impatient with Nat's pusillanimity. Charlotte suspected that James would positively welcome his nephew's withdrawing from the business as it would allow him to increase the involvement of his elder sons Alphonse and Gustave (who first begin to figure in the correspondence in 1846).[23] As Betty put it, the "old ties of fraternal union" for a time seemed "pretty close to falling apart."[24]

Nor were these the only sources of familial disunity. Even before the 1848 revolution, there had been complaints from Frankfurt about the attitude of the London house. It was, complained Anselm, "very unpleasant to be the most humble servant, to execute your order without even knowing by the Spanish correspondence what is going forward. Very true it is that we do not merit any consideration, & that since a long time ago [*sic*] we are ranged in a secondary line in the Community of the different houses."[25] As this implies, Anselm was assuming that he, as the eldest of the next generation, would be Amschel's successor in Frankfurt. Yet the collapse of the Vienna house changed everything, as it put pressure on him to take over permanently his father's place in Austria. In the same way, Carl wished his eldest son Mayer Carl to succeed him in Italy. However, the childless Amschel was even more determined that Mayer Carl should take over from him in Frankfurt, leaving his younger and less able brother Adolph to go to Naples. As James observed, such argu-

ments were not only between the elderly brothers but also between their sons and
nephews, who were all evidently vying for control of the Frankfurt house, since it
continued to be dominant over its Vienna and Naples branches: "Anselm is at odds
with Mayer Carl. Mayer Carl is at odds with Adolph."[26] Although notably partisan
in her eldest brother's favour, Charlotte's diary details some of the ill-feeling this
rivalry generated:

> Mayer Carl . . . is mature; a man of the world and an international citi-
> zen. He is in his prime and at the height of his by no means inconsider-
> able powers. He has certainly earned himself a greater degree of
> popularity than Anselm through his engaging manner, his vivacious per-
> sonality and witty conversation. Indeed he is a welcome and well liked
> figure in Frankfurt, far more so than my brother-in-law ever was, is or
> could be. I rather doubt that he possesses the solid breadth and depth of
> knowledge that Anselm has gained and I am in no position to assess
> whether he is an experienced businessman, or whether his judgement on
> important matters is sound and whether he is a good writer and speaker.
> But . . . Anselm is utterly condescending towards my brother, which is
> quite unjustifiable for one would have to scour whole kingdoms to find
> such a gifted young man. Perhaps he does not have the aptitude for
> thorough research and lengthy study required for the pursuit of the sci-
> entific branches of intellectual thought. Yet, as a banker and a man of
> the world, as a refined and educated member of European Society (for
> he is at ease with all nationalities and classes), it seems to me he is with-
> out equal. It is unjust and unworthy of Anselm to treat him with such
> disdain.[27]

Finally, it is important to bear in mind the anger felt in London and Paris towards
the Vienna house after the débâcle of 1848. At times, James talked as if even he
would not be sorry to sever his links with Vienna. "I have no interest in Vienna," he
wrote to New Court in December 1849. "While others speculate against the government there, our people in Vienna are not so smart and are unfortunately poor
businessmen. They always think they are doing business for the good of the state."[28]

Yet in the end the partnership was renewed in 1852 with relatively limited alterations to the 1844 system and continued to function with as much success as ever in
the following two decades. Why was this? The best explanation for the survival of
the Rothschild houses as a multinational partnership lies in the vital role played by
James in bridging the generation gap and binding the increasingly divergent
branches of the family together again. As Charlotte remarked when she saw her
uncle in Frankfurt in 1849, James had emerged from the crisis of 1848 with his lust
for life and business undiminished:

> I have seldom seen such a practically shrewd man, so worldly and canny,
> so mentally and physically active and indefatigable. When I reflect that
> he grew up in the Frankfurt Judengasse and never enjoyed the advan-
> tages of high culture in his childhood and youth, I am amazed and
> admire him beyond words. He has fun and takes pleasure in everything.
> Every day he writes two or three letters and dictates at least six, reads all
> the French, German and English newspapers, bathes, has a one-hour
> morning nap, and plays whist for three or four hours.[29]

And this was James's routine when he was *away* from Paris. The James whom the young stockbroker Feydeau encountered in the rue Laffitte was as much a force of nature as he had been in Heine's heyday; if anything, age made James only the more formidable.

For all his youthful vigour, James nevertheless remained deeply imbued with the familial ethos of his father's day. Even before 1848, he had been worried by the signs of dissension between the five houses. Disagreements about the accounts, he warned Lionel in April 1847, were leading "to a state of affairs that in the end everyone deals for himself and this then creates a great deal of unpleasantness." "It is only the reputation, the happiness and the unity of the family which lies close to my heart," he wrote, echoing the familiar admonitions of Mayer Amschel, "and it is as a result of our business dealings that we remain united. If one shares and receives the accounts every day, then everything will stay united God willing."[30] It was to this theme that James returned with passionate urgency in the summer of 1850—a letter of such importance that it deserves to be quoted at length:

> It is easier to break up a thing than to put it back together again. We have children enough to carry on the business for a hundred years and so we must not go against one another . . . We must not delude ourselves: the day when a [single] company no longer exists—when we lose that unity and co-operation in business which in the eyes of the world gives us our true strength—the day that ceases to exist and each of us goes his own way, then good old Amschel will say, "I have £2 million in the business [but now] I am withdrawing it," and what can we do to stop him? As soon as there is no longer majority [decision-making] he can marry himself to a Goldschmidt and say, "I am investing my money wherever I like," and we shall never stop reproaching ourselves. I also believe, dear Lionel, that we two, who are the only ones with influence in Frankfurt, must really aim to restore peace between all [the partners] . . . What will happen if we are not careful is that capital amounting to £3 million will fall into the hands of outsiders, instead of being passed on to our children. I ask you, have we gone mad? You will say that I am getting old and that I just want to increase the interest on my capital. But, firstly, all our reserves are, thank God, much stronger than when we made our last partnership contract, and secondly, as I said to you on the day I arrived here, you will find in me a faithful uncle who will do everything in his power to achieve the necessary compromise. I therefore believe that we must follow these lines of argument and do everything possible—make every sacrifice on both sides—to maintain this unity which, thanks be to the Almighty, has protected us from all the recent misfortunes, and each of us must try to see what he can do in order to achieve this objective.[31]

These were themes James harped on throughout 1850 and 1851. "I assure you," he told Lionel's wife Charlotte (whom he had identified as an ally), "the family is everything: it is the only source of the happiness which with God's help we possess, it is our attachment [to one another], it is our unity."[32]

It is in the light of James's campaign for unity that the partnership contract of 1852 should therefore be understood—not as weakening the ties between the houses,[33] but as *preserving* them through a compromise whereby the English partners dropped their demands for full independence in exchange for higher rates of return on their capital.[34] As early as 1850, James had outlined the terms of this compromise: in Nat's words, he proposed "that the rate of interest on the capital for us should be raised," provided always that the London house was more profitable than the others.[35] This was also the thrust of his letter to Lionel quoted above; and it was the system finally agreed to in 1852. The British partners received a variety of sweeteners: not only were they permitted to withdraw £260,250 from their share of the firm's capital, but the interest on their share (now 20 per cent of the total) was increased to 3.5 per cent, compared with 3 per cent for James, 2.625 per cent for Carl and 2.5 for Amschel and Salomon. In addition, the rules governing the joint conduct of business were relaxed: henceforth, no partner could be obliged by the majority to go on business trips, while investments in real estate were no longer to be financed from the collective funds. In return for these concessions, the English partners accepted a new system of collaboration. Clause 12 of the agreement stated that "to secure an open and brotherly co-operation and the advancement of their general, reciprocal business interests" the partners would keep one another informed of any transactions worth more than 10 million gulden (*c*. £830,000), and offer participations of up to 10 per cent on a reciprocal basis. Otherwise, the terms of all previous agreements not specifically altered by the new contract remained in force including, for example, the procedures for common accounting.[36] This undoubtedly represented a measure of decentralisation. But considering that the alternative (seriously discussed the following year) was the complete liquidation of the collective enterprise, it represented a victory for James.[37]

What the 1852 agreement did not do was to decide the succession in Frankfurt (other than to rule out Adolph): henceforth, Anselm, Mayer Carl and Wilhelm Carl were all to sign for the Frankfurt house. (It also gave Alphonse and Gustave the right to sign for the Paris house.)[38] Only after the deaths of James's brothers in 1855 did the new structure of the firm emerge (see table 1a). Despite the provisions of his

Table 1a. Personal shares of combined Rothschild capital, 1852 and 1855.

1852	£	£	PER CENT	1855	£	£	PER CENT
Lionel	464,770.75			Lionel	685,536.86		
Anthony	464,770.75	1,859,083.00	20.05	Anthony	685,536.86	2,742,147.44	25.80
Nat	464,770.75			Nat	685,536.86		
Mayer	464,770.75			Mayer	685,536.86		
Amschel		1,859,083.00	20.05				
Salomon		1,859,083.00	20.05	Anselm		2,742,147.44	25.80
James		1,847,083.00	19.92	James		2,727,987.43	25.67
Carl		1,847,083.00	19.92	M. Carl	805,540.66		
				Adolph	805,540.66	2,416,621.99	22.74
				W. Carl	805,540.66		
Total		9,271,415.00	100.00	Total	10,628,904.28		100.0

Note: 1855 figures estimated (in the absence of documented figures for the Frankfurt, Vienna and Paris houses) on the basis of figures for Naples and London. Between 1852 and 1855, the capital of the Naples house grew by 13.5 per cent, that of the London house by 22.8 per cent; I have applied the average of these figures (18 per cent) across the board.

Sources: CPHDCM, 637/1/7/115–120, Societäts-Übereinkunft, Oct. 31, 1852, between Amschel, Salomon, Carl, James, Lionel, Anthony, Nat and Mayer; AN, 132 AQ 3/1, Undated document, *c*. Dec. 1855, reallocating Amschel and Carl's shares.

will, all Salomon's share of the collective capital passed to Anselm (an outcome which, for reasons which are obscure, James challenged only half-heartedly on his wife's behalf). Carl's share was divided equally between his sons after the deduction of a seventh, which went to his daughter Charlotte. Finally, and decisively, Amschel's share was divided up in such a way that James and Anselm each received a quarter, as did the sons of Nathan and the sons of Carl.[39] The net effect of all this was to give close to equal power to Anselm, James and the English-born partners, while reducing the influence of Carl's sons. Their influence was further reduced by the decision to put Adolph in charge of the Naples house, and leave Frankfurt to Mayer Carl and his pious brother Wilhelm Carl.[40]

It was a compromise which worked in practice. After 1852, James was prepared to show a much greater degree of deference to his nephews' wishes than in the past. New Court no longer took orders from James—as can easily be inferred from the diminished length of his letters to London after 1848. Increasingly, he scribbled no more than a postscript to Nat's despatch and often concluded his suggestions about business—as if to remind himself that there was no longer a *primus inter pares*—with the telling phrase: "Do, dear nephews, what you wish." This was doubtless gratifying to Lionel. Yet the compromise of 1852 meant that the pre-1848 system of co-operation between the five houses was in fact resumed with only a modest degree of decentralisation. The balance sheets of the Paris and London houses reveal a rate of interdependence which was less than had been the case in the 1820s, but it was still substantial. To give just one example, 17.4 per cent of the Paris house's assets in December 1851 were monies owed to it by other Rothschild houses, principally London.[41]

Moreover, the London partners' assumption that their house would be more profitable than the others proved over-confident. Although the Naples and Frankfurt houses tended to stagnate (for reasons largely beyond the control of Adolph and Mayer Carl), it was James who made much of the running after 1852, expanding his continental railway interests so successfully that by the end of his life the capital of the Paris house far exceeded that of its partners. Anselm too proved unexpectedly adept at restoring the vitality of the shattered Vienna house. It turned out to be far from disadvantageous for the London partners to share in these continental successes. The new system thus inaugurated a new era of equality of status between the London and Paris houses, with Vienna reviving while Frankfurt and Naples declined in their influence.

As in the past, it was not only through partnership agreements and wills that the Rothschilds maintained the integrity of the family firm. Endogamy continued to play a crucial role. The period between 1848 and 1877 saw no fewer than nine marriages within the family, the manifest purpose of which was to strengthen the links between the different branches. In 1849 Carl's third son Wilhelm Carl married his cousin Anselm's second daughter Hannah Mathilde; a year later, his brother Adolph married her sister Julie; and in 1857 James's eldest son Alphonse married his cousin Lionel's daughter Leonora at Gunnersbury. To list the rest here would be tedious.[42] With a single exception in the years before 1873, those who did not marry other Rothschilds did not stray far from the Jewish "cousinhood."[43] In 1850 Mayer married Juliana Cohen—defeating a rival suit from Joseph Montefiore—while his nephew Gustave married Cécile Anspach in 1859.[44] If Wilhelm Carl had not married a Rothschild, he would have married a Schnapper—a member of his grand-mother Gutle's family.[45]

The brokering of these alliances was, as it had been for nearly two generations, a major preoccupation of the female members of the family. Charlotte made no bones about their rationale. As she enthused on hearing of her brother Wilhelm Carl's engagement to Hannah Mathilde, "My good parents will certainly be pleased that he has not chosen a stranger. For us Jews, and particularly for us Rothschilds, it is better not to come into contact with other families, as it always leads to unpleasant-ness and costs money."[46] The idea that either the pious groom or the musical bride was making a spontaneous choice was, in this case, nonsense. Charlotte's cousin Betty saw the match in a very different light, reporting to her son that "poor Mathilde only determined regretfully to marry Willy." Now she was "preparing her-self with a truly angelic resignation for the sacrifice of her young heart's dearest illu-sions. It has to be said that the prospect of being Willy's lifelong companion wouldn't entice a young woman brought up as she has been and blessed with a cul-tivated mind."[47] The question which remained to be resolved was whom Betty's sons Alphonse and Gustave should marry. It seems that Hannah Mathilde had in fact set her heart on the latter, while her sister Julie had hoped to marry Alphonse. But, after teasing her son on the subject, Betty reported that:

> Papa, frank and honest man that he is . . . brought up the subject with-out beating about the bush. He expressed all his regrets to the poor mother . . . and he undeceived her of illusions that the desire for success might encourage wrongly, and he asked her in her own interest and for the happiness of her daughter to look elsewhere.[48]

This was good news for Charlotte, who was planning a similar double match between Betty's sons and her daughters Leonora and Evelina. In her diary, she coolly weighed up the respective merits of the two putative sons-in-law:

> Gustave is an excellent young man. He has the best and warmest heart and is deeply devoted to his parents, brothers and sisters and relatives. He has a strongly developed sense of duty and his obedience could serve as an example to all young people of his generation. Whether he is tal-ented or not, I could not in all honesty say. He has enjoyed the great benefits and advantages of a good education, but is, he claims, stupid, easily intimidated and unable to string ten words together in the com-pany of strangers. They say he has acquired considerable skill in mathe-matics but I am ignorant of that subject and cannot pass judgement.
>
> His brother, Alphonse, combines the extraordinary energy and vital-ity of our uncle [James] with Betty's facility for languages. He is a good reader, listener and observer and he remembers everything he absorbs. He can converse on the topics of the day with an easy manner, without pedantry, but always in a direct, penetrating and amusing way, touching upon every subject in the most agreeable fashion. He cannot be relied upon for an opinion, since he never voices one, indeed, perhaps does not have opinions; but it is a pleasure to hear him, for he speaks without emotion in the most engaging and lively tone.
>
> Mrs Disraeli calls Gustave handsome; I do not know whether I agree with her. He is the only one of the Jacobean line who can boast this

advantage with his large, soft, blue-green eyes. In his early years they were apparently weak like all the Rothschild eyes, but now there is no trace of the childhood trouble, except a certain quality which one might almost call languishing. His eyebrows are finely drawn; his brow well formed, fair and clear; he has a full head of dark brown, silky hair; his nose is not oriental; he has a large mouth which, however, cannot be praised on account of its expression which is good natured at best and reveals neither understanding nor depth of feeling. Gustave is slim, his bearing is easy and his manners those of the highest society. I should like to see his profile at the altar.[49]

She was only half-successful: nine years later it was Alphonse's profile she saw at the altar, alongside her daughter Leonora. By that time, moreover, she had revised her opinion of the bridegroom. Now he seemed "a man, who perhaps for ten of fifteen years has run the round of the world—is completely blasé, can neither admire nor love—and yet demands the entire devotion of his bride, her slavish devotion." Still, she concluded, it was "better so—the man whose passions are dead, whose feelings have lost all freshness, all depth, is likely to prove a safe husband, and the wife will probably find happiness in the discharge, in the fulfilment of her duties. Her disenchantment will be bitter but not lasting." In any case, her daughter attached "much importance to a certain position in the world, and would not like to descend from what she fancies to be the throne of the R's to be the bride of a humbler man."[50] Such sentiments were doubtless based on Charlotte's own experience, and tell us much about the distinctive quality of such arranged marriages.

The extent to which parental choice was decisive should not, of course, be exaggerated. The fact that Charlotte failed to secure Alphonse's brother for her other daughter suggests that parents were less able to impose their choices of spouse on their children than had previously been the case. Anselm's daughter Julie also successfully repelled the advances of her cousin Wilhelm Carl, as well as those of a more distant relation, Nathaniel Montefiore.[51] On the other hand, her final "choice" of Adolph was strictly governed by her father and future father-in-law, who spent months drawing up the marriage contract;[52] and although such negotiations often involved sums of money being settled individually on the bride-to-be to give her a measure of financial independence, this should not be mistaken for some sort of proto-feminism.[53] There were limits to what the Rothschilds were prepared to inflict on their daughters, as became apparent when old Amschel announced shortly after his wife's death that he wished to remarry none other than his own grand-niece, the much sought-after Julie (who was not yet twenty).[54] The rest of the family—backed up by his doctors—closed ranks against this idea. But it is not known how far their opposition was actuated by fears for his health as opposed to the happiness of the young lady in question: James for one appears to have worried that, if Amschel's proposal were rejected too abruptly, he might withdraw his capital from the firm and marry a stranger.[55]

The Orthodox and the Reformed

As Charlotte emphasised, endogamy continued to be partly a function of the Rothschilds' Judaism: the family policy remained that sons and daughters could not marry outside their faith (even if they were socially so superior to their co-religionists that they could not marry outside the family either). The extent of Rothschild religious commitment in this period should not be underestimated: if anything, it was greater than had been the case in the 1820s and 1830s, and this was another important source of familial unity in the period after 1848. James continued to be the least strict in his observance. "Well, I wish you a hearty good Sabbath," he wrote to his nephews and son in 1847. "I hope you are having a good time and a good hunt. Are you eating well, drinking well and sleeping well as is the wish of your loving uncle and father?"[56] As the existence of such a letter itself testifies, he saw nothing wrong with being at his desk on the Sabbath. He and Carl also were conspicuously erratic in their attendance at synagogue (unlike their wives).[57]

Yet James remained as firmly convinced of the functional importance of the family's Jewish identity as he had been in the days of Hannah Mayer's apostasy. Although he very nearly forgot the date of Passover in 1850, he was nevertheless willing to cancel a business trip to London in order to read the Haggadah.[58] He was happy to receive the Frankfurt rabbi Leopold Stein's new book in 1860 (though the size of the donation he sent Stein is not recorded).[59] His wife Betty was as secular-minded as her husband, but she too had a strong sense that observance was a social if not a spiritual imperative. When she heard that her son Alphonse had attended the synagogue in New York, she declared herself "over the moon," adding:

> It's good thing, my good son, not only out of religious feeling, but out of patriotism, which in our high position is a stimulus to those who might forget it and encouraging to those who remain firmly attached to it. That way you reconcile those who might blame us even while they think as we do, and make sure you have the high esteem of those who hold different beliefs.[60]

That said, it was evidently something of a surprise to her that Alphonse had gone to the synagogue of his own volition.

Wilhelm Carl meanwhile remained the only Orthodox member of the younger generation. Continuing his uncle Amschel's campaign against the Reformist tendencies of the Frankfurt community, he supported the creation of a new Israelite Religious Community for Orthodox believers, donating the lion's share of the funds to build a new synagogue in the Schützenstrasse. Yet he opposed the outright schism advocated by the new community's rabbi, Samson Raphael Hirsch, who wished his followers to withdraw altogether from the main Frankfurt community. Orthodox though he was, Wilhelm Carl shared the Rothschild view that diversity of practice should not compromise Jewish communal unity.[61]

His English cousins also continued to consider themselves "good Israelites," observing holy days and avoiding work on the Sabbath. James once teased Anthony when he was visiting Paris that he liked to pick up his prayer books,[62] an impression of piety confirmed when his nephew dutifully fasted at Yom Kippur in 1849, despite fearing (wrongly) that it was medically inadvisable given the outbreak of cholera then sweeping Paris.[63] It was typical that he and Lionel had to supply Nat with *matzot* when he was in Paris during Passover.[64] Even when on holiday in Brighton, Lionel and his family celebrated Yom Kippur, fasting and praying on the Day of Atonement.[65] But the four London-born brothers were not Orthodox in the way that Wilhelm Carl was. In 1851 Disraeli unthinkingly sent Charlotte and Lionel a large joint of venison he had been given by the Duke of Portland:

> Not knowing what to do with it, with our establishment breaking up, I thought I had made a happy hit & sent it to Madame Rothschild (as we have dined there so often, & they never with us) it never striking me for an instant that it was an unclean meat, wh[ich] I fear it is. How[ever] as I mentioned the donor & they love Lords . . . I think they will swallow it.[66]

He seems to have been right, though it seems unlikely that this was a reflection of love for the aristocracy; the fact was that Lionel's family, like James's, did not keep strict kosher. Indeed, Mayer was such an enthusiast for venison that he defended stag hunting in a political speech at Folkestone in 1866![67]

On broader religious questions, the English brothers inclined towards the Reform movement, such as it was in England. When an attempt was made (in 1853) to exclude representatives of the Reform-inclined West London Synagogue from their places on the Board of Deputies because they had fallen foul of the conservative Chief Rabbi, Lionel spoke out against what he called "popery." "He had every respect for the ecclesiastical authorities," he declared, "but he was not going to be led by them as by a Catholic priest. They might be, and no doubt were, very learned men but they had no right to enquire of him whether he kept one day or two days of the festivals"—an important distinction between Reform and Orthodox practice.[68] Such views may explain why the Reform community in Frankfurt had appealed to Lionel for help in their struggle against the dominant Orthodoxy the previous year.[69]

This tendency towards Reform was more pronounced in the case of their wives.[70] This may have been because the traditional synagogue service had been a masculine affair: there is some evidence that Rothschild women had little or no knowledge of Hebrew.[71] Anthony's wife Louisa, for example, shared the Reform movement's aspiration to modernise Jewish forms of worship precisely because synagogue services compared unfavourably with church services. "What a pity one cannot go to church and hear a good sermon," she exclaimed in 1847, frustrated by her inability to understand Hebrew.[72] This did not imply leanings towards apostasy, however. Rather, she was determined that her children should "be better instructed and able to join their brethren in public worship." Accordingly, her daughters Constance and Annie were brought up on a strong blend of Jewish doctrine and Anglican forms. After a short family service at home on the Sabbath, she gave her daughters Bible lessons and spent the rest of the day reading Jewish and non-Jewish religious literature while they studied subjects like the "History and Literature of the Israelites." Yom Kippur was solemnly observed, as Constance recorded in her diary in 1861. Yet the Sabbath lectures her mother published in 1857—with chapters on "Truthfulness," "Peace in the Home" and "Charity"—contained much that could equally well have appeared in a contemporary Anglican book of homilies:

> Oh Lord, Thou hast made me so much happier, Thou hast vouchsafed to me so many more blessings than to thousands of Thy creatures, that I know not how I can ever thank Thee sufficiently. I can only pray to Thee

to make me charitable and compassionate towards those who suffer and are in want, and to prevent me from being selfish and from thinking only of my gratification. Place in my heart, O Lord, the wish and inclination to feed the hungry, to clothe the naked and to console the sorrowful, as long as I have the power and the means to do so, that I may thereby be less undeserving of all Thy bounteous goodness to me, and less unworthy of Thy favour and merciful protection, O my God, Amen.[73]

Raised on a diet of this sort of thing, it is not wholly surprising that, like their mother, Louisa's daughters preferred Westminster Abbey to the synagogue.[74] What is more unusual is that Charlotte, who had been raised in a far more Orthodox atmosphere in Frankfurt, should have felt similar inclinations. Her letters to her son Leo show that she frequently attended non-Jewish services and institutions. She saw no reason not to participate in the affairs of the Anglican Church in her capacity as a landowner. She heard the Bishop of Oxford preach at the consecration of Acton church (near Gunnersbury) in 1866, confessing that she had been "really spell-bound" by his sermon, though she was less impressed when the Bishop of London performed the same office for a church in Ealing.[75] In this she was far from unique: Mayer's wife Juliana took such a close interest in one of the livings in the gift of the Mentmore estate that she drove one incumbent to resign.[76] Charlotte was also attracted to the fashionable world of Anglo-Catholicism, witnessing (in the space of just over a year) a Catholic bazaar, the consecration of Nazareth House by Archbishop Manning, a service in a Carmelite chapel in Kensington and another at the House of the Sisters of Mercy. On each occasion, she owed her invitation to Catholic friends like Lady Lothian and Lady Lyndhurst.[77]

Charlotte constantly compared what she saw on these occasions with analogous Jewish gatherings and, although the comparisons were not always unfavourable to her own faith, there was a strong vein of criticism. Attending a prize-giving at the Jews' Free School, she was:

> painfully struck by the contrast of those engaged in the ceremony among Jewish children, and the prelates, patrons, friends and visitors, who witnessed a similar function in the [Catholic] House of Charity . . . Dr. Adler [probably the Chief Rabbi's son Hermann, the first minister of Bayswater Synagogue], after having said a few words rushed away, as if the plague had been in the building, while Mr. Green [Rabbi A. L. Green of the Central Synagogue, who also acted as her almoner] escaped by a side door, without even saying a single word to any one. There was not one single visitor, man or woman, a large open space filled with empty chairs and I felt so shy at occupying the vast area that I was obliged to retire to a corner near the singing class.—Whatever may be said of the genuflexions and outward, showy ceremonies of the Catholics, their works, their good works, are noble and sublime, and among us there really is no heartiness.[78]

In the light of this it seems less remarkable that explicitly Christian institutions appealed to members of the Rothschild family for financial assistance. These appeals were sometimes successful: in 1871, for example, a Catholic priest persuaded Charlotte to give £50 to his school in Brentford.[79]

As this suggests, it was still mainly through charitable work that the Rothschilds continued to give expression to their religious impulses. The traditional forms of male philanthropy were remarkably long-lived. In Vienna Anselm began each working day at 9.30 a.m. by going through all the begging letters, personally determining the sums to be paid to each supplicant; and even when he went for his daily constitutional to the Schönbrunn zoo, a bank clerk accompanied him to distribute coins to the beggars he encountered.[80] In Frankfurt Jacob Rosenheim acted as Wilhelm Carl's "beggars' secretary"; but Wilhelm Carl himself still made the decisions. As his son recalled:

> Every evening, often as late as eight or nine o'clock, my father would go to the Baron at his business premises on Fahrgasse, and sometimes also to the Grüneburg, in order to present him personally with a list, carefully drawn up by my mother, of the petitions—20 to 30 of them on average—received from all over the Jewish world, personal appeals for help, letters from the most esteemed rabbis in every country, the *yeshivot* and welfare institutions in the East and the West. In each individual case, the Baron personally decided on what seemed to him to be an appropriate amount. Incidentally, he also read with a certain amount of satisfaction every single letter of thanks received. Before it was presented to the Baron, information on each request had to be sought from one of the rabbis in the Baron's confidence who were located throughout the world. Each item of information was registered and copied verbatim into a book.[81]

The punctiliousness in each case is impressive. Yet there came a point when the volume of requests for aid could no longer be managed in this old-fashioned way, especially as the numbers of poor Jewish immigrants from eastern Europe began to rise. When a man like Lionel was dealing with millions, it was absurd to expect him personally to authorise contributions like the hundred pounds he paid in 1850 "towards the Fund for the erection of Almshouses for Indigent Foreigners"; or the comparable sum his uncle Amschel asked him to contribute to a Jewish girls' school in Frankfurt two years later.[82] Much of this work therefore began to be delegated. In London Asher Asher—a doctor from Scotland who worked as secretary of the Great Synagogue after 1866—acted as Lionel's unpaid "private almoner," virtually "the manager of the 'Charitable Department' of New Court," according to one contemporary source.[83] Likewise in Paris, Feydeau recalled "a special office . . . where several employees were exclusively occupied with recording the requests for help, studying them, and gathering information on the actual position of those seeking help."[84] Charity was turning into a chore scarcely distinguishable from the more humdrum aspects of banking. After 1859, some of this work could be passed on to, or at least co-ordinated by, the new Board of Guardians for the Relief of the Jewish Poor. In 1868, for example, one Emanuel Sperling, a father of four and "a highly respectable man well worthy of recommendation" was "desirous of opening a small shop for which purpose he has got a little towards the same"; Sophie Bendheim, the daughter of a distant member of the Davidson family, needed money for her daughter's dowry.[85] This, however, was never a substitute for the philanthropic activities of the family and firm.

The women of the family were in a position to be more actively engaged; indeed to some extent philanthropy became their work, performed as assiduously as their husbands' work at the bank. The Jews' Free School had been an important focus of Rothschild benefaction since Nathan's day; in the 1850s and 1860s it began to attract not just money but personal involvement in its affairs from Charlotte and Louisa (whose husband Anthony had become president of its board of governors in 1847).[86] When she first visited it in 1848, Louisa found it "an excellent institution" providing "gratuitous instruction" to "about nine hundred poor children taken from the very lowest classes," but its educational standards were low.[87] Her sister-in-law Charlotte despaired of "the little learners in Bell Lane" whom she described to her son as "indescribably dingy and dirty—and uncouth." "It is quite disheartening to be perpetually trying to improve those Caucasian[88] arabs," she declared in 1865, "and without ever being able to descry any real progress in them." Her weekly visits to Bell Lane were "far from agreeable to me" as "the humble classes of our community [are] terribly dirty and ragged in bad weather." On the other hand, she found it "impossible . . . to go among all the poor, dirty little children without becoming deeply interested in their progress and general improvement." By the 1870s, her efforts—which included arranging an inspection by Matthew Arnold—and those of her brother-in-law Anthony had transformed it, more than trebling the number of pupils, increasing its annual budget by a factor of twenty and raising the number of teachers twenty-five-fold.[89]

Other educational institutions in which Rothschild women took an interest included the Jews' College, founded in 1855;[90] the Sabbath schools of the Association for the Diffusion of Religious Knowledge;[91] and the Borough Jewish schools founded in south London by Mayer's wife Juliana in 1867.[92] There were also, as in the past, efforts to relieve the sick. In addition to being a member of the Jewish Ladies Benevolent Loan Society and the Ladies Benevolent Institution, Louisa established a Jewish Convalescent Home, which was supplied with food from a special kitchen financed by Charlotte in Artillery Lane.[93] In addition, Charlotte established a Home for Aged Incurables, reorganised the London Lying-in Charity and was President of the Ladies' Benevolent Loan Society and the Needlework Guild for the East End Maternity Home.[94] There was also a Rothschild-founded Day Nursery for Jewish Infants in Whitechapel and a Jews' Deaf and Dumb Home on Walmer Road, Notting Hill.[95] Finally, Charlotte sought to involve herself in the new Board of Guardians. In 1861, for example, she enabled Rabbi Green to present the Board with ten sewing-machines which were to be hired out or sold to poor immigrant women who wished to earn money as seamstresses. She later donated £100–£200 a year to a "Girls' Workroom" established by Green.[96]

In his sermon at her memorial service in 1884, Hermann Adler recalled that the principal theme of Charlotte's published *Prayers and Meditations* and *Addresses to Young Children* (originally composed for the Girls' Free School) had been "that those who suffer and stand in need of assistance should be near to us and our sympathy . . . that the rich must meet the poor by 'giving not only gold, but time, which is life.'" This she had very definitely done. Her dying words, he told the congregation, had been: "Remember the Poor"—and by this was primarily meant the Jewish poor.[97] However, Adler did not allude to an important distinction which Charlotte had made throughout her adult life between charitable "giving" and donations of a specifically religious character. In 1864, she had a revealing conversation with Rabbi Green when he

> asked for a new scroll of law for his synagogue. He says that formerly there were religious persons who had great generosity—and superstitious people, who though not very wealthy or liberal, gave to the Temple from feelings of awe and dread; but that superstition has been annihilated by civilization, and that the religous Jews have ceased to be generous—while the generous Israelites allow their bounty to flow into secular channels.—I dare say he is right.—I would infinitely rather give twenty pounds to a school than expend it for a *sepher* . . .[98]

Sincere concern for the material needs of the Jewish community, in other words, could be accompanied by a critical stance towards Judaism as an organised religion. It is also worth noting the first signs of disquiet within the Jewish elite at the rising rate of immigration from Eastern Europe. In 1856 Charlotte organised an "Amateur Concert in aid of the Funds of the Jewish Emigration Loan Society" at which her children Evelina and Alfred performed, and Louisa was a member of the Society's Committee.[99] The purpose of this organisation may easily be inferred. As we shall see, the more poor Jews immigrated to England from Eastern and Central Europe, the more members of the Jewish elite wished to see emigrating elsewhere.

Perhaps the most marked change in Rothschild attitudes towards charity in this period was James's. This was probably a reaction to the events of the 1840s, which had revealed two things: the extent of anti-Jewish feeling in French society as a whole, and the extent of his own personal unpopularity among the poor of Paris. Prior to 1848, James had been of all the five sons of Mayer Amschel the least publicly engaged in Jewish communal life. Though he had taken up the cudgels on behalf of the Jews of Damascus during his battle with Thiers in 1840, he had done relatively little for the Jews of Paris. That changed after the revolution. In 1850 James informed the Consistory of Paris of his intention to create a Jewish hospital at 76 rue Picpus to replace the inadequate "Maison centrale de secours pour israélites indigents de Paris" founded in 1841. Two years later, on December 20, 1852, the hospital—a spacious new building designed by Jean-Alexandre Thierry—was formally opened after what the *Univers Israélite* described as "one of the grandest [ceremonies] that Judaism has ever celebrated within our midst," attended by the Minister of Public Works, the Director of the Department of Religion and the Prefect of the Seine.[100] At around the same time, he also made a substantial contribution to the new Romano-Byzantine synagogue built by Thierry for the Consistory in the rue Notre-Dame-de-Nazareth. There were also substantial donations to establish two orphanages in the rue des Rosiers and the rue de Lamblardie (the latter named after Salomon and Caroline).

These benefactions coincided with increased Rothschild involvement in the institutions of French Jewry. In 1850, Alphonse became a member of the Central Consistory; two years later, Gustave was elected to the Paris Consistory and became its president in 1856. After 1858, the Consistory deposited its funds at de Rothschild Frères.[101] It seems rather as if James's self-conscious status as a political "outsider" under Napoleon III's regime gave him the confidence to assume the role of lay leader of the Jewish community which his brothers and nephews already played elsewhere. Yet he was also careful to dispense some money without regard to creed, establishing a more or less permanent soup kitchen in the rue de Rivoli.[102]

Perhaps nothing better illustrates the extent of Rothschild efforts on behalf of their poorer brethren than the sheer number and extent of the contributions made by the family to the new hospital in Jerusalem which had at last been established in the 1850s by Albert Cohn. The names of no fewer than eleven Rothschilds appear in a contemporary list of donors to the hospital and to related facilities: Charlotte set up "an industrial training institute" there, to which she sent an annual cheque; Anselm funded a small bank; Betty provided clothing for pregnant women and Alphonse and Gustave funded training in handicrafts for forty youths. The family also paid a total of 122,850 piastres in "voluntary contributions."[103] The fact that members of all branches of the family appear among the benefactors reminds us that although most of their charitable work went on at a national—or rather urban—level, the Rothschilds continued to feel a responsibility towards a wider, "universal" Jewish community.[104]

Lionel Stands

No history of the Rothschilds would be complete without a discussion of the decisive role played by Lionel in securing practising Jews the right to sit as Members of Parliament in the House of Commons. However, it is important not to consider this particular question in isolation or, for that matter, as a minor episode in the teleological "Whig" history of English constitutional progress. The institutional barrier which prevented Jews who were elected as MPs from taking their seats in the Commons—the Oath of Abjuration containing the words "upon the true faith of a Christian"—was only one of a number which members of the Rothschild family sought to challenge in the 1840s and 1850s.[105] Of comparable importance to them were the obstacles to matriculation at Oxford and graduation at Cambridge.

In addition, there were social institutions which, although they did not formally exclude Jews, had never admitted them before: penetrating these was as important as overthrowing formal legal handicaps. Given the structure of British politics in the nineteenth century, a seat in the House of Commons by itself was of only limited value; local political power was just as important and in some ways a prerequisite for parliamentary representation. Moreover, there was an important social difference between local power based on urban votes and that rooted in a rural constituency. For many of the most important political decisions were taken not at Westminster but in "the country"—those complex circuits of aristocratic country houses where the political elite spent such a large proportion of the year. Even in town, Parliament was far from being the sole political forum: an MP who was not also a member of one or more of the London clubs clustered around Piccadilly and Pall Mall led a truncated political existence. And of course gaining access to the House of Commons did not automatically open the doors of the House of Lords to Jews.

Why did the Rothschilds want to improve their access to these institutions of the British establishment? The strictly instrumental interpretation that they wished to increase their political influence in order to maximise their leverage over government will not do. To be sure, many non-Jewish City families were represented in the

House of Commons by this time (notably the Barings).[106] But by the 1840s the Rothschilds were firmly established as the pre-eminent private bank in the City; and despite the chilly relations which developed with the Bank of England after Nathan's death, there was little reason to doubt that, on the rare occasions when the British government required to borrow money, it would turn to New Court. Moreover, once they had gained access to the House of Commons, the Rothschilds appear to have made little use of its facilities—at least as a debating chamber. It is rather more convincing to argue that Lionel, influenced as he was by his mother, wished to win hitherto denied privileges for Jews as a matter of principle. His relatives on the continent never ceased to applaud Lionel's efforts to secure admission to Parliament: for James, his nephew was fighting a symbolic battle on behalf of *all* Jews, one which stood in lineal succession to the battles fought by Mayer Amschel in Frankfurt forty years before. That said, there is no mistaking the authenticity of Lionel's liberalism,[107] though at the time most politicians (including Lord John Russell) were more inclined to label him a Whig. It was not just the "Jewish question" which lured him and his brothers away from the Tories, but also the much more important cause célèbre of the 1840s, free trade, which became identified with the Liberal party in the wake of the Tory revolt against Peel in 1846.

Here, then, is one of the great paradoxes of 1848: at a time when the Rothschilds were widely vilified by continental liberals as props of reaction, they were playing a leading role in an archetypal liberal campaign for legal equality in Britain. After all, Jewish emancipation was one of the achievements of the Frankfurt parliament, though it was subsequently rescinded in Frankfurt itself in 1852.[108] Even Betty, that staunch Orléanist opponent of the revolution, had to admit it: "We Jews ought not . . . to complain of this great movement and relocation of interests. Everywhere emancipation has brought down the chains of the Middle Ages, and has given back to these pariahs of fanaticism and intolerance the rights of humanity and equality. We should congratulate ourselves on this . . ."[109]

Yet here too there is a need for qualification. Firstly, there were elements of the revolutionary movement, as we have seen, which were markedly anti-Jewish; indeed, violence against Jews was one of the phenomena which most disgusted the Rothschilds about the revolutions of 1848–9. Secondly, in some ways what was really at issue was the Rothschilds' status *within* the British Jewish community. Rivalry with other members of the Jewish elite—notably David Salomons—was without doubt a strong motivating force. The reality was that for most poor Jews in Britain (and even more so on the continent) the notion of representation in Parliament was as remote as the notion of study at Cambridge. For all the rhetoric of collective struggle for Jewry, the Rothschilds were to some extent pursuing their own interests as a family—specifically, their own claim to be the "royal family" of Judaism.

In the light of subsequent events, it is extraordinary to recall that in 1839 the *Allgemeine Zeitung des Judenthums* had launched a bitter attack against the Rothschilds, accusing them of positively harming the cause of Jewish emancipation:

> Well we know to our dismay that the repulsive attitude towards the Jews in Germany, which had almost disappeared completely at the time of the Wars of Liberation, increased with the increase in the House of Rothschild; and that the latter's great wealth and [that of] their partners

have adversely affected the Jewish cause, so that as the former grew so the latter sank all the further . . . We must sharply separate the Jewish cause from the whole House of Rothschild and their consorts.[110]

At the time, however, it did appear that the family had lost sight of the wider interests of European Jewry. It was not a Rothschild but one of their business rivals, David Salomons of the London & Westminster Bank, who in 1835 won an early victory for the cause of Jewish political rights in England by getting himself elected Sheriff of the City of London. In the process, he and his Whig supporters secured the passage of an act which abolished the requirement that an elected Sheriff sign a declaration containing the words "upon the true faith of a Christian."[111] It was not a Rothschild but Francis Henry Goldsmid who became the first Jew admitted to the Bar. It was not a Rothschild but an in-law, Moses Montefiore, who was knighted and then made a baronet, thus (as James put it) "raising the standing of the Jews in England."[112] It was not a Rothschild but Isaac Lyon Goldsmid who led the Jewish Association for Obtaining Civil Rights and Privileges.

However, the Rothschilds took a renewed interest in the question of emancipation after the Damascus affair in 1840. The precedent set then of using Rothschild influence to improve conditions for Jews in the less tolerant states of Europe continued throughout the 1840s. In 1842 James went to see Guizot "concerning the Polish Jews,"[113] while Anselm sought to orchestrate press opposition to new anti-Jewish measures proposed in Prussia.[114] In 1844 "execrable" new measures proposed by Nicholas I to reduce still further the Jewish Pale (permitted area) of settlement and to bring the Russian Jews' schools and communities under direct state control prompted Lionel to seek interviews with Lord Aberdeen and Peel in advance of a visit by the Tsar to London.[115] When Montefiore travelled to Russia to protest at the government's treatment of the Jews, Lionel again saw Peel to request letters of introduction for him to Count Nesselrode.[116] In the same vein, we have already seen how the Rothschilds sought to use the political crisis in Rome in 1848–9 to extract concessions from the Pope with regard to the city's Jews.

It was nevertheless in England—hardly a country renowned for its religious intolerance—that the most celebrated campaign for Jewish rights was fought and, eventually, won. The position of Jews in Britain at this time was in many ways anomalous, reflecting the relative smallness of the Jewish community by Central European standards. The total Jewish population of the British Isles had been just 27,000 in 1828; thirty-two years later (after decades of unprecedented demographic growth in the country as a whole) there were still only 40,000 Jews—around 0.2 per cent of the population, more than half of them living in London.[117] By continental standards, and compared with popular attitudes to Catholics (and especially Irish Catholics, hostility to Jews was muted. Yet there remained on the statute books, albeit mainly as dead letters, a variety of disabilities including prohibitions on Jews owning landed property and endowing schools. More important, as we have seen, a variety of public offices, of which the most important was membership of Parliament, required the Christological oath. It was the abolition of this oath which was to become the paramount objective of Rothschild political activity.

Under the influence of his wife Hannah, Nathan had taken up the question of Jewish political rights in 1829–30, in the wake of the successful passage of the

Catholic emancipation act. Rothschild disillusionment with the Tory party can be dated from this period, when it became obvious that the Whigs were far more likely to give their support to an equivalent measure for Jews. This political realignment continued after Nathan's death as a succession of emancipation bills introduced by Robert Grant were thrown out in the Commons in the face of largely Tory opposition. Hitherto overlooked records suggest that Nat played a supporting role in the unsuccessful 1841 campaign to allow Jewish councillors on provincial corporations to swear the same amended oath Salomons had been able to use as Sheriff of London.[118] Tory opposition to this measure in the Lords—which the Rothschilds monitored closely—did nothing to improve relations with the party.[119] In the wake of the Conservative election victory in 1841, the Rothschilds' old friend Herries warned the new Chancellor Henry Goulburn that he might face opposition from "the Jews and brokers" in the City:

> It may be as well to bear in mind that the said gentry may not be so propitious to you as in former time. The part which Jones Lloyd, Sam Gurney and the Rothschilds etc. took in the City election indicates no kind feeling toward the Conservative Party. But they will not allow their feelings to stand much in the way of their own interest although they will not forgive the rejection of the bill to enable the Jews to be Common Council men and those Leviathans of the money market have much more power to promote or to obstruct a financial measure than any other description of men even possessing larger capitals than themselves.[120]

A letter from a party activist confirms that Mayer had indeed been involved in registering voters in the City to boost the Liberal poll.[121] When Peel later asked Wellington to drum up support for his government, the Duke was equally pessimistic. "The Rothschilds," he warned Peel, "are not without their political objects, particularly the old lady [Hannah] and Mr Lionel. They have long been anxious for support to the petitions of the Jews for concessions of political privileges."[122] Though he was "now more of a Tory than when [he] was in London," Nat stressed that his support for Peel would be strictly conditional: "I trust he will be liberally inclined towards us poor Jews & if he emancipates us, he shall have my support."[123] For Nat, it was the Jewish issue alone which alienated the Rothschilds from Conservatism. As he wrote half-seriously in 1842:

> [Y]ou must know that altho' a staunch whig in England I am an ultra redhot conservative here, I fancy you wd adopt the latter way of thinking also if it were not that the little bit which has been removed from a part of the body, & which part Billy [Anthony] in particular has always considered of the greatest importance, prevented our exercising the same rights & privileges as others not in the same predicament.[124]

Altogether more Liberal in outlook, Anthony welcomed Peel's difficulties with his party in the Commons in the belief—correct as it turned out—that they would make him "a little more liberal & I trust that Sir Robert if he is so will do something for the poor Jews."[125] As for Lionel, he did not hesitate to lend his support to the Liberal candidate James Pattison at the October 1843 by-election in the City, urging Jewish voters to break the Sabbath in order to vote. These votes were crucial, as Pattison only narrowly beat his Tory opponent, who was none other than one of the Rothschilds' old rivals, Thomas Baring.[126]

Yet Lionel hesitated to follow David Salomons's example and involve himself directly in political activity. The most obvious explanation for this hesitation was purely practical: politics took up time which could not easily be spared by the senior partner of a bank as big as N. M. Rothschild & Sons. Perhaps Lionel shared James's view—expressed as early as 1816—that "as soon as a merchant takes too much part in public affairs it is difficult for him to carry on with his bankers' business."[127] On the other hand, the pressure from family members—including James—for him to do something to raise the family's political profile in England was considerable. James's notions of political activity remained rooted in his experience of the 1820s, when he and his elder brothers had energetically accumulated titles and decorations by ingratiating themselves with the monarchs of the various states with which they did business. He sought to encourage his nephews to do the same in England in 1838, telling Lionel that he had

> had a long conversation with the King of Belgium and he promised us that he will write to the Queen of England and he will arrange for his wife to write that you should all be invited to all the balls . . . The King has granted the four brothers [an] order . . . and if you, my dear nephews, are devotees of such ribbons then I will ensure that next time you will be the recipients, God willing, [though] in England these are not worn.[128]

Less old-fashioned was Anselm's hope "in a year or two to be able to congratulate one of you on a seat in Parliament & to admire your eloquent speeches."[129] When Isaac Lyon Goldsmid became the first Jewish baronet in 1841, Anthony wrote from Paris that he "should have liked Sir Lionel de R. much better & he ought to have tried."[130] Similarly, when Salomon was made a "citizen of honour" of Vienna in 1843, Anthony pointedly hoped that it would "produce an effect in Old England."[131]

The pressure mounted in 1845 as David Salomons scored another important point. Having won a contested City ballot for the aldermanry of Portsoken, Salomons was confronted with the oath "upon a true faith of a Christian"; when he refused to take it, the Court of Aldermen declared his election void. Salomons complained to Peel, who—as Anthony had predicted—now proved more sympathetic, instructing the Lord Chancellor, Lyndhurst, to draft a bill removing all remaining municipal disabilities as they affected Jews. The bill was enacted on July 31, 1845.[132] Lionel had in fact played a part in securing the passage of the act, having been one of the committee of five sent by the Board of Deputies to lobby Peel on the subject.[133] But Salomons got the glory, and it rankled with Lionel's competitive relatives. "I shall be glad to see [you] Ld M. of London & M.P. for the city," wrote his brother Nat. "You ought to be canvassing for the E[ast] Ind[ia Company] direction, my dear Lionel."[134] A year later, he was still harping on the same theme: "Our French fogies . . . all say you will soon be in the House of Commons & are preparing yourself."[135] When Salomons visited Paris shortly after his triumph, Hannah was frosty. "We must allow him," she wrote to Charlotte, "to enjoy the satisfaction of [the good cause's] success and ourselves fully to participate in the good which we so sincerely hope and trust may result to the community we belong to, from which I do not doubt individual merit and exertions will be duly appreciated."[136] Moses Montefiore's baronetcy in 1846 made Anthony hope that "perhaps when the Whigs come in . . . they will think they ought to give something to your Honour."[137] No sooner had Peel's government collapsed than Nat was urging his brother to "stand or state officially you will stand for the City," suggesting that he "engage some clever fellow to come & read with you in the evenings for an hour or so, to be a little more at home on the different questions of political economy."[138]

Nor was it only members of his own family who urged Lionel to be more politically active. In 1841 a political associate of the Irish leader Daniel O'Connell invited him "as one of the most influential of your honored nation" to attend a public meeting ("in Exeter Hall in the Anchor Tavern") at which he proposed to discuss "the political position of the Jews."[139] Two years later, he was being offered assistance on the assumption that he himself would want to contest the City of London by-election.[140]

Still Lionel remained reluctant. While others wasted no time in entering the breach made by Salomons—among them his brother Mayer, who became High Sheriff of Buckinghamshire in February[141]—Lionel did nothing. Even when he himself was offered a baronetcy by the new Prime Minister, Lord John Russell, he stubbornly refused to accept it—to the dismay of his relatives.[142] His stated reasons for doing so suggest that Lionel had a trait of petulance: he was reluctant to accept an honour which had already been bestowed on two other Jews, and would be content with nothing less than a peerage. Prince Albert reported him as saying: "[Y]ou have nothing higher to offer me?"[143] This was bluntness worthy of his father, but his mother Hannah was incensed:

> I do not think it good taste for you to refuse it, as your little friend [presumably Russell] remarks what [?more] can she bestow[?] The Peerage cannot be bestowed at present without taking the Oath and that I suppose you would not do. A Personal Compliment from the Highest Personage should be esteemed and may lead to other advantages but to repudiate it might create anger—and in accepting it you do not do away with your original Title. The Arms may be splendid. The previous granting to the other 2 gentlemen I think has nothing to do with yours—and decidedly does not reduce the Compliment—this is my opinion— excuse my candour.[144]

His brothers, any one of whom would have accepted, were baffled. As Nat cheerily wrote, "If I were you I would accept an English Baronetage, it's better than being a German Baron.—Old Billy thinks Sir Anthony would sound very well & if you do not wish it for yourself you might get it for him—We have all got very pretty names & Sir Mayer of Mentmore wd even shine in a romance."[145] James too weighed in:

> I wish you, my dear Lionel, a lot of luck that your nice Queen has, thank God, taken such a liking to you. Do be very careful that your Prince Albert does not become jealous of you. Meanwhile I would urge you to accept it for one must never reject [such an honour] and one must never let such an opportunity pass by. A Minister can easily be replaced. Previously I could have become anything over here whereas now it is virtually impossible.[146]

But Lionel was unmoved. In the end, the only way out of the impasse was for Anthony to accept the honour.[147] Even his final capitulation—when he agreed to stand as a Liberal candidate in the general election of 1847—was made only after "hesitation."[148]

Lionel's decision to stand for Parliament—he was adopted as a candidate by the Liberal London Registration Association on June 29, 1847—was a watershed in Rothschild history. As a result of his decision, the Rothschild name was to become inextricably linked to the campaign for Jewish political rights; he devoted much of the next decade to a succession of gruelling electoral and parliamentary battles. Why did this most reluctant of public figures do it, when he might easily have left the field to Salomons—or for that matter to Mayer, who simultaneously stood (against his eldest brother's wishes) in Hythe?[149] The obvious answer is that familial pressure finally proved irresistible. A second possibility is that he was talked into standing not by his own relations but by Lord John Russell, who was himself one of the sitting City MPs and who may have hoped to secure Jewish votes for himself. A third is that Lionel did not expect to win; that what ended up as a *cause célèbre* was intended to be a token gesture. One contemporary at least thought he would lose and that he had merely been drafted in by the Whigs to "pay the whole cost of their expenses."[150] And it is noteworthy that none of the other Jewish candidates was elected: it was a close contest, and the Whigs and Radicals would have had only a single-figure majority in the Commons had it not been for the Tory split.

The complex electoral politics of the Victorian City of London precluded confidence in victory. The constituency, which stretched as far east as Tower Hamlets, was a large one (nearly 50,000 votes were cast in 1847) which returned four MPs. On this occasion, there were nine candidates—four Liberals, one Peelite, three Protectionists and an independent—and the campaigning was intense, with around twelve public meetings in the space of a month. Lionel's platform was at first sight unremarkable: in addition to the obvious issue of religious "liberty of conscience," he declared himself in favour of free trade.[151] He evidently did not follow Nat's advice "to go a little farther than my Lord John" and "be as liberal as possible."[152] On closer inspection, he took stances which may even have counted against him: he argued for lower duties on tobacco and tea and the introduction of a property tax, a popular stance with the unenfranchised poor, but one which was hardly calculated to win over a propertied electorate. Despite an explicit offer of Catholic support from an enterprising priest named Lauch—which appears to have been accepted—Lionel declared himself against increasing the grant to the Maynooth Catholic college (though he hedged on the more general principle of state aid to denominational schools).[153] Nor were Jewish votes necessarily as important as might be thought: not many Jews were as yet qualified or registered to vote. Although Lionel received an offer of support from at least one Jewish Conservative and was assured by his mother that that "the Jews . . . will go up in a body all nicely dressed and vote for you,"[154] the Peelite Masterman still managed to secure election despite his declared opposition to emancipation.[155]

On the other hand, Lionel had two advantages. The press played a bigger role in London than in most parts of the country, and his contacts with newspapermen were rapidly developing. To be sure, a specifically Jewish press was in its infancy. In 1841 he and others had invested in Jacob Franklin's *Voice of Jacob*, though this was soon supplanted by the *Jewish Chronicle*.[156] But Lionel had a far more influential backer in the form of John Thadeus Delane, the twenty-nine-year-old editor of *The Times*, who was prevailed on to help him draft his election address. For his part, Delane believed he had secured Lionel's victory: he found Charlotte "in a state of almost frenzied delight and gratitude" after the result and was "overwhelmed with thanks" by Nat and Anthony.[157] The *Economist* also lent its support.[158] On the other hand, the opponents of emancipation had arguably just as influential a journalist on their side. The historian J. A. Froude recalled Thomas Carlyle remarking as they stood in front of 148 Piccadilly:

> I do not mean that I want King John back again, but if you ask me which mode of treating these people to have been the nearest to the will of the Almighty about them—to build them palaces like that, or to take the pincers for them, I declare for the pincers . . . "Now Sir, the State requires some of these millions you have heaped together with your financing work. You won't? Very well"—and the speaker gave a twist with his wrist—"Now will you[?]"—and another twist, till the millions were yielded.

Somewhat improbably, Carlyle claimed that Lionel had offered him generous remuneration if he would write a pamphlet in favour of the removal of disabilities. Carlyle supposedly told him "that it could not be . . . I observed too that I could not conceive why he and his friends, who were supposed to be looking out for the coming of Shiloh, should be seeking seats in a Gentile legislature." He expressed the same view in a letter to the MP Monckton Milnes: "A Jew is bad, but what is a Sham-Jew, a Quack-Jew? And how can a real Jew, by possibility, try to be a Senator, or even a Citizen of any country, except his own wretched Palestine, whither all his thoughts and steps and efforts tend?"[159] Carlyle's attitude stands in marked contrast to that of Thackeray, who underwent something of a conversion on the subject as a result of social contact with the Rothschilds.[160]

As the alleged approach to Carlyle suggests, the second and perhaps more important advantage Lionel enjoyed was money. According to Lord Grey, the Whig Secretary for War, he made "no secret of his determination to carry his election by money."[161] Nat's subsequent letters from Paris suggest that his brother had indeed "cashed up" "large sums."[162] In the end, this may well have turned the scale. Lionel was elected third in the poll with 6,792 votes, compared with Russell's 7,137, Pattison's 7,030 and Masterman's 6,772, which beat the other Liberal, Larpent, by just three votes. His Catholic agent Lauch believed that he had saved the day for Lionel; and his motives for supporting a Rothschild were nakedly mercenary.[163]

To the rest of the family, this was the political victory they had so long thirsted for. It was, wrote Nat, "one of the greatest triumphs for the Family as well as of the greatest advantage to the poor Jews in Germany and all over the world."[164] His wife called it "the beginning of a new era for the Jewish nation, having a most distinguished champion like you."[165] "The breach has been made," exulted Betty, "the obstacle of imputation, prejudice and intolerance is distinctly foundering."[166] Congratulations even came from Metternich (who perhaps failed to see it as a victory for that liberalism which would drive him into English exile less than a year later).[167] Yet all this euphoria overlooked the fact that, if he wished to take his seat as an MP,

Lionel would still have to swear the oath "upon the true faith of the Christian"—unless, of course, the government could pass the measure which it had proved impossible to pass eleven years before, namely a bill doing away with the oath. Russell had already pledged to introduce one.[168] In truth, Lionel's victory would be complete only once a majority of both Houses of Parliament had voted in favour of such a measure.

Disraeli

The issue raised by Lionel's election divided the British political elite along fascinating and far from predictable lines. Not the least unexpected development was that Russell's bill to remove parliamentary disabilities attracted support not only from his own side of the House, but also from both factions of the divided Tories. When he introduced the bill in December 1847, the arch-Peelite Gladstone and the Protectionist leaders Lord George Bentinck and Disraeli all spoke in favour. Of these, Disraeli was the most personally interested, though his motivations and conduct were more complicated than might be imagined.

Disraeli had by now known the Rothschilds for nearly a decade. His earliest recorded social encounters with the family had been in 1838, and the acquaintance had become good enough to guarantee Disraeli a friendly reception when he visited Paris in 1842.[169] By 1844–5, he and his wife Mary Anne were dining with the Rothschilds frequently: in May 1844, twice in June 1845 and again later that summer at Brighton.[170] By 1846, Lionel was helping Disraeli speculate in French railways and later assisted him with his tangle of debts (in excess of £5,000 at this time). There was more to this friendship than his appreciation of their money and their appreciation of his wit, however. This was Disraeli's most creative period as a novelist: *Coningsby, or, The New Generation* was published in 1844, *Sybil, or, The Two Nations* in 1845 and *Tancred, or, The New Crusade* in 1847. The contribution to these works made by his relationships with the Rothschilds is widely acknowledged, but still underestimated.

Having been baptised in large part because his father Isaac had fallen out with his synagogue and fancied himself as a country gentlemen, Disraeli remained fascinated by Judaism all his life. His enemies sought to use his origins against him; but Disraeli boldly turned what others saw as a weakness into a strength. Particularly in the fiction of the 1840s, he set out to reconcile what he regarded as his "racial" Jewishness with his Christian beliefs, arguing in effect that he enjoyed the best of both worlds. There is no question that contact with the Rothschilds had a substantial influence on his characterisation of Judaism. Lionel and Charlotte were unquestionably an attractive couple, he rich and influential, she intelligent and beautiful; but it was their Jewishness which most fascinated Disraeli—and indeed his wife. What made them doubly attractive to the childless Disraelis was their brood of five. They were, Disraeli wrote (inviting them to Grosvenor Gate to watch a parade in Hyde Park in June 1845), "beauteous children."

Three months later, the family had a bizarre visit from a hysterical Mary Anne, who flung herself into Charlotte's arms. After a preamble to the effect that she and Disraeli were in a state of exhaustion ("I have been so busy correcting proofsheets, the publishers are so tiresome . . . poor Dis' has been sitting up the whole night writing") and were therefore about to depart for Paris, Mary Anne astonished Charlotte by announcing that she wished to make her six-year-old daughter Evelina the sole beneficiary of her will:

> Mrs Disraeli heaved a deep sigh and said: "This is a farewell visit, I may never see you again—life is so uncertain . . . Disi and I may be blown up on the railroad or the steamer, there is not a human body that loves me in the world, and besides my adored husband I care for no one on earth, but *I* love your glorious race . . ."
>
> . . . I tried to calm and quiet my visitor [Charlotte wrote], who, after having enumerated her goods and chattels to me, took a paper out of her pocket saying: "This is my Will and you must read it, show it to the dear Baron, and take care of it for me."

When Charlotte gently told her that she "could not accept such a great responsibility," Mary Anne opened the paper and read it aloud: "'In the event of my beloved Husband preceding me to the grave, I leave and bequeath to Evelina de Rothschild all my personal property.' . . . 'I love the Jews [she went on]—I have attached myself to your children and she is my favourite, she shall, she must wear the butterfly [one of Mary Anne's jewels].'"

The will was returned the next morning after "a scene, a very disagreeble one," presumably between Disraeli and his wife.[171] Yet the couple's interest in the family showed no sign of waning. When Leo was born in 1845, Disraeli expressed the hope (in a letter from Paris) that "he will prove worthy of his pure and sacred race, and of his beautiful brothers and sisters." "My dear," exclaimed Mary Anne on seeing the child, "that beautiful baby may be the future Messiah whom we are led to expect—who knows? And you will be the most favoured of women."[172]

There was always an undertone of frustrated attraction in Charlotte's relationship with Disraeli, as well as a jealous impatience with his wife Mary Anne. It was an attraction Disraeli did not deny. "Amid the struggles of my life," he told her in March 1867, "the sympathy of those we love is balm, and there is no one I love more than you."[173] There is some reason to think that this was more than Disraelian hyperbole. On one occasion when Charlotte called on the Disraelis, there was evidently some kind of scene involving Mary Anne; Disraeli hastened to apologise (writing "in Cabinet"):

> I think . . . though I deeply regret the inconvenience to which you were subjected, that it was, on the whole, better you did not meet yesterday, for, from protracted want of sleep & other causes, she was in a state of great excitement, so that I myself never see her in the evening now.
>
> She . . . sends you many loves . . . I wd. also send you my love, but I gave it you long ago.[174]

The oddity about all this was Mary Anne's highly demonstrative affection for Charlotte—perhaps a way of over-compensating for any jealousy she may have felt. When Mrs Disraeli was ill in 1869, "She murmured to me to write to you," Disraeli scribbled in a note to Charlotte. The Rothschilds responded by sending the invalid delicacies from the Piccadilly kitchens.[175] (After Mary Anne's death, however, it was Charlotte's turn to feel jealous as Disraeli spent increasing amounts of time "at the feet of Lady B[radford]."[176] She responded by sending him "six large baskets of English strawberries, 200 head of gigantic Parisian *asperges*, and the largest and finest Strasburg *foie gras* that ever was seen," a none too subtle reminder that her resources would always exceed those of the "wealthy old lady.")[177]

But perhaps the most singular aspect of their relationship is its religious ambiguity. As Charlotte recalled, Disraeli's attitude to his own Jewish roots was always ambivalent. "Never shall I forget," she wrote in 1866, "Mr. Disraeli's look of blank astonishment when I ventured to assert that through the Montefiores, Mocattas and Lindos, Lady [Louisa] de R[othschild] had the great and delightful honor of being his cousin; but heaven descended is what Mr. Disraeli affects to be, though London is full of his relations, whose existence he completely ignores."[178] Yet the two found a good deal of common ground when they discussed religious questions. In 1863 he sent her a copy of Ernest Renan's newly published and hugely contentious *Life of Jesus*. She found Renan's attempt to demythologise Christ "delightful," though she had reservations about its portrayal of his Jewish background:

> It reads like a beautiful poem written by an ardent poet inspired to reveal the truth, to reveal it with tenderness, with reverence & with glowing zeal. For enlightened Jews there will not[,] I believe, be any novelty of appreciation in the book as regards the principal figure[,] the great founder of Christianity, of the religion which has ruled the world these eighteen hundred years; but many of our co-religionists will be deeply pained at having been painted by Renan in colours so stark & so repelling. When prejudices are believed to be waning it is doubly disturbing to see a long persecuted nation held up to the scorn of calm readers & earnest thinkers as incorrigibly sordid, cold, cunning and— even stubborn, hard-hearted & narrow-minded. A great writer apparently so fair & just, in the communication of his opinions—whose judgement is so correct, whose feelings seem so pure & noble, should not have condescended to heighten the dazzling brilliance of his great picture by introducing such deep shadows—as if he had felt it required to calumniate the Jews in order to atone to the religious world for the liberties taken with the greatest & highest of all subjects of human interest.[179]

Ten years later, Disraeli thanked her for sending him a copy of her *Addresses*. "I have read your little volume with sympathy and admiration," he wrote, "the tone of tenderness which pervades the Addresses and their devout and elevated feelings must touch the hearts of all of every creed. I had the gratification to read one aloud last evening (on the holiness of the Sabbath). Its piety & eloquence deeply touched my auditors . . ."[180]

Disraeli's novels need to be read in the light of all this. In *Coningsby*, the character of Sidonia is, as Lord Blake has said, a cross between Lionel and Disraeli himself.[181] To be more precise, he has Lionel's background, profession, religion, temperament and perhaps even looks ("pale, with an impressive brow, and dark eyes of great intelligence"), though his political and philosophical views are Disraeli's. Thus we are told that his father had made money in the Peninsular War, then "resolved to emigrate to England, with which he had in the course of years, formed considerable commercial connections. He arrived here after the peace of Paris, with his large capital. He staked all on the Waterloo loan; and the event made him one of the greatest capitalists in Europe." After the war, he and his brothers lent their money to the European states—"France wanted some; Austria more; Prussia a little; Russia a few millions"—and he "became lord and master of the money-market of the world." The younger Sidonia has all the skills of a banker: he is an accomplished mathematician and "possessed a complete mastery over the principal European languages," skills honed by travels to Germany, Paris and Naples. He is formidably dispassionate, a quality detailed at considerable length (for example, "he shrank from sensibility, and often took refuge in sarcasm"). We are even told that "his devotion to field-sports . . . was the safety valve of his energy," and are treated to a detailed description of what can only be one of the Rothschild hotels in Paris. Interestingly, Sidonia is also the hero's rival in love: he wrongly suspects his beloved Edith of being the object of Sidonia's desires, though it transpires that the cold-hearted Sidonia is himself the object of another's unrequited love.

In this context, the most intriguing passages in *Coningsby* are those which deal with Sidonia's religion. We are told early on that he is "of that faith that the Apostles professed before they followed their master" and later that he is "as firm in his adherence to the code of the great Legislator as if the trumpet still sounded on Sinai." He was "proud of his origin, and confident in the future of his kind." In one important respect, Sidonia is more Disraeli than Lionel, as he is said to be descended from Spanish Marranos—Sephardic Jews who had outwardly conformed as Catholics while remaining Jews in secret—and Disraeli liked to fantasise that his own family were Sephardi. But much of the rest is manifestly Rothschild-inspired. Thus as a young man Sidonia is "shut out from universities and schools, those universities and schools which were indebted for their first knowledge of ancient philosophy to the learning and enterprise of his ancestors." In addition, "his religion walled him out from the pursuits of a citizen." Yet "no earthly considerations would ever induce him to impair that purity of race on which he prides himself" by marrying a Gentile. It is only when Sidonia's views on his "race" are expounded that Disraeli takes over from Lionel:

> The Hebrew is an unmixed race . . . An unmixed race of a first rate organisation are the aristocracy of Nature . . . In his comprehensive travels, Sidonia had visited and examined the Hebrew communities of the world. He had found in general, the lower orders debased; the superior immersed in sordid pursuits; but he perceived that the intellectual development was not impaired. This gave him hope. He was persuaded that organisation would outlive persecution. When he reflected on what they had endured, it was only marvellous the race had not disappeared . . . In spite of centuries, of tens of centuries of degradation, the Jewish mind exercises a vast influence on the affairs of Europe. I speak not of their laws, which you still obey; of their literature, with which your minds are saturated; but of the living Hebrew intellect.

Yet even here the Rothschild influence is detectable. When Disraeli seeks to illustrate his point about the extent of Jewish influence, he draws with extraordinary directness from recent Rothschild history when he has Sidonia say:

> "I told you just now that I was going up to town tomorrow, because I [have] always made it a rule to interpose when affairs of State were on the carpet. Otherwise, I never interfere. I read of peace and war in news-

papers, but I am never alarmed, except when I am informed that the Sovereigns want more treasure . . .

"A few years back we were applied to by Russia. Now, there has been no friendship between the Court of St Petersburgh and my family. It has Dutch connections, which have generally supplied it; and our representations in favour of the Polish Hebrews, a numerous race, but the most suffering and degraded of all the tribes, have not been very agreeable to the Czar. However, circumstances drew to an approximation between the Romanoffs. I resolved to go myself to St Petersburgh. I had, on my arrival, an interview with the Russian Minister of Finance Count Cancrin; I beheld the son of a Lithuanian Jew. The loan was connected with the affairs of Spain; I resolved on repairing to Spain from Russia. I had an audience immediately on my arrival with the Spanish Minister, Senor Mendizabel [*sic*]; I beheld one like myself, the son of a Nuevo Christiano, a Jew of Arragon. In consequence of what transpired at Madrid, I went straight to Paris to consult the President of the French Council; I beheld the son of a French Jew [presumably Soult].

". . . So you see my dear Coningsby, that the world is governed by very different personages from what is imagined by those who are not behind the scenes."

Leaving aside the Disraelian fantasy that these eminent figures were themselves Jewish, this is unmistakably Rothschildian in inspiration.

There is even a pointed and very topical allusion to the Jews being politically "arrayed in the same ranks as the leveller and the latitudinarian, and prepared to support the policy which may even endanger his life and property, rather than tamely continue under a system which seeks to degrade him. The Tories lose an important election at a critical moment; 'tis the Jews come forward to vote against them . . . Yet the Jews, Coningsby, are essentially Tories. Toryism, indeed, is but copied from the mighty prototype which has fashioned Europe."[182] It is easy to see why Hannah enjoyed the book. As she wrote to Charlotte, "in dwelling upon the good qualities of Sidonia's race; in using many arguments for their emancipation he cleverly introduced many circumstances we might recognise and the character was finely drawn . . . I have written a note to him expressing our admiration of his spiritual production."[183]

If *Coningsby* contains a coded dedication to Lionel, then *Tancred* has one to his wife. The scene in London is once again set with copious Rothschild allusions. We pay a visit to "Sequin Court," as well as to Sidonia's lavishly decorated house. There are topical allusions to Sidonia's efforts to acquire a French railway called "The Great Northern." Once again, Sidonia is a mouthpiece for Disraelian theory—which now sought to redefine Christianity as essentially a variant or development of Judaism:

"I believe [Sidonia declares] that God spoke to Moses on Mount Horeb, and you believe that he was crucified, in the person of Jesus on Mount Calvary. Both were, at least carnally, children of Israel: they spoke Hebrew to the Hebrews. The prophets were only Hebrews; the apostles were only Hebrews. The churches of Asia, which have vanished, were founded by a native Hebrew; and the church of Rome, which says it shall last for ever, and which converted this island to the faith of Moses and of Christ . . . was also founded by a native Hebrew."

It is the character of Eva, however, who makes the boldest pronouncements along these lines. As a Syrian-Jewish princess, of course, she bears little superficial resemblance to Charlotte; however, the description of her physiognomy suggests that she provided Disraeli with some kind of model. In the same way, though it seems improbable that Charlotte's views bore any resemblance to Eva's, we should not rule it out. She has, for example, a Rothschildian aversion to the idea of mixed marriage and conversion. "The Hebrews have never blended with their conquerors," she exclaims and later: "No; I will never become a Christian!" Similarly, Disraeli's pet theme—the common origins of Judaism and Christianity—has its echoes in her own writings. "Are you of those Franks who worship a Jewess," asks Eva when she meets Tancred for the first time (in an oasis in the Holy Land), "or of those others who revile her . . ?" Jesus, she reminds him, "was a great man, but he was a Jew; and you worship him." So: "Half of Christendom worships a Jewess, and the other half a Jew." Another Rothschildian passage has Eva ask Tancred:

> "Which is the greatest city in Europe?"
> "Without doubt, the capital of my country London."
> . . . "How rich the most honoured man must be there! Tell me, is he a Christian?"
> "I believe he is one of your race and faith."
> "And in Paris; who is the richest man in Paris?"
> "The brother, I believe, of the richest man in London."
> "I know all about Vienna," said the lady, smiling, "Caesar makes my countrymen barons of the empire, and rightly, for it would fall to pieces in a week without their support."

Where Disraeli left Charlotte behind was in his contrived (and to contemporaries outrageous) argument that, in "supply[ing] the victim and the immolators" at the crucifixion of Christ, the Jews had "fulfilled the beneficent intention" of God and "saved the human race."[184] Nor would she have accepted his argument (in *Sybil*) that "Christianity is completed Judaism, or it is nothing . . . Judaism is incomplete without Christianity."[185]

The arguments outlined in his fiction informed Disraeli's attitude to Russell's disabilities bill. He was prepared to support the bill, but on Tory terms, telling Lionel, Anthony and their wives two weeks before the first debate that "we must ask for our rights and privileges not for concessions and liberty of conscience." This disconcerted the Liberals round the table: Louisa described Disraeli as talking in "his strange, Tancredian vein" and "wonder[ed] if he will have the courage to speak to the House in the same manner."[186] He did;[187] and Charlotte was initially enthusiastic: "It was not possible," she told Delane in March 1848, "to express oneself with greater intelligence . . . power, wit or originality than our friend, Disraeli."[188]

Parliament and Peers

The problem for Disraeli was that what sold as fiction was well-nigh disastrous as practical politics. Less than a year before, he and the Protectionist leader Bentinck had divided their party and ousted Peel as Tory leader; yet in supporting Russell's bill they were risking yet another split between the front and back benches. Neither of them initially appears to have anticipated the extent of the trouble they were letting themselves in for. Bentinck was especially insouciant, telling Croker in September 1847:

> I have always, I believe, voted in favour of the Jews. I say I believe, because I never could work myself into caring two straws about the question one way or the other, and scarcely know how I may have voted, viewing it quite differently from the Roman Catholic question, which I have ever considered a great national concernment . . . The Jew matter I look upon as a personal matter, as I would a great private estate or a Divorce Bill . . . [L]ike the questions affecting the Roman Catholics, with the Protectionist party it should remain an open question. I shall probably give a silent vote, maintaining my own consistency in favour of the Jews, but not offending the larger portion of the party, who, I presume, will be the other way. Disraeli, of course, will warmly support the Jews, first from hereditary prepossession in their favour, and next because he and the Rothschilds are great allies . . . The Rothschilds all stand high in private character, and the city of London having elected Lionel Rothschild one of her representatives, it is such a pronunciation of public opinion that I do not think the party, as a party, would do themselves any good by taking up the question against the Jews.[189]

As for Disraeli, he confidently assured Bentinck and John Manners on November 16 that "the peril is not so imminent . . . & the battle will not be fought until next year."[190]

Both were much too sanguine. In fact only two other Protectionists joined them in voting for the bill (Milnes Gaskell and—probably from a conversionist standpoint—Thomas Baring). No fewer than 138, led by diehards like Sir Robert Inglis, voted against, plunging the party into fresh turmoil. "Must I . . . cheer Disraeli when he declares that there is no difference between those who crucified Christ and those who kneel before Christ crucified?" Augustus Stafford demanded to know. Bentinck resigned, leaving the leadership of what he now called "the No Popery, No Jew Party" in the hands of Lord Stanley.[191] It is understandable that Disraeli thereafter sought to tone down his views when the matter was debated in the Commons: the remarkable thing is that a man so widely regarded at the time and since as "conscience-less" (Dickens's phrase) did not quietly drop his support for emancipation altogether. The frequent criticisms of his conduct—especially by Charlotte and Louisa—were unfair; for Disraeli continued to vote and occasionally speak on the same side he had taken in 1847.[192] The uncharitable view would of course be that his financial dependence on Lionel at this period precluded a U-turn; that was what Charlotte suspected. In May 1848 she had another embarrassing scene with Mary Anne, who claimed that Lionel was not replying to Disraeli's letters. One of these revealed "that her husband was still deeply in debt and was being hounded terribly by the money-lenders and implored my husband for help and support."[193] After yet another confrontation between the two women, Lionel resolved to lend Disraeli a further £1,000.[194]

There was division within the Peelite camp too. When Russell introduced his bill in December 1847, another who spoke in favour was Peel's austere High Church protégé Gladstone, who had earlier been an opponent of Jewish emancipation. Although he found the decision "painful" (and confided to his dairy the thought that it might force him to leave Parliament), Gladstone's logic was typically rigorous: having admitted Catholics, Quakers, Moravians, Separatists and Unitarians to the Commons and having admitted Jews to local government, to maintain the effective prohibition on Jewish MPs would be inconsistent.[195] Peel himself spoke in favour during a later debate in February 1848, and nine other supporters joined him in the "ayes." But their colleague Goulburn—formerly Peel's Chancellor—spoke against, seeing the election of an ineligible candidate as a revolutionary challenge to Parliament; and forty other Peelites voted with him. On the second reading, the Peelites split again, 29 for and 43 against.[196] The Tory and Peelite opposition did not suffice, however, to stop Russell's bill: it was initially approved prior to its first reading by a majority of 67; secured a second reading by a majority of 73; and a third reading by 61 votes.

But it was in the Lords that support was wanting. A few Whigs expressed their support after relatively gentle persuasion. Unlike a bank such as Coutts, however, the Rothschilds had relatively few aristocratic debtors—Lady Ailesbury was a rare exception[197]—and so their leverage in this quarter was limited. Whig grandees like the Duke of Devonshire and the Marquess of Lansdowne could be counted on, while the Marquess of Londonderry was won over by early 1848; but the Earl of Orford had told Hannah when she met him at the Duke of Bedford's that he was opposed (though he assured her Lionel would "gain" in the end).[198] Lord Ashley, the future Earl of Shaftesbury—responsible for some of the most important social legislation of the period—was another opponent. And among the bishops there was predictably dogged resistance. When Russell's bill was debated in May 1848, it was strongly opposed by Wilberforce, Bishop of Oxford, and he was joined by the Archbishops of Canterbury and Armagh and sixteen bishops. Only the Archbishop of York and four Whiggish bishops voted in favour. With Lionel, Anthony, Mayer, Hannah and her sister Judith Montefiore watching from the gallery, the measure was rejected by a majority of 35.[199]

Charlotte's diary gives a vivid account of the impact of the debate and result on the family. She and Louisa were still waiting for their husbands to return from Westminster when, at 3.30 a.m.:

> the men came into the room, Lionel with a smiling face—he always has so much firmness and self-control—Anthony and Mayer crimson in the face . . . they said the speeches were scandalous and I was advised not to read a word of them. I went to sleep at 5 and woke again at 6; I had dreamt that a huge vampire was greedily sucking my blood . . . Apparently, when the result of the vote was declared, a loud, enthusiastic roar of approval resounded . . . throughout the House. Surely we do not deserve so much hatred. I spent all day Friday weeping and sobbing out of over-excitement.[200]

Some idea of the flavour of the temporal lords' arguments against emancipation can be found in the letters written on the subject by the Queen's uncle, the Duke of Cumberland—now King of Hanover. In part, he shared the episcopal view that "the idea of admitting persons who deny the existence of our Saviour" was "horrible." But his anxieties were partly social in nature, predicting that "the whole of the riches of the country would by degrees come into the hands of the Jews, manufacturers

and calico-makers," and citing the example of Amschel's entertainments in Frankfurt to illustrate Jewish social pretensions.[201] He knew whereof he spoke, having dined at Hannah's just a few years before.[202] There was not a great deal to choose between this two-faced snobbery and the crude caricatures published on the subject during the period. *One of the benefits of the Jewish emancipation* depicted an old clothes-dealer bringing home a sucking pig to his wife and exclaiming: "Dare mine dear, see vot I've pought you! tanks to de Paron Roast-child & de Pill" (see illustration 1.ii).

Consequently, Lionel seems to have resolved to adopt a method which the older generation of Rothschilds had used to great effect (for rather less lofty purposes) in the 1820s and 1830s. On December 23, 1846, Nat wrote to his brother in terms which are unambiguous:

> I regret much to observe that you think it necessary to use certain means to secure some votes in the House of Lords which are not peculiarly commendable, I must say I should have preferred to have seen it otherwise, after the late *procès de corruption* which we witnessed here one fights rather shy of being party to anything of the sort. To come however to the point, on this occasion our worthy uncle & yr humble servant are of opinion that we must not be too scrupulous and if it be necessary to ensure the success of the measure we must not mind a sacrifice—We can not fix the *amount*, you must know better how much is required than we do, I hope that as you say half the sum demanded will

suffice, at all events our good Uncle has authorised me to write that he will take it upon himself to satisfy all the Family that whatever you do is for the best and that you may put down the *sum* to the house—of course you will not cash up until the bill passes the Lords, and you must not make any bargain or care about who gets it—The thing is this in our opinion, you place so much at the disposal of the individual in question upon the bill passing and you know nothing more about it—I wd not give money to support a petition nor for any other purpose that does not intimately concern us—all we have to do is to give the money in the event of the case being won to the lucky jockey—I think you can not be sufficiently cautious in managing this job & I therefore do not see how you can propose a subscription to yr friends—On what plea? & what do you suppose they will give? if merely a trifle it will not be worth while, if on the other hand they will cash up & not ask for particulars of course I wd take their money as they are as much benefited as ourselves.[203]

In short, Lionel was proposing to buy votes in the Upper House. Still more striking is the revelation that he sought to win the support of Prince Albert (whose influence in the Lords was considerable) in a similar fashion. Of course, Albert was probably already sympathetic. Lionel had been in touch with him from the moment he embarked on his political career in 1847, and by 1848 Nat was able to record his "delight . . . that Prince Albert is so favourably disposed towards you and that he will support our bills." But he also advised Lionel to "pay him now & then a visit & coax him a little." "You should now work the court party," he wrote on February 14, "get yr. friend P. A. [Prince Albert] to use his influence and then perhaps [the bill] will go thro'."[204] What this meant in practice is one of the most intriguing, but hitherto overlooked, episodes in the emancipation story.

By this time the Rothschilds' early links to Prince Albert—in their capacity as postmen to the European elite—had developed into more serious financial dealings. In 1842, for example, James invested 100,000 francs in Nord shares for Albert's adviser Baron Stockmar.[205] Three years later, when Albert was planning a trip to Coburg to discuss financial matters with his brother, Stockmar relayed Lionel's request "that the house of Rothschild might have the honour to act as banker in Germany for any financial requirement which Your Majesty might have on this journey."[206] In 1847 the Rothschilds gave Albert's impecunious Bavarian relative Prince Ludwig von Oettingen-Wallerstein a £3,000 loan which Albert personally guaranteed; he thus became the debtor when Prince Oettingen defaulted after a year, leaving only an unsaleable art collection as security.[207] This explains why Nat expected his brother to "cash up" in order to be sure of Albert's support, though he and his uncle became vehemently opposed—on financial grounds—to making any payment after the outbreak of the revolution in Paris.[208] In May, Albert summoned Anthony to the Palace to "request a loan for his brother the duke of Coblenz [should be Coburg] and [for himself?] a loan of [£]13 or 12,000" (later raised to £15,000).[209] Nat made his opposition abundantly clear:

[Y]ou ask my advice respecting a loan of £15/ [thousand] to P. A. [Prince Albert]. I think there is not the slightest reason to consent to it, you will find yourselves in the same position with regard to him as we are with L. P. [Louis Philippe]—If I do not mistake my dear Brother he already owes you £5,000 which we paid here to the Bavarian minister [Prince Oettingen], I really do not think you are authorised to advance so large a sum considering the state of things & you should in my opinion tell him so—There is not the slightest reason to make compliments with him & I am convinced that whether you give the cash or not it will not make the slightest difference in the fate of the Jews bill—I can only repeat that I am decidedly against the advance & under the present circumstances I do not think you are authorised to consenting to it.[210]

It is not clear whether Lionel deferred to his brother's wishes. We know that Albert bought the lease of Balmoral Castle and its 10,000 acres for £2,000 just ten days after Nat wrote his letter; but there is no indication in the Royal Archives of Rothschild involvement in this.[211] On the other hand, Lionel did see Albert and Stockmar at Windsor in January 1849.[212] And it is suggestive that in July 1850— just eleven days before Lionel's famous attempt to take his seat by swearing a modified oath on the Old Testament—he contributed £50,000 to subsidise Albert's pet but chronically under-funded project for a Great Exhibition of the "Industry of All Nations."[213] Three years later, it was apparently pressure from "the Court"—that is, Albert and Stockmar—which induced Lord Aberdeen to drop his opposition to emancipation in order to form a coalition between Peelites and Whigs.[214] The evidence is circumstantial, but it does not seem unreasonable to infer that something had indeed been done to "get . . . P.A. to use his influence."

Yet whatever Lionel attempted in this direction proved insufficient: it was probably never realistic to imagine that opposition in the Lords could be overcome by paying sweeteners to the "court party." As Russell rather acerbically put it, "You have such an abominable habit of assigning to anything a money value that you seem to think even principles may be purchased. Now throughout this country the parties hostile to your Bill all are [a] great section of the High Church Party and the Low Church Party to a man. Now get one of their organs to fight your battle if you can, for their opposition is a conscientious one."[215] Persuasion, the Prime Minister argued, rather than bribery was the only way forward. Although another bill was brought forward by Russell in the summer of 1849 and approved in the Commons, it was once again (as he had foreseen) thrown out by the Lords by 95 votes to 25.[216]

This prompted Lionel finally to "accept the stewardship of the Chiltern Hundreds"—to force a by-election in the City—a move he announced in a statement "To the Electors of the City of London," published in *The Times:* "The contest is now between the House of Lords and yourselves. They attempt to retain the last remnant of religious intolerance; you desire to remove it . . . I believe that you are prepared to maintain the great constitutional struggle that is before you."[217] His more radical friends—notably the MPs J. Abel Smith and John Roebuck—had in fact urged him to force a by-election when the first Russell bill had been rejected over a year before; so the move itself was not unexpected.[218] It was the confrontational language of Lionel's address which provoked the "storm" of criticism described by Charlotte.[219]

To understand why this was, it is important to bear in mind the broader European context in which these events took place. On January 1, 1848, Alphonse had written to Lionel to express the hope that the New Year would witness "the triumph of religious equality over the [rotten?] principles of superstition and intolerance."[220]

Needless to say, it witnessed a good deal more than that. But although the 1848 revolution did give Jews in some European states legal equality (if only temporarily),[221] its net effect on the campaign for emancipation in Britain was probably negative. As the letters which arrived from Paris, Frankfurt and Vienna indicated, the revolution precipitated isolated but alarming outbreaks of popular anti-Jewish violence, for example in parts of rural Germany and in Hungary.[222] At the same time, however, many of the more radical liberals who considered themselves the leaders of the revolution were themselves Jews—hence Mayer Carl's view that "the Jews themselves provoke anti-Semitism."[223] The association of the emancipation issue with the continental revolution was therefore doubly damaging. Lionel's address suggested to many of his Whig and Tory supporters that the Rothschilds too were throwing in their lot with radicalism—even Chartism—at the very moment when the radicals were denouncing the Rothschilds for financing the defeat of the Hungarian revolution![224]

Whatever reservations he may have awoken among his supporters, Lionel's ploy worked as an electoral gambit. He trounced his Tory opponent, Lord John Manners—who seems to have been persuaded to stand as a token gesture[225]—by 6,017 votes to 2,814.[226] Having thrown in his lot with the radicals, however, Lionel now had little alternative but to follow their next piece of tactical advice: to present himself at the Commons to claim his seat. This was essentially to follow the examples of the Catholic O'Connell and the Quaker Pease and represented Lionel's most confrontational step yet; Peel explicitly warned him against it. Small wonder he hesitated, spending fully a year trying to persuade Russell to bring in another bill. But at a crowded and boisterous meeting of City Liberals in the London Tavern on July 25, 1850, he publicly attacked the government for failing to "carry on measures of reform and improvement" and "to further the cause of civil and religious liberty."[227] At 12.20 the next day, following the resolution passed unanimously at that meeting, he appeared before the table of a rowdy House of Commons and, in answer to the Clerk's question whether he desired to subscribe the Protestant or Catholic oath, replied: "I desire to be sworn upon the Old Testament." As the Tory diehard Sir Robert Inglis rose to protest, the Speaker directed Lionel to withdraw and there followed a debate, primarily concerned with procedure.[228] After the weekend, it was decided to ask Lionel directly why he wished to be sworn on the Old Testament, to which he replied: "Because that is the form of swearing which I declare to be most binding upon my conscience." He was once again asked to withdraw and, after a densely argued debate, it was agreed (by 113 votes to 59) that he should be allowed to do as he requested.[229] The next day (July 30), Lionel again appeared and was duly offered the Old Testament. The oaths of allegiance and supremacy were administered, but when the clerk reached the words "upon the true faith of a Christian":

> The baron then paused, and after a second or two said: "I omit these words, as not binding upon my conscience." He then placed his hat upon his head, kissed the Old Testament, and added, "So help me, God." This act was followed by loud cheers from the Liberal side of the house. He also took up his pen, with the object, we presume, of signing his name to the Parliamentary test-roll; but Sir F[rederick] Thesiger rose and much excitement prevailed on all sides, in the midst of which the

Speaker said the hon. member must withdraw. (Loud cries of "No, no"; "Take your seat"; "Chair" and "Order.") The baron, however, withdrew.[230]

Though anti-climactic, this was probably a wise decision. Granted, it amounted to another defeat. When the debate resumed on August 5, a government resolution was passed that Lionel could not take his seat unless he swore the abjuration oath in full, and it was nearly a year before the government could introduce a bill designed to amend the oath as required.[231] But when David Salomons sought to force the pace following his victory in a by-election at Greenwich, he was no more successful and cut a rather less dignified figure. Having taken his seat without having sworn the three oaths in full, Salomons was ordered by the Speaker to withdraw, but refused; when a motion was passed requiring him to withdraw, he still refused and indeed spoke and voted against it; and only finally left the House when the Speaker asked the Serjeant-at-Arms to remove him.[232] The net result was the same: as a further vote confirmed, neither he nor Lionel could take their seats until they swore the abjuration oath. Salomons's only achievement was an act of June 1852 which did away with the archaic penalties which might in theory have been inflicted on him for his unlawful conduct following a successful court action against him.[233] The electorate seemed to deliver their verdict on his tactics when he was defeated resoundingly in the 1852 general election; Lionel, by contrast, won again.[234] The waiting game resumed, for it soon became apparent that emancipation remained as divisive in the Commons and as unpalatable in the Lords as ever. *De facto*, Lionel acted as a kind of seatless MP, lobbying from outside the chamber when issues affecting Jews arose in Parliament (for example, state funding of Jewish schools in 1851–2 or the exemption of rabbinical divorces from the jurisdiction of the civil Divorce Court in 1857).[235] But *de iure* there was deadlock. Yet another bill was defeated in the Lords; and in 1855 there was even an ingenious attempt by the Rothschilds' old foe Thomas Duncombe to force another City by-election on the ground that by floating the government's Crimean War loan Lionel had "entered into a contract for the public service."[236]

"A Real Triumph"

It was not until after the 1857 election—which saw Lionel once again returned for the City, this time ahead of Russell, who had quarrelled with the Liberal caucus—that battle was rejoined in parliament. With a comfortable majority behind him, Palmerston felt it was "due to the City of London with reference to the election of Baron Lionel de Rothschild, to give Parliament early in this session an opportunity of again considering the question of admission of Jews, and that such a proposal would have the best chance of success by being proposed by the Government."[237] A bill was duly introduced on May 15 and gained a resounding majority of 123 on its third reading. To the satisfaction of its proponents a number of senior Tories now signalled a change of heart, notably Sir John Pakington, Sir Fitzroy Kelly and most important Lord Stanley, the son of the Earl of Derby, the party leader.[238] In the Lords too the new Bishop of London expressed support; and altogether 139 members of the Upper House voted in favour. Yet once again—to Lionel's disappointment—they were in the minority. When the government shrank from overruling the Lords by a unilateral resolution, instead introducing a new Oaths Validity Act Amendment Bill, Lionel decided once again to resign his seat and fight a by-election on the issue. He was returned unopposed, having launched another strong attack on "the men who went but very seldom among the people, who knew not the wishes of the people, and who, in fact, attended to very little but their own pleasure and amusement."[239]

It was not this renewed appeal to people versus peers which finally broke the deadlock, however, but—paradoxically—the advent of a minority Conservative government. For now Disraeli, as Chancellor of the Exchequer and leader of the party in the Commons, was at last able to repay his debts to the Rothschilds by persuading the reluctant Derby that the Lords must compromise. He did this by giving the Opposition a free hand in the Commons. On April 27, 1858, Russell's Oaths Amendment Bill had been mauled in the Lords at the committee stage, the crucial fifth clause being struck out. Two weeks later, a motion proposed by Russell "disagreeing" with the Lords was passed by a majority of 113. Even more startling, the House also passed (by 55 votes) a motion proposed by the maverick Duncombe that Lionel be appointed a member of the Commons committee set up to explain the "reasons" for its disagreement. Russell then moved that these reasons be relayed through a conference with the Upper House. The Lords' consent to this was the decisive turning point. On May 31, the Earl of Lucan proposed what proved to be the solution: that the Commons should be allowed to change its own oath of admission by resolution, provided this was first legalised by act of Parliament. This allowed the Lords to spell out their "Reasons" for disagreeing with the Commons and Derby—albeit "sulkily and reluctantly"—declared his support for it on July 1. On the 23rd, the compromise became law in the form of two acts, one merging the three oaths of allegiance, supremacy and abjuration for all offices which had hitherto required them; the other permitting Jews to omit the words "upon the true faith of a Christian" if the body to which they sought admission consented. On Monday July 26, Lionel appeared once again in the Commons. For the last time, he was obliged to withdraw as the House debated the two resolutions necessary for him to take the shortened oath—essentially a final opportunity for diehards like Samuel Warren and Spencer Walpole to record their opposition to "the intrusion of the blasphemer."[240] The critical resolution having been passed by 32 votes, Lionel was at last sworn in as a member using the new oath—and the Old Testament. Rather piquantly, given the means to which he had earlier resorted, the first piece of legislation on which he voted immediately after taking his seat on the Opposition front bench was The Corrupt Practices Prevention Act Continuance Bill.[241]

Lionel's admission to Parliament was, as James wrote, "a real triumph for the family."[242] At the general election held the following year, his brother Mayer joined him in the Commons (along with David Salomons); and in 1865 his son Natty was elected.[243] As Charlotte pointed out with glee, in a close vote (as in July 1864) Palmerston's government could be "saved by the Jews."[244] Lionel's election also had a wider resonance for the Jewish community as a whole: the Board of Deputies published resolutions expressing its "sincerest gratification . . . respect and gratitude"[245] and, henceforth, the anniversary of Lionel's admission to the Commons would be prize-giving day at the Jews' Free School—though Lionel pointedly underlined his own commitment to religious toleration by endowing the City of London school with "its most valuable [open] scholarship in honour of his taking his seat."[246]

But the political significance of the triumph has seldom been properly understood. Lionel had triumphed as a Liberal; and the long campaign had forged political and social links with a small but influential group of Liberal MPs. According to his diary, Gladstone dined with him or his brother Mayer four times and corresponded or met with members of the family on at least another four occasions in the period 1856 to 1864.[247] Other Liberals whose names recur in Charlotte's letters of the 1860s as regular visitors to 148 Piccadilly include Charles Villiers, the MP for Wolverhampton (who was President of the Poor Law Board from 1859 to 1866) and Robert Lowe, Chancellor in Gladstone's first ministry.[248] Yet it was not without significance that Lionel's first act after signing the roll and shaking hands with the Speaker was to shake hands with Disraeli, whose contribution in this final phase of the battle may well have been decisive. Relations between Disraeli and the Rothschilds had been improving steadily since the early 1850s, and Lionel had in fact been in close communication with Disraeli during the decisive weeks of 1858. In January he had dined at Gunnersbury (along with Cardinal Wiseman and a host of Orléanist exiles).[249] In May, Disraeli was heard to remark after the government had narrowly avoided defeat over policy in India: "What does the Baron say about it? He knows most things!"[250] Two months later, on July 15, Lionel went to see the Chancellor in his office, "as we had not seen him since our Bill was in the House of Commons." He found him:

> in excellent spirits, said everything was going on as well as possible . . . I told him I hoped that our Bill would pass next Monday. They would manage to have the Queen's assent obtained immediately. I could not get him to [illegible] it as he said it depended upon others if it would not wait till the [commission] at the end of session for all Bills, or if they could get a commission on purpose so as to enable me to take my seat before the House is up. I dare say I shall be able to manage it . . . Dizzy said again today, that it was by the greatest chance possible that we had [illegible] this division for us instead of against us on the 2nd reading of our Bill—he worked all he could for us—so he said.[251]

Lionel responded to this by asking Disraeli "if he would dine with Johnny [Russell] and Co.", but:

> like a sensible fellow he refused, saying that his presence as Minister would spoil the party. I am glad I asked him, as he cannot say that we in any way neglect him. I told him that we were very anxious to have the royal assent to the Bill in time to enable me to take my seat this year, but you know what a humbug he is. He talked of what is customary, without promising anything . . . Mrs. Dizzy dined at Mayer's and went over the old story again, saying how much Dizzy had done for us and how angry he was once because we would not believe it.[252]

The undertone of scepticism in Lionel's accounts of these encounters should not be taken to mean that Disraeli did not do all he could in 1858. On the contrary: his influence must surely account for Derby's grudging capitulation. The closeness of relations between the two men immediately after Lionel's admission to Parliament confirms that the Rothschilds no longer had any reason to doubt Disraeli's bona fides.[253] Despite the formidable political constraints under which he had to work, the creator of Sidonia and Eva had not failed his "race."

Cambridge

It is instructive to compare the outright battle over the admission of Jews to Parliament in this period with the pragmatic fudge which allowed them to study at Cambridge. Here too the Rothschilds played a pioneering role. Indeed, their success in circumventing such religious restrictions as remained at Cambridge may explain why they were so taken aback by the intransigence of the House of Lords. It is illuminating to compare their tactics in the two cases.

The Rothschilds, it should be stressed, did not *need* to go to Cambridge, much less Oxford, any more than they needed to sit in the House of Commons. The education of Rothschild children remained for most of the nineteenth century a much more cosmopolitan affair than the ancient English public schools and universities could provide. Thus the family continued to rely on private tutors and to send children abroad for a substantial part of their studies, to ensure above all that they maintained the family's multilingualism. As for learning about banking, the only way to do that was in a bank; if Cambridge offered anything, it was distraction from the priorities of the family business. Moreover, as in the 1820s and 1830s, the Rothschilds continued to attach almost as much importance to the education of daughters—unlike the public schools and universities, which of course remained overwhelmingly masculine until the late twentieth century. Anthony's daughter Constance and Lionel's son Natty had German drummed into them with more or less equal vigour. Charlotte in particular was a vehement advocate of formal study for her daughters and nieces.[254] However, Mayer's attendance at Cambridge had set a precedent which Charlotte was determined all her sons should follow. The trouble was that the position of Jews at Cambridge remained a grey area: formally excluded from taking degrees until 1856, they could nevertheless become members of the university—provided they were willing to fulfil the obligation to attend chapel imposed on undergraduates by all colleges.

It is curious that—unlike the oath of abjuration—this was an essentially Christian duty which the Rothschilds were prepared in principle to perform, provided their attendance at chapel was minimalistic and passive. As we have seen, Mayer had attended Trinity on just that basis in the 1830s; and when Arthur Cohen, a cousin on his mother's side, resolved to read mathematics at Cambridge in the autumn of 1849—just after Lionel's by-election victory over Manners—he assumed a similar arrangement would be possible. Through J. Abel Smith, one of Lionel's most active political supporters, Mayer sought to persuade the Master of Christ's, James Cartmell, to bend the chapel rules for Cohen's sake, arguing that (as Cartmell put it) "if I admit Mr Cohen, no one, except myself, need know what his religious creed is." Mayer also told Cartmell "that Mr Cohen is ready to attend divine service in the college chapel." The Master, however, was unpersuaded. "It would be a breach of good faith to the Society," he argued, to conceal Cohen's religion, while "it would be most repugnant to my feelings and contrary to my notions of what is right, to exact from Mr Cohen an outward compliance with a form of worship, the basis and spirit of which he entirely disclaims and disbelieves."[255]

To Mayer, this suggested that a precedent might be set "for pointed exclusion of the members of one religious community from the benefits of a Cambridge University education." He and Moses Montefiore therefore turned to none other than Prince Albert—then Chancellor of the University—asking him to put Cohen's case to the Master of Magdalene, who was also Dean of Windsor. Royal pressure succeeded where Rothschild pressure had failed in the 1830s, when Mayer had been forced to leave the college over the question of chapel attendance.[256] Cohen was duly admitted on the basis of a deal with the Dean who, as Cohen was able to report, "inform[ed] me that on Wednesday and Friday the Chapel only lasts 10 minutes [and] advised me to attend on these days instead of the other days, and at the same time communicated to me that my attendance on Sacrament Sundays would not be required."[257]

Similar arrangements had to be negotiated at Trinity when the next generation of Rothschild men went up, beginning with Natty in 1859. By this time, the acts of 1854 and 1856 meant that Jews were now able to take degrees (except in theology). But the problem of religious obligations persisted at the college level. Although Natty's tutor Joseph Lightfoot (who became Hulsean Professor of Divinity in 1861) "promised to do all he can about Chapel" the Master William Whewell remained "the stumbling block in the way of reform."[258] In 1862, as Natty reported to his parents, "the Trinity Dons . . . made themselves very unpopular by threatening to gate everyone who refuses to take the sacrament in Chapel; the consequence of this new rule is that a very large number absented themselves from chapel today, and will get into trouble for breaking an important college rule."[259] Natty plainly felt that little of substance had been achieved by the reforms of the 1850s. "In order to effect anything in the way of reform here," he complained,

> it will be necessary to wait some time for as long as the universities are looked upon as seminaries for the Church of England or as part of the established church itself, it will be impossible to do anything more . . . [W]hat certainly ought to be done away with is the necessity to take orders after seven years or the total abandonment of the fellowship . . . [I]t is very hard for a conscientious individual . . . to be deprived of his fellowship, because he will not declare himself a member of the Church of England. I never could see why a national institution like this which is the stepping stone to legal and political preferments as well as ecclesiastical ones should be ruled by priests as if it were a Jesuit's seminary or a Talmud school . . .[260]

Nor was attendance at chapel the only compromise they had to make at Cambridge. The second-year examination known as the "Little Go" required a detailed knowledge of William Paley's *Evidences of Christianity*. An irate letter from Charlotte to Leo shows how much of an obstacle this presented, but also suggests that she felt he should be able to overcome it:

> [Y]our unaccountable mistake at the examination vexed and annoyed me greatly.—Of course you did not, could not, intend offering an insult

to the Reverend examiners, and no person acquainted with you could have supposed you capable of such an utter want of feeling for the clergy, and of such a complete want of respect for a faith, which though not your own, and indeed unknown to you, ought nevertheless to be held in respect, as the worship of the Almighty by millions of human beings.—But the mistake is nevertheless very reprehensible, and indeed unpardonable. In whatever light it may be viewed, it cannot do otherwise than create a bad impression.—A young man, who appears in the Senate-house, and cannot object to be examined in the evidences of Christianity, ought to make himself acquainted with the subject.—Had I not known you to be surrounded by Revd. instructors, I should have offered some advice, but I really thought you would have had the good, natural, common sense to ask your tutors for a sketch, an outline, if not a history of the Christian faith.—You will pass for the most ignorant, most thoughtless, and most shallow of human beings. I am grieved at it, but I am sorry there is nothing to explain away.[261]

For his part Leo was baffled by "the mysteries of theology and . . . various doxies": when he dined with a group of disputatious dons one night he felt "so mystified that I did not dare open my lips." (A friend who was also present feared "they might forget my presence and make some attack upon the Jews.")[262] Even in the more youthful environment of the debating chamber, the Rothschilds were made to feel ill at ease. Natty recalled how his "blood boiled with rage" one night at the Union when a speaker "quoted as a solitary instance of the too great power of the House of Commons the passing of the Jew Bill. I had hoped that the day was gone by for all [distinctions] of this kind and if I had spoken at once, I might have aroused religious passions, not so easy to quell as arouse."[263]

The Rothschild presence at Cambridge was therefore a qualified victory compared with the victory Lionel wished to achieve in the House of Commons. (It was not in fact until 1871 that the final religious tests were abolished at the ancient universities.) There is a marked and not easily explicable contrast between the willingness of his brother and sons to attend college chapel services and study Paley, and his refusal to swear an oath which included a declaration of Christian faith. Presumably if undergraduates had been required to take the sacraments it would have been a different story.

Great Exhibitions and Crystal Palaces

Monuments to military victories are not usually built before a battle is won. The Rothschilds, however, began building monuments to their political ascendancy some years before Lionel was finally able to take his seat at Westminster. That, at least, is one way of interpreting the extraordinary burst of architectural activity between 1850 and 1860, when the Rothschilds built no fewer than four immense country houses for themselves, and rebuilt a fifth: at Mentmore, Aston Clinton, Ferrières, Pregny and Boulogne.

Of course, Nathan and his brothers had begun to acquire country residences from the earliest days of their prosperity, as we have seen. By the time of the 1848 revolution, their houses and estates at Ferrières, Suresnes, Boulogne, Gunnersbury, Schillersdorf and Grüneburg had been in the family for years. Nor did the 1850s witness a complete change in attitude towards these rural retreats. When purchasing new land in Buckinghamshire after 1848, notably the farms at Aston Clinton, the London partners remained as economically rational as their father and uncles had been before them: unless the agricultural land paid 3.5 per cent on the purchasing price, they were not interested. "If you think that Aston Clinton is worth [£]26,000," wrote Lionel to Mayer in 1849, "I have no objection to yr. offering it, but I think we ought always to be able to rely on 3 1/2 clear of all charges, it is not like a fancy place, you must consider it entirely as an investment."[264] When he visited Schillersdorf in 1849, he commented that it was "a magnificent property and although [Uncle Salomon] paid a little dear for it, it will if well managed pay him a good interest."[265]

In buying land when they did—in the wake of the great agricultural crisis of the mid-1840s—the Rothschilds were going in at the bottom of the market. It was in 1848 that the Duke of Buckingham was finally declared bankrupt, and a year later Mayer was receiving estate agents' reports from Ireland, advising him of the favourable opportunities there. "Potatoes failing all directions and free trade ruining everybody," ran one such tip; "Ireland completely ruined, now is the time or at least it is fast approaching for buying estates on the sly. When the Parliamentary Title be obtained acknowledge the purchase and resell at a very advanced premium."[266] In fact, he and his brothers had no interest in such carpet-bagging: their interest in real estate, as their mother remarked, reflected the fact that by December 1849 the yield on consols had fallen to 3.1 per cent. It was "the most proper time" to buy land "when the funds lie so high as they are at present for altho the interest may be reduced on funded property land will always be an equivalent."[267] Such investments cannot be seen as symptoms of a declining entrepreneurial spirit. The same is true of the French Rothschilds' purchases of wine-growing estates: Nat's purchase of Château Brane-Mouton in 1853 (which he renamed Mouton-Rothschild) and James's long battle to gain control of Château Lafite near Pauillac were informed by a shrewd assessment of the demand for good-quality clarets. James was an old man when he finally secured control of Lafite in 1868 (for £177,600), but almost immediately he began bidding up the price of the new vintage.[268]

Yet there is a difference between spending £26,000 on farmland and spending an equivalent sum on a palatial new house. It is easily forgotten how few English landowners built themselves new "stately homes" in the nineteenth century: what had been affordable a hundred years before was now out of the question.[269] For the Rothschilds, on the other hand, money was no object. When the London partners withdrew £260,250 from the firm's joint capital in 1852—primarily to finance their building projects—it represented less than 3 per cent of the total. Yet the quoted price for the new house at Mentmore was just £15,427. For the immense amount of work he undertook for the Rothschilds between 1853 and 1873, the builder George Myers was altogether paid just £350,000.[270]

The fact that they could afford it, however, does not explain *why* they decided to spend their money on big houses which plainly did not pay a return on the investment. The banal explanation—and it may be sufficient—is that the Rothschilds liked to spend time in the country; and the advent of railways meant that they could do so without neglecting their work in the City. The London and North Western Line allowed Lionel and his brothers to commute easily between Mentmore and

Euston: Lionel could have "a gallop" in the country and still be down in time for an evening debate in the Commons. The Strasbourg–Ligny line, opened in May 1849, did the same for James and his sons at Ferrières.[271] There is, however, a supplementary and perhaps necessary explanation. The new houses staked a claim to aristocratic status. As early as 1846, Lionel had intimated that he regarded a baronetcy as beneath him, and embarked on his campaign to enter the House of Commons only when it was clear that a peerage was not going to be forthcoming. But this was not some symptom of "feudalisation"—of decadent bourgeois submission to anachronistic upper-class values; for it must not be forgotten that Mentmore was being built at the time when Lionel was openly challenging the legislative role of the House of Lords. The Rothschild bid for noble status in Britain was uncompromising and nothing expressed this more tangibly than the houses the family built for themselves. They were more than mere imitations of eighteenth-century country houses. They were advertisements for Rothschild power, five-star hotels for influential guests, private art galleries: in short, centres for corporate hospitality.

Their very choice of architect was significant. Joseph Paxton had been known to the family since the 1830s and had advised Louise on her Günthersburg house in the 1840s; but it was his design of the Crystal Palace for the Great Exhibition which seems to have convinced the family to entrust him with something more than mere alterations. Work began on Mentmore in August 1851, the year of the Exhibition, and for all its Elizabethan inspiration—Paxton had Wollaton and Hardwick houses in mind as models—it was by the standards of the day an innovative building with its huge glass-roofed hall, hot running water and central heating. It cannot really be understood as a family home for Mayer, his wife and his daughter. Boasting twenty-six rooms on the ground floor alone, it was essentially a hotel where numerous guests could be entertained and accommodated. Those guests were supposed to be reminded of their host's global influence: indeed, the trophy-like heads of the European sovereigns (in this instance by the Italian sculptor Raphael Monti) were becoming something of a Rothschild trademark. But Mentmore was also an art gallery, intended to link the modern power of the Rothschilds with more historically venerable antecedents—hence the three massive lanterns originally made for the Doge of Venice, the Gobelin tapestries and the collection of antique furniture from sixteenth-century Italy and eighteenth-century France.[272]

In building Mentmore, Mayer had set a standard for the rest of the family. Aston Clinton, altered for Anthony between 1854 and 1855 by Paxton's son-in-law George Henry Stokes, was a botched job by comparison. Attempting to enlarge the existing house, Stokes failed altogether to realise Louisa's "dream," though she hoped that "in time I may grow attached to this little place which I thought at first sight the ugliest on earth."[273] By contrast, James set out determinedly to trump Mentmore at Ferrières. To the chagrin of the French architectural profession, to say nothing of the local stonemasons, he called in Paxton and Myers. It was a commission they more than once regretted accepting, for James felt no compunction about rejecting Paxton's first design after seeking a second opinion from the French architect Antoine-Julien Hénard; while friction between the English and French workers on the site led to a strike and finally violence over pay differentials.[274] The final result—which was not completed until 1860—was an eclectic mixture of French, Italian and English styles. Sophisticates like the Goncourts loathed it: "Trees and waterworks created by spending millions, round a château costing eighteen millions, an idiotic and ridiculous extravagance, a pudding of every style, the fruit of a stupid ambition to have all monuments in one!"[275] Bismarck thought it looked like "an overturned chest of drawers." The poet and diplomat Wilfrid Scawen Blunt called it "a monstrous Pall Mall club decorated in the most outrageous Louis Philippe taste";[276] while the anti-Semite Edouard Drumont dismissed it as "an incredible bric-a-brac shop."[277]

It was nevertheless a state-of-the art affair: James famously moved the kitchens a hundred yards away from the house to prevent his guests from smelling the cooks at work, building a small underground railway to connect them with the basement beneath the dining room. And like Mentmore it was part advertisement (with Charles-Henri Cordier's caryatids symbolising Rothschild dominance over the four quarters of the globe), part hotel (with over eighty rooms), and part gallery (with the great hall functioning as James's increasingly cluttered "personal museum"). It was all on a hypertrophic scale—as Evelina said, "the place was too regal to be without sentinels"—yet it had an exotic, theatrical quality due largely to the interiors by the stage-designer Eugène Lami, who gave the smoking room its faintly kitsch Venetian frescoes.[278] Château Pregny, built by Stokes for Adolph in 1858, was a modest affair in comparison. Overlooking Lake Geneva, this Louis XVI-style building was primarily intended as a show-case for Adolph's collection of paintings and *objets d'art*—exotic rock crystals, precious stones and wood carvings.[279] The work done on the house at Boulogne by Armand-Auguste-Joseph Berthelin in 1855 was similar in quality, though Berthelin took his inspiration from the Versailles of Louis XIV.[280]

The 1850s and 1860s also saw substantial transformations in the gardens around the Rothschild houses. At Ferrières, under Paxton's direction, there was a new pond with ornamental bridges, as well as elaborate greenhouses and winter gardens. Though her daughter Evelina preferred the grounds of Gunnersbury and Mentmore,[281] Charlotte's descriptions of Ferrières in this period gush with enthusiasm about

> the shrubs and trees and flowers, hot houses and greenhouses, and . . . the brilliant and excellent contents of the latter.—Ferrières is, in my opinion, fairyland, and lacks nothing but an extensive and picturesque view . . . Uncle James collects ducks, swans and pheasants from all parts of the world . . . [A]s an ensemble—with orangeries, conservatories, crystal palaces, vineries—hot and green houses, orchards, fruit and flower gardens, farms, zoological treasures—animals wild and tame . . . Ferrières is unsurpassed . . . [It is like] the Palace of Aladdin, [with] its fairy gardens, wondrous aviaries, marvellous carp streams and crystal palaces full of luscious fruit and glowing flowers.[282]

At Boulogne the landscape gardener Poyre built an elaborate water garden with cascades and romantic rockeries, while James added "geese with curled feathers," white ducks, Egyptian donkeys and a talking parrot to his collection of exotic fauna.[283] At Pregny too there was a menagerie for Adolph's collection of Patagonian hares, kangaroos and antelopes.[284] Even the older houses had their gardens redesigned: though he rarely went there, Anselm turned the grounds of Schillersdorf into a Silesian version of Regent's Park. He also added a lake to attract wild duck and a large number of English-style cottages for the estate workers—an early example of Rothschild paternalism in the country, just as the various animal and bird collections showed the first stirrings of the later Rothschilds' passion for zoology.[285]

Nor were the family's residences in the great European cities neglected. Lionel acquired the house next door to 148 Piccadilly from the MP Fitzroy Kelly and commissioned Nelson & Innes to rebuild a new and much larger house on the site of the two houses, moving to Kingston House in Knightsbridge while the work was in progress.[286] To get an impression of the finished building (which was demolished a century later when Park Lane was widened for traffic), one need only walk into one of the grander London clubs: the basement was set aside for the male servants' quarters and wine cellar, the ground floor was a spacious hall, the staircase a mass of marble leading to the huge reception rooms on the first floor, leaving the second floor for the private rooms and the garret for the maids. The kitchens were moved under the terrace in the garden.[287] The various hotels in Paris were on a similar scale and shared the same basic structure.[288]

And of course the task of filling all these houses with appropriate furniture and ornaments was never complete. A not untypical shopping expedition by Charlotte in Paris yielded a list of possible purchases including a marble group for £2,000; four small statues; a crystal chandelier; four busts of Roman Emperors; "two marvellous vases of rosso antico, most beautifully carved, and exhibiting Neptune surrounded by tritons and sea-nymphs" for 5,000 guineas; and a table for £150.[289] A year later the London art dealers were offering her, among other things, a painting by Rubens, "a wonderful chimney-piece by Inigo Jones, a beautiful Sir Joshua [Reynolds], representing a lovely woman . . . and last though not least Mr. Russell's long promised Japanese or Chinese collection."[290] Snobs like the Goncourts liked to sneer at the Rothschilds' reliance on art dealers: one of their malicious stories describes Anselm offering an optician 36,000 francs if he could invent "a lorgnette which could give him the ability to see with the eyes of a man of taste"; another imagines James throwing in a dress for the dealer's daughter to secure a Veronese at a good price.[291] The reality was that the Rothschilds were now among the elite of art collectors; perhaps even at its head.[292] "A trumpery little Raphael [for] 150,000 f[ran]cs—the Cuyp 92.000 f[ran]cs," reported Nat to his brothers from a Paris auction in 1869. "One must have plenty of money now to buy pictures"—or, as his cousin Gustave put it, "money to be spent in a moment."[293] But who had that kind of money if not the Rothschilds?

After all this, the rebuilding of the bank offices at New Court in the early 1860s seemed an afterthought. To be sure, Charlotte thought the new building "quite marvellous, and intended for magnificent business."[294] It remained to be seen how far politics—not to mention art and architecture—would henceforth distract the younger generation of Rothschilds from fulfilling that intention.

TWO

The Era of Mobility
(1849–1858)

[M]oi, je serais charmé de faire une niche à ce juif qui nous jugule.
CAVOUR[1]

The 1850s were a difficult time for the Rothschilds: that, at least, is the traditional view. Firstly, Louis Napoleon Bonaparte, of whom James had always been suspicious, overthrew the republican constitution and proclaimed himself Emperor, his uncle's lineal successor. Secondly, James's financial rival Achille Fould—the younger brother of Benoît, Heine's "chief rabbi of the Rive Gauche" railway—became Finance Minister. According to an often quoted account by the comte de Viel-Castel, Fould told Napoleon: "It is absolutely necessary that Your Majesty free yourself from the tutelage of Rothschild, who reigns in spite of you."[2] Thirdly, the formation of new "universal" banks like the Crédit Mobilier—the brainchild of James's former associates the Pereires—threatened the dominant position of the Rothschilds not only in France, but throughout Europe. Finally, the 1850s were a time of international instability: for the first time since 1815 the Rothchilds' nightmare of major wars between the great powers became a reality, first in the Crimea (Britain and France against Russia over Turkey) and then in Italy (France against Austria over Italy).

Yet this account is misleading in two respects. Because historians have relied too heavily on biased sources like the diaries of Count Hübner, Apponyi's successor as Austrian ambassador, it overstates the difficulties which James experienced under Napoleon's regime. Moreover, it is too Francocentric: such difficulties as James experienced should not be seen in isolation at a time when the other Rothschild houses were prospering.

Two Emperors

It was malice on Hübner's part to portray Betty's relationship with General Changarnier as a romantic one. In fact, her recently rediscovered letters to Alphonse during his absence in America reveal that her first impressions of him were less than favourable. The general struck her as a "thin, ugly man of medium height and with nothing military about him but his moustaches. At first sight he seems old and worn out."[3] When he dined with them in January 1849, he "was as good company as possible and most desirous to please," but "in this respect he was only partly successful. I don't find in him the spirit of openness and loyalty which I have so often heard him praised for; on the contrary, he gave the impression rather of being a two-faced man . . ."[4] Disraeli was told by Hannah that Changarnier was rather straitlaced: when invited to dine at the Rothschilds along with a celebrated opera singer, he refused and "lectured [Betty] for inviting a public singer to her table."[5] Nor by this stage had Betty ruled out some kind of accommodation with Louis Napoleon. The President, she told her son in April, was "doing well. Every day he gives certain proofs of [his belief in] the principle of order and legal authority." So reassured was she that she "finally broke the ice and appeared in the President's salons. Without appearing to affect to a political sulk, it would have been difficult for me to remain away any longer."[6]

On the other hand, there is no question that Changarnier said the right things to reassure a woman who, more than other members of the family, had reacted strongly against the revolution. "He is," she wrote approvingly, "a reactionary of the right sort . . . The other day he was talking about the symbol of the third virtue on our flags, and he said to me, 'I hate fraternity so much that if I had a brother, I would call him my cousin.' " Soon she was assuring Alphonse, "My friend Changarnier will hold the madmen in check," and adding that the family was "protected by our worthy Changarnier." "In our excellent Changarnier," she declared in June, "we have a sure friend, who is too well acquainted with what is going on not to let us know [of trouble] immediately. I would not be able to tell you how honourable this man is, what a noble heart and loyal soul he has, how open-minded he is, this former hero, uniting knightly courage that brings strength of purpose and resolve which must succeed."[7] If she said this sort of thing in public, it is perhaps not so surprising that Hübner detected an amorous as well as a political attraction. Her aunt Hannah herself commented discreetly that Changarnier was "much devoted to the family, thinks a great deal of the talent and abilities of Betty, appreciates the courage and manner of acting of the family during the time of the revolution and appears to study their welfare."[8] For his part, James commented—with a mixture of admiration and bemusement—that although Changarnier was willing to give him sensitive political information (for example, over French policy in the Don Pacifico affair), he would never speculate himself on such news: "Now Charganier has never got mixed up [in speculation] and he has never said to me that he wants to speculate. In fact I am sure that if I were to propose something to him or to his adjutant, he would no longer receive me nor accept my invitations. He is the most singular fellow I know!"[9] Bonaparte, by contrast, was more than happy to speculate—but not with James.

Throughout 1850, James struggled to reconcile the two men, increasingly conscious that it was Napoleon who had the upper hand, and that this could spell trouble for him. "The President probably thinks that I have wronged him," he reported in January 1850, "so it seems that I too do not stand very high in his regard, particularly as Fould will do me no favours. Thank God I have no need of him."[10] As this suggests, it is also true that he distrusted Fould (the fact that he had married a Gentile did not help).[11] Still, the nature of their rivalry should not be misunderstood—they saw one another often, and one detects a grudging respect: to have one brother a banker and the other a Finance Minister was, as James acknowledged, no mean strategy.[12] James plainly felt himself at a disadvantage in business and in politics: "Unfortunately," he grumbled, "I see with annoyance that business is being taken away from us and we are not what we used to be."[13] But it is wrong to suggest that his failure to secure the issue of rentes which took place at the end of 1850 was a symptom of his waning financial influence.[14] In fact, James had prepared a bid, but stayed away from the auction because of the death of Nat's four-year-old son Mayer Albert, whose funeral coincided with the Finance Minister's auction. Even as he mourned, James could not resist gloating that his absence would make Fould's auction "a fiasco": "Now they see that one cannot push Rothschild aside, as Fould wanted to do."[15]

In truth, James's principal concern was more diplomatic than financial. He feared that the President's erratic foreign policy might lead to friction, if not war, between France and the other powers, whether Britain (over the Don Pacifico affair) or Prussia (over Germany). Chirac's story about James attempting to tone down French policy in late 1850 at a meeting with Napoleon and Changarnier has the ring of truth about it. "Come now, let's see, vat is it about, this quarrel ofer Germany?" James allegedly said. "Let's come to some arrenchment, for heafen's sake, let's come to some arrenchment." Napoleon, so the story goes, merely turned his back on him.[16] James did indeed see Napoleon on a number of occasions in 1850 and 1851; but he never claimed to have any success in influencing his policy.[17] On the contrary, he grumbled that the President "like[d] nothing more than to play the little soldier"; he was "an ass . . . who would end up turning the whole world against him."[18] In particular, the possibility of French meddling in the quarrel between Austria and Prussia which flared up in the second half of 1850 filled him with foreboding.[19] Though he continued to dread ending up "in the hands of the reds," James would not have been entirely sorry if Louis Napoleon had been "chased away like Louis Philippe" over his foreign policy blunders.[20]

All this explains why, as the likelihood of a Bonapartist coup d'état increased, James was nervous. As early as October 1850, he began to remit gold to the London house, explaining to his nephews that "I would rather have all my gold over there earning 3 per cent on deposit than put it in rentes or keep it in the cellar, when a man like that [Napoleon] might take my money away for being a friend of Changarnier's. I'm not afraid but I like to be careful. Politically, this is a wretched country."[21] At the same time, James increased his political exposure by remaining in contact with Changarnier even after the latter's dismissal from his army and National Guard commands. In October 1851 James told his nephews that "our General" had "great hopes." "I suspect that before they are realised," he added uneasily, "Paris may be bathed in blood. I have sold all my rentes."[22] It was thus not unreasonable for James to fear that he too might be arrested along with Changarnier and the other republican leaders when the coup was launched on the night of December 1–2. Symbolically, he had fallen downstairs and sprained his ankle a week before "Operation Rubicon" (as the coup was codenamed), so he was quite literally prostrate when the Bonapartists struck.[23] Small wonder his letters to London immediately after the coup say nothing about politics; as James explained, he had reason to fear that they were being intercepted.[24] Fortunately for the historian, Betty was less discreet when she met Apponyi, so we have a good idea of her furious reaction:

> She believes that the President has only succeeded in coming to the rescue of the reds, that he will be obliged to adopt a see-saw policy and that he will finally end up as the instrument of [their] demagogy. "In order to continue down the path the President has chosen, he is obliged to frighten us with demagogy [meaning the far left]; consequently he cannot destroy it completely; I therefore fear that, far from saving society, on the contrary, he will destroy it by applying his personal rule."[25]

Yet James was never a man to confuse his political preferences with his business interests. Beyond his liking for Changarnier, he felt no loyalty to the Republic, and accepted the new situation with (as Hübner put it) "great resignation."[26] Pereire brought a reassuring account of the situation to an impromptu gathering of bankers at the rue Laffitte. Those present did not

> exactly blame Louis Napoleon for having decided to have done with [the constitution] before 1852; the thing was regarded as more or less inevitable; it was only worrying that it was a dangerous gamble. The arrest of several generals was reported; there were fears that this might lead to divisions within the army, which, so it was said, would be the end of France, whoever was the victor. M. Pereire was bombarded with questions. He described what he had seen: the good humour of the officers; the good spirit of the soldiers, the great development of the military forces, the indifference of those who read the proclamations, the tranquillity of Paris, despite the surprises of the morning. The great financiers listened with pleasure to this reassuring news.[27]

Moreover, it soon became apparent that, in smashing the republican left and signalling his support for an expansionary credit policy, Napoleon was generating a climate of financial optimism. The price of rentes tells its own story. On the eve of the coup, 3 per cent rentes were quoted at 56 and 5 per cents at 90.5. Immediately after, prices leapt to 64 and 102.5 respectively; and by the end of 1852—when Napoleon proclaimed himself Emperor on the first anniversary of the coup–3 per cents stood at 83—a capital gain of nearly 50 per cent from Republic to Empire (see illustration 2.i). Figures for gross investment in railways tell the same story: after a perod of stagnation between 1848 and 1851, investment increased by a factor of five in the period to 1856.[28] James had for some time been conscious that economic and political events were out of synchrony: even the war scares and domestic alarms of the pre-coup period had not been as destabilising as he himself had anticipated.[29] "To listen to the politicians," he remarked in 1850, "you would think all was lost; to listen to the financiers is to be told quite the opposite."[30] But from December 2 onwards, politics and economics were brought back into harmony by a government that consciously identified its own health with that of the bourse.[31]

The Napoleonic regime was thus far from an ideal outcome for James, who would probably have preferred Changarnier to pave the way for an Orléanist restoration. But once it was apparent that Napoleon had no intention of penalising him personally, he could live with it. He had already summarised his position—presciently—in October 1850: "In the end we shall have an Emperor, which will end with war, for if I wasn't so afraid of war, then I would be an imperialist myself."[32] After the coup, he was quick to recognise that his rivals would steal a march on him if he was identified too closely with the defunct republic.[33] While Betty could express her "demoralisation" with Napoleon by retreating into internal exile at Fer-rières, her husband had (once again) to move with the times: "I think Napoleon is gaining strength," he reported to London, just three weeks after the coup, "despite the fact that the great and the good will not accept his invitations. Do you think that we too should stay away completely?"[34] It was a rhetorical question. Even the Roth-schild women could not sustain their social boycott indefinitely. Indeed, their mood began to soften even before the end of December. "At the Rothschilds," observed Apponyi waspishly after an encounter with Nat's wife Charlotte and Betty, "the mood of calm stems from the enormous amounts of money they are making at the moment as a result of the boom in all the bonds and shares they have in their port-folio."[35]

It was at least the fifth change of regime since James had settled in Paris, and it was evidently becoming hard for him to take such events seriously. "My good nephews, how would you like a French constitution for two sous? They're being sold in the streets for that here." An absolute government was "not very good; but here you can do what you like and it's all forgotten."[36] As early as October 1852, James could breezily report that he was "on the best footing with the Emperor and every-one"; this was fully two months before Napoleon actually proclaimed himself Emperor.[37] It was also just days before Napoleon's famous Bordeaux speech in which he declared: "The Empire means peace" ("L'Empire, c'est la paix"). This seemed to rule out the rash infringements of Belgian neutrality or challenges to Prussian rule in the Rhineland which had caused most concern in the previous two years, and explains why the other powers recognised Napoleon as Emperor with only token quibbles.

Of course, it was not that easy: in January 1853 James was still having difficulty getting to see the new Emperor.[38] But he had two routes into the new court. Firstly, he remained Austrian consul-general, and made a point of wearing his scarlet uni-form to remind anyone who had forgotten his diplomatic status.[39] In August 1852 he had been able to relay an anodyne message to Napoleon from the new Austrian Emperor Franz Joseph; and, although Hübner did his best to undermine James's claim to represent Vienna in Paris, he had no chance of dislodging him as long as the Rothschilds remained Austria's bankers.[40] The second way James sought to ingrati-ate himself with Napoleon was by championing the cause of the half-Spanish, half-Scottish adventuress Eugénie de Montijo, who more snobbish Parisians assumed would merely be Napoleon's next mistress. Napoleon had been introduced to her in 1850 and by the end of 1852 was infatuated; when his plans foundered for a diplo-matic marriage to Princess Adelaide of Hohenlohe (one of Queen Victoria's nieces) he impulsively resolved to marry her—to the dismay of his ministers.

This decision was still a secret, however, on January 12, when Eugénie arrived at a ball at the Tuileries on the arm of none other than James—who, noted Hübner, had long been "under the spell of the young Andalusian, but now more than ever, for he was one of those who believed in a marriage." One of his sons—presumably Alphonse—escorted her mother. When the party entered the Salle des Maréchaux, intending to find seats for the ladies, the wife of the Foreign Minister Drouyn de

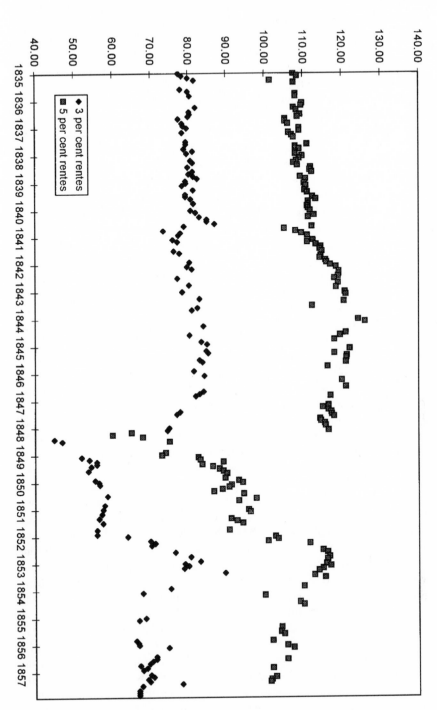

2.ii: The weekly closing price of French 3 per cent and 5 per cent rentes, 1835–1857.

Lhuys haughtily informed Eugénie that the seats in question were reserved for the wives of ministers. Napoleon overheard this, came across to the two women and offered them seats on the imperial dais. After two hours, the Emperor and Eugénie disappeared into the cabinet impérial, to return later arm in arm. Three days later he proposed; on the 22nd the engagement was made public; a week later the wedding took place. "I prefer a young woman whom I love and esteem," declared Napoleon. "One can love a woman without esteeming her," commented Anselm's wife Charlotte shortly after this, "but one only marries a women one honours and respects." This compliment—a rather strained one given the Rothschild family's habitual distinction between romantic love and marriage—was duly relayed to the imperial couple.[41]

The significance of this should not be exaggerated, of course; on the other hand, it is easy for the modern reader to forget how seriously contemporaries took the complex rituals of nineteenth-century court life—especially, it might be said, at the court of an unpredictable parvenu who owed his throne to a coup d'état and his legitimacy to carefully managed plebiscites.

The Crédit Mobilier

Of course, it was not at the Tuileries or at Compiègne (where Napoleon did his hunting), but at the bourse and in the railway boardrooms that James's fate in the Second Empire was really decided. Here, the Second Empire witnessed what is usually portrayed as one of the great corporate battles of the nineteenth century: the fight to the finish between the Rothschilds and the Crédit Mobilier.

Partly because of the coincidence of the foundation of the Crédit Mobilier (November 20, 1852) and the formal proclamation of the Second Empire (December 2), the significance of the new bank has often been misunderstood. For example, it is portrayed by many writers as a primarily political challenge to the dominance of the Rothschilds over French public finance—Napoleon III's response to Fould's challenge to "free himself" from Rothschild tutelage.[42] A second misconception is that the Crédit Mobilier represented a revolutionary new kind of bank, in contradistinction to the "old" private bank personified by the Rothschilds.[43]

In fact, there was nothing fundamentally new about the idea of creating a bank on the basis of publicly raised share capital. Since 1826, joint-stock banks had been legal in Britain, and banks like the National Provincial and the London & Westminster Bank—both established in 1833—had revealed the possibilities of the new form long before the Pereires turned to banking; by the time the Crédit Mobilier was founded there were around a hundred joint-stock banks in England and Wales, twice the number of London-based private banks. Nor is it true to say that British joint-stock banks eschewed lending to industry (though they tended not to go in for long-term investment, they often extended overdrafts and discounted bills in ways which were long-term in effect). Long-term industrial investment was not really what the Crédit Mobilier did anyway, *pace* the claims of economic historians like Alexander Gerschenkron and Rondo Cameron that it promoted industrialisation not only in France but throughout the continent.[44] There were precedents for what the Pereires attempted in France too, the earliest (if one ignores John Law's Banque Générale) being Laffitte's Caisse Générale du Commerce et de l'Industrie. Nor, as Landes has argued, were the Rothschilds and other established Paris banks especially old-fashioned in their response to the Crédit Mobilier's challenge: they too saw the rationale of the joint-stock form for longer-term investments.[45] Although their capital differed from the Pereires' in being entirely their own, the French and Austrian Rothschilds used it in much the same way as the Crédit Mobilier used its bondholders' and depositors' money—and in the long run more successfully. To make a simple but usually overlooked point: the Crédit Mobilier was not even *bigger* than the Rothschilds. Its initial capital was 20 (later 60) million francs; that of de Rothschild Frères in 1852 was in excess of 88 million francs; and that of the combined Rothschild houses no less than 230 million francs. Of the Crédit Mobilier's initial capital, the Pereires themselves accounted for only around 29 per cent.[46]

In reality, it was not so much what they did as they way they did it which convinced contemporaries, and in turn historians, that there was a profound difference between the Rothschilds and the Crédit Mobilier. (Only someone unfamiliar with Paris could lump "Rothschild, Fould and Pereyre [*sic*]" together as Bismarck did.)[47] The Pereires continued to use their old Saint-Simonian rhetoric about the collective benefits of industrial investment, even as they speculated in rentes and railway shares and pocketed the profits for themselves. The Rothschilds, by contrast, made no secret of the fact that they were speculating and profiting, and regarded their contributions to the wider communities to which they belonged as a charitable activity, distinct from their business.[48] When Castellane met Anthony for the first time in 1850 he was rather shocked by the latter's complaint that "in London you can make [money] on everything, on cotton as well as rentes, as much as you like, but here [in Paris] you can hardly speculate on anything but rentes."[49] That was not the way the Saint-Simonians talked: for them it was a matter of mobilising the savings of all France in the pursuit of a steam-driven utopia. It was a difference in style vividly captured by the stockbroker Feydeau in his memoirs. Unlike the Pereires, he argued, James was "simply a solid, intelligent and astute 'capital merchant' ":

> The sole task of maximising the return on his colossal fortune constituted for him a round-the-clock occupation. Each liquidation at the end of the month was a combat which he fought for the security of his house, the eminence of his name, the affirmation of his power. He kept abreast of the slightest pieces of news—political, financial, commercial and industrial—from all quarters of the globe; he did his best to profit from these, quite instinctively, missing no opportunity for gain, no matter how small.[50]

As we have seen, doing business with a man like James was a thankless task for small fry like Feydeau. But one needed only to go the offices of the Crédit Mobilier to encounter

> the most striking contrast possible with the house of Rothschild. At the Pereires' there were no hard words to be feared and no outbursts to dread. Acidulously polite men, ulcerated by hatred, always concentrating, hard and tense like bars of iron, inflexible in their ideas, filled with admiration for themselves, they were always to be found surrounded by friends, all cupping their ears in order to find out the line their patrons were taking, which shares they were working on, if they were buying or selling. The employees of the Crédit Mobilier lay in wait for you on the stairs to interrogate you to see if you had an order. Everyone wanted to

get rich, and at any price; each, necessarily, was trying to work in the same direction as his masters.[51]

James evidently relished this contrast, and on one occasion, with that sardonic humour which was to become his trademark under the Second Empire, commissioned Feydeau to undertake a speculation on his behalf—in the form of a purchase of a thousand Crédit Mobilier shares. He did this no fewer than five times, astonishing his broker by actually paying for them in full at the liquidation. When Feydeau expressed his incredulity, James feigned surprise:

> Vat do you mean, my young friend? . . . I do not mock you at all. Listen: I haf the greatest possible confitence in the chenius of Messrs Pereire. They are the greatest financiers on this earth. I am a family man, and I am happy to infest a part of my little fortune in their affairs. I only regret one thing, and that is that I cannot entrust all off my capital to such clefer men.[52]

Contemporaries—notably the financier Jules Isaac Mirès after his fall from grace—sometimes attributed this difference in style to the different cultural backgrounds of the two families. The "Jews of the North," he suggested, having originated in the harsh, restrictive atmosphere of Germany, were "cold" and "methodical" in their selfish pursuit of wealth, and indifferent to the interests of the state; whereas the "Jews from the Midi" not only had "more noble" "Latin" instincts, but had also benefited from France's more tolerant treatment of the Jews, and so did business in a more altruistic, public spirited way.[53] Others conceived of the difference in more political terms: Rothschild represented "the aristocracy of money" and "financial feudalism," while his rivals stood for "financial democracy and an economic '1789.' "[54]

In reality, the competition between the two had its origins in the prosaic realm of railway concessions. To say the least, the republic had been an unhappy interlude for the railway enthusiasts. Investment and construction had stagnated as the politicians argued interminably about which concession should be granted to whom; interest rates were high, the bourse depressed, employers wary of labour unrest. Only one major line got under way (the Ouest from Versailles to Rennes). One of the most immediate consequences of Napoleon's coup was that it ended all this. The very day after the seizure of power, the concession for the Lyon–Mediterranean line was granted, followed two days later by the Paris–Lyon to a consortium of which both the Paris and London Rothschilds were members. The Nord company's concession was also renegotiated on terms which were singularly favourable to the company. The Empire was a bonanza for rail entrepreneurs: altogether no fewer than twenty-five concessions were awarded between 1852 and 1857, and a further thirty followed in the years to 1870.[55]

In all this, an influential role was played by Napoleon's illegitimate half-brother the duc de Morny, who saw the new regime principally as an opportunity to enrich himself and argued strongly in favour of merging the many small railway companies into a few big lines. James was in touch with Morny in early 1852, and liked what he heard. Interestingly, the French house's balance sheet drawn up at this time shows that James held shares in various railway companies worth more than 20 million francs (around 15 per cent of the Paris house's total assets).[56] The value of these shares was now rocketing as investors reacted to the new regime's encouragement: Apponyi estimated that James made 1.5 million francs in a single week in April 1852 "without having to pay out a penny."[57] Given the enormous increases in capital achieved by the Paris house in the 1850s, the figure does not seem improbable. It is worth noting that of all the big six French lines the Rothschild-controlled Nord was the most intensively utilised and most profitable: although it accounted for only 9 per cent of total French network in terms of length, it carried 14 per cent of freight and more than 12 per cent of all passenger traffic. The ratio of fares and freight rates to costs was 2.7: in the 1850s and the volume of traffic more than doubled between the 1850s and the 1860s.[58]

Increasingly, however, James and the Pereires were at odds. The first signs of dissension had manifested themselves in 1849, when the latter had sought to raise money for their proposed Paris–Lyon–Avignon project without reference to the Rothschilds. The process continued apace in 1852, though it is far from easy to say exactly when the decisive breach occurred. An important step towards divorce was taken when James decided to participate in the Paris–Lyon line syndicate, taking around 12 per cent of its stock (other shareholders included Bartholony, Hottinguer and Baring and, although not named as a concessionary, Talabot seems to have played a leading role).[59] This signified an unambiguous rejection of the Pereires' rival scheme. In an illuminating series of letters, James explained his reasons for doing so to his nephews:

> Regarding Lyon, it would be very damaging for the Nord if it were to be left out and if two other companies were to make it, so I said to Hottinguer, we will take as big a share as any other house and if Baring is going to arrange a subscription in London, it should be done jointly with you. In short, I do not want a major operation to take place under a new government without our name being on it. If such an operation were to succeed without us, then people would say "We don't need Rothschild any more." As we can take as much as we like, it is better that we remain part of this camaraderie . . . The gentlemen concerned are very popular with the ministers.[60]

A passing reference to one of the brothers as "an ass" suggests that relations with James were now rapidly deteriorating.[61]

But the partnership was not yet over. Indeed, Isaac Pereire was deputed to act as James's representative on the new Paris–Lyon company's board. Moreover, his brother Emile continued to play a leading role as chairman of the Nord board, and was involved in the renegotiation of the Nord's concession—the other major railway deal clinched in January 1852. The company raised 40 million francs by issuing bearer bonds and used the money to take over the Boulogne–Amiens line and to build new branch lines (for example, to Maubeuge); in return, its concession was extended for ninety-nine years, with an option to the state to buy the company out in 1876.[62] It was not until later in the year that the split came, when James offered his support to Talabot once again.

Talabot's aim was now to merge the new Paris–Lyon company with his lines to the south—Avignon–Marseille, Marseille–Toulon and smaller lines in Gard and Hérault—creating a grand Compagnie de la Méditerranée along lines very similar to those originally envisaged by the Pereires. James's decision to take 2,000 shares in this ambitious but financially stretched entity left the Pereires out in the cold.[63] (The fact that Morny was another shareholder must cast doubt on the simplistic notion that the Pereires had the new regime's backing against the Rothschilds.) The final blow came when James refused to provide similar financial support for the Pereires' Midi company: although his subscription of 3.3 million francs was far from negligible, Alphonse's resignation from the board was a vote of no confidence.[64] The Crédit Mobilier was therefore founded by the Pereires in response to *their* exclusion from what looked like a new Talabot–Rothschild axis backed by the regime in the person of Morny.

The Pereires did not have to look far for models on which to base their alternative source of railway finance: two successful semi-public banks had already been launched before the Crédit Mobilier was conceived. The first was the Foulds' Crédit Foncier, a mortgage bank established with governmental backing in March 1852 to provide long-term loans to landowners by selling mortgage bonds—an extremely popular nineteenth-century form of investment—to savers. By the end of 1853 it had increased its capital to 60 million francs and had issued loans totalling 27 million.[65] It is worth pointing out that James was as hostile to the Crédit Foncier as he was to the Crédit Mobilier, arguing in October 1853 that the interest at which it lent its money was too high and the obligations it issued were viewed with too much suspicion in rural areas for it to perform its intended purpose. Far from supporting agricultural proprietors, it was being used to finance urban property development, much of it of a speculative nature:

> From the outset we have seen these problems clearly and it is for that reason that we have refused to become involved in the affair, although overtures have repeatedly been made to us . . . The Crédit Foncier . . . involves itself in risky operations and it is these which up until now have made its profits . . . It is not a soundly established enterprise.[66]

The other new bank was the Caisse des Actions Réunies, an investment trust established with 5 million francs' capital by Mirès, then the editor of the *Journal des Chemins de Fer*, in 1850. Although Mirès did not transform the Caisse into the more ambitious Caisse Générale des Chemins de Fers until 1853, he subsequently claimed that it had given Benoît Fould the idea for a much bigger venture:

> I said to myself, if M. Mirès, on his own, could create such a society, a society made up of more considerable people would represent a powerful financial organisation, destined to conduct simultaneously major financial operations and industrial enterprises. On my return [from Baden] I looked for suitable men to involve in this project and I found no one more suitable . . . than MM. E. and I. Pereire . . . And that was how the Crédit Mobilier was born.[67]

Another version has the Interior Minister Persigny more or less forcing the idea of the Crédit Mobilier through against the unbending opposition of Achille Fould—though this was probably an attempt by the Foulds to disclaim responsibility after the Crédit Mobilier had failed.[68] In fact the Foulds and Pereires were equal partners, with a majority shareholding between them.[69]

What was new about the Crédit Mobilier? It was not, despite the original intentions of the Pereires, permitted by the Banque de France to call itself a bank. Essentially, it was an investment trust, set up by a Pereire-led group with a capital of 20 (later 60) million francs, the prime function of which was to attract the savings of smaller investors into railways. Many investors had burnt their fingers in the 1840s when numerous railway companies had issued a multitude of highly volatile shares. The Crédit Mobilier simplified matters: it offered its investors standardised bonds of varying duration and used their money to invest in stocks and shares as its directors saw fit. In short, it was an intermediary between the bond market and the share market, a deposit bank which issued bonds rather than non-transferable certificates of deposit. The final statutes of the bank published on November 20 were the result of a compromise between the more cautious government ministers and the Pereires: current accounts and money raised from the sale of short-term bonds were not to exceed double the firm's paid-up capital, twice the level demanded by the Finance Ministry; money from long-term bonds was not to exceed 600 million francs, ten times its capital.[70]

The Crédit Mobilier is usually seen as a direct challenge to the power of de Rothschild Frères.[71] It is true that there soon developed a fierce commercial rivalry between the two firms. James was also irked by the social pretensions of his erstwhile subordinates—especially when they bought the 8,200 acre estate of d'Armainvilliers next to Ferrières, the Palmer vineyards next to Château Mouton and even the house next door to Nat's in the rue du Faubourg-Saint-Honoré![72] Nor had he made any secret of his reservations about the new bank. As he wrote—in a personal letter to Napoleon on November 15—it would at once be excessively powerful and excessively vulnerable to crises, a line of argument which was less contradictory than Persigny later made it sound.[73]

The first objection James raised was the classic conservative objection to joint-stock companies, that the directors would be "anonymous" and "irresponsible," and might abuse their power over other people's money. But James went further in predicting that the new bank would be in a position to establish "a redoubtable domination of commerce and industry." "By the sheer volume of their investments," he warned, the directors of this company would "make the law in the market, and a law which will be beyond control and beyond competition . . . and concentrate in their hands the greater part of the national wealth . . . That would be a calamity . . . The bank when it is fully active will be stronger than the government itself." At the same time, its very strength would rest on foundations of sand; and this was precisely what made the prospect of a calamity so real. For whereas the bank would offer investors bonds paying fixed interest, its own investments in shares would be "variable, doubtful, uncertain." In a moment of crisis, the bank would lead the economy "to the edge of an abyss." Taking it for granted that the new bank would maintain an inadequate reserve, James predicted that if it got into difficulties the government would have to choose between "a general bankruptcy" or the suspension of gold and silver convertibility.[74] These were exaggerated fears designed to intimidate Louis Napoleon; but they were not entirely without foundation, as we shall see.

Yet the fact that James was opposed to the Crédit Mobilier should not be taken to mean that it was directed against him. It may be that the Pereires were sincere in offering James shares in their new venture; his refusal is not proof of *their* antagonism towards him. Nor should too much be read into the fact that the bank's charter was published in the *Moniteur Universel* while James was away from Paris. The fact that some of the Rothschilds' closest associates in Italy and Germany—Torlonia, Oppenheim and Heine—were among the shareholders also weakens the anti-Rothschild thesis: these people had too much to lose from incurring James's wrath.

In truth, the Crédit Mobilier, with its overt claims to be a financial "centre" acting in the public interest, was more of a challenge to the Banque de France. The new institution had been created, declared Pereire in 1854, "out of the necessity to introduce into circulation a new agent, a new fiduciary money, bearing its own daily interest"—an indication that he saw its bonds as performing a quasi-monetary function.[75] Above all, as the more astute contemporary commentators discerned, it was a response to the Banque de France's tight lending policy in the wake of the 1848 revolution: prior to 1852, the Banque refused to lend money against railway shares and lent against rentes at the relatively steep rate of 6 per cent. As the yield on rentes had fallen to 3.6 per cent by November 1852, the advent of the Crédit Mobilier becomes more intelligible.[76] So does James's opposition: in 1852 de Rothschild Frères held Banque de France shares valued at 1,131,078 francs, which were depressed by the launch of the Crédit Mobilier. We see here the beginning of an alliance between Rothschilds and the Banque which would be consummated when Alphonse became a regent of the Banque in 1855.

The Crédit Mobilier began with a bang. Its 500 franc shares opened at 1,100 and touched 1,600 four days later. At their peak in March 1856 they were trading at 1,982 francs. Those were massive capital gains for the original shareholders which it is hard to believe James did not envy. The dividends too looked healthy, rising from 13 per cent in 1853 to 40 two years later (implying earnings of 4 and 10 per cent).[77] Such results seemed to discredit James's prophecies of disaster. Nor were they the products of creative accounting. For these were the glory years of French railway building: between 1851 and 1856 gross investment increased by a factor of five; more than twice as much track was opened in the 1850s as in the 1840s. Moreover, the ratio of fares and freight charges to operating costs was at its all-time peak.[78] The Crédit Mobilier's raison d'être was to enable the Pereires to take a share of this buoyant market; and in this it succeeded.

Yet the extent of its success should not be exaggerated. It is true that, with the funds they were able to raise through the Crédit Mobilier, the Pereires were able to build up shareholdings in a substantial network of railway companies, exerting a dominant influence over the Midi (Bordeaux–Cette), the Paris–Lyon *via* Bourbonnais line and the Ouest (which merged the Paris–Rouen, Rouen–Havre, Dieppe–Fécamp and Versailles–Rennes lines). But the Rothschilds continued to control the Nord and had the biggest single shareholding in the Paris–Lyon, which later fused with the Grand Central to form the Paris–Lyon–Mediterranean in 1857, not to mention their smaller stakes in the Midi and the Ardennes-et-Oise.[79] Between them the Pereires had eight seats on the boards of various French railway companies; the Rothschilds had fourteen.[80] Besides, there were numerous other new players, notably Morny himself (who launched the Grand Central Company in 1853), not all of whom can be considered Pereire allies. The lines of battle were far less distinct than has often been claimed: Charles Laffitte was the Pereires' partner in the Ouest, but was also a substantial shareholder in the Nord.[81] The duc de Galliera was a founder of the Crédit Mobilier but also a member of the board of the Nord.[82] The

Pereires may have been predominant in the lines which fused to become the Est, but it was N. M. Rothschild & Sons in London which placed bonds worth £2.5 million in London for the company in 1854.[83]

One thing is sure: Mirès' later claim that by 1855 James had "abdicated" in the face of competition from the "new" bank is untenable.[84] In fact, it was the Crédit Mobilier which risked overstretching itself. It was an exaggeration to say, as James did, that its capital was "insignificant," but there is a case for saying that the Crédit Mobilier was undercapitalised in relation to the Pereires' aspirations.[85] As early as 1853, the company sought to issue bonds worth 120 million francs in an attempt to increase the funds at its disposal, but the government exercised its power of veto. When the Pereires tried again in 1855, they were again thwarted by the government.[86] As a result, the Crédit Mobilier increasingly found itself relying on some 60–100 million francs of more conventional deposits, mainly from associated businesses like railway companies. These constraints may explain the marked discrepancy between its founders' stated intentions and the reality of its investment strategy. In fact, its portfolio was characterised by a relatively high turnover, with its total assets fluctuating between as little as 50 million francs in 1854 and as much as 266 million francs a year later.[87]

If the Pereires had confined their activities to France then it is doubtful whether the celebrated "war" between them and the Rothschilds would ever have amounted to much more than a skirmish. But they did not. What made the Crédit Mobilier seem genuinely threatening to James was its potential to expand outside France and to become a pan-European phenomenon. On April 2, 1853, the Cologne bankers Abraham Oppenheim and Gustave Mevissen of the Schaffhausenscher Bankverein were granted a licence by the Grand Duke of Hesse-Darmstadt to open a discounting and issuing bank. They called the new bank the Darmstädter Bank für Handel und Industrie and, with its projected capital set at 25 million gulden (around 54 million francs) and its Pereire-style charter, it obviously aimed to be the German Crédit Mobilier. This was effectively a challenge to the Rothschilds in their ancestral home: Darmstadt is less than twenty miles to the south of Frankfurt, and the only reason Oppenheim and Mevissen chose to establish their new bank there was that the authorities in both Frankfurt and Cologne had refused to grant them a licence. Among the nine directors, four were from Frankfurt, including the Rothschilds' old rival Moritz Bethmann.

But what was more worrying was the direct involvement of the Pereires and Foulds in the new venture. As we have seen, Abraham Oppenheim himself had been one of the original shareholders in the Crédit Mobilier (he had 500 shares), and he sent his brother Simon to Paris to drum up French interest. The agreement he made was generous: of the initial 40,000 shares, the founder-directors retained 4,000; a further 4,000 were issued by Bethmann in Frankfurt, 10,000 were sold at par to Crédit Mobilier shareholders and the remainder were held jointly by Oppenheim, Mevissen, Fould and the Crédit Mobilier. But it proved the only way of ensuring the success of the new venture. Had it not been for French purchases of the shares when they were offered to the public in May, the price might very well have fallen below par (a weakness which was inevitably blamed on Rothschild machinations). The effect of these purchases was to give the Crédit Mobilier a majority shareholding.[88] It was not long before there was talk of establishing similar satellites in other countries. As early as July 1853, James felt obliged to warn the Piedmontese banker Bolmida against establishing a Crédit Mobilier in Turin, warning him that the "disagreeable possibilities" of such a bank would outweigh the "positive advantages."[89] The Pereires' first attempt to establish a Spanish Crédito Mobiliaro was also in 1853, while the idea of a Belgian Crédit Mobilier was floated not much later. By 1854 even Austria did not seem immune to Pereire penetration.[90] These moves raised the alarming possibility that the Crédit Mobilier might take on the character of a multinational, challenging the hitherto unique position of the Rothschilds in European finance.

Again, however, the story should not be oversimplified. It was not only the Pereires who realised the possibilities of joint-stock banking in the 1850s. There were a number of imitations in London (for example, the Crédit Foncier and Mobilier of England, the International Land Company and the International Financial Society), though they made little headway. In 1855 and 1856 alone, thirteen such banks were established in German states, including David Hansemann's Disconto-Gesellschaft, the Berliner Handelsgesellschaft, the Vereinsbank and the Norddeutsche Bank (the last two both in Hamburg). Nor should we ignore the equally important newcomers who adopted the more traditional private and merchant banking structure, for in many ways these posed a more enduring threat to the Rothschilds' pre-eminence. In London, the dominant position of Baring Brothers and N. M. Rothschild (especially in the acceptance market) was being challenged by the growth of existing merchant banks like Schröders and Frühling & Goschen, and the advent of newer firms, notably C. J. Hambro & Son (1839), Overend Gurney and Kleinwort & Cohen (1855). In Frankfurt too, M. A. Rothschild & Söhne was encountering new competition from Erlanger & Söhne, founded by the converted Jew Löb Moses Erlanger, as well as from Jacob S. H. Stern, Lazard Speyer-Ellissen, Moritz B. Goldschmidt (1851) and Gebrüder Sulzbach (1856).[91] In Paris, a new force was the firm of Lazard Frères, founded in 1854.

Apart from the boom conditions of the early 1850s, one reason for the proliferation of new banks was the revolution in communications brought about by the advent of the telegraph. Though the original discovery can be traced back to the eighteenth century, and successful demonstrations of its application happened in the 1830s, it was not until after 1848 that the telegraph had a real impact on international finance. By 1850 lines were in commercial operation in the United States, England and Prussia, France and Belgium; but it was the Dover–Calais submarine link in 1851 which was the real watershed. Even before the cable had been laid, Julius Reuter[92] wrote to New Court: "Should you favour our service for the transmission of the Berlin and Viennese exchange rates we would pledge ourselves not to give the service to any other London house and moreover we would refund you for any cable not arriving at the fixed time."[93] However, any such monopolistic arrangement had long since vanished on the Continent and did not last long in London.

This explains the somewhat unexpected hostility of James to an innovation he might have been expected to embrace. Throughout the 1850s, he repeatedly complained that "the telegraph is ruining our business." The fact was that the telegraph made it much easier to do what the Rothschilds had managed so ingeniously before, namely to conduct financial business between affiliated houses over long distances.

Many of their rivals now sought to imitate their example with the assistance of "the wires": by the 1860s, Frankfurt families like the Speyers, Sterns and Erlangers had all established branches in London and Paris and, in the case of the Speyers, in New York as well. "It appears," James complained in April 1851, "that yesterday a great many German scoundrels sold [French] railway shares in London with the telegraph . . . Since the telegraph became available, people work much more. Every day at 12 they send a despatch, even for trivial deals, and realise [their profit] before the bourse closes the same day." Once, the Rothschilds had been able to steal a march on their rivals with their unrivalled system of couriers and carrier pigeons; but now "anyone can get the news." James could see that there was no alternative but "to do the same," but it still struck him as a "crying shame that the telegraph has been established." It meant that even when he went to take the waters for his summer holiday, there was no respite from business: "One has too much to think about when bathing, which is not good."[94] Such complaints were still being echoed by James's son as late as the 1870s:[95] although the Rothschilds had no option but to make use of the new technology, they always regretted the way it tended to broadcast financial news, and continued to write letters to one another in their accustomed fashion right up until the First World War.

The Gold Rush

The significance of such grumblings should not be exaggerated, however. The reality was that, although they were facing increased competition in Europe, the Rothschilds remained in a league of their own as an authentically global operation. Indeed, it was in the continents beyond the reach of the telegraph that they made some of their biggest advances in the 1850s. There was no telegraph link from Europe to North America or India until 1866; no link to Latin America until 1869; and no link to Australia until 1873. In these regions, the Rothschilds' traditional system of semi-autonomous agents, corresponding regularly but not in daily contact, remained unsurpassed. The European agents continued to do their work, of course: Weisweiller and Bauer in Madrid; Samuel Lambert, having succeeded his father-in-law Richtenberger in Brussels; and newer recruits like Horaz Landau who served in Constantinople and then Italy. But their role as intelligence-gatherers was now less important than it had been, though of course confidential political information remained at a premium and could be obtained if an agent was well enough connected. It was the more remote agents, however, whose role was of greater strategic significance in this period.

The 1848 crisis had exposed the difficulty of conducting business across the Atlantic, particularly when a single agent occupied such a position of independent power in New York. It had partly been with the idea of replacing Belmont with a full Rothschild partner that James had sent Alphonse there in October that year. Betty's letters to her son demonstrate how serious this intention was. He should, she advised, be patient until he had acquired enough experience of American affairs but then

> you can speak the language of the big boys; respectfully first of all, and, if politeness does not work, then with energy and the dignity which befits your status and rights, and which will put the man in his place. If

after that Mr B. still wants to play the lord and let you take it or leave it, well then you'll be in a position to take up your glove and show this gentleman the door . . .[96]

Matters evidently came to a head in the spring of 1849. "The situation with Belmont is no longer tenable," she wrote on March 24. He had

too little merited one's trust for one to leave him even a pretence of it without failing one's own interest and one's dignity . . . The question is then: wouldn't it be a great help to the future of our family to set up a House in New York, a House which would bear our name . . . America's future appears so grandiose to those who choose to reflect on it that I hold fast to the thought with pride, I confess, that you, my son, will be the one to lay the foundations of a House that will bring honour to our name . . . [Y]our career would take off . . . and you will leap to the head of a great House with one step.

Her plan, she told him in May, was "to see you established in America for anything . . . and deliver this great future from the stupidity and greed of an agent . . . So I repeat: stay in the New World; if the worst comes to the worst, if the old world should fall, which God will not permit, it would become a new fatherland for us."[97]

The idea continued to be discussed after her son's (supposedly temporary) return to Europe in 1849. "Alphonse . . . has made up his mind to return," reported Lionel having seen his cousin at Wildbad; "we have spoken in general terms about the American business, but that is all. Uncle James and Alphonse both think a great deal of money is to be made in America and wish to continue that business, so that in any case he will go back."[98] Alphonse himself spoke of "putting affairs over there on a more convenient footing" when he returned to America, and Castellane was in no doubt that he would soon leave Paris again "to found a house in New York."[99] Even in New York, it was "everywhere known that Baron Alphonse is coming to the States."[100]

Yet it never happened; an omission which was arguably the Rothschilds' single greatest strategic mistake. It is not easy to say why this was. One possibility, strongly suggested by Betty's letters, is that Alphonse could not bring himself to relinquish the comforts of Parisian life for the less sophisticated ways of New York. It was the mother who had to persuade the son, and she sought to make the idea more appealing to him by suggesting that, after an initial period of two years, the day-to-day running of the projected new house would be entrusted to "a temporary agent up to the time when someone from the family, or later, your brothers, wanted to devote a stay of a few months to it from time to time . . . Once the House was founded you could quickly come back to us, dear son, while at the same time overseeing the man who would come to replace you from afar."[101] Nor were the London partners much enthused, though they continued to suspect Belmont of "speculating with our money."[102] According to Betty, Lionel and his brothers took "a dim view of this project." They were "worried that Paris is getting too much out of it, and would rather see an agent there. But this agent could only be Davidson who works very much in their interest."[103]

Perhaps the most convincing explanation, however, is that Belmont at last succeeded in persuading James that he could not be replaced. By now he was a well-established figure in the US, whose social standing and political influence were growing almost as rapidly as his personal fortune. In 1849 he was able to announce his engagement to Caroline Perry, daughter of Commodore Matthew Galbraith Perry of the United States Navy and, as Belmont emphasised, a member of "one of our best families."[104] Four years later, in an unexpected role-reversal, it was Belmont who came to Europe—as the American ambassador to the Hague.[105] These signs of worldly success (which a young, French-educated Rothschild would have taken time to equal) may finally have convinced James to let Belmont be. Even Betty acknowledged that Belmont had "created for himself a strong and independent position; he knows inside-out all the country's resources; he holds the key to all the wheeling and dealing in the commercial world." "I would incline to the view," her husband reluctantly concluded in 1858,

> that we should leave the management of American business entirely in Belmont's hands, as we can have complete confidence in him and he understands business there so completely, and if we do so we shall no longer have to put up with endless complaints and questions as to whether or not we will accept bills from this or that banker.[106]

Only seven years before he had been complaining bitterly that Belmont did not let him "see the books" of the New York agency.[107]

Of course, Belmont was only in charge of the East Coast business; that principally meant bond issues by established north-eastern states like New York, Pennsylvania and Ohio and major railways like the Illinois Central. Of increasing allure in the 1850s, however, was the West Coast, where Benjamin Davidson had been sent from Mexico, armed with a blanket credit of £40,000, on the news that gold had been struck in California.[108] Once again, the Rothschilds had misgivings about entrusting their interests to a single individual in so remote a market—"where civilisation is at a very low ebb [and] where affairs are attended with personal risk"; so it was decided to send a clerk named May from the Frankfurt house to join Davidson in San Francisco. James approved of May: he was "a good little chap . . . clever and a Frankfurt Jew. I always have a great deal of confidence in such people."[109] But he was soon disillusioned. Just over a year later, a row blew up when May and Davidson decided to spend between $26,000 and $50,000 on a new house. Davidson's brother leapt to his defence, pointing out that the Californian agency had made profits of £37,762 in just two years; that its running costs were justifiable given the high cost of living in San Francisco; and that prior to acquiring the new house he had been living in a "shanty built over his vault, like a pig in a sty—which he left to go out & get his meals in fear and trembling lest a cry of fire should call him back & that he should find himself burnt out."[110]

As in the case of similar disputes with agents, this seems to have blown over, leaving both Davidson and May *in situ*. Ten years later, they were both still there; indeed, it was now May who requested to be allowed to return home—in a letter which sheds light on the Rothschilds' relations with their American agents:

> I am growing every day older, I am now in my 36th year, and it is time for me to make up my mind whether I should continue to lead this solitary life and spend the remainder of my days far away from my family, or whether I should return and settle at home. This is no Country where

a man and particularly a European, even if he should have the least pretensions to civilization and sociability, can remain for many years, it is
all very well as long as one is young but the riper age brings on other
ideas. You must not suppose . . . that I have accumulated so much
wealth in this country, which determined me to withdraw from the
business . . . it is true that the position which you had been kind enough
to give me and which kindness I shall never forget and makes me all my
life grateful to you, has been to me a great advantage, but . . . your interests have never in the least suffered by it and . . . your business had
always to be considered first and cared for above all.[111]

Later in the 1850s, it was decided to send another Davidson—Nathaniel—to
take Benjamin's place in Mexico, which, for all its political instability, still promised
important business opportunities: not only loans to the chronically insolvent state,
but also investments in mercury and coal mines and an iron foundry.[112] The importance of this continuing Mexican presence increased in 1860–61, when Mexico
became the object of French imperial ambitions. Scharfenberg meanwhile remained
in Cuba, which momentarily acquired a political importance when the American
government sought to buy it from Spain—a scheme in which Belmont had a hand,
but which foundered in the face of political opposition in the US.

Finally, mention should also be made of another traditional Rothschild sphere of
interest in the Americas: Brazil. This had been a hobby-horse of Nathan's in the
1820s, but for two decades business between London and Rio had been limited,
partly because successive governments had not had recourse to the London capital
market.[113] That changed with the outbreak of war with Argentina and Uruguay in
1851, the costs of which forced Brazil to issue a £1.04 million loan through N. M.
Rothschild the following year. The rapid growth of the country's railway network
also created new financial needs. The 1851 loan was quickly followed by a £1.8 million issue for the Bahia and San Francisco Railway Company; another loan of £1.5
million to the government which was also to finance railways (both 1858); a £2 million issue for the São Paulo Railway Company (1859) and another government loan
of just under £1.4 million.[114] A currency crisis in 1860 and a slide in the price of
Brazilian bonds necessitated a period of consolidation; a new loan of £3.8 million in
1863 therefore mainly served to convert earlier debts dating from the 1820s and
1840s.[115] However, the outbreak of war with Paraguay in 1865 put Brazilian
finances under renewed pressure and it was only after protracted negotiations with
the Brazilian minister Moriera that Lionel agreed to a new loan of just under £7 million.[116] As the war drew to a close in 1869–70, there was talk of yet another loan. It
was just the beginning of an exceptionally monogamous financial relationship
between the Brazilian government and the London house which, between 1852 and
1914, generated bond issues worth no less than £142 million.[117]

Brazil and the United States had been areas of Rothschild activity for decades;
Asia was more or less *terra incognita* by comparison. But here too the 1850s were a
time of expansion. In the wake of the "Opium Wars" of 1839–42 (so called because
the pretext for fighting them was a Chinese bar on opium imports from British-controlled India), Hong Kong had been annexed by Britain and five other Chinese
"treaty ports" opened to European traders. This accelerated the process whereby

Chinese teas and silks were exchanged for Western silver and Indian opium, and created attractive new opportunities for British business (simultaneously eroding the power of Chinese merchants like Wu Ping-chien, whom one historian has called the Rothschild of the Orient).[118] By 1853 the London house was in regular correspondence with a Shanghai-based merchant firm, Cramptons, Hanbury & Co., to whom it made regular shipments of silver from Mexico and Europe.[119] Silver was evidently the prime concern, though the bank was also interested in Indian opium, some of which found its way westward to Constantinople, and by the later 1850s it was in regular correspondence with a Calcutta firm, Schoene, Kilburn & Co. Peripheral crises like the Chinese rebellions of the 1850s and the Indian Mutiny of 1857 thus had a resonance in New Court which previous Asian upheavals had lacked. For the first time, the bank was becoming involved in the commerce of the British Empire, a field it had previously left to others.[120] It was thus a pardonable exaggeration to say that "the entire universe paid tribute [to Rothschild]; he had his offices in China, in India, in even the least civilised countries."[121] This was the great difference between the Rothschilds and the Eurocentric Pereires.

The great flow of silver to the East which was such a feature of the mid-nineteenth-century world economy helps explain why discoveries of gold in California and Australia in the 1840s aroused such excitement. The impact of these discoveries can hardly be overstated. In 1846 world gold production was around 1.4 million troy ounces fine, of which more than half came from Russia. By 1855 total production had risen to 6.4 million ounces, with around half the increase from North America and half from Australia. We have already seen how the Rothschilds sought to involve themselves in the Californian gold rush by sending Benjamin Davidson north from Mexico. They were also interested in the Australian fields. No sooner had gold been discovered in New South Wales and Victoria in 1851 than the Rothschilds were being urged "that a branch of your House accredited here with an ample supply of coin at the commencement would form the basis of one of the most extensive and moneyed establishments in either hemisphere."[122] This advice was not followed to the letter: as in the case of Shanghai and Calcutta it was at first thought sufficient to rely on a separate firm as Melbourne correspondent, though in this case the firm was run by Jacob Montefiore and his son Leslie.[123] However, family ties proved no guarantee of competence. As if to confirm Mayer Amschel's hallowed disdain for in-laws, Montefiore & Co. went bankrupt in 1855 owing a substantial sum to the London house, and a proper Rothschild agent, Jeffrey Cullen, had to be sent out to act as fireman.

The Cullens had worked for N. M. Rothschild since the time of Waterloo, so Cullen had a good idea of what his employers wanted: even before he had wound up the Montefiores' tangled affairs, he was eagerly asking for consignments of mercury and other goods in demand in the colony (above all alcohol, whether beer, whisky or port). "If you should make me a consignment of this," he wrote, unconsciously echoing the tone of Nathan's letters as a young textile dealer, "you may rest assured of my using all my endeavors to do the business in such a way as to give you satisfaction." By September he was asking for "a credit of £5,000 or £10,000 by every mail ship" and, in order to enable him to visit the gold diggings in person, the assistance of "a good Financier, as there is not such a thing in the whole Colony, even the heads of the Government are grossly ignorant of their business and upon more than one occasion I have been sent [for by] the Treasury, to explain some trifling matter of monetary affairs."[124]

If Cullen was at the periphery of the Rothschilds' nascent gold and silver empire, at its centre lay the various refineries and mints which the family acquired in this period. James had operated his own refinery in Paris since as early as 1827, moving it to a new building in Quai de Valmy and establishing a *société en commandite* under the direction of Michel Benoît Poisat in 1838. At the same time, he went into partnership with Dierickx, the Master of Paris Mint in 1843, a relationship which lasted until 1860.[125] The new gold discoveries led to an immense increase in the activity of both refinery and mint. It was, in James's words, "a revolution in the money market." Thus, when Lionel resolved in 1849 to involve the London house directly in the gold-refining business, he was following his uncle's lead.

In Nathan's day, there had been four private refiners in London—Browne & Wingrove, Johnson & Stokes, Percival Norton Johnson and Cox & Merle—in addition to the Royal Mint's own refinery. Of these, Browne & Wingrove had done the lion's share of the Bank of England's refining. However, the discoveries in California and Australia greatly increased the volume of gold coming to the Bank: in 1852 gold purchases reached a peak of £15.3 million, over two-thirds of which was in bar form—far more than Browne & Wingrove could handle. It was to fill this gap that Lionel proposed to lease the Royal Mint's refinery, which since 1829 had been using the sulphuric acid system of parting under its Master, Mathison. From September 1849 he began telling his political allies J. Abel Smith and Lord John Russell "repeatedly" that "a change in the system of the Mint" was necessary, a recommendation duly adopted by a Royal Commission set up to examine its activities. "I hope," he told his brothers, "the ministers will have courage enough to make the alterations and that we shall be able to get it—it would be a capital business." As Nat said, "with such large arrivals of specie from California & Mexico it is more necessary than ever."

Mathison predictably sought to resist this "privatisation," but in vain; and fortunately for the Rothschilds Percival Norton Johnson did not listen to his new partner George Matthey, who urged him to enter a bid.[126] In January 1852, therefore, Anthony acquired the lease for the refinery, and by December Lionel was in a position formally to ask the Governor of the Bank, Thomas Hankey (another political ally), "to be permitted to present directly to the Bank of England my gold and silver bars, refined and melted under my responsibility." In its first year of activity, the refinery processed over 300,000 ounces of Australian gold and 450,000 ounces of Californian.[127] It was a sign of its importance that Gladstone—that most ardent of bullionists—paid a visit there in 1862, directly after an "expedition" to the Bank of England.[128] As Flandreau has shown, their control of refining and minting capacity on both sides of the Channel enabled the Rothschilds to operate a unique "system" of arbitrage, with the London house buying American or Australian gold on the French house's account, relaying these via the London bullion brokers to Paris. The Paris house meanwhile bought silver for New Court, which relayed it via London or Southampton to the East. Not only was this profitable; by the late 1850s it was becoming an integral part of a bimetallic international monetary system.[129]

Public Finance and the Crimean War

For decades, the Rothschilds had regarded a major European war as the greatest of all dangers to their own financial position—worse even than a revolution. In March 1854 war came. Implausibly, the Crimean War had its origins in a dispute between Catholic and Orthodox monks about the so-called Holy Places in Jerusalem. In reality, it was a revival of the old question about how much power Russia should exercise over the waning Ottoman Empire—in particular, the Danubian principalities of Moldavia and Wallachia—and the Black Sea. This time, in contrast to 1840, France and Britain united: the former in order to break up the Holy Alliance, the latter for no reason other than to give the Tsar a beating, which a liberal public felt he deserved for his conduct in suppressing the Hungarian revolution in 1849. The Tsar, who five years before had been the arbiter of Central Europe, found himself deserted by the other members of the Holy Alliance: Austria flirted with the Western powers and all but joined in the war, Prussia continued her policy of impotence and irrelevance. Piedmont jumped on the anti-Russian bandwagon in the belief that any war would weaken the Austrian position in Italy.

Considering how quickly the Russians gave into the demands of this coalition, it was a strangely prolonged war. The first serious military action came in the summer of 1853 when the Tsar ordered troops into the Danubian principalities and the British and French navies approached the Dardanelles. By the time fighting broke out between Russia and Turkey in October, the Russians had effectively dropped their overblown claim to be sole protectors of Christians in the Ottoman Empire; so France and Britain had to go to war over the principalities and the Black Sea. But in June 1854, the Tsar promised the Austrians that he would evacuate the principalities; the war could then only be about the Black Sea. It was therefore to revise the 1841 Straits convention "in the interests of the Balance of Power of Europe" that French and British troops landed at the Crimea, with the practical objective of capturing Sevastopol. As early as November 1854, the Russian government agreed to this point (again for fear of Austria joining in) but because France and Britain had still to decide what it actually meant, the war dragged inconclusively on. Attempts to find a negotiated agreement following Nicholas I's death in March 1855 foundered. Instead, the Russians rashly decided to resist any restrictions on their naval power in the Black Sea, goading the Western powers to finish the war off. Sevastopol fell on September 8; the French suggested some new war aims; and finally at the Congress of Paris (February–April 1856) the crisis was concluded. The Black Sea was neutralised; Russia lost a chunk of Bessarabia (modern Moldova); and France and Britain agreed to guarantee the future independence of Turkey. In practice, these terms would last as long as Russia took to recover from her defeat—about twenty years, as it turned out, for it had been a traumatic and costly exposure of the Tsarist system's administrative deficiencies. The most enduring achievement of the victors was the creation of Rumania by the fusion of the Danubian principalities, which was achieved in 1859—something they had not set out to achieve.

The precise causes and significance of the Crimean War did not concern the Rothschilds much. Why should they? A dispute between Roman and Greek monks over Christian relics held no interest for the builders of the Jerusalem Jewish hospital. Nor did they have any railway interests in the Danubian principalities. As for the international status of the Black Sea, the London house had already taken a conscious decision not to involve itself in grain exports from Odessa for purely economic reasons.[130] What mattered was that a war—any war—between the great powers was bound to have a disruptive effect on the international financial markets. And so it did, as table 2a shows.

Table 2a: The financial impact of the Crimean War.

	PEAK PRICE	DATE	TROUGH PRICE	DATE	PERCENTAGE CHANGE
British 3 per cent consols	101.38	Dec. 1852	85.75	Apr. 1854	−15
French 4.5 per cent rentes	105.25	Feb. 1853	89.75	Mar. 1854	−15
Austrian 5 per cent metalliques	84.62	Dec. 1852	64.25	Dec. 1854	−24
Prussian 3.5 per cent bonds	94.50	Dec. 1852	84.25	Dec. 1854	−11

Note: British and French figures are weekly closing prices as quoted in London; Austrian and Prussian figures are end-of-year prices as quoted in Frankfurt.
Sources: *Spectator*; Heyn, "Private banking and industrialisation," pp. 358–72.

To diplomatic observers, the Rothschilds looked worried, and understandably so. Their correspondent in St Petersburg had reassured them in June 1853 there would be no war, and had been believed.[131] When the British Foreign Minister Clarendon saw Lionel on September 27—shortly after the government's instructions to Admiral Dundas to pass the Straits had been leaked—he told him "he never remember[ed] such a day" in the City.[132] In January 1854, with the Western navies finally entering the Black Sea, Hübner found James "completely demoralised."[133] Amschel gave the same impression. When Bismarck heard the news of the Russian ambassador's recall from Paris in February 1854, he "considered whom I could best frighten thereby. My eye fell on [Amschel] Rothschild. He turned as white as chalk when I gave him the news to read. His first remark was, 'If only I had known it this morning'; his second, 'Will you do a little business with me tomorrow?' I declined the offer in a friendly way, thanking him and left him to his agitated reflections."[134] John Bright, one of the most vociferous opponents of the war in London, heard Lionel remark gravely on March 31 that "a country with £800,000,000 of debt should have considered much and seriously before it involved itself in another war."[135]

Yet far from weakening the Rothschilds' position, the Crimean War had precisely the opposite effect in that it emphatically reasserted the Rothschild houses' primacy in the field of public finance. Indeed, it demonstrated that the Rothschilds had for years been exaggerating the financial dangers of war. In reality, wars—and especially short wars of the sort which characterised the period from 1854 to 1871—created financial opportunities which they, with their distinctive multinational structure, were especially well placed to exploit. Even for those powers which did not directly fight in it, the Crimean War increased military expenditure above the level of revenues available from taxation (see table 2b), and therefore forced all concerned—even parsimonious Britain—to go to the bond market. Although their rivals, including the Crédit Mobilier, tried, none could challenge the Rothschilds' traditional pre-eminence in that market.

It made life easier, of course, that an old rival—Barings—had the misfortune to be banker to the losing side. In 1850, it had seemed a setback when the Russian government entrusted a new £5.5 million loan to Baring.[136] Heavily oversubscribed, it had opened at a 2 per cent premium and left Joshua Bates and Thomas Baring with a commission of £105,000.[137] But two years later, as diplomatic relations deteriorated, Barings found itself in an exposed position, denounced by Palmerston in the Commons as the Tsar's "agent" and widely (though erroneously) believed to have participated in the 1854 Russian war loan.[138]

Table 2b: Increases in public spending, 1852–1855 (millions of national currencies).

	AUSTRIA (GULDEN)	BRITAIN (POUNDS)	FRANCE (FRANCS)	RUSSIA (ROUBLES)
1852	310	55	1,513	280
1853	321	56	1,548	313
1854	407	83	1,988	384
1855	441	93	2,309	526
percentage increase	42	69	53	88

Source: Mitchell, *European historical statistics*, pp. 734f.

This helps to explain the near monopoly enjoyed by Rothschilds over British war finance. As Chancellor when the war began, Gladstone had pledged himself with characteristic rigour against "the system of raising funds necessary for war by loans," on the grounds that it "practise[d] wholesale systematic deception upon the people." Britain was still burdened by a substantial debt left over from the Napoleonic Wars: as Lionel had said, the national debt on the eve of war stood at around £782 million, and although in relation to gross national product the debt burden was steadily falling (from 250 per cent in 1820 to around 115 per cent in 1854), contemporary politicians were unaware of this. Gladstone therefore proposed to finance the war by increasing income tax—first from 7d in the pound to 10½d, finally to 14d—and some consumption taxes. It was not enough, however, and by the time he resigned from office (to be replaced by Sir George Lewis), the government had run up a £6.2 million deficit for the year 1854 (financed by the sale of treasury bills) and faced a shortfall nearly four times as large in the following year. Lewis imposed a further £5.5 million of new taxation, but the 1855 deficit remained £22.7 million. The government had no alternative but to turn to the City; with Barings under a cloud, that could only mean New Court.

In 1855 the London house took the whole of a loan worth £16 million. In February the following year—by which time the war was, of course, over—it submitted the only tender for another loan of £5 million; and in May it secured a final tranche of £5 million. In both the 1855 loans, Lionel at first offered fractionally less than the minimum set by the Chancellor, but had no hesitation in accepting the government's terms. It is hard to say how meaningful this bargaining was: the terms agreed were only slightly higher than the current market yield on consols, so there was no question of unjustifiable profits being made by the bank. Lionel was probably seeking as much to strike a patriotic posture as to make a profit, with a view to strengthening the case for his own admission to Parliament. On the other hand, the 1856 loans were heavily oversubscribed (by a factor of nearly six in February and eight in May). Palmerston saw this as a sign of City confidence in the government; it might equally well have been proof that the Chancellor was being over-generous in the aftermath of victory.[139]

In France the revival of Rothschild influence over public finance actually pre-dated the war. On March 14, 1852, Napoleon announced a large conversion opera-tion, intended to cut the cost of debt service by reducing the interest due on the greater part of the national debt from 5 to 4.5 per cent.[140] Investors had twenty days to choose between accepting the new 4.5 per cents or redeeming the 5 per cents for cash. The move was justified by the government in macroeconomic terms as part of a strategy to lower interest rates and boost business activity. However, faced with a sudden slump in the price of 5 per cents (from 103 to 99 in just ten days) and fear-ing that an unexpectedly high number of bondholders would demand the redemp-tion of their rentes rather than conversion, the new Finance Minister Jean Bineau was forced to turn to the bankers. It was Hottinguer and de Rothschild Frères rather than the Pereires who took the largest share in the subsequent support operation, whereby the banks bought up 5 per cents to push the price back above par; and the Banque de France which facilitated their purchases by extending its discounting facilities against rentes.[141] The manoeuvre achieved its object, and the great major-ity of rentiers accepted the new bonds.[142]

Two years later, when France and Britain issued their ultimatum to Russia to withdraw from the Danubian principalities, James naturally expected to be called on once again by the French Treasury. On March 4, 1854, he told Prince Albert's brother Ernest II, Duke of Saxe-Coburg-Gotha, "that for a war with Russia any sum was at command; he would furnish at once 'as many millions as were desired'."[143] By now, however, the Crédit Mobilier had entered the lists, and when the government three days later announced its intention to borrow 250 million francs, a contest between the two seemed inevitable. Mirès later claimed the credit for persuading Bineau and Napoleon to sell the bonds directly by public subscription; perhaps he did. Yet he exaggerated when he claimed that this and the subsequent 500 million franc war loan of 1855 had "liberated the French government from a tyranny incompatible with the dignity of a dynasty born of universal suffrage."[144] For by April 1855, with another 750 million francs needed, the new Finance Minister Pierre Magne had to inform Napoleon that the domestic market was reaching satu-ration point.[145] As a result, a substantial share of the 1855 loan was issued in London, and Napoleon elected to revert to the French government's traditional banker there. Although the Crédit Mobilier took a substantial share of this issue, the Rothschilds were once again in charge: while the Paris house handled some 60 mil-lion francs, the London house received subscriptions totalling 208.5 million.[146]

The Rothschilds' role in assisting the Banque de France in the post-war monetary crisis—in part a consequence of the government's short-term borrowing from the Banque during the war—merely underlined James's ascendancy. Writing in April 1856, James could not conceal his glee at the regime's difficulties: "The Emperor is excessively displeased to see that the birth of a prince and the conclusion of peace are not having a better effect on public credit, and that it might be said that he has been forced to make peace for want of money." Indeed, the money market was so tight that, if James were to make a business trip to Brussels, people might say that he was taking all his capital there.[147] Not for the last time, James was subtly mocking the regime's financial dependence on him.

The other combatant power to whom the Rothschilds lent money was Turkey. Here too there was competition, though this is understandable as the Rothschilds had not hitherto established a serious financial relationship with the Porte (with the exception of the Greek indemnity payment). The first Turkish war loan of 1854 was taken by Goldschmidt, Bischoffsheim (a minor City house, Palmer, MacKillop & Dent, also seems to have been involved, though James somewhat paranoiacally suspected the long arm of the Crédit Mobilier). It was a failure. Attracted by descriptions of Turkey's copper mines and perhaps thinking of Turkey as Nathan had previously thought of Spain, James therefore resolved to take over.[148] In Horaz Landau, who had been sent as the Rothschild agent to Constantinople shortly before the Crimean War, he chose an able negotiator; when the Turks found themselves in need of more funds in 1855 the Rothschilds were ready and waiting.

In February 1855, during a temporary lull in the fighting, Landau began skilfully to weave his way between the Sultan's minister Fuad Pasha and the Western diplomats, proposing a new loan, this time guaranteed by France and Britain, while at the same time drip-feeding short-term advances to the government—a classic Rothschild tactic. In August the London house was able to inform Landau that a £5 million loan to Turkey had been secured with an Anglo-French guarantee, thus allowing much more generous terms to be offered than would otherwise have been possible.[149] No sooner was the war over than Alphonse was despatched to Constantinople to discuss the possibility of establishing a new bank there, once again encountering competition from a minor English house (this time Layards). However, the onset of the 1857 economic crisis—combined with a realisation that the risks involved in Turkish finance were greater than had initially been anticipated—led to something of a retreat from Constantinople in the succeeding years.[150] Although Landau continued to agree to small advances, the idea that "the national bank of Turkey [might] become a branch of the House of Rothschild" (as *The Times* put it in 1857) was shelved.[151]

Austria did not fire a shot in the Crimean War. She had to make substantial military preparations, however, if only to back up her tougher diplomatic communications to Russia regarding the Danubian principalities; and because of the fragility of her financial and monetary system in the wake of 1848–9, the effect was roughly equivalent to that of outright war on the French economy (if not greater). As tables 2a and 2b show, Austrian bonds were actually worse affected by the war than French; and Austrian expenditure rose by only slightly less, despite the policy of non-intervention. This was the first act in a "tragedy" of financial weakness which in many ways provides the key to the disasters which befell Austria in the decade after 1857. Past and present military expenditure weighed heavily on the Austrian budget, so that defence spending and debt service accounted for 60–80 per cent of the total. Although attempts were made to economise, fresh military crises invariably nullified these. Taxes were raised and state assets were sold; still the government had to borrow to meet its outgoings. When it borrowed short from the National Bank, the exchange rate—decoupled from silver in 1848—depreciated: between mid-1853 and mid-1854 the gulden fell from 9 per cent below par to 36 per cent below. When the government borrowed long from a frail bond market, the effect was to crowd out private investment. Between 1848 and 1865 the total funded public debt rose from 1.1 billion gulden to 2.5 billion, an average annual increase of around 80 million, but with disruptive peaks as in the mid-1850s. Constantly haemorrhaging fiscal and monetary policy thus combined to constrain economic growth, so that the tax base stagnated and the downward spiral continued.[152]

Could anything have been done to remedy this? In November 1851 the Austrian Finance Minister Krauss wrote a letter to James "in which he lamented a good deal and demanded his counsel, requesting him to shed some light on the situation." On being shown this letter, Apponyi urged James "not just to shed some light, but to take a torch, as only you can, and try to rid us of all our monetary wastepaper."[153] James and his partners tried. Though the Rothschilds might justifiably have closed down the Vienna house after 1848, instead Anselm set about rebuilding what his father had built only to destroy. It was a thankless task, the more so as Anselm's wife refused to settle in a city she disliked intensely. A rather lonely figure, he at first went through the motions of following in his father's footsteps: going to see the returned Metternich, making public donations to causes favoured by the Emperor[154]—even siding with Austrian foreign policy in a half-hearted sort of way. But Anselm was haunted by the memory of his father's downfall, and all his efforts to shore up Austrian finances were, one senses, premised on a sense of inevitable failure. When he called on Metternich in December 1853, Anselm's mood was bleak:

> Austria's financial condition, he stated . . . was inevitably approaching a crisis, unless we hit upon the right method of avoiding it . . . Rothschild declared that he had expected better things of Herr Baumgartner [Krauss's successor as Finance Minister], but that Baumgartner had no sense of reality and was not equal to his task . . . The conversation at this stage was interrupted by a visit from the Nuncio. Rothschild took his leave and as I went with him to the door he said to me, "You mark my words, we are on the eve of a crisis; if something is not done to avert it, it will be upon us before the new year!"[155]

Still, there were successes which kept alive the tradition of Rothschild influence at Vienna, albeit in shadowy form. In 1852 the London and Frankfurt house jointly issued Austrian 5 per cents worth £3.5 million for Baumgartner.[156] In April 1854, faced with a run on the currency, the government turned once again to Anselm, who managed to persuade the other houses to participate in a further credit of 34 million gulden, though nearly half of this was provided by Fould.[157]

In short, the bond issues generated directly or indirectly by the Crimean War were largely handled by the Rothschilds. Table 2c (which only gives the figures for the London house) provides an overview.

2c: Principal bond issues by N. M. Rothschild & Sons, 1850–1859.

	COUNTRY	NOMINAL AMOUNT ISSUED (£)	COUPON (PER CENT)	PRICE
1852	Austria	3,500,000	5	90.00
1855	Britain	16,000,000	3	100.00
	France	30,000,000	4.5 or 3	89.46 or 63.23
	Turkey	5,000,800	4	102.62
1856	Britain	8,890,000	3	90.00
	Britain	5,400,000	3	93.00
1859	Austria	6,000,000	5	80.00

Source: Ayer, *Century of finance*, pp. 42–9.

Of all the great powers, Prussia played the smallest part in the Crimean crisis—to the point that the British delegation at the Paris Congress demanded her exclusion from the peace negotiations. However, Prussian expenditure was in fact rising rather rapidly in this period: in total it was around 45 per cent higher in 1857 than it had been ten years before. Though the Prussian state had more robust sources of revenue than the Austrian, it too still needed to borrow. Here too the Rothschilds were able to rebuild their financial influence. As early as 1851, James went in person to Berlin for talks with the Prussian Finance Minister Bodelschwingh about a new issue of 4 per cent bonds.[158]

Relations with Berlin in the early 1850s were to some extent disrupted by a silly quarrel precipitated by Bismarck over the German Confederation's long-standing deposit (the "fortress money") with the Frankfurt house. As the Prussian delegate to the Confederation, Bismarck saw it as his role to make life as difficult as possible for his Austrian opposite number Count Thun. A proposal by Thun that the Confederation should borrow 260,000 gulden from Amschel on the security of the fortress money, to pay for the now obsolescent German navy, gave him the perfect opportunity. The sum of money involved was insignificant: the real question was whether or not the restored Confederation could be made to work in the old, Austrian-led way. No sooner had Thun, as presiding delegate, secured approval for an initial advance (in January 1851), than Bismarck announced that Prussia regarded this as an illegitimate use of federal funds (despite the fact that the money was not actually being drawn from the fortress account). To his horror, Amschel found himself caught in a crossfire of peremptory instructions from Austrian and Prussian representatives.

Thun threatened to take the Confederation's business to another banker; Bismarck said he would transfer the Prussian delegation's account to Bethmann. Despite all his attempts to ingratiate himself with Bismarck, and despite an explicit instruction from Bismarck's deputy Wetzel not to pay the money, Amschel felt he had little alternative but to accede to Thun's instructions, which were formally in order. A sense of the intemperate tone used by both sides in the ensuing row can be gained from Thun's letter to Schwarzenberg of January 12, in which he denounced Prussia for having

> recourse to such a disgustingly contemptible means as to appeal to a Jew against the Diet. I feel that their action has made the position so acute that an understanding and reconciliation will no longer be possible. The Diet naturally could not accept the position, and if Rothschild had not agreed to pay the money, I could not have left the matter in suspense for another twenty-four hours, even if war would have been the inevitable result.

"I confess," he wrote to Bismarck himself, "that so long as I live I shall blush to think of it. The evening when Councillor Wetzel showed me the protest [to Rothschild], I could have cried like a child at the disgrace to our common fatherland." Bismarck gave as good as he got, however:

> It is not our fault if, as you say, the Diet has been dragged in the mud though arguments with a Jew; it is the fault of those who have exploited the Diet's business connection with a Jew in order, in an unconsti-

tional manner, to divert moneys that were in the Jew's keeping from the object to which they had been assigned.

As for Amschel, Bismarck portrayed him in his report to the Prussian Minister President Count von Manteuffel as so "anxious to please the Austrian Government in every possible way . . . that he immediately informs the Austrian Delegate of every remittance that he receives for the Prussian Delegation to the Diet":

> On one occasion Count Thun actually informed me that the House of Rothschild had been instructed to make such a payment before I had received any official intimation to that effect. The conduct of the House of Rothschild in connection with this protest has caused me to ignore all invitations from the Herr von Rothschild resident here, and in general to give him to understand that his action has been highly displeasing to the Prussian Government . . . I cannot but regard it as highly desirable that the business relationship in which the Prussian Delegation to the Diet has hitherto stood with the House of Rothschild should be broken off, and that the business should be transferred to another firm here.

Both Thun and Bismarck had in fact overplayed their hands. Thun was reprimanded by Schwarzenberg for summarily sacking a Prussian official at the Federal Treasury who had also protested at the proposed Rothschild loan; while in Berlin both Bodelschwingh and the President of the Seehandlung made it clear that Bethmann was no substitute for the Rothschilds, who not only held large deposits for the Seehandlung but had also taken a substantial share of the 1850 Prussian loan.[159]

These were arguments which Bismarck could understand: much as he enjoyed goading Thun, he always grasped the importance of economic self-interest in politics. Within months of the resolution of the naval dispute (it was agreed to sell the ships off), he had changed his tone completely, and was now speaking up on behalf of the Rothschilds against an Austrian-backed protest by Frankfurt Catholics against the laws of 1848 and 1849 which had conferred full citizenship rights on the town's Jews.[160] Now, when the Frankfurt house requested the title of "court banker" to the Prussian court—a request which Manteuffel was inclined to grant because "Rothschild will thus be to a certain extent diverted from his fervent efforts to improve the Vienna currency, and will be favourably inclined towards a railway loan we are thinking of raising"[161]—Bismarck was in favour, playing down the row over the naval loan with characteristic cynicism:

> The Rothschilds have never been really guilty of anti-Prussian sympathies; all that happened was that on the occasion of a dispute that occurred between ourselves and Austria . . . they were more afraid of Austria than of us. Now, since the Rothschilds cannot properly be expected to show such courage as would lead the *iustum ac tenacem propositi virum* [man of firm and righteous will] to resist such *ardorem civium prave iubentium* [popular clamour for wrong] as Count Thun developed on that occasion, and as the other members of the family have since apologised for the attitude of Baron Amschel, whom they described as senile, I feel that, in view of the services which this financial power is able to render, their mistake on this occasion may be consigned to oblivion.[162]

Indeed, he went so far as to propose that Mayer Carl be granted a Prussian honour—the Red Eagle of the Third Class—on the ground that this would woo the Rothschilds away from Austria. This generated one of those Ruritanian debates so typical of Central European bureaucracies: would Rothschild goodwill be more forthcoming if the honour were withheld a little longer? Should the honour be redesigned so that the traditional crucifix motif was replaced by some other symbol more suitable for a Jew? But the bottom line was that the Prussians needed the Rothschilds: Manteuffel overruled Bodelschwingh and the title of court banker was granted, to the chagrin of Bethmann, who remained merely Prussian consul.[163]

This had the intended effect. Mayer Carl shortly afterwards hinted to Bismarck that "he would be exceedingly grateful if he could be shown a possibility of placing his money at 3 1/2 per cent." When it seemed possible that Prussia too would be drawn into the war in the spring of 1854, Manteuffel sent his adviser Niebuhr to negotiate a 15 million thaler loan with the Rothschilds. It is true that this project fell through, despite prolonged negotiations at Heidelberg, where James and Nat travelled to join Mayer Carl and Niebuhr, and again at Hanover in June. Bodelschwingh was also able to block the proposal that the interest of all extant Prussian loans be paid through the Frankfurt house. However, Mayer Carl returned to the field in 1856, placing 7 million thalers of a new Prussian loan. Moreover, Bismarck now endorsed the idea of entrusting Prussian interest payments in typically realist style: "We may, of course, assume that the bank has its own reasons for making such a proposal, for it is not going to undertake all the work involved out of devotion to Prussia. The fact, however, that its advantage is identical with ours does not seem to me to furnish any reason why we should ignore ours."[164] The request was finally granted in 1860, when Bodelschwingh left office. Bismarck defended Rothschild interests in other ways too. When Mayer Carl took exception to being awarded the Order of the Red Eagle—in its third- and then second-class versions, but with an oval design in place of the usual cross—Bismarck was quick to deny allegations that he had nevertheless presumed to wear the Christian version. In 1861 James too received a Prussian order.[165]

By the end of the 1850s, then, the Rothschilds had reaffirmed their position as Europe's pre-eminent lender to governments. Britain, France, Turkey, Austria and Prussia had all issued bonds through one or more of the Rothschild houses. Nor does the list end there. Other important clients of the period included Belgium (though here business had to be shared more than in the past with the new Banque Nationale),[166] Hesse-Nassau, whose finances the Frankfurt house more or less monopolised,[167] and the Papacy. Here the Rothschilds had made an early move, in the hope of securing concessions to the Roman Jews in return for financing the Pope's restoration to the city. The negotiations proved much more difficult than had been anticipated, however, for the Vatican strenuously refused to allow the loan to be made formally conditional on even limited measures of Jewish emancipation, though the Pope did give James a separate guarantee that the ghetto would be abolished.[168] The financial terms proved difficult to agree too. While Carl was prepared to advance the Pope only 10 million francs before his return to Rome, the Pope demanded much more. Even Carl's demand that the loan be secured by a mortgage on ecclesiastical lands was rejected.

The final terms—which James himself had to hammer out—were exceptionally generous, given the Papal record of insolvency and instability. Altogether, 5 per cent bonds with a nominal value of 50 million francs were purchased in advance of the Pope's return (April 1850), followed by two more instalments of 28 million francs.[169] Further loans followed in 1853 (26 million francs of 8 per cent bonds at 95) and in August 1857, when an ambitious attempt was made to consolidate the Papal debt and to stabilise the Roman currency. New 5 per cent bonds were floated on the Paris market with a total value of 142.4 million francs—equivalent to around 40 per cent of the total Papal debt (around 350 million francs).[170] The paradox of Rothschild relations with the Papacy was that substantial profits could be made as long as the Holy See did not reform its finances; but if it could not reform its finances, it was unlikely to reform its treatment of the Jews. Given the choice between boycotting the Vatican—thus losing their monopoly over the Pope's external borrowing—and accepting defeat over the Jewish question, the Rothschilds opted for the latter.

Besides Russia, which was avoided for obvious reasons, there were two exceptions to this rule of financial dominance. One was Spain, which issued a loan through Mirès in 1856,[171] though it is doubtful whether the Rothschilds had any desire to re-enter the market for Spanish bonds which they had quit so long ago in preference for the system of advances against mercury. The more important exception—though it was only a partial exception—was the Kingdom of Piedmont–Sardinia.

In 1849 James had managed to secure control of a substantial loan to Piedmont, using methods which dismayed the ambitious young financier and aspirant politician Cavour. Having trebled its national debt by its two abortive attempts to drive Austria out of Italy, Piedmont was a natural target for Rothschild financial penetration. Cavour could only watch in disgust as James returned in 1850 to negotiate another loan with the Piedmontese Finance Minister Constantino Nigra. Cavour's critique of Nigra's "deplorable" dependence on James should be read with some caution: the reality was that Piedmontese credit at this juncture was weak, not that James was deliberately driving down the price of its bonds. On the other hand, there is no doubt that James saw Piedmont rather as a farmer might regard an undernourished cow to be fattened and then milked. The 1850 loan, he gleefully reported to his nephews, was "the most beautiful deal I've ever made." Apart from his 2.5 per cent commission, it was essentially an investment in the future: of the new issue of 5 per cent rentes totalling 120 million lire, James took 20 million à forfait (that is, bought them outright) at a price of 85, agreeing to sell a further 60 million in Paris on the government's behalf and leaving the rest in Nigra's hands. In fact, he quickly passed on more than half of the first 20 million to the local bankers in Turin, intending to sit on the rest and await the recovery in Piedmontese credit, which he confidently expected.[172]

Cavour's chance soon came. In October 1850 he became Minister for Agriculture, Trade and Shipping, and made his first tentative attempt to challenge the nascent Rothschild monopoly two months later, when he got wind of a further issue of rentes (to reimburse the Turin central bank for its reparations payments to Austria). Eagerly, Cavour sought to find buyers for the new issue in Frankfurt and Vienna, urging his friend De La Rue to approach Goldschmidt and Sina. "It would delight me," he declared, "to play a trick on that Jew who has us by the *jugular*."[173]

With Cavour's appointment as Finance Minister in April 1851 came the opportunity to attempt a complete break. The financial position was daunting: in addition to the 25 million lire owing to James for the various short-term advances with which he had been "drip-feeding" Nigra, he faced a budget deficit of some 20 million lire and other debts totalling 68 million. Cavour therefore had to move swiftly to break the Rothschild grip. Having raised 18 million lire on the Turin money market to tide him over, he ordered his ambassador in London to look for a new banker willing to fund a substantial new Piedmontese loan. "We must at all costs extricate ourselves from the painful position in which we are placed with regard to the House of Rothschild," he insisted. "A loan concluded in England is the only means whereby we can regain our independence . . . If we do not speedily succeed in concluding a loan with London, we shall find ourselves compelled again to pass through the Caudine forks of the Rothschilds."[174] To assist the ambassador, Cavour despatched his old rival Count Revel. Revel found Baring reluctant, but the newer house of Hambro was willing to do the business, issuing £3.6 million of Piedmontese bonds at 85.[175]

There is no question that, as soon as James realised what was afoot, he did everything in his power to stymie the new loan. Cavour firmly believed that James was behind a negative report on Piedmontese finances in *The Times;* he was undoubtedly selling Piedmontese bonds with all his energy. Indeed, this was the occasion of one of the rather crude (but to contemporaries somehow devastating) word plays which were to become his trademark under the Second Empire: "L'emprunt est ouvert, mais non couvert" (literally "The loan has opened, but it is not subscribed").[176] James came close to winning: the bonds went to a discount in Paris and Cavour had some anxious hours. Yet in the end it was beyond him to buck the market indefinitely, especially as he himself had been responsible for making the market for Piedmontese bonds in the first place. "We can do what we like," he told his nephews, "but we cannot stop the Piedmontese from rising, as it was we who issued them at 85."[177] Nor was James so economically irrational as to carry on selling when "the world" was set on a rise. By the end of 1851, his own holding of Piedmontese bonds was not much changed at around a million francs: Cavour was wrong when he claimed that James had "sold the lot."[178]

Yet it had never been Cavour's intention "immediately to break with Rothschild, but merely to show him that we can do without him."[179] For his part, James could not help but admire Cavour; the man, as he put it in one of his very rare compliments to a politician, had "character."[180] Cavour underlined his point in 1852, when Alphonse was sent to Turin offering to take the remainder of Nigra's 1850 rentes (some 40 million lire) at 92. As soon as the Piedmontese parliament took his hint that he had no need of the money and rejected the offer, he was able politely to turn Alphonse away.[181] But he fully expected to have to turn to the Rothschilds again in the near future; all he had really been trying to achieve was an improvement in his bargaining position. Thus, when James returned in January 1853 to repeat his offer of the previous year, Cavour—now Prime Minister—was able to bid him up from an initial offer of 88 for the 40 million to 94.5. When Cavour then raised the subject of yet another loan, he made simultaneous approaches to Hambro, to Fould in Paris and to James, who despatched Alphonse once again to Turin. For Cavour, this competition was invaluable: the escalating Crimean crisis was driving the price of all bonds down, Piedmontese included: Hambros could offer no more than 65 for the new 3 per cent bonds, Fould would go little higher—but Alphonse, determined to win back his father's pet client, offered 70 and a commission of 2 per cent. As Cavour said, "the rivalry of Fould was worth several millions," and James subsequently grumbled about the "considerable loss" he had incurred.[182] At the same time, Cavour needed James to help pay the interest on the Hambro loan during the early phase of the Crimean crisis, until he was bailed out by the British government subsidy paid when Piedmont joined in the war against Russia.

"To do Rothschild justice," Cavour remarked with wonderful understatement in January 1855, "it must be said that he never asks for money. That is his better side."[183] What Cavour had demonstrated was that the state which shopped around in the more competitive financial markets of the 1850s was more likely to see that better side. That James was once again in favour at Turin was revealed when, to the dismay of the Pereires, he emerged as the main foreign shareholder in the new Piedmontese investment bank. "Pereire is simply furious," wrote Cavour in February 1856, whereas "Rothschild seemed delighted. He says that he wants to make an Italian credit, 'Because, do you see, you must have Italy. Hurry up, for if peace is concluded [between Russia and the Western powers], it is necessary to be in a position to act immediately.' " The new bank, he and Cavour agreed, should be "an Italian affair instead of a Piedmontese affair."[184] With astonishing prescience, James was already preparing to finance the next European war—the war he foresaw between Austria and Piedmont. It was the second time he had hinted to Cavour that he would back him in such a conflict.

The Counter-Attack

The Rothschilds had faced competition during economic upswings before; it was when the downturns came that they tended to see off their rivals. The 1850s were no exception. At a certain point, the demands on the international capital markets from new banks and railway companies, combined with the borrowings of states involved in the Crimean War, could no longer be sustained; and definitely could no longer be reconciled with monetary stability. A slowing-down was detectable even before the war ended; the crash came in August 1857 when the Ohio Life and Trust Co. stopped payments, triggering a domino-like succession of American bank failures. The crisis spread swiftly across the Atlantic to Glasgow and Liverpool, where at least four banks failed, as well as to Hamburg, and might have claimed the Anglo-American house of Peabody & Co. in London had it not been for an £800,000 loan from the Bank of England.[185] As far as can be established, none of the Rothschild houses was badly affected by this crisis. The profits of the London house for 1857 were well down (to a negligible £8,000), but they were still profits; the Naples house did rather better, though it had a bad year in 1858.

French monetary policy in this difficult period was in many ways the key to the Rothschild counter-attack against the pretensions of the Pereires; this has seldom been understood. A vital turning point in their rivalry was the election of Alphonse de Rothschild as a regent of the Banque de France in 1855. Viewed strictly in terms of the Rothschilds' importance as shareholders in the Banque, it was natural for a member of the family to become, in effect, one of its directors. The Paris house held over 1,000 Banque shares in 1852; Plessis has shown that this number tended to rise, reaching peaks of 1,499 in 1857 and 1,616 in 1864. Moreover, individual family members held up to 200 shares in their own private portfolios. Even allowing for the high level of concentration of share ownership, this made the Rothschilds probably the Banque's biggest shareholders.[186]

Nevertheless, Alphonse's election was controversial for a number of reasons. First, despite their large stake, the Rothschilds had not been admitted to the Banque's Assemblée Générale prior to 1855 (presumably because James remained technically a foreigner). Second, although the convert d'Eichthal had been a regent before him, Alphonse was the first Jew to become a regent. Third, and most important, his appointment coincided with a potentially crucial debate about the future of the Banque itself. This explains why the meeting of January 22, 1855, at which Alphonse's name was put forward as a prospective regent, was the best attended in the period: Mirès and the Pereires were among the 138 members who voted and— quite exceptionally—the election had to go to a second round before Alphonse obtained an undisputed majority over the other two candidates. Although the regents were not quite the *haute banque* caste of French political legend, Alphonse's election was an important watershed, finally putting the Rothschilds on a par with the Mallets, Davilliers and Hottinguers. More to the point, it gave the Rothschilds a representative in the Banque at a critical juncture. Alphonse may have made more formal contributions to the Banque's deliberations in the 1860s. But a Rothschild influence over French monetary policy in the 1850s is unmistakable, and proved crucial in the Rothschild–Pereire conflict.[187]

The question, in essence, was how far the Banque should become more like the Bank of England in the way that it influenced the French money market. It had done much to strengthen its own position during the 1848 crisis, killing off the regional banks of issue; but it remained a relatively small entity—its capital of around 70 million francs in 1852 was rather less than that of de Rothschild Frères— and the Crédit Mobilier's pretensions posed a serious threat. The climax of the banking and railway boom in 1855, combined with the fiscal demands of the Crimean War and a bad harvest, placed the Banque under a severe strain. In August 1855, to replenish its depleted reserves, the Governor was forced secretly to buy 30 million francs of gold and 25 million francs of silver from de Rothschild Frères.[188] A year later, the situation deteriorated so much that the Governor had to request permission to suspend the convertibility of the currency. A substantial number of the regents favoured this move, but Alphonse was not one of them. Supported by the Finance Minister Magne, he and his father successfully argued for an increase in the discount rate and larger purchases of gold and silver—including a further 83 million francs from the Rothschilds themselves—in order to maintain cash payments.[189] Between 1855 and 1857 the Paris house provided the Banque with gold worth 751 million francs, purchased through New Court at a premium of around 11 per cent.[190]

The debate on the renewal of the Banque's charter thus took place at a time when the Governor was increasingly dependent on the Rothschilds to replenish his reserves. Though Alphonse was absent from the Banque during the first half of the year, it seems likely that his father played some part in these debates, arguing against the Pereires' schemes for a radical restructuring of the Banque designed to make it more accommodating to the new investment banks with their large portfolios of shares. The final outcome of the debate was essentially a victory for the conservatives: in return for accepting 100 million francs of rentes from the government, the Banque was allowed to double its capital and was freed to raise its discount rate above 6 per cent when monetary tightening seemed necessary. Priority, in other words, was given to maintaining exchange rate stability rather than the liquidity of the domestic financial markets; and this was to prove a real constraint on the Crédit Mobilier.[191]

It was while this institutional battle was being fought (in 1856) that James launched the Réunion Financière—essentially a loose confederation of private banks and allied railway financiers like Bartholony, Pillet-Will, Blount and Talabot—with the intention of challenging the Pereires at their own game.[192] In fact, his plan of using the Réunion as the basis for a new joint-stock bank similar to the Crédit Mobilier[193] was thwarted by Magne, who imposed a temporary ban on new company formations in early 1856 as part of his effort to cool down the economy and free capital for the government's own pressing financial needs. This seemed to Mirès (whose plans were also affected by the ban) like a victory for the Pereires, and there is no denying that the Réunion group controlled a smaller amount of railway capital than the Pereires and their allies (49 million francs to 94).[194] But the signal had been given: from now on, the French Rothschilds at least were prepared to contemplate the adoption of Pereire-style investment banking.[195]

In fact, it soon became apparent that the restrictions imposed on the domestic capital market, combined with the more restrictive discount policy of the Banque de France, imposed a bigger constraint on the Pereires than on the Rothschilds. Nothing illustrated this more starkly than the Pereires' failure to prevent the fusion of the Grand Central line with the Rothschild-controlled Paris–Orléans line in June 1857, a setback which prompted anguished allegations from the Pereires about a conspiracy against them and their undertakings. "To reduce us to impotence," they complained to Napoleon, "they say we are all-powerful."[196] The reality was that, as the financial crisis of 1857 intensified, it was the Pereires who suffered more. Of all the railway lines, it was the Nord which proved most resilient in the crisis; the Banque de France's advances to the other railway companies and the Franqueville conventions (whereby the government guaranteed dividends and subsidised the building of unprofitable branch lines) were responses to the weakness of the "new" bank, not the "old."[197]

This explains why the Pereires tended to come off second best in the great pan-European race for railway concessions after 1856–7. That the railway business became genuinely international in this period is often underestimated as a factor in international relations. It is a myth that railways favoured nationalism by creating integrated national markets: the railway map of Europe very quickly spilled over state borders to become a transnational network, and much of the capital invested in railways in Spain, northern Italy, the Habsburg Empire and Russia was either English or French. This internationalisation of the railways coincided with a dawning awareness among military planners that they could play a vital strategic role in transporting armies as well as goods and travellers. The control of the railways thus became a political as well as a financial question, and one of considerable significance in the events leading up to the "unifications" of Italy and Germany.

The pattern repeated itself with variations in Belgium, Spain, Piedmont, Naples,

Austria, the Danubian principalities, Russia and even Turkey. First there were competing attempts to establish Crédit Mobilier-style banks in these economies; then, or simultaneously, there was scramble involving much the same people to grab railway concessions. In Belgium the Rothschilds' old friend King Leopold positively encouraged James to establish a Crédit Mobilier-style bank, but James dropped the idea as soon as he was sure that the Pereires had no intention of doing so themselves; he acted only when it was necessary to thwart his rivals. In truth, existing Belgian financial institutions like the Société Générale rendered the Pereires more or less superfluous. James was therefore free to extend the influence of the Nord company over important sections of the Belgian rail network, acquiring control of the Namur–Liège line and forming a consortium with the Société Générale for the Mons–Hautmont line. He was also indirectly involved as a director of the Est line in its acquisition of the Luxembourg railways—a vital link between the Belgian ports of Ostend and Antwerp and the Rhineland.[198] In Switzerland there was more of a contest: the Pereires built up a large shareholding in the Western line along Lake Geneva, but the more important Central and North-East lines remained in Swiss hands until the Réunion Financière bought a stake in the latter and merged it with other lines to the south to create the United Swiss Railway Company.[199] In Naples there was a momentary alarm when it seemed that the King might be about to grant the Pereires a bank charter, but this soon passed; the Bourbon regime had an intense suspicion of economic innovation and made even the construction of railways in Sicily well-nigh impossible.[200]

Elsewhere the Pereire threat was more serious, and elicited a succession of decisive Rothschild responses. In Spain, they succeeded in establishing the Crédito Mobiliaro Español following the legalisation of joint-stock banking in December 1855. They were not the only French bankers to do so: Adolphe Prost (of the Compagnie Générale des Caisses d'Escompte) set up a Compañia General de Crédito and the Rothschilds responded by setting up the Sociedad Española Mercantil e Industrial. The banks were broadly similar in their size and objectives. The Pereires dreamt of financing a railway connection from their own Midi line's Bayonne terminus, across the Pyrenees and through Madrid to Cadiz in the south-west. The Rothschild response was swift: in partnership with the ubiquitous Morny, James secured the Madrid–Almansa concession from the marqués de Salamanca in 1855 and two years later created the Madrid, Zaragoza and Alicante Railway Company, the first stretch of which (Madrid–Alicante) was opened in May 1858. Morny simultaneously snapped up the concessions to link Madrid to Portugal via Ciudad Real and Badajoz, as well as the routes to Málaga and Granada via Córdoba. This left the Pereires with only the head and the tail of their original design: the Bayonne–Madrid link, which was constituted as the Norte de España in December 1858; and the Córdoba–Seville link, which they built in partnership with Charles Laffitte. Although this meant that the Rothschild group failed to secure the connection between Spain and France, the point here is the slowness with which the Pereires moved; plainly their difficulties in 1857 put a brake on their schemes outside France. It is also striking that James was now collaborating with Morny and even Mirès (who secured the Pamplona–Zaragoza line), and perhaps equally striking that they were collaborating with him.[201]

The Rothschild victory in Piedmont was even more clearcut, though in some ways it was a Pyrrhic victory. There was a moment in December 1855 when it seemed that Cavour and the Pereires (whom he thought "astonishingly able") were going to strike up an alliance, which would have been a serious blow for James. But the Pereires evidently wanted too much—"a monopoly," as Cavour complained. James was more subtle, and it was he who gained the main foreign shareholding (33 per cent) in the new Cassa del Commercio e delle Industrie in Turin, established in February 1856 as the sole chartered joint-stock bank in Piedmont. In fact, James's plans for "an Italian bank" in Turin proved to be premature; the coincidence of the 1857 financial crisis and the death of the bank's director Luigi Bolmida plunged it into difficulties and by 1858 it was all but defunct. Nevertheless, we can infer what Bolmida and James had been trying to achieve from an Italian account of a visit by James to Turin in April 1857, shortly after Bolmida's death. "He wanted," according to this, "to resume Bolmida's projects which consisted essentially of obtaining from M. de Cavour the granting to the Piedmontese Crédit Mobilier [that is, the Cassa del Commercio] of all the state railways in order to create in turn a Grand Central [line] and to secure for himself the concession for the grand railway of the two Rivieras." As in Spain, in other words, a new bank was a means to the end of expanding the Rothschild railway empire: James was evidently hoping not only to gain control of the Victor Emmanuel Railway Company, formed by Charles Laffitte and Alexandre Bixio in 1853 to link Turin to France and Switzerland, but also to secure the concession to link Marseille to Nice and Genoa.[202] Though he managed only the latter (in partnership with the French financier Gustave Delahante), the extent of James's victory in Piedmont should not be understated. Moreover, we can see that, as in northern France and Belgium, James was building up a railway network which crossed borders in what were soon to become strategically vital areas: Savoy and Nice, which Napoleon III coveted, and the Piedmont–Lombardy border. Significantly, the natural railway routes from northern Italy across the Alps ran not from Turin but from Austrian-controlled Milan or Venice.

This explains a good deal of the Rothschild strategy in Austrian territory. The Pereires had stolen a march on the Rothschilds in January 1855, when they persuaded the financially pressed Austrian government to sell them a section of the state railway network (the Prague–Brünn line in Bohemia and the line running east from Marchfeld into Hungary), another early privatisation.[203] Though the Rothschilds still controlled Salomon's Nordbahn, they had shown little interest in Austrian railways since 1848, which had increasingly been built and controlled by the state; but the Pereires' coup galvanised Anselm. The Pereires had managed to create a formidable consortium: the board of their new Imperial and Royal Chartered Austrian State Railway Company (Staatsbahn for short) included Morny, Fould, Ludwig Pereira and the Vienna bankers Sina and Eskeles (who already controlled the Vienna–Raab line).[204] Moreover, they appeared to have secured a bargain: the lines which they acquired for just 77 million gulden had cost 94 million gulden to build. They had also done Napoleon III's foreign policy a favour: the purchase was widely seen as cementing the Austro-French alliance of December 1854, and was actively encouraged by Hübner in Paris. It was, complained Anselm, a "disgraceful business"—so disgraceful, indeed, that he immediately set about trying to imitate it. When the Pereires proposed to the government the creation of a Crédit Mobilier in Vienna—with the obvious intention of buying up the remaining state lines—he and James agreed to organise a rival bid. Given that the lines in question were those which would link Vienna to Trieste (the Südbahn) and Milan to Venice (the Lombard), it is easy to see their concern.

The Rothschilds had four decisive advantages. Firstly, the entente between Austria and France proved to be short-lived. Secondly, as the financial position in France deteriorated, the government ruled that foreign securities could not be issued on the bourse; for the Pereires this was a lethal blow—James, by contrast, could still count on New Court and the London market. Thirdly, the Rothschilds were able to assemble a group of grand names (notably Count Chotek and the princes Schwarzenberg, Fürstenberg and Auersperg) to act as their partners, as well as the banker Leopold Lämel, an influential figure in Prague. Finally, they very probably had sight of the Pereires' bid thanks to the Minister of Commerce Baron Bruck, which enabled them to draw up a similar but more attractive alternative, with nearly double the capital (100 million gulden to the Pereires' 56.6 million) and a more overtly Austrian orientation. By the end of October 1855, the issue was settled. On November 6 the Imperial and Royal Austrian Credit Institute for Commerce and Industry (Creditanstalt) was formally chartered; a month later the first shares were issued, of which the Rothschilds and their partners retained at least 40 per cent.[205]

With its branches in Prague, Budapest, Brünn, Kronstadt and later Trieste and Lemberg, the Creditanstalt swiftly established itself as the dominant financial institution of the Habsburg Empire, a position of unrivalled pre-eminence it retained until the eve of the First World War. Nothing did more to re-establish the Rothschilds' economic influence in Central Europe. Yet the extent to which the Creditanstalt represented a moral victory for the Pereires' methods can hardly be overstated. In order to beat them, James—after all his earlier criticisms of the investment bank as a concept—had been obliged to join them, as he admitted to Count Orlov, the new President of the Russian Council of State:

> Every time we have been consulted by government, we have indicated with the utmost force the dangers posed by these credit institutions, but when our views have not prevailed . . . we have had no option but to participate in these enterprises, which after all are excellent for those who undertake them . . . It was impossible for us to abstain completely . . .[206]

In almost all respects, the Creditanstalt was modelled on the Crédit Mobilier; if anything, its charter gave it even more latitude to invest in or lend money against every conceivable kind of asset—industrial shares, state bonds, land and even commodities—and to raise money in every conceivable way—issuing shares and bonds, accepting deposits. The key to the Rothschild revival in Vienna was thus the unabashed adoption of the methods of their arch-rivals.

In the short run, the Creditanstalt secured the Rothschilds the dominant position they had sought in the developing Central European railway network. In 1856 the Pereires were once again defeated in the contest for the crucial Lombard and Central Italian lines, the defection to the Rothschild side of their former ally Galliera proving fatal to their efforts. It was now that the Rothschilds' access to the London capital market also began to tell: when the new Imperial Lombardo Venetian and Central Italian Railway Company was launched, £1.2 million of its total £6 million shares were taken by an English group led by the London house, which also issued bonds for the company worth £3.1 million. The Paris house provided just under half the total funds required, the Creditanstalt the rest. This gave the Rothschilds and their associates control of more than 600 miles of Italian railways, of which 260 miles were already in operation.[207]

Of equal interest were the lines running westwards from Austria into Bavaria. The Frankfurt house had been involved in one of the earliest South German railways, the so-called Taunusbahn connecting Frankfurt to Wiesbaden, which in 1853 had been extended to Nassau. In 1855 it added to its railway interests by joining a consortium with Hirsch, d'Eichthal, Bischoffsheim and others to finance the Bavarian Ostbahn, linking Nuremberg to Regensburg, Munich and Passau on the Austrian border.[208] There were also moves to extend this line northwards through Schweinfurth to Bebra.[209] It was therefore logical for the Rothschild group to secure the concession to link Vienna, Linz and Salzburg (the Kaiserin Elizabeth-Westbahn): this time the Paris and Vienna houses provided 30 million of the 60 million gulden capital.[210] The lines to the Habsburg east were more problematic. Here too the Pereires established an early lead, securing the eastward extension of the Vienna–Budapest line to Szeged and Timisoara (the Franz Joseph Orientbahn), which connected with the state-owned Südbahn. But once again lack of funds proved their undoing. In addition to acquiring the Hungarian Danube Steamship Company (Danagözhajózái Társaság), the Rothschild group struck south into present-day Slovenia and Croatia, acquiring (through Talabot) the line to Agram (Zagreb) and Sisak. There also appears to have been some co-operation with the Oppenheims, who acquired the concession to link Villach and Klagenfurt in Austria to Maribor in Slovenia.

By August 1858 the thought of "une affaire gigantesque" linking these various strands to Vienna and Trieste by swallowing up both the Franz Joseph Orientbahn and the Südbahn was making James "tremble." He did it nonetheless: a month later, for 100 million gulden, he and Talabot bought the Südbahn from the Austrian government, then merged it with the Lombard and the Franz Joseph lines to form a single railway giant: the South Austrian Lombardo Venetian and Central Italian railway company. There was also talk of building a rail link from Habsburg Transylvania to Bucharest in the now autonomous principalities of Wallachia and Moldavia.[211] It seemed only a matter of time before the network of lines in which the Rothschilds had an interest would stretch to Constantinople and the Black Sea coast.

At this point a note of qualification needs to be sounded: from the moment the Creditanstalt was created and the process of railway mergers began, there was an inevitable dilution of Rothschild control. It cannot be assumed that all the steps described above were initiated or even wholly endorsed by James or Anselm. James patently had reservations about the project for a line to Bucharest, the purpose of which (to judge by the proposed route along the Habsburg frontier) was manifestly more military than commercial. In the summer of 1858, Anselm actually threatened to resign from the board of the Creditanstalt "because he [did] not approve [of] the way in which business is being conducted"—a threat he carried out the following year.[212] This did not signify a lasting break between the bank and its founder, for his son Nathaniel took his place in 1861; but it suggests that we should beware of equating Rothschild and Creditanstalt, just as we need to be cautious in using phrases like "the Rothschild group" to describe the loose coalition of investors who took over the Austrian rail system—or, for that matter, the Rothschilds and their business associates in France.[213]

There was only one major European region which the Rothschilds relinquished to their rivals: Russia. In the wake of the Crimean War, tentative advances were made to the new Tsar's government regarding the possibility of developing the embryonic rail network. However, James seems to have been content to let the Pereires take the initiative here, having received pessimistic reports of the likely profitability of new lines. This pessimism was vindicated when Barings sought to raise some £2.8 million in London for a new Grande Société des Chemins de Fers Russes to link Warsaw and St Petersburg. The issue was a flop and earned the firm yet more opprobrium from the Russophobe press.[214] Curiously, James seems briefly to have revived the idea of establishing a Rothschild house in St Petersburg in 1858; but when he casually suggested that Alphonse or Gustave might spend "a few years" setting up "an establishment in Petersburg," it was only because he felt that "it might contribute to the emancipation of the Jews"—not because he was attracted by business possibilities there.[215]

By the end of 1858, then, the challenge posed to the Rothschilds' position not only within France, but right across the European continent, had been quashed. This had largely been possible because, while the Pereires' resources remained fundamentally Parisian, the Rothschilds were an authentic multinational, with a business empire which expanded during the 1850s as far afield as the new goldfields of California and Australia. The Rothschilds' superior resources made it possible for them to reimpose their dominance over European public finance in the period of the Crimean War. At the same time, their alliance with the Banque de France ensured that when the downturn came in 1856–7, the convertibility of the currency was maintained and reforms which might have eased the Pereires' overstretched position were rejected. The contest for control of the Central and Southern European railway networks which followed was therefore an unequal one. Yet in order to secure the crucial railway lines linking Austria to Germany, Italy, Hungary and the Balkans, the Rothschilds had to imitate the Pereires by establishing their own versions of the Crédit Mobilier in Turin and, more important, in Vienna. The increasing complexity of the Rothschild business empire makes it harder to consider it as a single, integrated entity after this period, though there is no question that James himself considered it still to be one. Before 1859 the Rothschilds had been fortunate in one signal respect: they had lent to the winning side in the Crimean War, not to the loser. The real test would come in the period 1859–70, when they would find themselves repeatedly on both sides of decisive conflicts which were to recast the map of Europe.

THREE

Nationalism and the Multinational
(1859–1863)

[T]he loss of Lombardy . . . is a loss of his rail roads and his dividends on his loan!   THE EARL OF SHAFTESBURY, 1859[1]

On the evening of Thursday January 14, 1858, the Austrian ambassador in Paris was dining at Alphonse de Rothschild's house in the rue Saint-Florentin when a clerk from the Rothschild office arrived with an urgent message. James, who was also present, left the room and returned almost at once—"quite pale," according to Hübner—to inform the assembled company that Italian terrorists had made an attempt on the lives of Napoleon III and the Empress Eugénie.[2] Did James discern that this would be the catalyst for yet another French intervention in Italian affairs, this time decisively on the side of "the revolution" and against Austria? It seems unlikely; it would have been more logical to expect the unscathed Emperor to react against the Italian nationalist movement—and that was the course he initially appeared to take.

Yet even as he acquiesced in the execution of his own would-be assassin, Felice Orsini, Napoleon chose to use him as the channel for a strange communication of sympathy with the nationalist cause: two letters, supposedly by Orsini, were made public before his execution, the first of which declared that "until Italy regains her independence, there can be no certainty of peace for Your Majesty or for Europe." If he himself did not draft this call to arms, Napoleon undoubtedly intended to answer it. Almost immediately he made overtures to the Piedmontese government; and on July 20 met Cavour at Plombières to discuss nothing less than a redrawing of the map of Italy: in return for Savoy, Cavour suggested, Napoleon should help Piedmont to create a Kingdom of Upper Italy "from the Alps to the Adriatic," which would then form an Italian federation with the Papal states, the Two Sicilies and the remaining states of central Italy. It was not, in fact, until January 1859 that France and Piedmont reached a formal agreement along these lines, symbolised by the marriage of Victor Emmanuel's daughter Clotilde to Napoleon's disreputable cousin Prince Jérôme (Nice was also sacrificed to France for the greater good). But the diplomatic manoeuvres of the intervening months, accompanied as they were by repeated attacks on Austria in the French press, gave James increasing cause for concern—or so it appeared.

On December 5, James went to see Napoleon to complain about the effect on financial confidence of an article in the previous day's *Moniteur* which, unbeknown to him, had been inspired by Jérôme. Napoleon, after an uncomfortable silence, assured him that he had "no intention of making changes in Italy"; despite his objections to Austrian policy, he "protested his pacific intentions."[3] A month later, however, the most Napoleon would say to Hübner was "that if relations [between France and Austria] were not as good as he desired, that would not affect in the slightest his sentiments towards his sovereign"; this did nothing to reassure James, who visited the ambassador the next day with the English ambassador Cowley in a state of "great alarm." There was, Hübner reported, panic at the Paris bourse. So James went to see the Emperor once again, who now assured him that he had not intended to offend Hübner. James "returned quite satisfied, and caused the funds to rise on the bourse."[4] Yet just three days later the market slumped back on the announcement of the marriage between Jérôme and Clotilde; Napoleon himself admitted that, though France was behind him, he did not have the bourse on his side. When James went hunting with the Emperor on January 23, the latter pointedly complained about Austrian military reinforcements in Italy and warned that Austria "might attack Piedmont."[5] And so the guessing game continued: the following weekend, James asked whether he should undertake a loan to Austria. Napoleon did not object; but James assured Hübner in February that de Rothschild Frères had "refused decidedly to give money to the Piedmontese until all danger of war had disappeared," despite a direct request from Jérôme.[6] On March 10 there was another panic at the bourse amid rumours that an English attempt at mediation had failed; once again Hübner detected James's alarm.[7] But when Cavour himself came to Paris two weeks later, following Russian proposals for a congress and an Austrian demand for Piedmontese disarmament, it appeared that the crisis was once again abating. "So, M. le baron," he was heard to ask James, "is it true that the bourse would rise by two francs the day I resign as Prime Minister?" "Oh, monsieur le comte," replied James, "you underestimate yourself!"[8] It was at around this time that James delivered himself of another *bon mot*, a barbed allusion to Napoleon's famous speech at Bordeaux seven years before:

> The Emperor does not know France. Twenty years ago a war might have been proclaimed without causing any great perturbation. Hardly anybody but the bankers held stock exchange or commercial securities, but today everybody has his railway coupons or his three per cents. The Emperor was right when he said "The Empire meant peace," but what he does not know is that the Empire is done for if we have a war.

"Entente fous," he concluded darkly, à la Nucingen, "bas de baix, bas d'embire."[9]

It was the same in London, where Disraeli—who owed his ministerial office to Palmerston's resignation over the Orsini affair—was kept closely informed of developments by Lionel. On January 14, he wrote to Derby, relaying information which doubtless came from New Court:

> The alarm in the City is very great: "the whole of the Mediterranean trade is stopped." The reduced value of securities is not less than 60 millions sterling, the greater part in France. Another such week will break the Paris bourse. "And all because one man chooses to disturb every-

thing." Only one feeling in the City—that the Government will have nothing to do with the affair. "Though the thing were settled in a few days, months will pass before confidence is again restored, and we were on the eve of immense prosperity."[10]

Lionel himself called in his election address on April 16 for "a strong government," whether Liberal or Tory, capable of responding to the "critical" events on the continent. This could be interpreted as an endorsement of the Palmerstonian line of strong support for Piedmont against Austria; but there were some Liberals who suspected Lionel of studied ambiguity, to conceal his own pro-Austrian sympathies. It was the first of many hints that, in the realm of international relations, the Rothschilds still had more in common with the Tories than with the Liberals. Shaftesbury (an opponent of emancipation, and therefore hardly unbiased) described Lionel on the eve of the battle of Magenta as "almost frantic, the loss of Lombardy to [that is, by] Austria is a loss of his rail roads and his dividends on his loan! . . . Strange, fearful, humiliating, but so it is, the destinies of this nation are the sport of an infidel Jew!"[11]

The Finances of "Unification"

Between 1859 and 1871 a succession of military conflicts in Europe and in the Americas confronted the Rothschilds with new and apparently insoluble dilemmas. Each was presented by one side as a war of unification—the unification of Italy, of the United States, of Germany—and so historians tend to regard their outcomes as in some sense predestined, if only by the "law" of political economies of scale. In reality, they were wars between multiple states, the outcomes of which were far from easy to foresee. Nationalism was not the decisive factor: the "unification" of Poland failed in 1863; the "unification" of Denmark failed the following year; the "unification" of the slave states the year after that; and the "unification" of Mexico in 1867. Nor was it unitary nation states which the politicians intended to create, but federations: Cavour originally planned a North Italian federation; in America, the war was a war about federalism; and in Germany Bismarck resolved in 1866 "to stick more to the confederation of states [model], while in practice giving it [the North German Bund and later the German Reich] the character of a federal state with elastic, inconspicuous but far-reaching forms of words." Moreover, all the conflicts could have turned out differently if there had been intervention by one or both of the world's two superpowers, Britain and Russia. As it happened, both elected to stay on the sidelines provided events in Europe had no implications for events in the Near East, to which they attached more significance; but this non-intervention was never wholly certain.

The choices faced by the Rothschilds were indeed far from easy. When Piedmont went to war with French support against Austria, which side should the Rothschilds support, given their financial involvement with all three states? When the states of the Union and the states of the Confederacy went to war in America, whom should the Rothschilds support? Imports of Southern cotton and tobacco were as much a part of their transatlantic business as investment in the Northern states and railways. When Prussia and Austria fought Denmark, it was perhaps less problematic, though the ties between the British and Danish crowns at times discomfited the London

Rothschilds. But when Prussia fought Austria and other members of the German Confederation, yet more conflicts of interest arose; as they did again when war broke out between Prussia and France in 1870.

The traditional inference drawn from all this is that the wars of the 1860s must have cost the Rothschilds dear.[12] To be sure, the diplomats' diaries from the period are full of references to anxious Rothschilds blanching at this or that piece of bad news: the descriptions quoted above of their responses to the Italian war of 1859 are typical. James himself famously reiterated his family's traditional aversion to war when he told Bleichröder in 1862 "that it is the principle of our house not to lend money for war; while it is not in our power to prevent the war, we at least want to retain the conviction that we have not contributed to it."[13] And it seems at first sight logical to infer from the repeated convulsions of the international financial markets that when war did come, it was damaging to the Rothschild balance sheets. Even more persuasive, the unifications of first Italy and then Germany seem to have sounded the death knell for two of the five Rothschild houses. The Naples house was wound up in 1863, just three years after Garibaldi's redshirts took Sicily from the Bourbons, paving the way for the annexation of their ancient kingdom by the House of Savoy. The firm of M. A. von Rothschild & Söhne limped on for three decades after the Prussian annexation of Frankfurt; but its decline (at least in relative terms) seems to date from 1866, the moment at which Berlin forcibly staked its claim to be the new financial centre of Germany.

There is, however, a defect in this argument, namely that it is substantially contradicted by the available evidence of the Rothschild banks' economic performance in this period. As table 3a shows, the 1860s and 1870s were two of the London house's three most profitable decades for the entire period before 1914 (the 1880s was the other).

Taking all five houses together, their average annual profits rose to unprecedented levels in the years 1852 to 1874 (see table 3b). The later periods 1874–1882 and 1898–1904 were more profitable, but compared with what had gone before, the "unification years" were golden ones.

Of course, such averages may be misleading, as they lump together periods of war and peace. But even when annual figures are analysed more closely, the results are unexpected. Illustration 3.i shows that the years 1859–61—the years of the wars of Italian unification—were in fact the most profitable years in the history of the Naples house.

Table 3a: Profits at N. M. Rothschild & Sons, 1830–1909 (decennial averages).

PERIOD	ANNUAL PROFITS (£)	PROFITS AS A PERCENTAGE OF CAPITAL
1830–39	65,915	4.9
1840–49	17,808	1.8
1850–59	102,837	4.9
1860–69	221,278	7.0
1870–79	468,308	9.8
1880–89	366,819	7.5
1890–99	244,463	4.6
1900–09	265,407	3.3

Source: RAL, RFamFD/13F.

Table 3b: Average annual profits of the combined Rothschild houses, 1815–1905 (£ thousand).

PERIOD	PROFITS
1815–18	479
1818–25	330
1825–28	85
1828–36	209
1836–44	221
1844–52	219
1852–62	1,304
1862–74	1,096
1874–82	1,912
1882–87	785
1888–96	952
1898–1904	1,558

Source: Appendix 2, table d.

Admittedly, the figures for the London house lend more support to the theory that the wars of the period were detrimental to the Rothschilds. In order to make a comparison, illustration 3.ii compares annual profits at New Court with those of two leading City rivals, Barings and Schröders, in each case calculating profits as a percentage of capital at the end of the previous accounting year. This indicates quite strongly that the years 1863–7—the years of the wars of German unification—*were* bad years for the London house; its most profitable years were years of peace: 1858, 1862 and 1873. It was Barings (and to a lesser extent Schröders) who seemed to thrive in the war-torn mid-1860s—though for Barings these high profits probably had more to do with the return of peace in America than with war in Europe. Nevertheless, it would be absurd to argue that there was no connection between the overall profitability of the period as a whole for the Rothschilds and the recurrence of military conflict. For, as we shall see, it was primarily by financing the European states' preparations for war and the international transfers which tended to follow the wars of the period that the Rothschilds were able to boost their profits in the years of peace. Far from damaging their position as the world's leading multinational bank, the wars of the mid-nineteenth century generated unprecedented business for the Rothschilds, just as fifty years before it had been war which had set them on their way to fortune and notoriety.

The wars of the 1850s and 1860s were fought by states which were, by and large, strapped for cash; this more than anything else explains the importance of the role played by bankers in the period—and the substantial profits they could make. Tax bases remained narrow. Indeed, it might be argued that they were especially restricted in this period, as more and more states followed the British example of trade liberalisation—Austria cutting tariffs and signing a trade agreement with the Prussian-led Zollverein in 1853, France signing a free trade treaty with Britain in 1860—for in the short term the effect of tariff reductions was to reduce revenue until increased trade volumes filled the gap. The Austrian state had the greatest difficulty in rationalising the tax system of its disparate territories and, despite heroic efforts by Bruck in the 1850s, at no point in the period was the budget balanced.[14] The Prussian state, by contrast, had a relatively efficient system of raising revenue, with profitable state enterprises filling its coffers;[15] but the political conflict between the Liberal-dominated parliament and an increasingly conservative monarch made finance almost as problematic. The question of who should determine the military budget—Landtag or crown?—was one of the two fundamental questions Bismarck was appointed to resolve. In addressing the other—who should rule Germany?—Bismarck had to increase the size of that budget substantially. The financial expedients he adopted to circumvent the Prussian parliament were as crucial to the achievement of German unification as the battles of Sadowa and Sedan.

Even more than in the previous decade, politicians seeking to raise money by means other than taxation had the advantage of a rapidly growing and diversifying international banking system. If the 1850s had been the decade of the Crédit Mobilier and similar investment banks, the 1860s saw the proliferation of more enduring institutions, joint-stock deposit banks. In Britain this had relatively limited significance for the Rothschilds, because the majority of deposit banks concentrated almost exclusively on the kind of domestic financial business which the London Rothschilds had always eschewed. Nevertheless, in the wake of the liberalisation of English company law in 1856 and 1862 there were a number of efforts to establish joint-stock banks with foreign ambitions, of which the Anglo-Austrian Bank—set up in January 1864 by George Grenfell Glyn—posed perhaps the most serious challenge to Rothschild interests.[16] These were the kind of newcomers who, in the words of Lionel's eldest son Natty, did "a great amount of rash business, so much so that Uncle Muffy [Mayer] would do very little or hardly anything with them."[17]

In France James had to contend with four important new competitors established in this period: the Crédit industriel et commercial (founded in 1859), the Société de dépôts et comptes courants (1863), the Société Générale (1864) and the Crédit Lyonnais (which opened its Paris branch in 1865).[18] In fact, not all of these were strictly speaking rivals. The Société Générale, for example, was established by a group including Talabot, Bartholony and Delahante, who were already linked to the Rothschilds through various railway ventures, and the new bank often acted in concert with the Rothschilds.[19] Relations with the Crédit Lyonnais were also cordial.[20] If anything, the new banks posed a more serious threat to the Crédit Mobilier, which was itself increasingly acting more like a deposit bank after the limited success of its ambitious investment schemes in the 1850s.[21] Even so, their existence served to broaden the bases of French finance, and this could only imply a relative diminution of Rothschild power in Paris. James chose not to involve himself directly in the Société Générale, though he was explicitly invited to "put himself at its head"; plainly, his own desire to establish a joint-stock bank in Paris had waned since the days of the Réunion Financière.[22] In Austria too there were new joint-stock establishments to rival the Rothschilds' Creditanstalt.[23] The idea of establishing an Austrian version of the Crédit Foncier in Vienna was more or less dismissed by James and Anselm when it was first suggested in 1863.[24] However, this left the field open to the Belgian financier Langrand-Dumonceau, who aimed to create an international network of mortgage banks and other institutions, and sought to cast himself as the Catholic alternative to the Jewish Rothschilds.[25]

All this gave the warring states more choice than had been the case in the past: if the Rothschilds refused to provide them with funds, they could turn to others. There was therefore no longer any real possibility of a Rothschild veto over bellicose

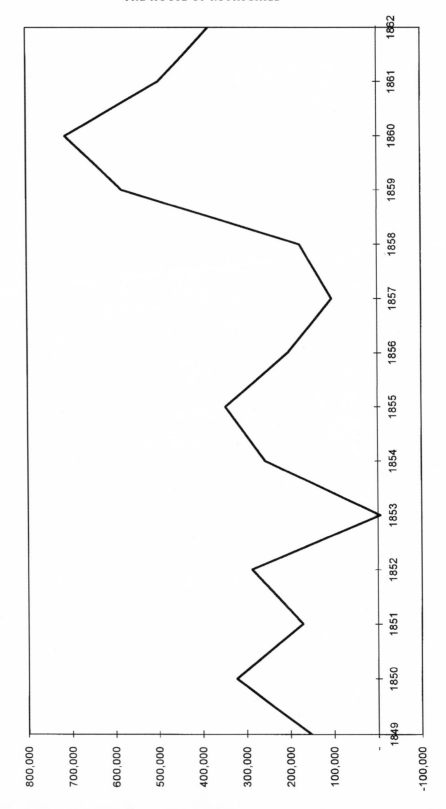

3.i: The profits of the Naples house, 1849–1862 (ducats).

3.ii: Profits as a percentage of capital at N. M. Rothschild & Sons, Barings and Schröders, 1850–1880.

policies (if such a thing had ever really existed). Governments might finally lose wars for want of funds, but that did not prevent them from starting them. If there are economic explanations for the defeats of Austria, the Confederacy and France, one is that they were less able to exploit the new sources of finance than Piedmont, the Union and Prussia; or rather that the financial markets were less willing to lend to them. For this was an era in which the increasing integration of the international monetary system gave bankers as a group an unprecedented power, even if no single bank could claim to be as powerful as the Rothschilds had been in the decades before 1848. The combination of free trade and the development of bimetallism as an international monetary system tended to reduce the politicians' freedom of manoeuvre; small miscalculations—diplomatic as much as fiscal—could lead to swift punishment from investors, the most obvious manifestations of which were, of course, a fall in the price of a government's bonds or a run on its currency, testing the monetary authority's commitment to currency convertibility. Table 3c illustrates the financial gravity of the 1858–9 crisis for Austrian bonds by comparing their performance with those of Britain and France. The fact that the bonds of one of the great powers could lose more than half their value as a direct result of a military defeat speaks for itself.

Table 3c: The financial impact of Italian unification.

	PEAK PRICE	DATE	TROUGH PRICE	DATE	PERCENTAGE CHANGE
British 3 per cent consols	98.00	Dec. 1858	89.62	June 1861	−8.6
French 3 per cent rentes	72.00	Dec. 1858	60.00	May 1859	−16.7
Austrian 5 per cent metalliques	81.88	April 1858	38.00	May 1859	−53.6

Note: British and French figures are weekly closing prices as quoted in London; Austrian and Prussian figures are end-of-year prices as quoted in Frankfurt.

Sources: *Spectator;* Heyn, "Private banking and industrialisation," pp. 358–72.

From Turin to Zaragoza

To the diplomats and politicians, the Rothschilds looked worried in 1859. In reality, they were calculating carefully to ensure that both sides in the conflict paid them for their financial services—a point which historians relying primarily on the diplomats' letters and diaries have naturally overlooked. Thus, while he urged Napoleon to preserve peace, James had no hesitation in subscribing to the French 500 million franc loan of 1858, which was widely regarded as a "war loan."[26] At the same time, the London house took the lead in organising a £6 million loan to Austria in January 1859, designed to consolidate the fiscal and monetary stabilisation achieved by Bruck since his appointment as Finance Minister in 1855.[27] Piedmont was more problematic. In the summer of 1858, after protracted negotiations, James had helped to organise a 45.4 million lire (nominal) Piedmontese loan for Cavour (sharing the bonds between the Paris house and the Turin National Bank) after the government had realised that a public subscription on the domestic market stood little chance of success.[28]

When Cavour sought to raise a further 30–35 million on the French capital market the following December, however, the situation had changed. He now tried to mend his broken bridges to the Pereires, threatening to deny James that "monopoly over our rentes which he has sought for so many years." "If, having divorced

Rothschild, we marry Messieurs Pereire," mused Cavour, "I believe we shall make a happy couple together." But this time the strategy of playing the two rivals off against one another failed: neither party was willing to accept the terms Cavour envisaged, and he was forced to retreat to a limited public subscription, issuing 1.5 million francs of rentes at a substantially lower price than he had proposed to sell them to the banks (79 compared with 86). This outcome reflected not so much a Rothschild refusal to finance war as a general reluctance, which was shared by the Crédit Mobilier, to attempt any large scale bond issues in the wake of the poor performance of the Austrian loan. Yet it should be noted that, despite what James said to Hübner, the Rothschilds did participate in Cavour's last pre-war bond issue, taking 1 million lire when he sold a further 4 million.[29]

Thus when war finally broke out at the end of April 1859[30]—following a rash ultimatum issued by Austria in the mistaken belief that Russia and Prussia would take her side—the Rothschilds had played at least some role in the financial preparations of all three combatants. To say simply that they sought to prevent the war— to assume that its outbreak was therefore a blow to them—is to make the same mistake which Hübner and others made at the time: to judge James by his words rather than his deeds.[31] He could not stop the war and he knew it; his aim was to minimise his losses on business already undertaken, and to seek to maximise his profits on whatever new business the war might generate. The classic illustration of this is the telegram sent from the London to the Paris house on April 30, 1859—the day Austrian troops crossed the border into Sardinia—which reads: "hostilities have commenced Austria wants a loan of 200,000,000 florins."[32]

The war, in any case, stopped of its own accord. No sooner had Austria suffered what looked like a fatal blow at Solferino (June 24) than Napoleon hastily made terms, fearful—and understandably so—of what might follow Prussia's mobilisation in the Rhineland. At Villafranca (July 12), he struck a compromise with Franz Joseph which seemed to leave Cavour high and dry: Austria retained Venetia and the fortresses of Lombardy, and secured a vague commitment that the other Italian rulers—now menaced by nationalist insurrection—would be restored. Only when it was evident that this was enough to avert a crisis on the Rhine could the conspiracy to unite Italy resume. By the end of December 1859 Napoleon seemed ready to ditch the Pope (whom French troops still notionally defended); by January 1860 Cavour was back in office; and on March 23 the two men updated the Plombières project. In return for Savoy and Nice, France would support a succession of plebiscites in the Italian states, the outcome of which was a foregone conclusion. Now two questions arose. Could Cavour control the revolution he had begun? Only when Garibaldi's thousand had run out of steam in Naples and Cavour's army had swept through the Papal states was it clear that he had succeeded, and that the new Italy would be a monarchy in the image of Piedmont. The other question was whether the great powers would intervene once again to preserve the Metternichian order, as they had done repeatedly in Italy. But Prussia would rescue Austria only in return for hegemony in Germany, which Austria refused; while Russia would break with France only in return for the revision of the 1856 Black Sea clauses, which Britain refused.

It is not easy to say what the Rothschilds collectively thought of the new Kingdom of Italy, formally proclaimed in 1861. James had on two occasions hinted to

Cavour that he favoured unification; while some younger members of the family in England were evidently caught up in the prevailing mood of Italophile enthusiasm: Anthony's teenage daughters Constance and Annie "translated in one short half hour Garibaldi's hymn of liberty into English poetry" in 1860.[33] On the other hand, James was perturbed by the role played by Garibaldi. This was not to be wondered at, as his invasion of Naples in September 1860 put the Rothschild house there in an acutely difficult position. Adolph opted to flee with the Bourbon King Francis II to Gaeta, north of Naples, but it soon became obvious that neither James nor Anselm was prepared to grant the exiled monarch the loans (of 1.5 and 2 million francs respectively) which he requested.[34] Adolph's embarrassment may partly explain his sister Charlotte's animus against Garibaldi, the "Italian rebel" whose "senseless reception" by the Whig elite when he visited England in 1864 she so deplored.[35] Like her later denunciations of Bismarck in 1866, these comments also reveal how far the woman who had enthusiastically hailed the revolutions of 1848 had come to share her uncle James's attitudes in the intervening years.

James's concept was authentically supranational; he was more or less deaf to the rhetoric of nationalism, which he saw as part of a regrettable tendency to democratise international relations—hence his suspicion of Garibaldi, whose every move seemed to weaken the bourse. In his eyes, it was a sign of Napoleon III's weakness that he had to take account of popular feeling within France in making his foreign policy; just as later it was a sign of Bismarck's unreliability that he was prepared to exploit German nationalist sentiment for Prussian ends. There was too much of 1848 in the events of 1860 and 1866 for his taste. On the other hand, James was no inflexible reactionary, wedded to the treaties of 1815. He preferred to think of states as businesses—not such an unreasonable elision considering how many Italian politicians (Cavour and Bastogi, for example) had banking backgrounds. Thus, where historians (following contemporary intellectuals) have seen nation-building, James saw mergers and demergers, and this illuminates his response to Austria's predicament after 1859. Piedmont's hostile takeover of Italy made sense and had succeeded; Austria was as financially weak in the wake of defeat as before; therefore she should sell her rights over Venetia or Holstein to the powers which could afford them—Italy and Prussia. It faintly puzzled him that the Austrian Emperor preferred to suffer further military defeats rather than to commercialise Habsburg decline in this fashion. After all, it made no difference to James whether Venetia was governed from Vienna or Turin or Florence; he continued to think of the map of Europe in terms of railways rather than borders. Indeed, as Shaftesbury quite rightly divined, the most important consequence of the Italian war for the Rothschilds was that it transferred a substantial part of the territory over which their Imperial Lombardo Venetian and Central Italian railway line ran from Austria to the new Kingdom of Italy. The crucial clauses of the Treaty of Zurich (November 1859) confirmed the validity of the existing concessions granted by Austria in Lombardy, substituting the new Italian state in the contracts where appropriate, and the same principle was applied to concessions granted by the old Italian states in July 1860. Formally, separate companies administered the tracks on either side of the Italian–Austrian border; in practice, the same shareholders still met in Paris to discuss the affairs of the whole north Italian network under James's chairmanship.[36]

It is in this light that we should understand the Rothschild response to Italian unification. James's initial reaction was to offer his services to vanquished and victors alike. As early as August 1859, the Austrian government was surprised to see the Paris house issuing bonds for Tuscany, though this was in fact the balance of an earlier transaction.[37] In March the following year, James intimated through Anselm that he would be glad to help the Austrian Treasury too as it struggled to finance its deficit. Typically, he took advantage of Habsburg weakness to spell out the first of many conditions. He would subscribe up to 25 million of the planned 200 million gulden loan, provided no other foreign bank were involved. "The Minister has always wanted to avoid entrusting this operation to our houses," he wrote menacingly, "and he has no idea how much he damages his own credit and jeopardises the success of the undertaking. The public has now grown accustomed to our houses patronising all Austrian [loans?], one way or another." If the operation were not entrusted exclusively to the Rothschilds, the public would assume "that we are withdrawing and have lost our confidence in Austria's finances, which will make a very bad impression."[38]

In August he sent a similar signal to Turin, where a new loan of 150 million lire was issued in August 1860. Although he took some 17.5 million lire of the new 4.5 per cent rentes (at a price of 80.5), James felt that he should have been given more. It was, he declared, "a land where there is money to be made and they have work for us":

> I am far from saying that we should propose a new business or say that we would be willing to make their rentes rise. No, for if Garibaldi carries on, I will certainly not be for a rise, and if he remains quiet, I will still feel like selling a bit . . . If we now . . . have to sell 1 million rentes in order to show our strength, I have nothing against that.[39]

As we shall see, the Rothschilds were able to use the aftermath of the Italian war to reassert their influence in France too, though such veiled threats proved unnecessary there.

James even sought to resuscitate his long-standing relationship with the Papacy, the interest on whose bonds he had rather hastily ceased to advance in December 1860.[40] If this was done on the assumption that Cavour and Garibaldi would soon be establishing a new Italian capital in Rome, James soon realised his mistake: despite Napoleon's willingness to leave the Papal states to Cavour, it proved politically impossible for him to withdraw French troops from Rome itself. On this question, the Emperor remained the prisoner of his own Ultramontane supporters.[41] When the chronically insolvent Vatican was forced to turn back to the rue Laffitte in 1863, the Rothschilds were therefore ready to oblige, albeit on a small scale. From its very inception in the 1830s, this relationship had always seemed implausible. Given the aggressively reactionary stance of Pius IX in this period, it now seemed quite bizarre, and it is no wonder the Papal nuncio in Paris was mocked: "The thesis is to burn M. de Rothschild: the hypothesis is to dine with him."[42] But the reality was that those like Langrand-Dumonceau who dreamt of replacing "Juda" with "a Catholic financial power" did not have the Rothschilds' financial strength; and that strength was sorely needed as the Vatican's credit steadily sank during the 1860s.[43] Moreover, at least some members of the family were notably respectful of Catholic sensibilities. Charlotte, as we have seen, was favourably impressed by the forms of worship and charitable institutions of the English Catholics; while in 1867 James showed himself sensitive to Catholic sentiment when he refused to ratify a major Italian loan which was to be secured on the temporal possessions of the clergy.

The decision to withdraw from the 1867 loan also needs to be seen in the context of growing Rothschild disenchantment with the financial policy of the new Italian state. As early as December 1861, James began to have doubts about the stability of the new state's finances. The Finance Minister, he complained, seemed intent on "ruining" his own credit, attaching more importance to new military expenditures (in the anticipation of further battles to complete the unification process) than to the government's existing liabilities.[44] Throughout the 1860s, James never wholly abandoned his earlier optimism about the new state's long-term economic prospects: Italy, as he put it, was "our hobby horse."[45] The problem was that, as long as the new government aspired to get its hands on Rome and Venetia, its military expenditures were likely to be inflated. The fact that there was serious resistance in southern Italy to the imposition of what was essentially Piedmontese rule further widened the gap between the new state's expenditure and its revenue. Between 1859 and 1865 the new government borrowed no less than 1,875 million lire: current revenues from tax and other sources covered only half its expenditures. Inevitably, this had an impact on both Italian bonds and the new currency. The Italian rente, which James predicted in 1862 would rise to "75 . . . if not 80,"[46] declined to a nadir of 54.08 in 1866—below the price of Roman bonds. On May 1, 1866, a year after joining the bimetallic Latin Monetary Union with France, Belgium and Switzerland, and on the eve of renewed war with Austria, Italy had to suspend the convertibility of the lira.[47]

The new Italian state was thus something of a financial disappointment. The Rothschild letters of the 1860s abound with abuse of the new Kingdom: the Italians were "rabble," successive ministers were "asses" and "imbeciles," Italy itself was no more than a "would-be great power." In September 1864 Alphonse struck his cousin (and mother-in-law) Charlotte as "preoccupied because the house is overburdened with Italian stock. He says that the Kingdom of Italy cannot last"; he also anticipated growing "hatred between Naples, Sicily, Tuscany and Piedmont."[48] James had confidently anticipated something like a greater Piedmont; instead, as Alphonse commented sourly in 1866, Italy's credit was approaching that of Spain or Mexico. "These Italians really are rogues," he wrote angrily on hearing of a new tax on foreign capital, "and I at least can give myself the credit for having always considered them as such despite the lyricism of the discourses in their favour pronounced in England and France."[49]

On the other hand, a weak government could still be a source of good business. Despite James's grumblings, the Rothschilds had helped to replenish the National Bank's dwindling reserves of precious metal on a number of occasions beginning in September 1862.[50] Six months later the London and Paris houses arranged a major rente issue worth some 500 million francs (nominal).[51] It was not long before more was needed, however, and 1864 saw prolonged wrangling between the government and its bankers over the price at which it was prepared to sell its treasury bills. Having more or less committed themselves to a further issue of 150 million rentes, the Rothschilds were dismayed to see the Italian government selling short-term paper at prices which could only weaken the market for its bonds. Only in order to prevent a further slide did James and Lionel agree to an advance of 17–18 million lire in gold.[52]

Although the inability of the Italian government to balance its budget and the resulting decline in the price of its bonds was somewhat embarrassing to its principal foreign bankers, all these transactions were far from unprofitable. Yet James and Lionel were not content with the resulting commissions. In addition, they sought to use the government's recurrent cash-flow difficulties to force it to make concessions to their railway company. True, their hopes of a "fusion" of the Lombard line and all the incomplete lines south to Livorno, Rome and Naples were frustrated by political opposition in the new Italian parliament to foreign control of the national railway network; the deputies were naturally keen that Italy should have her own railways as well as her own state. But by 1865 the government's financial needs overrode such economic nationalism: for 200 million lire it was agreed to sell the existing state-owned lines to the Lombard company. This put the company's own finances under considerable pressure, necessitating short-term advances from both the Rothschilds and Talabot's Société Générale while it sought to raise the necessary funds by issuing new bonds.[53] However, in conjunction with similar acquisitions in Austria and Switzerland, it represented a strategic investment.

The year 1865 also saw renewed debate about the construction of railway lines through the Alps. While others debated the relative political merits of the Fréjus (France), Lukmanier/St Gotthard (Switzerland) and Brenner (Austria) passes, James could look on with equanimity, as he had almost all the options covered. For, while others unified nations, the Rothschilds were quietly unifying Europe. As James put it to Landau in December: "All these questions are connected." "It is effectively beyond doubt," he enthused in a letter to the banker d'Eichthal, "that the Brenner line . . . will be the premier route through the Alps, at the very centre of Europe, and that it will divert to its profit the greater part of the general traffic of the Orient, the Mediterranean and the Adriatic towards the West of Europe . . ."[54] This was James's map of Europe: a railway map.

The parallel Alphonse drew with Spain is a useful one, for there was indeed a superficial similarity between the Rothschilds' dealings with Spain in this period and their dealings with Italy. Here too railways were the key, with the Zaragoza line playing the same role in James's Spanish calculations as the Lombard line in Italy. Like the Italian government, the government in Madrid continued to run budget deficits—as it had done more or less without interruption since the 1820s. In both cases, Rothschild financial assistance tended to be made conditional on railway concessions. There were three differences between Spain and Italy, however. First, political instability was worse in the former: a military coup against the absolutist pretensions of the crown in 1854 had been followed by a full-blown revolution, but the old differences between Moderados and Progresistas—each with their own general—had led to a constitutional crisis in 1856. The Moderado regime of General Leopoldo O'Donnell was overthrown in 1863 by another royal coup. Three years later there was an abortive *pronunciamento* by yet another general. Sometimes, this political chaos could be made light of. As James put it in December 1864: "Nothing new here. Just a change of government in Spain."[55] But by February 1867 he was presciently warning his sons to expect "a 1792" in Spain.[56] "In general," reflected

Alphonse later the same year, "Spain marches in the opposite direction to other countries. Spain is calm when the rest of the world is in trouble, and makes revolutions when the rest of the world is in repose."[57] Spain was "the country of surprises, where one cannot even count on tomorrow coming."[58]

The second difference between Spain and Italy was, as Nat never ceased to remind his brothers, that Spain had a much longer history of insolvency: each time the Spanish government approached the bond market, it encountered the disgruntled holders of old "passive" debts on which previous governments had defaulted. The acute deflationary crisis which gripped Spain in the mid-1860s hardly helped to increase Spanish creditworthiness. Finally, the Spanish railways were much less profitable than those of Italy. By the mid-1860s, when government subsidies dried up, the Zaragoza line had debts to the Paris house of as much as 40 million francs and was running an annual deficit of 1.5 million. The letters of the Paris house are full of laments about this financial "nightmare."[59]

All this helps to explain the relatively cautious attitude of James and his nephews when approached by successive Spanish governments for loans in the 1860s. A small advance was agreed in 1861–2;[60] but a larger operation foundered in 1864, prompting attempts by rivals like the Pereires and Barings to step into the breach.[61] Two years later James was prepared to countenance a new advance of 8 million francs only in return for tax breaks or subsidies for his railway company (an objective which temporarily seemed to bring Rothschild and Pereire interests into harmony).[62] However, a rival group of French banks led by Fould and Hottinguer stole a march by offering the Madrid government a new bond-issue worth some 79 million francs. This was followed in 1867 by a further loan arranged by the Société Générale (with Barings in a supporting role) which was intended to convert the so-called "passive" debt on which interest payments had been suspended.[63] Although the competition annoyed James, history was merely repeating itself: the English Rothschilds were as reluctant as ever to encumber themselves with new Spanish bonds, preferring to continue the system of modest advances against the output of the Almadén mines.[64] Other forms of guarantee offered—the salt monopoly, the tobacco monopoly or colonial revenues from Cuba—did not have the appeal of mercury: the English Rothschilds always preferred metals, and the more precious the better.

The French Rothschilds, by contrast, were mainly concerned to secure concessions for the ailing Zaragoza line, and were willing to flirt with the possibility of further advances and even a new loan to this end:[65] as Anthony rightly said, "railroads are always at the bottom of the Baron's business."[66] The tortuous negotiations of 1867 revolved around the ban on Spanish bonds at the French bourse which had been imposed in 1861 in an attempt to combat capital export. The French premier Eugène Rouher intimated that he was willing to end this suspension—thus allowing a new Spanish loan to go ahead—provided the Spanish government set its financial house in order. The question was whether this reordering would include the kind of perks for the Zaragoza line sought by James; though quite why the Spanish government should borrow between 10 and 100 million francs purely in order to hand it over to French-controlled railway companies was never entirely clear.[67] The negotiations, which were initiated on behalf of the Narváez government by the banker Salamanca, were still dragging on inconclusively when the revolution broke out—by which time Narváez was dead and Salamanca bankrupt. "A little security and stability in the political system," grumbled Alphonse, "would be more efficacious than any subsidy."[68] It was not to be: in September a coalition of generals led by Juan Prim launched a successful revolution which overthrew Queen Isabella. Indeed, one reason for the failure of the various loan negotiations prior to this was probably the various bankers' sense of impending upheaval.[69] As Alphonse acknowledged, Weisweiller had "long anticipated the Catastrophe."[70]

Napoleon at Ferrières

That Alphonse was able to count on strong support from the French government in his negotiations with Spain is in itself noteworthy. For perhaps the most unexpected consequence of the Italian war was its impact on relations between the Rothschilds and Bonapartist France. Superficially, the French role in Italian unification was one of the high points of Napoleon III's reign, and the Second Empire never looked more outwardly impressive than it did in the early 1860s. When Lionel visited Paris in April 1861, he was dazzled by the transformation of the city being wrought by Georges Haussmann. "I must say," he commented half-seriously on seeing some of the wide, new boulevards which had replaced the cluttered alleys of the old town, "I wish we had a man like the Emperor for three months just to make a few alterations in old London."[71] Yet behind this veneer the Empire was developing serious weaknesses. In part, these were diplomatic. Nothing did more to alienate English Liberal opinion than Napoleon's acquisition of Savoy and Nice in March 1860; this intimation of "vast conceptions" akin to those of his uncle undid all the diplomatic good done by the Anglo-French trade treaty signed in the same month. To James, Anglo-French antagonism could only imply trouble for France; that had been the lesson, as he saw it, of Louis Philippe's demise. "The most revolutionary developments of French internal policy," he told the new Austrian ambassador, Richard Metternich in October 1859, "would not affect the financial world here as profoundly as a breach with England."[72] "It is a great pity," remarked Mayer Carl in March the following year, "that the favorable impression of the treaty should suffer by all these unfortunate speeches [about Italy] which lead to nothing good [and] are at liberty to spoil the good understanding which ought to exist between England and France for the general security of Europe."[73] "The great financiers of Paris and especially the Rothschilds" were, according to one diplomatic observer the following month, "engineering a panic and are shrieking from the housetops that war between the two great sea powers is inevitable."[74]

This diplomatic estrangement had an economic dimension too. The approach of civil war in America led to a drain of gold from Europe across the Atlantic, beginning in 1860. This affected both London and Paris; but, while the Bank of England relied principally on increases in Bank rate to defend its reserves, the Banque de France was not quite converted to strict imitation of Threadneedle Street practice. Partly in order to avoid further increases in its discount rate—which some of the regents opposed—the Governor of the Banque therefore authorised purchases of gold in London in November 1860. Unfortunately, his agent made the mistake of withdrawing over £300,000 directly from the Bank of England itself, a confrontational step which Alphonse deplored. An agreement to swap 50 million francs of Bank of England gold for the equivalent in Banque de France silver provided only a temporary respite for the Banque, which was coming under additional pressure from the abnormally large French trade deficit and the financing needs of the government.

These difficulties forced the government to turn to the Rothschilds. In October 1861 an elaborate transaction was agreed whereby de Rothschild Frères and five other Paris banks (Hottinguer, Fould, Pillet-Will, Mallet and Durand) drew three-month bills on the London house and on Barings to the value of £2 million, with the aim of reducing the premium on sterling bills and halting the gold flow across the Channel. At the same time, the Banque sold rentes (though it appears to have partly negated the deflationary effect of these open market operations by issuing 50 million francs' worth of small denomination notes).[75] None of these devices really resolved the Banque's difficulties, however, which continued into 1862–4 as gold and silver were diverted to Egypt and India, the principal suppliers of cotton to the European textile industry in the absence of the blockaded American South.[76]

For the Paris Rothschilds, tight money meant a revival of influence; or rather, it meant a decline in the influence of a number of rivals. In 1861 Jules Mirès was arrested for fraud, a downfall James relished: "Rothschild is triumphant," observed Mérimée, "and says that he is the sole baron of industry."[77] The early 1860s also saw the first intimations of the Crédit Mobilier's mortality. Having invested heavily in real estate through their subsidiary the Compagnie Immobilière, by 1864 the Pereires found themselves struggling to balance their books.[78] As these stars of the 1850s waned, Alphonse waxed as the voice of economic orthodoxy at the Banque de France. The Crédit Mobilier, argued Alphonse in October 1864, was the "principal author" of the monetary crisis and the "sole remedy lay in the energetic resistance of the Banque." "The suspension of convertibility," he feared, was the Pereires' last hope of survival. "This situation is really quite critical, for it is a struggle to the death between the old system and the new system of business, between the Crédit Mob. and the banks of state."[79] The testimony he and his father gave to the monetary Enquête of 1865 was therefore an advance obituary for the earlier ambitions of the Pereires to supplant the Banque with a more expansionist system of credit. "You wish to establish a dozen banks?" James asked the commission, alluding to Pereires' requests for monetary relaxation:

> You wish to give them the right to issue notes? Where will the confidence be then? Suppose I am at the head of a small bank which has a little money, but needs a lot. I would not take precautions, I would say: Let come what may! Some other bank is going to have to come to the rescue. That is what all the little banks will do which will be established and which will look towards the Banque de France, as if towards a mother bank which is obliged to pay for the follies of others.[80]

Monetary policy, he and Alphonse argued, could be a matter for the Banque alone; confidence would evaporate if the convertibility of its notes were threatened; its conduct should resemble as far as possible that of the Bank of England, with the important exception that silver should continue to enjoy equal status with gold in the Banque's reserve.[81] The Pereires sought to strike back, blaming their difficulties on the Banque's high discount rate and the drain of French capital abroad orchestrated by the Rothschilds. As Emile Pereire put it in November 1865:

There are people at the Banque who wish me ill . . . [But] it was not me who financed the Zaragoza and Alicante railways; it was not me who financed the Lombard lines; it was not me who was responsible for the 1,500 million of Italian loans, Belgian loans, Austrians, Romans, Spanish; and yet the signature which these operations all bear is among those which accuse us of having impoverished the national wealth for the benefit of foreigners![82]

But the Rothschilds could follow the death throes of the "Mob." with detached *Schadenfreude.* James even indulged in a casual speculation in Crédit Mobilier shares, though he was probably not responsible (as some contemporaries believed) for their last great rise and fall in 1864.[83] The "old" bank had become the new; the "new" bank had become the old.

In fact, the monetary difficulties of the early 1860s were not solely due to uncontrollable global economic forces; they were partly a consequence of the government's fiscal policy. The Italian war had necessitated an increase in public borrowing: in 1859, for example, the Banque had to lend the Treasury 100 million francs against rentes and also discounted treasury bills worth 25 million. These sums, however, were just a small fraction of the regime's total borrowings throughout the 1850s, which—even without the costs of the Crimean and Italian campaigns—had totalled approximately 2 billion francs.[84] The decision of the former Minister of State Achille Fould to set himself up as the leading critic of this policy paved the way for an unlikely political realignment which would have been unthinkable a decade earlier.

It was a rapprochement of erstwhile foes visible at first only in the countryside. As early as November 1860 it was reported that the Emperor was "hunting at St Germain with Messrs Fould and Rothschild"; the following October rumour had it that "Messrs Fould, de Germiny [the Banque Governor] and Alphonse Rothschild have held long conferences on the financial situation with the Emperor at Compiègne."[85] A month later, however, came the announcement in Paris of Fould's return to office as Finance Minister—an announcement conspicuously welcomed by the Rothschilds and the bourse as a whole.[86] "I am glad to note that . . . your good friend . . . Fould has followed your wise counsel not to reduce the Banque's discount rate," wrote James in a letter to Alphonse just a few weeks later. Alphonse should "go to Fould and quite openly and freely chat with him a bit" and intimate that "we would very much like to work hand in hand with him."[87]

Substantial proof of this new harmony between Rothschild, Fould and Bonaparte came in January 1862 with the conversion of the (relatively few) 4.5 per cent rentes into 3 per cents. Although James, who was wintering in Nice, had some minor reservations about the transaction, in the end Fould was able to count on complete Rothschild support, not only at the Banque de France but at the rue Laffitte itself. In the first phase, the Paris house lent the government 30 million francs (for four months at 5 per cent interest) to push up the price of 3 per cents. In addition, Alphonse agreed to purchase 85.9 million francs of thirty-year government debentures, which were also to be gradually converted by the government into 3 per cent rentes. The conversion was a success for the government; for his part, James was delighted to have reasserted the Rothschilds' traditional predominance in French public finance.[88]

The famous visit of the Emperor to hunt at Ferrières on December 16, 1862, needs to be seen in this context. Historians have often represented this as symbolising the reconciliation of Bonaparte with (if not his surrender to) the old Orléanist *haute finance*,[89] and so it seemed. Accompanied by Fould, his Minister of State (and cousin) the comte de Walewski, the English ambassador Earl Cowley and Generals Fleury and Ney, Napoleon travelled by rail to Ozouer-la-Ferrières, where he was met by James's four sons at 10.15 a.m. Having walked across the green velvet carpet embroidered with golden bees which had been rolled out across the station platform, the Emperor and his party were then transported to the château itself in five carriages decked out in the Rothschild colours of blue and yellow. On his arrival, imperial flags were flown from all four towers. The rest of the family (including Anthony, Natty and his sister Evelina) were then introduced in the main hall, and the Emperor paused to admire the pictures by Van Dyck, Velasquez and Rubens hanging there. He then stepped outside to plant a commemorative cedar tree in the gardens, after which he was served a lavish breakfast. "The service of silver plate made from models which were immediately destroyed to preserve it unique," reported *The Times* in reverent tones, "was accompanied by the celebrated service of Sèvres porcelain, every plate of which bears an authentic picture by Boucher." The hunting itself was also pronounced a success: some 1,231 head of game were reported killed. The afternoon concluded with a buffet in the hall, accompanied from the gallery by the senescent Rossini's specially composed "Chorus of Democratic Hunters" (*sic*), a piece of nonsense scored for tenors, baritones and basses, accompanied by two drums and a tam-tam. At 6 p.m., the imperial party returned to the station, their way illuminated by "keepers, huntsmen and other persons employed on the domain, holding torches."[90]

Yet the extent to which this most ostentatious of all displays of Rothschild hospitality represented a genuine reconciliation with Napoleon is doubtful. Although quite favourably impressed by the Emperor himself, Natty captured something of the uncomfortable reality of the day in his account to his parents:

> I must say it was one of the most disagreeable rides I ever had as the road [from the station] was like a pane of glass . . . If it had been in England the populace would have been much more enthusiastic; as it was the cries of Vive l'Emperor were for the greater part uttered by paid agents . . . After breakfast, which lasted some time and would have been excellent if it had only been warm, the sportsmen adjourned to the Park. There was an enormous show of game, but as most of the shots had drunk 10 or 12 different kinds of wine they shot very badly. Altogether some 800 pheasants were murdered; they ought to have killed 1500.[91]

Moreover, according to one account, James could not resist a barbed parting shot as he bade the Emperor farewell. "Sire," he supposedly said, "mes enfants et moi, nous n'oublierons jamais cette journée. *Le* mémoire nous en sera cher": with the masculine article, "mémoire" means "bill," suggesting a pun at the Emperor's expense (in both senses).[92] Like the Goncourt brothers, for whom Napoleon was just the latest French sovereign "to pay a state visit to money,"[93] the contemporary German cartoonists who portrayed Napoleon as hunting the golden calf or fat "bags" of money were wide of the mark (see illustrations 3.iii and 3.iv); but they all sensed the essentially bogus nature of the occasion. The Ferrières reception was nothing if not a bid for Anglo-French reconciliation—hence the presence of Cowley and no fewer than four English Rothschilds.[94] Yet no such reconciliation ever came. On the contrary, each diplomatic crisis seemed to drive France and England further apart.

Publicly, the Bonapartes and Rothschilds were now on friendly terms, and James and his relatives were regularly invited to court social functions. In January 1863, for example, he was spotted by the Goncourts at a soirée given by the Emperor's cousin Princess Mathilde.[95] A few months later, Alphonse went to Compiègne once again to discuss monetary policy with the Emperor, noting with satisfaction that "HM appears to understand the necessity to take rigorous measures."[96] He and his wife returned there just four months later for an evening of charades—a favourite imperial pastime—in which Leonora appeared as "Judith with the head of Holofernes," complete with "three or four millions in diamonds on her head and neck."[97] The following year, Fould specifically asked James to discuss the monetary situation with the Emperor, fearing that the Pereires might yet persuade Napoleon to abandon convertibility.[98] Instead, James sent Alphonse, whose only complaint was that the Empress was rather garrulous and "wanted to know too much about the Jews."[99] In November 1865 Leonora was again asked to join the amateur theatricals at Compiègne. She and her husband, along with Gustave and his wife Cecile were also present at the Emperor's celebrated fancy-dress ball in February 1866, at which the Empress somewhat ominously appeared as Marie-Antoinette.[100]

Yet contemporaries could not help noticing the ambivalence of the relationship. Compared with James, Napoleon was still young: he was fifty-four when he visited Ferrières, James seventy. Yet the Emperor's health was indifferent, depriving him of energy at critical moments, whereas James—though his eyes were deteriorating and his hands increasingly arthritic—had lost little of his prodigious vigour. When Charlotte called to see her uncle in the rue Laffitte in 1864, she "found him at luncheon, eating first beefsteak with potatoes and then an enormous helping of lobster. One must be well or nearly so to venture upon such heavy diet." She was equally impressed by his "excessively exhausting" lifestyle, "perpetually oscillating between Paris and Ferrières," not to mention Boulogne, Nice, Wildbad and Homburg. He remained the dominant force in the Paris house until the last year of his life, indefatigably corresponding and rushing from one meeting to the next, driven by a work ethic his younger relatives could not hope to match. In August 1867 Anthony gave a pained account of a visit by James to London:

> This morning I needed to go to the Ex[change]—at 9.00 comes the Baron[,] I must go with him to the P[rince] of W[ales]—to the Duke of Cambridge & then the V[ice]roy of E[gypt] then the Sultan so that one is as confused & then if one is not at the office [one is] blown up [told off] so it is quite impossible to write as one ought.[101]

Nevertheless, James still found time to build up an unrivalled collection of wildfowl at Ferrières and to conduct a protracted flirtation with the comtesse Walewska, the minister's wife. Nor should the long periods he spent each year at such spas be taken as a sign of failing strength: for it was precisely when he went to take the waters that he seemed "more juvenile, more frisky than ever," "din[ing] at the public

3.iii: *Das goldene Kalb* (1862).

table, and speak[ing] with every lady, provided she is pretty and young."[102] When the French press carried exaggerated reports that his sight had failed altogether in 1866, James was:

> irate and most impatiently anxious to give the flattest contradiction to all the penny-a-liners, who had lamented his supposed blindness. So he made a point of going the round of the theatres with his sons, of sending countless glances to all the actresses, as many to the fair occupants of stalls and boxes, and of ending his day by playing whist and winning at the clubs, and giving a faithful account of all the partridges, pheasants and chevreuils [deer] brought down by his own unerring gun.[103]

Supremely self-confident, and perhaps now a little reckless in his old age, James felt free to give vent to that sardonic humour which in the past he had tended to suppress. Some of his jokes were the stuff of stock exchange lore: "At the bourse, there comes a time when, if you want to succeed, you have to speak Hebrew";[104] "You ask, do I know what causes the bourse to rise and to fall? If I knew that I would be a rich man!"[105] Asked by an eager young broker if he thought installing a turnstile and charging admission to the bourse would affect the price of rentes, James, deadpan, responded: "My fiew is that it vill cost me twenty sous a day."[106] But his most famous jokes—like the pun on "mémoire" at Ferrières—subtly mocked the Emperor. "L'Empire, c'est la baisse" defies translation: literally "the Empire means a falling market," this pun on Napoleon's famous claim that the Empire meant "la paix" was to prove a damning epitaph for Napoleon's regime.

3.iv: *Ferrières: Auf der großen Jagd bei'm Rothschild* (1862).

Small wonder, then, that contemporaries reverted to the old Orléanist joke that he and his family were the real rulers of France. Those most malicious of contemporary diarists, the Goncourt brothers, pictured a gathering of seventy-four Rothschilds at Gustave's wedding:

> I imagine them on one of those days Rembrandt invented for synagogues and mysterious temples, lit by a sun like the golden calf. I see all those male heads, green with the sheen of millions, white and dull like the paper of a banknote. A fête in a bank cavern . . . Pariah kings of the world, today they covet everything and control everything, the newspapers, the arts, the writers and the thrones, disposing over the music hall and world peace, controlling states and empires, discounting their railways as the usurer controls a young man, discounting his dreams . . . Thus they rule in all walks of human life, including the Opéra itself . . . It isn't the captivity of Babylon, but the captivity of Jerusalem.[107]

To the Goncourts, James was "a monstrous figure . . . the most base, [with] the most terrifying frog-like face, his eyes bloodshot, eyelids like shells, a mouth like a purse and drooling, a sort of golden satyr."[108] But those, like Feydeau, who saw James in his "natural element"—his office—could not help but be impressed by the sheer life force he exuded:

> He had the singular and precious ability to concentrate his thoughts, to become inwardly absorbed, even in the midst of the most infernal brouhaha. Often, when about to conclude the most important transactions, he would close his door and receive no one; often too, he used effortlessly to conduct the most important and the most trivial operations at one and the same time, charging one of his sons, usually the

eldest, to receive in his main office the clerks from the bourse, while he, huddled in a corner of the same room with some minister or ambassador, happily discussed the conditions of an operation involving hundreds of millions . . . He sometimes broke off in the middle of discussing the terms of a loan which stood to earn him several dozen millions, to exact from some hapless courtier, who could not but agree, a concession which can only have been worth about fifty francs on some miserable little deal . . . This financial genius had the redoubtable ability to see everything and do everything himself . . . This Titan . . . read all the letters, received all the despatches, and found time in the evening to perform his social duties despite devoting himself to business from five in the morning. And you had to see how everything in his immense banking house ran like clockwork! What marvellous order throughout! What obedient employees . . . !109

Thus, even as Napoleon began to loosen his own grip on political power, James became more and more the absolute monarch of Parisian finance. Before this "holiest of holies of money," as the Goncourts put it, "all men were equal, as absolutely as before Death itself."110

The question remains: how far did Rothschild power actually undermine the Bonapartist regime, as some contemporaries believed it did? If James seemed at least ambivalent towards the imperial regime in public, in private he and his family remained downright hostile. His French relatives, Natty felt, were "more ridiculously Orléanist than ever, finding fault with every thing and every body connected with the emperor," a view echoed by Benjamin Davidson after an encounter with Betty.111 James at first gave the shift towards a more parliamentary constitution a cautious welcome, but half expected Napoleon to resort to another *coup d'état*.112 When Alphonse resolved to follow his uncle Lionel's example and stand for election it was as an opposition candidate—though James had reservations about making Rothschild opposition so "overt."113

But why were the Rothschilds opposed to a regime which, by the 1860s, was scarcely unfavourable to their business? More important than lingering Orléanist sentiment, James and his sons saw a fundamental contradiction between the supposed new era of sound finance under Fould and the Emperor's foreign policy, which remained as adventurous—and in their eyes dangerous—as ever. The early 1860s saw a succession of international crises in which Napoleon seemed tempted to "make mischief"; and each time he showed signs of doing so, the expectation of increased military expenditure and yet more government deficits tended to depress the price of rentes.114 As early as July 1863, there was talk of a new French loan, for example;115 the recurrent monetary difficulties of the Banque could also easily be attributed to the effects of imperial foreign policy on financial confidence. Even before the Italian war, as we have seen, James had formulated his theory of Bonapartist politics: "No peace, no Empire." The events of the subsequent years only made him the more sure of this, and his letters abound with references to the connection between financial weakness and diplomatic room for manoeuvre. "There won't be no war [*sic*]," he assured his nephews in October 1863. "As I said, the Emperor should speak terribly peacefully. He has to if he wants to get money [and] if indeed a loan is to be made."116 "I believe," he wrote in April 1865, "that the weak bourse will help to keep the Emperor in a more peaceful frame of mind."[117] And again in March 1866: "We will maintain the peace for some time, as the great man [Napoleon] cannot [afford to] make war."[118] His recurrent anxiety was that internal political weakness might nevertheless tempt Napoleon to gamble on foreign adventure.[119] The more Napoleon confirmed this fear, the more James foresaw financial trouble: that was what he meant when he said that the Empire had come to mean "la baisse" rather than "la paix."

The Roots of British Neutrality

Distrust of Napoleon provides one of the keys to understanding the Rothschild response to the events of the 1860s. There is, however, a point of equal importance to be made about the political and diplomatic role of the British Rothschilds in the same period, namely their acceptance of what amounted to a policy of non-intervention in the conflicts not only of the European continent but also of the American.

It is not at all easy to plot the course of the British Rothschilds' political engagement in the 1860s. Having secured admission into the House of Commons, Lionel never addressed his fellow MPs, but it is an error to suppose that he was politically inactive. He attended the House frequently—even being carried into a debate on one occasion when immobilised by arthritis—and saw senior political figures and journalists so frequently at New Court and Piccadilly that his wife could write in 1866: "Politics interest your father to the exclusion of all other topics."[120] Naturally enough, Lionel remained a Liberal, having for so long enjoyed the majority of that party's support in his campaign for admission to parliament, as did his bucolic younger brother Mayer. He was a Liberal on economic policy too, as much a convinced free trader as his friends Charles Villiers, the brother of the Liberal Foreign Secretary Clarendon, and the future Liberal Chancellor, Robert Lowe. But ties of friendship inclined him in the direction of Disraeli, if not Disraeli's party; he and Charlotte were also friendly with other Tories, including General Jonathan Peel (Sir Robert's brother, though not a Peelite) and Lord Henry Lennox, MP for Chichester.[121] It was typical of Lionel that in 1865 he asked Delane to tone down his attacks on Russell's government in *The Times*, while at the same time welcoming the government's most effective critic—Disraeli—to New Court.[122] In April 1866, in the thick of the debate over Russell's Reform Bill, the Rothschilds had "the two great rivals at dinner—the whig [Gladstone] on Saturday, the tory [Disraeli] on Sunday. Natty says that the two entertainments represent Scylla and Charybdis—and that we are sure to have crossness and ill-humour on one of the two days, if not on both."[123]

Natty—Lionel's eldest son, and of all the British Rothschilds the most politically engaged—also steered something of a zig-zag course. His earliest recorded political remarks indicate an enthusiastic Liberalism, combining hero-worship of Gladstone, cynicism about Disraeli and a Cobdenite enthusiasm for free trade. But he was also warm in his praise for Palmerston, and never seems to have regarded trade treaties as a substitute for military readiness (a view doubtless reinforced by his own military training and service with the Buckinghamshire Yeomanry).[124] When he first visited the Commons (to hear the Reform Bill debates in 1866) "he found the great Mr. Gladstone's oratory heavy and pompous, while he thought that Mr. Disraeli sparkled delightfully." Lowe's arguments against Reform appear to have swayed him; yet Bright—its most passionate proponent—remained a hero.

It says much about the ambiguity of Rothschild politics that when pro-Reform demonstrations were held in London in July 1866, Evelina locked away her Sèvres vases and refused to venture outside; yet when "some conservative gentleman said to Natty, who was defending the foolish reformers, that he was sorry all our windows had not been smashed . . . your brother replied we were perfectly safe, as the people knew us to be their friends; they cheered the house, and Natty and Alfy in the crowd." When Lady Alice Peel told Lionel "that the soldiers ought to have shot twenty or thirty of the rabble, which would very soon have put an end to the riot," he gave a characteristically oblique reply: "You may say anything to me, Lady Alice, but I advise you not to go about London with such suggestions." Charlotte blamed the Tory Home Secretary Spencer Walpole for provoking the violence by excluding the demonstrators from Hyde Park; but she nevertheless accepted that "if a Tory government can but be induced to bring in liberal measures, there is no earthly reason why it should not prove as useful as the Whig administration."[125] Lionel "wished every success to Mr Dis." in government—but this was partly because he had no desire to fight yet another general election if the Tory ministry foundered. He can hardly have been reassured when Disraeli told him in February 1867, on the eve of the new parliamentary session, that "when we meet again, I shall be either a man or a mouse, but we shall not resign, depend upon it, without making an appeal to the country." Throughout the long process of amendment and passage of Disraeli's Reform Bill, the Rothschild door remained open to politicians of all hues: Charlotte eagerly read John Stuart Mill (who went so far as to advocate female suffrage), gave tea to the Gladstones and dined with the Disraelis. Lionel dutifully attended the debates and voted on amendments, conferring often with "our friend" Disraeli, but marvelling ironically "to see the same members in such high spirits in passing a measure which last year they opposed in the most violent manner."[126]

The basis of the British Rothschilds' increasingly bipartisan approach to politics remained, as in the past, foreign policy. Furnished with impeccable political intelligence from the Paris house, they were able to command the attention of any government, Liberal or Tory. Sharing James's objective—to restrain Napoleon III from aggression which might lead to a general war—they generally sought to shape British policy accordingly (by contrast, it is remarkable how little the British members of the family worried about Prussia). Yet there is no missing a slight loss of interest in continental affairs in this period. Anselm no doubt exaggerated, but his analysis of March 1866 says much about the letters he had been receiving from New Court:

> Do not have any illusions; the political influence of England in continental affairs can be considered as nil; it is not by constantly keeping one's sword in its sheath, or one's armoured vessels in the peaceful waters of ports that one makes the most of oneself, that one makes oneself feared. Anyway, it is clear that Reform Bill and the bovine epidemic are dearer to the heart of John Bull than the duchies [of Schleswig and Holstein].[127]

The shaft was well aimed: there is no doubt that Mayer spent more time in 1866 worrying about the effect of the rinderpest sweeping his herds at Mentmore than about the unification of Germany. Dramatic events—the failure of Overend,

Gurney (May 10), the fall of the Russell government (June 26), the Reform riots in London (July 23)—distracted British attention from events on the continent at a crucial moment.[128] Whatever qualms Lionel may have had about Bismarck, he had no strong desire for British intervention on the continent; and even if he had, it is unlikely that he could have done much to overcome the isolationism of successive Foreign Secretaries. As long as Gladstonian principles of fiscal rectitude prevailed, British budgets were balanced so that even when defence expenditures were increased, they were financed by taxation not borrowing: in only four years between 1858 and 1874 did the government run a deficit, and in each case it was tiny. The long-run trend was for the national debt to be paid off, not increased: between 1858 and 1900 it fell from £809 million to £569 million (perhaps Gladstone's most tangible achievement). A government that did not borrow money was a government the Rothschilds could advise, but not pressurise.

The American Wars

The habit of British non-intervention may be said to have begun with Russell's emotive welcome to Italian unification, which more or less negated his and Palmerston's suspicions of French policy. The outbreak of the American Civil War, by diverting British attention to the security of Canada, established the pattern which was to persist for more than a decade. Rothschild attitudes towards the American conflict have often been misunderstood; in fact they illustrate the essentially passive role played by Lionel in foreign affairs in this period. Because Belmont (as the Democrats' national chairman) was a leading supporter of Stephen A. Douglas, Lincoln's opponent in the presidential election of 1860, he—and in turn the Rothschilds—incurred opprobrium from both sides in the war which broke out the following year. Northern Republicans reviled "the Douglas National Chairman" as a trimmer on the issue of slavery; so did Southern Democrats, but from the opposing point of view.[129]

According to one of his biographers, Belmont struggled throughout the conflict to bolster Rothschild support for the Union: his nightmare was that his "masters" in Europe would lend financial support to the South.[130] But he and the Rothschilds were still repeatedly accused of Confederate sympathies, especially in the wake of General George McClellan's nomination as Democrat candidate in 1864, because he favoured a negotiated peace with the South rather than what Belmont called Lincoln's "fatal policy of confiscation and forcible emancipation." "Will we have a dishonourable peace, in order to enrich Belmont, the Rothschilds, and the whole tribe of Jews, who have been buying up Confederate bonds," thundered the *Chicago Tribune* in 1864, "or an honourable peace won by Grant and Sherman at the cannon's mouth?" "Let us look at a few undeniable facts," wrote the *New York Times* that October. "The notorious undenied leader of the Democratic Party at [the] Chicago [convention] was the agent of the Rothschilds. Yes, the great Democratic party has fallen so low that it has to seek a leader in the agent of foreign Jew bankers." It was an argument developed in lurid terms by a Pennsylvanian supporter of Lincoln at a rally the following month:

> The agent of the Rothschilds is the chief manager of the Democratic Party! (Cries of "that's so" and cheers) . . . What a first rate Secretary of the treasury he would make, if Mr McClellan happened to be elected!

(Laughter) There is not a people or government in Christendom in which the paws, or fangs, or claws of the Rothschilds are not plunged to the very heart of the treasury . . . and they would like to do the same here . . . We did not want to borrow and the Jews have got mad, and have been mad ever since (Cheers). But they and Jeff Davis and the devil are not going to conquer us (Prolonged applause).[131]

Was there any truth in the allegation of support for the South?[132] There was evidently some sympathy for the Southern cause in the rue Laffitte, if not at New Court. This owed at least something to the reports from James's third son Salomon, who had been sent across the Atlantic in 1859 (rather as Alphonse had been in 1848) as part of his business education, and remained there until the outbreak of war in April 1861. Although appalled in a Dickensian way by most aspects of American political life, Salomon was inclined to sympathise with the South, and argued in his last despatch to Paris that Europe should recognise the Confederacy in order to halt the war.[133] Quite apart from the argument that the South should be allowed to determine its own laws—which swayed such unlikely supporters of the slave states as Gladstone—the disruption to the European economy caused by the Northern blockade of Southern cotton exports provided a persuasive argument in favour of a swift peace, if not a Southern victory. At least one of the London house's American correspondents—the house of Chieves & Osborne in Petersburg, Virginia—repeatedly urged "that England should at once recognise the Southern Confederacy upon the score of interest and humanity [*sic*]."[134] And Belmont himself (contrary to Katz's account) explicitly told Lionel when he visited London in 1863 that "soon the North would be conquered."[135] However, much as they deplored the outbreak of war, the Rothschilds adopted a posture of neutrality in the early stages of the war, arguing against intervention by either Britain or France.[136] In 1863, the American consul-general in Frankfurt informed *Harper's Weekly* after a conversation with Mayer Carl that

> here the firm of M. A. Rothschild a[nd] Son are opposed to slavery and in favor of the Union. A *converted Jew*, Erlanger, has taken the rebel loan of £3,000,000 and lives in this city; and Baron Rothschild informed me that all Germany condemned this act of lending money to establish a slaveholding government, and that so great was public opinion against it that Erlanger a. Co. dare not offer it on the Frankfort bourse. I further know that the Jews rejoice to think that none of their sect would be guilty of loaning money for the purpose above named; but it was left, they say, for apostate Jews to do it.[137]

It was indeed Erlanger, in conjunction with the American James Slidell, who issued the first "cotton guaranteed" Confederate loan in March 1864; and the only London bank which would consent to become involved was not N. M. Rothschild but J. Henry Schröder & Co., which had never previously issued a government loan. The London house informed Belmont that "the Confederate Loan was of so speculative a nature that it was very likely to attract all wild speculators . . . It was brought out by foreigners, and we do not hear of any respectable people having anything to do with it . . . We ourselves have been quite neutral and have had nothing to do with it."[138] By 1864 at the latest, James was involved in financing Northern imports from

Europe, criticising Belmont for his reluctance to assist the Lincoln government and urging his sceptical nephew Nat that Northern bonds represented a good investment.[139] When the charge of having financed the South was repeated in 1874, Belmont was able to state with only slight exaggeration that "some nine years ago, the late Baron James de Rothschild, in Paris, showed . . . by his books, in my presence, that he was one of the earliest and largest investors in our security during the war." The idea that the Rothschilds backed the South was mere legend, like the later allegations against Belmont that he sought to delay the payment of American aid to the Fenians.[140]

What is undeniable is that compared with rivals like Barings and the London-based Americans George Peabody and Junius Spencer Morgan, Rothschild interest in American finance—Northern and Southern—was limited and continued to be so for the rest of the century. While newcomers like the Seligmans could operate with a family member in New York, the Rothschilds remained at one remove from the American market, the more so as Belmont devoted increasing amounts of his time and energy to politics (accumulating powerful enemies in the process).[141] Moreover, the Civil War had done much to disillusion even James about the United States. Although he had been optimistic about increasing transatlantic business after the conclusion of peace in 1865, he was haunted by the fear of a resumption of political "disturbances." In 1867, his last word on the subject was to sell American funds because "I have the deep conviction that although America is a country beyond all calculation, one should not have any illusions that the battle which is being rejoined is not only directed against the President but against the South."[142]

Although James's sons continued to take an interest in the cotton market, Alphonse expressly told his cousins in January 1868 that "we do not wish to speculate on some Negro revolt in the South or anything of that sort."[143] He was equally lukewarm about American railways.[144] There was a similar though milder reaction in London. When the American financier Jay Cooke visited London in 1870 in the hope of finding takers for $5 million of Northern Pacific Railroad bonds, he got short shrift from Lionel.[145] Rothschild involvement in the US economy increasingly was confined to bond issues for states or the federal government. Even this proved problematic: the resumption of post-war business got off to a bad start when the London house invested in $500,000 of Pennsylvania state bonds. Within a year, it was apparent that the state intended to pay off its creditors with depreciated dollars; but when Belmont protested, he elicited a crudely anti-Semitic response from the state's Treasurer, William H. Kemble: "We are willing to give you the pound of flesh, but not one drop of Christian blood."[146] A New York state loan in 1870, issued by the Paris, London and Frankfurt houses in partnership with Adolph Hansemann, was more successful and led to another successful issue in 1871.[147] However, the Rothschilds always preferred to deal with the central government, and from 1869 onwards they lobbied President Ulysses S. Grant for the chance to assist him in the task of stabilising federal finances. The London house was among the five issuing houses for the 1871 refunding loan, a process repeated two years later and again in 1878.[148] To be sure, the Rothschilds continued to be denounced by Belmont's opponents as the "European Shylocks," whose sole purpose was to revalue the bonds of the various American states by putting the United States on to the gold standard.[149] But the reality was that the Civil War had led not only to a temporary decline in British continental influence, but to a permanent decline in the Rothschilds' transatlantic influence.

The best argument of all against meddling in other people's civil wars was provided by events south of the Rio Grande. Although Napoleon III failed in his attempts to influence the outcome of the American Civil War, he did manage to intervene in the affairs of the American continent in another way. The French invasion of Mexico was one of the least successful ventures in imperialism of the entire nineteenth century. In part, it sprang from Napoleon's belief that Mexico must be preserved from complete American annexation. In part, it was a way of giving the former Austrian Governor of Lombardy a new job, though the Archduke Maximilian accepted the Mexican throne only under pressure from his ambitious Saxe-Coburg wife Charlotte and against the advice of his brother, the Emperor Franz Joseph. Only superficially was the invasion about money. The initial French, British and Spanish expeditions to Mexico in 1861 were prompted by the new Progressive government's refusal to maintain interest payments on the country's foreign debt; and throughout the succeeding years the interests of the bondholders were frequently cited to justify what was being done. But in reality most of the bondholders were British, and the French had to inflate their own claims or (as Morny did) acquire other people's. The decision of Britain and Spain to pull out in April 1862 and the subsequent despatch of 30,000 more French troops swiftly turned the Mexican affair into a costly fiasco. It was possible to occupy the country and install Maximilian, but the French Treasury could not sustain an open-ended commitment: hence the Convention of Miramar stipulated that the new Mexican regime owed France 270 million francs—40 million for the bondholders and other private interests, the rest for the costs of the invasion. This in turn could be paid only by raising a new Mexican loan in Europe; and this required the new regime to be secure. But as soon as the American Civil War ended and the US signalled that she did not regard Maximilian as the legitimate ruler of the country, the occupation became untenable. In 1866 Napoleon was obliged ignominiously to withdraw his troops, leaving the hapless Maximilian to face a firing squad the following year.

It has been suggested that the Rothschilds were opposed to the Mexican adventure.[150] The reverse is true. The Rothschilds had interests in Mexico, as we have seen. Indeed, Nathaniel Davidson was concerned that he stood to lose at least $10,000 as a result of the Juarez government's refusal to recognise legal agreements made by its conservative predecessor, particularly with regard to Church lands, on the security of which Davidson had lent some $700,000. The San Rafael ironworks he had acquired were also under threat.[151] Davidson therefore welcomed the arrival of European forces at Vera Cruz, and only regretted that they did not move more swiftly to overthrow Juarez.[152] He hastened to assist the French expedition's paymaster by discounting bills and providing him with several million dollars of gold from California.[153] There was an indirect interest in Maximilian too: his wife was the daughter of King Leopold of the Belgians, a long-standing Rothschild friend who had entrusted her legacy to the Paris house as long ago as 1848.[154] As soon as the French government brought up the question of a Mexican loan, the Rothschilds therefore made no secret of their interest.[155]

To be sure, James was always sceptical about the likely success of such a loan. "I don't quite understand," he mused in August 1863, "how an Austrian Prince can go under the title of Emperor with French troops, and if they don't stay, who can guarantee that taxes will continue to be collected and [interest paid on] the loan." He correctly foresaw too that the ending of the American Civil War would weaken the French position. Even if the loan were taken in commission, James had no desire to be associated with bonds which might easily be rendered worthless if the whole adventure ended in a débâcle.[156] But these doubts should not be taken to mean that he was against the loan; it merely explains his uncharacteristic eagerness to act in tandem with Barings, thus spreading the risk, and the pains he and Alphonse took to secure the agreement of the London bondholders to their terms.[157] Ultimately, he was sorry to lose the Mexican loan to rivals like the Crédit Mobilier and Glyn's and made an energetic effort to hang on to it. He regarded the idea of a new Mexican bank as potentially "a golden deal" and was disappointed when that too had to be abandoned.[158] Even without the loan, the Rothschilds found themselves exposed, thanks to Davidson's over-enthusiastic discounting of bills not only for the French army but for Maximilian himself. When the French withdrawal was announced—to Davidson's horror—they were left with bills on Maximilian's doomed regime worth some 6 million francs.[159]

There had therefore been legitimate, if ultimately disappointed, commercial reasons for supporting the Mexican adventure. However, there was a more subtle and perhaps more important subsidiary argument in favour: squandering money and men in distant Mexico distracted France from Central Europe. The private correspondence makes this manifest: as James put it bluntly in June 1863, sending money and troops to Mexico was "not good for the Treasury, but it avoids war over Poland" (see next chapter).[160] The ramifications of this weakening of France, however, would prove far greater than he would ever know. Alphonse's assessment, following the news of Maximilian's death was not overdone:

> One should not deceive oneself: the tragic death of poor Maximilian is an event which could have very serious consequences. In the country [France] there reigns a general discontent stemming from the frivolity with which questions of internal as well as external policy are treated. From this there comes a general malaise, an uncertainty about the future which influences all transactions.[161]

This malaise was the "baisse" against which James had all along warned.

FOUR

Blood and Silver
(1863–1867)

We aren't working for the King of Prussia.
JAMES DE ROTHSCHILD, 1865.[1]

When Otto von Bismarck accepted Amschel's invitation to lunch with him in Frankfurt in June 1851, he can hardly have been aware whose example he was following. Thirty years before, Metternich too had "taken soup" with Amschel; it had been the beginning of a long and mutually beneficial friendship between the Austrian Chancellor and the house of Rothschild. They attended to his private finances (often on preferential terms) and acted as a swift and secret channel of diplomatic communication; he in turn provided them with sensitive political news and gave them a privileged position not only in Habsburg finances but in Austrian society. It was evidently Amschel's hope that Rothschild relations with Bismarck would follow the same pattern; and for a time that seemed a not unrealistic expectation.

Although Bismarck's anti-Austrian policy had briefly brought him into conflict with the Rothschilds during his time as Prussian envoy in Frankfurt, neither side had taken this personally, and Bismarck had subsequently entrusted his private financial affairs to the Frankfurt house, which also acted as the Prussian delegation's official banker. M. A. Rothschild & Söhne remained his bankers until 1867. Like Metternich, Bismarck was not a rich man before 1866; unlike him, however, he never sought to borrow on a large scale from the Rothschilds, though he ran up a modest overdraft in 1866, when his expenditures (27,000 thalers) exceeded his salary as Minister President (15,000 thalers) and the income from his estates (around 4,000 thalers)—a debt easily cleared when he was awarded a gift of 400,000 thalers by the Prussian Landtag as a reward for his victory over Austria. Before that time, Bismarck relied on the Rothschilds primarily to provide him with current account facilities, using the Paris house to pay his substantial expenses (10,550 francs) when he visited Biarritz in 1865, for example. Bismarck expected an annual statement of his account at the beginning of each year "so that I can make my calculations as [I set my clock] by the sundial."[2] In addition, because his account was often in surplus—as in June 1863, when he was in credit to 82,247 gulden—the Rothschilds paid him interest (at 4 per cent) and occasionally made investments on his behalf. At some point before 1861 they bought shares for him in the Berlin Tivoli brewery, a firm in which the Frankfurt house had a major stake (other major shareholders were the Oppenheims of Cologne).

As Fritz Stern has shown, after 1859 Bismarck delegated an increasing amount of his private financial affairs to Gerson Bleichröder, who had taken over his father Samuel's Berlin banking business on his death four years before.[3] But this did not necessarily signify a breaking of the Rothschild connection. Bleichröder had for some time been one of the principal bankers in Berlin with whom the Rothschilds did business, and it was apparently Mayer Carl who first recommended him to Bismarck. Moreover, Bleichröder was at pains to make available to the Rothschilds whatever scraps of political information he could pick up in Berlin. In March 1861, for example, he more or less accurately forecast that further Liberal election successes would lead to a complete breakdown in relations between crown and Landtag "on the army question" followed "in three months" by "another dissolution and at the end a change in the electoral law, with a reactionary minister or the entire abolition of the chamber." His information steadily improved after Bismarck returned from St Petersburg to Berlin, after which the phrase "according to personal information from Herr von Bismarck" began to feature in his correspondence. At first, Bleichröder assumed that the "reactionary" and "unpopular" Bismarck would not last long. Gradually, however, he established a closer relationship with the beleaguered premier, not least because Bismarck wished to use him as a channel of communication to James in Paris. As Bismarck's aide Robert von Keudell put it, James "always had free access to the Emperor Napoleon, who allowed him to speak openly not only on financial but on political questions as well. This made it possible to send information to the Emperor through Bleichröder and Rothschilds for which the official route seemed inappropriate." Meetings with Keudell and Bismarck himself became increasingly regular; soon Bleichröder's letters were full of allusions to his "good source."[4]

Nor did Mayer Carl in Frankfurt neglect his increasingly influential client. We have already seen how by 1860 he had secured, partly thanks to Bismarck, the title of Prussian court banker and a minor decoration. In the hope of obtaining a rather better mark of honour, Mayer Carl wrote to Bismarck in 1863 in the kind of elaborately sycophantic language which his English and French cousins had long since been able to disdain:

> Your Excellency knows my old, proven and unbounded devotion to your person and knows how attached I have always been to Prussian interests, even though my great and protracted services have not . . . been noticed in any prominent fashion . . . I now turn to you, full of confidence in Your Excellency as a noble, magnanimous and all-powerful representative and do not doubt that Your Excellency in just appreciation of the facts known to Yourself will kindly think of me and grant me a dignified token of the all-highest recognition . . . May heavenly Providence always watch over Your Excellency and may you experience only days of brightest joy and of boundless good fortune in the circle of your family, may it be my lot always to enjoy Your Excellency's high

favour and gracious protection and to be able to count myself among your most faithful admirers and servants.[5]

Yet it was not to be. Where the financial relationship between the Rothschilds and Metternich had flourished, their links to Bismarck withered. Despite his position of semi-dependence on the Rothschilds, whose disfavour would have been injurious to what was still a small firm,[6] it seems that Bleichröder was able to poach Bismarck's account from the Frankfurt house. To begin with, he did no more than collect Bismarck's official salary in Berlin and disburse some of his domestic expenditures. Even before Bismarck returned to Berlin in 1862, however, Bleichröder began to offer his services as an investment adviser, complaining on his putative client's behalf when the Tivoli company failed to pay a dividend. Soon he was offering Bismarck a succession of Prussian railway and bank share options, as well as providing him with regular reports from the Berlin bourse. By the end of 1866, he had achieved his objective: it was Bleichröder not Rothschild who handled the investment of Bismarck's 400,000 thaler gift, and at some point after July 1867 Bismarck closed his account in Frankfurt and remitted the balance (57,000 thalers) to Bleichröder. "It is not necessary to let the Jews get the upper hand," Bismarck later declared, "or to come to depend on them financially to such an extent as is regrettably the case in several countries. My relations as a minister with Jewish high finance have always been such that the obligation has been on their side and not on mine."[7] This was true: Bleichröder was always deferential to Bismarck in a way that (for all Mayer Carl's florid avowals) the Rothschilds would never have been if Bismarck had continued to bank with them. The path Bismarck led Prussia down after 1862 was simply too uncongenial to Rothschild interests in Austria, in Italy and in France.

For their part, as we shall see, the Rothschilds soon came to regard Bismarck with a mixture of antipathy and admiration. He was a "madcap," declared James in March 1866.[8] At around the same time, Anselm memorably likened him to "a wild boar foaming with rage."[9] Bismarck, wrote James a month later, was "a fellow who just wants war."[10] "The terrible Bismarck," exclaimed Charlotte, "is inexorable; he is the great highway robber of the second half of the nineteenth century."[11] Yet perhaps even more telling than these denunciations are the expressions of admiration which the Rothschilds also evidently felt for "the white revolutionary." As early as 1868, Charlotte could regard "a Bismarck intelligence" as a desideratum in a son-in-law.[12] Alphonse, who of all the Rothschilds had most reason to hate Bismarck, could refer to him with only a hint of bitterness as "the great master of the world" and "the man behind the curtain . . . wire-pulling the puppets of the whole European political show."[13] When Bismarck finally fell from power in 1890, Alphonse's comment was a singular tribute to an old adversary: with Bismarck gone, he wrote, "the European countries certainly cannot be said to dwell on solid fundamental principles."[14] Bismarck never really felt the same respect for the Rothschilds, alluding to them on a number of occasions in more or less anti-Semitic terms. But nor did he underestimate their financial acumen.[15] Perhaps he also recognised in them something of his own hard-nosed "realism." In later life he defined his own view of political principles as similar to Amschel's who, he recalled jokingly, had been in the habit of asking his chief clerk: "Mr Meier [*sic*], if you please, what are my principles today with regard to American hides?"[16]

German Unification: The Financial Background

In one sense, it is easy to see why Bismarck was able to avoid "depending" on the Rothschilds or any other bankers in a way that no Austrian politician of the period could. Financially, Prussia was in a different league. Table 4a gives some bald figures for the nominal increases in expenditure for three of the principal combatants in the period. The figures for France and Prussia are in fact quite similar; but the Austrian figures—which show expenditure nearly trebling between 1857 and 1867—testify unambiguously to the Habsburg monarchy's unsustainable military commitments. It was the army and the defence budget which caused this growth, not (as might be imagined) inflation, which was comparatively restrained (prices rose by just 5 per cent, surprisingly little in view of the substantial monetary expansion of those years).[17]

Table 4a: Public expenditure in the era of unifications, 1857–1870.

	FRANCE		AUSTRIA		PRUSSIA	
	million francs	index	million gulden	index	million thaler	index
1857	1,893	100.0	371	100.0	122.8	100.0
1867	2,170	114.6	943	297.5	171.0	139.3
1870	3,173	167.6	422	113.7	212.9	173.4

Sources: Mitchell, *European historical statistics*, pp. 370–85; Schremmer, "Public finance," pp. 458f.

The attitudes of bankers, however, were more directly determined by the way military spending was financed. Here Prussia's advantage over both her principal rivals was more pronounced. Between 1847 and 1859 the total Austrian debt increased by a factor of 2.8; for Prussia the equivalent figure was just 1.8. More important, Prussia started the period with an exceptionally low debt burden: in the 1850s public debt as a proportion of national income was around 15 per cent and as late as 1869 was still less than 17 per cent; the equivalent figure for France rose from 29 per cent in 1851 to 42 per cent in 1869. Figures for the cost of debt service make the difference equally apparent: in 1857 the Austrian state was spending 26 per cent of its ordinary revenue on debt service, compared with a figure of just 11 per cent for Prussia. For the Bonapartist era as a whole, the equivalent figure for France averaged 30 per cent; even at its peak in 1867 the Prussian debt service burden was less (27 per cent).[18] This meant that, from the point of view of a prospective lender, Prussia was a good credit risk; France slightly less so; Austria a downright bad one. Again, these differentials can be illustrated with reference to bond prices. The price of Austrian 5 per cent metalliques touched twin troughs of around 42 (a price not seen since the Napoleonic period) in 1859 and 1866. Prussian 3.5 per cents, by contrast, never fell below 78 (see table 4b).

To make the difference clear, throughout the period between 1851 and 1868 the yield spread between Prussian and Austrian bonds ranged between 2.7 and 8.6 percentage points, averaging almost exactly 5 per cent (see illustration 4.i). The gap is less pronounced for Prussia and France, but it is still there: on average between 1860 and 1871, it was just over one percentage point. As Talleyrand observed (with par-

Table 4b: The financial impact of German unification.

	PEAK PRICE	DATE	TROUGH PRICE	DATE	PERCENTAGE CHANGE
British 3 per cent consols	93.75	Nov. 1862	86.25	May 1866	−8.0
	94.12	May 1870	90.75	Aug. 1870	−3.6
Prussian 3.5 per cent bonds	91.25	Dec. 1864	78.25	Dec. 1870	−14.2
French 3 per cent rentes	71.00	May 1862			
	65.05	Mar. 1864	−8.4		
	69.40	Sept. 1865	60.80	Apr. 1866	−12.4
	76.98	May 1869	50.80	Jan. 1871	−34.0
Austrian 5 per cent metalliques	60.00	Dec. 1864	42.38	Dec. 1866	−29.4

Note: British and French prices are as quoted in London; Prussian and Austrian prices as quoted in Frankfurt.
Sources: House of Commons, *Accounts and papers*, vol. XXVII and XXXI; *Economist*; Heyn, "Private Banking and
   Industrialisation," pp. 358–72.

donable exaggeration) in January 1865, "Prussia stood above par in politics as on the bourse."[19] Thus while it is still possible to explain the outcomes of the various conflicts of the period 1858–71 in terms of the shrewd diplomacy of statesmen or the bold strategy of generals, a financial explanation is necessary too, if not sufficient. Another way of putting this is that Austrian policy failed precisely because it was financially unsustainable: unable to afford the military effort necessary to achieve victory in both Italy and Germany, the Austrians should have accepted the option of selling their territory in one, to enable them to afford to defend the other. This was essentially the strategy advocated by James and his nephews. By seeking to defy financial reality, Austria ended up losing on both fronts.

Nevertheless, it would be wrong to suggest that Bismarck's victory was financially predetermined. Bismarck's access to state revenues in the crucial years 1862–6 was technically illegal in the absence of parliamentary approval, and even his own "gap theory" (*Lückentheorie*) could not easily justify increases in expenditure much above the last approved budget. On average, expenditure in the years 1863–6 exceeded the sanctioned ordinary expenditure of 1861 by some 38 million thalers per annum.[20] Bismarck risked being held personally liable for raising funds without parliamentary sanction, and in January 1864 the Liberal-dominated Landtag rejected his request for a loan of just 12 million thalers. From this point, he had no option but (as he put it) to "take [funds] wherever he could find them." But that, as we shall see, was easier said than done, and Bismarck was bluffing when he assured the Austrian chargé d'affaires in the summer of 1864 that he had reserves of 75 million thalers. Indeed, it is arguable that the market's confidence in Prussian finance in this period was to some extent overdone. In the immediate aftermath of the war against Denmark, Bismarck advocated cuts in defence spending as a way of raising money; if this could be achieved, he reasoned, "Nobody would be able to form an opinion about the financial strength of Prussia."[21] That puts the high quotation of Prussian bonds in a rather different light.

In any case, the struggle for mastery in Germany was as much diplomatic as military: money furnished the sinews of war, but the role of money in the diplomacy of the 1860s proved relatively limited, as James found out to his chagrin. Regardless of Austrian weakness, there were a number of occasions when Bismarck's ambitions could have been thwarted if not wrecked altogether: the element of contingency in the diplomacy of the 1860s should never be forgotten. Had Russian policy been less

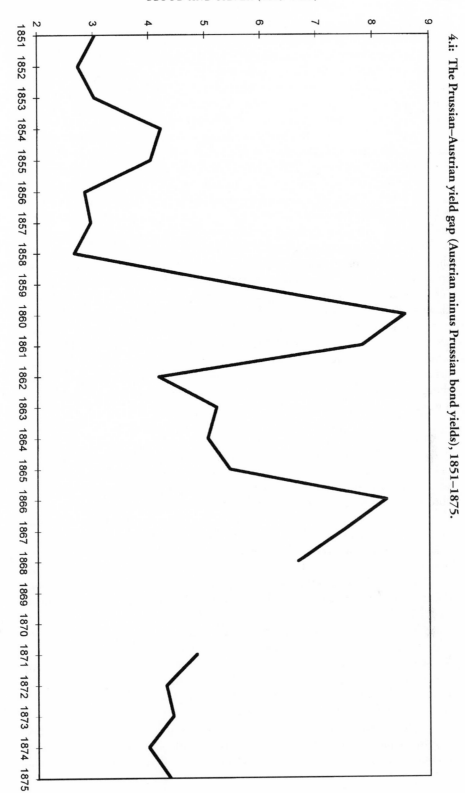

4.i: The Prussian–Austrian yield gap (Austrian minus Prussian bond yields), 1851–1875.

hostile to Austria, for example, Bismarck would have been vulnerable to the pressure from the East which had forced Prussia to accept the restoration of German dominance in Germany at Olmütz in 1849. Had British policy not been so passive, the crises over Poland and Denmark might have turned out less advantageously to Prussia. Had Napoleon III not replaced Thouvenel with Drouyn de Lhuys, French policy might have been more consequential: instead of acting primarily in the interests of Italy (over Venetia if not over Rome), Napoleon might have anticipated the threat posed to France by an expansionist Prussia. Nor should the Austrian attempts to reform the German Confederation be dismissed as mere pipe-dreams. Each time Austria raised the subject—in February 1862, in January 1863 and, most dangerously for Bismarck, in August of the same year—Prussia's position looked precarious. Austria had more support among the other German states. And Franz Joseph might conceivably have made up his mind to exchange Venetia or Holstein for cash and a "fig-leaf" of territory rather than face another war and another defeat.

Ultimately, it was the mistakes of others which gave Bismarck his opportunities: the Danish decision to annex Schleswig and Holstein in November 1863, the Austrian appeal to the Confederation over the duchies in June 1866 and, later, the superfluous French demand for a permanent renunciation of the Hohenzollern claim to the Spanish throne in 1870. Even the military outcomes were more balanced than is often assumed: when war broke out in 1866, Austria seemed to have secured the support of mighty France as well as the other major German states, while Prussia's sole allies were, as one Prussian official observed with only slight exaggeration, "the duke of Mecklenburg and Garibaldi." Well drilled and well armed though the Prussian infantry were, their breech-loading "needle-guns" did not guarantee victory at Königgrätz.

Dress Rehearsal: Poland

The crisis precipitated by the Polish revolt against Russian rule in January 1863 provided a sort of dress rehearsal for the wars of 1864 and 1866: in so far as Russia waged war against Poland, she was able to do so swiftly and, despite much fuss abroad, without foreign intervention. The financial implications were less straightforward. From the Rothschild point of view, the rising was singularly unwelcome. For the first time in forty years, the Rothschilds had managed to secure a major Russian loan in April 1862. It seemed a tremendous coup: an issue of 5 per cent bonds worth £15 million, of which £5 million were taken directly by the Paris and London houses at 94 and the rest sold to the public on commission. But the bonds did not do as well as James had hoped and the London, Paris and Naples houses were left holding Russian paper worth at least £2 million on the eve of the Polish rising.[22] James's hope had been that prices would rise provided Russia did not become embroiled in war; but the crisis in Poland confounded this expectation. What made the crisis so alarming was not so much Bismarck's somewhat heavy-handed offer of support to the Tsar (which won him no friends anywhere)[23] as Napoleon III's attempts to stick up for Poland, which threatened—as in 1830—to precipitate a Franco-Russian war. Bismarck was lucky: if Britain had supported France more warmly, or if Alexander II had been persuaded to back down, his position would have been exposed. As it was, Drouyn's attempt to resurrect the Crimean coalition was a disastrous failure, simultaneously alienating both Russia and Britain.

At the time, Disraeli offered a characteristically imaginative interpretation of events which has often been repeated since as evidence of Rothschild power. On July 21 he warned Mrs Brydges Williams—one of his many middle-aged female admirers—that "a war in the centre of Europe, on the pretext of restoring Poland, is a general war, and a long one," adding: "The Rothschilds, who have contracted two loans this year, one to Russia and the other to Italy . . . are naturally very nervous." Three months later he was still pessimistic:

> The Polish question is a diplomatic Frankenstein, created, out of cadaverous remnants, by the mystic blundering of Lord Russell. At present, the peace of the world has been preserved, not by the statesmen, but by the capitalists. For the last three months, it has been a struggle between the secret societies and the European millionaires. Rothschild hitherto has won; but the death of Billault [the President of the French Senate, and one of the Emperor's close advisers during the crisis] may be as fatal for him as the poignard of a Polish patriot; for, I believe, in that part of the world they are called patriots, though in Naples only brigands.[24]

This was pure fantasy. In reality, the crisis had been beyond any Rothschild control; all James and Lionel could do was fume as inept French diplomacy drove down the price of Russian and Italian bonds. As James put it after hearing a torrid account from the Russian ambassador of Napoleon's desire to "turn the whole map of Europe around," it was "devilishly disagreeable to be issuing a loan right now"; but he did not believe for a moment that there would be a war—only "bad bourses" and "hot water." This relative optimism reflected the fact that James was better informed than Disraeli: he knew that both the French and the Austrian governments were divided on the issue (in the French case, Walewski for war, Persigny and Fould against), and for this reason calculated that the crisis would blow over. His only real flicker of doubt came on June 17, when a second Anglo-French note to Russia and an interview with Drouyn persuaded him to sell £25,000 of Russian bonds. By the end of July, after long discussions with Prince Altenburg at Wildbad, the "old bourse man" (as James called himself) was sure peace would be preserved.[25] In London, too, Lionel was confident on the basis of "West End" (that is, political) intelligence of "better times." "Nothing in Poland," he told his son Leo. "We shall not interfere for the Poles who are not a bit better than the Russians."[26]

The most serious consequence of the Polish crisis was to set back Rothschild plans of establishing a long-term relationship with Russia. The financial costs of suppressing the Polish rising were sufficiently heavy to jeopardise the payment of the interest on the newly issued bonds, forcing James and Lionel to put up around a million pounds on the security of yet more Russian bonds, while at the same time disinclining them to offer any more bonds to the market.[27] This seems to have confirmed Nat's habitual pessimism about Russian finances, and for the rest of the 1860s he opposed involvement in any other Russian bond issues.[28] There were other reasons for keeping at a safe distance from St Petersburg too: pro-Polish sentiment was strong in Paris and in London, and both Charlotte and Alphonse cited this as an argument for leaving Russian business to others. "I am so glad that the Barings, and not the Rothschilds have taken the Russian loan," wrote Charlotte in April 1864, following the announcement of a new bond issue by the Rothschilds' old rivals. "If our house had negotiated it, most assuredly there would have been a great outcry against those horrid jews for helping the cruel Russians to crush the poor Poles."[29]

For the rest of the 1860s, Russia reverted to her traditional bankers, Hope and Baring, who also issued a major £6 million loan in 1866.[30] James, however, still itched to be involved. He was "heartily sorry to have lost the country" when there was "pure wine" to be made there.[31] As early as February 1867, he began to contemplate the possibility, which he had previously rejected, of involving himself directly in Russian railways, a subject he discussed at some length when the Tsar and his Prime Minister Gorchakov visited Paris in 1867. However, he remained convinced that the Russian government should act as the borrower by issuing conventional rentes in Paris and London, rather than trying to issue railway bonds, and the discussions came to nothing, as did another project for a Russian mortgage bank.[32] It was not until after his death that the Rothschilds finally agreed to issue a Russian railway loan.

Schleswig–Holstein

As far as James was concerned, Austria's defeat in Italy in 1859 was a decisive turning point: he would never again regard Austria as a great power in financial terms. In his eyes, the main question thereafter was how to wind up Austria's presence in Italy rather as a bankrupt enterprise might be wound up: an insolvent empire, he reasoned, needed to liquidate its unsustainable commitments—to rationalise itself. It was mysterious to James that this diagnosis was rejected not only by the Austrian government but also to some extent by his own nephew Anselm, who (like his father before him) increasingly identified himself with the Habsburg regime, especially after his appointment to the Reichsrat Imperial Council Finance Committee in 1861.[33] In many ways, James was right about the extent of Austrian weakness; but because the Austrians themselves resolutely denied the fact, he was inclined to overplay his hand.

No sooner had hostilities broken out in 1859, as we have seen, than the Austrian government issued a frantic plea for a loan of 200 million gulden; James responded as if Austria were at his mercy, insisting that no other foreign banks be involved. Yet there were too many rival banks eager to lend to Vienna for such a monopoly to be easily achieved. Bischoffsheim and Goldschmidt were able to secure the first tranche of the new loan, which was issued as a lottery loan. James retaliated by selling Austrian securities and refusing to co-operate when Anselm advanced the government 11 million gulden due to it from the loan of 1859. "We have got nothing from the Austrian sterling bonds," he wrote angrily, "including a price at which we can sell them." James felt "ill" at the thought of advancing money to Vienna when the government had provided no real security and even spoke darkly of instigating legal proceedings against the Austrian government to protect "our money." Relations reached a nadir in 1862, with protracted wrangles about the commission still due for the 1859 bonds, and talk of suspending the interest payments due on them.[34] When the possibility of a new Austrian loan of 50 million gulden was raised in 1862, James was indifferent:

> I don't think much will come to us, so we should tell Anselm to let us know by telegraph 24 hours in advance how much we are going to take,

because in Vienna nothing ever runs entirely according to plan. I must say it's all one to me, but I am keen that Anselm should not be able to say that we are leaving him in the lurch and not supporting his house.

Only when Anselm threatened to form a consortium including Erlanger and others did the other Rothschild houses hastily agree to participate in what was effectively a second issue of 1860 premium bonds. This threat was a sign of the growing distance between the Vienna branch and the other Rothschild houses, and irritated Mayer Carl and James.[35] The pattern repeated itself a year later when the Austrian Finance Minister Brentano sought to raise another loan. Again Anselm infuriated James by agreeing to act in partnership with the two rival syndicates formed to bid for the loan, which included the Crédit Mobilier, its London imitator the International Financial Society and the new Anglo-Austrian Bank established earlier in the same year by George Grenfell Glyn. In fact, this loose consortium ended up merely advancing £4 million to Brentano. When the government sought to fund this advance by issuing 70 million gulden of bonds the following year, the Creditanstalt was one of only two bidders, and offered to subscribe just 19 million.[36]

Primarily, then, Rothschild financial support for the Austrian government was renewed in an effort to preserve family unity *contra mundum*; James remained pessimistic throughout about Austrian bonds, selling heavily in the summer of 1862 and again the following year.[37] The unexpected resurfacing of the Schleswig–Holstein question in November 1863 merely reinforced his pessimism: he could see no advantage for Austria in siding with Prussia against the Danish annexation of Schleswig and Holstein, especially as their joint invasion was not sanctioned by the German Confederation's Diet in Frankfurt. True, Denmark was technically in breach of the Treaty of London; but the war which broke out in February 1864 seemed to most members of the family an absurdity: Charlotte called it "a mere freak on the part of Kings and Emperors and royal Dukes!" If anything, she was inclined to sympathise with the Danes, a widespread sentiment in both London and Paris.[38] For his part, James saw only increased expenditures which Austria could ill afford and which therefore made the latest tranche of her bonds even harder to sell—though needless to say he was quick to see the possibility of a loan to Denmark, assuming an indemnity would be imposed on her.[39]

What especially alarmed James was the fact that no sooner had the Danes been defeated than the alliance between Austria and Prussia evaporated: united against Denmark (and against foreign arbitration of the sort attempted ineffectually by France and Britain), they still could not agree between themselves what should become of the duchies.[40] Various combinations were discussed when the two monarchs met at Schönbrunn, but William would not agree to give up Prussian land in return for both Schleswig and Holstein, while Franz Joseph still rejected the old Prussian demand for military hegemony in North Germany. Increasingly, the Austrians inclined towards the German liberals' favourite solution: that the duchies should pass to the Duke of Augustenburg. However, in February 1865 Bismarck intimated that he would agree to this only if the duchies were made wholly dependent on Prussia, a *démarche* which (coming just months after he had vetoed the Austrian application to join the Zollverein) raised the prospect of another, more serious war—between Austria and Prussia. This anxiety merely made the Austrian position worse.[41] The curious thing is that the Rothschilds chose this moment to take up the £3 million balance of the 1859 sterling loan, including £500,000 *à forfait;* once again, the only rationale for this foolhardy commitment was the need to thwart the ambitions of another rival, Langrand-Dumonceau, who was touting a scheme for an Austrian Mortgage Bank and a loan secured on crown lands.[42] To all intents and purposes Austria was broke when Belcredi took over from Schmerling as Chancellor in July 1865, with a deficit of 80 million gulden and no apparent means to cover it other than yet more advances from the banks.[43]

Austria fell into further disrepute in James's eyes with the decline into insolvency of the Esterházy family, on whose behalf the Frankfurt and Vienna houses had been raising loans since the 1820s. Between 1861 and 1864, no less than 6.3 million gulden had been raised through the issue of bonds secured on Esterházy lands. Then, in June 1865, Paul Esterházy was forced to suspend payments on premium bonds bearing his name, prompting a storm of public criticism directed at the banks which had issued the bonds.[44] At a time when Móric Esterházy increasingly directed Austrian foreign policy as Minister without Portfolio, the collapse of his own family's finances neatly paralleled the collapse of those of the Empire itself.[45] The embarrassment this fiasco caused the Rothschilds might have served as a warning.

Privatisation and Diplomacy

Why then go on doing business with Vienna? The answer to this question is that James believed he had a solution to the Austrian problem. From as early as December 1861 he had begun to contemplate a transaction which, as he saw it, offered not only financial advantages but also diplomatic advantages to the Austrian government, as well as a substantial commission for himself: the sale of Venetia to Italy.[46] The Gastein compromise of August 1865, which temporarily gave Austria Holstein and Prussia Schleswig, did not preclude an analogous deal whereby Austria could sell Holstein to Prussia. Indeed, Bismarck had suggested this at Schönbrunn the year before, and the Gastein agreement seemed to set a precedent by transferring Lauenburg from Austria to Prussia in return for a payment of 2.5 million Danish thalers.[47] The question seemed to be simply whether a price could be found acceptable to all parties. If this could be achieved, the territories disputed between Austria and her enemies to the north and south would be transformed into mere real estate, as marketable as the over-encumbered private estates of the Esterházys.

To understand what the Rothschilds were attempting to do in the tortuous but decisive negotiations of 1865, it is important to realise that there was in fact a degree of symmetry about the Prussian, Italian and Austrian positions. Each state was strapped for cash. The prospective buyers of disputed territory would therefore be able to raise it only by borrowing. But neither was in a position to do so easily, Prussia because of the constitutional conflict, Italy because of her increasingly low credit-rating. To the Rothschilds, the answer seemed to be obvious: both should privatise state assets—preferably railways—using the receipts to buy Holstein and Venetia respectively. At the same time, Austria's financial position was so precarious that even selling one or both of these territories was unlikely to balance the budget. Austria had already sold off most of her state railways, so privatisation was not the answer here; instead, James reasoned, the already private railway lines should seek tax breaks from the government as part of the price of financial assistance. This was the essence of James's vision in 1865: a complex of interdependent transactions designed to liquidate Austria's unsustainable empire without the need for an economically disruptive war.

The Prussian case is the best known. Prussia was financially stronger than Austria; but in the short term the constitutional crisis and the Danish war created a cash-flow crisis. Once it was apparent that the Landtag would not sanction any kind of loan to the government, Bismarck had to fulfil his threat to resort to other sources. One option which had immediately presented itself in early 1864 was a loan of 15 million thalers from a consortium of bankers led by Raphael Erlanger. To Bleichröder this was alarming: he knew the hostility James felt towards upstarts like Erlanger, and hastened to reassure him that this offer had been "totally rejected," though in fact the Seehandlung did some sort of deal with Erlanger shortly after this. The trouble was that the Rothschilds wanted Bleichröder to stop Erlanger without being willing to lend to Berlin themselves. When Bleichröder suggested that the government raise money by mortgaging some 20 million thalers of 4.5 per cent bonds already authorised by the Diet to pay for Silesian railways (but as yet unsold), James referred him to Mayer Carl; but the latter passed the buck back, replying that the Paris house would "remain completely aloof" from such a deal—a refusal which Bleichröder felt it wise to conceal from Bismarck: "On the contrary, I tried to make him believe that your esteemed Houses would cheerfully lend their support to Prussian finance operations." The government was by now deeply divided on the finance question, the Finance Minister Bodelschwingh opposing the diversion of the railway bonds to military ends, and pressing Bismarck to recall the Diet in the hope of securing an authorised loan. But any hope that the victory over Denmark would relax the mood of the Liberals in the Landtag was dashed in 1865, when the government's conduct was denounced as illegal and all its requests for funds firmly rejected.

This raises an important question: how, if Austria had accepted the idea of selling Holstein to Prussia, would Prussia have paid for it? As early as November 1864, Bismarck was promising "magnificent money equivalents"; if the equivalents "were high," Esterházy told the Prussian ambassador Werther, "he would not reject the offer." It was here that the Rothschilds sought for the first time to act as brokers, with Bleichröder and Moritz Goldschmidt of the Vienna house corresponding back and forth in search of a price which both sides would accept. As Goldschmidt said, the sum in question "would have to be fat to overcome the immense reluctance against a cash settlement, which would not be very honourable," a view echoed by the Austrian Finance Minister Plener. It soon emerged that the figure the Prussians had in mind was 40 million gulden (around 23 million thalers). But where was this to come from? Bleichröder might claim that Prussia's "coffers were full," but Bodelschwingh had told the Diet that the war against Denmark had already cost 25 million thalers, half of which had been met from the state "treasure" (meaning reserve funds); according to Bleichröder, that left around 37 million thalers in the reserve.[48] Not much would have remained of that if Prussia had bought Holstein.

The other possibility was that Prussia might sell state property of her own to raise the requisite funds. There were in fact two options, both of which Bleichröder had already suggested before 1864. The first related to the railway between Cologne and Minden (near Hanover), "the backbone of rail transport in north-western Germany"; the second, more ambitious scheme related to the crown lands in the middle Saar, and in particular to the coal mines there. The Prussian state had originally put up around a seventh of the Cologne–Minden line's 13 million thalers capital, but under a deal struck with the Prussian Commerce Minister Baron August von der Heydt it had guaranteed the interest on the entirety and, in return, had the right to buy out all the other stockholders in 1870. In December 1862 Bleichröder proposed to von der Heydt's successor von Itzenplitz that the government sell what amounted to its "share options" back to the company for 14 million thalers. The other possibility, raised by Bleichröder in November 1863, was that the government should sell the crown lands in the Saar to a specially created joint-stock company, retaining a majority shareholding, but receiving cash for the company for the rest. Such a sale had in fact been rumoured as early as 1861, though reports that the French Rothschilds had offered 20 million thalers for the mines were unfounded. Apart from the obvious advantages of giving the government the cash it required, privatisation had the additional rationale that if, as Bismarck thought probable, France demanded the Saarland as "compensation" for Prussian territorial expansion elsewhere, the mines would remain in Prussian hands. From the point of view of Bleichröder, privatisation would extend the already substantial industrial empire in the Rhineland of the Oppenheims, with whom he also had close business links.[49]

It would indeed have been a coup if, by these means, the Rothschilds and their associates in Prussia had been able to resolve the quarrel between Austria and Prussia. But there was a catch. If money were made available to Prussia, Bismarck might well be tempted to use it not to pay for Holstein but to wage war on Austria. In fact, the Prussian government was thinking along precisely these lines even before the Gastein treaty. When an agreement was reached on the Cologne–Minden deal on July 18, 1865, whereby the government relinquished its share options for 13 million thaler, Bismarck at once informed the Crown Prince: "The financial means for complete mobilisation and for a one-year military campaign are available; the amount is circa 60 million thalers." "We have money," crowed the War Minister Roon, "enough to give us a free hand in foreign policy, enough, if need be, to mobilise the whole army and to pay for an entire campaign . . . Whence the money? Without violating a law, primarily through an arrangement with the Cologne–Minden Railroad, which I and even Bodelschwingh consider very *advantageous*." It did not take long for the Austrian chargé Chotek to report that Prussia had "such an important supply of money as one usually keeps in readiness in anticipation of war."[50] On the other hand, the Cologne–Minden sale was still not enough to guarantee victory; Roon was still thinking in terms of the diplomatic leverage Prussia would gain from her apparent readiness for war, rather than of actually fighting. In August, Bismarck too advised Bleichröder against selling securities on his account "because of some premature fear of war." "The conditions of our financial and military preparations," he commented after Gastein, "made it desirable not to force the break prematurely."[51] In particular, Bismarck had cause to fear that if Austria also succeeded in raising money any conflict would be, at least in financial terms, too evenly matched for comfort. His objective in the summer of 1865 was therefore plain: to prevent by any means at his disposal the Austrian government from successfully floating a loan.

Austria manifestly did need a loan in 1865; and it was probably to encourage the government to come to him that James bought £300,000 of Anglo-Austrian bonds at the relatively generous price of 78.9 in mid-August.[52] At first, it is true, he was reluctant to make a major new loan. On September 9 he actually told the Finance Ministry official Baron Becke, sent to negotiate with him in Paris, that it was "impossible for us to make a loan." But Becke's reaction impressed him: "The man was completely thrown and said, 'That means the government must go bankrupt.'" This was a shocking threat, recalling the collapse of Austrian finances in the Napoleonic Wars, and it did not fail to move one who remembered those days. James hastily proposed a compromise: a year's advance of 1 or 2 million pounds, to be made by the London and Paris houses in partnership with Barings (whom he knew the Austrians had also approached), with a possible loan to follow.

This uncharacteristic willingness to work in tandem with Barings—as well as with the Société Générale and the Crédit Foncier, who were also approached— shows that James did not underestimate the risks involved in lending to Vienna. Nevertheless, he wished to show Becke "that we are not against Austria" by "doing something." The reasons are not hard to divine. Apart from anything else, the Rothschilds continued to hold substantial amounts of Austrian bonds: as James put it, "we have too much money [invested] in this government." If Austria really did declare bankruptcy, those bonds would depreciate drastically: "The good man just wants money to pay the interest payments and I can see the necessity of doing this. Baring is also very committed to Austria, so that he has an interest in it too." Moreover, the terms of such an advance *in extremis* could only be profitable: "Clearly the man will allow one to make as much money from him as one could wish, and Austria is after all always a great state."[53]

Initially, James toyed with the earlier Langrand-Dumonceau idea of a loan secured on crown lands. But the financial difficulties of the Lombard line—which had just necessitated a cash injection of 63 million francs from the Paris house and the Société Générale—suggested another possibility to his fertile business imagination. According to the terms of the company's charter, it would have to begin paying a levy to the Austrian state in 1868. Now James saw a way of boosting the company's ailing stock market quotation: an exemption from the levy which, as Alphonse put it, "weighs so heavily on the future of our Lombards."[54] Finally, the loan negotiations offered a way to exert pressure on Austria to come to the kind of accommodation with Prussia and Italy which would avert war. Alphonse discussed with the Italian ambassador the possibility of an exchange of Venetia—for cash or for the Danubian principalities (Rumania)—on September 16; three days later, James expressed the hope that the "Italian question" could be "decided," and suggested inserting the familiar Rothschild clause that the loan should be conditional on peace being maintained.[55] By September 23 he was thinking even more radically:

> One could tack on a trade treaty with England and perhaps France . . . Really, one could do a golden deal. The[se] people want us to make money out of them. Conditions we prescribe: a Chamber which approves [the loan] and reduction of the army. I think that with a constitution the people have to enjoy better credit than hitherto.[56]

Just three days later, he and Alphonse seemed to have secured "all that we want" after "a long conversation" with Becke:

As for the trade treaty, there will be no difficulty about linking it to the loan . . . An understanding seems equally likely on the question of the tax on the Lombard line. In the end one would obtain the most favourable conditions [if we agreed to a loan] today, as the government has elbow-room. It needs money to consolidate its political position and wants to succeed at all costs.[57]

We know from the reports of the Austrian diplomat Mühlinen how desperate Becke was to secure James's co-operation at this stage. In Becke's view, Austria's "financial fate" was "in his [James's] hands," and he did not hesitate to offer inducements of a more personal nature:

[I]f we don't succeed with him, we won't accomplish anything of conse-quence with the others. We must then, make the sparks fly, and espe-cially flatter old man James. Anything pleasing to his conceit is worth 1 or 2 per cent . . . How would it be if we gave him a "grand cordon?" It was the cross of Stanislaus that made the Russian loan. Has he the iron crown of the first class? If not can we let him hope for it?[58]

By October 3, the deal seemed only to lack signatures.[59]

A Meeting at Biarritz

Then, suddenly, there were delays. Of course, there had always been arguments against the deal. In part these were financial: the tightening of the Paris money market in the summer of 1865 had at first inclined Alphonse to think that the issue of a new Austrian loan was "an impossible thing at the present time."[60] When Anselm had unexpectedly revised Austria's needs upwards to 150 million gulden, his French cousin had been irate. He found it

difficult to understand how a man who has as much experience of busi-ness . . . versed as he is in Austrian finance [as] a member of the Reichs-rat finance commission, could fail to warn us that Austria is on the edge of the abyss; that he should permit us to keep all our [Austrian] securi-ties, that he should even constantly encourage us to buy more, and then all of a sudden he comes along and tells us calmly that if Austria is unable to make a loan of 150 million gulden, she will have no option but to declare bankruptcy.[61]

According to Alphonse's calculations, the government in fact needed 49 million gulden (£6.9 million) just to meet its impending debt repayments.[62] Nat had no doubts: any new Austrian bonds would be nothing more than "rubbish."[63] At the crucial moment in early October, Mayer Carl added his doubts:

I only regret that as far as the continent is concerned & particularly Ger-many the prospect for such [is] all but very encouraging—Money is very dear and likely to become more still & our public has lost so much by the Anglo Austrian that you cannot rely upon a market . . . I must con-fess that I have not the least confidence in the Austrian government which has always taken us in & . . . [is] not to be relied upon . . . I have written so often & so fully to Paris on the subject that I really do not know what to do but I am afraid that this time if you come to an

arrangement you will be just as much taken in as our friend & cousins.
Our public sells daily large quantities of Austrian stock.[64]

There was also, as Mayer Carl pointed out, a political counter-argument. The constitutional wrangling between Austria and Hungary, which resulted in the prorogation of the Reichsrat in September 1865, seemed to raise exactly the same problem in Austria as already existed in Prussia: was the government legally entitled to raise a new loan? This was an argument which worried the London banks more than the French.[65]

The question which historians have hitherto been unable to answer is whether or not the ultimate failure of the Austrian loan talks was—as the Austrians themselves claimed—the result of a secret agreement between Bismarck and James intended to deny the Austrians Rothschild support. Bismarck undoubtedly set out to stop the loan. As early as June 19—referring to "the opportunities which a complication of the foreign situation could yield"—Bismarck had "noted that it might be advisable by proper financial operations to weaken the present inclination of the money market towards an Austrian loan." Indeed, he underlined the passage in a diplomatic report which quoted an Austrian official saying that "because of its lack of credit the Austrian government would temporarily have to give up its great power position." "Through our money operations," he told Roon, Prussia needed "to paralyse those intended by Austria." It may have been partly with this object in mind that he suggested to Bleichröder an operation whereby the Rothschilds might buy Prussian bonds from the Seehandlung which could then advance the proceeds to the government, thus notionally circumventing the parliamentary prohibition on unauthorised loans.[66]

Does this ulterior motive explain why the deal fell through? Perhaps: it seems unlikely that Mayer Carl's refusal to take 9 million thalers of 1859 Prussian bonds, offered him in July by the Seehandlung at par, was uninfluenced by political considerations, given that he was prepared to go as high as 99.5, and that within a week they were being sold at par to Berlin bankers and were trading at 101.[67] James and Alphonse were undoubtedly becoming suspicious of Prussian intentions. On August 4, before the Gastein compromise, James echoed his son's "dissatisfaction with German politics." He refused to believe that war would break out "as Austria is weak enough to give in," but accused Bismarck of contemplating "a wild coup" and expressed growing "distrust" of Bleichröder. Accordingly, he gave instructions to sell 400,000 thalers of Prussian securities. This worried Bleichröder so much that, at the suggestion of a friend, he rushed to see James at Ostend "to tell me," as James put it drily, "how well everything was going."[68] James's assessment of the Prussian situation reveals how little he thought of both Bismarck and Bleichröder at this juncture: "Bismarck is absolutely not to be trusted, as his domestic position is very bad. Bleichröder thinks it could come to a revolution. That is sheer nonsense. I don't believe a word of it, as a man does not risk his own country for the sake of holding onto office."[69] And when Bismarck tried again, James understood perfectly what he was aiming to do. Even before the two met in Baden-Baden on September 2, James had already concluded that the decision to increase the Seehandlung's discount rate was "a political move, designed to prevent Austria from getting a loan and to force her to sell the duchies [Schleswig and Holstein]."

Yet this meeting saw a change in James's tone. "Bismarck told me yesterday," he informed his nephews after their meeting, "that the Austrians are at present not all willing to sell them. But in the end they will give in."[70] For the first time, Bismarck advanced the argument that, if James did lend money to Austria, it would reduce rather than increase the pressure on the Emperor to accept the sale of Holstein. This did not stop the negotiations between the Rothschilds and Becke from nearing a successful conclusion; but when Bismarck visited Napoleon III at Biarritz a month later, he redoubled his efforts to sabotage the loan—and this time he seemed to succeed. On October 6 James reported to his nephews that he had put off further discussions with Becke "as it is not possible at the present moment to think of a major transaction. It is said here that Bismarck spoke in a very bellicose and proud way to Drouyn de Lhuys."[71] The next day, after hunting at Ferrières, James spent two hours closeted with Bismarck (who complimented him on the quality of his wine). An uneasy Mühlinen reported back to Vienna:

> I do not know what passed between them, but I do know that the evening before at Ferrières, the old baron was very well disposed and drank to the success of all our wishes . . . while after the visit in question the negotiations took a turn for the worse. The rumour spread that Monsieur de Bismarck has offered 80 million thalers for Holstein. One of Rothschild's sons, Alphonse, went so far as to tell one of my colleagues that we ought to accept the proposition and then we wouldn't need the loan.[72]

Once again, it soon emerged, Bismarck was telling James that to lend to Austria would undermine the chances of a peaceful sale of contested territory; Mühlinen was wrong only about the price Bismarck had in mind for Holstein (Bleichröder had proposed a mere 21 million thalers, two-thirds of the proceeds of the Cologne–Minden deal).[73] A few days later (on or before October 15), as Mühlinen reported to the Austrian Foreign Minister Mensdorff, James repeated the Bismarckian message, though he was careful to deny its source. He also threw in for good measure the Italian proposal, secretly advanced at around the same time, that Venetia also be sold:

> Towards the close of our conversation James Rothschild said to me suddenly: "Why do you not accept the offer that is said to have been made to you? Let them buy Holstein." . . . I replied to the baron in the presence of his two sons that I could not countenance his insinuation. Although I had no instructions on the subject, I believed that I must state to him my personal opinion that the Imperial Government was not contemplating that contingency. The baron interrupted me to state that it was just a stock exchange rumour like that about the sale of Venetia and that it had not come from any minister or diplomat. I replied that I had but too much reason to infer the source of these fine projects [namely, Bismarck] which had been reaching me for some time on all sides. Since he had just mentioned Venetia, I felt an additional obligation to act with vigour against those who were attempting to mislead the public as to the intentions of my government. Never could it attempt even a discussion on the basis that people were trying to establish, by bringing forward Holstein, in order to arrive at the famous scheme for

the purchase of Venetia . . . I was convinced that rather than permit the integrity of the empire to be meddled with, Austria would stake her last man and her last florin . . . [I]f foreign capital was going to put itself at the service of our enemies, it would be the first to suffer; it would not prevent us from finding at home the means to ward off the blows that they wanted to deal us.[74]

For days James prevaricated, racked with doubts and gout.[75] In Vienna the delay even became a matter for ribald public comment. Evelina reported that when her father-in-law Anselm went to the theatre "to see a new piece, in which the principal actor is made to say: 'Wir brauchen Geld, Geld, Geld' . . . the whole audience turned round to look at Uncle A. who felt uncomfortable in consequence of being stared at by the modern argus, the public."[76]

Yet Bismarck had not achieved his object; for on October 18 James and his London nephews resolved to go ahead. Two days later, terms seemed to have been agreed for an advance of 49 million gulden or a loan of 90 to 150 million at a price of 68, with a subsidiary deal freeing the Lombard line of the projected tax for twenty years, in return for which James renounced the government guarantee on the bonds of the Trieste and Venice rail networks.[77] The Rothschilds' private correspondence shows that the railway tax-break—the value of which Alphonse put at 1.4 million gulden a year and Mühlinen at a total of 28 million—was in fact the crucial issue, so much so that James now made it the *sine qua non* not just of a loan but also of an advance. The Lombard concession had become, as Alphonse said, "the capital point"—"le tout qui nous intéresse sérieusement." What he and his father did not realise was that by raising the question of Holstein and Venetia they had unwittingly overstepped the mark in the eyes of the Austrian government. By the time Alphonse woke up to the fact that Vienna was becoming, as he put it, "fidgety," it was too late. At the suggestion of the Vienna banker Samuel Haber, Mühlinen and Becke had established contact with a group of Paris banks including Hottinguer, Mallet and Fould, led by the Crédit Foncier. Where James had been making (as Mühlinen put it) "unacceptable propositions" and demanding "real concessions—tax exemption for the Lombard," the rival banks offered "much more than Rothschild and without asking anything in return." "It may be objected," wrote Mühlinen frankly, "that this latter consortium does not have the prestige of Rothschild–Baring. I admit it, and it is for that reason that for seven weeks we have done the impossible at the price of listening to some pretty hard things from the lips of Baron James in order to go along with him." On November 14 he and Becke concluded with the Crédit Foncier consortium. Thus, far from acting in concert with Bismarck to sabotage the Austrian loan, James had merely overplayed his hand. When he and Alphonse realised that the Crédit Foncier had outbid them, they were astounded: it struck Alphonse as "so fantastic that I can't believe it; those gentlemen must have famous chutzpah to risk such a difficult affair." James was furious with the "Austrian scoundrels," and accused Becke of having been bribed; Anselm and Ferdinand were "very much disgusted with Mr de Becke's behaviour," which they considered "both ungentlemanly and unbusinesslike." Indeed, Anselm went so far as to threaten to resign from the Reichsrat, though James advised against this ("as the Austrians won't reappoint a Jew in a hurry").[78]

The question remains whether it was his insistence on tax-breaks for the Lombard line, as the Austrians claimed, which had proved the fatal stumbling block. On reflection, James concluded that the Austrians were merely using his Lombard demands as a pretext for what was essentially a political decision in favour of a purely French loan. There are reasons to think he was right about this. For the terms of the Crédit Foncier loan were in fact markedly worse than the package James had envisaged: the rival consortium bought bonds with a face value of around 150 million gulden at an effective price of 61.25 so that, after commissions, the Austrian government received just 90 million gulden. As James said, this was usurious when the market quotation for Austrian bonds was 70. By comparison, the Rothschild price for the loan had been a modest 68 or, if one factors in the cost of the Lombard concession, 67.1. It seems more plausible that it was James's allusion to the possible sale of Holstein and Venetia which persuaded the Austrian negotiators to look elsewhere. When Franz Joseph was informed by his officials in Paris that James regarded the proposed loan as conditional on the recognition of Italy as a kingdom, he scrawled in the margin: "There can be no talk of that."[79] The fact that Lord John Russell also endorsed the idea of selling Venetia may have added as much to their suspicions as James's meeting with Bismarck. A loan issued by a purely French consortium with the approval of Napoleon and Drouyn seemed to have fewer strings attached; indeed, it seemed to raise the possibility of luring France into a defensive alliance against Prussia and Italy. When Goldschmidt heard that Becke had accepted the Crédit Foncier's offer, he concluded that "in the Holstein purchase business there is *absolutely nothing* to be done."

In the final analysis, therefore, it was the fundamental Austrian refusal to sell either Holstein or Venetia which was the key—not Bismarck's intrigues, nor James's private railway demands. This intransigence is usually blamed on Franz Joseph's antiquated sense of Habsburg honour (even he himself later called Austrian policy "very honourable, but very stupid"). Yet it is worth asking how stupid it was to reject the various offers made for Holstein and Venice. If 49 million gulden was needed just to satisfy Austria's creditors in the period to February 1866, the 40 million gulden being offered by Prussia for Holstein perhaps was "too little." It was not unreasonable for Goldschmidt to suggest that Prussia sugar the pill with either a piece of Silesia (Bismarck himself contemplated the county of Glatz) or the little enclave of Hohenzollern in Württemberg, the ancestral home of the Prussian royal family. (Had not Victor Emmanuel sacrificed his ancestral home of Savoy to France?) Perhaps too Mensdorff was right when he argued that to sell parts of a multinational empire might set a worse precedent than to risk losing them by force of arms. At least in a war there was a chance of victory, however slender.

The Road to Königgrätz

We are never more angry with others than when we know we are at fault ourselves. James knew that in raising on Bismarck's behalf the questions of Holstein and Venetia he had unwittingly scuppered what would have been a useful deal for the Lombard line. Yet, as he and his relatives went back to the drawing board to devise what was to prove a costly and difficult new rights issue for their railway, they did not blame themselves.[80] Nor did they blame Austria, as they might well have. Indeed, negotiations for new advances to Vienna began as early as February 1, 1866.[81]

Instead, and with unusual vehemence, they blamed Prussia. For the sake of form, James had sent Bismarck a case of burgundy in November as a memento of his visit to Ferrières; but the Rothschilds' private view of the Prussian Minister President would take years to recover from the failure of the Austrian loan. On January 16, 1866, Mayer Carl wrote an angry letter from Frankfurt which was little short of a call to arms:

> The state of things in this part of the world becomes daily more complicated and the behaviour of Prussia assumes a character unheard of in the annals of history and everybody is of [the] opinion that the Prussians deserve a good lesson for the scandalous manner in which she [sic] trifles with the whole of Germany: her way of acting is quite unprecedented & it is useless to form an opinion of what may or will happen but the fact is that Germany at large is opposed to the policy of a Government whose ambitious views must be put an end to.[82]

It was a sentiment echoed by Lionel's youngest son Leo in Cambridge: "It seems so brutal of the Prussians that they cannot be satisfied and that they are still anxious to ruin all the minor powers."[83] In Vienna Goldschmidt too was becoming impatient with Bismarck's belligerence. James's mood was not improved when the Prussian ambassador Goltz candidly—and surely without his government's authorisation—warned him that war with Austria was likely because "Austria has given Prussia a negative answer about Holstein, that she absolutely refuses to sell her rights [there]."[84] For Alphonse, Prussia was the "spectre at the feast": he saw no hope of the financial markets stabilising so long as Bismarck, with his "policy of annexation," remained in power.[85] All this helps explain why James was so hostile to the proposition—rejected on March 14 after an approach from Bleichröder's associate Lehmann and a two hour interview with Goltz—that the Rothschilds form a syndicate to buy the government's remaining 80,000 Cologne–Minden shares for 20 million thalers.[86]

This refusal is often cited as evidence of a general Rothschild policy "not to lend money for war"; in this case, myth and reality more or less correspond. That famous phrase is in fact taken from a letter of 1862; but James said more or less the same on this occasion. As he told his nephews in London: "I refused Bleichröder's associate, on the grounds that we cannot give money to make war. Only when we know for sure that the two governments have come to an agreement will we see what is to be done."[87] James believed with good reason that Bismarck's position had been seriously weakened by the Landtag commission's ruling that the earlier Cologne–Minden deal was illegal.[88] Now, he reasoned, Prussia was in real financial difficulties. Had Bismarck wanted the 20 million thalers to make a new offer for Holstein, then James might possibly have been interested; but Goltz had tipped him off that Bismarck now intended a violent solution to the German question. Even Bleichröder admitted this: the most he could say was that "if it had to happen, a rupture [between Austria and Prussia] would not break out before the month of April or May."[89] Under the circumstances, to have bought the Cologne–Minden shares would not only have defied the explicit will of the Landtag—and we should not underestimate the Rothschilds' regard for parliamentary sanctions—but would also have amounted to funding Prussian war preparations. Small wonder Bismarck scolded Goltz in a letter of March 13 for showing his hand at such a delicate moment:

> We wish to postpone making full preparations for war in order first to carry though the financial operations which would necessarily become more difficult when the situation becomes more tense owing to an increase of armaments. In this connection, I would mention in confidence that we had entered preliminary negotiations with the House of Rothschild . . . It is in the nature of things that the House should not welcome the possibility of war, and should do everything possible to prevent war from breaking out; I am able more particularly to assure Your Excellency that Baron Rothschild informed our agent [Bleichröder] that a few weeks ago he would not have been averse from carrying through a transaction with Prussia, and that he would perhaps have done so with real pleasure, but that the altered circumstances, and especially a conversation which he had had with Your Excellency, now prevented him from doing so. I feel I ought to mention this fact, since it shows how careful one must be in dealing with Rothschild.[90]

Anthony, who happened to be in Paris, was dismissive of the Prussian proposal: Prussia might be "very anxious" for war, but "their money is as bad as ever . . . the whole country is against it and the Prussian Minister . . . has been for the last 2 hours asking the Baron . . . to advance to the gov. for 20 Million of Thalers upon a lot of Railroad Rubbish."[91] On March 17 Goltz informed the King bluntly "that the House of Rothschild is determined to bring its whole influence to bear to prevent Prussia from going to war."[92] As the Crown Prince put it, "Rothschild is moving heaven and earth [against] Bismarck."[93] On this occasion, the cartoonists were right: on May 20 the Munich *Punsch* ran a cartoon on its cover entitled "Rothschild's Readiness for War" which portrayed James clinging on to his money-bags and declaring: "I'm not giving anything! I don't have any money! The only pleasure I get is neutrality. And you surely won't deny me one pleasure?" (see illustration 4.ii).

We know that in the end James failed to stop the war; but that should not blind us to the vulnerability of Bismarck's position at this juncture. When the Prussian ministers met in Berlin on the same day Goltz wrote his letter, their options were alarmingly narrow, as the terse minutes of the meeting indicate: "The procurement of money creates difficulties. The placing of the Cologne–Minden shares can be done only at a loss. Sale of Saarbrücken suggested. Third possibility is to call the Diet and get a loan, but then great German programme and a great German parliament." The last option seemed to imply capitulation to the Liberals.[94] This was the time of the so-called "Coburg cabal"—a conspiracy to secure Bismarck's dismissal which supposedly involved Queen Victoria, Russell, Disraeli and the Rothschilds. On March 20 James eagerly relayed rumours from Berlin "that Bismarck is leaving the ministry and peace will be preserved."[95] Two days later Disraeli told Mayer that Bismarck "ought to be hung!"[96] When Gustave heard that "Bismarck, to extricate himself . . . considers convoking an all-German Parliament" it struck him as "the limit" and "unbelievable"—further proof of his desperation.[97] The Prussian premier, wrote Mayer Carl, had "got himself into a terrible mess and thinks that the sword is likely to bring everything round."[98] As this suggests, the Rothschilds continued to worry that internal pressure might merely increase Bismarck's desire for war—this

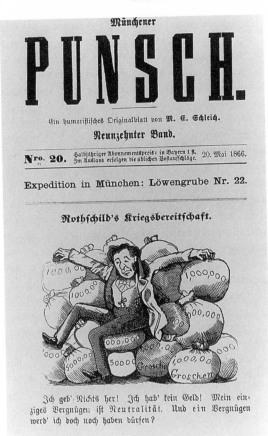

Münchener

PUNSCH.

Ein humoristisches Originalblatt von M. E. Schleich.

Neunzehnter Band.

Nro. 20. Halbjähriger Abonnementspreis: in Bayern 1 fl. 20. Mai 1866.
           Im Auslande erfolgen die üblichen Postaufschläge.

Expedition in München: Löwengrube Nr. 22.

Rothschild's Kriegsbereitschaft.

Ich geb' Nichts her! Ich hab' kein Geld! Mein ein-
ziges Vergnügen ist Neutralität. Und ein Vergnügen
werd' ich doch noch haben dürfen?

4.ii: M. E. Schleich, *Rothschild's Kriegsbereitschaft, Ein humoristisches Originalblatt*, Münchener Punsch, 19, Nr. 20 (May 20, 1866).

was the period when they abused him most vitriolically as a "madcap" and "foaming like a wild boar." In James's words, "one never knows what he is about to do and if he can only get the King's support he will declare war as if it were nothing."[99]

Even if Bismarck did win the King's backing, however, the question remained how was he to pay for such a war. Bodelschwingh was down to his last 40 million thalers; and on May 2 the Cabinet ruled out the sale of the Saar mines.[100] Under the circumstances, it did not seem unreasonable to hope for Bismarck's fall.[101] The disarmament proposals put forward by Austria on April 7 merely added to his difficulties: two weeks later, he had to accept them. As for his decision to don the mantle of revolutionary nationalism by proposing a parliament for the Confederation elected by universal suffrage, this seemed to run counter to everything Bismarck had stood for since 1848. As late as April 27, Bleichröder still did not rule out the possibility that Prussia would give in and Bismarck would resign.[102] The second and third weeks of May saw the Prussian government in disarray: an assassination attempt against Bismarck, the dissolution of the Landtag, crisis on the Berlin bourse, and Roon's calculation that the cost of mobilising nine army corps would be 24 million thalers with a further 6 million per month as long as it remained on a war footing.[103] On May 18 emergency credit institutes had to be set up and currency convertibility suspended; three days later, when the Seehandlung attempted to sell treasury bills in

Paris, James once again intimated his opposition to Goltz.[104] As late as June 9—fully a week after Bodelschwingh's successor had failed to sell the Cologne–Minden shares to a consortium led by Bleichröder and Oppenheim—Lehmann was sent back to Paris "to ask us if we want to make an advance of gold bars or silver to the Bank, either on Cologne–Minden shares or on drafts on the Seehandlung."[105] Once again he was turned away. As Alphonse put it, the deal would have yielded "a pretty profit"; but James was "little disposed at this moment" to oblige a government which Lehmann himself portrayed as tottering.

Not content with denying Bismarck money, James also sought to deny him something he believed Prussia needed just as much: an alliance with Italy. The Italian position was in many ways similar to both the Prussian and Austrian. Rothschild confidence in Italy's financial stability had declined sharply since the 1850s and James was still selling Italian bonds in August 1865. He and his sons were genuinely shocked when the Italian government announced a deficit of 280 million lire in September 1865.[106] Yet there were good reasons for continuing to do business with Italy. Firstly, if the transfer of Venetia from Austria to Italy was to be achieved peacefully, Italy would require financial assistance to make the purchase. Secondly, and perhaps more important, Italy now controlled a large area of territory covered by the Lombard company's rail network. The year 1866 therefore saw a second opportunity to secure concessions for the company in return for a loan to the government. The danger was that Italy, like Prussia, might use any money made available to her for war rather than a peaceful purchase of Venetia.[107] When the Italian government approached James for short-term advances totalling 35 million lire in September 1865, he was therefore not averse to obliging;[108] but he continued to watch carefully for evidence of Italian disarmament before going any further.[109]

News of a 150 million lire bond issue in early 1866 at first seemed of minimal significance, as the government initially asked Landau to take just 14 million. In March, however, the government made a new approach, offering the Lombard company a new and more generous contract in return for an advance of 125 million lire. This seemed to give the Rothschilds the leverage they needed, though the announcement shortly afterwards of a tax on government bonds suggests that the Italians intended to use sticks as well as carrots to secure Rothschild co-operation.[110] If the Italians could only be persuaded to adopt a peaceful policy—and ideally to use the proceeds of a loan to purchase Venetia from Austria—then Bismarck would be diplomatically isolated.[111] Nigra, the Italian ambassador, alarmed James by telling him that Italy would join Prussia in the event of a war with Austria.[112] However, on March 22 the Italian government unexpectedly invited Landau, the Rothschild agent, to act as an intermediary "to relay propositions for [the purchase of] Venetia and thus to avoid war." Alphonse's assessment of this proposition is revealing:

> It is to be feared that such an initiative on our part might be very ill received and might make our position in Vienna very delicate. We have already made insinuations in this regard on several occasions and we have been given to understand that we should never broach the subject, which awakens all H.M.'s sense of amour propre. Perhaps in the critical circumstances in which Austria finds itself, however, the G[overnmen]t [may?] modify its ideas . . . The one thing which can be inferred from

the Italian G[overnmen]t's démarche is that it has decided to take part in the war if it happens but has not yet signed a treaty with Prussia.[113]

The Landau initiative was part of a British-backed bid to pressurise Austria and Italy into a peaceful agreement over Venetia. Other possibilities floated at the same time included the exchange of Venetia for Rumania, where a revolt had overthrown the elected Prince Nicholas Cuza, and the exchange of Holstein for Glatz (again).

In the first instance, these efforts failed because, once again, the Austrians would not hear of selling out. Even before he relayed the Landau proposal to Esterházy, Anselm urged that Landau should not accept the Italian mission, in the belief that the proposed sale of Venetia would be rejected out of hand. If Landau came to Vienna bearing such dishonourable proposals, he would bring the Rothschilds further into disrepute as "partisans of Italy":

> The Cabinet here is afraid of nothing. If the need arises, it will take the bull by the horns[?]; without the assistance of France, and I hope it will lack this support, the Italian army will exhaust itself in vain effort against the forts of the quadrilateral. The question of the duchies [of Schleswig and Holstein] is generally considered a question of honour, that of Venetia a question of material existence. [The government] turns a deaf ear to an offer of money on the part of Prussia; it would be more deaf than ever to such an offer from Italy, whose pockets in any case are empty.[114]

Esterházy's rejection of the Landau offer and Prussian allegations of Austrian troop movements only served to confirm this gloomy assessment.[115] By the time the British government formally proposed the sale of Venetia for £40 million, it was too late.[116] The Italian announcement of a domestic bond issue worth 250 million lire could now only be construed as a measure to finance military preparations.[117] On April 8 the Italians secretly signed an agreement with Prussia, binding for just three months, to go to war against Austria if Prussia did, in return for which they would get Venetia. This gave the Italians the confidence to withstand a barrage of Rothschild criticism—criticism which was only intensified by the Italian government's decision to impose a levy on all bondholders. Accusing the Italians of having "dealt a death blow to the credit" by their foreign and financial policy, James issued an unveiled threat: if the Italian government attempted to raise another foreign loan, "I declare to you in the most formal manner that I, who have been the patron of Italian funds in Paris, would repudiate completely all new dealings with Italy and that I would refuse henceforth to charge myself with the payment of the interest on the Italian debt . . ."[118] He was equally furious with Bismarck: the Italian alliance convinced James that he was "a fellow who just wants war. I do declare the fellow is too bad and I will stand by Austria with the greatest pleasure in order to topple that wretched Bismarck."[119]

Yet it was neither Prussian aggression, Austrian intransigence nor Italian insouciance which finally defeated the efforts to avert war. In fact, for all their talk of honour, once the politicians in Vienna grasped the imminence of war they bent over backwards to find a compromise. On April 9 the Austrian ambassador in Paris, Metternich, intimated to James that Austria would "give in" if France sided with Prussia. It was a message he repeated the next day, as James recorded:

> It looks as if Austria is, like all the powers, in need of money, which makes me continue to believe in peace . . . Metternich says that Austria will offer anything to keep the peace, and in the end will probably give in . . . Austria needs 8–10 million gulden. Will do everything we want and accept all conditions. It will sicken me if they are forced to give in to Prussia.[120]

As that final comment suggests, James was increasingly sympathetic to the Austrian position. But the crucial point is that he expected an Austrian capitulation. And indeed that seemed to be on the cards, even after Bismarck had made his obviously unacceptable Gablenz proposals to give Schleswig and Holstein to a Prussian prince. It was not until May 28 that Austria finally rejected this "compromise"; and only on June 1 that she asked the Confederation Diet in Frankfurt to settle the question— the breach of the earlier Austro-Prussian accord on the duchies which gave Bismarck his *casus belli*.[121] Even then, Austrian troops withdrew from Holstein without a fight.

In the end, it was French policy which prevented a peaceful outcome. From an early stage, the Rothschilds had realised that the role of France would be decisive: if she acted as honest broker between Austria and Italy, James reasoned, then an agreement might be reached; but if she encouraged the Italians to throw in their lot with Bismarck, war seemed almost inevitable.[122] It was perhaps the most important decision of Napoleon III's career; and, characteristically, he tried to have it both ways. In Vienna Anselm was given to understand that France would side against Prussia in the event of war; James and Alphonse too began to think in these terms, though they suspected Napoleon of merely wanting "to fish in troubled waters" rather than to deter Prussia.[123] They were right: far from urging restraint, Napoleon was in fact secretly advising the Italians to accept Bismarck's offer. Indeed, it was the realisation that Napoleon was fomenting war rather than discouraging it which prompted James to make his final, vain bid to preserve peace. The irony is that his success in reversing French policy may well have had precisely the opposite effect.

James did not need to invent a financial crisis to bolster his arguments against war: the European stock exchanges were already sliding into full-scale panic. This was only partly because of the fear of war: as it happened, the diplomatic crisis also coincided with a banking crisis in both England and France, which had its roots in the return of the international cotton market to normality following the end of the American Civil War. The Rothschilds were themselves affected by this crisis, but much less severely than the joint-stock and investment banks: indeed, the principal victims of the crisis were to be the London bank of Overend, Gurney and the Crédit Mobilier. For Lionel and his sons, the crisis was bad enough to keep them at New Court during the Sabbath and the "immense city failures" dominated conversation from the House of Commons to Lady Downshire's ball.[124] To James, however, the fall in share and bond prices was almost welcome; unlike his rivals, he was "praise God in debt to no one"—indeed, he sent the London house £150,000 to ease its difficulties—and the crisis provided him with an ideal diplomatic lever.[125] His aim was to persuade Napoleon III that the negative economic consequences of war would outweigh any international (and hence domestic political) gains it might bring.

He began his campaign on April 8, the very day of the secret Prussian-Italian alliance. As Natty reported, "he had a long conversation with the Emperor at the Tuileries last night and tried to impress on His Majesty the necessity of remaining at Peace."[126] It was an argument James repeated when he saw the Emperor again three days later, in an effort "to persuade him that war would be the greatest misfortune for the economy"—a view seconded by Pereire.[127] As Alphonse reported, Napoleon sought to reassure him:

> Prussia *thinks* she can count on the support of France. But there is nothing in that, and even as she secretly encourages Bismarck in his adventures, France will preserve her freedom of action, and reserves the right to act according to the circumstances. The Emperor would like to see the question of Venetia resolved. If Austria agrees, he would march firmly with her, and Prussia would pay the price of her follies.[128]

Two weeks later, having been assured by Walewski that war was unavoidable, James went to see Napoleon yet again "to preach peace."[129] He now found the Emperor "very preoccupied," as Alphonse recorded:

> He said that he considered the question closed and that he did not think that Bismarck could remain in office, and that as for himself, he had not wanted to get mixed up in the quarrel because all he would have done would have been to exacerbate it by his intervention . . . But he received that instant . . . the news that Austria was putting its army on a war footing in Italy . . . My father asked him why he did not intervene to bring about an understanding between Austria and Italy. The Emperor replied that this could take place only through war, as Austria did not wish to listen to any proposals, and that he had proposed the [Danubian] principalities, but they had wanted Silesia.[130]

As this indicated, Napoleon was still inclined to side with the Italians, insisting that they had yet to begin military preparations. It was his old game of backing the revolution wherever it might break out, and when he said as much, denouncing the treaties of 1815 in a speech at Auxerre on May 6, the Rothschilds were appalled. The effect of the speech on the Paris bourse was devastating. It marked, wrote Alphonse the next day, "a new era and one can no longer even conjecture what will happen now in the world, and what revolutions Europe will have to endure before returning to equilibrium."[131] At a ball given by the Empress at the Tuileries that night, Mérimée noticed that "the faces of the ambassadors were so long, that one would have taken them for people condemned to death. But the longest of all was that of Rothschild. They say that he lost ten millions the evening before."[132] It was in fact after the Auxerre speech—which caused renewed panic on the Paris bourse—that James coined his famous epigram: "L'Empire, c'est la baisse."[133]

It is conceivable that, had Napoleon been consistent in backing Italy and (by implication) Prussia against Austria, the Austrians might still have backed down. Yet at the eleventh hour—perhaps partly because of James's badgering—Napoleon seemed to come to Austria's rescue. The diplomatic compromise was foreshadowed economically. First the Crédit Foncier offered another cash advance, as requested by Metternich.[134] Then the Lombard company's annual general meeting in Paris on April 15 was a "brilliant success"—which also seemed to reaffirm the economic links between France and Austria.[135] The crucial development came in the course of May, when Austria unexpectedly offered to cede Venetia to *France* (which might then hand it over to Italy) in return for support against Prussia. Although Napoleon dithered, reverting to his hobby-horse of a Congress, this remarkable and often misunderstood initiative bore fruit on June 12, when Austria and France signed a treaty guaranteeing French neutrality. Throughout the negotiations, James played an active role in promoting French "goodwill towards Austria," regularly seeing Rouher, the British ambassador Cowley and Napoleon himself. Typically, he had his own private anti-Italian agenda, enlisting the French government's support in his private quarrel with Italy over the tax on rentes. He also held out as an incentive to the Austrians the prospect of renewing the existing Rothschild short-term credits in Vienna, though the Austrians retorted with quibbles about their contract with the Lombard line.[136]

Bismarck had told Bleichröder on May 23: "The Emperor [Napoleon] can still make peace if he wants."[137] This was not quite true; for in bolstering the Austrian position Napoleon was in fact contributing decisively to the outbreak of war. The treaty of June 12 was predicated on the assumption that, with France neutral, Austria could not only defeat but dismantle Prussia and Italy: in return for relinquishing Venetia, Austria intended nothing less than the restoration of the Bourbons in the Two Sicilies, the Pope in central Italy and even the old duchies of Tuscany, Parma and Modena. Prussia would be reduced to the frontiers of 1807, losing Silesia to Austria, Lusatia to Saxony, and her Rhine provinces to Hanover, Hesse-Darmstadt, Bavaria and Württemberg.[138] Although Bleichröder had been talking as if the war had already begun since May 4,[139] it was only really after June 12 that Austria decided to fight rather than capitulate. Indeed, James himself regarded the war as not having begun until June 13.[140] Thus it was French policy—at once encouraging Italy and Austria to fight—which turned what might have been a phoney war over Schleswig–Holstein into a full-scale war over the future of Germany and Italy. Without his intending it, James's efforts to secure peace by shifting Napoleon from a pro-Italian to a pro-Austrian position had tempted the Habsburg regime to stand and fight on both fronts.

Silver Linings

The Rothschilds had tried to stop the war of 1866; they had failed. The costs of this failure for Austria were high: contrary to the expectations of most contemporaries—the Rothschilds included—she and her German allies were decisively defeated by Prussia in the field, a defeat which counted for infinitely more than the Austrian victories over Italy. This time, the Rothschilds had backed the losing side. Moreover, the ramifications of the battle of Königgrätz seemed and were immense. "Casca il mondo," said the Papal nuncio, and with reason. Bismarck's alliance of Prussian conservatism with democracy, *kleindeutsch* Liberalism, Italian nationalism and even the Hungarian revolution truly turned the world upside down.

The dismay of the Austrian Rothschilds was understandable: "In consequence of the terrible news from the battlefield," Anselm's son Nathaniel wrote after Königgrätz, "I feel so deeply upset and depressed that I am hardly able to write."[141] Nor was this just pained patriotism—though Anselm affirmed the existence of this with his donation of 100,000 gulden for the care of the wounded.[142] (He also firmly resisted efforts to distinguish between Jews and non-Jews in the Austrian army).[143] Until the preliminary peace had been signed at Nikolsburg on July 26, there seemed every chance that the Prussian army would continue southwards to Vienna itself.[144] As it was, Rothschild properties in the vicinity of the battlefields came directly under Prussian control. Communications to the Rothschild-owned ironworks at Witkowitz were cut off, so that the workforce could not be paid.[145] It was reported that Schillersdorf had been occupied—allegedly by members of the Prussian-backed Hungarian legion—and "a great part of the game" plundered.[146] In fact, when Ferdinand arrived there in September, he found a handful of Prussian cavalry officers; on the day they left, he reported crossly, "they cantered their horses all over the gravel paths in the park. One of them had a hedge put up under *my* window, and kept jumping over it backwards and forwards. All the English servants were looking on and laughing at his want of skill."[147]

In Frankfurt too there was horror; and again this reflected the direct threat posed to the town itself by Prussian arms. From an early stage, Mayer Carl had recognised the vulnerability of Frankfurt "in the centre of it all" and his hopes of remaining on "good terms with both parties" were soon shattered.[148] He himself could not help siding with the majority of German states and the Confederation itself against Prussia. "Now that hostilities have begun," he wrote on June 11, "we must hope that Prussia will get a famous licking and be well punished for her unaccountable conduct which is considered by everyone as quite unheard of in the annals of ancient & modern history."[149] By June 20 preparations were under way "to keep the Prussians at a distance" from Frankfurt;[150] but it was obvious when they prepared to attack the city on July 8 that resistance would be futile, and Mayer Carl hurriedly sent his daughters off to France.[151] On July 17, after another decisive Prussian victory over troops of the Confederation, the town was occupied.[152] "In a great state of perturbation and anxiety," Mayer Carl's wife Louise described to her sister-in-law Charlotte:

> the insolence of the Prussians, of their actual robberies, for it seems they go into all the shops, select the most beautiful and most costly articles and never think of paying for anything. In Willy's house on the Zeil the soldiers occupied every room, with the exception of Matty's [Hannah Mathilde's] dormitory, and would drink nothing but Champagne at their meals![153]

If it were true that by now the Rothschilds were beginning to be assimilated into their respective national milieus, such feelings would presumably have been much less pronounced in neutral London and Paris. But they were not: the entire family seems to have identified itself with the Austrian–German side. When the Italians received what James called "a real hiding" from the Austrian army at Custozza, he was delighted: "It will do them good," was his verdict, "and will make it easier to arrive at peace."[154] As for Prussia, Mayer Carl's fears that the French house might belatedly succumb to Bleichröder's appeals for assistance were surely unfounded: James exclaimed that he "heartily wished Austria to give the damned Prussians a good licking, as they have messed everything up."[155] The news of Austrian losses on the eve of Königgrätz therefore made him "half crazy." "I declare," he told his nephews, "I am wholly [pro-]Austrian this time, as the war is just too unjust."[156] Even his eight-year-old granddaughter Bettina was "very angry with Mr Bismarck for having taken Venice [sic]." "Will it depend upon Mr Bismarck," she asked her English grandparents, "whether you go to Gunnersbury or some other place?"[157]

But what could be done? Whereas a number of those close to the Emperor continued to urge an anti-Austrian policy on him, Alphonse had discerned as early as April the dangerous implications of a German war for France.[158] Napoleon's indecision—his encouragement of both Italy and Austria to fight—had left him not the arbitrator he had hoped to be, but a mere spectator. On July 1 Alphonse astutely summed up the contradictory nature of French policy:

> If the Austrians win, our government will align itself with them, if they lose we will fall on them . . . It is probable that two observation corps will be formed before long, one on the Rhine and the other on the Alps. As a precautionary measure rather than with a predetermined objective, because the Emperor is said to be very uncertain, and adopts a cold and reserved tone in his relations with Prussia. France is playing for big stakes, in effect. The preponderance of the Prussians in Germany would be an immense danger which would not even be compensated for by the acquisition of the Rhineland provinces . . . So all public sympathies are for the Austrians, though because no one knows what the Emperor thinks, people dread their success as much as they wish for it, for L. Napoleon's friends are agitating a great deal in favour of Prussia.[159]

Alphonse rightly discerned that if Napoleon could not make up his mind to join the war on the Austrian side—or lacked the military readiness to do so—he was in no position to demand "compensation" from a victorious Prussia.[160] In the Rothschilds' eyes, the various French bids for territory in Germany, Belgium or Luxembourg were bound to come to nothing; the most that France could do was to persuade the defeated Italians to accept Venetia without demanding anything else.[161] Itching as he was for "Prussia the aggressive to receive a hard lesson at the hands of imperial France," James's verdict was damning: "If I were Emperor, I would be ashamed of myself."[162] For him and his sons, a French war against Prussia had merely been postponed: in the end, Napoleon would be "forced to go to war with Prussia, as these people think Europe belongs to them."[163] Any peace between France and Prussia would only be "bastard peace."[164]

The English Rothschilds too were dismayed by the Prussian victory. To Charlotte, the war of 1866 was not about the unification of Germany, but its division—indeed its defeat—by Prussia. On July 10 she even predicted that Prussian ambition would ultimately necessitate British intervention:

> The Prussians . . . are not at all likely to be moderate in the hour of their triumph. In that event, namely if they wish to swallow up all Protestant Germany, France, perhaps without drawing her mighty sword, will ask for the Rhenish and catholic provinces of the new northern Empire, and without wishing to interfere, and quite in spite of Lord Derby's unstatesmanlike speech to the effect that the great continental events cannot possibly interest us, we may be drawn into an armed interven-

tion, to prevent the civilized world from being absolutely divided between France and Prussia.[165]

Of course, as Alphonse said, Napoleon might have acted more decisively if there had been such English support for a French intervention to check Prussia. But it was not to be. Bismarck's terms—which gave Prussia military control of Germany north of the Main but guaranteed an "international independent existence" for the South German states—were seen as moderate enough in London to preclude a concerted intervention.[166] As Charlotte remarked, in response to a plea from Louise "to ask Mr. Delane for a powerful article in the *Times*": "[W]hat does Count Bismarck care for an article in our English papers[?]—He has vanquished the world, even now he would not have consented to peace, had he not obtained for himself an empire quite as large as he can possibly wish for and rule over without fear of revolution and aggression."[167] The most that Charlotte could do was to join "a committee of ladies, who are willing to collect subscriptions for the poor Austrian soldiers."[168]

Yet, for all this, the political significance of Königgrätz outweighed its financial significance; if anything, the swift end to the conflict permitted a general financial recovery, abruptly ending the tight monetary conditions of the preceding months. With this in mind, we should not exaggerate the *financial* costs of war to the Rothschilds. As we have seen, a sense of the impending storm had prompted James to cut his losses and minimise his exposure weeks before the fighting began. As early as April 9, he gave his London nephews some advice which deserves to be as famous as his more pacific axioms. He told them to sell whatever securities they could, even at a loss. "I am very much afraid of war," he wrote, "and would rather make a sacrifice in order to keep and maintain my holdings of cash because *in a war there is money to be made from having money*."[169] A week before, James had already instructed Bleichröder to start selling Rothschild securities in Berlin as soon as he believed war was certain (though he was angry when Bleichröder started to do so prematurely).[170] On April 10 he was able to report to London that he had "paid off all his Lombard bonds" and would "watch any war with equanimity."[171] "Now my good nephews," he wrote, contemplating the "full-scale panic" on the Paris bourse, "the world will not come to an end, and if war does come one will find other ways of making money." In the final analysis, that was James's first principle: not peace at any price, but profits under any circumstances, peace or no peace.

James's assessment as the war began was the product of a lifetime's experience of financing war and peace: "In the long run, all securities must fall since everyone will need loans. Italy wants one and no power can sustain war for two months. Perhaps it will therefore be quite short."[172] His son Alphonse could also see the strictly economic benefits of war, even as he deplored its political implications. As he reminded his cousins in London, receipts on the Lombard line had never been better than during the war of 1859–60 and were likely to soar again as the Austrian government paid the company to transport its troops to Italy.[173] This ability to distinguish between politics and private interest was a family characteristic. Chided before the war began for being "too devoted an Austrian," Anselm retorted that he was "far more a devoted pro-Rothschild."[174]

Moreover, whatever their emotional engagement, the extent of the Rothschilds' financial commitments to the defeated states was in reality limited. Throughout June they assisted the government in Vienna with small advances and sales of "Anglo-Austrian" bonds in Frankfurt; but that was all.[175] Mayer Carl systematically spurned requests for loans from the other German states which sided with Austria. He refused a 3 million gulden loan requested by Baden in April;[176] a 12 million gulden loan requested by Bavaria in May;[177] and a plea for funds of any sort from Württemberg on June 17—despite the fact that only four months before he had been vying with Erlanger to secure a loan to Stuttgart. Only after much deliberation did the Paris and Frankfurt houses agree to advance the Kingdom a paltry 4 million gulden—and that for just six months.[178]

To be sure, James continued to ignore all Bleichröder's arguments in favour of lending to the victor, Prussia: in August he "turned down flat" a request from the Prussian ambassador for 20 million francs.[179] But in the case of Italy James hedged. Under the terms of long-standing agreements, the Rothschilds were supposed to pay the interest on Italian rentes in Paris as well as to pay the government sums relating to the Lombard line; because of the war they seem to have delayed doing either, despite increasingly urgent requests from Florence.[180] On the other hand, James refused to sell his substantial holdings of Italian rentes until late in the day, rightly assuming that Italy would be on the winning side, but failing to see that she might nevertheless be defeated herself. Ironically, then, probably the biggest losses suffered by the French house as a result of the war were on Italian rentes. It was scant consolation to able to exert a measure of financial leverage over Italy during the armistice and peace negotiations, though Alphonse's terse formulation on July 8 was a classic of its kind: "Certainly as long as peace is not concluded, Italy cannot count on us for money; once peace is signed, then we shall see." Once again, the Rothschild position was: "One cannot give money to continue the war." The trouble was, as Alphonse and his father knew only too well, that the most profitable business would be the one concluded before peace was agreed, as after that Italian rentes would rally.[181] James was "tempted" when the Italian government offered to accept advance payment of 100 million lire of future payments from the Lombard line at a discount of as much as 40 per cent. But (unusually) he elected not to act without Napoleon's express approval, and deferred to his wish that nothing be done before an armistice had been agreed, cancelling Landau's premature offer to advance 25 million lire against rentes.[182] The Italian government responded by repeating its demands not only for Venetia but also for an indemnity and the Tyrol, and turning successfully to other banks (the Crédit Foncier and the Sterns). It was therefore diplomatic rather than financial pressure which induced them to rest content with Venetia—and indeed to pay Austria 86 million francs for it.[183]

Partly thanks to James, Bismarck had fought the war without the means to pay for it. As he later said, he felt on the eve of Königgrätz "that he was playing a game of cards with a million dollar stake that he did not really possess." This was only too true, and had he lost he really would have seemed "the greatest scoundrel in the world."[184] Victory, however, promised to solve the fundamental financial crisis of the Prussian state which had brought Bismarck to power in the first place and which had bedevilled the preceding four years. For convention had it that the victor in war could levy indemnities on the vanquished.

The vanquished included, of course, the Liberal enemy within the Prussian

Landtag. Bismarck's espousal of the *kleindeutsch* programme split the Liberals; victory over Austria isolated those "Progressives"—who appeared to care more about parliamentary sovereignty than national unity. Their defeat in the elections held on the same day as Königgrätz was almost as important to Bismarck as his triumph over Austria on the battlefield. Yet in one fundamental respect—which is sometimes overlooked—Bismarck too had to compromise. When von der Heydt replaced Bodelschwingh as Finance Minister on the eve of war, he insisted that Bismarck acknowledge that the preceding years' financial policy had been "without legal basis" by seeking an indemnity act from the Landtag after the war. (An erstwhile Liberal and businessman, von der Heydt himself had resigned as Finance Minister in 1862 rather than breach the constitution.) In agreeing to this, Bismarck effectively abandoned his original commitment to William I that he would assert the monarch's unqualified control over the military budget; for, although the military budget of the North German Confederation and later the Reich was never voted on annually, it was still voted on periodically. It was this "resolution of the internal question" (heralded by Bleichröder in his letters to Paris and voted through by an overwhelming majority in September) which allowed Prussia to return to financial normality.

However, Bismarck never intended that Prussian taxpayers alone should pay the costs of victory. From the outset, he fought the war against the other German states in an almost piratical spirit. James heard as early as June 28 that Bismarck had "sent all his generals after [the King of Hanover] in order nicely to take his money, his person and his soldiers."[185] Perhaps the most revolutionary act of Bismarck's entire career was the annexation of Hanover and the deposition of its ancient ruling house; his motivation was at least in part financial. The Kingdom of Saxony was left intact, but Bismarck still imposed an occupation levy of 10,000 thalers per day (using the money to fund a hastily formed Hungarian legion) and then a final indemnity of 10 million. So long as Bismarck was only expropriating princes, of course, the Rothschilds could afford to look on with equanimity. Indeed, they found themselves reminded of the distant days when the Elector of Hesse-Kassel had been forced to hide his considerable private fortune from the armies of Napoleon I. When the Saxon minister Vizthum was despatched to Munich to arrange the transfer to neutral territory of his government's gold and silver reserve (which had hastily been moved there from Dresden), he decided to send the silver—around a million thalers of silver coins which had been packed into bottles—to the Paris Rothschilds. James wanted to convert the money into francs when it arrived in Paris—in return for a commission. But Vizthum was able to remind him of the legend of the Elector's treasure, which the Rothschilds themselves had done so much to propagate: "The King of Saxony is showing similar confidence in you and I am sure that you will not disappoint him."[186] Not that James was outwitted: when Prussia fixed the Saxon indemnity at 10 million thalers, he urged Bleichröder to secure a share of the loan required by the Dresden government to pay the money.[187]

In the same way, the 30 million gulden "war contribution" levied on Austria was advanced by a consortium of thirty banks, including the Vienna house and the Creditanstalt; and there was soon talk of further loans and advances—though, as Alphonse observed, it remained unclear for some time whether Austria would "recover or die."[188] Württemberg too had to issue a 14 million gulden loan to pay her indemnity; this time the Frankfurt, London and Paris houses took the lion's share (10 million), though they had to squeeze their own profit margins to outbid the ubiquitous Erlanger.[189] As in the past, post-war indemnity transfers were a lucrative source of business, even if the profits had to be shared with others. Typically, when the Duke of Hesse-Nassau received 8.8 million thalers in compensation from Prussia, Mayer Carl was on hand to advise him how best to invest it.[190] And of course the upheaval, like that over Schleswig-Holstein, had the effect of enlivening the art market: it was at this time that Adolph was able to buy the Grand Duke of Baden's collection of crystal.[191] The Esterházys were not the only eminent Central European dynasty reduced to selling off the family jewels in 1866.[192]

This was routine. However, when it became obvious that Frankfurt too would be obliged to pay an indemnity, there was more cause for concern. After all, Frankfurt did not have a princely house: it had the Rothschilds. Any reparations demand imposed by the Prussians would inevitably require personal sacrifices by the town's richest citizens. Even before the Prussians had made their demands known, Adolph was fretting about the implications. "The Prussians' behaviour at Frankfurt does upset me," he wrote to London from the safety of Geneva,

> also I shall probably lose the income from the lease of my house there; who else would take such a big place as my late father's in Frankfurt when there will be no more diplomatic corps in that town? and I cannot give it to somebody who might convert it so as to use it as an inn or an Hotel. In addition we shall have to pay taxes. All this is depressing for me and makes me grumpy.[193]

When the Prussians presented their bill—in the first instance 6 million thalers demanded by Manteuffel, the commander of the Prussian forces, and then a further and apparently additional demand from Bismarck himself for 25 million thalers— the family was appalled. On behalf of the Frankfurt Chamber of Commerce, Mayer Carl immediately protested at the size of this sum and telegraphed in the same sense to Bismarck.[194] To Alphonse, the indemnity on Frankfurt was "barbaric"—"like something out of the thirty years war"—and he fully believed reports that the Prussians intended to starve the town into submission.[195] Charlotte even heard rumours—spread by "that horrid fellow Mr. Erlanger'—"that Uncle Charles [Mayer Carl] had been put into prison. This I hope and believe is not the case, but the Prussians are perfect monsters."[196] When James heard the same rumour, he leapt to his feet and exclaimed: "A Rothschild? It's impossible!"[197] Anselm also signed a petition against "the colossal war tax" on Frankfurt, though he doubted whether it would achieve anything as "Prussian rule by club now prevails."[198]

In fact, Mayer Carl's efforts to achieve "some arrangement . . . to . . . prevent this dreadful calamity" were partially successful. On July 25 he travelled to Berlin where he appealed to "the King of Prussia to be rather less severe upon the poor Francforters"; just over a week later he was invited back and had two meetings with Bismarck on August 6 and 7.[199] The terms of the compromise he struck showed once again that, to the Rothschilds, questions of money were more important than questions of borders: in return for accepting annexation by Prussia, it was agreed that Frankfurt would pay only the initial 6 million thalers for the costs of occupation. What Charlotte called "the transformation of the good, old prosperous town of our ancestors into an insignificant addition to Prussian greatness" was patently less of a sacrifice than 25 million thalers.[200] According to one account, "Uncle Charles . . . won the 76,000 hearts of the town during the height of the Prussian exactions"; and as a candidate for election to the parliament of Bismarck's new North German Confederation he took care to remind voters that he had "manfully stood up" to Manteuffel in 1866 when his political opponent, the Liberal journalist Leopold Sonnemann, had fled the town.[201] He won by a landslide, defeating the Democrat candidate by 6,853 to 311, and duly fulfilled his electors hopes by recouping a further 4 million thalers.[202]

Yet there was still a price which the Rothschilds were made to pay for their refusal to assist Bismarck financially. On August 14, just over a week before the final Peace of Prague, James finally followed Bleichröder's advice and made an offer to issue a Prussian loan.[203] The response from Berlin was brusque.[204] Without ceremony, the Seehandlung informed Mayer Carl that the Frankfurt house would henceforth no longer be entrusted with issuing Prussian bonds in South Germany.[205] In September 1865 James had proudly declared that the Rothschilds "did not work for the King of Prussia"; now, it seemed, the King of Prussia did not need the Rothschilds.

FIVE

Bonds and Iron
(1867–1870)

[W]e will be forced to go to war, not because of the external
danger but rather because of excessive liberties granted too soon
and too quickly. JAMES DE ROTHSCHILD, FEBRUARY 1, 1867[1]

O n November 15, 1868, at the age of seventy-six, James de Rothschild, the last of Mayer Amschel's five sons, died. Despite occasional bouts of illness—he complained most frequently of "sore eyes"—he had continued to exhibit a quite phenomenal vitality until the last year of his life. In February the previous year, he had spoken of "wanting to retire," and assured his sons (in terms which recalled his Napoleonic youth) that "having retired from the field of battle, it is necessary to leave all imaginable powers in the hands of the generals."[2] But it never happened. It was only in April 1868 that his strength began to fail. "Uncle James has been very ailing," reported Ferdinand, "he hardly goes to the bureau and sits half the day in his armchair." Even in these last days James continued to intimidate his younger relatives. "He rather upbraided me for not writing to him," added Ferdinand nervously, "but until now, I am happy to say, has not yet blown me up."[3] When the crisis came, it was characteristic that James himself kept his relatives informed of his condition. "The most terrible pains are making me faint-hearted," he grumbled in early October. "My eyes are poorly and I am suffering very much."[4] Yet as late as October 31, although bed-ridden, he still had the energy to dictate a letter to his son Edmond on the subject of a loan to Spain.[5] On November 3, despite having passed a "really extraordinary" number of large gall-stones and despite Alphonse's assurances that it was "becoming difficult to talk seriously with him about business," James gave his last recorded instruction: to sell rentes.[6] Like his brother Nathan, whom he so closely resembled as a businessman, James died a bear.

For his sons, the world had abruptly lost its axis; for his nephews, the cessation of James's letters marked the end of the long era in which, for all their hard-won autonomy, "the Baron" had been *primus inter pares*. "At least we have the consolation of seeing this grief shared by all, the big and the small, the old and the young," wrote Alphonse:

> No one was more popular than our excellent father, and no one more deserved to be so. To the most rare and precious qualities of spirit he added a gaiety, an affability in every communication, which won over people's hearts and attached them to him for ever. He left us still full of . . . youthful spirit, in the full enjoyment of his faculties, surrounded by respect, affection and, I believe I can say, general admiration.[7]

James's funeral on November 18 was indeed an event in French public life as well as a watershed in the family's history. The contingents from Frankfurt (Wilhelm Carl and his sister-in-law Louise) and London (Anthony, Leo, Natty and Alfred) could not fail to be impressed by the crowds who turned out on the day of their uncle's interment. "All Paris came to pay their respects," reported Leo, "and the whole courtyard was full as all these strangers & friends alike passed before the house. The funeral cortege started & the boulevards were lined with spectators . . . it was a public funeral which our Uncle's greatness & popularity had earned for him & this spontaneous outburst of sympathy gratified all our relatives."[8] "I never saw such an assembly of people as came to the rue Laffitte this morning," reported his eldest brother Natty; "4,000 people passed through the Drawing room, they say there were 6,000 people in the court yard and from the Rue Laffitte to Pere la Chaise [the cemetery] the wheels are lined 5 deep on both sides . . ."[9]

This was no mere family hyperbole. Even *The Times's* Paris correspondent Prévost-Paradol was impressed: "Before 10, the Rue Laffitte was full of people from all parts of Paris [come] to offer their condolence to his family. I do not remember to have ever seen, no matter on what occasion, the Boulevards from the corner of that street along to the Porte St. Denis more crowded and it required the exertions of several sergents de ville to keep a passage open."[10] There were diplomats (including the Austrian ambassador Metternich), leaders of the Jewish community, including the three Chief Rabbis, as well as representatives of the Banque de France, the bourse and the Compagnie du Nord. Above all, there were throngs of lesser bankers—men like Gerson Bleichröder and Siegmund Warburg, who journeyed to Paris to pay their last respects to the chief of the "power of powers."[11] Though the family had declined the military honours due to a recipient of the Great Cross of the Legion of Honour, and though his gravestone bore an austere inscription—simply the letter "R"—James's funeral still struck Alfred as "more like that of an Emperor than of a private individual."[12]

In fact, the Emperor of the French himself was not present, merely sending his master of ceremonies, the obscure duc de Cambacérès. Otherwise, there were no senior political figures in evidence. Moreover, among the telegrams of sympathy sent by heads of state from the Austrian Emperor Franz Joseph to the American President Ulysses S. Grant, there was also one from the exiled Orléans royal family whose throne Napoleon III had to all intents and purposes usurped. The significance of this was not lost on contemporaries. As Prévost-Paradol put it in a subtly worded obituary in the *Journal des Débats*, James had represented "financial royalty": towards political royalty, by contrast, he had been "compelled to observe in the midst of ever-recurring political dissensions, a prudent neutrality." Although "nobody could ever reproach him with not having at all times very punctually paid to Caesar what was due to Caesar," he had been "a citizen of the world rather than belonging to any nationality in particular."

> With all this, he had his preferences . . . Certainly for him the most pleasing period was the Restoration . . . and the Orléans Government was also dear to him . . . [But] with his strong good sense he knew that real security exists only under a free Government. He took a serious view of business; he placed no trust in vain theories, and he disliked risky ventures. It was just that which set him apart from the present time and gave him an old-fashioned air in the midst of a generation less risk-averse in business as well as in politics.[13]

This was, of course, a thinly veiled dig at the Bonapartist regime—the kind of press criticism which the more liberal press law introduced in 1867 had made possible. It was also close to the mark: James had indeed remained ambivalent, if not hostile, to the Second Empire to the last, and this explains the conspicuous absence of political figures at his funeral.

James's death marked the end of an era in more ways than one. He was the last of the generation which had been born in the Frankfurt Judengasse. Having inherited the mantle of his brother Nathan in 1836, he had helped steer the family firm through the worst storm in its history in 1848. While conceding greater autonomy to the London house, he had largely checked the centrifugal forces generated by conflicts of temperament and interest within the family. He had transformed the Paris house, adding to its original accepting and issuing functions a new role as an industrial investment bank with its own railway "empire." In 1815 the capital of the Paris house he founded had been £55,000; by 1852 the figure was £3,541,700 and just ten years after his death £16,914,000.[14] What made this achievement so remarkable was the fact that James had managed to withstand not only periodic financial crises, but also a succession of severe political crises: 1830, 1848 and 1852. And he had exerted for nearly four decades a unique influence over French foreign policy and European international relations in general. Nothing quite like this was possible again after 1868. Ferrières and the Gare du Nord—the two most grandiose monuments he left to posterity—are not out of scale.

As an individual, he was without question one of the richest men in history. According to *The Times*, his personal fortune as disbursed to his heirs by his will amounted to 1,100 million francs (£44 million).[15] The *Kölnische Zeitung* came up with the even higher figure of 2,000 million. These figures—which do not even include his extensive rural and urban real estate in the rue Laffitte, Ferrières, Boulogne and château Lafite—are so enormous as to be scarcely credible. (Expressed as a percentage of French gross national product, 1,100 million francs is equivalent to a staggering 4.2 per cent.) However, surviving documents enable us to calculate a more realistic figure. James's will specified cash payments or annuities to his relatives and a handful of minor legatees (including his manservant) totalling approximately 20 million francs, of which the greater part (16 million) went to his wife Betty. In addition, an unspecified residue, including James's share of the combined capital of the Rothschild houses was divided between his three sons, his daughter Charlotte and his granddaughter Hélène.[16] Unfortunately, no figures for the firm's capital have survived for the years between 1863 and 1879, and the 1863 figure is an estimate by Gille. However, bearing in mind that James's personal share had been put at 25.67 per cent in 1855, we can estimate the value of his share eight years later at £5,728,000, or around 143,200,000 francs. It is impossible to put an exact price on James's real estate, but the fact that the contents of Ferrières were valued at 20 million francs while the Lafite estate had cost 4.1 million francs would suggest a rough figure of around 30 million francs.[17] Adding all these figures together, a total of around 193 million francs (£7.7 million) would seem reasonable, though this must be an underestimate (we do not know how big a securities portfolio James had amassed apart from his share in the family partnership; nor is it possible to attach a cash value to his huge art collection). "It seems to me," joked Mérimée irreverently, "that it must be more disagreeable to die when one has so many millions."[18]

There was one other thing which James sought to bequeath his heirs: the culture he himself had inherited from Mayer Amschel. In many ways, his will is the last authentic expression of that distinctive ethos which had been the foundation of the Rothschilds' success. Here was the old appeal to fraternal unity, urged on his sons "as a duty, the fulfilment of which will bear the happiest of fruits." He explicitly urged them:

> never to forget the mutual confidence and fraternal accord which reigned between my beloved brothers and me and which became the source of fruitful happiness in happy days, just as it was a refuge in times of trial. That fraternal union alone, [which was] the dying wish of my worthy and revered father, has been our strength and has been our protective shield, [and along with] our love of work and practice of probity, has been the source of our prosperity and public reputation. May the wish which I in my turn express here therefore be religiously taken to heart by each of my children, as the most precious legacy of my fatherly love . . .

Here too was the old principle (enshrined since in the earliest partnership contracts) that his sons should "not do business outside the [family] house, whether in public funds, commodities or other securities"; though James elaborated on this point in more detail than had perhaps seemed necessary in previous decades:

> A house cannot be well managed, its unity cannot be preserved, unless all the associates work in the same interests and in the same way. I have left, I hope, each of my children a sufficiently independent fortune for them not to need to run after dangerous enterprises. I urge them not to give their names to all the affairs which are offered to them so that the name they bear will always be as respected as it is at present. I urge them not to put all their fortune in paper and as far as possible to hold current securities which can be realised at short notice.

That last injunction takes us close to the heart of Rothschild business philosophy: invest some of your property in real estate and favour high liquidity in your securities portfolio. Yet, echoing once again his father's words more than a half a century before, James ended with a ringing reminder to his children of the connection between their business and their religion, urging them: "never to discard the holy traditions of our forefathers. It is a precious heritage which I leave to you and which you will pass on to your children. The will of God has given man his religion at the same time as his life; to obey this decree of providence is our first duty; to desert one's faith is a crime. Love the God of your ancestors and serve him with good deeds: may I be accepted into his bosom and watch over you from the heaven above as I have watched over you on earth."[19]

Guided by—one might even say thanks to—these hallowed principles, James had outlived most if not all of his rivals. Most piquant of all was his final triumph over those sorcerer's apprentices, the Pereires. The Crédit Mobilier had been in difficulties for some time, partly because of the activities of its property offshoot the Crédit Immobilièr, partly because of its own unsuccessful attempts to involve itself in Austrian and Spanish government finance. The first sign of trouble came in early 1866, when it doubled its nominal capital with a major rights issue and sought to raise a further 80 million francs for the Immobilièr.[20] The financial crisis of that year, exacerbated as it was by pre-war tensions in Central Europe, proved fatal. Despite the Pereires' efforts to push up the price of Mobilier shares from the low of 420 francs in June 1866, by the end of the year they were barely able to pay a dividend.[21] As usual, Emile Pereire blamed the "hostility" of "the Rothschild group," and pleaded with his friends in the government for assistance.[22] But a loan of 29 million francs from the Crédit Foncier did not suffice[23] and in April 1867, as the full extent of the Immobilière's losses became apparent, the Pereires had no alternative but to throw themselves on the mercy of the Banque de France—the institution which they had once dreamt of supplanting—with a request for a 75 million franc loan. Predictably, they were given short shrift, not least by Alphonse in his increasingly influential capacity as a regent. At a special meeting on September 14, he argued strongly that only 32 million francs should be made available, and that this should be "to facilitate the liquidation of the Crédit Mobilier."[24] When the bank's shares touched a nadir of 140, the Saint-Simonians' flagship was sunk.

The Pereires' decline and fall evoked no sympathy whatever from the Rothschilds. To the bitter end, James remained implacably hostile to the very principle of the Crédit Mobilier. "On a given day," he told Landau in March 1867, "all these financial societies will agree among themselves, absorb all business activities and will leave us nothing, as they say colloquially, but the bones to gnaw on."[25] He categorically opposed all efforts to rescue the Crédit Mobilier.[26] To others, however, it seemed that it was the Pereires themselves who were being left with only the bones. Ten days after the decisive meeting at the Banque, Napoleon III's *de facto* deputy Rouher observed: "The Pereires are really to be pitied; they did not deserve the ferocious hatred with which they are being pursued."[27] It was true. Once the Crédit Mobilier was effectively defunct, the Rothschilds proceeded to buy up the Pereires' private assets with an unforgiving ruthlessness. As we have seen, the Pereires' purchases of town and country houses near to Rothschild properties had always rankled with James. It is easy to imagine the Rothschild *Schadenfreude* in 1868, when Adolph bought the hôtel at 47 rue de Monceau from Isaac Pereire's son Eugène for just £42,000—£17,200 less than the Pereires had paid for it; and in 1880, when Edmond bought the Pereire château d'Armainvilliers. As if to twist the knife still further, Alphonse declined to buy any Pereire paintings when their collection went on sale in 1872: "No very celebrated works," he remarked dismissively, "simply a few

THE PERIOD.

People of the Period.—BARON LIONEL DE ROTHSCHILD.
(THE MODERN CROESUS.)

5.i: *Baron Lionel de Rothschild (The Modern Croesus), The Period* (July 5, 1870).

honourable mediocrities."[28] It is tempting to read this as an oblique epitaph for the Pereires themselves.

By contrast, James's death seemed to leave the Rothschilds in a position of unrivalled supremacy. "There is after all only one less Rothschild," declared the author of one panegyric in 1868: "The Rothschilds carry on."[29] In 1870 the British magazine *The Period* used a now familiar image when it portrayed Lionel as the new Rothschild "king" upon his throne of cash and bonds, accepting the obeisances of the rulers of the world—among them, the Emperor of China, the Sultan, Napoleon III, the Pope William I and Queen Victoria (see illustration 5.i).

Yet the Crédit Mobilier's failure did not represent a generic failure of joint-stock banking: on the contrary, the years after James's death saw no slackening in the proliferation of such banks. And as international financial markets grew larger, more competitive and better integrated, the relative importance of the Rothschilds' concentration of private capital was already declining, immense though it was. Two years before James's death, the French journalist Emile de Girardin commented:

> The great [private] banking houses have lost their influence. They can still, when the political and monetary circumstances do not go against them (which is becoming rare) determine the great [financial] movements, but . . . from now on the universal suffrage of speculation will prevail over the influence of this or that [private] banker.[30]

The reign of the "banquiers," he suggested, was coming to an end; "the reign of the institutions, of the great financial companies" was beginning.[31]

If 1868 marked a turning point in French financial history, did it also mark a political turning point? It is tempting to argue that it did—that James's death, following hard on the heels of the Crédit Mobilier's collapse, sounded a kind of financial death-knell for the regime. "L'Empire, c'est la baisse," James had said in 1866; was not its political demise also legibly imminent after the Prussian victory over Austria? It would be convenient for the historian's narrative if this were true—if "the orthodox bankers" really had "delivered a deadly blow to the already tottering credit of the Second Empire."[32] In reality, the most pronounced feature of the period between 1866 and 1870 was the optimism of the French financial markets. There undoubtedly had been a *baisse* tendency between 1863 and 1866. From a peak of 71.75 in late October 1862, the rente had fallen to a low of 64.85 in November 1864. But thereafter its trend was upwards: the crisis precipitated by the Austro-Prussian conflict, which James had cited as an argument for a change in French policy, was in many ways just a temporary check. Prices touched their lowest point (60.80) on April 28, 1866, almost two months before war broke out; they actually rose from 63.03 to 68.45 in the week which saw the battle of Königgrätz. There were ups and downs thereafter—often linked to fears about Napoleon's health[33]—but the general trend is unmistakable. The closing price on the week ending May 21, 1870, was 75.05, a level not seen since the Empire's halcyon days in the 1850s. Seldom has a débâcle been so blithely unanticipated by the bond market as that of 1870.

How are we to explain this? The plain answer is that the Second Empire after Königgrätz was a foolish rentier's paradise. This was because monetary conditions, for primarily international reasons, eased. An improvement in the French balance of payments, combined with the creation of the Latin Monetary Union, led to an influx of gold and silver into the Banque de France's reserve, allowing the discount rate to be lowered to 3 per cent in August 1866 and 2.5 per cent in May 1867.[34] At the time there was much gloomy comment about the contemporaneous decline in industrial activity—investment in railways tailed off sharply after 1862—but the so-called "strike of the billion" (a reference to the Banque's unprecedented reserves) had its positive aspect in rising bond prices.[35] A new issue of rentes worth 340 million francs in the summer of 1868 was heavily oversubscribed.[36] The harvests of 1868 and 1869 were good too. All this is important because it helps to explain why France, though she lost the war in 1870, was able to win the peace in 1871–3.

The financial markets' buoyant mood in the late 1860s was further encouraged by the liberal reforms introduced by Napoleon. The first tentative steps away from dictatorship had been taken in 1860 and 1861, which saw modest increases in the power of the hitherto rubber-stamping Legislative Assembly; but it was not until 1867 that Napeolon III began to move rapidly towards a "Liberal Empire." Deputies in the Legislative Body were given the right to question ministers; and in 1868 restrictions on the press were lifted. In the short run, this merely opened the lid of a Pandora's box of criticism, at its most vitriolic in the pages of Henri Rochefort's *Lanterne*. Perhaps the unfettered opposition's greatest success was in exposing the extraordinary financial irregularities perpetrated by Georges Haussmann, the prefect of the Seine, to pay for his grandiose reconstruction of Paris, that most tangible achievement of the imperial regime. In the elections of May 1869, despite the best efforts of Rouher, only 57 per cent of votes were cast for the government compared with figures in excess of 80 per cent in the 1850s.

In all this, the Rothschilds played an important though somewhat ambivalent part. As early as December 12, 1866, Disraeli told Stanley he "had received from one of the Rothschild family alarming news as to the state of France. It was thought that people were getting tired of the empire."[37] James viewed the liberalisation of the Empire with scepticism from the outset: "I find it very difficult to believe," he told his children in January 1867, "that these liberal alterations can do much good for credit or for the country; indeed, it is a sign of great weakness."[38] In a remarkable letter to his sons, James set out what was in effect his political testament:

> You are going to say that your father is changing his way of thinking, and that he is on one side very liberal, in the way I have written to you on the question of Spain, and on the other anti-liberal vis-à-vis France. Let me begin by telling you that, strictly speaking, you are right, but there is within me on one side a man who is political and a liberal and on the other side a financial man, and unfortunately [a country's] finances cannot progress without liberties, but [they progress] even less with too many. I turn my thoughts to the past, and to all that we saw during fifteen years of Louis Philippe's reign, when the government allowed [deputies] to address the house as freely as possible, and granted complete freedom of the press. Where did that lead us? To the overthrow of the government and all the changes and revolutions which have happened since. For unfortunately France is a country of vanity, where an orator can address the house to show off his talent in pretty speeches without thinking about the real interest of the nation. Now I believe that liberties are necessary in this sense, that people should have the right to publish simple articles and that they should be allowed to speak frankly about things which everyone talks about, but it is a long way from that to all the liberties which the Emperor is willing to grant. I tell you candidly that it is a very serious and hazardous thing and that willy-nilly we will be forced to go to war, not because of the external danger but rather because of excessive liberties granted too soon and too quickly. A man who has been in prison a long time cannot easily breathe the air he is eager to enjoy, and when he comes out he takes in too much at once and it takes his breath away and I fear that that is what will happen with the freedom of the press . . . I only hope that the law will include in its terms the restrictions which will be necessary to halt the evil that that otherwise might well lead us to war.[39]

Alphonse shared some of his father's pessimism, though his point of view was not so strictly economic. As he saw it, "one of these days the liberal movement [would] simply become irresistible"; but he predicted "conflicts" and further political upheavals to come.[40] At the end of 1866, he told his mother-in-law Charlotte that he was (as she recorded):

> convinced that the Empire cannot last, but will be succeeded ere very long by a republic—a republic gratefully accepted by the whole of France as a state of transition, which will allow the most urgent reforms

to be introduced, and allow time for the selection of a ruler, King or
Emperor from the ranks of the numerous living representatives of the
Bourbon and Orléans families.[41]

When his in-laws expressed the hope that Napoleon would continue his liberal
policy, he responded bleakly: "What is necessary above all is that one have a policy,
for in truth they do not know where they are going, or with whom they are going."[42]
But that did not restrain him from active opposition to the Bonapartist regime now
that the opportunity presented itself. In the summer of 1867 he stood for election to
the local council of Seine-et-Marne on an anti-government platform.[43] Interestingly, James expressed "a little vexation that his son is counted among the members
of the opposition," and was inclined to deprecate the path of "open opposition."
Indeed, he explicitly assured Napoleon that "he was not of the side of the opposition."[44] But at the same time he did not restrain his son. "No minister," he told his
son, "will take it upon himself to put us into the Opposition."[45] In other words, he
regarded Alphonse's activity as a way of putting pressure on the government, in the
belief that no French government could afford to risk alienating the Rothschilds.

Nor did James object to the activities of Gustave's friend Léon Say, whose articles
in the *Journal de Débats* in 1865 in many ways initiated the campaign against
Haussmann's Parisian regime and provided the basis for Jules Ferry's famous pamphlet, *Les Comptes fantastiques d'Haussman*.[46] As a member of the boards of both the
Zaragoza and the Nord railways, Say was widely regarded as a Rothschild man, if
not a Rothschild "servant."[47] Although he evidently had political ambitions of his
own, there is no doubt that in attacking Haussmann he was grinding a Rothschild
axe. Since 1860, when the Rothschilds had carried out a minor funding operation
for the city of Paris, Haussmann had relied partly on the Crédit Foncier to finance
his building operations as well as on contractors who were willing to accept IOUs in
the form of deferred payments and "delegation bonds."[48] In exposing the irregularities in the prefect's accounts—which added up to some 400 million francs of unauthorised debt—Say was therefore dealing an indirect blow to the Crédit
Foncier—much to Alphonse's satisfaction.[49] The Rothschilds had no hesitation in
taking a share of the new loan floated to liquidate Haussmann's less orthodox liabilities.[50] Not surprisingly, then, Alphonse was (tentatively) pleased by the Liberal
opposition's apparent success in the May 1869 elections, even if the "Reds" did
rather too well for Gustave's taste and Nat was mildly alarmed by outbreaks of working class "hub bub."[51] "It seems to me," Alphonse wrote to London in July 1869,
"that if France wants liberty, she is a lot less revolutionary than before, the conservative sentiment is a lot more developed than it was a few years ago, and I have confidence that we will come though this crisis without tumultuous events and without
deep troubles." Admittedly, there were signs of working class discontent, but he was
confident that a broadly based parliamentary regime would be able to cope with
these.[52]

This sense of liberal victory undermines the widely held assumption that the
Second Empire was sliding politically towards revolution even before the outbreak
of war in 1870. On the contrary, by embracing the opposition, Napoleon seemed to
turn the collapse of the "Rouhernement" to his own advantage. On January 2,

1870, it was announced that the erstwhile Republican orator Emile Ollivier was to form a new liberal government—a move anticipated by Nat as early as the previous July.[53] Alphonse was not much enamoured of Ollivier, but he remained fundamentally bullish. "Paris is full of the joys of its new ministry," he reported in early January 1870. "All one sees are contented people and the bourse manifests its liberal sympathies by a resounding rally. All the men in the ministry are wise and sensible, if not of a very exceptional talent. They can count for the moment on a large majority in the Chamber, and there is therefore good reason to believe that confidence in the future will be maintained."[54] According to Disraeli, who was in touch with Anthony that same month, "the Rothschilds . . . were now very confident that things would go smoothly; they thought the Emperor had outmanoeuvred the Orleanists by adopting a constitutional system, and might look forward with confidence to the future of his son."[55] Even the unruly scenes caused by Rochefort at Victor Hugo's funeral did not perturb Alphonse unduly: "When a government has public opinion with it, it is very strong." "The impotence of the democratic party," he assured his cousins, was "beyond doubt."[56]

In the course of the next three months the constitution was remodelled along parliamentary lines, and on May 8 the new regime was endorsed by 68 per cent of voters. The decision to resort to yet another plebiscite initially annoyed Alphonse—it struck him as "a true puerility" and fresh proof of the ineptitude and mediocrity of the new ministers, awakening as it did fears of a second coup by the Emperor or a socialist insurrection in the big cities.[57] But he welcomed the result "as a great victory for the party of order and the liberal party over the party of disorder"—a verdict apparently endorsed by a new upward surge at the bourse.[58]

The problem was that the price of liberalisation was military weakness. Napoleon himself grasped the implications of Königgrätz when he called for reform of the lax system of military service in order to double the size of the army. Charlotte reported as early as August 1866 that the Emperor was "revolving in his head endless plans and projects for new breechloaders and needle guns, and murderous cannon." Four months later, James heard of the Emperor's plans to increase the army.[59] But by giving the opposition its head in the Legislative Body he ensured that his Army Bill would be emasculated. As events in Prussia a decade before had demonstrated, liberals tended not to relish the prospect of increased military service, much less the taxes needed to pay for it. The arguments against higher spending seemed all the more plausible in view of the large sums which had already been squandered in Mexico, and which continued to be absorbed by the colonisation of Algeria.[60]

All the government's efforts in this direction therefore encountered stiff political opposition.[61] The Rothschilds themselves were against French rearmament: as James saw it, it would "make a very bad impression and people will believe in war."[62] He and his sons therefore shed no tears when the Army Bill was whittled down.[63] Like most contemporaries, they seem to have believed that France was already strong enough to take on Prussia if, as Alphonse put it, Bismarck made "the biggest mistake of all, to give France a pretext to pick a quarrel with him, when the occasion for it seems favourable."[64] When the organisers of the Paris Exhibition (among them Alphonse) found it hard to borrow works of art from the provinces, a joke did the rounds "that the Prussians might come, and carry them away." The significance of this is precisely that it was regarded as a joke.[65] As James said, there were "inexplicable contradictions" in the French situation: "[W]e have just put on an Exhibition, we ought to direct all our capital to industrial projects to improve the country; instead we're forced to borrow to pay for [defence] expenditures."[66] When the Finance Minister Magne announced a loan in January 1868, its object was as much to stimulate the economy as to finance rearmament.[67] Alphonse repeatedly cast doubt on the wisdom of French rearmament in his letters to his cousins: indeed, he seems to have been an early subscriber to the (erroneous) theory that arms races cause wars.[68] Mayer Carl took a similar view in Berlin; he too saw French rather than Prussian policy as to blame.[69] Alphonse reported enthusiastically from Paris in December 1869 that the Minister of Finances had reported "a very prosperous situation with a surplus of 60 millions of which the greater part will have to be used for public works and the rest for reductions in taxes and the improvement of the position of the minor functionaries."[70] A month later, the talk was of new government subsidies for railway construction.[71]

This fundamental military weakness would not perhaps have mattered if the regime had been capable of pursuing a wholly passive foreign policy. But it was not. And it was as Napoleon cast around for some way of matching Bismarck's triumph in Germany that the full extent of French weakness became apparent—or should have done.

Latin Illusions

Throughout the nineteenth century, there was a tendency—there are too many exceptions to speak of a rule—for diplomatic ties to be cemented if not actually built on movements of capital. Britain, the first economy capable of generating large enough balance of payments surpluses to allow sustained capital export, had secured most of its allies against Napoleon this way; and after 1815 the formal and informal British Empire was erected on an increasing stream of overseas lending. France was the other nineteenth-century power to export capital on a large scale; indeed, the value of foreign government loans issued in Paris in the years 1861–5 came close to equalling that issued in London. As we have seen, many of the new banks and railways established in countries like Spain, Italy and Austria after 1850 were based on French capital. This process reached its peak in the 1860s. But whatever its economic rationale (and there were many who questioned even that) its diplomatic or strategic benefits proved to be limited. If the Prussian challenge to French power on the continent was to be met, France needed reliable allies. Increasingly, Britain invested outside Europe: between 1854 and 1870 the proportion of British foreign investment which went to the continent fell from 54 to 25 per cent; by 1900 the figure was just 5 per cent.[72] This helps explain Britain's increasing diplomatic "isolation." Anthony spoke for both Cobdenite Liberals and isolationist Tories when he declared in the immediate aftermath of the Austro-Prussian war:

> We want peace at any price. It is the desire of all our statesmen. Take, for instance, Lord Derby. He owes his income of £120,000 to the fact that his estates in Ireland and Lancashire are being covered with factories and factory towns. Is he likely to support a militarist policy? They are all in the same boat. What do we care about Germany or Austria or Belgium? That sort of thing is out of date.[73]

On the continent, meanwhile, French capital tended to flow to states which were either unable or unwilling to reciprocate with anything more than interest (and in some cases not even that).

The striking feature of European economic development after 1866 was the increasing regional segmentation of the capital market. France continued to invest heavily in and to trade with Belgium, Spain and Italy: this helps to explain the viability of the Latin Monetary Union established by France, Belgium, Italy and Switzerland in 1865.[74] Austria, after the calamity of 1866, reorientated herself politically and economically towards Hungary and the Balkans. The proliferating banks of Prussian North Germany, meanwhile, began to invest substantial sums in other German states, Scandinavia and Russia. The implications for French foreign policy were as profound as they were unnoticed. For French capital was flowing to two states which were negligible quantities in the balance of power—Belgium and Spain—and to Italy which, because of the Roman conundrum, could never commit herself unequivocally to Bonapartist France. To be sure of checking Prussia, France needed Russia; or, failing that, an Austria willing to reopen the question answered so decisively at Königgrätz. Diplomacy may partly explain why neither of these alliances was achieved: as long as Bismarck could keep Russia and Austria–Hungary vaguely interested in the idea of a reconstituted Holy Alliance, France was forced to bid high for the support of either; and both Austria and Russia demanded a price Napoleon hesitated to pay—support against the other in the Near East.[75] Yet the French bargaining position would have been much stronger if either Austria or Russia had been recipients of substantial amounts of French capital. Without that, France had only her military power to offer; and that, as we have seen, was doubtful.

The Rothschilds' role in this process was vital, if to a large extent unconscious. The English Rothschilds shared the prevailing Palmerstonian view that France, not Prussia, was the power which threatened European equilibrium. In August 1866, a week before the Peace of Prague was signed, Charlotte expressed a widespread view when she told her son: "[W]e have known long and well that the Emperor Napoleon was the instigator of the war, and hoped to profit by it."[76] Lionel did not hesitate to pass on the criticisms of French policy he received from his uncle and cousins to Disraeli.[77]

Nothing did more to reinforce British Francophobia than Napoleon's inept efforts to revive the idea of some sort of territorial "compensation" for France, supposedly as a reward for her neutrality in 1866. Twice in that year, Napoleon had raised this issue only to back down. In March 1867 he tried again. Egged on by Bismarck to present Europe with a fait accompli, he struck a deal with the King of Holland to buy the Duchy of Luxembourg from him: yet another of those abortive real estate transactions which were such a feature of the 1860s. Luxembourg was an anomaly—the personal possession of the Dutch King, it had been a part of the post-1815 German Confederation and its fortress had been garrisoned by Prussian troops. It was also a member of the Prussian Customs Union. The prospect of its annexation by France therefore aroused the ire of the German National Liberals (whom Bismarck tipped off) and seemed to raise once again the spectre of a Franco-Prussian war. James and Alphonse had not been involved in the negotiations between Paris and the Hague, but when they got wind of them they were predictably appalled, and bombarded London with frantic requests for English media-

tion. Less than two months after he had made it, James's prediction that political liberalisation would lead France into a war seemed alarmingly close to being realised.
Even when Napoleon once again backed down, the possibility that Prussia would
opt for war could not easily be dismissed: Mayer Carl's assurances of Bismarck's
pacific intentions were flatly contradicted by Bleichröder from Berlin. The war scare
ended only when both sides agreed to submit the matter to an international conference in London; there it was decided to neutralise Luxembourg on the model of Belgium since 1839.[78] Even then, the compromise merely seemed a postponement:
Anthony was alarmed by the evidence of military preparations on both sides of the
Rhine when he visited the continent later that summer.[79] Mayer had formed the
impression as early as September that the other German states would side with Prussia "in the event of a French action."[80]

The more encouraging aspect of the 1867 crisis was the apparent revival of the
old Rothschild system of informal diplomacy. James and Alphonse saw the Emperor
and Rouher repeatedly during April; Bleichröder and Mayer Carl relayed (admittedly contradictory) information from Bismarck; and Lionel passed it on to Disraeli,
who sent it to Lord Stanley, who in turn passed it on to the Queen. Any British
response was then transmitted back through the Rothschilds to Bleichröder's
"friend."[81] It was still apparently the case, as Stanley informed the Queen, that New
Court's "information as to what is passing on the Continent is generally quite as
early and quite as accurate as that which can be obtained through diplomatic channels."[82] The decision to refer the matter to a conference in London was partly
mapped out through these unofficial channels, with crudely coded telegrams
between Berlin and London establishing the basic framework for negotiation. In
many ways, Alphonse's wish for effective English mediation had therefore been
granted. Yet subsequent events prevented this process being repeated in 1870.
Firstly, the Conservative government fell in London. Although Leo was friendly
with the Foreign Secretary Clarendon's son, and although Lionel and Charlotte saw
Gladstone occasionally, relations were far less intimate than when Disraeli was in
office.[83] Secondly, James's death and Alphonse's increasing identification with the
opposition meant, as Alfred observed in April 1868, that "the rue Laffitte [seldom]
hears any news from the French Ministers."[84] Thirdly, the French government further antagonised British opinion in 1869 by embroiling itself in a scheme to acquire
control of some crucial Belgian railways.

Once, this would have been a deal which would have greatly interested the Rothschilds. But their influence in Brussels had been waning for some years. This was
partly because of the death in 1865 of their old friend and client Leopold I; relations
were never so close with his son.[85] More important, the Belgian banks (especially the
Banque Nationale and the Société Générale) were now sufficiently strong to dispense with the Rothschild assistance they had relied on since the 1820s. When the
Belgian government raised a 60 million franc loan in 1865, the Paris house was
offered only 4 million francs. Two years later, when a further 60 million was issued,
the Rothschilds' share was only slightly more (6 million)—a figure Alphonse
regarded as "almost derisory."[86] There was no Rothschild involvement in the French
government's abortive railway purchase, which was widely interpreted as having a
strategic objective: to allow the swift movement of French troops into Belgium in

the event of a war with Prussia.[87] In London this was regarded as the diplomatic equivalent of sacrilege: preserving the neutrality of Belgium was becoming the holy of holies of British continental policy.

Nowhere was the incompatibility of French finance and diplomacy more obvious than in Spain. It was over the political future of Spain that France ultimately went to war with Prussia in 1870; historians rarely trouble to explain why this was. The answer lies in the sustained penetration of the Spanish economy by French capital in the 1860s, and the growing assumption of Bonapartist politicians that this entitled France to an informal imperial influence over the country. Far from disrupting the plans of the various French banks interested in Spanish finances, mines and railways, the revolution of September 1868 seemed to invite increased French involvement. Indeed, it was only after the revolution that it proved possible to reach an agreement on a loan to Madrid along the lines envisaged by James since 1866: not for the first time, the shift to a parliamentary regime seemed to encourage the Rothschilds, even if it was forcibly achieved. Though he died just days before it was concluded, the Spanish loan of 1868 was James's last great coup, as Say wrote at the time in the *Journal des Economistes*. The Paris house took 3 per cent bonds worth 100 million francs (nominal) at a price of 33, reopening the Paris market to Spanish paper; in return, the Spanish government paid subsidies worth 30 million francs to the Zaragoza company.[88] This was the first Rothschild bond issue for Spain in decades, and was intended to be the beginning of a sustained effort to put the country "back on its feet."

Enthusiasm for the new parliamentary regime was short-lived, however, in Paris as in Spain. Apart from the usual post-revolutionary centrifugal tendencies, the new regime had to fight a long and costly war to retain control of Cuba: this precluded financial stabilisation. The classic Rothschild solution—the sale of the island to the United States—proved politically impossible, though Alphonse found the Prime Minister Prim personally sympathetic to the idea.[89] This meant a return to the old pattern of declining bond prices, ad hoc advances on mercury or tobacco, continuing losses on "that devil of a railway": in short, business as usual.[90] Yet, as in the 1860s, other banks were eager to challenge the Rothschilds' traditional dominance in Madrid.[91] In particular, there was a vigorous campaign by the Banque de Paris, whose director Delahante envisaged "capitalising the revenue of the mines of Almadén, of [the copper mines of] Rio Tinto and a lot of other state properties and, in a word, more or less substituting himself for the state administration." Although he presented this as a venture which he and the Rothschilds might undertake together, Alphonse had little doubt that Delahante dreamt of substituting himself for the Rothschilds too; in any case, a fresh outbreak of political instability and a further deterioration of the monetary situation put paid to the scheme.[92] The culmination of this struggle came in 1870, when the Rothschilds narrowly managed to defeat an attempt by Delahante to gain control of the Almadén mines. Symbolically and financially, that would have been a heavy blow.[93]

Even after this victory, rival French banks continued to vie with the Rothschilds for influence in Madrid. But they had only partial sucess. In 1871 a consortium led once again by the Banque de Paris successfully issued a new Spanish loan, allowing the Rothschilds only "a very small slice."[94] Something similar happened the following year, prompting over-confident talk at the Crédit Lyonnais of "Rothschild" having "lost Spain."[95] On the other hand, long-term lending to Spanish governments remained as risky a business as ever. The years 1866 to 1882 saw a Spanish debt explosion: the public debt rose from 4.6 billion pesetas to 12.9 billion pesetas. The bulk of the new debt was taken by foreign lenders: the percentage of total debt held abroad rose from just 18 per cent in 1867 to 44 per cent in 1873. This was an unsustainable increase: as a percentage of GNP, total debt rose from around 70 per cent to a peak of 180 per cent in 1879.[96] The collapse of the constitutional monarchy in 1873 knocked down Spanish bonds to below 18, compared with prices of above 30 in 1868, and the position deteriorated still further in the succeeding years. While their rivals retreated to lick burnt fingers, the Rothschilds were more than content to continue the traditional system of advances against the output of the Almadén mines, the value of which was as dependable as the value of Spanish paper was not.[97] This continued to be a reliable source of income until the 1920s. The early 1870s—when political uncertainty was at its height and bond prices were slumping—saw a dramatic leap in the price of mercury from a norm of £6–8 per bottle to a peak of £22 in 1873. Fearing that such prices would encourage other producers to open uneconomic mines, the Rothschilds hastily stepped up the output of the mines: between 1873 and 1887 production very nearly doubled.[98]

So well did the Almadén system seem to be working—Alphonse described it as a "milch cow"—that the possibility was raised in 1872 of extending it to the Spanish government's copper mines at Rio Tinto.[99] The republican interlude of 1873 put this plan on hold; but the Bourbon restoration at the end of the following year led to the sale of the mines to a British company for £3.7 million (rather more than the Rothschilds thought they were worth).[100] It was only later that the Rothschilds became interested in Rio Tinto as major shareholders—an involvement which proved exceedingly profitable as world demand for copper soared. The same, however, cannot be said of the French house's continued involvement with the Zaragoza railway. Despite steadily swallowing up smaller lines like the Córdoba—Seville, the "MZA" (Madrid–Zaragoza–Alicante) never paid a dividend to its shareholders. The prolonged rivalry between it and the Pereires' Norte network, which lasted into the 1920s, must rank as one of the least profitable of Rothschild campaigns—despite state subsidies totalling £24 million, compared with a total French investment of £70 million.[101]

More than anything else, this sustained economic interest in Spain explains the French government's political interest in the country in the wake of the 1868 revolution. No sooner had Queen Isabella been ousted than speculation began about a possible successor from one of the other European royal houses. Shrewdly, the Rothschilds took care not to drop the Bourbons: indeed, the Paris house's direct involvement in the finances of the royal family seems to date from the weeks immediately before the revolution which overthrew them.[102] But a Bourbon candidate was out of the question in the short term, despite Napoleon III's preference for Isabella's son, Alfonso, the Prince of Asturia. As usual on such occasions, there was a Saxe-Coburg candidate, Ferdinand.[103] But several other names were discussed in the long interregnum between the revolution and the final acceptance of the throne by Amadeo of Savoy (the son of the Italian King Victor Emmanuel) in October 1870.[104] One of them was Leopold of Hohenzollern-Sigmaringen, a relative of the Prussian King. It was, of course, the French effort to prohibit his candidature, implying as it seemed a new Prussian threat from the south, which precipitated the fateful war of 1870.

If Belgium and Spain were non-powers, Italy was at least a contender. James had sought with little success to exert financial pressure on the Italian government during the 1866 crisis: in the end his plan that Italy should buy Venetia from Austria was realised, but only after the war he had hoped to avert. In the period after the Peace of Prague, the possibility of an anti-Prussian alliance between France and Italy was raised more than once, with Austria as a possible third. Bismarck called such a combination "conjectural rubbish"; nevertheless, it should not be dismissed out of hand. In February 1869 Nat heard it alleged that "his Majesty will determine upon war, in order to divert public attention from internal affairs" and that the Italian ambassador in Paris was returning to Italy "with a political motive, viz that of inducing his Government to make an offensive [and] defensive treaty with this country."[105] Two months before, the Italians had in fact secretly offered their neutrality in the event of a war, proposing the Tyrol as the price. And when war broke out in 1870, Victor Emmanuel seriously considered joining France against Prussia; it was unusual for him to be overruled, as he was on this occasion, by his ministers.

From a financial point of view, Italy was biddable. The costs of war—both external and internal—had pushed up spending from 916 million lire in 1862 to 1,371 million in 1866; but revenue lagged drastically behind, rising from just 480 million to 600 million, so that by 1866 more than half of all expenditure was being financed by borrowing. In the four years after 1861, the national debt more than doubled to around 5,000 million lire (approximately 55 per cent of GNP).[106] Not only did the price of Italian rentes slump from around 66 to just above 50 in 1867; in 1866 the convertibility of the lira had to be suspended, leading to a marked currency depreciation. Against sterling, for example, the Italian currency fell some 12 per cent between 1862 and 1867.[107] Italian politics continued to perplex foreign observers (Cavour's "disciple" Quintino Sella was about the only post-risorgimento figure the Rothschilds had a good word for; the arch-intriguer Urbano Rattazzi was their *bête noire*).[108] As in Spain, there was nevertheless considerable competition between French bankers for a share of whatever financial operation the Italians chose to make to extricate themselves from their financial difficulties. The beginning of 1867 saw the latest steps in this direction by the maverick prophet of Catholic finance, Langrand-Dumonceau, with the Rothschilds hard on his heels.[109]

Yet bedevilling any possible alliance between Italy and France was the question of the relationship between the Italian Kingdom and the Roman Catholic Church. The diplomatic key to this was the status of the city of Rome itself which, despite the agreement struck with France in 1864, Italian politicians continued to covet. But the ramifications of the enmity between the Italian state and the Pope also extended to the realm of finance. When the Italian government proposed to raise money through the sale of ecclesiastical properties, there was considerable interest from foreign banks.[110] In the course of several months of negotiations, a syndicate emerged—made up of the Rothschilds, the Société Générale and the Crédit Foncier, with Langrand tagging along—to advance the government money ahead of the sale: the talk was of a loan of 600 million lire in return for a 10 per cent commission and Church lands supposedly worth over 1,000 million.[111] But as it emerged that the sale of Church lands was vehemently opposed by the Pope and, more important, that the Italian government wished to transfer at least some of the reponsibility for the act of expropriation to the bankers, the Rothschilds began to draw back.

This withdrawal was partly for business reasons, it is true: there were various aspects of the proposed deal which James disliked, not least the need to share it with "swindlers" like Langrand.[112] But the principal reason, as the private letters to London show, was that James was loath to incur the wrath of the increasingly influential Ultramontane party in France. This sensitivity to Catholic opinion was an intriguing feature of James's later years. He had already shown signs of it in 1865, when he argued against selling Spanish bonds on the ground that "to act against the government and minister [of] a Catholic country like Spain, where Jews are not even allowed to have synagogues, could do no good in the long run."[113] Now he used the same argument again:

> As a Jew, I don't like to go against the clergy as that could hurt Jews everywhere . . . It [was] not just because of the small share [we had], but because the deal was impossible, impossible to do. I, a Jew, should force the clergy to sell their property? . . . I remain a financier and [do] not [want to get involved with] politics which will turn the clergy against us.[114]

Even the pragmatic Alphonse agreed that "to associate oneself with a political act, which might well be convenient, but which is neither just nor equitable, would, I believe, be to sacrifice one's good reputation to the love of gain, and to stir up against the Jews of Italy all the passions of the Middle Ages."[115]

The Roman obstacle proved insuperable. Renewed negotiations with the Crédit Foncier and the Rattazzi government about a more straightforward advance of 100–120 million lire in July 1867 were blown off course by the renewed crisis over Rome that autumn.[116] In a piece of sheer *opéra buffe*, Rattazzi encouraged Garibaldi to make a second attack on Rome, then had him arrested, and then resigned when the French despatched new troops to Rome. Garibaldi then escaped from his island retreat at Caprera, only to find the population of Rome apathetic and the Italian regular army siding with the French: his volunteers were duly defeated at Mentana, just as they had been at Aspromonte five years before.[117]

In the wake of this fiasco, which momentarily raised the spectre of a war between France and Italy, the Church lands issue resurfaced, but once again James and Alphonse declined to become involved, despite the obvious frustration of the London partners.[118] As usual, there were business reasons for this reserve: talk of a tax on Italian rentes annoyed James, as did the Crédit Foncier's increasingly independent style of negotiation.[119] But fundamentally it was the religious problem which was decisive. "We are in a Catholic country," declared Alphonse regretfully, "and one cannot go against the religious prejudices of the country where one lives, especially when one belongs to another faith oneself."[120] Nat agreed: it would be "a very difficult matter for our Paris house to go into the Ecclesiastical business." "The Church people," he argued, "would tear us to pieces if they could and nothing in the world would make us so unpopular. For my part let the profit be what it may I most sincerely hope we may have nothing to do with it."[121] Pointedly, Alphonse reminded his London cousins that "in almost analogous circumstances" they had "refused to make the Russian loan, because of liberal sentiment in England, which in those days sincerely pronounced itself in favour of Poland and against Russia."[122] Moreover, there was also now the added political complication of the French presence in Rome. In February and March 1868 Alphonse and James were in close consultation with Napoleon and Rouher, who saw an understanding over Rome as the precondition for a loan of any sort to Italy.[123] Such an understanding was never achieved.

Even more than the closure of the Naples house in 1863, the abortive negotiations of 1867–9 were the turning point in the history of the Rothschilds in Italy. Mayer Carl was right when he complained that it was "a great pity that all our enemies & those who constantly oppose us everywhere should get hold of such a profitable business."[124] True, the sales of Church land raised less money than had been intended; their main effect was to depress Italian land prices. And the Rothschilds continued to be the dominant force in the management of the Italian external debt until the 1880s: between 1861 and 1882 over 70 per cent of interest payments on foreign held rentes went through the Rothschild houses.[125] It was also to the London house that the Italian government turned for a 644 million lire stabilisation loan when it was decided to resume specie payments in 1880–81.[126] Yet Alphonse would never wield the influence over Italian governments which James had enjoyed in the 1850s and 1860s.

From the point of view of French diplomacy, the difficulties raised by the sale of the Italian Church lands were more ominous. For the Roman imbroglio not only precluded Rothschild involvement in the sale of Church lands; it also effectively ruled out the possibility of an anti-Prussian partnership between France and Italy. Each time the French Rothschilds retreated from the Church lands business, it was German bankers like Erlanger, Oppenheim, Hansemann and Bleichröder who stepped into the breach.[127]

Another sign of the declining influence of French capital in Italy was the gradual disintegration of what had been one of James's proudest creations: the South Austrian Lombardo Venetian and Central Railway Company. Compared with the Zaragoza line, the Lombard was a success story: it actually paid dividends to its shareholders.[128] Its future prospects also seemed rosy: the Austrian Brenner pass was opened for rail traffic in 1867, and in 1871 the Fréjus tunnel was opened, sharply reducing journey times from Italy to France. When members of the English family travelled on the Lombard network they were suitably impressed by these developments.[129] Moreover, there seemed no reason why the Lombard should not continue to extend its geographical reach. In 1867 it secured control of a number of Roman lines for a modest advance to the Italian government of 11 million lire.[130] Two years later, the company's bonds were boosted by talk of extending its network into the Balkans and towards Constantinople.

Yet there were undeniable problems. Natty and his uncle Anthony both complained about overmanning on the Italian part of the network. More seriously, the company's financial needs seemed insatiable. The amounts of money absorbed by the Lombard company, even after government subsidies, were staggering. According to Gille, the French house poured over £5 million into the company between 1864 and 1870, with more being needed each year.[131] Ayer's figures indicate that the London house issued Lombard bonds with a nominal value of £24.6 million between 1866 and 1871. The issue price of these bonds tells its own story: in the first issue of 1866 the price was 93 per cent of par; further issues later the same year were for an average price of 79; in 1871 the price was down to 43.[132] In 1874 alone, payments made by the London house on the company's account totalled £893,000.[133] In the 1860s cash-flow crises were more or less an annual event.[134] Inevitably, the financial weakness of the company gave its major shareholders less political leverage than they had enjoyed in the past. Straddling the Austrian–Italian border as it did, paying substantial sums on a regular basis to the governments on each side, the line had once given James real political influence. By the late 1860s that had ceased to be the case. The old game of advancing moneys due to the government could still be played;[135] but increasingly the various states dictated to the company.

In 1868, for example, the Italian government threatened to cut off the railways' subsidies as part of its programme of retrenchment, and two years later it proposed a tax which Alphonse feared would consume all the profits generated by the Italian side of the network.[136] The Austrian government meanwhile sought to force the company to construct an uneconomic branch line in the politically sensitive Tyrol.[137] The Prussian government's efforts to promote an alternative link from Germany to Italy via the St Gotthard pass sowed confusion in Rothschild ranks: Mayer Carl voted against the proposed subsidy only to be berated by his relations who had hoped the new pass would boost Lombard bond prices.[138] There was similar disarray when the Austrian government announced its determination to enforce the financial separation of the Austrian Südbahn from the less profitable Italian network, which had been repeatedly postponed since 1866.[139] It was the end of an era. In 1875 the Rothschilds sold the Italian network to the government for 750 million francs (£30 million); henceforth Italian railways would be the preserve of the Italian political elite.[140]

These financial and political pressures gave rise to new kinds of friction between the various Rothschild houses, precipitating periodic "wars of words" between London, Frankfurt, Vienna and Paris. The Paris house was regarded by the others as excessively sanguine about the Lombard company's finances and susceptible to pressure from other major shareholders like Talabot. Alphonse retorted by accusing Anselm of putting the interests of the Creditanstalt before the collective Rothschild interest. This, however, was just part of a more profound process of divergence which by the 1870s seemed to call into question the fundamental rationale of the Rothschilds' traditional multinational partnership, so eloquently reiterated by James in his will. Though not unrelated to personal differences, as we shall see, this divergence of interests was primarily due to the changing patterns of capital formation, which were gradually allowing Central Europe to emancipate itself from Western European influence. Gradually, the interests of the various houses were becoming more and more geographically distinct. The ultimate failure of France to find any way of effectively counterbalancing Prussian power also had its roots in this process.

The Isolation of Austria–Hungary

An alliance between France and Italy, even if it had been secured, would have been of little strategic value if Austria had not been a party to it. Superficially, a Franco-

Austrian alliance was the most likely combination to emerge after 1866; indeed, as we have seen, it had already emerged during 1866, and may even be regarded as one of the reasons Austria risked war against Prussia. After the Austrian defeat, there were repeated French attempts to resuscitate the idea: in April and August 1867, in the summer of 1868, in December the same year, in March and September 1869. To the duc de Gramont—the French ambassador in Vienna who became Foreign Minister in April 1870—such an alliance seemed not only attainable; he believed it had been attained. Gramont treated the abortive agreement of 1869 as if it had been genuinely as well as "morally signed" (Napoleon's wishful phrase). A French general was even sent to Vienna to discuss joint military operations. But the fundamental stumbling block all along was that the new Austro-Hungarian Dual Monarchy had different priorities from the old Austrian Empire. As Lionel informed Disraeli in 1867, the idea of revanche in either Germany or Italy was not seriously entertained in Vienna,[141] much less in Budapest: the future now seemed to lie in the Balkans. The problem for France was that the Austrian Prime Minister Beust's interest in Bosnia–Hercegovina implied conflict with Russia, not Prussia. Unless France were willing to favour Austria against Russia over the Eastern Question—for example, over the Cretan revolt against Turkish rule—there was no reality to the Austro-French alliance.[142] And so it proved. There was only really one occasion—at the end of 1868—when the Vienna Rothschilds reported a serious intention on the part of Beust to fight another war against Prussia, and that plainly had more to do with events in Rumania and Crete than with France.[143]

So much for the diplomatic foreground; but these events make little sense in the absence of an economic background. The key, once again, lies in the regionalisation of the European capital market. In the 1850s and 1860s, as we have seen, Austria's recurrent fiscal deficits had been partly financed by English and French capital. After the débâcle of 1866, James sought to resume business as before. Although he declared that he "really no longer had any great confidence in the ailing credit of Austria," in practice he began to offer cash advances almost at once.[144] Indeed, he made a personal visit to Vienna in the summer of 1867 to try to negotiate a new issue of "Anglo-Austrians"—sterling bonds of the sort which had been issued in 1859.[145] Yet to other members of the family this seemed premature at a time when the *Ausgleich* between Austria and Hungary had yet to be finalised. Mayer Carl was especially sceptical about the financial viability of the new system of Austro-Hungarian "dualism," which gave Hungary almost complete financial autonomy save for a relatively low contribution to a "common" Austro-Hungarian defence budget; he was prepared to contemplate issuing new Austrian bonds only if the price were extremely low.[146] This wariness was shared by Natty in England.[147]

Their reservations were only confirmed by the efforts of the Austrian government to secure rival offers from the Crédit Foncier and other Paris houses in November 1867. As Alphonse complained, "In truth, it is pretty difficult to deal with the Austrian government, which is always so pressed for money that it approaches everyone simultaneously," making it "almost impossible to bring any association to a happy conclusion."[148] To cap it all, even as these talks were going on, the government announced a new tax on all securities and a compulsory conversion of the interest on existing government bonds from 5 to 4.5 per cent—a measure denounced somewhat intemperately by Alphonse as "impractical financial Jacobinism" and *de facto* "bankruptcy," which could only undermine Austrian credit.[149] There were similar difficulties with the Hungarian government's fledgling attempts at borrowing in its own right.[150]

These problems need to be seen in the context of a breakdown of communication—and confidence—between the Vienna house and the other Rothschilds branches. In 1867, to his uncle's great indignation, Anselm negotiated an Austrian crown estates loan with a Vienna syndicate and even allowed the Société Générale to issue the new bonds in Paris.[151] This was the first sign of a new policy of semi-autonomy on his part, which ran parallel to the divergence of railway interests described above. The Hungarian General Credit Bank (Magyar Altalanos Hitelbank) set up by the Vienna house and the Creditanstalt in 1867 was part of the same trend: Anselm pursued new business opportunities in Hungary with only the most perfunctory nods towards Paris and London.[152] When Austrian bonds were suspended in London following the forced conversion of 1868, Anselm was indignant, siding with the government against what he regarded as an awkward minority of English bondholders, and reproaching Lionel for not taking the same line.[153] Fresh proof of his Austro-Hungarian orientation came in February 1870, when he announced the conclusion of a new 30 million gulden Hungarian lottery loan. His partners were exclusively Austrian and Hungarian banks, and he offered Lionel a risible participation of just 250,000 gulden.[154] It was not until 1871 that another Rothschild house (Frankfurt) secured a worthwhile share in a Hungarian loan, a mortgage on the state railways; and not until 1873 that the London house participated in a Hungarian bond issue.[155] Symptomatic of the widening gap between the houses was the diminishing frequency of communications from Vienna to London: Anselm's son Albert sought to revive the traditional practice of regular correspondence in 1871, supplying detailed reports of Austrian economics and politics—which reveal, among other things, his father's closeness to Beust—but these soon tailed off.[156]

Predictably, Anselm's independent course angered the other houses. James complained that he "informed [them] of all transactions not before but after they were agreed," despite the fact that "many of them were better suited in their own interests to the foreign, and preferably the Parisian, rather than the Austrian market." Mayer Carl accused him of "always advocat[ing] the interest of the government & never our own," an echo of earlier complaints about Anselm's father Salomon. Alphonse, on the other hand, grumbled that "despite his good relations with the government" Anselm was "often ill-informed about what goes on in Vienna."[157] Above all, Anselm seemed to be "allow[ing] all the business to go into other hands" (Mayer Carl). "In giving his support to all these new banks," argued Alphonse, "our good uncle is encouraging competition against our houses in every market in Europe."[158] To such complaints Anselm responded in terms which say much about the growing dissension within the family. He had established the Hungarian Credit Bank without out reference to Paris, he wrote, because he did not wish merely to be regarded as "an agent or a reporter for the [Rothschild] house." On numerous occasions in the past, Anselm complained, he had been "wholly left out" of transactions undertaken by the other Rothschild houses. In the case of a recent Lombard bond issue, he had been:

fobbed off with empty, vacuous private letters, with letters which say nothing more than the better or worse state of the [Paris] bourse and withhold [details of] the . . . often interesting negotiations and advance transactions with Italy, Spain and so on. If I can be accused of acting with a certain sensitivity, I admit it, but one must give vent to one's natural feelings if they are not sufficiently taken into account . . . The fact that I do a lot of business hand in hand with the Creditanstalt is quite true and perfectly understandable. It was I more than anyone else who brought it into being . . . and I therefore have a certain affection for the bank, which in any case, thanks to its capital of 50 million gulden . . . has now become a financial power here which commands respect and which has to be reckoned with.[159]

In April 1869 Ferdinand relayed to Lionel a similar message from his father:

He is very pleased with the business he has been transacting. The Vienna house holds about 14,000 Credit[anstalt] shares on which there is a profit of £100,000. He is now transacting the sale of a bridge at Pesth with the Hungarian Govt [on] which he hopes to make £20,000.—He says there is an immense deal of business transacted at the bourse at Vienna, that the public follow him blindly, and that he is very satisfied with his position among his brother financiers.[160]

This did not convince Anthony: when he visited Vienna in September 1869 his impression was of a speculative bubble fuelled by the National Bank's lax monetary policy.[161] Anselm further antagonised the French and English houses when the Creditanstalt became involved in a projected Banque de Paris loan to, of all places, Spain; his argument that he could not determine the lending policy of a joint-stock bank in which he was a large but not the controlling shareholder did not wash in Paris.[162]

Nothing revealed more starkly the way Rothschild interests were diverging than the plan to extend the Austrian railway network through the Balkans to Turkey, which Anselm took up enthusiastically in early 1869.[163] To his chagrin, the other Rothschild houses were deeply sceptical—partly on the ground of Turkish financial unreliability, partly because they considered their existing railway interests quite burdensome enough—and in the end Anselm had to withdraw from involvement, leaving the field to the Belgian banker, Baron Maurice de Hirsch.[164] "The Turkish railways have no interest for us," agreed Alphonse and Lionel emphatically.[165] Anselm had been forced to listen to harsh words from his relatives in the years since 1866; but here he could with justice rebuke them. The plan for a rail link to Constantinople had been "a grand European enterprise in which the financial forces of France and England" could have combined with those of Austria. When Alphonse later objected to his becoming involved in the new Banque Austro-Ottomane, Anselm pulled no punches:

I simply do not understand the feeling of aversion felt [by the Paris house] towards this enterprise which in no way prejudices the interests of our houses, and least of all those of the Paris house, which as you very well know maintains no agent at Constantinople and, so far as I am aware, scarcely has any business dealings with the Ottoman government. If it were otherwise, I would undoubtedly have abstained out of consideration for the other houses from even an indirect interest in the company which—it should be said in passing—is going very well and has already concluded several considerable advances to the government. The proof is that its shares stand at 40 to 45 per cent above par.

The Vienna house, he continued angrily,

> finds itself in a quite distinctive and abnormal situation; all the major transactions in London, Paris and Frankfurt are handled jointly by the houses there. As for Vienna, now and then we are allowed some scraps and it is certainly not with those that I am in a position to meet my constantly increasing costs and the pretensions which people expect on account of my surname. I have a certain ambition, which is certainly not reprehensible, to march if not side by side with the other houses then at least not too far behind them—and up until the present, with the help of God, this plan of campaign has not gone badly.[166]

If the London and Paris house shirked the challenge of the Balkans and Turkey, could they reproach him for acting alone elsewhere? It was essentially the same question Beust had asked Napoleon III; and there was no real answer.

The Economic Origins of the German Reich

Whatever their views on Balkan railways, there was one East European question which did interest the other Rothschild houses in the 1860s and 1870s: the condition of the Rumanian Jews. The Jewish population of the country had been rising for some time as a result of immigration from the Russian Empire. In 1866 there was a pogrom in Bucharest prompted by debates in the legislature on Jewish emancipation, and similar outbreaks of violence recurred in subsequent years. In Iasi (usually called Jassy at the time) the Jews were the objects of especially severe and sustained persecution. The Rumanian government seemed indifferent. Not for the first time, the Rothschilds therefore sought to use their international political influence on behalf of their "poor co-religionists."[167] In Paris James urged the French government to protest formally to the regime in Bucharest. In London too the Rothschilds mobilised official criticism of "the terrible jew-hunt at Jassy," though Lionel doubted the wisdom of sending Moses Montefiore on yet another foreign mission, as proposed by the Board of Deputies.[168] But it was above all in Berlin that the Rothschilds concentrated their efforts. This might at first seem strange; but it must be remembered that in April 1866 a Prussian prince (the second son of Charles Anthony of Hohenzollern-Sigmaringen) had become King Carol I of Rumania, and it was naturally assumed, as Goldschmidt put it to Bleichröder, that "Prussia has primacy and greatest influence with the governing Prince in Bucharest."[169] Ferdinand too hoped that Mayer Carl would use his influence in Berlin "in favour of the unfortunate Jews."[170] According to the Prussian ambassador in London, no fewer than "twelve Rothschilds [had] requested most urgently" Prussian intervention.[171] Mayer Carl also seems to have written directly to the Rumanian Prince's father.

In fact, Bismarck did instruct his consul general in Bucharest to investigate the situation and "if appropriate to make forbearing remonstrances to the authorities."[172] But he was reluctant to do more without the support of Russia, which continued to regard the erstwhile Danubian principalities as within its sphere of influence. Given that many of the Rumanian Jews had fled even worse conditions to the east, it was no surprise that the Russian Foreign Minister Gorchakov flatly declined "to consider as a crime the measures that the Rumanian government has taken against the national plague of the Jews there," adding: "If all Jews were Rothchilds and Crémieuxs, then the situation would be different, but under prevailing conditions one could not blame the government if it sought to protect its people against such bloodsuckers."[173] Mayer Carl himself reported that the elder Hohenzollern "complains bitterly about the Austrian Newspapers which are continually attacking his son and I am particularly sorry . . . most of these papers are in the hands of Jews."[174] In October 1869 Alphonse had a personal audience on the subject with the Rumanian Prince, who struck him as a "very nice boy, who appears to have intelligence and energy," and who promised "to take the poor Jews under his protection":

> But it's always the same story: the Jews regard themselves as foreigners, they are full of ignorance and prejudice and they refuse to give them the rights which alone can assimilate them to the other citizens and allow them to apply their intelligence to something other than a more or less illicit form of commerce.[175]

It is doubtful whether these efforts (which were repeated in 1872, 1877 and 1881) achieved much: as late as 1900, the Rothschild houses and the Hungarian Credit Bank had to refuse participation in a Rumanian petroleum deal proposed by the Disconto-Gesellschaft because of the Bucharest government's continuing ill-treatment of Jews.[176] Their principal significance is as evidence of the readiness of the Rothschilds to repair their relations with Bismarck, so badly damaged by the events of 1866.

The speed with which these relations were restored is a testament to Mayer Carl's acumen, as well as to Bismarck's appreciation that the Rothschilds, for all their efforts to thwart his German policy, could still be useful to him. Their political rapprochement may be said to have begun in February 1867, when Mayer Carl was persuaded—apparently by Bismarck, among others—to stand for election to the parliament of the new North German Confederation, which was to meet in Berlin. It must be said that he had his reservations about following his English cousins into parliamentary politics. "He will not consent," reported Natty; "he says one party here wish to get him out of the way so as to be able to transact all the business and that the others will not be thankful to him if he went to Berlin where he would have to give his advice about the German Currency and ever so many things in all of which the Prussian interest is opposed to that of Frankfurt."[177] But, as Charlotte wrote:

> [T]he town of Frankfurt will not hear of another representative, he will be elected in spite of all his protestations and he may see himself obliged to yield in the end especially as it is not likely that the German parliament will remain assembled during many months of the year . . . Mr. de Bismarck and Mr. de Savigny [Karl Friedrich, who had been involved in drafting the Confederation's constitution] have written to him to implore him to accept the proffered honor, saying that his ability,

knowledge, and experience will be much appreciated at Berlin. It is impossible to receive more flattering proofs of regard and admiration.[178]

To the English Rothschilds, Mayer Carl's near-unanimous election was a family triumph in the tradition established by Lionel. In itself, it was "a post of honour"; the significance lay in the fact that he had "obtained five thousand three hundred votes, out of five thousand six hundred . . . in a town where fifty years ago, at the entrance of the public gardens there stood in huge characters a very ugly prohibition to the effect that: 'Jews are forbidden to enter.' " What more symbolic triumph could be imagined than that a Rothschild should be "unanimously chosen by the jew-hating city of Frankfort to represent its interests in the bosom of the German parliament"?[179] For Mayer Carl, on the other hand, there were practical considerations. Now he had a good reason to make the regular visits to Berlin which would keep him in "contact with all the great men and master minds of Germany." A Rothschild presence in Berlin was also welcome to Bismarck. Not only did he encourage Mayer Carl's candidature; when he visited Paris in the summer of 1867 he also held out a well-chosen olive branch to James in the form of the grand ribbon of the red eagle—"a great honour," as Alphonse noted, "and the highest distinction which a Jew has ever received in Prussia."[180] Bismarck went still further that November when he elevated Mayer Carl to the Prussian Upper House—in effect, a life peerage, nearly twenty years before the English Rothschilds finally secured their hereditary peerage.[181] On at least one occasion he even urged Mayer Carl to buy a house in Berlin so that he could spend more time there—advice which Mayer Carl contemplated taking in 1871.[182] The two were soon on very familiar terms: at a concert at the royal palace in Berlin in 1867 Bismarck jokingly told Mayer Carl "that if England wants a King for Abyssinia he could recommend the ex-monarch of Hannover."[183] As the venue of this encounter indicates, Mayer Carl was also considered *hoffähig* (presentable at court): in March 1869 he had "a long chat with the crown Prince who takes great interest in everything and is very well informed," followed by an audience with the Queen.[184] A year later, he was invited to a small party by "their majesties" to meet the Tsar's brother, Grand Duke Michael; and he attended a theatrical performance at the palace that April.[185]

To Mayer Carl, this transformation of Bismarck from the ogre of Königgrätz into his friend "old B" was not merely flattering but useful: from April 1868 onwards he began to have access to the kind of first-hand political news from Berlin which had previously been Bleichröder's sole preserve. For Bismarck, that was the whole point: through Mayer Carl he could be assured of a direct line of communication not only to Paris but also to London. A classic illustration of their new relationship in action came in April 1868, when Mayer Carl was in Berlin for the opening of the "Customs parliament" which brought together democratically elected candidates from the entire Zollverein in 1868.[186] Intended to pave the way for South German accession to the North German Confederation, the parliament turned out to be an embarrassment for Bismarck because of the anti-Prussian mood of the majority of South German members; this may explain his decision to float a proposal for Franco-Prussian bilateral disarmament through the Rothschilds.

On the morning of April 23, Mayer Carl sent a telegram to the London house: "Tell your friend [Disraeli] that from the 1st of May army reduction here has been decided upon, and will continue on a larger scale if same system is adopted else-where."[187] He elaborated on this message in a letter sent the same day:

> I think that the step taken by old B will have a good effect and that the French Emperor will be invited to discontinue his armaments which would be a capital thing . . . Everything depends now on France & if your friends use their influence it will lead to a new aspect of things. The army reduction is to take place on the 1st of May & I don't think [but] that it must have a great effect . . . as nothing is more wanted than a simple proof of Prussian peace.[188]

Disraeli seized on this, passing the telegram on to Stanley with a characteristically over-excited covering note:

> This appears to me important: Charles [Mayer Carl] is virtually Bis-marck. A few days ago, B. was all fury against France, and declared that France was resolved on war etc.: but on Monday the Rs. wrote to Berlin that they understood England was so satisfied with Prussia, so con-vinced, that she really wished peace etc., that England would take no step, at the instance of France, which would imply doubt of Prussia etc. This is the answer. I can't help thinking, that you have another grand opportunity of securing the peace of Europe and establishing your fame.

Sight of Mayer Carl's letter two days later merely encouraged the Chancellor:

> I feel persuaded it's all true. They [Rothschilds] have a letter this morn-ing in detail, explaining the telegram, and enforcing it. The writer, fresh from Bismarck himself, does not speak as if doubt were possible: gives all the details of the military reductions to commence on 1st May, and the larger ones which will immediately be set afoot, if France responds.[189]

Disraeli's encouraging response had promptly been relayed back to Berlin.[190] True to form, however, Stanley was lukewarm. He understood Disraeli to intend "that we might represent this to the French, as our doing, and possibly induce them to give some promise of disarmament in their turn: when the result being made public, England in general would reap much credit, and the ministry in particular be strengthened"; but he "doubted the feasibility of this combination, ingenious as it is." Still, he did not question the quality of Mayer Carl's intelligence, noting in the margin of Disraeli's first letter on the subject: "They [Mayer Carl and Bismarck] see one another daily."[191] There were similar communications between Berlin and London in March 1869. "Old *B*," reported Mayer Carl on March 15, "is not with-out certain apprehension about the Belgian Question, but still he thinks that noth-ing is likely to take place which might endanger the preservation of peace: he says that all depends upon the French Empereur and that nobody can foresee what alter-native plans he may have." Four days later, "B. . . . sat next to me to-day in the house [and] gave me the same information but he would like to know what old Nap's plans are & if there is any truth in the alliance with Austria & Italy."[192]

These exchanges raise an obvious question: was the Machiavellian Bismarck using Mayer Carl to feed misinformation about Prussian intentions to London and

Paris? There is no question that Mayer Carl began to identify himself with Prussian interests as early as April 1867—witness his new use of "we" and "us" as shorthand for the Prussian government. When challenged over his vote against the St Gotthard tunnel subsidy in 1870, he replied that he had withheld his support "as I find myself in the Reichstag not as a representative of the House of Rothschilds but as a representative of the people, and from this point of view I am against any subsidy for foreign railway purposes so long as the state is still struggling with a deficit of its own."[193] "[T]here is a famous difference between Prussia and all these other rubbishing [*sic*] countries," he exclaimed on the eve of the Franco-Prussian War, one of many indications that he too was succumbing to that gruff chauvinism which 1866 had done so much to foster in Prussia.[194] But this should not be understood as the familiar old story of German-Jewish bourgeois "capitulation" before the Junker *Machtmensch*; nor can it be assumed that Bismarck was seeking to hoodwink the Rothschilds. Bismarck may have expected that the question of South German accession to his new Confederation would one day lead to conflict with France; but he cannot be accused of forcing the pace towards war at any time before March 1870. As he put it in February 1868: "That German unity could be furthered by violent events I too regard as probable, but . . . to induce a violent catastrophe is quite another matter . . . German unity is not at this moment a ripe fruit."[195] The signals Bismarck sent to Paris through Bleichröder were also peaceful;[196] and when, in the autumn of 1868, Alphonse heard from Berlin that "war was inevitable in the spring," Mayer Carl was dismissive: "I would not attach much importance to what Bleichröder says as he mainly repeats what he hears from people who are often *à la baisse* and he himself is always black when he thinks it suits our purpose."[197]

Mayer Carl had good reason to believe that Bismarck's intentions were peaceful at least in the short term, for all his intelligence about Prussia's financial position pointed in that direction. That impression was reinforced by the spate of new private sector financial opportunities in Prussia which followed the 1866 war.

Rothschild involvement in Prussian finance resumed as early as January 1867, when Mayer Carl managed to secure the participation of the Frankfurt and Paris houses in a 14 million thaler issue of 4.5 per cent state railway bonds.[198] This was to be the first of many transactions done jointly with the Disconto-Gesellschaft, whose director Adolph Hansemann was rightly identified by Mayer Carl as the coming man in the new and rapidly changing world of Prussian–German finance. Despite all the ill-feeling of 1866, Mayer Carl almost at once secured readmission to the Prussian loan consortium: it was as if all the harsh words of 1866 had never been uttered. There followed participation in two further loans intended to meet Prussia's post-war military expenses, one for 30 million thalers in March 1867 and another for 24 million in August.[199] May 1868 saw yet another loan of 10 million thalers.[200] In November of the same year there was the offer of a 20 million thaler railway loan; in May 1869 a further 5 million.[201] In each case, the Frankfurt house shared its allocation equally with the London and Paris houses. "You can be quite sure," Mayer Carl assured Natty on Christmas Day 1869, "that no Prussian loan or loan for the North German Confederation will or can be made without my knowing it or having a share in the business . . . You know that I am on the very best terms with Camphausen & that Hansemann is my great friend; I am therefore not afraid that anything will take place without our knowing it."[202] When Camphausen attempted to consolidate the Prussian debt in 1870, Mayer Carl was able to boast that "our house at Frankfurt will be *the only firm* entrusted with the new arrangement."[203]

These borrowing operations, as Mayer Carl knew full well, were to some extent a consequence of the government's continuing budgetary difficulties. It is not easy to unravel Prussian financial policy in these years because of the disruptive effects of war and politics on the official statistics. But the available figures are unambiguous. According to published budgets, total public expenditure in Prussia had increased from 130.1 million thalers in 1860 to 168.9 million in 1867: the growth of the army and navy budgets accounts for about 40 per cent of the difference. However, these figures tell only part of the story, for actual expenditures were much higher. Between 1863 and 1868, budget targets were consistently overshot: altogether around 246 million thalers more was spent than intended. Here again military spending (including ordinary, extraordinary and off-budget figures) was the key: as a percentage of total spending it rose from 23 per cent in 1861 to 48 per cent in 1866.[204] These expenditures were met by short-term borrowing (selling treasury bills to the Berlin banks), which was funded after 1866 by the bond issues described above. The increase in public debt was steep: from 870 million thalers in 1866 to 1,302 million just three years later.[205] As we have seen, the fiscal strain of war on Prussia was much less than it had been for Austria for two main reasons. Firstly, Prussia began the wars of unification with a relatively low debt burden; secondly, economic growth meant that in macroeconomic terms the increase in debt was modest—less than 2 per cent of national income according to one estimate. Nevertheless, the contemporary bond markets (which lacked such modern data) were perturbed: the years 1864 to 1870 saw a sharp fall in the price of Prussian bonds, from 91.25 to 78.25.

Mayer Carl had no doubt that Bismarck remained strapped for cash. "Here there is such a want of money in the treasury," he reported in May 1868, "that the government would be quite miserable if they thought that a war was likely to take place."[206] The government's attempt to issue bonds secured on the tobacco monopoly in the autumn of 1868 was a failure.[207] "Money here is tight," he reported in April 1869, "[and] the last Prussian loan is flat."[208] Nowhere are the connections between public finance, private interest and foreign policy more visible than in Mayer Carl's letters of May the same year:

> *May 10:* Here the Government is very hard up and old B particularly cross as nearly all the new taxes will be rejected [by the Confederation parliament] . . .
>
> *May 23:* Old B makes long speeches & coaxes all the members of the opposition but . . . will not succeed to make the liberals vote for the new taxes. Meanwhile the Government is very much embarrassed and I should not be astonished if we come to have a new Finance Minister which would be a capital thing as the present man [von der Heydt] is a great *Bosche* and not a friend of the House . . .
>
> *May 25:* [T]he feeling in the house is a very disagreeable one . . . but Heaven knows how the Government is to get out of the financial mess. As far as peace is concerned it is a capital thing and our friends on the border of the Seine will not be displeased to hear of our difficulties . . .
>
> *May 31:* The King I am happy to say is thank heaven much better

but old B has had a violent bilious attack & is very cross . . . All my friends urge me to speak and to attack the Government about the new financial measures but I need not tell you how unpleasant it is for me, particularly as what one says is to be published all over the world and is generally misinterpreted . . .

June 3: Old B says that he is ill, but I think that he is merely very much put out as all his new schemes have turned out to failure and the liberal party is determined to oppose every measure which is not likely to bring a change in the system . . .

June 5: Old B is quite well again & fancies that his scheme will be accepted in the Zoll Parliament, but I am quite certain that the duty on Petroleum will be rejected as all the liberals are determined to vote against it & the only consequence will be that he *must resort to liberal measures.*

June 10: Old B is so much disgusted with the opposition he met with, that he talks of resigning but it is an old trick & nobody believes in it . . .[209]

The most convincing proof of the government's financial difficulties was the rejection that autumn of its proposal for a 100 million thaler lottery loan secured on the Prussian railways.[210] Only after Camphausen had replaced von der Heydt at the Finance Ministry did Mayer Carl become more optimistic about the financial future.[211]

Yet even as Bismarck tried and failed to secure adequate—and more important, politically uncontrolled—tax revenues for Prussia and the new Confederation, private finance in Germany was booming. This was the first phase of what became known as the *Gründerzeit*—the founders' era, after the large number of new joint stock companies established between 1866 and 1873. "You have no idea what a competition there is now in business," reported Mayer Carl in March 1870; "it is more than a mania and a regular disease like Cholera."[212] In this hectic period, Mayer Carl's association with Hansemann brought him shares in numerous transactions: loans to the cities of Danzig and Königsberg and to the Silesian, Magdeburg and Cologne–Minden railways.[213] Here too there was cause for optimism about the international situation; for one of the most ambitious new banks established in this period was the Preussische Central-Boden-Credit Aktiengesellschaft, a Prussian mortgage bank modelled on the French Crédit Foncier. Originally Abraham Oppenheim's scheme (though not according to Mayer Carl), the project was taken up by Hansemann in earnest in 1870 and brought to a successful conclusion. The domestic political appeal of the project from Bismarck's point of view was obvious: here was a way to reconcile the East Elbian landowners to the new liberal era— through cheap credit. As Mayer Carl commented, "The King's great wish is to have a Prussian Crédit Foncier to please the new nobles who are in great awe of it." For our purposes, however, it is the international significance of the scheme which is noteworthy: for it was from the outset intended to be a Franco-Prussian undertaking, the Paris Crédit Foncier taking a leading share, along with the Banque de Paris and the French Rothschilds.[214] Once again, it is probably unnecessary to infer a Machiavellian motive on Bismarck's part. Although he was well aware of the imminent Spanish crisis when Bleichröder informed him of the Crédit Foncier's new issue on June 26, his silence on the subject was not designed to syphon off French capital on the eve of war; Bismarck simply wished the French Rothschilds to continue playing their now well-established role in Prussian finance. The real significance of the issue is the immense success it enjoyed in Paris: surely the ultimate folly of the Bonapartist bourse.[215]

An unexpected revelation in this context is the extent of hostility between Mayer Carl and Bleichröder at this time. Contrary to Fritz Stern's impression, the Rothschilds were increasingly impatient with Bleichröder and regarded Hansemann as their principal business partner in Berlin. Beginning in the autumn of 1868, Mayer Carl complained repeatedly about Bleichröder, whose pretension to be the Rothschilds' "agent" in Berlin he dismissed contemptuously. "I think it quite ridiculous of Bleichröder to write to you & to Paris wishing you to entrust your interests to him," he told New Court during the negotiations for a new Prussian loan in 1868: "[H]e has nothing to do with it."[216] A year later he denounced Bleichröder as "an old fool who wants everybody to think & believe that he is our agent whilst he does business with any one who gives him 1/8 commission."[217] "I do not see much of him," he remarked in March 1870,

> He is very jealous of Mr. Hansemann and as he does business with every body whilst he wants to make the rest believe *that he is our agent* I do not care much about him. He also makes a great fool of himself and runs after fine people, titles and orders, things which have also become a regular mania amongst the members of the Jewish tribe . . . Bleichröder is a fool who cares merely for personal distinctions and has not the least influence in these quarters.[218]

It was same story a few weeks later:

> Mr Bleichröder takes good care to make every body believe that he is the *agent* of our house and many persons fancy that whatever he does is for our a/c [account] & with our consent. If you have any business with Berlin I should strongly advise to apply to Mr Hansemann who is first-rate and particularly honest. We do all our business with him & I need not tell you that we have every reason to be particularly satisfied with his services.[219]

And again in October:

> You know that we chiefly employ Mr Hansemann for all we have to do at Berlin and never apply to Bleichröder who is a regular busybody & wants the whole world to believe that he is our agent & that nothing can be done without him. Mr Hansemann is very honest & would never think of doing anything without us whilst I am not quite sure that Mr Bleichröder deserves to be viewed in the same light.[220]

The final reason for Mayer Carl's confidence in Bismarck's pacific intentions was a sense that there was no need for war to bring about the accession of the South German states: economic forces seemed to be completing the process of unification unprompted. The period 1867–70 saw Mayer Carl busy not only with Prussian finance, but also with the finances of other German states, including the South German states still outside the Bismarckian Confederation. He participated in a succession of loans to the Kingdom of Württemberg, for example (9 million gulden out of a total of 15 million in 1867, 25 million in 1868);[221] as well as in bond issues for Baden,[222] Bavaria[223] and Saxony.[224] In addition, he was able to arrange loans for a number of smaller German states, notably Brunswick,[225] Saxe-Meiningen,[226] Saxe-Coburg-Gotha[227] and the city state of Hamburg.[228] Often the sums and profits involved in these loans were trifling; but Mayer Carl was a firm believer that "every little helps" and "1/2 an egg is better than an empty shell." In any case, the real significance of this activity lay in its geographical range: to all intents and purposes an integrated German capital market now existed, with its principal centres in Frankfurt, Berlin and Hamburg, serving an emerging North and South German confederation—the nascent Reich. It is telling that most of these loans were for railway construction, not military purposes: the South Germans might bark at Prussia, but they evidently had no intention of biting. To Mayer Carl, shuttling back and forth between Frankfurt and Berlin, the evidence of German economic unification was unmistakable. Why go to war for it?

The Russian Option

With hindsight, only an alliance between France and Russia could really have prevented the unification of Germany on Bismarck's terms. The obvious diplomatic opportunity for such a combination came in June 1867 when Gorchakov and the Tsar visited Paris "to do business"; but subsequent differences of opinion over the Cretan revolt proved an insuperable obstacle to an understanding. Another obstacle—and here there is a marked contrast with the period after 1887—was the failure of the Paris capital market to establish a dominant position in Russian finances. As we have seen, James had tried and failed to "establish a new Rothschild foothold" in St Petersburg on a number of occasions. Semi-official advances were made to the Paris house in the autumn of 1867;[229] but when James met the Financial Minister Reutern in August 1868, he drew a blank. In the course of a long discussion, James proposed to undertake "a large financial operation," meaning a large issue of government bonds to finance new railways. But Reutern was uninterested. The government had "no financial operation in view" and certainly had no desire to borrow money in order to leave it on deposit—at a lower rate of interest—with James. Reutern wished to minimise state intervention in Russian railways, not to have the state finance the railways itself. All he could offer James was involvement in the privatisation of the line from Moscow to Odessa. Although there were desultory negotiations on this subject it was not what the Rothschilds wanted. In James's eyes, direct involvement in private undertakings "in regions so remote from our sphere of action" was too risky.[230]

This general feeling of wariness only intensified after James's death. As the Frankfurt house put it in late 1868, "Up until now we have not had much luck with Russia and with all these things we seem to arrive like the mustard after dinner is over, which is neither agreeable nor honourable."[231] Even when the Russian government seemed to change its mind in early 1869, Mayer Carl felt nervous at the thought of a large loan: "[I]t is impossible to pay close attention to a business of such magnitude by the ordinary way of correspondence . . . [but] we have nobody to send to Petersburg and till now we have had so little luck with the Northern Barbarians that we ought to be careful & not let the cat out of the bag for others to reap the harvest [*sic*]."[232] He declined to go to St Petersburg; as did Alphonse, who suspected that a highly publicised Rothschild visit was merely designed to pressurise Russia's traditional bankers, Baring and Hope.[233] The project was still in a state of limbo as 1869 drew to a close.[234] Rather as in the United States, the Rothschilds refused repeatedly to establish a familial representation in St Petersburg. In August 1871, Gorchakov urged Mayer Carl that "we ought to have a house at Petersburg," telling him "that one has no idea how much business there is to be made in Russia. '*C'est une mine d'or*' were his words."[235] This advice was never heeded. Alphonse even opposed the indirect involvement of Anselm or Mayer Carl in an Austro-German joint-stock bank to be established in St Petersburg by the Creditanstalt.[236]

Such caution, however, was not shared by other bankers in Berlin. "The Berlin Bourse is a capital market for Russian securities," reported Mayer Carl in May 1868 with detectable incredulity, "and the public buy almost nothing else." Bleichröder was assiduous in promoting the idea of a Russian Crédit Foncier, which was to be the counterpart of the Hansemann–Rothschild—Oppenheim Prussian mortgage bank.[237] Bleichröder and Hansemann were also much more enthusiastic about Russian railways than the Rothschilds.[238] This needs to be seen as part of an early movement of German capital eastwards: the 1860s also saw a variety of proposals emanating from Berlin and Hamburg for loans to Sweden and Finland (which, though ruled by the Tsar, had its own parliament and enjoyed considerable autonomy).[239] The continental Rothschilds were never more than half-hearted participants in these ventures—for example, taking a 5 per cent stake in the 50 million rouble Russian mortgage loan of 1867, but refusing an option when more such bonds were issued two years later and blowing hot and cold thereafter.[240]

Rather curiously, given their reservations about lending to Russia in 1863, it was the London Rothschilds who proved most convinced of the value of Russian business. Natty was critical of Mayer Carl for failing to go to Moscow at the time of the abortive 1869 negotiations,[241] and it seems to have been at his instigation that the London house pressed the matter to a conclusion that December.[242] The issue of £12 million of Russian 5 per cents at a price of 80 was one of the most ambitious Rothschild undertakings of this period, and a resounding success in all the markets where subscriptions were opened: it was heavily oversubscribed in Paris and Berlin. As Mayer Carl declared, it was "decidedly the greatest success of the day and the Russian Government ought to be particularly grateful to you and will never think of applying to any body else, which I hope will send a large number of other transactions."[243] It was indeed the first of a succession of five major Russian bond issues in the years up to 1875 (totalling £62 million nominal),[244] though the connection to St Petersburg remained a somewhat fragile one.

The Rothschilds wanted the Russian government to confine itself to such bond issues and to end the practice of guaranteeing private railway company bonds, but this proved difficult to achieve as long as Bleichröder and others were willing to invest directly in Russian railways.[245] "[I]t is a great pity," complained Mayer Carl on more than one occasion, "that the Russian Government should allow all these Railways to issue their bonds which are all taken up by the public and spoil our market."[246] Moreover, as early as October 1870, with the Russian denunciation of the 1856 neutralisation of the Black Sea, Anglo-Russian relations began to deteriorate over the Eastern Question.[247] The Balkan revolts of 1875 led to yet another breakdown in Rothschild–Russian relations, despite the hopes which Alphonse had expressed when he and Edmond visited St. Petersburg the year before.[248] The crucial financial realignments which brought France and Russia and ultimately England together to check the new Germany lay more than a decade in the future.

II

Cousins

SIX

Reich, Republic, Rentes
(1870–1873)

I hope that now the world will at least appreciate what Germany is.   MAYER CARL VON ROTHSCHILD, SEPTEMBER 1, 1870[1]

[I]t ought to be added that the French rente is a security which can always find buyers . . .
ALPHONSE DE ROTHSCHILD, AUGUST 22, 1870[2]

The Franco-Prussian war of 1870–71 was, on the face of it, a disaster for the Rothschilds. For the first time, Rothschild houses found themselves on directly opposing sides in a major European war they could do nothing to prevent. In his memoirs, Moritz Goldschmidt's son remembered Anselm in 1870 exclaiming petulantly: "I won't stand for its coming to war! I won't stand for it, even if it costs me thousands of gulden—I won't tolerate it!"[3] Still war came. The Paris partners elected to "remain at their posts" in the rue Laffitte, even as the Prussian army swept towards the French capital: despite an early awareness of French unpreparedness and the Bonapartist regime's culpability in precipitating the war, Alphonse and Gustave nevertheless identified themselves with *la patrie*. They lent the French war effort their financial support and sought to use their influence in London to further the aims of French diplomacy. At least two of the younger French Rothschilds—their brother Edmond and Nat's son James Edouard—served in the Garde Mobile. The great symbol of this identification was the occupation of Ferrières by the Prussian army. The arrival there of Bismarck and William I in September 1870 seemed to signify with stark force the advent of a new era in which Rothschild financial power must bow down before Prussian "blood and iron."

In Frankfurt, meanwhile, Mayer Carl identified himself even more unequivocally with victorious Prussia, and not only with Prussia but with the new German Reich proclaimed in the aftermath of the French defeat. Here too there was a potent symbol, for Mayer Carl was chosen as one of the parliamentary delegates sent from the Reichstag of the North German Confederation to "pay homage" to the Prussian King on the eve of his proclamation as the "Emperor William" in the Galerie des Glaces at Versailles. Mayer Carl did not, however, stay for the ceremony itself; there is no Rothschild among the cheering soldiers and uniformed officials in Anton von Werner's great depiction of the occasion, *The Proclamation of the German Empire*.[4] Again, the Rothschilds seemed dwarfed by the new and ostentatiously military power of Germany.

Yet perhaps the most striking aspect of the French defeat—apart from the speed with which it was achieved—was the speed with which it was overcome. For a time in 1870 it seemed as if the collapse of the Bonapartist regime would plunge France—or rather Paris—into a revolutionary turmoil comparable with 1792 or 1848. The vain efforts of Republicans like Gambetta to prolong the war by means of a *levée en masse* seemed to jeopardise all the material achievements of "bourgeois society." The peace terms, when they were finally accepted in January 1871, seemed crushing not only in territorial terms—the loss of Alsace and Lorraine—but in financial terms—an indemnity of 5 billion francs. All this could have turned the Third Republic into the Weimar Republic of the nineteenth century. Instead, a dramatic financial recovery enabled the French to pay their reparations bill ahead of schedule, thus ending the German occupation of northern French territory in 1873. In the same year, stock market crashes in Vienna and Berlin plunged all of Central Europe into economic depression, raising doubts about the internal stability of the Bismarckian system. The Rothschilds played a decisive role in this financial *revanche*. As a result, their power in Paris—and in Europe itself—seemed to emerge enhanced rather than diminished.

There is no question that the Rothschild intelligence system failed badly over the question of the Spanish throne. They knew well enough that one of the candidates being considered by the Cortes in Madrid was Leopold of Hohenzollern-Sigmaringen. But they failed to grasp the significance of Bismarck's support for his candidacy, which he decided upon as early as February. We know that Bismarck concealed this decision from Bleichröder, allowing his personal banker to continue to believe that "the political realm offers no cause for disquiet" until perhaps as late as July 5.[5] Interestingly, he seems nevertheless to have dropped a hint to the Rothschilds. According to a letter to New Court dated April 5, "Old B" told Mayer Carl, "that the news from Spain are [*sic*] so bad and that the financial state of that country looks particularly queer."[6] But if this was a coded warning of an imminent Spanish crisis, Mayer Carl failed to decipher it.

Equally, Alphonse failed to appreciate the significance of the duc de Gramont's appointment as French Foreign Minister in May. Gramont's belief in the existence of a *de facto* Franco-Austrian alliance made him willing to take far greater diplomatic risks than his predecessor, who had considered English support the essential precondition for any reckoning with Prussia; but when Alphonse heard of Gramont's appointment, he commented: "We will be delighted by it from every point of view, because it is necessary to have at the head of this ministry a man of experience who is wise enough not to want to try to win fame for himself by some brilliant stroke."[7] A more erroneous character assessment would be difficult to imagine; though the fact that the Duke's son later married a Rothschild (Mayer Carl's daughter Margaretha) raises the possibility that he was already a family friend. On July 2 Mayer

Carl saw Benedetti, the French ambassador in Berlin, who was leaving (along with the usual throng of grandees, politicians and bankers) to take the waters at Wildbad. He was, Mayer Carl reported to New Court, "very glad to be able to rest a little after all the fatigue of the great Capital. He seems in very good spirits and says that everything is in perfect order and that peace is assured."[8]

The Rothschilds were not alone in their complacency: the under-secretary at the British Foreign Office greeted the new Foreign Secretary Lord Granville on July 12 with the unfortunate observation that "he had never during his long experience known so great a lull in foreign affairs." But Mayer Carl's letter of July 2 gives us a valuable clue to why bankers in particular were taken unawares by the Spanish crisis. Not only was it the holiday season; as he reported routinely, the Frankfurt bourse, like its Paris counterpart, was "in very good spirits." It was the eve of the Prussian Crédit Foncier flotation—that symbol of Franco-Prussian economic co-operation—and Mayer Carl's main concern was that "everything [should] go well." He became concerned about "this Spanish fuss" only on July 7, and even then was confident that it would not "not come to a serious disturbance of peace."[9] An early City of London pessimist like Henry Raphael seemed to be making an uncharacteristic mistake by selling at such a time.[10] Yet, unbeknown to the Rothschilds, both the Prussian and the French governments were already bent on a major diplomatic confrontation, if not outright war.

There is no question that Bismarck set out to back the Hohenzollern candidacy with the intention of provoking France. As early as July 8, he spoke of "mobilising the whole army and attacking the French." This was at least partly because he saw a foreign policy crisis as a way out of the internal deadlock over the financial question and the South German opposition to unification on Prussian terms. On July 10, for example, he confessed that "politically a French attack would be very beneficial to our situation." Bismarck's difficulty was in overcoming the reluctance of Leopold's father Karl Anton and, more important, the unwillingness of William I to quarrel with France over the issue. In fact, Leopold had declined the candidacy on April 22, and it was only after much persuasion that Bismarck overturned this. A further difficulty arose when a cipher clerk in Madrid incorrectly decoded the Spanish envoy's message conveying Leopold's acceptance; this meant that instead of remaining in session to elect Leopold, the Cortes was dissolved, creating an unforeseen delay.

It was a war of crossed wires: when they met at Bad Ems on July 9, William intimated to Benedetti that he would not be opposed if Leopold once again withdrew, but the more conciliatory part of the latter's telegram to Paris was rendered indecipherable by climatic interference during transmission. Still, when Benedetti returned to pester William the next day, he was granted an audience. Although William refused to ask Leopold to withdraw, on the ground that it was purely a matter for the Hohenzollern-Sigmaringens, he instructed Werther, his ambassador in London, to assure Gramont of Prussia's peaceful intentions. On July 12 Karl Anton declared that his son would not, after all, be a candidate. At their meeting outside the Kurgarten the next morning, William famously declared to Benedetti: "Eh bien, voilà donc une bonne nouvelle qui nous sauve de toutes difficultés." That afternoon he went further, telling the ambassador that he approved Leopold's withdrawal "in the same sense and in the same degree in which he had given his approval to the acceptance," that is, "entirely and without reservation."

While all this went on at Ems, Bismarck was to some extent "out of the loop," though he was already preparing the German press for some sort of *démarche*. He regained control of events only on July 13, when he received the famous telegram from Ems relating the gist of William's encounters with Benedetti. Bismarck's rewriting of this telegram for publication in the press correctly stated the King's view that he could not undertake "in perpetuity never again to give his consent" to a renewed Hohenzollern candidature, but made it seem that William had subsequently refused to see Benedetti because the French demand had been offensive to him. This was not at all the sense of the original, and was calculated to affront Gramont. Bismarck proceeded to use the doctored telegram as the basis for an anti-French propaganda campaign directed at both domestic and foreign opinion.[11]

Thus Bismarck made Prussia's policy more aggressive than his supposed master would have wished. Nevertheless, the blame for the war cannot be laid exclusively at Prussia's door. The French had been signalling their opposition to a Hohenzollern candidacy from March 1869 onwards. When the news of it broke in Paris on 2–3 July, the immediate reaction was bellicose. Gustave summed up the French mood. The markets were "cool," but:

> you cannot imagine the effect which this news this morning has had on the public as much as on the government, not to allow at any price that the prince should be named King of Spain and that in order to prevent this one will not recoil from war with Prussia. Never, it is said here, and it is the opinion of the Emperor, will there be a better occasion to make war on a more popular issue than this.[12]

Accordingly, on July 6, the French government approved a highly inflammatory declaration drafted by Gramont to be read in the Legislative Body. As Gustave discerned, Gramont's "violent" language was a true reflection of the government's position: nothing less than an "absolute veto by the king" of the Hohenzollern candidacy would satisfy them, and if Leopold were to accept the crown it would be regarded as "a declaration of war." "Here," he repeated, "one is all ready to make war, and one considers that one will never have a better and more popular occasion to do so."[13] When Gustave saw the French Prime Minister Ollivier, he was warned that France would use "every means" to stop the candidacy, "even war, and under such circumstances it will be a war of enthusiasm as in 89."[14] "The Emperor is going to get what he wants," Gustave predicted, "war imposed by a parliamentary vote."[15]

The crucial French step in this direction was Gramont's insistence on July 12— after Leopold had withdrawn—that Benedetti demand from William a gratuitous and uncalled-for "assurance that he shall not again authorise this candidacy." It was never likely that William would give such an assurance and Gramont's repeated insistence that Benedetti ask for it was obviously designed to provoke Berlin, as was the request for a letter of apology to Napoleon. In the same reckless way, instead of resting content with William's last conciliatory words to Benedetti, Gramont seized on the Ems telegram as a *casus belli* and secured French mobilisation on the afternoon of July 14—though not before Napoleon had once again dusted off his dog-eared solution to all diplomatic difficulties: a congress. It was too late. On July 15 Ollivier and Gramont presented the Chamber with a version of the events at Ems just as distorted as Bismarck's, and war was declared. It was not until after the news of this reached Berlin that William agreed to Prussian mobilisation. "France is determined to pick up [*sic*] a quarrel," concluded Mayer Carl. It is hard not to agree, even if it was a quarrel which was welcome to Bismarck and fatal for France.[16] According to Gustave, the French view was "that if we have to have war, if it is inevitable, it is better to have it now rather than in six months."

It was the fact that France not only appeared to be more aggressive than Prussia but actually *was* the aggressor which determined British non-intervention. As in the Luxembourg crisis of 1867, the Rothschilds acted as a channel of communication between London and the potential belligerents. On July 5 Napoleon had asked Alphonse to relay a message to Gladstone asking for his support in securing the withdrawal of the Hohenzollern candidature. Natty delivered this to Gladstone at his home at 11 Carlton House Terrace early on the morning of July 6 and, finding him on the point of leaving to see the Queen at Windsor, drove with him to the railway station. According to Morley, "For a time Mr. Gladstone was silent. Then he said he did not approve of the candidature, but he was not disposed to interfere with the liberty of the Spanish people to choose their own sovereign."[17] This has sometimes been interpreted as a blow to the French Rothschilds' hopes; but it seems just as likely that this is what they wanted to hear. A lukewarm response was what was needed if the increasingly reckless Gramont was to be restrained. Gustave wanted England "to preserve the peace":[18] that meant putting pressure on France as much as on Prussia.[19] "We hear that your government has put a good deal of pressure on ours to accept [a compromise]," he wrote on July 11, "but in the meantime *unfortunately* the public mood and the Chamber are becoming aroused."[20] Thus, when the Hohenzollern candidature was withdrawn on July 12, the Paris house sent another telegram to London stating optimistically: "The French are satisfied." Gladstone saw it late that night. This was the cue for Granville to telegram to Lyons, the ambassador in Paris, that France should indeed "accept as satisfactory and conclusive the withdrawal of the candidature of Prince Leopold."[21]

British pressure had some effect in Paris: when Lyons delivered his message, General Leboeuf's demand that reservists be called up was rejected by the council of ministers, and it was decided not to regard Gramont's demand for a guarantee of non-renewal as an ultimatum. At this point the Rothschilds' informal mediation appeared to have contributed once again to the maintenance of peace. "Half an hour later," wrote Gustave on hearing of William's unqualified endorsement of Leopold's withdrawal on July 12, "and war would have been declared, although it may not be in accordance with the ideas of the Emperor, who wanted war, but he is obliged to be satisfied with that response. Thus peace is made, or rather the war is adjourned, for I do not believe that relations between the two countries will remain good."[22] Mayer Carl's relief was less qualified: "[E]verything is settled in a satisfactory manner and the dreadful calamity of a European war is spared. Thank God for that . . ."[23] Disillusionment the following day was profound; and they had no doubt where the blame lay. On the very day war broke out, Gustave raised the possibility that France might revive her earlier designs on Belgium.[24] Nothing did more to discredit the French case in London.

The financial consequences of the crisis have been neglected by historians but deserve attention; for they too help to explain British non-intervention. In the first months of the war, German and French financial markets were more or less equally affected. Things were bad in Paris: the price of rentes had begun to slide as soon as the news broke of the Hohenzollern candidature, from 74.83 on June 4 to 71.25 on July 9; the outbreak of war saw a sharp fall to 67.05.[25] But these figures were little different from those in Frankfurt and Berlin, where the recently issued Prussian 4.5 per cent bonds slumped from 93.5 to 77.3—if anything, the German crisis at the outbreak of the war was worse. Though the flight for liquidity was enough to plunge a number of banks on both sides into difficulties, the Rothschilds were more or less untroubled. Apart from a substantial sum (35 million francs) owing to Russia, the French house seems to have had relatively few problematic liabilities, and the Frankfurt house almost none. Even if he had missed a Bismarckian hint, Mayer Carl had "taken [his] precautions in time."[26] As accurate news of the first French reverses at Spicheren and Froeschwiller filtered back, of course, it was the French market which collapsed, while the German markets rallied.[27] The British market, by contrast, was barely affected throughout: the biggest fall was 3.6 per cent between May and August 1870. The contrast with 1866, when the war between Austria and Prussia coincided with an acute financial crisis in London, is marked. (What seems to have happened in 1870 is that French capital began to flow to London from a fairly early stage in the conflict—one of the best indicators that, for all the government's rhetoric, there was a vein of pessimism in Paris.) It is not without significance that Gladstone himself bought consols worth £2,500 at a price of 90 on 18 July: a private and well-founded vote of confidence in British non-intervention.[28]

The English Rothschilds therefore viewed events on the continent with something more like neutrality than had been the case in 1866, when Prussia had seemed the villain of the piece. True, there was a flicker of Francophile sentiment on the news of the French defeat at Sedan, prompted by the presence in London of Alphonse's wife Leonora; hence, perhaps, Lionel's request for details of Prussian atrocities and his later role in transferring money raised abroad for French war-wounded and prisoners-of-war.[29] And before Sedan the London house did more for the French war effort than for the Prussian: French purchases of biscuits and salt pork in England were financed by the London house, though the government's bills were discounted on less than generous terms. In addition, New Court initially offered to subscribe to any French war loan and to send gold if it were required by the Banque de France, though these offers were not taken up as the French government financed the first phase of the war by selling treasury bills on the domestic market. By the time the government brought out a proper war loan in late August, however, the London house was less keen.[30] When the Government of National Defence sought to raise a £10 million loan in London in the autumn of 1870, it was to the minor American firm of J. S. Morgan & Co. that it had to turn.[31]

By contrast, offers from Mayer Carl of Prussian war bonds, which were ignored at the outset of the war, led to talk of a subscription of 1 million thalers by the London house in October.[32] The following month, Hansemann was sent to London to arrange an issue of five-year treasury bonds worth 51 million thalers; the short duration of the bonds was a signal of the intention to impose reparations on France, though not necessarily the extent of any indemnity. Mayer Carl made a persuasive case for Rothschild participation in this operation:

The position of the Fft House is not pleasant as the Government has the right to expect our support and is sure not to forget it if we do not assist them and leave the task to *others*. On the other hand we do not mean to do any thing that might be disagreeable to you or place you in a false position towards our Paris friends. I hope therefore that if Mr Hansemann pays you a visit you will receive him kindly and tell him exactly what you would like me to do . . . [I]f we lose the opportunity of showing ourselves useful to [the government] others will jump at the opportunity of putting us aside and I *in particular* must suffer from the effect . . . I should not have troubled you with all these details if the chief question was not to get the money *from England:* and to hear from you how this could be managed to conciliate the interest of our houses with the views & wants of the Government. I own that I should be very sorry if Schröder who I dare say represents Erlanger & all that clique were to take hold of the Prussian business as I have every reason to believe that all the other Prussian houses who are interested in the [North German] Confederate bonds would join him, delighted at the idea of having turned us out.[33]

The London house hesitated to be publicly identified with the new loan, but evidently put Hansemann in touch with the Bank of London; Mayer Carl likewise used the Seehandlung as a kind of front for his participation. New Court also helped to replenish the Seehandlung's silver reserve—one of the main objectives of the loan.[34]

These financial factors partly explain why Britain declined to play the mediating role which the French Rothschilds hoped for. From the outset of the war, Alphonse and Gustave urged the British government to intervene to broker an early peace, hoping that they and their cousins once again could act as the channel for pacific communications.[35] But the only thing which would have prompted such an intervention would have been a French victory, with its implicit threat to Belgium; and once that possibility evaporated Gladstone and his ministers were more or less content to let events take their course. The other potential danger—that Russia and Austria–Hungary would also become embroiled in a "general war"—was never real: Gorchakov and Beust stuck to their policy of non-intervention (agreed as early as September 1869), announcing their neutrality on July 13 and 20 respectively. Even Disraeli's criticism of Gladstonian inaction was a mere reflex action: he saw no real reason to resist the "German revolution," and as for saving Napoleon III, had he not just dedicated his novel *Lothair* to the Orléanist duc d'Aumale? It was especially irksome for Alphonse that *The Times*—whose editor Delane's friendship with Lionel was well known—came out strongly against France in its early coverage of the war. In particular, the paper's publication of the draft treaty Benedetti had given Bismarck in 1866 seemed to confirm suspicions that France had designs on Belgium.[36] In October 1870 Gladstone himself published an anonymous article in the *Edinburgh Review* in which he declared that the "new law of nations . . . censured the aggression of France."[37] There were those who believed that the Rothschilds were responsible when *The Times* changed its tune in the same month, arguing for intervention to prevent the annexation of Alsace and Lorraine.[38] But in truth any Rothschild attempts to find a basis for English mediation were bound to come to nothing. The assumption that the war would be long and indecisive may also have encouraged a policy of wait-and-see in London.[39]

For the Rothschilds on the continent, neutrality was never an option. Mayer Carl had no hesitation in subscribing 1 million thalers to the initial Prussian war loan; when this public subscription raised only half the 120 million thalers sought by the government—another sign of German nervousness in the early stages of the war— he readily joined the Hansemann-led syndicate to underwrite a further 20.7 million thalers (of which the Frankfurt house took 3 million).[40] Once news of Prussian successes began to reach Frankfurt, he could not resist basking in Bismarckian reflected glory. "I should think that the people at Paris will be rather astonished," he wrote gleefully after Froeschwiller, "particularly as they most likely did not fancy that the Germans could lick them so easily. Here and all over the country there is a great enthusiasm and I need not tell you that everybody is quite delighted." "I have not the least doubt," he wrote a week later, "that the German troops will be victorious and that a durable peace will be made. Meanwhile there is a good deal of business and every one speculates thinking that we are likely to have a great life."[41]

As the military news got better, so his tone became more strident: "I think that the French have no chance of success," he exclaimed on August 27, "and will learn to know what it is to compete with the German nation and with one Million of men."[42] Like so many Germans, he was exhilarated by the news of Sedan and eagerly increased his holdings of government bonds.[43] "There is not the least doubt," he declared on November 23, "that the [German] Government is called upon to be first fiddle in the future European concert";[44] "Germany strong and united will be able to do more for the peace of the world than any other nation."[45] To be sure, he and his family had no illusions about the human costs of the conflict: his English-born wife Louise and their children worked "day and night" in the hospital they established for wounded soldiers.[46] But he had no doubt about the justice of the Prussian cause. Despite his grumblings about the discomfort of the journey, Mayer Carl was only too proud to be invited along with other parliamentarians to "pay homage at Versailles to the German Emperor."[47]

Identification with one's native land cut the other way in Paris. James's sons, unlike their father, were French citizens and they were punctilious in their patriotism. On July 19, for example, Alphonse resigned his post as consul-general of the North German Confederation in France.[48] They subscribed for at least 50 million francs of the August war loan.[49] From the outset, he and Gustave expressed the hope that "the first clash would be favourable to French arms." At first this was primarily because they believed it would precipitate English diplomatic mediation;[50] but as the war proceeded, anti-Prussian feeling began to generate a less dispassionate patriotism. By the time Ferdinand arrived in Paris, he found his cousins "very excited and pour[ing] out volumes of wrath on the Prussians, Bismarck and Cie." "They are all extremely French in their views and feelings," he reported to London, "plus catholique que le pape."[51] Edmond and Nat's son James Edouard, as noted above, served in the Garde Mobile;[52] and Alphonse did his bit guarding the ramparts of Paris on the eve of the Prussian siege, as did Nathan James, who may have fought in Trochu's abortive "sortie" to the south of Paris on November 30.[53] On August 6 Mérimée heard of "a Rothschild" leaving Paris in August "with his bag and a baguette on his back, travelling in a third class compartment of the Nord railway, in which his house has twenty million shares."[54] Though it is undeniable that Anselm returned to Vienna before Sedan and James Edouard's brother Arthur was in Brussels in late 1870, that story has the whiff of malicious gossip. In reality, the Rothschilds stood their ground and risked their lives in the crisis, unlike many wealthy Parisians.

The difficulty for those in France was that from a very early stage they were confronted with alarming intimations of defeat. Anselm happened to be in Paris when the war broke out, and he made no secret of his views: "The French are full of enthusiasm but the Prussians have a better military organisation and their army is much superior in number."[55] Alphonse too was pessimistic. "The wine is poured," he declared on July 20, "and it is unfortunately necessary to drink it. It will be pretty bitter."[56] An early sign of French mismanagement in Rothschild eyes was the response of the government to the economic consequences of the war. Talk of the suspension of gold convertibility by the Banque de France and heavy-handed attempts to prevent specie from leaving Paris infuriated Alphonse, who favoured relying on increases in the discount rate.[57] On August 4 some 2 million francs of silver which the Rothschilds were sending to Belgium in exchange for gold on behalf of the government were seized by the police in the belief that they were being smuggled out of the country.[58] By the 12th, the Banque had effectively been forced by the government to suspend convertibility and this was followed by a moratorium on bills of exchange: the only reason Alphonse did not resign his post as regent over these measures was, as he put it, that it would be "to desert one's post at the moment of combat."[59] More alarming still was the request of a "senior military personage" to send a small packet of his securities for safekeeping in London house. As Alphonse commented, "Such a recommendation on his part, as you may imagine, has awakened our suspicions, and we intend to follow his example . . ."[60] They began to do so three days later.[61] On August 11 James Edouard sent over his collection of rare books and drawings.[62] As the crisis deepened, securities were sent to Lambert, the Rothschild agent in Brussels.[63] On the day of Sedan, at Bleichröder's recommendation, the Paris house sold the shares it held in the Cologne–Minden railway—at a handsome profit.[64]

Measures to stop capital flight were, however, the least of Alphonse's worries. From a remarkably early stage—well before news of reverses at the front—he and his brother feared that war would trigger a revolution in Paris. As early as July 19, Gustave was reminded of 1848; a week later, his brother was detailing the steps being taken to combat the "desperate efforts" of "the Left" to stage a "coup de main" in Paris.[65] At that stage he was still confident that the government had the situation under control; but by the first week of August he felt that in its efforts to combat capital flight the government itself was allowing itself "to be drawn down the revolutionary slope. Once it was the nobles who were regarded as suspect; today it is businessmen."[66] "The danger comes from the interior rather than from the Prussians," he wrote sombrely on August 3. "We have no military force here [in Paris], and if by some mischance we were to suffer some reverse, who knows to what excesses the fury of the populace could lead." The Finance Minister seemed unable to resist "the propensities of certain members of the Cabinet who believe themselves back in the time of the French Republic." If a military victory did not come soon, warned Alphonse on August 6, "the revolutionary party would gain the upper hand."[67] Just three days later, revolution no longer seemed merely possible, but distinctly likely in the absence of a military victory. When the Legislative Body met there were calls not just for Ollivier's resignation but for the abdication of the Emperor, who was frantically trying to mobilise a new army at Châlons. As far as Alphonse could see, the fall of the Empire was now "a *fait accompli*."[68]

This prescience of revolution is easy to explain. To the Rothschilds (as to Metternich), modern history's most important lesson had always been that a French revolution might lead to a European war, and that conversely a war involving France might lead to a French revolution. This fear had influenced Rothschild calculations time and again since 1815, but had never been exactly fulfilled. In 1830 and 1848 there had been revolutions without wars. In 1855 and 1859 there had been wars without revolutions. In 1870 history at last fitted the Rothschild model. Indeed, that may be why the Rothschilds came out of the 1870–71 crisis so unscathed.

At the same time, there was also a genuine desire on Alphonse's part for a limited republican revolution to get rid of the Bonapartist regime, which his parents had always viewed with such suspicion and which he himself had overtly opposed during its final liberal phase. Alphonse's letter to London of August 13 indicates that he was already in contact with moderate republic leaders—"certain persons who under the present circumstances could be called on to exercise an influence on events"—and that they had reassured him of their commitment to maintaining order.[69] At least one member of the new Government of National Defence—Crémieux—was an old Rothschild associate, and Alphonse was quick to reassure his cousins of the new regime's good intentions. "As the republic has been proclaimed," he reported on September 4, "it is probable that popular anger will be disarmed and that there will be no serious disorder on the street."[70] Any possibility of a Bonapartist restoration or regency (something Bismarck would not have been averse to) Alphonse vehemently opposed.[71] There is some evidence, admittedly, that he and Gustave would have welcomed a monarchist restoration, whether of the Bourbon or Orléanist dynasties.[72] But in the immediate crisis of military defeat, they embraced the Republic without equivocation, even if privately they hoped it would be a transitional regime.

Bismarck at Ferrières

The most poignant symbol of the French Rothschilds' share in the French defeat was without doubt the occupation of the château and park at Ferrières. This was an eventuality which Alphonse had anticipated with trepidation even before Sedan.[73] On September 14, a week after the advance on Paris had begun, it happened.

It was at Ferrières that the first tentative and unsuccessful steps towards peace were taken by the new French government; and at Ferrières that Bismarck and Moltke openly quarrelled over strategy. Therein lies its principal historical importance. Yet the occupation of Ferrières can be seen to have had another significance: the "irony" of having the Prussian King and his Junker Chancellor installed at the château which was the most extravagant statement of Rothschild and therefore Jewish wealth. For Stern, the "raucous" conduct of the Germans was an expression of anti-Semitism with ominous significance.[74] The difficulty is in deciding how improperly by contemporary standards the occupiers actually behaved.

The first Prussians to arrive, according to an account later written by the estate manager Bergman for Alphonse's wife Leonora,[75] were Generals von Eupling and Gordon and their respective staffs. Relations with the Rothschilds' domestic staff certainly got off to an unpromising start. On September 17 General Gordon ordered the head butler to arrange dinner for fifteen; when thirty-two guests turned up there was not enough food to go around (though sixty-five bottles of wine were consumed) and Gordon had one of the servants locked up in the stables overnight as a punishment. The next morning Gordon left, and the 19th saw the arrival of William I, accompanied by Bismarck, the Chief of the General Staff Moltke, the Minister of War Roon, numerous other senior officers and around 3,000 men. (Others who stayed there included the Grand Dukes of Baden and Mecklenburg-Strelitz.) To some at least of these uninvited guests, Ferrières was a revelation. With its Mentmorian exterior and exotic interiors, it seemed "fairylike, magnificent"; yet the fact that it was the creation of a Jew—of the "Judenkönig," as Roon called him—tempered their admiration with disdain. The initials JR—James de Rothschild's—which recurred on the ornate walls and ceilings were translated with laboured humour as "Judaeorum Rex."[76]

Perhaps mindful of James's efforts to thwart his plans in 1866, Bismarck himself seems to have taken an especially malicious pleasure in the situation. "Here I sit under a picture of old Rothschild and his family," he wrote to his wife on September 21 from what had been James's suite of rooms. "Negotiators of every sort hang on to my coat-tails like Jews round a market trader"—a significant choice of image.[77] It was Bismarck who threatened to beat a servant who refused to serve him wine from the Rothschild cellars.[78] And it was Bismarck who went out shooting pheasants in the château grounds, grumbling that the gun he was given was too small, with too few cartridges and inadequate shot.[79] It was probably also Bismarck who arranged for a complaint about Rothschild inhospitality to be placed in the German press.[80] Later, when asked whether he would be prepared to negotiate peace terms with a republican regime, Bismarck replied snidely that he would recognise "not only the Republic, but, if you want, a Gambetta dynasty . . . Indeed, any dynasty, whether Bleichröder or Rothschild."[81]

On the other hand, Bismarck's feelings of animosity were not shared by his royal master. "Folk like us can't rise to this," William was heard to comment on seeing Ferrières; "only a Rothschild can achieve it." Anxious not to give offence to the family, he specifically ordered that there should be no requisitioning from the estate and that game and wine cellars should be left intact. As Bergman reported, "The sojourn of the King went off well, he had his own kitchen and kitchen staff, the estate had to provide for everything necessary, game, fruits and flowers; he gave 2,000 francs for the staff of the château." He also took "good care to obtain a written statement that after his departure nothing was missing in the château" and left seventy-five men behind to guard it. No doubt there were some departures from these royal self-denying ordinances. "The soldiers billeted at La Taffarette [part of the estate]," grumbled Bergman,

> fished all the ponds, but that wasn't enough for them, so they decided one night to open the sluice-gates in order to find lots of fish stranded the next morning. When I was given warning of this, I went with several of my men and a locksmith arrived to close the gates, but at that very moment the cavalrymen arrived to water the horses. Terrible disap-

pointment, no water! The soldiers thought it was I who had had the
water drained and they dragged me to the General.

After the King's departure on October 5, several houses and the château cellars were
"pillaged" and blankets and mattresses were requisitioned for nearby field-hospitals.
On January 1, 1871, Bergman lamented:

> There is no more livestock on the farms, we have no coal, [though] we
> have still got some fire wood. The game of the outer park has been killed
> by the Prussians and by poachers; the grounds are reserved for the Prus-
> sians, the Commandant has it patrolled at night, the pheasants and
> flowers are reserved, the gamekeepers were disarmed the day the Prus-
> sians arrived . . . [T]here's no money left in our cashbox, we pay with
> bread coupons, the farms are used as barracks . . . In short they treat Fer-
> rières with respect, there are 25 officers at the château at present, they
> have their own cook paid for by the château but they are very hard to
> please. Finally the requisition expenses of the estate and of the village
> approximately amount to 200 to 250,000 francs . . . [T]he château [is]
> very dirty indeed.[82]

Yet we should not exaggerate the significance of an old retainer's hand-wringing.
Prussian troops remained at Ferrières until the end of August 1871.[83] Naturally, the
French Rothschilds were only too keen to find fault with the conduct of the occupiers. But when Anthony visited the château on September 1, "to see what the Prussians had done [and] whether everything was as it was when the poor Baron left it,"
he was pleasantly surprised. According to his account,

> there is not the least damage either to the House [or] the Park [or] the
> trees, there are as many pheasants in the Park as formerly—they have a
> great many more partridges & all their birds are there—not a thing
> injured in the gardens so that the King's orders were obeyed—they have
> even sent back all carriages that they took to Versailles—they drank all
> the wine that was in one cellar—the other one was finished up . . . They
> took a few little things not worth speaking [of], Bismarck took 250
> sheep. Of course the carpets [are] a little spoilt . . . but when one con-
> siders that all the Prussian Army passed by . . . I think it wonderful that
> not a thing should be hurt . . . & they all ought to thank His Majesty &
> hold their tongues . . . So much for Ferrières—& I think that with all
> their Houses—Boulogne & Ferrières—nothing damaged by the war[,]
> nothing taken by the communists, no person hurt or wounded[,] that
> they ought to thank God that they got off so well.[84]

Even allowing for his evident impatience at the griping of his French relatives,
Anthony's account would seem to explode the idea of Teutonic depredations. Gustave himself admitted that the estate was "in as fair a state of things as could be
expected" when he visited the château later the same month.[85]

On reflection, the notion that the Prussians indulged in looting and pillaging
may have been a construct inspired by the peace terms outlined by Bismarck at Ferrières. The French regarded these as excessively harsh; they were therefore inclined to
think of the German armies as ruthless plunderers at the local level too. The Rothschilds' role in the peace negotiations was so important that it was perhaps inevitable

that they began to equate the fate of France with the fate of Ferrières, and to exaggerate the burdens imposed on the latter.

We have already seen how quickly Alphonse and Gustave accepted the need for a moderate republican regime in the aftermath of the defeat at Sedan, while continuing to express forebodings about the danger of a full-blown Jacobin revolution in Paris. When reading their letters to London in 1870 and 1871, it is important to remember that their original objective had been to secure swift English intervention to end the war and establish a moderate peace. To some extent, therefore, warnings of impending revolution had a diplomatic purpose. As Alphonse wrote to London on August 8, "If Europe does not want France to become a hotbed of anarchy, it is necessary that it be ready and resolved to intervene seriously and without wasting time after the first big battle."[86] Five days later, he insisted that effective English peace-making was also the condition of political stability in a new French republic. Even at this early stage Alphonse was unequivocal about the kind of peace which would be acceptable, so much so that it becomes hard to distinguish his own views from those of the moderate Republican leadership. In fact, Alphonse's first letter to London on the subject predated the fall of the Empire by some weeks. On August 13—in a carefully phrased résumé which was obviously intended to relay republican views to Gladstone—he stated the terms which a new republican regime would be willing to accept on the assumption of a French defeat:

> Any dismembering of France would be opposed to the last and any pretensions of that nature raised by Prussia would encounter a desperate resistance. Even a war indemnity would be a difficult condition to accept, but influential forces would exercise themselves in that sense . . . for if we were beaten it is evident that it would be necessary to submit to a certain extent to the laws of defeat. It would nevertheless be necessary for the [other] powers to be ready to intervene *very swiftly*, and mediation to happen *immediately*, for otherwise any loss of time could only increase the mood of exasperation and compromise the results of mediation. One would therefore agree to give some money, but one would go no further.[87]

He repeated that formulation on September 4, the day the news reached Paris of the débâcle at Sedan:

> One will sign a peace without hesitation, no matter how miserable and humiliating it may be, if it can be obtained by a sacrifice of money. But no one here will dare to sign a peace that entails a cession of territory. You will say to us that in the present state to which we are reduced France cannot defend itself, that we have no more army and no ammunition. That may be true, but the public sentiment is so strong that the country would rather allow itself to be ruined and broken into pieces than have to cede territory. That would mean the destruction of France and I believe that the foreign powers have a big enough interest in not allowing the balance of Europe to be completely overthrown by Prussia to prevent such a fatal result. The moment to intervene has arrived. Any action must be immediate and energetic.[88]

Jules Favre's famous "not an inch of territory" statement of September 6 thus can have come as no surprise in London. Alphonse saw Favre that very day, and once again anticipated his argument: "One can consent to every sacrifice except that of a cession of territory . . . because a cession of territory will render all government impossible . . . I am perfectly convinced that the present government has only one thought: to make peace. But it is in the interest of Europe to intervene in order that this peace should not be ephemeral."[89] Later, Gustave was critical of Favre's tactics, blaming them on General Trochu;[90] yet it is evident from the Rothschilds' own correspondence that his brother had a major hand in them and regarded Favre's statement as "worthy and clever." Indeed, to judge by Alphonse's letters, it was he as much as Favre who was making French foreign policy in September 1870. On the 11th, for example, his letter to New Court contained threats and promises intended to secure English mediation which it is hard to believe were authorised by the government as a whole:

> It is in the interest of all Europe . . . to render peace possible and not to throw France into a state of anarchy such that an occupation, so to speak on a permanent basis, becomes necessary [as that] would inevitably lead sooner or later to the most serious complications and could even cause Prussia to lose the positive results of her victory. That is not a threat, it is the truth of the situation. No one will dare to sign a peace with cessions of territory, and it will be necessary for Prussia to govern the country, which will not be easy, for in every town in France which has not been occupied by the enemy, there will be revolutionary movements . . . Be assured that one will accept here all the conditions that will be demanded to obtain peace except a cession of territory. A war indemnity, part of the navy, even the French colonies and even more so Luxembourg.[91]

Alphonse was, of course, right to anticipate a German demand for territory as well as money. As early as August 15, Mayer Carl relayed to London the mood on the Frankfurt bourse: "I dare say France will lose her old German provinces, a large portion of her fleet & besides she will have to pay a very large amount of money: this is generally thought." A few days later he added more in the same vein: "The struggle is a national one and the great victories of the German arms claim everything that can possibly be expected. You have no conception of the enthusiasm which exists here & all over Germany and the humiliation of France must be exemplary to satisfy public opinion. Everything is getting up & the German loan is [at a] 7% premium and will no doubt go higher still as the French must pay for everything." "The Germans," he predicted darkly, "will take good care to impose conditions which will assure the peace for a long time."[92] By August 26 he was able to offer more detail:

> The French must be humiliated which is the only way for us to be preserved from further wars & I have no doubt that the French must give up Alsatia, the Lorraine, a good part of their fleet & at least one hundred Million Sterling as war contribution. Strasbourg & Metz must become Federal fortresses this is the general opinion & old *B* is sure to make the best of it.[93]

Mayer Carl also justified the annexation of Alsace–Lorraine on nationalist as well as strategic grounds: "[I]t is foolish to think that the German nation will give up the struggle without keeping those old German provinces which had been conquered . . ."[94]

But the new French government's hope that England would intervene to moderate the German demands was, for reasons described above, unrealistic. "We have received your letters," Alphonse wrote dolefully to New Court on September 6, "and we see with great regret that England is not disposed to intervene."[95] Not that he immediately abandoned hope of swaying British policy: he was in regular contact with the British ambassador Lord Lyons and was evidently involved in the diplomatic efforts of Thiers, who set off in search of support in London and St Petersburg.[96] Nor was it wholly unrealistic to hope for more sympathy from Gladstone, who strongly disapproved of the unilateral annexation of French territory and privately considered the transfer of Luxembourg to Prussia "an ingenious idea."[97] However, he was riled by a Rothschild letter on this subject which seemed to assume his support on this point and (fatally) to make "very cool assumptions . . . about the interests of Belgium." Indeed, by the end of September Gladstone had begun to suspect the Rothschilds of "twisting the words" of some of the intelligence they were relaying to him.[98]

Any possibility of effective intervention was buried when the Russians seized the opportunity presented by the crisis to reopen the question of the Black Sea's neutralisation.[99] At this point Alphonse ceased to discount rentes for the government, instead converting his remaining cash into drafts on the Banque de France which were sent to London for safety. With the Prussian army closing in on Paris and no sign of an imminent armistice, it was a moment for understatement in the great Rothschild tradition. "There is no need for me to say," he concluded, "that this extremity is most disagreeable for us, but the government has informed us in a proclamation that we are ready to be buried beneath the walls of Paris, and the prospect is not an alluring one."[100] On September 17, the day before Favre secured an interview with Bismarck at Ferrières, Lyons gave Gustave advance warning of the German position. Bismarck had told him "that he had no need of money, that they had more of that than they wanted, and that what really was required was to have Metz and Strasbourg . . . If that is refused, which is probable, he [Bismarck] will enter Paris, cut off our business communications and put the city to fire and sword without respite." "That will be agreeable," was Gustave's parting comment in what he plainly expected to be his last letter to London for some time. "Goodbye my dear cousins, the ambassadors, including Lord Lyons, are leaving this evening after which we are going to be living without knowing what will become of us—a very pretty prospect."[101] Favre's interviews on the 18th thus merely confirmed what the Rothschilds already fully expected. Although Favre went so far as to offer Bismarck 5 billion francs if France could retain Strasbourg and Alsace, "old B" responded memorably: "We will talk about the money later, first we want to determine and secure the German frontier."[102]

Communications were not wholly severed. Occasional letters were sent across the lines by balloon and were relayed by telegraph to London but it proved extremely difficult to send letters into Paris during the siege.[103] On December 10, for example, Alphonse received a letter from his cousins dated October 21;[104] and it was not until February 3, 1871, when a New Court courier arrived with a large hamper, that regular correspondence resumed. To all intents and purposes, then, the Parisians were

on their own for four harrowing months, and even after the armistice of January 28
communications remained erratic until June. Because they ceased to write letters in
the period of the Prussian siege, we know little about their experiences; but it seems
safe to assume that they endured at least a measure of the cold, hunger and terror
which everyone did who remained in the besieged city. When the food package
arrived from London in February, Alphonse and his relatives "fell like children on all
the excellent things you sent us."[105] Once again, Bismarck's mood was vindictive,
relishing the thought of the Rothschilds brought low. On January 30, two days after
an armistice had at long last been signed, he indulged in more anti-Rothschild jokes.
On hearing that a Rothschild was intending to leave Paris, Bismarck suggested he
should be arrested as a *franc-tireur* (sniper). "Then Bleichröder will come running
and prostrate himself on behalf of the whole Rothschild family," exclaimed Bismarck's cousin. "Then we will send both to Paris," jeered Bismarck, "where they can
join the dog hunt"—a reference to the wretched diet of those who had been trapped
in the city.[106]

"Le Pivot d'une Combinaison": Reparations

A fundamental question arises, and it is the question historians have much more
often asked about the peace terms which were formulated in the same place nearly
half a century later, when the tables were turned and Germany was the defeated
power. Were the peace terms excessively harsh? Another question—also more often
asked about the peace of 1919—is whether or not it was right to try to resist them
by continuing to fight, even at the risk of precipitating internal revolution and civil
war. The paradox is that the territorial demands—the cession of Alsace and Lorraine—were not unreasonable: Austria after all had surrendered territory following
both her defeats in 1859–60 and 1866. Yet these were the demands the French
found intolerable. The monetary demands, by contrast, were remarkably harsh. Yet
from the outset the French were more willing to countenance these. It was in many
ways futile for Gambetta to balloon out of Paris and drum up his *levée en masse*:
although the new armies raised did inflict unforeseen casualties on the Prussian
occupiers, they never stood a chance of winning a real victory over them. The price
of thus postponing peace was also high from the point of view of internal stability
and did nothing to modify the Prussian terms.

Yet the parallel with the experience of the Weimar Republic after 1919 is a suggestive one in four ways. Firstly, a futile attempt at military resistance may have
served to scotch or at least weaken the nascent "stab in the back" theory advanced by
the far left in Paris after Sedan. No one could doubt by 1871 that France had been
defeated "in the field"; without a myth of republican pusillanimity it was difficult
for the diverse factions of the Right to unite. Secondly, the descent of Paris into
anarchy and the subsequent repression of the Commune in the summer of 1871
may have had a salutary effect in banishing for generations the spectres of Jacobinism, Blanquism, Proudhonism and Marxism: moderate republicans were united by
their common aversion to the extreme left in a way which never happened in
Weimar Germany. Thirdly, the continuing occupation of large parts of France by
Prussian troops after 1870 gave the moderate republicans an incentive to pay reparations which was lacking for Germany in the 1920s; France tried to occupy
German territory after default, instead of occupying in advance of payment.

Finally, and crucially, a determined and sincere attempt to pay reparations could count after 1870 on the wholehearted support of the European capital market, led by the Rothschild houses. During the early 1870s the French paid substantial sums for their defeat—ironically, a good deal more than they had been willing to pay for adequate military preparation before the war. The financial markets rewarded them by advancing the money needed to make the fastest possible transfer of reparations at a relatively low cost: it was, quite simply, the biggest financial operation of the century, and arguably the Rothschilds' crowning achievement. By contrast, Germany in the early 1920s set out to avoid paying reparations and in the process inflicted not only hyperinflation on herself but massive currency depreciation on foreign lenders; the markets reacted by never trusting the German government again, and the subsequent attempt to pay reparations in a long series of small instalments failed miserably. The Third Republic survived for seventy years; the Weimar Republic for less than fourteen. The key to that difference may lie in the peace of 1871.

Of course, one should not lose sight of the differences between the two cases. The war of 1870 was short and cost far less in life and treasure than the war of 1914–18. Consequently, France embarked on paying reparations with a lower level of national debt and far less serious fiscal and monetary problems. Even so, the payment of the German indemnity remains one of the great financial feats of modern times.[107] Between June 1871 and September 1873, France paid Germany 4,993 million francs, around 8 per cent of gross domestic product in the first year, and 13 per cent in the second.[108] These figures need to be seen in the context of the existing level of national debt (which was a good deal higher than in 1815). As a percentage of GDP, French public debt was already 44 per cent in 1869, before the war, and 59 per cent in 1871, before most of the indemnity had been paid. So the total internal and external debt burden in 1871 was in the vicinity of 80 per cent of GDP. This was approximately half the size of the total debt burden Germany laboured under in 1921 (when the reparations total was belatedly fixed). On the other hand, the German reparations schedule in the 1920s was intended to stretch over decades, so that the annual burden of debt service and amortisation averaged less than 3 per cent of GDP during the 1920s. For France to pay an average of more than 10 per cent of GDP in two successive years was an astonishing achievement. Even more astonishing, the transfer was made with the minimum of exchange rate depreciation and domestic inflation. The history of how this was achieved deserves to be better understood.[109]

The Rothschilds first began to consider the question of the French indemnity as early as August 1870. As we have seen, Mayer Carl cited a figure of £100 million—2.5 billion francs—as a possible total. As early as November, Anselm was trying to work out how such a large sum could be paid. He suggested to Lionel that, following the precedent of 1815, new 5 per cent rentes would have to be issued, and envisaged the Rothschilds playing the role Barings had played then, as intermediaries for the transfer of money from Paris to Berlin.[110] This, as Lionel objected, was premature, though it proved quite prescient. According to Bismarck, Favre mentioned a sum of 5 billion francs when the two met in September, though this was intended to be conditional on the retention of Alsace–Lorraine. When the Germans insisted on territorial cessions, negotiations were once again suspended and war went on. It was not until February 1871 that work on the indemnity question could be resumed.

From the beginning, German bankers assumed that the spoils of their government's victory would include their control of the collection of reparations. Bleichröder believed he had stolen a march on his rivals when he was summoned (along with the industrialist Henckel von Donnersmarck) to advise Bismarck at Versailles;[111] and in the wake of this trip he badgered the Paris Rothschilds with proposals for floating a French loan on the Berlin market. Needless to say, Mayer Carl was against involving Bleichröder, arguing that any transaction should be handled in tandem with Hansemann and the Seehandlung.[112] However, Alphonse seems to have determined from an early stage to exclude as far as possible all the German bankers—including even his own cousins in Frankfurt and Vienna.[113] His plan was to create two allied and Rothschild-led syndicates in Paris and London, the former including all the older private banks (the so-called *haute banque*) but not the joint-stock banks; the latter to be composed solely of N. M. Rothschild and Barings. This strategy had a dual significance: it was designed to punish the German banks on what may be interpreted as patriotic grounds; but it was also designed to strike a blow for the "old" banks against their joint-stock rivals in France and England. To this end, earlier rivalries among the private banks were forgotten—in particular the rivalry between Rothschilds and Barings which dated back to the financing and transfer of the last French indemnity.

The first round of the struggle for control of the operation was fought over the payment of 200 million francs demanded by the German occupiers from the city of Paris in February. At this early stage, needless to say, tension between the French and German sides was high. If the Germans had been willing to accept French banknotes, the matter would have been straightforward: it was easy for the Banque de France to advance 210 million francs to the provisional city commissioners (one of whom, it should be said, was Léon Say). But, anxious that the French currency might depreciate, the Germans insisted on being paid in coin. This seemed so unreasonable to Alphonse that he assumed they were merely looking for a pretext to break off negotiations, end the armistice and march into Paris itself. In the end, despite the continuing difficulties of regular communication with London, Alphonse managed to hammer out a compromise: 50 million was to be paid at once in French banknotes; 50 million in gold or silver coin as soon as possible; and the remainder in commercial bills on London and Berlin. The operation was guaranteed by a Rothschild-led syndicate of French private banks and carried out with the assistance of the London house.[114] Most of the bills bought and handed over to the Germans (63 million out of 100) were in fact short-dated (one- or two-week) bills on London; the two bills for 2 million thalers which Alphonse gave to a dazzled Bleichröder were exceptional.[115] This was the first sign that Alphonse intended London rather than Berlin to be the nodal point of the reparations process. Indeed, Alphonse made a hurried visit to New Court on February 21–2 to discuss how the same operation could be repeated on a larger scale for the impending national indemnity.[116] As he had expected, the action of buying so much "London" weakened the franc slightly against sterling, though the Germans were protected against this depreciation under the terms of the agreement (as were the bankers: the Paris authorities had agreed to a fixed rate). At the same time, he foresaw the problems the Germans could create in London if they sought to convert their sterling bills into gold at one fell swoop.[117]

The Paris contribution was merely an appetiser; the final total of the indemnity to be imposed had still to be decided. This proved less than easy. Figures bandied around at Versailles ranged from 3 to 8 billion francs; a "peevish" Bismarck himself initially proposed to Thiers a sum of 6 billion, which Thiers—leaping to his feet "as if he had been bitten by a mad dog"—denounced as "une indignité."[118] Even when he reduced this to 5 billion, the French continued to dismiss the figure as "exorbitant." Still more galling to the French negotiators was Bismarck's assurance that Bleichröder and Henckel had "devised a procedure by which this tribute, so burdensome in appearance, will be paid by you without your being aware of it." As Favre remarked bitterly, the two German financiers "did their best to prove to us how much they wanted to carry out a colossal operation with our billions." It was in order to head this off that Thiers requested the return of Alphonse from London to represent the views of both the Paris and London Rothschild houses.[119] On February 25, with the two sides apparently deadlocked, Alphonse was summoned to Versailles. He was given an ominously frosty reception by the German Chancellor when he arrived that evening.

If Bismarck hoped that, as the son of a Frankfurt Jew, "Rothschild" would somehow be able to arbitrate, then he was disappointed. To be sure, Alphonse dissuaded the "exasperated" Thiers and Favre from "breaking off the negotiations and throwing themselves into the arms of Europe." But when the German representatives proposed to him an initial annual payment of 1.5 billion francs, half in specie, half in bills, he "declared that he had no brief to discuss these [technical] questions as the French negotiators were not in agreement even on the first principles" of the peace. After an hour of inconclusive discussion, Bismarck appeared: "He was pale with anger and demanded what proposals we had agreed on. I replied that I had not been able to examine the questions since the two governments were not in agreement on basic principles. I thought Bismarck was going to devour me; he shouted, 'But in that case peace is impossible!' "

Alphonse returned to discuss the next step with Thiers and Favre, but Bismarck was not finished: "A little later [he] reappeared with the following proposal. A billion payable within a year, the rest in three years . . ." It was now ten o'clock at night, and time for Alphonse to return to Paris. The final discussions, as he recalled in the letter he dashed off the next morning, had been "extremely lively and Bismarck had come close to saying that if war was resumed he would wage it horribly, as it had never been seen before."[120] Even Bleichröder confessed to being shocked at Bismarck's "monstrous brusquerie and intentional rudeness." Had anyone ever spoken in this fashion to a Rothschild?[121] With magnificent understatement, Alphonse summed up his position as "difficult":

> Under a political façade they really wanted me to intervene in order to be the pivot of a financial combination which appears ruinous . . . It is not necessary to make a group of bankers intervene directly in a political matter, thereby bringing upon themselves all the opprobrium of a negotiation, the moral responsibility of which they ought not to bear.

In one sense, Bismarck's bluster had worked. The next day, as Alphonse anticipated, Thiers and Favre agreed to the 5 billion franc figure. To be precise: under the terms agreed on February 26, France was to owe Germany 5 billion francs, with interest accruing at 5 per cent, less the value of the French railways in Alsace and Lorraine and not including the Paris indemnity and other occupation charges already levied.[122] The schedule of payment was tight: 500 million was due in the first month after the definitive peace treaty was signed (May 10); 1 billion by the end of 1871; then 500 million by May 1872; and a further billion due each March during the succeeding three years. These were terms which Alphonse could only regard as "disastrous" and "shameful": 5 billion, he exclaimed, was a "fabulous figure" and "scarcely possible to pay within three years." Rather like Keynes in 1919, he vehemently and repeatedly disputed the possibility of paying the sum demanded; at first he regarded even 2 billion as "absurd," though he was later prepared to contemplate 2.5 billion.[123] And like Keynes he warned cleverly that excessive reparations not only would plunge the defeated country into economic chaos but would disrupt the European economy as a whole: the difficulty of effecting such a large unrequited transfer would create turmoil on the international financial markets.[124] But unlike Keynes Alphonse failed to persuade anyone. When the French government reluctantly accepted the peace terms, there was no serious intention to default on the indemnity payments in the way that there was in Berlin throughout the 1920s. Indeed, within days of warning his English cousins of the impossibility of paying 5 billion francs, Alphonse himself was hard at work preparing the ground for the transfer of the first instalment.

The best explanation for this shift from despair to action is that Alphonse had in fact won important concessions at Versailles, though at the price of bearing the brunt of Bismarck's wrath. The retention of the fortress of Belfort was one. More important, the possibility was recognised of discounted payment in advance of the envisaged time-limit; and if that proved possible, the phased German evacuation of the occupied départements of north-eastern France would also be speeded up.[125] Above all, Alphonse ensured that, although the Germans fixed the reparations total and set a time-limit for its payment, it was agreed that—within certain limits[126]— the French would be free to organise the payment themselves. As he had explained to Thiers at Versailles, Bleichröder and Henckel wanted "to link a large financial operation to the conclusion of the peace treaty." But Alphonse's view was that:

> the two governments ought to agree on the size of the indemnity to be paid and the time in which it had to be paid, but that the French Government ought to reserve for itself absolutely the right to effect the payments as it saw fit. For otherwise that would lead to a confusion of particular interests with general interests and from every point of view that could have the most regrettable consequences.

Alphonse was his father's son; for this was a classic Rothschild stroke. It was presumably this which persuaded Thiers to drop his objections to the 5 billion figure the next morning. Moreover, it ensured that the Rothschilds rather than the German bankers secured control of the financing of the indemnity.

At least six technical questions had to be answered if the indemnity were to be paid and the occupation ended.[127] First, how far could payments be made without detrimentally affecting the French exchange rate in the way that the Paris payment had? Second, and closely related, should the Banque de France, which had suspended the convertibility of the franc into silver and gold during the war, aim to return to the bimetallic standard? Since Sedan, the French government had been relying heavily on short-term advances from the Banque against treasury bills to meet its financial needs.[128] Clearly, the initial payments to Germany would have to be funded in the same way; but further issues of money against treasury bills risked, as Alphonse repeatedly warned, a "descent into paper money," just as the need to convert francs into currency acceptable in Berlin risked an exchange rate crisis. The third question followed logically from this: how soon could rentes[129] be floated in French and especially foreign markets in order to raise the money needed for the indemnity (and for the government's own needs) in a non-inflationary way? Fourth, would it be possible to introduce new taxes and control internal government expenditure in such a way that the new debt incurred in this way could be serviced? This in turn raised the question of the form of any new taxation: should France now belatedly follow England in introducing an income tax; or should it revert to a policy of imposing duties on raw materials; or should the stock exchange itself bear some of the brunt of the costs of defeat in the form of a new stamp duty on securities transactions? Finally, what of those largest and most visible private concentrations of capital, the railways? Might their assets and revenues in some way be utilised, whether by taxing them or by using them as a guarantee for the debt to Germany?

These were extremely difficult questions for a government born of defeat to answer. From the point of view of the government's financial advisers, the Rothschilds, their implications were complex and ambiguous. The chance to control the great indemnity transfer held out the promise of large profits, but these might be negated if it all failed, or if the price of success proved to be taxes on the Rothschilds' own assets. Above all, it was an immense risk to become identified with paying such large sums of money to Berlin. The Jewish bankers and politicians who became identified with the policy of "fulfilment" in Germany in the 1920s paid dearly for doing so; it is extraordinary, with hindsight, how little contemporary criticism Alphonse incurred for playing a similar role in the 1870s (though in the 1880s, as we shall see, that changed).

Nothing illustrated the difficulties involved more starkly than the collapse of the new government's authority in the city of Paris itself between March and May 1871, just as preparations were getting under way for the payment of the first instalment of the indemnity. Although Alphonse repeatedly reassured his cousins that the majority of Frenchmen were conservatively inclined—a view endorsed by the monarchists' victory in the elections to the National Assembly held on February 8—the threat from the "parti rouge" in the capital had been real from the moment the perennial "red" Auguste Blanqui and the rest had emerged from hiding or imprisonment after the fall of the Empire. Twice they had led "the mob" to the Hôtel de Ville following military reverses: on October 31, 1870, and again on January 19. By March the stage seemed set for a re-enactment of 1848; even the cast was unchanged, with moderate republicans led by Thiers and Grévy and the radical left represented in the Assembly by Louis Blanc, Delescluze and Ledru-Rollin. When, on March 18 Thiers sought to disarm the National Guard—enlarged and at the same time politicised during the war—history duly repeated itself, though as another tragedy rather than a farce. Heavily outnumbered, the government troops opted to fraternise with the crowds. Rather than risk further defections, Thiers decided to pull all his forces out to Versailles,[130] leaving Paris in the hands of the Central Committee of the National Guard.

On March 26 a new municipal government was elected, the Commune—its name redolent of 1792—and this was soon under the control of the Blanquists and Jacobins. Fighting broke out in early April and another full-scale siege was soon in progress. Reading from their crumpled historical script, the Communards set up a Committee of Public Safety on May 1, revived the old revolutionary calendar and began to put one another on trial. This time, however, the Terror was inflicted on the revolutionaries rather than by them. In the Bloody Week which ended on May 28, around 20,000 people died, around half of them Communard prisoners lined up and shot at the orders of the army commanders in improvised "abattoirs."[131]

For the French Rothschilds, the advent of the Commune proved to be the most serious threat to property, if not to life, of the entire period between 1815 and 1940. On March 26 Alphonse advised Gustave to leave Paris for Versailles, but intended to remain in the rue Laffitte himself.[132] However, on his way back after paying his brother a visit on April 1, he was warned by the train driver that the Commune had ordered communications with Versailles to be severed and that the train he was travelling in would be the last into the city. He disembarked and returned to Versailles.[133] This was a sensible decision; if he had proceeded to the city centre he might well have ended up a hostage and would unquestionably have found himself caught up in some of the most brutal street-fighting of the nineteenth century. It was only by a hair's breadth that Rothschild offices and houses avoided being burnt down; to Alphonse's relief, the Gare du Nord also escaped serious damage, unlike the Banque de France and the Finance Ministry.[134] When Alfred visited Paris in late June, he was able to report cheerfully that:

> the various shots that found their way into this house, have only knocked off a corner of the ceiling in the smoking room and the only souvenirs of the revolution are a brush with which the blackguards were going to petrolize (a new verb) the house, and various photographs of these ruffians whose great pleasure was to be immortalized in various positions.[135]

Even so, Ferdinand was shocked by the effect of the crisis on his cousins' physical condition: he found Alphonse and Gustave "painfully green and yellow" when he met them in Paris in August—and disconcertingly secretive.[136]

From the point of view of the indemnity payment, the descent of Paris into civil war was a setback, bringing financial activity to a near standstill.[137] There were compensations nonetheless. Events in Paris could be portrayed as a threat to the governments of all countries, and further evidence of the unwisdom of a Carthaginian peace.[138] Moreover, once military discipline had been re-established within the regular army, it gave the government a chance "to get rid of all those vermin, veritable gallows fodder who constantly threaten society"—to "purge France and the world of all these rogues." Evidently, Alphonse shared the violent antipathy towards the Parisian "dangerous classes" which was at the root of the Bloody Week.[139]

It is tempting to add that there was one further benefit: the defeat of the Commune reinforced Thiers' position as President. But was this really advantageous? One of the puzzles of the early 1870s is the nature of the relationship between

Thiers and the Rothschilds. Early on, Alphonse referred to Thiers as "our friend" and seemed happy to see him as "master of the situation"; and there is no question that he stood four-square behind him and the moderate republicans during and immediately after the "war against Paris." To Alphonse, Thiers seemed the only man capable of reconciling republican Paris with the monarchist provinces.[140] But "our friend" was a Rothschild euphemism devoid of emotional content. In truth, Alphonse had reservations about Thiers which soon resurfaced. Thiers, after all, had been no friend of Alphonse's father in the days of Louis Philippe; and the old man evidently made Rothschild *fils* feel uneasy, perhaps on account of this. "It is really difficult to converse with him," complained Alphonse after one encounter, "especially for people like me whom he knew as children."[141] Was Alphonse just a little afraid of Thiers? Alfred noticed that he "rather dreaded calling upon the little President of the great Republic."[142] More often, Alphonse articulated this sense of unease by criticising Thiers' dictatorial tendencies (especially towards the Banque), or his fondness for political double-dealing. "A Proteus who, despite his great stature, always slips through our fingers" was his curious verdict.[143] As early as June 1871, Alphonse predicted that, if Thiers were to fall, he would most probably be replaced by the duc d'Aumale, paving the way for an Orléanist restoration.[144]

Nevertheless, Thiers had one quality which the Rothschilds did not underrate: he grasped the primacy of finance over all other factors under the circumstances of 1871–3. "Above all," Alphonse told Thiers in early June, "the political situation must be clarified and for the present it must be completely subordinated to the financial questions."[145] Subsequent events were to confirm that Thiers accepted this. Despite his seniority, the President generally deferred to Alphonse's advice on these financial questions. And despite repeated efforts by rival banks to challenge the Rothschilds' position, he never really questioned the need for their leadership in the payment of the indemnity. This in turn may explain why, as he later told Gambetta, Alphonse acted to keep Thiers in power when his position seemed to be threatened in late 1872. According to one account, Alphonse told Gambetta:

> that he liked M. Thiers but that Thiers had nonetheless unjustly accused him of having been his enemy. For a whole year, he refused to see him. Thiers said: "It was Rothschild who overthrew me." "He said that to me too," Gambetta interrupted. "It isn't true!" replied Alphonse de Rothschild vehemently . . . "I obviously had a certain influence with quite a large number of deputies and I enabled Thiers to hold on for six months longer than he would have lasted without me. I told my friends in the Chamber, 'Don't overthrow Thiers; that would be a national disaster . . . At least let the great loan operations finish, for on them depend the credit and fortune of France.' I never said anything else."[146]

Whatever their suspicions about one another, the two men were united by bonds of interest, though in the strictly financial sense of both words.

Could other banks have handled the indemnity payment just as well—perhaps even more cheaply? It is arguable. Three per cent rentes looked undervalued in the first half of 1871 at prices of 50–53 francs. Bleichröder was far from being the only European banker who saw the opportunity for netting large profits from the "great operation," not only in the form of commissions, but in the form of capital gains if the rentes could be taken firm at such low prices; given the track record of the rente as an investment since 1815, a substantial rise seemed inevitable. He and other German bankers swarmed around Paris in May, trying to secure a share of the action.[147] Nor were they alone. The Banque de Paris also attempted to outbid the Rothschilds, and there was also competition from J. S. Morgan, who had taken the risk of financing the French war effort in October 1870.[148]

However, none of the Rothschilds' rivals could claim to match their international reach as an issuing house: as Mazerat of the Crédit Lyonnais put it, "Rothschild's great European relations and the power of his capital resources create for him an absolutely exceptional role."[149] This was the key. In order to raise the maximum amount of hard currency from the issue, Thiers and the French Finance Minister Augustin Pouyer-Quertier wished to sell as many of the new rentes as possible outside France, and ideally in London. The fact that Alphonse could legitimately present himself as the spokesman not just of the Parisian *haute banque* but also of New Court was his trump card. "Our opinion, I have no doubt," he reported to London, "will have a very great influence over the decisions which the [Finance] Minister is in the process of taking and our attitude must necessarily be very influenced by yours." "The minister has addressed himself to no one other than us," he added later, "and I have no doubt that you can be assured of the conduct of the entire operation in England." Alphonse also recommended that the issuing of rentes in Germany be handled through the Frankfurt house, rather than by Bleichröder and Hansemann, "particularly as it seems to me that it would be difficult for the government to open a subscription directly through German bankers, whereas the house of Rothschild has a cosmopolitan name."[150] Small wonder the Rothschilds' rivals grumbled: as Mazerat put it, Alphonse had become "the pivot of all the financial combinations which are going to emerge. It is impossible to keep abreast of his projects."[151]

With the government thus committed to Rothschilds, all that remained to be agreed were the mechanics of the operation. Alphonse's letters of June 1871 give perhaps the best insight available into the way such negotiations were conducted.[152] The points at issue were numerous: the timing of the issue (before or after the elections of July 2?); the amount to be issued (2 billion francs or more?); the respective shares of the French, English and other markets; the interest and amortisation payable on the bonds; the issue price (figures discussed ranged from 80 to 85); the timing of subscription payments (how many monthly instalments?); the bankers' precise role (should they take the bonds firm or underwrite part or all of the issue?); the size of their commission, brokerage and other charges; and finally the exchange rate for interest payments to foreign subscribers (should this be pegged against future depreciation of the franc?).

The answers arrived at after days of haggling were as follows: subscriptions for 2.6 billion francs worth of 5 per cent rentes were to be opened on June 26 at an issuing price of 82.5, though with the timing of subscription payments such that the net price was around 79.5. The exchange rate for English interest payments was fixed at 25.30 francs to the pound. The two syndicates led by the Rothschilds in London and Paris were formally underwriting only 1,060 million of the total issue, in return for which they received a commission worth 2 per cent of the nominal value (21.2 million francs),[153] so that the effective price of their subscriptions was more like 77.5 (Alphonse calculated the figure as 77.7). There was, admittedly, a catch of sorts. Technically, the syndicates were underwriting not the first billion of the issue (as the Berlin bankers had expected) but the *second* billion. If the issue went badly, their chances of being left holding large quantities of rentes were therefore higher. On the other hand, if the issue went so well that the public bought the lot, the bankers would have to rest content with their commission. The Berliners thought this "flatly unacceptable."[154] However, the French government concluded a secret oral agreement with the Rothschild houses to the effect that they would be allowed to hang on to some or all of the rentes they underwrote.[155] The Rothschild share was therefore 410.5 million francs—more than a third of the total amount underwritten or 16 per cent of the total issue.[156] It is therefore a matter of straight-forward arithmetic to calculate the profits they earned. The commission alone was worth 8 million francs; but that overlooks the large capital gains involved. If the London and Paris houses held on to all the rentes for which they had paid an effective price of 77.7 and sold them all at the market's next peak in November 1871 (97.1), they would have made a profit of around 80 million francs (*c.* £3 million).[157]

It was typical that Alphonse regarded this as rather less than might have been achieved. It had proved impossible to achieve a complete Rothschild monopoly. Not only had the French joint-stock banks managed to secure a small share, but the markets other than London and Paris had been effectively "free for all," so that brokers began trading unofficially in Brussels even before the subscriptions were opened. "I confess it's a veritable muddle," grumbled Alphonse, whose opinion of the inexperienced Pouyer-Quertier had never been high, "but I assure you that it is not our fault; to prevent it we would have had to become Ministers of Finance ourselves."[158] Yet within a few days, as the full extent of the loan's success became apparent, such complaints faded. At first, subscriptions were said to be double the amount issued; by July 20 Alphonse estimated a factor of eight.[159] Not only that, but the French joint-stock banks had been successfully squeezed out, as they were again when the city of Paris issued a loan of its own through the Rothschilds not long after. As Mazerat of the Crédit Lyonnais complained:

> In all the affairs which have been contracted since the war, the house of Rothschild and, under its aegis, the *haute banque* group, have played an almost exclusive role . . . It was Rothschild and his friends, with the support of the Banque de France, which advanced the 200 million francs necessary for the city of Paris to pay its war contribution; it was the same group which reserved for itself the 2 billion loan and it was only as a favour that the credit establishments were able, at the last minute, to obtain for themselves an insignificant share of the commission of 20 millions which the Rothschild syndicate had earned for itself . . . Now the next loan for the city of Paris is announced on the same terms . . .

With Alphonse now one of the dominant regents at the Banque de France and the Rothschilds' "long-standing intimate friend" Say now Prefect of the Seine, the joint-stock banks saw themselves as the victims of political discrimination. On August 5 they therefore signed an agreement which was little short of an anti-Rothschild alliance. As Mazerat put it, deliberately casting aspersions on Alphonse's patriotic credentials, the joint-stock banks had united "as French establishments" to lay claim to "the place which they must legitimately take in French affairs."[160]

The objective of cutting the German banks out of the operation had also been achieved—though how far this was the fault of bad communications, timidity in Berlin or malice aforethought in Paris is hard to say.[161] It is worth noting that this exclusion extended not only to Bleichröder,[162] Hansemann and Oppenheim but to the Rothschild houses in Frankfurt and Vienna as well. Anselm applied for as much as 31 million francs of the new rentes and the Creditanstalt for 47 million, but by the time these applications reached Paris subscriptions were already closed.[163] Mayer Carl only just managed to secure a subscription for 2 million francs.[164] Not for the first time, the fault lines dividing the European capital market were breaking up the traditional co-operation between the Rothschild houses, leaving only an Anglo-French axis intact. That this did not concern Alphonse is plain. "I do not regret," he wrote with a hard-edged satisfaction, "having been able to demonstrate to these gentlemen, despite all our goodwill, that when we are engaged in a transaction, we can do without them, just as we can do without the Berlin types who have missed the chance to make a pretty nice profit."[165] Triumph though it was for the English and French houses, the first Thiers rente also marked a further step towards the disintegration of the Rothschilds as a united pan-European force.

This, of course, was only the first phase: there remained the question of how the money raised by the rentes issue should be transferred to the German government. The obvious way of proceeding was for the government to buy bills on London—the most popular of liquid financial instruments—and hand them over to Berlin. Something like a third of the first 1.8 billion francs was indeed paid in this way; to Alphonse's annoyance, it proved impossible to establish a monopoly on the French government's purchases of bills.[166] However, the Germans now began to make difficulties, insisting that they would rather receive gold or German thaler bills than long-dated sterling bills.[167] As usual, Bleichröder sought to inflate his own importance by relaying the views of his "friend" on this issue to Paris.[168] But Alphonse was unimpressed. "These gentlemen may be great [military] victors," he commented acerbically, "but they are certainly pretty bad financiers. They are locking up the money we remit them and do nothing to facilitate the payments."[169] The transfer difficulties precipitated a mild currency crisis in the last months of 1871, coinciding as they did with a poor harvest (and therefore a need for French grain imports), a speculative surge at the bourse and the first serious arguments about tax policy.[170] To protect its reserve, the Banque de France had to issue new small-denomination notes and pressurised the government to reduce its large floating debt. This burst the bubble on the bourse: the price of rentes peaked in November then fell about five percentage points in the first half of 1872 (see illustration 6.i). As a consequence of all this, discussions of the next payments due in Berlin by May 1872 had to be deferred until the New Year.[171]

The French government's difficulties gave the Rothschilds' rivals a fresh opportunity to tout for business. It was the Banque de Paris which led the challenge, acting as a front (so Alphonse suspected) for German interests, notably Henckel von Donnersmarck. The "Paribas"[172] director Soubeyran had got the better of Alphonse in the scramble for bills in the summer of 1871 and on the question of the 300 million francs due by May Alphonse was forced to give ground: after much wrangling, he and the other private bankers guaranteed half the sum, leaving the other half to the joint-stock banks.[173] This was but a foretaste of the bitter competition for control of

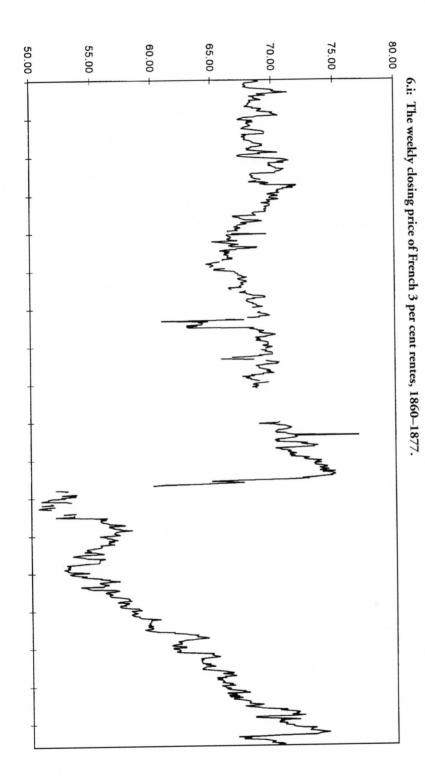

6.i: The weekly closing price of French 3 per cent rentes, 1860–1877.

the remaining 3 billion still to be paid. Once again Bleichröder kept trying to force the pace, having made contact with Pouyer-Quertier when the latter visited Berlin. He pestered Alphonse with more or less hare-brained schemes, all designed to secure for himself a bigger share of the next big operation: a new Franco-German joint-stock bank should be set up in Paris to handle the next loan; the 3 billion should be guaranteed by French railway shares (in other words, French railway shareholders would exchange these for rentes and hand over control of the French rail network to Berlin).[174] Like Henckel von Donnersmarck's proposal for a lottery loan,[175] all these German schemes were ultimately irrelevant: a sudden upsurge of patriotic feeling in France itself—an impatience to end the occupation as soon as possible—made it highly likely that the 1871 rente operation would be repeated. The only question was whether the Paris and London Rothschilds would be able to repeat their earlier coup of controlling the new issue.

At first, Alphonse was sceptical about the possibility of paying the 3 billion ahead of schedule in view of French political instability and the slight deterioration in Franco-German relations which happened in the spring of 1872.[176] By the end of June, however, fear that the Paribas group might steal a march on him galvanised him into action.[177] It was inevitable that the government would be less generous the second time around. In order to secure a repeat of the underwriting system, the bankers had to promise to provide the government with 700 million francs in hard currency. As Alphonse said, this was necessary only "in order to be able to justify a bigger commission."[178] The price of the issue was also set higher—it was offered to the public at 84.5, though the effective net price to the underwriters was 80.5.[179] It was probably also inevitable that the joint-stock banks would succeed in securing a larger participation. Yet once again Alphonse had the best of the bargaining. As in the previous year, only a billion of the total issue of 3.5 billion francs was guaranteed: of this billion, the Rothschild group (that is, the Paris and London Rothschilds, Barings and the *haute banque* firms) took 64.3 per cent, leaving slightly less than a third to the joint-stock banks; the same proportions applied to the 700 million franc foreign currency advance. The two Rothschild houses alone accounted for 282 million of the guaranteed billion and 197.5 million of the 700 million advance—28 per cent of the total in each case.[180]

Despite the fact that most of the transfer in 1872 and 1873 was paid in thaler bills,[181] the German banks continued to play a minor role. Bleichröder even came to Paris in person to combat what he saw as a sinister conspiracy to corner the German market by Hansemann, but neither was really on the inside track: altogether, German subscriptions amounted to just 3 million francs.[182] As for Mayer Carl, he could only grumble: "[W]e know nothing and have only the pleasure of seeing empty letters from our Paris friends with long phrases *pour tout potage*."[183] For the lucky insiders, the profits involved were once again substantial. The commissions amounted to 1.5 per cent on the guaranteed billion (15 million) and 25 million on the 700 million francs of foreign exchange, implying 11.2 million francs for the two Rothschild houses alone. That excludes the large capital gains made as the rentes rose rapidly above the purchase; it seems reasonable to assume that the Rothschilds themselves invested in the issue as well as underwriting it.[184]

Mayer Carl evidently would not have been sorry if the loan had flopped; in fact, as Alphonse had foreseen, the guarantee was even more superfluous than in the previous year, though even he was taken aback at the extent of oversubscription: a factor of around eight.[185] This struck him as "ridiculous," and in the short term that view seemed to be confirmed. Once again, transfer problems depressed the exchanges in late 1872 and rentes sagged to a new post-war low.[186] This time, it was the German government's objection to being paid in bills on Hamburg which caused the difficulty.[187] Yet the oversubscription of July reflected a far from unrealistic market assessment of the rente's medium-term prospects: in the three and a half years between December 1872 (81.5) and March 1877 (107.88), the 5 per cent rente rose more or less uninterruptedly by more than 25 percentage points, prices last seen on the very eve of the Empire's fall.

Nothing could better illustrate the lack of correlation between French financial and political strength in the crisis of 1870–71. We are bound to ask: if France could so swiftly "win the peace" by paying off reparations worth 5 billion francs in the space of just over two years, why had she been so woefully unable to win the war? Why were the French more willing to pay for defeat after the fact than to pay for the chance of victory before war broke out? The only logical conclusion is that the Bonapartist regime should have issued 5 billion francs of rentes to finance rearmament in the late 1860s; could have done so financially, but was unable to do so because of its own political deficiencies.

Soll und Haben

Thus were the spoils delivered to the victor. But what would the victor do with them? From an early stage in the indemnity transfer, Alphonse had expressed doubts about the financial competence of the recipients of reparations. "The Berlin market is in a shocking state," he exclaimed in December 1872. "Where then are the 5 milliards we have paid to these gentlemen? It is said no profit derives from ill-gotten wealth."[188] The crisis which swept through the Central European financial markets in the summer of 1873 seemed to vindicate him entirely. "Our 5 billions have cost them dear," he noted with satisfaction that September.[189]

On the other side of the political divide, Mayer Carl had also had some doubts about the sustainability of the Gründer boom, which resumed with a renewed vigour in the wake of Sedan. In particular, he was disturbed by the proliferation of new joint-stock banks throughout Germany. Of course, his objections to this trend were self-interested. "All these banks," he grumbled in January 1871, "are too glad when they have an opportunity of investing money and showing that they are the only parties who make loans and push us aside."[190] On the other hand, he was right to recognise symptoms of economic overheating, even if he had no real idea of their cause. "The wild speculation in all the new bank shares," he reported in October 1871, "continues to be the chief topic of conversation & nobody understands the mania shown in favour of all these new rubbishing schemes which absorb a good deal of money."[191] "The mania for starting new Banks and Crédit Mobiliers is becoming a regular nuisance," he added a month later, "and will no doubt end by a catastrophe as nobody knows what all these establishments are to do with the money of [their?] subscribers."[192] By May 1872 Mayer Carl was explicitly predicting "a monetary crisis which is not unlikely to take place in consequence of all the rubbishing shares which have been issued and what are floating about and seen to be perfectly unfallable [sic]."[193]

On the other hand, the sheer volume of business in the new Reich more than compensated for the nuisance of increased competition. Even as the new Reich was being proclaimed in January 1871, Mayer Carl was busy with a loan to Württemberg, though on this occasion he was defeated by "Erlanger and all his rubbishing banks."[194] He was more successful when Baden too turned to the capital market in the same year, and also arranged a small loan for the municipality of Ratisbon. Munich, on the other hand, eluded him.[195] Plainly, the old Rothschild dominance in South Germany was a thing of the past. It was therefore of vital importance to Mayer Carl to develop his links to Hansemann and the Disconto-Gesellschaft, and through him to the burgeoning Berlin market. Hansemann, he reminded his English cousins with Victorian over-emphasis, was:

> a *fine* and *great friend of the house* much more so than Bleichröder who is merely a *vain* and *ambitious* fellow hunting after *personal advantages &* *distinctions* which may be of service to him but which cannot be of consequence *to our personal* interests . . . Mr Hansemann is *so sincerely attached to me* that he would never do anything *directly* or *indirectly* to *injure* our interests which you may depend upon . . . Unless you keep up a *friendly understanding with him* you will never be able to do any business here with the Government as he is particularly in favour & his influence is greatly increasing. I can therefore only repeat what I said so often that if we want to act cleverly we ought to be on the best footing with Mr Hansemann & I have every reason to believe that he never does anything *without me* but that he expects the London & Paris houses to be equally on good terms with him.[196]

It was through Hansemann that Mayer Carl became involved in a number of profitable railways, including the Cologne–Minden line. "I am sure that you will be *more* than satisfied," he reported to New Court, which evidently had a share in this business, "& think that *old Charly* is not so stupid as he looks"—a nice indication of the sense of financial inferiority the Frankfurt partners were beginning to feel.[197] His involvement in South German railways also seems to have been linked to Hansemann.[198] It seems that in the early 1870s Mayer Carl was increasingly acting as a satellite of the Disconto-Gesellschaft, the more so with each fresh sign of neglect from London or Paris.

It would be too much to posit a direct causal link between the French indemnity and the crash which brought German finance to a standstill in 1873. After all, it was in Vienna rather than Berlin that the crisis began on May 8–9.[199] Nevertheless, there is no question that German fiscal and monetary policy in the period the indemnity was paid did nothing to check the post-war "mania." "I saw the Finance Minister in the [upper] house," wrote Mayer Carl in March 1872, "& he asked me if I could make use of money as he has so much that he did not know what to do with it."[200] This was a pardonable exaggeration: still, if we accept that the war had cost Germany 220 million thalers, it had in effect generated a budgetary surplus in the form of reparations worth 1.3 billion thalers (5 billion francs). The German government used this money in a number of ways which tended to fuel the stock market boom. Granted, 120 million thalers were put in a "war chest" in the Julius Tower to await the next war—as effective a sterilisation of the money as could have been achieved. But the Germans spent around 60 million on grandiose building projects in newly imperial Berlin, and much of the rest on reducing the debts of the Reich's member states and the North German Confederation. This created additional liquidity in an already buoyant economy.[201]

A related difficulty was the uncertainty about Germany's monetary arrangements. Within the new Reich in 1871 there were at least seven coin systems, mostly silver-based. However, the Liberal bankers like Ludwig Bamberger who took the lead in the monetary debate after 1870 favoured the adoption of an altogether new German currency based on gold, partly because of the fall in the price of silver relative to gold. The first legislative steps towards this were taken as early as October 1871, but it was not until July 1873 that a Coinage Law was passed, and not until March 1875 that a central bank, the Reichsbank, was created to manage the new currency.[202] By that time, the bubble had long since burst. The available statistics point to an increase in the money supply of around 50 per cent in the period 1871–3 and price inflation of a similar order. The crash of 1873 wiped out those gains and drove thousands of firms into bankruptcy.

Was this nemesis after the hubris of Versailles? Alphonse thought so. Yet the financial crisis of 1873 and the subsequent onset of the so-called "Great Depression"—the decline in primary product prices which continued into the 1890s—did not spell the end of French *strategic* vulnerability. As early as January 1874, just four months after the last German troops had left French soil, Thiers' successor the duc Decazes was accusing Germany of planning a new war against France. The following year, Bismarck's mouthpieces in the German press asked "Is war in sight?" unleashing panic on French markets.[203]

The alarm proved to be a false one; possibly Bismarck had never intended anything more than to beat the militarist drum for domestic political reasons. To the Rothschilds, however, what was crucial was the decision of Disraeli and Gorchakov to put aside their differences in Central Asia in the interests of peace in Europe. At least, that was how Disraeli presented it to them. "Last evening," reported Charlotte to her son, "[Dizzy] paid a flying visit to your father, and told him of his immense success in negotiating for the maintenance of peace on the continent."[204] The Prime Minister was, of course, indulging in his customary hyperbole. Still, the difference between his conduct and Gladstone's in 1870–71 can hardly have escaped Lionel's notice. The events of those years revealed two things: that conflicts between the great powers, though hazardous to them as a family, were not unprofitable to them as bankers; and that the key to international stability lay not in Paris, nor in Berlin—but in London.

SEVEN

"The Caucasian Royal Family"

*I could see how strangely like a Royal family the Rothschilds are
in one respect—namely, that they all quarrel with one another,
but are united as against the world.*

SIR CHARLES DILKE, MARCH 1879[1]

In Thomas Mann's 1901 novel *Buddenbrooks*, which depicts the decline and fall of
a Hanseatic merchant family and firm, decadence is detectable in the third generation and fatal in the fourth. It is certainly tempting to write the history of the
Rothschilds after 1878 with this model in mind. As Mayer Amschel's grandsons
died, so leadership passed to a fourth generation which seemed to lack the entrepreneurial drive and financial aptitude which had made the family firm rise and prosper. New educational opportunities distracted them from business. The process of
social assimilation into the traditional aristocracy transported them, physically and
emotionally, from City to country. "A new era has decidedly begun in business,"
Alphonse had written enthusiastically to his cousins in 1865. "Only the young generation which has had a college education is capable of comprehending the exigen-
cies of the times. It is the young generation therefore which should be entrusted
with the direction of the grand financial operations of the epoch."[2] But this young
generation struck contemporaries as epigoni.

The evidence is to hand for the construction of such a narrative. The deaths of
Nat (1870), Anselm (1874), Mayer (1874), Anthony (1876) and Lionel (1879) left
only their younger cousins in Frankfurt and Paris as representatives of the third generation. Of James's sons, Alphonse remained a formidable force in French finance
until his death in 1905, assisted by his younger brother Gustave, but Salomon James
had died at the age of twenty-nine and Edmond played only a minor role in the
business. Of the sons of Carl, Adolph withdrew from the business in 1863 and
Mayer Carl's health began to decline in the later 1870s, leaving the pious and financially unambitious Wilhelm Carl to preside over the last years of the Frankfurt
house after his brother's death in 1886.[3]

Even in old age and illness, those members of the third generation who had been
active partners in the business remained imbued with their father's work ethic. Nat

had been considered an invalid for many years before his death in February 1870: his servant marvelled how "for 18 years he has fought against what to others would have been an insupportable illness." Yet, just hours before his death, "he talked to Alphonse about American stocks and the Russian Loan and . . . a few seconds before he died he told his servants to bring him a cup of tea early in the morning as he wished to have the newspapers read to him."[4] Anthony too always remained first and foremost a banker, though he was overshadowed in the public mind by his more politically active elder brother. He invariably greeted friends and relations with the question "What's the news?"—a true banker's salutation.[5]

For much of his career, Lionel suffered so severely from attacks of rheumatic gout (arthritis would seem the appropriate modern term) that on occasions he had to be carried to the House of Commons gallery to attend debates on Jewish emancipation. "For more than twenty years," *The Times* observed, "he was wheeled from room to room of his house or from his carriage to his office in a chair constructed for the purpose." Yet, as the newspaper also recorded, "up to the last working-day before the day of his death he continued to be the mainspring of a business which had no parallel in magnitude" and it was "on his sagacity and assiduity that the direction of the business chiefly depended." Of course, the paper's recently retired editor Delane was a close family friend, so allowance should perhaps be made for the obituarist's enthusiasm; even so, his comments on Lionel's role and abilities were insightful and are borne out by the performance of the London house under his leadership:

> A business which mainly depends on the delicate and incessant variations of the money market in all parts of the world . . . requires . . . a sort of intuitive instinct for appreciating the effect of variations of exchange, which is, perhaps, hereditary, and cannot, like most forms of ability, be acquired to order. But this is only, as it were, the instrument of calculation, and the qualities upon which its due use depends are far higher. Everything must, of course, depend on obtaining information from all parts of the world, and upon forming a just estimate of it when obtained; and for this is needed not merely a knowledge of men in general, but an almost cosmopolitan knowledge of the peculiarities of various countries and nations. Nor is it sufficient for this capacity of judgement to be exercised on mere matters of commercial exchange. Political prospects are intimately involved in the estimate to be formed of any great monetary transaction, and to appreciate these a close acquaintance is requisite with the course of public affairs throughout the world and with the character of public men. Baron Lionel de Rothschild possessed these qualities in a very eminent degree, and they combined to render him, not merely a successful manager of his great house, but a very considerable figure in the social and political world. *Nothing diverted him from attention to the daily operations of his firm, and almost to the last he held in his hand the threads of all its intricate interests. He was as thorough in its management every day as if he was laying over again the foundation of his house's fortunes.*[6]

Disraeli had no reason to exaggerate when he called Lionel "one of the ablest men I ever knew."[7] He was also one of the richest: when he died he left £2,700,000 (all but £15,000 to his wife and children), to say nothing of the houses at Piccadilly and

Gunnersbury and one of the biggest private art collections of the era.[8] Equally, those who disliked Lionel testified to his devotion to business. The day before he died, he summoned the broker Edward Wagg to his bedside at 148 Piccadilly to tell him: "I have been looking at my fortnightly account and you have made a mistake in the addition."[9] More than three decades later, stories still circulated which implied an almost avaricious trait: the financier Horace Farquhar told Herbert Asquith maliciously (and probably untruthfully) how "the old Jew always used to have on his table in his office in New Court a little chest in wh. he hoarded his pearls, and in the intervals of business handled and fondled them."[10]

The eldest of the third generation, Anselm, shared many of these traits—in particular that asceticism which Max Weber identified as the mainspring of capital accumulation (though he sought its origins in Calvinism). He was a keen reader, an enthusiastic and expert collector of *objets d'art* (which he housed in a specially built gallery in the Renngasse) and an avid theatre-goer with his own box at the opera; but otherwise he lived austerely, occupying only two rooms in the Vienna palace he had inherited from his father, and vacating the castle at Schillersdorf in preference for a small cottage-style house on the estate. He seldom invited guests there.[11] As Hermann Goldschmidt recalled, "he lived the life of an immigrant and a miser. He was averse to any outward displays of wealth, travelled only by hansom cab and never had his own coach and four." So self-effacing and parsimonious was he that he also refused to have his portrait painted. For most of their married life, he and his wife lived apart (mainly, it seems, because she disliked living in Vienna); but unlike his father, Anselm scrupulously avoided sexual liaisons in Austria, confining himself to fleeting dalliances when he visited London and Paris. (His preferred vice was snuff.)[12] He too seemed to his sons to have boundless energy. When hunting for antiques in France and Holland in the summer of 1868, Ferdinand recalled, "he used to rise at 6 o'clock and remain on his legs until dusk, dragging the unfortunate two men [his secretary and his valet] with him shopping and sight-seeing.—I wish he had handed his constitution down to his sons."[13] A good deal of the running of the house was delegated to Goldschmidt—Anselm ignored as far as possible the other employees in the office, speaking French to accentuate his distance from them—but he remained the master, and an exacting one. When angry he would throw his pen across the room and spit.[14] Despite a painful bladder complaint, he too remained active in the business to the last.[15]

It was entirely in keeping with Anselm's old-fashioned style that he requested to be buried "with the greatest simplicity" in Frankfurt. "The funeral was as unpretending as if it had been that of a poor Jew," reported *The Times*. "The corpse was removed from the railway station in a mere carrier's van . . . As the hour of the funeral had been kept secret, comparatively few persons were at the ceremony."[16] Yet this was the man who had left in his will a sum in excess of 50 million thalers—double the assets of the Jesuit order, as Bismarck rather gratuitously pointed out.[17] The contrast could scarcely have been more marked with the funerals of James and of Lionel, whose interment at the recently established Willesden cemetery was attended by a throng of relations, Rothschild agents and brokers, MPs (including Sir William Harcourt and Thomson Hankey) and representatives of numerous Jewish organisations.[18]

The Fourth Generation

It might at first seem odd that it proved difficult to replace the third generation. After all, in an age of high fertility, the fourth generation was inevitably more numerous than the third, and one might have expected to find enough competent businessmen among the forty-four children born into it.[19] Contemporaries were certainly impressed by the sheer number of Rothschilds. In 1859 the Goncourts noted with astonishment that there were approximately seventy-four Rothschilds at dinner following the wedding of Gustave and Cécile Anspach.[20] It was Disraeli who famously declared "that there cannot be too many Rothschilds."[21] Was that not self-evidently true?

Part of the problem was an over-supply of daughters. Though it may seem absurd to us, the third generation was conscious of having difficulty in producing sons: this anxiety is not wholly unintelligible, as the ratio of male to female children in the fourth generation was 17:27. Moreover, no fewer than five of the male children died in infancy.[22] It was partly because none of Carl's sons themselves produced a male heir that the Naples and Frankfurt houses were wound up, the former in 1863, the latter in 1901.

Inevitably, the sons who survived were a step further removed from the ethos of work and calculation on which the family's fortune had been founded. Indeed, even their own mother had a fairly low opinion of the three young men who were now intended to take over the management of the London house. With that harsh candour which she liked to employ, Charlotte wrote as early as 1840 that Natty "was a thin, ugly baby, but that did not signify; he was a boy, and as such most welcome for his father and the whole family. I never could prefer him to his sisters, and nursed him not so well as he ought to have been nursed." By the time he was nine she had made up her mind that he "lack[ed] cordiality and frankness. He is reserved and shy and not generous; in fact he is the only one of my children fond of money for the sake of hoarding it . . . [H]e is constitutionally indolent." In the next six years there was an improvement—he seemed to apply himself to his studies—but "he remain[ed] shy" and Charlotte concluded bluntly: "[H]e will not be a clever, but a very well informed, highly cultivated man."[23]

Following in the footsteps of his Uncle Mayer, Natty went to Cambridge to read moral science (which included moral philosophy, political economy, modern history, general jurisprudence and the laws of England) in October 1859 and seems to have had no difficulty with his work.[24] But he struggled with the commoner's second year examination known as the "Little Go" because of its compulsory mathematical and theological elements.[25] His letters to his parents suggest that he devoted more time to riding with the drag hounds, amateur dramatics and attending debates at the Union (a familiar story), though unlike the rest of the family, he showed almost no interest in art and architecture.[26] If anything captured his attention, it was politics: from an early age he evidently enjoyed discussing political news with his well-informed father.

Though a good beginning for a prospective MP, it could be argued that all this was a poor preparation for a dynamic City career. In particular, Natty's lack of mathematical aptitude would seem to disprove *The Times*'s suggestion that the capacity for financial calculation was hereditary. His parents had expected more, as can be inferred from his self-justifying arguments in favour of hunting and the Amateur Dramatic Company:

> I have found my experience that in order to get on here at all it is absolutely necessary to take two hours at least of violent exercise *per diem*, so that if I do not go with the drag [hounds] I must do something else in the same way . . . The ADC takes up some time, but I have found I do not work one bit more if I do nothing but work and only destroy my health and make life up here a curse and a plague . . . I came up here unprepared and cannot expect to do much. If I am never seen, people will expect more and at the end of the time set me down for a greater fool than I am.

Natty managed to pass the Little Go, but despite intensive "coaching" and encouragement from the Master of Trinity, William Whewell, and the Hulsean Professor of Divinity, Joseph Lightfoot (later Bishop of Durham), he seemed unlikely to secure honours, and left Cambridge without taking his final examinations at the end of Michaelmas 1862.[27] After being elected to the Athenaeum (1860), entering the House of Commons as MP for Aylesbury (1865), becoming an officer in the Buckinghamshire Yeomanry and inheriting his uncle's baronetcy (1876), Natty seemed destined for a political rather than a financial career. Thus it was for the evidence he gave before a Commons committee that he first won applause in the City. Charlotte was evidently surprised.[28]

It may of course be asked why she and Lionel so desperately wished their sons to be academically successful: despite Alphonse's faith in "college education," there is no obvious reason why an honours degree from Cambridge would have been an advantage in the City. On the other hand, the proportion of City bankers educated at public school, Oxford or Cambridge rose markedly in the course of the nineteenth century.[29] Charlotte urged Leo to "find an hour or two in the course of the day to write English exercises . . . [as] it would enable you, even in the practical routine of New Court life to draw up contracts, make statements upon important financial transactions, and furnish those great papers, which should really not be drawn up by clerks." But her real aim, one suspects, was less to prepare Leo for "the real business of life . . . at New Court" than to give him the classical education she herself had missed and craved—and in so doing to add another trophy to the Rothschild collection. A degree, like a seat in the Commons, had no functional value to the Rothschilds as bankers, but was a prize in their campaign for complete social parity with the Gentile elite. "University honors," she lectured her youngest son in 1865, "are excellent credentials; if they do not prove the winner to be possessed of great gifts and remarkable talents, they prove that he has applied and exerted himself to acquire knowledge, that he has a firm will, energy, assiduity and perseverance, and those are valuable qualities." Two years later, she reverted to the same theme:

> distinctions achieved at the University must be a passport, a letter of introduction to the favorable opinion of the world.—In your own family, in business, in society, in the House of Commons, at home and abroad, and in all classes of the community—a man who has taken a good degree at Cambridge or Oxford is more highly thought of, and this

good opinion acts as an encouragement to every useful exertion throughout life.[30]

She and Lionel were furious when Leo lent some money to a friend, for this was a betrayal of social origins which Cambridge was partly supposed to efface:

> I always thought you had common sense, and never thought you silly enough to advance five hundred pounds to a stupid scamp, who has hardly as many shillings in the world that he can call his own. [D]angerous as it is for all individuals to lend money—it is far more so for any one, who bears the name of Rothschild.—Indeed I have not expressed myself correctly; it is absolutely impossible that any person, any member, great or insignificant[,] of our family should think, for one single instant of anything so absurd.—the loan of money is perfectly certain to change a friend into an enemy.—Nobody would think of returning money to a Rothschild, but would shun the lender in consequence, and probably for ever—and we might sacrifice enormous sums without doing any good, or giving any pleasure.—I have never in the whole course of my existence, lent any one a single six pence;—if a gift can be of service, well and good; is [*sic*] the petitioner too proud to accept five or ten pounds let him, if he can refund the money, give it to a charity. I have acted upon that principle all my life—and thank God, have no imprudence to regret . . .
>
> PS Why can't you lock yourself up . . . and keep away from all the idle, lazy, good-for-nothing young men, who infest Cambridge, and steal your precious time, your good intentions and your energy away[?][31]

But academic credentials eluded this generation. At best Natty did not disgrace himself at Cambridge; his younger brothers did rather worse. Charlotte may have been anxious that Alfred "should visit Cambridge and distinguish himself there," but after only a single year (1861–2) he was taken ill and never returned.[32] Efforts were made to introduce Alfred to the world of philanthropy and politics: under Anthony's supervision, he sat on a City committee "for the Relief of distress" in the hard winter of 1867. "I hope and believe that your brother will attend," wrote his anxious mother. "It will do [Alfred] good to accustom himself to popular meetings, and, in time, he may perhaps become reconciled to the idea of entering parliament, which, at present, seems so repugnant to his tastes."[33] In 1868 he became the first Jew to be elected to the Court of Directors of the Bank of England, another appointment he owed entirely to his family rather than his ability. But he conspicuously failed to make this the position of influence which Alphonse made his role as regent of the Banque de France.[34] Alfred lived the life of a *fin de siècle* aesthete, at once effete and faintly risqué. Max Beerbohm's cartoon—*A quiet evening in Seymour Place. Doctors consulting whether Mr Alfred may, or may not, take a second praline before bedtime*—captures the former quality (see illustration 7.i). So does Alfred's somewhat feeble *bon mot* when another Bank of England director (reflecting on Anselm's will) "suggested that in fifty years the Times would announce that your brother had left all Buckinghamshire. 'You make a mistake' was the reply to a very

7.i: Max Beerbohm, *A quiet evening in Seymour Place. Doctors consulting whether Mr Alfred may, or may not, take a second praline before bedtime.*

unseemly remark, 'believe me I shall leave a great deal more, I shall leave the world.'"[35]

Leopold (Leo) was, if anything, an even greater disappointment, if only because Lionel and Charlotte pinned their last remaining hopes for academic success on him. Despite—perhaps because of—a relentless bombardment of parental exhortations and reproofs throughout his Cambridge career, Leo had to postpone his Little Go, was marked down for his limited knowledge of Christian theology and scraped a third in his final exams. His mother feared that he would "pass for the most ignorant, most thoughtless, and most shallow of human beings" and was mortified to hear her friend Matthew Arnold say "that he cannot believe you are or ever will be a reading man, as you talked of going to Newmarket which he thought was a pity, as you seemed to him made for better things. I assure you I am not exaggerating—and that Mr. Arnold reverted three times to the race-course."[36] Lionel, who like Charlotte had hoped to see him in "Class I and very high up," later commented acidly: "Your examiners were quite right in saying you were a good hand at guessing."[37] It is hard not to sympathise with Leo and his brothers. "Dear Papa does not expect any so-called news from your pen," ran a typical letter from home in 1866,

> but he wishes to know how you spend your time, at what hour you separate yourself from your beloved pillow, when you breakfast, with a description of the breakfast-table and of the ingredients of that earliest

meal, how many hours you devote to serious conscientious studies, divided into preparations and lessons, what authors you are reading in Greek and Latin, in prose and poetry, how much leisure you devote to lighter reading such as modern poetry and history, how much, or how little to still lighter literature, such as romances and novels, in French and English—how much exercise you take.[38]

Any university teacher knows how counter-productive this kind of parental pressure can be. If Leo preferred to idle away his time in the company of "idle, lazy, good-for-nothing young men" like Cyril Flower,[39] it may partly have been a reaction against his mother and father's incessant lecturing. The more desperately Charlotte urged him to "study something—drawing, painting, music, languages"—the more his interests turned elsewhere, principally to horse-racing.[40] In the end, the only "English" Rothschild of this generation to secure a university degree (in law) was Nat's son James Edouard, who grew up and studied in France.[41] It can hardly be claimed that he was an advertisement for higher education. An ardent bibliophile who accumulated a large collection of rare books, obsessively excluding volumes with the slightest blemish, he is said to have committed suicide in 1881 at the age of thirty-six, perhaps the first Rothschild in whom the desire to accumulate valuable objects took on a dysfunctional character.[42]

Of course, Leo's devotion to the Turf had a precedent. His uncle Anthony had been a keen racegoer in his youth and his uncle Mayer was even more of an equine enthusiast. Indeed, it was said of Mayer in the 1860s that he was "so constantly away and amusing himself that his partners' and nephews' . . . softly modulated voices had become inaudible to him."[43] In "the Baron's Year" of 1871, his horses won four of the five "classic" races: the Derby, the Oaks, the Thousand Guineas and the St Leger. Eight years later, Leo himself was the owner of the Derby winner when his little-known horse Sir Bevys beat the Earl of Rosebery's Visconti into third place (though Leo had used the bogus name "Mr Acton" to conceal his identity). He nearly won the Derby again with St Frusquin in 1896 (the horse came second to the Prince of Wales's Persimmon) and did win it a second time in 1904 with St Amant. This was a symbol more of continuity than of decadence, then; the fact that he could earn as much as £46,766 in prize money in a single season may even be taken as a sign of traditional acumen.[44] At the same time, sport was now an integral part of City life—witness the cricket match between a Stock Exchange XI and Leo's own XI in 1880, a classic example of late-Victorian corporate hospitality.[45] Another novelty was Leo's enthusiasm for motor cars, the supreme rich man's toy of the *fin-de-siècle*.[46] There was also something new about the extravagance of having a racehorse like St Frusquin modelled in silver by Fabergé (with twelve bronze replicas for friends).[47]

The sons of Anselm evinced similar tendencies. The eldest, Nathaniel (b. 1836), studied at Brünn but quarrelled bitterly with his father, who considered him spendthrift and financially incompetent.[48] Ferdinand (b. 1839) showed even less interest in the family business, preferring to spend his time in England, where both his mother and wife had been born and raised. He was quite candid about his lack of the most important of Rothschild traits. "It is an odd thing," he wrote forlornly in 1872, "but whenever I sell any stock it is sure to rise and if I buy any it generally falls."[49] That left Salomon Albert (b. 1844), usually known in the family as "Sal-

bert." Albert had studied at Bonn as well as at Brünn "with great energy, perseverance, devotion and success" but, when his father was taken ill in 1866, seemed
"over-anxious, over-alarmed, dreadfully frightened at [the prospect of] his undi-
vided responsibility" for the Vienna house.[50] When Anselm finally died eight years
later, he left most of his real estate and art collection to Nathaniel and Ferdinand
and only his share of the family partnership to Albert, who regarded himself as
having been "not very well treated."[51] In short, Albert had to be forced into the business, *faute de mieux*.

In Paris, of course, it was the third generation rather than the fourth which came
to power after James's death in 1868. Yet here too there seemed to be a falling off.
Part of the problem was that James had been such a domineering father. Feydeau
commented that James had "never delegated the smallest part of his enormous
responsibility to his children or his employees." "What submissiveness on the part of
his sons," he marvelled ironically. "What a feeling of hierarchy! What respect! They
would not permit themselves, even with respect to the most minimal transaction, to
sign—with that cabalistic signature which binds the house—without consulting
their father. 'Ask Papa,' you are told by men of forty, who are almost as experienced
as their father, no matter how trifling the inquiry you address to them."[52] The
Goncourts noticed the same tendency.[53]

The eldest son Alphonse—who was forty-one when his father died—seems to
have withstood the years of paternal dominance the best, suggesting once again that
it was the first-born of the third generation who was most likely to inherit or imbibe
the mentality of the Judengasse. Educated at the Collège Bourbon, Alphonse had an
enthusiasm for art (and for stamp-collecting), but he never allowed these interests to
distract him from the serious business of the bank.[54] In March 1866, he was asked
by a friend after dinner "why, when he was so rich, he worked like a negro to become
more so. 'Ah!' he replied, 'You don't know the pleasure of feeling heaps of Christians
under one's boots.' " Like Lionel and Anselm, he took pleasure in austerity: when he
was observed in 1891 taking the train from Nice to Monte Carlo (where he "played
very little") it was his very ordinariness which was remarkable: "He waits for the
train sitting on a bench, like any common mortal, and smoking his cigar"—albeit
watched like a hawk by the conductor who stood ready to open the door of his compartment as soon as he showed any sign of boarding.[55] Gustave too shared many of
the attitudes of the older Rothschilds. As Mérimée remarked wryly when he dined
with him and his wife at Cannes in 1867, "he seemed to have a good deal of religion
and to think on the subject of money like the rest of his house." When he later
heard that Gustave had impulsively left for Nice, he had no doubt he had sub-let his
villa in Cannes at a profit.[56]

It was James's younger sons who struggled. The Goncourts observed in 1862 how
imperiously Salomon James (b. 1835) was treated by his father. After losing a million francs at the bourse, he:

> received this letter from the father of millions: "Mr Salomon Rothschild
> will go to spend the night at Ferrières, where he will receive instructions
> which concern him." The next day, he received the order to leave for
> Frankfurt. Two years passed in the counting house there; he believed his
> penance was over; he wrote to his father who replied: "Mr Salomon's

business is not yet finished." And a new order sent him to spend a couple of years in the United States.[57]

This was a caricature but one based on reality, as a letter from James to his elder sons in August 1861 indicates. Offering his sons 100,000 francs apiece of new Piedmontese bonds, he explicitly ordered that Salomon should have "nothing to do with realising them and should give the matter no thought at all, as I wish to avoid at any price giving him an opportunity to speak with brokers or coming once again into contact with the open market . . . I do not want to allow ideas of speculation to enter his head again."[58] He was never admitted into the partnership as an *associé*.[59]

Just three years later, Salomon was dead—killed, so the Goncourts heard, "by the stress of speculating at the bourse—a Rothschild dead from the stress of money!"[60] Alas for poetic justice, it seems to have been a horse rather than the bourse which precipitated his heart failure. As Charlotte reported:

> [P]oor Salomon's uncontrollable love of excitement was the result of the ever agitated condition of his heart and circulation. He was at the races last Sunday, and came home much fatigued, from having driven a spirited horse, which nearly pulled his arms off. In the middle of the night he woke covered with cold perspiration, and seized with a great difficulty of breathing; he rushed to the window for air—but the indisposition passed off—and he was I believe tolerably well unto Wednesday, when the fatal attack seized him. From the beginning the Doctors declared that there was no hope, for the poor patient began to spit blood, and the fluttering of his heart was most distressing; he was conscious until within a few moments of his end, and did not seem to be aware of his condition.[61]

The youngest son, Edmond (b. 1845), fared better; but as late as 1864 his eldest brother dismissed him as "a child, who ought not to go into the bureau for the next five or six years." A studious young man, Edmond passed his baccalaureate "not only satisfactorily but brilliantly" (to Charlotte's envious chagrin) and was rewarded by being allowed to visit Egypt—the beginning of a lifelong interest in the Middle East.[62]

In part, the seeming decadence of the new generation was a reflection of the sheer number of Rothschilds there now were, only a minority of whom were required to enter the partnership and work, but all of whom had the means to live like princes. Apart from anything else, that meant a great deal of work for architects. The acquisition of country estates and the building of country houses, as we have seen, predated the 1870s and 1880s by several decades. There was therefore nothing qualitatively new about the way that Natty and his wife Emma regarded their house at Tring; indeed, having been bought by Lionel for his newly married son, Tring in many ways represented a continuation of the older generation's aspirations.[63] Like Ferdinand's Waddesdon and Alfred's Halton—the other English properties bought or built on in this period—it seemed to contemporaries to represent just another addition to the family's territorial empire in and around the Vale of Aylesbury.[64] Nor could Natty resist the family habit of altering existing buildings beyond recognition: with the assistance of the architect George Devey, he managed to turn an elegant

Wren house into a rather stolid, institutional Victorian pile.[65] Leo did something similar to Ascott, which he acquired from his uncle Mayer, using the same firm of architects to remodel the house in the mock Tudor style.[66] Both Natty and Leo also followed the fashion for building picturesque new cottages for tenants and employees on their estates; indeed, Natty took pains to create a kind of paternalistic "welfare state" at Tring.[67]

It was the quantity rather than the quality of such Rothschild investments in real estate which was new. The more numerous French Rothschilds acquired, modernised or built from scratch at least eight new country houses in this period, including Edmond's S-shaped château d'Armainvilliers, built in the Anglo-Norman rustic style by Langlais and Emile Ulmann in the 1880s.[68] In Austria Nathaniel bought two new country estates: one at Reichenau, where the architects Armand-Louis Bauqué and Emilio Pio built the polychromatic château Penelope, and another at Enzesfeld near Vöslau, which he acquired from Graf Schönburg.[69] His brother Albert also bought Langau, an estate in the Kalkalpen mountains in Lower Austria,[70] and their sister Alice had two houses built: Eythrope on the Waddesdon estate and a villa in Grasse in the south of France. Finally, in the late 1880s, the remaining Frankfurt Rothschilds, Wilhelm Carl and Hannah Mathilde, built a villa at Königstein in the Taunus hills, also using Bauqué and Pio.[71] There were at least seven new town houses too.[72] Mention should also perhaps be made of the reconstruction of the original Rothschild house "zum grünen Schild" in 1884 at the time the remainder of the Judengasse was torn down: the Rothschilds consciously sought to preserve it as a monument to their ghetto origins.[73] As in the past, styles and architects were swapped within the family regardless of national borders. The only real difference between the third and fourth generations, perhaps, was the preference for French architects and styles of the 1870s and 1880s, compared with the Anglophilia of the 1850s—a trend exemplified by Destailleur's work for both Ferdinand and Albert.

Similarly, more Rothschilds meant more art collections. In fact, the previous generation had probably made more numerous acquisitions and accumulated bigger collections; but the division of these between their heirs gave each an incentive to acquire more. This was without question the period when the Rothschilds became the world's leading art buyers, driving up prices of the artists and genres they coveted to unprecedented heights at the major sales of the 1880s. The Blenheim, Leigh Court and Fountaine sales all saw big Rothschild purchases, to the disquiet of (among others) Sir James Robinson, Keeper of Queen's Pictures—though Charlotte herself believed that the Marlborough collection should be bought for the nation.[74] This mania for art had its grotesque side. In 1870 Ferdinand paid £6,800 for a damascened shield by George de Gys which had cost barely £250 twenty-eight years before. In 1878 Edmond paid between £24,000 and £30,000 for a Sèvres-clad commode designed for Mme du Barry, a mistress of Louis XV; it had cost her just £3,200. Two years later, Mayer Carl paid the Merkel family of Nuremberg £32,000 for a parcel-gilt and enamelled standing cup made in 1550 by the Nuremberg silversmith Wenzel Jamnitzer, making it the dearest work of art that had ever been sold. Yet by 1911, when much of his collection of silverware was sold, only fourteen out of eighty-nine lots fetched more than £1,500. Both Ferdinand and Gustave spent in excess of £7,000 on two oval enamel dishes at the Fountaine sale in 1884, while Ferdinand and Alphonse spent more than a quarter of a million pounds apiece for three (supposed) works by Rubens in the Duke of Marlborough's collection. It was the first time any picture in history had fetched more than £20,000.[75] Fifteen years later, Edmond went still further, spending £48,000 on the duc de Choiseul's ludicrously ornate bureau (previous owners included Talleyrand and Metternich).[76] Even Natty—reputedly uninterested in art—could not resist adding to the collection of eighteenth-century English works he had inherited from his father. In 1886 he paid around £20,000 for Reynolds's *Garrick between Tragedy and Comedy* in the sale of the 2nd Earl of Dudley's collection.[77] Leo too added to the thirty-six paintings he inherited from his parents, though his tastes were more eclectic, ranging from Boucher to Stubbs, from Franz Snyders to Hogarth (*The Harlot's Progress: Quarrels with her Protector*).[78]

What was qualitatively new was the priority which certain members of the new generation—Alfred, Nathaniel and Ferdinand in particular—gave their country houses, their gardens and their art collections. In itself, the house designed in the French seventeenth-century style for Alfred at Halton by William Rogers (built between 1882 and 1888) was no more spectacular than Mentmore; indeed, its main hall was smaller.[79] It was the novelties like the private circus ring, bowling alley, ice-skating rink, indoor swimming pool and Indian pavilion which struck visitors as faintly absurd. Nor was Alfred's collection of paintings and works of art more impressive than his father's. The Dutch masters, the eighteenth-century English and French paintings, the Sèvres porcelain, the French furniture, the silver—these had all been to the taste of the older generation. Although he bought over 160 new paintings in all (compared with the thirty-eight he inherited), they represented variations on his father's favourite themes (Greuze, Romney, Reynolds, Gainsborough, Cuyp). The only real shift was Alfred's evident preference for the French eighteenth century.[80] It was the fact that he published a lavishly bound and illustrated two-volume catalogue of the collection which was new; the fact that he accumulated such an immense amount of Sèvres (including sixty vases and objects and six full services); and perhaps also the enthusiasm for female portraits. Nor was Alfred the first Rothschild to show an interest in music (he composed six piano pieces entitled *Boutons des Roses* in honour of Mayer Carl's daughters); but he was surely the first to conduct his own orchestra. The older Rothschilds had not been above ostentatious displays, but it is hard to imagine any of them dressing up as a circus ringmaster, complete with top hat, blue frock coat and lavender gloves, or wielding a diamond-studded boxwood baton.[81] Small wonder some guests were repelled by "the hideousness of the things, the showiness! the sense of lavish wealth, thrust up your nose . . . the ghastly coarseness of the sight."[82] Sir Algernon West, Gladstone's secretary, dismissed it as "an exaggerated nightmare of gorgeousness and senseless and ill-applied magnificence"; his successor Edward Hamilton agreed. "The decorations," he commented, "are sadly overdone, and one's eyes long to rest on something which is not all gilt and gold."[83] David Lindsay was more contemptuous: Alfred, he recalled, had been "tinged with the tarnish of wealth."[84]

Designed by Destailleur in a style which mixed Renaissance and eighteenth-century French elements, Ferdinand's house at Waddesdon proved far from easy to build on the sandy and poorly drained terrain he had chosen; but the result was a triumph, arguably the greatest of the Rothschild houses. It had (and has) magnificent gardens, with fifty greenhouses and at least as many staff: the gardens alone cost his sister Alice £7,500 a year to maintain when she inherited Waddesdon in 1898, and a further £10,000 to maintain the other grounds, including the farm and dairy.[85] Inside, there was a glittering collection, including Dutch works by Cuyp, de Hooch and ter Borch as well as English paintings by Romney, Reynolds and Gainsborough (whom Ferdinand did much to make fashionable).[86]

Yet Waddesdon—a Loire château in deepest Buckinghamshire—was not to every taste. Gladstone's daughter Mary also felt "oppressed with the extreme gorgeousness and luxury" when she visited.[87] The Liberal Lord politician Richard Haldane, who acted as a Rothschild legal adviser for many years, mocked the preciousness of Ferdinand's hospitality. "I do love all seemly luxury," he declared in 1898. "When lying in bed in the mornings it gives me great satisfaction when a lacquey softly enters the room and asks whether I will take tea, coffee, chocolate or cocoa. This privilege is accorded to me in the houses of all my distinguished friends: but it is only at Waddesdon that on saying I prefer tea, the valet further enquires whether I fancy Ceylon, Souchong or Assam." David Lindsay remarked on the way "Baron Ferdinand['s] hands always itch with nervousness":

> [He] walks about at times petulantly, while jealously caring for the pleasure of his guests. I failed to gather that his priceless pictures give him true pleasure. His clock for which he gave £25,000, his escritoire for which £30,000 was paid, his statuary, his china, and his superb collection of jewels, enamels and so forth ("gimcrack" he calls them)—all these things give him meagre satisfaction; and I felt that the only pleasure he derives from them is gained when he is showing them to his friends. Even then one sees how bitterly he resents comment which is ignorant or inept . . . [I]t is in the gardens and the shrubberies that he is happy . . . It is only when among his shrubs and orchids that the nervous hands of Baron Ferdinand are at rest.[88]

Ferdinand's often neurotic letters to another close friend, the Earl of Rosebery, give a similar impression. Even by the standards of the period, this was a highly charged relationship, though it seems that Ferdinand's passionate feelings were not wholly requited. He summed his own personality up well when he told Rosebery in 1878: "I am a lonely, suffering and occasionally a very miserable individual despite the gilded and marble rooms in which I live."[89] Another friend, Edward Hamilton, wrote an ambivalent memoir following Ferdinand's death in 1898 which deserves to be quoted at length:

> There was no one of late years of whom I have seen more, or from whom I had received greater and more uniform kindnesses. He always had a room for me at Waddesdon and a cabin on board his yacht . . . Though presumably he had to buy his experience when he was young, I believe he was less "taken in" than almost any other collector. The only times when his taste sometimes failed was in his choice of presents to others . . . [He] was not open-handed like other members of the family, for he disliked parting with shillings . . . and had a horror of being *done* . . . He had rather an unfortunate manner, and was not infrequently gauche. He gave and took offence easily; but *au fond* was most kind-hearted and loyal as a friend. No man was more uniformly glad to see one . . . and gave one the heartiest of welcomes. Having lived so much alone, and having at his command everything that he wanted, he was

rather selfishly disposed, which is not to be wondered at. The spoilt child became the spoilt man . . . His leading characteristic was perhaps his impulsive and impatient nature. He was always in a hurry. He did not eat but devoured. He did not walk but ran . . . He could not wait for anybody or anything . . . There were some curious contradictions about him. He was very nervous about himself and sent for a doctor on the smallest provocation; but he often declined to follow the doctor's advice. He took great care of himself as a rule, and yet he would often commit imprudences. He was proud of his race and his family; and liked talking about his predecessors as if he had an illustrious ancestry and the bluest of bloods . . . I doubt if he ever was a really happy man.[90]

This gives a good flavour not only of Ferdinand's character but of the often ambiguous quality of the relationships between members of the family and members of the political elite.

Like Alfred and Ferdinand, Nathaniel devoted most of his energies to houses, art and his own delicate sensibilities. The Renaissance style *palais* he built in the Theresianumgasse was one of the great Rothschild town houses; according to one account, he ran out of money at an early stage and had to borrow a million gulden from his father. (This did not stop him later spending tens of thousands of gulden on imported roses from Naples.) Inside, it was almost entirely French in style (one of the reception rooms by the sculptor François-Antoine Zoegger was especially ornate) and the art collection was the familiar mix: paintings by Greuze, Reynolds, Rembrandt and Van Dyck and numerous articles of furniture associated with Marie-Antoinette: in short, "le goût Rothschild" epitomised.[91] Like Alfred, Nathaniel had his own orchestra; like Ferdinand, he lavished attention on his gardens, especially the park and hothouses at Hohe Warte created for him in 1884 by Bauqué and Pio and Jean Girette.[92] And—predictably—Nathaniel was an excessively sensitive soul. A hypochondriac, he was especially prone to insomnia. Indeed, according to Hermann Goldschmidt, it was his search for a place conducive to sleep which led him to buy both the Reichenau and Enzesfeld estates, though he stayed only one night in the latter, leaving by the first train when he heard of the locality's reputation for epidemics. When cruising in his 4 million gulden English-built yacht, he refused to sail too far from the coast for fear of drowning.[93]

This is not to disparage the Rothschilds' collective contribution to the arts in this period. As a trustee of the National Gallery and the Wallace Collection, Alfred put his connoisseur's expertise to public use, just as Ferdinand bequeathed some of the more unusual pieces which he had inherited from his father's *Schatzkammer* to the British Museum, along with some he himself had collected.[94] Alphonse too made a substantial public contribution to the museums of the Third Republic. Elected a member of the Académie des beaux-arts in 1885, he not only built up an impressive private collection of mainly Dutch masters, but also donated around 2,000 works—including pieces by contemporary artists like Rodin—to 150 different museums.[95] The point is that for Alfred, Ferdinand and Nathaniel the aesthetic had taken over from the ascetic. It was a transformation hinted at in Oscar Wilde's short story "The Model Millionaire, a note of admiration," published in 1887, which describes how an impoverished young man-about-town gives a sovereign to a miserable old beggar whose portrait an artist friend is painting. The "beggar" turns out to be a disguised "Baron Hausberg," "one of the richest men in Europe . . . [who] could buy all

London to-morrow without overdrawing his account . . . has a house in every capital [and] dines off gold plate." He is also the artist's patron, having commissioned him "to paint him a beggar." (Predictably, the Baron repays the young man's generosity by providing him with the £10,000 he needs to marry his beloved.)[96] Here a classic Rothschild anecdote is translated into the idiom of the *fin de siècle:* "the model millionaire" has become a benevolent artistic patron, far removed from the origin of his millions—even if it is a little hard imagining Alfred dressing up as a beggar, even for the sake of a practical joke.

Partners

The question nevertheless remains how far all these symptoms of "decadence" actually affected the performance of the Rothschilds as bankers. Anecdotal evidence suggests that they did. When the ambitious young Hamburg banker Max Warburg arrived to serve a part of his apprenticeship at New Court in the 1890s, he was firmly told by Alfred: "A gentleman is not to be found in the office before eleven and never stays beyond four."[97] According to a Rothschild employee who joined the bank after the First World War, Leo's routine was to arrive at 11 a.m., go to lunch at 1.30 p.m. and return home at 5 p.m.; Alfred generally arrived at 2 p.m., lunched at 3.30–4 p.m. and spent much of the remainder of the afternoon sleeping on a sofa in the partners' room.[98] Although he worked a good deal harder, Natty too gave the impression of being a reluctant banker. Asked if he had a formula for financial success, Natty habitually replied, "Yes, by selling too soon"—an attitude which has sometimes been seen as indicative of excessive risk-aversion.[99] He grumbled to Rosebery about having to remain at the office like "a solitary hermit" after the end of the London "season."[100] Competitors were scathing about New Court as they had never been before. Edward Baring commented that the Rothschilds had become "so unreasonable and lazy that it is difficult to ensure a business being properly carried through under their direction. They refuse to look into new things and their intelligence and capacity is not of a high order."[101] Ernest Cassel, one of the dynamic newcomers to the City in the 1890s, was even more dismissive: the brothers, he declared in 1901, were "absolutely useless & not remarkable for intelligence."[102]

To be sure, the London Rothschilds had an invaluable assistant in the "ever industrious" form of another young Hamburger, Carl Meyer, who became one of the confidential clerks in the 1880s. Meyer's letters to his wife suggest that outside the partners' room business at New Court continued to be conducted at a frenetic pace. "I have been working ever since this morning like a nigger," he told her in a typical series of letters from the mid-1880s:

> His Lordship [Natty] *asked* me to lunch with him in the private dining-room—so you may imagine how I have worked . . . I have been extremely busy again all day long and shall continue to be so if I want to get away on Friday evening. But it *must* be done . . . I have very little to tell you, except the old story that I can hardly hold my pen, so busy have I been all day long . . . I am really too beastly overworked.[103]

Meyer was a regular guest at the partners' lunches not for the sake of his small talk but because these were intelligence-gathering exercises to which other bankers, brokers and civil servants were invited.[104] Yet when he sought promotion to procurist in

1890 (asking for £6,000 a year, the right to sign for the firm and his own private office) he was turned down and his resignation was accepted in 1897. According to City gossip, the brothers felt he was getting "too big for his boots." He left to work with Ernest Cassel.[105]

This *de haut en bas* treatment of subordinates was endemic. In 1905 Carl Meyer heard that Alfred was "becoming more unbearable than ever to the staff and treats men of 30 years service like office boys." Stockbrokers also chafed at such treatment. As Alfred Wagg of Helbert Wagg recalled, "an interview with Lord Rothschild had to be amazingly rapid . . . He came in, placed a watch on his desk, and intimated that the interview would last five minutes, or three, or even less." On one occasion, Natty asked the broker Fred Cripps the price of Rio Tinto shares. Having heard the answer, he said: "You are wrong by a quarter of a point." To this Cripps not unreasonably replied: "Why did you ask me if you already knew?" "There was," he recalled, "an awful silence in the room. I was utterly crestfallen, and under cover of the stifled hush I rapidly retreated." Alfred Wagg had a similar experience in 1912, when he went to inform Natty that his firm was to leave the stock exchange:

> On arriving at New Court, I asked to see Lord Rothschild privately and he came to see me in a little room at the back of the building. I gave him the letter [explaining the firm's withdrawal], the terms of which couldn't have been nicer. He sat down and read it attentively. He then got up saying, "Well, you know your own business best," and walked out of the room. Not one word of good wishes or of regret that the hundred years of intimate connection between the two firms was to cease.

As we shall see, Fred Cripps was not wide of the mark when he commented on the quasi-royal quality of an "audience" with Natty: "One waited in an ante-room before being ushered into the presence, and then one filed through as though it were Buckingham Palace."[106] This kind of thing struck those on the receiving end as both anachronistic and out of proportion to the firm's relative financial importance.

Similar charges of complacency have been levelled against the French house for the same period. In 1875 Henri Germain of the Crédit Lyonnais remarked that Alphonse brought to business questions "a sort of dignity which was not conducive to success. He never puts himself out, he always waits for people to come and find him."[107] Palmade has argued that by this time the Rothschilds were "on the wane," yielding their primacy in French economic life to industrialists like Schneider.[108] A study published in 1914 observed that although the Rothschild name continued to figure in major loans issued on the French market, it was actually the deposit banks which now placed most of the new bonds. It retained its "moral" influence—especially where diplomatic factors were important—but the Paris house's real financial power was allegedly declining.[109]

There is evidence to support these views in the partners' own correspondence: repeated complaints about competition from rivals, for example. "Others have become Millionaires," grumbled Mayer Carl in 1869, "& . . . the public laughs at our constant stupidity." "The fact is," he continued morosely the following year,

> that all these associations [meaning joint-stock banks] are so strong and find every body to support them that *they do not want to us* [and] *are too glad if we leave it all to them* as the public does not care any more about

names & merely wants profit . . . It is useless to . . . fancy that our position is the same which it was 30 years ago. Unless we want to be perfectly isolated we must pull with others & I have no doubt that you are
of the same opinion as all these banks try to oppose us whenever they
can and do not mind what sacrifice they make to show that they are just
as powerful & influential than [sic] we are . . . [Y]ou have no idea how
great the competition is & how difficult our position becomes in consequence of all these new banks who merely want to show that they can
turn us out.[110]

Nor was this merely a temporary feature of the *Gründerzeit*. In 1906, Natty
inveighed—with more than a hint of envy—against his former pupil "Warburg at
Hamburg who resembles the frog in the fable & is swollen up with vanity & the
belief in his own power to control the European markets, & interest all big houses in
any & every syndicate."[111] There were also occasional expressions of complacency.
"I share your opinion, my dear Alfred," wrote Alphonse in 1891, "not to become
apprehensive of competition nor of threatening Finance Ministers. We should do
only business which suits us and under conditions convenient to us."[112] "We are
glad to go on in our old humdrum & jog trot way," wrote Natty in 1906 (in a letter
expressing criticism of the methods of the Crédit Lyonnais), "& are quite satisfied . . . No doubt Monsieur Germain was a very able administrator & wonderfully
good at organisation; but we here were old fashioned enough to believe that the
system on which he transacted his business was essentially vicious."[113]

Yet—as we shall see—it is not absolutely clear that the Rothschild houses *did* fare
all that badly after 1878 in terms of profits and capital (figures for which were, of
course, unavailable to contemporaries outside the partnership). In fact, the continuing effectiveness of key figures—in particular Natty, Alphonse and Albert—to some
extent compensated for the feebleness of the likes of Alfred, Ferdinand and
Nathaniel. To be sure, there were disagreements and even quarrels between the partners; but that was nothing new. If there was a problem it was that the world was no
longer ideally suited to the activities of a multinational private bank with bases in
London, Paris, Frankfurt and Vienna. Conflicts of interest between the various
houses had always been a feature of the Rothschild system; but from the 1860s they
became progressively more and more acute and ultimately ended in the disintegration of the partnership system in the early 1900s. Though personal factors played
some part in this, it was primarily a consequence of economic and political events
beyond their control: the segmentation of the European capital market, the political
effects of the wars of 1859–71 and the reorientation of British and French foreign
investment to extra-European markets.

The theory of the Rothschild system continued to be enunciated regularly.
"Where all four Rothschild houses act in their own names," declared Mayer Carl in
1862, "they truly need no associates."[114] The best response to increased competition, wrote Alphonse the following year, was "to tighten once again the ties which
unite our houses and pull together all our forces with a common thread."[115] "We
must stick together," James declared in 1865, "but in order to do that each must go
hand in hand with the other to be sure that there is no difference between the different parts of the business and that one house encourages the other and keeps it
accurately informed about its business and neither one nor the other tries to draw

everything to itself."[116] His will was perhaps the final expression of this philosophy of parternship by one who had imbibed it directly from Mayer Amschel; but it would be easy to cite a score of such affirmations of the old system in the years after his death.[117] As late as 1895, the mantra was still being repeated. "Each house does what it considers best," wrote Carl Meyer, "but on the other hand they know that the houses are all associated and for this reason no house would do a business which it knew would be against the interests of one of the other houses."[118]

Practice did not always conform to such confederal principles, however. The first obvious sign of fragmentation was Adolph's apparently unilateral decision to withdraw from the partnership and close down the Naples house in 1863 on the ground that the Naples market had been "deprived of its importance." This was an unprecedented event which shocked James and took months of negotiations to resolve. It was a sign of the new mood of suspicion that Adolph initially demanded three months to study the books of the various houses before accepting a definitive settlement, even threatening to open a new, independent bank if he did not get his way. He did. On September 22, 1863, he relinquished his partnership, withdrawing the sum of £1,593,777 as his share—more or less equivalent to the capital of the Naples house (£1,328,025) which was now wound up.[119] However, his efforts to carry on business in Italy in a semi-detached role were evidently stymied by James, who now denounced him as "riff-raff" and a "great lump"; he wanted to tell him "to go to the devil," he told his sons, "without doing him the honour of writing to him."[120] In particular, James was furious to hear that his nephew intended doing business in competition with the Paris house in the Turin market. Having abandoned his birthright, Adolph was now privately anathematised, though James was outwardly careful to conciliate his nephew lest he defect to the Crédit Mobilier.[121] In the end, Adolph avoided an outright breach by retiring from business altogether, selling the family residence in Naples and frittering away the remainder of his life on his collection of *objets d'art* at Pregny.[122]

A second sign of trouble was the increasing autonomy of the Vienna house under Anselm, which actually predated the 1863 agreement. When Adolph announced his withdrawal, Anselm seems to have sought to end the Vienna house's technical subordination to the Frankfurt house, though he was advised by the family lawyer Reinganum not to do this (in essence, the problem was that Anselm had a personal 25 per cent share in the combined capital, though the Vienna house itself remained relatively much smaller).[123] The persistence of this imbalance led to a steady deterioration in relations between Anselm and the rest of the family.[124] By 1867 James "regarded the association as illusory given the novel way in which our dear Uncle [Anselm] understands it."[125] Anselm felt obliged to defend himself, accusing the Paris house of treating him like a mere "agent or correspondent."[126] To reinforce his point, he repaid all the Vienna house's outstanding debts to the Frankfurt house two years ahead of schedule, precipitating further friction between himself and Mayer Carl.[127] This was followed by a similar accounting "divorce" between London and Vienna in 1870.[128]

Relations between Paris and the other houses also deteriorated somewhat, and not only because of the political upheaval of 1870–71. In February 1868 Nat felt obliged to warn his brothers in London that "on the day you should come to such an understanding [with other parties] on a matter of business negotiable on our place, the public would be entitled to believe that our long existing association has been severed."[129] A symptom of growing estrangement was the increasing secretiveness of the Paris partners.[130] Members of the other branches of the family continued to visit Paris quite regularly as of old—Anthony and Alfred in 1867, for example—but they found themselves marginalised in the office, following James from one meeting to another or signing routine letters.[131] Ferdinand was especially put out by his reception in 1871. "I assure you my dear Uncle," he told Lionel,

> when one has spent some little time in England and has become accustomed to the cordial and amiable and pleasant manner of the "London" family the great contrast of the Parisian relatives strikes one most forcibly.—Gustave seemed frightened out of his wits that I might discover some of his bureau-secrets and whenever I put a question to him—he answered it in the most evasive and round about manner.[132]

The feeling of distrust was not unreciprocated: criticisms of the Parisians' business methods were frequent. "In Paris," grumbled Mayer Carl in a typical letter to New Court, "they *will* take everything in hand and particularly things what [*sic*] they do not understand, the consequence being that they must be mismanaged and others reap the fruit of our exertion."[133] Admittedly, these complaints may have been prompted partly by envy of the relative growth of the Paris house. When Alphonse drew up his balance sheet following James's death, he was "delighted" (and the other houses not a little dismayed) to find that in the previous five years the Paris house had made "over four Millions sterling."[134] On the other hand, it gives an insight into Rothschild accounting practices that this came as a shock even to the French partners.[135]

These sources of conflict—as much as deteriorating Franco-Prussian relations—explain Mayer Carl's subsequent resolution not "to have anything to do with them," meaning his Paris cousins.[136] There was no mistaking his *Schadenfreude* when Ferrières was occupied by the Prussians and the rue Laffitte by the Communards. "[I]f the Paris house insists," he thundered in 1871, "upon not *paying attention to what I say they will face the consequences of their proceedings sooner* or later, *perhaps too late!*"[137] For his part, Alphonse felt that it was he who was trying to maintain the spirit of family unity against the separatist tendencies of the other houses.[138] And he could not resist the occasional dig at Mayer Carl's relatively poor financial performance. "I know only too well my dear cousin's habit of putting blame on all the other Houses," he wrote acerbically in 1882. "The best proof of his superior competence would be to present better balance sheets."[139] The upshot was that by the end of the 1870s co-operation between the four houses was not much greater than co-operation between each house and its local allies.[140]

All this made the revision of the partnership agreement—necessary as partners died—increasingly difficult. So bad had relations become by the time of James's death in 1868 that Alphonse sought to avoid holding a family summit to revise the contract, fearing acrimonious exchanges "the moment certain extremely heterogeneous elements of the family come face to face. Won't M[ayer] Carl and Anselm simply grab one another by the hair[?]" Even before the partners finally met in August 1869, the bickering began,[141] and when Nat died a year later Alphonse once again sought to avoid "striking a new balance sheet."[142] This time he was successful:

negotiations for a new agreement did not resume until 1874 and henceforth such matters were settled by post without the traditional family summits. Even so, acrimony was still liable to erupt. "If the policy which he pursues in Vienna is at all similar to his conduct towards his relatives of late," grumbled Natty to Alphonse following a row with Albert about Ferdinand's will, "the only thing I can say is I am astonished there is so little anti-semitic feeling in Vienna."[143]

The partnership agreements after 1874 had three notable features. Firstly, following the precedent set by Adolph, the partners now began to withdraw substantial capital sums from the partnership rather than living solely from fixed interest. This issue had first surfaced in 1869, apparently at the suggestion of the London partners, when sums of the order of £500,000 per house were discussed.[144] By 1872 the figure had been increased to £700,000 because (as Alphonse put it) "the Houses are so prosperous that a capital deduction cannot cause any harm."[145] Inevitably, Anselm was opposed to any reduction in the capital of the Vienna house.[146] His death, however, removed the principal obstacle and the new agreement of 1874–5 allowed no less than £8 million to be withdrawn from the combined capital of £35.5 million.[147] The 1879 contract following Lionel's death saw a repeat of the procedure: this time £4.7 million was withdrawn, reducing the combined capital to £25.5 million.[148] A further half million came out when James Edouard died in 1881, followed by £3.8 million later the same year.[149] The 1887 contract (following Mayer Carl's death the previous year) withdrew £3.4 million, the 1888 contract a further £2.7 million, and £2.8 million was withdrawn in 1898, followed by £1.1 million a year later;[150] £6.4 million was taken out when Wilhelm Carl died, £2 million when Arthur died, £1.4 million when Nathaniel died and £4.5 million when Alphonse died.[151] Altogether £41.3 million was withdrawn from the partnership between 1874 and 1905. If that money had remained in the business, its capital would have been more than double what it actually was in 1905 (£37 million). That the Rothschilds were able to afford such immense capital reductions is in itself remarkable; that they no longer ploughed their profits back into the family firm is, however, the more telling point.

Apart from the obvious need to settle the wills of deceased partners, the formal justification for this was the need to maintain some sort of equilibrium between the various partners' shares; yet this was not the effect. Under the terms of the 1863 contract, the shares had been equal: James had 25 per cent, as did Anselm (as Salomon's heir), the sons of Nathan and the sons of Carl. Under the terms of the 1879 contract, by contrast, the sons of James had 31.4 per cent; the sons of Anselm 22.7 per cent; Mayer Carl and Wilhelm Carl 22.3 per cent; the sons of Lionel 15.7 per cent and the sons of Nat 7.9 per cent. Because Nat's sons were French by birth and upbringing, they could be expected to side with the Parisians in any dispute, giving the French partners a considerably larger stake than the others, though not an outright majority. The vagaries of inheritance altered these figures somewhat, but without reducing the French predominance. By 1905 the French partners had some 46.8 per cent of the total capital, excluding Henri's 3.9 per cent; the Austrians 25.9 per cent; the English just 23.4 per cent. These figures nevertheless understated the greater size of the Paris house, which accounted for fully 57 per cent of the combined capital, compared with 22 per cent for Vienna and 20 per cent for London. The discrepancy between personal and institutional shares is explained by the fact that—again as a result of intermarriage and inheritance—the Austrian and English Rothschilds had substantial individual stakes in the Paris house. In this sense, the partnership did remain an integrated multinational entity until it was discontinued (at some point between October 1905 and July 1909).[152]

Secondly, it was necessary after 1874 to distinguish explicitly between active and "sleeping" partners as the number of partners increased (by 1879 there were twelve in all). For example, Lionel and Anthony were adamant that Nat's French-born sons James Edouard and Arthur should not inherit their father's full rights as partners with executive power in the London house.[153] It was also firmly asserted in the 1875 contract that, of Anselm's sons, neither Nathaniel nor Ferdinand would be allowed to play an executive role.[154] (Interestingly, this contract attempted to clip the wings of the Vienna house: it was stipulated that Albert would "not undertake any important transaction without having beforehand consulted with the other houses and having obtained the approval of at least one of them.")[155] Another "sleeping" partner was James Edouard's son Henri. However, no distinction was drawn between dominant and subordinate partners: in terms of his capital share, Alphonse always had equal status with his brothers Gustave and Edmond; similarly, Natty, Alfred and Leo were treated as equals in the partnership acts, though Natty was unquestionably in charge at New Court.[156] The same was true in Frankfurt, where Mayer Carl was the dominant partner, to the extent that he and his brother Wilhelm Carl were barely on speaking terms—they even erected a partition across the desk they shared to avoid seeing one another when signing letters.[157]

Finally, a seeming paradox should be explained: as the partnership between the various Rothschild houses became in practice looser, it was renewed more and more regularly. This has a prosaic explanation: the introduction of taxes on inheritance necessitated more precise methods of assessment of individual shares in the partnership, so that in 1899 it was decided for the first time to draw up combined balance sheets on an annual basis.[158] There was also probably a legal need to tighten up the somewhat imprecise and irregular form of the partnership: Lord Haldane later recalled how in around 1889 he had "rearranged the Rothschild partnerships which had got into a very vague relation, placing the whole family potentially at the mercy of one dishonest partner."[159] In its last decade, however, the partnership was in reality little more than an Anglo-French axis, with minimal links to Vienna. Typically, of the £28 million of bills discounted by the London house in 1906, £12 million were for the account of the Paris house. On the other hand, when the Vienna house issued a large Austrian loan in 1908, New Court was not even notified.[160] Under these circumstances, it is not entirely surprising that the partnership was not renewed after 1905.

This date, then—when the London, Paris and Vienna houses established by Nathan, James and Salomon became entirely separate entities—is the real watershed in Rothschild history, for it was at this point that the unique "confederal" system of a multinational partnership, dating back to the 1820s, finally came to an end. As early as 1868, a shrewd French journalist had divined what such a break-up would imply. "The five sons of Mayer [Amschel]," wrote Roqueplan, recalling the origins of the system,

> establish between themselves a sort of financial equilibrium which is not
> without a certain resemblance to the continental equilibrium dreamt of

by Richelieu. None of the places where the brothers are based is sacrificed to the others and the appeal made by everyone—states and individuals—to their credit and their capital obliges all who borrow to act with restraint, as they find themselves under supervision. This leads to a general *entente* and a middle way which soothes sources of friction, tempers ambition, diminishes miscalculations . . . The house of Rothschild . . . becomes the superintendent of the finances of Europe. *Divide up the house of Rothschild into a French house, an English, an Austrian, a Neapolitan, and its mediating influence disappears. You have [just another] national bank; you no longer have this universal bank house,* where the rivalries between the different European states come to be limited and resolved.[161]

Yet, although it is tempting to explain the problems which beset the Rothschild partnership system in personal terms, structural factors were probably more important. Throughout the period, the principal bone of contention between Vienna and the other houses was the willingness of Anselm to do business with rival banks, including associates of the Pereire brothers, the Crédit Foncier and even members of the hated Erlanger "clique."[162] Part of the difficulty was that the other houses regarded the Creditanstalt as effectively a subsidiary of the Vienna house, whereas Anselm insisted that it was not.[163] Similar conflicts arose with respect to the different railway companies in which the Rothschilds had large but not controlling interests.[164] The fact was that the development of joint-stock institutions—and indeed of other private banks—in all the major financial markets was bound to create conflicts of loyalty. The Rothschilds were no longer so dominant that they could underwrite major bond issues without assistance from other local banks. Increasingly, each house developed informal partners in its own market—Barings in London, the *haute banque* in Paris, the Creditanstalt in Vienna and the Disconto-Gesellschaft in Germany—and the volume of business done with these soon began to exceed the volume of cross-border business with other Rothschild houses. It was all very well to accuse the Frankfurt house of having becoming Hansemann's "satellite," but the Paris house was not offering sufficient business to keep Mayer Carl in its own orbit.[165]

In a similar way, it became progressively more and more difficult to rely on the traditional system of salaried agents. As the case of Becker & Fuld in Amsterdam illustrated, agents could not be expected to confine themselves solely to Rothschild business when so many other opportunities presented themselves; yet the more they did business on their own account, the more like competitors they became.[166] Natty might talk of "pulling up" agents by "adopt[ing] . . . a system similar to the one the Jesuits practise. First of all never leave a man too long in one place and then have a wandering Jew to spy & to report."[167] But there was no denying that the old agency system was obsolescent. Mayer Carl's reliance on Hansemann's Disconto-Gesellschaft and his animus against Bleichröder were part of the same trend.

Even within the offices of the Rothschild houses, the old ways were in decline. "Every moment," complained Mayer Carl in 1873,

> one of the clerks leaves the House, either to become the manager of a Bank or for the sake of establishing himself on his own account. Jews with their terrible ambition are the worst employees. I know they merely

want to poke their nose everywhere and try to find out as much as they can to cut their stick when it suits their purpose. There is not a good clerk to be had and I assure you it is a perfect nuisance . . . all these new Banks pay such salaries that no one thinks of coming forward.[168]

From its inception, the Rothschild system had ruled out the possibility that talented "outsiders" would ever rise above the status of "clerks" in order to prevent any challenge to the continuity of family control. Once joint-stock banks offered "careers open to talent," however, it became increasingly difficult to attract and retain able employees—hence Carl Meyer's departure.

Similarly, the decline of the Frankfurt house was not solely due to the failure of Mayer Carl and Wilhelm Carl to produce a male heir.[169] Nor can too much blame be laid at the door of the two brothers for failing to make the business a more successful one, though its results were disappointing and Wilhelm Carl was ready to throw in his hand as early as 1890.[170] It was also partly the consequence of the decline of Frankfurt as a financial centre relative to Berlin. In fact, the other partners contemplated opening a "resuscitated or new Frankfurt House" after Wilhelm Carl's death, but this plan was abandoned, possibly because of a dispute about taxation with the Frankfurt authorities.[171] As a result, the *fons et origo* of the Rothschild fortunes—the firm of M. A. von Rothschild & Söhne—was finally wound up in 1901. The Rothschilds remained a presence in Frankfurt, to be sure. Indeed, Minna's husband Max Goldschmidt managed to keep the Rothschild name going, albeit after a hyphen. But although "von Goldschmidt-Rothschild" was the town's (and indeed the German Reich's) wealthiest man before the First World War, and although members of the family accounted for five of its top ten taxpayers in 1911, the income on their capital was conspicuously low.[172] It was symbolic of the Rothschilds' waning power that most of the old bank's staff now went to work for the Disconto-Gesellschaft; while, under the terms of Wilhelm Carl's will, the office in the Fahrgasse built by Amschel and Salomon in the first flower of their prosperity became a museum for Jewish antiquities.[173]

In this context, it is significant that the 1860s and 1870s saw the last wave of Rothschild intermarriage: of the thirty-one members of the fourth generation who married, thirteen married another Rothschild.[174] Between 1849 and 1877, there were altogether nine such weddings, beginning with Anselm's daughters Hannah Mathilde (to Wilhelm Carl in 1849) and Julie (to Adolph in 1850); and followed a decade later by James's sons Alphonse (to Leonora in 1857) and Salomon James (to Mayer Carl's daughter Adèle in 1862). The wedding three years later of Anselm's son Ferdinand to Lionel's daughter Evelina was one of the supreme moments of Rothschild endogamy. The post-nuptial dinner at 148 Piccadilly was attended by 126 people including Disraeli, the First Lord of the Admiralty, and the Austrian and French ambassadors; and the subsequent ball was graced by the Duke of Cambridge. It was intended and interpreted as a renewal of the ties between the London and Vienna houses (Ferdinand's mother had, of course, been Lionel's elder sister Charlotte) and the couple planned to divide their time between Piccadilly and Schillersdorf.[175] Indeed, Anselm "deplored the non-existence of more Evys than one in order that all his sons might be equally well provided."[176]

It was also evidently a love-match, even if Ferdinand's passion for the wedding jewellery somewhat comically exceeded that of his betrothed.[177] In December 1866, however, while her husband was in Austria helping his father in the wake of König-grätz, Evelina died in childbirth.[178] It was one of the most painful events in the history of the English Rothschilds. "Henceforth my life can merely be wrought with sorrow and with anguish and with bitter longing," Ferdinand told Leo:

> Mine is a loss which years cannot repair, nor any accidental circumstances relieve. Ever since my childhood I was attached to her. The older I became, the more we met, the deeper I loved her and in later years she had so grown into my heart that my only wishes, cares, joys, affections, whatever sentiments in fact a man can possess were directly or indirectly wound up with her existence. I can find no consolation in the future. It may partly come from the past, in the recollection of those happy bygone days, when she lived, when we were so intensely happy.

"[C]rushed by the calamity which has fallen on a house of sunshine and happiness, which has made his life gloomy and desolate," he did not remarry, but increasingly relied on the company of his sister Alice, who remained a spinster.[179] He left two poignant memorials to his dead wife: a children's hospital named after her in the New Kent Road in Southwark and a mausoleum in the Jewish cemetery at Forest Gate.[180]

This tragedy did not deter Charlotte from seeking a spouse for her eldest son from within the "fairy circle." Initially, she hoped Natty "would fall in love or glide into that delightful feeling and make the excellent Baronet [Anthony] supremely happy by proposing to one of his daughters."[181] However, she was just as pleased when Natty expressed interest in Mayer Carl's daughter Emma, and they were duly married in Frankfurt in 1867. Although their engagement was a blow to Nat's son James Edouard, who had been earmarked for Emma by other members of the family, it was probably for the best. The austere Natty and the stern Emma were well suited to each other,[182] while James Edouard's marriage in 1871 to Emma's sister Laura Thérèse was also regarded as a good if unglamorous match. As Ferdinand reported: "There never was a happier couple than they are, they bill and they coo and they speak about their baby and their house, as if no one else had ever been married, and as if their Henri was the only Henri in the world. (I believe he is a fright.) I must say that I never saw a funnier looking little couple than they are; so short and fat and dumpy."[183]

All this goes to show that these marriages were not necessarily imposed by parental design, but were often based on genuine affection; it was just that the family's pattern of working, socialising and holidaying together narrowed the range of possible spouses. When Charlotte heard that Albert had become engaged to Alphonse's daughter Bettina in 1875, she commented that "no young man ever appears on the horizon without it being said that he seeks the hand of a cousin, and the surmise is not extraordinary as hitherto we have intermarried so very much."[184] They were wed the following year. The only alternative Albert had apparently considered was one of Mayer Carl's daughters.[185] Finally, in 1877, Alphonse's youngest brother Edmond married Wilhelm Carl's daughter Adelheid, having previously been rejected by her cousin Margaretha.

By this time, however, there were signs that the practice of endogamy could not be sustained for much longer. In 1874, Charlotte had heard that "there would not be the slightest use, at present, of invading the territory of the Austrian Rothschilds for matrimonial purposes"—though no reason was given for this. She also sympathised when Margaretha refused to marry Edmond: "[P]robably the idea of being the 8th Rothschild lady in Paris does not please her."[186] For reasons which were never made explicit, Edmond's marriage to Adelheid proved to be the last such pure Rothschild match.

A question inevitably poses itself: was this because the family became more aware of the genetic risks of such "inbreeding"? When Natty married Emma, after all, he was marrying the daughter of his father's sister and his mother's brother. In the eyes of a modern geneticist, such a pairing was ill advised (for reasons discussed in chapter 6 of volume 1). And it is tempting to explain the idiosyncrasies of some members of the fourth and fifth generation in genetic terms. Yet it seems unlikely that the Rothschilds gave up cousin marriage on medical grounds. Although Gregor Mendel's research into heredity began in the 1860s it was largely unknown until the early 1900s, while the theory of "eugenics" which became fashionable in the 1880s positively encouraged inbreeding at least within racial groups if not families. It was not science which ended Rothschild endogamy but a change in the family's attitude towards the rest of society—and especially society's elite.

Peers and Peerages

A major difference between the fourth generation and their parents was that a number of female Rothschilds now married outside the Jewish faith, without incurring the opprobrium which had fallen on Hannah Mayer when she had married Henry Fitzroy in 1839. The first of these marriages was between Anthony's daughter Annie and Eliot Yorke, third son of the 4th Earl of Hardwicke, in 1873.[187] Five years later, Annie's sister Constance married Cyril Flower, Leo's Cambridge friend (later Lord Battersea), and in 1878 Mayer's daughter, Hannah, married Archibald Primrose, the 5th Earl of Rosebery, already established as a rising star in the Liberal party, later Foreign Secretary (1886 and 1892–3) and Gladstone's successor as Prime Minister (1894–5). In the same year, Mayer Carl's daughter Margaretha married Agénor, duc de Gramont (the son of the former Foreign Minister) and in 1882 her youngest sister Bertha Clara married Alexandre Berthier, prince de Wagram, a descendant of Napoleon's Chief of General Staff.[188] Finally, in 1887, Hélène, daughter of Salomon James, married the Dutch Baron Etienne van Zuylen de Nyevelt.

This too could be interpreted as a sign that the original culture of the family—once so determinedly loyal to Judaism—was being diluted. That was the view taken by some Jewish contemporaries. "The rabbinical query is on every lip," wrote the *Jewish Chronicle* in October 1877, " 'If the flame is seized on the cedars, how will fare the hyssop on the wall; if the leviathan is brought up with a hook, how will the minnows escape?' "[189] In fact, none of the four women who did this converted to Christianity.[190] Constance apparently thought of doing so before her marriage, noting that she was "only Jewish by race, not by religion or doctrine." "My mind is not in the least impregnated by Jewish doctrine, I have not the feeling of pride in isolation," she wrote. "My Church is the universal one, my God, the Father of all mankind, my creed charity, toleration and morality. I can worship the great Creator under any name." Indeed, on one occasion she went so far as to declare: "I wish I could be a Christian. I love the faith and the worship." In the end, however, she decided that conversion would be "impossible" and "a falsehood," though she remained for the rest of her life "at the very outer gates of Christianity."[191] Annie too remained at least nominally attached to Judaism.[192] Hannah's commitment to her family's faith was probably stronger. Although she was married in a church and allowed her children to be raised as Christians, she continued to light candles on Friday evenings, to attend synagogue and to fast and pray on the Day of Atonement. Despite embracing her husband's Scottish cultural heritage, she was buried in the Jewish cemetery at Willesden rather than at Dalmeny.[193]

Nor was the family's approval of the matches unqualified. Mayer Carl cut Margaretha out of his will for converting to Christianity.[194] As late as 1887, Salomon James's widow Adèle disinherited her Hélène for marrying outside the faith, leaving her house in the rue Berryer to the French government fine arts administration.[195] Even Alphonse's grandson Guy was reminded by his parents "at every opportunity" that "the most important rule was the one forbidding marriage with a woman who was not Jewish, or not willing to be converted to the Jewish faith."[196] Charlotte's letters in the 1860s reveal the persistence of the assumption that Rothschilds should marry within the faith, if not the family. The ideal spouse for a Rothschild girl, she thought, was "some substantial Jew, belonging to a good family." Among the possible husbands she considered suitable for Annie and Constance—or indeed for their cousin Clementine—was Julian Goldsmid.[197] When she first heard that Anthony's daughters were being courted by non-Jews (Lord Henry Lennox, the MP for Chichester, was one of those mentioned), Charlotte was sure that "Uncle Anthony, in the event of proposals, is sure to say 'no' " and that their mother "would not say 'yes.' "[198] "Caucasian husbands," she noted, "would, of course, be much preferred to flat-nosed Franks as Mr. Disraeli calls the christian beaux."[199]

By late 1866 Charlotte seemed to accept that Constance would choose a Christian spouse.[200] But when Annie revealed that Eliot Yorke had proposed, her father came under strong pressure from Lionel and Natty not to give his consent. Mayer and his wife Juliana also expressed disapproval, which was apparently (and ironically) echoed by their daughter Hannah; as did James's widow Betty. "The sentiments of sadness fill me more at this moment than I can express," she wrote pointedly to Annie's mother. "They do not, however, stop me from assuring you of my greatest sympathy in your distress and that of my dear nephew Sir Anthony." It was only after the match had received support from Nat's widow Charlotte, Anselm and Alfred ("on behalf of everyone at Gunnersbury") that Anthony gave in to his daughter's entreaties. Even so, Constance recollected after the registry office ceremony, "Papa looked so sad. We all felt it dreadfully, Annie included."[201] In one way, subsequent events seemed to vindicate the doubters: though the marriage was apparently happy, Yorke died five years later.

Nor was the second such "mixed" marriage between Annie's sister Constance and Leo's friend Cyril Flower an unqualified success. The problem in this case was that the "wonderfully handsome" Flower was very probably a homosexual, celebrated for his female impersonations at Cambridge. In fairness, the earnest Constance seems to have enjoyed being married to one of the more "advanced" Liberal MPs of the day—she herself was a keen teetotaller—and doubtless welcomed his elevation to the peerage as Lord Battersea in 1892. But when he was offered the Governorship of New South Wales by Gladstone the following year, Constance refused to leave her mother (and her charitable work) for Australia and he had to turn down the appointment—a decision which his wife feared had "blighted my dear Cyril's career" and condemned them to "years of misery."[202]

The best known of all the mixed marriages of the period was that between Mayer's daughter Hannah and Rosebery. Here too there is evidence of some Rothschild opposition. Though rumours of a match had circulated since 1876, their engagement was not announced until both her parents were dead; and no male Rothschild attended the wedding, so that Disraeli gave the bride away.[203] And here too it might be thought that Rosebery gave up bachelorhood reluctantly. In the most malicious view, Rosebery was a misogynist who married a Rothschild primarily for financial reasons. She, after all, was one of the richest heiresses of the period, having inherited not only Mentmore and 107 Piccadilly but also £100,000 a year.[204] That made her an attractive prospect to an ambitious politician, despite the fact that (as her cousin Constance put it), she took "no interest in big subjects" and expressed herself (according to her husband) in a "childish" way.[205]

It has also been claimed that Rosebery harboured faint anti-Semitic prejudices. "One night at Mentmore," David Lindsay, the Earl of Balcarres, recalled many years later, "when Hannah Rothschild had had a house party in which her compatriots were unusually numerous, all the ladies had gathered at the foot of the great staircase and were about to go up with lighted candles. Rosebery standing aloof from the bevy of beauty raised his hand—they looked at him, rather puzzled, and then he said in solemn tones: 'To your tents, O Israel.' " Lindsay also heard that "within a week of Hannah's death he began to cut off subscriptions to Jewish charities, and before long all had been cancelled."[206] Finally, there is the connection alleged by the 9th Marquess of Queensberry, between Rosebery, his private secretary Lord Drumlanrig and the homosexual circle whose most notorious member was Oscar Wilde.[207]

Yet these arguments cannot be sustained. Apart from anything else, Rosebery already owned a large estate in Scotland (Dalmeny) as well as a house at Epsom (the Durdans), and had an income of more than £30,000 a year.[208] He of all people did not need to marry for money. Nor is there any doubt that Rosebery loved Hannah. Writing to Gladstone, he described his engagement as "the most momentous event of my life." The fact that his diary says so little about her has sometimes been interpreted as evidence of a lack of ardour but, given that he treated it mainly as a record of his political activities, the reverse is more likely. The number of references to dinners and lunches with members of the family in 1877 suggests an energetic courtship, while the complete silence of the 1878 volume for the months after the wedding suggests that Hannah gave him better things to do than diary-writing.[209] Balcarres misconstrued a simple joke; while Queensbury can be dismissed as the harbinger of the lunatic "sodomite conspiracy" theory advanced during the First World War by Noel Pemberton Billing.[210]

Moreover, there is good testimony that Rosebery relied on Hannah to provide the political "drive" which on his own he lacked. Lord Granville half-seriously urged her that "*if you keep him up to the mark*, [he] is sure to have his page in history"; while Edward Hamilton remarked on her "notable . . . faculty of getting other people to work and of quickening their energies."[211] Winston Churchill too described her as "a remarkable woman on whom he [Rosebery] had leaned . . . She was ever a pacifying and composing element in his life which he was never able to find again because he never could give full confidence to anyone else." Such comments lend some credibility to the suggestion that Hannah provided the model for the ambitious Marcella Maxwell in Mrs Humphry Ward's novels *Marcella* (1894) and *Sir George Tressady* (1909).[212] Churchill thought Rosebery "maimed" by Hannah's tragic and painfully protracted death from typhoid in 1890, a view which is borne out by his terse but plainly tortured diary entries.[213] Observing him at the funeral, Sir Henry Ponsonby saw that he "never spoke but remained close to the coffin till it was lowered into the grave. Lord Rothschild led him back to the chapel but he looked down the whole time . . . He wishes to show in public that he is able to put aside his sorrow, but in private he breaks down."[214] After her death, relations between Rosebery and other members of the Rothschild family remained close.[215]

It should also be stressed that there could be unease on the other side about such mixed marriages. Rosebery's mother, the Duchess of Cleveland, was strongly opposed to her son's choice of "one who has not the faith & hope of Christ" as his spouse. "No two persons of different religions can marry without making a very great sacrifice," she told her son, "and—pardon me for adding, grieving and disappointing those who love them best . . . You must also of course expect to be unkindly judged by the world."[216] Three days after his wife's funeral, Rosebery himself poignantly told Queen Victoria: "There is . . . one incident of this tragedy only less painful than the actual loss: which is that at the moment of death the difference of creed makes itself felt, and another religion steps in to claim the corpse. It was inevitable, and I do not complain; and my wife's family have been more than kind. But none the less it is exquisitely painful."[217]

Finally, it is important to remember that none of these marriages involved a male Rothschild. As the heirs to the capital of the partnership and to the religious legacy of Mayer Amschel, they had much less freedom of choice when it came to marriage. For this reason, the really problematic relationship was between Alfred and his mistress Marie ("Mina") Wombwell, née Boyer—not only a Christian but a married woman. Although he may have had an illegitimate child by her (the child's name Almina suggests a combination of "Al" and "Mina") we do not know if Alfred ever contemplated marriage; it is conceivable that he dismissed the idea in view of inevitable and insuperable family opposition (though another possibility is that Alfred was in fact a homosexual).[218] Alfred nevertheless committed a sin which his great-grandfather would have regarded as equally grave. He gave Almina a £500,000 dowry when she married the Earl of Carnarvon (in addition to settling his debts of £150,000) and left a large portion of his £1.5 million estate to them and their children (£125,000 and the house in Seamore Place).[219]

In short, the various "mixed" marriages described above should not be taken as evidence of a profound change in attitudes. Still, it is hard to imagine them happening while James still lived. The fact that all the marriages involved an alliance with aristocratic families (with the partial exception of Constance's to Cyril Flower, who was made a peer only later) is no coincidence. The social benefits of association of the English and French elite, it might be thought, were felt to outweigh the costs of religious compromise. But it would be wrong to imply a kind of strategy of social advancement. To some extent, as the *Jewish Chronicle* suggested, it was precisely the fact of the Rothschilds' social advancement which made such marriages happen: Constance had met Cyril Flower because her cousin had been to Cambridge; Hannah met Rosebery because her father was an established political and sporting figure (they are said to have been introduced by Mary Anne Disraeli at Newmarket) and because Ferdinand knew Rosebery well.[220] As Cassis has shown, a very high proportion of late nineteenth-century City bankers married the daughters of aristocrats (no fewer than 38 per cent of the private bankers in his sample and at least 24 per cent of all bankers and bank directors).[221]

The question of the relationship between the Rothschilds of this period and the aristocracy has often been discussed. The point is made that Natty's elevation to the peerage in 1885 represented the final triumph of the campaign for social assimilation which the Rothschilds had waged since the time of Mayer Amschel. At the same time, those who argue that a process of "feudalisation" sapped the entrepreneurial and/or liberal spirit of the bourgeoisie in the second half of the nineteenth century cite this as an archetype. The reality is more complex. The transition from baronet to hereditary peer had its roots in Rothschild relations with successive Prime Ministers as well as with members of the royal family; for social promotion was at once a reward for political or public service and a sign of royal favour. It is also worth noting that, as with the rights of Jews to take their seats in the Lower House of Parliament, England was in some ways behind some continental states.

The Austrian case illustrates the subtle gradations of status involved. Technically, the Rothschilds had first acquired noble status—the prefix "von" and a coat of arms—from the Habsburg Emperor as early as 1816, adding the title "Baron" (Freiherr) six years later. However, it was not until 1861 that a Rothschild—Anselm—was given the political equivalent of a peerage, a seat in the Reichsrat or imperial council.[222] And the ultimate social achievement—the right to be presented at court—did not come until December 1887, when Albert and his wife were formally declared *hoffähig*. As *The Times* reported, this was "the first time that such a privilege has been conceded in Austria to persons of the Jewish religion, and the event is causing a sensation in society."[223] It was only after this that members of the Rothschild family and members of the Austrian royal family began to mix socially in Austria itself.[224] Nathaniel in particular was accepted into Viennese aristocratic society in a way which had entirely eluded his father and grandfather, being addressed with the familiar "du" by such grandees as Count Wilczek, who regarded him as "an unusually charming man and a really noble [*sic*] character." The connection to the Metternichs also remained socially invaluable.[225]

According to contemporary gossip, Nathaniel had an affair with Baroness Maria Vetsera, who later became the mistress of Crown Prince Rudolph. Moreover, when Rudolph and Maria committed suicide together at the royal hunting lodge at Mayerling in January 1889, it was Nathaniel's brother Albert—as chairman of the Nordbahn—who received the first telegraph reports of the tragedy and had to relay the news to the imperial palace.[226] This may be apocryphal, but it is undoubtedly the case that Rudolph's mother, the Empress Elisabeth, became friendly with Adolph's widow Julie; indeed, she had just visited the Rothschild house at Pregny in Switzerland when she was murdered at Lake Geneva by an Italian anarchist in September

1898. When Franz Joseph celebrated his diamond jubilee in 1908 with a grand reception, Albert was there—one of the few who attended in civilian dress.[227]

In Germany, there was a similar progression from elevation to the peerage to social intercourse. Mayer Carl, as we have seen, had been appointed to the Prussian Upper House (Herrenhaus) in 1867 and was treated as *hoffähig* thereafter. Although he never ceased to disparage Bleichröder's social climbing—and was beside himself with glee when the latter's ennoblement did not confer on him the title of Freiherr[228]—Mayer Carl himself rarely omitted to mention his own encounters with Prussian royalty, no matter how inconsequential. He and his wife's work in establishing a hospital for the war wounded in Frankfurt in 1870–71 undoubtedly earned them royal favour. "I have just had an interview with the Emperor which lasted a whole hour," he gushed in December 1871, "and I need not tell you that we are on the best terms, particularly in consequence of what I gave the Empress for her hospital which seemed to please His Majesty beyond anything else. Louisa is a great favourite of the Empress and Her Majesty delighted in showing her how much she appreciated all she had done . . . which is a capital thing for our own interests." The Empress seems to have been especially friendly.[229] A still closer relationship later developed between Wilhelm Carl's wife Hannah Mathilde and Victoria, the widow of Kaiser Frederick III and daughter of Queen Victoria, who evidently enjoyed the faintly Anglophile atmosphere of the Rothschild house at Königstein.[230] Although Victoria's son William II was viewed with deep suspicion by members of the family and harboured quite strong anti-Semitic prejudices, his accession in 1888 did not harm the Rothschilds' position. In 1903 Wilhelm Carl's son-in-law Max Goldschmidt was given the title "Freiherr von Goldschmidt-Rothschild."[231]

In England, by contrast, the process happened in reverse, with the Rothschilds winning acceptability at court and intimacy with royalty some years before they were able to secure a seat in the House of Lords; for, despite the fact that it became legally possible for a Jew to become a peer in 1866, Queen Victoria proved strongly resistant to the idea in practice. The Rothschilds were considered presentable at court as early as 1856, when Victoria noticed the "extremely handsome" looks of Lionel's daughter Leonora at a royal drawing room.[232] The real social breakthrough, however, came at Cambridge in 1861, when Natty was introduced to the Prince of Wales (the future Edward VII) by the Duke of St Albans. A common enthusiasm for hunting in turn led to introductions for Alfred and Leo.[233] Horse racing played a similar role: Mayer was "delighted" when the Prince "[partook] of his cake, Mayonnaise and champagne" at the Derby in 1864 and again in 1866.[234] Soon members of the family were regularly being invited to court functions or to aristocratic gatherings at which royalty was also present.[235] In turn they entertained members of the royal family, principally—though not exclusively—the Prince of Wales.[236] In March the following year, he went out stag-hunting with Mayer at Mentmore and two months later he dined at Anthony's;[237] he and Princess Alexandra attended "an interminable banquet" at Lionel's in 1871 and the Prince dined at Ferdinand's along with Disraeli four years after that.[238] The Prince also attended the Rosebery–Rothschild marriage in 1878 (along with his uncle the Duke of Cambridge) and Leo's wedding to Marie Perugia in 1881—a remarkable gesture of royal religious tolerance.[239]

In addition to these more or less formal occasions, "Prince Hal" (as Disraeli called him) was also entertained in the more louche style that he preferred: Alfred, for example, could be relied on to produce opera stars like Nellie Melba, Adelina Patti and the actress Sarah Bernhardt at his dinners; another family friend from the emerging world of "show business" was the librettist Sir Arthur Sullivan.[240] Ferdinand too knew how to amuse the heir to the throne: when the Prince fell downstairs and broke his leg at Waddesdon in 1898, the story made the national newspapers.[241] As an ardent Francophile, he was a regular Rothschild guest on other side of the Channel too. In the summer of 1867, James entertained him at Boulogne.[242] He also visited Ferrières five years later (returning there in 1888);[243] and he lunched with Alphonse at Cannes in 1895.[244] Such contacts did not cease on his accession to the throne—rather the reverse.[245] Members of the Rothschild family were an integral part of Edward VII's cosmopolitan social circle, along with the Sassoons, the railway financier Maurice de Hirsch, Ernest Cassel, Horace Farquhar and others identified by Edward Hamilton as the "smart set."[246]

However, it would be quite wrong to portray the Rothschilds as in any way in awe of the royal family or, for that matter, especially eager for elevation to the peerage. Natty, for example, initially found the Prince of Wales's conversation "commonplace and very slow." "He is excessively fond of the chase," he told his parents,

> very fond of riddles and strong cigars and will I suppose eventually settle down into a well-disciplined German Prince with all the narrow views of his father's family. He is excessively polite and that is certainly his redeeming quality. If he followed the bent of his own inclination, it strikes me he would take to gambling and certainly keep away from the law lectures he is obliged to go to now.

Five years later, he had not changed his view, commenting drily "that war and peace, and the state of politics do not occupy H.R.H. half so much as his amusements."[247] His mother shared these sentiments. Though she thought the future King "most enchantingly agreeable" with "manners . . . not to be surpassed anywhere," she felt it was "to be deplored that he does not give a portion of his time to serious pursuits, nor any of his friendship or society to distinguished men in politics, art, science or literature." He had, she concluded (after he left the Commons gallery during a speech by Gladstone), "no taste for serious subjects."[248] When the Prince won a "large stake" on a Rothschild horse, Charlotte was tight-lipped: "[O]f course, I would infinitely rather he won than lost upon a Rothschild horse—but the future King of England should not go about betting."[249]

Nor was it only the Prince of Wales who came in for criticism. When Lady Alice Peel lent her Queen Victoria's privately printed Highland album, Charlotte was scathing:

> There is not a ray, indeed not the faintest glimmering of talent or even of pretty writing in the volume, which seems astonishing, as very great and illustrious statesmen pronounce the Queen to be remarkably clever . . . [T]he redeeming and truly interesting feature of the work is its extraordinary and almost incredible simplicity; there is not the remotest allusion to royalty or sovereign power; the most humble minded of Her Majesty's subjects might have written it; not a single word reminds the

reader that the writer rules over hundreds of millions of human beings, and that the sun never sets over her dominions . . . [I]n reality there is not a newspaper which is not ten thousand times more interesting.[250]

Ferdinand and Alice shared her dismay at the Queen's "allusions to the gillies, and the foot-note devoted to 'John Brown' [the Queen's 'Highland attendant'] and his curly hair."[251]

Such attitudes reflected the enduring streak of asceticism which had been inherited from the generation born in the Frankfurt ghetto. Indeed, having risen so far by their own efforts the Rothschilds considered themselves in many ways superior to the aristocracy, not least in financial terms. It was well known that the Prince of Wales and his brothers were inclined to live beyond their allowances provided by the Civil List; keeping up the family tradition of lending to future rulers, Anthony offered his assistance and by August 1874 the Queen was alarmed to hear of "a large sum owing to Sir A. de Rothschild" by her eldest son.[252] However, the Rothschilds' role between then and his accession twenty-seven long years later seems primarily to have been to keep the Prince out of debt, aside from a £160,000 mortgage on Sandringham which was discreetly hushed up.[253]

A less obvious sign of aristocratic, if not royal, financial dependency came when a son of the Duke of Argyll, Lord Walter Campbell, expressed the wish to enter the City as confidential clerk to the Rothschilds' stockbroker Arthur Wagg for a salary of £1,000 a year. Lionel cautiously "advised Lord Walter to go and speak to the Duke at Inverary, as that proud nobleman might not like his son to enter into partnership with an Israelite"; but Charlotte was gleeful because of the Campbells' royal connections: "The Waggs will be overjoyed, if the partnership should really take place, to be connected in business with the brother-in-law of Her Royal Highness the Princess Louise. This will be more extraordinary, if it occurs, than the invasion of Caucasian beauties into . . . London fashionable society."[254] Such links between the court and the City were commonplace by 1907, when Leo suggested as a possible director of Rio Tinto "the Earl of Denbigh, a very honourable man, Colonel of the City Artillery and formerly Lord in Waiting to the Queen and then to the King, a catholic peer with pleasant manners."[255]

For his part, Natty welcomed such signs of aristocratic compromise. As a strongly Liberal student, he had resented the unearned privileges enjoyed by aristocrats at Cambridge. "I cannot yet make out," he had complained to his parents, "why noblemen and their sons etc. can take their degree after seven terms and have no Little Go to pass. Both noblemen and fellow Commoners should be done away with, but I am afraid these things never will take place."[256] As late as 1888—after he himself had become Lord Rothschild—he commented sternly about "the harm which a few of the aristocracy do to their class by frequently displaying a want of sense and honour in money affairs and by resorting to gambling."[257] The Rothschilds did not think of themselves as becoming aristocratic, even if it appeared that they were; if anything, they wished the aristocracy to become more like them. As Charlotte said, it was better for a younger son of the Earl of Mayo to "earn [a] living in the city handsomely, but by great exertion, activity and labour, instead of starving in the West End."[258]

The key to the Rothschild attitude was that, as the nearest thing the Jews of

Europe had to a royal family, they considered themselves the equals of royalty. When Charlotte heard that Prince Alfred was to visit Bonn, where Albert was studying, she sought to arrange a meeting between "the gifted scion of the Caucasian royal family . . . and the clever scion of the royal family of England."[259] For other Jews, she declared a few weeks later, "un marriage d'ambition" meant a marriage to "a Rothschild or a Koh-i-Noor [a Cohen, an allusion to her mother-in-law's family] . . . since there are no jewish Queens and Empresses in the 19th century."[260] In a similar vein, Juliana and Hannah were "a queen and a Princess of Israel and of Mentmore."[261] Such notions explain the Rothschilds' tendency to compete with the royal family. Typically, Natty reported with satisfaction the superiority of his own horse to the Prince's when they hunted together at Cambridge.[262] Likewise, when Ferdinand went to Buckingham Palace, "he thought and said that no lady was to be compared to his wife—and no equipage to the one that conveyed" them there; and when an especially lavish supper was provided at Stafford House, it was "not royal but Rothschildian."[263] Invited to dine at the Palace, Mayer set out resolved "to find fault with every thing."[264] On at least one occasion, his sister-in-law Charlotte preferred a minor family engagement to a royal ball and sought to avoid attending royal drawing rooms, which she found "tiring and tedious in the superlative degree."[265] And when the Empress of Austria visited England in 1876, Charlotte was adamant that she had enjoyed her reception more at Waddesdon than at Windsor.[266] Contemporaries often used the phrase "Kings of the Jews" when they talked about the Rothschilds: the evidence of the family's own correspondence suggests it was not an unwelcome compliment.

Yet despite all this—perhaps even *because* of the family's pretensions—it proved impossible to persuade Victoria to elevate Lionel to the House of Lords. Rumours of such a promotion were current as early as 1863.[267] However, there were those at court who were hostile towards the Rothschilds, a hostility which they were able to express more freely after the death of Prince Albert in 1861. At the time of the Prince of Wales's marriage, Charlotte complained of the family's exclusion from the festivities. "Lord Sydney," she wrote bitterly, "though fed from time immemorial upon all the delicacies in and out of season by all the continental Rothschilds, and not disdaining our dinners either, never thought us worthy of being asked to court. When the poor Prince was alive, dear Papa used to apply to him—when forgotten or omitted. Now one would not like to trouble the Queen."[268] Another enemy at court was Lord Spencer, who advised that the Prince and Princess should not attend a Rothschild ball as "the Prince ought only to visit those of undoubted position in Society." "The Rothschilds are very worthy people," he added, "but they especially hold their position from wealth and perhaps the accidental beauty of the first daughter they brought out."[269] Nor did Sir Francis Knollys, the Prince's private secretary, give unqualified approval to the Rothschilds' intimacy with his master;[270] while the Queen's equerry Arthur Hardinge felt it necessary to take a visiting Russian royal to Westminster Abbey "as a corrective" after a Rothschild dinner "resplendent with Hebrew gold."[271] The Prince of Wales himself evidently resisted such pressures. When Natty and Alfred attended a royal levee in 1865, Charlotte was able to report triumphantly

> the Prince was gracious, as usual, smiled and shook hands—but H.R.H.
> has accustomed them to much kindness and cordiality; what amused

them, however, was the rebuke he gave to Lord Sydney, who fine gentleman and jew-hater as he is, announced Natty as Monsieur "Roshil"—
"Mr. de Rothschild" was the correction he received from royal lips.[272]

Another welcome ally in this period was Lady Ely, who invited Natty, Alfred, Ferdinand and Evelina to a select ball for the Prince and Princess of Wales in 1865.[273]

But neither she nor the heir to the throne was in a position to influence the
Queen on matters of royal patronage. That Victoria was reluctant to give "a title and
mark of [her] approbation to a jew" had been intimated to the Rothschilds as early
as 1867 by Disraeli,[274] though it should be emphasised that Lionel himself had no
desire to accept a peerage from Disraeli. "Our friend [Charles Villiers, the Liberal
MP for Wolverhampton] is famously intrigued about the paragraph in the papers
respecting my being raised to the Peerage," he remarked in a letter to his wife in
March 1868:

> Just the same as everything else, the Liberals would like to carry out
> everything themselves . . . He could not understand nor could they at
> Lady P[almerston]'s that I won't accept anything from the present Gov-
> ernment. They all fancy Dis is under great obligations to us—so the best
> thing is to hold my tongue and let them think what they like—it is only
> amusing to hear all their nonsense.[275]

That was prescient, for no sooner had he become Prime Minister than Gladstone
proposed Lionel as one of eleven new Liberal peers he wished the Queen to create.
The idea, as expressed by the Liberal leader in the Lords Earl Granville, was that the
Rothschilds now represented "a class whose influence is great by their wealth, their
intelligence, their literary connections, and their numerous seats in the House of
Commons. It may be wise to attach them to the Aristocracy rather than to drive
them into the democratic camp."[276] But the Queen would have none of it.[277]
Granville had to report regretfully that the Queen had "a strong feeling on the subject": "To make a *Jew* a peer," she told him, "is a step she cd. *not* consent to."[278]
Beaten, Granville advised Gladstone not to force the issue: "She will yield, but reluctantly, and there will be criticism enough reaching Her, to confirm her in her opinion that she was a better judge than her Govt, and make her more difficult on
another occasion." Gladstone was irked by what seemed to him an inconsistency,
and refused to find an alternative (Christian) "commercial man." "The merit of
Rothschild is that his position is well defined and separated," he argued with his
usual intellectual rigour. "Her argument is null and void. If it be sound, she has been
wrong in consenting to emancipate the Jews." Lionel, he argued, stood "so much
better for the promotion, than anyone whom we can put in his place." To exclude
him would be "to revive by Prerogative the disability which formerly existed by
Statute, and which the Crown and Parliament thought proper to abolish."[279] The
Prime Minister explored every available option—giving Lionel an Irish peerage, for
example—but was eventually forced to back down.[280] He sought to revive the idea
again in 1873, but was again overruled. As a result, Lionel died a commoner.

Was Queen Victoria an anti-Semite?[281] She certainly did admit to a "feeling of
which she cannot divest herself, against making a person of the Jewish religion, a
Peer." But the charge of racial prejudice seems unfounded in view of her affection
for Disraeli, who made so much of his Jewish origins.[282] In fact, her objections were

as much social and political as religious. As she put it in her journal, "I shall have to refuse on the score of his religion, as much as on that of his wealth, being in fact derived largely from money contracts &c., also pointing out the folly of the Whigs wanting to make such a number of Peers."[283] She elaborated on the second point in a letter to Gladstone of November 1, 1869:

> She cannot think that one who owes his great wealth to contracts with Foreign Govts. for loans, or to successful speculations on the Stock Exchange can fairly claim a British peerage. However high Sir [*sic*] L. Rothschild may stand personally in Public estimation, this seems to her not the less a species of gambling, because it is on a gigantic scale—and far removed from that legitimate trading which she delights to honour, in which men have raised themselves by patient industry and unswerving probity to positions of wealth and influence.—such men as the late Thomas Cubitt [the builder], or George Stephenson would have done honour to any house of Peers.[284]

This, however, can be dismissed as mere excuse-making, as at this date there were already three peers whose fortunes stemmed from banking.[285] A more plausible reason for her opposition can be inferred from Granville's allusion to "the present unfortunate antagonism between the Lords and the Commons." The Lords had been the principal source of opposition to the admission of Jews into Parliament and had consented to a fudged compromise only in 1858, giving the Commons the right to modify its own oath to new members. The Queen may have feared that making Lionel a peer would lead to a repeat of the constitutional wrangles of the 1850s. It is noteworthy that Gladstone had deliberately raised the possibility of a "Jew peer" at the same time as that of a Roman Catholic peer (in the person of Sir John Acton).[286] As Granville put it when the issue resurfaced in 1873, the idea of a Rothschild peerage was intended to "be a complement to that of the Catholic."[287] Much more was at stake here than a reward to a loyal Liberal MP for services rendered.

It is worth noting that all this went on without any encouragement from the Rothschilds themselves. Many years before, Lionel had turned down the offer of a baronetcy as beneath his dignity, but by the 1860s he was evidently unwilling to chase after a peerage. "Rothschild is one of the best I know," commented Gladstone as he broached the issue at Balmoral in 1873, "and if I could but get from him a Mem[orandum]. of certain services of his father as to the money during the war I think it wd carry the case over all difficulty. But though I have begged & they have promised for about 4 years, I have never been able to get this in an available form."[288] Nor can it be said that Lionel's son set out to acquire a peerage for himself after his father's death; on the contrary, as we shall see, his politics were increasingly at odds with those of Gladstone (so much so that Alphonse assumed it was Salisbury who had secured him the peerage in 1885). During the long debates between the Queen and her Prime Minister, the Rothschilds were entirely passive.

So what happened between 1873 and 1885 to "overcome the strong scruples" in the Queen's mind? As far as Gladstone's secretary Hamilton was concerned, the significance of a Rothschild peerage had not changed: "[I]t removes the last remnant of religious disqualifications." Natty himself echoed the sentiment when he thanked "the greatest champion of civil and religious liberty" for "bestow[ing] for the first time a peerage on a member of our faith";[289] and he doubtless relished re-enacting his father's triumph in the Commons when, on July 9, 1885, he was sworn in with his hat on his head and his hand on a Hebrew Old Testament. Gladstone's allusions to "really valuable public service" may help to explain why the Queen withdrew her opposition.[290] True, Gladstone was alluding to Nathan's role in the Napoleonic Wars; but, as we shall see, the Rothschilds' direct and enthusiastic involvement in British imperial finance can really be dated from Disraeli's period in office in the mid-1870s, and it seems plausible that this did not go unnoticed by the Queen—though it is too much to portray the peerage as a direct reward for financial services rendered in Egypt.[291] As we shall see, elevating Natty to the Lords may even have been Gladstone's attempt to "kick upstairs" an increasingly troublesome backbench critic of his foreign policy.

The Rothschild peerage also needs to be seen as part of a more general social sea-change. The aim, as Edward Hamilton put it, was "to give an addition to commercial strength to the House of Lords," and Natty's elevation coincided with Edward Baring's becoming Lord Revelstoke.[292] Cassis has also shown that a high percentage of City bankers were titled in the two and a half decades before the First World War and nearly a fifth of them acquired their peerages in the period after 1890. Most of the inherited peerages had been created only in the previous decade. (Lord Addington, Lord Aldenham, Lord Avebury, Lord Biddulph and Lord Hillingdon were all hereditary peers created at around the same time.)[293] The creations of 1885 were thus part of a veritable boom in City peerages.[294] Moreover, Natty was soon joined in the Lords by other Jewish peers: Lord Wandsworth (Sydney James Stern), Lord Swaythling (Samuel Montagu) and Lord Pirbright (Henry de Worms, himself a descendant of Mayer Amschel's eldest daughter Jeanette).[295]

That did not mean that Natty's elevation secured the "universal welcome" predicted by Gladstone;[296] as Hamilton observed, some people "turn[ed] up their noses at the Rothschild peerage." Such snobbery persisted; many of the adverse comments about Alfred and other members of the family cited above can be read as its typical expressions. For the Rothschilds, however, it was a moment to reassert familial pride. Unlike most other business peers, and to the delight of his relations, Natty retained his surname by taking the title of Baron Rothschild of Tring.[297] After 1885 any traces of prejudice within the royal family seem to have vanished. Members of the Rothschild family were involved in the various commemorations of the Queen's Golden Jubilee;[298] and in May 1890 the Queen herself paid a visit to Ferdinand at Waddesdon.[299] Indeed, the effete and fussy "Ferdy" became something of a royal favourite in his old age.[300] The Queen also visited his sister Alice's villa at Grasse several times while she was staying in the south of France in 1891.[301]

In other words, the fact that the Rothschilds formally joined the aristocracy and entered "court society" in this period should not merely be seen as a sign of "feudalisation" or docile assimilation to the values of the established European elite. Even those of the fourth generation who devoted themselves to their gilded palaces and manicured gardens remained conscious and proud of their family's Jewish identity. Ferdinand was typical in that he was (to quote Edward Hamilton again) "proud of his race and his family; and liked talking about his predecessors as if he had an illustrious ancestry and the bluest of bloods." He, Alfred and Nathaniel had ceased to be hard-working businessmen; but in becoming *fin de siècle* aesthetes they had not ceased to be Jews, just as Hannah had not ceased to be a Jew in marrying a Scottish earl. Assimilation is the wrong word to describe the Rothschilds' assertion of their own status as—in Charlotte's idiosyncratic phrase—"the Caucasian royal family." In the 1840s Georges Dairnvaell had commented that the Rothschilds were, after the Saxe-Coburgs, "the most numerous dynasty in Europe";[302] and the similarities between the two extended, cosmopolitan families had increased over the succeeding years. When Alfred visited Leopold II in Brussels in 1892, at least one of them saw it as a meeting of equals: "To me the King simply said: 'Votre famille m'a toujours gâté' ['Your family has always spoiled me'], upon which I replied: 'Pardon Sire, c'est Votre Majesté qui a toujours gâté notre famille.' Short and sweet."[303]

EIGHT

Jewish Questions

Gentlemen, if you do not give us your support, we will proba-
bly have to proscribe you . . . If you do support us, however, we
will make you greater than the modest founder of your house,
or indeed his proudest grandson, could ever have dreamt . . . We
will make you great as we shall take our first elected prince from
your house.

THEODOR HERZL, "ADDRESS TO
THE ROTHSCHILD FAMILY COUNCIL," 1895[1]

The relationship between the Rothschilds and the wider Jewish communities of Europe remained in many ways unchanged in the time of the fourth generation. The aristocratic marriages described in the previous chapter were, it must be emphasised, the exceptions. Most Rothschilds still married other Jews. Indeed, the really significant change in the period was that those other Jews were no longer other Rothschilds. In the third generation there had only been three such marriages, two of which were in fact to cousins through the female line. The first real Jewish outsiders to marry into the family were the Italian industrialist Baron Raimondo Franchetti, who married Sara Louise, daughter of Anselm, in 1858; and Cécile Anspach, who married Gustave the following year. The animosity felt by Betty and her daughter-in-law Adèle towards Cécile provides a good indication of how difficult it was for such outsiders to win acceptance by the family.[2] After 1877 that changed, and marriage to other members of the Jewish social elite rapidly became the norm. In 1878 Wilhelm Carl's daughter Minna married Max Goldschmidt, whose sister was Maurice de Hirsch's wife.[3] It gives an indication of how persistent the practice of endogamy was that Minna's son Albert married Edmond's daughter Miriam in 1910—by which time his father had taken the name von Goldschmidt-Rothschild on being ennobled.[4] Another family which established marital links to the French Rothschilds in this period were the Halphens: in 1905 Alphonse's son Edouard married Germaine Halphen and in 1909 Edmond's son Maurice married her sister Noémie.[5]

Perhaps the best example of a dynastic alliance was between the Rothschilds and the Sassoons, a family who had made their fortune in India and the Far East, some of whom settled in England in this period. In 1881—at a ceremony attended by the Prince of Wales and notable for the wide press coverage it received—Leo married Marie Perugia, daughter of the Trieste merchant Achille Perugia, whose other daughter married Arthur Sassoon.[6] Another link to the Sassoons was forged in 1887, when Gustave's daughter Aline married Sir Edward Sassoon, son and heir of Albert Sassoon.[7] And in 1907 Gustave's son Robert married Nelly Beer, whose family was also linked by marriage to the Sassoons. All the other marriages of this generation were to wealthy Jews of a comparable social standing.[8] This signalled the end of the marital exclusivism of the mid-nineteenth century and the integration of the Rothschilds—albeit as *primus inter pares*—into a wider "cousinhood" of wealthy Jewish families.[9]

The Rothschilds thus remained confidently Jewish; indeed, they became less remote from the Jewish community as a whole as a result of such marriages. True, there were flickers of religious uncertainty, and not only on the part of Constance. The tragic death of Alphonse's and Leonora's infant son René as a result of an infection (erysipelas) following his circumcision precipitated much soul-searching on Charlotte's part.[10] She was also shocked by the strictly kosher diet kept by Wilhelm Carl and his family: "To eat . . . as they do," she commented, noting their "wan and feeble" appearance, "means not to eat at all; it is worse than doing penance."[11] When they met in Frankfurt after a long separation, Natty thought his uncle Wilhelm Carl "too Caucasian in looks to be ornamental. His gait and manner and mode of speech are jewish, not his features."[12] Yet Natty's own fidelity to the religion of his forefathers was unshakeable. As an undergraduate, he dismissed Paley's *Evidences of Christianity* as "the most absurd conglomeration of words I ever broke my head over, so that there is no danger of my being converted as many up here have prophesied."[13] Leo had been forced to study more than his fair share of Paley too; but there is no mistaking the enthusiasm with which he described attending synagogue in Vienna with his uncle Anthony and cousin Albert in 1869.[14] When a new synagogue was built at St Petersburg Place, Bayswater, in 1877 it was Leo who laid the foundation stone, as his father had done seven years before when work was begun on the Central Synagogue.[15]

Like their grandfather and father before them, Natty and his brothers were not much interested in the finer points of theology or religious ritual. In 1912, for example, Natty was reported as saying that he did "not consider it the part of an orthodox Jew to discuss the shape and size of a *mikvah* [Jewish bathhouse]."[16] For them, religion meant the organisation and functioning of the Jewish community; and as Rothschilds, they regarded it as self-evident that they should act as the lay leaders of that community in England. The extent to which they were able to occupy this position in the late nineteenth century is remarkable. Natty was President of the United Synagogue from 1879 to his death in 1915 (though he took little interest in day-to-day matters).[17] Between 1868 and 1941, a Rothschild served without interruption as treasurer of the Board of Deputies: first Ferdinand (1868–74) then Natty (to 1879) then Leo (to 1917) then Lionel.[18] Natty was also honorary president of the Federation of Synagogues, president of the Jews' Free School, vice-president of the Anglo-Jewish Association and a member of the Sanitary and Legislative Committees of the Board of Guardians.[19] Leo succeeded him as president of the Free School and was also vice-president of the Poor Jews' Temporary Shelter (see below).[20] The Rothschilds also had influence over the *Jewish Chronicle* when it was owned by Asher Myers (though not after it was acquired by the Zionist Leopold Greenberg in 1907).[21] In France the Rothschilds built several new synagogues, including one in the rue de la Victoire (1877) and three others financed by Edmond between 1907 and 1913.[22] By comparison, the Viennese Rothschilds were less engaged with their fellow Jews.[23]

To be sure, Rothschild primacy was not wholly undisputed in what was, after all, less a single community than a number of more or less distinct communities (besides the United Synagogue, there were also the Sephardic Spanish and Portuguese, the Reform and a growing number of Orthodox congregations established by immigrants from Eastern Europe). The most often cited example of a challenge to Natty's position came with the creation in 1887 of the Federation of Synagogues, the brainchild of the bullion dealer and politician Samuel Montagu, which was intended to act as an umbrella for the Orthodox congregations. Natty had for some time been concerned about what he saw as the "spiritual destitution" of the East End,[24] and at the Federation's foundation he was made its president, but in December 1888 he was forced to surrender the office to Montagu after a confrontation at the United Synagogue Council over the admission of the Federation to the London Shechita Board (the authority overseeing ritual slaughter).[25] It would seem that what he wished to achieve was the imposition of the United Synagogue's authority over the newcomers—hence his original scheme for a large synagogue in Whitechapel Road to be linked to a "Jewish Toynbee Hall."[26]

The significance of this should not be exaggerated, however. In fact, Natty retained the title of honorary president and even performed the opening ceremony for the Federation's first synagogue in New Road in 1892.[27] Indeed, his desire to unite the various Jewish communities was more welcome to Montagu than to many members of the United Synagogue. It was to this end, following the death of the long-serving Chief Rabbi Nathan Marcus Adler in 1890—and despite opposition from Adler's son and successor Hermann—that Natty called a conference of the various synagogues, arguing "that the time had come when even the humblest portion of the Community . . . and certainly the most orthodox, should invite the other branches of the Community to join with us in attempting to unite us all. I will not say under one head, but under one spiritual Chief." However, it proved impossible to reconcile the competing claims for influence of the different communities; and a similar effort failed in 1910 for the same reason.[28] Still, Natty was powerful enough to secure the appointment of Joseph Herman Hertz as Chief Rabbi in succession to Adler in 1912, largely (according to one account) on the strength of Lord Milner's recommendation, though more probably because he saw Hertz as likely to appeal to both the Federation and the United Synagogue—to the Orthodox East End and the more assimilated West End.[29]

If his influence extended this far on an essentially religious question, it is hardly surprising that on more political questions relating to the Jewish community Natty was accorded quasi-regal status. As the scion of the richest of all Jewish families, a key figure in the City, an MP and then a peer, and as an unofficial diplomat with direct access to most senior politicians of the day, he had no equal. It might not be possible to get the various Jewish communities to agree on a single spiritual "Chief"; but there could be little doubt that Natty was their *de facto* temporal chief.

To appreciate the significance of this, it is necessary to appreciate the profound—and alarming—questions which were being raised about the position of Jews in Europe at this time. When Natty became a peer, Alphonse's reaction was revealing: "This news will have great repercussions in Austria and Germany," he wrote, "where anti-Semitism is still so virulent."[30] The late nineteenth century saw the transformation of what had previously been an incoherent and politically heterogeneous prejudice against Jews—sometimes harking back to the restrictions imposed on them under the *ancien régime*, sometimes looking forward to a utopia in which they and all other exploitative capitalists would be expropriated—into something more like organised political movements. It is no coincidence that the term "anti-Semitism" itself dates from this period: racial theories were developing which purported to explain the supposedly anti-social behaviour of Jews in terms of their genes rather than their religion. As political life became more democratised by the development of mass literacy and the widening of the franchise, the years after *c.* 1877 saw a great upsurge of anti-Jewish journalism, speech-making and, in some countries such as Russia, actual policy. The Rothschilds had little other than their religion in common with the Jews who came westwards from Eastern and Central Europe. As we have seen, they were part of a wealthy elite which had overcome virtually all of the social barriers which remained against Jews in Western Europe. Yet, having since the 1820s been the targets of political malcontents on both the left and right, it was probably inevitable that the Rothschilds would once again be identified as the personification of the "Jewish problem." This was the disadvantage of being "Kings of the Jews."

Anti-Semitism

Events in the mid-twentieth century tempt us to exaggerate the importance of anti-Semitism in the late nineteenth century. As an organised political movement it was minor compared with socialism; and it is a mistake to see every expression of hostility towards Jews as a manifestation of it, for these were as ubiquitous as votes for anti-Semitic candidates were sparse. The memory of National Socialism also inclines us to look first to the German lands for signs of anti-Semitism. Of course, there were some there (more in Austria than in Germany, where the Rothschilds' financial importance was declining); but traces can also be found in Britain, while Russia was the only major state which systematically discriminated against the Jews. Yet France, where Jews had enjoyed equal rights for longer than anywhere else, was also the country where the volume of anti-Semitic publication was greatest.

It is not without importance that Wilhelm Marr, the man who introduced the specifically racialist term *Antisemitismus* to German politics, had worked as a young man for the Wertheimsteins, a family closely linked to the Vienna Rothschilds. In an unpublished memoir, Marr recalled how he had been dismissed in 1841 despite working harder than many of the Jewish clerks in the firm. "It was," he recalled bitterly, "the 'goi' who had to bear the consequences of the economic crisis."[31] Such experiences seemed to find an echo in the economic difficulties of many Germans after the 1873 crash. A good example of the kind of anti-Rothschild polemic inspired by writers like Marr was *The Frankfurt Jews and the Mulcting of the People's*

Wellbeing published by "Germanicus" in 1880. The title speaks for itself: beginning with the now familiar garbled version of the Elector's treasure story, the author is primarily concerned to relate Germany's economic difficulties during and after the *Gründerzeit* to capital export (especially to Russia) encouraged by the Rothschilds and their lackeys in the financial press.[32] There is not a great deal to choose between this and the claim made by the Hessian Reichstag Deputy Otto Böckel in 1890 that the Rothschilds had cornered the world market in oil—a charge which was being repeated in Social Democrat pubs in Berlin five years later (illustrating how readily this rhetoric could still be used by the left).[33] Friedrich von Scherb's 1893 *History of the House of the Rothschild* developed this point in some detail, arguing that the Rothschilds' relentless profiteering had found a new target: having dominated state loans and then railway construction, they were now seeking to establish global monopolies of raw materials.[34]

By 1911, when Werner Sombart published his tendentious but influential book *The Jews and Economic Life*, such claims enjoyed a degree of intellectual respectability. For Sombart, "the name Rothschild" meant "more than the firm which bears it"; it meant "all the Jews who are active at the bourse":

> For only with their help were the Rothschilds able to achieve that posi-
> tion of supreme power—indeed one can justly say the sole mastery of
> the bond market—which we see them possessing for half a century. It is
> certainly no exaggeration that one used to be able to say that . . . a
> Finance Minister who alienated this world house and refused to co-
> operate with it more or less had to shut his office up. . . [N]ot only in
> quantitative terms, but also in qualitative terms, the modern bourse is
> Rothschildian (and thus Jewish).[35]

But it was not necessary to root anti-Semitism in this kind of bogus sociology: the racial differences between Jews and Germans could simply be asserted. Max Bauer's pamphlet *Bismarck and Rothschild* (1891), contrasted Bismarck, the embodiment of Teutonic, peasant virtue, with Rothschild, his cosmopolitan antithesis:

> The principle of his existence is not the calm growth of a constructive
> strength, but the hasty and nervous gathering of a dismembered mass of
> money . . . But [thinks Bismarck] just leave the Jew to his insatiable
> pleasure; once the five billion marks have been paid in full, it will be the
> German's turn to amuse himself in his own fashion! . . . Bismarck's phys-
> ical and spiritual form stands clearly and tangibly for all to see . . . But
> what physical notion does the world have of Rothschild? He is never
> seen, just as the tapeworm remains invisible in the human body. The
> "house" of Rothschild is a structureless, parasitical something-or-other,
> that proliferates across the earth from Frankfurt and Paris to London,
> like a twisted telephone wire. There is neither structure nor life in him,
> nothing that grows in the earth, nothing that strives towards God. Bis-
> marck's spirit is like a gothic building . . . These are the powers which
> stand antagonistically opposite one another in the political culture of
> our times: insatiable Jewry, that destroys life; and hearty Germandom,
> which generates life.[36]

There were similar publications in Austria;[37] but there, where the Rothschilds remained a major economic force, anti-Semitism was more politically effective than in Germany. It was in the years after the 1873 Vienna stock market crash that Karl Lueger conceived his "Christian Social" campaign against Jewish financial power.[38] A turning point in this campaign was Lueger's call in 1884 for the nationalisation of the Rothschild-owned Kaiser-Ferdinand-Nordbahn when the government proposed renewing the original charter granted to Salomon in 1836.[39] Lueger's demand that the government pay "attention for once to the voice of the people instead of the voices of the Rothschilds" was echoed by Georg Schönerer's German National Association, and their ire was only increased when Albert was awarded the Iron Cross in 1893 for his role in Austro-Hungarian monetary reform.[40] However, when Lueger himself came to power as Mayor of Vienna in 1897, he quickly discovered how difficult it was to dispense with the Rothschilds. By the late 1890s, critics like the conservative Karl Kraus (himself a Jew by birth) and the Social Democrat newspaper the *Arbeiterzeitung* were accusing Lueger of being "on good terms with the Rothschilds" and even working "hand in hand with the Jew Rothschild."[41] At the same time, in classic Habsburg fashion, the *Jüdische Zeitschrift* accused the Rothschilds of employing anti-Semites in preference to Jews![42] Rothschild power remained a byword even among those without a political axe to grind. To give just one example, the Tyrolean poet and professor of geology Adolf Pichler remarked in 1882 how "Rothschild" could "make the Mount Olympus of Austrian government bonds totter." It was, he added sarcastically, "a sublime spectacle."[43]

But it was in France that anti-Semitism was most articulate and all-pervasive. The outpouring of publications hostile to the Rothschilds which characterised the 1880s had no real parallel in nineteenth-century history; not even the great pamphlet war after the Nord railway accident in 1846 produced so many libels. This time the catalysing "accident" was the collapse of the clerically backed Union Générale bank in 1882. No sooner had the Union Générale folded than its founder Paul Eugène Bontoux began laying the blame on "Jewish finance" and its ally "governmental freemasonry." This refrain was taken up by sections of the press: the *Moniteur de Lyon* spoke of a "conspiracy orchestrated by a society of Jewish bankers from Germany" and a "German-Jewish conspiracy."[44]

Perhaps paradoxically, in view of his later role as a Dreyfusard, few writers did more to give this idea currency than the novelist Emile Zola. Although set in the Second Empire, his novel *L'Argent*—part of his vast Rougon Macquart cycle—was obviously inspired by the Union Générale débâcle (with occasional allusions to the Crédit Mobilier). And although the character of Gundermann was plainly not based on Alphonse, there is no doubt whatever that it was based, with one or two modifications, on his late father James. There is an eerie quality to this unflattering resurrection, for Gundermann lacks the redeeming humanity of Balzac's Nucingen, the other great literary creation James inspired. The best explanation for this is that Zola had not known James as Balzac had; over a decade after his death, he had to turn for inspiration to the memoirs of others—indeed, passages of *L'Argent* are lifted more or less verbatim from Feydeau. Gundermann is introduced early on as:

> the banker king, the master of the bourse and of the world . . . the man
> who knew [all] secrets, who made at his beck and call the markets rise
> and fall as God makes the thunder . . . the king of gold . . . Gundermann
> was the true master, the all-powerful king, feared and obeyed by Paris

and the world . . . One could already see that in Paris a Gundermann reigned on a more solid and more respected throne than the emperor.[45]

He is cool, calculating, dyspeptic (a fictional touch), ascetic, workaholic. Saccard, by contrast, is an impetuous young would-be financier with clerical sympathies who dreams of financing projects in the Balkans and Middle East which might eventually lead to the purchase of Jerusalem and the re-establishment of the Papacy there. In the hope of winning his support, he goes to see Gundermann in his "immense hôtel" where he lives and works with his "innumerable family": five daughters, four sons and fourteen grandchildren. Once again we enter the thronged offices of the rue Laffitte, where queues of brokers file past the impassive banker, who treats them with indifference or—if they dare to address him—outright contempt; where art-dealers vie with foreign ambassadors for his attention; and where (the debt to Feydeau is unmistakable) a small boy of five or six bursts in, riding a broomstick and playing a trumpet. This bizarre court confirms in Saccard's eyes "the universal royalty" of Gundermann.[46]

Saccard wants Gundermann's backing—yearns, in fact, to make money on the bourse just as he has. Yet as he contemplates "the Jew" he instinctively imagines himself "an honest man, living by the sweat of his brow" and is overwhelmed with an "inextinguishable hatred" for

> that accursed race which no longer has its own country, no longer has its own prince, which lives parasitically in the home of nations, feigning to obey the law, but in reality only obeying its own God of theft, of blood, of anger . . . fulfilling everywhere its mission of ferocious conquest, to lie in wait for its prey, suck the blood out of everyone, [and] grow fat on the life of others.

As Saccard sees it, the Jew has a hereditary advantage over the Christian in finance, and he foresees—even as he enters Gundermann's office—"the final conquest of all the peoples by the Jews."

When, inevitably, Gundermann dismisses his proposal, Saccard's antipathy becomes positively violent: "Ah the dirty Jew! There's one it would be a decided pleasure to chew between one's teeth, the way a dog chews a bone! Though certainly it would be too terrible and too large a morsel to swallow." "The empire has been sold to the Jews, to the dirty Jews," he cries:

> All our money is doomed to fall between their crooked claws. The Universal Bank can do nothing more than crumble before their omnipotence . . . And he gave vent to his hereditary hatred, he repeated his accusations against that race of traffickers and usurers, on the march throughout the centuries against the peoples [of the world], whose blood they suck . . . [bent on] the certain conquest of the world, which they will possess one day by the invincible power of money . . . Ah! that Gundermann! A Prussian at heart . . . Had he not dared to say one evening in a salon that if ever a war broke out between Prussia and France, the latter would be defeated![47]

In the end, of course, Gundermann triumphs: the Banque Universelle collapses and Saccard ends up in jail, leaving in his wake a trail of broken hearts and empty purses.

No one could accuse Zola of having failed to do his homework: not only was the portrayal of James's office carefully based on an eyewitness account, but the rise and fall of the Union Générale was described with some precision—the mopping up of clerical and aristocratic savings, the bidding up of its own shares and the eventual débâcle. But what Zola had also done was to give literary credibility to the idea that the Union Générale really had been destroyed by the Rothschilds, as well as to the canard that the French Rothschilds had pro-German sympathies. That such notions struck a chord in the France of the Third Republic is all too apparent. Guy de Charnacé's *Baron Vampire* is as wretched a book as *L'Argent* is powerful; but its message is not too different. The character of Rebb Schmoul, like Gundermann, is a German Jew with a distinctively racial gift for financial manipulation. A "bird of prey," he profits from the horrors of war, then metamorphoses into Baron Rakonitz, advising impecunious baronesses in return for their social patronage.[48] Such stereotypes were given added currency by the publication of Bontoux's own memoirs in 1888. Although Bontoux did not mention the Rothschilds by name, there was little doubt about whom he meant when he denounced "la Banque Juive," which, "not content with the billions which had come into into its coffers for fifty years . . . not content with the monopoly which it exercises on nine-tenths at least of all Europe's financial affairs," had set out to destroy the Union Générale.[49]

It was, however, another disappointed man—Edouard Drumont—who made perhaps the biggest of all individual contributions to French anti-Semitic mythology. Edouard Drumont had worked as a young man at the Crédit Mobilier and had devoted years to researching and writing a huge and rambling tome which purported to describe the full extent of Jewish domination of French economic and political life. First published in 1886 and so successful that it subsequently appeared in 200 editions, *Jewish France* took the notion of a racially determined and anti-French Jewish character and developed it into a pseudo-system. Thus "the Rothschilds, despite their billions, have the air of second-hand clothes dealers. Their wives, despite all the diamonds of Golconda, will always look like merchants at their toilet." Even the sophisticated Baroness Betty cannot conceal her origins as a "Frankfurt Jewess" when the conversation turns to precious stones.[50] In part, Drumont was merely updating the pamphlets of the 1840s (Dairnvaell was his main inspiration), so that much of his attention in the first volume is devoted to the idea of the Rothschilds' excessive political power. It is all here: their speculation on the outcome of Waterloo, their immense profits from the Nord concession, their antagonism to the more public-spirited Pereires. Goudchaux—a Jew—saves them from bankruptcy in 1848 and Jews in the Commune protect Rothschild properties from arson in 1871. The politics of the Republic are merely a continuation of this story: Gambetta is in league with the Jews and Masons, Léon Say—"l'homme du roi des juifs"—plays a similar role, and Cousin, President of the Supreme Council, is merely a cog in the great Jewish–Masonic machine which is the Compagnie du Nord. Even the fall of Jules Ferry can be attributed to the Rothschilds' malign influence.[51] Best of all, Drumont suggests that the Union Générale was in fact an elaborate Jewish trap, designed to mulct the clericals of their savings.[52]

Drumont's later *Testament of an Anti-Semite* (1894) further developed these poisonous ideas, partly in order to explain the limited political achievements of the anti-Semitic movement. Here he adopted a more pseudo-empirical style, calculating how much the Rothschilds' supposed fortune of 3 billion francs would weigh measured out in silver—and how many men it would require to move it!—and comparing the number of acres of land owned by the Rothschild family with the number owned by the religious orders. If the Boulangists had eschewed anti-Semitism, it was only because "Rothschild had paid [them] 200,000 francs for the municipal elections, on condition that the candidates would not take an anti-Semitic stance," and because the Boulangist leader Laguerre had personally received 50,000 francs.[53] If the French economy was depressed, it was because "Léon Say . . . had handed over the Banque [de France] to the German Jews," allowing the Rothschilds to lend out its gold to the Bank of England.[54] If France was internationally isolated, it was because the Rothschilds had handed over Egypt to England and financed Italian armaments with French capital.[55] This last charge of lack of patriotism was repeated a few years later in *The Jews against France* (1899).[56] "The God Rothschild," Drumont concluded, was the real "master" of France: "Neither Emperor, nor Tsar, nor King, nor Sultan, nor President of the Republic . . . he has none of the responsibilities of power and all the advantages; he disposes over all the governmental forces, all the resources of France for his private purposes."[57]

Drumont was only the most prolific of a group of anti-Semitic writers of the period who directed their fire at the Rothschilds. Another purveyor of similar libels was Auguste Chirac, whose *Kings of the Republic* (1883) mingled old chestnuts like the myths of the Elector's treasure and Waterloo with new claims about the Nord line and the Rothschilds' relationship with the revolutionaries of 1848 and 1870–71. Once again, there was both a racial and a national dimension to the argument: not only were the Rothschilds Jews, they were also Germans—hence their eagerness to despoil France by financing reparations payments in 1815 and 1871.[58] Chirac's later book, *The Speculation of 1870 to 1884* (1887), was a more sophisticated work which sought to explain the Rothschilds' recent profits by analysing the fluctuations of bond prices in the period before and after the Union Générale crisis—a not unreasonable enterprise in itself, but compromised once again by its intemperate and unsubstantiated allegations against the Rothschilds and Léon Say. Though superficially empirical, this was in reality just another diatribe against "the triumph of the feudalism of money and the crushing of the worker" and the control of the Republic by "a *king* named Rothschild, with a courtesan or maidservant called *Jewish finance*." The main allegation made here was that the Rothschilds had conspired to undermine French influence in Egypt for the benefit of England, as part of their historic mission to "kill France" by financial means. The outwardly unremarkable Alphonse was in truth "Moloch-Baal, that is to say the God *Gold*, marching towards the conquest of Europe and perhaps the world, possessing [real] power behind the royal names and political garb, having, in a word, all the profits and avoiding all the responsibilities."[59]

Predictably, such diatribes were accompanied by numerous hateful caricatures, of which the best known is probably Léandre's *God Protect Israel*. Here Alphonse is portrayed as an emaciated, half-slumbering giant who clutches the globe in claw-like hands and wears on his bald head a crown shaped like the golden calf (see illustration 8.i).

In a similar vein is Lepneveu's *Nathan Mayer or the Origin of the Billions* which portrays a bearded Rothschild with the body of a wolf lying on a bed of bones and

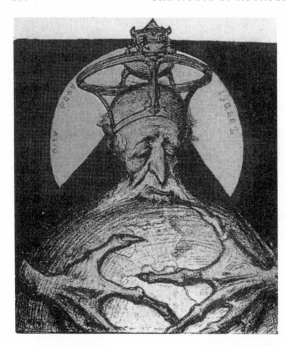

8.i: C. Léandre, *Dieu protège Israel, Le Rêve* (April 1898).

coins on the battlefield of Waterloo (see illustration 8.ii). More crudely, another cartoon (probably from the political left) portrayed "Rothschild" as a giant pig being pulled in a carriage by ragged workers with the caption: "What a fat pig! He grows fat as we grow thin."[60]

Though primarily conpiracy theorists, writers like Drumont and Chirac were also preoccupied with the Rothschilds' penetration of French high culture and society. In the second volume of *Jewish France*, Drumont devotes a long passage to the château and gardens at Ferrières. The art and furnishings, he concedes, are magnificent; what is lamentable is that so many jewels of French heritage should belong to Jews who can only jumble them together like so much "bric-à-brac." Nor is it only French culture which the Rothschilds can buy. "This château without a past," he comments, "does not recall the grand seigneurial lifestyle of the past"; yet the visitors' book now contains "the most illustrious names of the French nobility." A prince de Joinville—"a man in whose veins flow drops of the blood of Louis XIV"—abases himself before a mere "money-lender." At Rothschild marriages, the list of noble names is complete: "[A]ll the [ancient] arms of France . . . gathered to worship the golden calf and to proclaim before the eyes of Europe that wealth is the sole royalty which now exists." It is the same story at the costume ball given by the princesse de Sagan in 1885: "this miserable aristocracy" shamelessly rubs shoulders with Mme Lambert-Rothschild, Mme Ephrussi and the rest of "Jewry."[61] At heart a romantic Legitimist, Drumont regarded the Bourbon and Orléanist nobility as traitors to their Gallic race. It was a theme he returned to in his *Testament*, noting with dismay Charlotte's purchase of "an abbey founded by Simon de Montfort" (Vaux-de-Cernay), Edouard's election to the exclusive Cercle de la rue Royale and the presence of the usual grand names at a Rothschild garden party.[62] Chirac too commented sourly on the relationship between the Rothschilds and the elite of the

8.ii: Lepneveu, *Nathan Mayer ou l'origine des milliards,* cover of *Musée des Horreurs,* no. 42 (c. 1900).

Faubourg Saint-Germain, which had once disdained James and Betty but now accepted their children as social equals.[63]

It was one of the oddities of the Jewish experience under the Third Republic that a high degree of social assimilation coincided with very public expressions of anti-Semitism. Nor was it merely a matter of outsiders like Drumont carping while royalist aristocrats put prejudice aside; often the very people who socialised with the Rothschilds sympathised with the views propounded by Drumont and Chirac. The almost schizophrenic nature of attitudes towards the Rothschilds can be illustrated with reference to two important contemporary sources: the Goncourt brothers' journal and Proust's *A la recherche du temps perdu.* The Goncourts not only shared Drumont's views; they knew him well. Their journals for the period 1870 to 1896 are full of spiteful anecdotes about the Rothschilds' "Jewish" character—their materialism, their Philistinism and so on.[64] Yet the Goncourts were also themselves quite happy to accept Rothschild hospitality: discussing French engravings with Edmond in 1874 and 1887, dining with Nat's widow in 1885, dining with Leonora in 1888, dining at Edmond's in 1889. It was characteristic of the period that the Goncourts could quote Drumont approvingly less than a year after praising Rothschild cuisine; could dine with Drumont and listen happily to his talk of putting "Rothschild against a wall" in March 1887, then discuss engravings with Edmond that December; could dine at Edmond's in June 1889, then exchange anti-Semitic anecdotes with Drumont in March 1890, just months before his abortive anti-Semitic call to arms on May 1.[65]

This world of Parisian salons, in which Jews and anti-Semites routinely mixed, was dramatically polarised in 1894 when Alfred Dreyfus, a Jewish officer on the

French General Staff, was accused of being a German spy, court-martialled, found guilty on the basis of forged documents and sentenced to life imprisonment on Devil's Island. Alphonse's reaction to the allegations against Dreyfus was initially one of alarm at the effect the case would have in encouraging anti-Semitism, on the assumption that Dreyfus was guilty; but this soon turned to anger as the evidence accumulated to suggest that Dreyfus had been framed.[66] According to one clerical memoir, Alphonse was "irritated by the condemnation of Dreyfus and by the indifference of the French aristocracy."[67] However, other members of the family were less willing to be identified publicly as "Dreyfusards," preferring to try to minimise the schism within their own upper-class milieu.

Proust gives a flavour of the atmosphere of this time, with Dreyfusard sympathies being studiously concealed by members of the heterogeneous circle around the duchesse de Guermantes. To Bloch, a Jew of relatively undistinguished origins, the very name Rothschild inspires awe; when he realises that an old English woman whom he has been patronising at the duchesse's is "La baronne Alphonse de Rothschild" he is thunderstruck:

> At that moment there suddenly flooded through Bloch's arteries so many ideas of millions and prestige . . . that it was as if he had suffered a stroke, a mental spasm, and he exclaimed involuntarily in the presence of the amiable old lady: "*If only I had known!*"—an exclamation of such stupidity that it kept him awake for eight nights in a row.[68]

The *prince* de Guermantes, on the other hand, will not even receive a Rothschild—indeed, would rather let a wing of his château burn down than ask for water-pumps from the neighbouring Rothschild house.[69] In fact, he turns out to harbour secret Dreyfusard inclinations;[70] but he keeps these hidden because to be identified as a Dreyfusard carries a social price. The *duc* de Guermantes pays that price when he fails to secure election to the presidency of the the Jockey Club because his wife "was a Dreyfusard . . . received the Rothschilds, and . . . for some time . . . had shown favour to great international magnates who, like the duc de Guermantes himself, were half-German."[71] This in turn makes the Duke bitter:

> The Alphonse Rothschilds, although they have the tact never to speak about this abominable affair, are Dreyfusards in their hearts, like all Jews . . . If a Frenchman steals or murders I do not feel obliged to find him innocent simply because he is a Frenchman. But the Jews will never admit that one of their fellow citizens is a traitor, although they know it perfectly well, and could not care less about the frightful consequences (the Duke was naturally thinking of the damned election . . .)[72]

The Dreyfus affair exposed similar attitudes on the political left as well. When a Jewish journalist named Bernard Lazare published a pro-Dreyfus pamphlet, he was immediately attacked by the socialist Alexandre Zévaès in the *Petite République* as "one of the faithful admirers of His Majesty Rothschild."[73]

Such attitudes existed in England too. In June 1900 David Lindsay recorded in his diary his attendance at "Hertford House, where a large party invited by Alfred Rothschild and Rosebery assembled to meet the Prince of Wales." "The number of Jews in this palace," Lindsay declared,

was past belief. I have studied the anti-semite question with some attention, always hoping to stem an ignoble movement: but when confronted by the herd of Ickleheimers, Puppenbergs, Raphaels, Sassoons
and the rest of the breed, my emotions gain the better of logic and
injustice, while I feel some sympathy with Lüger [*sic*] and Drumont—
John Burns [the labour leader and future Liberal Cabinet minister], by
the way, says the Jew is the tapeworm of civilization.[74]

Yet Lindsay continued to accept invitations to Waddesdon and Tring. Similar sentiments were sometimes privately expressed by non-Jewish bankers in the City,
though none could avoid doing business with Jews.[75] There are also a number of
stereotypical Jewish financier-villains in late Victorian fiction: Trollope's uncouth
Melmotte in *The Way We Live Now* is not based on a Rothschild, but there is no mistaking the provenance of Baron Glumthal—"the great Frankfurt millionaire" with
the "slightest trace of a foreign accent" and the politically all-powerful "house" in
Charles Lever's *Davenport Dunn*.[76]

The difference between England and France is that anti-Semitism was more
likely to be given a political outlet on the left than on the right. Where Drumont
was a frustrated clerical legitimist, the English writers who explicitly attacked the
Rothschilds were as likely to be socialists or New Liberals like John Burns as radical
nationalists. A good illustration is John Reeves's book *The Rothschilds: The Financial
Rulers of Nations* (1887), which returns a typical verdict: "The Rothschilds belong
to no one nationality, they are cosmopolitan . . . they belonged to no party, they
were ready to grow rich at the expense of friend and foe alike."[77] Four years later, it
was the *Labour Leader* which denounced the Rothschilds as a

> blood-sucking crew [which] has been the cause of untold mischief and
> misery in Europe during the present century, and has piled up its prodi-
> gious wealth chiefly through fomenting wars between States which
> ought never to have quarrelled. Wherever there is trouble in Europe,
> wherever rumours of war circulate and men's minds are distraught with
> fear of change and calamity you may be sure that a hook-nosed Roth-
> schild is at his games somewhere near the region of the disturbance.[78]

Perhaps the most intriguing case of all is that of the left-leaning Liberal J. A.
Hobson, author of the classic *Imperialism: A Study* (1902). Like many radical writers of the period, Hobson regarded the Boer War as having been engineered "by a
small group of international financiers, chiefly German in origin and Jewish in race"
who were "prepared to fasten on any . . . spot upon the globe . . . taking their gains
not out of the genuine fruits of industry, even the industry of others, but out of the
construction, promotion, and financial manipulations of companies."[79] There is no
question that he regarded the Rothschilds as central to this group.[80] It is true that in
later years Hobson moved away from this anti-Semitic line of argument in favour of
a more orthodox socialist anti-capitalism. But such rhetoric had become part of the
political language of Edwardian radicalism. As we shall see, it was Lloyd George, the
most radical of pre-war Chancellors of the Exchequer, who singled out Natty for a
remarkable personal attack during the debates over his 1909 budget, though Lloyd

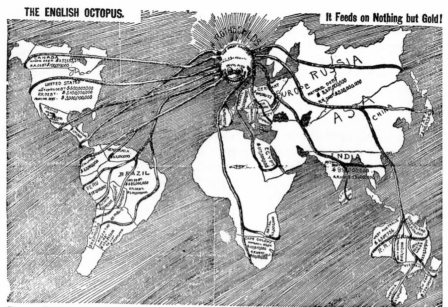

Denver Road.

8.iii: "Coin" Harvey, *The English Octopus: It Feeds on Nothing but Gold!* (1894).

George himself was denounced by the right for his own involvement with Jewish financiers (the Isaacs brothers) in the Marconi affair.

In America too there was anti-Rothschildism. Ever since the 1830s, the Rothschilds had been political targets in the United States, despite their relatively limited financial influence there. But even the attacks they had suffered during the Civil War paled alongside those during the brief heyday of the People's Party in the 1890s. The Populists were essentially opponents of American entry into the gold standard, mobilising the discontent of mid-Western farmers with the low grain prices of the 1880s. However, their critique of the "gold gamblers of Europe and America" and "the secret cabals of the international gold ring" had a strong anti-Semitic as well as anti-English component, due not least to the prominent role played by the London Rothschilds in the loans which facilitated the American transition to gold. Gordon Clark's book *Shylock: as Banker, Bondholder, Corruptionist, Conspirator* alleged that a deal had been struck between Hugh McCulloch, Secretary of the Treasury under Lincoln and Johnson, and James de Rothschild: "The most direful part of this business between Rothschild and the United States Treasury," he claimed, "was not the loss of money, even by the hundreds of millions. It was the resignation of the country itself INTO THE HANDS OF ENGLAND, as England has long been resigned into the hands of HER JEWS." In *Coin's Financial School* (1894), "Coin" Harvey depicted the world in the clutches of a huge, "English Octopus" bearing the name: "Rothschilds" (see illustration 8.iii). In the same author's novel *A Tale of Two Nations*, the mastermind of the English plan to "destroy the United States" by demonetising silver is a banker named "Baron Rothe." These allegations became something of an embarrassment when the Populist movement was absorbed by the Democrat Party. The Democratic presidential candidate William Jennings Bryan had to explain to Jewish Democrats that in attacking the Rothschilds he and the Populist leaders were "not attacking a race; we are attacking greed and avarice which know no race or religion."[81]

It might be asked how far such polemics could actually hurt the Rothschilds, secure as they seemed in their palatial residences. Yet the repeated identification of the Rothschilds as the architects of a Jewish capitalist conspiracy almost inevitably inspired acts of violence directed against members of the family. The least serious of these were the crude assault on Natty's son Walter, who was dragged off his horse by some unemployed workmen while hunting near Tring, and the "Jew hunts" experienced by his brother Charles at Harrow.[82] More serious were the two assassination attempts of the period. In August 1895 a crude letter bomb was sent to Alphonse at his home in the rue Florentin; in his absence it was forwarded to the rue Laffitte where it blew up and seriously injured his head clerk. "An Anarchist outrage on one of the Rothschilds is not greatly to be wondered at," commented *The Times*. "In France as elsewhere they are so wealthy and hold so prominent a place that they stand out as the natural objects which Anarchists would seek to attack, and when we take further into account the intense anti-Jewish feeling which exists in France, we are the more inclined to wonder that they have escaped so long."[83] Nor was the threat of assassination confined to France. In London in 1912 a man named William Tebbitt fired at Leo five times with a revolver as he was driving out of New Court, riddling his car with bullets and badly wounding the policeman on guard at the door.[84] Tebbitt appears to have been insane (Leo had apparently done him some kindness); but the attack was symptomatic of the vulnerability of the family at a time when handguns and hand-grenades were making assassination easier than it had ever been in the past.

Responses

The most elementary response to attack is to fight back. That was the response favoured by Alphonse's son Edouard and Gustave's son Robert, both whom responded to racial insults by demanding satisfaction on the field of honour.[85] But one could not duel with every anti-Semite. The question of how to respond to religious and racial intolerance had long preoccupied the Rothschilds; but the new forms of prejudice which characterised the *fin de siècle* called for new responses. These were not easy to formulate.

Because of their unique social position—simultaneously at the apex of the respective Jewish communities and in increasingly close contact with the European aristocracies—the Rothschilds were sometimes inclined to blame anti-Semitism not just on anti-Semites but on other Jews. In 1875 Mayer Carl told Bismarck: "As for anti-semitic feeling the Jews themselves are to blame, and the present agitation must be ascribed to their arrogance, vanity and unspeakable insolence."[86] To modern eyes, this seems a shocking statement, suggesting a kind of disloyalty to the wider Jewish community which is not at first sight easily reconciled with the Rothschilds' claim to be that community's lay leaders. Yet the fact that the man who tried to assassinate Leo was (as Natty put it) "of our own persuasion" is significant: there were profound tensions between Jews too in this period.

The two groups which gave the Rothschilds most concern were *nouveaux riches*—Jewish bankers and businessmen who had made their fortunes more recently than the Rothschilds—and, perhaps more important, *Ostjuden:* the much more numerous Jews of Eastern Europe (principally though not exclusively from the Russian Empire), 2.5 million of whom migrated westwards after the pogroms sparked off by the assassination of Alexander II in 1881 and the new discriminatory laws introduced the following year.[87] In the former category, Gerson Bleichröder was viewed with especial distaste, though it is reasonable to assume that part of Mayer Carl's grievance against Bleichröder had its origins in their business disagreements. Forwarding a letter from Bleichröder on the subject of German anti-Semitism in November 1880, Natty told Disraeli:

> There is no doubt that Bleichröder himself is one of the causes of the Jewish persecution, he has been employed so often by the German Government that he has become arrogant and forgets that he is very often merely "a Ballon d'essai."
> There are also a great many other reasons . . . among them the constant influx of Polish Russian and Roumanian Jews who arrive in a state of starvation and are socialists until they become rich.
> The Jews also are proprietors of half the newspapers particularly of those papers which are anti Russian . . . I hear also that Madame von Bleichröder is most disagreeable & haughty.[88]

As these comments suggest, the new poor were at least as great a source of embarrassment as the *nouveaux riches.*

The Rothschild response to anti-Semitism was not just (as Drumont alleged) to demand high levels of police protection and to fortify their houses; though they can be forgiven for doing so in the light of the assassination attempts described above. There was a long-standing family view about how best to deflect or mitigate anti-Jewish feelings. Ever since the time of Mayer Amschel, the Rothschilds had taken care to make charitable contributions not only to the Jewish communities where they lived, but also to non-Jewish "good causes" as part of a conscious strategy to win social acceptance. There is some evidence to suggest that members of the third generation had tended to neglect this tradition during the last decades of their lives. The younger Rothschilds, however, consciously revived it in the 1880s and 1890s, though in England the emphasis was now laid as much on public service as on financial donations; and in every case there was a new interest in the provision of housing for the poor, in addition to the traditional preoccupations with health care and education.

We have already seen how Ferdinand set up a hospital dedicated to his wife Evelina after her death. His brother-in-law Natty was also president of no fewer than three hospitals, treasurer of the King Edward VII Hospital Fund and chairman of the Council of the British Red Cross, as well as running what has been called "a two-tier health service" on his Tring estate.[89] In Frankfurt Mayer Carl and Louise established the Clementine Interdenominational Girls' Hospital following the death of their eldest daughter Clementine and also contributed towards the town's public baths. Finally, their unmarried daughter Hannah Louise was responsible for a large number of public foundations including the Baron Mayer Carl von Rothschild Carolinum Foundation, a medical foundation which came to specialise in dental care.[90] The Viennese Rothschilds also made major charitable contributions in this field:

founding a general hospital, an orphanage, an institute for the blind and one for the deaf and mute. Nathaniel left considerable sums to establish a sanatorium for nervous illnesses at Döbling and Rosenhügel and his house at Reichenau became a hospital.[91] And in France Adolph established an ophthalmological hospital in Paris after a surgeon in Geneva successfully removed a piece of metal which had lodged in his eye, while Henri set up a clinic at 199 rue Marcadet.[92] Education remained important too (as it had been since the days of the Philanthropin in Frankfurt). In addition to the Carolinum Foundation, Hannah Louise established the Carl von Rothschild Public Library (which later occupied the Rothschild house on Untermainkai)[93] and the Anselm Salomon von Rothschild Foundation for the Promotion of the Arts. Her sister Hannah Mathilde was also a major benefactor of the new Frankfurt University set up in 1910.[94]

It was a sign of the times, however, that the provision of cheap housing now became an object of Rothschild philanthropy. For the late nineteenth century saw an acceleration in the pace of urbanisation as millions of people throughout Europe left the countryside to find employment in cities. London, Paris, Vienna and Frankfurt were all affected in this way, albeit to varying degrees. Although there was heavy private investment in housing, contemporaries could hardly fail to notice the appalling conditions which prevailed in the "slums" of Europe's many East Ends: landlords had an obvious incentive to overcrowd their properties, and almost none to provide good sanitation (which at the very least required a measure of collective action by builders and property-owners).[95] One Rothschild response to this was to set an example by acting as model landlords themselves. Natty, Leo and Ferdinand also made a point of running their Buckinghamshire estates as models of modern paternalism, providing tenants with improved housing, running water, club houses and other facilities.[96] But these experiments in private welfare (not dissimilar to those adopted by some big German industrial concerns in the period) had no real applicability in the slum areas where the Rothschilds owned no land.

A first step to address the urban problem was taken by the Paris Rothschilds in 1874, when a fund was established known as l'Oeuvre des loyers (later Secours Rothschild) to pay 100,000 francs a year to the mayors of the Paris arrondissements to assist poor families unable to pay their rents.[97] Thirty years later, another bigger Rothschild Foundation "for the Improvement of the Material Existence of Workers" was set up with 10 million francs' capital to construct affordable working class housing blocks in the 11th, 12th and 19th arrondissements.[98] The model for this was in fact the English Rothschilds' Four Per Cent Industrial Dwellings Company, which had been set up in the 1880s (see below).

All this needs to be set in the context of the family's primary charitable function as benefactors *within* the Jewish communities, though the distinction, as we shall see, is not always easy to make. The continental Rothschilds continued to found specifically Jewish institutions. In 1870, for example, James Edouard established the hospital of Berck-sur-Mer, which specialised in bone disorders, while Edmond modernised the old Jewish hospital in the rue Picpus; in addition, he and Gustave each founded a new Jewish school.[99] In Austria Anselm established a Jewish hospital at Wahring in 1870;[100] while in Frankfurt the indefatigably philanthropic Hannah Mathilde founded a Jewish Children's Home, the Georgine Sara von Rothschild Foundation for Sick Foreign Jews, an Old People's Home for Jewish Women (in the old Rothschild house on the Zeil), a Jewish Home for Women in Bad Nauheim, as well as a Sanatorium for Poor Jews in Bad Soden, a spa town near her summer residence at Königstein.[101] In London the Jews' Free School remained a favoured institution, as did (albeit to lesser degree) the Jews' College.[102]

However, the influx of East European Jews created new problems which the established institutions could not address. Unlike many Non-conformists, British Jews felt no anxiety about the expansion of state support for secular education, providing they could maintain their own communal control over religious education.[103] At the same time, Natty and his relatives grasped the need for extra-curricular organisation. For example, Natty's wife Emma provided around 60 per cent of the annual costs of the Brady Street Lads' Club founded in Whitechapel in 1896 to keep young Jewish men out of mischief.[104] Her son Walter contributed £5,000 to the costs of the Hayes Industrial School set up in 1901 for Jewish young offenders, nearly a third of the total.[105] Two years later, the Rothschilds and Montefiores combined to create a similar school for girls with the explicit object of improving the religious education working class girls received.[106] The spirit in which all these efforts were conceived can be gauged from Lionel's declaration at the opening of the Hutchison House Club for Working Lads on June 28, 1905:

> We hope to catch the youth of the immediate neighbourhood, and to help them to rise in the world, to help them out of the temptations which they find in the street, the music-halls and the public houses. We want to instil into the boys ambition, the pride of being Jews and the pride in being Englishmen. [Cheers] We want to teach them the qualities of endurance and sportsmanship.[107]

It is hard to imagine a more clearcut call for cultural integration. As Natty declared in a speech to the United Synagogue council in 1891, the "paramount duty devolving upon the Jewish community" was "the task of Anglicising the numbers of their foreign brethren at present living in the East End of London."[108] Max Beerbohm's cartoon A Quiet Morning in the Tate Gallery hints at the difficulty the Rothschilds had in understanding "their foreign brethren." The curator is pictured "trying to expound to one of the Trustees the spiritual fineness" of a picture of a group of Orthodox rabbis in a synagogue. With his neat moustache, top hat and cane, the Trustee in question—Alfred—looks unconvinced (illustration 8.iv).

The housing question also called for new forms of benefaction. In May 1884 Natty was invited to join a Board of Guardians Sanitary Committee set up specifically to consider ways of providing better housing for the growing number of poor Jewish tenants living in East End districts like Spitalfields, Whitechapel and Goodmans Fields—areas which had been notorious for crime and prostitution even before the case of Jack the Ripper in 1888. A first step towards tackling the housing problem for immigrants was taken that year with the creation of the Poor Jews' Temporary Shelter, which offered accommodation for up to fourteen days for single men and helped families to find lodgings. But a new East End Enquiry Commission under Natty's chairmanship also proposed creating more permanent housing— "healthy homes . . . at rentals such as the poor can pay"—through the creation of a Dwellings Company of the sort which had proliferated since the 1860s and had been encouraged by Richard Cross's Artisans' and Labourers'' Dwellings Improve-

8.iv: Max Beerbohm, *A quiet morning in the Tate Gallery* (1907).

ment Act of 1875.[109] Apparently encouraged to pursue the matter by his dying mother, Natty sought to mobilise other wealthy Jews—including Lionel Cohen, the bullion-broker F. D. Mocatta, Claude Montefiore and Samuel Montagu—but in the end the Four Per Cent Industrial Dwellings Company set up in March 1885 had to rely on the Rothschilds for a quarter of its £40,000 share capital (another major donor was the Rothschild-supported Jews' Free School which lent the company £8,000 two years later).

The Industrial Dwellings Company was not strictly speaking a charitable foundation: its declared aim was to "provide the maximum of accommodation for the minimum rent compatible with the yielding of a nett 4 per cent per annum dividend upon the paid-up Capital," and the "ruthless utilitarianism" of the resulting flats has been condemned by a modern social historian. However, the differential between this fixed return and the much higher returns being reaped by purely commercial landlords was substantial and can be regarded as a kind of subsidy: the flats were unquestionably an improvement on the slums they replaced. Two months after the initial subscription was announced, Natty purchased a site at Flower and Dean Street (off Commercial Street in the heart of Spitalfields) from the Metropolitan Board of Works for £7,000. Designed by the Jewish architect N. S. Joseph, the austere seven-storey buildings were officially opened in April 1887 and were named after Charlotte. Inside, there was spartan accommodation for up to 228 families (in 477 rooms). The Company went on to build a similar estate in Brady Street and acquired a second site in Flower and Dean Street, where "Nathaniel Dwellings" were built in 1891–2.[110]

Of course, it would be quite wrong to regard all this purely as a response to the increase of anti-Semitism: as Jews, the Rothschilds regarded charitable work as a religious obligation and this impulse was reinforced by the voluntarist ethos of Victorian liberalism. To take the case of Anthony's daughter Constance, who was president of the National Union of Women Workers, an executive of Lady Somerset's National British Women's Temperance Association, an active member of the Society for the Prevention of Cruelty to Children as well as a Home Office-appointed prison visitor;[111] such activities were the sort of thing the wife of any ambitious Liberal MP was expected to go in for. In any case, like her aunt Charlotte, she evidently derived pleasure from such work. She was just as active, if not more so, with Jewish organisations: the Union of Jewish Women, the Ladies Conjoint Visiting Committee of the Board of Guardians and the Jewish Ladies Society for Preventative and Rescue Work (later renamed the Jewish Association for the Protection of Girls and Women), a society for rescuing "fallen women" (as unmarried mothers and prostitutes were euphemistically known) and preventing other working-class Jewish girls from falling in the same way.[112] This was a pattern of activity Charlotte had established in the 1850s and 1860s, and it evidently gave both her and Constance the kind of fulfilment which their male relatives could derive from the "counting house" or politics. Emma too was a compulsive philanthropist: in 1879 she recorded no fewer than 400 individual charitable donations and subscribed to 177 "good causes" in the Tring area, including the Church Girls Union, the Young Women's Christian Association and the Tring United Band of Hope![113]

Nevertheless, there undoubtedly was a "defensive" rationale at work. In part, it was important to demonstrate that rich bankers could be relied upon to make a *voluntary* contribution towards the amelioration of social problems. As we shall see, this was vital as an increasing number of politicians on the political left argued for direct state intervention to redistribute income and wealth; modest though the proposals of New Liberals were at the turn of the century, the Rothschilds shared that violent aversion, so widespread among the rich of the period, to any increases in direct taxation—especially those motivated by a desire to improve working class living standards. The Rothschild argument was that "capital" must be left free from taxation in order to accumulate; only then could economic growth, increased employment and higher wages be expected. In return, the rich could be relied upon to make their contribution towards the needs of the deserving poor on a voluntary basis. It is worth pausing to assess approximately how big a contribution was in fact being made here. Alphonse's will provides a good test case, as he made quite a large number of charitable bequests, with a total value of around 635,000 francs. Yet this was equivalent to less than 0.5 per cent of the value of his share of the Rothschild partnership (135 million francs) which was passed on tax-free to his son Edouard.[114] Of course, this takes no account of the substantial sums Alphonse contributed to charitable causes in his lifetime; and further research would be needed to establish the proportion of his income spent in this way. Nevertheless, it was always a weakness of the conservative argument against higher taxation that in general private charitability at the turn of the century tended to fall short of the traditional 10 per cent.

In the case of specifically Jewish philanthropy, of course, there was a further motive: the perceived need to accelerate the "Anglicisation" of the newly arrived East European Jews. Of course, there was never much chance of achieving the kind of rapid assimilation which the Rothschilds and their cousins had achieved in the late eighteenth and early nineteenth centuries. They, after all, had arrived in England already relatively well off and well educated; the majority arriving from Eastern Europe in the late nineteenth century were poor artisans. An especially alarming moment in this context was the great East End tailors' strike of 1888. To an ardent anti-socialist like Natty, the spectacle of a major industrial dispute within the Jewish community was hardly an agreeable one. Both he and Samuel Montagu hastened to offer their services as mediators, in the hope of splitting the difference between the two sides; though it is hard to believe that Natty had much insight into the labour relations of the East End.[115] Their intervention reflected the Jewish elite's anxiety to appease any nascent radicals within the East End: they had before them the example of Russia, where the Jews' persecution was often spuriously justified by numerical over-representation within the revolutionary movement.

One criticism sometimes advanced by critics of Rothschild philanthropy was that, far from promoting assimilation, the Industrial Dwellings Company merely encouraged the creation of new ghettos. Thus it has been pointed out that 95 per cent of the tenants in the Charlotte de Rothschild Buildings were Jews.[116] But this is misleading. At the Directors' meeting of February 18, 1890, it was agreed that "as far as possible, the proportion of Christian tenants to Jewish tenants should be from 33 to 40 per cent" in the company's Brady Street flats. In 1899 space was reserved in the company's East Ham property for the construction of non-Jewish places of worship "in order that the estate should in no way form a 'Ghetto.'" Though the Charlotte de Rothschild Buildings were mainly occupied by Jewish families, a third of the tenants in the Navarino Manions in Stoke Newington Buildings were not, according to figures for 1904. The company's Camberwell estate (Evelina Mansions) had no Jewish tenants at all in 1911.[117]

An alternative solution to the problems caused by immigration was, of course, to stop it. However, when the idea of restrictions on immigration surfaced for the first time in the 1880s, the Rothschilds and their circle were disconcerted. As N. S. Joseph, the architect of Rothschild Buildings put it, "The letters which spell exclusion are not very different from those which compose expulsion."[118] When the anti-immigration campaigner Arnold White wrote to Natty in 1891, his arguments for legislation were rejected (though not without a qualification): "I share with you the opinion that an influx of persons of foreign birth, likely to become a public charge by reason of physical incapacity or mental disease, is most undesirable and should be discharged. I have no reason to believe that such persons come here in number sufficient to justify legislation."[119] Nevertheless, by the turn of the century, a growing number of Conservative MPs were becoming convinced of the need for immigration controls and this put Natty—by now a staunch party man—in a difficult position. In the 1900 election, Natty was embarrassed when his agent in the East End endorsed two candidates (Sir William Eden Evans-Gordon in Stepney and David Hope Kyd in Whitechapel) who proved to be proponents of immigration control; and he felt obliged to disown the Unionist candidate in St George's in the East, Thomas Dewar, after an intemperate election address was reported in the *Jewish Chronicle*.[120]

When, at Evans-Gordon's instigation, the immigration question was referred to a Royal Commission, however, Natty made no secret of his opposition to "exclusion."[121] As a member of the Commission, of course, he was primarily concerned to

question witnesses. But when a number of these (including Arnold White) specifically claimed that it was Rothschild charity which acted as a "magnet" for poor
immigrants, he felt obliged to respond.[122] Natty dissented from the majority on the
Commission, whose report called for "undesirable" immigrants—including crimi-
nals, the mentally handicapped, people with contagious diseases and anyone "of
notoriously bad character"—to be barred from entry or expelled. In his minority
report, Natty argued forcibly that such legislation "would certainly affect deserving
and hard-working men, whose impecunious position on their arrival would be no
criterion of their incapacity to attain independence."[123] For him, the case of the
"little Jew who was first educated at the Jews' Free School" and who became Senior
Wrangler in Cambridge in 1908 was the ideal: the young mathematician's father had
"fled from Odessa some years ago. I believe he used to preach in a small synagogue.
He is now foreman in a small tailoring business where he receives high wages and
teaches in one of the small Cheders. Such a boy," he observed, "might have done
benefit to Russia. I hope he will do well here."[124]

His son Walter echoed this view. "Great Britain," he argued, "should be the
refuge for the oppressed and unjustly ill-treated people of other nations so long as
they were decent and hard-working."[125] But Natty's opposition to the bill introduced in 1904[126] and his support for a Liberal critic of the bill in the 1905 Mile End
by-election[127] could not prevent an act being passed later that year. This act established, he declared, "a loathsome system of police interference and espionage, of
passports and arbitrary power."[128] Nevertheless, he opposed petitioning for its
repeal—as other members of the Board of Deputies wished to do—on the ground
that a renewed debate might lead to a tightening of the rules; instead he pinned his
hopes on persuading governments to apply it leniently.[129] If nothing else, the passage of the Aliens Act in 1905 gave the lie to Arnold White's claim that "the Prime
Minister and the Cabinet of England alter their policy . . . at the frown of the Rothschilds."[130]

There were two other ways of taking the sting out of the immigration isssue. One
was to persuade the Russian government to end its discrimination against the Jews
in its territory. This was what many Russian Jews pinned their hopes on, in the belief
that the Rothschilds' financial leverage could force the Tsarist regime to mend its
ways. Indeed, stories from the Pale of Jewish settlement like "The Czar in Rothschild's Castle," credited "Rothschild" with positively supernatural powers, and
dreamt of him literally teaching the Tsar a lesson. Thanks to his possession of "King
Solomon's signet ring," Rothschild had become "the man who . . . controls the destiny of nations," living in a vast palace "where enormous hoards of gold were stored
and guarded by gigantic warriors." If the Tsar accepted an invitation to spend the
night in Rothschild's castle, he would be enlightened by pyrotechnical visions of the
history of the Jews. In such stories the myth of the Hebrew talisman lived on.[131] As
we shall see, however, exerting leverage in St Petersburg on this issue was more a
question of money than magic; and diplomatic factors made it difficult for the
Rothschilds to do much more than protest at anti-Jewish policies.

The other possible strategy was to get as many as possible of the new arrivals to
move on. This had in fact been the Jewish community's practice for some years. In
1867, the Board of Guardians wrote to New Court on behalf of "Haim Kohen
Hahamake," a "very deserving" Greek merchant who had lost £8,000 and who

wished to return to Greece; the Rothschilds sent £100. At around the same time, Alfred sat on the committee of an East End Emigration and Relief Fund.[132] In 1881–5 alone, some 2,301 families were sent back to Eastern Europe under such schemes.[133] Natty himself paid the costs of 200 families who wished to leave England for Canada in this period.[134] In 1891 he was one of the eight founding shareholders of Maurice de Hirsch's French-based Jewish Colonisation Association, an organisation for Jewish emigration from Russia to Argentina;[135] and personally offered "to spend £40,000 in transporting to S. Africa and establishing on good Agricultural Land with an easy access to the sea a carefully selected No. [between 400 and 500 familes] of Russian Jews . . . [to] be taken exclusively from a class who have proved themselves to be successful and persevering Agriculturalists."[136] This question of "re-exporting" immigrants resurfaced in 1905, when levels of emigration from Russia soared.[137] Natty's comments on the Royal Commission the previous year indicate that he still favoured "re-exporting" immigrants under certain circumstances.[138]

But could not the Jews return to their biblical place of origin? The notion that the Rothschilds would use their wealth to restore the Jewish kingdom of Jerusalem in the Holy Land dated back as far as the 1830s; and it too lived on in the Pale: "Was not Rothschild a fit prince to . . . restore scattered Israel to the Land of Promise [and] ascend the throne of David?"[139] However, although the family had taken an interest in the Jews of the Middle East since the time of the Damascus affair and continued to donate money to educational and other institutions for Jews in Jerusalem,[140] it was only much later that a Rothschild first seriously began to consider the possibility of founding Jewish colonies in Palestine. Edmond, James's youngest son, became interested in this idea in 1882 under the influence of Zadok Kahn and Michael Erlanger of the Central Committee of the Alliance Israélite Universelle. It was they who introduced him to Samuel Mohilever, Rabbi of the city of Radom (then in Russia) who wanted to resettle a group of Jewish farmers from Belorussia in Palestine; and Josef Feinberg, who wanted money for an already existing colony at Rishon le Zion ("First in Zion"), south of Jaffa (now Tel Aviv). When Edmond gave Feinberg 25,000 francs to drill for water at Rishon le Zion, other settlers in the area were encouraged to apply to him, including a group of Rumanian Jews at Samarin near Mount Carmel (later Zikhron Ya'aqov) who intimated that they expected not just money but leadership from the famous Rothschild.

Edmond responded enthusiastically. As he told Samuel Hirsch, head of the "Mikveh Israel" Agricultural College, his aim was "to create models of future settlements, something like settlement nuclei, around which further groups of immigrants could subsequently settle."[141] Every new settler at Rishon le Zion had to sign an agreement "to submit myself totally to the orders which the administration shall think necessary in the name of M. le Baron in anything concerning the cultivation of the land and its service and if any action should be taken against me I have no right to oppose it." On this decidedly authoritarian basis, Edmond instructed Mohilever's settlers to attempt viniculture at Eqron (later renamed Mazkeret Batya after his mother Betty). There were also experiments with silk manufacture at Rosh Pinna, as well as perfume and glass production, not to mention synagogues, schools and hospitals—every detail supervised by the Baron's "officials."[142] Although he insisted all along that he was engaged not in philanthropy but in creating economically self-sustaining settlements, Edmond's highly paternalistic approach inevitably generated what would now be called a "dependency culture." By 1889, despite investments totalling £1.6 million, there were numerous symptoms of economic failure.[143] Although he transferred the administration of the settlements to the Jewish Colonisation Association in 1900, tacitly accepting the need for greater local autonomy, he continued to act as their banker in his capacity as chairman of the JCA's Palestine Committee. By 1903 nineteen of the twenty-eight Jewish settlements in Palestine were subsidised partially or wholly by him.[144] Altogether he spent around £5.6 million on his settlements.[145]

Edmond's colonising ventures should not be equated with Zionism in the sense of a Jewish nationalism aiming at the creation of a Jewish state, nor should the English Rothschilds' interest in Jewish colonisation. In 1890, Natty attended (along with other luminaries of the London community such as Samuel and Cohen) the opening meeting of the Chovevei Zion Association of England, which united the various local Hovevei Zion ("lovers of Zion") groups which had been formed after 1883 in reaction to the Russian pogroms.[146] Leo also lent support to Israel Zangwill's Jewish Territorial Organisation, which sought to establish Jewish colonies in Mesopotamia (Iraq and Kurdistan).[147] But none of the Rothschilds of this generation favoured the notion of a Jewish state in the Middle East; indeed, Edmond explicitly advised the settlers to seek Ottoman citizenship.[148] Even less interested was Albert, who in 1895 received what doubtless seemed to be yet another half-mad demand for money—a billion francs, no less—from a more than usually verbose *Schnorrer*.

By 1895 the Viennese playwright and journalist Theodor Herzl had become convinced that the only "solution to the Jewish question" was for the Jews to leave Europe and found their own *Judenstaat* modelled on the independent nation states already founded by Greeks, Italians, Germans and other peoples in the course of the nineteenth century.[149] Having found a sympathetic listener in Hirsch, he made a succession of attempts to win the support of the Rothschilds, in the belief that they were about to "liquidate" their unknowably vast capital as a response to anti-Semitic attacks and that he could provide them with a "historic mission" in which to invest it.[150] But despite the mediation of the Chief Rabbi of Vienna, Güdemann, Herzel's sixty-six page Address "to the Rothschild Family Council" was never sent.[151] He did not even get an answer from Albert to his initial approach, and concluded bitterly that his Address "should not be laid before the Rothschilds, who are vulgar, contemptuous, egoistical people." Instead, he must wage "a battle against the powerful Jews" by mobilising the Jewish masses.

This switch from ingratiation to aggression was characteristic of a particular type of Rothschild correspondent. King Ludwig II of Bavaria responded in a rather similar way when the Rothschilds rejected his requests for loans to finance his mania for fairy tale castles: he instructed his servants to rob the Rothschild bank in Frankfurt.[152] Herzl, however, never gave up hope of securing Rothschild support. As early as May the following year, he was seeking to gain a hearing from Edmond through the Chief Rabbi in Paris, Zadok Kahn, even offering to resign from his own embryonic movement if Edmond would take over as leader. But when Edmond said that he regarded Herzl's talk of founding a state in Ottoman territory as a threat to his

Die Kinder Israels ziehen ins gelobte Land um eine Republique zu gründen.

8.v: Christian Schöller, *Die Kinder Israels ziehen ins Gelobte Land, um eine Republik zu gründen* (1848).

own colonisation programme, Herzl reverted to hostility. A year later, he was denouncing them as "a national misfortune for the Jews."[153] Even when he managed to secure an interview with Edmond in August 1896, it was only to be disillusioned further. By 1898, he had concluded that Edmond was slow-witted and that he would have to try appealing to the more financially powerful Alphonse—a view confirmed by his visit to Rishon le Zion that October.[154]

At first, he got no further in London. Natty refused even to see him in 1901 (despite the intercession of his cousin Lady Battersea) and he clashed when Herzl gave evidence to the Royal Commission on Alien Immigration in 1902; in the wake of that first encounter Natty made it plain that he would "view with horror the establishment of a Jewish Colony pure and simple." "Of one thing I am convinced," he declared: "that the dream of Palestine is a myth and a will-of-the-wisp."[155] Leo was also opposed to Zionism in Herzl's sense.[156] It was only when Herzl changed his strategy, arguing that any Jewish colony in Sinai could be a part of the British Empire, that Natty became interested, introducing him to Joseph Chamberlain. His support increased markedly in the last years of Herzl's life, though their plan for a British–Jewish colony in Sinai ultimately came to nothing because of diplomatic obstacles.[157]

Why did the Rothschilds give Herzl's original conception of a "Jews' State" such

8.vi: Anon., *Auszug der Juden aus Deutschland!, Politischer Bilderbogen*, Nr. 17 (1895).

short shrift? Part of the reason was that, despite his assurances that they would ben-efit financially and in other ways from supporting him—he even offered to make the first elected "prince" of the new state a Rothschild—Herzl's utopia had markedly socialist characteristics (notably a nationalised banking system) which were hardly calculated to appeal to them. Indeed, Herzl had an offputting tendency to mix protestations of altruism with threats to "liquidate the Rothschilds" or to "wage a barbaric campaign" against them if they opposed him. But there was another more important objection, and Herzl quite openly acknowledged it himself: if a Jewish nation state were to be created, it would very probably encourage anti-Semites to question the existing national identities of assimilated Jews. Natty was a Jewish Eng-lishman just as as Alphonse was a Jewish Frenchmen, and Albert a Jewish Austrian. They did not share Herzl's pessimistic and prophetic view—inspired by covering the Dreyfus affair for the *Neue Freie Presse*—that such national rights of citizenship would one day be revoked by anti-Semitic governments; far from seeing Zionism as an "answer to the Jewish question," they saw it as a threat to their position. To the Rothschilds, a cartoon like the one which depicted them—not for the first time—as part of a throng of Jews leaving Germany was deeply disturbing, even if they were pictured arriving at the dockside in their own private carriage (illustrations 8.v and 8.vi). Such a vision of mass emigration, whether to the Holy Land or (as the anti-Semitic cartoon wishfully suggested) to the bottom of the sea, represented nothing less than the negation of the social position their family had achieved since Nathan himself had arrived in England as an alien immigrant a century before: that of royalty in the eyes of many Jews, aristocracy in the eyes of most Gentiles, but at the very least subjects or citizens of the countries of their birth. With the benefit of hindsight, we can see that Herzl was a prophet. Less than half a century after his death, the German, Austrian and French Rothschilds had all fallen victim to just the anti-Semitic onslaught he had foreseen. But it is equally easy to see why, at the time, his vision seemed a fantastic and even dangerous one.

NINE

"On the Side of Imperialism" (1874–1885)

If the special interest of the investor is liable to clash with the public interest and to induce a wrecking policy, still more dangerous is the special interest of the financier . . . These great businesses—banking, broking, bill discounting, loan floating, company promoting—form the central ganglion of international capitalism. United by the strongest bonds of organisation, always in the closest and quickest touch with one another, situated in the very heart of the business capital of every State, controlled, so far as Europe is concerned, chiefly by men of a single and peculiar race, who have behind them many centuries of financial experience, they are in a unique position to manipulate the policy of nations . . . Does anyone seriously suppose that a great war could be undertaken by any European State, or a great State loan subscribed, if the house of Rothschild and its connexions set their face against it?

Every great political act involving a new flow of capital, or a large fluctuation in the values of existing investments, must receive the sanction and the practical aid of this little group of financial kings . . . As speculators or financial dealers they constitute . . . the gravest single factor in the economics of Imperialism . . . Each condition . . . of their profitable business . . . throws them on the side of Imperialism . . . There is not a war, or a revolution, an anarchist assassination or any other public shock, which is not gainful to these men; they are harpies who suck their gains from every sudden disturbance of public credit . . . The wealth of these houses, the scale of their operations, and their cosmopolitan organisation make them the prime determinants of economic policy. They have the largest definite stake in the business of Imperialism, and the amplest means of forcing their will upon the policy of nations . . . [F]inance is . . . the governor of the imperial engine, directing the energy and determining the work . . .

J. A. HOBSON, *IMPERIALISM: A STUDY* (1902)[1]

Decline is a relative concept. Compared with their commanding position in the international capital market before 1880, the Rothschilds unquestionably declined thereafter. Compared with rival banks, they were less profitable and grew less rapidly. Yet as table 9.i shows, the Rothschilds remained in absolute terms a formidable financial force even on the eve of the First World War. N. M. Rothschild & Sons was far and away the largest private bank in the City of London in terms of capital. This dominance is even more impressive if one recalls that the London house was still just one of four Rothschild houses. Illustration 9.i shows the combined capital of the Rothschild houses according to successive partnership contracts. Between 1874 and 1887 it rose from £34.4 million to £38.0 million, and reached a peak of £41.5 million in 1899. In 1904, the last year for which combined figures were drawn up, it was still £37.1 million. If capital had not been withdrawn after 1898, the total capital would have been in excess of £45 million. This made N. M. Rothschild not only the biggest private bank in London, but one of the biggest banks of any kind in the world. In 1881 seventy-one different credit establishments were quoted on the Paris bourse with a paid-up capital of 1.49 billion francs: the combined Rothschild houses alone had capital not far short of a billion francs and the Paris house—with capital of 590 million francs—was still one of the biggest French banks.[2] In 1913 the total share capital of the five German great banks (the Darmstädter, the Disconto-Gesellschaft, the Deutsche, the Dresdner and the Berliner Handels-Gesellschaft) totalled 870 million marks (£43 million)—not much more than the combined capital of the Rothschild houses a decade before.[3]

Of course, the Rothschilds' balance sheet was substantially smaller than that of the big joint-stock deposit banks. The biggest British "clearing" bank, the Midland, had deposits worth £125 million on the eve of the First World War, compared with an equivalent figure for the London house (assets minus capital) of just over £14 million.[4] For Deutsche Bank—the biggest German bank in 1914—the figure was £74 million.[5] But this does not compare like with like. The Rothschilds had never been interested in taking deposits. Their principal concern was to use their capital as the basis for large-scale bond market underwriting, attracting outside funds directly into new securities, rather than soliciting deposits.

The less impressive difference between the Rothschilds and their rivals was that the former were less profitable in relative terms. Table 9b allows a more systematic comparison with five other major City banks. It shows that the London house's average profits as a percentage of capital tended to decline from a peak of 9.8 per cent in the 1870s to just 3.9 per cent in the decade 1900–9. The Rothschilds, it seems, played safe: with their enormous accumulation of capital inherited from the previous generations, Natty and his brothers apparently felt under no pressure to aim at the kind of high returns achieved by Barings or Schröders, much less a joint-stock bank like the Midland. Figures for acceptances between 1890 and 1914 also show the London house lagging behind Kleinworts, Schröders and Morgan Grenfell, and even being overtaken by Brandts and Hambros after 1910. Annual acceptances by N. M. Rothschild for the period 1890–1914 averaged £2.7 million, compared with £5.6 million for Barings, £7.2 million for Schröders and £9 million for Kleinworts, the market leader.[6] In terms of assets, the available balance sheet figures show Barings and Schröders rapidly gaining on N. M. Rothschild in the decade before 1914. In 1903 assets at New Court had totalled £25 million, compared with £10.3 million at Schröders and £9.9 million at Barings. Ten years later, the Rothschild total was more or less unchanged, while Schröders had increased their balance sheet to £19.1 million and the figure at Barings had risen to £15.8 million.[7]

9.i: Combined Rothschild capital, selected years (£ thousand).

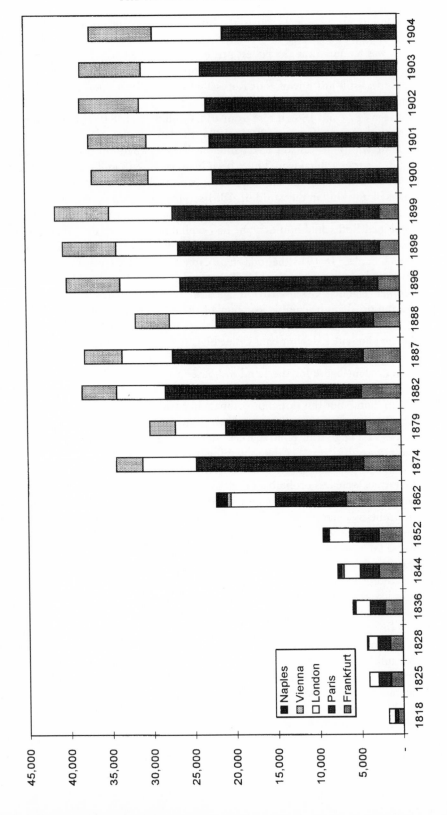

Table 9a: Capital and acceptances of N. M. Rothschild & Sons and other City merchant banks, 1870–1914 (£ million).

	CAPITAL	CAPITAL	CAPITAL	ACCEPTANCES	ACCEPTANCES	ACCEPTANCES
N. M. Rothschild	5.90	7.07	6.37	0.91	3.44	1.31
Baring Brothers	1.63	1.02	1.02	6.70	3.89	3.72
Wm Brandt Sons	0.18		1.00	0.10	0.70	0.72
Brown, Shipley	1.20		0.78		4.50	5.10
A. Gibbs & Sons			1.22		0.88	1.17
C. J. Hambro	0.63	0.04	1.00	0.98	0.84	1.34
Fr. Huth & Co.	0.50	0.60	0.75			3.30
Kleinwort, Sons	0.84	1.19	4.42	2.10	5.40	8.50
Lazard Brothers	0.60†	1.20	1.00			
J. H. Schröder	1.69	1.24	3.54	3.22	4.00	5.82
J. S. Morgan*	1.80†		1.00		4.20	
Seligman Brothers	1.35		3.00			

* from 1910 Morgan, Grenfell & Co.   †Estimate.

Sources: RAL, RFamFD/13F; Cassis, *City*, p. 33; *idem*, *City bankers*, pp. 31f.; Kynaston, *City*, vol. I, pp. 312f.; vol. II, p. 9; Chapman, *Merchant banking*, pp. 44, 55, 121f., 200f., 208f.; Roberts, *Schroders*, pp. 44, 57, 99, 527–35; Ziegler, *Sixth great power*, pp. 372–8; Wake, *Kleinwort Benson*, pp. 472f.

Another indicator of relative decline is the fact that, in terms of individual wealth, the Rothschilds ceased to be exceptional. Natty was the richest of his generation of English Rothschilds (leaving £2.5 million when he died in 1915); but at least thirteen British millionaires in the period 1890–1915 left as much as or more than him.[8] Across the Atlantic, Junius Morgan had already left that amount when he had died in 1890. When his son Pierpont died in 1913, the estimated net value of his estate, excluding his art collection, was $68.3 million (£14 million); including artworks, his fortune was closer to £24 million.[9] Small wonder the Morgans partner Clinton Dawkins felt like bragging in 1901:

> Old Pierpont Morgan and the house in the U.S. occupy a position immensely more predominant than Rothschilds' in Europe . . . Taken together, the Morgan combination of the U.S. and London probably do not fall very far short of the Rothschilds in capital, are immensely more expansive and active, and are in with the great progressive undertakings of the world.—Old P. Morgan is well over 60 . . . [but he has] behind him . . . young Morgan, under 40 with the makings of a biggish man, and myself.—The Rothschilds have nothing new but the experience and great prestige of old Nattie . . . Therefore, provided we can go on and bring in one or two good men to assist the next 20 years ought to see the Rothschilds thrown into the background and the Morgan group supreme.[10]

A number of qualifications need to be made, however. Firstly, if the figures for the period 1830–69 are taken into account, the performance of N. M. Rothschild & Sons after 1879 was not in fact markedly worse than it was for the period before. The 1870s were an exceptional decade; the period before and the period after did not greatly differ from one another. To speak of decline relative to the past is therefore misleading. Secondly, by continuing to play safe, the Rothschilds *were* safe. The story of Barings presents a profound contrast in this period. The figures in table 9b also reflect the extent of the rival bank's contraction as a result of the 1890 crisis; Barings' high profit rate was partly a function of its dangerously narrow capital base.

Table 9b: Profits at six major London banks as a percentage of capital, 1830–1909 (decennial averages).

	N. M. ROTHSCHILD	BARING BROTHERS	SCHRÖDERS	KLEINWORTS	J. S. MORGAN/ MORGAN GRENFELL	MIDLAND
1830–39	5.9	15.5				
1840–49	1.8	13.3				16.3
1850–59	4.9	21.3				17.9
1860–69	7.0	27.6	10.6			22.2
1870–79	9.8	11.9	11.6		15.1	21.9
1880–89	7.5	13.6	6.3	4.0	5.2	19.8
1890–99	4.6	13.6	7.5	4.1	7.8	24.3
1900–09	3.9	27.1	10.5	3.6	4.7	22.8

Note: definitions of both capital and profits varied from company to company.
Sources: RAL, RFamFD/13F; Roberts, *Schröders*, pp. 44, 57, 99, 527–35; Ziegler, *Sixth great power*, pp. 372–8; Wake, *Kleinwort Benson*, pp. 472f.; Burk, *Morgan Grenfell*, pp. 260–70, 278–81; Holmes and Green, *Midland*, pp. 331–3.

The Rothschild combination of relatively low profitability and longevity recalls Friedrich Gentz's illuminating point made as early as 1827 that one of the two fundamental Rothschild principles was:

> never to strive for excessive profits in their undertakings, to give each of their operations clear limits and, no matter how much human ingenuity and caution it may require, to insulate themselves from the play of happenstance. In this maxim lies one of the chief secrets of their strength. There is no question that, with the means at their disposal, they could achieve far higher returns on this or that operation. But even if doing so would not have compromised the safety of their undertakings, they would in any case have made less in the end than they do by distributing their resources over a larger number of transactions which constantly recur and are repeated no matter what the [economic] conditions.[11]

Nor should the fact that N. M. Rothschild fell behind Schröders and Kleinworts in the acceptance market necessarily be interpreted as a sign of decline: even if these figures are correct,[12] the Rothschilds were never as reliant on acceptances to generate their profits as other London merchants. As in the past, they concentrated their resources on the bond market and there they remained pre-eminent. Finally, the profits of the London house should not be looked at in isolation from those of other houses, a substantial part of which continued to be shared between the various partners. The profits of the combined Rothschild houses are difficult to calculate because of the large sums which were withdrawn as individual partners died, but illustration 9.ii presents appropriately adjusted figures. Once again, the impression is not one of decline: average annual profits slumped—by nearly half—in the depressed years 1874–9 (having exceeded £1 million between 1852 and 1874); but the years 1879–82 seem to have been the most profitable in the Rothschilds' history (average annual profits were in excess of £4 million), and although this could not be sustained, the trend between 1888 and 1904 was upwards (from £785,000 a year in the mid-1880s to £1.6 million between 1898 and 1904).

There is a useful parallel to be drawn here between the performance of the

London Rothschilds and that of the British economy as a whole. For years, economic historians have argued that the British economy after around 1870 suffered from relative decline, noting the more rapid growth of the American or German economies in the period and the decline in Britain's position as the dominant exporter of manufactures. While some have blamed this relative decline on "entrepreneurial failure" or even a culturally determined "decline of the industrial spirit," others have identified the City of London as an institutional culprit which impeded the modernisation of Britain's industry by encouraging excessive levels of capital export in the late nineteenth century. The Rothschilds had throughout the nineteenth century played a major role in encouraging this capital export, and continued to do so right up until 1914. The possibility therefore arises that Natty can be blamed not only for the decline of his own firm, but for that of the British economy as a whole.

The reality is that the decline of the British economy, like the decline of the Rothschilds before 1914, has been exaggerated. Capital exports were only starving British industry of investment if it can be shown that there was a capital shortage inhibiting firms from modernising their plant; there is little evidence to support this view. In fact, the high level of capital export from Britain was an integral part of the British economy's global role as an exporter of manufactures, an importer of food and other primary products, the lender of last resort in the international monetary system, a major exporter of skilled colonists and, not least, the imperial guarantor of law and order on most seas and vast tracts of land (9.5 million square miles in 1860; 12.7 million in 1909). To measure the costs and benefits of this system too narrowly—in terms of the prosperity of those Britons who remained within the British Isles—is to miss the point. Some 444 million people lived under some form of British rule on the eve of the First World War: contrary to the nationalist propaganda of the decolonisation era, British statesmen could not and did not make economic policy solely for the benefit of the 10 per cent who happened to live in the United Kingdom. While the profits of overseas expansion unquestionably flowed to a relatively small elite of investors, the broad "multiplier" effects of British-financed investment and trade were felt far beyond Britain herself. Nor should the costs of governing and defending the Empire be exaggerated; the tax and debt burden incurred by Britain was in fact small relative to the enormous extent of British power and the economic benefits generated by a secure empire of more or less free trade, free capital movement and free migration.

Already by the 1850s British overseas investments totalled in the region of £200 million.[13] In the second half of the century, however, there were three great waves of capital export. Between 1861 and 1872, net foreign investment rose from just 1.4 per cent of GNP to 7.7 per cent, before dropping back down to 0.8 per cent in 1877. It then rose more or less steadily to 7.3 per cent in 1890, before once again falling down below 1 per cent in 1901. In the third upswing, foreign investment rose to an all-time peak of 9.1 per cent in 1913—a level not subsequently surpassed until the 1990s.[14] In absolute terms, this led to a huge accumulation of foreign assets, rising more than tenfold from £370 million in 1860 to £3.9 billion in 1913—around a third of the total stock of British wealth. No other country came close to this level of foreign investment: the closest, France, had foreign assets worth

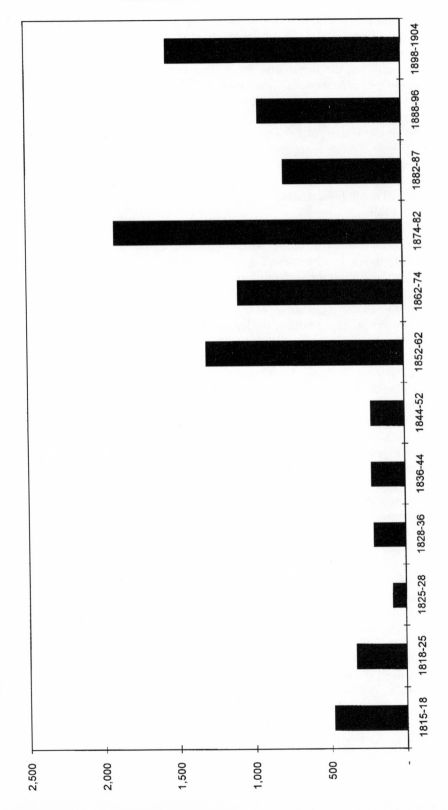

9.ii: Average annual Rothschild profits (combined houses), selected periods (£ thousand).

less than half the British total, Germany just over a quarter. Britain accounted for something like 44 per cent of total foreign investment on the eve of the First World War.[15] Although there was an inverse relationship between the cycle of foreign investment and that of domestic fixed investment, this high level of capital export should not, however, be understood in crude terms as a "drain" of capital from the British economy. It is also a mistake to see capital exports as in some sense "causing" the British trade deficit to widen.[16] In fact, the income earned on these investments more than matched the export of new capital, just as (when coupled with revenue from "invisible" earnings) it invariably exceeded the trade deficit. In the 1890s net foreign investment amounted to 3.3 per cent of GNP, compared with net property income from abroad of 5.6 per cent. For the next decade, the figures were 5.1 and 5.9 respectively.[17]

Why did the British economy behave in this way? The greater part of overseas investment was "portfolio" rather than "direct" in nature, in other words it was mediated by stock exchanges through sales of bonds and shares issued on behalf of foreign governments and companies. According to Edelstein, the explanation for the "pull" of foreign securities was that, even allowing for the higher degree of risk involved, their yields were rather higher (by around 1.5 percentage points) than those of domestic securities when averaged out over the period 1870–1913. However, this averaging conceals substantial fluctuations. Analysing the accounts of 482 firms, Davis and Huttenback have shown that domestic rates of return were sometimes higher than foreign—in the 1890s for example.[18] Their work also quantifies the importance in the eyes of investors of imperialism, as rates of return on investments in the Empire were markedly different from those on investments in foreign territories not politically controlled by Britain: as much as 67 per cent higher in the period before 1884, but 40 per cent lower thereafter.[19] Was the rising level of British investment abroad therefore an economically irrational product of imperialism—a case of capital following the flag rather than maximum profits? Much modern historiography tends to emphasise the non-economic motivations for the rapid expansion of the British Empire.[20] On the other hand, Davis and Huttenback show that imperial possessions were not the main destination of British investment taken as a whole: for the period between 1865 and 1914, only around 25 per cent of investment went to the Empire, compared with 30 per cent for the British economy itself and 45 per cent for foreign economies. Their work points to the existence of an elite of investors with a material interest in the Empire as a mechanism for stabilising the international capital market *as a whole*. Late-nineteenth-century imperialism was the political accompaniment to an economic process similar to the "globalisation" of the late twentieth century.

As leading members of that elite of imperial investors, the Rothschilds' role in British imperialism was substantial. Public issues of foreign securities in London between 1865 and 1914 totalled £4,082 million. N. M. Rothschild & Sons were either solely or jointly responsible for over a quarter of this total (£1,085).[21] No other bank could match this, though Barings tried in the 1860–90 period and Pierpont Morgan came close thereafter, with the Seligman brothers not far behind and Ernest Cassel a formidable rival from the turn of the century. Table 9c gives a breakdown of the geographical distribution and type of Rothschild loans issued for the period after 1852.

Table 9c: Loans issued by N. M. Rothschild & Sons, 1852–1914.

	TOTAL (£)	PERCENTAGE	OF WHICH PUBLIC SECTOR	PERCENTAGE OF TOTAL
Britain	11,941,582	8.7	96,266,582	86.0
Europe	90,034,413	45.6	54,929,413	94.1
Middle East	78,677,640	6.1	78,677,640	100.0
Latin America	189,003,610	14.6	175,898,990	93.1
North America	291,700,448	22.5	284,900,448	97.7
Australasia	5,000,000	0.4	5,000,000	100.0
Asia	20,200,000	1.6	11,500,000	56.9
Africa	7,200,000	0.5	3,700,000	51.4
of which Empire	77,547,580	6.0	65,347,580	84.3
Total	1,293,757,693	100.0	1,210,873,073	93.6

Sources: Ayer, *Century of finance*, pp. 14–81; RAL.

A comparison of the Rothschild figures with the data in Davis and Huttenback (see table 9d) reveals that N. M. Rothschild continued to be far more interested in government finance than in private sector issues. Only around 36 per cent of all "called up" capital between 1865 and 1914 was for governments; the equivalent figure for loans issued by the London Rothschilds in (approximately) the same period is over 90 per cent. (Almost all the rest was accounted for by foreign railway companies.) The extent of Rothschild dominance in government bond issues was astonishing. For the London market as a whole, foreign public sector issues between 1865 and 1914 amounted to £1.48 billion, of which close to three quarters were handled by the Rothschilds solely or in partnership. New Court also remained far more interested in Europe and far less interested in Britain than the London market as a whole, and was under-represented in African, Asian and Australasian issues. Perhaps the most striking difference of all, however, is that the Rothschilds were relatively uninvolved in imperial issues, which accounted for only 6 per cent of their business, compared with around 26 per cent for the British capital market as a whole. Given Natty's and Alfred's influential role in the politics of imperialism, this is a highly surprising finding, suggesting that they attached relatively little importance to the Empire as a field for their own private financial activities. To be more precise, they showed no preference for states (for example, Egypt) whose bonds were guaranteed by British financial control over states (for example, Brazil) which remained politically independent. It was therefore quite wrong to say (as Ernest Cassel said of Alfred) that the Rothschilds "would hardly take up anything that did not have the British government guarantee about it."[22]

In two respects only was the London house "representative" of the City as a whole. North and South American issues accounted for almost exactly the same proportions of its business as they did for the total market. And the Rothschilds shared the City's relative lack of interest in domestic private sector finance, which accounted for just over 1 per cent of all Rothschild issues (though the Rothschilds had the reputation of being especially indifferent to domestic industry). When Sir Edward Guinness sought to float his Irish brewing company on the stock market in 1886, the London house refused to handle the £6 million flotation, which was snapped up by Barings. The shares and debentures proved immensely popular (they were oversubscribed nearly twenty times) and Barings made a profit on the

Table 9d: Geographical distribution of all British capital called up, 1865–1914.

	£ THOUSANDS	PERCENTAGE
UK	1,487,519	31.8
Europe	349,974	7.5
North America	1,059,797	22.7
South America & Caribbean	631,235	13.5
Africa	310,198	6.6
Asia	442,518	9.5
Australia & Pacific	374,404	8.0
Unknown	22,800	0.4
Total	4,678,445	100.0

Source: Davis and Huttenback, *Mammon*, p. 46.

issue of around £500,000. Yet, when asked by a journalist if he regretted turning the business down, Natty replied: "I don't look at it quite that way. I go to the House every morning and when I say 'No' to every scheme and enterprise submitted to me, I return home at night carefree and contented. But when I agree to any proposal, I am immediately filled with anxiety. To say 'Yes' is like putting your finger in a machine: the whirring wheels may drag your whole body in after the finger."[23] This is often seen as epitomising the caution of the fourth generation. Thus, while others reaped substantial profits from financing the construction of the London underground rail network, the Rothschilds kept their distance.[24] Even the idea of a Channel Tunnel—which appealed to the French Rothschilds as a way of increasing the traffic on their Nord line—left Natty cold. "You can take it from me quite positively," he told his cousins in 1906, "that this measure [the Channel Tunnel Bill] would be rejected by an enormous majority in the House of Lords and it is certainly not worthwhile for you to waste your time or your money on it."[25]

There were some exceptions to this rule of abstention, admittedly. Perhaps seeking to emulate Barings' success with Guinness, Natty undertook four successive share and debenture issues for the Manchester Ship Canal between 1886 and 1891, worth a total of £13 million. But, as Edward Hamilton commented, the failure of the first of these issues led to "an invidious comparison" being drawn in the City between "Rothschild's water" and "Baring's beer." Even in partnership with Barings it proved impossible to make the second issue a success.[26] Similarly, having been pioneers of rapid communication in the early part of the century, the Rothschilds might have been expected to grasp the significance of an innovation like the telephone. Indeed, they themselves began to experiment with the telephone as a way of communicating between Paris and London as early as 1891. But a share issue of £488,000 the following year for the New Telephone Company was a trifling affair, and it is remarkable that the London and Paris partners continued to communicate with one another by handwritten letter just as their fathers, grandfathers and great-grandfather had done.[27]

All this helps explain why historians have often characterised the Rothschilds of this generation as "conservative" in their approach to finance.[28] (The obvious contrast is with the French house, which remained a major shareholder in railway lines like the Nord.) Yet this critique rests on a misunderstanding of the Rothschilds' *modus operandi* and their role in the process of late-nineteenth-century globalisation. There was, for example, one domestic industrial sector in which the Rothschilds did enjoy some success: predictably, perhaps, it was the sector most closely linked to government—defence. And of far greater importance than any involvement in domestic industry and transport were the Rothschilds' interests in foreign mining and the international market for metals and precious stones (which are discussed in the next chapter).

The Rothschilds' role in the economics and politics of imperialism should not therefore be caricatured as part of a wider teleology of decline. In many ways, imperialism did not represent a dramatic break with their past success. Foreign public sector investment remained their principal interest, with "home" government borrowing in second place, in so far as France, Austria–Hungary and to a lesser extent Britain were all forced to continue to issue new bonds to finance the rising costs of defending their empires. Here, in the international bond market, the Rothschilds had few if any real equals. Their role in foreign private sector finance (especially railways) was more modest, as was their acceptance business. But their international mining interests, as we shall see, were vast.

As in the past, the Rothschilds continued to have an interest in the continuation and expansion of a global economic system in which capital, goods and indeed people could move as freely and as securely as possible. However, if this could be achieved without political intervention, they were content: thus the long history of Rothschild involvement in Brazil shows that they did not regard formal imperial control as a precondition of profitable capital export. Only where important bonds appeared to be in jeopardy as a result of political instability in the borrowing territory did the Rothschilds support direct political intervention. Their mining interests in Spain and Mexico did not require foreign intervention, despite the recurrent instability of politics in those countries; whereas it is hard to imagine their investments in Burmese ruby mines or New Caledonian nickel mines in the absence of direct European control. The South African case illustrates the ambivalence of Rothschild attitudes to imperialism as personified by Cecil Rhodes: though strongly attracted to gold and diamond mining, they were suspicious of Rhodes's wilder schemes to extend British political influence north of the Cape colony. Nor is there any sign of a preference for railways in imperial territory.

Generally, the Rothschilds backed British empire-building only when they felt confident that this could be achieved without precipitating conflict with other European powers, or (less often) when they felt that a rival power would impose a more economically restrictive colonial rule if Britain did not act (it was usually assumed that a French or German regime would be more protectionist than a British one, though in reality French and German tariffs were not vastly higher). The desire to avoid international conflict explains the Rothschild preference for what might be called multinational imperialism, where economic interests were guaranteed by more than one European power. The classic illustration is the case of Egypt, where the Rothschilds sought to reconcile conflicting British and French political interests in the shared interests of bondholders of both nationalities. (The Rothschilds were less interested in Greece and Turkey, where such multi-national financial guarantees were also used.) In China too they favoured co-operation between the European powers.

There was, it should be stressed, a certain instinctiveness about all this: while critics like Hobson had theories of imperialism, the imperialists themselves did not.

"[I]t is a curious thing," wrote Natty to Paris in May 1906, "how investors & capitalists dread the stocks of their own countries particularly if they live in Europe." He had a hazy notion that investors were attracted to "exotics" by their higher yields, and that these reflected the higher risks of investing overseas; but his own preferences for particular regions or sectors appear to have been based in large part on unspoken assumptions.[29] Yet his assumptions about the *politics* of imperialism were far from unspoken: no member of the family before or since has been more politically active. Here there was an important discontinuity. In the past, the Rothschilds had tended to view politics through the prism of their own financial interests: nearly all James's interventions in the realm of diplomacy had been based on business calculations. This cannot be said of the members of the fourth generation. Economic self-interest was still paramount; but sometimes Natty and Alfred took positions for "purely" ideological or party political reasons which were unrelated to the portfolio of N. M. Rothschild & Sons, just as they had private interests in areas where imperial control was never a serious possibility. Natty in particular thought of himself as "wearing different hats": there was one for New Court and one for Westminster (or, as he would have said, one for the East End and one for the West End). The full-time politicians tended to think the same way, though in neither case was the distinction between private and public interest perfectly maintained.

In fact, the politics of imperialism took precedence over economic considerations more often than the Rothschilds themselves may have realised. Although it is undeniably true that they profited from high levels of capital export, in particular cases the fourth generation often allowed national political considerations to take precedence over the collective economic interest of the Rothschild houses. The fact was that the reorientation of British finance away from continental Europe made the Rothschilds' network linking London, Paris, Frankfurt and Vienna somewhat obsolescent. At the same time, colonial conflicts of interest between France and Britain presented the Rothschild houses with difficult choices. It was in this period that the various houses began to operate more and more independently of one another: these Anglo-French disagreements, and the Austrian indifference to the world outside Europe, help to explain why.

The Financial Politics of Empire: Egypt

The best-known example of Rothschild involvement in British imperialism is the case of Egypt. Famously, it was the London house which advanced £4 million to Disraeli's government in 1875, allowing the British crown to acquire a substantial shareholding in the Suez Canal Company. Quite apart from the romantic penumbra which surrounds this transaction, this is often seen as the first step down the road towards the British military occupation and financial control of the country after 1882, a process which the Rothschilds also helped to facilitate.[30] Yet the roads to and from the Suez share purchase were far from straight; in many ways the Rothschilds' role in Egypt illustrates the ambiguities and contingencies which lie behind a historical construct like "imperialism."

To understand the significance of the hectic events of 1875, it is necessary to know something of Middle Eastern finance. In the aftermath of the Crimean War, both the Sultan in Constantinople and his vassal the Viceroy or "Khedive"[31] in Cairo had begun to accumulate huge and ultimately unsustainable domestic and foreign debts. Between 1855 and 1875, the Ottoman debt increased from around 9 million Turkish lire to around 251 million. In relation to the financial resources of the Ottoman government, this was wholly unsustainable: as a percentage of current revenue, the burden rose from 130 per cent to around 1,500 per cent; as a percentage of expenditure, interest payments and amortisation rose from 15 per cent in 1860 to a peak of 50 per cent in 1875.[32] The Egyptian case was similar: between 1862, the date of the first Egyptian foreign loan, and 1876, the total public debt rose from 3.3 million Egyptian pounds to 76 million, roughly ten times total tax revenue; in addition, the Khedive Ismail owed around 11 million pounds on his own private account. The 1876 budget showed debt charges at more than half (55.5 per cent) of all expenditure.[33]

It is worth setting these figures into some sort of comparative perspective, if only to establish an approximate notion of what constituted sustainable borrowing in the nineteenth century. For most of the century (until 1873), the British national debt had been more than ten times total public tax revenue; while debt charges accounted for around 50 per cent of gross expenditure from 1818 until 1855.[34] However, the trend for Britain from the 1840s until 1914 was more or less uninterruptedly downwards, so that by the eve of the First World War, total debt was just over three times total revenue and debt charges accounted for a mere 10 per cent of total expenditure. Moreover, the British economy grew at historically unprecedented rates. In the Turkish and Egyptian cases, debt ballooned in the two decades to 1875 relative to the state budgets, yet economic activity stagnated. Compared with other major borrowers on the international market (such as Brazil or Russia), Turkey and Egypt were out of control. Brazilian and Russian debts were never much more than three times greater than total tax revenue, while debt service typically accounted for less than 15 per cent of total spending. In fact, the closest parallel to the Middle Eastern experience was that of Spain, which also defaulted in the 1870s (see tables 9e and 9f). In the context of the general financial crisis which afflicted all the European markets after 1873, a Middle Eastern debt crisis was thus inevitable.

Table 9e: National debt as a percentage of tax revenues, selected years and countries, 1869–1913.

	BRITAIN	FRANCE	TURKEY	EGYPT	SPAIN	BRAZIL	RUSSIA
1869	1,060.7	587.1	608.1		1,033.4	205.2	
1879	905.5		1,758.5	1,074.5	1,628.2	167.4	
1889	693.2		871.3	976.5	784.4	177.3	
1899	501.5		1,044.7	883.2		398.7	
1909	438.5		1,015.8	599.5		282.9	
1913	331.0	650.8		532.1			258.3

Sources: Mitchell, *British historical statistics* pp. 396–9, 402f.; Crouchley, *Economic development*, pp. 274ff.; Shaw, "Ottoman expenditures and budgets," pp. 374ff.; Issawi, *Economic history of the Middle East*, pp. 100f., 104ff.; Levy, "Brazilian public debt," pp. 248–52; Mitchell, *European historical statistics*, pp. 370–85, 789; Martin, *Rothschild*; Carreras, *Industrializacion Espanola*, pp. 185–7; Gatrell, *Government, industry and rearmament*, pp. 140, 150; Apostol, Bernatzky and Michelson, *Russian public finances*, pp. 234, 239; Hobson, "Wary Titan," pp. 505f.

Strategic considerations had served to start the ball of indebtedness rolling. It was to support the Ottoman military position during the Crimean War that the first British loans to the Porte were made in 1854 and 1855 (the second of these through the London Rothschilds) and the Banque Ottomaine (later the Imperial Ottoman

Bank) was set up in 1856. Both these loans were formally secured on all the Ottoman government's tax revenues from Egypt. However, European loans to the Middle East after 1860 were principally based on economic calculations. In the case of Turkey, European railway promoters (led by Hirsch) envisaged an expansion of the Austrian railway network through the Balkans to the Bosphorus, thus opening up Turkish markets to new kinds of European commerce; while the French entre-preneur-cum-visionary Ferdinand de Lesseps saw that to realise the ancient dream of a canal between the Mediterranean and the Red Sea would create a vital artery of international trade, shortening the sea route between London and Bombay by more than 40 per cent. The artificial stimulus to Egyptian cotton exports provided by the American Civil War also played a part. Despite the obvious importance of the Suez Canal to British trade with India and the traditional importance attached by British diplomacy to strengthening the Ottoman Empire, it was not primarily British investors who financed the Turkish and Egyptian deficits. In Turkey the lead before 1875 was taken by French banks (notably the Société Générale); in Egypt by the Frankfurt-born financiers Hermann and Henry Oppenheim and the French broth-ers Edouard and André Dervieu.[35] In the short run, this was presumably profitable business for the issuing houses: by 1877 the Turkish debt had reached 251 million lire, of which, after commissions and discounts, the Treasury in Constantinople had received just 135 million. Far from promoting Middle Eastern economic develop-ment, however, the hapless bondholders were merely bankrolling chronically profli-gate governments. Millions were squandered by the Sultan Abdul Aziz on his luxurious European tour of 1867;[36] still more by his successor Abdul Mejid on the new Dolmabahçe palace, a cross between a seraglio and a Victorian railway station. And even the private undertakings like Hirsch's railways and Lesseps's canal proved less profitable than had been anticipated. Indeed, the concessions granted to Hirsch and Lesseps cost the two governments substantially more money than they received.[37]

Table 9f: Debt service as a percentage of expenditure, selected years and countries, 1860–1910.

	BRITAIN	TURKEY	EGYPT	SPAIN	BRAZIL	RUSSIA
1860	41.2	15.2		60.1	9.3	
1865	39.3			48.4	6.7	
1870	40.4			29.0	8.0	
1875	37.1		55.5	31.3	9.9	
1880	34.5	28.8		50.7	10.2	
1885	32.8			72.4	10.7	
1890	27.0	11.9		77.6	6.2	
1895	23.1	19.7		37.5	12.2	
1900	16.1	19.3		38.9	15.8	14.2
1905	16.6			40.5	17.9	9.6
1910	13.3	33.4		56.2	21.8	15.7

Source: as table 9e.

The Rothschilds' abstention from involvement in the Middle East between 1855 and 1875 therefore looks prudent with hindsight. We know, for example, that Lesseps approached James seeking support for his canal project as early as June 1854—five months before he secured the necessary concession from the Khedive—

but was rebuffed.[38] Landau, the Rothschild agent in Turin, had a brother in Alexandria who worked in tandem with the Oppenheims and sought to lure the Rothschilds into lending to the Egyptian government in the mid-1860s, but in vain. Though the ageing James was tempted, this was one of the rare occasions when his nephew Nat's risk-aversion prevailed—and with good reason.[39] Although Lionel was directly approached by an Egyptian representative who came bearing gifts in 1867, he politely demurred.[40] By 1869, even as the canal was formally opened, Alphonse was predicting the collapse of the Suez Canal Company and the assumption in London was that the Egyptian government would not be far behind it.[41] The London and Paris Rothschilds took an equally dim view of Turkish financial prospects: Anselm's interest in extending the Südbahn through the Balkans was evidently not shared by his cousins.[42] When the Egyptian Finance Minister Ismail Sadyk Pasha sought financial assistance from the Rothschilds in 1874, the request was firmly turned down.[43] The most they were willing to do was to make sure Verdi got his fee for conducting the world première of Aïda at the Cairo Opera House in 1871.[44]

By the beginning of 1875, there was still no obvious reason for the Rothschilds to alter their view. Lesseps, on the verge of bankruptcy, had been touting around the idea of selling the canal to one or more of the European powers since 1871, but the Ottoman government vetoed all the schemes mooted, the Gladstone ministry had shown no interest and the future of the canal had become entangled in complex legal wrangles about its tolls. Disraeli's return to power in February 1874 was the first crucial change which brought the Rothschilds into play. Always a romantic on Oriental matters[45]—but also realistic in discerning the approach of a new "Eastern crisis" and the future strategic importance of Egypt—Disraeli asked Lionel to reopen the question of a British purchase of the canal, and Natty was duly despatched to Paris.[46] For their part, the Rothschilds were keen, seeing the chance to repeat for the Egyptian canal what they had previously managed for European railways, namely the financing of a major asset sale. Yet, as Gustave reported, French political opposition to the idea of a British purchase seemed insuperable.[47] When Disraeli proposed instead a direct offer through the Rothshilds to buy the Khedive's canal shares, this opposition took on a financial dimension, reflecting the close links between the Crédit Foncier, the Société Générale and the Anglo-Egyptian Bank.[48]

It was the declaration of Turkey's bankruptcy by the Ottoman prime minister Mahmud Nedim Pasha on October 7 which transformed the situation by suddenly weakening the position of both the Khedive and his French bankers.[49] With Turkey bankrupt, it would be no easy matter for Egypt to borrow more money; yet Ismail needed—so he said—between three and four million pounds to meet payments due by the end of November. Schemes were devised by both the French banks and Dervieu to advance the Khedive money on the security of his canal shares, but the rival syndicates soon became deadlocked. This gave Disraeli his chance. A request for assistance from the British Treasury to "reorganise and control" Egyptian finances on November 10 had already signalled the readiness of the Khedive to turn to London as a last resort. Four days later, Frederick Greenwood, the editor of the *Pall Mall Gazette*, heard from Henry Oppenheim—recently settled in London—about the negotiations with the Anglo-Egyptian Bank and Dervieu, and suggested (not quite correctly) to the Foreign Secretary Lord Derby that the Suez Canal shares were about to pass into French hands.[50] In fact, the Crédit Foncier did now propose to buy the shares for 50 million francs (£2 million) and indeed acquired an option to do so, but the French Foreign Minister, the duc de Decazes, chose not to proceed without Derby's blessing and this was flatly denied. The Khedive therefore had little option but to sell to Britain, and on November 23 offered to relinquish his shares for £4 million, pledging to pay an additional 5 per cent on the purchase money until the pawned coupons were restored and dividend payments resumed. Derby and the Chancellor Sir Stafford Northcote were against accepting the offer, arguing that the canal should be controlled by an International Commission; but, when the matter was discussed in the five Cabinet meetings held between November 18 and 24, Disraeli eventually prevailed.[51]

Four million pounds was a huge sum in 1875: the cost of the purchase was equivalent to 8.3 per cent of the entire UK budget net of debt charges.[52] Moreover, as Disraeli told the Queen in his letter of November 18, there was "scarcely breathing time" as the Khedive required the money "by the 30th of this month." The difficulty was that Parliament was not sitting and it was unclear whether the government could raise the money from the Bank of England without its authority.[53] This explains why it was that on November 24 (or possibly the day before), as soon as he had the Cabinet's agreement to buy the shares, Disraeli sent his principal private secretary Montagu Corry to see Lionel, an episode which Corry was later heard to recount with all the narrative verve of his master:

> Disraeli had arranged with him that he should be in attendance . . . just outside the Cabinet room and, when his chief put out his head and said "Yes," should take immediate action. On this signal being given he went off to New Court and told Rothschild in confidence that the Prime Minister wanted £4,000,000 "to-morrow." Rothschild . . . picked up a muscatel grape, ate it, threw out the skin, and said deliberately, "What is your security?" "The British Government." "You shall have it."[54]

This was partly fantasy. In all likelihood, the Prime Minister had already privately discussed the matter with Lionel, so the decision was not a split-second one (Disraeli himself later told the Prince of Wales that the Rothschilds had "4 & 20 hours to make up their minds").[55] The terms agreed were that money was to be advanced to the British government—to be held at the disposal of the Egyptian government (beginning with £1 million on December 1 and the rest by January)—in return for a commission of 2.5 per cent; the government was also to be charged 5 per cent per annum interest until the money was repaid (though this was effectively passed on to the Khedive, who had to pay the Treasury 5 per cent interest until the shares once again yielded a dividend). On November 25 the contract was signed by the British consul-general, General Stanton, and the Egyptian Minister of Finance;[56] and four days later Lionel telegraphed to the Egyptian government that he would hold £2 million at its disposal from December 1 (double the first instalment originally envisaged), £1 million from December 15 and the last million from January 1, 1876.[57] By January 5, N. M. Rothschild & Sons had paid the full amount due (£3,976,582 2s 6d), much of it directly to the Egyptian government's creditors.[58] Parliament voted the payment of £4,080,000 on February 21 (the bulk of it raised by the creation of 3.5 per cent Exchequer Bonds), and the advance was repaid from the proceeds in the course of March, along with the commission of £99,414.[59] The interest due (£52,485) was finally paid on June 2.[60]

Two different accounts of this quite unprecedented transaction have passed into the historical record. The first is Disraeli's, as relayed in his letters to Queen Victoria at Balmoral. Ownership of the shares, he told her, "wd. give the possessor an immense, not to say proponderating, influence in the management of the Canal. It is vital to Her Majesty's authority & power at this critical moment, that the Canal should belong to England."[61] Having succeeded, he was triumphant and quite happy to share the glory with Lionel:

> It is just settled: you have it, Madam. The French Government has been outgeneraled. They tried too much, offering loans at an usurious rate, & with conditions wh: would have virtually given them the government of Egypt.
>
> The Khedive, in despair & disgust, offered Yr Majesty's Government to purchase his shares outright—he never would listen to such a proposition before.
>
> Four millions sterling! and almost immediately. There was only one firm that cd do it—Rothschilds. They behaved admirably, advanced the money at a low rate [what appears to be "five percent" scored out], and the entire interest of the Khedive is now yours, Madam.
>
> Yesterday the Cabinet sate four hours and more on this & Mr Disraeli has not had one moment[']s rest today; therefore this despatch must be pardoned, as his head is rather weak. He will tell the whole wondrous tale tomorrow.
>
> He was in Cabinet today, when Yr Majesty's second tel: arrived, wh. must be his excuse for his brief & stupid answer—but it was the crisis.
>
> The Govt. & Rothschilds agreed to keep it secret but there is little doubt it will be known tomorrow from *Kairo*.[62]

He was even more extravagant in his account to Lady Bradford:

> We have had all the gamblers, capitalists, financiers of the world organized and platooned in bands of plunderers, arrayed against us, and secret emissaries in every corner, and have baffled them all, and have never been suspected. The day before yesterday, Lesseps, whose company has the remaining shares, backed by the French whose agent he was, made a great offer. Had it succeeded, the whole of the Suez Canal would have belonged to France, and they might have shut it up . . . The Fairy [Queen Victoria] is in ecstasies . . .[63]

To add to the impression of a diplomatic triumph at the expense of France, Disraeli later told the Prince of Wales that Lionel had not been able to "appeal to their strongest ally, their own family in Paris, for Alphonse is *si francisé* that he wd. have betrayed the whole scheme instantly."[64] According to Lord John Manners, Disraeli had been "much elated" by his coup and "anticipate[d] a great revival of English influence abroad in consequence."[65] It also suited Bismarck to portray what had happened as a blow to French prestige;[66] and the idea that Disraeli had outwitted the French government with Rothschild support was, as we have seen, later taken up by French anti-Semites like Chirac.

The opposing interpretation—to be precise, the Opposition interpretation—was confused, suggesting that Disraeli had, if nothing else, outwitted the Liberals. Gladstone was immediately up in arms. "I am aware of no cause," he wrote to Granville, "that could warrant or excuse it, except its being necessary to prevent the closing of the canal. But . . . the closing of the London and North Western [railway] would be about as probable." Even if the purchase had been done "in concert with the other Powers" it was "an act of folly, fraught with future embarrassment"; if it had been done unilaterally, it was "an act of folly fraught with personal danger." He foresaw "grave consequences."[67] According to Gladstone, the proper course of action would have entailed parliamentary consultation and the involvement of the Bank of England. But Granville's letter to Gladstone on November 28 was little more than a succession of half-baked questions. "As regards my first impressions," he wrote, "which I mistrust, it appears to be very foolish." But he was uncertain why. Was it "without precedent . . . that the Gov should become part shareholders of a private undertaking over which by normal means they can have no control?":

> Is it not enough of a political measure, to induce and justify other countries in taking precautionary means [?]
> Is it not possible that Lesseps and the Rothschilds have duped the Govt into giving this great impetus to the value of the Suez Canal shares, by threatening them with a purchase by French Capitalists[?]
> Is it the intention of the Gov to buy in the open market another 100,000 shares at enhanced prices, in order to have an effective control[?] If they do so, cannot the remaining Shareholders still get them into endless difficulties[?]
> Will it not give rise to all sorts of international difficulties, & questions[?]
> Is the canal to remain subject to the discretionary powers, which we have always maintained, belonged to the Sultan[?]
> Ought so great a responsibility to be taken without immediately consulting Parliament[?]

"I suppose," he concluded after starting these decidedly lame hares, "that the quieter we keep about the Suez Canal at present the better."[68] This was a view echoed by Lord Hartington, who was now formally the leader of the Liberals following Gladstone's resignation and who discerned the popularity of Disraeli's coup.

It therefore fell to the former Chancellor, Sir Robert Lowe, to give full vent to Gladstone's instinctive sense of disapproval. In what Disraeli sarcastically predicted would be "a great invective against a stock-jobbing Ministry," Lowe argued that the Rothschilds' total charges—£150,000 for a loan of £4 million for three months—amounted to 15 per cent per annum interest, a figure more appropriate for an Egyptian government than a British one.[69] (This view was evidently shared by some at the Treasury, including the Secretary to the Treasury W. H. Smith.)[70] Liberal critics also took up Granville's suggestion that the purchase of the shares had given rise to "gambling on the Stock Exchange"—that is, speculation in Egyptian bonds by those in the know, namely the Rothschilds. This was subsequently given credence by Disraeli's solicitor Philip Rose, who believed the Rothschilds had "benefited largely," having "bought to the extent of millions of Eyptian stock."[71] Disraeli himself heard rumours that they had made "at least 1/4 of a million," though Montagu Corry heard from another source that "the Rothschilds had not made the slightest use of the intelligence, as they considered themselves standing in the position of the Government."[72] Another Opposition claim was the old chestnut that, as an MP, Natty was prohibited from profiting from a government loan; this was more easily rebutted by the argument that Natty was not yet a full partner in the bank, while Lionel had lost his seat in Parliament in 1874.[73]

The truth lies somewhere between these two extremes. Politically, it was not quite true to suggest that Britain had secured control and thwarted the French government in the process. According to Wolf, the French government had decided against attempting a French purchase and therefore saw the British intervention as a welcome solution to the Egyptian crisis. Nor did ownership of 44 per cent of the Canal Company's original shares give Britain control over the canal itself (especially as the shares had no voting rights until 1895 and had only ten votes thereafter). On the other hand, the Khedive's pledge to pay 5 per cent in lieu of dividends on the canal shares gave the British government a new and direct interest in Egyptian finances.[74] Disraeli was wrong to suggest that the Canal Company was in a position to close the canal to British shipping; in law, that was not the case. On the other hand, there was no guarantee that the law binding the company to keep the canal open to all shipping would always be respected, and, as Disraeli rightly said, the ownership of the shares gave Britain an additional "leverage"—a stronger justification to retaliate—in the event of a threat to her communications. This view was accepted by *The Times* and by other bankers (including Lord Overstone), and with hindsight it seems justified.[75] If the French government had been entirely content with the purchase, it would not have been necessary for the Rothschilds to maintain such strict secrecy between November 23 and 25.[76] Gustave's letter of December 31 indicates that there had initially been "panic" in Paris at the thought of a British takeover of Egypt. Two weeks later, his elder brother relayed a veiled warning from the French government: "Should England now accentuate even more her policy of intervention in the Egyptian affairs by coming to the rescue of the Khedive by means of another financial operation and by taking hold of the Country's principal revenues, the position of the French Govt. might become very delicate . . ."[77]

Financially too, the Liberal criticisms were ill-founded. As Disraeli pointed out in a withering response to Gladstone and Lowe in the Commons,[78] Lowe's arguments understated the opportunity-cost to the Rothschilds of immobilising at such short notice so large a sum even for three months, especially when (as the Rothschild letters from Paris and Frankfurt confirm) the possibility of a French or Russian diplomatic reaction could not be ruled out.[79] When it was suggested by the stockbroker Arthur Wagg that the Rothschilds should have provided the money free of charge, Lionel was dismissive. "Arthur Wagg," he retorted, "you're a young man and will learn better. I've made £100,000 out of the deal, I wish it had been £200,000."[80] As he pointed out to Corry on February 19, there had been a real risk involved: the Khedive might have insisted on payment in gold; "unforeseen events" might have tightened the money market; another government "accustomed to do business with the Rothschilds might have called upon that Firm to undertake a transaction involving large ready money payments, and finding the Firm unable to meet the demand, have transferred the business to other hands." Nor was it guaranteed that the Bank of England would have been willing to furnish the money, had it been approached. As Corry told Disraeli after his interview with Lionel, that was:

> a point . . . which could only have been determined by the full Board, at the obvious sacrifice of dispatch and secrecy . . . Baron Rothschild imagines that the Government might, possibly, have *compelled* the Bank to find the four millions (and at a lower rate of commission). But this would have been a violent act, before the commission of which, he maintains, they were bound to use every endeavour to obtain the money from independent Firms. He declares too, without hesitation, that the Bank of England could not have found the required sum without grave disturbance of the money market.

It was, Lionel concluded, "the entire absence of such disturbance" which provided the best "vindication of the commission charged."[81]

These arguments cannot be dismissed as mere special pleading. Rothschild profit and loss accounts also refute the charge of large-scale speculation in Egyptian bonds suggested by Granville and Lowe: the 1875 accounts show a sale of £12,682 of 1873 Egyptian bonds, but even if these had been bought at 55 and sold at 76 on November 26, the total profit would have amounted to just £3,505. The real financial significance of the transaction may have been the breathing space it gave to the French banks like the Crédit Foncier whose holdings of Egyptian bonds were much larger. In this sense, the purchase of the canal shares was far from being a blow to French interests.[82] Finally, the purchase of the shares proved a much better deal for the British taxpayer than the critics anticipated. By January 1876 they had risen from £22 10s 4d to £34 12s 6d, a 50 per cent increase. The market value of the government's stake was £24 million in 1898; £40 million on the eve of the First World War; and £93 million by 1935 (around £528 a share).[83] Between 1875 and 1895, the government received its £200,000 a year from Cairo; thereafter it was paid proper dividends, which rose from £690,000 in 1895 to £880,000 in 1901.[84]

Another Eastern Question

As Overstone and others realised, the purchase of the canal shares was merely the prelude to a large-scale British involvement in Egyptian finance and, ultimately, government; it also signalled a renewed British determination to exert influence on the Eastern Question as a whole. As early as July 1876, it was rumoured in Berlin that "the English Government had purchased the suzerainty of Egypt for £10 million."[85] However, it would be wrong to portray the road from 1875 to the military occupation of 1882 as a straight one; and it would be equally misleading to suggest that the Rothschilds were eager to go down it. In the immediate aftermath of the Suez coup, Derby despatched the Paymaster-General Stephen Cave to Egypt in a belated response to the Khedive's earlier request for British financial assistance. Cave's first objective was to establish some kind of control over Egyptian finances, if only to ensure that the 5 per cent interest due on the newly acquired canal shares continued to be paid.[86] The corollary, it soon emerged, was that the Rothschilds should assist with the consolidation and conversion of the Egyptian regime's multiple debts—a view strongly advanced by Charles Rivers Wilson, comptroller-general of the National Debt Office and the British government's representative on the Suez Canal council.[87] However, their private correspondence shows what reluctant imperialists the Rothschilds were. From an early stage, they advised against the publication of Cave's report and emphasised to Disraeli "the difficulties of putting ourselves at the head of a large financial operation."[88] Their reluctance was partly based on narrow financial considerations: although happy to speculate in small amounts of Egyptian bonds, Lionel and Alphonse plainly felt that Cave and Rivers Wilson were underestimating how difficult it would be to stabilise Egyptian finances while Ismail remained Khedive.[89]

There was a further political reservation, however. Lionel and Alphonse continued to attach more significance to maintaining harmonious relations between the great powers—in this case France and England—than to imposing foreign financial control on Egypt. Indeed, it was through Alphonse that the British government was first informed of the French President MacMahon's compromise proposal: a multinational commission to oversee Egyptian finances, on which England, France and Italy would be equally represented.[90] From Paris, Alfred relayed Decazes' "anger" at Derby's prevarications and warned the government not to "throw cold water" on the French proposal; Lionel relayed Disraeli's reponse: "[T]hey want the French to make a good plan and not one that will put money into their pockets and without doing the Khedive any good."[91] The difficulty was that there was a conflict of interest between those who held interest-bearing Egyptian bonds and those—mainly the French and Egyptian banks—who had been advancing money short-term to the Khedive. In essence, the bondholders refused to accept that the short-term lenders had an equal claim and so vetoed a generalised writing-down of all Egyptian debts by 20 per cent—a position endorsed by the British government.[92] This paralysed the new Caisse de la Dette Publique which had been set up in May.[93] In the absence of Anglo-French accord, the Rothschilds simply refused to take on the task of restructuring the Egyptian debt, and it was left to a commission of inquiry to fix the consolidated debt at £76 million (a figure which did not include £15 million of private debts secured on the Khedive's lands and a substantial floating debt which may have been as much as £6 million).[94]

It was not until 1878 that these difficulties seemed to have been overcome, with the creation of a committee composed of the Caisse representatives, Lesseps, Rivers Wilson and one Egyptian, and their recommendation that an "international" government be appointed under Nubar Pasha, with Rivers Wilson as Finance Minister and the Frenchman Eugène de Blignières as Minister of Public Works.[95] Simultaneously, the English and French Rothschilds agreed to float an £8.5 million loan, to be secured on a large tract of the Khedive's domain lands.[96] Apart from the confidence it gave investors, the significance of this lies in the impression it gave of Anglo-French amity, the *Journal de Débats* going so far as to describe it as "almost equivalent to the conclusion of an alliance between France and England."[97] This was undoubtedly the impression the Rothschilds wished to convey. However, like investors' confidence in Egypt, it proved ephemeral.

British and French policy in Egypt cannot be viewed in isolation; it was in truth merely a sub-plot in the bigger story of the Ottoman debt crisis which, as we have seen, had been a precondition of the sale of the Suez Canal shares by the Khedive. The Ottoman debt crisis too needs to be seen in the context of great-power diplomacy; it had after all been precipitated by a revolt against Ottoman rule in the provinces of Bosnia–Hercegovina and Bulgaria. This was a "Christian" cause which Russian diplomats sought to exploit for foreign political reasons, and British Liberals sought to exploit for domestic political ones. If the Rothschild role in Egypt had been politically sensitive, their position in the Balkan crisis of 1875–8 was much more so. Their sympathy with Disraeli naturally inclined them to support his essentially pro-Turkish policy; but their financial commitment to Russia ran directly counter to this.

Russia had been pursuing a "forward" policy towards Turkey from October 1870, when the Tsar had repudiated the Black Sea clauses of the 1856 Treaty of Paris. True, the ending of the neutralisation of the Straits—one of the few concrete results of the Crimean War—had to be sanctioned by the other powers at an international conference in London; and Bismarck's policy of reconciling Germany, Austria and Russia under the banner of the "Three Emperors" League" (*Dreikaiserbund*) tended to restrain Russia's Balkan policy in the early 1870s. However, some kind of confrontation between Russia and Britain over Turkey was a strong possibility, especially with Disraeli dreaming about breaking up the Three Emperors' League. No sooner had the revolt broken out in Bosnia–Hercegovina in the summer of 1875 than Disraeli began to accuse Russia, Austria and Prussia of fomenting the disintegration of the Ottoman Empire. In reality, both Andrássy, the Austro-Hungarian Foreign Minister, and Gorchakov, his Russian counterpart, would have been content with a six-power agreement to impose "effective measures" on Turkey, and Derby would probably have accepted this (as France and Italy did). But Disraeli was not interested.

On May 26, 1876, Lionel wrote to Disraeli: "I hope very soon to be able to congratulate you on the conclusion of an arrangement, which will ensure peace for a good many years owing to an energetic and determined policy."[98] In truth Disraeli's "energetic policy" of sending the fleet to Besika Bay and seeking to split the Three Emperors' League came close to embroiling Britain in war. The Sultan abdicated in May 1876, Serbia and Montenegro joined the anti-Turkish revolt the following month and the "Bulgarian atrocities"—in which up to 15,000 Bulgarian Christians were allegedly killed by Ottoman irregulars known as Bashi-Bazouks—gave Gladstone a perfect opportunity to emerge from retirement, filled with righteous indignation. When Disraeli met the Russian ambassador Shuvalov at a dinner at Lionel's on June 9, his unease at Britain's diplomatic isolation was evident.[99] Indeed, when the Indian Secretary, Lord Salisbury, went to Constantinople to attend the international conference called by Derby, he came close to agreeing with the Russian plenipotentiary Ignatiev that Turkey should grant autonomy to a partitioned Bulgaria; while Disraeli's crude attempt to buy Austria out of the Three Emperors' League—"How much money do you want?" was his blunt question—came to nothing. Lionel's letter to Disraeli of September 8, one of a series which offered the Prime Minister encouragement as well as City intelligence, confirms that he was having "a very difficult uphill fight."[100] If Britain and Russia had indeed gone to war in June 1877, the responsibility would have been as much Disraeli's as Gorchakov's, and perhaps more so. As it was, he lost two senior ministers (Derby and Lord Carnarvon) over the issue.

To the Rothschilds, the prospect of such a war was alarming in the extreme for one good reason. Between 1870 and 1875, the London and Paris Rothschilds had jointly issued Russian bonds worth a total of £62 million, thus finally securing that influence over Russian finances which had eluded them for so long. It had been a profitable business: the price of Russian 5 per cents had risen from 85 in March 1870 to 106 in August 1875, a 24 per cent increase. The Eastern crisis of 1875–7 more than wiped out this improvement, driving the price down to 74 in October 1876 and 68 in April the following year when Russia declared war on Turkey. The effects were felt on most government bonds and on all the major European bourses.[101] Natty himself later called the 1878 banking crisis, which began with the collapse of the City of Glasgow Bank and culminated in the failure of the West of England Bank, the biggest "ever known in the history of English banking."[102] The dilemma which faced Lionel and Natty (as he prepared to succeed his ailing father) was acute: should they support Russia, at the risk of seeing the Ottoman Empire humiliated and even broken up, with all that might imply for Egypt and for Britain herself?

They chose Turkey, leaving the 1877 Russian loan to a consortium of German bankers led by Mendelssohn, with the French joint-stock banks—notably the Comptoir d'Escompte and the Crédit Lyonnais—vying for a share.[103] The Rothschilds, Disraeli was able to assure the Queen in August, were "extremely hostile to the present Russian policy, & have refused to assist the Czar in his present exigency."[104] This was a real sacrifice, as it more or less excluded the Rothschilds from Russian finance for a decade and a half. It cannot merely be explained in terms of their economic interests in the Ottoman Empire, because these were almost non-existent at the moment of crisis in 1877. The major railway concessions in the Balkans were largely in the hands of Hirsch; they continued to spurn requests for financial support from Constantinople;[105] and the first big loan to Egypt was over a year away. The only credible explanation is therefore a non-economic one.

There is little doubt that Gladstone's and Lowe's attacks on the Rothschilds' role in the Suez Canal share purchase had done much to undermine Lionel's sense of party-political loyalty. More important, the Rothschilds regarded a Slav nationalist triumph in the Balkans as undesirable from the point of view of their "co-religionists." From the moment he published his pamphlet *Bulgarian Horrors and the Question of the East* in September 1876, Gladstone had made his campaign against Disraeli's policy a religious crusade. By its very nature, this appeal on behalf of the Balkan Christians was of limited interest to the Rothschilds (and other wealthy Jews like the Goldsmids), especially when it reminded voters of Disraeli's Jewish origins—and those of his supporters.[106] As Derby commented, "Gladstone . . . deplores the influence of 'Judaic sympathies,' not confined to professing Jews, on the eastern queston: whether this refers to Disraeli, or to the Telegraph people, or to the Rothschilds . . . is left in darkness."[107] Lionel was scathing about "all these public meetings" where the Turks were attacked but nothing was said "about the cause of the insurrection & disturbances."[108] His concerns were quite different, as can be seen from the letter he wrote to Disraeli which was read aloud at the Congress of Berlin: it was the persecution of Jews in Eastern Europe (particularly Rumania) to which he wished to draw attention.[109] Alphonse sought to exert similar pressure on Bismarck through Bleichröder.[110] Article 44 of the final Treaty of Berlin, which guaranteed religious toleration for all faiths in the Balkans, manifestly counted for more in the Rothschilds' eyes than the convoluted compromise over Bulgaria.

Lionel therefore gave Disraeli's policy his unequivocal backing. "[H]ow truly I rejoice," he wrote at the end of March 1877, "at the success of a patriotic and just policy—Owing to your great firmness and statesman-like views we have arrived at a point when we may confidently expect soon to be able to congratulate you on the prospects of a general peace."[111] Natty too assured Montagu Corry of his firm "Turkish" sympathies.[112] Throughout the crisis, they sent Disraeli regular summaries of their intelligence from the continent and offered to act as a channel of informal communication to Vienna. In August, for example, Disraeli informed the Queen that he had "made up his mind to consult Messrs. Rothschild confidentially on the matter" of Russian undertakings to Austria with regard to the neutrality of Serbia and Bulgaria. "They are intimately connected with Austria and the Austrian Imperial Family. Baron Rothschild consented to telegraph to the head of the family at Vienna, & requested, that, before any advance was made, he shd. obtain from Count Andrassy an explicit declaration on the matters in question . . . Two days after th[e]y. received a reply . . . [containing information] different from the impression then afloat.[113] Such was the Rothschilds' intimacy with the Prime Minister that other key diplomatic actors—including the Russian ambassador and the British Foreign Secretary himself—felt positively marginalised. "Schou. [Shuvalov] tells L[ad]y D[erby]. that he finds the Rothschilds acquainted with everything that goes on," complained Derby in December 1877:

> even more so than the ministers: he is convinced that they are in daily communications with the Premier, hear all that passes, & use it for their own purposes. From other sources I am certain that the leakage of cabinet secrets, of which we have so often complained, is mainly in that quarter: for when Ld B[eaconsfield]. goes out of town there is generally but little gossip of that kind . . . the Rothschilds no doubt get their news direct from himself.[114]

Nor did the Disraeli–Rothschild relationship go unnoticed by the Liberal leadership. "The Rothschilds are behaving abominably," Granville reported to Gladstone in August 1877, three months after Gladstone had moved his "Resolutions [for] a vital or material alteration of the declared policy of Her Majesty's Government" in the Commons.[115] Four months later, Granville was incensed to hear "that N. Rothschild (a red hot Turk) ridicules the notion of Dizzy intending war. He says that the Turks have placed themselves in his hands (a charming trust to have) and that Russia will yield." According to Natty, "Dizzy does not mean to go to war against the Straits being opened to all vessels of war."[116] That was not what he later told the historian J. A. Froude, whom he unsuccessfully tried to persuade to write a biography of Disraeli "in accordance with his (Ld R's) views." Looking back, Natty admitted "that he (Ld B[eaconsfield]) had determined in favor of war: that it was necessary to his policy: that the Queen pressed him on . . . and that he was checked only by the opposition which he met with both in and out of the cabinet."[117]

Whether bluffing or not, Disraeli was lucky. Firstly, Bismarck chose not to support Gorchakov and Ignatiev, fearing that too complete a Russian success would fatally demote Austria–Hungary from great-power status.[118] Secondly, the Russians stumbled militarily when their advance was checked at Plevna in December 1877. Thirdly, they overplayed their hand in trying to create a new "Big Bulgaria" by the treaty of San Stefano while reneging on their earlier undertaking to let Austria–Hungary have Bosnia–Hercegovina. All this made Salisbury's task when he succeeded Derby as Foreign Secretary in the spring of 1878 a good deal easier than it might have been. By concluding a series of bargains with Russia (which secured Bessarabia and Batum), Turkey (which surrendered Cyprus to Britain in return for a guarantee of her Asian territory) and Austria (which was allowed to occupy Bosnia—Hercegovina and the Sanjak of Novibazar between Serbia and Montenegro), Salisbury paved the way for Disraeli's diplomatic "triumph" at Berlin.

How far Berlin really represented a victory is in fact debatable: the division of Bulgaria into three—Bulgaria, which became autonomous, Eastern Rumelia, which remained under Turkish suzerainty and Macedonia, which remained part of the Ottoman Empire—did not have the look of a lasting solution; and Turkey had been made to surrender all but a vestige of her power in the Balkans. To be sure, Russian troops were withdrawn from the Balkans by the end of 1879, and Disraeli had undoubtedly reasserted British leadership in the diplomacy of the Eastern Question. He also had the satisfaction of seeing Russia at odds with Germany and Austria–Hungary. The Rothschilds' warm praise for Disraeli was not wholly unjustified.[119] Nevertheless, the open-ended nature of the settlement was confirmed within less than a year of the Congress of Berlin.

In April 1879 the Khedive dismissed the "international" government, which had predictably made itself unpopular with Egyptian taxpayers. The result was a sharp drop in the new Rothschild-issued bonds. It has often been suggested that from this point onwards Natty agitated for a British military intervention in Egypt.[120] This is incorrect. Natty accepted Rivers Wilson's argument for "the immediate removal of the Viceroy by a firman from the Porte, supported by the Powers, and at the same time the nomination of his eldest son," Tewfiq. But he opposed the idea of suspending the 1877 loan, which the former minister believed would help bring this enforced abdication about,[121] declaring that he and his French cousins "object[ed] strongly to Wilson's proposal to withdraw the loan, which they would consider a very dishonourable proceeding."[122] Once again, their objective was one to which Gladstone could scarcely have objected: a concerted action in partnership with the other interested powers to depose Ismail and replace him with Tewfiq. However, the old conflicts between the different creditor interests soon resurfaced. Naturally, the Rothschilds' first priority was to re-establish the security of their 1877 bonds, an object not shared by the holders of earlier Egyptian paper.[123] It took until December 1879 to secure the consent of the Austrian and Greek governments to a compromise which ring-fenced the domain lands on which the Rothschild loan was secured, without demoting the other creditors' claims.[124] Nevertheless, the new regime—effectively under the control of a new Anglo-French-dominated Commission of Liquidation, was to prove almost as short-lived as its predecessor. Within a matter of months, the system of "dual control" was to fall apart, never to be restored.

From Investment to Invasion

Gladstone lost no time in fulfilling the Rothschilds' worst expectations following his election victory in the spring of 1880. He came to power in the wake of another

Turkish declaration of bankruptcy,[125] and almost immediately sought to organise some kind of economic sanction on behalf of that large and disparate group of Turkish creditors of which he himself was a member (see below). In addition to withdrawing British military consuls from Turkey and compelling the Porte to make the concessions to Greece and Montenegro which had been agreed at Berlin, he contemplated seizing the port of Smyrna. This appalled the Rothschilds, not least because, as Natty pointed out to Disraeli, the revenues of Smyrna were already hypothecated to the guaranteed loan which the Rothschilds had issued in 1855. Warning Disraeli that only Russia and perhaps Italy were likely to support this policy, Natty predicted international complications arising from Gladstone's "arrogance": "In the stock exchange they say tickets for the European Concert are very much offered."[126] "If the other powers disagree," he told Bleichröder on October 8,

> nobody knows what will happen. As passionate and irritable a man as Gladstone may do anything. If he goes on alone with Russia and Italy, this would make the worst impression and be very unpopular. There is only one man who could manage this damned business—it is Prince Bismarck who has to put into order the Egyptian business. It is desirable that he should take matters in hand.[127]

When Granville called on the German ambassador Count Münster that morning he found Alfred already there. "He and Alfred Rothschild looked rather sheepish at being found together," Granville told Gladstone. "I asked what did R. want to know. Münster said he came to tell me that he knows it is Smyrna."[128] Natty felt sure that "Gladstone would like to go it alone" but was confident that he would not be able to do so "without asking the other ministers [foreign ambassadors] for their advice. England will not act without Germany, and never alone with Russia—I have good reason for my opinion. The best informed people tell me that Bismarck is stronger in foreign policy than ever before."[129]

As it turned out, Gladstone was able to secure his objective without needing to occupy Smyrna. On December 20, 1881, the Sultan promulgated the Decree of Muharrem which reduced the Turkish debt and annual charges[130] and established a new Administration of the Ottoman Public Debt. Formally, this was a pre-emptive action agreed with the bondholders to prevent direct intervention by the great powers under the terms of the resolutions passed at the Congress of Berlin. In practice, the various national representatives on the Administration were appointed with government approval; and, with the chair of the Administration being taken alternately by a British and French representative, it looked at first sight like an extension of the Egyptian system of "dual control" (though with anomalies like the farming out of the tobacco monopoly to a consortium including the Vienna Rothschilds, the Creditanstalt and Bleichröder).[131] Not for the last time, Gladstone had ended up delivering a solution to which the Rothschilds could hardly object. Despite Alphonse's continuing reservations about the stability of Turkish finance,[132] they themselves issued two major loans under the new dispensation, one in 1891 for £6.9 million and another three years later for £9 million (in partnership with the Ottoman Bank). Significantly, both were secured on the Egyptian tribute, like their previous Turkish loan of 1855.[133]

To understand the Decree of Muharrem, it is necessary to appreciate the shifting diplomatic relationships between the other European powers at this time. In the wake of the Russo-Turkish war, Bismarck had struggled to restore the Three Emperors" League between Germany, Austria—Hungary and Russia, beginning with a secret defensive alliance with Austria in October 1879. Although this was in fact directed against Russia, he then encouraged the Russians to seek some kind of understanding with Austria, which culminated in the second *Dreikaiserbund* of June 1881. Essentially, this was a pact of neutrality if one of the three was involved in a war with a fourth power, but the terms with respect to the Balkans were its more important aspect. Conflict with Turkey herself was excluded from the terms of the alliance, but Austria—Hungary effectively gave Russia a free hand in "unifying" Bulgaria, while the Russians accepted the possibility of an Austrian annexation of Bosnia—Hercegovina (which she had occupied since the Congress of Berlin). In addition, Austria established what amounted to a protectorate over Serbia, recognising King Milan in 1881, and two years later securing a German commitment to the defence of Rumania against a Russian attack. At the same time, a quite distinct Triple Alliance was formed in May 1881 between Germany, Austria and Italy, which was partly directed against French Mediterranean expansion (signalled by the occupation of Tunis in 1881), but also bought Italian neutrality in the event of an Austrian war with Russia. There was plainly a contradiction between the Three Emperors' Alliance and the Triple Alliance; but in the absence of conflict between Austria and Russia, it was a latent contradiction, and the *Dreikaiserbund* was renewed with little difficulty in March 1884. So swiftly were the agreements struck at Berlin in 1878 overhauled.

Where did this leave Britain and France? The answer was potentially isolated if their relations deteriorated in Egypt—unless of course a pro-Russian policy were adopted by one or both. The chances of an Anglo-Russian understanding were whittled away as Russian influence extended through Central Asia towards Persia, Afghanistan and the North-Western frontier of the Raj. Despite the immense political differences between the Republic and Tsardom, Franco-Russian rapprochement was a more realistic possibility, and fear of such a constellation was in many ways the key to Bismarck's elaborate system. In essence, he was able to cast Germany not just as a broker in colonial disputes but even as a potential ally.

The English Rothschilds were evidently attracted by this. Rothschild policy after 1880 therefore became increasingly subject to a subtle Bismarckian influence, with Bleichröder at last able to play the role of intermediary which he had previously been denied. Bismarck, once the bane of financial stability, became in the 1880s its apparent guarantor. When the British ambassador Lord Ampthill called on Bleichröder in 1882 he reported seeing a telegram from the Paris Rothschilds asking for immediate news of the Kaiser's health. "I asked Bleichröder what effect French financiers expected from the Emperor's death upon the Paris Bourse. 'A general *baisse* of from 10–15 per cent,' he replied, 'because of the uncertainty of Bismarck's tenure of office under a new reign.' "[134] A year later, the German ambassador in London was told by Natty that an Anglo-German understanding was what "most reasonable Englishmen, except for a few ministers" wanted.[135] The fact that after 1881 a rising proportion of Turkish debt was absorbed by the Berlin capital market—with the Deutsche Bank playing a leading role—helps to elucidate this Germanophile tendency.[136]

The disadvantage of an Anglo-German rapprochement from the Rothschild point of view was that it was likely to imply a deterioration in Anglo-French relations. In fact, that was already on the cards when a nationalist military revolt led by Arabi Pasha against the Khedive Tewfiq's supine regime paralysed the system of "dual control" in Egypt. The flexing of French muscles in both Morocco in 1880 and Tunis the following year may explain the reluctance of the Gladstone ministry to embark on the policy of concerted Anglo-French intervention. It had little to do with Gladstonian squeamishness about intervention in Egyptian affairs *per se*, for within a remarkably short space of time he had given the order to shell Alexandria (July 1882) and overthrow Arabi (September).

The Rothschilds' role in this astounding sequence of events was essentially to mediate between the British and French governments. It was already difficult enough in London because of the suspicion between Natty and Gladstone; the political position in France might have made it a good deal harder, had it not been for the ramifications of the Union Générale banking crisis.

The rise and fall of the Union Générale have already been touched upon as the inspiration for Zola's novel *L'Argent*. It is now time to relate it to the complex politics of the Third Republic and the Eastern Question, in which, for a brief period, it played a role as important as that played by the Suez Canal. At root, the Union Générale was a product of the effort, initiated by Langrand-Dumonceau and taken up by Hirsch in the late 1860s, to build a rail link—the Orient line—through the Balkans to Constantinople, an effort which ran into trouble when Turkey defaulted and the Treaty of San Stefano transferred parts of the original Turkish concession to the newly independent Balkan states.[137] Paul Eugène Bontoux was an obscure French railway engineer who had worked for both the Staatsbahn and the Roth-schild-owned Südbahn before beginning to build his own Austro-Hungarian business empire in the mid-1870s. Initially, he wished to channel French capital into a range of Central European businesses. By the time he quit the Südbahn in 1878, however, he had become convinced of the need to establish a new financial institution to challenge the dominant position of the Rothschild–Creditanstalt group in Vienna. If the first step was the relaunching of the Union Générale in 1878 with a capital of 25 million francs, then the creation of the Österreichische Länderbank in 1880 was the second. With the support of the Austrian Chancellor Taaffe, Bontoux acquired interests in Austro-Hungarian railways and coal mines and sought to replace Hirsch in the development of the rail links to Belgrade, Constantinople and Salonica.[138] Later he diversified, so that the Union Générale ended up with a wide range of shareholdings throughout Europe.[139]

Yet the Union Générale was always more than just another investment trust on the Crédit Mobilier model. Like Langrand-Dumonceau before him, Bontoux used Ultramontane and anti-Rothschild rhetoric to mobilise the savings of self-consciously conservative Catholic investors. The Legitimist Pretender, the comte de Chambord, was among those who invested in Union Générale shares.[140] The scale of the enterprise should not be exaggerated: at its peak its assets amounted to little more than 38 million francs.[141] However, Bontoux's practice of increasing its nominal capital well beyond the genuine subscriptions he was able to raise meant that the Union Générale was a speculative house of cards, with insufficient capital for the kind of long-term investments and short-term deposits which made up its balance sheet. By December 1881 shares with a nominal price of 500 francs stood at 3,000, but the bank's supposed profits were anticipated rather than real and, despite Bontoux's denials, a substantial proportion of Union Générale shares (over 10,000, worth some 17 million francs) were held by the bank itself.[142] By the end of 1881, as the Banque de France began to push up interest rates, the speculative bubble was close to bursting. In the two weeks after January 4, the share price fell from 3,005 to 1,300 and on January 31 the Union Générale was forced to suspend payments. After his conviction for financial malpractice and flight to Spain, Bontoux repeatedly claimed that he was the victim of a "Jewish plot"; but there is no evidence to support this allegation. In fact only a large loan from the major Paris banks, to which the Rothschilds contributed 10 million francs, averted a domino-like financial collapse on the Paris market.[143] (As we shall see, this form of collective rescue was to be used again in London when Barings crashed eight years later.)

The historical significance of the Union Générale crash lies mainly in its timing. For in November 1881—on the eve of the crash—Léon Gambetta had become the French premier, committed (as it appeared) to a policy of external adventure and internal radicalism. Although the proximate cause of his fall a mere two months later was a defeat in the National Assembly on the issue of electoral reform, it was arguably the financial crisis of January which really scuppered him, wrecking his plans for a large-scale debt conversion and railway nationalisation.[144] The evidence remains circumstantial, but there is no question that the fall of Gambetta (and the return of Say to the Finance Ministry) was welcome to the Rothschilds from an international point of view. On January 25 Alphonse had written to Natty warning him that Gambetta was unwilling to co-operate with England over Egypt on the terms proposed by the British ambassador Lord Lyons and casting doubt on the Anglo-French commercial treaty also under discussion. Natty passed the letter on to Dilke (now parliamentary under-secretary to the Foreign Office) with the cryptic comment that it was "unsatisfactory."[145] The very next day Gambetta was forced to resign. Less than a fortnight later, Alphonse met Lyons at the French Foreign Ministry and asked him "what he would like me to say to M. de Freycinet with regard to the Egyptian question? After quite a moment of reflection he replied: 'Tell him to effect the treaty of commerce.' "[146] It seems that Natty and Alphonse were acting, as their fathers had before them, as an unofficial channel of communication to the new French government, Natty writing to Paris "in the sense [Dilke] indicate[d]" and Alphonse replying with the assurance that "there is no one in the whole French Cabinet who understands the importance of the commercial treaty with England better" than Say.[147] Despite their habitual suspicion of Rothschild motives, Granville and Gladstone could not deny that this information was "interesting."[148]

Even more interesting were the strong indications from Alphonse that the French government would not object to firm action by Britain to get rid of Arabi Pasha. As Alphonse argued, there would be too much opposition in the French Chamber for the French government to participate in full-scale "armed intervention"; what he and Say evidently wished was for Britain to go ahead on her own.[149] This information reached London at a time when Gladstone was still hoping to arrive at a multilateral solution via a conference at Constantinople, despite pressure from members of his Cabinet (notably Hartington) for unilateral military action. When British ships bombarded Alexandria in July—a month after riots in the city had seemed to strengthen the case for military action—Alphonse was delighted, noting that "England can now no longer withdraw until law and order are re-established all over the country; this is the best guarantee . . . to all those with legal interests in Egypt." He took "the greatest satisfaction" from the news of General Wolseley's victory at Tel-el-Kebir less than two months later.[150] It is difficult to avoid the conclusion that the Rothschilds encouraged the British government to override Gladstone's conscientious scruples and (as the Cabinet minute of July 31 put it) forcibly to "put down Arabi." That decision was taken on the same day Gambetta's successor Freycinet was defeated in the Chamber for proposing joint Anglo-French occupation of the canal zone.[151] By September 7 Granville had more or less accepted Natty's view that in Egypt "it was clear that England must secure the future predominance."[152] It is doubtful that this change of heart would have been possible in the absence of strong indications that France would acquiesce, and these the Rothschilds were happy to provide. In only one respect did Alphonse and Natty view the Egyptian occupation differently: for the former, it was intended as a signal to Bismarck of Anglo-French unity, while the latter was keen to act in accord with the German Chancellor.

If the Rothschilds had wished to set a trap for Gladstone, they could hardly have done better than to lure him into the occupation of Egypt. Gladstone himself had accurately prophesied the complications which would arise from such an action; now he found himself beset by them.[153] Firstly, it was not at all obvious how the Khedive's government was to be reconstituted. Secondly, there was the long-standing financial question as to which creditors should have precedence. Thirdly, there was the domestic political difficulty that Gladstone had played into the hands of the Opposition by adopting imperialism so reluctantly. Finally, and perhaps most important, he had handed the other European powers a stick with which to beat Britain.

The French acquiescence in the English takeover of a territory in which France had by far the greater economic stake was always bizarre; it did not last long. Within less than a month of Wolseley's victory, as Gustave reported to Natty and Natty to Granville, rumours began to circulate in Paris that the British government was trying to buy Suez Canal shares on the open market with the intention of acquiring a majority holding. This seems to have been what Natty wanted the government to do; but Gladstone remained deeply suspicious of anything which resembled Disraeli's original share purchase of 1875—he still felt aspects of the transaction were being concealed from him—and in any case it proved impossible to reach an agreement with Lesseps and the French shareholders in the Canal Company.[154]

The canal was only a part of the Egyptian problem. Perhaps not surprisingly, for reasons discussed below, Gladstone regarded Egyptian finance as a "holy subject"; but he was still determined to resolve the issue through the "concert of Europe." In the era of Bismarckian *Realpolitik* this was an impossibility. Bleichröder was soon relaying signals from Berlin which seemed to imply a sudden German change of heart over English policy in Egypt, and the London conference on which Gladstone pinned his hopes ended in stalemate in the summer of 1884.[155] Isolated, Gladstone had no alternative but to entrust the restructuring of Egyptian finance to the classic City combination of Rothschild and Baring. On August 4 the First Lord of the

Admiralty, Lord Northbrook—a member of the Baring family, though never a partner in the bank—was despatched to Egypt to enquire into the country's finances. As
Randolph Churchill pointed out indignantly in the Commons, his cousin Evelyn
Baring (later Lord Cromer) was already in Cairo as consul-general.[156] "Therefore,"
thundered Churchill,

> two members of the great house of Baring are to be entrusted, so far as I
> can make out, with the sole disposal and almost unlimited control of
> England's political and financial interests in Egypt . . . I should like to
> point out, in this connection, that there literally would be no difference
> whatever in sending out two members of the house of Rothschild to
> sending out two members of the house of Baring. The two are almost
> equal in greatness and in their great pecuniary interest in the East; and it
> stands to reason that if Her Majesty's Government had proposed—sup-
> posing a member of the house of Rothschilds, by circumstances and his
> public position, fitted to undertake the task—to send out such a
> member, there would have been a great cry of displeasure from the
> House of Commons and the country. But there would have been no dif-
> ference between the position of Rothschilds and Baring . . .[157]

Given Northbrook's political track-record (he was a former Viceroy of India)
Churchill was scoring a cheap point, and his claim that "the public service of this
country has hitherto been uniformly free from the least connection with the commercial and financial private enterprises of the City of London" was, of course, nonsense. But it is of some interest that he believed a Rothschild involvement in
Egyptian policy would have aroused more public objection than a Baring involvement.

What Churchill did not know was that, the very day after Northbrook was sent
to Egypt, Natty gave Granville an assurance that his firm would provide a short-
term loan of £1 million to meet Egypt's immediate deficit, though he pointedly
demanded to know "what will Govt. do to help to secure his debt?" The need to
renew this loan gave the Rothschilds precisely the kind of financial leverage over
policy which Churchill erroneously attributed to the Barings: talking darkly of an
impending Egyptian bankruptcy, Natty told Granville on December 26 that he was
willing to renew the loan only for two weeks, in order to speed up negotiations with
the other powers.[158] Even as he tightened the screw, Natty seems to have enjoyed
tormenting the government with conflicting and irreconcilable messages from
Berlin and Paris. "Our only chance is to come to terms with Bismarck," he told
Hamilton in August.[159] On September 1, he warned Granville that "Bismarck is
very angry, [and says] that he will defend the rights of the German . . . bond holders, that he will oppose illegal action on the part of the Egyptians and give us an ultimate [sic] ratio, the Mandate of Europe to France, & in his opinion we should not
like to face this." But when he dined with Gladstone three months later, he "scoffed
at the French computation of Egyptian Land Revenue," strongly endorsing the estimates in Northbrook's report the previous month which had called for a sole British
control of Egyptian finance.[160]

It is hard not to sympathise with Gladstone as he was inexorably driven towards
a *de facto* British protectorate: so ubiquitous did the Rothschilds seem that he

accused them of leaking critical information to the French government—at a time when Hartington was supplying Natty with details of Northbrook's report to pass on to Bismarck.[161] There was probably something in this: in October the French premier Jules Ferry told Bismarck's son Herbert "that England was agitating the great financial houses, and especially the Rothschilds, and was giving them to understand that the Egyptian Loans would become valueless, and the bondholders would lose everything, if the British Government were to be driven to extremities . . . The financiers were now really anxious and were trying to modify the French Government's attitide towards England."[162] Small wonder Rosebery hesitated to join the Cabinet at this critical juncture: he doubtless imagined another fierce speech on the subject of financial families from Churchill.[163] Even as it was, Churchill made a wild speech about "a gang of Jewish usurers in London and Paris seducing Ismail Pasha into their net" and alleged that "Gladstone had delivered the Egyptians back into the toils of their Jewish taskmasters."[164]

Finally, and fatally, there was the question of where to stop Britain's new jurisdiction. To the south of Egypt, religious revolt was raging in the Sudan under the leadership of the Mahdi. Again the Rothschilds encouraged British intervention, and again Gladstone found himself unable to resist the combination of imperialist sentiment at home and the over-ambition of "the man on the spot," in this case "Chinese" Gordon. All concerned overestimated British power, the French Rothschilds cheerfully repeating a bourse story "that Gordon Pasha carried along £100,000 in Bank of England notes, the best English weapon to put an end to the revolt."[165] Far from reporting on the logistics of withdrawal from Sudan, as he had been instructed to do, Gordon sought to take on the Mahdi. The news reached London of his probable death on February 5, 1885. It was this crisis which finally persuaded Rosebery to join the government,[166] a decision welcomed by Natty in revealing terms: "[Y]our clear judgments and patriotic devotion will help the Govt. and save the country. I hope you will take care that large reinforcements are sent up the Nile. The campaign in the Soudan must be a brilliant success and no mistake."[167]

There can be no question that the Rothschilds benefited directly from the British occupation of Egypt. As Gustave said, British control was good news for most (though not all) Egyptian bondholders as "Egyptian credit obviously would benefit should England become jointly liable for Egypt's external obligations."[168] Not only that, but it created a secure new form of bond for the Rothschilds themselves to issue: after 1884 all Egyptian bond issues were effectively underwritten by Britain. Between 1885 and 1893, the London, Paris and Frankfurt houses were jointly responsible for four major Egyptian bond issues worth nearly £50 million. The fact that these issues were handled by the Rothschilds, in partnership with Bleichröder and in one case the Disconto-Gesellschaft, had a diplomatic significance. In March 1885 it was agreed that the first of these loans would be guaranteed by all the interested powers, but Bismarck made ratification of this agreement conditional on German banks—meaning Bleichröder—being given a share in it. This ruled out the option of issuing the bonds through the Bank of England (as happened with issues for India and other colonies), and made a Rothschild operation the obvious solution. One of Salisbury's first tasks on forming a minority administration in the summer of 1885 was to break the news to the Bank that he was "entrusting the issue of the English portion of the Loan to the agency of N. M. Rothschild, because that firm is one with the Houses of the same name in Paris and Frankfurt, and is in similar relations with the House of Bleichroeder in Berlin."[169]

More important than any guarantee was the success with which Evelyn Baring stabilised Egyptian finance.[170] The loans of 1890 and 1893 were conversion loans, issued to lower the interest on the Egyptian debt.[171] Nor can this be portrayed in Egyptian nationalist terms as a triumph of foreign investors over Egyptian interests: under Baring, there were substantial infrastructural investments (railways and, most famously, the Aswan dam built between 1898 and 1904); yet the absolute debt burden fell from a peak of £106 million in 1891 to just £94 million in 1913 and with it per capita taxation. Put another way, at the beginning of the period the debt burden had been ten times current revenue; by the end the figure was just five.[172] So strict was the British financial control that the Rothschilds were soon complaining that their commissions on Egyptian business were being squeezed.[173] This may partly explain why the Rothschilds increasingly abandoned the field to Ernest Cassel after Baring left Egypt in 1907, though a more likely explanation is that Natty feared British control was slipping in the face of resurgent Egyptian nationalism.[174]

The heaviest cost of the shift to formal British control was paid not by bondholders or taxpayers but by British foreign policy. Between 1882 and 1922, Britain felt obliged to promise the other powers no fewer than 66 times that she would end her occupation of Egypt, but all attempts to extricate Britain from Egypt foundered in the face of the irreconcilable views of the other powers. In September 1885 Natty was asked to take soundings in Berlin about Drummond Wolff's idea of replacing British troops with Turks in Egypt. Bismarck's son Herbert replied on his father's behalf with a resounding negative.[175] The idea floated by the Foreign Office in 1887 of "Neutralisation of Egypt under English Guardianship" was equally foredoomed to fail; the French insisted the Sultan say no.[176] In practice, a "veiled Protectorate" (Milner's phrase) had been established and a momentous precedent set—just as Gladstone had warned would happen at the time of the Suez Canal share purchase.

The ultimate irony is that one of the principal beneficiaries of the operation proved to be none other than Gladstone himself. In late 1875—possibly just before his arch-rival's purchase of the Suez Canal shares—he had acquired £45,000 (nominal) of the Ottoman Egyptian Tribute loan of 1871 at a price of just 38. As the editor of his diaries has shown, he had added a further £5,000 (nominal) by 1878 (the year of the Congress of Berlin); and in 1879 a further £15,000 of the 1854 Ottoman loan, which was also secured on the Egyptian Tribute. By 1882 these bonds accounted for no less than 37 per cent of his entire portfolio (£51,500 nominal). Even before the military occupation of Egypt—which he himself ordered—these proved a good investment: the price of 1871 bonds rose from 38 to 57 in the summer of 1882, and had indeed reached 62 the year before. The British takeover brought the Prime Minister still greater profits: by December 1882 the price of 1871 bonds had risen to 82. By 1891 they had touched 97—a capital gain of more than 130 per cent on his initial investment in 1875 alone.[177] Small wonder he once described Turkish state bankruptcy as "the greatest of all *political* crimes."[178] When we speak of Victorian hypocrisy, Gladstone's repressed attitude towards sex often springs to mind; but it was his attitude to imperial finance which was truly hypocritical. It had been heroic hypocrisy on his part to denounce the purchase of the Suez Canal shares by Disraeli on behalf of the government when he was making one of the most profitable private speculations of his career on the back of it. The Eastern Question was one of the main causes of the schism between the Rothschilds and Gladstone in this period; it is tempting to conclude that Gladstone's double standards—contrasting so markedly with Disraeli's romantic hyperbole—were at the root of the rift.

TEN

Party Politics

Dizzy was here . . . [O]ur friend [is] in very good spirits and not at all put out on account of the violent attacks in the House. What do you say to the visitor who is now with dear Ma whilst I am writing—this I have just heard, that the famous Mr Gladstone is with her drinking tea and eating bread and butter, I doubt whether he will come to see me.

LIONEL TO LEO AND LEONORA, MARCH 1876[1]

There is no question that the debates over Egypt and Turkey in the 1870s did much to alienate the Rothschilds from Gladstone. It would be wrong, however, to suggest that there was an outright break with the Liberal party or an unqualified acceptance of Conservatism. There is a nice symbolism in the fact that Disraeli could call on Lionel on the same day in 1876 that Gladstone had tea with Charlotte. Nor was that an isolated coincidence. Four years later, Ferdinand wrote a letter to his friend and relation by marriage the Earl of Rosebery, describing a similar occasion: "Lord B[eacons]field[2] is staying with [Alfred]—the other day he had to be sent to dinner with Natty, as Gladstone came to dinner to meet the Duke of Cambridge. (Private.)"[3] Until 1905 there was always something of a "revolving door" quality to Rothschild politics: although members of the family (in particular Natty) became more and more closely identified with Conservatism—or rather with Liberal Unionism—channels of communication to the Gladstonians were never closed. Nor were relations with the Conservative leadership after Disraeli always completely harmonious. The politicisation of the Jewish immigration issue after 1900 provided a salutary reminder of why the family had become Liberals in the first place.

Undeniably, the Rothschilds of the fourth generation thought about politics in more ideological terms than their parents and grandparents—most obviously over Ireland, but also over the "social question" (or questions) posed as European cities grew ever more crowded. These were the issues which did most to divide them from Gladstone. However, it was not until after the turn of the century that Natty gave up on the Liberals entirely. Like his father and grandfather before him, he continued to believe that, on matters of finance and diplomacy, the Rothschilds should be heeded no matter which party was in power. This partly explains the rather similar relationships he had with politicians as different in political orientation as Rosebery, Lord Randolph Churchill and Arthur Balfour. In the intimate world of late Victorian politics, the Rothschilds met such men frequently: in the City (to talk finance over lunch at New Court) and in the West End (to talk politics over dinner in the clubs and houses of Piccadilly). They and numerous other members of the political elite, Liberals and Tories alike, were regular guests at the Rothschild country houses (especially Tring, Waddesdon and Halton). It was in this milieu that many of the most important political decisions of the period were taken. And when the Rothschilds could not speak to their political friends, they wrote to them—luckily for the historian, because Natty's decision that his own correspondence be destroyed posthumously has left little in the Rothschilds' own archives. Although the letters from Paris still allow us to infer a good deal about what was going on at New Court, much of what follows is therefore based on the papers of the politicians themselves, leaving the historian to wonder how much of the Rothschilds' political role remains irrevocably hidden from posterity.

From Gladstone to Disraeli

Part of the family in fact never ceased to be Liberal. To the end of their lives, both Mayer and Anthony remained firm if ideologically unsophisticated Liberals. Mayer relished defending his Hythe seat against the Tory squirearchy, drumming up votes from the Folkestone fishermen,[4] while Anthony continued to lean to the Cobdenite wing of the party. It was Anthony who was heard to declare in September 1866: "The sooner we are rid of the colonies, the better for England"—a surprising sentiment, it might be thought, for a Rothschild of this period, and an expression of uncompromising economic liberalism.[5] Nor should it be forgotten that Anthony's daughters Constance and Annie remained firmly attached to the Liberal party throughout their lives and that Mayer's daughter married the man who would succeed Gladstone as Liberal Prime Minister.

Even Lionel's sons began their political careers as avowed Liberals; and when their cousin Leo took to the hustings for the first time in 1865, he explicitly asked voters "whether you would rather be ruled by Palmerston, Russell and Gladstone or Derby, Disraeli and Malmesbury"; the former grouping plainly had his support. Standing as a Liberal for Aylesbury in the same year, Natty "drove over to Missenden and [was] met by a large party who promenaded me through the town and over the hills and far away like a tame bear." Asked by Non-conformist voters if he would support the abolition of Church rates, he gave a categorical "yes."[6] This was a position which recalled the doctrinaire liberalism he had evinced as an undergraduate at Cambridge.

It is also important to note that there continued to be frequent contacts between members of the family and Gladstone right up until the end of his political career. His accession to the premiership for the first time in December 1868 did not change a pattern of intercourse which had begun in the 1850s. Lord Granville relayed Rothschild views about the 1868 election to Gladstone when he stayed at Mentmore the following year,[7] while Gladstone himself dined with Lionel and Charlotte at 148 Piccadilly in 1869 and 1870.[8] There were also frequent "business" meetings with Lionel. In April 1869, for example, the two men met to discuss the budget and, as we have seen, Gladstone had several important interviews with members of the family during the Franco-Prussian war of 1870–71. He also called on Lionel at New Court in July 1874 and again a year later (though his diary does not reveal why).[9] It was only after the Suez share controversy that these meetings apparently ceased—though Lionel still passed on the occasional bit of gossip via Granville.[10]

Even after Suez, Gladstone maintained a more than merely social acquaintance with Lionel's wife Charlotte. In 1874 he sent her his portrait and a year later recorded in his dairy a conversation with her "on the state of belief." This led to an exchange of letters lasting until August the following year in which Charlotte sent Gladstone a succession of scriptural commentaries by Jewish authors, evidently to assist him in his theological researches.[11] Charlotte appears to have declined mentally after her husband's death; but Gladstone continued to call on her at Gunnersbury—visits her son described as "almost the last pleasure my dear mother enjoyed before her illness" and death in 1884.[12] Despite their political differences, he and Natty dined together in 1884 and 1885, and met on a number of other occasions (principally to discuss Egyptian matters) during Gladstone's third ministry. Out of office, the Grand Old Man was just as welcome to dinner, and visited Tring in February 1891.[13]

Nor did Gladstone feel any inhibitions about resuming with Natty's wife Emma the scholarly correspondence he had earlier conducted with her mother-in-law. In August 1888, for example, he wrote to her asking for her help in tracing "a popular but able account of the Mosaic law compared with other contemporary or ancient systems in its moral and social aspect on a number of points—the comparison being greatly in its favour." Emma was no theologian (she preferred to discuss English and German literature) but she was evidently pleased to be addressed by such an eminent figure and did her best to assist him and to find common ground. Thanking him for a signed copy of one of his scriptural works, she observed "that though our needs differ on so many points, the Christians and the Jews agree in their fidelity to those Holy Scriptures of which you say 'they arm us with the means of neutralising and repelling the assaults of toil in and from ourselves!' " A shared enthusiasm for Goethe provided further matter for correspondence.[14] Gladstone also socialised with Ferdinand and his sister Alice as well as with Constance and her husband Cyril Flower, to whom he offered a peerage and the Governorship of New South Wales during his fourth and final ministry.[15] In 1893, Annie too had the pleasure of seeing "the G.O.M." ("Grand Old Man"); in a letter to her sister, she described gleefully how "his old face lights up with vehemence and fire when he talks of the vile Turks."[16] Much to the consternation of the radical press, Gladstone accepted an invitation to Tring in the same year, despite the extent of his political differences with Natty by this time.[17] A reciprocal visit by Natty and Emma to Hawarden in 1896 suggests, however, that the subject of politics was now being avoided. When Emma and Gladstone corresponded after this visit it was on the subject of the maximum circumference of a birch tree. It seems that "Mr G." and her husband had finally found a shared enthusiasm—for trees.[18]

Yet these continuing personal contacts cannot disguise the Rothschilds' unmistakable drift away from Gladstone's politics. Plainly, this had much to do with the uniquely intimate relationship between the Rothschilds and Disraeli. In his early years, as we have already seen, he had romanticised them in his novels, had cultivated them socially and had turned to Lionel on occasion for tips on French railway share speculations. These were unsuccessful, and Disraeli's finances—a tangled mess of debts and usurious interest payments—reached their nadir at the end of the 1850s. It should be stressed that, contrary to contemporary rumour, the Rothschilds did not bail him out.[19] In 1862–63 a wealthy Yorkshire landowner named Andrew Montagu offered his assistance, and an arrangement was reached whereby he bought up all Disraeli's debts in return for a £57,000 mortgage at 3 per cent on Hughenden, considerably reducing Disraeli's annual expenditure. Not long afterwards, he inherited £30,000 from Mrs Brydges Williams, one of those devoted elderly ladies whose affections he excelled at winning, and he also made around £20,000 from his novels. It was claimed after Disraeli's death that the Rothschilds paid off the mortgage on Hughenden before his nephew Coningsby inherited it, but there was no obvious need for them to do this.[20]

In the early days, familiarity with Disraeli had bred a degree of contempt, not least because of his idiosyncratic attitude towards his father's faith. By the 1860s, however, his political standing was sufficiently high for disrespect to give way to admiration. Charlotte's letters during the Reform Bill period repeatedly pay tribute to his political abilities. "Mr Disraeli" was "delightfully agreeable," she wrote typically in 1866: "[W]e listened to him with intense admiration, dear Papa and I . . . It was a great treat to hear him, and even Mrs. Disraeli's presence was unable to mar the pleasure."[21] Lionel too perceptibly warmed to Disraeli as he neared the top of the greasy pole. During the Reform debates of 1867, the two were notably close, dining together regularly after the House rose and exchanging political confidences. The tone of these letters suggests an almost complete absence of party-political friction: Disraeli definitely did not treat Lionel as a Chancellor of the Exchequer would be expected to treat an Opposition MP, while Lionel's political commentary in his surviving letters is so neutral that it would be hard to infer his party allegiance in the absence of other evidence.[22] Only occasionally did Disraeli prove evasive. In August 1867, for example, he "called after the Cabinet on Saturday but," as Charlotte noted with disappointment, "Papa's utmost endeavours could not penetrate through the great man's official reserve;—he would not tell Papa a word, and the fate of the Reform Bill is in the clouds."[23] Mayer too was impressed by Disraeli's bold leadership in this period, as was his nephew Natty.[24]

When Disraeli finally secured the cherished premiership, Mary Anne confided in the Rothschilds at once, and the French Rothschilds wrote to express their delight at the success of the "extraordinary man."[25] Though realistic about the minority administration's chances of survival, Lionel was critical of Delane for attacking the new Prime Minister in *The Times*. Disraeli for his part was remarkably candid with Lionel about his intentions with regard to the composition of the Cabinet, though he continued to keep him guessing about his legislative programme. On the Irish Church question, Lionel remarked in March 1868, "I fancy he has no fixed ideas and, like the Reform Bill, will be guided by circumstances." "[T]here is no knowing," he added two days later, "what Dis will do to keep on the top of the tree." It seems that Lionel was now actively assisting Disraeli in his efforts by "leaking" information about Opposition intentions. "Yesterday the Diz's were our only visitors," he told his wife on March 9. "[H]e did not tell me much and wanted to know all the reports. When I told him that they [his Liberal sources] said many of his supporters would go against him in this Irish Question, he said that whatever he brought forward would be supported on his side by everyone. I recommended him to give some good evening parties."[26] When Disraeli was defeated in the 1868 election, Lionel remained supportive. "[I]n that great parliamentary struggle in which you play so prominent a part," he wrote in March the following year, "if the tide has turned for a moment, it will only be an opportunity for you to display additional power of eloquence, and talent, and you will allow me to say that we shall always rejoice in your success, and feel personally grateful for the friendly feelings, which on every occasion you have evinced towards us."[27] Symbolically, he named a racehorse after a character in Disraeli's novel *Lothair*, dashed off in the wake of defeat, while Anthony provided "a battalion of pheasants, and some hares."[28]

Their relationship continued on the same footing while Disraeli was in Opposition. Disraeli was invited to 148 Piccadilly at least three times in 1870 and there were all kinds of other social contacts. He offered critical thoughts on one of Constance's books, while Alfred offered him rooms in London when his own were unavailable.[29] "[P]ray consent to spend some time under this roof," wrote Charlotte from Gunnersbury in September 1873. "The sooner you come and the later you stay after the 1st of October which is our great fast & day of atonement, the better we shall all be pleased and the more grateful we shall feel."[30] In addition to hospitality, Lionel could always offer valuable news from the other side of the political lines: inside information about the contents of a Liberal bill for example, or the editorial line Delane was planning to take in *The Times*. "Baron Rothschild . . . is a Liberal," Disraeli explained to Lord Bradford in a revealing aside, "and . . . knows everything."[31] Small wonder the Liberals feared that Disraeli would pre-empt them by giving Lionel a peerage when he returned to power in 1874.

The closeness of the friendship between Disraeli and the Rothschilds in these years can hardly be exaggerated; it is tempting (though not quite accurate) to say that he was treated as one of the family, especially after his wife Mary Anne's death in 1872. It was Disraeli who gave Hannah away when she married Rosebery in 1878; and when the Prime Minister made his will that December, he nominated Natty as one his executors along with his lawyer Sir Philip Rose.[32] Following Lionel's death the following June, his sons replied to Disraeli's condolences by telling him that their father "looked upon you as his 'dearest friend.' "[33] It is hard to think of anyone who was closer to him in these later years.

Lionel's sons continued their father's gravitation towards "Beaconsfieldism," though like him they continued to sit on the Liberal side of the Commons. By the time Disraeli's "jingo" policy on the Eastern Question was being put to the vote in the Commons in 1878, the Liberal leadership had more or less written Natty off. Gladstone's loyal lieutenant Sir William Harcourt suggested that, in common with many other "commercial men . . . who find their pecuniary interests greatly damaged by the present state of things," the Rothschilds had "gone Tory altogether."[34] Much as William Harcourt expected, Natty defied the official party line of abstention when the government sought emergency credits in February, and again two months later when Sir Wilfrid Lawson pressed an amendment opposing the calling out of the reserves in April, voting with the government on both occasions. He also opposed Lord Hartington's two resolutions on the movement of Indian troops (May

Lionel de Rothschild, by Moritz Daniel Oppenheim, c. 1858.

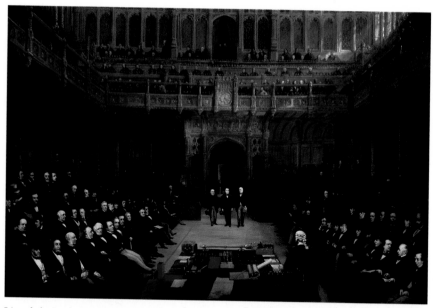

Lionel de Rothschild being introduced into the House of Commons by Lord John Russell and J. Abel Smith on July 26, 1858, by Henry Barraud, 1874.

Lionel de Rothschild in the last year of his life, signed WFH, 1879.

Photograph of James de Rothschild in old age, c. 1866.

Mayer de Rothschild, undated and unsigned miniature.

Alphonse de Rothschild, by Guth, *Vanity
Fair,* September 20, 1894.

The house at Ferrières, built for James de Rothschild by Joseph Paxton and others. Bismarck thought it looked like "an overturned chest of drawers."

"Pillars of the City—A Scene on 'Change,'" by Lockhart Bogle, the *Graphic,* May 9, 1891, showing the 1st Lord Rothschild ("Natty"), with his back to the pillar, his bulky son Walter and, between them, Carl Meyer.

Natty de Rothschild as Master of Hounds, by John Charlton, 1884, the year before Natty's elevation to the peerage. Tring Park is in the background.

Ferdinand de Rothschild, c. 1890.

The house at Halton, designed for Alfred de Rothschild by William Rogers and built between 1882 and 1888.

Walter, the 2nd Lord Rothschild, with his carriage and zebras.

Leopold de Rothschild, by Dighton, c. 1885.

Alfred de Rothschild, by Julius Luz, c. 1880.

Lionel de Rothschild, c. 1930.

Louis von Rothschild, c. 1930, shortly before the Creditanstalt crisis.

Anthony de Rothschild seated at his desk in the "Room," by William Dring, 1948.

"Conversation Piece": in the "Room," c. 1960. Background (*left to right*): Leopold de Rothschild, Edmund de Rothschild, Philip Shelbourne, Jacob Rothschild. Foreground (*left to right*): Michael Bucks, Evelyn de Rothschild, David Colville.

23) and the Treaty of Berlin (August 2).[35] This, it has sometimes been argued, was the political crossroads for the Rothschilds and other wealthy Jews, the moment at which their loyalty to Liberalism, forged in the prolonged campaign for Jewish emancipation, finally yielded to the appeal of Disraelian imperialism.[36] It would be more accurate to see it as the first overt step away from Gladstonian Liberalism by a largely aristocratic or county-based Whig group numbering around forty.[37]

As Disraeli's government crumbled in 1879–80 under Gladstone's fierce onslaught on "Beaconsfieldism" (remembered in the history books as the Midlothian campaign after the Scottish county seat which Gladstone was persuaded to contest at the election), Natty increasingly acted as a Tory in Liberal clothing. On one occasion, as he told Monty Corry in obvious embarrassment, he "got into the House just as the division was taking place & as I did not receive a hint from anyone found that I had voted in the majority wh was a censure on the Govt. I write this to you although you know I wd sooner have cut off both my hands than do such a thing."[38] He made amends in March 1879 when he warned Disraeli that Sir Charles Dilke intended moving a Liberal vote of censure over the government's South African policy in the wake of the Zulu victory at Isandhlwana and that "a good many conservatives would abstain from voting." This sort of information—gathered, as Natty put it, "from conversations in West End clubs and in the City"—may seem trivial now; but it was really the only way for a Victorian Prime Minister "to hear the opinions of the public" (meaning the political elite).[39] By December 1879 Natty was obliquely affirming his new political allegiance by referring to the Liberal leader as "that archfiend Gladstone," ending his New Year greetings to Disraeli with the wish "that he [Gladstone] will do you good and himself harm."[40] Ferdinand echoed this sentiment when he told Rosebery: "I wish your Mr G. at the bottom of the sea."[41]

After the Liberal election victory in 1880, Alfred offered Disraeli a suite of rooms in his house at 1 Seamore Place, while Natty continued to furnish the latest news of Liberal infighting—though one suspects that the aim now was more to cheer an old man than to kindle the fires of effective Opposition.[42] When *Endymion* was published, containing yet another fictionalised version of the Rothschilds in the form of the "Neuchatels," Natty was fulsome in his praise (perhaps recognising that one of the differences between Sidonia and Adrian Neuchatel was the difference in social standing between himself and his father):

> One of these days "When the flag of St George's waves over the plains of Rasselas" and Cyprus is a flourishing colony, "those who have failed in literature and arts" will no longer talk of your works as the dreams of a poet or the imagination of a visionary but will acknowledge as I have always done that you are one of the greatest British statesman.

It was, he declared, a "magnificent addition to British literature."[43] The venerable author continued to stay with Alfred—"the best and kindest host in the world"—until January 1881, when he moved into the house at 19 Curzon Street which he had bought with the proceeds of *Endymion;* and Alfred was one of the guests when he entertained there for the first and last time on March 10, 1881.[44] When Disraeli died in the early hours of April 19, it fell to Natty to carry out his last wishes that he be buried alongside his wife at Hughenden and that his funeral "be conducted with the same simplicity as hers." This meant politely declining the public funeral which Gladstone (through gritted teeth) proposed.[45]

Politics in "Bucks"

Disraeli had been, as Alphonse said, "the best and the truest friend of our Family."[46] But it was not just this friendship which lured the Rothschilds away from the Liberal party. Of equal importance were ideological differences between Gladstonian Liberals—some of them distinctly Radical—and more conservatively inclined Whigs. These manifested themselves most obviously at elections.

When the Rothschilds had first begun to establish themselves as a political force in Buckinghamshire during the 1850s, elements of the established Whig leadership in and around Aylesbury had been quite hostile. Lord Carrington referred to them caustically as the "Red Sea" while Acton Tindal talked of resisting the "circumcision" of the Aylesbury party. In 1865 Natty was returned unopposed for the seat, but there remained obvious differences with Tindal (for example over the abolition of Church rates).[47] Three years later, however, it was the Rothschilds who all at once seemed to be on the right of the party. The Radical League secretary George Howell was more or less foisted upon them in Aylesbury, ending the cosy arrangement whereby a Rothschild and a Tory had been returned unopposed for the two-member constituency.[48] In the City, Lionel found himself embarrassed by association with the Liberal candidate in Tower Hamlets, a convert from Judaism named Joseph d'Aguilar Samuda. This may have been one of the reasons that he lost his seat—an unusual defeat in an election which saw an increase in the Liberal vote overall.[49] Six years later, Lionel lost again. This time, however, the reason was the rift which had opened up between him and Gladstone on fiscal policy. As *The Times* later recalled, Lionel pointed out ("at perhaps the only great election meeting which he attended"),

> that Mr Gladstone's proposal to abolish the Income-tax &c. would deprive the country of £9,000,000 a year and that the surplus would not reach more than half that amount. For the other half there must be more new taxes. When his audience shouted "No" and "Economy," he replied that economy had not got so far as to save four millions and a half a year. Baron de Rothschild's opinion was that new taxes must be imposed, and that they must be imposed upon property. He suggested license duties, such as are paid by commercial men in Austria.[50]

That advocating higher taxes can have negative electoral consequences is no modern discovery. Lionel was nevertheless vindicated by Northcote's budget of 1874, which retained the income tax, albeit with a higher threshold and lower effective rate for incomes below £400 a year.

The party political tensions between the Rothschilds and Gladstone came to a head in 1876, when Disraeli's elevation to the Lords necessitated a by-election in his Buckinghamshire constituency at the very height of Gladstone's "atrocitarian" campaign. Gladstone was eager for a Liberal victory and evidently saw the Bulgarian question as a means to that end: he sent the Liberal candidate Rupert Carington "250 little ones" (copies of his pamphlet) and followed the campaign with keen interest. When a friend of Granville's sounded out Lionel five days before the ballot, he found him violently in favour of Dizzy, & Derby—but talked as if he was in favour of Carrington [*sic*] but how impossible it was under the present system of voting to know how votes would go—Gave an instance 3 of his tenants, could not tell whether they would vote with him or the rector. His belief was that F[remantle] [the Tory candidate] would win by 5 or 600.[51]

This proved an accurate forecast.

Two years later, the rift widened still further when the second Aylesbury seat was won by the Liberal candidate George W. E. Russell—the nephew of Lord John. In a good example of the anti-Semitic undertone of the campaign against "Beaconsfield-ism," Russell had, as Granville admitted to Gladstone, "attacked Dizzy as a Jew, a Jingo & something else beginning with a J" (the other word was "Juggler"). When this was reported in the local Conservative *Buckinghamshire Herald* (despite Russell's attempts to retract the word "Jew") Natty was furious and took "the first opportunity of throwing dirt" at Russell when he next saw Gladstone.[52] That leading Liberals were willing to act in this way makes it difficult to claim that the Rothschilds' gravitation toward Disraeli was governed purely by differences with Gladstone over foreign policy.

Diplomatic factors were undoubtedly important in their own right. It was a matter of "regret" in the eyes of the French Rothschilds when the Liberals won in 1880 because they regarded Conservative governments as more likely to "maintain the prestige and the influence of old England";[53] and "Mr Gladstone's disregard for foreign policy" was the main reason they fervently wished Salisbury to remain in power at the end of 1885.[54] It is true that, when Ferdinand decided to enter politics in 1885, he insisted that he wished to stand as a Liberal. But he intimated to the radically inclined Dilke that he had qualms about the party's foreign policy and implied that his political allegiance might be conditional on the Liberals sticking to an imperialist line. This letter deserves to be quoted at length as an illustration of the Rothschilds' political ambivalence in this period:

> I am not as you think by nature a conservative. Conservativism has been the ruin of several foreign countries and liberal politics have been the making of England. To liberalism we—you—owe everything. On no point and in no manner do I incline towards Toryism in any form. On the other hand though I may not be competent to express decided opinions on such matters I deplore for the sake of the country which I have adopted and I love truly the restricted policy of the present Govt. who have sacrificed if not the interests yet the magic powers of the English flag and name to the narrow issues of Parliamentary reforms. I am perhaps "plus catholique que le Pape" but I would cheer the Union Jack planted on every island of the Polynees, on every crag of the Himalayas, on every minaret of the East (this is a metaphor). You (I mean the Govt.) have to come [to] it [imperialism] after all in the long run. *Vide* the present expedition to Khartoum and augmentations to your colonies . . .
>
> If I ever succeed in entering the House of Commons I mean to support the liberal Government of the day . . . [But] if I find that after all in the future politics shape themselves in a manner which might be disqui-

eting to my sympathies (I use on purpose a strong expression) I shall give up the game and retire into the usual obscurity of my existence.[55]

The significance of this letter becomes apparent when it is remembered that Ferdinand became a parliamentary candidate for the new single-member constituency of Mid-Buckinghamshire only because his cousin Natty had been made a peer. It has already been suggested that one reason Gladstone chose to elevate Natty at the end of his second ministry was to replace him in the House of Commons at the impending election; and it should by now be intelligible why he might have wished to do so. On October 29, 1884, Hartington's secretary Reginald Brett wrote a letter on the subject to Lord Richard Grosvenor, the Liberal Chief Whip and patronage secretary, which illuminates this point. Brett began by suggesting "that some special civility should paid by you or Mr Gladstone to Natty Rothschild. He is not a very robust Liberal, but I suppose there is not much object in letting him drift, and still less in driving him over to the Tories." This was an oblique suggestion that the idea of a Rothschild peerage be resuscitated. But he then went on to warn Grosvenor that replacing Natty in the Commons with Ferdinand would be unlikely to have the effect the Liberal leadership desired:

> If it is thought that the Rothschilds can be played off one against the other, and that because Ferdinand may be a more acceptable or more pliant colleague, he can be put forward at Natty's expense, a very great mistake is made.
> The Rothschilds have held together for generations, and discipline in their family is differently understood from what it is in that of the Russells. If the Liberal party breaks with Natty, it breaks with the whole clan, and there is I imagine nothing to be gained by such a proceeding.[56]

Ferdinand's letter to Dilke more than confirmed that diagnosis: if he was to take Natty's place, the Rothschild line on foreign policy would remain the same. As its recipient sourly commented, "F. Rothschild wants to get into Parliament and I told him that he is a Tory and ought to stand as a Tory . . . He will never get in as a Liberal nowadays, I'm sure."[57] This proved more or less correct: although Ferdinand initially stood as a Liberal (even expressing support for temperance in pursuit of the Non-conformist vote), by 1890 he was describing himself in the House as "a drastic and ardent supporter of the [Salisbury] government."[58]

The visitors book Ferdinand kept at Waddesdon provides a fascinating insight into the ambiguity of his politics. A survey of the more regular political visitors between 1881 and 1898 gives a slight predominance to the Liberals: Edward Hamilton leads the field with no fewer than fifty-two visits, followed by the Liberal leader Hartington (ten visits), the Liberal Home Secretary and Chancellor Harcourt (nine), Rosebery (nine) and Dilke (two). Other Liberal visitors included Gladstone, Reginald Brett, the historian Lord Acton, his colleague James Bryce (later Chancellor of Duchy of Lancaster and President of Board of Trade), the future leader of the party Herbert Asquith, Lord Carrington (who became Governor of New South Wales) and the Earl of Dalhousie (who became Secretary of State for Scotland). However, two of the most regular visitors were Liberal Unionists: the Attorney General Henry James, who visited seventeen times, and Joseph Chamberlain, who was a guest at Waddesdon on twelve occasions, often accompanied by his son Austen. And there were almost as many Tory visitors as Liberals: Harry Chaplin (President of the Boards of Agriculture and later Local Government) who stayed at Waddesdon twenty-six times; Lord Salisbury's nephew and successor Arthur Balfour (eight visits); George Curzon, Salisbury's Assistant Private Secretary and Under-Secretary of State for India (also eight); the President of the Board of Agriculture Walter Long (five); Lord Randolph Churchill (twice); the Under-Secretary of State for War Earl Brownlow (also twice); and the Under-Secretary of State for Foreign Affairs Sir James Fergusson.[59]

As Ferdinand's letter to Dilke indicated, it was not just imperial issues which were shifting the Rothschilds away from Liberalism. Of increasing importance was their suspicion of the social policies advocated by radical urban-based Liberals like Chamberlain and Dilke himself. "[I]f I do not call myself a radical," Ferdinand explained,

> it is that I consider it unworthy of great leaders of men like Chamberlain and yourself to court popularity with the masses by advocating such trivial measures as the abolition of the game laws for instance and stimulating an unhealthy desire for social and pecuniary equality the disastrous results of which have been only too well illustrated in France, instead of governing the people on broad principles and leading them into wider issues.[60]

Even Chamberlain's talk of compulsory purchases of land by local authorities to provide allotments for the working class alarmed Natty.[61] The Rothschilds' drift away from Gladstonian Liberalism reflected not only discontent with his lukewarm imperialism, but also mistrust of his party's domestic political tendencies. One reason why the Irish question came to play such a decisive role in the politics of the 1880s and 1890s was precisely that proposals to improve the lot of Irish tenants awakened fears for the security of landed property in the minds of English landowners like the Rothschilds.

Unionism

Although some contemporaries tended to think of it as the first of England's colonies, Ireland had been an integral part of the United Kingdom since the seventeenth century, with Irish MPs sitting in the Westminster House of Commons since 1800. It was not a place the Rothschilds knew well. They had no economic interests there; indeed, few members of the family had even set foot there. Anthony holidayed there with his daughters in 1865 and was favourably impressed by the natural beauty of some of the estates he visited.[62] Ferdinand, who went there three years later, was less keen on the "extremely wild" landscape but found the people "most hospitable"—though he was bemused to be mistaken for a Catholic in Dublin.[63] For most Rothschilds, however, it was *terra incognita*. Writing in 1865, Charlotte made it sound as remote and alien as the furthest-flung colony: a country of endemic "mismanagement," of uncouth manners, rampant drunkenness and senseless violence.[64] If Natty ever went there, no record of his visit appears to have survived.

Yet Ireland proved to be of all the issues of the period the one which most influenced his political conduct. This was for two reasons. Not only did attempts to strengthen the position of Irish tenants relative to their landlords seem to threaten the rights of all property-owners; the idea of giving Ireland "Home Rule"—that is, some form of devolved legislature and government—also seemed to threaten the integrity of the United Kingdom and to imply a general decentralisation of power throughout the Empire. It was this dual significance of the Irish question which brought together such improbable political allies as the "Young Whig" Natty de Rothschild, the "Tory Democrat" Lord Randolph Churchill and the Radical Liberal Joseph Chamberlain, thereby shattering Gladstonian Liberalism and recasting post-Disraelian Conservatism.

The first sign of a Rothschild revolt on Ireland came in 1880, when Natty joined a group of mainly aristocratic "Young Whigs" in voting against Gladstone's Irish Land Bill, which sought to compensate tenants who had been ejected by landlords for non-payment of rent. Their objection was the principled one that nothing should infringe the sanctity of contract: as far as Natty was concerned, as he told Disraeli, the measure implied nothing less than "confiscation."[65] Natty was one of the six most consistent opponents of the Liberal leadership's policy, voting twice against the Compensation for Disturbance Bill and twice for hostile amendments. This put him in the company of Whig grandees like J. C. Dundas, C. W. Fitzwilliam and Albert H. G. Grey (later the 4th Earl Grey).[66] When, in the wake of the December 1885 election (which gave Parnell's Irish Nationalists the balance of power at Westminster), Gladstone began to consider the more radical solution of Home Rule, it was predictable that Natty would align himself with the scheme's opponents.

With hindsight, Gladstone's conception—"the management [by] an Irish legislative body of Irish as distinct from Imperial affairs"—was a sane one, and might conceivably have taken the sting out of Irish nationalism at a time when opposition to "Rome Rule" in Ulster was embryonic. It envisaged an Irish parliament with only very limited powers, leaving defence, foreign policy and customs in the hands of the "Imperial" government, while removing or at least reducing the Irish representation at Westminster. If the Tories had been more far-sighted they might have offered Parnell something similar themselves (as indeed they thought of doing). However, opposition to Home Rule had more to do with the internal dynamics of British party politics than with Irish aspirations; at least, that is the impression given by what has survived of Natty's correspondence on the subject.

Natty had been dismayed by Gladstone's renewed ascendancy over the Liberal party, which he had hoped to see led by Hartington (the quintessentially Whig heir to the Duke of Devonshire). In a cryptic letter on November 29, he told Hartington: "Gladstone's name might well be changed to Ichabod," enclosing an explanatory note from the Old Testament: "Eli's grandson was called Ichabod or 'The glory is departing from Israel' being born after the defeat of the Israelites by the Philistines. Samuel Chap. IV, Verse 21."[67] Five days after Gladstone's son had hinted at his father's intentions for Ireland (on December 17, 1885), Natty had a meeting with Randolph Churchill at which he briefed him, for Salisbury's benefit, on the likely Liberal split, explaining "that John Morley and Chamberlain were separated and that the former who had no money and only desired an official salary had definitely signified perfect obedience to the G.O.M. . . . that Parnell had got Gladstone tight and that the latter had committed himself."[68] The aim of this meeting was plain enough. Both Churchill and Sir Drummond Wolff (one of the other key figures in Churchill's would-be "Fourth Party") were already thinking of "negotiating for a coalition [with the Whigs] through Rothschild," though Churchill's ideas for increased political "fusion" or integration of Ireland with the mainland already struck many Whigs as alarmingly radical.[69]

The unanswered questions were which of the Whigs would be willing to desert Gladstone, and what the secessionists' relationship would be with the Conservatives, who remained in office until January 30. Throughout the crucial months leading up to the decisive defeat of the Home Rule Bill on June 8, the Rothschilds acted as political go-betweens. On January 8, for example, Churchill was able to give Salisbury fresh intelligence from the Liberal camp courtesy of Cyril Flower, who had just heard Gladstone denounce Churchill as "an unprincipled young blackguard or something very analogous thereto"; and from Natty, who had told Brett "that Harcourt and Dilke were . . . of the opinion that Mr Gladstone would abandon Home Rule and come round to his colleague's views."[70] In order to encourage the dissidents, Alfred informed Hartington that Salisbury would be willing to serve as Foreign Secretary in a coalition led by him; there was, he was able to reassure Churchill, "no truth whatsoever in the respect of Hartington's surrender; quite the contrary."[71]

By March attention had switched to the position of Chamberlain, who for some time had been itching to break with Gladstone. At a dinner at Reginald Brett's, Balfour met Chamberlain along with two key Whig figures, Albert Grey and Natty. As Balfour told Salisbury, it was "openly assumed" by all present "that Ch[amberlain] was going to leave the Govt," Gladstone having communicated enough of his Irish scheme "to convince Joe that he at least could not swallow it!" In the course of the discussion, Natty and Grey confirmed that there were plans afoot to hold "a big Anti-Home Rule Meeting in the City," though neither Natty nor Chamberlain felt this would be helpful.[72] The meeting nevertheless went ahead at the Guildhall on April 2; and at a second meeting at the Westminster Palace Hotel the following month Natty openly declared himself. It was his election on to a Liberal Unionist General Committee at this meeting which marked his final political break with Gladstone.[73] Other prominent Jewish MPs who joined him included his cousin Ferdinand and Francis Goldsmid, but it was not really their Jewishness which was the decisive factor: the City establishment—including George Goschen, Revelstoke and many others—was overwhelmingly Unionist.[74]

As Alphonse suggested, the Rothschild desideratum was in fact "a Hartington–Salisbury ministry": a coalition, in other words, of Liberal Unionists and Conservatives.[75] However, this proved far from straightforward to achieve. Churchill and Natty were unsuccessful in their efforts to involve Harcourt in their schemes;[76] while at a meeting at Waddesdon on June 13—five days after Home Rule had been defeated in the Commons—Chamberlain told Balfour that he regarded a Liberal Unionist–Conservative coalition as "impossible." The most he was willing to offer was "a definite and complete understanding with Hartington, and an adequate though less complete understanding with me" ensuring "a sufficient unity of action by means of consultations behind the Speaker's Chair."[77] This was essentially Hartington's view when Natty approached him three days later.[78]

The common goal of "getting rid of Gladstone" was achieved with a vengeance.

The result of the general election of July that year was a "smash" for Gladstone and Home Rule: 316 Conservatives were elected and 78 Liberal Unionists, against just 191 Gladstonians and 85 Irish Nationalists. The defeat was especially heavy in Scotland—"the old man['s] . . . dung hill"—where Natty had urged both Churchill and Chamberlain to campaign. The swing away from the G.O.M. was also pronounced in rural constituencies like Ferdinand's at Aylesbury.[79] But Unionist harmony—captured by Brett's memorable image of Churchill, Natty and Chamberlain "conduct[ing] the business of the Empire in great measure *together*"—was short-lived. It was easy to get "a large party of liberal unionists" to shoot together at Mentmore; less easy to get them to work together in government.[80] As early as December, Salisbury, Churchill and Chamberlain were at odds over the government's County Councils Bill; and Churchill himself resigned as Chancellor over the defence budget that same month.[81] By February the following year, Natty was disillusioned with the government's policy in Ireland—a combination of coercion and a new Land Act which he considered "most rotten." "You will find your old colleagues worn out by nocturnal vigils and a growing demand for a strong Government in Ireland," he reported to Churchill. He predicted that if the government did not "take care, a feeling will spring up that some form of Home Rule is preferable to the present disorder and discontent."[82]

Natty's real loyalty at this stage seems to have been to Hartington. What Natty, Churchill and Chamberlain agreed on, Brett told Hartington, was "the maintenance of the [Liberal] Unionist party. And on this account your wishes and opinions seem to be the prime factor in all their calculations . . . the essential thing, as Randolph says, is 'to keep the Gladstone gang out of office.' "[83] Employing a true landowner's mixed metaphor, Natty suggested to Churchill in March that the Unionists would be content provided measures were enacted which they initiated or supported:

> Hartington is not Little Bo Peep and has not lost his sheep [meaning his supporters], he and Joe support the Govt most enthusiastically and energetically, both in regard to the Crimes Bill and the Great Purchase scheme which is to come at a later period. There are some horses remaining on the Turf whose parentage is doubtful, their dams having been covered by 2 or 3 stallions [that is, some legislative measures with a number of different sponsors in the Commons]. I should say, if I were asked, that the parentage of these . . . measures is dubious, but one of the sires is certainly Joe.[84]

When Edward Hamilton dined with Natty in August, he was told categorically that "Hartington will be Prime Minister very soon, and the Prime Minister of the real 'Liberal' party, of which the so called Conservatives are now the proper representatives. Hartington would never again be made to do the dirty work of the Radicals. He had repented 'eating dirt' out of feelings of party loyalty." However, Natty also revealed his own growing doubts about Chamberlain, who was still talking as if the old Liberal factions could be reunited:[85]

> As to Chamberlain, he would never be a big man. He was a Radical wolf in Tory sheep's clothing. He was the typical democrat—a spendthrift and a Jingo—a great contrast to R. Churchill who was quite a Peelite

about economical and foreign matters. As to Mr. G., he was hopeless—
never knew his own mind two years or even two months running; and a
continual danger to the State.[86]

Small wonder a loyal Gladstonian like Hamilton bridled at this (though he could
not deny Natty's "wonderful knowledge of what is going on"). But it is intriguing
that Hamilton's next engagement was dinner at Mentmore with Rosebery, whom he
now regarded as a future Liberal leader in the Lords, if not more.

What was at issue, in other words, was nothing less than the fate of the Liberal
party, with Hartington pulling one way, Chamberlain another, and Rosebery stuck
in the middle trying to salvage something from the Gladstonian wreck. Certainly,
Natty's hope of somehow bringing Churchill and Hartington together on a "real"
Liberal ticket was doomed by the former's deteriorating physical and mental health;
but at this stage it still seemed possible to avoid an outright takeover of the Liberal
Unionists by the Conservatives.[87] Why else did Natty propose to give Hartington
money for Liberal Unionist election costs in 1890, and encourage Lord Derby to do
the same?[88] Nor was it unrealistic to assume, as Natty did in 1888, that Gladstone
had been "ousted from power for good" and that "with Mr G. gone, Home Rule
would die a natural death."[89] Even Gladstone's political resurrection after the Liberal victory in 1892 proved fleeting; and Rosebery's succession could be cautiously
celebrated in the belief that his commitment to Home Rule and reform of the
House of Lords was only skin-deep.[90]

Churchill and Rosebery

Perhaps the most remarkable aspect of Natty's role in the complex party politics of
the 1880s was its remoteness from his concerns as a banker. For the first time, it
might be said, a Rothschild was engaged in politics as a vocation for its own sake,
with only the most tenuous connection between the debates over Ireland or social
policy and his own interests as a wealthy landowner.

Nevertheless, it is important to bear in mind that, while all this was going on,
Natty continued to spend most of his working day at New Court; and as a banker
his primary political concern was with foreign rather than domestic policy. Even as
we try to uncover and reconstruct his role in the debates over Home Rule, we should
remember that it was the diplomacy of imperialism which mattered more to him.
How far were the Rothschilds able to use their political connections to influence foreign policy in this period? One way to approach this question is to consider their
relationships with the two politicians of the post-Disraeli era to whom they were
probably closest: Randolph Churchill and Rosebery. And here it is necessary to say a
brief word about the most important of all Victorian Britain's imperial possessions:
India.

Before 1880 the Rothschilds had not been much interested in India, though they
did some business with firms there. When their relatives Gabriel and Maurice
Worms had returned from Ceylon in 1865 after an absence of twenty-five years,
Charlotte had been appalled not only by their appearance—"old, hideous anglo-
caucasian Indians"—but also by their descriptions of life on a tea plantation. With
its naked coolies, intense heat, snakes, elephants, porcupines and pearl-eating
insects, it might have been another planet; the fact that the Worms had called one of

their plantations "Rothschild" was a compliment, not a sign of the family's financial involvement in the Raj.[91] After 1880, however, that changed. Between 1881 and 1887, Charlotte's sons were responsible for issuing Indian railway shares worth a total of £6.4 million.[92]

The departure of the Liberals and the appointment of Churchill as Secretary of State for India by Lord Salisbury in the summer of 1885 seemed to herald a blossoming of the Rothschilds' interest in India. Contradictory as he was throughout his meteoric political career, Churchill now lost no time in establishing precisely the kind of relationship with Natty and his brothers in relation to India which he had earlier accused Gladstone's government of having with the Barings in relation to Egypt. While planning the issue of a loan for the Indian Midland Railway, Churchill specifically told the Viceroy, Lord Dufferin, "If I am at the office next year . . . when the loan is brought out I shall fight a great battle against [Bertram] Currie to place it in the hands of the Rothschilds, whose financial knowledge is as great as that of the Bank of England is small, and whose clientele is enormous."[93]

Churchill's biographer Roy Foster suggests that the Rothschilds did indeed help place the new company's shares. Contemporaries also assumed that Churchill's decision to annex Burma—announced on New Year's Day 1886—was linked to his growing intimacy with the Rothschilds. As Edward Hamilton observed sardonically, "Jingoism is . . . popular so long as it brings profit."[94] Certainly, they applied to take over "all Burmese railways and construct lines to the frontier" within a week of the annexation being announced, Churchill assuring Salisbury that they were "as keen as nuts."[95] The fact seems to speak for itself that in 1889 the Rothschilds were responsible for the immensely successful Burma Ruby Mines share issue—when the throng of would-be subscribers grew so large that Natty reputedly had to climb up a ladder to get into the bank, and the shares went to a 300 per cent premium.[96] Did not Brett tell Hartington in 1886 that "Churchill and Natty Rothschild seem[ed] to conduct the business of the Empire in great measure *together*, in consultation with Chamberlain"?[97] Did not Hamilton later observe (to Rosebery) that what had got Churchill "into trouble" was his "excessive intimacy" with "a certain financial house"? And did not Lady Salisbury "launch out" in conversation with Herbert von Bismarck and Rosebery "against Randolph who communicated everything to Natty Rothschild" and "hint that people did not give great financial houses political news for nothing"?[98] The evidence of an excessively close relationship seems compelling, especially in view of the precariousness of Churchill's personal finances. As is now well known—though his earlier biographers suppressed the fact—he died owing the London house "the astonishing sum of £66,902," though he had also made some money on mining shares by following Rothschild advice.[99]

Yet on closer inspection it seems that Churchill's stints at the India Office and the Exchequer were of only limited importance to the Rothschilds in their capacity as bankers and, equally, that their importance to Churchill as his bankers only really mattered after he had left office. The Burma Ruby Mines issue was for just £300,000 and it came out four years after Churchill had ended his brief tenure at the India Office. Similarly, it was not until 1896 that the Rothschilds issued £2 million of shares in Burmese railways; their initial approach to the Indian Finance Committee ten years before had been rejected. At the Exchequer in Salisbury's second government, Churchill sought their advice on financial policy (appointing Natty to a commission to enquire into public expenditure). But it is not easy to represent Churchill's ultimately self-destructive and ultra-Gladstonian opposition to military expenditure as in any way beneficial to Rothschild interests: indeed, his views on Egypt and monetary policy rapidly diverged from those of Natty.[100] Nor were the Rothschilds involved in his fateful decision to resign in December 1886. When Reginald Brett asked if he could tell Natty the news, Churchill "said no, because he is furious with Alfred Rothschild, who it appears is talking strongly against him. 'He complains that I did not consult the Rothschilds. After all I am glad to have them as friends, but I am not yet Rivers Wilson and am not yet in their pay.' "[101] To Natty, Churchill's resignation seemed a mere "freak of temper," though Churchill himself insisted that it was "a simple miscalculation . . . that he did not know that Salisbury had 'the king up his sleeve,' in other words that he was ready to fill up the vacancy by appointing Goschen."[102]

As that suggests, it was only after he had left office that he began to borrow large sums from the family: up until 1888 his overdraft was just £900 and it was not until 1891 that it ballooned to £11,000.[103] Although Natty continued to encourage Churchill to believe that he might one day return to office, it is unlikely, in view of the former Chancellor's increasingly erratic behaviour, that he sincerely believed this himself. As Edward Hamilton put it in August 1888, "R. Churchill turns to N. Rothschild for everything . . . but Rothschild, who is R.C.'s chief mentor, is giving R.C. up as a hopeless politician."[104] Indeed, it seems right to regard Natty's bankrolling of Churchill after 1886 as primarily an act of friendship as syphilis inexorably took its toll; for politically and financially he was now more a liability than an asset. The loose cannon went off again in 1891 when Churchill returned from a Rothschild-assisted expedition to Mashonaland only to denounce publicly the region's economic prospects—a gaffe which infuriated Natty, as we shall see. It was less calculation than kindness to the increasingly pathetic Churchill which prompted the Rothschilds to take an interest in the career of his ambitious son, though no doubt they were gratified when young Winston opposed the Aliens Bill in 1904 as Liberal MP for Manchester.[105]

The case of Rosebery could hardly be more different, though similar questions arise about the extent of Rothschild influence. Was it politically significant that the man who was served as Foreign Secretary in Gladstone's third and fourth ministries and succeeded him as Prime Minister in 1894 was married to a Rothschild? As with Churchill, some contemporaries thought so. "It is not nice at this juncture," the Liberal periodical *Justice* commented after Gladstone's visit to Tring in September 1893, "when the foreign secretary is closely connected by marriage with the same intriguing [*sic*] financial house, to see Mr Gladstone hobnobbing with Lord Rothschild."

There is no question that, almost from the moment he married Hannah, the more political members of the family took an interest in Rosebery's career. In September 1878—just six months after the wedding—Ferdinand revealed to Rosebery the extent of this interest:

Natty as usual talked a good deal about you and endeavoured to pump me about your racing and political doings. He wanted to know amongst other things if you would accept subordinate office in the event of it's [*sic*] being offered to you when the liberals come in again. I pleaded ignorance on every score.—Alfred appeared this morning at 11 and seemed very well up on my proceedings . . . he already knew that we had been to the play together last night—What a pity that the Inquisition has been abolished. What touts my relations would have been![106]

In the case of Churchill, private financial ties really came after his time in office; in the case of Rosebery, however, they came before it. In November 1878 Ferdinand suggested to Rosebery: "If you have a few spare thousand pounds (from £9–10) you might invest them in the new . . . Egyptian loan which the House brings out next week."[107] A letter from Natty of 1880 sheds further light on the kind of "good advice about investments" Rosebery was receiving from his in-laws. "I am happy to say," he wrote archly, "I never know before hearing what the Ministers are going to do. I can only tell you that I bought 100,000 for New Court today and I s[houl]d. advise you to tell Mr May [either Rosebery's broker or a Rothschild clerk] to pay for yours."[108]

This might seem to explain why, when Gladstone offered him the post of Commissioner of Works and a seat in the Cabinet as Lord Privy Seal in 1884, Rosebery initially refused. Citing the impending decisions to be taken by the government regarding Egyptian finance, he told Granville: "You can guess the extreme delicacy of my relation to that question, for although I am not a member of the House of Rothschild, I am allied to it as closely as possible by kinship and friendship, and I feel therefore strongly the difficulty of entering the Cabinet at the moment . . ."[109] Yet when the murder of General Gordon persuaded Rosebery to accept Gladstone's offer, neither he nor the Rothschilds made any effort to break off their financial relations. In the fortnight after he joined the government, he saw members of the family on at least four occasions, including two dinners with Natty.[110] And in August 1885, only two months after Gladstone's resignation had temporarily removed him from office again, Rosebery was allotted £50,000 of the new Egyptian loan issued by the London house. Interestingly, "in accordance with [Rosebery's] wishes the Egyptian money [was] paid into the Bank to the credit of Hannah."[111]

The pattern repeated itself when Rosebery became Foreign Secretary in 1886. This time it was Natty who expressed public reservations, telling Reginald Brett in January that Rosebery was "out of the question" as a possible Liberal Foreign Secretary "owing to his connection with the House of Rothschild."[112] Over dinner at Gunnersbury in 1887, he baffled Edward Hamilton—who had expected him to "crack Rosebery up [praise him] . . . *out of a feeling of pride for so near a connection by marriage*"—by running him down: "Rosebery was no platform speaker. His speeches were watery; his reputation as Foreign Secretary had been over-rated—he had indeed ruined it by his despatch about Batoum [Batum] which was a rasping bark with no intention or power to bite; Bismarck was greatly disappointed with him."[113] But this should not be taken at face value. As before, Rosebery and the Rothschilds remained in close contact on diplomatic questions (notably Afghanistan); and Alfred wrote encouragingly from New Court that "from all sides & even distant climes we hear nothing but great satisfaction at the nomination of the new Minister of Foreign Affairs."[114] When Rosebery left office once again following the defeat of the Home Rule Bill, it was Natty who encouraged him to keep his political hand in by becoming chairman of the new London County Council.[115] He also discussed industrial relations with Alphonse shortly before returning to government in 1892—discussions which foreshadowed his intervention in the miners' strike the following year.[116] It also seems unlikely (as the German ambassador claimed) that the Rothschilds discouraged Rosebery from returning to the Foreign Office:[117] such correspondence as remains from this period suggests that they continued to supply him with financial and diplomatic news (for example, about Egypt). The French Rothschilds welcomed his elevation to the premiership following Gladstone's resignation,[118] and Alfred took the unusual step of acting on the Prime Minister's behalf in a dispute with the Bank of England over a box of securities allegedly mislaid by the Bank's former Chief Cashier. (His intercession resulted in an out-of-court compensation payment of no less than £20,000.)[119] Natty regretted Rosebery's subsequent resignation of the premiership, not least because it represented a victory for Harcourt—"more pompous & boisterous than ever and more perfidious"—and his increasingly progressive fiscal policy.[120]

Rosebery had stuck it out alongside the Gladstonians for longer than Natty; but his formation of the imperialist Liberal League in 1902 indicated that his sympathies had never been that far removed from the Unionists; and his political career after he broke with the Liberal party altogether in 1905 closely paralleled Natty's (both opposed Lloyd George's budget in 1909, for example, and the Parliament Bill which reduced the power of the House of Lords).

As with Churchill, however, the question remains whether the Rothschilds got anything material out of their relationship with Rosebery. The answer is that by and large they did not. To be sure, the surviving correspondence shows the Rothschilds supplying Rosebery with financial and diplomatic information; but there are few direct requests for ministerial action one way or another, barring some very minor patronage business once Rosebery had honours in his gift. Nor does recent research on Rosebery's foreign policy indicate anything which could be described as a Rothschild influence.[121] It is therefore tempting to conclude that the fears expressed by more Radical Liberals about Rosebery's links to the "intriguing" Rothschilds were groundless. Yet there was at least one occasion when Rosebery undoubtedly did give them advance warning of an important diplomatic decision. As Foreign Secretary in January 1893, he used Reginald Brett to communicate to New Court the government's intention to reinforce the Egyptian garrison. "I saw Natty and Alfred," reported Brett,

> and told them that you were much obliged to them for having given you all the information at their disposal, and therefore wished them to know [of the reinforcement] *before reading it in the papers* . . . Of course they were delighted and most grateful. Natty wished me to tell you that all the information and any assistance which he can give you is always at your disposal.[122]

It may be that this was an isolated incident; on the other hand, the possibility cannot be discounted that such inside information was more often communicated orally, or in letters which have not survived.

Conservatism in France

There were undoubtedly parallels between the English Rothschilds' political activity and that of their French cousins. Of course, as Alphonse never tired of noting in his letters, the French Republic was a very different political environment, in which both left and right adopted more extreme positions than in Britain.[123] Moreover, the French Rothschilds had developed a much greater degree of ideological neutrality (or flexibility) as a result of the frequent regime changes they had lived through. At heart, Alphonse and his brothers were, like their mother, Orléanists: there are enough positive references in their letters to the idea of a monarchical restoration to confirm that.[124] But like their father, they were quite prepared to work with republican politicians. The distinction they drew was between moderate or conservative republicans and radical or "red" republicans. They were not sorry to see Thiers replaced as President of the Republic by Marshal MacMahon in 1873 and lamented MacMahon's fall four years later after the abortive coup of May 16,[125] whereas the Republican victory in the elections which followed revived memories of the Commune in Alphonse's mind.[126] Only the appointment of their old friend Léon Say as Finance Minister in December reassured Alphonse. Although Say's readiness to sell the new 3 per cent rentes directly to the public reduced their traditional underwriting commission, the Rothschilds were keen subscribers.[127] They were no less supportive of the government's loan of mid-1881, subscribing over 100 million francs.[128]

If "respect" for landed property was the touchstone of conservativism in the eyes of Natty, the French Rothschilds attached a similar importance to the private French railway companies in which they, of course, continued to hold a major stake. In the early 1870s, when there was a spate of new branch-line construction, Alphonse worried that the Nord company was being bypassed in favour of other companies.[129] Later, it was the more serious threat of railway nationalisation—that old objective of 1848—which preyed on his mind.[130] As in England, "socialism" became a shorthand for any threatened state intrusion on hitherto unrestricted property rights.[131]

It is in this light that the Rothschilds' attitude towards Léon Gambetta, the Republican hero of the war of 1870, becomes intelligible. The Rothschilds were perfectly prepared to encourage Gambetta, despite his reputation dating back to the Belleville programme of 1869 as a *fou furieux*, provided he concentrated on giving France an imperial policy. There is a famous account of a dinner during Gambetta's brief premiership (1881–2) at which he and Alphonse were spotted

> chatting amiably in a window alcove, the two sovereigns—Gambetta, the actual master of France, and Rothschild . . . Gambetta wanted to make a naval demonstration: five gunboats to the port of Tunis, five companies to disembark and say nicely to the Bey: "Accept a protectorate, or hop it." It was done in a matter of 24 hours . . . Alphonse de Rothschild then began to speak, and to speak very knowledgeably about Italian and English politicians. Gambetta listened with mingled admiration and astonishment: he had not suspected Alphonse de Rothschild of possessing such a well-developed and lively intelligence. Between them, the two men considered Depretis, Cairoli, Sella, Disraeli, Gladstone, Crispi, Hartington, Granville . . . [When the time for toasts came] Gambetta drank "To a restored France!" Alphonse de Rothschild

responded "To the man who will restore her!" The words were vague and could just as well have applied to [General de] Galliffet as to Gambetta. But Gambetta did not hesitate to take them as referring to himself. He searched for some moments for a suitable response, which eluded him, and then replied very simply, "Ah! I would be willing." If only the electoral committee of Belleville had been there to see their Gambetta in the company of these princes and marquises.[132]

The point of this anecdote was, of course, to suggest that Gambetta had sold out on achieving power. However, the domestic policies which Gambetta was simultaneously pursuing—though far from socialistic—were less palatable to the Rothschilds than the conquest of Tunis. Firstly, Gambetta envisaged a massive conversion operation of some 6 billion francs of 5 per cent rentes. It was a sign of *haute banque* opposition to this that Say refused to accept the portfolio of Minister of Finance under Gambetta. Indeed, according to police reports, Alphonse told journalists in December 1881: "I want an all-out campaign; it is necessary to demolish Gambetta before he demolishes us."[133] We have already seen how the collapse of the Union Générale contributed to that demolition. Secondly, Gambetta seemed to intend some kind of railway nationalisation. It was only after his fall that an agreement was reached which granted the companies a further thirty years before the state exercised its right to repurchase the lines.[134] A politician of the left like Gambetta might be almost as ready as a politician of the right to pursue imperialist policies; but the Rothschilds, for primarily domestic political reasons, preferred their imperialism to be conservative. On the other hand, they were wary—with good reason—of the chauvinistic tendencies of the French right. They disliked the agitation in support of General Boulanger following his dismissal as Minister for War in May 1887, which (like Bonapartism before it) combined domestic political radicalism and a foreign aggressiveness which the Rothschilds saw as incommensurate with France's strength; it was only after the "useless" and "incompetent" General's fall in 1889 that they began to act as his private bankers.[135]

The rise of trade unions and socialist parties was apparently viewed with more alarm by the French Rothschilds than by the British, though this probably reflected France's greater historical susceptibility to revolutionary politics. In 1892 Edmond wrote with alarm of the increasingly vocal socialist attacks on the "plutocracy" and warned of impending "anarchy," while Alphonse predicted that the "socialist epidemic" would be more "dangerous" in France than in England.[136] When he discussed industrial relations with Rosebery in 1892, Alphonse stressed that he was opposed to any intervention by the state in labour disputes.[137] He evidently regarded Rosebery as something of a conundrum, noting wryly after their meeting: "[T]here are no radicals in our country living in grand manors and with a yearly income of £100,000."[138] "For my part," Alphonse told the writer Jules Huret in 1897, "I don't believe in this working-class movement":

> I am sure that, generally speaking, working people are very satisfied with their lot, that they don't complain at all and that they are not in the least interested in what is called socialism. There are obviously ringleaders who try to make a lot of noise and attract a following but such people have neither hold nor influence over honest reasonable, hard-working labourers. One has to distinguish between good and bad workers. Those

who demand the eight hour day are the lazy, incapable ones. The others, the steady serious fathers of families, want to be able to work long enough to provide for themselves and their family. But if they were all compelled to work only eight hours a day do you know what the majority of them would do? Well, they would drink! . . . What else would you expect them to do?

It may be that Huret misquoted Alphonse, but his letters to London suggest that this was more or less what he thought: an uncompromising, not to say crass, *laissez-faire* view of the labour market of the sort routinely expressed by many industrialists of the period. Equally run-of-the-mill was Alphonse's defence of economic inequality:

I have never understood what is meant by "haute banque." What does it mean the "haute banque"? There are richer men and poorer men and that's all there is to it! Some are richer today and will be poorer tomorrow . . . Everyone is subject to such variations—everyone without exception! And no one can boast of being able to escape them. As for these agglomerations of capital, it is money which circulates . . . [and] bears fruit. It's the wealth of nations! If you frighten it away, or threaten it, it will disappear. And, on that day, all will be lost. That will be the end of the prosperity of the country. Capital *is* labour! Apart from some unfortunate exceptions . . . each man . . . has that share of the available capital that his intelligence, energy and industry merit.[139]

This complacent apologia spoke volumes for the social and political isolation of the Rothschilds as the new century approached—and with it a new era in which political power would no longer be so easily confined to the dining rooms of clubs and country houses.

ELEVEN

The Risks and Returns of Empire
(1885–1902)

[T]ake Constitution Jesuits if obtainable and insert English Empire for Roman Catholic Religion.
CECIL RHODES TO LORD ROTHSCHILD, 1888.[1]

In 1889 the Chancellor of the Exchequer George Goschen undertook to convert £500 million of 3 per cent consols into 2.5 per cents—an operation involving nearly half the national debt. The conversion seemed to symbolise the extraordinary virtuous circle which had been established in Britain whereby imperial expansion was combined with fiscal retrenchment. With the national debt falling steadily towards its lowest absolute level since the Napoleonic Wars, the Victorians appeared to have achieved empire without overstretch.

Goschen's conversion also testified to the continuing dominance of N. M. Rothschild & Sons in the London bond market. Loyal though he was to his old master Gladstone, Edward Hamilton (now at the Treasury) had no hesitation in recommending that Goschen "take Rothschilds . . . into his confidence" as well as Barings. Hamilton was surprised when Natty refused to "look at" the Treasury's offer of 20–25 million 2.5 per cents at a price of just over 99, dismissing "the possible margin of profit" as "wholly out of proportion to the risk run" and persuading the more accommodating Revelstoke to insist on a price no higher than 97.5. To Hamilton, this seemed bizarrely tight-fisted at a time of steadily falling interest rates.[2] It was only a year later that Natty's prudence would become all too intelligible.

The Risks of Informal Empire: The Barings Crisis
Historians have long debated how far "trade followed the flag" in imperialism, or vice versa. In Egypt the flag had followed debt (though debt had followed trade); but the transition from investment to invasion was not an inevitable one. In other overseas markets, the interests of European investors were never the pretext or justification for the imposition of external political control. The classic illustration of this point is the case of Latin America where, after the promulgation of the Monroe doc-

trine, European imperial influence was more or less bound to be "informal" and therefore largely economic rather than "formal" and political. (The exceptions to the rule were the British, French and Dutch colonies of Guyana.) The events of 1890—which saw Baring Brothers brought to the verge of bankruptcy by bad loans to Argentina—illustrate the disadvantage of the informal approach to empire. Had Argentina been a Middle Eastern or Asian state, her political instability might well have prompted political intervention in the interests of a major bondholder like Barings. The peculiarly neutralised status of Latin America precluded such a solution.

The story of the Barings crisis has been told often enough; in the context of a history of the Rothschilds, three questions need to be addressed. First, is there any truth in the contemporary claim that "the finger of the Jew"—meaning the Rothschilds—in some way triggered the downfall of their oldest rival? Second, what calculations ultimately prompted Natty to participate in the rescue of Barings? And third, why was it that no similar disaster befell the Rothschilds themselves? For their commitments to the neighbouring and no less politically unstable state of Brazil were comparable in scale to Barings' Argentinian commitments.

Barings' involvement in Argentina grew steadily in the decades after 1850, and was on the whole so successful—profits averaged 13 per cent of capital between 1880 and 1889—that by the late 1880s a fatal overconfidence had set in. Others saw the clouds gathering. As early as 1888, the *Bankers Magazine* was expressing doubts about the stability of the Argentine Confederation; the *Statist* was warning of an "inevitable" crash by mid-1889. Though Randolph Churchill later claimed that Natty had told him (probably in 1889) that Barings were "all right and nothing the matter with them,"[3] this was mere discretion on a delicate subject; in truth, the Rothschilds anticipated the Barings crisis at least two years before it broke. As Alphonse remarked in October 1888, Argentina "would have to grow rapidly very rich indeed" to be able to service her accumulating debt burden.[4] Gustave predicted an imminent "crash in Argentine funds with a bad reaction on all the other markets," and hoped—vainly as it proved—that the prospect of this might "calm down the zeal of Messrs. Barings, the Banque de Paris and others with regard to all of this Argentine business."[5] (In fact, they themselves were not wholly uninvolved in Argentina: in 1889 Wilhelm Carl was appointed the government's financial agent in Frankfurt.)[6] The rise in the Bank of England discount rate from 4 to 6 per cent in the second half of 1889 was seen as a sign of "nerves" on the part of the Governor, William Lidderdale, about the Latin American situation. Indeed, the fear of a gold drain in the event of a crisis there prompted Goschen to propose the issue of one-pound notes.[7]

There were numerous different Argentine securities in the Baring portfolio by 1890, including many *cedulas*, bonds issued by Argentine banks against mortgage loans to landowners. The fatal deal was the huge £2 million share issue which Barings floated for the Buenos Aires Water and Drainage Company, set up to modernise the city's water and sewerage system. Not only did the bank fail to place more than £150,000 of these with the public—despite resorting to "market devices" which were subsequently the subject of much criticism—but when John Baring visited Buenos Aires at the end of 1889, he was alarmed to find work on the new water system progressing slowly, the company the object of fierce political criticism, and householders avoiding paying the hard currency rates which were supposed to guarantee shareholders a respectable dividend. Even if political conditions had remained stable Barings would have got into trouble; but the crisis was precipitated in July 1890 when the Finance Minister resigned over President Miguel Celman's inflationary policies. The exchange rate slumped and a revolution supported by naval officers forced Celman to flee. "Anarchy" loomed, and with it default.[8]

Yet the scale of the problem remained hidden until the eleventh hour. When Edward Hamilton dined with Natty on October 8—the day after Bank rate was raised once again to 6 per cent—the latter "confessed to being very uneasy about the present state of things in the City"; but Hamilton added that "nobody knows exactly why an uneasy feeling should prevail: beyond that there is a sort of general apprehension that certain big houses are not in a very comfortable or easy position, mainly due to the Argentine crisis & the general fall in securities . . ."[9] The initial estimate by Bertram Currie of Glyn, Mills when he was approached by Revelstoke for an immediate loan on October 13 was that there was a gap between Barings' acceptances and the bills in its portfolio of £1 million, which could easily have been filled: Currie immediately advanced three-quarters of the sum.[10] As late as November 2, the mood of the handful of bankers who knew about this loan—including Natty—was relatively sanguine.[11] It was only later that the size of the hole was revealed. When the books were scrutinised by Currie and the former Bank of England Governor Benjamin Buck Greene, they found the difference between bills payable (£15.8 million) and bills receivable (£7 million) to be far larger than had previously been indicated.[12] And that was only part of the problem. Barings' total liabilities were close to £21 million (including large Russian government deposits which had begun to be withdrawn in late 1889), whereas the bank's assets included £4 million of Argentine securities held jointly with the Buenos Aires firm of Samuel Hale & Co.

Considering that the capital of Baring Brothers in 1890 was just £2.9 million, these were disastrous figures: a ratio of capital to liabilities of just 14 per cent should be compared with an average figure for N. M. Rothschild of 39 per cent for the 1880–89 period. To have accumulated a portfolio of Argentine securities larger than the firm's entire capital was folly on a grand scale. It was, as Lidderdale put it, "haphazard management, certain to bring any firm to grief." *The Times* agreed, when the crisis finally became public: Barings had "gone far beyond the bounds of prudence."[13] Under the circumstances, it is not therefore surprising that Natty initially argued for letting Barings go under when he was approached by Everard Hambro on the morning of November 8; dismissed Lidderdale's suggestion that Rothschilds could somehow influence the Argentine government to support "the enormous mass of discredited South American securities which were weighing on the Stock Market"; and opposed Currie's suggestion that they and "three or four others should lend the Barings four millions to tide over their difficulties." It was not a matter of enmity—though there was undoubtedly some personal and professional rivalry between Rothschild and Revelstoke—so much as genuine dismay at the extent of the bank's insolvency.[14]

It was also nonsense to suggest (as Revelstoke's brother Colonel Robert Baring did) that the Rothschilds were in any way responsible for the Russian government's massive cash withdrawals from Barings which brought the crisis to a head.[15] There is no question—as the letters from Paris to New Court show—that the Rothschilds intended to make "the greatest efforts to forestall a catastrophe," provided these did not jeopardise the position of any other bank.[16] As this suggests, Natty was unwilling to make any commitments until he was sure that not only the Bank of England but also the Treasury were willing to give their support to a rescue operation. The fact was, as Natty explained to Reginald Brett on November 29, that some of the Russian deposits withdrawn from Barings had ended up at New Court. "They now have a large sum belonging to the Russian Government," Brett reported:

> No doubt they are alarmed at the Barings' speculations in Argentine, as the Barings formerly held all the securities of the Russian Government. The moment there was a suspicion of the Barings' house, Staal received a telegram ordering him to withdraw the Russian deposits. Had Natty supported B. Currie's original proposals, that order would have extended to the Rothschilds—it might have commenced a run upon them—a debacle.[17]

There was thus an element of self-interest in Natty's calculations.

Credit is usually given to the "the Sinbad of Threadneedle Street"—as Goschen's successor Harcourt called the Governor of the Bank—for saving Barings from oblivion and the City from "a panic of unparalleled dimensions." This, as Lidderdale himself acknowledged, is to understate Natty's role in persuading the government to act.[18] Goschen's initial reaction—seconded by the First Lord of Treasury, W. H. Smith—was to refuse Lidderdale's request for £1 million, arguing that "la haute finance" would have "to find its own solution." The most he was prepared to offer, he told Lidderdale on November 11, was authorisation to suspend the Bank Act if the drain on the Bank's reserve grew too great (an offer which was refused).[19] But, as Goschen warned Salisbury, "the Rothschilds [were] sure to put the screws on"; and when the Prime Minister sent for Natty on November 12 they were put on with a vengeance. The Barings, Natty told Salisbury contemptuously, were finished; at most the partners would be left with £10,000 a year apiece and might "prefer to cut up their remaining capital and retire into the country on 4 per cent a year . . . each." The danger was that their losses were so great as to threaten "a catastrophe [which] would put an end to the commercial habit of transacting all business of the world by bills on London." Natty subsequently made a similar point to Brett: if Barings had "been allowed to collapse, most of the great London houses would have fallen with them."[20] His conclusion was that nothing but government intervention could avert a crisis greater even than that of 1866. As would happen again in 1914, a crisis on the London acceptance market was presented as a crisis for the City as a whole, and hence for the country.

The most Natty was willing to do in the absence of government support was to help the Bank of England find the gold it would need as news of the crisis spread. In time-honoured fashion, he had already sent an immediate request to Alphonse for a three-month loan of £2 million in gold from the Banque de France to its counterpart in Threadneedle Street.[21] On November 12 Lidderdale asked Natty to arrange for a further £1 million to be sent; this too was immediately done, with consols accepted by the Banque as security pending an appropriate issue of treasury bills.[22] The effect was to ease pressure on the Bank, helping to boost its reserve from the low point of £11 million on November 7 to £16.6 million a month later.[23] As Alphonse pointed out, however, this could not be "considered as a solution of all the difficulties."[24] The key remained to bring Salisbury on board, which meant overcoming the opposition of Goschen. Already on November 12 Natty had gained half a point: after his meeting with Salisbury, the Cabinet agreed to pass a bill of indemnity if the Bank of England were forced to violate its charter by lending to Barings on "Argentine securities . . . *provided they obtained Gladstone's consent.*"[25] This helps explain why Natty had found his interview with Salisbury "rather satisfying": he felt he was overcoming the government's obduracy. The next day, apprehension of "some serious contingency" (as the banker John Biddulph Martin put it) began to spread, and "the many rumours that had been in circulation concentrated themselves with more and more persistence on the name of Baring Bros.," though when Biddulph left the City "everything [was still] going on as usual."[26] It was only on Friday the 14th that dangerously large numbers of bills on Barings began to be brought to the Bank of England for discount; and it was this which decisively strengthened the case for direct government action. That afternoon, with Goschen on his way to a routine speaking engagement in Scotland, Salisbury and Smith agreed to bear half of any loss arising from Barings' bills taken in by the Bank during a twenty-four period beginning at 2 p.m. that day.

The next move was to set up a guarantee fund to spread the costs of any loss which might be left when Barings' assets were finally liquidated.[27] This was achieved at a meeting in the Governors' Room at the Bank between members of the Bank's Committee of Treasury and the leading merchant bankers. Again the negotiations were delicately balanced. Lidderdale opened the bidding by saying that the Bank itself would pledge £1 million on condition that at least £3 million was guaranteed by other City firms.[28] Currie promptly offered £500,000 on condition that Rothschilds do the same. Once again, the fate of Barings was in Natty's hands. According to Tom Baring (no unbiased party) he hesitated and was only "shamed" by Currie into agreeing. Currie himself recorded more reliably that Natty "hesitated and desired to consult his brothers"—that old Rothschild device to buy time—"but was finally and after some pressure persuaded." That pressure, according to Edward Hamilton, took the form of Lidderdale telling Natty: "We can get on without you."[29]

Perhaps they could have; but Natty's assent, however reluctantly given, made the task immeasurably easier: thereafter, the guarantee fund grew rapidly as all the leading merchants joined the list of contributors, followed by the joint-stock banks the following day. By the end of the twenty-four-hour "window," £10 million had been accumulated (the figure later rose to £17 million, though only £7.5 million was actually needed)—proof, as Alphonse commented,

> that the English houses perfectly understand their responsibility and by preventing the catastrophe threatening the house of Baring they are acting in their own self-interest, in as much as the house of Baring just now is the keystone of English commercial credit. The downfall of this house would bring forth a terrific calamity for English commerce all over the world.[30]

More important, the news of the government guarantee and the formation of the syndicate reassured holders of bills endorsed by Barings that they would get their money.[31] Still, this was far from being the happy ending of the story; and the ramifications of the Barings crisis show just why Natty had hesitated at the crucial moment. The possibility still existed of a general Argentine default, which would at a stroke have wiped out the value of a fifth of Barings' assets. Even as things stood, Argentine securities were down to 40 per cent of their March 1889 value by July 1891. Natty now found himself chairman of a committee of bankers entrusted with the task of defending the interests of all British bondholders in Buenos Aires.[32] Although he favoured the imposition on the government of a programme of currency stabilisation based on the hypothecation of customs revenues, a more piecemeal approach ended up being adopted.[33] In 1892 it was agreed to advance the government a new loan in order that it should buy the waterworks and thus liquidate one of Barings' most onerous obligations; but that merely increased the Argentine external debt to £38 million and a further loan in 1893 pushed the total up still further.[34] The condition of this second loan—the so-called Romero agreement—was financial control over the Argentine rail network. It was not in fact until 1897 that the Argentine government fully resumed interest payments.[35]

This delay inevitably slowed down the winding up of the old Barings' partnership which, as Alphonse pointed out, was the key to "the whole question": "[I]t is not enough to have prevented a momentary suspension of the house of Baring," he wrote on December 29, "worse has yet to be forestalled by the liquidation of the . . . affairs that have caused the embarrassment."[36] In April 1893, with the sale of Barings' assets proceeding more slowly than expected, the bankers' guarantee had to be extended (albeit on a reduced scale) to November the following year.[37] Although Cecil Baring remarked that Natty was "very humane" when a new company—Baring Estate Co.—was set up to liquidate the remaining Argentine bonds, there is no doubt that the Rothschilds resented the continuing claim on their resources which the Barings guarantee entailed. It was only in 1894 that the reconstituted Barings finally repaid the advances made by the guarantors.

All this helps to explain why Natty's standing in official circles was enhanced by the Barings crisis. It was not just that Revelstoke was brought low; the Rothschilds themselves had played a pivotal role in averting a potentially acute financial crisis. Before the crisis, Edward Hamilton had been rather disdainful of the Rothschilds. In April 1889, at the time of a minor Treasury operation in exchequer bills, he had written in his diary: "Though I always think it well to keep clear of them in the East End I actually lunched in New Court."[38] When the Liberals came back in, however, Natty was closely consulted by the new Chancellor Harcourt on the complex question of stock exchange stamp duties.[39] Ten years later, on the eve of the next Liberal government, Hamilton named Natty—along with Ernest Cassel and the second Lord Revelstoke—as one of the "first counsellors" and "representative [City] men" to whom any new Chancellor of the Exchequer should be introduced.[40]

What had happened in 1890 was that a bank which, according to the formal rules of the financial market, should have failed was bailed out by a collective intervention initiated by the Bank of England, underwritten at the critical juncture by the government and paid for by a broad coalition of other City houses under the leadership of Currie and Rothschild. For the government and hence the taxpayer, it was a cheap solution: cheaper, at any rate, than sending a gunboat or an invasion force, as might conceivably have been done if Argentina had been a Middle Eastern defaulter. The price the banks paid was low too: it amounted to little more than the cost of tying up money in advances to Barings' creditors, which was much less than the cost of letting Barings fail. Yet one question remains: why did the Rothschilds themselves not also go the way of Barings? For in many ways they were as heavily engaged in Latin American finance. Comparing Barings' experience with that of the Rothschilds in Brazil helps to clarify the relative costs and benefits of informal empire.

On November 1890 Natty had told Salisbury that he "was quite indifferent . . . he had no liabilities." This was sheer bluff. In reality, the Rothschilds had been grappling for some time with their own Latin American debt crisis. We have already seen how Lionel revived the old Rothschild connection with Brazil in the 1860s. There was a lull in Brazilian government borrowing in the 1870s after the end of the Paraguayan War—the only major issue was a £5.3 million loan in 1875—but the 1880s saw a fresh bout of activity in which once again the Rothschilds acted as the government's sole issuing agent in London. Altogether, the Rothschilds were responsible for Brazilian government bond issues totalling £37 million between 1883 and 1889, as well as £320,000 for the Bahia–San Francisco railway company.[41] In addition to helping consolidate the existing floating debt and convert earlier bonds to a lower rate of interest, this money was used to finance interest payments to existing railway companies and to subsidise shipping companies, so that it was at least partly being used for developmental and especially infrastructural investment.[42] All seemed to be proceeding well—slavery was abolished in 1888 and the currency regained its gold parity the following year—when the Emperor Pedro was overthrown by a republican revolution backed by the army. This appears to have taken the Rothschilds completely by surprise.[43] As in Argentina, there was a run on the currency and a slump in the overseas quotation of Brazilian bonds. By 1893 the country was in a state of civil war, with both the navy and monarchists in the south of the country defying the new government. Signs of stabilisation in 1895 were illusory: in 1896–7 a new revolt flared up among the peasants of the north-east.

Why did this not lead to a Rothschild crisis in parallel to the Barings crisis? One obvious answer is that in absolute terms the London house lost "only" around £740,000 between 1890 and 1893. This was partly because the Rothschilds did not hold large quantities of Brazilian bonds themselves: in 1886, for example, they accounted for just 2.4 per cent of the London house's total assets.[44] Secondly, as mentioned above, the Rothschilds maintained a far higher ratio of capital to liabilities than the Barings: even at its lowest point in the period (1890) it was still 19.5 per cent. They were therefore better placed to cope with crises of the sort which happened in 1889. Finally, and perhaps most obviously, the capital of the London house was £5.9 million in 1890, compared with £2.9 million for Barings, to say nothing of the capital of the other Rothschild houses. The losses they suffered were therefore relatively much smaller.

Rothschilds were not Barings; nor was Brazil Argentina. Despite the political instability of the decade after 1889, it was not in fact until 1898 that the government declared a moratorium on its external debt. The ability of the government to maintain debt service until this point had surprised Alphonse,[45] but it was really not so remarkable. Compared with many other major debtor states of the period, Brazil was not highly geared: even at its peak in 1898–9, total public debt was just 400 per cent of tax revenue. Interest and amortisation of the external debt generally consumed a relatively small percentage of total government expenditure: the average figure of 10.5 per cent for the years 1890–99 was markedly lower than comparable figures for other borrowing states.[46] In fact, it was not until *after* the 1898–1900 stabilisation that a real debt problem began to develop. Between 1890 and 1914, the London house issued a staggering £83 million of Brazilian public sector bonds and a further £5.8 million of private sector securities. In addition, Natty and his brothers became heavily involved in a parallel expansion in Chilean borrowing, issuing Chilean bonds worth £33 million between 1886 and 1914. These accumulations of debt far exceeded the economic growth which these countries were capable of achieving, even with world demand rising for their staple exports (coffee and rubber in the case of Brazil, guano and copper in Chile). Between 1890 and 1913, the total Brazilian debt (in sterling) rose by a factor of 3.5; real gross domestic product grew just 2.7 times. Moreover, the rapid expansion of coffee production in the state of São Paulo—it quadrupled between 1870 and 1900—led to a crisis of excess supply.

Plainly, the Rothschilds had substantial financial leverage over Brazil. When the government suspended service on its existing bonds in 1898, the London house effectively dictated the terms of the necessary rescheduling (which essentially postponed all sinking fund payments until 1911).[47] The new Funding Loan issued by Rothschilds to consolidate the state's various obligations was secured, Ottoman fashion, on the customs receipts and the government was compelled to pursue a rigorous programme of retrenchment, spelt out in a stern letter from New Court to the President-Elect Campos-Salles, which was published in *The Times* for all to read.[48] This policy led to a rapid appreciation of the currency (the milreis) from 7¼d to 16d in 1913, a trend which intensified the already acute crisis in the coffee industry by pushing up Brazilian costs as world market prices were falling.

However, there were limits to the amount of control which could be exercised through such informal imperialism. For one thing, growing competition in the international capital market inevitably began to erode the dominance which the Rothschilds had enjoyed for most of the nineteenth century over Brazilian external finance. By 1906 the Rothschild position was under attack in both Chile (from the Speyers and Deutsche Bank)[49] and Brazil (from Schröders). When in 1905 the state of São Paulo sought financial assistance for a coffee-stockpiling scheme which it was hoped would shore up the falling price of the state's main product, Alfred dismissed the "valorisation" scheme out of hand as "an artificial & mad speculation" which would end in disaster.[50] Natty was equally dubious about the federal government's simultaneous effort to regulate the milreis–sterling exchange rate by creating a new Caixa de Conversão.[51] However, Schröders and Kleinworts put together a syndicate of New York, Hamburg and Le Havre coffee merchants and proceeded to buy up no fewer than 8 million bags between the autumn of 1906 and May 1908—equivalent to more than half annual world consumption.[52] When Schröders sought to enlist Natty's support for the £15 million loan needed to liquidate the syndicate's advances to São Paulo, Natty's immediate response was blunt: "Certainly not for that damned swindle." Had he persisted in his refusal, Schröders would have been dangerously exposed: without Rothschild backing, there could be no guarantee from the Brazil-

ian federal government, and without that the loan might well have failed, leaving
Schröders with a sixth of its capital in advances to São Paulo and nothing but coffee
beans as collateral. Natty chose to draw a somewhat Jesuitical distinction between
directly financing the valorisation scheme and lending to the Brazilian state (even if
it then used the money to pay for the valorisation scheme).[53] Having made
Schröders squirm, he finally agreed to take a share in the loan,[54] but his instinct that
such schemes were unlikely to have an enduring success was right. In 1910 competition from the East Indies caused a sharp collapse in the price of rubber which no
amount of stockpiling could cushion and the resulting foreign exchange crisis overwhelmed the Caixa de Conversão.[55] The effect of the crisis was to puncture the
already declining market for Brazilian bonds, leaving 94 per cent of the £11 million
loan issued by Rothschilds in 1913 with the underwriters.[56] A new loan was about
to be agreed, which would have been conditional on foreign control of the Banco de
Brasil, when war broke out in Europe in 1914.[57]

Informal imperialism—by definition—generally lacked the ultimate sanction of
government intervention. It was a very different thing, as French investors found in
1888–9, to put money into a canal in Panama as opposed to one in Egypt, where
French influence had been considerable, even if ultimately subordinate to that of
Britain.[58] The choice in Latin America seemed to be between American control or
no control. When the Brazilian government appeared to be contemplating the
annexation of Trinidad in 1895, for example, Natty urged Salisbury's principal private secretary Schomberg McDonnell to make diplomatic representations in order
that Brazil should submit her claims to arbitration. McDonnell told Salisbury "that
it was for the Rothschilds to prove . . . the policy of withdrawing and that, if they
could effect this, the main difficulty in the way of arbitration would be removed . . .
There is no doubt the Rothschilds can do this; but they naturally want to make us
do it." In practice, that meant that it was up to Natty whether he wished to cable the
Brazilian Minister of Finance on the subject; as far as the government was concerned, Brazil was literally the Rothschilds' affair.[59] The limits of the British bankers'
influence became manifest when not only Brazil but also Argentina and Chile began
to spend substantial sums on their navies. Despite warnings of "financial ruin," it
proved impossible to arrest the Latin American arms race—not least because British
shipbuilders were the recipients of lucrative orders as a consequence of it.[60] As Natty
rather ingenuously remarked when seeking to rein in Brazilian railway building, "it
is always a delicate matter to question the policy of a government."[61]

"Staunch Monometallists"

The enormous levels of capital export from Britain which characterised the late
nineteenth and early twentieth centuries were to some extent facilitated by the
development of a global monetary system: first the bimetallic (silver and gold)
system and then, from the mid-1870s, the gold standard, which fixed the exchange
rates of most major currencies in terms of gold and hence tied them to sterling, the
world's reserve currency. Until recently, the role the Rothschilds played in this
process has generally been understated and often misunderstood.

It has traditionally been assumed that the Rothschilds were firm proponents of
the transition from bimetallism to the gold standard. Indeed, to American Populists,
the Rothschilds personified the "international gold ring" which they believed was

behind the demonetisation of silver. It is easy to see why this was. They still had their refining and broking business;[62] and, as we shall see, their interests in gold mining grew rapidly in the last two decades of the century. Moreover, many of the bond issues handled by the Rothschilds in this period were linked to the recipients' adoption of the gold standard. This was most obvious in the case of the United States, where they and their agent August Belmont played a major role in financing the resumption of specie payments (which had been suspended during the Civil War).

In July 1874 the London house, in partnership with the New York banker Joseph Seligman, agreed to underwrite a US bond issue worth $45 million of 5 per cents with a six-month option on $123 million. When this proved unsuccessful, Junius Morgan's group and the First National Bank of New York was brought into the syndicate for a second issue of $25 million, of which the Rothschilds took 55 per cent.[63] Altogether, N. M. Rothschild was involved in issuing no less than £267 million in US bonds in London and New York between 1873 and 1877. These loans were designed not only to stabilise American finances but also to enable the US to adopt the gold standard in the foreseeable future. However, when the 45th Congress met in October 1877, a bill was drawn up which would have restored the "free" coinage of silver and its status as legal tender—a measure which Belmont furiously denounced as "open theft" and "blind and dishonest frenzy." Only when it was stipulated that silver would be allowed to circulate in strictly limited quantities and would not be used to pay off the interest due on outstanding bonds did the Rothschilds relent. The Secretary of the Treasury John Sherman then negotiated a new loan of $50 million in gold coin through Belmont in 1877 which allowed the adoption of the gold standard to go ahead at the beginning of 1879.[64] This was accompanied by a further bond issue, though this time Junius Morgan's ambitious son Pierpont sought to exclude the Rothschilds, to the irritation of Lionel and Natty who (as he told Herman Hoskier of Brown, Shipley & Co.) refused "to join any American Syndicate and be at their mercy or command, and would only take it up if we were given the lead to work it our own way with a group of friends around us."[65] Continuing doubts about the American commitment to gold may help to explain why the Rothschilds played such a small role in the great boom in American railway shares and bonds of the post-Civil War era.[66]

The issue was still politically open as late as March 1893, when Grover Cleveland attempted to raise a $50–60 million gold loan to maintain convertibility at a time of rapidly diminishing US gold reserves. Though Morgans were willing to act jointly, Natty, Alfred and Leo hesitated: Alfred remained "greatly opposed" even after Cleveland secured the repeal of the Sherman Silver Purchase Act which had continued to give silver a limited circulation. Finally, an agreement was reached which proved highly lucrative (a tribute, perhaps, to the brothers' negotiating skills, rather than proof of the Morgan view that they were excessively cautious). $62.3 million of US 4 per cent bonds were taken by the bankers at 104.5 and sold to eager investors for 112.25 (the price later rose to 119). Tales of profits of $6 million being made in the space of twenty-two minutes were grist to the Populist mill, of course, and helped ensure that William Jennings Bryan rather than Cleveland was chosen as the Democrats' presidential candidate in 1896. However, Bryan's defeat by the Republican William McKinley set the seal on the American transition to gold.[67]

The American stabilisation was part of a wider process. In 1868 only Britain and a number of its economic dependencies—Portugal, Egypt, Canada, Chile and Australia—had been on the gold standard. France and the other members of the Latin Monetary Union, Russia, Persia and some Latin American states had been on the bimetallic system; most of the rest of the world, including most of central Europe, had been on the silver standard. Forty years later, only China, Persia and a handful of Central American countries were still on silver. The gold standard was, in effect, the global monetary system, though in practice a number of Asian economies had a gold exchange standard (with local currencies convertible into sterling rather than actual gold) and a number of "Latin" economies in Europe and America did not maintain convertibility at all.[68] In a number of major European states—Germany (1871–3), France (1878) and Russia (1897)—the Rothschilds played a key role in facilitating the monetary transition, though in Italy Hambros rather over-ambitiously stole a march in 1881–2.[69] Thereafter, the London and Paris houses acted as vital auxiliaries to their respective central banks, sending specie across the Channel in large quantities at times of crisis in one or other market. This in itself was a profitable business. At the same time, the gold standard ensured that foreign bonds denominated in gold-based currencies were proof against exchange rate fluctuations and therefore marketable to more cautious investors, who might otherwise cling to consols and "home rails." Monetary integration encouraged the growth of the international bond market because convertibility "signalled a country's commitment to sound budgets, balanced external payments and sustainable volumes of foreign borrowing."[70] It was thus good for the Rothschilds' main business.

It is not to be wondered at, then, that the English Rothschilds were often heard to defend bullionist orthodoxy in the renewed bimetallist debates of the early 1890s. For example, Alfred "strongly opposed . . . any radical change as regards the metallic circulation of Great Britain" in a private report he wrote for the Governor of the Bank of England in 1886;[71] and four years later Natty firmly opposed Goschen's proposal to introduce a one-pound note, a reform which in fact represented an innocent modernisation of the 1844 system and a sensible response to the growing demands on the Bank of England. When Gladstone and his Chancellor of the Exchequer Harcourt were casting round for a suitable British delegate to veto American bimetallist plans at the International Monetary Conference held at Brussels in 1892, Alfred thus seemed the ideal choice. As Harcourt put it,

> The name of Rothschild will carry a weight which no other could command in the monetary world.—I have not the advantage of knowing Alfred's opinions on these subjects, but I take it for granted that he is a good staunch monometallist (What Mr Gladstone calls a "sane man') who will uphold to the death the single gold standard . . .[72]

Alfred duly assured Harcourt that he "could have found no stauncher supporter of Monometallism than myself" and that he was "strenuously devoted towards maintaining our financial supremacy to which England owes her overwhelming mercantile supremacy."[73]

Yet Alfred proved incapable of sticking for long to his allotted role as "sane man." In November he surprised everyone (not least his fellow delegate Bertram Currie) by coming up with his own compromise plan. Though mocked by his enemies in the

City and Treasury and probably doomed to fail given the highly polarised mood at the conference, this was in many ways a reasonable attempt to reconcile the bullionists and bimetallists by raising and maintaining the price of silver through a five-year international purchasing agreement without actually giving silver equal status with gold. Had it been adopted, Alfred argued, "time would have been given to the South African mines to prove whether their yearly output would have been sufficient to satisfy the additional demand of the whole world, and time would have been given to India to introduce a gold standard with a gold currency."[74] In the eyes of the "brutal monometallist" Currie, however, this was far from being the "Monometallism with honour" or "euthanasia of Bimetallism" which Harcourt had urged them to bring home; indeed, Alfred's project had won qualified support from some bimetallists at the conference, though not enough to become a practical proposition.[75]

Moreover, when the issue resurfaced in 1897, there were rumours that Natty too had softened his stance under the influence of Arthur Balfour, who harboured bimetallist urges. He declined to sign a City memorandum against bimetallism circulated by Currie and signed by most of the other leading merchant banks. And, rather to the embarrassment of the new Chancellor Sir Michael Hicks Beach, he was once again willing to contemplate limited concessions to the silver bugs: the reopening of the Indian mints, the conversion of a fifth of the Bank of England's reserve into silver and the raising of the legal tender limit for silver from £2 to £4 (as opposed to the American bimetallists' target of £10).[76]

How are we to explain this mild heterodoxy? One historical point to recall is that Natty's grandfather had been among the critics of the excessively rigid bullionist theory. But Alfred and Natty were doing more than echoing the past. They were also reflecting the views of their French partners who were (in Alphonse's phrase) "extreme" believers in bimetallism.[77] As regent of the Banque de France, Alphonse had defended the bimetallic system throughout the 1860s against attacks from proponents of paper money (the Pereires) and the Latin Monetary Union. In some ways, this was a monetary conservatism—a banker's "conventional wisdom"—which mirrored that of his English relations. Just as Natty saw the one-pound note as a threat to the British status quo, so too Alphonse vehemently opposed the introduction of a twenty-five franc coin in 1870.[78] But, as Flandreau has shown, the Rothschilds' apparently contradictory position was a logical one. Bimetallism only ceased to work because the French government took the political decision in 1873 not to facilitate the German demonetisation of silver by continuing to convert it freely into gold.[79] Prior to 1873 it had worked because "bimetallic arbitrages [by private agents in bimetallic countries] pegged the gold–silver exchange rate within an interval reflecting the costs associated with melting one metal and coining the other one." The Rothschilds were the key arbitrageurs in this system, which depended on Britain operating the gold standard and France the dual standard. It therefore made sense for the English Rothschilds to favour gold and the French bimetallism *for their respective countries;* the English Rothschilds never favoured the demonetisation of silver for the world as a whole.[80] Even after the battle for silver was lost, Alphonse continued to argue that bimetallism had offered a more flexible system for Anglo-French monetary policy than gold.[81] Finally, the English Rothschilds had their own private reasons for wishing to avoid the complete demonetisation of silver, given their interests in mercury (the main use of which was in silver refining), even if their private stake in the gold industry was vastly greater.

An Empire Underground

The difficulties experienced by bankers who dealt in Latin American bonds were not new: in many ways they resembled problems the Rothschilds had previously encountered in the 1820s and in Spain and Portugal in the 1830s. Nor was the Rothschilds' response to these debt crises altogether new. In the 1830s they had acquired control of the Almadén mercury mines in the belief that some kind of tangible asset was necessary if money was to be advanced to a state as unstable as Spain. What happened in the 1880s reflected not dissimilar calculations, but the Rothschilds now involved themselves in mining on an unprecedented scale. Indeed, it is not too much to say that the decision of the London and Paris houses to develop what can justifiably be described as a mining empire was the most important change in their mode of operation since their decision to become involved in railway finance in the 1830s. For just as James had seen that controlling a pan-European railway network was as important as financing the nascent nation states of the mid-century decades, so Natty and Alphonse understood that investing in mines was as important as issuing bonds for Europe's overseas colonies and economic satellites. Like the railways before them, the mines offered higher rates of return than state bonds; while as assets they were less liable to lose their value (the risks of punitive taxation and even expropriation were real but generally lower than the risks of a government default). Claims that the Rothschilds were a declining force after 1880 rarely take account of this profoundly important change of direction.

We have already seen how the London house was able to re-establish control over the output of the Almadén mercury mines in the 1870s. These continued to provide a steady source of outcome until the 1920s: between 1871 and 1907, for example, the London house made around £900,000 from the mines, 8 per cent of their total yield.[82] The Rothschilds' role in Almadén was relatively passive, however, to judge by the partners' correspondence, compared with their involvement in the far more dynamic business of gold mining.

Beginning in the 1840s, the London house had taken a keen interest in the discoveries of gold in the New World, which had prompted them to acquire their own refinery in London in 1852. In California and Mexico, in particular, the Davidson brothers had been encouraged to involve themselves closely in the development of the most promising mines. By the 1870s they had acquired new business associates in the area. One was the consultant mining engineer Hamilton Smith, whose report on the El Calleo gold mines in Venezuela in 1881 persuaded the Rothschilds to invest there too. It was very probably Natty who encouraged Smith to settle in London in 1885 and to establish a partnership with another mining expert, Edmund de Crano. A year later, they became the managing directors of a new company, the Exploration Company.[83] This was to be a crucial vehicle for the Rothschilds' mining ambitions.

At first the Exploration Company acted as a consultancy, advising its shareholders on mining propositions; but in 1889 it was relaunched as a joint-stock company with a nominal capital of £300,000, and increasingly it acted as a company promoter (in other words, it floated mining companies on the London stock exchange, charging a fee of 20 per cent on nominal capital). In essence, it was a way for respectable City firms to conduct what was widely regarded as a highly speculative kind of business, without directly risking their good names. In addition to the Rothschilds, the twenty founding shareholders of the company included Lord Revelstoke, Everard Hambro, Henry Oppenheim and Arthur Wagg; Horace Farquhar was chairman until 1896. By that time the company's capital had increased to £1.25 million and its market value to £2.24 million, making it, as the banker Harry Gibbs put it, "the strongest institution of its kind in the world." For the founders, who were entitled to half the surplus after 10 per cent had been distributed and who retained control of the company by dint of their inflated voting rights, it was an immensely profitable investment. Altogether between 1889 and 1903, it issued shares with a nominal value of £20.7 million for twenty-three companies.[84] Between 1889 and 1895, it paid a total of 265 per cent in dividends on its initial paid-up capital of £30,000, quadrupling the value of its shares, though the dividends fell to 80 per cent in the subsequent decade and just 40 per cent in the period 1905–14. That the Exploration Company was a Rothschild creation is obvious. Together Natty and his brothers held 30 per cent of the stock (though their share declined as the company grew), and from 1889 to 1897 the company actually had its offices in St Swithin's Lane.

In addition to the profits they made from their investment in the Exploration Company itself, the Rothschilds reaped substantial returns from the various mining companies it promoted. The 1886 balance sheet of the London house shows a total shareholding in mining firms worth just £27,000; within a few years the figure was much larger.[85] In 1891 the Rothschilds held 5,000 £1 shares in Consolidated Gold Fields of South Africa, later increasing their stake to 13,000 shares.[86] When Julius Wernher and Alfred Beit—the pre-eminent "Randlords"—floated Rand Mines in February 1893, the Rothschilds were allotted 27,000 out of 100,000 shares; and when the same company raised a further £1 million in 1897, they took £35,000 of the bonds. This gave them a substantial stake in the huge "Corner House" group which accounted for around 37 per cent of the gold produced from the Rand between 1902 and 1913. The profits to be made from such investments were huge. Shares in Rand Mines rose from a low of £15 10s in 1897 to a peak of £45 in 1899.[87] Similarly, the London and Paris houses bought shares worth £100,000 in the new Marievale and Nigel Gold Mines Estates before it was floated on the stock market in 1895, immediately selling them at a 25 per cent profit. They also had a "call" on 50,000 £1 shares which were worth £4 when the company was floated.[88] The French house was apparently less successful, complaining in early 1894 that its profits on some mining shares were only narrowly in excess of its losses on others.[89]

Gold mines were the Exploration Company's first love: understandably, given the dramatic expansion of South African gold production following the new discoveries on the Witwatersrand and the successful application of deep mining technology.[90] In 1892 the Company launched the Consolidated Deep Level Co. and the Geldenhuis Deep; this was followed by the flotation of Rand Mines and Goldfields of Mashonaland in 1893, and then Jumpers Deep Levels and the Transvaal and General Association in 1894. In all this, the Rothschilds took a keen interest. In early

1892 Carl Meyer was sent to the Transvaal to investigate the various gold mines. His report was euphoric. The fields, he declared, had "an enormous future before them":

> [T]he country altogether will for the next 10 or 20 years offer greater scope for European capital than South America and similar countries. Here is a fine country, lovely climate, inhabited by Dutch and Anglo-Saxons [*sic*], only beginning to be developed and replete with every mineral as well as adapted for every branch of agriculture. I feel that it would pay for the Houses of Rothschild to have a clever representative here who would be able to do plenty of good business.[91]

Although no such "clever representative" was sent, the Rothschilds' indirect participation in the South African gold boom through the Exploration Company has often been underestimated.[92] Nor did the Company confine itself to South Africa. In 1894 it launched the West Australian and General Association as a regional subsidiary, and this in turn led to flotations for the New Zealand Exploration Company in 1896—though neither of these proved as profitable as their South African counterparts.

The acquisition of major stakes in such a wide range of gold mines was a bold move, predicated on important assumptions about the future of the world gold market. As Alphonse said, the Rand conjured up visions of an "Aladdin's grotto." At first sight, it is odd that he expressed no fears about a possible over-supply of the metal (as he would have done had the Rand contained untapped reserves of mercury or copper).[93] The explanation for this is straightforward: the demand for gold seemed likely to remain buoyant as more and more countries adopted it as the basis for their monetary systems. So long as that continued, an increase in the supply of gold would not depress the price, but merely lead to monetary expansion and a general increase in the prices of all assets.[94] It was on the back of such expectations that the so-called "Kaffir boom" in South African mining shares of 1893–4 took off. Small wonder the English Rothschilds encouraged the spread of the gold standard.

The Rothschilds were not monometallists; they were multimetallists. Of increasing importance to them in the same period was copper: a base metal, but one in growing demand in the last quarter of the century with the rapid development of electrical engineering. The French Rothschilds may have been indirectly involved in the first major attempt to corner the copper market by the Société des Métaux and Comptoir d'Escompte in the late 1870s, but it seems more likely that they moved into copper after that bubble had burst in 1889.[95] In the late 1880s the London and Paris houses added to their Spanish interests by acquiring a controlling interest in the Rio Tinto mines, which at that time accounted for more than 10 per cent of total world copper production.[96] This was an investment of the first importance: by the early 1900s the price of "Tintos" was a benchmark cited almost as often in correspondence between London and Paris as the price of consols and rentes had been half a century before.[97] The London Rothschilds also acted as the company's banker in 1895, issuing debentures worth £3.6 million (for a £110,500 commission).[98]

This was only part of a wider advance into copper mining and marketing, probably driven by a need to defend the Rio Tinto investment against falling prices as new sources of copper were discovered elsewhere. Also in the 1880s the Paris house acquired a 37.5 per cent stake in the Boleo Company, a Mexican copper mine; and after 1895 the Exploration Company was the principal source of finance for the Montana-based Anaconda Mining Company. These interests gave the Rothschilds a position of real power on the world copper market. Along with Leonard Lewisohn in New York and Brandeis, Goldschmidt & Co. they were members of a marketing syndicate which, beginning in 1895, succeeded in pushing the price of copper back to £50 a ton by direct purchases and output restrictions.[99] Nor did they hesitate to add to their copper interests as new sources were discovered. In 1903 the Exploration Company raised £1 million for the Otavi Minen und Eisenbahn Gesellschaft in German South-West Africa.[100] The French Rothschilds also took an interest in the utilisation of copper, investing in companies like the Compagnie Générale de Traction de Paris.[101]

The Rothschilds were equally interested in the extraction of precious stones. Their involvement with De Beers—perhaps the most famous of all their mining ventures—will be discussed below; but it is worth noting that it was not the only investment of this sort they made. In 1889 they also floated the Burma Ruby Mines company after a prolonged tussle to secure a seven-year mining concession from the British government, which had annexed the territory three years before.[102] This proved another profitable enterprise: the price of rubies was still rising strongly four years later (in marked contrast to the price of diamonds).[103]

The French house generally deferred to the expertise of the London partners when it came to gold and precious stones. Typically, it was through the London-based Exploration Company that de Rothschild Frères became shareholders in the Compagnie Française des Mines d'Or et Exploration (CONFRADOR) in 1895. However, Alphonse and his brothers had their own mining interests which developed just as rapidly in the same period. In the 1880s, for example, the French house began to expand its interest in Spanish silver-bearing lead, which it bought from an agent in Cartagena and purified into merchant lead and silver at its Le Havre refinery. Advised by their equivalent of Hamilton Smith—a graduate of the Paris School of Mines named Jules Aron—Alphonse and his brothers invested 250,000 francs in their French refinery and switched to a system of direct purchase from the Spanish producers, though they were reluctant to follow Aron's advice to invest directly in a Spanish refinery. It was not until 1880–81 that he was able to persuade them to establish the Peñarroya Mining and Metallurgical Company, which leased the lead mining empire from its Spanish owner. By 1913 the company produced no less than 80 per cent of Spanish silver and 60 per cent of its lead. With a 40 per cent stake in Peñarroya and an exclusive selling agency, the French house became one of the biggest single players in the international lead market.[104] At the same time and in much the same way, Alphonse and his brothers acquired a 25 per cent interest in the Nickel Company set up by the Australian entrepreneur John Higginson on the French-owned Pacific island of New Caledonia.[105] The strategy here was ambitious—by 1884 the company had acquired most European nickel refineries—but the discovery of nickel mines in Canada in 1891 shattered the dream of a nickel monopoly, and forced "Le Nickel" to halve its capital value and enter into a loose market-sharing agreement with the American–Canadian International Nickel Company. The third major mining investment of the period was the Mexican Boleo (copper) Company mentioned above. All told, by around 1900 the French house had an investment in these mining companies with a nominal value of 11.5 million francs (£460,000) and a market value twice as great, equivalent to around 4 per cent of the firm's total capital.[106]

Similar in style was the French Rothschilds' involvement in the Russian petroleum industry. This had been an interest since the 1860s, when the French house had begun to import petrol from America, and in 1879 they had gone into partnership with the refiner Deutsch de la Meurthe to manufacture kerosene in Spain and later to establish a new refinery at Fiume. The search for oil to supply this refinery led to the first Rothschild soundings of the rapidly growing Russian oilfields around Baku. (The Austrian house also had some interests in the Galician oil industry, but no collaboration seems to have been contemplated.)[107] When the Paris house's proposal of a partnership with the Nobel Brothers Petroleum Co. was rebuffed in 1883–4, the Paris partners took the decision to buy another firm, the Batum Oil Refining and Trading Company (usually known by its Russian acronym BNITO). They also built up a substantial fleet of over 2,000 oil tank cars as well as "immobilising vast capital" in a refinery at Novorossiysk and an oil depository at Odessa.[108] McKay has estimated the value of the Paris house's investments in Russian oil by the turn of the century at around 58 million francs (£2.3 million).[109] At peak, around a third of Russian oil output was Rothschild-controlled.[110]

The 1890s were a period of frantic growth in the world market for oil. The Rothschilds' Russian kerosene was sold in Europe (in much the same way as Spanish lead) through their Industrial and Commercial Caspian and Black Sea Kerosene Company (Société Industrielle et Commerciale de Naphte Caspienne et de la Mer Noire). Later, they also went into partnership with a Russian shipping firm (Pollack & Co.) and the International Bank of St Petersburg to form a new company called Mazout in order to expand their sales to the Russian domestic market. This meant they were competing not only with the Nobels, but with the American giant Standard Oil. A similar competition developed in the Asian market. In 1891 the London-based brothers Marcus and Samuel Samuel acquired the right to market BNITO's kerosene east of Suez, using their pioneering tanker ships—the origin of the Shell Transport and Trading Company formed in 1897. Their principal Asian rival was the fast-growing Royal Dutch company, based in the Dutch East Indies.

As competition drove prices down, the customary efforts were made to end the "oil wars" by forming a profit-sharing cartel (1893–5).[111] However, the negotiations with Standard Oil came to nothing and the tendency was for the Rothschilds to participate in the gradual merger between Shell and Royal Dutch. The Rothschilds took a third share of the Asiatic Petroleum Co. created by the two oil firms in 1902, and in 1911 exchanged their entire Russian operation for shares in Royal Dutch and Shell, making them the largest shareholders in each. Even at the time, this seemed a good deal as the Rothschild stakes in BNITO and Mazout were valued at £2.9 million, while their new shares in Royal Dutch/Shell promised healthy returns.[112] Just six years later, the wisdom of the Rothschild retreat from Baku would become clear.

Mercury, gold, copper, lead, silver, diamonds, rubies and oil: by 1900 the Rothschilds occupied a remarkable position in the world market for non-ferrous metals, precious stones and petroleum. Not only did they raise capital for new mining companies directly or through the Exploration Company; they also invested substantial sums of their own in mining shares and took a close interest in efforts to cartelise or otherwise regulate the international raw-materials market. This was hardly the strategy of a business in decline. On the contrary, the London and Paris houses had shrewdly discerned a way of developing one of their traditional lines of business in response to fundamental structural changes in the world economy.

Rhodes and the Rothschilds

Aside from its generally high profitability, part of the appeal of the mining empire the Rothschilds acquired in the 1880s and 1890s lay in its apparent freedom from political control. Once a concession had been granted or a piece of territory sold, mining companies seemed to enjoy something close to complete autonomy, especially when the mines were in remote locations, as they often were, or in parts of the world with relatively rudimentary state structures. Yet this kind of imperialism could never entirely be separated from the formal imperialism of national flags and dotted lines in maps; least of all in the mind of Cecil Rhodes.

The origins of the Rothschilds' relationship with Rhodes can be traced back to 1882, when Natty sent the firm's former San Francisco agent Albert Gansl to Kimberley—the main diamond mining centre—to report on the affairs of the Anglo-African Diamond Mining Company, which had a claim in Dutoitspan, one of the four major "pipes" in the area (the others being Kimberley, Bultfontein and De Beers). Within a few months, Gansl had concluded that the numerous small companies—there were more than a hundred altogether—were ruining one another by over-production, and argued strongly for amalgamation. However, despite the creation of an Amalgamation Committee in London and plans to issue shares worth £3.5 million in a merged diamond company, the scheme foundered on the jealousies of the shareholders and directors of the rival firms.[113] In addition to the difficulty of reaching agreement on the value of existing shares (which, in an amalgamation, would have been exchanged for new ones), the slump in diamond prices in 1882–3 probably also put the Rothschilds off. The French Rothschilds certainly grumbled about their losses on the Anglo-African shares which their London cousins had recommended.

It was the Exploration Company which, albeit indirectly, revived the Rothschilds' interest in diamonds when it recruited another American engineer, Gardner Williams, to report on mining prospects in South Africa. By this time, the process of amalgamation was further advanced than it had been five years before: the Kimberley claims were virtually under the sole control of Kimberley Central, which had a market value of around £2.45 million in 1887 and a yield of 1.3 carats per load. The next biggest operation was the De Beers Mining Company, which was worth around £2 million and had a slightly lower yield.[114] The question in the mind of Cecil Rhodes—a director and major shareholder in De Beers, and a promiscuous Kimberley company promoter—was which of the two would succeed in merging with the Compagnie Française, one of the last independent firms on the Kimberley pipe.

Rhodes had begun to realise that, given the limited financial resources of both De Beers and Central, the key to victory in the impending takeover battle lay in London, and that whoever secured the financial backing of a major City house would win. Identifying Williams (whom he had first met on a steamer to London in 1885) as his entrée to New Court, he hastily offered him the job of general manager at De Beers;[115] and two months later set off for London for his first interview with the famous Lord Rothschild. Natty drove a hard bargain. On August 4, Rhodes cabled to Kimberley the details of a plan which would give De Beers the money to buy the Compagnie, but at a steep price. Essentially, Rothschilds advanced £750,000 in cash in return for 50,000 new De Beers shares at £15 each, plus £200,000 in debentures. For this, they received a commission of £100,000, but also half the difference between the £15 price paid for the De Beers shares and their London market price on October 5, 1887. According to Turrell, this implied an additional £150,000, so that "the Rothschild syndicate was paid £250,000 for advancing £750,000 for the purchase."[116] After negotiations in Paris which dragged on into September, the directors of the French company accepted the merger terms, which converted French shares into De Beers shares at a ratio of 100:162.[117]

Yet this was far from being a victory for Rhodes. It is true that a counter-bid by the Central for the Compagnie was seen off, but it would seem that this was achieved only by a promise to sell the Compagnie to the Central for £656,000. Because all but £100,000 of this was paid in the form of Kimberley Central shares and stock, historians used to think Rhodes had cleverly acquired a stake in the Central; in fact, all that had happened was that the Central had acquired the Compagnie at a bargain price, and it was generally expected that De Beers would now be swallowed by the Central. Rhodes envisaged buying up stocks in the remaining independent mines in Bultfontein and Dutoitspan and completing the De Beers–Kimberley Central merger, but to do this he needed the agreement of the chairman–director of the Kimberley Central, Francis Baring-Gould, and its biggest shareholder, the ebullient Barney Barnato. Had both resisted—as legend has it they did—Rhodes would in all likelihood have lost.

In the event, only Baring-Gould proved hard to get; Barnato saw the opportunity to make a killing, and secretly committed himself to Rhodes.[118] In November de Crano wired from Kimberley that Rhodes needed a new loan of £300,000 to buy up Central shares, suggesting strongly to the Rothschilds that, if they did not provide the money, Rhodes's associate Alfred Beit would do so.[119] It was at this point that Natty acquired 5,754 shares in De Beers for himself, making him one of the company's biggest shareholders (Rhodes himself had only 4,000).[120] This strategy continued throughout 1888, while Rhodes and Natty sought to overcome the resistance of Baring-Gould.[121] On March 13, 1888, Rhodes formally registered De Beers Consolidated with a capital of £3.1 million and a further £1.5 million in debenture stock,[122] but still Baring-Gould and a minority of Central shareholders held out. Apart from the prospect of hefty profits on both Central and De Beers shares, which soared in the first half of 1888, a decisive factor in bringing Barnato round was the offer of a "life governorship" of the new company, an extraordinary concession which Natty evidently disliked.[123] Even so, the merger continued to be impeded, first by a legal challenge from Central shareholders who objected to the blanket terms of the trust deed defining the new company's objectives, then by a fearful fire in the De Beers mines, which killed 202 men.[124] It was not until January 1889 that the liquidation of Kimberley Central was finally concluded, by which time De Beers had acquired 93 per cent of its rival's capital, so that the final purchase of the Central cost less than a tenth of its valuation at £5.3 million.[125] Thereafter, it was a relatively easy matter to mop up the remaining small companies.[126]

Throughout this protracted struggle, Natty's main role had been to help Rhodes find the money for his share purchases, issuing £2.25 million first debenture stock so that De Beers could pay off its old debts and acquire leases in Dutoitspan and Bultfontein.[127] The total cost of the merger was plainly more than he had expected; but like many others Natty was not immune to Rhodes's melodramatic charm. "The whole case depends whether you have any confidence and trust in myself," Rhodes appealed to him on one occasion in 1888. "Perhaps someone else can do it better. I really do not know. You know my objects and the whole case is a question of trust[.] I know with you behind me I can do all I have said. If however you think differently I have nothing to say."[128] This relationship continued after the merger was completed. It was the Exploration Company, for example, which issued £1.75 million De Beers Consolidated Mortgage Debentures in 1889, 17.8 per cent of which were taken by the London Rothschilds; and in 1894 the London house itself issued De Beers debentures worth £3.5 million.[129] All this meant that the Rothschilds had acquired a substantial stake in the new firm and thus a substantial financial hold over Rhodes, who felt more than a little uneasy at the high level of gearing the takeover battle had necessitated.[130] Carl Meyer's appointment to the board of the new De Beers was the most visible sign that Natty intended to keep a weather eye on its progress. By 1899 N. M. Rothschild & Sons were the second biggest shareholder in De Beers (with 31,666 shares), only slightly fewer than Barnato's nephews the Joel brothers (33,576). Rhodes had only 13,537; Beit 11,858.[131] It was to prove a superb investment.

As the smoke dispersed in the boardrooms, the question immediately arose as to how the new De Beers Consolidated—which now controlled 98 per cent of South African output—was to establish its authority over the international diamond market.[132] Schemes for a syndicate had been discussed since 1887, though it was not until March 1890 that De Beers concluded an agreement with a combination of five friendly firms led by Wernher, Beit & Co.[133] As this was the kind of thing the Rothschilds had traditionally done to maintain the price of mercury and were also doing with copper, the syndicate soon received Natty's blessing, though the Rothschilds' own participation in it was limited.[134] The one strategy which the Rothschilds firmly opposed was any kind of hoarding of diamonds by De Beers. As Natty told Rhodes in July 1891, he had "no right to speculate in diamonds, but were bound to sell as best you could." "[A]s regards the disposal of the diamonds," he concluded, "the more I think of it the more I feel convinced that you cannot do better than follow the ordinary laws of supply and demand and avoid, as far as possible, all artificial means, combinations, accumulations, etc, etc." When it transpired that the Kimberley directors had nevertheless covertly established a "secret reserve" to bolster their depressed share price—one of a number of acts of defiance by the men on the spot—Carl Meyer denounced it as "immoral."[135] In the event, the device proved superfluous: from 1896 onwards the diamond market rallied, and De Beers' annuals dividends reached 40 per cent (£1.6 million) over the next five years, pushing the share price up after the initial sticky start. As Natty told Rhodes in 1900, "The history of the De Beers Company is simply a fairy tale. You have established a practical monopoly of the production of diamonds, you have succeeded in establishing a remarkably steady market for the sale of your productions, and you have succeeded in finding machinery capable of carrying this through."[136] In other words, what more did Rhodes want? Nevertheless, Rhodes continued to chafe at the restrictions imposed on him regarding the sale of diamonds, travelling to London in 1898 to complain about the marketing syndicate's excessive profits.[137]

Establishing De Beers as the dominant power in the Kimberley diamond fields had little or no political ramifications, given that Kimberley and the surrounding land (Griqualand West) had been annexed by Britain in 1871. But from the outset Rhodes's ambitions extended far beyond British territory. It was not just the gold discoveries on the Boer-controlled Witwatersrand which whetted his appetite to expand British influence north of Cape Colony. In fact, Rhodes had been rather unsuccessful in his investments on the Rand and his company, Consolidated Gold Fields, was soon looking further afield for as yet undiscovered gold reserves (when it was not investing in De Beers shares). To be precise, he wanted to strike northwards beyond the Transvaal into the kingdom of the Matebele King Lobengula.

In January 1888, Rhodes wrote a long letter to Natty seeking his support for the new concession he had just secured from Lobengula to develop the "simply endless" gold fields on the other side of the Limpopo River. It is clear from this that, though he hoped the Rothschilds would "take a share" in the venture, Rhodes was more interested in their political influence than their money. There was, he reported, "a good deal of opposition at home to the size of our concession," principally from the rival Bechuanaland Exploration Company, established by Lord Gifford and George Cawston, as well as from the Portuguese government. He was especially worried to hear talk of replacing his pliant friend Sir Hercules Robinson as the British high commissioner in Cape Colony, for reasons which made his own long-term objectives absolutely plain:

> I feel the danger of any new change of policy and he [Robinson] has managed so well during the last 8 years, for whilst keeping the confidence of the Africaner [*sic*] party, he has steadily fought out the expansion Northwards and completely surrounded the [Boer] Republics, it is almost entirely due to him that we have extended from the Vaal River to the Zambezi and if you look at the map, you will see that by his policy he has completely shut in the Transvaal Republic so that it cannot expand. If we leave matters now quietly to work, with the development of the gold in the Transvaal, we shall gradually get a united S. Africa under the English flag. The [gold] diggers eventually will never endure a purely Boer Government, the whole matter is simply a question of time, but it would all be ruined if we had a new man with a brand new policy of antagonism to the neighbouring republics and basing his policy on the Mackenzie pro-native ideas it would lead to endless friction. There are endless questions now cropping up—for instance the future of Swazieland [*sic*] and the mode of dealing with the Matabele King all of which if not ably handled may lead to endless rows and I think Sir Hercules with his eight years['] experience is still the best possible man.[138]

Later the same year, Rhodes wrote to Natty in a similar vein, now imagining De Beers as "another East India Company . . . with the enormous back country daily developing," and outlining more of his "visionary dreams":

> [T]he Matabele king . . . is the only block to Central Africa, as, once we have his territory, the rest is easy, as the rest is simply a village system with a separate headman, all independent of each other . . .

> [T]he new East Africa Company at Mombassa . . . should work down
> through Tanganyika to the Zambesi to join our development from the
> South, getting in between the Germans and the Congo State . . . All I
> want is at present to stop being cut off . . . There is another connecting
> link in the Lake Company, or Nyanza, which trades up the Shire from
> the Zambesi, but of course the key is Matabele Land, with its gold, the
> reports as to which are not based solely on hearsay . . . Fancy, this Gold
> Field [in Matabele Land, which] was purchasable, at about £150,000
> two years ago, is now selling for over ten millions. I proposed to Beit and
> Robinson we should buy the whole length, about 30 miles and leave out
> nothing, and the documents were actually drawn [up], but, unfortu-
> nately, I had to leave, and after I left the plan fell through.[139]

It is difficult not to see a direct line from these schemes to the fiasco of the "Jameson
Raid" in December 1895, and perhaps even to the outbreak of war with the Boers in
1899. Rhodes was bent on a programme of encirclement and expansion which was
incompatible with the independent existence of the Boer republics; and he expected
Natty to support him.

So convinced was he that Natty would help realise his vision that in June 1888 he
revised his will in order to leave him all his property bar 2,000 De Beers shares
(which he left to his brothers and sisters).[140] To leave several hundred thousand
pounds to one of the richest men in the world might seem perverse; but in a letter
accompanying the will Rhodes intimated to Natty that this money should be used
to found what his biographer has called "a society of the elect for the good of the
Empire." "In considering question suggested take Constitution Jesuits if obtainable," Rhodes scribbled, "and insert English Empire for Roman Catholic Religion."[141] It is highly unlikely that Rhodes (much less Rothschild) had ever read the
Jesuit constitution drafted by St Ignatius in 1558; this was just shorthand for the
kind of dedicated brotherhood which was his ideal. What is striking is that—like
that other very different visionary of the period, Theodor Herzl—Rhodes saw the
legendary Lord Rothschild as the one man with resources capable of making his
dream a reality.

It is usually assumed that Rhodes's expansionist aspirations must have been
shared by the Rothschilds: why else tell Natty so much about them? There is, however, a need for caution. To be sure, Natty and his brothers were not opposed to the
idea of an enlarged British South Africa. When Rhodes joined forces with Gifford
and Cawston of the Bechuanaland Company to create a new Central Search Association—to spearhead his plans for Matabeleland—Natty was a major shareholder,
and increased his involvement when this became the United Concessions Company
in 1890.[142] He was also a foundation shareholder when Rhodes established the
British South Africa Company in 1889, and acted as the company's investment
adviser free of charge.[143] More important, as a letter of January 1892 shows, Natty
had no illusions about Rhodes's ambitions. "[O]ur first and foremost wish in connection with South African matters," he told Rhodes, "is that you should remain at
the head of affairs in that Colony and that you should be able to carry out that great
Imperial policy which has been the dream of your life.—I think you will do us the
justice to admit that we have always loyally supported you in the carrying out of that
policy, and you may rest assured that we shall continue to do so."[144]

Indeed, Natty would no longer willingly listen to criticism of Rhodes. When the increasingly unstable Randolph Churchill returned from South Africa in 1891 denouncing the prospects of Mashonaland and declaring in the press that "no more unwise or unsafe speculation exists than the investment of money in [mining] exploration syndicates," Natty was incensed—especially as he had financed Churchill's trip.[145] Sir William Harcourt's son Lewis ("Loulou") described in his diary an extraordinary confrontation between Natty and Churchill at Tring in early 1893, when the latter:

> attacked Rhodes & S Africa & Mashonaland most bitterly, said the country was bankrupt & [Cecil] Rhodes a sham and that Natty knew it and Rhodes could not raise £51,000 in the City to open a mine etc. All this was to Natty's face and made him furious—so much so that he went out of the room for a few minutes to cool himself.[146]

Nor did the Rothschilds have any qualms about Rhodes's use of force against the Matebele and other black African tribes who got in his way. Writing from Paris in October 1893, Arthur de Rothschild made the classic imperialist connection between "a little spurt in the shares of the Chartered Co." and "a sharp engagement having taken place with the Matabeles, 100 of them having been killed, whilst there was, I am happy to say, hardly a single casualty on our side." The senior partners in the Paris house were equally enthused, not least by Rhodes's autocratic style of governing the Cape after he became its Prime Minister in 1890.[147]

Yet there was always a substantial gap between Rhodes and Rothschild with respect to the *means* of extending British influence from the Cape. Philosophically, Rhodes was always closer to Liberal imperialism than to the policy of the Salisbury governments, which tended to subordinate the ambitions of white colonists on the periphery to the diplomatic interests of the metropolitan government. He was in favour of Home Rule, for example, the litmus test of late-Victorian politics.[148] Having expected so much from Natty, Rhodes was quickly disillusioned. He was frustrated by the Rothschilds' inability to persuade the Portuguese government to cede Delagoa Bay, the principal sea port on the Mozambique coast and therefore the strategic key to the future of the Transvaal.[149] Negotiations on this subject dragged on, but although Natty talked optimistically of buying the land from Portugal, diplomatic obstacles proved insuperable.[150] Rhodes felt Salisbury had "treated [him] very badly over the Portuguese business," a charge which Natty was at pains to dispute. "You must not forget," he explained to the impetuous empire-builder,

> that at that time public opinion all over Europe was very much in favour of Portugal, and it would hardly have been wise for Lord Salisbury to incur the reproach, on the part of friendly Powers, that this country was going to crush weak little Portugal for the sake of a no doubt important but underdeveloped region in Central Africa. After all, could you have expected more, or as much from a Liberal Government?[151]

When Rhodes tried again with a direct approach to the Portuguese envoy Luiz de Soveral, he felt Natty's support was lukewarm.[152] "It appears that you take Soveral's view that nothing can be done," he complained in May 1893:

I thought that you would do all you could as for several years you have felt and rightly so, that the Delagoa is the key of our position in S. Africa . . . I am afraid that we are going to buy Delagoa Bay. We want it and are prepared to pay for it. With the growth of the Transvaal the longer we wait the more we shall have to pay and with the completion of the Delagoa line we shall probably never get it.[153]

In this, as in much else, he was moving too rapidly for the Rothschilds, who grew weary of explaining that the Portuguese government had no intention of selling the territory in question.[154] As early as February 1891, Rhodes confided in Reginald Brett that he regarded Natty as "honest but without sufficient brains."[155] It was not long before he revised his will once again, appointing a second trustee of his fortune alongside Natty. "The thought torments me sometimes," he declared, "that if I die all my money will pass into the hands of a man who, however well-disposed, is absolutely incapable of understanding my ideas. I have endeavoured to explain them to him, but I could see from the look on his face that it made no impression . . . and that I was simply wasting my time."[156]

For his part, Natty was perturbed by the cavalier way in which Rhodes set about using De Beers Consolidated to advance his designs in Matabeleland. The first bone of contention was Rhodes's determination that De Beers should be a major shareholder in the British South Africa Company, usually referred to in correspondence as "the Charter." Natty's view was "that De Beers should not hold so speculative a security," a view strongly supported by Carl Meyer, always "a great pessimist about the Charter."[157] In January 1892 Natty spelt his views out in "perfectly frank" terms:

[Y]ou are the only judge as to whether the Cape Government ought to take over the Northern Territories; that is not our business and we do not wish to offer any opinion on the subject. You must know how far your Charter would meet with the approval of Her Majesty's Government. But what we do say is, that if that is your policy, and you require money for the purpose, you will have to obtain it from other sources than the cash reserve of the Debeers [sic] Company. We have always held that the Debeers Company is simply and purely a diamond mining company . . . and if it became known that the Debeers Company lent money to the Chartered Company, some Debeers shareholders might move for an injunction, and get up an agitation to turn out the Board and put in their own nominees, which would be most undesirable. Apart, therefore, from the question whether it is right or wrong to use the funds of the Debeers Company in this way it would be very injudicious, and might do a great deal of harm to the credit and reputation of the Company and its Directors.

To Rhodes's complaint that the Charter Company needed money, Natty replied:

that sooner than let the Debeers Company subsidize the Chartered Company, we would prefer your getting a small export tax on diamonds; no doubt there would be some grumbling at first, but eventually the trade will get accustomed to it. And this raises the point if the time has come for you to consider whether the Cape Government should take over the Diamond Mines and buy out the shareholders; not, of course, at the high figures of a few years ago, but at a fair and equitable

price. Let that idea pass through your fertile brain and tell me what you
think of it.[158]

It is not difficult to imagine what Rhodes thought of the idea of submitting De
Beers and the Charter to such direct political control.

In such negotiations, Natty was always careful to avoid antagonising the volatile
Rhodes: "[Y]ou know I do not like to interfere in their [De Beers'] internal administration," he assured him in July 1892, "and only hope that the company will be
able to pay good dividends in the future and gradually diminish their indebtedness."[159] There were in fact a number of occasions when Rhodes was able to disregard "orders" from London (for example when he insisted on buying the Premier or
Wesselton mine). But Natty did not disguise from Rhodes that the big De Beers
shareholders on the London board held the purse strings.[160] Such conflicts between
the London board and the life governors flared up again in 1899, when Rhodes
wished De Beers to invest money in Rand gold mines and railways at a time when it
was having to borrow to pay its dividend. Natty's opposition to this and his criticism
of the system of life governorships prompted Rhodes to complain that "the whole of
my policy in connection with De Beers has been opposed by the London board
almost ever since it was created" and to subject Carl Meyer to "violent abuse." Yet he
could not get around the fact that Natty together with "the majority of the French
shareholders . . . represent[ed] the larger portion of the Company's capital," and in
the end they were able to insist on the the abolition of life governorships.[161] It is also
worth noting that Rhodes himself owed the Rothschilds substantial sums on his
own account: in mid-1895, when he was premier of Cape Colony, he owed them as
much as £16,515, though he was by this time a millionaire in his own right, mainly
thanks to his holdings of De Beers shares.[162] This was far more than Randolph
Churchill owed them when he was in office.

Quite apart from the specific role of De Beers, Natty's vision of South Africa's
future differed in many essentials from that of Rhodes. It is hard to believe, for
example, that Rhodes welcomed his offer in 1891 to subsidise the passage and settlement of hundreds of families of Russian Jews fleeing Tsarist persecution.[163] A
more serious source of friction was Natty's refusal to recognise that Rhodes's plans
ruled out peaceful coexistence with the Boer republics. In May 1892 Rhodes was
curtly informed that the London house was contemplating floating a £2.5 million
loan for the Transvaal government to enable it to expand its own railway network, a
possibility which had been raised earlier that year by President Paul Kruger during a
visit by Carl Meyer to Johannesburg. Kruger, Meyer had reported to New Court,
was "a queer old Boer, ugly, badly dressed and ill-mannered, but a splendid type all
the same and a very impressive speaker." And he added a political observation: "The
relations between the old Boer party and the new mining industry population are
getting much better than they have been hitherto." It was not by chance that these
talks had taken place while Rhodes was himself in London.[164]

It is, of course, arguable that the aim of the 1892 loan was to establish an informal imperial control over the Transvaal—something Rhodes might have been
expected to welcome. When Natty raised the issue with Lord Salisbury he pointedly
stressed that he had been able to whittle down Kruger's original plan for a larger loan
to acquire the Portuguese Delagoa Bay line.[165] And when he wrote to Rhodes on the

subject he emphasised that "in drawing up the contract we were careful to reserve to ourselves a voice in future borrowings, as you suggested," and that he intended pointing out "the necessity for coming to an arrangement with the Cape Railway when the time comes": "We also told them that we cannot agree to their borrowing more money for the Natal extension, and as you will see from the prospectus, we insisted upon the money being spent exclusively within the limits of the Republic. Naturally we shall never let them think that we are acting at your suggestion."[166]

As this indicates, Rhodes's first thought had been that by building their own railway links southwards, the Boers would be in a position to dictate terms to the gold mines. Natty evidently wished to reassure him, but as he himself admitted, "we could not very well dictate to the Government what tariff they were to charge when the line will be completed." As Chapman has shown, the Boers had no intention of being intimidated by their new bankers. When New Court wrote its customary admonition that the money raised "be used with the very greatest prudence and economy" and "that every expenditure . . . be subjected to a strict and efficient control," Pretoria replied fiercely that no "control can be allowed, that the Government prior to the several drawings being made cannot state for which purpose the money will be used, and further that the Government cannot consent to the money remaining deposited with you until it is required."[167] The success of the Transvaal bonds on the London market was therefore a blow to Rhodes. The issue was predicated on peace between the Cape and the Boers, whereas by late 1895 plans were already afoot in Cape Town to overthrow the Kruger government in the name of the non-Boer "Uitlanders" in the Transvaal.[168]

The Jameson Raid—an abortive invasion by what was, in effect, Rhodes's private army in Bechuanaland—appalled the Rothschilds, who had no inkling of the plans for a coup. Although Rhodes had discussed the idea of fomenting Uitlander revolt with Joseph Chamberlain—who had joined Salisbury's government as Colonial Secretary in the summer of 1895—he apparently had said nothing of the kind to Natty; and he in turn was not sufficiently close to Chamberlain to be tipped off (as was *The Times*'s Africa correspondent).[169] In the wake of the débâcle, Natty sought to patch up relations between London and Pretoria, urging Kruger to come to London in terms which could hardly have disavowed Jameson more explicitly. "By accepting invitation without conditions," he assured Kruger, "you will obtain the independence of the Republic. We hope nothing will be done to strengthen hands of opponents of Transvaal Government here and it is also absolutely necessary to prevent the growth of hostile feeling to Boer Government, for up till now public opinion has been in your favour and everything will be done to make your task easy."[170] Hobson was in the wrong when he claimed the "financiers" had profited from Jameson's escapade: the opposite was true.

The Pitfalls of Formal Empire: The Boer War

The failure of the Jameson Raid merely postponed the conflict with the Boer republics, however. Within a year of arriving in South Africa as high commissioner in 1897, Alfred Milner became convinced that the only way to establish British control over the republics' external policy was by war. He readily took up the cause of Uitlanders' franchise, and Chamberlain felt bound by party political considerations to back him up. These two had sufficient leverage to dissuade Natty from issuing a second Transvaal loan in November 1898;[171] but it was awkward from Milner's point of view that the informal diplomacy of the Rothschilds nevertheless aimed at defusing the quarrel with Pretoria. In June 1899 Alfred telegraphed directly to Kruger in terms which cannot have been dictated by the Colonial Office, though Chamberlain had been consulted beforehand:

> [N]either the Country nor the Government wants war, but one can never foretell what may happen and what public opinion might force the Government to do . . . The crux of the situation is that the Uit-landers should have some direct and immediate representation in the Volksraad parliament whereas the defect of Your Excellency's proposi-tion is that every change is postponed for so long a time that it does not in any way affect the present situation.[172]

Kruger was not deaf to such appeals. On July 6 Chamberlain heard from New Court advance news of a concession from Kruger: the Uitlanders were to be offered a "seven years' retrospective and retroactive franchise" which "would be accepted with acclamation by the non-British Uitlanders who it is feared expect Lord Salis-bury to go to war."[173] Natty was able to confirm this to McDonnell twelve days later, prompting Chamberlain to describe the crisis as "ended."[174] As late as August 25, Carl Meyer still "persist[ed] in believing that a modus vivendi [would] be found *for this time*—though I admit Kruger is trying the Govt's patience and . . . there is a smell of gunpowder in the air which is dangerous."[175] This was also the view taken by Cecil Rhodes, who remained confident until the eleventh hour that "the Boers [would] give in at last."[176] As it became apparent that this time Kruger did not intend to back down, the Rothschilds made one last effort to achieve a peaceful solu-tion. At the suggestion of Hartington (now the Duke of Devonshire), a telegram was sent to Samuel Marks, a business associate in Pretoria, which—without the authorisation of either Chamberlain or Salisbury—effectively reformulated British policy:

> Government of Great Britain are anxious Peace. If agree to 5 Years Fran-chise without conditions Government of Transvaal have no reason to fear friendly discussion subsequently arranging details. Positive no fur-ther demands shall . . . be sprung. War occur now it is his [Kruger's] fault not Government of Great Britain . . . We are assured by N M Rothschild & Sons Government of Great Britain and England or the British do not wish interfere integrity Transvaal . . . Most strongly urge you to do utmost secure franchise *without conditions*. In our opinion only way war can be prevented.[177]

It was a proposal which was not only rejected by the Boers but which would in any case probably have been repudiated by Salisbury. He feared that such "subterranean negotiations" might lead to "serious entanglement" and asked Natty "very earnestly" to desist from "any further communication of this kind with Pretoria."[178]

The Rothschild view was not based on any deep sympathy for Boer self-govern-ment: as Natty told McDonnell, Samuel Marks was confident that, if peace were preserved, "In 15 years the Transvaal will be British." "Kruger is the last of the old Boer Toryism," argued Marks's partner Lewis, and "he is also the last President of the kind that the Transvaal will ever have."[179] Moreover, once war had broken out,

Natty unhesitatingly involved himself in the war effort, suggesting that Boer supplies through Delagoa Bay be immediately cut off.[180] The obligatory patriotic
rhetoric came readily when local soldiers returned to Buckinghamshire from the
war, while Alfred contributed in his own way by organising a spectacular gala
evening at Covent Garden.[181] Natty also remained on good terms with Milner and
wrote warmly to congratulate him—albeit "in my wife's name"—"on having firmly
established His Majesty's Dominions in South Africa."[182] Yet privately he deplored
the "wretched guerrilla warfare" the British army found itself having to wage.[183]
Within two months of peace being concluded, Alfred was promoting reconciliation
between British and Boer generals around his dinner table.[184]

Natty was especially unnerved by the claims of Radical writers like Hobson that
the war was being fought on behalf of those who had financial interests in the gold
and diamond fields, advising Rhodes to:

> be careful in what you say regarding the conduct of the war and your
> relations with the military authorities. Feeling in this country [is] run-
> ning high at present over everything connected with the war and there is
> a considerable inclination, on both sides of the House, to lay the blame
> for what has taken place on the shoulders of capitalists and those inter-
> ested in South African Mining. It would be a great pity to add fuel to the
> fire and you would only be playing into the hands of the opposition
> which I am sure you want to avoid. I hope, therefore, that you will be
> careful in your utterances and if you have any complaints to make
> against the War Office underlings, you will no doubt have opportunities
> to do so privately.[185]

This helps explain Natty's letters to Balfour two months later urging him privately
that "a good War Minister . . . gives his generals twice as much as they ask for":

> There was a clever article in the "Daily News" the other day which
> ended by saying that, unable as His Majesty's Ministers were to make
> peace, they were still more unable to carry on war . . . It will be far
> cheaper in the long run to make a big effort now, than to run the risk of
> the war dragging on for another year . . . I think it right you should
> know both what the public feeling is on the subject and also the anxiety
> which is felt by some out in Africa that there is a desire to save money
> and [we may] thus in the end be forced to incur a much larger expendi-
> ture.[186]

In short, Natty agreed with Rhodes's criticisms of the way the war was being waged;
but he viewed public expression of such criticisms by anyone with large private
interests in the mines of Kimberley and the Rand as highly impolitic.

Yet there was a certain irony in this Rothschild warning against false economy in
wartime; for the Boer War was in the process of exposing the Rothschilds' declining
influence over that area of British policy where it had once been greatest: finance.
The Boer War was the first time since the Crimean War that Britain had been forced
to finance a war by a major net increase in the national debt. But whereas in the
1850s it had been taken for granted that the Treasury would turn to N. M. Rothschild & Sons to meet its borrowing requirement, that was no longer assured half a
century on. Natty assumed from the outset, as he told Edward Hamilton, that the

Chancellor Sir Michael Hicks Beach "would send for me when he is ready." But his recommendation that consols be issued with a Rothschild guarantee was rejected in favour of Ernest Cassel's argument for a "much more dignified" open market sale of Exchequer bonds at a price of 98.5. The "Khaki loan" was heavily oversubscribed and Hamilton discerned with some glee "the jealousy with which the Rothschilds regard Cassel." When the need for a further loan arose in July, Natty fell in behind Cassel (and against the Bank of England), arguing for a second bond issue, this time for £10 million. But Hamilton struck a second blow against Rothschilds by agreeing with Clinton Dawkins of J. P. Morgan and Lord Revelstoke of the revitalised Barings to make an advance placing of half the sum in the US. This infuriated Natty, who had been drumming up subscriptions on the assumption that the London market would have to place the full amount.[187] True, a third issue of £11 million was sold without recourse to the American market, but when the government steeled itself for a much bigger issue of £60 million in consols it once again called on Morgan. Half the total was taken by Morgan, N. M. Rothschild and the Bank of England (£10 million apiece) at a firm price of 94.5. What is more, Morgan secured a commission two times higher than the London banks'.[188] The modest amount left to smaller firms generated a good deal of resentment among "*English* circles in the City" who felt, according to Horace Farquhar's brother Granville, "furious at finding every dirty German Jew in, and themselves left out."[189] But the fact was that the distinctly un-German and un-Jewish figure of Pierpont Morgan was the principal victor: for the first time in over a century, the British government had been forced to borrow a large sum from a foreign power to wage a war in its own empire. It was an early sign of that shift in the centre of financial gravity across the Atlantic which would be such a decisive—and for the Rothschilds fateful—feature of the new century.

Morgan flexed his muscles again in the spring of 1902, when it was decided to raise a new £32 million loan. Natty—who Dawkins suspected still had "a lot of the last Consol issue . . . on his hands at a loss"—argued for issuing a new Transvaal Guaranteed Loan, but Dawkins, backed up by a visit from Morgan himself, prevailed on Hicks Beach to stick to consols. Although the Americans agreed to take only £5 million—leaving Rothschilds with £7 million and Cassel and the Bank with £2 million apiece—they also found themselves able to dictate the issue price (93.5). It was a sign of the ill-feeling generated by this new American rival that Natty pointedly refused to give Morgan's London house a share of his allocation.[190] Even after the war, the Rothschild bargaining position looked weak. Although the 1903 Transvaal loan for £30 million was sold without American assistance, Natty's request for a 2.75 per cent coupon was overruled by the Treasury as too low and it was decided to exclude applications for less than £2,000—a change of policy which Alfred angrily denounced as "most un-English."[191]

Nor did victory in the Boer War represent an unqualified assertion of metropolitan authority in South Africa. Although the Boers were ultimately forced to make peace, it was Cape Town (and Kimberley) rather than London which benefited from the British victory. The final conflicts within the De Beers company between the London board and Rhodes were a microcosm of this. Even as the war in the Transvaal got under way, Rhodes was being exhorted telegraphically by Natty "to extinguish floating debt and free mortgaged consols no dividend even if earned could be

paid before this done . . . we therefore suggest take advantage of favourable opportunity to create fifty thousand more shares which would be readily absorbed by
existing shareholders."[192] Natty followed this up eight months later with a detailed
critique of Rhodes's accounting methods—and in particular his habit of accumulating large surpluses which he and the other life governors "used for every kind of
purpose, some connected with the mines and some with outside investments and
ventures."[193] And Natty continued to oppose Rhodes's ambition to break the power
of the diamond-marketing syndicate in London.[194]

Nevertheless, Rhodes left his successors at De Beers in an almost unassailable
position. Annual dividends rose from around £1.6 million (40 per cent a share) in
the period 1896 to 1901 to £2 million from 1902 to 1904. Even Natty had to admit
that these were "brilliant results."[195] Moreover, political attacks on the use of Chinese labour in the South African mines—which the Liberals turned into a major
campaigning issue in the 1906 election—served to widen the gap between London
and Cape Town.[196] Finally, the Rothschilds' control over De Beers was dealt a damaging blow when the Inland Revenue sought to extend the tax liability of the company from the dividends of the British shareholders to the net profits of the
company as a whole, a move which necessitated the formal dissolution of the
London board and confirmed the supremacy of Kimberley over the European shareholders. As an alarmed Natty put it, "if the London Office is closed pure and simple,
the De Beers Co. would be a Wernher Beit Co. and ultimately he would acquire the
control and you would know absolutely nothing now [about] whatever takes
place."[197]

It was nevertheless the Rothschilds' reduced role in the financing of the Boer War
which was the most ominous development. Just over a decade before, at the time of
the Goschen conversion and the Barings crisis, N. M. Rothschild had seemed as
financially dominant as ever. Now the dawn of a new century had brought the first
unambiguous indication that the Rothschilds' dominance was coming to an end.
Did the Rothschilds themselves sense this? There is one telling piece of evidence to
suggest that perhaps they did. On New Year's eve at the end of December 1900,
there was, as Edward Hamilton recorded in his diary,

> a Rothschild gathering at Mentmore to see the 19th century out. I think
> we mustered 24 in all—R. [Rosebery] & his 3 unmarried children, the
> Crewes, Natty & his two sons, the Leos & their three boys, the Arthur
> Sassoons . . . Rosebery after dinner proposed "prosperity to the House of
> Rothschild" in a touching little speech, which elicited tears from Natty
> and Leo.[198]

TWELVE

Finances and Alliances
(1885–1906)

At the present moment, [Alfred] is suffering from megalomania, the German Emperor having offered him a high decoration for the part he had played in establishing a better feeling between England and Germany.
SCHOMBERG MCDONNELL TO LORD SALISBURY, JANUARY 1899[1]

No doubt politics and finance often go hand in hand . . .
LORD ROTHSCHILD[2]

The history of Europe between 1870 and 1914 has often been written as a history of imperial rivalry, leading to the formation of a polarised alliance system and ultimately a calamitous war. Yet there are reasons to be sceptical about this narrative. For if there was a war which imperialism should have caused it was the war between Britain and Russia which failed to break out in the 1870s and 1880s; or the war between Britain and France which failed to break out in the 1880s or 1890s. These three powers were, after all, the real imperial rivals, coming into repeated conflict with one another from Constantinople to Kabul (in the case of Britain and Russia), from the Sudan to Siam (in the case of Britain and France). Few contemporaries would have predicted they would end up fighting a war on the same side.

Nor should it be assumed that there were insuperable forces generating an ultimately lethal "Anglo-German antagonism." Indeed, from the Rothschilds' point of view, precisely the opposite outcome seemed not only desirable but possible: an Anglo-German understanding (if not an outright alliance) seemed a logical response to the imperial differences between Britain, France and Russia. There is always a strong temptation for the historian to be condescending to diplomatic intitiatives that fail, by assuming or seeking to prove that they were bound to do so. The efforts to secure some kind of understanding between Britain and Germany in the years before the outbreak of the First World War have very frequently been the object of such condescension. The fact that Alfred de Rothschild played such an important role in trying to broker an Anglo-German alliance has only encouraged the tendency to dismiss the enterprise as futile. As we have seen, Alfred was not greatly admired by his contemporaries, and his reputation as a dilettante has inclined later writers to assume that everything he did lacked seriousness—as if he genuinely imagined that an alliance could be achieved "by the simple expedient of inviting Chamberlain and Hatzfeldt (or Eckardstein) to dinner."[3] The role of Baron Hermann von Eckardstein, the first secretary at the German embassy, has also tended to be discounted by historians, following the disparaging remarks of contemporaries like Edward Hamilton, who dismissed him as "a sort of unofficial go-between on Anglo-German affairs at the beck and call of the firm of Rothschild."[4] At best, the idea of an Anglo-German alliance has been seen as appealing too narrowly to the bankers of the City of London, particularly those of German and Jewish origin—a view which, of course, Germanophobe contemporaries did not hesitate to express.[5]

Yet the ultimate descent of the relationship between Britain and Germany into the disastrous war of 1914–18 should not be retrospectively "over-determined." In many ways, the arguments for some kind of understanding, if not a full alliance, were founded on common international interests. This is not to resuscitate the old argument about "missed opportunities" in Anglo-German relations which could have averted the carnage of the trenches, a line which has all too often rested on the wisdom of hindsight and unreliable memoirs; it is merely to suggest that the failure of the Anglo-German entente to develop was a more contingent than predetermined outcome—something which cannot be said of all the diplomatic combinations of the pre-1914 period.

Wars Not Fought

From the moment Egypt was occupied, Britain found herself at a diplomatic disadvantage when trying to check analogous expansion by her imperial rivals. In one case, that of Germany, there was no real attempt to do so; but in the case of Russia and France British diplomacy was less pliant.

The German Chancellor's map of Africa was, as he said, subordinate to his map of Europe; nevertheless, he enjoyed pretending (as his son told Gladstone) that "there is and can be no quarrel about Egypt if colonial matters are amicably settled." Natty relayed a similar message from the German ambassador Count Paul von Hatzfeldt to Randolph Churchill in September 1886.[6] The obvious place to look for colonial compensations was in sub-Saharan Africa, where the Belgian King Leopold II had established a vast private empire through his International Association of the Congo. British interests lay further south, but it seemed prudent to establish some kind of indirect strategic foothold by encouraging the reliably Anglophile Portuguese to claim some territory in the Lower Congo: it was the Rothschilds' tacit approval of this strategy which disinclined them to assist Leopold in his activities.[7] Beginning in 1884, Bismarck used Egypt as the pretext for a series of audacious German interventions in the region, menacing Britain with a Franco-German "League of Neutrals" in Africa, asserting German control over Angra Pequena in South-West Africa and claiming all the territory between Cape Colony and Portuguese West Africa. The British response was to appease Germany by accepting the South-West African colony and conceding further territorial acquisitions in the

Cameroons and East Africa. The issue of Zanzibar raised by Hatzfeldt in 1886 was typical: Germany had no economic interest worth talking about in Zanzibar (and indeed exchanged it for Heligoland in the North Sea in 1890); but it was worth asking for such territory so long as Britain was embarrassed by her position in Egypt.

There were at least two regions where Russia could legitimately stake comparable claims: in Central Asia and the Balkans. In neither case was it entirely credible for Britain to resist. For this reason, the Rothschilds were inclined to press for a British policy of conciliation and concession—despite their own growing hostility towards the anti-Semitic Tsarist regime.

In April 1885, in the dying days of Gladstone's second ministry, an Anglo-Russian conflict threatened to break out following the Russian victory over Afghan forces at Penjdeh. Natty at once sought to avert war by sounding out (at Reginald Brett's suggestion) the Russian ambassador Count de Staal. When Staal asked what Britain would be "satisfied" with as the basis for a diplomatic compromise, Natty suggested "the immediate recall of the Russian forces from the debated country," but added: "Do this, and you will get a boundary line not unlike the one which you Russians have drawn for yourselves." Staal duly responded with a proposal of this sort to Brett, who forwarded it to Gladstone. Usually sceptical about Natty's initiatives, even Edward Hamilton had to admit that it was "something to have got anything out of the Russian Embassy, however unofficially it may be put forward."[8] In classic Rothschild fashion, Natty sought to accelerate the process of pacification by inviting Staal to dine with a group of Liberal and Tory politicians, among them Harcourt, now Home Secretary, Brett, Drummond Wolff and the rising Conservative star Arthur Balfour.[9] When Churchill took over the India Office in the summer of 1885, he hastened to tell him the good news that the Russians wished to settle the Afghan frontier issue, and Churchill was able to announce an agreement in a typically flamboyant speech at Sheffield on September 3.[10] This, however, was premature. No sooner had the Liberals returned to office in January 1886 than Alfred had to warn Rosebery that:

> affairs in Afghanistan are looking very bad for England. The Russians have completely got round the Afghans and . . . the position of the English Boundary Commission is one of actual danger. The Afghans are openly hostile to us and whilst our Commission is almost unguarded the Russians have 30,000 men close at hand and are pushing on their railway as fast as possible.[11]

The crisis abated once again, but the Rothschilds continued to keep a close watch on the North-Western frontier. Indeed, in 1888 Edmond travelled under Russian escort to Samarkand, ostensibly to look into "commercial conditions" but more probably to assess the extent of the Russian military threat to Kabul.[12]

It was a similar story when a crisis blew up over Bulgaria in 1885. To the Rothschilds, there seemed no very good reason for Britain to get mixed up in the affairs of Bulgaria at this time of growing diplomatic isolation. If Britain had a right to run the affairs of Egypt, then Russia had every right to prevent the Bulgarian King Alexander from unifying Bulgaria and Eastern Rumelia on his own terms, as he sought to do in September 1885. The only reasons for opposing Russian intervention were dynastic (one of Queen Victoria's daughters was married to Alexander's brother Henry) and moralistic (the fate of the Bulgarians had been an emotive issue since Gladstone's atrocitarian campaign, and the Russian kidnapping of Alexander aroused fresh indignation). Though Natty accepted the need to "keep the Prince of Bulgaria on the throne and keep the minor states like Serbia from helping themselves," he immediately discerned that Russia meant "to meddle in the Balkans."[13] His attitude, in essence, was that Britain should tolerate this.

In this, Natty was at one with Bismarck; and in many ways the Rothschilds' interest in the project of Anglo-German rapprochement has its origins in this period. Writing to Randolph Churchill in September 1886, he evidently relished relaying the German ambassador Hatzfeldt's objections to British policy over Bulgaria:

> [H]e said here you are illogical and by your want of logic are running great risks. Your statesmen and yr press say you have no direct interest in the Danube or the Balkan Peninsula, you recognise Russia's rights and you ask her not to interfere in Egypt and to remain within her sphere in Asia but today our agent in Sophia renews his telegrams that Sir [Frank] Lascelles [the consul-general in Bulgaria] is continually and continuously intriguing and manoeuvring against Russia, if this goes on you may be astonished at finding your hands forced in different parts of the world. Your conduct in Bulgaria is inexplicable[,] we shall not and cannot support such a policy and you must not be astonished if to bother you Russia listened to France.[14]

Churchill, Natty evidently hoped, would take a more Bismarckian line than the Foreign Secretary Lord Iddesleigh (as Stafford Northcote had become). When the latter—variously dismissed by Natty as an "old goat" and a "cackling . . . old hen"—sent Alexander Condie Stephen to New Court to request a £400,000 loan for the anti-Russian regime at Sofia, Natty was incredulous. "[N]aturally I refused," he told Churchill; "was there ever such folly?" Churchill responded by blocking Stephen's appointment as envoy to Sofia (even sending a telegraph to Salisbury in Foreign Office cipher signed "Iddesleigh").[15] To reinforce the argument for passivity, Natty went so far as to relay (via Balfour to Salisbury) Hatzfeldt's warning of a possible German attack on France—the implication being that a simultaneous Anglo-Russian conflict would risk a general war.[16] Natty's letters to Reginald Brett and Rosebery after the Liberals came back in took the same line: Russian policy in Bulgaria should be tolerated—and increasingly Natty justified this argument with reference to the wishes of Germany. Bismarck, he told Rosebery in November, was "put out with the French for pushing themselves forward as the protectors of Russia in Bulgaria." A month later, he reported that Bismarck had "isolated France and I should not be in the least astonished if he made England and Russia staunch friends." "My own belief," he concluded the following February, "is that there will be no war . . . France has been flirting with Russia. The result as anyone could have foreseen is that Bismarck will let Russia do what she likes in the Balkans."[17]

Not for the last time, the Rothschild hope that Britain and Germany could cooperate was not fulfilled. This was partly because it suited Salisbury better to negotiate a new Triple Entente with Italy and Austria to preserve the status quo in the Mediterranean and the Black Sea. Though an unimpressive pair of allies for Britain, this sufficed to deter Russia from drastic action when a new Bulgarian king was elected who was also distantly related to English royalty (he was Ferdinand of Saxe-

Coburg, the son of one of Prince Albert's cousins) but, more important, had an Austro-Hungarian military background. At the same time, so Salisbury argued, the Triple Entente created an indirect link to Berlin through the German Triple Alliance, of which Italy and Austria were also members. It was an uneasy equilibrium, which logically implied (despite all Bismarck's efforts to preserve some vestige of the Three Emperors' League) a Russo-French rapprochement, though it remained to be seen how easy that would be to achieve and whether its existence would reinforce or weaken the case for Anglo-German co-operation.

Of all the other imperial powers, it was France which reacted most aggressively to the British takeover in Egypt: indeed, in many ways it was the Anglo-French antagonism which was the most important feature of the diplomatic scene in the 1880s and 1890s. As in the past, this was more awkward for the Rothschilds than any other international division for the obvious reason that the two Rothschild houses which still worked closely together were in London and Paris. But it was not easy to see what could be done. In 1886, at the time of the French expedition to Tonkin in Indo-China,[18] the French Rothschilds uneasily predicted to Herbert von Bismarck "that the next European war will be between England and France."[19] They hoped briefly that the return of Rosebery as Foreign Secretary in 1892 might improve matters; but it rapidly became apparent that, despite his reluctance to confirm Britain's anti-French Mediterranean agreements with Austria and Italy, Rosebery was inclined to continue the previous government's Francophobe policy. He was dismayed by rumours (which were vehemently repudiated by the French Rothschilds) that France intended some kind of takeover of Siam following a naval confrontation on the River Mekong in July 1893.[20] And the following January, Rosebery responded to Austrian worries about Russian designs on the Straits by assuring the Austrian ambassador that he "would not recoil from the danger of involving England in a war with Russia," adding that, if France sided with Russia, "we should require the assistance of the Triple Alliance to hold France in check."[21]

Predictably, it was Egypt and her southern neighbour the Sudan which proved the main cause of Anglo-French antagonism—so much so that a war between England and France seemed a real possibility in 1895. As we have seen, Rosebery tipped off the Rothschilds about the government's intention to reinforce the Egyptian garrison in January 1893. In January and February 1894, Alfred reciprocated by passing on to Rosebery alarming reports they had received about the growing mood of hostility to British rule in Cairo.[22] It was now increasingly apparent that the French government intended to make some kind of bid for control of Fashoda on the Upper Nile. Fearful that French control of Fashoda would compromise the British position in Egypt, Rosebery—who became Prime Minister in March—hastily concluded an agreement with the King of the Belgians to lease the area south of Fashoda to the Belgian Congo in return for a strip of the Western Congo, with the obvious intention of blocking French access to Fashoda. In the difficult negotiations which ensued, the French Rothschilds sought to mediate, assuring their English cousins that the French government was not "full of Anglophobes," but warning them that British policy in Africa seemed intolerably "aggressive" in Paris.[23] It was no use: attempts by the French Foreign Minister Gabriel Hanotaux to reach some kind of compromise over Fashoda failed and when an expedition led by the French explorer Marchand set off for the Upper Nile, Rosebery's Under-Secretary at the

Foreign Office, Sir Edward Grey, denounced it as "an unfriendly act." It was at this critical moment (June 1895) that Rosebery resigned, leaving Britain in a position of unprecedented diplomatic isolation.

Fortunately for the incoming Salisbury government, the contemporaneous defeat of Italy by the Abyssinian forces at Adowa took the wind out of French sails, for reasons which Natty spelt out to McDonnell for Salisbury's consideration. "The French are in desperate alarm lest the defeat of Italy should lead to a revival of the Three Emperors' Alliance," he argued, "the French Government [is therefore] too weak to give us any real trouble." But he warned Salisbury that "if the powers combined to reopen the question of evacuation [of Egypt], it would be impossible for the Government to resist."[24] This was an encouragement to act swiftly. Exactly a week later, the order was given to reconquer the Sudan.[25] When Hanotaux's successor Théophile Delcassé reacted to Kitchener's victory over the Sudanese dervishes at Omdurman by occupying Fashoda, the Rothschilds egged Salisbury on to call the French bluff. Kitchener should be ordered to "to take Marchand prisoner," Natty told McDonnell in September. At the height of the crisis two months later, Alfred assured him "that the French will yield and that there will be no war. He thinks," added McDonnell, "the French army [is] in a very rotten state; but has a great opinion of the French navy . . . (this is a pious opinion which Lord R[othschild] thinks is nonsense). *M. de Staal* [the Russian ambassador] also told Lord R. this morning that he thought there would be no war."[26]

Did Natty consciously put British strategic interests in Egypt ahead of his Paris cousins' sensibilities? Possibly; but a more plausible explanation is that the French Rothschilds were, as in 1882, content to see British dominance in Egypt asserted, even at the expense of French pride. There is no evidence that Alphonse favoured Delcassé's confrontational strategy. In any case, the Rothschilds knew enough to recognise the weakness of the French position. As the Russian ambassador indicated to Natty during the Fashoda crisis, St Petersburg would never support Paris on African issues—any more than Paris would support St Petersburg over the Black Sea Straits.

Fashoda is of interest because it reminds us of a war between the great powers which did not happen, but might have. Similarly, it is important to remember that in 1895 and 1896 both Britain and Russia toyed with the idea of using their navies to force the Straits and assert their direct control over Constantinople. In the event, neither side was sufficiently sure of its naval power to risk such a step; but had it been attempted, a diplomatic crisis as serious as that of 1878 would have been almost unavoidable. Here too there was an unrealised war, this time between Britain and Russia. If nothing else, all this goes to show that, if we are to explain why a war eventually broke out in which Britain, France and Russia fought on the same side, imperialism is unlikely to provide an answer.

The Franco–Russian Entente

Of all the diplomatic combinations which arose in this period, the Franco-Russian entente was the most logical both strategically and economically. France and Russia had common foes: Germany between them and Britain all around them. Moreover, France was a capital exporter, while industrialising Russia was hungry for foreign loans. Indeed, French diplomats and bankers began to discuss the possibility of a Franco-Russian entente based on French loans as early 1880.[27]

Nevertheless, it is important to realise how many obstacles there were to such an alignment. There were, to begin with, financial difficulties. Recurrent instability on the Paris bourse—the Union Générale crisis of 1882 was followed by the failure of the Comptoir d'Escompte in 1889 and the Panama Canal crisis in 1893—cast doubt on France's basic capacity to cope with large scale Russian operations. On the Russian side too there were problems. It was only in 1894–7 that the rouble was finally put on the gold standard, so that exchange fluctuations further complicated negotiations up until that point.[28] The bond markets also remained wary of Russian bonds. The price of Russian 5 per cents oscillated with unusual rapidity in the 1880s, dropping sharply at the end of 1886, recovering in the first half of 1887, then falling again to a nadir of 89.75 in early 1888, only to leap up to a peak of 104.25 in May 1889. There was another steep drop in 1891, however. Between March and November, the new 4 per cent Russians fell over 10 per cent from 100.25 to just 90. It was only after that crisis that a steady appreciation set in, culminating in August 1898 (105) (see illustration 12.i).

There were also serious diplomatic difficulties in the way of a Franco-Russian alliance. Firstly, Bismarck's diplomacy appeared, at least outwardly, to hinge on maintaining the links between Germany, Austria and Russia which he had first forged in the Three Emperors' Alliance. The rise of General Boulanger served to rekindle Franco-German animosity, but it did not lead Russia to side with France: the Russian ambassador in Berlin, Count Peter Shuvalov, merely spoke of Russian neutrality in the event of a war between Germany and France. The Russian objective in the early 1880s was to separate Germany and Austria–Hungary, not to risk alienating Bismarck for the sake of France. The secret Reinsurance Treaty signed between Germany and Russia in June 1887 may have been practically meaningless (it guaranteed Russian neutrality unless Germany attacked France and German neutrality unless Russia attacked Austria); but it at least indicated a desire in both Berlin and St Petersburg to maintain some sort of diplomatic connection. Moreover, as mentioned already, there were important limits to what France and Russia could offer one another. France was never willing to back Russian policy with respect to Turkey; Russia was never willing to back French policy in the Sudan.

Finally, there were political obstacles, and not just because of the obvious difference between Republican France and Tsarist Russia. The assassination of the "Tsar Liberator" Alexander II in March 1881 and the accession of his reactionary son Alexander III led to a marked deterioration in the treatment of the Empire's four million Jews, most of whom continued to be confined to the so-called Pale of Permanent Settlement in Poland and western Russia. Under Alexander II there had been some relaxation in the restrictions on Jewish residence and occupation; but a wave of pogroms in 1881 and 1882 encouraged the Tsar and his new ministers in the belief that "the people" had to be protected from the "pernicious activity" of the "in many ways harmful" Jews. In the wake of the May Laws of 1882, which imposed new restrictions on where Jews could live and the business they could do, there was a sustained campaign against them. Educational opportunity, the right to own land, access to the professions, the right to reside in villages or outside the

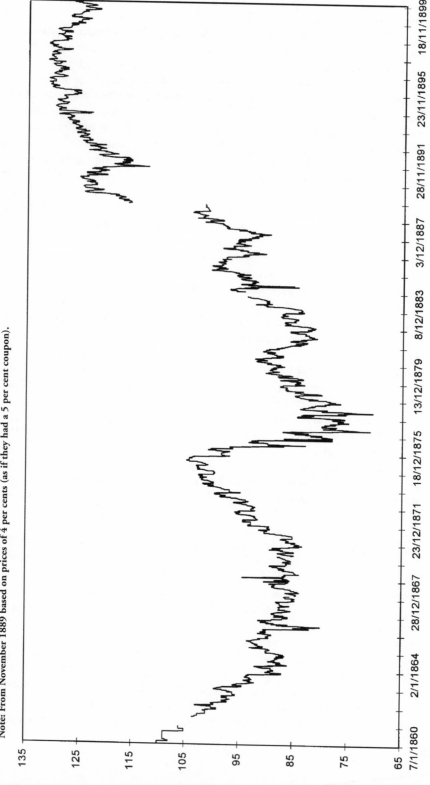

12.i: The weekly closing price of Russian 5 per cents, 1860–1900.

Note: From November 1889 based on prices of 4 per cents (as if they had a 5 per cent coupon).

Pale—all were curtailed. Jews responded in various ways: around two million emigrated, as we have seen. Among those who remained, most struggled on as best they could, but some were attracted by the revolutionary politics of organisations like the Socialist Revolutionaries, the Social Democrats and the specifically Jewish Bund: enough to convince Tsarist ministers that they were right to regard the Jews as a menace. When new pogroms occurred at Kishinev in 1903 and more generally in 1905—accompanied by the kind of ritual-murder claims which had sparked off the Damascus affair more than sixty years before—there was enough evidence of official indifference, if not complicity, to confirm the impression abroad that the Tsarist regime was the most anti-Semitic in the world.

The Rothschilds were dismayed by all this. As early as May 1881, the Austrian, French and British partners began to discuss what practical steps could be taken "on behalf of our unfortunate co-religionists."[29] The marriage of Alphonse's daughter to the Russian Jewish banker Maurice Ephrussi may have served to increase their interest in this question. Thus it was rumoured in diplomatic circles that the Rothschilds had secured the dismissal of the French ambassador in St Petersburg, Appert, when he informed the new Madame Ephrussi that she would not be considered presentable at court by the Tsar.[30] What made Rothschild Russophobia matter was that de Rothschild Frères were still regarded by other French banks (and indeed by the Russian Finance Minister) as the Russian government's preferred agent in Paris, without whom no major operation could be assured of success.[31] When Shuvalov informally approached the Paris house in 1882 on behalf of the Finance Minister Bunge, Gustave did not beat about the bush: "[W]e can but reply that we wish for nothing more than to conclude a financial operation with the Russian Government, however we are unable to do so in view of the persecution of our Russian co-religionists."[32] That was to be a more or less constant refrain from the London partners too in the coming years.

This explains the limited success of Elie de Cyon (alias Ilya Fadeyevich Tsion), a Russian Jew of strongly Germanophobe views who sought to act as a go-between between the French and Russian governments at a time when rumours of a German attack on Boulangist France were at their height. His aim, as he later described it, was to achieve Russia's "economic emancipation from Germany and the transfer of the market in Russian bonds to Paris." Although he found the Tsar's adviser Michael Katkov sceptical about the danger of war when he visited him in Febraury 1887 (on the ground that Bismarck's sabre-rattling was merely an electoral ploy), Cyon aroused his interest by communicating "the result of my discussions with several representatives of the Parisian *haute banque*, who were all very well disposed [towards Russia]." His trump card, as he thought, was that:

> one of the Rothschilds brothers, with whom I had long conversation on the subject towards the end of January, [had] once again assured me that their house was always at the service of our [Russia's] ministry of finance, [and was ready] to resume the relations which had been forcibly interrupted twelve years before, at the moment when France was obliged to devote all her capital to her own internal needs.[33]

Cyon then made a similar claim to the new Russian Finance Minister I. A. Vyshnegradsky, who expressed doubts about the likelihood of "obtaining the co-operation of the house of Rothschild, without which the Paris market did not have much value." Vyshnegradsky intimated that until he had convincing evidence of Roth-schild goodwill—he suggested the Paris house might offer to convert the mortgage bonds issued by the Russian Crédit Foncier—he was unwilling to make a direct gov-ernmental approach to the rue Laffitte.[34] According to Cyon's account, he then returned to Paris and began negotiating along these lines with the Rothschilds, talks which were ultimately crowned with success. Although in April—at the peak of the Boulanger crisis—Katkov informed him that the terms being discussed were unac-ceptable, Cyon rushed back to St Petersburg and secured the government's approval. On May 5 Vyshnegradsky and an unnamed Rothschild representative signed an agreement reducing the interest on mortgage bonds totalling around 108 million marks.[35] Cyon later published a letter from the Paris house congratulating him on his achievement, and expressing "satisfaction that we have felt at being able to profit from this occasion to renew direct relations with the Russian Imperial Minister of Finance."[36]

The significance of Cyon's activities should not be exaggerated, however. While he protested his altruistic motives, the Rothschilds themselves regarded him as "a man of dubious honorability" and commented shrewdly: "Nothing proves that he did not begin by presenting himself there in our name just as he presents himself here in the name of the minister, by virtue of a dual mandate which he has volun-tarily taken upon himself."[37] More to the point, Cyon very probably misrepresented in his memoir the nature of the mortgage bond operation. It must be remembered that the months of April and May 1887 witnessed the culmination of the Boulanger crisis. It is apparent even from Cyon's own account that Bismarck, recognising what was afoot, sought to interfere in his negotiations. Nor was Cyon able to conclude the deal without securing the consent of Bleichröder in Berlin: after all, the original mortgage bonds had been floated by Bleichröder, not by the Rothschilds, though the Paris house had taken a share in the issue.[38] Given that more of the mortgage bonds were in German hands than in French, Cyon had really done nothing more than secure Rothschild approval of a transaction which was between Berlin and St Petersburg. This was easily given as it meant nothing; it did not represent the deci-sive shift of Russian finance to Paris. What is more, when that shift began to happen in September 1887, the Rothschilds were not involved.

It was a financial reorientation which was encouraged by the low price of Russian bonds and propelled by Bismarck's decision to prohibit their use as collateral for Reichsbank loans (the famous "Lombardverbot"). The striking thing—*pace* Cyon—is that, far from leading the Paris market, the Rothschilds followed it at some dis-tance. It was a syndicate of rival banks including Mallet and Hottinguer which proposed creating a French bank in St Petersburg.[39] The first major loan floated for the imperial government—for 500 million francs—was underwritten by a syndicate of deposit banks including the Banque Paribas, the Crédit Lyonnais, the Comptoir d'Escompte and Herman Hoskier of the British firm Brown, Shipley.[40] This occurred in the autumn of 1888, by which time the rise of Russian bonds seemed well established.

What made the French Rothschilds change their minds about Russia? From an early stage they had admitted that it would be harder for them to take positive action in response to Russian anti-Semitism (beyond assisting Russian Jews to emigrate) than for their English cousins. The problem was partly, as Gustave explained, that religious "intolerance" was a more delicate subject in France than in England, because of the efforts of the Republican government to restrict clerical influence over education; in addition, however, he and his brothers had to take into consideration "our Government['s] relations with the Russian Government."[41] The French Rothschilds may also have been more susceptible to the argument which the Russians themselves liked to advance, that "there might be some reasonable improvement in this question of the Jews inside Russia and that . . . our attitude respecting the financial operations with the Russian Government could contribute to such an improvement."[42] Secondly, the fall of Boulanger in May 1887 and the Republican victory in the 1889 elections seemed to be the harbinger of a more stable period in French politics.[43] Thirdly, Alphonse had been genuinely alarmed in early 1888 by Bismarck's attempts (as he put it) to build a "golden bridge for Russia, in order to break up, if not the alliance, at least the existing friendship presently between our country and Russia." If anything was calculated to change his attitude towards Russia, it was the prospect of "a quadruple alliance of England, Russia, Germany and Austria" which would leave France out in the cold.[44] Finally, there were strictly financial reasons for a change of policy. The crisis on the French market caused by the crash of the Comptoir d'Escompte enhanced the Rothschilds' reputation in Russia: it appeared to be Alphonse who had intervened at the Banque de France to avert a complete collapse. The bonds which the Russian government now proposed to convert into 4 per cent paper had mainly been issued through the Rothschilds in the early 1870s. Under these circumstances, it is not wholly surprising that the Paris house agreed to undertake two major Russian bond issues in 1889 with a total face value of some £77 million. Rather less easily explained is the readiness of the London house to join in these operations, and to take a share in a third £12 million issue in 1890.[45]

True to past form, this new Rothschild–Russian connection was to prove a highly unstable one. Right away there was controversy in St Petersburg about the terms of the first loan: had Vyshnegradsky agreed to excessively generous terms in return for a private share of the business? As Girault has shown, the cost of the 1889 loan to the Russian Treasury was indeed slightly higher than that of the non-Rothschild loan the previous year; on the other hand, by reducing the margin between the price they paid for the bonds and the price at which they sold them to the public, the Rothschilds were able to attract more subscribers. Similarly, Vyshnegradsky's "cut" was in reality intended for Hoskier, who had arranged the 1888 loan and insisted on being involved again.[46] It is also worth bearing in mind that some German bankers, notably Bleichröder and Hansemann, acted as more or less equal partners in what was effectively a syndicate, so that the idea of a straightforward switch of Russian borrowing from Berlin to Paris is misleading. Indeed, the second loan of 1889 seems to have been initiated by the Germans—prematurely in the eyes of Alphonse—and by 1891 Bleichröder was keenly anticipating another major loan (of around £24 million) in which he expected to take a substantial share.[47]

Having re-established their financial links to St Petersburg, the Rothschilds now sought to exert pressure on the Russian government by renewing their criticism of its anti-Jewish policies. In May 1891 the French house unexpectedly withdrew from negotiations leading up to the issue of the new loan which Bleichröder had been anticipating.[48] At the time, it was assumed in the Russian press that this was because "Messrs Rothschild of Paris [had] made certain demands upon the Russian Government regarding the Jews of Russia" and had pulled out when these were rejected. According to one newspaper, there had been "a strong pressure" on Alphonse "by the Israelite and Judaeophile party in England which, as it appears, has been irritated by certain administrative measures taken in Russian towards a portion of the Israelite population."[49] It has been suggested that this was merely a pretext: the real aim was not to force the Russian government to treat Russian Jews better, but to agree to a more binding military alliance with France than had hitherto been contemplated in St Petersburg.[50] Another possibility is that the French premier Ribot regarded the Rothschild syndicate as too "German" precisely because of Bleichröder's involvement.[51] If either of these interpretations were true, it would be a classic illustration of the persistence of Rothschild financial power in the sphere of international relations. On close inspection, however, neither is persuasive.

In the first place, there were a number of non-financial reasons for closer Franco-Russian ties, not least the increasingly unfriendly attitude of the German government following the accession of William II in 1888 and the dismissal of Bismarck two years later. The assurances of William and the new Chancellor Caprivi that Germany would support Austria in the event of a war with Russia and their blunt refusal to renew the secret Reinsurance Treaty made financial inducements superfluous: logically, France and Russia were likely to gravitate towards one another, even if the Russian Foreign Minister Giers was in less of a hurry to conclude a binding military alliance than the Tsar himself.

Secondly, the Rothschilds' sense of outrage at the Russian government's continuing anti-Semitism seems to have been as genuine as ever. In August 1890 Natty's son Walter wrote to Bleichröder urging him to "use your powerful influence at St. Petersburg to prevent the Government from putting into force the old cruel and senseless laws . . . which are so harsh and oppressive that they may be the cause of many Jews becoming violent Nihilists."[52] It may be that Vyshnegradsky had made some kind of promise that the persecution of the Jews would be eased and that his failure to honour this was genuinely taken amiss.[53] For their part, the London Rothschilds felt that "Alphonse could not have done otherwise" in view of the "mediaeval barbarities" which had been committed.[54] Nor is there any reason to doubt Edmond's sincerity when he decried "the never ending horrors to which our poor co-religionists are subjected in Russia."[55] In another private letter to his London cousins, Alphonse likened Alexander III's religious intolerance to that of Louis XIV and Philip II of Spain and expressed deep scepticism about the attempt by the arch-reactionary Konstantin Pobedonostsev to strike a more conciliatory note in September 1892.[56] It is hard to believe that the Russian and French press would have overlooked a diplomatic significance to the Rothschilds' withdrawal from the 1891 loan if there had been any; instead there was agreement that the religious issue was the cause of the breach.

Finally, the Rothschilds had strictly financial reasons for blowing hot and cold towards Russia. The large short-term deposits of Russian gold with the London house during the Barings crisis in 1890, for example, obliged the English partners to be circumspect in their political criticisms; by 1891 that constraint had been removed.[57] The growing investments of the French Rothschilds in the Russian oil industry also need to be taken into account. Indeed, Girault has suggested that it was really disagreements about Russian trade policy—specifically its protective tariffs on imports of rails and its new tax on oil exports—which led the Rothschilds to pull out of the 1891 loan.[58] The catastrophic Russian famine of 1891, which was at least to some degree exacerbated by Vyshnegradsky's policies, may have played a part too. Above all, it is important to notice that the renewed slump in Russian bond prices predated the Rothschild withdrawal from the loan by over a month. That in itself provides a plausible explanation for the decision.

If there was a political subtext to the 1891 "incident" it related to French domestic politics and the difficulties of the Panama Canal Company, which helped to topple the Ribot government later the following year. The Rothschilds had kept a safe distance from the Panama affair, as we have seen; but there is some evidence to suggest they also viewed with hostility the far from disinterested efforts of Ribot to keep it afloat.[59] The diplomatic significance of this governmental crisis in France was that it delayed the ratification of a Franco-Russian military convention, under which Russia agreed to assist France in the event of German aggression, until the beginning of 1894. Continuing political instability in France acted as an impediment to diplomatic convergence. Alphonse himself expressed pessimism to Witte's agent Raffalovich about the ability of the French market to continue its support of Russia if the government continued with its protectionist policy and tax increases.[60]

It was the appointment of Witte as Finance Minister which persuaded the Rothschilds to resume financial relations with Russia. Once again the treatment of the Jews was a key issue. In October 1892 the German ambassador in Paris, Count Münster, gave an assessment which may not have been far wide of the mark:

> Whereas I have hitherto always assumed that His Majesty the Emperor of Russia will never bind himself to the Democratic Republic, or enter into a treaty of alliance, I am now no longer quite certain whether some agreements have not been entered into. The Rothschilds, who have so far always asserted that nothing of the kind existed, no longer so definitely deny this; and they have suddenly changed their attitude towards Russia and are negotiating a 500,000,000 [franc] loan. The Rothschilds who have so far been Royalists, have approached the Republic, and are now hand in glove with the Government whereby they regain their influence. The prospect of making a profit and, according to Alphonse Rothschild, the hope of attaining better conditions for the Jews in Russia, have induced the House here to enter into negotiations for a loan . . . That the wife of the new Finance Minister, Witte, whom Russian ladies here have described to me as being an intelligent and very intriguing Jewess, is of great help in bringing about an understanding with the Jewish bankers, seems to me to be not improbable. The Paris Bourse is afraid of being overshadowed by the Bourse of Berlin, and the big Jews believe that if they can earn money they can best help the small Jews, with the result that although the French market is saturated with Russian securities, the French give their good francs for bad roubles.[61]

The fact that the Rothschilds privately alluded to the Jewish origins of Witte's wife lends credibility to this interpretation.[62] However, there were once again economic considerations at work. The loan which Münster heard discussed in 1892 did not in fact come off, and it was not until 1894 that the Rothschild-led syndicate issued a 3.5 per cent loan worth around £16 million (400 million francs).[63] This was followed by a 3 per cent loan for the same amount in 1896, for which Alphonse was awarded the Grand Cross.[64] By that time, the rise in Russian funds was beginning to look sustainable, though the second loan was only placed with investors slowly— even with the timely assistance of a visit by the Tsar to Paris.[65] The Rothschilds may also have been attracted by Witte's stated objective of putting Russia on to the gold standard, which accorded with their global interests in gold mining and refining. Indeed, there had been talk at New Court in 1891 of making an approach to Baron Gunzberg, the owner of the Lena gold mines.[66]

There remains, however, a paradox. Confidential Rothschild correspondence shows that the London house participated in the 1894 loan and did not oppose the 1896 loan.[67] Yet Münster and others had the strong impression that "the London House [would] have nothing to do with" Russian finance, an impression which was strongly confirmed five years later. To Münster, this was merely a proof of "how cunning these great Jews are. They always have a back door open." More recently, historians have tended to argue that the British Rothschilds felt more strongly on the question of their co-religionists' rights than the French.[68] The archival evidence, nevertheless, suggests that more subtle considerations were involved. Essentially, the Rothschilds drew a distinction between Franco-Russian rapprochement, which they favoured, and Anglo-Russian rapprochement, which they were against. This might seem contradictory, but it was in many ways a rational application of the principle of the balance of power. In Natty's eyes, an alliance between France and Russia might be acceptable; but its corollary was some kind of understanding between Britain and Germany. This explains the hostility he and his brothers expressed towards Russia when Witte was considering the possibility of floating a loan in London.

This initiative originated in the fatigue of the Paris market. As we have seen, the price of Russian bonds peaked in August 1898 and when Witte visited Paris later that summer Alphonse indicated that he would be unwilling to contemplate a new Russian loan in the face of rising yields across the board.[69] This refusal was made after consultation with Natty, who in turn had asked Salisbury, observing that "it would neither be in accordance with the interest nor the inclination of Ld. Rothschild to encourage M. de Witte, unless Y[our] L[ordship] thought it desirable that he should do so." In a reply which perfectly illustrates how the bond market and diplomacy interacted, Salisbury agreed:

> that, as matters stand, it is not in our interest to encourage the borrow-
> ing operations of Monsieur de Witte. But it may by some unforeseen
> turn of events, become so: & therefore it would not be prudent to show
> reluctance to help him too manifestly. The most useful condition to
> bring him to is a belief that he has still a chance of getting our assis-
> tance.[70]

This hint was duly taken, and in January 1899 the Russians broached the idea of a loan in London.

To understand the Rothschild response to this approach, it is necessary to bear in mind the role of Germany, whose policy towards Russia was in a state of flux at this period. Despite the anti-Russian signals of the early Wilhelmine years, the German banks had been positively encouraged by the German Foreign Office to participate in the 1894 and 1896 Russian loans, precisely in order to prevent a French monopoly on Russian finance.[71] Indeed, by 1898 the German government was beginning to think in terms of a return to the Russo-German option. Thus, when the idea of a Russian loan in London was floated in 1899, it was closely linked to a parallel suggestion of a diplomatic deal between Russia and Germany, the implication being that, if Britain refused to lend to Russia, she should turn to Berlin. The dilemma for the Rothschilds was acute: on the one hand, they were against an Anglo-Russian rapprochement, but nor did they wish to see Berlin and St Petersburg reconciled in such a way that their own pet scheme for Anglo-German rapprochement fell by the wayside. This explains why the proposal split the London partners along lines summarised by McDonnell for Salisbury:

> The question will then arise whether or not the English market shall be permitted to raise a loan [of] probably £15,000,000 . . . for Russia, Mr Alfred Rothschild, who is violently Russophobe, says *No:* on no account.
>
> Lord Rothschild is less decided: he thinks that his House could make or mar such a loan: if they brought it out, it would not be particularly lucrative: and his inclination is adverse to the operation.
>
> But if the London market remains closed he is afraid that Russia may learn her own financial strength . . . [A]s a last resource [*sic*] Russia can find the money herself, though it would involve the depletion of her war chest.[72]

Natty was relieved to learn three days later that the proposed Russo-German agreement had foundered—partly, he claimed, because of the German "desire to combine with England (and possibly with America and Japan) for commercial purposes in China." He warmed to this theme a week later, gleefully reporting that "Germany meanwhile is evidently alarmed at Russia's recent proposal: she has sent a large order for Maxim guns and for quick firing field guns to Messrs Vickers of Sheffield."[73] "No one here," he told the German ambassador in May, "would think of lending them [the Russians] money which would be used for armaments directed against England, and he regarded it as certain that all the efforts by Witte and his local agents in the city would remain unsuccessful." Hatzfeldt attributed this "to the anti-Russian feeling by the family because of the Jewish question" (noting that this was not shared by other City houses); but diplomatic considerations were as important, if not more so.[74] Between August 1899 and May 1901, the Russians reverted to Paris, with Delcassé's broadening of the terms of the entente "to maintain the balance of power in Europe" reinforced by a new 4 per cent 425 million franc loan, floated by the old Rothschild-led consortium in May 1901. Again, it was symbolic of the interdependence of diplomacy and finance in the alliance system that Delcassé's visit to St Petersburg in 1899 was followed by Edmond's in 1901.[75] Hatzfeldt's report to Holstein on this loan speaks volumes for the continuing influence of the Rothschilds in international relations: "It is not easy to see how, even with the best will in the world, the French will find the necessary money, as they have already invested [so much] money in Russian bonds. But if Rothschild considers it possible, then it probably is possible." The new German Chancellor, Prince Bernhard von Bülow, noted in the margin: "Yes."[76]

Italy
The alliance between Russia and France was far from being the only diplomatic development of the pre-war decades which had a financial subtext. The case of Italy—the only other power as reliant as Russia on foreign finance to fund her deficit—was not so very different. Italy had become closely tied to the Paris capital market even before her unification, thanks to James de Rothschild's shrewd backing of Cavour and Piedmont and his ambitious schemes to link north Italy to the rest of Europe by rail. However, by the late 1880s the financial influence of France in Italy was declining relative to that of Germany. In both Paris and Berlin this tendency was seen in strongly political terms at a time when Italy was closely aligned with Germany and Austria through the Triple Alliance and at odds with France over the Mediterranean and trade policy. In July 1889, for example, the German ambassador in Rome complained that "the so-called Rothschild group" (which as usual included Bleichröder and the Disconto-Gesellschaft) had been "able to present itself as the principal group" in Italian business, despite the fact that its "relations must be called French rather than German." His hope was that a purely German group of banks led by the Deutsche Bank and the Berliner Handels-Gesellschaft would be able to take over Italy's bond-issuing business, and this was duly agreed with the Italian Prime Minister Francesco Crispi in September 1889.[77] Conversely, the French government wished de Rothschild Frères to refuse any request for financial assistance from Rome. In October 1890 there was delight at the Quai d'Orsay when Alphonse reported the following exchange between Padoa, the Rothschild agent in Rome, and the Italian Finance Minister, who had evidently been discomfited by the German group's terms for supporting the price of Italian bonds:

> The minister did not conceal the distress in which the Italian Treasury found itself. He spoke bitterly about the exigencies of the Germans and their bad faith. He demanded forcefully that the Rothschild representative should himself decide to buy secretly six million [lire of] Italian 5 per cent rentes [that is, 120 million lire nominal] from the government's pension fund. M. de Rothschild's response was negative . . . [His letter] explains that it would be impossible for him to involve himself in a clandestine operation and that unfortunately the rapprochement which seems to be developing between the two countries is not sufficiently advanced to permit a public operation.

Needless to say, the French Foreign Minister Ribot "enouraged M. de Rothschild to maintain this attitude. Our policy . . . must consist in being friendly towards Italy, not to make difficulties for her, to avoid needlessly offending her, but also not to make our bourse available to her and not to open our market to her until she has properly learnt the lesson she is learning at the moment about the benefits of the Triple Alliance."[78]

With the lira exchange rate and bond prices sliding sharply between 1890 and

1894, the French had good reason to gloat over the Italians' predicament. However, it proved harder to break the link between Rome and Berlin than Ribot had anticipated. In 1891, following Crispi's fall from power, a rather unsubtle attempt was made to woo his successor the Marquis di Rudinì. When the latter approached Padoa for a loan of 140 million lire, the suggestion was made that this would be forthcoming if Italy altered her policy over North Africa and tariffs in a pro-French sense. Rudinì recalled that his first impulse on hearing this suggestion was "to take the dirty Jew by the neck and kick him downstairs," but he restrained himself on the grounds that such conduct "would have been unbecoming in a Marquis di Rudinì."[79] The Triple Alliance with Germany and Austria was renewed three months later, and in the years up until 1896 the German role in Italian finance continued to grow at the expense of the French.[80] Partly for this reason, Alfred's claim that Italy was about to desert the Triple Alliance in 1897 was viewed with scepticism by McDonnell and Salisbury.[81]

Anglo–German Amity

If France and Russia could be brought together partly on the basis of floating Tsarist bonds on the Paris bourse, it is worth asking what economic factors might have contributed towards an Anglo-German rapprochement. An encouraging precedent seemed to be set by the 1890 agreement between Britain and Germany, which gave Britain Zanzibar in return for the North Sea island of Heligoland and a narrow strip of land affording German South-West Africa access to the Zambezi River. Nor should the failure of this and other colonial agreements to develop into an alliance be seen as leading necessarily to war.[82]

It was over China that some form of Anglo-German co-operation seemed most likely to develop. Since 1874, the date of the first foreign loan raised for Imperial China, the Chinese government's principal source of external finance had been two British firms based in Hong Kong, the Hong Kong & Shanghai Banking Corporation and Jardine, Matheson & Co.[83] The British government, in the person of Sir Robert Hart, also controlled the Imperial Maritime Customs. In March 1885, however, Alphonse heard rumours of "the great master of the world"—Bismarck—"wishing to meddle in the Chinese question."[84] The intelligence was soon confirmed when Hansemann approached New Court and the Hong Kong & Shanghai Bank with a proposal to divide Chinese government and railway finance equally between the British and German members of a new syndicate.[85] The Rothschilds had no objection to this: as Alphonse said, it was "much to be desired that the excessive growth of German activities and ambitions should be directed to the Far East and we shall not feel uneasy about their conquest in that direction."[86] The only concern at this stage was that Hansemann might aim at something more than a 50:50 partnership. Relaying information about a visit to Germany by the Chinese ambassador in London, Natty urged the Foreign Secretary Lord Iddesleigh to take "such steps as will tend to secure for English manufacturers a fair proportion of any future contracts with the Chinese Goverment."[87] Reassurance came, however, when Hansemann involved Wilhelm Carl in the negotiations which culminated with the creation of the Deutsch-Asiatische Bank in February 1889, a joint venture involving more than thirteen leading German banks including the Frankfurt house. When one of the younger Oppenheims travelled to China to investigate its economic prospects on behalf of this group, the London Rothschilds actually financed his trip.[88]

The period between 1888 and 1893 saw a series of important changes of personnel in Berlin which threw German foreign policy into confusion and put the idea of Anglo-German co-operation in China temporarily on the back-burner. The first was the succession of William II as Kaiser in 1888, following the belated death of his grandfather and the premature death of his father after just ninety-nine days on the throne. For the French Rothschilds, this was nothing less than a "nightmare" given the new Kaiser's reputation for instability and bellicosity.[89] Indeed, Gustave went so far as to make a remarkable prediction:

> Should the Emperor Frederick III die and his son Prince William ascend to the throne there would be no change of policy as long as M. von Bismarck is alive and carries on; however, should he retire voluntarily or die, it is believed that nothing could then prevent Prince William from pursuing his warlike objectives and this would mean a world war.[90]

In fact, as Alphonse anticipated, Bismarck's departure was involuntary: by March 1890 the differences between the Chancellor and the new monarch on both foreign and domestic policy could no longer be bridged and Bismarck was forced to resign.[91] "[C]apricious, adventurous and imperious, confident in his destiny," William seemed to pose a threat to a European order of which the Rothschilds had come to see Bismarck as the custodian. "[I]n the interest of world peace," Alphonse told Bleichröder, "we deeply regret his departure, because we are convinced that to a large extent its maintenance in the last years was his doing."[92] The sense of discontinuity was heightened three years later when Bleichröder himself died.[93]

It is tempting to see these anxieties as prescient, and it is undeniable that German foreign policy after 1890 became clumsy and often self-defeating in a way that it had never been under Bismarck. In the context of the 1890s, however, it would be more accurate to say that Alphonse and Gustave were tending to idealise Bismarck—who only two decades earlier had seemed to them the personification of caprice and adventure—and to demonise the Kaiser. As early as September 1891, the French partners were admitting that their fears of William had been exaggerated; in truth, the defects of Wilhelmine foreign policy may have owed as much to the influence of the excessively devious Friedrich von Holstein—the *éminence grise* at the Foreign Office—than to the Kaiser, whose power was always a good deal more institutionally circumscribed than he himself realised.[94] Nor was the death of Bleichröder an irreparable loss: as we have seen, the Rothschilds had tended to rate Hansemann above him, and the essentially diplomatic function Bleichröder had played was carried on without much interruption by Paul Schwabach.[95] It did not therefore take long for the idea of an Anglo-German overseas partnership to resurface.

As usual, the key was imperial rivalry between Britain on the one hand and France and Russia on the other. By raising the spectre of increased Russian influence in the Far East, the Japanese defeat of China in 1894 created a perfect opportunity for co-operation between Berlin and London; and as before it was the Rothschilds and Hansemann who were the driving forces. In essence, Natty and Hansemann sought to promote a partnership between the Hong Kong & Shanghai Bank and the new Deutsch-Asiatische Bank which they hoped, with suitable official backing from their respective governments, would prevent Russia from gaining an excessive influence over China. To be sure, the aspirations of the bankers were far from being the same as those of the diplomats and politicians. Holstein, for example, wanted Germany to side with Russia and France rather than with Britain, and joined in their objections to the Japanese annexation of Liaotung at Shimoneseki in April 1895. Other officials in the Wilhelmstrasse wrongly suspected the Rothschilds of wanting to exclude the German banks from the Chinese market. Nor was Ewen Cameron of the Hong Kong & Shanghai Bank convinced of the necessity of giving up his firm's traditional monopoly in Chinese finance. But events bore out the wisdom of the Hansemann–Rothschild view.[96] The announcement in May 1895 that China would finance her indemnity payment to Japan with a Russian loan of £15 million—as opposed to the multinational loan favoured by Natty and Hansemann—was, as Alphonse remarked, "a bitter pill" for both the British and German governments.[97] The loan of course could not be financed by Russia herself, given that Russia was an international debtor; in effect, it was a French loan, issued by the Banque Paribas, Crédit Lyonnais and Hottinguer, but the benefits were divided evenly between Russia and France, the former gaining the right to extend its Trans-Siberian Railway through Manchuria, the latter securing railway concessions in China. There was even a new Russo-Chinese bank, founded by the Russian banker Rothstein with predominantly French funding, and a formal Russo-Chinese alliance in May 1896.[98] The only British financial success was a £1 million gold loan issued by the Chartered Bank of India, Australia and China, which had been arranged by Ernest Cassel.[99]

In the wake of this reverse, Hansemann's proposal that the Hong Kong & Shanghai Bank should join forces with the Deutsch-Asiatische looked a good deal more attractive, and an agreement between the two banks was signed in July 1895. For Natty, the main aim of this alliance was to end competition between the great powers by putting Chinese foreign loans in the hands of a single multinational consortium, as had been done in the past for Greece and Turkey, though with an implicit Anglo-German predominance. After much diplomatic manoeuvring, this was finally achieved when a second Chinese loan (this time for £16 million) was issued in 1898.[100] There continued to be difficulties, admittedly. Natty was unable to persuade Salisbury to give the loan a government guarantee, with the result that the British share of the loan proved embarrassingly hard to place.[101] The diplomats also remained suspicious of one another's territorial ambitions, especially when Britain seemed willing to risk war with Russia over Port Arthur in March 1898.[102] A few months later, a bitter dispute broke out between Cameron of the Hong Kong & Shanghai Bank and Hansemann over a railway concession in the Shantung province.[103] However, by August these tensions had been substantially dispelled thanks in large part to the efforts of Alfred and Natty.

At the height of the Port Arthur crisis in March, Alfred held a dinner attended by Chamberlain, Balfour, Harry Chaplin, Hatzfeldt and Eckardstein, at which the Germans had a chance to voice their grievances about China in a "friendly, private, and quite unofficial conversation . . . on strictly neutral territory." This occurred on the very day that the majority of the Cabinet overruled Chamberlain on the question of Port Arthur, agreeing to rest content with the "territorial or cartographic consolation" of Wei-hai-wei (the harbour opposite Port Arthur).[104] A similar conciliatory function was performed by Natty with respect to Hansemann, whom Cameron had enraged by accusing him of breaching the Deutsch-Asiatische Bank's contract with the Hong Kong & Shanghai. At a conference of bankers and politicians in London at the beginning of September it was agreed to divide China into "spheres of influence" for the purpose of allocating rail concessions, leaving the Yangtse Valley to the British banks, Shantung to the Germans and splitting the Tientsin–Chinkiang route.[105] Interviewed by McDonnell in January 1899, Natty assured the Prime Minister of Germany's sincere "desire to combine with England (and possibly with America and Japan) for commercial purposes in China."[106]

Disputes about railways continued—Hansemann and Carl Meyer crossed swords on the subject at the end of 1899—but the pattern of collaboration had been established.[107] When the Germans sent an expedition to China following the Boxer Rising and the Russian invasion of Manchuria in 1900, they used the Rothschilds to assure London that "the Russians won't risk a war," and in October Britain and Germany signed a new agreement to maintain the integrity of the Chinese Empire and an "Open Door" trade regime.[108] This was without doubt the high watermark of Anglo-German *political* co-operation in China; but it is important to recognise that business co-operation continued for some years to come. Further disagreements (prompted by the intrusion of the so-called Peking Syndicate into the Hoangho region) were resolved at another bankers' conference arranged by Natty and Hansemann in Berlin in 1902.[109] As late as 1905, when the *Times* correspondent in Peking attacked the cosy arrangement between the British and German banks, Natty complained to his editor.[110]

The dinner at Alfred's at the time of the Port Arthur crisis in March 1898 illustrates the way minor imperial issues could be seized upon as the basis for much more ambitious diplomatic proposals. Easy though it is to dismiss such "amateur negotiation," Balfour's account suggests that it was on this occasion that new life was breathed into the idea of an Anglo-German alliance, ten years after Bismarck had first bruited it:

> [B]etween the courses . . . there was an infinity of talk, out of the nebulous friendliness of which I really gathered very little except that the Germans . . . felt aggrieved at our protest about Shantung railways. This took place on Friday the 25th [of March]—the day on which, at an afternoon Cabinet, the Government took their courage in both hands and (Joe [Chamberlain] dissenting) agreed on the Wei-hai-wei policy. The next incident was that Joe informed me that he had been asked to meet Hatzfeldt under like conditions. I raised no objection and (again I believe at Alfred's) another unofficial and informal conversation took place. Joe is very impulsive: and the Cabinet discussion of the preceding days had forced on his attention our isolated and occasionally therefore difficult diplomatic position. He certainly went far in the expression of his own personal leaning towards a German alliance; he combated the notion that our form of Parliamentary government rendered such an alliance precarious (a notion which apparently haunts the German mind), and I believe even threw out a vague suggestion as to the form which an arrangement between the two countries might take.[111]

The response from the German Foreign Secretary Prince Bernhard von Bülow, Balfour recalled, was "immediate":

> [H]is telegraphic reply (paraphrased to Joe at a second interview) dwelt again on the Parliamentary difficulty,—but also expressed with happy frankness the German view of England's position in the European system. They hold, it seems, that we are more than a match for France, but not more than a match for Russia and France combined. The issue of such a contest would be doubtful. They could not afford to see us succumb,—not because they loved us, but because they know that they would be the next victims—and so on. The whole tenor of the conversation (as represented to me) being in favour of a closer union between the countries.[112]

This was the start of a protracted period of diplomatic toing and froing between Berlin and London in which the Rothschilds played a pivotal role. Not only did key meetings take place in the "neutral" dining room of Seamore Place; Hatzfeldt sent his son to spend weekends at Tring "in order to stay as much as possible 'au courant' of Rothschild's news,"[113] while Alfred and Paul Schwabach soon came to be regarded by Bülow as a "safe and useful . . . channel" for diplomatic communication.[114]

It is usually argued that Hatzfeldt and Chamberlain were talking at cross purposes: where the former wanted Britain to join the German-Austrian-Italian Triple Alliance, the latter had in mind a more limited "Treaty or Arrangement between Germany and Great Britain for a term of years . . . of a defensive character based upon a mutual understanding as to policy in China and elsewhere."[115] But one might conceivably have led to the other, as happened with the Anglo-French entente which came later. Another familiar objection is that colonial disputes elsewhere—over Portuguese Mozambique and the Samoan Islands, for example—militated against Anglo-German rapprochement. But this is not persuasive for the same reason: Britain's relations with France were bedevilled by as many if not more colonial flashpoints and, as we shall see, most of the points at issue between London and Berlin had been amicably settled by 1903.

Many historians cite the German naval programme initiated in 1897 as the key to the "rise of the Anglo-German antagonism." Bülow, so the argument runs, wished to keep a "free hand," which meant in practice that he wished to build a navy capable of challenging Britain's maritime supremacy. There is, of course, no question that Tirpitz's navy was regarded as a direct threat in London. And as we shall see, even so keen a proponent of good relations with Germany as Natty was not immune to the dreadnought mania of the period. Yet it is too easily forgotten that Britain won the maritime arms race. As early as 1905, with the completion of the First Sea Lord "Jackie" Fisher's initial naval reforms, the Director of Naval Intelligence could confidently describe as "overwhelming" Britain's "maritime preponderance" over Germany. This was quite right: the number of German battleships only increased from thirteen to sixteen between 1898 and 1905, whereas the British battle fleet rose from twenty-nine to forty-four ships. This did not maintain the 1889 two-power standard, but it sufficed to check a purely German threat. Although naval "scares" recurred thereafter, the Germans were in fact never able to reach the target set by Tirpitz of a navy big enough to make an Anglo-German naval war too risky for the western power to contemplate. By 1912 the naval race was effectively over because the Germans—economically strong but fiscally weak— could not afford to match the British rate of construction.[116] In the light of all this, the project of an Anglo-German alliance was far from an idle dream.

It is important to remember that it was not only in China that British and German interests seemed to be complementary. The protracted haggling with Portugal over the future of her African colonies (and especially Delagoa Bay) finally produced an agreement in 1898 whereby Britain and Germany jointly lent money to Portugal secured on her colonial property, but with a secret clause dividing the Portuguese territory into spheres of influence.[117] Nor were the Rothschilds unrealistic in urging compromise in London with respect to German claims in West Africa: there was no real conflict of interest there.[118] The Samoan crisis which blew up in April 1899 was resolved by the end of the year, with Alfred and Schwabach acting as unofficial intermediaries.[119] The two countries even co-operated over Venezuela's external debt in 1902.

Another more strategically important region where Anglo-German co-operation seemed viable was the Ottoman Empire. The Germans had begun to show an interest in Turkish finance even before 1889, when the Kaiser made the first of his visits to Constantinople. The year before, Gustave heard a rumour that the German government wished to establish a Turkish administration of the public debt "the same as in Egypt, however, with Germany predominant."[120] So long as Russia seemed to menace the Straits—as the Rothschilds were convinced was the case—the prospects for some sort of Anglo-German co-operation in the region remained good.[121] Thus the two countries worked closely together following the military defeat of Greece by Turkey in 1897, hammering out the details of a new financial control over Athens.[122] In revealing terms, Natty urged McDonnell that

> the right policy for England at the present moment is to come to terms with Germany on the Greek question; we must look facts in the face as they are, we have an avowed Franco-Russian Alliance and although the Egyptian question may not be raised at present we must play the game of those whose sentiments, if not their acts, are hostile to this country. I am in no sense a philo-German, nor do I believe in the divine right of Kings but I am sure that the right thing now would be to settle the Greek things as soon as possible and to come to terms with old Hatzfeldt.[123]

A better known opportunity for cooperation came in 1899—a year after the Kaiser's second visit to the Bosphorus—when the Sultan agreed to the proposal for an Imperial Ottoman Baghdad Railway, the brainchild of Georg von Siemens of the Deutsche Bank (hence the "Berlin–Baghdad railway"). Siemens and his successor Arthur von Gwinner always intended to secure British as well as French participation in the venture; the problem was the lack of interest in the City, which had largely lost faith in the future of the Ottoman regime.[124] Remembering the example of the Suez Canal, Natty advised the government itself to "take a part of the ordinary shares" in the enterprise, but the Foreign Secretary Lord Lansdowne was sceptical, preferring to tempt private finance with subsidies.[125] In March 1903, an agreement was drawn up for an extension of the line to Basra which would have given the British members of a consortium—led by Sir Ernest Cassel and Revelstoke—25 per cent; but the fact that German investors would hold 35 per cent prompted a barrage of criticism in right-wing journals like the *Spectator* and the *National Review*, and Balfour—now Prime Minister—chose to pull out.[126] To those whose memories extended back to the 1870s, this was a bizarre decision: on that basis, Disraeli's purchase of the Khedive's Suez Canal shares would have been disavowed because French shareholders were in a majority.

It should be stressed that in all this the Rothschilds were acting with singular disinterestedness. They did no business whatever in Samoa, Venezuela or West Africa. Their involvement in Chinese finance was also limited and had ceased altogether by the time of the revolution which overthrew the last Emperor in 1911 (though Carl Meyer remained a useful contact on the Hong Kong & Shanghai board).[127] Even the Ottoman Empire did not much concern them in this period, save where the colonisation of Palestine was concerned.[128] Edward Hamilton thought Natty had stayed out of the proposed Baghdad consortium out of "timidity"; but Natty's allusions to "the terrible Turk" and "the Turkish mess" in his correspondence with Paris reflected a genuine (and not unjustified) scepticism about the Ottoman regime's stability. "I always dread the reopening of any Eastern Question," he exclaimed in May 1906, and, as long as there was a chance of such a reopening, he and most other City bankers generally gave Constantinople a wide berth.[129] "If the [British] Government calls on us for definite object," Natty explained to his cousins a year later, "we shall always be ready to examine any business that is brought before us and will do our best to bring it to a successful issue if possible, but I should be very sorry to hear if nolens volens our name was to be associated with the various kinds of cat[']s meat which abound in the Ottoman Empire . . . [N]o prudent person can be particularly anxious to endorse all the Ottoman cat[']s meat."[130] Though Natty enthusiastically welcomed the Young Turk revolution of 1908, his enthusiasm stopped short of lending to it: the efforts of Ernest Cassel "to direct the policy of the Ottoman Empire" by financial means were the subject of scathing comment at New Court.[131] Perhaps it was a fundamental weakness of the projected Anglo-German entente that its foundations were supposed to be laid in ground the Rothschilds themselves regarded as infirm.

There was one region of potential Anglo-German conflict where the Rothschilds very definitely did have an interest, however: South Africa. Apart from its deleterious effect on mining shares, what made the Jameson Raid especially deplorable in the eyes of the Rothschilds was the damage it did to Anglo-German relations: William II's telegram congratulating Kruger on repelling the invaders "without appealing to the help of friendly powers" did lasting damage to Anglo-German relations, and it is significant that the Rothschilds relied on the Warburgs as intermediaries in trying to conciliate Kruger.[132] When Alfred sought to join in the continuing debate on the Uitlanders' franchise in 1897, he proposed to involve Germany in the negotiations with Kruger—a suggestion swiftly dismissed by Chamberlain.[133] German expressions of sympathy for the Boers during the war between Britain and the Transvaal Republic were a further cause of tension between London and Berlin. Was it here therefore over South Africa that the idea of an Anglo-German alliance came to grief?

Perhaps: a crucial part of the Rothschild argument against war was that "a certain person in Berlin"—meaning the Kaiser—would be "very cross" if the Boers were to be attacked.[134] The point of the 1898 agreement with Germany over Portuguese Mozambique was partly that it was supposed to discourage the Germans from siding with Kruger, but the possibility of outright war seemed to cast doubt on that arrangement. Alfred was in close touch with Hatzfeldt during the crisis, assuring him in September that, despite the expectations of war in the City, there were as yet "no definite grounds for this panic"; but this was empty reassurance.[135] Renewed German talk of a "continental league" against Britain at the end of 1899 and the British interception of German mail steamers in South African waters in January 1900 unquestionably stalled progress towards an Anglo-German understanding. Indeed, attacks on British policy in the German press became so violent that Alfred felt bound to protest to Eckardstein about what he called a "'pinprick' policy"— "and, although a pin is not a very impressive instrument, repeated pricks may cause a wound . . ."[136] At the same time, Alfred attempted to exert pressure on *The Times*, whose Berlin correspondent Saunders was taking an increasingly strident Germanophobe line. Alfred invited the paper's manager, Charles Moberly Bell, to dine with him in June 1902 and intimated that the King himself was concerned about the tone of Saunders's reports. When Bell reported his conversation to his correspondent, Saunders exploded in terms which illustrate the way Rothschild Germanophilia could be represented as unpatriotic—and worse:

> I know the power of German influence dynastic, racial &c., including the Rothschilds. It is not *business*. It is *dining, shooting, toasts, finance, honours, marriages, dynastic friendships*. It is not hard steel, like Joe Chamberlain, or even Lansdowne, It is not *English* . . . I regret that you told Alfred Rothschild that you would give him your decision *in writing* . . . What you write will go to the Emperor. He wants to explore your counsels . . . *They* want to bind both England and you.[137]

Yet the Boer War did not do as much damage to Anglo-German relations as Alfred feared. German banks like M. M. Warburg had no qualms about applying for a share of the 1903 Transvaal loan.[138] Perhaps more important, in undermining British self-confidence the war strengthened the arguments for ending diplomatic isolation.[139] Indeed, it was actually during the war—in the early months of 1901— that Alfred was involved in a renewed effort to bring Chamberlain and the new Foreign Secretary Lansdowne into contact with German representatives on the basis of (in Chamberlain's words) "co-operation with Germany and adherence to Triple Alliance."

The territory which was now brought into the discussions in earnest—Chamberlain had first raised it in 1899—was Morocco. Because of later events, it is easy to assume there was something inevitable about disagreements between Britain and Germany over Morocco; but that seemed far from likely in 1901. Indeed, French designs in the entire north-west African region (further advanced by a secret deal with Italy in 1900) seemed positively to favour some sort of joint action. Britain was already concerned by Spanish fortifications at Algeciras, which seemed to pose a threat to Gibraltar, that vital Mediterranean gatepost. Indeed, Balfour had requested that Rothschilds refuse any loan requests from Spain in 1898.[140] The possibility of a joint Franco-Spanish "liquidation" of Morocco was a real one. The obvious alternative was to divide Morocco into British and German spheres of influence, with Britain taking Tangier and Germany the Atlantic coast. This was the basic thrust of a draft agreement discussed in May and again in December. The talks continued sporadically into 1902, with Holstein once again using the "safe and useful . . . channel Schwabach-Rothschild."[141] It was in fact German lack of interest in Morocco—as expressed unambiguously by both Bülow and the Kaiser in early 1903—which prevented any such scheme being realised.

So why did the idea of an Anglo-German entente fail? Why was it with France rather than with Germany that Britain concluded a wide-ranging colonial agreement in April 1904? One rather unsophisticated answer relates to the personalities involved. Edward VII's Francophilia is occasionally cited, while Eckardstein somewhat implausibly blamed "the fact that the 'haute finance' has drawn closer to France and Russia" on "the allegedly discourteous treatment . . . of Alfred Rothschild . . . by H[is] M[ajesty]" (the Kaiser) during a state visit to Britain.[142] The crucial stumbling block was probably Salisbury's fundamental lack of enthusiasm and even suspicion, which was echoed by his private secretary McDonnell. He was deeply sceptical when Alfred and Natty themselves began to agitate for an Anglo-German combination against Russia, telling Salisbury that Alfred was "suffering from megalomania" having been offered a decoration by the Kaiser for his contribution to Anglo-German amity.[143] Alfred accepted the honour (Order of the Crown, First Class), though he felt obliged to write a long letter to Salisbury, protesting (rather too much) that any "services rendered . . . were the result of my being absolutely imbued with the *sole desire of doing that which I considered was in the interests of my country* and I therefore exerted my best efforts to try to bring about a better feeling between England and Germany on several occasions when the relations between these two countries were seriously strained."[144] By July McDonnell was reporting Alfred's initiatives in the form of facetious stage directions:

The German Emperor
The usual autumn farce is about to be played.
Act I
Eckardstein, the heavy friend of England, has been to tell Alfred Rothschild that the Emperor is convinced that war between us and the Transvaal is inevitable . . . Two days later Eckardstein reappears on the stage and tells Rothschild that the Emperor is furious because the Queen has slighted him by not inviting him to Windsor: that H.I.M. desires nothing more than to be friends with us; but unless we give him speedy evidence of our good will by deeds not words, he will ally himself with Russia and France, all the preliminaries having been arranged for such an alliance.[145]

When Eckardstein repeated this threat in October, Salisbury drily minuted: "I think I have heard all this before."[146] The Germans evidently detected the Prime Minister's scepticism. Asked by Alfred to provide "a short memorandum on the questions at issue (Samoa, Morocco) which he could give to Mr Balfour," Hatzfeldt told Berlin he doubted "if he could attempt to influence foreign questions, or do so successfully. My feeling is that Lord Salisbury is quite determined to enter into no special arrangements with us at present."[147] It was not until after Salisbury's departure that Holstein felt Alfred could "once again be used in political matters," telling Bülow in July 1902: "He is on good terms with Balfour and Chamberlain; Salisbury used to cut him."[148]

Chamberlain was also temperamentally ill suited to a policy of conciliation. In public, he had talked grandly of "New Triple Alliance between the Teutonic race and the two great branches of the Anglo-Saxon race"; but he seemed oblivious to the limits on what Bülow could say in reply. In his Reichstag speech of December 11, 1899, the German Chancellor had expressed his readiness and willingness "on the basis of full reciprocity and mutual consideration to live with [England] in peace and harmony." Yet inexplicably Chamberlain regarded this as the "cold shoulder" and although, as Eckardstein lamented, "the great mass of people saw in it no sharpness or coolness towards England, on the other hand I have had to face for a few days the assaults of newspaper proprietors, Cabinet Ministers, the Rothschilds, as well as the Royal Family."[149] When difficulties arose, Chamberlain lost patience, telling Alfred petulantly: "If they are so short-sighted and cannot see that it is a question of the rise of a new constellation in the world, they are beyond help."[150] The conclusion is therefore tempting that the opportunity for some kind of Anglo-German entente comparable with that agreed with France in 1904 was needlessly thrown away. There were other factors, however, which counted for more than mere personal foibles.

The Rationale of the Entente

There were several reasons why an entente with France ultimately came to seem preferable to one with Germany. The first was that the French had a bigger and better concession to offer Britain than anything Germany might have offered: namely final acceptance of the British position in Egypt. After more than twenty years of recurrent friction, this was a major diplomatic climb-down by Delcassé, and it is easy to see why Lansdowne hastened to commit it to paper. From a financial point of view, Cassel was by now a more important force in Egypt than the Rothschilds—it was he who raised the money for the Aswan dam and other infrastructural improvements after 1897, thereby winning the confidence of Lord Cromer.[151] Still, the Rothschilds added their voice to the argument for Anglo-French compromise over Egypt when Natty's son Walter told Cromer that "our cousins in Paris" were prepared to support his plans for redeeming part of the Egyptian debt only "with the agreement of the French Government."[152] The price of this agreement was that France acquired the right "to preserve order in Morocco and to provide assistance for the purpose of all administrative, economic, financial and military reforms which it may require"—a concession which the French regarded as giving them the same position of *de facto* power in Morocco as Britain had enjoyed in Egypt since 1882. In the subsequent rows about Morocco, the Germans were often in the right; but the fact was that Britain had opted for France and so was bound to back French claims even when they went beyond the formal status quo.

A second (and probably more important) reason why the entente with France came about, however, was the dramatic alteration in the Asian balance of power. If Britain had continued to feel menaced by Russia in the East—if Russia had defeated Japan in 1904, for example—then the arguments for an Anglo-German entente might ultimately have prevailed. But the advent of Japan as an effective counterweight to Russian ambitions in Manchuria introduced a new variable into the equation. The German government had always felt uneasy about the prospect of an arrangement with Britain which conceivably could have meant Germany fighting a war against Russia in Europe for the sake of British interests in China. This explains the assurances given by Bülow and the Kaiser in 1901 of German neutrality in the event of an Anglo-Russian conflict in the Far East. Japan, by contrast, had every reason to look for a European ally. When the Russian government refused to compromise over Manchuria, Tokyo turned readily to London and in January 1902 a defensive alliance was concluded. This was the real watershed which marked the end of British isolationism: for at this stage French policy was still based on the assumption of military and financial support for Russia in Asia, if necessary against England.

Historians have sometimes wondered why the Rothschilds were slow to seize the opportunity of lending to Japan, the most economically dynamic and self-consciously "Western" of all the Asian countries. It is true that N. M. Rothschild and Parr's had jointly underwritten a loan for the construction of Japan's first railway between Edo and Yokohama in 1872, but the connection subsequently lapsed and it was Barings who took the lead when Japan returned to the City in 1898.[153] When, in the wake of the Anglo-Japanese alliance, the Japanese government sought a loan of £5.1 million, Natty was emphatically told that Lansdowne regarded it "as a matter of political importance that Japan should be able to raise in this country rather than elsewhere the money which she requires . . . and on reasonable terms." But he declined to play a leading role and the initiative passed back to Barings and the Hong Kong & Shanghai Bank.[154] The issue was a success. Given the Rothschilds' continuing aversion to Russia, it seems curious that Natty missed this chance: 1903, after all, was the year of the pogrom at Kishinev (near the Rumanian border) in which forty-five Jews died, and the Germans were quite right to expect this to intensify Rothschild Russophobia.[155] A fresh wave of anti-Jewish violence in 1905 prompted Natty, as one of the four members of the Russo-Jewish Committee, to denounce in a letter to *The Times*:

> the unspeakable calamities [which] have befallen the Jews in Russia. They have again become the victims of outrages to which there is probably no parallel in history. At numerous places they have been mercilessly struck down and massacred. Fiendish savagery has characterised the attitude of the ferocious mobs which have been allowed by the official protectors of life and property to perpetrate their work of murder, mutilation and pillage.[156]

To start the process of fund-raising for the victims, New Court matched the £10,000 donation already made by Jacob Schiff of Kuhn, Loeb & Co. in New York. In addition, Natty pressed Balfour—who had now succeeded Salisbury as Prime Minister—to protest on behalf of "the Jewish victims of law and lawlessness in Russia" and to urge the Russian government "to put an end to the atrocious attacks on the Jews."[157]

The explanation for the Rothschilds' initial hesitation about Japan would seem to be threefold. Firstly, the Anglo-Japanese alliance was a blow to the strategy of rapprochement with Germany; indeed, it may even be said to have made that strategy redundant. Secondly, the Rothschilds did not imagine that Japan could by herself take on Russia: in December 1903 Leo had a bet with the Duke of Devonshire that there would be no war between Russia and Japan—to the amusement of the Japanese ambassador Hayashi, who told Eckardstein that the Duke would win the bet. Even when Hayashi approached Alfred less than a month before hostilities broke out, the Rothschilds still declined to make a firm financial commitment.[158] Thirdly, when the war began, the Paris Rothschilds found themselves struggling to support the price of Russian bonds, which predictably slumped on the outbreak of hostilities, and fell precipitously as the Russian campaign disintegrated.[159] It was therefore only after the war broke out that the Rothschilds took an interest in Japan, participating in a new £5 million loan as part of a consortium led by Kuhn, Loeb and M. M. Warburg.[160] This coincided with an "absolute" refusal "to have anything to do with a Russian loan," as Walter informed Herbert Gladstone.[161] Even the French Rothschilds now refused their assistance to St Petersburg, albeit less irrevocably. As Alphonse told the German ambassador in Paris in August 1904:

> The Paris House of Rothschild is hostile to Russia, and at the present time is standing somewhat aloof from Russian operations . . . Russia had made fine promises regarding the future treatment of his co-religionists, if only the money were forthcoming, but . . . his attitude was that these were empty promises. Since, however, as a good Frenchman he feels that he is more or less called upon to support the Russian Alliance (and that is what I infer), he will possibly soften in the end and open his purse, however unfavourable a view he may take of the present situation.[162]

The Japanese victories at Port Arthur, at Mukden and, decisively, at Tsushima in May 1905 vindicated the decision to back Japan against Russia on economic as well as religious grounds. In the aftermath of the war, the new ties between Britain, the US and Japan were reinforced not only diplomatically but also financially. In 1906 both the London and the Paris houses were involved in another £25 million loan, which this time also attracted subscriptions in France and Germany; and they jointly undertook a further £11.5 million loan the following year. Natty was by now confident of "the future prosperity of Japan, both financially & economically," assuring his initially more sceptical Parisian relatives that "their dense & intelligent population, their loyalty zeal & intelligence, will soon bring them to the front rank both in commerce & manufacture."[163] On the other hand, he could hardly deny that "the success of Japanese financial undertakings [was] owing to intermediaries who initiated the world into the value of Japanese Bonds when hardly anyone would look at them."[164] It was Jacob Schiff who was now the "welcome & much honoured guest at Tokio" and who had "incense . . . poured on his devoted head"; and it was "his dear nephew Warburg at Hamburg" who, following the success of the Japanese loan in Hamburg, "resemble[d] the frog in the fable & [was] swollen up with vanity & the belief in his own power to control the European markets, & interest all big houses in any & every syndicate."[165] They, along with Revelstoke, had appreciated Japan's potential long before the Rothschilds latched on. It was not quite true to claim, as Natty did in May 1907, that "We have always had great faith in Japan, faith in their military and naval prowess which the late war amply justified, faith in the resources of the country and still greater faith in the wisdom of the Japanese rulers."[166]

Nor were the wider diplomatic implications of the Japanese victory entirely congenial to the Rothschilds. By discrediting Russia as an imperial power—and plunging the country into revolution—the war removed at a stroke one of the strongest arguments for Anglo-German rapprochment. But it did not (as the Germans had hoped it might) force France to "choose between Russia and Germany or England." Natty himself saw the 1907 loan to Japan as a way of forging a colonial entente between France and Japan. "I never for one moment thought that the Japanese had any designs on the French Colonies or were imbued with those ambitious designs which were attributed to them," he explained in two illuminating letters to his cousins:

> But as a matter of course in order to obtain the object the French Government had in view, it was necessary that a quid pro quo should be offered to the Japanese Government and you can flatter yourself and flatter yourself most justly that by introducing two loans to the French Capitalists you brought about this desired consummation . . . No doubt politics and finance often go hand in hand, & if a capitalist is directly interested in the stocks of a country, he is naturally anxious that that country should increase in prosperity & development, which can only occur in times of peace & tranquillity.[167]

Such a rapprochement between France and Japan, coming as it did in the wake of the Anglo-Japanese alliance, implied a convergence of British and French interests; and this was more or less impossible to reconcile with the Rothschilds' earlier goal of Anglo-German amity.

It was not, in fact, in the Far East that this contradiction made itself most apparent, but in Morocco, where previously the auspices for Anglo-German harmony had been quite good. "Lord Rothschild told me yesterday it was stupid of us to believe England had warlike intentions," the German ambassador Count Metternich informed Bülow in January 1905. "Such never existed here, and this Government especially wished to maintain good relations with us. Mr Balfour had said this to him a few days before."[168] But the very fact that such an assurance had to be given was proof itself of how rapidly the two countries were drifting apart. The new pro-French orientation of British policy was confirmed when the Kaiser landed at Tangier on March 31 and demanded an international conference to reaffirm Morocco's independence. Far from supporting the German arguments for an "Open Door" in Morocco, Lansdowne worried that the crisis might topple Delcassé and end with a French retreat. The British concern now seemed to be to bolster the French position in Morocco, in order to see off a German bid for an Atlantic port. This Francophile tendency became even more pronounced following the Liberal election victory which brought Henry Campbell-Bannerman to power in January 1906. To Natty, this spelt the end for German policy in Morocco: "[N]o sane person can believe that the Emperor of Germany will wish to oppose the wishes & feelings of a united Europe," he told his cousins in Paris on January 3, "& much less can he hope for any success at all, now that a Liberal Government in England fully endorses the Anglo French entente."[169] Natty vaguely hoped for "a compromise which would please both sides & wound the vanity of neither," and sought to quell fears at the rue Laffitte that Bülow might be contemplating a military solution.[170] But on the substantive issues—the internationalisation of the Moroccan police and a proposed

Moroccan bank—he regarded Germany as isolated: as he told Edouard in late February 1906,

> [O]ur Government is supporting yours on the various questions connected with Morocco, & in fact I may go so far as to say that they think the French proposals both reasonable & moderate . . . your Government has the firm support of ours, and . . . Mr Rouvier's wishes find a warm re-echo in Sir Edward Grey's mind. And no doubt the feeling of this perfect entente will considerably help towards the solution, and probably the feeling of this entente is what most rankles in the minds of those who direct the policy in the Wilhelmstrasse.[171]

Natty declared that he regarded the German police proposals as "most dangerous [and] certain to meet with failure" as they "could never be approved of here." Yet when this was relayed by Metternich to Berlin, the Kaiser minuted bluntly "darin stehe ich fest"—"he was determined," in other words, "to hold out on the police question."[172] This sort of intransigence tended to erode Natty's patience with the German government, and particularly with "His Teutonic (or Satanic) Majesty." "If the very conciliatory attitude your Government is now taking does not produce the desired effect," he told his French cousins, "it will be for the single reason that they are determined on the Banks of the Spree, that no oil should be poured on the troubled waters."[173] "The line taken at Berlin, or rather the official language of the Wilhelmstrasse," he wrote a fortnight later, "is somewhat circular: they say Germany has made so many sacrifices, & has shown her good will so much, that it devolves on France to hold out the olive branch & make some concession, but they do not tell us what sacrifices Germany has made." If a "modus vivendi" was to be found, he added, it would have to be "satisfactory to Teuton arrogance, without interfering with Gallic rights." In the end, Natty hailed the outcome of the Algeciras conference as "gratifying to French political interests, but also to the financial interests of your country." In addition to averting war, he concluded, it had "proved the value of the Anglo French Entente & . . . demonstrated the solidarity of a Franco Russian Alliance; & personally I should very much doubt the desire of the Emperor of Germany to make war upon France for no reason at all."[174] This was a very different kind of language from that which had been current at New Court ten years before.

The improvement in France's diplomatic position was not a purely diplomatic phenomenon, however. As Natty repeated time and again, it was firmly based on financial strength. The entente with Japan mentioned above was not the only French diplomatic initiative reinforced by bond issues on the Paris capital market. In the wake of the Russo-Japanese War, there was a brief moment when it seemed that monarchical diplomacy might undo the achievements of a decade of French foreign policy. This was the meeting between William II and Nicholas II at Björkö in July 1905 at which the two emperors agreed a European defensive alliance—a realignment which would have transformed the international scene if it had been formally ratified. But, as A. J. P. Taylor put it, "the Paris bourse made a stronger appeal than monarchical solidarity."[175] Russia, in dire financial straits after Tsushima, desperately needed fresh loans to help reconstruct her military capability, and the Paris market was still capable of tapping a deeper pool of savings for foreign issues than that of Berlin, where the insatiable needs of German industry and German government were paramount.

Italy too could be wooed in this way. The conversion of Italian rentes in the summer of 1906 was undertaken by a consortium led by the French Rothschilds, and although seven Berlin banks were members of the syndicate, the German share of the 1 billion franc operation was smaller than the French, and the diplomats in both Paris and Berlin interpreted that as a French success. The agreement was only signed on June 26, after the Algeciras conference had ended; throughout it, Italy had consistently sided with France, marking the effective end of the Triple Alliance which had bound her to Germany and Austria–Hungary.[176]

These aspects of pre-war financial diplomacy are quite well known. What is less obvious is the role of finance in underpinning the Anglo-French entente. The Rothschild archives show how close co-operation was between London and Paris in the period after 1905, especially with respect to monetary policy. As in the past, the Rothschilds acted as private helpmeets to the Bank of England and the Banque de France, facilitating that co-operation between the two financial centres which was so vital to the stability of the pre-war gold standard. Sometimes the role they played had a directly political significance, as when the Rothschilds brokered the secret purchase by the Bank of England of shares in the Constantinople Quay company in 1906–7 (part of a joint Anglo-French bid to acquire a controlling interest in the concern).[177] To Natty, it was self-evident that—even when they were primarily diplomatic in their inspiration—such complex transactions could not be left to the Foreign Office mandarins. "[A]lthough they may be diplomatists," he observed acidly, "[they] are certainly not men of business."[178]

More often, however, the Rothschilds' cross-Channel role was a matter of equilibrating the gold reserves of the two central banks, ensuring that British and French monetary policy did not come into conflict. In November 1906, for example, when Bank rate stood at 6 per cent and large quantities of gold were being withdrawn from London by Brazil, India and other large holders of sterling balances, Natty and Edouard arranged advances of gold sovereigns worth £600,000 from the Banque de France.[179] This "policy of courtesy & of aid" was extremely welcome in London, and as Natty observed: "It is very important to know that in the future, if at any moment it should be thought necessary & imperative, a helping hand will be ready to come forward from the other side of the Channel to the rescue of the Old Lady in Threadneedle Street."[180] No sooner had this letter been sent than Natty was asked by the Bank to seek a further delivery of £400,000 in sovereigns. This too was promptly arranged, and topped up with a further £600,000 in the course of the month.[181] These exchanges of gold for bills—which totalled £1.4 million in all— may well have averted a further increase in Bank rate, and indeed allowed the Bank to cut it in stages back to 4 per cent by April 1907. The point to be emphasised is that the Rothschilds had stepped in after direct negotiations between the central banks had broken down.[182]

The great test of Anglo-French monetary co-operation came in the second half of 1907, when the crisis which had been gathering in the United States broke, sending waves throughout the international economy. As early as March, Natty and Edouard had exchanged uncharacteristically harsh words following the Banque de France's decision to raise its own discount rate: plainly Edouard was unimpressed by his relative's request for a further "2 or 3 millions" of French gold for Threadneedle Street. "I regret very much," Natty hastened to write in response, "that you should have considered us such ninnies as to suppose that the Bank of France would come forward and stem any depression which might be caused by over-speculation in America."[183] Natty knew when he was in a tight spot: in the course of April and May, he mutely bowed to French requests that the sovereigns borrowed the previous December be returned to Paris.[184] But in August the position in London began to deteriorate. Natty was forewarned (and so was able to alert his cousins) about the Bank's decision to put Bank rate back up to 4.5 per cent, but he later complained that his advice to tighten policy still further had been ignored.[185] By the end of October, with the American crisis in full spate, Bank rate had to be raised again, and Natty was once again deputed to ask for French gold to replenish the Old Lady's reserves. This time, he was in no mood for cousinly prevarication: Robert's objections to a repeat of the previous year's lending were, he wrote impatiently, "singularly fallacious." The French Rothschilds felt that a crisis which (in their view) had its roots in President Roosevelt's misguided attacks on Wall Street did not concern the Banque de France. "It would be just as wise," retorted Natty, "to lay down as a rule that in no case the fire brigade was to extinguish a fire if it originally arose out of the action of an incendiary."[186]

On November 4 the Governor, William Campbell, raised Bank rate to 6 per cent and sent for Natty—a testament to the key role the Rothschilds still played in the money market. It was, Natty told his cousins, "unanimously decided to ask me to telegraph to you and ask you to use your best endeavours to renew with the Bank of France the operation which you did last year, and which was so successful then." This was no sooner requested than done, this time to the tune of £3 million, of which the Rothschilds provided £400,000. Although Bank rate went up another percentage point on November 7—and remained there until the New Year—this once again did much to stabilise the London market: as Campbell wrote to the Paris house, their assistance had "prevented my taking even more stringent means to protect our Gold Reserves."[187] It was a further proof of the enduring value of the Rothschilds' cross-Channel link that when J. P. Morgan directly approached the Banque de France for assistance for the American market, he was rebuffed—a vindication of Natty's view, expressed in a blunt telegram to Morgan on November 6, that the Americans should set their own house in order.[188] By contrast, Campbell could count on being able to borrow further gold from Paris through the Rothschilds if the Bank's reserve fell any lower.[189] Conversely, his counterpart in Paris could discreetly hint that a British rate cut would be welcome once the crisis was over in January 1908; he could rely on the Rothschilds to give him advance warning of any such reduction.[190]

The crisis of 1907 was the most serious financial crisis before 1914 itself and it revealed the economic dimension to the Anglo-French entente. Nor did such co-operation end as market conditions eased. In July 1908, for example, the Banque de France bought consols worth over £1 million through New Court. Later the same year, the Bank of England consulted Natty about the possibility of large scale withdrawals of gold from the London market by French banks.[191] It was a matter of routine that, when the London money market tightened again in late 1909, the Rothschilds discussed the possibility of yet another swap of bills for French gold.[192]

At the height of the 1907 crisis, Natty wrote an uncharacteristically long and reflective letter to his Paris relatives in which he spelt out the functioning of the gold standard as he understood it, and the crucial role performed by the Anglo-French relationship. The key, he argued, was that "the whole trade of the world is carried on by bills on London." There were always "running on London between £300 and £400 Millions of drafts, of which probably more than half are for foreign account." According to the classical theory, "When the Bank is obliged to raise the rate of discount owing to an efflux of gold . . . the rate of exchange rises automatically and gold comes back to the Bank of England." But this had profound implications for the rest of the world—and particularly the Banque de France. The conclusion Natty drew was one with which modern historians of the gold standard would agree—namely that central bank co-operation was essential to the stability of the system:

> Our excellent brother in law Alphonse used often to talk this question over with me . . . He was always afraid that unless the Bank of France and others acted generously on these occasions the exchange on London would rise to such a height that large quantities of gold in circulation would find its [sic] way to London and that that would create greater inconvenience and would be far worse than any step which the Bank of France or other great institutions thought right in a moment of crisis to take. I have troubled you with these details as I wish to impress on you as far as I can how intimately and of necessity all countries are bound together.[193]

In other words, the world's principal creditor economies, France and Britain were "bound together" by a common interest in monetary stability. The Rothschild contribution to this system was all the more important if, as Natty believed, the Bank of England was failing to build up its gold reserves to a level commensurate with its global role.[194] He and his French cousins thus continued to see themselves as auxiliaries to their respective central banks; even if they themselves were no longer, as they had been in the past, the lenders to the lenders of resort.

The Anglo–Russian Antagonism

Yet it would be quite wrong to conclude that the final political and military consummation of the Anglo-French entente in 1914 was in some sense economically determined. These financial considerations undoubtedly helped to elevate the Anglo-French relationship above the Anglo-German relationship in British eyes; but that was far from meaning a defensive alliance, guaranteeing British intervention in the case of a continental war. In fact, prior to August 2, 1914, there was never any guarantee that Britain would support France militarily if war broke out (though the Foreign Secretary Sir Edward Grey gave personal assurances which encouraged the French to expect such support).[195] In June 1908 Natty himself felt obliged to point out to his Paris cousins that "there was no question of alliance, offensive or defensive . . . and nothing would be so unwise as to make use of that word." To be sure, he was "equally certain that an unwarranted attack by Germany on France would arouse sympathies and feeling which no government could withstand"; but he insisted that "Germany [had] no idea of an unwarranted attack."[196]

This raises an important point. Historians usually talk as if Germany's relatively rapid economic growth before 1914 implied an equal growth of German international power. Informed contemporaries knew better. The combination of a decen-

tralised federal system and a relatively democratic imperial parliament meant that
the Reich found it extremely difficult to finance its increased armaments expenditure after 1897 by raising taxes. This helps explain the relatively high level of
German government borrowing in the pre-war period, though in fact much of the
borrowing was undertaken by the federal states and local authorities to finance non-
military expenditures. The high level of public sector borrowing in itself put a strain
on the German capital market; the fact that it coincided with very high levels of private sector investment (mainly to finance the rapid growth of the electrical engineering and chemical sectors) compounded the difficulty. The resulting upward
pressure on German interest rates—most apparent in the rising yields on German
bonds—was widely seen by contemporaries as a sign of German financial weakness.

By now, Natty was no longer sympathetic towards "the German octopus" (or
"Deutschland über alles," as he sometimes called it). He was, he told his cousins in
April 1907, "no admirer of German statesmanship and I am never enamoured of
their policy, nor do I trust what they choose to call Weltpolitik." He was especially
hostile to the efforts of Admiral Tirpitz to narrow the naval gap between Britain and
Germany. Yet he was quick to discern the limits of German power. "There is no
doubt," he observed, "that the foreign policy of Germany has resulted in her isolation and also that there has been a comparative failure of securing by political means
what is euphemistically called commercial and industrial enterprise and which
would be better designated under the term financial concessions [overseas]."[197]
Moreover, he knew perfectly well that the Germans could not afford a prolonged
naval race, and this financial weakness made the "scaremongering" notion of a
German threat to British security seem fundamentally implausible. "[T]he German
Government is very hard up," noted Natty in April 1906, as yet another Reich loan
was put on the market.[198] Nor did he overlook the difficulties experienced by the
Reichsbank during 1907, which were in many ways more serious than anything
experienced in London. "Germans are scientific and symmetrical in everything," he
wrote (with more than a hint of irony), "and their Bank act has been held up to the
admiration of the world by those speculators who grumble at high rates of interest
here as a marvel of scientific simplicity and elasticity." But although "elastic conditions [had] enabled them to inflate their currency . . . the length of their [tether?] has
been reached as the German Government has Treasury Bonds and Treasury Notes to
issue."[199] Natty was especially struck by the German need to sell bonds on foreign
capital markets, an expedient which neither Britain nor France had to resort to in
peacetime.[200]

Of course, the Rothschilds saw that financial constraints might positively
encourage the German government to pursue an aggressive foreign policy, because
by "rattl[ing] the sword in the scabbard" the Kaiser and Bülow hoped to "defer the
realisation of many socialistic dreams."[201] Yet such sabre-rattling could only "incur
fresh military and naval expenditure on a grand scale" and thus worsen the internal
position. This explains why Alfred renewed his old links to the German court when
the Kaiser visited England in December 1907. As Natty observed shrewdly, "it is
hardly likely that the German Emperor will want to be quarrelsome . . . [when] he
has his hands full with all his socialists."[202] The impression of an over-stretched
Reich was promptly confirmed by a huge Prussian bond issue in April 1908 and by
the Reich budget, which showed "a large deficit . . . due to an ambitious naval pro-

gramme, to the necessity of increasing the pay of all their civil servants, and to what they practically call 'miscalculations' in their old age pension scheme."[203] Small wonder the Rothschilds, like the Warburgs in Hamburg, expected the German government to seek some sort of agreement limiting naval construction.[204] The second Moroccan crisis in 1911—when the German government sent the *Panther* to Agadir—underlined the vulnerability of the Berlin market to withdrawals of foreign capital.[205] To the bankers, Germany seemed weak, not strong.

Nor could it be taken for granted that a Liberal government would ever be able to bring itself to fight on the same side as Russia in a war. Here too the Rothschilds sought to resist the tendency for Europe to divide into "armed camps" by opposing the idea of an Anglo-Russian entente. Perhaps if the 1905 revolution had led to an enduring liberalisation of Russia, their attitude might have been different. The French socialist leader Jaurès hoped that the Rothschilds would use their financial power to force Russia down the road of parliamentarisation, recalling how "in 1848 the Rothschilds, as creditors of the King of Prussia, had imposed on him the budgetary control of a Landtag and the granting of a constitution for the sake of their loans."[206] Natty did indeed express the hope in January 1906 that "wise counsels will prevail at St. Petersburg & that a liberal régime may be instituted."[207] But the Rothschilds were sceptical when the post-revolutionary government approached the Paris house in the hope of securing financial assistance in exchange for promises of reform.[208] In the hope of overcoming the English partners' hostility, an informal approach was made by one Dr Brandt, a minor figure at the Russian embassy in London (whom Natty described as "an ugly hump-backed Russian Jew, evidently full of his own importance") who "came here in order to explain to us the position of Russian Jews & to point out to us how their fate might be ameliorated":

> The Jew, said Dr Brandt, is an object of horror & detestation to everyone in Russia. The Emperor & the Court hate him, hatred which is shared by Witte & the Ministers, the Russian people loathe him, & the Duma, which is about to be elected, will reflect the wishes of the Court & the opinion of the Russian people. You cannot emigrate 5 millions of Russian Jews, & if you do not do something, you may have, & probably will have a "Red letter" Saturday, a second Saint Barthélémy, & nearly the whole Jewish Russian population sacrificed to the fury & orthodoxy of the holy Russian people. As far as I understood him, the remedy is a very simple one. Make a big loan for Russia, & something may be done for the Jews!

But Natty had heard this tale too many times before: "I told him not precisely in the words that I am using to you, but words to the same effect: that he was putting the cart before the horse, namely, that when the Russian Jew has liberty & equal rights, Russian finance would improve & the Treasury difficulties would be considerably less."[209]

It was the same story when the somewhat more plausible figure of Arthur Raffalovich called on Alfred the following month:

> He said that 6 months ago his Master, Mr de Witte & the Emperor, were anxious, most anxious to ameliorate the fate of the Jewish population in Russia, but that now public opinion in Russia was excited and

the Emperor & the Imperial Family, as well as the Ministers, were both hurt & grieved at the fact that the Russian Jews had attempted to defy a just & paternal government, that the Hebrew population were the authors of the Socialistic & Revolutionary movement, & that when everything was quieting down in Russia, they alone of his numerous subjects had refrained from sending congratulatory addresses expressing their loyalty & devotion to the Throne & their love for the country that treats them so well! He naturally supposed that we wished to ameliorate the fate of our coreligionists, and that there was only one way of doing so, namely, by our consenting to place ourselves at the head of an International Syndicate who would be prepared to accommodate the Czar with untold millions, anything between £60 to £120,000,000! Should we agree to the proposal, he gave us his word of honour that those reforms we have at heart would be immediately effected, & on our answer, the fate of our coreligionists depended, and the responsibility lay with us, & not with the governing power at St Petersburg.[210]

Again Natty was unbending. Similar promises had been made when the Paris house had arranged large loans for Vyshnegradsky, but had not been kept. Nor had Witte given Edmond and Edouard any reason to believe in a real change of policy in St Petersburg when they had last seen him in Paris. "[T]aking all the circumstances into consideration," Natty replied, "we could & would not help Russia in her need until she had done for our co-religionists that which would make them happy & contented subjects of the Czar & prosperous citizens of the Russian Empire." He added for good measure that "it was absurd to suppose that the Jewish population hated the Czar. A large number of alien emigrants only [prayed?] to go home & dwell in their own country . . . & I also told him that when the Cesarewitch was born, strange to say, in the ghettos of London & New York, the health of the Czar was drunk, and blessings invoked on the new born babe." This was Raffalovich's cue to produce a draft message to be sent back to Russia which Natty "slightly altered, as I was particularly desirous that he should only lay stress on the Jewish Question." A final approach by a Russian purporting to speak on behalf of "our co-religionists" was dismissed out of hand:

> [W]e should not think of associating ourselves with it until the fate of our co-religionists in that country was assured. We know from very good sources that that their present position is as bad as it has ever been; & probably much worse. The Jewish population live in dread of fresh outrages at any moment, & particularly when our Passover holiday occurs. The Liberal Party in Russia are also very anxious & the prospect of a huge Loan being made in Paris or Berlin fills them with dismay. They think that the money, which is often called the "sinews of war," will be in this case a fresh emblem of oppression.[211]

"We can have no direct or financial interest in the Russian Loan" was Natty's last word.[212]

Perhaps as a way reinforcing his case for consumption in the rue Laffitte, Natty also added a financial objection: he suspected that Russia was heading for a financial crisis and might even have to abandon the convertibility of the rouble. The difficulty with this was, as he himself conceded, "that there are a great many people in the world who look at Russian finance with very different eyes from what we do. A friend of mine who was staying with me on Sunday, who is a prominent Radical in this country . . . told me on Sunday that the Russian Government were rapidly getting the better of all their troubles & disorder. He acknowledged that their finances were at present in an awful state; but, with a chuckle, he said, time & the resources of the country will bring them through."[213] Both Revelstoke and Morgan had been in St Petersburg before the revolution broke out in 1905 and it was predictable that once order was restored they would resume negotiations for a Russian loan. With the blessing of both Asquith and Grey, they arranged to place £13 million of a massive £89 million Russian bond issue on the London market.[214] The main source of financial support for Russia remained France, of course: as Natty might have realised, French banks and bondholders had already put too much into Russia to risk the collapse of the currency and the devaluation of their own investments. But in Berlin too there were eager takers, led by Mendelssohn. To make matters worse, it was widely reported in the financial press that the Rothschilds had covertly subscribed to the loan.[215]

Natty sometimes maintained that he opposed lending to Russia on "purely financial" grounds, quite apart from his religious scruples. He was firmly convinced that the new Russian loan would fail outright or that those who subscribed to it would soon lose out as a result of "renewed discontent [and] rioting which may be sporadic in various places but which will become general." The political situation in Russia, he warned, remained "in a very critical and parlous state" and he predicted "periodic outbreaks of dynamite outrages, of bomb throwing and assassination." He even went so far as to compare the election of the first Duma to the calling of the Estates General in 1789.[216] Although in the medium term Natty was right to foresee another and much bigger Russian revolution, it might be thought that, at least in the short term, there was an element of wishful thinking in all this; even as he made the pessimistic argument, Natty could not conceal his envy of the "very magnificent profit" which he assumed Barings were making.[217] Yet it soon became evident that the Rothschilds had been justified in refusing the loan on purely financial grounds: although it was relatively firm to begin with, by July the price of the new bonds had slumped and Revelstoke was left holding a large parcel at a loss.[218] "As we have been wise enough to eschew Russian finance for some considerable time," Natty was able to gloat, "& lucky enough not to be inveigled by false promises into taking any part in the Russian Loan, the fall in Russian securities only affects us indirectly & only so far as [it] may have a considerable effect on the price of other securities.—We are naturally more affected by the fate of our unfortunate co-religionists in Russia & by the barbarities which are again being practised."[219]

Nevertheless, the persistent political instability of Russia did not mean, as Natty fervently hoped, that "all these beautiful detailed accounts in the papers, of understandings between England and Russia are myths & inventions."[220] In June 1906, as news reached London of more "hideous slaughter" of Russian Jews, Natty went to see the Foreign Secretary to "ask him if international action cannot be taken, & on this ground, [that] the continuance of this monstrous policy will send fugitives in hundreds if not in thousands to countries where they are not wanted, & where there are already many seeking work." But Grey was evidently not much moved by this argument; he attached a good deal more significance to strengthening the diplomatic links between Britain, France and Russia which he regarded as essential if German ambitions were to be kept in check. The most he was prepared to offer Natty was "unofficial & verbal communications to be made to the effect that a recurrence of these outrages would alienate public opinion & prevent the good feeling which ought to exist between the two countries."[221] Although Natty was pleased to see that "my friend" seemed "very nervous about the future of Russia," this was self-delusion. Grey was already much too firmly committed to the policy of Anglo-Russian entente to be distracted by the plight of the Russian Jews.

As the extent of the government's commitment to Russia emerged, there were moments when Natty and his brothers tempered their Russophobia. They donated a thousand guineas to a Russian Relief Fund established by Revelstoke in 1907 without specifying that their contribution should be for Jews only. They did not do anything positively to worsen the Russian financial position, for, as Leo said, "however much we may dislike the great Northern power, no one can wish to see a financial disaster on the Banks of the Neva." At times, Natty even began to speak as if he felt the post-revolutionary reforms might endure.[222] When the Anglo-Russian entente was formally announced in September 1907, he was lukewarm, but worried that excessive criticism in the Radical press might encourage the Russian belief that the newspapers were in Jewish hands and might therefore "be very prejudicial to the fate of our Russian co-religionists." "Some of our co-religionists will not be over pleased with this rapprochement," he admitted a few weeks later, "but I always tell them the cause of the Jews in Russia will not be improved if it is supposed that they stir up enmity between England and Russia."[223] He even seemed prepared to countenance the idea of a Russian loan on the London market (though in the end the loans of 1907 and 1909 were left to Revelstoke and Cassel).[224]

Yet this was a momentary wavering. Taking advantage of a chance meeting at Epsom racecourse in June 1908, Leo buttonholed the King on the eve of his visit to St Petersburg. The upshot of their meeting was a long and carefully worded letter signed by all three English brothers. Blaming the recent pogroms on organisations like the Octobrists and the Union of the Russian People—though without denying the involvement of "a certain number of Jews . . . in the Anarchical movement"— the Rothschilds complained that little had been done to punish the culprits and that there had consequently been:

> a recrudescence of the persecution of the Jewish population artificially hidden under legal devices. The Jewish population is again terrified and naturally there are fears both in Russia and elsewhere that emigration may take place on a large and unprecedented scale, which would have the double effect of depriving Russia of industrious and sober workmen and this extra influx of immigrants would certainly disorganise the position and condition of all workmen in many parts of the world.

Through his private secretary Sir Francis Knollys, the King "promised to take the matter into his serious consideration and [to] consult with Sir Charles Hardinge, who accompanies him and with the English Ambassador in St Petersburg what is the best course to pursue."[225] In the end, it was decided that the ambassador (Sir Arthur Nicolson) should raise the issue with the new Russian premier Stolypin;[226] but Natty regarded the latter's response as "most unsatisfactory":

[I]t is quite true that he promises legislation in a year or two, but it will be very mild legislation and in fact Mr Stolopine [*sic*] not only blames the Jews themselves for everything which has taken place, but he declares most positively, which is particularly ridiculous, that if the Jews had equal rights they would soon hold all the land in Russia and be masters of the country and that the pogroms in fact were risings of unfortunate debtors against modern Shylocks.[227]

The King (or "Meilach," as Natty liked to call him, recalling the old days of Hebrew codewords) put a more positive gloss on this response, insisting "that in a short time something will be done for the Jews and he was assured that there would be no Russian Loan this year which he considered a good sign."[228] But when the charge of ritual murder was revived in 1912 during a trial at Kiev any hopes of progress on the "Jewish question" were scotched, and Natty had to resume his campaign, corresponding publicly on the issue with Cardinal Merry del Val and drawing up a formal letter of protest which was signed by various political grandees including Rosebery and Cromer.[229] Natty continued to hope that the Anglo-Russian entente would founder—if not over the treatment of the Jews, then on some traditional bone of contention like the Straits—but he underestimated Grey's willingness to appease the Tsarist regime, and the City's willingness to absorb new Russian bonds.[230] From their low point in August 1906 of 71.5, Russian 4 per cents rose to a peak of 96.25 in December 1910, ensuring handsome profits to compensate Revelstoke and the other Russophiles for their losses on the first post-revolutionary loan.

Austria

It is tempting to conclude, then, that the direction of capital flows in pre-1914 Europe made the Triple Entente with France and Russia the most likely diplomatic combination for Britain. In that sense, the Rothschilds had been swimming against a powerful economic tide in trying to broker some kind of Anglo-German understanding, or in trying to keep Britain and Russia apart. Yet they did not give up. There remained one other possibility which had not been tried since the 1850s—namely, a renewal of the financial links between London and Austria–Hungary. Of course, the London house had been much involved in Hungarian finance in the 1870s and 1880s, so the once vital link between the London capital market and the Habsburg monarchy had not wholly faded from memory. But by the turn of the century Austro-Hungarian finance had become more introverted, reflecting the somewhat autarkic character of the post-1867 Habsburg economy—essentially a protectionist Central European customs and monetary union. As we have seen, the links between the Vienna house and the other Rothschild houses had tended to weaken after Anselm's death: indeed, the surviving records of the Austrian bank suggest that such links were more or less non-existent by 1900. Moreover, the highly decentralised Austro-Hungarian financial system meant that arms expenditure remained relatively low compared with the other great powers, so that in theory there was less need for foreign loans than in Russia. Nevertheless, stagnating tax revenues, the increased military costs arising from naval construction[231] and the annexation of Bosnia–Hercegovina, as well as the rising cost of governing a fissiparous, multi-ethnic conglomerate, led to recurrent deficits on both the Austrian and Hungarian budgets. "Notwithstanding all the new taxes," ran one report to Holstein in the late 1880s, "the balancing of the budget is known to be a *pium desiderium.* Meanwhile they continue to borrow merrily from Rothschilds."[232]

Throughout the 1890s and into the early 1900s, new issues of Austrian and Hungarian rentes were more or less monopolised by a Rothschild-led consortium whose other members were the Creditanstalt, the Bodencreditanstalt and the Ungarische Creditbank. Indeed, even after 1900 the group was involved either solely or in partnership with Austrian and Hungarian issues worth around 2.8 billion crowns (*c.* £120 million).[233] This so-called "Rothschild group" offered, even if it did not always deliver, access to foreign capital markets. Could the polarisation of European politics have been arrested by increasing British or French holdings of Austro-Hungarian rentes? The question is not wholly unrealistic. In 1907 and again in 1910 the idea of issuing a major Hungarian loan in Paris was seriously discussed, though in the end it foundered in the face of political opposition.[234] In 1914 the London Rothschilds, in partnership with Schröders, successfully arranged two separate bond issues by Austria and Hungary worth a total of £19.5 million.

There were four reasons why the loans of 1914 were too little and came too late to extricate Austria–Hungary from the Dual Alliance with Germany. Firstly, despite repeated efforts to broaden the international market for Austrian and Hungarian rentes, investors in Paris and London were markedly less keen than those in Berlin. For most of the period, such external finance as was required came from Germany, and specifically Mendelssohn and the Darmstädter and Deutsche Banks.[235] Indeed, so close were the links between the Vienna Rothschilds and these Berlin banks that in 1910 the British consul general in Budapest regarded the Rothschild group as "the chain which binds the Dual Monarchy . . . *nolens volens* to Germany." Secondly, the Rothschild group began to fall apart. Previously, Albert's dominance had been more or less uncontested: as Alexander Spitzmüller of the Creditanstalt recalled, although he had "absolutely no well-defined influence," his advice was hard to ignore when major decisions were being taken. This reflected the distinctive system of interlocking directorships which was such an important feature of Austro-Hungarian business. Albert, Spitzmüller later recalled, was "represented on the board of directors by many personalities from the world of business who were close to him . . . [H]e used to make his influence, through the occupation of places on the board of directors, a sort of tyranny . . . [and] always appeared to me to be a peculiar mix of gentleman and brutal potentate." The situation was similar at the Bodencreditanstalt, where Albert "did not have a determining role but his word had weight." In the eyes of Julius Blum, Albert was always the master of the Rothschild group. But under the leadership of Theodor von Taussig and his successor, the Bodencreditanstalt increasingly pursued a more independent course, as did the Creditanstalt when Spitzmüller took command in 1910. By the time of Albert's death in 1911, the group had ceased to exist.

Thirdly, and partly because of this disunity, the Austrian and Hungarian governments succeeded in freeing themselves from the dominance of the Rothschild group by tapping new sources of domestic finance. After 1897, a share of any new issues of rentes had to be allotted to the Postal Savings Banks. Six years later, the Austrian Finance Minister Böhm-Bawerk allowed the big non-Rothschild banks like the Wiener Bankverein to participate in a major conversion operation; and in 1908 both Austria and Hungary finally adopted the system of public subscription for new bond issues which by this time was virtually the norm in most West European states. The last vestiges of the Rothschild group's monopoly were swept away in January 1910 when a new Austrian issue of rentes was sold exclusively to the Postal Savings Banks, leading to the creation of a new and much more broadly based consortium. Despite Albert's attempt to boycott the new system, the Bodencreditanstalt broke ranks;[236] and although his son and successor Louis was able to construct a new Rothschild-led group embracing the Creditanstalt, the Wiener Bankverein and the Länderbank, it was never able to re-establish the previous group's role in public finance.

The fourth reason why there was never much likelihood of reviving the old, financially based partnership between Britain and Austria was purely political. "[A]s a matter of course," wrote Natty to Paris in April 1906, "we do not know if our dear cousin Salbert [Albert] is on speaking terms with the new Hungarian Government."[237] This was symptomatic of the extreme difficulty of operating in a political system as decentralised and volatile as the Austro-Hungarian. Natty visited Vienna in 1907, but seems to have gleaned little from the visit; and subsequent communications during the crisis-ridden year which followed from Albert were anodyne— sometimes even omitting to mention important financial news.[238] Although the Austrian ambassador in London hoped that Rothschild influence over *The Times* and *Daily Telegraph* might moderate the British response to the annexation of Bosnia in October 1908, he was exaggerating Natty's influence and the scope for generating pro-Austrian sentiment.[239] The truth was that in both London and Vienna the political influence of the Rothschilds was on the wane. "I openly recognise," Albert told Sieghart in 1910, "that I overestimated the influence of the Archduke Franz Ferdinand." It was a telling admission, suggesting that Albert had shared Franz Ferdinand's hostility to the policy of compromise with Russia in the Balkans favoured by Count Aerenthal, the Austrian Foreign Minister between 1906 and 1912. That, in reality, was the right option for Vienna: the more policy came to be characterised by hostility to Russia and subservience to Germany, the closer Austria– Hungary edged towards the disaster of a great power war over the Balkans. The Rothschilds, who had never cared much for that turbulent region,[240] could do little to prevent this.

In the final analysis, therefore, there were economic forces at work which at least made some combinations of powers more likely than others. To put it simply, there was an important difference between those countries which were net creditors (Britain and France), those which were self-financing but not capital exporting (Austria–Hungary and to some extent Germany), and those which had to borrow large amounts from abroad (Russia and Italy). These financial factors had a bearing on diplomacy. Of all the great powers, Russia relied most heavily on foreign lending in the period before 1914; and the predominance of France as Russia's main source of external finance had as its corollary a diplomatic rapprochement between the two powers, despite the fact that they had less in common in terms of their internal politics than any other two-power combination, and despite the fact that for most of the nineteenth century they had been diplomatically at odds. This Franco-Russian entente was one of the defining diplomatic developments of the 1890s; and the Rothschilds played a central role in it—despite their strong antipathy towards the Tsarist regime's anti-Jewish policies. A similar financial gravitation attracted Italy and Turkey towards Germany (though it was not strong enough to ensure diplomatic loyalty from Italy in 1914).

No such financial relationship drew Britain and Germany together, however, despite the strong desire of Alfred in particular to build some kind of Anglo-German entente. Nor did it prove possible to restore the old financial ties between Britain and Austria. In truth, neither Germany nor Austria–Hungary needed much in the way of outside capital; they could manage together, and so they did. By contrast, and despite their colonial disagreements, London and Paris were gradually drawn together after 1900, not just by shared Germanophobia, but also by their common interest as international financial centres in monetary stability: here too the Rothschilds played a key role as agents mediating between and bolstering the Bank of England and the Banque de France. What remained undetermined was the extent of Britain's military commitment to France, not to mention the extent of her diplomatic commitment to Russia.

With hindsight, it is possible to see that the ideal diplomatic constellation from the Rothschilds' point of view had been the Crimean coalition of Britain and France against Russia, with Austria and Prussia more or less neutral, but inclining to the West; but this was not to return until almost a century after the Crimean War, under the very different circumstances of the Cold War. The constellation which finally emerged in 1914, by contrast, was almost the worst of all possible worlds.

Natty's political marginalisation in the period after around 1905 lies here. On the one hand, he was a keen proponent of increased naval expenditure; on the other, he was reluctant to pay for it. In March 1909 he spelt out this ultimately untenable position in a speech to the Institute of Directors and the Naval and Military Defence Committee of the London Chamber of Commerce:

> At the present time we were threatened with a great increase of taxation. He [Natty] did not know if the revenue would come up to expectation, but a large expenditure had been incurred, and he supposed a good deal more would be be necessary, because all would agree that the Fleet must be maintained in the highest state of efficiency. (Cheers). That being the case, heavier burdens would be thrown on the entire community, and an institute of this kind might be able to say a few words to the Chancellor of the Exchequer with the object of preventing the incidence of taxation from disturbing the commercial arrangements of the country more than was necessary. (Cheers).[15]

A month later, he told a large City audience at the Guildhall "to pledge their support to the Government in any financial arrangements that might be necessary to maintain our naval supremacy"; yet he failed to spell out which arrangements he had in mind.[16] Natty knew full well that "the two absorbent questions . . . namely the Budget and the Navy estimates," were "closely allied"; but he underestimated the political and constitutional implications of this alliance.[17]

In Germany, by contrast, where the Reich was conventionally restricted to financing itself (and hence the German army and navy) exclusively from indirect taxes, the tendency was for tariffs to rise; but working-class dissatisfaction with the combination of "dear bread" and "militarism" was so successfully exploited by the Social Democratic Party (SPD) that the government was soon forced to contemplate introducing property taxes at the Reich level.[18] Here again, Natty misread the implications of increased "militarism." In 1907 he interpreted Prince Bülow's election victory over the SPD as a victory for what the strategy historians have dubbed "social imperialism":

> The elections which took place in Germany at the end of the last week are a striking example of how national sentiments and imperialistic tendencies have more than anything else contributed to the rout of socialistic ideas, in all probability the Kaiser and his favourite henchman Prince Bülow will go ahead with their Welt-Politik, will rattle the sword in the scabbard, will incur fresh military and naval expenditure on a grand scale, expenditure which no doubt will be felt in England and in France and must in the state of European finance defer the realisation of many socialistic dreams.[19]

In reality, the 1907 result was an ephemeral victory obtained by uniting the so-called "bourgeois" parties in the wake of the successful war against the Herero in South-West Africa. By the time of the next general election in 1912, that unity had crumbled precisely because of disagreements about the funding of military expenditure. Contrary to the assumptions of many on the German right, spending more on the army and navy tended to strengthen the position of the Social Democrats by focusing voters' attention on the regressive way in which defence spending was financed.

The other way of paying for the rising costs of domestic and foreign policy was, of course, by borrowing. As table 13c shows, this was an option favoured in some countries more than in others. Both Germany and Russia borrowed heavily in the period after 1890, roughly doubling their national debts in the period to 1913; however, when adjustment is made for the depreciation of the rouble in sterling terms, the debt burden in the Russian case rose by just two-thirds, a significantly smaller increase. In absolute terms, France borrowed a lot too, though from a starting point of higher indebtedness than Germany (hence the lower percentage increase). Britain was unusual among the great powers in reducing the level of her national debt between 1887 and 1913. This achievement is all the more impressive when one remembers that the cost of the Boer War drove up government borrowing—by £132 million in total—in the years between 1900 and 1903.

Table 13c: National debts in millions of national currencies (and sterling), 1887–1913.

	FRANCE (FRANCS)	BRITAIN (POUNDS)	GERMANY* (MARKS)	RUSSIA (ROUBLES)
1887	23,723	655	8,566	4,418
	(£941)		(£419)	(£395)
1890	–	618	10,540	4,905
			(£516)	(£572)
1913	32,976	625	21,679	8,858
	(£1,308)		(£1,061)	(£937)
percentage increase†	39	–5	153	137

* Germany = Reich plus federal states.
† Increase in sterling terms.
Sources: Schremmer, "Public finance," p. 398; Mitchell, *British historical statistics*, pp. 402f.; Hoffmann *et al.*, *Wachstum*, pp. 789f.; Apostol, Bernatzky and Michelson, *Russian public finances*, pp. 234, 239.

These were not unsustainable burdens at a time of unprecedented economic growth. Indeed, in all four cases total debt tended to fall in relation to net national product, as table 13d shows. By modern standards, only France had a high ratio of debt to net national product and the tendency was for the burden to diminish.

Table 13d: National debt as a percentage of net national product, 1887–1913.

	FRANCE	BRITAIN	GERMANY*	RUSSIA
1887	119.3	55.3	50.0	65.0
1890	–	44.6	51.2	77.1
1913	86.5	27.6	44.4	47.3

* Germany = Reich plus federal states.
Sources: as table 13c and Hobson, "Wary Titan," pp. 505f.

Nevertheless, contemporaries were disturbed by the absolute increase in government borrowing. This was because of the decline in bond prices—or rise in yields (see table 13e)—which manifested itself after around 1890.

The principal cause of this decline was in fact the acceleration of inflation, a monetary phenomenon caused by the increase in gold production and, more important, the rapid development of banking intermediation, which was increasing the use of paper money and cashless transaction methods (especially inter-bank clearing). Contemporaries, however, interpreted rising bond yields as a form of market protest against lax fiscal policies. This was only really true in so far as public sector

Table 13e: Major European bond prices, *c.* 1896-1914.

	PEAK PRICE	DATE	TROUGH PRICE	DATE	PERCENTAGE CHANGE
British 2.75 per cent consols*	113.50	July 1896	78.96	Dec. 1913	-30.4
French 3 per cent rentes	105.00	Aug. 1897	80.00	July 1914	-23.8
Russian 4 per cents	105.00	Aug. 1898	71.50	Aug. 1906	-31.9
German Imperial 3 per cents	99.38	Sept. 1896	73.00	July 1913	-26.5

* For 1913 2.5 per cent price recalculated on a 2.75 per cent coupon.
Source: *Economist* (weekly closing prices).

bond issues were tending to push up the cost of borrowing across the board by "crowding out" or competing with private sector claims on the capital market. Nevertheless, the accusation of fiscal incontinence was repeatedly levelled at most governments—even the British—by critics on both the left and right. Table 13f shows that rising yields were a universal phenomenon; of more interest, however, is the fact that there were pronounced differences or "spreads" between the yields on the various countries' bonds. These yield spreads genuinely did express market assessments not just of fiscal policy but more generally of political stability and foreign policy, given the traditionally close correlations between the perils of revolution, war and insolvency. Perhaps predictably, because of the experience of 1904-5 and her more general problems of economic and political "backwardness," Russia was regarded as the biggest credit risk among the great powers. More surprising is the wide differential between German yields and those for British and French bonds, which were remarkably similar. This cannot be explained in terms of the greater demands by the German private sector on the Berlin capital market, as these are *London* prices (and in any case investors were generally choosing between different governments' bonds, not between industrial securities or bonds). It seems investors shared the view of the better-informed political observers of the time that Wilhelmine Germany was financially less strong than its Western rivals.

Table 13f: Bond yields of the major powers, 1911-1914.

	BRITISH CONSOLS	FRENCH RENTES	GERMAN 3 PER CENTS	RUSSIAN 4 PER CENTS	GERMAN-BRITISH YIELD SPREAD	RUSSIAN-BRITISH YIELD SPRREAD
Mar 1911	3.08	3.13	3.56	4.21	0.48	1.13
July 1914	3.34	3.81	4.06	4.66	0.72	1.32
Average	3.29	3.36	3.84	4.36	0.55	1.07

Source: *Economist* (average monthly London prices).

"Too Much Lord Rothschild"

By the turn of the century, the Rothschild identification with the Conservative party was more or less complete. Dorothy Pinto (who later married Edmond's son James) recalled how "as a child I thought Lord Rothschild *lived* at the Foreign Office, because from my schoolroom window I used to watch his carriage standing outside every afternoon—while in reality of course he was closeted with Arthur Balfour."[20] The two men had their differences, to be sure: in 1901, for example, Natty wrote to complain about a speech Balfour had made in the Commons which had made inaccurate criticisms of De Beers, and they seem to have disagreed on the question of immigration controls.[21] But for most of Balfour's three-year term as Prime Minister they worked closely together.

There was a danger to this proximity. As Edward Hamilton commented, even before Salisbury retired in July 1902 Natty had "become so strong a party man, he will now be 'out of it' whenever the other side comes in."[22] This was astute. In the past, the Rothschilds had been adept at maintaining lines of communication with both government and Opposition. By the early 1900s, however, a new generation of Liberals had come to the fore with whom Natty and his brothers had virtually no social or political contact. Had Rosebery retained the Liberal leadership, there would have been no problem, but after his resignation as Prime Minister in 1895, and as Liberal leader the following year, his influence waned. As president of the imperialist Liberal League, he was profoundly out of sympathy with the more Radical "New" Liberal wing of the party which filled the majority of ministerial posts when the party regained power in 1906. By that time Rosebery had left the party altogether, having denounced both the Anglo-French entente and Irish Home Rule the year before.[23] As the husband of Hannah's daughter Peggy, Rosebery's son-in-law the Earl of Crewe was naturally part of the broader Rothschild familial circle, but there is little evidence that he was politically close to Natty.[24] True, it was a matter of course that Herbert Asquith, the new Chancellor, was invited to dine with the Lords Rothschild and Revelstoke at the Lord Mayor's annual dinner. But neither Asquith nor the City grandees had any illusions about their deep differences of opinion. As Natty put it, "the City Magnates who were present . . . came to the very easy conclusion that Mr Asquith did not understand much about business. The frigid way in which his remarks were listened to will, I hope, be a damper to some of his rash & enthusiastic advisers."[25] He and his brothers were not wholly excluded from the corridors of power; but their views, frigid or otherwise, carried little weight. Once, the Rothschilds had mixed with politicians regardless of party allegiance in order to obtain the best possible political intelligence and to influence financial and foreign policy. Now Natty was himself a politician, making remarkably frequent public speeches and donating substantial sums to the Tory party machine. He had become so overtly partisan that he was effectively cut off from both intelligence and influence under a Liberal administration.

An electoral landslide on the scale of the Liberal triumph in 1906 usually owes as much to the exhaustion and disunity of the vanquished party as to the programme of the victor. Central to the Conservatives' demise were the rising costs of their imperial policies after 1899, and their inability to agree on a way to pay for them. It was not just a question of beating the Boers and building new battleships. The administrative and even physical deficiencies exposed by the war in South Africa prompted widespread criticism—even a sense of national crisis—on both left and right. The Conservatives lacked a coherent response. It was typical that, when asked by Chamberlain to chair a Treasury committee to consider improving the piecemeal system of old-age pensions, Natty made little secret of his scepticism about the possibility of some kind of state contributory system on the German model, and he was even more hostile to any idea of non-contributory handouts to the elderly.[26] Following Chamberlain's conversion to the idea of increased protectionist tariffs as a solution to Britain's domestic and imperial problems, the Rothschilds' response was as ambivalent as that of the party as a whole.

For most of the second half of the nineteenth century, the family had been firmly committed to free trade. Alphonse's vitriolic comments on American and French tariff policy in the 1890s show that such attitudes were alive and well even at the turn of the century. "France is going to die from suffocation under protectionism," he warned in 1896. "The best of socialisms is the free exchange of international production, and were M. Jaurès (the socialist leader) to preach nothing else we would unanimously be of his opinion."[27] But by 1903 his London cousins were wavering in their allegiance to "the sacred principles of free trade." On July 3, Natty confessed to Edward Hamilton that he was "rather taken by Chamberlain's plan"—a remarkable volte face for a man who had once dismissed the Colonial Secretary as "a Radical wolf in Tory sheep's clothing . . . the typical democrat—a spendthrift and jingo."[28] When Chamberlain resigned from the Cabinet over the issue on September 17, Natty defended both him and Balfour against the complaints of the Duke of Devonshire who "ought to have known at the Cabinet what Chamberlain intended doing, but . . . was either asleep or woolgathering."[29] On October 7, the day after Chamberlain's curtain-raising call for a policy of "imperial preference" at Glasgow, his keen supporter Harry Chaplin dined with Alfred and two other "City men":

> I asked in an innocent way what they thought of the Glasgow Speech in the City and they all burst out at once. Only one opinion!!!!! Some well-known and prominent Free Traders and others who had always been opposed—come round entirely, general satisfaction, followed by a boom—Consols going up 1 or 3/4—the precise details in City matters I can never remember and it doesn't matter. Alfred R, whom I asked afterwards privately, more than confirmed all this. He has been in the City today, and entirely agreed that there is no doubt as to the impression you have made in those circles, and after all, the City is very important.[30]

In reality, Chamberlain's proposals divided the City elite. Lining up behind Chamberlain and alongside the Rothschild brothers were Cassel, Clinton Dawkins of J. S. Morgan, Everard Hambro (who became honorary treasurer of the Tariff Reform League), the Gibbs family, Robert Benson, Edward Stern and Philip Sassoon. Influential names, no doubt; but the opponents included not only Felix Schuster, the increasingly authoritative governor of the Union Bank of London and one of the City's staunchest Liberals, but also Conservative Free Traders like Lord Avebury and Sir James Mackay (later Lord Inchcape).[31] These were formidable opponents, and it may have been their rejection of Chamberlain which persuaded Natty to row back from his initial support. By the time "Joe" addressed a public meeting at the Guildhall in January 1904, it was becoming apparent that, as Dawkins put it after the speech, "banking opinion [was] on the whole against him"—perhaps understandably, when he tactlessly told his audience that "banking was not the creator of our prosperity, but its creation . . . not the cause of our wealth but the consequence." Significantly, when the Duke of Devonshire addressed a free trade meeting in the same venue two weeks later, Natty was on the platform.[32] This would seem to bear out Hamilton's snide comment (in relation to another fiscal question) that Natty now thought "it necessary to consult every broker" and had "no idea of having an opinion of his own."[33]

Perhaps Natty was not confused; it seems more likely that, like Balfour himself, he was sitting on the fence for tactical reasons, in the hope of maintaining a semblance of party unity. Either way, he could do nothing to limit the damage done by Chamberlain's campaign. Natty had "no doubt," even before the voting began in January 1906, that "Sir H[enr]y Campbell-Bannerman [would] have a majority."[34] What the Rothschilds were not prepared for was the scale of the Conservative rout: the Liberals not only increased their share of the vote from 45 to 49 per cent, but— more important—won an immense majority in the Commons, taking 400 out of 670 seats to the Conservatives' 157. Given the Liberals' proximity to the Labour and Irish Nationalist parties on key issues, their MPs (30 and 83 respectively in number) could be regarded as pro-government too. Contrary to Leo's expectation, even Balfour lost his seat (though it was quickly agreed to install him in place of Alban Gibbs as one of the two City members). It was, as Natty lamented even before the final results were in, a "disastrous" result—"unexpectedly bad."

Why had it happened? Besides the obvious point that "the country has had 20 years of Unionist Government & naturally wanted a change," Natty offered a long list of factors:

> Education, the Religious Question connected with it, Ultra protestantism, in some cases orders from the Catholic Hierarchy to their labouring men to vote Radical & for Socialists, Chinese Labour [in South Africa], the Temperance Question, dissatisfaction of the Jewish voters with the Alien Immigration Act, and last but not least the Taff Vale decision . . . that Trades' Unions could be sued for damages caused by a strike, that their funds were not as supposed, inalienable.[35]

But the key was surely the Tory split over tariffs. Even within the Rothschild family, there was division, with Natty's son Walter winning Mid Bucks as a Unionist Free Trader, and even going so far as to vote with the Liberal government against the Chamberlainites in March 1906,[36] while in the City of London constituency itself, the Conservative vote split evenly between the Tariff Reformer Gibbs and the Free Trader Sir Edward Clarke. In analysing the results, Natty sometimes sought to play down the significance of the tariff issue. Walter's large majority, he insisted, was merely a sign of local "loyalty" to the family, rather than a vote for free trade; while the City result "in no way represented . . . a feeling for Tariff Reform, & certainly not for Chamberlainism."[37] But privately he could not deny that the split had been fatal, and his comments on the subject show where his sympathies really lay. "One thing however I feel quite certain of," he remarked bitterly, "[and] that is that a great many of the Free fooders, & Free traders, like the Duke of Devonshire, are by no means satisfied with the situation they have helped to create."[38] Natty was obliquely critical of Chamberlain too, contrasting his ambition to "build up a new party & a new policy" with Balfour's pragmatic desire simply to "increase the power of the opposition just at present." Both he and Leo agreed that "the late Prime Minister" would have to stay on as Tory leader "because his views on the fiscal question are more in accordance with those of the country than Mr Chamberlain's."[39] But they felt closer on the issue of principle to Chamberlain than to Devonshire. Natty's support for a strategy of "sit[ting] & watch[ing] the course of events" rather than "propound[ing] a policy" was tactical rather than ideological; he evidently hoped that under Balfour's leadership unity on the tariff issue might ultimately be attainable.

Thus in 1910—by which time Balfour had come off the fence in favour of protection—Natty was able to be more open about "the advantages of Tariff Reform." "[T]he subject is the most popular one for the moment," he told his French cousins, "and probably will turn the election."[40]

Such political misjudgements became a regular feature of Natty's correspondence in the Liberal era. He was, it should be remembered, no longer a young man: he was in his seventieth year when he wrote those lines. But the belief that an election could be won on a protectionist platform was not the greatest of his political miscalculations. On a wide range of issues, the Liberals could confidently be expected to disagree among themselves. On Chinese labour in South Africa, they did so almost at once, to his great glee.[41] On education, as Natty said, it was indeed difficult to produce "a measure acceptable alike to the Dissenters, the Church, & the Non Conformists."[42] There were Liberal businessmen who were bound to oppose a trade union bill which placed the unions "under a different law from the rest of the community."[43] Above all, there was little reason to expect the issue of Home Rule to be any easier for Campbell-Bannerman than it had been for Gladstone.[44] Yet Natty was wildly over-optimistic in thinking that such divisions might make the government "a very short lived one, & the Unionist Party may be again restored to strength & power much more quickly than they expected." Of course, the Conservatives could only really recover from the nadir of 1906, and it was reasonable to draw encouragement from local and by-election results.[45] But there were a few subjects which were very likely to unite the Liberals: and one of them was the question of taxation.

Natty was not unaware of the significance of this. "[T]he chief bone of contention besides the Education question," he predicted even before the voting had begun in 1906, "will be the Budget, which is to be of a very Radical character."[46] From an early stage, he recognised that the vociferous contingent of Labour MPs— "the gentlemen who wear red neckties, & are sorry they cannot doff the Phrygian Cap"—would put pressure on the government to consider measures such as "a large & comprehensive scheme of old age pensions, & a square meal once a day for every child in school." Although he was inclined to think that the government would "not do anything rash or violent," he grasped that any measures which implied an increase in government expenditure must imply some kind of increase in the burden of direct taxation: after all, the Liberals had been elected as unequivocal Free Traders, and so could hardly be expected substantially to increase indirect taxation.[47]

To begin with, the fiscal issue lay more or less dormant: the government inherited a surplus and Natty did not expect "any rash experiments in finance . . . the difficulties connected with a graduated income tax may be hinted at & the taxation of site values talked of, but probably everything will go on in the same humdrum fashion." "No doubt there are a good many crude ideas in the air about new forms of taxation or confiscation," he airily told his cousins in Paris. "I could not say that the Government would not be inclined to adopt them if they thought they were feasible or likely to bring grist to their mill." But they would not, because such measures "would defeat their own object & be illusory sources of revenue, besides doing a great deal of harm."[48] Natty was more or less dismissive of Asquith's first budget, which had disappointed some commentators who had been hoping for more radical retrenchment. At first, it had been hoped by the likes of Schuster and Holden "that Mr Asquith was going to put on extra taxation in order to buy up the National

Debt; and now they heap coals of fire on the Chancellor of the Exchequer's head"
because his budget reduced taxation.[49] Natty put this down to the fact that the
deposit banks had large holdings of consols, the price of which they wished to see
pushed up; for his part he was more alarmed by Asquith's decision to set up a Commons Committee "on the incidence of the Income Tax, & various schemes for grad-
uating that obnoxious impost." But even the prospect of a graduated tax and a
surcharge for higher incomes did not worry him much at this stage "as the number
of millionaires was very few, they already paid very heavy death duties and a great
many of them might send their fortunes to America or elsewhere, where they could
not be taxed."[50]

Considering the size of the government's majority in the Commons, Natty's
equanimity was strange. It had two bases. Firstly, he retained the old Rothschild
faith that an excessively radical fiscal policy would be punished by the financial markets: capital would be sent abroad to avoid higher taxes and consols would fall,
embarrassing a Radical Chancellor into compromising. The already low price of
consols when the Liberals came to office seemed to reinforce that argument; it was
even more gratifying when they dropped two percentage points in the summer.
Natty outlined his views on the subject in a series of letters to Paris:

> As English securities were dull, I hope it will give the Chancellor of the
> Exchequer food for reflection & will convince him of the folly of the
> greater part of the Government's Radical programme . . . 87¾ [is]
> the lowest price Consols have been since the war. It is . . . an ironical
> answer to Lloyd George who boasted at Manchester the other day that
> the Rise in Consols was a proof of the Confidence the country had in
> His Majesty's Ministers . . . This state of affairs should have a salutary
> effect at both the Treasury & the Local Government Board; because,
> whether they like it or not, it would be quite impossible for the County
> & Municipal Authorities to borrow money, & without money they
> cannot carry on their Socialistic programme & destroy private enter-
> prise. The Chancellor of the Exchequer will, I suppose, also learn that
> the Socialistic taxation he talked of is not conducive to public credit . . .
> [N]othing is more likely to defeat socialistic legislation than the depreci-
> ation of Home Securities.[51]

Nor did Natty see this as a peculiarity of British politics. His letters to Paris in
this period constantly allude to the parallel between British events and the attempts
by left-of-centre French governments to introduce income tax or to increase state
control over the railways. He saw it as a general rule of democratic politics in a capitalist economy: financial "nervousness on account of the socialistic tendencies of
modern legislative bodies . . . is very disagreeable but it is perhaps the best cure for
the socialistic tendencies." And again: "the fear of socialistic legislation is the real
cause of the depression in both hemispheres."[52] Natty constantly hoped that "the
small bona-fide holders of English securities . . . many of [whom] helped to put a
radical government in power" would turn against the government's fiscal policy *en
masse*.[53] Indeed, he went so far as to outline his argument in an interview with the
left-leaning *Daily News* in October 1907—one of the first occasions a journalist had
ever been admitted to New Court, and a calculated bid to reach a wider audience.
The message was straightforward: " 'Stocks are low,' said Lord Rothschild, 'because

Governments all over the world are hitting at capital.' "[54]

This marked the start of an escalating campaign of public opposition to the government's fiscal policy. When the government proposed radical reform of the licensing laws—a sop to the Temperance lobby—Natty chaired a meeting of brewery debenture holders to protest at the negative financial consequences.[55] When Lloyd George became Chancellor and hinted at the need to "rob henroosts" to pay for the new non-contributory pensions, he harped on the same old theme.[56] The culmination of his campaign came with the unveiling of Lloyd George's so-called "People's Budget" of 1909, the key features of which were an increase in tax on "unearned" income to 1s 2d in the pound, the introduction of a super-tax on incomes above £5,000, an increase in inheritance tax and levies on land values.[57] With the exception of the last item (which implied the first systematic survey of land values for centuries), none of these changes was actually unprecedented: differentiated taxation had been introduced by Asquith in 1907, the principle of graduation had always been implicit in the existence of an income tax threshold and Goschen—a Conservative Chancellor—had been the first to tax inheritances in 1889. Yet the apparently radical *intent* of the budget as a whole galvanised Natty into a kind of high-profile political engagement which went beyond even his father's campaign for Jewish admission to the Commons.

No sooner had the Finance Bill been introduced than he organised the letter to Asquith signed by twenty-one leading City figures (representing fourteen City houses, including Barings, Gibbs, Hambros and J. S. Morgan), which warned that the new taxes—particularly the "great increase and graduation of the death duties"—would not only "prove seriously injurious to the commerce and industries of the country" by eating into capital, but would also "discourage private enterprise and thrift, thus in the long-run diminishing employment and reducing wages." He then called and chaired a protest meeting "representative of all interests in the City, and independent of political associations" at the Cannon Street Hotel on June 23, which passed a resolution that "the main proposals in the Budget weaken the security in all private property, discourage enterprise and thrift, and would prove seriously injurious to the commerce and industries of the country."[58] His own speech at this meeting took a somewhat different tack, arguing that the Chancellor had no historic right to raise a surplus for unspecified purposes and that the taxes on land were an underhand ploy to "establish the principles of Socialism and collectivism." But, speaking later in the Lords, Natty reverted to his original economic critique, assuring fellow peers that both capital flight and increased unemployment in the building trade were due to the damage Lloyd George had done to "credit" and "confidence."[59] He was still peddling the same line when it was confirmed that the Tories had failed to secure a majority in the first 1910 election.[60]

Just as he believed firmly in the power of the City's banking elite, Natty also remained confident that the House of Lords would be able "to alter considerably or to throw out" any excessively radical measures.[61] As early as January 1906, he had consoled himself with the thought that "it doesn't matter what takes place in the House of Commons, as the House of Lords will put it all right."[62] "The Lords play with loaded dice," declared Leo on the eve of the Liberals' second session in early 1907, so that if "very many extreme measures [are] brought in . . . it is doubtful if they will be passed, at all events in the shape in which they were introduced." Even if these included, as he expected, "the abolition of the House of Lords, Home Rule for Ireland, a licensing bill, increased taxation with many other socialistic measures," the Prime Minister would have to "put a good deal of water into his wine."[63] Nor did they take seriously the possibility that the Lords' right of veto might be challenged. "I do not think," declared Natty blithely later that summer, "that the House of Lords is in any peril whatsoever." Talk in the Commons of "materially diminishing its power & influence" was "looked upon as a farce, & will probably be forgotten in a few days"; he mentioned it to his cousins only "to show how weak our Government must be, if they seriously introduce a plan which has no chance of ultimate success, & which exposes them to the ridicule of everyone, with the exception of their immediate followers."[64] Natty thus felt no qualms about voting with the other Tory peers to throw out the government's Licensing Bill in November 1908;[65] and he and his brothers were delighted when their relative and friend Rosebery joined the campaign against the People's Budget, denouncing it as "the end of all, the negation of faith, of family, of property, of Monarchy, of Empire"—in short, "revolution."[66] The link between City opposition and the peers' opposition was deliberately symbolised when Natty presented the Budget Protest League's petition—carrying 14,000 signatures—to the Lords on November 22.[67]

Yet Natty overestimated the power of both the City and the House of Lords. For one thing, it was not at all convincing to blame the "low price of English funds" on the government's "socialistic doctrines."[68] As Lipman has shown with reference to the period 1859 to 1914, there was a difference between the average yield of consols under Conservative governments and the average yield under Liberal governments, but it was very small (less than ten basis points), and is much better explained by changes in inflation and the international situation.[69] Consol prices did indeed fall under Campbell-Bannerman and Asquith, from a peak of 90.4 in February 1906 to a pre-war low of 71.8 at the end of 1913. But it was difficult to blame this slide on Liberal fiscal policy, and it did not have the effect of constraining Asquith or his more radical successor Lloyd George. "Politics," as Natty occasionally had to admit, "but little influence our Stock Exchange." Possibly some bears in the market were "influenced by the fear of prospective legislation, a temperance measure and various wild schemes which are spoken of in connection with old age pensions"; but "the chief anxiety of the City and the Stock Exchange [was] always the money market," and that was much more influenced by the state of gold reserves, the Bank's discounting policy and aggregate new debt creation in the global economy as a whole.[70]

Time and again, the markets refused to back up Natty's condemnation of Liberal fiscal policy by falling when they were supposed to. There was no negative reaction to Asquith's 1907 budget, despite the fact that Natty denounced it as "immoral" and tending towards "the gradual extinction of all private fortunes."[71] In truth, he later had to acknowledge, it was "very doubtful if the markets are at all affected by political news just now. The prices improve or decline according to the financial news of the day, the state of the money-market and the news which is received from other financial centres."[72] "[I]n the long run," he conceded in early 1908 as the markets once again refused to be moved by the Licensing Bill, "very easy money always tells."[73] The 1908 budget was also roundly condemned by Natty, but "all the markets [were] good" after its presentation, and the stock exchange seemed not to care about the new Chancellor's explicit warnings of "further and heavy increased taxation on what he calls the idle rich." A slight drop in the price of consols later that summer and a sustained decline in the second half of the year offered some support for Natty's interpretation, but neither was solely caused by Lloyd George's talk of "robbing henroosts." Indeed, the clearer Lloyd George's intentions became, the less consols fell: prices actually rose in the first five months of 1909. The most that can be said is that the City discounted the People's Budget six months before its publication and even then the effect was modest and ephemeral.[74] The *Westminster Gazette* cruelly summed up the absurdity of Natty's position when its cartoonist depicted him "escaping to the Antarctic region disguised as a Penguin" to avoid Lloyd George's taxes (see illustration 13.i).

Only when a tax measure threatened to bear directly on financial transactions was the argument plausible that fiscal policy was depressing the stock market. Thus Natty was on strong ground when he—along with a large number of other City representatives Lloyd George consulted—argued against an increase in the stamp duties on domestic and foreign bills of exchange on the ground that it would cause "a large diminution of business" and therefore of revenue. This argument was ultimately accepted by the Chancellor and the original scale of duties was altered to reduce the charge on "transactions of average magnitude" (defined as those greater than £1,000).[75] Here the bankers had real leverage. But Lloyd George's more important proposals apparently caused "no perturbation in the minds of the public" (meaning investors in aggregate): despite Natty's campaign, the markets as a whole were "firm" in the wake of the 1909 budget. Indeed, a loan by the London County Council which was issued just after the budget was heavily oversubscribed.[76] Nor can Natty's claims that the markets improved on the news of the Lords' rejection of the budget be taken seriously. As the *Economist* put it, the stock exchange had "now persuaded itself [that] its own interests will not be greatly affected. Prices have, therefore, been left very much to purely market influences."[77] So long as the markets seemed neutral, it was just as plausible for supporters of the government to argue that the Lords' rejection would cause a financial crisis.

The key to the ultimate failure of Natty's opposition to Liberal finance lies here: although Liberal tax policy was unprecedentedly progressive, it was entirely orthodox in that the aim of increased taxation was to balance the budget and indeed to reduce the national debt. Lloyd George inherited a deficit when he became Chancellor, largely the result of the 1907 economic downturn, the new pensions scheme and increasing defence expenditure. The principal objective of the People's Budget was to reduce that deficit; and, for the majority of investors interested in consols, that was the crucial thing. How the money was raised was less important, and Natty's claim that any surplus would be squandered on "socialistic expenditure which would pander to the lower classes" was absurd. To write about "the destruction of capital" and "firm and brilliant markets" in one and the same letter was to encapsulate the contradiction in the argument.[78]

Natty also exaggerated the strength of the Lords on fiscal questions. As he himself admitted, "the House of Lords cannot amend [a Finance Bill], but can only reject en bloc, [and] that is a very serious thing to do."[79] If a budget were rejected principally because it increased tax on the very social group which was over-represented in the Lords—the wealthy elite—then a good case could be made for a constitutional

13.i: *Potted Peers: Lord Rothschild,* "The whole of the British capital having been exported to the South Pole as a result of the Budget Revolution, Lord Rothschild flies from St Swithin's Lane and succeeds in escaping to the Antarctic regions disguised as a Penguin," *Westminster Gazette* (1909).

reform. As early as December 1906, Lansdowne indicated that he did not wish to see a head-to-head confrontation with the government when he argued that the Trades Disputes Bill was "a test question at the last election." When "the conflict between Lords and Commons" began in earnest over peers' amendments to the Education Bill, Natty was right to feel nervous and wrong to assume that the resulting "agitation" would "damage the Government a good deal."[80] If, as he suspected in February 1907, the government wished to provoke the Lords into rejecting "very popular measures" in order to fight a new election on the constitutional issue, the stakes would be high indeed.[81] It was all very well to sneer at "the much pampered and not over-worked British workman"; but there were now enough lower-income voters enfranchised to make the position of "those who have got something"—a typical Natty euphemism for the very rich—politically vulnerable.[82]

It must be added that Natty's arguments against higher income taxes and death duties have not worn well. "[D]iminished incomes," he reasoned, "mean a diminution of money to spend and a diminution of employment, increased death duties mean a diminution of capital and less Income Tax, increased Income Tax means less money to save and less Capital liable to death duty." As a justification for leaving the rich in peace to enjoy their largely unearned and inherited wealth this was weak stuff. In an increasingly democratic system, a policy of "making the Income Tax . . . still more disagreeable to the capitalists & to the wealthy" had undoubted and not easily refutable attractions. Even if Natty was not wholly wrong that relatively modest increases in death duties represented the thin end of a wedge, he was doomed to lose the debate—especially when he admitted the force of the argument that "the burden of taxation should fall on the shoulders of those best able to bear it."[83] In just the same way, the Rothschilds' arguments against land reform to increase the number of small proprietors in the British Isles were economically reasonable, but sounded at the time like the special pleading of big landowners.[84] It was to stretch the antiquated principle of virtual representation too far to justify the Lords' opposition to government measures on the basis of Opposition by-election successes. To be sure, the Liberals saw their commanding majority in the Commons shrink as a consequence of the 1910 elections.[85] But in the end it was the Lords who lost their power to veto finance bills. And of course Lloyd George's taxes were ultimately put in place. "I cannot suppose," Natty mused in January 1910, "that . . . the masses . . . can have any sympathy for the rich men who are to be taxed."[86] It was as if this had only just dawned on him.

To make life easier for the Liberals, Natty had also unwittingly handed the government the perfect stick with which to beat him even before the People's Budget was unveiled. It would undoubtedly have been hard for the government to justify new taxes if the surpluses which had characterised its first two years in office had continued. And it might just have been credible to oppose higher direct taxes if the budget had been unbalanced by "Old Age Pensions and various other sops which [the government's] democratic supporters are clamouring for."[87] But the reality was that a large part of the hole Lloyd George was trying to fill was due to the increased defence spending; and this was something Natty and his associates in the City had vehemently supported. Natty had publicly endorsed Richard Haldane's programme of army reforms (though he privately opposed the conversion of the old militias into the Special Reserve).[88] He and Leo had been even more enthused by the decision to increase expenditure on the navy (not least because it put the Radicals' noses out of joint).[89] But Natty's involvement in the campaign for eight rather than four dreadnoughts in early 1909 was a grievous tactical blunder. When he explicitly admitted that "a large expenditure had been incurred, and he supposed a good deal more would be be necessary" if the navy were to be kept "in the highest state of efficiency," he was giving Lloyd George the perfect opening.[90] And when the Chancellor hit back at "the inevitable Lord Rothschild" in a speech at the Holborn Restaurant—the very day after the anti-budget meeting at which Natty had accused him of "Socialism and collectivism"—he did not miss his chance:

> Really, in all of these things we are having too much Lord Rothschild. We are not to have temperance reform in this country. Why? Because Lord Rothschild has sent a circular to the Peers saying so. (Laughter.) We must have more Dreadnoughts. Why? Because Lord Rothschild said so at a meeting in the City. (Laughter.) We must not pay for them when we have them. Why? Because Lord Rothschild said so at another meeting. (Laughter and cheers.) You must not have estate duties and a supertax. Why? Because Lord Rothschild signed a protest on behalf of the

bankers to say he would not stand it. (Laughter.) You must not have a tax on reversions. Why? Because Lord Rothschild, as chairman of an insurance company, has said it would not do. (Laughter.) You must not have a tax on undeveloped land. Why? Because Lord Rothschild is chairman of an industrial dwellings company. (Laughter.) You ought not to have old-age pensions. Why? Because Lord Rothschild was a member of a committee that said it could not be done. (Laughter.) Now, really, I should like to know, is Lord Rothschild the dictator of this country? (Cheers.) Are we really to have all the ways of reform blocked simply by a noticeboard, "No thoroughfare. By order of Nathaniel Rothschild?" (Laughter and cheers.) There are countries where they have made it perfectly clear that they are not going to have their policy dictated merely by great financiers, and if this sort of thing goes on this country will join the rest of them. (Cheers.) Apart from purely party moves . . . there is really no move against the Budget at all.[91]

This was characteristically strong, not to say demagogic stuff (especially if the other countries alluded to implicitly included Russia);[92] but it struck the Rothschild campaign at its weakest point. Natty had wanted more dreadnoughts. How did he propose they should be paid for, if not partly from his own pocket?

Lloyd George knew when he had an opponent on the run. Speaking at a meeting at Walworth Hall in London on December 18, he warmed to his theme:

> Who clamoured for additional Dreadnoughts? He [Lloyd George] remembered a great meeting in the City, presided over by Lord Rothschild, who demanded that eight Dreadnoughts should be instantly laid down. The Government had ordered four, and Lord Rothschild would not pay (laughter). There had been a very cruel king in the past who ordered Lord Rothschild's ancestors to make bricks without straw (loud laughter). That was a much easier job than making Dreadnoughts without money.[93]

As has often been pointed out, there was a fairly unmistakable anti-Semitic connotation to this last jibe (reminiscent of Thomas Carlyle's allusion many years before to King John's treatment of the Jews and of Gladstone's swipes at Disraeli during the Bulgarian agitation).[94] On this occasion, the lack of taste did not much diminish the effectiveness of the attack. Nor did Natty have much of an answer when a Jewish member of the government—the Chancellor of the Duchy of Lancaster Herbert Samuel—reminded him of the House of Lords' ignominious role in opposing his own father's admission to Parliament. Natty's unconvincing response at an election meeting in the East End was that he was opposing "the new bureaucracy which the Government wish to introduce in this country"—a bureaucracy "similar" to the one which members of his audience had "fled from Russia to escape"![95] As they trundled around the country from one speaking engagement to the next, the abuse he and Lloyd George hurled at one another grew steadily cruder; the difference was that Lloyd George was winning the argument.[96] Never in the history of the house of Rothschild had a partner put himself in such a politically exposed position.

Yet within five years, the tables were turned. Lloyd George's "ruinous financial policy" might not frighten the markets as much as it financed the Rothschilds;[97] but by the summer of 1914 the Liberal government's majority in the House of Commons had been so whittled away at by-elections that the Chancellor suffered a humiliating defeat: the rejection of his Finance Bill. "Mr Lloyd George," Natty gloated on July 10, "is . . . even a discredited person in the eyes of the Government's own supporters."[98] Moreover, the Chancellor was about to be engulfed by a financial crisis of such magnitude that he would be driven to seek the assistance of none other than the despised Lord Rothschild.

The cause of the crisis was an unforeseen and little regarded event in Sarajevo.

"Hatred Let Loose"

War was not a certainty in 1914; neither imperialism, nor the alliance system, nor any other impersonal forces made it inevitable. But it was a possibility. The question was what kind of war there would be. Another Balkan war? A continental war involving Russia and Austria, and therefore probably also France and Germany? It is important to remember that the third possibility—a world war involving the British Empire—was, of all the possible scenarios, one of the least likely. To most observers in London, including the Rothschilds, a civil war in Ireland seemed a more imminent danger.

Even as the financial and constitutional conflict between Lords and Commons had raged in 1909 and 1910, Natty had not lost sight of the old questions of land reform and Home Rule in Ireland.[99] By putting the Irish MPs in a pivotal position at Westminster—the two big parties were almost exactly matched—the 1910 elections resurrected the Irish question.[100] Partly for that reason, Natty became suddenly more cautious in his attitude to the constitutional question. He was willing to do a great deal to get the Conservatives back into power, even offering to lend to a minority Balfour government if it was denied supply by the Liberals in the Commons—an extraordinary proposal.[101] But like Lansdowne and Balfour he feared a drastic inundation of Liberal peers. No sooner had Parliament reconvened than the previous year's battle over the budget was put to one side as a lost cause; the older and more bitter question of Ireland, by contrast, seemed as winnable as ever—provided the Unionist majority in the Lords could be preserved.[102] There was therefore a need to restrain the "hot-headed young bloods and old bloods too, who do not weigh the consequences of their action."[103]

The question which has sometimes been asked is whether Natty was himself hot-headed on the subject of Ulster. Was he in any way associated with those in the Conservative party who encouraged the Ulster Unionists to contemplate armed resistance to Home Rule? According to one account, he "personally contributed at least £10,000 to support the Ulster Volunteer Force resistance."[104] The evidence in the Milner papers on which this assertion based is, however, problematic: it is not inconceivable that Natty was the individual identified by the letter "D" on a list of contributors to an Ulster defence fund. What makes it seem unlikely is that in his letters to his Paris cousins Natty was anything but militant. "It is very unpleasant, disagreeable, I may even say painful," he told his cousins on March 19, 1914,

> to read of warlike preparations being made on both sides and sailors and artillery men spoken of as if England was going to embark on a real and serious military campaign. Hitherto at the crucial moment common

sense and good will on both sides have proved to be such very strong factors that the danger has been averted and the problem has been solved.
Will history repeat itself on this occasion? I earnestly hope so.

A few months later, he insisted that the view of "the great majority of Unionists can
be summed up in a few words—'It is our imperative duty to do everything which
will in all probability prevent Civil War' "[105] By the beginning of July, he was optimistic: "[T]he 'Peace barometer' is decidedly rising," he was able to report to Paris;
there was now "a belief in City circles that civil war will be avoided in Ulster" and
that "the Ulster question will be settled, at all events for the time being." Natty "sincerely hoped" this would be the case and that "the shadow [of civil war] which has
been hanging for so many months over the Country" would be lifted.[106]

The truth was that, quite apart from the damage he had done to his relations with
the Liberals, Natty was no longer being kept closely informed by the Conservative
leadership by 1914. Balfour had been a close friend; his successor, the Glaswegian
Bonar Law, was not—hence Natty's "pain" when Balfour decided to resign the leadership in November 1911.[107] Natty barely knew Law and a handful of meetings in
1911 and 1912 did not change that.[108] Personal and perhaps political differences
can also be detected. According to the Conservative chairman Sir Arthur Steel-Maitland, the family contributed "£12,000 a year and large sums at Elections and subscribe[d] very largely to the L[iberal] U[nionist]s also," as well as controlling at least
one parliamentary seat at Hythe. But the Rothschilds' favoured candidate for this
seat—Philip Sassoon—no longer met with the leadership's approval.[109] When Herbert Gibbs approached Natty about raising additional funds in the City for Central
Office in October 1911, Natty did not even reply; when Gibbs suggested that Bonar
Law be invited to explain his financial policy to the City, Natty opposed the suggestion.[110]

This froideur was more than merely personal. Under Bonar Law, the Conservatives not only became more aggressive on the Ulster question; they also became
more aggressive on matters of foreign policy, and especially where Germany was
concerned—a mood encouraged by the increasingly Germanophobe Tory-support-
ing press. It may seem odd that a man who in 1909 advocated an enlarged dreadnought programme should still have cherished hopes of preserving peace between
Britain and Germany; but Natty evidently did. (He had after all emphasised that "in
advocating a very strong Navy [he] had no intention of urging an aggressive
policy.") In 1912, Natty published a heartfelt essay in a collection entitled *England
and Germany* which reveals his enduring Germanophilia: "What have we . . . not got
in common with Germany?" he asked. "Nothing perhaps except their army and our
navy. But a combination of the most powerful military nation with the most powerful naval nation ought to be such as to command the respect of the whole world,
and ensure universal peace."[111] With the benefit of hindsight this seems almost
pathetic. Yet 1912—the year the Germans effectively abandoned the naval race—
saw the beginning of a renewed effort to promote Anglo-German co-operation by
Paul Schwabach, who remained in regular communication with the Rothschilds up
until August 1914.[112]

Even in 1914 there seemed little reason to expect the calamity of a war between
Britain and Germany. Sir Edward Holden might fret about the size of the German

"war chest" in the Julius tower at Spandau, and urge the City banks to pool their gold to give the Bank of England an adequate reserve in case of war; but Natty dismissed these as "very ridiculous ideas."[113] When he saw the German ambassador at Tring in March, "he said most decidedly that as far as he could see and as far as he knew, there was no reason for fear of war and no complications ahead."[114] June and July 1914 were dominated at New Court by Ulster worries and Brazilian loan negotiations. It was just another symptom of the good financial relations then prevailing between Britain and Germany that Max Warburg was in London on three separate occasions to finalise his firm's role in the operation.[115]

It has been suggested that the Rothschilds failed to grasp the significance of the July crisis—until, that is, it became the August war. As Cassis has observed, of twenty-five letters between New Court and the rue Laffitte between June 29 and July 23, only five mention the diplomatic ramifications of the assassination of the Archduke Franz Ferdinand at Sarajevo—"a sad example," as Natty observed somewhat otiosely, "both [*sic*] of Servian brutality, the hatred of the Greek Church for those of the Catholic Faith and last but not least of the morals and doctrines of the anarchical party."[116] As early as July 6, however, Natty was wondering nervously: "Will the Austrian Monarchy and people remain quiet? or may a war be precipitated, the consequences of which no one can foresee?"[117] Eight days later, he reported "a considerable amount of anxiety in some circles about Austro-Servian relations."[118] It is true that even on July 22, Natty remained confident, "rather fancy[ing] the well founded belief in influential quarters that unless Russia backed up Servia the latter will eat humble pie and that the inclination in Russia is to remain quiet, circumstances there not favouring a forward movement."[119] That, however, was not a wholly unreasonable assumption at that stage. Nor was the "general idea" he relayed the following day "that the various matters in dispute will be arranged without appeal to arms."[120] Before the details of the Austrian ultimatum to Serbia were known, it seemed quite likely that the Serbs would "give every satisfaction."[121] Natty was not complacent. As he told his cousins on July 27, "[N]o one thinks and talks about anything else but the European situation and the consequences which might arise if serious steps were not taken to prevent a European conflagration." But it was "the universal opinion that Austria was quite justified in the demands she made on Servia and it would ill-become the great Powers if by a hasty and ill-conceived action they did anything which might be viewed as condoning a brutal murder," even if "as usual from time immemorial" Austria had "not acted with diplomatic skill." He was confident that Asquith's government would leave "no stone . . . unturned in the attempts which will be made to preserve the peace of Europe and in this policy, although the . . . two rival parties in the state are more sharply divided than they have ever been, Mr Asquith will have the entire country at his back."[122]

Throughout the critical days from June 28 until August 3, Natty hoped for a diplomatic resolution of the crisis. He can undoubtedly be accused of naivety in believing that the German government did not want war. "It is very difficult to express any very positive opinion," he told his French relatives one June 29, "but I think I may say we believe you to be wrong, not you personally, but French opinion, in attributing sinister motives and underhand dealings to the German Emperor[;] he is bound by certain treaties and engagements to come to the assistance of Austria if she is attacked by Russia but that is the last thing he wishes to do." It was quite true that "the Czar and the Kaiser [were] corresponding directly over the wires in the interests of peace"; where Natty erred was in thinking that the Kaiser's ministers (and more particularly his generals) sincerely wished the war to be "localised."[123] "The Powers are still talking and negotiating between themselves and endeavouring to localize the bloodshed and misery," he reported hopefully on July 30. "[C]lumsy as Austria may have been, it would be ultra-criminal if millions of lives were sacrificed in order to sanctify the theory of murder, a brutal murder which the Servians have committed."[124] It is not difficult to infer from the tone of these letters that he was having difficulty persuading the Parisians of this view. His last attempt the next day, which implied that it was up to France to restrain Russia, shows the extent to which Natty was still a Germanophile at heart; it also deserves to be quoted as a last vain expression of faith in Rothschild financial leverage:

> [T]here are persistent rumours in the City that the German Emperor is using all of his influence at both St. Petersburg & Vienna to find a solution which would not be distasteful either to Austria or to Russia. I am convinced also that this very laudatory example is being strenuously followed here. Now I venture to ask you what the French govt is doing at the present moment and what is their policy? I hope and trust M. Poincaré who is undoubtedly a "persona gratiosus" with the Czar is not only pointing out to but also impressing upon the Russian Govt 1) that the result of a war, however powerful a country their ally may be, is doubtful, but whatever the result may be, the sacrifices and misery attendant upon it are stupendous & untold. In this case the calamity would be greater than anything ever seen or known before. 2) France is Russia's greatest creditor, in fact the financial and economic conditions of the two countries are intimately connected & we hope you will do your best to bring any influence you may have, to bear upon your statesmen even at the last moment, to prevent this hideous struggle from taking place, and to point out to Russia that she owes this to France.[125]

At the time, however, this was not so ingenuous as it may seem now. For one thing, similar attempts at mediation had averted war often enough in the past (over the Morocco, for example). At the same time, Natty's comments indicate that he for one had no illusions about the likely duration and intensity of a war. Given the widespread belief among historians that people in August 1914 expected a short war, this is an important point. Even more important, he was by no means unique in the City. Nothing testifies more clearly to the extent of pessimism in the financial world than the severity of the financial crisis precipitated by the July crisis.

The Vienna stock exchange had begun to slide as early as July 13, but the crisis was not really detectable in London until July 27—the day before the Austrian declaration of war on Serbia. "All the foreign Banks and particularly the German ones took a very large amount of money out of the Stock Exchange to-day," Natty informed the Paris house, "and although the brokers found most of the money they wanted if not all, the markets were at one time quite demoralized, a good many weak speculators selling à nil prix and all the foreign speculators selling Consols . . ."[126] That this was only the beginning became apparent the next day when—in a development which took Natty wholly by surprise—the Paris house sent a coded telegram requesting the sale of "a vast quantity of Consols here for the French Govt & Savings banks." He refused, first on the purely technical ground that "in the actual state of our markets it is quite impossible to do anything at all as prices are quite nominal and very few transactions of any importance have taken place"; then adding that the more political argument that it would produce "a deplorable effect . . . if we were to send gold to a Continental Power for the purpose of strengthening itself at a moment when 'War' is in the mouths of everyone."[127] Despite his assurances to the French Rothschilds that their telegrams were being kept strictly secret, Natty at once warned Asquith of what had happened. With heroic understatement, Asquith called this "ominous."[128] The possibility was now dawning that an acute liquidity crisis emanating from the acceptance houses could threaten the entire British financial system.

On July 29—the day after the rue Laffitte's request for gold—consols plunged from above 74 to 69.5 and continued to fall when the market re-opened. By the 30th the Bank of England had advanced £14 million to the discount market and a similar amount to the banks, but was forced to protect its reserve by pushing up Bank rate from 3 to 4 per cent. Already, as Natty reported, there was "talk in a rather loose way" of closing the stock exchange.[129] Firms who did a large continental acceptance business—like Kleinworts and Schröders—were in desperate straits, with around £350 million bills of exchange outstanding and an unknowable proportion of them unlikely to be honoured.[130] When Bank rate was doubled to 8 per cent on July 31—followed by a further 2 per cent hike the following day—it suddenly became apparent that writers like Bloch, Angell and Hobson had been wrong: the banks could not stop a war, but war could stop the banks. To avert a complete collapse, the stock exchange was closed on the 31st, a step which not even the worst crisis of the preceding hundred years had necessitated. The next day (as in 1847, 1857 and 1866), Lloyd George gave the Governor of the Bank a letter permitting him to exceed, if need be, the note-issue limit set by the Bank Charter Act. Fortuitously, August 1 was a Saturday and the following Monday a Bank Holiday; further breathing space was provided by extending the holiday for the rest of the week. The stock exchange remained closed "until further notice."[131]

The financial crisis was inevitable; what remained uncertain until August 3 was whether Britain would actually enter the war. We can infer what the City expected to happen if Britain stayed out. Between July 18 and August 1 (the last day when quotations were published), the bonds of all the major powers slumped, but some fell further than others. Russian 4 per cents fell by 8.7 per cent, French 3 per cents by 7.8 per cent—but German 3 per cents by just 4 per cent. In the absence of British intervention, the City was putting its money on Moltke, just as it had in 1870. The Parisians remembered 1870 too. In August, fearing a second siege of Paris, Edouard sent his family to England. (Although they later returned, he felt nervous enough during the second battle of the Marne to send them away again, this time to his Lafite estate.) At the same time, he moved the bank's offices temporarily to Bordeaux.[132]

But the British decision to tip the balance in favour of France by intervening—taken by a deeply divided Cabinet after long hours of debate—was not one the Rothschilds or any other bankers could influence. On July 31 Natty implored *The Times* to tone down its leading articles, which were "hounding the country into war"; but both Wickham Steed and his proprietor Lord Northcliffe regarded this as "a dirty German-Jewish international financial attempt to bully us into advocating neutrality" and concluded that "the proper answer would be a still stiffer leading article tomorrow." "We dare not stand aside," Saturday's leader duly thundered. "Our strongest interest is the law of self-preservation."[133] As Schwabach lamented to Alfred on August 1, British intervention now seemed likely, "though at this precise moment there seem to be no grounds for it . . . [But] you and I are conscious of having tried, with all our might, to improve relations between our countries."[134] Natty even sent a personal appeal for peace to the Kaiser, who minuted irrelevantly that he was "an old and much respected acquaintance of mine. Some 75 to 80 years old." This too was in vain: before a reply could be sent communications were interrupted.[135] On August 3 Grey addressed the Commons to the effect that Britain would not "stand aside"; as Natty put it to his cousins, the German invasion of Belgium was "an act which England could never tolerate."[136] Of course, there were other, more compelling reasons for the government's decision: the belief that if Germany defeated France, Britain's own security would be at risk, and perhaps also a desire to keep the Unionists out of power. Still, it is understandable that the Rothschilds, who had been so much involved in the events leading up to the treaty of 1839, should have emphasised Belgian neutrality as the reason for British intervention.

There was no euphoria in New Court. There they rightly foresaw, as Natty put it, "the greatest military fight in the annals of the world," a "horrid war," the duration of which no one could foresee.[137] "No Government has ever had a more serious and painful task before it," Alfred wrote to Paris. He could not think of the "military & moral spectacle which we have before us with its painful details looming in the distance . . . without shuddering."[138] For once, he and his Liberal cousin Annie were in agreement: "[T]he awful tragedy of a European war" struck her as "almost unthinkable." "One cannot help wondering," she exclaimed, "where is the use of diplomacy, of arbitration, of that worn-out sentence, the 'resources of civilization,' if war is to be the only arbitrator!"[139] It was symbolic of the way in which the war was going to sever the Rothschilds' traditional familial links to the continent that she and her husband were holidaying in Bergen at the end of July, while Natty's son Charles was in Hungary with his wife—herself a Hungarian by birth.

Was there any consolation? Of all the Rothschilds, Annie's sister Constance was unusual in catching right away the euphoric, anti-German mood which swept the country after war was declared. She also welcomed the war as an apparent solution to the Ulster crisis:

> *August 5:* . . . Edward Grey is doing well, Redmond made a very fine speech. For the present, the Irish peril is at an end. Both North and South combine to come to our aid. A generous people! We hope that Lord Kitchener will be given command of the Army, at all events of the organization.
> *August 7:* Kitchener Secretary of War, Thank God.
> *August 13:* Hatred *let loose.* Splendid behaviour of the Belgians. Cruelty of the Germans.
> *September 9:* . . . Last night's news were better. *If only* the Russians could get quickly to Berlin.
> *September 30:* Home Rule Bill on the Statute Book. Great disgust

evinced by Carson and Bonar Law, but splendid and dramatic scene in the House of Commons! Hope and pray that Covenanters and Nationalists will fight side by side.[140]

There is no sign that Natty or his brothers felt any such relief, however: after all, their views on Ireland were diametrically opposed to those of their ardent Gladstonian cousin. The only possible consolation for the partners at New Court was that, having failed to avert the calamity, they could at least perform the traditional Rothschild role of financing the war effort.

But were they able to do so? Certainly, they were soon called upon by the politicians to assist with the financial consequences of war much as they had been in previous crises. In his *War Memoirs*, for example, Lloyd George poetically recalled how the war had reconciled him with his erstwhile enemy:

> One of those whose advice I sought was Lord Rothschild. My previous contact with him was not of a propitiatory character . . . However, this was not the time to allow political quarrels to intrude into our counsel. The nation was in peril. I invited him to the Treasury for a talk. He came promptly. We shook hands. I said, "Lord Rothschild, we have had some political unpleasantness." He interrupted me: "Mr Lloyd George, this is no time to recall those things. What can I do to help?" I told him. He undertook to do it at once. It was done.[141]

Lloyd George saw many City bankers in the first week of August, but few impressed him. Sir Edward Holden was one; Natty seemingly another. "Only the old Jew made sense," he was heard to comment to his private secretary—though "old Jew" became "great Prince of Israel" in the memoirs.[142] Writing in *Reynolds Weekly Newspaper* in 1915, he enlarged on Natty's contribution:

> Lord Rothschild had a high sense of duty to the State, and although his interpretation of what was best for the country did not always coincide with mine, when the war fell upon us he readily and cheerfully forgot all past differences and encounters . . . He was prepared to make sacrifices for what he genuinely believed in. It will therefore surprise no one who knew him that he was one of those who recommended the double income tax, with a heavier super-tax, for the war expenditure.

Asked many years later by his son to name his "ideal cabinet," he named Natty as Chancellor of the Exchequer, alongside Winston Churchill and Jan Smuts.[143] Haldane left a rather similar impression in his memoirs. Learning (while standing in for Grey at the Foreign Office in 1915) "that a steamer had started from South America and that, although neutral, there was reason to suppose that she contained supplies intended for the Germans," Haldane

> motored to Lord Rothschild's house in Piccadilly, and found him lying down and obviously very ill. But he stretched out his hand before I could speak, and said, "Haldane, I do not know what you are come for except to see me, but I have said to myself that if Haldane asks me to write a cheque for him for £25,000 and to ask no questions, I will do it on the spot." I told him that it was not for a cheque, but only to get a ship stopped that I was come. He sent a message to stop the ship at once.[144]

If all this sounds rather too good to be true—and especially Lloyd George's image of a heretic recanting his opposition to super-tax—the clue lies in Haldane's reference to Natty's physical condition. In fact, both Lloyd George and Haldane were applying something of the obituarist's rose tint to their recollections. The reality was that the war had plunged the Rothschilds—and indeed the entire City—into a profound crisis. Keynes's analysis at the time was succinct: "The [clearing] banks . . . are depending on the accepting houses and on the discount houses; the discount houses are depending on the accepting houses; and the accepting houses are depending on foreign clients who are unable to remit." Table 13g shows the extent of the problem and reveals that Kleinworts and Schröders were especially exposed; but N. M. Rothschild was affected too.[145] It was not wholly persuasive when Natty assured Lloyd George on August 6 that he was "perfectly disinterested" in the debate between the Chancellor, the Governor of the Bank and the clearing banks.[146]

Table 13g: The London acceptance market: liabilities on acceptances at year end, 1912–1914 (£ million).

	Barings	Kleinwort Sons	Schröders	Hambros	N. M. Rothschild	Gibbs	Brandts	Total of "big seven"	All acceptances
1912	6.58	13.36	11.95	3.45	3.49	1.38	3.19	43.40	133
1913	6.64	14.21	11.66	4.57	3.19	2.04	3.33	45.64	140
1914	3.72	8.54	5.82	1.34	1.31	1.17	0.72	22.62	69

Source: Chapman, *Merchant Banking*, p. 209.

The dispute which caused Lloyd George to seek Natty's advice was a technical one: the big clearing banks wanted a full suspension of gold convertibility as had happened in Britain in 1797, and as had already happened officially or practically in Russia, Germany and France in 1914. This would have allowed them to supply their clients with liquidity at a rate lower than Bank rate (which went back down to 6 per cent on August 6). The Treasury and Bank preferred to follow post-1844 convention and to avoid suspension if at all possible. The compromise which Natty helped to broker was that convertibility should be maintained but Bank rate lowered by a further 1 per cent.[147] A week later, the acceptance market was relieved by a further decision that the Bank would discount all bills accepted before August 4 at the new lower rate. This was a success; there is no mistaking the relief behind the congratulations which Alfred and Leo sent to Lloyd George on August 13. Their "very great appreciation of the most successful manner with which you dealt with a difficulty quite unparalleled in the history of the finances of this Country" was understandable, even if allusions to the Chancellor's "masterly eye" and "masterly hand" were a bit rich coming so soon after the denunciations of 1909–10.[148] Natty wrote in rather more measured tones more than two weeks later after Lloyd George had effectively rejected his recommendation (on August 27) that the moratorium be ended and the stock exchange reopened.[149]

Yet the real significance of Natty's role—compared with his role in the less serious crisis of 1890—was the changed balance of power in the City it revealed. "They can play you a nasty trick," he told the Governor of the Bank at one stage during the negotiations in Lloyd George's office. "They are very powerful."[150] Once that might have been said of the Rothschilds themselves. But Natty was referring to the clearing banks. It is also striking that, despite the steps taken to stabilise the acceptance market, N. M. Rothschild & Sons lost close to £1.5 million in 1914—an immense sum equivalent to 23 per cent of its capital. In terms of their capital, none of the other major City banks was so drastically affected by the outbreak of war.

To be sure, there was no shortage of cross-Channel business as the British Treasury began to subsidise the French war effort, though communications were difficult during the first week of the war.[151] Indeed, it was not until early 1915 that regular and reliable communications could be established through the diplomatic telegraph service.[152] Nevertheless, an initial loan of £1.7 million from Britain to France was quickly agreed through the Rothschilds, and this was followed by advances against Treasury bills totalling £8 million between October 1914 and October 1917.[153] In the grand scheme of inter-Allied finance, however, this was small beer. All told, France borrowed £610 million from Britain during the war; but even this sum was dwarfed by the £738 million borrowed from the United States, and most of the money lent by Britain was in fact recycled from the £936 million of American money she herself had to borrow. The key to the financing of the war, as very soon became apparent, lay not in London or in Paris but in New York: that transatlantic shift of the financial centre of gravity which had been first been intimated during the Boer War now became a reality. In this regard, it was not without significance that when Edouard had telegraphed J. P. Morgan on August 1 to request a loan to the French government of $100 million he had drawn a blank.[154] Morgan had not forgotten the way his London subsidiary had been refused a share of the South African loan twelve years before. Far more than Lloyd George's death duties and other taxes, it was the Rothschilds' poor representation on Wall Street which now condemned them to a period of contraction far more rapid than anything they had hitherto suffered. "In this very painful episode," Natty wrote to Paris at the outbreak of war, "it is at all events satisfactory to know that you and ourselves are standing shoulder-to-shoulder."[155] "United on the battlefields, we are also united in finance!" telegraphed Edouard to New Court the following year.[156] But these rallying calls to arms had a very hollow ring; what united the Rothschilds after 1914 was decline—and it was a decline that was to continue for at least half a century.

III

Descendants

FOURTEEN

Deluges
(1915–1945)

This is indeed a time of terror *and tribulation.*
CONSTANCE, LADY BATTERSEA, TO HER SISTER ANNIE YORKE, 1916[1]

What Churchill called "the world crisis" of the First World War coincided with, and intensified, a deep crisis within the Rothschild family. Between the death of Alphonse in 1905 and that of Alfred in 1918, the generation which had dominated Rothschild finance since around 1875 disappeared. In Paris Gustave died just six years after his elder brother, leaving only Edmond as the last and least business-minded of James's sons; and although he lived until 1934 he was already sixty-nine in 1914. In Vienna Anselm's last surviving son Albert died in 1911. Lionel's three sons Natty, Leo and Alfred died within a few years of one another in 1915, 1917 and 1918. These deaths seemed to many observers to mark the end of an era.

"The death of Lord Rothschild is an event which not even the war can overshadow," declared the *Western Morning News*:

> This prince of financiers and friend of King Edward probably knew more of the inner history of European wars and diplomacy in general than the greatest statesman we have ever had. Every great stroke of policy by the nation in the last half-century has been preceded by the brief but all-significant announcement, "Lord Rothschild visited the Prime Minister yesterday." It was one of the signs for which those behind the scenes looked when big decisions were pending.[2]

It was, in the words of the *Financier and Bullionist*, "an open secret . . . that he was the confidant of Kings and Cabinet Ministers, and that his invaluable advice was constantly sought and as constantly acted upon."[3] There were enough senior politicians at the funeral at Willesden to confirm such claims about Natty's influence. Three Cabinet ministers attended: the Chancellor Lloyd George, the President of the Local Government Board Herbert Samuel and the Lord Chief Justice Lord Reading, as well as the former Tory leader (and future Foreign Secretary) Arthur Balfour.[4] "To me," Balfour confided to Lady Wemyss, "Natty's death is a greater blow than most people would suppose, I was really fond of him; and really admired that self-contained and somewhat joyless character. He had a high ideal of public duty and was utterly indifferent to worldly pomps and vanities."[5] The Chief Rabbi was unequivocal in his memorial sermon a few weeks later: Natty had been quite simply the "foremost Jew of the world."[6]

None of those who came to praise Natty, however, could claim that he had been a great banker. The City editor of the *New Witness* came close to damning Natty with faint praise:

> He made less mistakes than any financier of his age. His instinct was always right. His sense of honour was acute, he could not do any-thing that he did not approve just because his firm was likely to make money . . . To be head of the greatest business house in the greatest busi-ness city in the world; to be consulted by kings and rulers and to control imperial policies and yet to die without an enemy. Is not that a great achievement?[7]

Possibly; but the fact remained that N. M. Rothschild & Sons under Natty's leader-ship had begun to underperform relative to its City rivals—the victim, perhaps, of his own political preoccupations and the complacent attitude towards business he shared with his brothers. Indeed, to some observers, Natty's death prompted pes-simistic reflections about the future of the Rothschilds as a financial force. "In Eng-land," reflected the *Daily News*,

> the Joint Stock Banks have entered the field, and there is no longer any question of a Rothschild predominance, still less of a Rothschild monopoly. Not less noteworthy, the whole business of public loans has declined in importance. Modern financial institutions make their vastest profits as well as exercise their weightiest influence in financing industry and commerce. The house of Rothschild has not ignored this form of enterprise, but it has not engaged in it with the same zeal as the great banking houses or companies of the United States and Germany. The effect of these and other tendencies has been to reduce, relatively . . . the part of the Rothschilds in the money world.[8]

The liberal *Nation* was more blunt: Natty's tastes, it remarked with disdain, had been "largely those of an English country gentleman . . . Did this later conservatism of habit have anything to do with the fact that much of the new business of the world did not get into the Rothschilds' hands? Certainly, one could not pick out the great financier in any member of the English branch. Great farmers, great collectors, great organizers of social life—yes. But hardly a modern money king."[9]

The Fifth Generation

That phrase was well chosen if it was intended to suggest a comparison with Natty's grandfather, who had pulled off his most celebrated (and mythologised) coup in the previous world war almost exactly a century before. Natty had been no Nathan. It was symptomatic of the increasingly sclerotic condition of the bank at the time of his death that Joseph Nauheim, one of the bank's senior clerks, could argue *against* the introduction of double-entry book-keeping when this was proposed by a committee set up "to enquire into the system of accounts . . . to consider what steps, if any, could be adopted to expedite the preparation of the Balance Sheet, and whether any improvements could be introduced into the system of account-keeping with a view to mak[ing] it more efficient and up to date." It is quite astonishing that a firm with the resources of N. M. Rothschild was still using the single-entry system in 1915. Yet Nauheim opposed the committee's recommendations—which ranged from the rationalisation of the system of classifying accounts to the abolition of knife erasers and the standardisation of book sizes—on the ground that the changes would be too time-consuming.[10] The committee's report is unusual for another reason: it is one of the earliest Rothschild documents to have been typed rather than handwritten. In fact, there was only one typewriter at New Court in 1915.

The real problem, however, lay with the next generation. Writing in the 1870s, Walter Bagehot had foreseen the problem when he asked how long the "large private banks" would be able to hold their own against the joint-stock banks:

> I am sure I should be very sorry to say that they certainly cannot, but at the same time I cannot be blind to the great difficulties which they must surmount. In the first place, an hereditary business of great magnitude is dangerous. The management of such a business needs more than common industry and more than common ability. But there is no security at all that these will be regularly combined in each generation . . . [If] the size of the banks is augmented and greater ability is required, the constant difficulty of an hereditary government will begin to be felt. "The father had great brains and created the business: but the son had less brains and lost or lessened it." This is the great history of all monarchies, and it may be the history of great private banks.[11]

It certainly appeared to be the history of the fifth generation of Rothschilds. In 1901 Clinton Dawkins put it bluntly: "The coming generation of the Rothschilds *est à faire pleurer.*"[12]

Natty's eldest son Walter had begun collecting animals, stuffed and live, at the age of six[13] and was already a knowledgeable zoologist when he went to study natural science at the University of Bonn and then at Cambridge.[14] In this, he had the more or less unqualified encouragement of his parents; as a twenty-first birthday present his father built him a museum at Tring to house his collection.[15] But the expectation persisted that he would follow in his forefathers' footsteps and enter the bank, a notion abandoned only in 1908 when it was discovered that "poor fat Walter" had been speculating wildly and disastrously on the stock exchange.[16] The sin of financial incompetence was compounded when it emerged that he was vainly trying to pay off a former mistress who had been blackmailing him—one of several scandalous liaisons which belied his awkward manner and bear-like appearance.[17] Although an indefatigable scientist who described 5,000 previously unclassified species in over a thousand publications, Walter was the last person capable of leading the family firm through the storms which loomed ahead, as much out of place in a bank as his zebras were when he drove them as a four-in-hand down Piccadilly.[18] Even as an MP, he contrived to antagonise both Arthur Balfour and Herbert Gladstone in a single speech.[19]

His brother Charles was better able to accept the burdens of City life and dutifully prepared to inherit a partnership at New Court; it was he who chaired the committee on the modernisation of the bank's accounting system. But Charles too was a scientist at heart.[20] A dedicated amateur botanist and entomologist who published 150 papers and described 500 new species of flea, he was also one of the country's first modern conservationists who delighted in the woodland around Ashton Wold, where he built himself a picturesque retreat.[21] After Natty's death, it was decided that Charles should succeed his father as senior partner; but two years later he succumbed to the Spanish influenza which swept Europe in 1917–19, contracted *encephalitis lethargica* (a neurological condition caused by the virus) and after a long, debilitating illness took his own life in 1923.[22]

This reorientation of intellectual ability away from business and into science (or the arts, in a case such as Aby Warburg) was a common phenomenon among business families of the *fin de siècle*, and especially Jewish families, reflecting the great widening of educational opportunities for Jews of that class and generation. In the cases of Walter and Charles, it is tempting to suggest a further genetic explanation. Throughout the nineteenth century, numerous members of the Rothschild family had evinced predispositions towards collecting and gardening. In Walter and Charles, these tendencies fused to produce an exceptional aptitude for zoological and botanical classification. Their cousin Lionel, Leo's eldest son, had similar inclinations, devoting much of his life to horticulture (though he also had a fondness for fast cars and boats).[23] His younger brother Anthony was also academically inclined, in a quite different direction: at Cambridge he secured a Double First in history (despite reputedly hunting five days out of seven) and it was often said of him in later years that he would have been happier as a don than as a banker.

The French house suffered similar problems as the old generation made way for the new. Edmond's son Jimmy had settled and married in England before the war; he showed no interest in banking, dividing his time between helping his father with his Palestinian schemes, the untaxing duties of a backbench Liberal MP and the Turf. An even less likely prospect—as it then seemed—was Edmond's second son Maurice who at the age of twenty-six had inherited an immense fortune, including the château at Pregny, from his second cousin Julie (Adolph's widow). He appeared content to devote his wealth to collecting works of modern art by the likes of Picasso, Braque and Chagall—an investment strategy much underrated at the time. There was therefore a certain piquancy about Jimmy's decision in 1913 to commission (for his London dining room) a series of panels by Diaghilev's set-designer Léon Bakst on the theme of *The Sleeping Beauty*. A number of family members acted as models for these, including Jimmy's wife Dorothy, his sister Miriam, Edouard's wife Germaine, Robert's wife Nelly and Edmond's wife Adelheid—as well as the Marquess of Crewe and his wife, Hannah Rosebery's daughter Peggy.[24] Was the choice of subject mere whimsy? It is tempting to suggest that it was an appropriate one; for, in the eyes of many contemporaries, the Rothschilds themselves seemed to be lapsing into a deep slumber.

The other branch of the family which had settled in France—the descendants of the English-born Nat—ceased altogether to play a part in the bank. Although still formally a partner, Nat's grandson Henri was another of the fifth generation's scientists. A qualified if misanthropic doctor, he had his own private laboratory, published extensively on the subject of infant nutrition and took an interest in the Curies" work on the medical use of radium. He also dabbled in the theatre, as a sponsor of the famous 1909 tour by Diaghilev's Ballet Russe, and as an amateur playwright using the *nom de plume* "André Pascal." With his Parisian château de la Muette, his mock-Tudor villa at Deauville and a yacht suggestively called *Eros*, Henri lived not to make money, but to spend it. His various attempts at entrepreneurship (he tried at various times to manufacture cars, mustard, soap and canned pheasant) were commercial failures.[25]

This meant that most of the responsibility for the running of de Rothschild Frères after 1905 devolved on Alphonse's only son, Edouard. He, however, was scarcely swashbuckling in his approach to business. Fastidious and ostentatiously old-fashioned—he still wore a frock coat at the Nord line's annual general meeting—he argued against offering investment advice to clients: "If they make a profit, they'll consider it their due; if they lose money, they'll say that they were ruined by the Rothschilds."[26] Edouard also had his share of extra-mural distractions, though they were rather more conventional than Henri's: bridge when in town, shooting at Ferrières and horse-racing at Longchamp.[27]

In Vienna too, the Rothschilds of the fifth generation tended to neglect the "counting house" for high culture or high life. After the death of Albert in 1911, control of the bank passed almost entirely to his second son Louis, despite the fact that he was not yet thirty; rather as Anselm before had handed power to Albert, effectively sidelining his other two sons. It has been said that Louis brought a modernising spirit to the Vienna house, involving it in such unfamiliar fields of activity as the New York Interborough Rapid Transit Company.[28] But he was no slave to work: the archetypal playboy bachelor (he married in his sixties), he was an accomplished rider and mountaineer who also found time to dabble in anatomy, botany and art.[29] Freed almost entirely from business responsibility, his brothers were in a position to indulge their enthusiasms still more. The elder, Alphonse, trained as a lawyer but after the war settled down to the life of a gentleman scholar, specialising in classical literature; the younger brother Eugène's most notable achievement was to write a monograph on Titian.

The Impact of War

Was any European family unaffected by the First World War? It seems doubtful. Not even the continent's richest could avoid sacrificing blood, time and money in the great slaughter of those years.

On the face of it, the Rothschilds were swept along by the patriotic fervour which historians usually see as the typical "mood" of 1914. Although they were all in their thirties when the war broke out, all three of Leo's sons (as officers in the Bucks Yeomanry) itched to fight for their country. The second son, Evelyn, saw action early on the Western Front and was invalided home in November 1915. Within a matter of months, he was back in the trenches and in March 1916 was mentioned in despatches. He was then sent to Palestine, where he met his younger brother Anthony, who had earlier been wounded at Gallipoli and ended the war as a major with the General Staff. To his frustration, Lionel was obliged to remain at New Court, where he sought an outlet for his bellicose urges in organising Jewish recruitment in the City. At least four of the French Rothschilds ended up in uniform. Jimmy was seconded to the British 3rd Army as an interpreter and, like his English relations, served in Palestine towards the end of the war. Henri concealed his chronic albuminuria and became an officer in the medical corps, but was invalided out by the effects of a typhus vaccination. His elder brother James served as a pilot in the Balkan theatre and Gustave's son Robert acted as interpreter on the Western Front. Of the Austrians, Alphonse and Eugène served as officers in the 6th Dragoons on the Italian front.[30] In practice, therefore, Rothschild did not fight against Rothschild: the English and French Rothschilds who fought were active only on the Western Front and in the Middle East, though James might conceivably have found himself flying over his Austrian cousins had he been deployed further west. Only one Rothschild was killed—Leo's son Evelyn in November 1917, from wounds sustained in a cavalry charge against Turkish positions at El Mughar—though the war claimed two other close relatives: Hannah Rosebery's son Neil Primrose, who was also killed in Palestine,[31] and the son of Charles's Hungarian sister-in-law.

Even for members of the family who were far from the Front, the war was a traumatic experience. Alfred and his cousins Constance and Annie—the last of Nathan's grandchildren—lived in terror of German air raids. At his insistence, the Dividend Office gallery at New Court was packed with sandbags to protect the Bullion Room below and a personal shelter was built for his use in the corner of the Drawn Bond Department. A special system was also designed to relay official air-raid warnings from the Royal Mint refinery (temporarily converted to munitions production) to New Court, and Alfred even had a wire net erected above the roof of his own house in the hope of intercepting falling bombs. Constance's war-time letters to her sister are full of anxious references to the same danger. "I hope if there are Zeppelins about," she wrote in January 1915, "that the airmen may be blinded and frozen [by the snow] . . . The Subway is ready for us . . . I always wear my pearls (as I do not want to lose them in a *débâcle*) and at night have a fur cloak at the foot of the bed, a shawl and warm slippers, and next to me, candles and matches."[32] Even when she was out of London she was "full of nervous forebodings . . . one thinks that one hears Zepps. at all hours of the evening and night, and there are constant explosions and gun-firing out at sea."[33] These fears were, of course, somewhat exaggerated as aerial bombardment was as yet in its infancy. Alfred died naturally—a month after the war had ended. Constance lived until 1931.

Nevertheless, those who remained at home endeavoured to do their "bit" for the war effort. As early as September 1914, Constance made her house at Aston Clinton available to Belgian refugees (whom she lectured on the wickedness of German war aims and the virtue of Temperance),[34] and helped to run a small hospital for the Red Cross. "The servants have all conformed to some necessities of this economising time," she boasted, apparently oblivious to the irony of delegating sacrifice to the domestics. "Lester has no men-servants under him. A bright, neat pretty little parlour-maid has taken their place . . . My Iron-room a canteen! . . . Cricket pavilion much used and liked as billiard-and reading-room—Tennis pavilion used as library for the village."[35] With slightly more self-awareness, she even welcomed the introduction of food rationing in 1917. "I fancy there will be some difficulty in large establishments and in public places like restaurants, etc.," she reflected, "but in small (!!) households like mine, the experiment will be *quite* interesting. Oh! dear, what strange experiences we are having!"[36]

While Charles continued to work at the bank, he served on the committee of the Volunteer Munitions Brigade and offered his services as a financial expert to Lloyd

George's new Ministry of Munitions.[37] In the same spirit, Alfred forwarded a petition to Lloyd George urging that cotton be declared contraband to prevent its reaching Germany.[38] His estate at Halton became a military camp and in 1917, at his suggestion, its beech woods were felled to provide pit props.[39] In all this, a general enthusiasm for Lloyd George's dynamic approach to the war effort is detectable. In October 1915—more than a year before he became Prime Minister—Constance was already dismissing his predecessor Asquith as "simply *played* out, not a bit up to the situation! . . . I think there is a rising tide of anger against the Government. If Mr. A. were to resign there is only one man to take his place, *Lloyd George*." "Oh dear," she exclaimed two months later, "we want a very different PM."[40] Alfred too seems to have become a devotee.[41] By contrast, Jimmy remained a loyal Asquithian and was one of the circle of his friends who rallied round immediately after his fall a year later.[42]

Yet the fact that members of the family were now fighting on opposite sides inevitably brought back to the surface the old questions about loyalty and identity which had first been raised by the wars of German unification. Five of Mayer Carl's seven daughters—all of whom had been raised in Frankfurt—had married French or English nationals: Adèle to James's son Salomon, Emma to Natty, Laura Thérèse to Nat's son James Edouard, Margaretha to the duc de Gramont and Bertha to the prince de Wagram. Wilhelm Carl's daughter Adelheid had married her French second cousin Edmond; and the Viennese Albert had married Alphonse's daughter Bettina. In each case the national loyalties of bride and groom were—at least in terms of their place of birth—to opposite sides in the war. The problem was compounded in the cases of three of the children produced by these marriages. In 1907 Natty's son Charles had married a Hungarian, Rozsika von Wertheimstein; three years later, Edmond's daughter Miriam had married a German relation, Albert von Goldschmidt-Rothschild; and in 1912 Albert's son Alphonse had married an Englishwoman (also a distant relation), Clarice Sebag-Montefiore. At the time, all of these marriages had made sense in the terms of the European Jewish "cousinhood"—indeed, Miriam and Albert *were* cousins (his mother was Minna von Rothschild). Yet in 1914 the claims of the fatherland trumped those of the cousinhood. When the war broke out, Albert left his wife in Paris and returned to Germany.

Moreover, there was a mood of public hostility towards "the enemy" which made even German names and accents suspect in London and Paris (and English and French names suspect in Berlin and Vienna). Although the Rothschilds did not follow the British royal family in Anglicising their no less German surname, one of their clerks—a man named Schönfelder—elected to become "Fairfield," a reaction perhaps to pressure from "patriotic" employees. It became impossible to converse in German during the lunch-break at New Court following the appearance there of a poster (published by the *Daily Mail*) bearing the legend "Intern Them All."[43] Walter resigned from Tring council when, in his absence, a resolution was passed in the same spirit. It was a similar story in France, where the Rothschilds were accused in the Chamber of Deputies of profiting from French military reverses and helping to supply the Germans with contraband nickel from New Caledonia.[44]

Matters were further complicated by the question of religion. Committed assimilationists as they had been for three generations, the London Rothschilds hastened to reinforce the patriotism of the British Jewish community, in which they contin-

ued to play a leading role.[45] The text of a poster produced by the British Board of
Deputies' Jewish Recruiting Committee gives a flavour of the mood of the time:

> THE COUNTRY'S CALL FOR MEN HAS BEEN NOBLY RE-
> SPONDED TO BY JEWS OF ALL CLASSES. ARE YOU HOLD-
> ING BACK? On the VICTORY OF THE ALLIES depends THE
> CAUSE OF FREEDOM AND TOLERATION which is the cause
> of England. Apply at the Recruiting Office at MESSRS. ROTH-
> SCHILD'S, NEW COURT ST SWITHIN'S LANE, E.C. and Major
> Lionel de Rothschild M.P. will enlist you. THERE MUST BE NO
> JEWISH SLACKERS. JEWISH YOUNG MEN! Do your duty to
> your faith and your Country. All British Born Jews ENLIST NOW.
> DON'T FORGET—Ask advice of Major LIONEL DE ROTH-
> SCHILD M.P. at the Jewish Recruiting Committee.[46]

As might be inferred from the tone of this, however, there were those who were
inclined to question the commitment of Jews to the war effort. Thus one of the
war's many bitter ironies: German-born Jews who had settled in Britain or America
were viewed with suspicion because of their birthplace; those who had remained in
Germany were viewed with suspicion because of their faith.

An obvious source of embarrassment for assimilationists like Lionel and his
father was the fact that Liberal England was fighting on the same side as Tsarist
Russia, the object of so much Rothschild-led criticism for its treatment of Jews.
When the Jewish author Israel Zangwill denounced the entente with Russia in a
letter to *The Times*, Natty publicly distanced himself and the Board of Deputies. He
even disowned the proposal of the American Jewish leader Oscar S. Straus that
Britain should press her ally to grant the Jews civil and political rights, arguing that
their lot would inevitably improve after the war as (in the words of the *Jewish
Chronicle*) "the militarism of Russia's next door neighbour . . . has in the main been
responsible for the reactionary spirit in Russia."[47] But this was not a line which went
down well among the more recent Jewish immigrants from the Russian Pale, and
not all the members of the family adhered to it.[48] In early 1915 Leo was one of those
who lobbied Kitchener and other ministers on the subject of Russian Jewry in
advance of the visit of the Russian Finance Minister, P. L. Bark. The message was
duly relayed to Petrograd: in his report to the Council of Ministers, Bark attributed
to "the all powerful Leopold de Rothschild" the fact that Kitchener "repeated constantly that one of the most important conditions for the success of the war is the
amelioration of the lot of the Jews in Russia."[49] In Paris, Edmond appears to have
made similar representations to Protopopov, the last Tsarist Minister of the Interior.

This and other injunctions to the Romanov regime to reform itself were, of
course, in vain; but the advent of a new parliamentary republic in Russia proved to
be anything but a solution to the problem. At first, there was optimism at New
Court that the provisional government's Finance Minister, an obscure Ukrainian
businessman named Mikhail Tereshchenko (who at once wrote "asking us to continue . . . and extend . . . our business relations"), would prove "a friend of the
Jews."[50] Later, the Rothschilds subscribed a million roubles to the "freedom loan"
issued by Kerensky to keep Russia in the war.[51] The Bolshevik Revolution of October dashed these hopes. French bondholders were effectively expropriated as Lenin

repudiated the imperial debt, while Russian Jews found their plight positively worsened as the country descended into a barbaric civil war. As late as 1924, in the period of the New Economic Policy, Rothschild views of Soviet Russia remained so hostile as to preclude even the acceptance of a deposit from one of the new Soviet state banks.

The paradox was that, to many commentators, the revolutions which swept westwards from Petrograd in 1917–19 appeared in large part to be the work of Jews, though the number of Bolshevik leaders who were of Jewish origin tended to be exaggerated. A few members of the family did in fact welcome the fall of the great Central and European monarchies. Writing to her sister on November 7, 1918, as the German and Austrian revolutions gathered momentum, that inveterate Liberal optimist Constance confessed to feeling:

> quite giddy when I read the morning papers with all the wonderful news. Everything topsy-turvy; a gigantic cataclysm, rather a kind of "Alice in Wonderland" or "Through the Looking Glass" effect. I seem to be always seeing Emperors and Kings and their Consorts running, and their thrones toppling over. Is it not wonderful![52]

But for those Rothschilds who were still closely involved with the family firm, such optimism was impossible in the face of such an explicitly anti-capitalist revolution. Even Constance had to acknowledge that the revolution might be "somewhat disastrous from a financial point of view" for the Vienna house. And there was also the faint but conceivable possibility that the "revolutionary element in this country" might draw inspiration from the continent.[53] Walter ghoulishly warned his eight-year-old nephew (and future heir) Victor that when the war was over he would be "put up against a wall and shot."[54] The few remaining Frankfurt Rothschilds identified much more closely with the deposed Hohenzollerns than with the new Weimar Republic, judging by the friendship which persisted between Hannah Mathilde and members of the deposed German royal family.[55]

"Dear Lord Rothschild": The Balfour Declaration

Perhaps the most profound conflict of identity which the war exacerbated, however, related to the future of Palestine and, specifically, to the Zionist aspiration to establish a Jewish nation state there. As we have seen, none of the Rothschilds had wholly embraced the projects of Herzl and Weizmann, although Edmond's colonisation schemes were in some ways compatible with Zionism. By pitting England, France and Russia against the Ottoman empire—an unprecedented combination in modern times—the war seemed to weaken his reservations about the Zionist dream of a Jewish state in Palestine. As he said in 1917, he had always expected:

> that a time might come when the fate of Palestine could be in the balance, and I desired that the world should have to reckon with the Jews there at such a time. We did a good deal in the last ten to fifteen years; we meant to do still more in the years to come; the present crisis has caught us in the middle of our activities, still one has to reckon with the facts and now we have to use the opportunity which will probably never return again.[56]

In the same way, the war did much to move the British Rothschilds closer to Zionism, though the extent of their conversion has often been overstated because of Walter's role as the addressee of the 1917 Balfour declaration. The enthusiasts in London were Jimmy and Charles's wife Rozsika, whom Jimmy introduced to Weizmann in July 1915. Through her, Weizmann met a wide range of influential figures, including Lady Crewe, Lord Robert Cecil (the Under-Secretary at the Foreign Office) and General Allenby, later the "liberator" of Jerusalem. Charles himself became directly involved following the Foreign Secretary Grey's March 1916 proposal for a Jewish Commonwealth in Palestine. Plainly, however, the best way of associating (in Weizmann's words) "the name of the greatest house in Jewry . . . with the granting of the Magna Carta of Jewish liberation" was to secure the backing of Walter; for as "Lord Rothschild" he was the heir of Natty's quasimonarchical status within British Jewry. It was with this aim in mind that a declaration of Jewish objectives in Palestine was laboriously drafted and redrafted between November 15 and January 26.

Walter's reasons for becoming involved were complex. Shortly before his death, his father had further revised his views on the issue in the light of Herbert Samuel's Cabinet memorandum on "The Future of Palestine" (January 1915), which argued that Palestine should become a British protectorate, "into which the scattered Jews would in time swarm back from all quarters of the globe, and in due course obtain Home Rule."[57] This had as much to do with British imperialism as with Zionism; and Walter generally followed his father in regarding the two as now being complementary. Shortly before an important meeting with Sir Mark Sykes at the Foreign Office, Walter wrote to Weizmann, opposing the idea that power in Palestine might be shared between England and France. "England must have sole control," he argued, and the Development Company which he envisaged running the Palestinian economy was to be firmly "under the tutelage and control of the British administration." This was the way the editor of the *Manchester Guardian* C. P. Scott was thinking too: talk of a system of Anglo-French dual control over post-war Palestine had to be resisted, he argued, if there was not to be a repeat of the unhappy experiment with dual control in Egypt.[58] It was presumably this line of argument which attracted Walter's cousin Lionel. According to Constance that March, even he was "convinced that we shall march upon Jerusalem, and found our protectorate there. When I suggested that Zionism was at an end, on account of Russia's new and wonderful move [revolution], he said certainly not . . ."[59] If nothing else, Lionel realised that the Revolution was unlikely to benefit Russian Jews in practice, despite the Bolsheviks' anti-clerical rhetoric.

Other members of the London and Paris Jewish "establishments" were more cautious, however; and Lionel himself soon changed his tune. In London the opposition to Zionism was led by Lucien Wolf, secretary of the Conjoint Foreign Committee of the Anglo-Jewish Association (after 1918, the Joint Foreign Committee) and head of the Board of Deputies' "Special Branch," who argued that Zionism would tend to fuel anti-Semitism and endanger the position of assimilated Jews in Western Europe. Wolf had influential supporters, including the Liberal Minister Edwin Montagu (who returned to the Cabinet in July 1917) and the Conjoint Committee presidents Claude Montefiore and David Alexander, who wrote a strongly anti-Zionist letter to *The Times* on May 24, 1917, supposedly expressing the "Views of Anglo-Jewry."[60] Shortly before his death, Leo intimated that he agreed with Montefiore and Alexander's view "that it was advisable to adopt a conciliatory tone towards Zionism, whilst maintaining the cardinal points of our own position, viz., that we would not concur in any proposals which implied the idea of nationality for the Jews in Palestine, or the granting of privileges detrimental to the other inhabitants."[61] After Leo's death, his widow Marie continued to take this line, as increasingly did Lionel. In Paris a similar line was taken by the secretary of the Alliance Israélite, Jacques Bigart.[62]

In the end, as Miriam Rothschild has shown, Walter prevailed—and in doing so revealed himself to be a good deal less unworldly than had hitherto been supposed. He shot back a letter to *The Times* in response to the Montefiore–Alexander letter of May 1917, denying that a Jewish state would undermine the loyalty of Jews to their countries of birth and residence. He then secured (narrowly) a vote of censure against Montefiore and Alexander at the Board of Deputies, which led the latter to resign, and got himself elected vice-president of the Board on July 20.

The final outcome naturally depended on the balance of forces within the Cabinet, but this too Walter was able to influence. Against the Zionists were Montagu, now elevated to the India Office, and another old India hand, the former Viceroy Earl Curzon, who argued that Palestine's economic resources were too limited to sustain a Jewish state and that any step in that direction would antagonise the Arabs of the region. It was crucial, therefore, to secure more weighty support, and to this end Walter bent the ears of Lloyd George—now Prime Minister—and the Foreign Secretary Balfour, the latter of whom suggested that they submit a declaration for the Cabinet to consider. After much drafting and redrafting, this was duly done on July 18. Matters moved slowly: pressing military questions inevitably took precedence over post-war pipe-dreams, and it was also now felt necessary to take soundings in Washington.[63] Even at the crucial meetings in October 1917, the future of Palestine was close to the bottom of the Cabinet's crowded agenda. Finally, however, Lloyd George was converted to the idea of a British-controlled Palestine; he and two other members of the inner War Cabinet—the South African Jan Smuts and Milner—began to worry that (as Walter had persuasively warned) the Germans might get their own pro-Zionist declaration out first, in a bid to win Jewish support in the United States and Russia.[64] Tipped off by Balfour that Montagu was still holding matters up, Walter sent another memorandum to the Foreign Office on October 3, which Balfour followed up in Cabinet the next day.[65]

Three weeks later, the Cabinet at last authorised Balfour "to take a suitable opportunity of making the following declaration of sympathy with the Zionist aspirations":

> His Majesty's Government view with favour the establishment in Palestine of a national home for the Jewish people, and will use their best endeavours to facilitate the achievement of this object, it being clearly understood that nothing shall be done which may prejudice the civil and religious rights of existing non-Jewish communities in Palestine, or the rights and political status enjoyed by Jews in any other country.

This text—which had been prepared by Leo Amery, assistant secretary to the War Cabinet—was sent by Balfour to Walter on November 2. Thus the origins of the state of Israel can indeed be traced back to a letter to Lord Rothschild. To underline the Rothschilds' contribution to this historic breakthrough, a huge celebration was held at the Covent Garden opera house on December 2 at which both Walter and Jimmy spoke. It was, Walter told the excited audience, "the greatest event that has occurred in Jewish history for the last eighteen hundred years."[66] "The British government," declared Jimmy, "had ratified the Zionist scheme":

> What was wanted from the Jewish people was no longer schemes but deeds, and he hoped that in the near future cohorts of modern Maccabees would be fighting their way through the hills of Judaea. The Jewish claim was one for justice and that also was the basis of the claims of the Arabs and Armenians, claims which Jews fully endorsed and were pledged to support. Britain stood as the foster mother of the new-born Jewish nation and he looked forward to the day when the nation, steeled in adversity but proud in hope, had proved itself by dint of its work to be a real daughter.[67]

Yet such portentous rhetoric was far from agreeable to other members of the family. Leo's widow Marie angrily denounced Walter as a traitor to the assimilationist principles of the family. Within a week of the issue of the declaration, Lionel took the lead in establishing a League of British Jews "to uphold the status of persons professing the Jewish religion; to resist the allegation that Jews constitute a separate political nationality" and "the tendency . . . to fix upon the Jews the acceptance of a nationality other than, and in addition to, that of the country of our birth or where we have lived and worked." He was joined in this enterprise by Sir Philip Magnus and Lord Swaythling, respectively the president and president-designate of the United Synagogue, Reform Synagogue and Federation of Synagogues, as well as another influential anti-Zionist Robert Waley-Cohen. As Waley-Cohen put it in a pointed dig at the Zionists, the aim was to enable "Jews of British nationality, who are at home in this country, and who are proud of their British nationality, to voice their views independently of the Jews of foreign origin who are residing in this country but who feel no strong attachment to their British nationality."[68]

In a similar spirit, the Joint Foreign Committee accepted the Balfour Declaration only with the explicit reservation "that nothing in the letter shall be held to imply that Jews constitute a separate political nationality all over the world or that Jewish citizens of countries outside Palestine owe political allegiance to the government of that country."[69] It is revealing that around this time Waley-Cohen and Swaythling wrote to Lionel proposing the establishment of a Jewish college as "a permanent War Memorial . . . to the Jews of the British Empire who have fallen in the War" in order to "carry on and interpret the Jewish and British traditions and give them their place as the permanent ennobling forces in the lives of future generations of Jewish citizens of the British Empire."[70] Even Edmond had moments of doubt, fearing that putting the Zionists in charge in Palestine would be "handing over control of the National Home to European Bolsheviks."[71]

These disagreements became increasingly acrimonious during the Paris peace conference of 1919. While Walter sought to exclude Montefiore from the Jewish delegation,[72] Weizmann countered the assimilationists' argument by warning of "subversive and anti-institutional forces in the Ghettos" which would gain the upper hand if the Zionists were thwarted. It was the assimilationists who had the better of the arguments at Paris. In the absence of Walter, who was supposed to represent pro-Zionist Anglo-Jewry, Wolf succeeded in exerting a dominant co-ordinating influence over the various Jewish groups present, especially over the question of Jews' rights and minority status in the new successor states of Central and Eastern Europe.

In fact, the Balfour Declaration was less revolutionary than the Zionists claimed and the assimilationists feared. Balfour himself "hope[d] that the Jews will make good in Palestine and eventually found a Jewish state." Like Lord Robert Cecil, his philo-Semitism had an almost Disraelian quality: as he put it in 1917, the Jews were "the most gifted race that mankind has seen since the Greeks of the fifth century."[73] But he regarded the Declaration as envisaging "some sort of British, American or other protectorate"; it "did not necessarily involve the early establishment of an independent Jewish state, which was matter for gradual development in accordance with the ordinary laws of political evolution."[74] Any idea of "a Jewish Government of Palestine," he assured Curzon in January 1919, was "certainly inadmissible."[75] Moreover, Curzon's fears about friction between Jews and Arabs proved all too well founded. Despite the hopes expressed in December 1918 when Walter gave a dinner for the Emir Feisal (attended also by Weizmann, Milner, Cecil, Crewe and T. E. Lawrence) and the agreement between Weizmann and Feisal which was signed the following month, trouble was not slow in coming. Jews and Arabs clashed violently as early as 1921 (which led the British authorities to limit immigration) and again in 1929. Walter was inclined to blame such problems on the high commissioner, Herbert Samuel, whose decision to appoint Haj Amin al Husseini as Grand Mufti of Jerusalem he especially deplored.[76] On the other hand, his efforts to reconcile the Zionists and the assimilationists were undermined when radicals at the World Zionist Conference in July 1921 called for the nationalisation of all land in Palestine.

By 1924 Walter was beginning to tire of the whole vexed question. Although he had been the first signatory of the Palestine Foundation Fund (Keren Heyesod) in 1920, he declined an invitation to chair the opening of the Hebrew University in 1925. Jimmy remained more active, briefing both Lloyd George and his Conservative successor Bonar Law about the problems not only of Palestine but also of Syria. In 1919, for example, he urged Lloyd George not to allow the Treasury to cut off funds needed for the economic development of Haifa, for fear of alienating the Arab population.[77] As soon as he heard of Lloyd George's fall in October 1922, he hastened to offer his expertise on Palestine to Bonar Law.[78] Jimmy's father Edmond also continued his involvement with Palestine, reorganising the old Palestine Committee of the Jewish Colonisation Association as the Palestine Jewish Colonisation Association—an autonomous organisation under his (and later Jimmy's) control.[79] However, Edmond worried that British policy ran the risk of "alienating public opinion in France by favouring the Arabs regarding Syria at the expense of the French . . . His only anxiety was the enormous importance of keeping the Anglo-French Alliance intact, as very powerful Catholic influences were doing their best to undermine it."[80] Even on this issue father and son disagreed: a good illustration of the way the question of Palestine's future tended to divide the Rothschild family.

The Doldrums

Yet it would be a mistake to explain the Rothschilds' *economic* difficulties after 1914 exclusively—if at all—in terms of the conflicts of loyalty engendered by the war. The diminution of Rothschild influence had as much to do with the war's economic consequences as with the generational changes of 1905–18 and the contemporaneous fragmentation of allegiances.

Although there is no question that the Rothschilds gained in one or two isolated respects from the war—which boosted demand for Vickers' guns, New Caledonian nickel and De Beers' diamonds—its net effect was unquestionably negative. It is only a slight exaggeration to say that the world in which the Rothschilds had thrived came to an end in 1914. For one thing, the war finally killed off what remained of co-operation between the Vienna house and its former associates in London and Paris. More seriously, it severed the ties between the Rothschilds and German banks like Bleichröders, Warburgs and the Disconto-Gesellschaft. The overseas trade which they and other acceptance houses had financed with scarcely an interruption for a century was suddenly disrupted, first by a paroxysm of panic in the major financial markets, then by blockades and submarines. The monetary system based on the gold standard—around which so much Rothschild business revolved—ceased to operate, as most of the major combatants suspended the convertibility of their currencies into specie and imposed exchange controls. The railways they had helped to build across Western Europe were used to transport troops into battle. Moreover, the costs of the four-year slaughter accelerated the process—discernible in the pre-war decade—whereby the European tax systems became more progressive. For the first time, the Rothschilds found themselves paying high taxes on their income and inheritances.

Table 14a shows the exceptionally sharp contraction experienced by the London house in the war years. It was in 1915 that N. M. Rothschild & Sons were at long last overtaken in terms of capital (by the Midland Bank), after nearly a century of being by far and away the country's largest bank. By 1918, Kleinworts too had grown larger than N. M. Rothschild, and Schröders were not far behind. The available balance sheets reveal that Barings' assets outstripped those of N. M. Rothschild in the years 1915–18, and although Schröders was also hard hit by the war, its balance sheet contracted less sharply than Rothschilds. A closer look at the Rothschild balances suggests a very sharp contraction in the bank's holding of British government bonds.[81]

Table 14a: The capital of six major British banks, 1913–1918 (£).

	N. M. ROTHSCHILD & SONS	BARING BROTHERS	SCHRÖDERS	KLEINWORTS GREENFELL	MORGAN	MIDLAND
1913	7,844,642	1,025,000	3,544,000	4,406,160	1,053,201	4,349,000
1914	6,367,906	1,025,000	3,535,000	4,423,149	924,490	4,781,000
1915	4,618,511	1,025,000	3,095,000	4,399,534	1,127,367	4,781,000
1916	4,521,846	1,025,000	3,054,000	4,332,986	1,185,942	4,781,000
1917	4,720,609	1,025,000	3,104,000	4,507,339	1,413,702	5,189,000
1918	3,614,602	1,025,000	3,159,000	4,669,483	1,454,205	7,173,000

Sources: RAL, RFamFD/13F; RFamFD/13E; Ziegler, *Sixth great power*, pp. 372–8; Roberts, *Schroders*, pp. 527–35; Wake, *Kleinwort Benson*, pp. 472f.; Burk, *Morgan Grenfell*, pp. 260–70, 278–81; Holmes and Green, *Midland*, pp. 331–3.

Table 14b confirms that a large part—but not all—of the explanation for this contraction lies in the heavy losses suffered by the Rothschilds in 1913–15. Barings and the Midland did far better; and if profits are expressed as a percentage of capital, the differentials are even wider (though Schröders did even worse overall). The other explanation for the bank's contraction in terms of capital must be the effect of the three partners' deaths; in particular Alfred's decision to bequeath such a large part of his estate outside the family explains the capital reduction of more than £1 million in 1918, despite moderately good profits for the third year running.

Table 14b: Profits at five major British banks, 1913–1918 (£).

	N. M. ROTHSCHILD	BARING BROTHERS	SCHRÖDERS	MORGAN GREENFELL	MIDLAND
1913	−92,962	359,673	428,000	−108,917	1,311,000
1914	−1,476,737	78,813	379,000	−229,742	1,192,000
1915	−117,195	1,094,436	69,000	438,782	1,211,000
1916	213,320	764,192	77,000	185,942	1,637,000
1917	230,123	589,913	35,000	177,508	1,968,000
1918	208,673	413,008	36,000	191,748	3,314,000

Sources: as table 14a.

A puzzle remains, however. For in many ways the First World War was financed in ways which were little different from those which had paid for the wars of the nineteenth century. Indeed, in strictly financial terms the scale of the war relative to the available economic resources was not that much greater than the cost of the Napoleonic Wars, though the latter were fought less intensively over a longer period. Governments raised some money by introducing new taxes, but mostly they resorted to borrowing. To give just three examples: the German national debt increased by around $19 billion between 1914 and 1919, the French by $25 billion and the British by $32 billion, so that by the end of the war national debts amounted to close to 200 per cent of GNP in each case. When bond yields became prohibitively high, all the combatant governments asked their central banks to print money in return for treasury bills. This was possible on a large scale because, as in the Napoleonic period, the convertibility of paper notes into gold had been suspended to prevent banking crises; as then, the result was inflation, with prices doubling or trebling. Why then did the Rothschilds fail to capitalise on the financial opportunities of the First World War? After all, it had been the Napoleonic Wars which had given Mayer Amschel and his sons their crucial business opportunities a century before.

The answer is plain enough. The defeat of France in the Napoleonic Wars had been financed to a large extent by British loans and subsidies to Austria, Russia and Prussia. With their establishments in Frankfurt, London and Paris, the Rothschilds had been in a uniquely good position to facilitate these transfers. The defeat of the Central Powers in the First World War also involved transfers (amounting to $9.7 billion) from Britain to her allies; but only in the case of France were the Rothschilds really in a position to play a part, and even then a minor one. Once they had been the principal agents for international transfers between Allied powers; now, with the British war effort so dependent on American credits, it was J. P. Morgan who succeeded N. M. Rothschild as the linchpin of war finance—confirming what a strategic error it had been not to establish a Rothschild house on the other side of the Atlantic.

There were also resemblances between the post-war periods after 1815 and after 1918. In both cases, there was an attempt to make the loser pay for part of the costs of the war. In both cases, wartime inflation had so reduced the internal debt of the loser state that it was better able to make such payments than was generally admitted or realised. After 1815 copious amounts of British capital stood available to finance the restored continental regimes; after 1918, it was American capital which the various "successor states" of Central Europe—not only Germany but also Austria, Hungary and Czechoslovakia—could draw on. Nevertheless, in both cases the new regimes in the defeated states proved unstable. The Weimar Republic, like restored Bourbon France, lasted just fifteen years. Britain, like Austria in the 1820s, lacked the financial resources to "police" post-war Europe. America, like Britain in the 1820s, gradually withdrew from continental commitments, despite being well able to afford them. The biggest differences between the 1820s and the 1920s were that Britain wrote off most of her allies' war debts, unlike America after 1918; the reparations burden imposed on France in 1815 was substantially less as a proportion of national income (around 7 per cent) than that imposed on Germany in 1921 (around 300 per cent); and, finally, the regimes which had to deal with the problems of the 1920s were democratic. This meant that bankers, bondholders and direct taxpayers were no longer politically over-represented as they had been in the 1820s. It was partly for this reason that Morgans could not play in the 1930s an analogous role to that played by the Rothschilds in the 1830s, using their financial influence via the bond market to discourage aggressive foreign policies. The economic and political crises of the 1930s exposed the limits of financial power in a way without parallel in the nineteenth century.

All this provides some excuse for the Rothschilds' inter-war difficulties. Yet, if the period had given the bank a much smoother ride, it is debatable how much more successful it would have been. The bank which Ronald Palin joined as a young clerk in 1925 seemed to belong to the age of Dombey & Son.[82] Save at lunchtime, when a green blind was drawn across the glass door, the partners could be seen at their desks in the panelled and upholstered splendour of "The Room," but to Palin they seemed "a higher order of creation" with whom communication was minimal.[83] They had their own entrance, their own dining room, and their desks were fitted with a row of bell-pushes which could be used to summon any member of staff. There was even a special office on the top floor called the Private Accounts Department ("Whores and Jockeys" to the staff) which handled the partners' private affairs. In the words of Lionel's son Edmund, who joined the bank in 1939, "The family who sat in the Room and the staff who occupied the General Office or sat in the Front Hall were two races apart."[84]

At the top of the hierarchy of clerks was the general manager, an office occupied for most of the inter-war years by the Hungarian-born Samuel Stephany, and the various departmental heads and senior clerks like the Nauheim brothers. The New Court office layout had a haphazard quality: located above the Room were the offices of the staff manager and the chief accountant, as well as the Control Department and the Private Accounts Department. The "General Office" was in fact a cramped public counter reached through a narrow back hall, which also contained the Cashiers and Bullion Department. In spite of its name, the Stock Department handled the business of bills of exchange and was divided into a Bills Receivable and a Bills Payable department. There, at rows of high sloping desks, clerks laboriously numbered and cancelled bills, then presented them for acceptance to the "walks" man. Even more cumbersome was the mode of operation of the Dividend Office, which dealt with issues and interest payments on foreign bond issues as well as dividends on the bearer shares of the bank's small number of corporate clients like Royal Dutch. It was, in Palin's words, "a time-and-motion student's nightmare," with its old-fashioned machines for cancelling coupons in the Coupon Department, its Brunsviga calculating machine and its actuarial tables. Speed was at a heavy discount. According to one anecdote, when the future Dividend Office chief Lionel Stewart was asked by one of the partners to tell him what 1 per cent of a hundred million was, he replied immediately: "One million." "Don't guess, boy," he was rebuked. "Go away and work it out." The maxims of the general manager Stephany were intended to foster the same mentality. "Anyone can make a mistake," he was fond of saying. "The man who never made a mistake never made anything. But Heaven help the man who misses a mistake when checking." Another piece of Stephany advice to younger employees was: "Never copy a total, always *make* it."[85]

This emphasis on punctiliousness would be more comprehensible had it not been combined with the most leisurely working practices imaginable. The chief of the Coupon Department, George Littlehales, lived in Mersea, for example, and rarely arrived at work before noon. At one o'clock he went to lunch; at 2.30 he set off again for home. As a junior clerk, Palin "rarely arrived much before 10.30 in the morning and could always count on two free days at the weekend." It was characteristic of the New Court order of priorities that there were three tape machines in the partners' waiting room: one for stock exchange prices, one for general news and one for sporting news. Like dons, the senior clerks had their own dining room and butler, while their juniors perpetuated the ambience of a minor public school, bestowing nicknames (Littlehales was known as "the Egg"), playing practical jokes and looking forward impatiently to the lunch break ("Children's Hour"). Long-serving Rothschild employees like George Tite and Shirley Snell lived like P. G. Wodehouse characters who had been obliged by a deficiency of inherited wealth to finance their leisure pursuits in the City. Tite summed the inter-war atmosphere up perfectly when he told Palin: "This, my boy, is the best club in London. We really ought to be paying a subscription instead of receiving a salary." In fact, he and his colleagues received more than just their salaries. In addition to his basic pay of £100 a year, paid quarterly, Palin received "lunch money" of £48 a year; "poundage" (notionally a payment from the Inland Revenue for the work of collecting income tax on foreign dividends); "touchings" from the partners on birthdays and anniversaries; one-eighth per cent brokerage on allotments of bonds and shares to applicants they had introduced to the bank; as well as holiday money.

This relatively generous remuneration perhaps explains why Rothschilds still managed to recruit talented figures like Michael Bucks (later general manager) and Peter Hobbs (later investment manager), who both joined the firm at around the same time as Palin. Generally, however, the system of recruitment was feudal in style. One senior employee had joined the bank as a porter on the strength of his mother's years of domestic service for the Roseberys. Palin himself was introduced to the firm because his father knew a director of the Bank of England. His interview consisted of being asked by the staff manager to spell "parallel" and "acknowledgement." Many employees were from families which had worked at New Court for generations: the Williamses and the Mercers, for example (typically, the young Ernest Mercer was referred to as "Mercer's son's brother's son"), while Rothschild couriers were still recruited from Folkestone families who had worked for Nathan himself. The first women employed at New Court were the unmarried daughters of two rabbis. They were confined to segregated offices at the top of the house and given lunch in a separate room in the basement (a practice which continued, like that of Saturday closing, until the 1960s). Palin's verdict does not seem unduly harsh: Rothschilds had become "an organisation . . . managed largely by amiable eccentrics who did very little work and that without much seriousness and by antiquated methods."[86] It seemed to be sinking into "genteel inactivity."[87]

Nor was this air of stagnation peculiar to the London house. When Edouard's son Guy joined the Paris house in 1931, he was struck by the way "the past clung to everything and everyone." His training took the form of learning to quote interest rates in fractions instead of decimals, which he was taught by a clerk whose other function was to read him selections from the newspapers in the morning. "The staff," Guy later recalled, "were imbued with the grandeur of 'the name' and of the responsibilities [it] imposed. Vestiges of the previous century were encountered at every moment and in every corner, even some that no longer had any reason for being," like the trifling account kept for the Vatican which dated back to the time of Baron James. Just as the London partners insulated themselves from the day-to-day running of business in the Room, Edouard and Robert passed their working hours in the vast "grand bureau," using the identical system of bell-pushes to communicate with their employees. "The bare-walled . . . ill-lit . . . depressing and drab" offices which housed the clerks "also recalled the past in their haphazard arrangement and their odour of stale tobacco and mustiness. After decades of underemployment, everyone worked slowly, without supervision or discipline." Guy quickly realised that "Rothschild Frères was more of a family secretariat than a working bank," whose main activity was "gently prolonging the nineteenth century."[88]

Yet such impressionistic accounts understate the extent of Rothschild activity in the 1920s and 1930s. It would perhaps be more historically accurate to regard the memory of "immobility" as a consequence of the two great economic traumas of the inter-war period, rather than a cause of problems peculiar to the Rothschilds.

In some ways the 1920s and 1930s were no less active periods for N. M. Rothschild & Sons than the previous two decades had been. If one adds together the nominal amounts of bond and share issues which the bank underwrote, the total for 1920–39 is only 5 per cent lower than the period 1900–19. The difference was twofold. Firstly, the bulk of inter-war business was done in partnership with other City firms, principally the Rothschilds' erstwhile rivals Barings and Schröders, rather than with the Paris and Vienna houses.[89] Other examples of collaboration include the Rothschilds' entry into the Chinese loan consortium in 1919 (a field still dominated by the Hong Kong & Shanghai Bank),[90] and their involvement with the purchase of various German-owned Turkish railway companies (via Swiss intermediaries) in conjunction with Schröders, Lloyds, the Westminster Bank and the

National Provincial Bank.[91] For reasons which are not wholly clear, it seems to have proved very difficult to resume the traditional co-operation between the three Rothshild houses after the war; and this may help to explain why the links which still remained with Paris and Vienna ultimately proved so problematic. The second difference was that the bond issues of the 1920s proved to be among the most disastrous investments of modern times because of the successive economic and political crises which afflicted the borrowing countries. Table 14c gives a geographical breakdown of the Rothschilds' major inter-war loans and share issues, which shows that British and European issues predominated, followed by Latin American and Asian—primarily Japanese (though here the Rothschilds were members of a large group led by the Westminster Bank, so the figure in the table substantially exaggerates their role).

Table 14c: Major bond and share issues in which N. M. Rothschild & Sons participated, 1921–1937.

REGION	TOTAL VALUE OF SECURITIES ISSUED (£)	PERCENTAGE OF TOTAL
Britain	38,112,921	21.3
Europe	38,607,700	21.5
Latin America	55,438,251	30.9
Japan	43,500,000	24.3
Other	3,500,000	2.0
Total	179,158,872	100.0

Source: RAL.

Closer examination reveals, however, that the Rothschilds were involved in lending to some of the most unstable regimes of the inter-war era. This was the unintended consequence of a rather uncritical resumption of pre-war patterns of business activity.

It was, of course, logical enough for a firm with such close historical links to Central Europe to play a leading role in financing the new states established in the ruins of the Habsburg and Hohenzollern empires. Unfortunately, even the most stable of these proved to be less than easy to deal with. Czechoslovakian bonds worth around £10 million were issued by a Barings-led consortium of N. M. Rothschild, Schröders and the New York firm of Kidder Peabody in 1922 and 1923; but the first tranche of bonds dipped below par because of an ill-timed attempt by the City of Prague to issue its own paper.[92] The Rothschilds appear to have eschewed the disastrous German bond issues of the early 1920s, most of which were reduced to near-worthlessness by the hyperinflation of 1922–3; but they were drawn back to the German market (partly under the influence of Max Warburg, then at the height of his powers), raising £835,000 for the Prussian province of Westphalia and combining with Barings and Schröders to float major loans for the cities of Hamburg and Berlin in 1926 and 1927. In addition, the London house joined the Vienna house as shareholders in the Warburgs' ambitious International Acceptance Bank (IAB), founded in 1921 to help finance the yawning post-war German trade deficit; and were later involved in another Warburg project, the London-based Industrial Finance and Investment Corporation Ltd.[93] Hungary was perhaps the most important Central European client of the period: here it was New Court which took the lead, issuing loans for £7.9 million in 1924, £2.25 million in 1925–26 and £1.6 million in 1936.[94]

Finally, there was Austria. In addition to the £3 million government loan of 1930, which was handled jointly with Barings, Schröders and Morgan Grenfell, the London house was indirectly interested in the Austrian economy—perhaps more than it realised before 1931—through its sister house in Vienna. Louis perhaps rather resembled Max Warburg in his over-optimistic assessment of the Central European economy in the 1920s. He elected to hold on to the Witkowitz ironworks once they became part of an independent Czechoslovakia (though he might have acted differently had they gone to Poland).[95] More important, he increased Rothschilds' involvement in the bank founded by his grandfather some six decades before: the Creditanstalt. In July 1921, he accepted the post of president of the Creditanstalt board (*Verwaltungsrat*), and it was in conjunction with the Creditanstalt that the Vienna house involved itself in concerns like the IAB and the Dutch-based Amstelbank.[96] It was a former Creditanstalt director and supervisory board member, Wilhelm Regendanz, who managed to persuade the London Rothschilds to issue £2 million bonds for an Austrian firm, the Vorarlberger Illwerke at Bregenz, the failure of which was an early warning of what lay ahead for the Central European economies.[97]

When the Bodenkreditanstalt got into difficulties in October 1929, it was to Louis that the Austrian government turned. He obliged by agreeing to what amounted to a merger of the two banks. On Wednesday October 18, the Paris house wrote to congratulate him on his action. "Thanks to your decisiveness and courageous attitude," wrote Edouard, "you saved Vienna's finances and avoided events that could have been extremely serious for your country and that would certainly have had repercussions in other financial capitals and markets."[98] Had he known what the following Tuesday would bring, he would have been offering anything but congratulations. Neither he nor Louis realised that history was about to repeat itself: just as Louis's great-grandfather Salomon had bailed out Arnstein & Eskeles on the eve of the 1848 crisis, so Louis's decision to bail out the Bodencreditanstalt was to bring the Vienna house to the brink of ruin.

It seemed equally logical for the London house to continue its traditionally close relationship with Latin America and above all with Brazil and Chile.[99] During the war, the American ambassador in Brazil had commented that "the Rothschilds have so mortgaged Brazil's financial future that . . . they will place every obstacle in the way of her entering into banking relations with any other house than their own or with any other nation than England."[100] This was a pardonable exaggeration. The London house issued bonds with a nominal value of more than £28 million for the Brazilian federal government in the inter-war years, plus an additional £17.5 million for Brazilian states and railways. (The total figure for Chile was around £10 million.) In the case of Brazil, financial (and political) stability hinged in large part on the world market for coffee; the 1922 loan of £9 million—in conjunction, once again, with Barings and Schröders—was specifically designed to finance the government's coffee price-support scheme and placed control of coffee exports in the hands of a committee of City banks (a repeat of what had been attempted, despite Rothschild reservations, in 1908).[101]

Doubts about the reliability of the Banco de Brasil persisted, however, and when the Brazilian government approached New Court for another £25 million loan in 1923 "to liquidate the floating debt and set Brazilian finances in order," Lionel asked Edwin Montagu to lead a mission to Brazil in the hope of imposing "some palatable form of foreign financial control" on the Banco de Brasil.[102] Unfortunately, the best that Montagu and his colleagues could come up with was a suggestion that the London banks might buy the Brazilian government's shares in the Banco, which Lionel rejected on the ground that it would be "most unpopular in Brazil for the national bank to be owned by foreigners."[103] In any case, the Bank of England's temporary embargo on foreign loans undercut the planned loan, and three years later—after a spat between Brazil and Britain over the admission of Germany to the League of Nations—the Brazilian government turned instead to Wall Street.[104] The London house nevertheless continued to exercise control over the coffee support scheme, which was transferred to the São Paulo state goverment in 1924, and resumed its dominant role in Brazilian federal bond issues when Brazil returned to the gold standard in 1927.[105] The Rothschild agent in Brazil, Henry Lynch (known locally as "Sir Lynch" after his knighthood), remained a key figure in the country's finances throughout the period. In Chile the stability of government finance was also linked closely with a staple export—nitrates for use in fertilisers and explosives.

In addition to this traditional bond market business, the Rothschilds maintained their pre-war interests in mining. Their influence as the principal shareholders in Rio Tinto became even greater as the firm expanded its interests from copper and pyrite to embrace sulphur-recovery, cinder-treatment and silica gel, and its geographical range from Spain to Belgium, Rhodesia and the Americas.[106] Key members of the board such as Lord Milner, Sir Arthur Steel-Maitland (the managing director of the Company in 1920) and Sir Auckland Geddes (who succeeded Milner as chairman in 1925) worked closely with New Court as the firm tried to cope with the volatility of the inter-war raw-materials markets.[107] In South Africa the London and Paris houses together remained major shareholders in De Beers, though increasingly its direction was determined by Ernest Oppenheimer's Anglo American Corporation (founded in 1917), which had acquired an even larger stake than the Rothschilds.[108] The only reverse was in Spain, where the Almadén mines were nationalised in 1929; but that had ceased to be a major source of revenue even before the war.

All this business hardly constituted immobility. The firm's familiar circle of stockbrokers—Cazenove, Messels, Panmure Gordon and Sebags—were kept occupied,[109] as were the firm's lawyers.[110] The trouble was that activity was not always matched by profitability. For when the world economy plunged into the great deflation of 1929–32—with prices, production and employment levels falling by unprecedented amounts—the areas of greatest Rothschild involvement were among the worst affected.

It is arguable, of course, that this greatest crisis of the capitalist system was caused by "structural" factors beyond the control of bankers and politicians alike. The legacy of the First World War was one of over-capacity and distorted markets for many staple agricultural and industrial products. But there can be no doubt that misguided fiscal and monetary policies—allied with the impossible tangle of international war debts and reparations obligations—did much to exacerbate and perpetuate the slump. In the early 1920s, too many countries sought to evade difficult political choices by running excessive public sector deficits and financing them with the help of the printing press: inflation and hyperinflation were the results, and in their wake financial instability as investors (especially bondholders) demanded higher yields to compensate them for the risk of more inflation. Austria was one of the states which experienced high post-war inflation. In the aftermath, the Vienna house had a hand in stabilising the new schilling, thwarting the efforts of inflation enthusiasts like the financier and industrialist Camilio Castiglione; but it is probable that, like virtually every Central European bank in the 1920s, its post-inflation balance sheet was long on deposits and short on reserves. From the mid-1920s onwards, the prevalent policy error was a fixation with unsustainable exchange rates, as governments sought vainly to imitate the gold standard system of the pre-1914 period, ignoring the absence of many of the essential preconditions for its earlier success. The result was that, especially after 1929, politicians sought to balance budgets and tighten monetary policy in the teeth of recession, subordinating all other policy objectives to the maintenance of gold equivalence.

There is no question that the Rothschilds had a hand in this, though the error was so widespread as to constitute a near-universal "conventional wisdom." Perhaps the London house's continuing importance in the international gold market was a factor. When the war-time ban on gold exports from London was lifted, N. M. Rothschild took on the role of intermediary between the bullion market and the Bank of England, to which the South African mine companies agreed to ship all their gold (roughly half of world output). The system adopted was that N. M. Rothschild advanced £3 17s 9d per standard ounce to the producers on receipt of the refined gold and then sold it at "the best price obtainable, giving the London market and the bullion brokers a chance to bid," pooling any premium and remitting it to the mines every six months.[111] Thus was born the so-called "Fix," whereby the world market price for gold was set every morning at 11 a.m.—beginning on September 12, 1919—following an auction conducted at New Court.[112] The choice of venue reflected the London house's dual role: as refiners and agents for the South African producers (the biggest seller).[113] It thus played a pivotal role in the stabilisation of the Indian and British currencies after the war.[114]

Yet it is hard to believe that this was the only reason the Rothschilds adhered to the reconstituted gold exchange standard. Ultimately, they liked gold for the same reason that the rest of the City liked gold: they feared that, if the pound were allowed to float, London would see its central role as the world's financial capital pass irrevocably to New York. Nor was their faith in the gold standard unthinking: in 1931 Walter argued—rightly—that the breakdown of the system in the Great Depression had "nothing to do with the rights or wrongs of Capitalism or Socialism, but . . . is owing to the greed of [certain] countries for gold. What they have succeeded in doing is to injure their own trade by withdrawing the means of barter from the rest of the world."[115] This was fair comment: the biggest difference between the pre-1914 gold standard and the gold exchange system of the 1920s was that two of the most important players—the United States and France—bent the rules by "sterilising" additions to their reserves in order to avoid domestic inflation. Without central bank co-operation, the system could not survive.

Compared with Britain, France compromised. So long as French tax-payers persisted in believing that the budget would be balanced by reparations which the Germans were determined not to pay, there was no chance of restoring the franc to its pre-war exchange rate. Indeed, it was only after protracted debate that the currency was pegged at 20 per cent of its old external value in 1928. This was a compromise which Edouard vehemently and vainly opposed in his capacity as one of the twelve regents of the Banque de France. In the summer of 1924 he was openly critical of the Left Cartel government led by Edouard Herriot for what he saw as its soft line towards striking railway workers—an important preoccupation for de Rothschild Frères in their role as major Nord shareholders. Early the following year, with the franc depreciating rapidly, he led a delegation from the Banque to discuss the currency question with Herriot. Though Edouard tactfully laid part of the blame for the weakness of the franc on "the clerical right and Communist extremists," he was also critical of excessive public sector pay settlements and called for a coalition of the Left Cartel with the more right-wing National Bloc it had replaced, with the aim of balancing the budget. However, the appointment of Emile Moreau as Governor of the Banque in June 1926 led to a diminution of Rothschild influence, for, while Edouard continued to dream of a return to pre-war parity, Moreau more realistically argued for stabilisation at something closer to the existing rate.[116] This division came close to outright conflict the following spring.[117] Edouard had a powerful supporter in the industrialist François de Wendel as well as leverage when the French government sought to raise money in London in 1927,[118] but he was asking the politically impossible. Even a new government led by Poincaré and empowered to balance the budget by decree could do no more than peg the franc at 25.52 to the dollar. Under Poincaré, the 3 per cent rente rose from 48.25 francs to 67.60; by contrast, Rothschild influence declined.

Edouard's position was not strengthened by the chequered political career of his cousin Maurice (Edmond's second son). In 1919 Maurice had been elected to the Chamber of Deputies on Clemenceau's National Bloc ticket for the constituency of Hautes-Pyrénées. From the outset he had made the most of his family background, using the slogan "My name is my platform" on election posters and, in order to secure the clerical vote, shamelessly assuring the clergy at Lourdes that he would "organise special trains for pilgrims, and on political and religious matters [press for] freedom of teaching in religious schools [and] the recall of teaching nuns." "Governments can do nothing," a local priest was given to understand, "without his family. The Rothschilds are, thanks to their banks, the finance ministry—the real one, the one that we can't do without."[119] These tactics evidently worked in 1919, but five years later they could not avert defeat at the hands of Herriot's Left Cartel. Undaunted, Maurice changed his political allegiance, accepting an invitation from the socialist newspaper owner Louis Cluzel to stand in a by-election for the Hautes-Alpes constituency. He won; but this time his electioneering methods were challenged. In a report to the Chamber, he was accused of spending 1.6 million francs (around £15,000) in order to secure victory, paying 5,000 francs to one small town to enable it to buy uniforms for its fire brigade, and even sending out 200 letters each containing twenty francs to individual voters. A motion calling for the election to be annulled was only narrowly defeated by 180 to 178, but when a committee of enquiry concluded that Maurice's contributions had been essentially charitable and therefore legitimate its report was resoundingly rejected (by 209 votes to 86). The election had to be re-run and although Maurice won (as he did again in April 1928) his reputation—and by association that of his family—had scarcely been enhanced.[120] Venal parliaments and gold-hoarding central banks bear at least some of the blame for the 1929–32 world crisis; the French Rothschilds were represented in both.

The Crash

It is usual, though slightly misleading, to regard Wall Street's "Black Thursday"— October 24, 1929—as marking the start of the Great Depression. In fact, there had been signs of declining economic activity in Europe for over a year. On the other hand, it is hard to overstate the knock-on effects of the unprecedented collapse of the American stock market, which wiped $30 billion off stocks worth $80 billion in the space of a month and drove the Dow Jones Industrials index from its peak of 381 on September 1929 to a final trough of 50 in May 1932. This asset-price deflation led to immense flows of American capital out of Europe. This in turn led to a generalised monetary contraction which central banks and governments worsened by trying to hang on to their gold exchange rates. One way of doing this was to increase interest rates; another was to cut public spending or put up taxes; a third was to raise tariffs in an effort to reduce imports. The principal effect of such policies was to push up unemployment to undreamt-of heights, as firms laid off workers, investors fled into liquidity, consumers tightened their belts and international trade dried up. This in turn generated a political reaction—sometimes violent— against the whole complex of institutions which seemed to be to blame.

For the Rothschilds, the first great crisis of the Depression came in Brazil. As commodity prices slid further in the global deflation, the government turned once again to the London house for assistance. Armed with the now familiar list of conditions, Stephany and Palin were despatched to Rio in February 1930, but their negotiations were undercut by the coup of Getulio Vargas—among the first of many shifts to dictatorship triggered by the Depression.[121] The following year the Treasury sent Sir Otto Niemeyer in the hope of imposing some kind of stabilisation package on the new regime, but in September Vargas suspended payments on foreign debt, following the precedents set in 1898 and 1914. Now the most that could be done was to negotiate some kind of rescheduling agreement. After protracted conferences with the Council of Foreign Bondholders, an agreement was reached with Vargas in March 1932 which secured preferential treatment for the oldest and best-secured loans. It was not until 1934, however, that a complete restructuring of the Brazilian debt was arranged with the principal foreign banks (the Rothschilds, Paribas and Dillon Read). By issuing new bonds, the government was able to pay around £6–8 million annually between 1932 and 1937, though it was not until 1962 that all the sterling bonds were finally liquidated.[122] It was a similar story in Chile, where a new Compania de Salitre de Chile (COSACH) was set up in 1931 to rationalise the nitrate industry on the basis of a loan worth £2 million issued jointly by N. M. Rothschild, Barings, Schröders and Morgan Grenfell. The scheme was doomed to fail as exports continued to decline. In January 1933 COSACH was liquidated and a moratorium on debt service announced. It took twenty years before an agreement was reached between the bondholders and the new Chilean Nitrate and Iodine Sales Corporation.[123]

It was in Europe, however, that the worst blow fell. On May 11, 1931, Creditanstalt officials showed the Austrian government the bank's annual balance sheet for 1930, which it was due to publish a few days later. It revealed losses of 140 million schillings (around £4 million) compared with paid up capital of 125 million schillings. Given that its balance sheet was as large as total central government expenditure, these were horrific figures; and as they were four months old the actual losses were probably closer to 160 million schillings. Under Austrian law, a bank whose losses exceeded half its capital had no option but to close down.[124] The prospect for the Vienna house, which held around 16.7 million schillings of the Creditanstalt's capital, was therefore grim. It was not much better for the 130 foreign banks (including de Rothschild Frères) who between them accounted for more than a third of its liabilities. However, the Austrian government was fearful that the collapse of the Creditanstalt would devastate between 60 and 80 per cent of Austrian industry (an exaggerated figure—in terms of capital, probably no more than 14 per cent of Austrian limited companies would have been affected). It was also pointed out that most of the losses were attributable to the merger with the Bodencreditanstalt which the government itself had insisted on. Accordingly, it was decided to replenish the Creditanstalt's capital with 100 million schillings in return for a 33 per cent shareholding. As part of the rescue package, the Paris house lent the Creditanstalt a further 136 million francs for six years.[125]

Yet this did not suffice to avert a financial panic which quickly spread from Vienna to Hungary, Germany and throughout the entire European economy. The National Bank did its utmost to keep the Austrian banking system liquid by discounting bills, but it was slow to raise its discount rate and public confidence spiralled downwards: memories of hyperinflation ten years before inclined Austrians to assume that the schilling would soon go the way of the crown before it, and there was a general flight into foreign currency and goods. Because of diplomatic complications, it took three weeks to organise a £3 million loan to the National Bank from the Bank of International Settlements and when this was exhausted the Austrians had to rely on a short-term loan of £4.3 million from the Bank of England. In July a similar crisis struck the Darmstädter und Nationalbank in Germany. In September a run on the Bank of England ended the pound's brief return to the gold standard.

The Creditanstalt crisis thus quickly became part of a general breakdown of the post-war monetary system. From the Rothschilds' point of view, however, it represented the final break between the Vienna house and the London house. When Lionel became chairman of a hastily constituted Austrian Creditanstalt Committee, set up to represent the foreign depositors and shareholders, he declared that to put any more money into the still haemorrhaging bank would be "inexpedient." Given the close links between the Creditanstalt and the Vienna house, this amounted to a refusal to bail Louis out. By 1933 the Paris Rothschilds were inclined to take the same view. Edmond advised Edouard that it would be "dangerous" even to look at the Vienna house's accounts "because it suggests involvement or support from the Paris house." His argument shows that the memories of 1848 had not faded:

> What is happening in the Vienna bank does not concern us. We advanced funds, it's a question of honour for Vienna to reimburse them . . . This matter of honour in our families has always been the overriding point of view. One need only recall the sale of the silverware [in 1848]. The Vienna house is not our business and in sum, as one of the heads of

the Paris house, I do not wish to give them any money, not a penny more.[126]

Edmond at least had no desire to "sell the silverware" a second time. Louis therefore had little option but to turn once again to the Austrian government.[127] In September 1933 he finally wound up his involvement in the Creditanstalt, which now effectively became a state-controlled concern, absorbing the Wiener Bank-Verein and part of the Niederösterreichische-Escompte-Gesellschaft.[128]

There is little doubt that the Creditanstalt crisis was the single most serious blow to the Rothschilds' position of the post-war period, biting deep into the capital of all three houses. Yet it is worth adding that the impact of the 1929–31 crash could have been worse. They were fortunate too that their involvement with the Swedish financier Ivan Kreuger—whose financial empire was literally based on matches—was not greater. In 1929 the London house had joined forces with the Boston bank of Lee, Higginson & Co. to issue shares for Kreuger totalling $10 million. Three years later, the Swede committed suicide and his empire collapsed, taking Lee, Higginson down with it.[129] At least the Rothschild houses survived the slump. The same could not be said of the bank which had been acquired by Max von Goldschmidt-Rothschild and his sons Albert and Erich in 1920. Goldschmidt-Rothschild & Co. (formerly A. Falkenberger) was handed over to the Reichs-Kredit-Gesellschaft in 1932—one of the lesser casualties of the German banking crisis.[130]

Under these circumstances it is not wholly surprising that the London house sought to increase its involvement in domestic corporate finance, especially as the British economy enjoyed a modest but nevertheless real recovery after the 1931 devaluation. Before 1914 N. M. Rothschild had been hesitant to involve itself in the domestic economy, and it was not until 1928 that this changed with a succession of issues of debenture stock—in partnership with Barings and Schröders—for various London underground railway companies. Two years later, the London National Property Co. raised £2 million through Rothschilds to finance the purchase of Shell-Mex House in the Strand, which it then let to the Shell Transport and Trading Co., and a year later the Woolworths retail chain was persuaded by Philip Hill to issue £9.36 million shares through New Court. Other early corporate clients included the brewers Charrington & Co.

These were ventures into unfamiliar terrain for a bank which had been almost exclusively concerned with overseas business for more than a century, and inevitably there were teething troubles. News of the London National Property issue leaked into the press, occasioning an ugly confrontation between Stephany and the veteran City editor of the *Financial News*, whom he accused of "picking up rumours in railway lavatories."[131] Although heavily oversubscribed, the Woolworths share offer was nearly wrecked by a minor City panic the weekend before the lists closed. With the letters of acceptance still waiting to be sent out, last-minute withdrawals began to pour in on the Monday morning. Staff had to work all night behind locked doors, completing and sending out acceptance letters before any more subscribers could pull out.[132] Of course, by comparison with the Paris house, with its extensive investments in railways and electricity companies, the London house remained a minor force in the world of domestic corporate finance.[133] But an important step had been taken in a direction which would prove vital to its recovery after 1945.

The extent of the Rothschilds' relative decline in the inter-war period should not therefore be overstated. The generation of Rothschilds who grew up in those years detected no waning of the family's wealth: indeed, the mores of the previous century were preserved as if in aspic. Guy and his sister Jacqueline had one English nanny each, though the two women disliked one another so intensely that they refused even to lunch together. The children thus grew up in a bizarre isolation not only from their parents, whom they lunched with once a week, but also from one another. They were isolated from the outside world too. As a schoolboy, Guy was driven to and from the *lycée* by one of his father's chauffeurs with a footman to provide additional protection. Much of his time was spent not in Paris but at one or other of the family's country houses. Each year the entire household progressed from Ferrières (November to January) to Cannes (February or March) and then on to Chantilly (Easter and July to September).[134] Similarly, Edmund's youth was divided between the house his father leased at 18 Kensington Palace Gardens and his 2,500 acre estate at Exbury in Hampshire.[135] Here and on the other great family estates, their parents pursued their expensive pastimes much as their grandparents had done before them. While Lionel indulged his passion for horticulture with the aid of up to 400 gardeners at Exbury, Edouard had his beloved racehorses at Chantilly. Maurice's wife Noémie meanwhile moved with the times by building an Alpine sports complex at Megève. As they came into their money, therefore, the younger Rothschilds felt no embarrassment about consuming conspicuously. For Guy, the 1930s meant golf, American cars, dancing at Biarritz and baccarat at Deauville. Philippe built himself a seaside villa at Arcachon, the better to entertain other men's wives, and helped his father to squander yet more money by building his own theatre in the rue Pigalle (a suitably louche location).[136]

Yet there were signs that the grandeur was beginning to fade. In 1922, Jimmy had rather unexpectedly inherited Waddesdon when Ferdinand's unmarried sister Alice died;[137] but when Harold Nicolson stayed there in July 1939 he was unimpressed (as he complained to Vita Sackville-West):

> Hardly a thing has been changed since the old Baron [Ferdinand]'s time. There are marvellous pictures and Sèvres, but execrable taste. Jimmy hates anything being altered, and the lavatories still have handles you pull up instead of chains you pull down. There is no running water in the bedrooms, and although it is very luxurious as regards food and drink and flowers, it is really less comfortable than our mud-pie in the Weald.[138]

Was this merely aesthetic conservatism, or were the huge running costs of the great houses beginning to pinch? Certainly, some of the old Rothschild houses had to be relinquished altogether. Halton was sold to the Royal Air Force after the war for £112,000, Aston Clinton was turned into a hotel and Gunnersbury became a public park. Tring would also have gone if the Museum of Natural History could have been persuaded to accept it as a gift.[139] The first Rothschild house in the West End, 107 Piccadilly, was demolished to make way for a hotel ballroom in 1929; nine years later, Alfred's grand house at 1 Seamore Place went the same way to allow the extension of Curzon Street. The lease on 148 Piccadilly was surrendered and its contents auctioned off in 1937.[140] Three of the French Rothschilds' houses were also given up.[141] Perhaps the most poignant symbol of the times was Walter's decision to sell almost all his Tring collection of stuffed birds (apart from 200 ostriches, rheas and cassowaries) to the American Museum of Natural History for $225,000 (less than a dollar per specimen).[142]

In 1935 the *Jewish Chronicle* ventured to suggest (with perhaps a hint of relief) that the Rothschilds' "heyday" was "waning": "The age of rationalisation and of multiple stores, of chemicals and oil has dawned . . . the sway of the former ruling families [is] no longer absolute."[143] Once there had been a certain grudging, deferential respect for the Rothschilds' grandiose way of life. Now, in the straitened circumstances of the 1930s, it came to seem faintly absurd—witness the two anecdotes most often related about Lionel. "No garden, however small," he is said to have proclaimed in a speech to the City Horticultural Society, "should contain less than two acres of rough woodland." Confronted with a canteen of cutlery (to be given as a wedding present to an employee), he was mystified. "Well, that's not much good," he exclaimed. "You could never have more than twelve people to dinner."[144] There are similar jokes about the French Rothschilds' luxurious bathing habits and their diet of puréed pearls in Albert Cohen's surreally comic novel *Mangeclous*.[145] Even a sympathetic writer like Cecil Roth detected the intimations of decline. His book *The Magnificent Rothschilds* (1938) could be read as an epitaph not only for the third and fourth generations (the last of whom had died the previous year), but also for the family's magnificence: "All had passed away . . . It was a different world."[146]

In the light of all this, perhaps it is understandable that the most intellectually gifted of the next generation of Rothschild men turned his back on the family business. In part, this was a vote of no confidence in the profession of banking, understandable given the "moribund, boring, rather painful" aspect of the City in the 1930s.[147] But it may also have been due to the influence on Victor at Cambridge of that generation of Apostles which included Anthony Blunt and Guy Burgess, whose political sympathies were inimical to capitalism *per se*. Years later there would be speculation about Victor's relationship with the Cambridge spies, culminating in the false allegation that he was the "fifth man" (a last, hitherto unexposed Soviet "mole" within the British secret service). His relationship with Blunt and Burgess after both had been recruited by the NKVD remained close enough to furnish circumstantial evidence for such claims. Not only did they rent his house in Bentinck Street during the war; it was also Victor who, in August 1940, recommended Blunt to MI5 (less than a year after he had been discharged from an intelligence course at Camberley because of his Marxist beliefs). And in Paris in 1944 Victor strongly seconded Kim Philby's argument that the Soviets should have been given the "Ultra" intercepts.[148] Yet it seems that Rothschild knew nothing of his friends' treachery at this time. Though unquestionably left of centre in his politics in the 1930s and 1940s, Victor found communism "rather dull," as he confessed to Keynes, an Apostle of the older generation.[149] (Nor was he a homosexual, one of the "weaknesses" which attracted the Russians to Blunt and Burgess.) When he finally discovered in 1962 that Philby was a communist, he had no hesitation in passing the information on to his former MI5 colleagues.[150]

At any event, Victor's decision to eschew finance left a gap which his cousins were too young to fill. After an undistinguished Cambridge career, Edmund, the elder of Lionel's two sons, embarked on a round-the-world trip in October 1937 which he did not complete until May 1939. Although the tour included visits to a number of important Rothschild agents (for example, in Brazil and Chile), it was far from obvious that he had a financial vocation.[151]

The French house lost a partner too at this time, though under very different circumstances. The death of Edmond in 1934 transformed overnight the balance of power in the rue Laffitte. Because Edmond's eldest son Jimmy had made over his share to his father, his brother Maurice—the maverick politician—now stood to inherit fully a third of the equity, to say nothing of half Edmond's 33 per cent stake in château Lafite.[152] Possibly because of his political activities, possibly because of his involvement with a disreputable property company, his cousins Edouard and Robert decided to buy him out. Maurice, however, refused to go quietly. After the three partners had failed to reach agreement over an unprofitable Moroccan company in which de Rothschild Frères had invested 80 million francs, Maurice sued, citing his grandfather James's stipulation "that the three branches of the family descended from him always be represented." Only in September 1939, after arbitration, was the buy-out settled. Subsequent developments have perhaps cast doubt on the wisdom of this splitting of the French family's resources. At the time, however, Maurice seemed dispensable, especially as Guy had now settled into the partners' bureau. In any case, more and more of the day-to-day management of the Paris house and its vast business empire was being entrusted to outsiders, notably the former civil servant and Minister of Public Works René Mayer.[153]

The Flood

The great irony is that it was precisely at this time of their greatest weakness that the myth of Rothschild power reached its zenith. Propelled into power by the miseries of the Depression, both the radical left and the radical right in France, Germany and Austria directed propaganda of unprecedented intensity against the family. This combined assault from both ends of the political spectrum was, of course, nothing new: the Rothschilds had been attracting such opprobrium for more than a hundred years. What was new was the fact that for the first time rhetoric was translated into political action.

In France the events of 1934 did much to revive hostile interest in the Rothschilds. The suicide of a minor-league fraudster named Stavisky in January exposed yet another of those financial scandals which were such a characteristic feature of the Third Republic. The following month—partly as a consequence of the government's botched attempts to get to the bottom of the affair—there was an attempted right-wing coup by a loose coalition of "leagues" ranging from the now somewhat grey-haired Action Française of Charles Maurras to the more youthful Croix de Feu, a veterans' association led by Colonel François de la Rocque. Although the coup failed, it forced the government of Edouard Daladier to resign. Later that year, at the Radical party's annual congress, Daladier launched a tirade against the "two hundred families"[154] who, he alleged, were "masters of the French economy and therefore of French policy." "These are forces," he added with the hint of a threat, "that a democratic state should not tolerate." The hint was enlarged upon a year later by the Communist newspaper L'Humanité which alleged links between the Rothschilds and La Rocque. In fact, La Rocque was on the payroll of the industrialist Ernest Mercier and Robert de Rothschild had no objection to being seen alongside him at the rue de la Victoire Synagogue on June 14, 1936. But virtually all other elements of the French right—including writers like Céline and Pierre Gaxotte (editor of *Je suis partout*)—were anti-Semitic. In January 1939 Maurras" journal *L'Action Française* accused the Rothschilds of fomenting war between France and Germany to defend the position of German Jews.[155]

It was the left which had the first opportunity to carry out its threats. In 1936 the Radicals, socialists and communists united to form the Popular Front government, pledged to achieve, among other things, "the liberation of the State from the grips of financial feudalism by establishing the nation's sovereignty over the Banque de France through the dismissal of its board of directors." Robert rightly foresaw "difficult days, weeks, months, as all skies—internal, financial and external—are terribly black."[156] Once in power, the Popular Front achieved much less than its more radical supporters had hoped. True, the new government sought to dilute the power of the "two hundred families" by giving the Banque de France a new council in which shareholders were outnumbered by "experts." But it did not nationalise the Banque outright. Even the termination of the private railway companies' concessions for the seven principal railway lines could hardly be portrayed as confiscation. When the state took over the operation of the Nord line, the Compagnie du Nord did not cease to exist; on the contrary, it received in return 270,000 shares in the new Société Nationale des Chemins de Fer, a guaranteed annual royalty on its revenues and a seat on its board. It is arguable that, thanks partly to the hard bargaining of René Mayer, the companies came out ahead, as the state took over from them debts totalling 6 billion francs, while the companies were able to retain their non-rail assets.[157]

An altogether more ruthless coalition had come to power in Germany in 1933, dominated by the National Socialist German Workers' Party. Hostility to the Rothschilds had been a feature of Nazi propaganda from the movement's infancy (see introduction to volume 1) despite the fact that the Frankfurt house had been wound up when Hitler was barely twelve years old. It was a hostility which was soon translated into action. At first the attacks were largely symbolic: in December 1933 the Frankfurt Rothschildallee was renamed Karolingerallee, while the Luisenplatz and Mathildenstrasse lost the plaques identifying them with members of the family. It was not until April 1938, with the "Ordinance on the Registration of Jewish Assets," that Rothschild property came under direct attack. In the wake of the orchestrated anti-Semitic demonstrations of the following November (Reichskristallnacht), nearly all the myriad Rothschild charitable and educational foundations—of which there were around twenty—were dissolved, with the exception of the Carolinum Dental Clinic, which had become part of Frankfurt university. The largest of these, the Baron Wilhelm Carl von Rothschild Foundation, was "Aryanised" under pressure from the city authorities, so that all references to its founder were expunged. At the same time, the Reich Association of Jews in Germany was forced to sell the Mathilde von Rothschild Paediatric Hospital, the Georgine Sara von Rothschild Foundation for Infirm Foreign Israelites and the Rothschild residence at Grosser Wollgraben 26 to the Frankfurt municipality. The Gestapo also confiscated the A. M. von Rothschild Sanatorium for Lung Diseases in the Black Forest.[158] At least four other Rothschild-founded institutions suffered the same fate.[159]

The private property of the few family members still resident in Germany was expropriated by similar methods, though there was in fact relatively little of it left by

1938. Before the process of confiscation began, Max von Goldschmidt-Rothschild's sons Albert, Rudolf and Erich sold the family houses at the Grüneburg and König-stein and opted to emigrate (Albert to Switzerland, where he committed suicide in 1941 when faced with the threat of expulsion).[160] But Maximilian—now 95—was too old to leave. He stayed on in the house in the Bockenheimer Landstrasse, with the garden which his wife's great-uncle Amschel had acquired over a century before in the earliest days of Jewish emancipation in Frankfurt. Or rather he was allowed to occupy a room in the house; for in a tragic fulfilment of Amschel's nightmare—dating back to the nights in 1815 when he first slept in the "free air" of the garden—Maximilian was forced to sell the property to the city of Frankfurt for just 610,000 reichsmarks (less tax). In the aftermath of Kristallnacht he was also obliged to sell his art collection to the city for 2.3 million reichsmarks (again less tax) and to donate a further 25 per cent of his remaining assets to the Reich as an "atonement payment" (Göring's characteristic device to make the Jews pay for the damage to property caused by Nazi vandalism). When Maximilian died in 1940 the rest of his property was confiscated. Five years later, when Allied bombers destroyed not only the house where he had spent his last days but also the old Fahrgasse office building and the old *Stammhaus* in the Börnestrasse, they were thus destroying relics which had ceased to belong to the Rothschilds. The pseudo-legal obliteration of the Roth-schilds from the town of their origin preceded the partial physical obliteration by some years.[161]

It had not been difficult to foresee what the rise of Nazism meant for the Roth-schilds in Vienna—the city so inextricably associated in Hitler's mind with the threat posed by Jewry. When the Duke of Windsor stayed with Eugène at Schloss Enzesfeld immediately after his abdication for the sake of Wallis Simpson, he is said to have discussed with his host the idea of a book about the persecution of the German Jews.[162] Not long after that, Eugène left Austria for England, followed later by his eldest brother Alphonse. Louis elected to stay at the bank; but he took the precaution of transferring ownership of the Witkowitz ironworks to the Alliance Assurance company (in which the London house still had a controlling interest).[163] He also transferred rights of disposal over all his Austrian assets to the New York bank of Kuhn, Loeb & Co. This was inadequate insurance. The day after the Austro-German *Anschluss* of March 11, 1938, as cheering crowds welcomed Hitler's troops into Vienna, Louis attempted to leave the city. His passport was confiscated, and the next day he was arrested and taken to the Gestapo headquarters at the Hotel Metropol on Morzin-Platz (where he found himself rubbing shoulders with the former Austrian Chancellor, Kurt von Schuschnigg, whose attempts to appease Hitler had so disastrously failed, and the socialist leader Leopold Kuntschak). The process of confiscating Rothschild property began at once. SS men were seen looting artworks from Louis's palace almost immediately after his arrest.[164] On March 30 the firm of S. M. von Rothschild was placed under compulsory administration by a new Austrian Credit Institute for Public Enterprises and Works at the orders of the Vienna Gauleiter's economic adviser Walter Rafelsberger, who was charged with the systematic confiscation of all Jewish assets in Austria. It was then put under the tem-porary control of the German firm of Merck, Finck & Co. and finally sold to them in October 1939.[165]

The next target was the Witkowitz ironworks, which Göring had already identified as a potentially profitable addition to his burgeoning industrial empire centred around the Reichswerke Hermann-Göring. Of course, Witkowitz remained on Czech territory and, as Göring's emissary Otto Weber soon discovered, was no longer owned by the Vienna house but by the Alliance. In addition, the Witkowitz board had safeguarded against sequestration the company's stake in the Swedish Freya ore mines as well as £200,000 in foreign currency. Louis therefore had a real bargaining position. When Himmler sought to ingratiate himself by sending some ornate French furniture to the prison, he was able to send it away complaining that it made his cell look like a "Cracow bordello."[166] Although Louis had to hand over most of his Austrian assets to secure his own release, the family was able to insist that a price be paid for Witkowitz (albeit a discounted price). But such legal niceties were ultimately bound to be swept aside by Nazi *force majeure*. Eugène's hopes of selling the ironworks to the Czechoslovak state for £10 million were dashed when Hitler bullied the Prague government into accepting partition in March 1939. With the works effectively under German control, Göring's commissioner Hans Kehrl, assisted by the Deutsche Bank board member Karl Rasche, turned up the pressure. A new supervisory board was set up, including Kehrl, Rasche and Paul Pleiger (the Reichswerke's general director). At the same time, Fritz Kranefuss—Himmler's adjutant and a supervisory board member of the Dresdner Bank—informed Rasche on the basis of Sicherheitsdienst intelligence that the transfer abroad of the ownership of Witkowitz had been illegal under currency laws. Finally, in July 1939, it was agreed to sell the plant for £2.9 million. However, the outbreak of war gave the Germans the perfect excuse not to pay. As a result, Witkowitz joined the lengthening list of Rothschild properties confiscated without compensation by the Nazi regime. In January 1941 Göring was able to take the process a step further when 43,300 Witkowitz shares were seized from the vaults of the Paris house (though even this did not give him a technical controlling interest).[167] (It was not until 1953 that the communist government established in Czechoslovakia in 1948 finally paid compensation to the Rothschilds—amounting to £1 million—for the works.)

Yet it was not their industrial investments which Hitler and his lackeys really coveted so much as their investments in art—the Old Masters, the Sèvres, the Louis Quinze bureaus—which were the most dazzling fruits of the family's financial success. In fleeing Austria, Alphonse had left behind one of the great European private collections; and attempts to buy it by Lord Duveen (possibly bidding on behalf of the original owners) were in vain. For the acquisition of so many old masters had given Hitler the idea of establishing a new German gallery at Linz, to give the Reich its Louvre. In June 1939 he authorised Hans Posse to begin work on the project, putting the best works seized from Austrian Jews into a "Führer Reserve" for this purpose.[168] It was the beginning of one of the greatest art thefts in history.

Up until the outbreak of the war in 1939, the corollary of the expropriation of the Jews was their emigration from German territory. (It was significant in this respect that the Rothschild palace in the Prinz Eugenstrasse was occupied by Adolf Eichmann's Central Office for Jewish Emigration, which worked closely with Rafelsberger's Asset Transactions Office.) Naturally, many (though not all) German and Austrian Jews wanted to get out, while the Nazis had no objection to their leaving, provided they could be mulcted in the process. Leading German Jewish bankers—notably Max Warburg—saw little alternative but to facilitate this process.

However, for Jews like the Rothschilds who remained outside the area of German control, this created a number of acute dilemmas. As early as June 1933, Lionel became one of the five presidents of a new Appeal Council of the Central British Fund for German Jewry (later the Council for German Jewry), to which the London house made an initial donation of £10,000.[169] Five years later, in early 1938, it was reported that the Council had raised £1 million, including a further Rothschild donation of £90,000; this was followed by £50,000 in November. It was not obvious, however, how best to use this money to help the German Jews. There were disagreements within the Board of Deputies over the idea of a boycott of German goods, for example, which may have precipitated Walter's resignation as vice-president. When James G. McDonald and Felix Warburg addressed a meeting of Jewish businessmen in January 1934, they found little enthusiasm for the alternative strategy of encouraging emigration from Germany. The following year McDonald returned with a more coherent plan (devised by Max Warburg) for a new bank with £3 million capital to finance the emigration of German Jews to Palestine. But despite Lionel's initial "almost amazing enthusiasm" the scheme foundered when details leaked prematurely to the press.[170] Both Anthony and Lionel were even more wary of a later Warburg scheme for an Anglo-American Jewish political bureau, arguing that "one can endanger his [*sic*] English citizenship if one becomes too strongly active in Jewish world actions."

Lionel's nephew Victor also became involved in the Central British Fund. "But for an accident of birth," he told a meeting of the Zionist Federation in October 1938, "I might be a refugee, or I might be in a concentration camp, or I might be a guest in the Hotel Metropol, Vienna."[171] However, the rest of his speech was a (somewhat muted) defence of the government's policy of restricting Jewish immigration to Palestine.[172] He struck a similar note of ambivalence when he addressed a meeting of the Earl Baldwin Fund for Refugees at the Mansion House that December:

> I know that children have been shot dead. I have interviewed people who have escaped from the concentration camps, and I can tell you that their experiences make the many horrors we read about nowadays seem like some nursery game. I have been the unhappy recipient of so many heart-rending letters from children, of documented reports and personal accounts from observers that it is difficult for me to believe that I shall ever become again the rather care-free and happy scientist that I was before all this began.

"The slow murder of 600,000 people," he told his audience, "is an act which has rarely happened in history." Yet he went on: "In spite of humanitarian feelings, we probably all agree that there is something unsatisfactory in refugees encroaching on the privacy of our country, even for relatively short periods of time." As for increasing migration to Palestine, the British government's position there was "appallingly complicated."[173] In March 1939, after visiting the United States to meet American refugee organisations, Victor appealed for a further £160,000 for the Council for German Jewry to promote emigration from Germany. Again there were qualifications. "No matter what doubts we may feel," he argued, "we can only make an impression on this immense problem if we can get an orderly exodus and some slight financial concessions from the German side"; he remained pessimistic about the possibilities of "mass colonisation of hundreds of thousands of people."[174] Even in 1946, speaking in the House of Lords, Victor defended the policy of restricting immigration to Palestine, despite the fact that "he himself had had a 75 year old aunt clubbed to death by the SS outside an extermination camp."[175]

Rather different anxieties beset the Rothschilds in France, where more than a thousand Jews arrived in the first year of the Nazi regime by crossing the border. Although Robert gave his support to an informal agency set up to assist these refugees—which in 1936 was reconstituted as the Committee of Assistance to Refugees—he worried about the effect of the influx on the established Jewish community in France. In May 1935 he made remarks to the general assembly of the Paris Consistory (of which he had become president two years before) which could only be construed as a criticism of the newcomers. "It is essential," he declared, "that foreign elements assimilate as quickly as possible . . . Immigrants, like guests, must learn how to behave and not criticise too much . . . and if they aren't happy here, they'd do better to leave."[176] This was the old assimilationist lament about new Jewish immigrants.

The only logical solution was therefore to find some alternative territory for the Jews to go to. The Nazis themselves thought of Madagascar. Interestingly, Guy Burgess's first assignment (when he was still a freelance intelligence agent) from MI6's D Section was—as he faithfully reported to Moscow in December 1938—"to activate Lord Rothschild" in an attempt to "split the Jewish movement" and "create an opposition towards Zionism and Dr Weitzmann [sic]."[177] At around the same time, the Paris house forwarded to New Court a proposal to purchase 200,000 acres of Brazil's Mato Grosso "for colonisation purposes"; and another to settle Jews in Sudan's Upper Nile Valley between Malakhal and Bor—supposedly "a huge territory . . . with no population and where Jews might organize themselves an important colony."[178] Kenya, Northern Rhodesia and Guiana were also considered. Only at the eleventh hour, it seems, did the Rothschilds recognise the need to admit refugees into Britain and France. In March 1939 Edouard's wife Germaine turned an old house at the edge of the Ferrières estate into a hostel for around 150 refugee children. After the German invasion, they were evacuated south and later dispersed, some escaping to the United States. A more secure refuge was found at Waddesdon for thirty children who were rescued from an orphanage in Frankfurt shortly before the outbreak of war.[179]

By 1939, of course, numerous members of the Rothschild family were themselves refugees. The German invasion of France in May 1940 increased their number substantially. Even before the fall of Paris, Robert had already reached the safety of Montreal, taking with him his wife Nelly and daughters Diane and Cécile. It was not until July, however, that his cousin and senior partner Edouard—now in his seventies—opted to leave France, finally reaching the United States after a circuitous journey through Spain and Portugal. (He too was accompanied by his wife Germaine and daughter Bethsabée, his elder daughter Jacqueline having already settled in America with her second husband.) Their former partner Maurice also ended up in Canada, while his ex-wife Noémie and son Edmond took refuge on the estate at Pregny. The other French Rothschild of that generation, Henri, was already resident in Portugal. Finally, Alain's pregnant wife reached the US via Spain and Brazil, while Guy's wife Alix took the route through Argentina, though she later rejoined her husband.

That left the men of the younger generation to fight. Robert's sons Alain and Elie were both taken prisoner by the Germans and ended up spending much of the war in a POW camp in Lübeck (and, in the case of Elie, Colditz). Edouard's son Guy was luckier. As a cavalry officer in charge of a hastily motorised platoon, he saw heavy fighting in Northern France (for which he was awarded the Croix de Guerre), narrowly eluding capture by the Germans on at least two occasions. After the French capitulation, Guy returned to the part of France left unoccupied by the regime, settling in the small Auvergne spa town of La Bourboule, where the offices of de Rothschild Frères had been moved. But in 1941, increasingly aware of the Vichy regime's readiness to echo and even anticipate German anti-Jewish measures, he decided to leave, securing the necessary papers after an initial abortive attempt to get out through Morocco.[180]

Both Henri's sons, James and Philippe, had rather similar experiences. The former served in the air force (as he had in the First World War) before escaping through Spain to Britain. Philippe was prevented by illness and a skiing injury from taking a part in the fighting, but endured perhaps the most difficult escape from France. Having been arrested in Morocco on his first attempt, he finally ended up crossing the Pyrenees on foot and flying to England from Portugal.[181] Many of the French Rothschilds then elected to return to the continent with General de Gaulle's Free French (though it should be emphasised that there were elements within de Gaulle's army which were far from philo-Semitic).[182] Guy's decision to join de Gaulle nearly cost him his life when the ship taking him back across the Atlantic was torpedoed. He survived, was given a job with de Gaulle's Mission Militaire de Liaison Administrative and returned to France with General Pierre Koenig in 1944. James also joined the Free French, as did his brother Philippe, his wife and elder daughter.

As had happened in Austria, the victorious Germans wasted no time in laying hands on the family's assets. The Paris house had managed to send some things abroad before the invasion of France (its shares in Royal Dutch were deposited with a Montreal bank, for instance, though these were then frozen as enemy assets when France fell). In addition, some family members were able to take jewellery with them when they fled: according to one report, Edouard arrived in New York with precious stones worth $1 million. However, the bulk of the family's wealth remained within relatively easy reach of the occupiers. On September 27, 1940, as the Germans began the process of identifying Jewish-owned companies, Field-Marshal Keitel issued a specific instruction to the Military Government in Occupied France to confiscate "possessions of the Palais Rothschild," including any which had been handed over to the French state. The following month, the Germans ordered that administrators be put in charge of Jewish firms. The Luftwaffe and later a German general occupied the Rothschild house at 23 avenue de Marigny.[183]

Yet the Germans soon found themselves in competition with the puppet Vichy regime they themselves had called into being. Even before Keitel's order, the Pétain regime issued a decree which declared that all Frenchmen who had left mainland France after May 10 had "removed themselves from the responsibilities and duties of members of the national community": accordingly, their assets were to be confiscated and sold, the proceeds going to the Vichy state. This was explicitly applied to Edouard, Robert and Henri. Soon after this, Pétain laid claim to the Rothschild offices in the rue Laffitte for a government welfare agency and showed every sign of intending to treat other buildings belonging to the family in a similar fashion, putting them all in the hands of a new Public Property Office.

In some ways, it made little difference to the Rothschilds whether it was the Germans or the Vichy regime which stole their property. The latter was motivated by anti-Semitism too, as evidenced by the decrees Pétain issued on October 3, 1940 and June 2, 1941, which drastically restricted the rights of French Jews, and the constant vitriolic attacks on the Rothschilds in pro-German papers like *Paris-Soir* and *Au Pilori*.[184] Nor can it seriously be argued that Vichy officials were somehow more lenient in their treatment of Rothschild property than the Germans would have been. Maurice Janicot, who ran Pétain's Public Property Office, is said to have prevented the Germans from clearing the cellars of Lafite, for example; but a lack of buyers seems the most likely explanation for his failure to sell Elie's Neuilly stable of horses, Alain's house on the rue du Cirque and Miriam's houses in Boulogne and Paris. As can be seen from his statement to the German authorities in May 1941— to the effect that de Rothschild Frères now belonged to the Vichy state—the aim was to pre-empt the Germans, not to protect the Rothschilds. The attempt by Pétain's Commissariat for Jewish Questions to convert the Institut de biologie-physico-chimique founded by Edmond in 1927 into a laboratory for the eugenicist Alexis Carrel says much about the fundamental compatibility of Vichy and the Third Reich.[185]

If Vichy had managed to beat the Germans to the assets of the Paris house, the Germans beat Vichy in the race to loot the private art collections of the French Rothschilds. This was partly because so much of it could not be moved out of the occupied zone in time. In the panic of May and June 1940, Miriam hastily buried part of her collection among sand dunes at Dieppe (the pictures hidden there were never recovered); while Edouard's collection was dispersed and hidden at his Reux estate, near Pont l'Evêque in Normandy, and at his stud farm at Meautry. Robert's collection from Laversine and elsewhere was hidden at Marmande in the south-west, while Philippe's pictures were mostly in Bordeaux. All these caches were soon discovered. Even more readily accessible was the huge collection at Ferrières (though the Boucher tapestries were so well concealed that the occupiers did not realise they were still there); Henri's collection at the château de la Muette; Maurice's at the château d'Armainvilliers; and the paintings in the major Paris residences (Maurice's at 41 rue du Faubourg Saint-Honoré and Robert's at 23 avenue de Marigny).

It was Alfred Rosenberg—the Nazi racial theorist and "Führer's Delegate for the Total Spiritual and Philosophical Development of the NSDAP"—who took the lead in tracking down and plundering these collections, arguing that "the Rothschilds are an enemy Jewish family and all their machinations to save their possessions should leave us cold." Within a remarkably short space of time he had rounded up 203 private collections including most of those listed above: a total of 21,903 works. These were then stored at the Jeu de Paume, where Göring duly arrived in November 1940 to act as Hitler's "buyer." The Reichsmarschall grabbed a number of choice items for himself, including some Dutch and French works from Edouard's collection, and a Memling Madonna for his wife; but the most prized

Rothschild possessions—Vermeer's *Astronomer*, Boucher's *Madame de Pompadour* and thirty other masterpieces including portraits by Hals and Rembrandt—he earmarked for Hitler. Needless to say, these were not purchases in any meaningful sense: the valuations of the pictures he selected for himself and his master were absurdly low.[186] Göring returned on similar sprees in February and March 1941, acquiring among other things a Rothshild-owned marble group depicting (fittingly) the Rape of Europa, which was transported to the grounds of his pseudo-Nordic hunting lodge, the Carinhall. On March 20 Rosenberg was able to report that he had completed his mission, sending a train loaded with stolen treasures to Neuschwanstein castle in Bavaria. When the files of his Einsatzstab were scrutinised after the war, the Rothschilds turned out to be the most important single source of plunder: altogether 3,978 items taken from nine different locations were identified as belonging to members of the family.[187] The Vichy authorities did less well, though they did turn up Maurice's collection (valued at 350 million francs) at Tarbes, and a truckload of paintings belonging to Robert, Maurice and Eugène.

As the war drew to a close, most of the stolen works were found by the advancing Allied armies, though a few pieces—a Watteau, for example, and the Rape of Europa taken by Göring—have never been recovered. The Memling Madonna was found when Göring offered it as a bribe to his American captors.[188] But a great deal more could have been lost. Only the intervention of the SS Intelligence Chief Kaltenbrunner prevented the fanatical Gauleiter Eigruber of Oberdonau from blowing up the Alt Aussee salt mines (southeast of Salzburg) to stop the many paintings hidden there from being returned to "International Jewry."[189]

If Hitler had successfully launched "Operation Sealion" in the summer of 1940, when Britain was at her most vulnerable, a similar fate might have befallen the English Rothschilds and their remaining private collections—a worse fate probably, as the invasion of Britain would have made the ultimate defeat of Germany infinitely harder to achieve. He did not, and they survived. Yet it was a tenuous kind of survival. Of the fifth generation, only Anthony lived to see the Allied victory, serving as a private in the Home Guard; Charles and Walter had both died before the war began, and Lionel died in January 1942. The next generation was too busy fighting to think of the bank; or too young, in the case of Lionel's second son Leo (born in 1927) and Anthony's own son Evelyn (born in 1931), who spent the years from 1940 to 1943 in America. Lionel's elder son Edmund refused to do as his father had felt compelled to do in the First World War: that is, to sit out the war in St Swithin's Lane. As an artillery officer in the Bucks Yeomanry, he served with the British Expeditionary Force in France, narrowly escaping capture at Cherbourg, and subsequently fought in North Africa and Italy with the 77th (Highland) Field Regiment.[190] Victor began the war in the commercial section of MI5, later becoming involved in bomb disposal (for which he was awarded the George Medal) and the Prime Minister's personal security. This brought him into close contact with Churchill and his private secretary Jock Colville and probably explains why he was entrusted with the highly sensitive investigation into the death of the head of the Polish government-in-exile, General Wladyslaw Sikorksi, in July 1943. Another Rothschild link to Churchill was forged when Jimmy became Under-Secretary to the Ministry of Supply in March 1945 (though it was to prove the briefest of ministerial careers).

All this had little immediate significance for the family firm, however. For the Second World War even more than the First was financed in ways which left little room for the Rothschilds to play their traditional role. The sinews of war had ceased to be flexed by bankers and bondholders; a new Keynesian age was dawning, in which governments would manage economic life more directly, controlling the allocation of scarce factors of production, manipulating the level of aggregate demand and treating money as little more than a convenient unit for national accounting. In this age, the firm over which Anthony presided in the war years seemed an anachronism. New Court itself lay almost empty. More than half the clerical staff and all the current records were moved to Tring, out of reach of the Blitz. Others—the younger men like Palin—were called up. Only a few old hands like Philip Hoyland remained, using the basement as a bomb shelter. It was only by good luck that the offices escaped serious damage when they were hit by incendiary bombs on the night of May 10, 1941, during a ferocious bombardment of the City which destroyed the nearby Salters Hall and literally "surrounded New Court by fire."[191] Other Rothschild properties were also commandeered for war use. The Royal Mint refinery was converted to artillery-parts production. Exbury was taken over by the navy (and temporarily renamed HMS *Mastodon*).[192] And Charles's and Rozsika's house at Ashton Wold was used by the Red Cross and the Ordnance Corps. Inevitably, these buildings also suffered some damage, not all of it through enemy action. In Evelyn Waugh's *Brideshead Revisited*, such wartime depredations seem to herald the dissolution of an older, Catholic aristocracy. As she contemplated what remained of the gardens at Ashton before leaving for war work at Bletchley, Victor's sister Miriam felt that her own family too was waning: "The Holocaust; the war; my parents' deaths; the end of the garden. Nothing seemed to matter any more."[193]

Two members of the family died as a consequence of the Nazi policy of genocide. The aunt to whom Victor referred in his speech in the Lords in 1946 was his mother's eldest sister Aranka, who perished at Buchenwald.[194] The other victim was Philippe's estranged wife Lili. "Why should the Germans harm me?" she had asked him in 1940. "I am from an old French Catholic family." Despite reverting to her original title, the comtesse de Chambure, she was arrested by the Gestapo in July 1944 and sent by the last transport to Ravensbrück where, her husband was later told, she was brutally murdered.[195] It is thus the blackest of ironies that the only person named Rothschild killed by the Nazis was not a Jew and had disowned the family name.

Only a few months later, Major Edmund de Rothschild led his battery of the 200 (Jewish) Field Regiment—part of the Jewish Infantry Brigade Group formed in November 1944—into the town of Mannheim "through an archway which still bore the repulsive legend *Judenrein*." As they drove into the town, people began to shout: "Die Juden kommen! Die Juden kommen!" ("The Jews are coming!") A few months later, he paid a visit to Hitler's mountain retreat, the "Eagle's Nest." "Seeing a mass of broken Sèvres porcelain," he later recalled, "I wondered if it had been stolen from one of my cousins" homes."[196] It probably had.

The first important strength of the family is unity.
SIR EVELYN DE ROTHSCHILD, 1996

The visitor to New Court today enters a black and white marble building in the modern style. The entrance hall, however, is dominated by William Armfield Hobday's 1820 portrait of Nathan Rothschild and his family. That portrait would not hang there if the firm of N. M. Rothschild & Sons were not conscious of—proud of—its history. Nor would this book have been written. It is worth asking, however, what exactly the relevance of a bank's past is to its present and future. For most of the nineteenth century, N. M. Rothschild was part of the biggest bank in the world which dominated the international bond market. For a contemporary equivalent, one has to imagine a merger between Merrill Lynch, Morgan Stanley, J. P. Morgan and probably Goldman Sachs too—as well, perhaps, as the International Monetary Fund, given the nineteenth-century Rothschilds' role in stabilising the finances of numerous governments. Today, by contrast, the bank occupies a relatively small niche in the international financial services business, dwarfed by such products of corporate hypertrophy as HSBC, Lloyds–TSB and the projected banking Behemoth Citigroup. Is looking back, then, anything more than an exercise in nostalgia? That is the question this epilogue seeks to answer. It should not be read as a history of the bank since 1945, but as an essay on the role history has performed in ensuring its post-war survival and its present success.*

Continuation

The history of N. M. Rothschild & Sons might have ended in the 1940s. That it did not owed much to Anthony de Rothschild. After his brilliant youth at Harrow and Cambridge, and his distinguished record in the Great War, he had dedicated himself

---

*The reader is reminded that this section of the book is not based on archival research but on published sources and interviews. Neither it nor chapter 14 therefore provide anything more than a sketch of a future history of the Rothschild banks since 1915—a task for another historian some years hence. Partly for this reason, I have kept endnotes to a minimum.

to conserving his heritage as a Rothschild. Like so many of his ancestors, he was a keen collector, with a particular enthusiasm for Chinese ceramics, and a devotee of first growth clarets.[1] He had been elected to the Jockey Club in 1925 and kept up his father's stable of horses and house at Newmarket. He had married (in 1926) Yvonne Cahen d'Anvers, whose family had been associated with de Rothschild Frères since the 1850s (he had even met her at his relative the Marquess of Crewe's residence when the latter was ambassador in Paris). His role in the Jewish community also echoed that of previous generations: like his uncle Natty, he was chairman of the Four Per Cent Industrial Dwellings Company; like his father and his great-uncle Anthony before him, he was president of the Jews' Free School. Yet the greatest challenge Anthony faced was in preserving his family's most fundamental role: as bankers.

To this task he brought a certain austere diligence. Every day, he commuted by train from Leighton Buzzard (the nearest station to his house at Ascott) to Euston and on to New Court. After lunch in the partners' dining room, Harold Nicolson described being "hurried out" at 2.30 p.m., "as then the work begins again and the great wheels of the Maison Rothschild revolve." In truth, however, the war had substantially reduced the size of N. M. Rothschild's "wheels"—and Anthony's approach to business was not calculated to make them revolve at great speed. "They know where we live," Ronald Palin remembered him as saying. "If they want to do business with us let them come and talk to us." As a watchword for the post-war world, this was perhaps too fatalistic. Edmund found life at New Court distinctly sedate when he returned from the war: the partners arrived at the Room between 10 and 10.30 a.m. and spent the morning perusing the incoming mail "to see if there was anything likely to result in some business":

> It was our practice in those days for all letters, cheques, bonds, bills of exchange and other such papers to be signed by a partner . . . In consequence, there was always a mass of documents waiting to be signed . . . if ever, before putting my signature to a document, I ventured to say to Tony . . . "I'm afraid I don't quite understand this," his reply was invariably the same: "No. You wouldn't."

Apart from a short and unhappy New York apprenticeship at Guaranty Trust and Kuhn, Loeb & Co. (where he "was made to feel very much the poor relation"), Edmund received little financial training before he became a partner. His younger brother Leopold, who became a partner in 1956, also did a tour of duty at Kuhn, Loeb, as well as at Morgan Stanley and Glyn, Mills; but Anthony had advised him *not* to read economics at Cambridge precisely because he was expected to become a partner. Nor was the former Lloyd's treasurer David Colville—who now came to New Court as a kind of *de facto* partner—strictly speaking new blood: his step-grandmother was the Marchioness of Crewe, daughter of Hannah Rosebery. Much of the day-to-day running of the business was left to Hugh Davies, who had succeeded Samuel Stephany as general manager, and his assistant Michael Bucks—both men who had worked their way up through the clerical ranks at N. M. Rothschild.

Not that these things made the firm unique in the clubbish, not to say somnolent, City of those days. Part of the problem, of course, was that post-war Britain retained many of the economic controls of wartime, not least restrictions on what had always been the basis of Rothschild business: capital export. Under the Bretton

Woods system, there was little scope for traditional international bond issues. This was, moreover, the zenith of British socialism, and although the Attlee governments owed a good deal more to Liberals like Beveridge and Keynes than to Marx, they were scarcely friendly towards the City. Consider the following views of one Labour party supporter, interviewed in January 1948:

> I do not believe that people should be allowed to have a lot of money unless they have earned it; being the son of a rich man is not a good enough reason . . . We have come to associate Conservative rule with the following conditions: unemployment, under-nourishment, unpreparedness, unpopularity abroad, unequal . . . education and opportunities, undeveloped resources and lack of opposition to Fascism . . . The only time when some of these wrongs were put right was during the war when conditions and the Labour members of the Cabinet forced the State Control of basic industries and commodities on the Government . . . The war showed up the stupidity of the old Tory idea that people will only work for private gain and therefore that private enterprise is more efficient than state enterprise . . . The old days of unrestrained private enterprise for private profit are, I hope, gone for-ever . . . Having a lot of money does not automatically mean that one is happy . . . The fact that under a Socialist Government the rich will not have so much money and advantages which they have not earned may be inconvenient to the rich; but this is unimportant, and I think that you will find that many rich people . . . will not be unduly worried about this prospect.

The fact that these were the words not of Aneurin Bevan but of the 3rd Lord Roth-schild may help to explain why he kept his distance from New Court throughout the 1940s and 1950s. When he finally left academic life for the private sector in 1959, it was to direct scientific research at Royal Dutch Shell (admittedly a firm with which the Rothschilds had historic links).

A restructuring of the old partnership had been in preparation since 1941, when Rothschilds Continuation Ltd had been created to act as a legal successor in the event of one of the two remaining partners being killed in the war: the new company became a partner in its own right. In 1947 N. M. Rothschild took a further step away from its original form with the creation of £1 million of voteless prefer-ence shares and £500,000 of ordinary voting shares. In retaining 60 per cent of the ordinary shares, Anthony ensured that he was the dominant partner; after him in the hierarchy came Edmund and Victor, who were each allocated 20 per cent (though Victor received a larger proportion of the voteless preference shares). It was a shift in the balance of power within the family which would have profound conse-quences in the next generation.

The point to emphasise, however, is the firm's contraction in terms of capital. On the eve of the First World War, the capital of the London house had been close to £8 million. A reduction to £1.5 million—especially allowing for the pound's forty per cent loss of purchasing power in the intervening period—signalled a dramatic decline, due in large part to business setbacks and unprecedented taxation. When Lionel died, he left an overdraft of £500,000, but his children also had to pay death duties totalling £200,000.

Anthony's strategy was to rebuild the firm's traditional overseas business. This was not easily done, given the fact that the direction of post-war capital flows was mainly from the United States to Europe. True, Edouard and Robert had by now set up Amsterdam Overseas (in conjunction with Peter Fleck of the Dutch company Pierson, Heldring & Pierson) to act as a New York base for Rothschild operations; but this does not seem to have generated much business for New Court. Initially, a great deal of labour went into untangling the various pre-war debts on which countries like Chile and Hungary had defaulted. New issues—like the 1951 offering of £5 million of 3.5 per cent stock for the International Bank for Reconstruction and Development (usually known as the World Bank)—were rare, and had to be shared with other City houses. The old Rothschild predominance in the South African gold market had already been reasserted three years previously when the international gold market reopened: once again, the world gold price was formally set in New Court's "fixing room." However, with the international gold pool aiming to hold the price of gold at $35 per ounce, this had lost much of its importance. Under these circumstances, the firm had to concentrate on documentary credit and acceptance business. This was far from unprofitable, but it had previously been the bank's second or third string.

The most ambitious—and at the same time the most traditional—project of the post-war years was in Canada, more or less unknown territory for the Rothschilds. Joseph Smallwood's scheme to develop the resource-rich province of Newfoundland (of which he was premier) was probably the most important financial opportunity generated by the bank's continuing links with Winston Churchill[2]—links strengthened by the fact that his private secretary was David Colville's brother Jock. Churchill had returned to Downing Street in October 1951 and was immediately attracted by Smallwood's scheme, which he hailed as "a grand imperial concept but not imperialistic." In that sense, the British Newfoundland Corporation Ltd ("Brinco") was something of an echo of past glories, a reminder of the role N. M. Rothschild had played in the heyday of the British Empire. Indeed, Lord Leathers, Churchill's Minister for Co-ordination of Transport, Fuel and Power, went so far as to ask: "You did Suez, so why can't you do Newfoundland?" Yet despite this Anthony was hesitant—so much so that the members of the consortium very nearly turned to German banks instead. It was largely owing to the efforts of Edmund that N. M. Rothschild remained on board, and even then it was felt necessary to bring in other City firms, including Schröders,[3] Hambros and Morgan Grenfell. The final agreement reached in March 1953 leased 60,000 square miles of land to the Brinco consortium for twenty years and, after surveys had effectively ruled out the exploitation of the region's mineral and timber resources, it was decided to construct a hydroelectric plant at Hamilton Falls. It was characteristic of the late-nineteenth-century flavour of the enterprise that, when the consortium privately distributed two million Brinco shares, Churchill himself bought 10,000.

In the years which followed, however, it proved impossible to sustain the "imperial" tie, partly because the Bank of England was obliged to restrict overseas investment to counter the perennial post-war weakness of sterling, but also because the Canadian government wished to diminish the "foreign" control of Brinco. The Rothschilds were not consulted about the first public issue of "Churchill Falls" shares and, although they nevertheless agreed to take up to $7 million of the shares issued, they were discouraged from doing so by the Canadian banks. The obstructiveness of the Quebec government was especially damaging, as it controlled the overland cable route to New York, potentially the plant's biggest customer. Although N. M. Rothschild participated in a subsequent issue of debentures for the Commonwealth Development Finance Co. in 1963 and a major loan to Newfoundland eight years later, the project never really extricated itself from this political tangle.[4] The Churchillian strategy proved a wrong turning in the era of decolonisation.

By the later 1950s, however, there were signs of a change of direction at New Court. In 1955 Anthony suffered a stroke which incapacitated him and forced him to retire; he died six years later. The partnership had meanwhile been doubly reinforced. After Cambridge, the navy and spells at Rio Tinto in New York and the Toronto arbitrage firm R. D. Smith & Co., his son Evelyn joined the bank in 1957; while Victor's elder son Jacob joined the firm six years later, after Oxford and stints with the accountants Cooper Brothers, Morgan Stanley and the investment partnership of Herman Robinow and Clifford Barclay. "We've been through difficult times because of the war," Leopold recalled Anthony saying. "It's up to you young people to go out and look for new business."

It was now that the first steps were taken to narrow what Palin called "the great gulf that separated the partners from even the most senior members of the staff." A century and a half of tradition ended in July 1960, when David Colville became the first non-family member formally to be made a partner (though he had already occupied a desk in the Room for some time). In September 1961 the general manager Michael Bucks was similarly elevated, followed in April 1962 by the experienced tax lawyer Philip Shelbourne, who helped to create the new Finance Department (responsible for corporate business). Since Jacob's arrival brought the total number of partners close to the legal maximum of ten, other long-serving senior executives had to be content with the status of "associates" until the 1967 Companies Act raised the maximum number of partners to twenty. The transformation was completed in September 1970 when the partnership was finally incorporated, bringing to an end the era of unlimited liability. A new board was constructed with four non-executive directors and twenty executive directors, and decision-making passed from the partners to a new executive committee.

This "New Court revolution" in the management structure had a physical counterpart. In October 1962, at Evelyn's suggestion, the old offices in New Court were finally demolished. It had already been necessary to expand across St Swithin's Lane to Chetwynd House; now the firm had to spend nearly three years in City Gate House, on the south side of remote Finsbury Square, while the present six-storey building was constructed. The new offices symbolised the new generation's determination to modernise the bank. Still, it was typical of the outside world's exaggerated impression of the bank's importance that a Japanese newspaper reported the construction of a new *sixty*-storey building. In reality, the London house was still relatively small. Its issued share capital when it was incorporated was just £10 million (with around £2 million of reserves), and its balance sheet showed assets totalling just £168 million. In terms of deposits N. M. Rothschild was also smaller than its City rivals. Nor did it have as many outside interests as the Paris house. All this helps to explain Jacob's declaration in 1965: "We must try to make ourselves as much a bank of brains as of money."

In the first instance, this meant moving into investment banking. In July

1961Rothschild Investment Trust (RIT) was set up with £3 million capital, two-thirds of which was raised from outside investors. Under Jacob's leadership, it thrived: initial pre-tax profits were in excess of 20 per cent of capital. By 1970 it had been joined by four other publicly quoted Rothschild investment trusts. Thereafter RIT took on something of a life of its own following its merger with three Eller-man-owned investment trusts in 1974, investing widely in everything from oil and gas to hotels and auctioneers. Despite the economic shocks of the early 1970s, its gross receipts reached nearly £7 million by the end of the decade and its net assets were close to £100 million, compared with just £6 million in 1970. For Jacob, who only turned forty in 1976, it was a remarkable achievement. Yet it is important to emphasise that from its very inception RIT was moving in a different direction from its parent company. As early as 1975, N. M. Rothschild had reduced its stake to just 9.4 per cent. When Saul Steinberg's Reliance Group acquired a quarter of RIT for £16 million in 1979, it seemed likely that the link to New Court might be broken altogether.

The first steps were also taken into the asset management business. In 1959, fol-lowing the example of Philip Hill, Higginson and Robert Fleming, the bank became trustee of the National Group's Shield Unit Fund, one of the first unit trusts. Direct asset management business soon followed, all of which (in compliance with the Financial Services Act of 1986) was later devolved to a new subsidiary company, N. M. Rothschild Asset Management.

A third important growth area was corporate finance. Apart from a couple of minor share issues in the late 1940s, little had been done in this line under Anthony. Ironically, in view of the bank's later role in privatisation, he and Colville had refused to become involved in steel "denationalisation" when the Churchill govern-ment proposed it in 1953, regarding the idea as dangerously political. Nor was N. M. Rothschild involved in the famous battle for the British Aluminium Co. of 1958–9, which is usually seen as ushering in the new era of takeovers and mergers. That changed in the 1960s, however, with a concerted effort to improve the bank's relations with industry. In 1964 a branch was even opened in Manchester—the first Rothschild office in the city since 1811—followed two years later by one in Leeds. Admittedly, the bank's first taste of corporate finance proper was discouraging. In February 1961 N. M. Rothschild advised Odhams Press in its resistance to a takeover bid from the *Daily Mirror*. The *Mirror*—advised by S. G. Warburg—won. But two years later, as advisers to the state-owned South Wales steel group Richard Thomas & Baldwins, a New Court team successfully trumped a rival bid for White-head Iron and Steel. By 1968 N. M. Rothschild could claim to be eighth equal in the City takeover league, having organised five deals with a total value of £370 mil-lion. Two years later, it was ranked fifth in a league table of issuing houses, having raised a total of £20 million for its client companies in the course of the year.

These were treacherous waters, however—and shark-infested. In 1969 N. M. Rothschild had its first encounter with the ebullient and fraudulent financier Robert Maxwell, when it advised Saul Steinberg's Leasco in Steinberg's £25 million bid for Maxwell's Pergamon Press. The deal fell through when the bidders uncovered irreg-ularities at Pergamon on a scale which prompted a Board of Trade enquiry into Maxwell. Sime Derby's takeover of Clive Holdings during the "Barber boom" of the early 1970s proved equally problematic when Dennis Pinder, the Sime Derby chairman, was accused of insider dealing and arrested in November 1973. However, when Jim Slater resigned from the ailing Slater Walker bank in October 1975, it was to N. M. Rothschild that the Bank of England turned for assistance in averting a full-scale secondary banking crisis—a tribute to the Prime Minister Edward Heath's confidence in the bank's new chairman, Victor, who had belatedly taken up an active role in the family firm that April, and was soon energetically rationalising its antiquated management structure.

There were two other important areas of domestic activity in this hectic period. Firstly, N. M. Rothschild kept an eye open for investment opportunities for itself, especially in growing areas such as media and telecommunications. The bank invested in ATV, one of the first independent television companies, and in the less successful British Telemeter Home Viewing, an abortive early pioneer of "pay-television." In addition, Evelyn sat on the boards of Beaverbrook Newspapers, the *Economist* and later The Telegraph plc. The old links to Alliance Assurance were also reinforced when Sun Alliance acquired a stake in Rothschilds Continuation, and Gresham Life was acquired for £6.9 million in 1973 (it was sold for £15 million six years later).

By this time, remarkably, most of N. M. Rothschild's balance sheet was domestic. Nevertheless, it remained an international bank at heart. It retained its long-standing interest in gold, even after the breakdown of the gold pool as a consequence of the pressures brought to bear on the dollar by the Vietnam War. Although the Royal Mint Refinery was sold, the bank continued to be a major bullion dealer, operating not only in the London market but also in New York, Hong Kong and Singapore, and laying the foundation for its present pre-eminent position in the Australian natural resources market (at the time of writing, Rothschild Australia accounts for around a third of the N. M. Rothschild group's profits). At the same time, its traditional business of channelling British capital into overseas investment promised to revive following the removal of the Interest Equalisation Tax in 1963 and the development of the "Eurobond" market. Here past ties could be an asset. When Portugal issued bonds worth $15 million in 1964, for example, it could cite precedents as far back as the 1820s for turning to N. M. Rothschild. In Latin America, under the direction of Leopold, the bank helped raise £3 million for the Inter-American Development Bank and £3 million for Chile in 1965; while three years later it organised two major loans totalling £41 million to its old client Brazil—funds which were used for major infrastructural projects like Chile's first atomic reactor and the Rio-Niteroi bridge. In 1966 N. M. Rothschild led a large syndicate raising the first tranche of funding for a trans-Alpine pipeline between Trieste and Ingolstadt, also old Rothschild territory. When Hungary became the first Eastern-bloc economy to borrow from Western banks in 1968, the decision to turn to New Court had numerous historical precedents. Pre-1914 links to Japan were also renewed by Edmund, who made several visits there between 1962 and 1969, arranging "Eurodollar" bond issues (in partnership with Nomura Securities) for a number of Japanese companies including Hitachi and Pioneer.

Above all—and the importance of this in shaping Rothschild attitudes can hardly be overstated—it was to the countries of the developing European Economic

Community that the bank looked. It was at around this time that Guy, the head of the Paris house, was being touted in some quarters as "EEC banker Rothschild." The same might equally well have been said of his London relatives.

A first tentative step in this direction was taken in 1960, when N. M. Rothschild and Warburgs placed £340,000 shares in the August Thyssen steel company on the London market—the first German shares to be quoted in London since the war. A year later the bank committed itself to join the Common Market Banking Syndicate (set up in Brussels in 1958) as soon as Britain signed the Treaty of Rome. The expectation was clearly that this would happen sooner rather than later. In September 1967 a Channel Study Group was formed (along with Morgan Grenfell, Lazards and Barings) in an effort to revive the old Victorian dream of a tunnel under the English Channel. Although this plan foundered like its predecessor, N. M. Rothschild maintained its interest in the project and acted as adviser to the European Channel Tunnel Group which initiated the present "Chunnel" in 1981. Another Europe-inspired project was the £20 million New Court European Investment Trust set up in 1972—at the time the European Communities Bill was going through parliament—in the hope of attracting British investors to continental securities. Most far-sighted of all was the Rothschild plan for a new currency called the "eurco" ("European Composite Unit"), based on the values of nine major European currencies. This forerunner of the later ecu and euro was primarily a practical response to the problem of sterling's depreciation relative to the deutschmark: the idea was to offer investors fifteen-year bonds with a face value of 30 million Eurcos (around £15 million) and an 8.5 per cent coupon. This experiment was a success: when bonds worth 20 million Eurcos were issued for Metropolitan Estates and Property, they were heavily oversubscribed. In the light of subsequent debates it is ironic that the *Daily Telegraph* welcomed the idea as "an encouraging grassroots move towards monetary union."

The logical way of advancing Britain's financial integration with the continent was to establish some kind of cross-Channel institutional link. In 1966, for example, N. M. Rothschild and the National Provincial Bank joined forces to create a new European bank with £1 million capital, and something similar was attempted two years later with the Manufacturers Hanover Trust Co. and the Riunione Adriatica di Sicurtà. However, the obvious strategy was to rebuild the old cross-Channel links between the British and French Rothschilds. The question was whether the two halves of this old partnership were any longer compatible.

The French Rothschilds' post-war experience had been very different from that of their English relatives. The older partners had not long survived the end of the war: Robert died at the end of 1946, Edouard three years later. Despite the upheavals of the years after 1940, the new triumvirate—Guy and his cousins Alain and Elie—found themselves the heirs of a substantial portfolio. In June 1946 de Rothschild Frères' assets were revalued (to take account of franc's depreciation) at 250 million francs (around £1 million); but that figure did not include the family's stake in the Compagnie du Nord and their investments in multinational companies like Rio Tinto, Peñarroya and Le Nickel. When new legislation allowed Guy and his partners to pool all their assets in a single investment fund, the Société d'Investissement du Nord (1953), the total capital came to 4 billion francs (around £4 million). The range of their financial interests was enormous—by 1964 the Compagnie du

Nord had stakes in 116 different enterprises ranging from cold storage to construction—but as in the past, mining and minerals remained in the forefront. Although there were setbacks associated with decolonisation in Mauritania and Algeria, Guy's ambitious strategy in this field bore fruit in the late 1960s as Le Nickel absorbed Peñarroya and various other mining companies. When the aluminium company Henry Kaiser pulled out of a planned expansion of Le Nickel, Guy sold half the company to a government corporation and created a new umbrella for Rothschild mineral interests, IMETAL. It was not long before this too was expanding, acquiring (after a struggle) two-thirds of the Pittsburgh-based Copperweld, and a stake in the British Lead Industries Group.

Guy's other main objective in this period was to compete with the French joint-stock banks which had been outstripping de Rothschild Frères since the First World War by attracting deposits, increasing shareholder equity and developing branch networks. Although the Paris house had increased its deposits by a factor of seven in the first two decades after the war, its balance sheet totalled just 421.5 million (new) francs (£31 million) when it was published for the first time in 1965, compared with a figure of 20 billion francs for the Crédit Lyonnais. Narrowing that gap became possible with the ending of the legal distinction between *banques d'affaires* and deposit banks in 1967. After exactly 150 years, de Rothschild Frères became Banque Rothschild, a limited-liability company with capital of around £3.5 million and a new modern office in place of the historic building in the rue Laffitte. The aim, as Guy put it, was to "collect more and more liquidities from the broadest possible clientele in the widest possible area." Formally, the new structure implied a dilution of family control: the three partners held only 30 per cent of the shares, while the Compagnie du Nord (which itself had around 20,000 shareholders) now owned the rest. But as long as the Rothschilds dominated the Nord, this "democratisation" was only notional. In 1973 Elie modestly assured an interviewer: "You can't compare the power of the Rothschild bank of 1850 with that of 1972. At that time . . . we were the first. Today, we're not so stupid as to think we're something other than what we really are, the fifteenth." But this was still something of an understatement, given the size of the Compagnie du Nord, which had effectively become the parent of the bank: between 1966 and 1968, its capital increased rapidly from 52.8 million to 335 million francs (around £25 million). Banque Rothschild drew additional strength from its links to James Goldsmith (who joined its board), acquiring 72 per cent of his Discount Bank for £5 million and going on to acquire three other banks to bring its total number of branches to twenty-one, employing around 2,000 people. When Banque Rothschild absorbed the Compagnie du Nord completely in 1978, its assets totalled 13 billion francs (around £1.3 billion).

The French Rothschilds would have been still bigger had it not been for the persistence of the split which had excluded Maurice from the Paris house in the 1930s. The supposed black sheep had made good in New York during the war, speculating on commodities so successfully—and inheriting so fortunately—that he was probably the richest of all the Rothschilds by the time of his death in 1957. Although his son Edmond had served a financial apprenticeship at de Rothschild Frères, working for the Transocéan company, he soon chose to set up his own venture capital company, Compagnie Financière, backing (*inter alia*) the immensely successful Club Méditerranée holiday company.

Nor was the Rothschild revival in France purely financial. Although (as in England) some of the family's numerous houses had to be sold or given to the state after the war,[5] Guy and his cousins did not take long to resume the traditional Rothschild role at the summit of Parisian "society." Guy and his second wife in particular began to appear as often in the gossip or racing columns as in the financial pages: it was she who urged him to reopen Ferrières and to throw lavish fancy-dress parties like the Proust Ball (1971) and the Surrealist Ball (1972). The other French branch of the family was meanwhile devoting most of its attention to the vineyards at Mouton, which Philippe inherited when his father Henri died in 1947, along with the neighbouring château d'Armailhac (acquired in 1933). The older Lafite vineyards remained the joint property of James's male descendants, though they were mainly managed by Elie and later Alain's son Eric. (The protracted battle between the Mouton and Lafite branches of the family over the classification of the former's produce attracted almost as much publicity as the parties at Ferrières.)

There was also a political dimension to the French Rothschilds' high profile. The recruitment of the former civil servant Georges Pompidou to run the ailing Transocéan subsidiary in 1954 was unremarkable at the time: as Deputy Commissioner of Tourism, Pompidou was no more than a minor civil servant. However, Pompidou combined his ascent to the post of general manager with careful cultivation of General de Gaulle, then in his self-imposed political retreat. When the political crisis over Algeria brought de Gaulle back to power as President of a newly constituted Fifth Republic, Pompidou left Banque Rothschild to run de Gaulle's staff office for six months before returning to the bank after the constitution had been revised. He went back into politics as de Gaulle's second Prime Minister between 1962 and 1968. Though probably of limited significance, Pompidou's past links with the rue Laffitte did much to sustain the myth of Rothschild power on both the left and the right. The irony is that his period as President—following de Gaulle's departure in 1969—coincided with a deepening crisis at Banque Rothschild.

Despite the structural differences between Banque Rothschild and N. M. Rothschild, the process of restoring the links between the Paris and London Rothschilds began as early as 1962, when the French house invested £600,000 in a new company chaired by Guy and obviously intended to promote Rothschild reunion: Rothschilds Second Continuation. There followed a succession of joint ventures. The Paris house took a 60 per cent stake in Five Arrows, a holding company set up to manage the English Rothschilds' mining interests in Canada. The London house then joined Warburgs and two other firms as members of the French Rothschilds' property syndicate Cogifon. The following year both houses collaborated in setting up the European Property Company and in 1968 Guy de Rothschild became a partner at N. M. Rothschild, while Evelyn was appointed a director of Banque Rothschild. An important development in this context was the transformation of the New York affiliate Amsterdam Overseas into New Court Securities, the shareholders of which included not only Banque Rothschild but also Edmond's Geneva-based Banque Privée. When the National Provincial scaled down its involvement in 1969 (following its absorption into the National Westminster Bank), a much larger entity was created along similar lines: Rothschild Intercontinental Bank (RIB), which brought together not only the London house (with a 28 per cent share) and the Paris

Banque Rothschild (with 6.5 per cent), but also Edmond's Banque Privée (2.5 per cent), as well as Pierson, Heldring & Pierson and two continental firms with historical links to the Rothschilds: Banque Lambert of Brussels and Sal. Oppenheim jnr of Cologne.

RIB was conceived as part of a wider global strategy. In 1971 it was brought in to float a $100 million loan to Mexico. Efforts were also made to revive Rothschild connections in Asia. In 1970, for example, N. M. Rothschild set up Tokyo Capital Holdings with Merrill Lynch and Nomura and floated loans for the Philippines and South Korea. In 1975, however, RIB was sold to the American financial giant Amex International (for £13 million). The global strategy appeared to falter.

One possible explanation for this lies in the changed economic circumstances of the early 1970s, which were characterised by inflationary problems in Western economies, exacerbated by the Organisation of Petroleum Exporting Countries' decision to quadruple oil prices in November 1973. The oil crisis had its advantages for bankers in that the oil exporters deposited a large proportion of their vastly increased incomes with Western banks, which were then able to "recycle" the money by lending on to the struggling oil importers. However, the Rothschilds were at something of a disadvantage in this business. In 1963, the Arab League—which included a number of key OPEC members—had formally blacklisted all Rothschild banks because of the family's links with the state of Israel. This ban was repeated in 1975. The identification of the Rothschilds with Israel meant that they could not play a prominent role in recycling Arab "petrodollars" (though it was possible for them to be indirectly involved).

In many ways, the Arab League blacklist reflects the persistence of the Rothschild myth. In fact—as in the past—Zionist sentiment was not uniformly strong in all branches of the family. Jimmy never ceased to hope for reconciliation between Britain and the Israeli politicians who had overthrown the Palestinian mandate (proposing that Israel be admitted to the Commonwealth in 1955) and left £6 million in his will to finance a new building for the Israeli parliament and the Weizmann Scientific Institute in Tel Aviv, while his widow Dorothy set up the Yad Hanadiv educational foundation, which Jacob and others continue to support. One Rothschild—Guy's sister Bethsabée—actually settled in Israel. Like that of his grandfather and namesake, Edmond's commitment to the new state was especially strong. He visited Israel in 1958 to discuss the financing of an oil pipeline from the Red Sea and even flew to Jerusalem during the 1967 Six Day War to make public his support of the Israeli government. By comparison, the London Rothschilds were more discreet, though they were reported to have donated to the Jewish Palestine Appeal in 1967.

On the other hand, a growing number of Rothschilds—including for the first time male members of the family—were now marrying out of the faith. Guy's first wife had been in the Rothschild tradition: Alix Schey von Koromla was a Goldschmidt-Rothschild on her mother's side (so his third cousin once removed) and both were active in the French Jewish community before the war. In 1957, however, he divorced, remarrying Marie-Hélène van Zuylen de Nyevelt—a slightly less distant cousin (her grandmother Hélène had been the daughter of James's son Salomon), but a Catholic. He resigned the presidency of the Jewish Consistory soon after, though he remained president of the Fonds Social Juif Unifié until 1982.

Other members of the family in France and England subsequently followed his example in marrying non-Jews, though when Edmond married a Catholic (Nadine Lhôpitalier) she converted to Judaism, as did Maria-Béatrice Caracciolo di Forino when she married Eric in 1983. When Guy's son David also married a Catholic, Olimpia Aldobrandini, they compromised: their son Alexandre has been brought up as a Jew, but not their three daughters. He himself sees no contradiction between marrying out of the faith and devoting a substantial proportion of his time to Jewish institutions like the Joint Campaign for France and Israel and the French Founda-tion for Judaism. But in this respect at least the power of familial tradition was undoubtedly on the wane.

The N. M. Rothschild Group

By the end of the 1970s, N. M. Rothschild and Banque Rothschild were approach-ing very different crossroads. In Britain the election of Margaret Thatcher's govern-ment, with its strong commitment to market deregulation, heralded profound changes in the City of London, notably the abolition of exchange controls in 1979 and the ending of restrictive practices on the stock exchange in 1986 (the so-called "Big Bang"). The question was how best to respond to these changes. To Jacob, the success of Rothschild offshoots like RIT and RIB appeared to point towards an alto-gether new kind of bank, bearing little resemblance to the firm founded by Nathan. In his eyes, traditional London merchant banks were now too small to hold their own. On the one hand, he later argued, there were giants like Amex which made even the biggest UK clearing banks seem small. On the other were the City mer-chant banks: Kleinwort Benson (with market capitalisation of £235 million), Hill Samuel, Hambros and Schröders. He might have added—near the bottom of his list—N. M. Rothschild & Sons Limited. For when Jacob sold his shares in the bank for £6.6 million, that implied a total valuation of just £60 million. (The annual report suggested an even smaller figure of £40 million.) By this time, RIT had effec-tively outgrown its parent: it was valued at around £80 million.

Ever since the mid-1970s, Jacob had wanted to merge N. M. Rothschild with another, younger merchant bank: S. G. Warburg (the founder of which had served part of his banking apprenticeship at New Court in the 1920s).[6] This Rothschild–Warburg combination would then have expanded to offer the widest possible range of financial services. But the plan—codenamed "War and Peace"—was opposed not only by Evelyn but also by Jacob's own father Victor. An alternative strategy (known to insiders as "Pandora") was to merge N. M. Rothschild and RIT, so that the origi-nal bank ceased to be a private, family-controlled operation. This too foundered in the face of Evelyn's and Victor's opposition. For them, the preservation of family control took precedence over expansion.

All this helps to explain Jacob's departure from New Court in 1980. Given that RIT still held 11.4 per cent of Rothschilds Continuation (now valued at £57 mil-lion) compared with N. M. Rothschild's stake of 8.2 per cent, it was bound to be a painful divorce; there was also the need to distinguish between two now separate entities both bearing the name Rothschild. After long and difficult discussions, it was agreed that a new business called J. Rothschild & Company would manage the assets of RIT (henceforth to be known only by its acronym). It was a serious rift within the English branch of the family.

What was the alternative strategy envisaged by Evelyn, who had taken over the chairmanship of N. M. Rothschild from Victor in June 1976? Some observers doubted whether there was one; indeed, it was suggested by some that Jacob's departure would prove a fatal blow to N. M. Rothschild. Yet a strategy there was; one which, in essence, involved playing to the bank's traditional strengths.

From its very inception, N. M. Rothschild had specialised in meeting the financial needs of governments, though it had been primarily associated with government loans; only occasionally (as when state railways were sold off) had it been involved in sales of government assets. In the 1980s, however, this was to become one of the bank's most important areas of activity, as the Thatcher government—eager to "roll back" state involvement in the economy and to reward Conservative supporters with reductions in direct taxation—discovered the fiscal benefits of what became known as privatisation.

The origins of the Rothschilds' involvement in privatisation can in fact be traced back to the period before Margaret Thatcher's premiership. Though his contribution was only indirect, Victor's role as the head of Edward Heath's Central Policy Review Staff (or "think tank") between 1970 and 1973 brought the Rothschilds back into the kind of direct communication with politicians which had been integral to their success in the nineteenth century. This may partly explain why in July 1971 the Heath government entrusted N. M. Rothschild with the sale of the Industrial Reorganisation Corporation. A year later came the more difficult task of selling the bankrupt Rolls Royce Motors on behalf of the receiver. Having failed to secure any offer above £35 million, the bank took the risk of offering the shares to the public for £38.4 million. Amid threats of a "work-in" by employees and renationalisation by the Labour spokesman Tony Benn, the flotation proved less than easy; but valuable lessons were learnt. The following years saw a proliferation of contacts between N. M. Rothschild and the political world. In August 1976 Miles Emley was seconded from the bank to advise none other than Tony Benn as the Department of Energy began to sell its stakes in the North Sea oil fields, beginning with a tranche of BP shares the following year. Less than twelve months later, the former Minister of Agriculture and later Lord President Christopher Soames joined the bank as a non-executive director, while Sir Claus Moser left the Government Statistical Service to become vice-chairman in 1978. Such recruits from the public sector brought expertise and "contacts" to New Court which were to be useful as the volume of government business grew.[7]

The traffic also moved in the opposite direction, from New Court to the public sector and government. Shortly after the Thatcher government came to power in 1979, executive director Peter Byrom was appointed by Keith Joseph to the board of British Shipbuilders. Of particular importance was the role of John Redwood, who had joined N. M. Rothschild from All Souls, and who laid much of the political foundation for privatisation in his book *Public Enterprise in Crisis*, published in 1980. In August 1983 Redwood quit the N. M. Rothschild Equity Research Team to join Mrs Thatcher's Downing Street Policy Unit, returning three years later as director of overseas privatisation. He and Michael Richardson, who joined N. M. Rothschild from the stockbrokers Cazenove in 1981, can (and do) claim much of the credit for turning the idea of privatisation into a political reality, though the firm's involvement predated their arrival.

It would nevertheless be misleading to claim that N. M. Rothschild led the way in the Thatcher government's asset sales. In fact, the bank was passed over when the new government sold a further tranche of BP shares in October 1979 and again when it sold its stake in Cable & Wireless. However, N. M. Rothschild did manage the sale of the National Electricity Board's shares in Ferranti in July 1980; and, more important, it also handled the first true privatisation in February 1982 when the high technology company Amersham International was sold—the first time a wholly government-owned concern had been floated on the stock market. Partly for this reason, the flotation aroused political controversy. Geoffrey Howe's decision as Chancellor was to sell the shares at a fixed price of 142 pence each, but when the issue was oversubscribed more than twenty-three times, pushing the share price up to 193 pence, the Labour party launched an ill-judged attack. Calling for a public enquiry, the Shadow Chancellor Roy Hattersley unwisely implied that there was more than a coincidental "correlation between contribution to the Tory party and the receipt of business from Government." He was obliged to eat his words when it was confirmed that N. M. Rothschild had made no contribution to the Conservatives. Such attacks continued when the BNOC (Britoil) sale went ahead in 1982, despite the fact that this time the shares were offered by tender with a minimum price. It did not go unnoticed that the head of Britoil was a former N. M. Rothschild director (Philip Shelbourne), though the bank was only one of six underwriters, and it was Warburgs who advised the Energy Secretary Nigel Lawson. A year later, in December 1983, N. M. Rothschild acquired a 29.9 per cent stake in the stock exchange jobber Smith Brothers, paving the way for the creation of a jointly owned stockbroker, Smith New Court.[8] Jacob, it seemed, was not the only Rothschild able to prepare for Big Bang.

Despite being passed over for the British Telecom contract, N. M. Rothschild scored its biggest success in 1985–6 when it won the "beauty contest" to advise British Gas on its £6 billion sell-off. This was to be perhaps the most effective of all the Conservative government's attempts to promote its ideal of a "share-owning democracy," personified by the advertisers' ubiquitous "Sid." By guaranteeing a minimum £250 shares to all applicants and limiting overseas and institutional investors to just 35 per cent of the total, it was hoped to avoid the persistent problem of oversubscription. When the flotation went ahead on December 3, a total of four million investors applied for £5.6 billion worth of shares. A remarkable feature of the operation was the exceptionally low underwriting commissions charged on domestic purchases by N. M. Rothschild and the other banks involved, which ranged from 0.25 per cent on the first £400 million to just 0.075 per cent on £2.5 billion. It was widely believed that the banks had undercharged the government by accepting such low rates; though as a bid for privatisation market-share it was probably astute.

The risks involved in such massive operations should not be underestimated. N. M. Rothschild was subsequently criticised by the National Audit Office for advising the government to sell the Royal Ordnance to British Aerospace for £190 million in 1985, on the ground that it was worth more. But the experience of the final BP sale two years later showed the extreme difficulty of such valuations. In April 1987 N. M. Rothschild had won the contract to handle the sale of the government's remaining 31.5 per cent stake in BP (worth around £5.7 billion) and to issue £1.5 billion new shares. The plan was to offer most of the shares to ordinary UK investors at a fixed price of 120 pence, auctioning the remainder to institutions and overseas buyers. By September there was confident talk of 20 per cent gains for investors and minimal underwriting charges for the government. Then, on the very eve of the sale, came the stock market crash of October 19, 1987. The bank argued for calling off the sale, rightly anticipating that the share price would go into free-fall. But the Chancellor of the Exchequer Nigel Lawson insisted on pressing on and was persuaded only with difficulty to create a "floor" of 70 pence above which the Bank of England agreed to maintain the price. This still implied heavy losses: Smith New Court lost more than £8.5 million.[9]

Yet the proponents of privatisation at New Court were undeterred. In 1987 the bank was among those appointed to advise the Electricity Council on the privatisation of the twelve regional electricity boards, successfully opposing the Energy Secretary Cecil Parkinson's plan for an "exploding" or "packaged" privatisation whereby the boards would have been sold as a single unit. In the same year it took on the task of privatising the ten water authorities. The following year brought the £2.5 billion British Steel sell-off. There was renewed controversy in 1991, when N. M. Rothschild was appointed to advise on the privatisation of British Coal, for the bank's report that only fourteen pits were suitable for stock market flotation led directly to Michael Heseltine's announcement in October 1992 that the remaining pits would have to be closed, with the loss of up to 44,000 jobs. The bank has since been involved in the privatisation of British Rail and Northern Ireland Electricity, and has advised the government on the sale of housing association loans and student loans.

It is inconceivable that a programme as radical as privatisation could have been implemented without close contact between the government and the City. It is equally inconceivable that such contacts could have been overlooked by the government's critics. After Margaret Thatcher's deposition in 1990, political support for the Conservative government dwindled rapidly; and the links between New Court and Westminister inevitably became the target of fresh Opposition criticism. In the wake of the 1992 election, which the Conservatives narrowly won, it was conspicuous that not only the Chancellor Norman Lamont, but also his junior minister Tony Nelson and the Environment Minister John Redwood were former N. M. Rothschild employees, while others (Oliver Letwin and later Robert Guy) sought election as Conservative candidates. But it was the appointment of former ministers (and senior civil servants) to positions at New Court which prompted the most public comment. Peter Walker, the former Secretary of State for Wales, became a non-executive director of the bank's Welsh subsidiary and of Smith New Court. Norman Lamont joined the N. M. Rothschild board after being replaced as Chancellor in 1993. Sir Clive Whitmore, the former permanent secretary at the Home Office, also joined the board, as did Sir Frank Cooper, the former permanent secretary at the Ministry of Defence; and Lord Wakeham, the former Energy Secretary who had earlier commissioned N. M. Rothschild to assess the viability (and potential for privatisation) of British Coal.

Yet the undoubted success of privatisation as a policy has done much to deflect criticism of these appointments. Not only has the Labour party entirely abandoned the idea of renationalising privatised industries; scores of foreign governments have also hastened to follow the British example. In doing so, many have turned to N. M.

Rothschild as the leading expert in the field. In 1988 alone, the bank handled eleven privatisations in eight different countries. In 1996–7 it advised the Brazilian government on the sale of its stake in the Companhia Vale do Rio Doce iron ore mines, Zambia on the privatisation of its copper industry and Germany on the £6 billion flotation of Deutsche Telekom (an operation since repeated for its Australian equivalent Telstra). Viewed as a whole, this immense transfer of assets from the public to the private sector has been one of the most important developments of the late-twentieth-century world economy, comparable with the creation of a truly international market for government debt in the nineteenth century, which distributed government liabilities in a similar way. N. M. Rothschild's contribution to the privatisation revolution is strongly reminiscent of its earlier role as the leading architect of the modern bond market.

Nevertheless, advising governments about privatisation has only been a part of the bank's corporate finance business since 1979. Probably of greater overall importance to the firm's profits has been its continued success within the private sector. In 1996 N. M. Rothschild was—for the second year running—ranked fifth in the *Acquisitions Monthly* league table of mergers and acquisitions advisers, handling twenty-four deals with a value of more than £9 billion. This was not far behind the market leader, Barings. Seven years before, it had ranked eleventh.

As in the 1960s and 1970s, the 1980s saw the growth of new offshoots of N. M. Rothschild. Of these, one of the most important was Rothschild Asset Management, which came to act as the umbrella for the bank's various offshore investment funds. By 1987 the Rothschild group as a whole could claim to have funds totalling over £10.3 billion under its management, of which around £4.3 billion were handled by RAM. It was unfortunate for Victor's younger son Amschel that his appointment as chief executive in January 1990 coincided with the onset of an international economic recession, for this weakened RAM's performance. When the profits of the parent bank and RAM were added together, the gap between N. M. Rothschild and its rivals seemed to be widening fast. On the other hand, Smith New Court recovered from the 1987 stock market crash to see profits hit record levels in the early 1990s. When it was decided to sell the Rothschild stake in Smith New Court to Merrill Lynch in 1995, it fetched £135 million, compared with £10 million which had been paid for it less than a decade before. (The business of securities marketing which it performed is now conducted jointly by N. M. Rothschild with the Dutch bank ABN AMRO.) Mention should also be made of Biotechnology Investments, a specialist venture capital fund set up under Victor Rothschild's direction in the early 1980s. Another initiative of which he would have approved was the bank's membership of a consortium led by Tattersall's which bid—unsuccessfully—to run the new National Lottery in 1992. As chairman of the 1978 Royal Commission on Gambling, he had recommended the creation of just such a lottery.

The last development of the 1980s was the transformation of New Court Securities—the Anglo-French Rothschild affiliate in New York—into Rothschild Incorporated, which rapidly built up a formidable list of corporate clients under the direction of its chief executive Bob Pirie and his successor Hank Tuten.[10] In the early 1990s Rothschild Inc. has managed to make almost as much money, if not more, acting for the creditors of recession victims like Olympia & York and the "junk bond" specialist Drexel Burnham Lambert.

By the end of the 1980s, after a decade of sustained growth under Evelyn's chairmanship, N. M. Rothschild & Sons had done much to disprove the Cassandras who had predicted that it had no future in the modern financial world. With share capital of £152 million, a balance sheet valued at £4.4 billion, dividends totalling £12 million and net profits of £5 million, the bank was no giant. But with 600 employees, 39 executive and 26 non-executive directors, it did not pretend to be. Moreover, the question remains open whether it was in fact necessary to become a "giant" to survive the 1980s. The experience of Jacob Rothschild after his break with New Court suggests that it may not have been.

To begin with, Jacob appeared intent on achieving his vision of a new kind of financial conglomerate. In 1981 RIT merged with Great Northern Investment to form RIT & Northern. In the space of three years he acquired 9.6 per cent of the new breakfast television company TV-am, 50 per cent of the (unrelated) New York merchant bank L. F. Rothschild, Unterberg, Towbin and 29.9 per cent of the City broker Kitcat & Aitken, and merged with the Charterhouse Group to form Charterhouse J. Rothschild, with a market capitalisation of £400 million—more than double the size of N. M. Rothschild. In a speech in 1983—three years after he had left New Court—he predicted that, as international financial deregulation continued, "the two broad types of giant institutions, the worldwide financial service company and the international commercial bank with a global trading competence, may themselves converge to form the ultimate, all-powerful, many-headed financial conglomerate." His own empire was beginning to approximate to that description.

Yet almost as quickly it unravelled. The turning point came in April 1984, when Jacob unveiled plans for yet another merger—with Mark Weinberg's insurance company Hambro Life. In the face of City criticism of its complexity, the deal was abandoned, causing a slump in Charterhouse J. Rothschild shares. Within a matter of months, Jacob sold off his stakes in Charterhouse and Kitkat & Aitken. In 1987 it was the turn of L. F. Rothschild to go (it subsequently filed for bankruptcy); and a year later he separated RIT Capital Partners as an investment manager from the core company J. Rothschild Holdings. This process of "down-sizing" continued in 1990 with the division of JRH into two separate companies: the unit trust Bishopsgate Growth and St James's Place Capital. Plainly, this meteoric performance had much to do with the economic cycle, and particularly the 1987 stock market crash (though Jacob and his shareholders realised a substantial profit on his various acquisitions). But it also reflected specific setbacks like the failure of the £13 billion bid he made in 1989 (along with James Goldsmith and Kerry Packer) for the tobacco giant BAT, which sharply reduced pre-tax profits. Although there have been new ventures since, Jacob (who succeeded his father as the 4th Lord Rothschild in 1990) has increasingly redirected his energies towards public work—notably as Chairman of the National Heritage Memorial Fund between 1992 and 1998.

An even more marked contrast is with the experience of the French Rothschilds in the 1980s; the moral—that size is not always an advantage—is similar. With Guy's retirement as chairman of the bank and of IMETAL in 1979 and Alain's departure from his last business post (as chairman of Discount Bank) the following year, a new generation was coming to the fore under Elie's chairmanship, in particular Guy's son David, who had begun his business career at Peñarroya in 1968 and, as chairman of the Compagnie du Nord, had presided over its merger with Banque

Rothschild. But this change at the top came at a time of mounting crisis. Profits at Banque Rothschild had slumped from 20 million francs in 1976 to 8.5 million in 1977 and the following three years were not much better: profits for 1980 were 18.3 million (£1.9 million). For a firm of the size of N. M. Rothschild, these figures might have been respectable. For Banque Rothschild—the tenth largest deposit bank in France with deposits of some 3.4 billion francs (£346 million)—they were more than disappointing.[11] The combination of size and weakness proved fatal when, in May 1981, the socialist François Mitterrand defeated Giscard d'Estaing in the French presidential election—a victory repeated the following month when his party won an overall majority in the National Assembly.

Since their 1973 pact with the Communists, the socialists had been committed to nationalising "the totality of the bank and financial community, particularly merchant banking and financial holding companies," a policy which, according to opinion polls, only 29 per cent of the electorate opposed. Now Mitterrand was in a position to fulfil that commitment; indeed, with four communist ministers in his government, he was bound to. Frantically and belatedly the Rothschilds attempted to demerge their industrial and banking interests, but the government vetoed this move and proceeded to take all banks with deposits above 1 billion francs into public ownership. Thirty-nine banks, including Banque Rothschild, were caught in the net. The bank founded by James de Rothschild thus became the state-owned Compagnie Européenne de Banque. To be sure, this was not Nazi-style expropriation. Compensation was paid in relation to share values at the end of 1980 and dividends distributed, adjusted for inflation: in the case of Banque Rothschild the sum due amounted to just 450 million francs (£41 million), of which the family received a third, in proportion to its share of the bank's equity. Indeed, some observers saw nationalisation as a blessing in disguise for an ailing firm. But Guy in particular was bitter about this second political assault in just over forty years: "A Jew under Pétain, a pariah under Mitterrand," he wrote in an angry article which appeared on the front page of Le Monde, "for me that's enough."

The twist in the tale was that Henri Emmanuelli, one of the ministers in the government responsible for nationalising the Banque Rothschild, was a director of the Paris branch of Edmond's Swiss-based Compagnie Financière, run jointly with his son Benjamin. Whether Edmond felt any Schadenfreude at the fate of the bank which his father had left on such bad terms is uncertain. What is beyond dispute is that, of all the Rothschilds, he was the most financially successful in the 1980s. In 1992 his Compagnie Financière had assets of around £1.1 billion, while his Banque Privée had an estimated £10.8 billion under management in 1995.

Had the various Rothschild banking concerns lost all contact with one another, it would have been difficult for the Paris Rothschilds to recover from the blow of nationalisation. Yet within three years of the destruction of Banque Rothschild, a new Paris house had been established. The parent company of the new Paris house was a holding company called Paris-Orléans Géstion which had been set up by David and Eric outside the structure of Banque Rothschild prior to nationalisation. Along with David's half-brother Edouard, the two cousins now decided to establish a small fund management company as a subsidiary of Paris-Orléans (which also owns the wine business, Domaines Barons de Rothschild). It took three years to persuade the reluctant Finance Minister Jacques Delors to grant a banking licence, and even then the government had the gall to prohibit the use of the family name, so that the new venture had to be launched in July 1984 as "PO Banque." The owner-ship of the firm revealed the extent to which this was a genuinely multinational Rothschild entity: Rothschilds Continuation Holdings (see below) put up 12.5 per cent of the capital, Edmond's Compagnie Financière 10 per cent and Rothschild Bank AG (Zurich) 7.5 per cent. The use of the five arrows symbol and the phrase "Groupe Rothschild" on the firm's stationery underlined the point. It was a success: in its first two years, its share value trebled and by 1986 it was managing some £273 million of its clients' funds, with capital of more than £4 million.

The electoral defeat of the French socialists and the advent of "cohabitation," with the Gaullist Jacques Chirac as Prime Minister in March 1986 under an increas-ingly conservative Mitterrand, allowed a full-scale revanche. Following the British example, the new French bank involved itself in privatisation, advising the govern-ment on the flotation of Paribas and, in October 1986, reclaiming the family name by becoming Rothschild & Associés Banque (later reverting to the old partnership structure as Rothschild & Cie Banque). Since then the new Paris house has become increasingly involved in French corporate finance. With capital of 150 million francs (£19 million) and around 15 billion francs (£1.9 billion) under management it is also one of the five leading corporate finance banks in France: a "boutique" in City terms, but a dynamic one.

This second renaissance in Paris was only part of a broader effort instigated by Evelyn to recreate something like the system of international partnership which had been the Rothschilds' greatest strength in the nineteenth century—in his words, to "get back together as a family." The creation of Rothschilds Continuation Holdings AG as the Swiss-based parent company for an expanding "Rothschild merchant banking group" was in this sense pregnant with historical significance. For the first time since before the First World War, formal steps were being taken to unite the disparate family interests which three-quarters of a century of political instability had fragmented. Here, it might be said, lay the key to Evelyn's strategy: his belief that the Rothschilds could combine the traditional virtues of the family firm with a genuinely global reach by constructing a modern version of the old Rothschild system: at the centre, a closely knit group of family-controlled companies, with an expanding network of agencies and associates with varying degrees of autonomy.

The structure of the group at the time of writing can be simplified as follows. At the top of the "pyramid" is Rothschilds Continuation Holdings AG, a Zurich-based holding company, the principal investments of which are the following nineteen firms, here grouped geographically:

- N. M. Rothschild & Sons Ltd, Rothschilds Continuation Ltd, N. M. Roth-schild Corporate Finance Ltd and Rothschild Asset Management Ltd (UK)
- N. M. Rothschild & Sons (CI) Ltd and Rothschild Asset Management (CI) Ltd (Channel Islands)
- Rothschild & Cie Banque and Rothschild & Cie (France)
- Rothschild Bank AG (Switzerland)
- Rothschild Europe BV and Rothschild Asset Management International Holdings BV (Netherlands)
- Rothschild North America Inc. and Rothschild Asset Management Inc. (US)

- N. M. Rothschild & Sons (Australia) Ltd, N. M. Rothschild Australia Holdings Pty Ltd and Rothschild Australia Asset Management Ltd
- N. M. Rothschild & Sons (Hong Kong) Ltd and Rothschild Asset Management (Hong Kong) Ltd
- N. M. Rothschild & Sons (Singapore) Ltd

The N. M. Rothschild group is thus a multinational entity (more than 50 per cent of its assets are now held outside the UK) with a wide geographical reach—again reminiscent of the system of houses which had been developed by Mayer Amschel's sons after 1815. But it is also controlled by the family through another Swiss company—Rothschild Concordia AG—which has a majority (52.4 per cent) stake in Rothschilds Continuation Holdings AG. Closely linked to this structure is the Paris-Orléans holding company which controls 37 per cent of Rothschild & Cie Banque in Paris, around 40 per cent of Rothschild North America, 22 per cent of Rothschild Canada and 40 per cent of Rothschild Europe. The financial involvement of the Compagnie Financière is smaller; but the appointment of Edmond's son Benjamin to the boards of Rothschilds Continuation Holdings AG and Rothschild Bank AG suggests that this may increase.

In addition to the companies listed above, there are also smaller subsidiaries reminiscent of the old agencies of the nineteenth century. Another historically charged move was the announcement in May 1989 that the London and Paris Rothschilds would be opening a subsidiary in Frankfurt: Rothschild GmbH. Two months later came the launch of Rothschild Italia SpA. By September 1990 similar operations were in place in Spain (Rothschild España SA) and Portugal. Nor is this network confined to Europe. In 1997 there were offices in Argentina, Bermuda, Brazil, Canada, Chile, Colombia, Czech Republic, Indonesia, Isle of Man, Japan, Luxembourg, Malaysia, Malta, Mexico, New Zealand, Poland, Russia, South Africa and Zimbabwe.

It goes without saying that there are important differences between the structure of the present group of Rothschild houses and the system operated by the five Rothschild houses at their zenith in the mid-nineteenth century. But in many respects the resemblances are close. The subsidiaries in Europe, the Americas and Asia perform functions similar to those performed by the Rothschild agents a century and a half ago, often in the same places. Perhaps most important—and in contrast to most large financial institutions—both ownership and leadership of the group are shared between the key family members. In the nineteenth century, the five brothers and later their sons bound themselves and their houses together with occasional partnership contracts. Today six members of the family have between them a total of thirty-seven board seats (including chairmanships and vice-chairmanships) on fifteen of the principal component companies of the N. M. Rothschild group. In the nineteenth century, the family partners were only notionally equals: in terms of capital shares and even more in terms of leadership there tended to be a dominant partner. The same is true today, with Evelyn the key figure as chairman of Rothschild Concordia AG, Rothschilds Continuation Holdings AG, Rothschild Bank AG, N. M. Rothschild & Sons Ltd and Rothschilds Continuation Ltd, as well as being a director of a number of other companies in the group. And, as in the past, the question of the succession is of crucial importance as Evelyn approaches retirement. A marker in this respect was the appointment of David as deputy chairman of N. M. Rothschild & Sons in January 1992. At a time when other old City families were losing control of the firms they had established, the Rothschilds were reasserting their dominance. Five months later, Evelyn made the line of succession explicit when he told *Le Monde:* "If something happens to me, there is David. If something happens to him, there is Amschel. Working as a family has always been our trademark." The death of Amschel in July 1996—following a meeting to discuss merging the Rothschilds' international asset management operations—was a tragic blow; but it still seems reasonable to assume that, when Evelyn decides to retire, David will succeed him in the key positions. David now travels regularly to London—a journey which can now be done a great deal more easily and swiftly than in the days when James had to undertake it.

The integration of the diverse Rothschild businesses has not been without its problems, of course, not least the crisis which hit the Rothschild Bank in Zurich in 1991–2. In the wake of the nationalisation of Banque Rothschild, Elie had become chairman of the Zurich bank, appointing Alfred Hartmann as general manager and later deputy chairman. The first sign of trouble came in 1984, when the bank was censured by the Swiss Banking Commission for its involvement in an illegal 50 million Swiss franc loan. Six years later, there was further embarrassment when the Zurich bank bought shares in Suchard on the eve of a Rothschild-backed bid for the company by Philip Morris. In July 1991, in a bid to stop the rot, N. M. Rothschild acquired 51 per cent of the company and Evelyn took over as chairman. What he discovered there invites a comparison with the experience of Anselm after his arrival in Vienna in 1848 (or perhaps Lionel's when he was confronted with the Creditanstalt crisis). Initially, it was announced that 63.5 million Swiss francs of the bank's hidden reserves would have to be liquidated to cover losses on bad loans of around 100 million Swiss francs (£40 million). Compared with the firm's capital of 185 million francs (£74 million), these were alarming figures. But the process of cleaning out the Augean stables had only just begun. In September 1992 it emerged that a senior executive at the bank, Jürg Heer, had authorised a number of large and illegal loans, principally to two German-Canadian property financiers. Total losses on these transactions were initially estimated at 200 million Swiss francs (£80 million), a figure which later had to be revised upwards to 270 million Swiss francs— more than the firm's entire capital. Had Rothschild Bank AG been a wholly independent entity, that would probably have been the end of its existence. However, as part of the wider Rothschild structure, it could be salvaged with an injection of 120.5 million Swiss francs, and most of the lost money was subsequently recovered.

The Zurich crisis was a reminder of the dangers of a multinational structure with a family firm at its core: small mistakes can have grave consequences. Yet compared with the disaster which engulfed the Rothschilds' historic rivals Barings in 1995— when a "rogue" dealer's illegal speculations in Singapore bankrupted the firm—the Zurich crisis was trifling. The fate of Barings, which was subsequently bought by ING, is the extreme case of what can go wrong for a traditional City merchant bank. It has not, however, been alone in passing into non-British ownership. S. G. Warburg has been bought by the Swiss Bank Corporation, Morgan Grenfell by Deutsche Bank, Kleinwort Benson by Dresdner Bank and the Hambros Banking

Group by Société Générale. Of the elite of City firms which used to make up the Acceptance Houses Committee, Rothschilds is one of only four which have succeeded in retaining their independence.[12]

Once again historical parallels come to mind. Throughout the nineteenth century, the single most important reason why the Rothschilds were able to withstand the financial crises, revolutions and wars which swept so many of their competitors into oblivion was that a crisis in one house could be contained and resolved with the assistance of the others. The rescue of the Paris house in 1830 and the Vienna house in 1848 are the two classic examples. The reconstruction of Rothschild Bank in Zurich recalls those earlier episodes.

The development of the N. M. Rothschild group thus needs to be understood partly as a way of defending the tradition of Rothschild independence in a world of ever-larger financial giants, not as a strategy for becoming one of those giants. At the time of writing, Rothschilds Continuation Holdings has shareholders' equity (capital, reserves and accumulated profits) of £460 million, or total capital resources of around £800 million if a broader definition is used. In addition, the Paris-Orléans holding company has capital of around £100 million. Of course, this puts the group a long way behind the biggest bank in the world, HSBC, which has total market capitalisation of around £55 billion; but such a comparision does not compare like with like. A better comparison is with Schröders, one of the few other independent City merchant banks, which is only slightly ahead; or with the firm which was incorporated as N. M. Rothschild & Sons Limited in 1970. An increase in capital and reserves from £12 million to £460 million is no mean achievement: it represents growth, adjusted for inflation, of nearly 400 per cent. The question which remains is how the family-controlled "mini-multinational" structure which Evelyn has created over the past decades will fare as international financial markets become characterised by ever higher levels of integration.

The modern financial world is often said to be quite different from the financial world of the past. Transactions, it is argued, are far larger than ever before and are executed with unprecedented speed thanks to advances in electronic communication. Public and private systems of regulation lag behind innovations like derivatives. The reserves of central banks are dwarfed by the vast turnover on the international foreign exchange markets. In the era of "globalisation," nation states themselves are obsolete; family firms even more so. The future belongs to vast international corporations. Yet the reader of this history may be inclined to question such crude assumptions. To be sure, compared with the period between 1914 and 1945—and perhaps also with the period before 1979—the financial world has completely changed. But compared with the hundred years before the First World War, the 1980s and 1990s looks less exceptional. Relative to the world's demographic and economic development in the nineteenth century—and certainly relative to the very limited financial resources of nation states—international capital movements in the nineteenth century were very large. Compared with what had gone before, nineteenth-century communications dramatically accelerated the speed at which business could be done. Regulation lagged far behind innovations on the bond market and stock market. Markets were volatile; trivial errors could have devastating consequences for individual firms. For most of the nineteenth century, there can be no doubt that the kind of firm which stood the best chance not only of prospering but of surviving more than a decade or two was a firm like the one founded by Mayer Amschel Rothschild and led from the ghetto to greatness by his Napoleonic son Nathan. It was rooted in a distinctive ethos of familial solidarity (*concordia*), a religiously rooted morality (*integritas*) and hard work (*industria*)—an ethos which proved remarkably durable despite the fissiparous tendencies of all large families, the corrupting effects of social assimilation and the myriad temptations of wealth. At the same time, its multinational structure gave it a unique degree of flexibility, enabling it to withstand even the worst economic and political crises.

A modern financial corporation may be able to replicate this flexibility. Perhaps, through the various spin-offs of bureaucratic rationalisation we call "management," it can even improve on the original. But it cannot easily replicate the ethos of the earlier kind of structure; for no amount of corporate rhetoric can turn its widely dispersed multitude of shareholders, directors, executives and employees into a family. Francis Fukuyama and others argue that one of the weaknesses of modern Western institutions like the corporation is that they do not elicit trust and loyalty from individual employees or investors. Perhaps the family firm does that better, even if a price is paid in forgone economies of scale.

It is a moot point whether or not bankers benefit—as bankers—from knowing their own history; as A. J. P. Taylor once said, men learn from history only how to make new mistakes, and too much knowledge of financial history can induce excessive risk-aversion in a professional investor. At least one senior figure in the N. M. Rothschild group has observed that he is a good deal more interested in the future of the Rothschilds than in their past; he is right to be. On the other hand, the history of N. M. Rothschild & Sons and the other Rothschild houses has a contemporary relevance—indeed utility—to him and his colleagues in one respect: the name Rothschild is in many ways as big an asset as any which appears in the balance sheets of the Rothschild group. It is a brand name like no other in international finance; and if nothing else this book shows why that is.

Moreover, the past has a more subtle influence on the present, quite apart from its value as source material for corporate publicity. It is something to live up to—a reputation to preserve—and that is often as good a motivation in business as the more prevalent, and sometimes more short-sighted, profit motive. One of the more surprising findings of this study has been the relatively low rate of return on capital achieved by the Rothschild houses in the second half of the nineteenth century, a phenomenon partly explained by the relatively high ratio of capital to liabilities which they maintained. Part of the secret of long-run success in banking is, of course, not to go bust; the Rothschilds' relative risk-aversion is one reason for their financial longevity. This has its roots in the psychology—to be precise, the longer time horizon—of a family firm, which has the interests of future generations as well as present shareholders to consider.

In 1836, following the death of Nathan Mayer Rothschild, his brothers, sons and nephew bound themselves together in a new partnership agreement. In doing so, they recalled how their father Mayer Amschel had told them nearly thirty years before "that acting in unison would be a sure means of achieving success in their work"; how he had "always recommended fraternal concord to them as a source of divine blessing." It was a principle they exhorted future generations of the family to remember:

May our children and descendants in the future be guided by the same aim, so that with the constant maintenance of unity the House of Rothschild may blossom and grow into full ripeness . . . and may they remain as mindful as we of the hallowed precept of our noble ancestor and present to posterity the godly image of united love and work.[13]

It is remarkable that, two centuries after Nathan first arrived in England, those words should still have a meaningful resonance.

Exchange Rates

Fortunately for the economic historian, the nineteenth century was characterised by a protracted process of currency convergence. After the pound returned to its pre-1797 Newtonian gold parity in the 1820s, other major currencies one by one established more or less stable exchange rates with it. It should be stressed that the gold standard proper was a late-nineteenth-century affair. Until the 1870s, France remained on a bimetallic (gold and silver) standard, along with the other members of the Latin Monetary Union (Belgium, Switzerland and Italy). Russia, Greece, Spain and Rumania were also bimetallist, as were most American countries including the United States. Most German states were on pure silver standards, as were the Scandinavian counties, Holland and most of Asia. Only Britain, Portugal, Canada, Australia and Chile were strictly speaking on the gold standard in 1868.[1] However, despite these differences, European exchange rates were relatively stable. The French, Belgian and Swiss francs were more or less consistently equivalent to one-twenty-fifth of a pound (that is, £1 = *c.* 25 francs: in fact, the franc–sterling exchange rate fluctuated between around 25.16 and 25.40 francs). The Prussian thaler was equally stable at around 6.8 thalers to the pound. The Austrian, Italian, Russian, Greek and Spanish currencies were not so stable, however, and were subject to periods of inconvertibility and depreciation. Table a gives some approximate sterling exhange rates for major European currencies at mid-century, though these should be used with some caution.

Table a: Sterling exchange rates of major currencies (per pound), mid-nineteenth century.

PRUSSIAN THALERS	FRENCH FRANCS	AUSTRIAN GULDEN	NEAPOLITAN DUCATS	ROMAN SCUDOS	RUSSIAN ROUBLES	SPANISH REALS	TURKISH PIASTRES
6.8	25.2	9.6	5.8	4.7	6.3	504.0	114.5

Source: Rothschild correspondence.

The process of German unification was decisive in the shift from bi-metallism to the gold standard. The German decision to establish a gold-based mark rather than extending the silver thaler to the rest of the German Reich had a knock-on effect in France, which was reluctant for political reasons to smooth the German transition to gold by continuing to accept silver.[2] Even so, until the very end of the century, a number of major currencies were not consistently on a metallic standard and were subject to periods of depreciation against sterling (this applies to the rouble and the

dollar). It was not until the last two decades before the First World War that most of
the world's economies were members of the informally constituted system of fixed
exchange rates known as the gold standard; only China, Persia and a few Latin
American economies remained on silver. Table b gives the pre-1914 parities once
most currencies had joined (strictly speaking, the currencies of Italy and Austria
were not legally convertible into gold, but their exchange rates were relatively stable
nonetheless).

Table b: Sterling exchange rates of major currencies (per pound), 1913.

	GERMAN MARKS	FRENCH FRANCS	ITALIAN LIRE	AUSTRIAN CROWNS	RUSSIAN ROUBLES	AMERICAN DOLLARS
1913	20.43	25.22	25.22	24.02	9.45	4.87

Source: Hardach, *First World War*, p. 293.

Selected Financial Statistics

A private partnership of the sort formed by the five Rothschild houses was under no obligation in the period covered by these statistics to produce balance sheets or profit and loss accounts. The figures for the capital of the five houses produced in tables d and e are taken from the surviving partnership agreements. The profit and loss accounts for N. M. Rothschild & Sons are based on summaries (the purpose of which is not known) which begin in 1829. The accounts are simple: on one side all the year's sales of commodities, stocks and shares are listed, on the other, all the year's purchases and other costs; the difference is recorded as the annual profit or loss. Table f gives the "bottom line" data and also figures for net appropriations (withdrawals and new capital) by partners. The balance sheet figures in table g are based on a similar series of summaries dating from 1873.

Nineteenth-century banks did not draw up balance sheets or profit and loss accounts in a standardized ways, so comparisons with other banks for which figures are available must be made with extreme caution.

Table c: Combined Rothschild capital, 1818–1904 (selected years, £ thousand).

	1818	1825	1828	1836	1844	1852	1862	1874	1879	1882
Frankfurt	680	1,450	1,534	2,121	2,750	2,746	6,694	4,533	4,225	4,735
Paris	350	1,490	1,466	1,774	2,311	3,542	8,479	20,088	16,815	23,589
London	742	1,142	1,183	1,733	2,005	2,500	5,355	6,509	6,102	5,922
Vienna			25	110	250	83	457	3,229	3,115	4,137
Naples			130	268	463	661	1,328			
Total	1,772	4,082	4,338	6,008	7,778	9,532	22,313	34,359	30,258	38,384

	1887	1888	1896	1898	1899	1900	1901	1902	1903	1904
Frankfurt	4,407	3,173	2,600	2,327	2,294					
Paris	22,974	18,878	23,793	24,254	24,947	22,328	22,665	23,136	23,736	21,086
London	6,149	5,674	7,296	7,545	7,704	7,779	7,641	8,057	7,196	8,429
Vienna	4,507	4,154	6,443	6,382	6,507	6,845	7,021	7,196	7,367	7,621
Total	38,038	31,880	40,131	40,507	41,452	36,953	37,327	38,388	38,298	37,136

Note: Because of rounding, figures in columns will not always add up exactly to totals.
Sources: CPHDCM, 637/1/3/1–11; 1/6/5; 1/6/7/7–14; 1/6/32; 1/6/44–5; 1/7/48–69; 1/7/115–20; 1/8/1–7; 1/9/1–4; RAL, RFamFD/3, B/1; AN, 132 AQ 1, 2, 3, 4, 5, 6, 7, 9, 10, 13, 15, 16, 17, 19; Gille, *Maison Rothschild,* vol. II, pp. 568–72.

Table d: Rothschild partners' shares of capital, 1852–1905 (percentages).

SEPT. 1852		DEC. 1855		SEPT. 1863	
Lionel		Lionel		Lionel	
Anthony		Anthony		Anthony	
Nat		Nat		Nat	
Mayer	20.0	Mayer	25.8	Mayer	25.0
Amschel	20.0	Anselm	25.8	Anselm	25.0
Salomon	20.0	James	25.7	James	25.0
James	19.9	Mayer Carl		Mayer Carl	
Carl	19.9	Adolph		Adolph	
		Wilhelm Carl	22.7	Wilhelm Carl	25.0

SEPT. 1879		OCT. 1882		JUNE 1887		OCT. 1887		APRIL 1888
Natty		Natty		Natty		Natty		
Alfred		Alfred		Alfred		Alfred		
Leo	15.7	Leo	17.1	Leo	20.4	Leo	29.5	22.5
James Edouard								
Arthur	7.9	Arthur, Henri	7.1	Arthur, Henri	6.6	Arthur, Henri	6.6	7.3
Albert		Albert		Albert		Albert		
Ferdinand		Ferdinand		Ferdinand		Ferdinand		
Nathaniel	22.7	Nathaniel	17.1	Nathaniel	23.0	Nathaniel	23.0	25.3
Alphonse		Alphonse		Alphonse		Alphonse		
Gustave		Gustave		Gustave		Gustave		
Edmond	31.4	Edmond	34.3	Edmond	31.8	Edmond	31.8	35.0
Mayer Carl		Mayer Carl		Mayer Carl				
Wilhelm Carl	22.3	Wilhelm Carl	24.4	Wilhelm Carl	18.1	Wilhelm Carl	9.1	10.0

DEC. 1896		JAN. 1898	JAN. 1899	DEC. 1899	
Natty				Natty	
Alfred				Alfred	
Leo	17.5	23.1	18.0	Leo	18.0
Arthur, Henri	7.3	6.8	7.5	Arthur, Henri	7.5
Albert					
Ferdinand				Albert	
Nathaniel	25.3	23.6	23.1	Nathaniel	23.1
Alphonse				Alphonse	
Gustave				Gustave	
Edmond	35.0	32.6	36.0	Edmond	36.0
Wilhelm Carl	14.9	13.9	15.4	Wilhelm Carl	15.4

Table d: Rothschild partners' shares of capital, 1852–1905 (percentages) *(cont'd.).*

DEC. 1900		JAN. 1901	JAN. 1902	OCT. 1904	JULY 1905	
Natty					Natty	
Alfred					Alfred	
Leo	21.3	21.3	21.3	22.5	Leo	23.4
Arthur, Henri	8.9	8.9	8.9	3.7	Arthur, Henri	3.9
Albert					Albert	
Nathaniel	27.3	27.3	27.3	28.9	Nathaniel	25.9
Alphonse					Edouard	
Gustave					Gustave	
Edmond	42.5	42.5	42.5	44.9	Edmond	46.8

Notes: 1855 figures are estimated on the basis of figures for Naples and London.
Sources: CPHDCM, 637/1/7/115–20, Societäts-Übereinkunft, Oct. 31, 1852; AN, 132 AQ 3/1, undated document, c. Dec. 1855; AN, 132 AQ 2, Partnership act, no. 2, Sept. 1879; Oct. 24, 1882; June 28, 1887; April 2, 1888; Nov. 23, 1899; Dec. 24, 1900; Dec. 16, 1901; Nov. 27, 1902; July 24, 1903; Gille, *Maison Rothschild,* vol. II, pp. 568–72.

Table e: N. M. Rothschild & Sons: profit and loss accounts, 1849–1914 (£).

	PROFIT/LOSS	NET APPROPRIATIONS	CAPITAL (END OF CALENDAR YEAR)
1849	334,524		1,952,018
1850	52,713		2,004,731
1851	54,891		2,059,622
1852	-30,969*		1,799,372
1853	276,814*		2,075,436
1854	45,092		2,120,528
1855	88,372		2,208,901
1856	60,355		2,269,255
1857	8,128*		2,261,127
1858	406,736		2,667,863
1859	66,242		2,734,105
1860	116,659		2,850,764
1861	135,775		2,986,539
1862	1,420,638		4,407,178
1863	-26,148	-500,000	3,881,029
1864	8,036		3,889,066
1865	-615		3,888,450
1866	37,615		3,926,065
1867	70,571		3,996,637
1868	306,235		4,302,872
1869	144,012	-600,000	3,846,885
1870	409,085		4,255,970
1871	597,180		4,853,150
1872	356,864	-700,000	4,510,014
1873	1,999,214		6,509,228
1874	137,192*		6,646,420
1875	834,713	-1,577,299	5,903,834
1876	-*		5,903,834
1877	194,464*	-2,203,295	3,899,147
1878	143,080*	246,381	4,145,527
1879	11,286		4,156,813
1880	639,686		4,796,499
1881	933,508		5,730,007

Table e: N. M. Rothschild & Sons: profit and loss accounts, 1849–1914 (£) *(cont'd.)*.

	PROFIT/LOSS	NET APPROPRIATIONS	CAPITAL (END OF CALENDAR YEAR)
1882	-26,713	-600,000	5,103,295
1883	-76,207		5,027,087
1884	3,351		5,030,438
1885	-160,261		4,870,177
1886	1,228,234		6,098,412
1887	-101,634		5,996,778
1888	14,697	-475,000	5,536,475
1889	1,213,525		6,750,000
1890	-77,063	-750,000	5,922,937
1891	-100,589		5,822,349
1892	-361,940		5,460,408
1893	-203,155	-400,000	4,857,254
1894	50,243		4,907,497
1895	107,500		5,014,997
1896	2,058,648		7,073,645
1897	-556	-569,129	6,503,959
1898	814,228		7,318,187
1899	157,315		7,475,502
1900	449,850	-243,352	7,682,001
1901	-40,878		7,641,123
1902	415,675		8,056,797
1903	-861,114		7,195,683
1904	1,233,343		8,429,027
1905	742,317	-1,537,281	7,634,063
1906	664,025		8,298,088
1907	-1,396,414		6,901,674
1908	1,093,439	-512,719	7,482,394
1909	353,830	7,698	7,843,922
1910	470,673	-390,000	7,924,595
1911	264,451	-264,452	7,924,595
1912	193,010	-180,000	7,937,605
1913	-92,962		7,844,642
1914	-1,476,737		6,367,906
1915	-117,195*		4,618,511
1916	213,320*		4,521,846
1917	230,123*		4,720,609
1918	208,673*	-679,129	3,614,602

Notes: Profit and loss figures were calculated as difference between total outgoings and total income.
* Not entirely clear from books.
Sources: RAL, RFamFD/13F; RFamFD/13E.

Table f: N. M. Rothschild & Sons: balance sheets, 1873–1918 (£, end of calendar year).

	ASSETS	LIABILITIES	CAPITAL
1873	15,595,035	9,085,807	6,509,228
1874	14,755,232	8,108,812	6,646,420
1875	18,487,727	12,583,893	5,903,834
1876	13,389,106	7,476,272	5,903,834
1877	13,389,489	7,291,198	6,098,297*
1878	13,592,698	7,351,321	6,241,377*
1879	13,022,317	8,865,504	4,156,813
1880	10,857,738	6,061,239	4,769,499
1881	12,177,367	6,447,359	5,730,007
1882	12,511,291	7,407,997	5,103,295
1883	12,734,390	7,707,303	5,027,087
1884	13,491,790	8,461,352	5,030,438
1885	11,446,012	6,575,835	4,870,177
1886	14,126,858	8,028,446	6,098,412
1887	16,984,901	10,988,123	5,996,778
1888	19,638,633	14,102,158	5,536,475
1889	23,986,545	17,236,545	6,750,000
1890	30,433,369	24,510,432	5,922,937
1891	22,080,046	16,257,697	5,822,349
1892	18,395,602	12,935,194	5,460,408
1893	16,424,287	11,567,033	4,857,254
1894	18,530,735	13,623,238	4,907,497
1895	19,260,482	14,245,485	5,014,997
1896	19,004,363	11,930,718	7,073,645
1897	17,280,561	10,776,602	6,503,959
1898	16,698,744	9,380,557	7,318,187
1899	17,273,769	9,798,267	7,475,502
1900	17,222,588	9,297,235	7,925,353*
1901	18,661,398	11,020,275	7,641,123
1902	20,000,321	11,943,524	8,056,797
1903	25,078,358	17,882,675	7,195,683
1904	25,492,080	17,063,053	8,429,027
1905	33,960,845	26,326,782	7,634,063
1906	30,590,780	22,292,692	8,298,088
1907	28,485,025	21,583,351	6,901,674
1908	24,367,808	15,885,415	8,482,393*
1909	26,420,446	18,222,693	8,197,753*
1910	29,435,027	21,120,432	8,314,595*
1911	26,059,641	17,870,594	8,189,047*
1912	26,003,274	17,885,669	8,117,605*
1913	25,011,664	17,167,022	7,844,642
1914	20,621,650	14,253,744	6,367,906
1915	17,834,043	13,215,533	4,618,510
1916	16,345,942	11,824,096	4,521,846
1917	12,465,925	7,745,315	4,720,610
1918	12,701,677	9,087,075	3,614,602

Notes: Assets: debits consisting of bills receivable not due, bullion on hand, stocks, shares and account balances. Liabilities: credits consisting of bills payable under acceptance, dividends due to the public and balances of accounts.
* Differs slightly from figure in profit and loss accounts.
Sources: RAL, RFamFD/13A/1; 13B/1; 13C/1; 13D/1; 13D/2; 13/E.

Abbreviations used in notes

AN	Archives Nationales, Paris
BL	British Library, London
CMR	C. M. von Rothschild (the Naples house)
CPHDCM	Centre for the Preservation of Historical Documentary Collections, Moscow
deRF	de Rothschild Frères (the Paris house)
DNB	Dictionary of National Biography
HSM	Hessisches Staatsarchiv, Marburg
HoL	House of Lords Record Office
IfS	Institut für Stadtgeschichte, Frankfurt
MAR	M. A. von Rothschild & Söhne (the Frankfurt house)
NLS	National Library of Scotland
NMR	N. M. Rothschild & Sons (the London house)
RAL	Rothschild Archive, London
RA	Royal Archives, Windsor Castle
SMR	S. M. von Rothschild (the Vienna house)

ONE   *Charlotte's Dream (1849–1858)*

1 RAL, RFamP/D/1/1, ff. 317–26, Charlotte Diary, May 21, 1848.
2 *The Times*, Oct. 31, 1845, p. 6. See also Berghoeffer, *Meyer Amschel*, p. 174; Corti, *Reign*, pp. 287f.
3 Corti, *Reign*, pp. 362f. The anecdote was also told about Amschel.
4 Prawer, *Heine*, p. 360. For Heine's condolences to Gutle's granddaughter Betty see RAL [formerly CPHDCM], 58–1–403/7, Heine to Betty, May 16, 1849.
5 Greville, *Memoirs (Second Part)*, vol. II, pp. 171ff. According to Greville, Gutle frequently went on such excursions and went "constantly to the opera or play." She was clearly not as ascetic as Börne and others liked to think.
6 Bodleian Library, dep. Hughenden 141/3 f. 21, Lionel de Rothschild to Disraeli, Sept. 13, 1850; Wiebe *et al.* (eds), *Disraeli letters*, vol. V, p. 364. Surprisingly for a Rothschild, she died intestate leaving a fortune of £800,000.
7 RAL, XI/109/71/2, Mayer Carl, Frankfurt, to his cousins, London, May 8, 1849. See also RAL, Moscow 224, Betty, Paris, to Alphonse, New York, May 10.
8 RAL, RFamP/D/1/3, ff. 56–70, Charlotte Diary, June 18, 1849. Details of Gutle's will in RAL, XI/109/71/4, James, Paris, to his brother [Amschel], Frankfurt, May 8.
9 RAL, RFamP/D/1/2, ff. 132–3, Charlotte Diary, Aug. 21, 1849.

10   Bismarck, *Gesammelte Werke*, vol. XIV/1, pp. 214, 219.

11   *Ibid.*, pp. 225, 228. Cf. Darmstadter, *Bismarck*, p. 115; Corti, *Reign*, pp. 313–16. Amschel subsequently offered to lease him the house in the Bockenheimer Landstrasse, though Bismarck declined, rightly detecting in Amschel's overtures an attempt to curry favour. According to that other arch-reactionary the King of Hanover, Amschel did this sort of thing "whenever any foreign Prince or Minister or man of distinction comes to Frankfurt." At his dinners there was "great grandeur and sumptuousness as to show of plate and luxuries, but he amuses the company by telling them where he bought his fish and meat, and the immense sums he has sacrificed on the occasion . . . shewing every moment le parvenu and the narrow minded lender and discounter of bills of exchange": Cox and Whibley (eds), *Letters of the King of Hanover*, p. 121.

12   RAL, T28/14, Amschel, Berlin, to Carl, undated, *c.* Sept. 1814.

13   RAL, XI/109/70/1, Mayer Carl, Frankfurt, to his cousins, London, Jan. 12, 1849; CPHDCM, 637/1/275/50–90, Amschel's Will, Feb. 6.

14   CPHDCM, 637/1/122/34, Salomon, Frankfurt, to Anselm, Vienna, June 30, 1853; CPHDCM, 637/1/122/37, same to same, July 2; CPHDCM, 637/1/122/40, July 11. Cf. Hansert, "Dynastic power," p. 171.

15   CPHDCM, 637/1/309, Charlotte to her mother Betty, undated, 1854.

16   On the formal commemoration of Amschel's death see Heuberger, *Rothschilds*, p. 177.

17   RAL, XI/109/68B/2, Nat, Paris, to his brothers, London, July 12, 1848.

18   RAL, RFamP/D/1/2, ff. 63–4, Charlotte Diary, Aug. 14, 1848.

19   RAL, Moscow 224, Betty, Paris, to Alphonse, New York, Jan. 18, 1849.

20   RAL, XI/109/73/2, Lionel Davidson, Paris, to Mayer, London, Nov. 22, 1849.

21   RAL, XI/109/67/1, Nat, Paris, to his brothers, London, June 27, 1848.

22   RAL, Moscow 224, Betty, Paris, to Alphonse, New York, Jan. 18, 1849.

23   RAL, RFamP/D/1/2, ff. 306–8, Charlotte Diary, Dec. 13, 1848.

24   RAL, Moscow 224, Betty, Paris, to Alphonse, New York, Jan. 18, 1849.

25   RAL, XI/109/65A, Anselm, Frankfurt, to Nat, Paris, Jan. 9, 1848.

26   RAL, XI/109/75, James to Lionel and Anthony, London, undated, *c.* May 23, 1850; RAL, XI/109/76, James, Paris, to Anthony, London, Aug. 13.

27   RAL, RFamP/D/1/1, ff. 47–50, Charlotte Diary, April 1848. See also RAL, RFamP/D/1/2, ff. 82–3, Aug. 14.

28   RAL, XI/109/73, James, Paris, to his nephews, London, Dec. 12, 1849.

29   RAL, RFamP/D/1/3, ff. 5–6, Charlotte Diary, June 18, 1849.

30   RAL, XI/109J/J/47, James, Paris, to his nephews, London, April 21, 1847; same to same, April 25.

31   RAL, XI/109/75, James to Lionel and Anthony, London, undated, *c.* May 23, 1850.

32   RAL, XI/109/78, James, Paris, to his nephews (postscript to a letter by Nat), London, March 31, 1851.

33   Gille, *Maison Rothschild*, vol. II, pp. 565–8; Plessis, *Banque de France*, vol. II, pp. 109–13; Landes, *Bankers and pashas*, pp. 30f.

34   RAL, XI/109/81, James, Paris, to his nephews, London, June 4, 1852.

35   Davis, *English Rothschilds*, pp. 137f.

36   CPHDCM, 637/1/7/115–20, Societäts-Übereinkunft, Oct. 31, 1852, between Amschel, Salomon, Carl, James, Lionel, Anthony, Nat and Mayer; AN, 132 AQ 1, Prorogation en nom collectif, undated, 1853.

37   CPHDCM, 637/1/6/33, Untitled agreement between Amschel, Salomon, Carl, James and Lionel, Oct. 31, 1852; AN, 132 AQ 1, Gutachten über Liquidation von Handlungsgesellschaften, Reinganum, Frankfurt, 24pp., Oct. 23, 1853.

38   Plessis, *Banque de France*, vol. II, pp. 42–5.

39   AN, 132 AQ 3/1, undated document, *c.* Dec. 1855, reallocating Amschel's and Carl's shares; CPHDCM, 637/1, James, Paris, to Anselm, Feb. 7, 1857; AN, 132 AQ 5902, James, Munich, to Betty, July 22, 1858.

40   Corti, *Reign*, pp. 360f.; Heuberger, *Rothschilds*, pp. 80ff.

41   CPHDCM, 637/1/131–11, Bilan deRF, Dec. 13, 1851.

42   In 1862, James's son Salomon James married Mayer Carl's daughter Adèle. In 1865, Anselm's son Ferdinand married Lionel's daughter Evelina. In 1867, Lionel's son Nathaniel ("Natty") married Mayer Carl's daughter Emma. In 1871, Nat's son James Edouard married Mayer Carl's daughter Laura Thérèse. In 1876, Anselm's youngest son Salomon Albert ("Salbert") married Alphonse's daughter Bettina. Finally, in 1877, James's youngest son Edmond married Wilhelm Carl's daughter Adelheid.

43   The exception was Anselm's daughter Sarah Louise, who married a Tuscan aristocrat, Barone Raimondo Franchetti in 1858.

44   Davis, *English Rothschilds*, pp. 65, 91f. She brought with her a dowry of £88,000. Cf. Capdebièle, "Female Rothschilds."

45   RAL, RFamP/D/1/2, ff. 173–4, Charlotte Diary, Sept. 4, 1848.

46   RAL, RFamP/D/1/2, ff. 234–7, Charlotte Diary, Oct. 9, 1848.

47   RAL, Moscow 224, Betty, Paris, to Alphonse, New York, May 16, 1849.

48   RAL, Moscow 224, Betty, Paris, to Alphonse, New York, Jan. 30, 1849. See also same to same, Dec. 7, 1848.

49   RAL, RFamPD/1, Charlotte Diary, March 20, 1848; RAL, RFamP/D/1/2, ff. 306–8, undated, *c.* Dec. 1848.

50   Davis, *English Rothschilds*, p. 64. Her fears may have been confirmed by the couple's somewhat perfunctory honeymoon, which attracted adverse press comment: Plessis, *Banque de France*, vol. II, pp. 254f.

51   RAL, RFamP/D/1/2, ff. 134–57, Charlotte Diary, Aug. 21, 1848. See also RAL, XI/109/73/3, Mayer Carl, Frankfurt, to Lionel, London, Nov. 9, 1849.

52   RAL, XI/109/72/3, Lionel, Frankfurt, to Anthony, Paris, Sept. 21, 1849.

53   Thus Nat and his wife wished to settle £10,000 in consols on Anselm's daughter Hannah Mathilde on the occasion of her marriage to Wilhelm Carl: RAL, XI/109/72/3, Charlotte de Rothschild [Nat's wife] and Nat, Frankfurt, to Mayer, London, Aug. 30, 1849. See also AN, 132 A Q 5902, James, Paris, to Lionel, London, Feb. 4, 1857.

54   RAL, RFamP/D/1/2, ff. 132–3, Charlotte Diary, Aug. 21, 1848, pp. 262–80; RAL, XI/109/72, James, Homburg, to Anthony, Paris, Aug. 10, 1849; RAL, T8/175, Lionel, Wildbad, to Mayer, London, Aug. 11; RAL, XI/109/72/2, same to same, Aug. 25.

55   RAL, XI/109/75, James to Lionel and Anthony, London, undated, *c.* May 23, 1850; RAL, XI/109/76, James, Paris, to his nephews, London, June 30.

56   RAL, XI/109J/J/47, James, Paris, to his nephews and son, London, March 4, 1847.

57   RAL, XI/109J/J/46B, James, Wildbad, to Lionel and Carl, July 16, 1846.

58   RAL, XI/109/74, James, Paris, to his nephews, London, March 22, 1850.

59   Leo Baeck Institute, New York, AR 3264, Leopold Stein collection, James, Paris, to Ober-Rabiner Leopold Stein, Feb. 10, 1860.

60   RAL, Moscow 224, Betty, Paris, to Alphonse, New York, Dec. 30, 1848.

61   Liberles, "Aristocrat and synagogue."

62   RAL, XI/109/63/1/75, Nat, Paris, to his brothers, London, Sept. 11, 1847; RAL, XI/109/72, James, Homburg, to Gustave and Anthony, Paris, July 28, 1849.

63   RAL, XI/109/72/3, Anthony, Paris, to Mayer, London, Sept. 19, 1849.

64   RAL, XI/109/94, Nat, Paris, to his brothers, London, undated, *c.* 1868.

65   RAL, RFamC/21, Charlotte, Brighton, to Leopold, Cambridge, Oct. 10, 1864.

66   Wiebe *et al.* (eds), *Disraeli letters*, vol. V, p. 459. Venison can be kosher, but not if killed in a hunt as this almost certainly was.

67   RAL, RFamC/21, Charlotte to Leo, Nov. 19, 1866. Macaulay reported after dining at Lionel's in 1859 that "pork in all its forms, was excluded"; instead he was served "Ortolans farcis à la Talleyrand . . . accompanied by some Johannisberg which was beyond all praise": Pinney (ed.), *Macaulay letters*, vol. VI, pp. 227f.

68   Feldman, *Englishmen and Jews*, pp. 68f. The Montefiores had links with the West London Synagogue, so there was a familial interest too.

69   RAL, T6/281, D. M. Hess, Frankfurt, to Lionel, London, Nov. 12, 1852.

70   See on this point Disraeli, *Endymion*, pp. 133–5.

71   See e.g. RAL, RFamC/21 Charlotte, Brighton, to Leopold, Cambridge, Nov. 21, 1864.

72   RAL, RFamP/D 4, Louisa *Journal*, Sept. 11, 1847.

73   Heuberger, *Rothschilds*, p. 123.

74   RAL, RFamP/D 4, Louisa *Journal*, May 8, 1848; Oct. 11. Cf. Endelman, *Radical assimilation*, pp. 81f., 84f.; Heuberger, *Rothschilds*, p. 123.

75   RAL, RFamC/21, Charlotte, London, to Leo, Cambridge, May 15, 1866; same to same, May 30.

76   RAL, RFamC/21, Charlotte, London, to Leo, Cambridge, June 21, 1868. "I hope," noted Charlotte, "the differences may yet be settled, as in these times of religious excitement, quarrels between Christian clergymen and Jewish patrons of livings would be very disagreeable."

77   RAL, RFamC/21, Charlotte, London, to Leo, Cambridge, May 16, 1865; same to same, May 28, 1866; July 20; July 26.

78   RAL, RFamC/21, Charlotte, London, to Leo, Cambridge, July 27, 1866. Cf. Black, *JFS*, pp. 60ff.

79   RAL, XI/109/94, James Dawson, Hon. Secretary of the Royal Naval Scripture Readers' Society, London, to [Lionel?], May 1, 1868; RAL, RFamC/21, Charlotte, London, to Leo, Switzerland, Sept. 13, 1871.

80   Goldschmidt, *Erinnerungen*, pp. 70ff., 92f.

81   Heuberger, *Rothschilds*, p. 128; Kaplan, *Making*, p. 202.

82   RAL, XI/109/77, Secretary of the Society of Friends of Foreigners in Distress, London, to Lionel, Nov. 25, 1850; RAL, XI/109/81, Amschel, Frankfurt, to Lionel, London, April 25, 1852.

83   Newman, *United Synagogue*, pp. 50f.

84   Feydeau, *Mémoires*, pp. 151ff. Cf. IfS, S2/8184, cutting from *Didaskalia*, April 2, 1857.

85   See e.g., RAL, XI/109/94/3, Secretary of the Board of Guardians for the Relief of the Jewish Poor, London, to Ferdinand, May 25, 1868; RAL, XI/109/102/3, Form donating £100 to the Board of Guardians, Aug. 28, 1870; RAL, XI/64/0/1876, Gerson Bleichröder, Berlin, to Lionel, London, Dec. 5, 1876.

86   Black, *JFS*, pp. 56f.

87   RAL, RFamP/D 4, Louisa Journal, May 8, 1848.

88   Charlotte's frequent use of the word "Caucasian" to mean Jewish is an unusual feature of her correspondence. The word was coined by the eighteenth-century anatomist Johann Friedrich Blumenbach to describe one of five racial types he discerned on the basis of measuring skull shapes. As the others were Mongoloid, Ethiopian, American and Malayan, he clearly intended the category to include all European and Middle Eastern peoples.

89   Black, *JFS*, p. 57. Cf. RAL, RFamC/21, Charlotte to Leo, Feb. 13, 1865; same to same, Feb. 22; March 14; Nov. 17; Nov. 28; Adler, *"Remember the Poor,"* p. 10.

90   Hyamson, *Jews College*, pp. 25, 48.

91   Black, *Social politics*, pp. 8–11.

92   Finestein, *Jewish society*, p. 320.

93   Lipman, *Social service*, p. 63.

94   *Ibid.*, pp. 267f.; Marks, *Model mothers*, pp. 110f.

95   Black, *Social politics*, pp. 8–11, 181f.

96   Lipman, *Social service*, pp. 67f.

97   Adler, *"Remember the Poor,"* pp. 5, 8f.

98   RAL, RFamC/21, Charlotte, London, to Leo, Cambridge, June 4, 1864.

99   RAL, uncatalogued leaflet, June 5, 1856.

100 Muhlstein, *Baron James*, p. 204.

101 Prevost-Marcilhacy, *Rothschild*, pp. 142f.

102 Blount, *Memoirs*, p. 101; Feydeau, *Mémoires*, pp. 151ff.

103 Lewnsohn, *Treue Anhänglichkeit*, pp. 10–15. According to Loewe the hospital was in fact founded by Betty in memory of her grandson Mayer Albert, who died in 1850: Loewe (ed.), *Montefiore diaries*, vol. II, pp. 68f. Cf. RAL, RFamC/21, Charlotte to Leo, Oct. 29, 1864; same to same, Sept. 18, 1871.

104 These efforts were not universally appreciated. According to *The Times*, "The Synagogue of that city [Jerusalem], whose members are known for their deep aversion to every innovation, and to progress in general, have pronounced a sentence of excommunication against all Israelites who should participate either as collectors or donors, in the subscription now open in Europe for the purpose of . . . establishing at Jerusalem . . . an extensive hospital and schools for adults and children of both sexes. Among the persons visited with this anathema are the heads of the different branches of the firm of Rothschild, who have subscribed 100,000 f. towards that charitable undertaking": *The Times*, Dec. 13, 1844, p. 5.

105 An act of 1707 also made it possible for voters to be made to swear the same oath, though this was not rigorously enforced: Salbstein, *Emancipation*, p. 50.

106 Cassis, *City bankers*, p. 269; *idem*, *City*, pp. 168ff.

107 For an early example, see Corti, *Reign*, pp. 158f.

108 *Ibid.*, p. 329; McCagg, *History*, p. 149; Macartney, *House*, p. 142. It was not fully achieved in Frankfurt until 1864.

109 RAL, Moscow 224, Betty, Paris, to Alphonse, New York, April 4, 1849.

110 Heuberger, *Rothschilds*, p. 120.

111 Salbstein, *Emancipation*, pp. 115–25. On the willingness of some local corporations to omit these

words without statutory sanction see RAL, T23/102, XI/109/36/1/23, Montefiore to Lionel, Oct. 21, 1838.

112 RAL, XI/109J/J/37, James, Paris, to his nephews, London, Nov. 12, 1837.

113 RAL, XI/109J/J/42, James, Paris, to his nephews, London, Feb. 13, 1842.

114 RAL, XI/109/42a/3/21, Anselm, Frankfurt, to Lionel, undated, *c.* May 1842.

115 RAL, T18/255, Peel to Lionel, undated, *c.* Jan. 1844; RAL, T118/237, same to same, Jan. 31; RAL, XI/109/46/1/88, Nat, Paris, to his brothers, London, undated, *c.* Feb.; BL, Add. MS 40540 f. 186, Lionel to Peel, Feb. 20, 1844; f. 188, same to same, Feb. 23; f. 184, July 16. See also RAL, XI/109/46/1/34, Anselm, Frankfurt, to his cousins, March 5; RAL, XI/109/47/1/58, same to same, June 9; RAL, RFamC/1/36, Hannah, Paris, to Charlotte, June 14; RAL, RFamC/1/37, Hannah, Paris, to Lionel, June 15; RAL, XI/109/54a/2/118, Anselm to his cousins, Nov. 17, 1845. Cf. Loewe (ed.), *Montefiore diaries*, vol. I, p. 317.

116 BL, Add. MS 40584 f. 396, Lionel to Peel, Feb. 10, 1846; f. 398, Peel to Lionel, Feb. 12; RAL, T42/19, Montefiore, St Petersburg, to the Barons de Rothschild, London, April 9.

117 Salbstein, *Emancipation*, p. 124.

118 He appears to have sought to persuade the mayor and aldermen of Dover—a town he knew well as a regular cross-Channel commuter—to sign a petition on the subject to be submitted to Parliament: RAL, XI/109/40/1/39, illegible, Dover, to NMR, Feb. 14, 1841; RAL, XI/109/40/1/40, unsigned letter to "Mr N. M. Rothschild Esq.," Feb. 17; RAL, XI/109/40/1/42, illegible, Dover, to NMR, Feb. 24; RAL, XI/109/40/1/44, Joh. March, Dover, to NMR, Feb. 24; RAL, XI/109/40/1/43, F. Franklyn, Dover, to "Baron N. Rothschild," March 8. The mayor was unable to secure enough support to oblige Nat, but assured him that he would be "pleased to see you a Knight of the Shire, as I feel your Tory principles highly qualify you for that high station."

119 RAL, T23/212, XI/109/40/1/31, W. [Note?], House of Lords, to NMR, June 14, 1841; RAL, T23/213, XI/109/40/1/32, T. A. Carter, Blenheim Palace, Woodstock, to Lionel, June 20.

120 RAL, T37/169, Herries to Goulburn, Sept. 12, 1841. Cf. Davis, *English Rothschilds*, p. 70.

121 RAL, XI/109/42, Moses Lepen, Ebenezer Square, Houndsditch, London, to "Mayer de Rothschild," London, Jan. 3, 1842. It is significant that Mayer had also been elected a member of Brooks's Club in 1841: Endelman, *Radical assimilation*, p. 75. It was not until 1852 that his brother Anthony also became a member: RAL, T6/286, H. Banderet, Brooks's Club, to Anthony, March 6, 1853. Cf. Davis, *English Rothschilds*, pp. 100f. The brothers were also members of the more overtly political Reform Club. In the same way, Alphonse became a member of the exclusive Paris Jockey Club in 1852 as well as the Cercle de l'Union: Plessis, *Banque de France*, vol. II, p. 241; Palmade, *Capitalism*, p. 218.

122 Wolf, "Rothschildiana," p. 276.

123 RAL, XI/104/1/5/118, Nat, Paris, to his brothers, London, undated, 1841.

124 RAL, XI/109/43a/2/105, Nat, Paris, to his brothers, London, July 9, 1842.

125 RAL, XI/109/48/1/5, Anthony, Paris, to his brothers, London, undated, June 1844.

126 Salbstein, *Emancipation*, p. 110.

127 RAL, XI/109/5B, James, Paris, to Nathan, London, Sept. 7, 1816.

128 RAL, XI/109J/J/38, James, Brussels, to his nephews, June 23, 1838.

129 RAL, XI/104/1/2/37, Anselm, Frankfurt, to his cousins, London, March 21, 1841.

130 RAL, XI/104/1/5/119, Anthony, Paris, to his brothers, London, Aug. 29, 1841.

131 RAL, XI/109/45a/1/17a, Anthony, Paris, to his brothers, undated, 1843.

132 Salbstein, *Emancipation*, pp. 132ff. In the same year the old law against Jews owning property was repealed.

133 RAL, XI/109/54a/2/118, Lionel to Anthony, March 12, 1845.

134 RAL, XI/109/51b/2/49, Nat, Paris, to Lionel, London, undated, *c.* March 1845.

135 RAL, XI/109/57/4/67, Nat and Mayer, Paris, to Lionel, London, undated, *c.* July 1846.

136 RAL, RFamC/1/44, Hannah, Paris, to Charlotte, undated, *c.* August 1845. Salomons was duly re-elected as an alderman, this time for Cordwainer Ward, in December 1847 and went on to become Lord Mayor of London in 1855.

137 RAL, XI/109/57/1/4, Anthony, Paris, to his brothers, London, undated, *c.* June 1846.

138 RAL, XI/109/57/1/53, Nat, Wildbad, to his brothers, July 8, 1846; RAL, XI/109J/J/46B, James, Wildbad, to Lionel, London, July 16.

139 RAL, XI/109/40/1/51, Thomas O'Brien, 15 Shaftesbury Terrace, Chelsea Square, to Lionel, London, March 10, 1841.

140   RAL, XI/109/44/4/31, Saul Myers, London, to Lionel, Sept. 26, 1843.

141   Wiebe *et al.* (eds), *Disraeli letters*, vol. IV, pp. 273f.; Davis, *English Rothschilds*, pp. 94f. He promptly initiated a week of lavish dinners at the White Hart Hotel, drafting in a contingent of French chefs in a calculated appeal to the stomachs of his county neighbours. The local press reproduced the menu, commenting in awe that it had been "served in the best possible taste."

142   He was one of three names submitted by Russell to the Queen: the others, as she noted in her journal, were a Colonel Fergusson and "another, whose name I cannot remember"—suggesting that Victoria did not attach much significance to the issue: RA, Queen Victoria's Journal, Nov. 14, 1846. He was in fact Frederick Currie, Secretary to the Government of Bengal. Lionel may have regarded these minor imperial functionaries as unsatisfactory company to keep.

143   RA Y148/6, Albert, Osborne, to Stockmar, Dec. 3, 1846.

144   RAL, RFamC/1/99, Hannah, Frankfurt, to Lionel, London, undated, *c.* Oct. 1846. Cf. Davis, *English Rothschilds*, p. 78; Mace, "From Frankfurt Jew," pp. 184f.

145   RAL, XI/109/58b/2/58, Nat, Paris, to his brothers, London, undated, *c.* Oct. 1846; RAL, T7/64, Anthony, Paris, to Lionel, London, Oct. 1.

146   RAL, XI/109J/J/46, James, Paris, to his nephews, London, Nov. 18, 1846. See also RAL, T7/86, Anselm, Frankfurt, to Lionel, Nov. 24, 1846.

147   *The Times*, Dec. 19, 1846. Unusually, the Rothschilds stipulated that the title would revert to Lionel's eldest son if Anthony failed to produce a male heir: Rothschild, *"You have it, Madam,"* p. 5.

148   RAL, XI/109/61/2/119, Nat, Paris, to Lionel, London, *c.* May 1847; RAL, T/158 [XI/109/63], same to same, undated, c. June. Nat refers to "difficulties" made by the Liberal party, though it is unclear what these were.

149   Alderman, *Jewish community*, p. 23; Davis, *English Rothschilds*, p. 80. Isaac Goldsmid and his son Francis also stood as Liberal candidates.

150   Davis, *English Rothschilds*, p. 72.

151   Salbstein, *Emancipation*, pp. 141–4; Davis, *English Rothschilds*, pp. 72f.

152   RAL, XI/109/63/2/33, Nat, Paris, to Lionel, London, undated, *c.* July 1847.

153   RAL, XI/109/62/1/39, James Lauch, St Bonifacius German Institution, London, to Lionel, July 8, 1847.

154   RAL, T6/215, E. Aby, 26 New Bridge, Blackfriars to Baron Lionel, undated, *c.* July 1847; RAL, RFamC/1/114 [ex XI/109/63], Hannah to Lionel, undated, *c.* July.

155   According to one estimate after the poll, only 500 of London's 17,000 Jews were registered to vote: RAL, T6/208, F. Herz and F. Berkeley to Lionel, Aug. 15, 1847.

156   Cesarani, *Jewish Chronicle*, pp. 8f.

157   *The Times* Archive, TTA JTD 2/76, Lionel to Delane, undated, June 1847; TTA JTD 2/77, same to same, July 30; RAL, XI/109/71/2, Delane to Lionel, May 8, 1849. Cf. Dasent, *Piccadilly*, pp. 137f. and 138n.

158   RAL, XI/109/71/1, James Wilson to Lionel, April 30, 1849.

159   Heffer, *Carlyle*, pp. 263f.; Modder, *Jew in the literature of England*, pp. 171f. It is worth noting that at this time Carlyle was romantically entangled with Lady Harriet Ashburton, the wife of Alexander Baring: *ibid.*, pp. 292f. However, Carlyle does not appear to have made his opposition to Lionel public, leaving that to papers like the *Morning Herald*, which referred to Lionel as a "foreigner," and one of the Tory candidates, who declared Lionel's proper place was as "one of the princes of Judah, in the land of Judah": Finestein, *Jewish society*, p. 100.

160   RAL, RFamP/D/1/2, ff. 134–57, Charlotte Diary, Aug. 21, 1848. In particular, he appears to have had a soft spot for Anthony's wife Louisa, to whom he apologised for his earlier attacks in 1848. He dined with the Rothschilds in February 1850 (finding the women "very nice") and by 1856–7 was in occasional friendly correspondence with Louisa: Thackeray, *Letters*, vol. II, pp. 644f.; vol. III, p. 626; vol. IV, p. 29. She appears in *Pendennis* as "a Jewish lady . . . with a child at her knee, and from whose face towards the child there shone a sweetness so angelical that it seemed to form a sort of glory round both. I protest I could have kneeled before her too . . .": Thackeray, *Pendennis*, p. 23. Cf. Cohen, *Lady de Rothschild*, pp. 33–7.

161   Salbstein, *Emancipation*, p. 144.

162   RAL, XI/109/66/2, Nat, Paris, to his brothers, London, May 26, 1848; RAL, XI/109/67/2, same to same, undated, *c.* May; undated, *c.* June.

163   RAL, XI/109/62/1/201, James Lauch, St Bonifacius German Institution, London, to Lionel, July 30,

1847. Lauch's letter deserves quotation for the flavour it gives of the politics of the day: "To be candid—I will agree in what every body says viz: that you, dear Baron! *were returned* by the *Catholics* whose accession to your righteous cause *determined* your victory . . . it was a great wisdom on your part, two months ago to send for me and *not to* be ashamed humbly to ask me the favour to give you my assistance in the approaching struggle! I resolved—*even if you should not help me as I wanted it for my institution* to assist *you faithfully* and *fervently*—to *honour in your eyes* my quality of a Catholic Priest . . . My great plan from the beginning was to determine the Catholic Electors to vote for you *in a body*—and you cannot imagine what pains and troubles I had to come *to this* always acting upon them by *different agencies* and *seldom personally* influencing, to prevent prejudices to take hold of them. We *succeeded just when I began* to despair—because we had a most powerful opposition to *overcome* or to *elude* . . . All this whilst I was in *hourly* danger of being arrested for debts or seeing execution carried out on the premises of the *Institution*; likewise *every word* I have written to you on this head is perfect and sacred truth . . . Now I say all this to you only to add: *that you owe me nothing, that I expect nothing* and that the Catholic Agents *expect nothing from You*, That I take upon myself *every expense* . . . Honest and honoured I have *nothing* to ask *at this or any time*, but *that favour which I asked you now a year ago*, when neither you nor I thought of an election Struggle—*I have done my duty to you* . . . and my heart *doubts not one moment* that you will do yours to me." Lionel does not seem to have obliged on the scale Lauch had hoped for: RAL, XI/109/62/2/41, same to same, Aug. 5—though he seems to have put him in touch with the exiled Metternich: RAL, XI/109/69B/1, same to same, Dec. 10, 1848.

164   RAL, XI/109/62/1/2, Nat, Paris, to Lionel, London, undated, *c.* July 1847; RAL, XI/109/63/2/87, same to same, undated, *c.* July.

165   RAL, T7/129, Charlotte, Paris, to Lionel, London, undated, *c.* Aug. 1847.

166   RAL, T7/128, Betty, Bern, to Lionel, Aug. 4, 1847. See also RAL, T7/127, Louise, Naples, to Lionel, Aug. 2; RAL, XI/109/62/2/14, Anthony, Paris, to Lionel, Aug. 2; RAL, T7/99, Salomon, Vienna, to Lionel, Aug. 4; Cohen, *Lady de Rothschild*, p. 41.

167   RAL, T7/100, Salomon, Vienna, to Anselm, Frankfurt, Aug. 5, 1847. See also RAL, T40/1 XI/109/62, S. Bleichröder, Berlin, to Lionel, Aug. 5.

168   Bodleian Library, Oxford, MS Eng. Lett. d.307 ff.16–18, Russell to Lionel, April 24, 1847.

169   Wiebe *et al.* (eds), *Disraeli letters*, vol III, p. 237.

170   Monypenny and Buckle, *Disraeli*, vol. II, p. 225; RAL, RFamC/1/44, Hannah, Paris, to Charlotte, London, undated, *c.* Aug. 1845.

171   Cohen, *Lady de Rothschild*, pp. 47ff.

172   Weintraub, *Disraeli*, pp. 243ff.; Monypenny and Buckle, *Disraeli*, vol. II, p. 333; Ridley, *Young Disraeli*, pp. 312f.; Hardwick, *Mrs Dizzy*, p. 158f.

173   RAL, RFamC/2/7, Disraeli to Charlotte, March 28, 1867.

174   RAL, RFamC2/9, Disraeli, to Charlotte, Nov. 23, 1867.

175   RAL, RFamC2/8, Disraeli to Charlotte, Nov. 19, 1869. Cf. Monypenny and Buckle, *Disraeli*, vol. V, pp. 223, 227.

176   RAL, RFamC/21, Charlotte, London, to Leo, July 27, 1874; Charlotte to Leo and Leonora, Trouville, Aug. 3; same to same, Aug. 11.

177   Monypenny and Buckle, *Disraeli*, vol. V, pp. 303f.

178   RAL, RFamC/21, Charlotte, London, to Leo, Cambridge, Nov. 19, 1866.

179   Bodleian Library, dep. Hughenden 141/3 f. 70, Charlotte, Burton, to Disraeli, Aug. 26, 1863.

180   RAL, RFamC/2/45, Disraeli, Bosbury House, Ledbury, to Charlotte, Oct. 17, 1870.

181   Blake, *Disraeli*, p. 202. For absurd suggestions that Sidonia is James, Adolph or Alfred see Rintoul, *Dictionary*, p. 790. Davis's scepticism seems unwarranted: Davis, *English Rothschilds*, p. 87.

182   Disraeli, *Coningsby*, pp. 114–17, 120f., 202, 213ff., 214–21, 249ff., 336f., 348. Disraeli's political views are given to Sidonia at pp. 236–40, 302f.

183   RAL, RFamC/1/35, Hannah to Charlotte, June 3, 1844. Like the good Liberal she had become, however, she "could not perfectly comprehend his meaning about the government of the country."

184   Disraeli, *Tancred*, pp. 115, 118–24, 133–4, 140, 145f., 186–96. The last point is repeated in Disraeli's *Lord George Bentinck*: see Salbstein, *Emancipation*, pp. 97–112.

185   It is worth noting that Disraeli made a second sketch of Charlotte's character over thirty years later as Mrs Neuchatel in *Endymion*. Interestingly, he alludes to that peculiar bitterness in her character which became more pronounced as she grew older and hints at unhappiness in her marriage to Lionel: "Adrian had married, when very young, a lady selected by his father. The selection seemed a good one. She was

the daughter of a most eminent banker, and had herself, though that was of slight importance, a large portion. She was a woman of abilities, highly cultivated . . . Her person, without being absolutely beautiful, was interesting. There was even a degree of fascination in her brown velvet eyes. And yet Mrs. Neuchatel was not a contented spirit; and though she appreciated the great qualities of her husband and viewed him even with reverence as well as affection, she scarcely contributed to his happiness as much as became her . . . [But] Adrian . . . was so absorbed by his own great affairs . . . that the over-refined fantasies of his wife produced not the slightest effect on the course of his life." Inexplicably, Disraeli decided to make the Neuchatels Swiss by origin, so that Judaism is not touched upon. But their history (as custodians of émigrés' wealth during the French wars) and the description of "Hainault house" make the model unmistakable. See esp. pp. 129–35, 146f., 162ff.

186   RAL, RFamP/D 4, Louisa Journal, Dec. 1, 1847. Cf. Cohen, *Lady de Rothschild*, p. 44.

187   On Disraeli's courageous but disastrous "Tancredian" speech of December 16, which was punctuated with cries of "Oh!" from his own side, see Somervell, *Disraeli and Gladstone*, p. 83; Maurois, *Disraeli*, pp. 179f. One cynical observer considered the speech "obviously addressed to Rothschild's money bags and . . . a bad selection from his novels": Conacher, *Peelites and the party system*, p. 188.

188   RAL, RFamP/D/1/1, Charlotte Diary, March 20, 1848.

189   Jennings (ed.), *Correspondence and diaries of Croker*, pp. 137f.; Pool (ed.), *Croker papers*, pp. 213f. According to Bentinck, Disraeli was counting on the Rothschilds acquiring Stowe from the bankrupt Duke of Buckingham "with all its Parliamentary influence"; he also believed Russell's conduct to be aimed at uniting the Whigs and Peelites. The King of Hanover attributed Bentinck's attitude to "his former haunts on the turf, and thus his connection with the Hebrews": Cox and Whibley (eds), *Letters of the King of Hanover*, p. 129.

190   Wiebe *et al.* (eds), *Disraeli letters*, vol. IV, p. 319f. Disraeli misunderstood the constitutional position, thinking that "if Rothschild were to go to the table & ask for the Roman Cath[olic] oath, wh: they co[ul]d not refuse him, that he co[ul]d take his seat. The words 'faith of a Christian' only being in the oath of abjuration, from wh: the Romans were relieved" in 1829. As late as April 1848 he expressed the vain hope that the acceptance of the Jewish bill would unite the Conservative factions: RAL, RFamP/D/1/1, ff. 151–75, Charlotte Diary, April 24.

191   Salbstein, *Emancipation*, pp. 170f.

192   See e.g. RAL, RFamP/D 4, Louisa Journal, Feb. 18, 1849; Cohen, *Lady de Rothschild*, pp. 42, 46.

193   RAL, RFamP/D/1/1, ff. 44f., Charlotte Diary, March 1848; RAL, RFamP/D/1/1, ff. 239–41, May 8. When the Disraelis accepted an invitation from the Goldsmids she concluded that they must "glauben . . . an die Vernichtung unserer Macht," but such fears had been dispelled by May.

194   RAL, RFamP/D/1/1, ff. 315–6, Charlotte Diary, May 19, 1848. See also RAL, RFamP/D/1/1, ff. 329–334, May 28. There was evidently a good deal of ill feeling between Mary Anne and Charlotte by this stage. While Lionel and Disraeli talked in the latter's study after dinner, Mary Anne complained that her husband had "sich für uns und unsere gerechte Sache während fünf Jahren seines Lebens aufgeopfert u. nur Undank sei ihm für die großen Bemühungen seines Geistes, seiner Feder u. seiner Lippen zu Theil geworden. Ich ärgerte mich, und konnte daher nicht schweigen, sagte ihr Mr. Disraeli habe nichts verloren und nichts eingebüßt." A few weeks later, Lionel suggested that his wife ask Mary Anne "why Mr. Dizzy cannot come up to speak with me whenever he sees me; is there any reason why I should cross the room always to speak with him, he [gives] himself such airs": RAL, RFamC/4/49, Lionel, Paris, to Charlotte, London, July 16. This was the nadir of Rothschild–Disraeli relations. See also RAL, RFamP/D/1/2, Charlotte Diary, Aug. 1; Davis, *English Rothschilds*, p. 88.

195   Matthew (ed.), *Gladstone diaries*, vol. III, p. 676.

196   Conacher, *Peelites and the party system*, p. 49.

197   RAL, XI/109J/J/46B, James, Wildbad, to Salomon, Nat and Alphonse, July 26, 1846; RAL, XI/109/65B/2/56, Nat, Paris, to his brothers, London, undated, *c.* Feb. 1848. More usually, the Rothschilds invested money on behalf of grandees like the Earl of Mar, and so technically were his debtors: RAL, T6/177, Earl of Mar, Alloa, to NMR, Feb. 11, 1846.

198   RAL, T7/50, Hannah to Lionel, Dec. 14, 1847; RAL, XI/109/65B/2/42, Nat, Paris, to his brothers, London, undated, *c.* Feb. 1848; RAL, RFamP/D/1/1, ff. 265–9, Charlotte Diary, May 14, 1848.

199   Salbstein, *Emancipation*, pp. 145–59.

200   RAL, RFamP/D/1/1, ff. 317–26, Charlotte Diary, May 21, 1848. See also in a similar though less febrile vein, RAL, RFamP/D 4, Louisa Journal, May 30.

201   Cox and Whibley (eds), *Letters of the King of Hanover*, pp. 116, 120f., 185f. Curiously, his sister the

Duchess of Gloucester was wholly sympathetic to the Rothschilds' case: RAL, XI/109/69A/1, Charlotte, Gunnersbury, to Lionel, Garboldisham, Oct. 9, 1848.

202   Loewe (ed.), *Montefiore diaries*, vol. I, p. 317.

203   RAL, XI/109/64b/1/153, Nat, Paris, to his brothers, London, Dec. 23, 1847.

204   RAL, T51/29, Dr Meyer, Buckingham Palace, to Lionel, May 19, 1847; RAL, XI/109/65B/2/56, Nat, Paris, to his brothers, London, undated, *c.* Feb. 1848; RAL, XI/109/65A/79, same to same, Feb. 14.

205   RAL, XI/109J/J/42, James, Paris, to his nephews, London, Nov. 24, 1842.

206   RA, Y153/66, Stockmar, Coburg, to Prince Albert, May 27, 1845. This offer was accepted.

207   Weintraub, *Albert*, p. 173. Oettingen had previously borrowed 100,000 gulden from the Frankfurt house in 1835; the second loan was negotiated from the London house while he was in London in the Bavarian diplomatic service.

208   RAL, XI/109/67/2, Nat, Paris, to his brothers, London, undated, *c.* March 1848.

209   RAL, RFamP/D/1/1, ff. 239–41, Charlotte Diary, May 8, 1848.

210   RAL, XI/109/66/2, Nat, Paris, to Lionel, May 10, 1848.

211   Weintraub, *Albert*, p. 191. Cf. RA, PP Prince Albert's accounts, 1848; RA, PP Vic Ledger 331, Royal accounts, Aug. 1852. I am grateful to Sheila de Bellaigue for her assistance on this point.

212   RAL, RFamP/D/1/2, f. 338, Charlotte Diary, Jan. 4, 1849.

213   Vincent, *Disraeli, Derby and the Conservative party*, p. 27; Weintraub, *Albert*, pp. 223ff. The idea had originated in June 1849. Lionel agreed to serve as one of two Treasurers when a Royal Commission was set up to rescue it in January the following year. At this stage, he and Anthony made an initial contribution of £1,000. For the role played by Sir Moses Montefiore, see Loewe (ed.), *Montefiore diaries*, vol. II, pp. 20f.

214   Salbstein, *Emancipation*, pp. 188f.

215   RAL, XI/109/70/2, Russell to Lionel, Feb. 13, 1849. In this fascinating letter, Russell sets out his own reasons for supporting emancipation—"I believe this country stands in need of God's blessing and that blessing is granted only to the nations who uphold his chosen people in this their second dispensation"—and contrasts them with the motives of the Radicals who were simply "glad to fight at your expense one of their political questions." See also RAL, XI/109/71/2, same, Carlton Club, to same, May 8: "Do not take it into your head that I want to compromise you with your own party—a Whig you are and a Whig you must remain."

216   RAL, RFamP/D/1/1, ff. 215–20, Charlotte Diary, May 7, 1848. Cf. Salbstein, *Emancipation*, pp. 175ff.

217   *The Times*, June 28, 1849, p. 8. Cf. RAL, XI/109/71/3, Sidney Smith to Anthony, June 4.

218   RAL, RFamP/D/1/1, ff. 329–34, Charlotte Diary, May 28, 1848; RAL, RFamP/D/1/1, ff. 338–42, May 29; RAL, RFamP/D/1/1, f. 343, June 1; RAL, RFamP/D/1/1, ff. 346–52, June 4; RAL, XI/109/67, James, Paris, June 2.

219   RAL, RFamP/D/1/3, ff. 5–6, Charlotte Diary, June–July 1849.

220   RAL, XI/109/65A, Alphonse, Paris, to Lionel, London, Jan. 1, 1848.

221   RAL, RFamP/D/1/1, Charlotte Diary, April 4, 1848; RAL, XI/109/65B/2/7, Charlotte [wife of Anselm] to Lionel, May 1.

222   RAL, XI/109/65B/1/81, Anselm, Frankfurt, to James, Nat and Alphonse, Paris, March 12, 1848; RAL, XI/109/65B/1/82, Mayer Carl, Frankfurt, to his cousins, London, March 12; RAL, XI/109J/J/48, Salomon, Vienna, to his brothers and nephews, March 22. As Salomon commented drily on hearing of attacks on Jews in Pressburg: "Schöne Freiheit." See also RAL, XI/109/67, Anselm, Vienna, to Amschel, Frankfurt, April 28; RAL, XI/109/66/2, Anselm, Vienna, to his cousins, London, May 3; RAL, XI/109/67, Anselm and Salomon, Vienna, to Amschel, Frankfurt, May 4; RAL, XI/109/72, James, Homburg, to Gustave and Anthony, Paris, July 29, 1849; RAL, XI/109/72/2, Anselm to James, Aug. 20.

223   RAL, XI/109/67, Anselm and Salomon, Vienna, to Amschel, Frankfurt, April 17, 1848; Mayer Carl, Frankfurt, to James, Paris, May 2; same to same, May 4; Anselm and Salomon to Amschel, May 4; same to same, May 19.

224   RAL, XI/109/72/1, Nat, Gräfenberg, to his brothers, London, July 17, 1849; RAL, XI/109/72/1, Lionel, Frankfurt, to Mayer, London, July 28; RAL, XI/109/72/4, James, Paris, to the Marquess of Londonderry, undated, *c.* July; RAL, XI/109/72/4, Lionel, Wildbad, to Mayer, London, Aug. 4. There was apparently an attempt to involve the Chartists by one of Lionel's supporters: RAL, XI/109/73/3, B. Hall to Lionel, Dec. 30: "I have been sometime playing a deep game with Feargus O'Connor and Mr

Reynolds the great Chartist leaders & think it most important that their interest should be indicted to carry your Bill."

225 Wiebe *et al.* (eds), *Disraeli letters*, vol. V, p. 196 and n. Manners had in fact dined with Lionel before being asked to stand, but Mayer seems to have guessed that he would be; evidently Disraeli was keeping Lionel informed of his party's intentions. As Disraeli saw it, the erstwhile Puseyite Manners needed to stand primarily in order to convince the rest of the Protectionists of his political reliability: *ibid.*, pp. 292f. Manners was only one of numerous Conservatives who were happy to dine with the Rothschilds while repeatedly voting against their admission to Parliament: see also RAL, XI/109/71/4, Nat, Paris, to his brothers, London, undated, *c.* April 1849.

226 RAL, XI/109/71, James, Paris, to his nephews, London, June 26, 1849; RAL, XI/109/72/1, Louise, Frankfurt, to Lionel, July 6. For Lionel's address to the City voters after his victory, see RAL, RFamC/4/442, July 20. There was an abortive attempt to challenge the result by means of a petition.

227 *The Times*, July 26, 1850, p. 5. Also present at the meeting was Thomas Hankey, Deputy Governor of the Bank of England. Some people were already treating Lionel as if he were a sitting MP: see RAL, XI/109/76, Secretary of The Provident Clerks' Mutual Life Assurance Association and Benevolent Fund to Lionel, July 19.

228 *The Times*, July 27, 1850, pp. 2f.; July 29, p. 3.

229 *The Times*, July 30, 1850, pp. 2–5. Cf. Wiebe *et al.* (eds), *Disraeli letters*, vol. V, p. 340; Salbstein, *Emancipation*, pp. 178f.; Loewe (ed.), *Montefiore diaries*, vol. II, p. 21. On this motion, Disraeli voted with the majority, i.e., against his own party, though before the debate he introduced a petition against the admission of Jews to Parliament from some of his own constituents in Buckinghamshire, made virtually no contribution during the debate and supported a hostile motion from his own side that Lionel be asked directly whether he would be sworn to the three oaths. It was narrowly defeated.

230 *The Times*, July 31, 1850, pp. 2–4, 8.

231 *The Times*, Aug. 2, 1850, p. 4; Aug. 5, p. 4; Aug. 6, pp. 2–4. This time Disraeli bravely reaffirmed his belief in the justice of emancipation, after a judicious defence of the House of Lords against Radical attacks.

232 All this was watched from the gallery by Louisa: Cohen, *Lady de Rothschild*, p. 43.

233 Salbstein, *Emancipation*, pp. 179–87.

234 RAL, XI/109/82, Lionel, Election Address to the Electors of the City of London, May 27, 1852. Cf. Loewe (ed.), *Montefiore diaries*, vol. II, p. 29.

235 Williams, *Making*, pp. 206f.; Alderman, *British Jewry*, pp. 67f.; Salbstein, *Emancipation*, p. 119.

236 *The Times*, June 27, 1855, p. 9; July 17, p. 7; July 18, p. 9; July 31, p. 10. The matter had to be referred to a select committee, which found in Lionel's favour.

237 Davis, *English Rothschilds*, pp. 84f.

238 They joined Disraeli, Milnes Gaskell and Tom Baring in voting against a spoiling amendment by Thesiger: Salbstein, *Emancipation*, p. 224.

239 *Ibid.*, p. 227. Ironically, Lloyd George would direct very similar abuse at Lionel's son Natty when he led opposition to the "People's Budget" in the Lords.

240 Steele, *Palmerston*, p. 144. On August 12, Warren wrote to Bishop Wilberforce: "Had you seen the air and gesture with which the Jew motioned away the tendered New Testament at the Bar of the House, your blood would have run cold, as [Edward] Hamilton told me his did."

241 *The Times*, July 27, 1858, p. 7. Cf. Salbstein, *Emancipation*, pp. 231ff.; Finestein, *Jewish society*, p. 167; Corti, *Reign*, p. 366; Davis, *English Rothschilds*, p. 86; Weintraub, *Disraeli*, pp. 372f. This was not the end of the story, as it was unclear whether the resolution would need to be renewed at each new parliamentary session. Duncombe therefore sought to convert it into a permanent standing order, and this was done in August 1860, though not before the Lords had modified the terms of the bill to make it clear that a revocable privilege rather than an entitlement was being granted.

242 AN, 132 AQ 5902, James, Carlsbad, to Nat, Paris, July 9, 1858.

243 Loewe (ed.), *Montefiore diaries*, vol. II, pp. 86f.; Davis, *English Rothschilds*, pp. 100f.; Alderman, *Jewish community*, p. 23; *idem, British Jewry*, pp. 67f.

244 RAL, RFamC/21, Charlotte, London, to Leo, Lucerne, July 8, 1864.

245 Loewe (ed.), *Montefiore diaries*, vol. II, p. 78.

246 *The Times*, July 25, 1873, p. 12; June 4, 1879, p. 10.

247 Matthew (ed.), *Gladstone diaries*, vol. V, pp. 132, 292, 387; vol. VI, pp. 46, 20, 101, 210, 292.

248 A dissertation could be written about Charlotte's "salon" at Piccadilly, if that is the right word to describe the various different social circles which her letters describe. The most important was of course the Rothschild family itself and related families (especially the Cohens and Montefiores). Occasionally admitted into this quite intimate milieu were the senior clerks and agents' families (the Davidsons, Bauer, Weisweiller, Scharfenberg, and Belmont); and members of closely connected City families like the Waggs and Helberts. Apart from Gladstone and Disraeli, her political friends included not only the Liberals mentioned above but also Conservatives like Bulwer Lytton, the novelist and MP for Hertford-shire, and Lord Henry Lennox, MP for Chichester and Disraeli's first Commissioner of Public Works. Also clearly part of the political circle was the editor of *The Times*, Delane. Overlapping but distinct was the diplomatic circle, composed of ambassadors and the members of the exiled Orléanist royal family. Socially on a par with this group were Charlotte's grand lady friends like the duchesses of Sutherland, Newcastle and St Albans.

249 Monypenny and Buckle, *Disraeli*, vol. IV, p. 109.

250 *Ibid.*, p. 147.

251 RAL, RFamC/4/54, Lionel to Charlotte, July 15, 1858.

252 RAL, RFamC/4/55, Lionel to Charlotte, July 16, 1858.

253 The Rothschilds visited Hughenden on October 11, Disraeli visited Gunnersbury three weeks later, and on January 4 the Foreign Secretary Malmesbury complained that "Disraeli *never reads a word of my papers*" which go round and knows nothing but what the Jews at Paris and London tell him": Monypenny and Buckle, *Disraeli*, vol. IV, pp. 186f., 224.

254 RAL, RFamP/D 4, Louisa *Journal*, Jan. 30, 1849; CPHDCM, 637/1/317, school report on Natty by Dr Classen, Direktor of Frankfurt Gymnasium, Oct. 5, 1854. Natty studied for three years there. On the education of female Rothschilds at this period, see Davis, *English Rothschilds*, pp. 64, 90f.; Heuberger, *Rothschilds*, p. 100.

255 RAL, XI/109/73/1, Cartmell to Smith, Oct. 14, 1849.

256 RA, F35A/47, Mayer [spelt Meyer here], New Court, to Prince Albert, Oct. 22, 1849; RA, F35A/48, Dean of Windsor, George Neville Grenville, Butleigh, to Colonel Charles Phipps, Oct. 26.

257 RAL, XI/109/73/1, Arthur Cohen, Magdalene College, to Mayer, Nov. 21, 1849. Davis, *English Roth-schilds*, pp. 105ff.; Endelman, *Radical assimilation*, p. 78. Cohen went on to distinguish himself: having been president of the Union and Third Wrangler, he became a successful barrister, representing Britain at the International Court of Justice at the Hague, a Liberal MP and, in 1906, a Privy Councillor.

258 RAL, RFamC/3/62, Natty, Cambridge, to his parents, London, undated, *c.* 1860; Davis, *English Roth-schilds*, pp. 116f.

259 RAL, RFamC/3/83, Natty, Cambridge, to his parents, London, Feb. 16, 1862.

260 RAL, RFamC/3/83, Natty, Cambridge, to his parents, London, Feb. 1, 1860.

261 RAL, RFamC/21, Charlotte, London, to Leo, Cambridge, Oct. 27, 1864.

262 Endelman, *Radical assimilation*, p. 78.

263 RAL, RFamC/3/82, Natty, Cambridge, to his parents, London, undated, *c.* 1860.

264 RAL, XI/109/69A/1, Nat, Paris, to his brothers, London, Oct. 3, 1848; RAL, XI/109/70/4, same to same, March 30, 1849; RAL, XI/109/71/1, April 10; RAL, XI/109/72/3, Lionel, Frankfurt, to Mayer, Sept. 23.

265 RAL, XI/109/73/1, Lionel, Freiwaldau, to Mayer, London, Sept. 10, 1849.

266 RAL, XI/109/72/3, J. G. ["Paddy"] to Mayer, London, Sept. 22, 1849.

267 RAL, XI/109/73/3, Hannah, Frankfurt, to Lionel, London, Dec. 11, 1849.

268 Heuberger, *Rothschilds*, pp. 171ff.; Muhlstein, *Baron James*, p. 211. Cf. Kindleberger, *Economic growth*, p. 45.

269 Beales, *Castlereagh to Gladstone*, p. 89. The dukes of Sutherland were a rare exception.

270 Spencer-Silver, *Pugin's builder*, pp. 173–9. Natty thought his parents had underpaid Myers: RAL, RFamC/3/57, Natty, Cambridge, to his parents, London, undated, *c.* 1861.

271 Prevost-Marcilhacy, *Rothschild*, p. 89; Davis, *English Rothschilds*, p. 92f.

272 Prevost-Marcilhacy, *Rothschild*, pp. 89ff., 104, 111–13, 139, 337ff. For Henry James's impressions of the interior, see Davis, *English Rothschilds*, pp. 164f. Mayer also bought Palace House at Newmarket in 1857, but this was primarily to provide a base for his stud farm and the house was left largely unaltered until George Devey's work in 1867–8.

273 Prevost-Marcilhacy, *Rothschild*, pp. 100f., 336f.; Davis, *English Rothschilds*, p. 99.

274 RAL, RFamC/21, Charlotte, Paris, to Lionel, Natty and Alfred, Sept. 18, 1864: "Alphonse complains of

his French workmen, while the great Baron calls all the English people, who built his castle[,] thieves and pickpockets."

275 Muhlstein, *Baron James*, p. 208.

276 Allfrey, *Jewish Court*, p. 40.

277 Drumont, *France juive*, vol. II, pp. 108–18.

278 RAL, XI/109/86, Evelina, Paris, to Lionel, undated, *c.* 1860. Cf. Prevost-Marcilhacy, *Rothschild*, pp. 74f., 93–7, 105ff., 122–36, 140, 308ff.; Plessis, *Banque de France*, vol. II, p. 238; Rothschild, *Whims*, pp. 7–28.

279 Prevost-Marcilhacy, *Rothschild*, pp. 101f., 136, 349f.

280 *Ibid.*, pp. 98ff., 117–21, 137f., 307f.

281 RAL, RFamC/6/16, Evelina, Paris, to Charlotte, London, Sept. 12, probably 1860. I am grateful to Lionel de Rothschild for this reference.

282 RAL, RFamC/21, Charlotte, Ferrières, to Lionel, Natty and Alfred, London, Sept. 29, 1864; Charlotte to Leo, Nov. 16; same to same, Sept. 19, 1865; Oct. 27.

283 RAL, RFamC/21, Charlotte, Boulogne, to Leo, Cambridge, Sept. 21, 1864.

284 Rothschild, Garton and Rothschild, *Rothschild Gardens*, pp. 158ff.

285 Prevost-Marcilhacy, *Rothschild*, pp. 137f., 141.

286 Even this temporary residence struck Macaulay as "a paradise": Lionel told him he had offered £300,000 for the house and its eight or ten acres of garden, but had been refused: Pinney (ed.), *Macaulay letters*, vol. VI, pp. 227f.

287 Dasent, *Piccadilly*, pp. 138f., 144, 289; Prevost-Marcilhacy, *Rothschild*, pp. 110, 335f.; Spencer-Silver, *Pugin's builder*, pp. 179ff.; Davis, *English Rothschilds*, p. 99.

288 The Paris houses of the 1850s and 1860s were Nat's at 33 rue du Faubourg-Saint-Honoré, which he acquired in 1856; Alphonse's at 4 rue Saint-Florentin; Gustave's at 23 avenue Marigny; Salomon James's at 3–5 rue de Messine; and Adolph's at 45–9 rue de Monceau, bought from Eugène Pereire in 1868: Prevost-Marcilhacy, *Rothschild*, pp. 103, 152ff., 218, 221f., 231, 259, 312f., 315f., 322f.

289 RAL, RFamC/21, Charlotte, Paris, to Lionel, Nathaniel and Alfred, London, Sept. 20, 1864.

290 RAL, RFamC/21, Charlotte, London, to Leopold, March 15, 1865; same to same, Oxford, Sept. 15; Sept. 19.

291 Goncourt, *Journal*, vol. I, pp. 922f., 1050.

292 See Hall, "English Rothschilds as collectors," pp. 275f., on Lionel's collection of "silver, silver-gilt, enamels, ivories, mother-of-pearl, rock crystals and hardstones carved and mounted, mounted tusks, horns, shells and nuts, Renaissance jewels, snuff boxes, Venetian and Flemish glass, majolica, Palissy and Henri II wares"—altogether 743 items when an inventory was made in 1882. Hall calls this "the greatest assemblage of such objects ever accumulated by a private individual."

293 RAL, T10/138, Nat, Paris, to his brothers, London, March 15, 1869; RAL, T10/146, Gustave to his cousins, London, March 16.

294 RAL, RFamC/21, Charlotte, London, to Leopold, Oct. 16, 1865. Cf. Kynaston, *City*, vol. I, p. 245.

TWO   *The Era of Mobility (1849–1858)*

1 Cavour, *Nouvelles lettres*, pp. 407f.

2 Viel-Castel, *Mémoires*, vol. IV, p. 139. Cf. Corti, *Reign*, pp. 279–82.

3 RAL, Moscow 224, Betty, Paris, to Alphonse, New York, undated, *c.* Nov. 20, 1848; same to same, Dec. 6.

4 RAL, Moscow 224, Betty, Paris, to Alphonse, New York, Jan. 11, 1849.

5 Wiebe *et al.* (eds), *Disraeli letters*, vol. V, p. 322.

6 RAL, Moscow 224, Betty, Paris, to Alphonse, New York, April 26, 1849.

7 RAL, Moscow 224, Betty, Paris, to Alphonse, New York, Feb. 7, 1849; same to same, May 3; June 14.

8 RAL, RFamC/1/178, Hannah, Paris, to Lionel, London, June 13, 1850.

9 RAL, XI/109/74, James, Paris, to his nephews, London, Feb. 13, 1850; same to same, March 9.

10 RAL, XI/109/74, James, Paris, to his nephews, London, Jan. 13, 1850. See also AN, 132 AQ 5902, James to Alphonse, Jan. 3; RAL, XI/109/75, James to his nephews, April 17; same to same, April 22; Oct. 23.

11 Grunwald, "Europe's railways," pp. 170, 208 and n.

12 RAL, XI/109/74, James, Paris, to his nephews, London, Jan. 31, 1850. See also Castellane, *Journal*, vol. IV, p. 203; RAL, XI/109/79, James to his nephews, Oct. 26, 1851.

13   RAL, XI/109/74, James, Paris, to his nephews, London, Feb. 2, 1850.

14   Gille, *Maison Rothschild*, vol. II, pp. 56f.

15   RAL, XI/109/76, James, Paris, to his nephews, London, Sept. 30, 1850; same to same, Dec. 12; Dec. 14; Dec. 21; Dec. 23; Dec. 29.

16   Bouvier, *Rothschild*, pp. 132f.

17   RAL, XI/109/74, James, Paris, to his nephews, London, Feb. 1, 1850; same to same, May 23.

18   RAL, XI/109/74, James, Paris, to his nephews, London, Feb. 25, 1850.

19   RAL, XI/109/77, James, Paris, to his nephews, London, Nov. 17; same to same, Nov. 19; Nov. 22; Nov. 23; Nov. 24; Nov. 25; Nov. 29. Cf. Corti, *Reign*, pp. 284f. The crisis blew over when Frederick William IV agreed at Olmütz to abandon the so-called "Erfurt Union" created by his minister Radowitz and to restore the old Metternichian Confederation, which then imposed "executions" (i.e. binding decisions) in Holstein (to the advantage of the Danes) and Hesse-Kassel (to the advantage of the unpopular Elector).

20   RAL, XI/109/75, James, Paris, to his nephews, London, May 13, 1850; RAL, XI/109/79, same to same, Nov. 18, 1851.

21   RAL, XI/109/77, James, Paris, to his nephews, London, Oct. 28, 1850. See also RAL, XI/109/79, same to same, Oct. 23, 1851: "[K]ommt ja etwas, was zwar erst in einiger Zeit geschehen wird, so ist besser man hat nicht alles in einer Stadt"; and Nov. 24.

22   RAL, XI/109/79, James, Paris, to his nephews, London, Oct. 11, 1851. See also Hübner, *Neuf ans*, vol. I, p. 12.

23   Apponyi, *Vingt-cinq ans*, vol. IV, p. 329f. He had fallen down the stairs at Princess Lieven's.

24   RAL, XI/109/79, James, Paris, to his nephews, London, Dec. 12, 1851.

25   Apponyi, *Vingt-cinq Ans*, vol. IV, p. 372. See also Cohen, *Lady de Rothschild*, p. 58.

26   Corti, *Reign*, p. 286. For examples of his ambivalence towards the republican regime, see RAL, XI/109/79, James, Paris, to his nephews, London, Oct. 29, 1851; same to same, Nov. 6; Nov. 20.

27   Bouvier, *Rothschild*, pp. 132f.; Plessis, *Banque de France*, vol. III, p. 79.

28   Caron, "France."

29   RAL, XI/109/74, James, Paris, to his nephews, London, Jan. 15, 1850.

30   RAL, XI/109/74, James, Paris, to his nephews, London, Jan. 15, 1850; same to same, Jan. 20.

31   RAL, XI/109/79, James, Paris, to his nephews, London, Dec. 3, 1851; same to same, Dec. 5; Dec. 6. James regarded the rise of funds after the coup as having been orchestrated by Napoleon's supporters, i.e. the Foulds.

32   RAL, XI/109/77, James, Paris, to his nephews, London, Oct. 28, 1850.

33   RAL, XI/109/79, James, Paris, to his nephews, London, Dec. 19, 1851.

34   RAL, XI/109/79, James, Paris, to his nephews, London, Dec. 26, 1851.

35   Apponyi, *Vingt-cinq ans*, vol. IV, p. 388.

36   RAL, XI/109/80, James, Paris, to his nephews, London, Jan. 15, 1852; RAL, XI/109/81, same to same, June 23.

37   RAL, XI/109/82, James, Paris, to his nephews, London, Oct. 1, 1852.

38   Hübner, *Neuf ans*, p. 97.

39   *Ibid.*, p. 120.

40   Corti, *Reign*, pp. 290, 353f.

41   Hübner, *Neuf ans*, pp. 100f. Cf. Bertaut, *Bourse*, pp. 264–72; Corti, *Reign*, pp. 350–53; Corley, *Democratic despot*, p. 139.

42   See e.g., Woodward, "Economic factors," p. 101; Corti, *Reign*, pp. 291f.; Bouvier, *Rothschild*, pp. 146–8; Gille, *Maison Rothschild*, vol. II, pp. 93–101; Girard, *Travaux publics*, p. 82; Lefèvre, *Chemins de fer et politique*, p. 21; Blanchard, "Railway policy," p. 107; Agulhon, *Republican experiment*, pp. 181f.; Landes, "Old and new," p. 113; Kemp, *Economic forces*, p. 167f. The Viel-Castel passage quoting Fould does not in fact refer to the foundation of the Crédit Mobilier at all but to that of the Crédit Foncier, a mortgage bank: *Mémoires*, vol. IV, p. 139. However, the fact that Isaac Pereire's son Eugène married Achille Fould's daughter has encouraged the assumption that the Crédit Mobilier was prefigured.

43   Clough, *France*, p. 173; Palmade, *Capitalism*, pp. 122–4. Cf. Gerschenkron, *Economic backwardness*.

44   Kindleberger, *Financial history*, pp. 88, 93, 108f.

45   Landes, "Old and new," pp. 114–20, 124f.; Bergeron, *Rothschild*, p. 83; Kemp, *Economic forces*, pp. 163–5; Palmade, *Capitalism*, pp. 128–36.

46   Ribeill, *Révolution ferroviaire*, p. 117.

47 Bismarck, *Gesammelte Werke*, vol. XIV/1, p. 415.

48 Landes, "Old and new," pp. 112f.; Palmade, *Capitalism*, pp. 139–48.

49 Castellane, *Journal*, vol. IV, p. 203.

50 Feydeau, *Mémoires*, pp. 128–41.

51 *Ibid.*, pp. 458–59.

52 *Ibid.*, pp. 110–21.

53 Mirès, *A mes juges*, pp. 74–89. Cf. Plenge, *Crédit Mobilier*, pp. 63f.

54 Anon., *M. Mirès et M. de Rothschild*, pp. 6ff.

55 Ribeill, *Révolution ferroviaire*, pp. 469–73.

56 CPHDCM, 637/1/131–11, Bilan deRF, Dec. 31, 1851.

57 Apponyi, *Vingt-cinq ans*, vol. IV, p. 449.

58 Ribeill, *Révolution ferroviaire*, p. 54; Lévy-Leboyer, "Capital investment," p. 257.

59 Gille, *Maison Rothschild*, vol. II, pp. 166–9; Palmade, *Capitalism*, pp. 139–48, 154; Cameron, *France and Europe*, pp. 213ff.; Bouvier, *Rothschild*, pp. 134–6, 146–8; Girard, *Travaux publics*, p. 87; Corti, *Reign*, p. 287.

60 RAL, XI/109/79, James, Paris, to his nephews, London, Dec. 21, 1851; same to same, Dec. 22; Dec. 24; Dec. 25.

61 RAL, XI/109/79, James, Paris, to his nephews, London, [postscript to a letter from Nat], Dec. 16, 1851.

62 Bouvier, *Rothschild*, pp. 133f.; Gille, *Maison Rothschild*, vol. II, p. 160f.; Agulhon, *Republican experiment*, pp. 181f.

63 Gille, *Maison Rothschild*, vol. II, pp. 169–73; Girard, *Travaux publics*, pp. 95ff.

64 Cameron, *France and Europe*, pp. 134–44; *idem*, "France," p. 115; Ribeill, *Révolution ferroviaire*, p. 118.

65 Braudel and Labrousse, *Histoire économique*, vol. III, pp. 377–80.

66 Gille, *Maison Rothschild*, vol. II, pp. 107–9.

67 Dupont-Ferrier, *Marché financier*, pp. 113–16. See also Cameron, *France and Europe*, pp. 131f.; Grunwald, "Europe's railways," pp. 184ff. See also Marion, *Histoire financière*, vol. V, pp. 343–8.

68 Aycard, *Crédit Mobilier*, pp. 46–8.

69 Corti, *Reign*, pp. 292f.; Braudel and Labrousse, *Histoire économique*, vol. III, pp. 393–7.

70 Cameron, *France and Europe*, pp. 134–44; Braudel and Labrousse, *Histoire économique*, vol. III, pp. 382f. The capital took the form of 120,000 shares with a nominal price of 500 francs each.

71 See e.g. Colling, *Roman de la finance*, pp. 75–7; Plenge, *Crédit Mobilier*, pp. 75f.

72 Prevost-Marcilhacy, *Rothschild*, p. 83. Persigny was told by Lionel that the purchase of d'Armainvilliers angered James more than the founding of the Crédit Mobilier: Gille, *Maison Rothschild*, vol. II, p. 116. On James's resolve never to encounter the Pereires at the train station which the two estates shared, see Goncourt, *Journal*, vol. I, p. 1156.

73 Gille, *Maison Rothschild*, vol. II, pp. 115f.

74 *Ibid.*, pp. 101–3, 121; Brogan, *French nation*, pp. 125–30.

75 Marion, *Histoire financière*, vol. V, pp. 343–8.

76 Plessis, *Banque de France*, vol. III, pp. 149–54.

77 Palmade, *Capitalism*, pp. 139–48; Corti, *Reign*, p. 292.

78 Caron, "France"; Lévy-Leboyer, "Capital investment," p. 257.

79 Ribeill, *Révolution ferroviaire*, p. 120.

80 *Ibid.*, pp. 157f.

81 Cameron, *France and Europe*, pp. 213–17; Gille, *Maison Rothschild*, vol. II, pp. 169–73; Schnerb, *Rouher*, pp. 77–82.

82 Plessis, *Banque de France*, vol. II, p.197.

83 Ayer, *Century of finance*, pp. 44f.; Davis, *English Rothshilds*, pp. 138f.

84 Gille, *Maison Rothschild*, vol. II, pp. 183f.

85 Bouvier, *Rothschild*, p. 148.

86 Gille, *Maison Rothschild*, vol. II, pp. 107, 98–200; Palmade, *Capitalism*, pp.139–48.

87 Palmade, *Capitalism*, p. 148; Braudel and Labrousse, *Histoire économique*, vol. III, pp. 382f., 397–400, 442f.; Cameron, *France and Europe*, pp. 145f.; Kemp, *Economic forces*, p. 167f.

88 Stürmer *et al.*, *Striking the balance*, pp. 136–40; Cameron, *France and Europe*, pp. 148–51; Kitchen, *Political Economy*, pp. 92f.; Stern, *Gold and iron*, p. 10.

89 Gille, *Maison Rothschild*, vol. II, p. 224.

90   *Ibid.*, pp. 252f; Cameron, *France and Europe*, p. 166.

91   Jurk, "Other Rothschilds," pp. 44ff.

92   Born Israel Beer Josaphat, Reuter had begun his career as a clerk in his uncle's bank at Göttingen, where he met the telegraph pioneer Karl Friedrich Gauss. In 1840 he started work for Charles Havas's Paris-based *Correspondance Garnier*, which translated foreign press reports into French and in 1850 moved to London, where he established the Reuter agency. Cf. Read, *Power of news*, p. 18.

93   RAL, T6/271, Reuter, Aachen, to NMR, April 27, 1850.

94   RAL, XI/109/75, James, Paris, to his nephews, London, April 1, 1850; RAL, XI/109/77, same to same, Nov. 19; RAL, XI/109/78, same to same, April 8, 1851 [postscript to a letter from Nat]; AN, 132 AQ 5902, James, Carlsbad, to his nephews and sons, July 11, 1858.

95   RAL, XI/109/88/1, Mayer Carl, Frankfurt, to his cousins and nephews, London, May 4, 1866; RAL, XI/109/97/1, Alphonse, Paris, to his cousins, London, March 7, 1869; RAL, T11/7, same to same, April 2; RAL, T12/107, April 18, 1876.

96   RAL, Moscow 224, Betty, Paris, to Alphonse, New York, Dec. 30, 1848; same to same, Feb. 20, 1849; March 7.

97   RAL, Moscow 224, Betty, Paris, to Alphonse, New York, March 24, 1849; same to same, April 4; May 16; May 24.

98   RAL, XI/109/72/2, Lionel, Wildbad, to Anthony, Paris, Aug. 15, 1849.

99   RAL, XI/109/73/1, Alphonse, Paris, to Anthony, Oct. 17, 1849; Castellane, *Journal*, vol. IV, p. 203.

100 RAL, T6/268, P. A. Curtis, New York, to NMR, April 1, 1850.

101 RAL, Moscow 224, Betty, Paris, to Alphonse, New York, March 24; same to same, April 4, 1849.

102 RAL, XI/109/73/2, Alphonse, Paris, to Anthony, London, undated, *c.* Nov. 1849.

103 RAL, Moscow 224, Betty, Paris, to Alphonse, New York, April 4, 1849.

104 RAL, XI/109/73/1, Belmont, New York, to NMR, Oct. 1, 1849. It was Perry who a few years later opened Japan to international trade, though this does not seem to have aroused much interest in New Court.

105 Katz, *Belmont*, p. 33; Glanz, "Rothschild legend," pp. 15–19.

106 AN, 132 AQ 5902, James de Rothschild, Carlsbad, to his sons, July 19, 1858.

107 RAL, XI/109/78, James, Paris, to his nephews, London [postscript to an undated letter from Nat], *c.* May 1851.

108 RAL, XI/109/71/2, Lionel Davidson, Paris, to NMR, May 2, 1849; RAL, XI/109/71/2, Benjamin Davidson, Valparaiso, to NMR, May 4; AN, 132 AQ 5417/1M21, NMR to deRF, Nov. 23.

109 RAL, XI/109/74, James, Paris, to his nephews, London, Feb. 7, 1850; RAL, XI/109/74, same to same, Feb. 21; AN, 132 AQ 5420/1M24, NMR, London, to Benjamin Davidson, San Francisco, March 8.

110 RAL, XI/109/78, James, Paris, to his nephews, London, [postscript to an undated letter from Nat], *c.* May 1851; AN, 132 AQ 5423/1M27, L. Davidson, Mexico to NMR, May 21; RAL, XI/109/79, James to his nephews, Oct. 1; RAL, T6/282, John Luck, San Francisco, to NMR, April 29, 1852.

111 AN, 132 AQ 5463/1M69, I. May, San Francisco, to NMR, Feb. 18, 1862.

112 AN, 132 AQ 5433/1M37&38, Nathaniel Davidson, San Rafael, to NMR, Nov. 17, 1853; AN, 132 AQ 5443/1M48, same, Mexico, to same, Dec. 30, 1856; AN, 132 AQ 5452/1M58, same to same, Dec. 2; AN, 132 AQ 5453/1M59, same to same, April 18, 1859; AN, 132 AQ 5455/1M61, Sept. 1; Dec. 6.

113 Levy, "Brazilian public debt," pp. 214–20.

114 Gille, *Maison Rothschild*, vol. II, pp. 410–13.

115 RAL, RFamC/4/223, Lionel, London, to Leo, Cambridge, Oct. 12, 1863; RAL, XI/109/86/1, Lionel, Brighton, to Anthony, undated, *c.* 1864.

116 RAL, XI/109/87/1, Nat, Paris, to Mayer, London, undated, *c.* 1865 (three letters); RAL, RFamC/21, Charlotte, London, to Leo, Cambridge, Feb. 13; same to same, May 4; RAL, XI/109/87/1, Lionel, Wiesbaden, to his brothers and Natty, London, Aug. 19; same to same, Aug. 20; Sept. 2; same, Paris, to same, Sept. 5; RAL, RFamC/21, Charlotte to Leo, Sept. 13; same to same, Aug. 20, 1866. Cf. Gille, *Maison Rothschild*, vol. II, pp. 458ff.

117 Ayer, *Century of finance*.

118 Fernández-Armesto, *Millennium*, p. 293.

119 RAL, T6/287, Cramptons, Hamburg & Co, Shanghai, Nov. 1, 1853; RAL, T6/299, same to same, April 12; RAL, XI/115/9B, July 12, 1856; RAL, T6/303, July 31; RAL, XI/115/9B, Sept. 5; Oct. 6.

120 RAL, XI/109/80, James, Paris, to his nephews, London, Jan. 15, 1852; RAL, T6/306 and 308,

Schoene, Kilburn & Co., Calcutta, to NMR, May 16, 1857; RAL, T6/325, same to same, Nov. 25; RAL, T6/318, April 9, 1858.

121 Feydeau, *Mémoires*, pp. 143–8.

122 RAL, T6/278, W. H. Burlow, Sydney, to NMR, June 20, 1852. AN, 132 AQ 5429/1M33, NMR to deRF, Jan. 3, 1853.

123 AN, 132 AQ 5420/1M24, NMR to deRF, Aug. 22, 1853.

124 RAL, XI/115/9A, Jeffrey Cullen, Melbourne, to NMR, April 7, 1855; same to same, April 18; May 1; Sept. 29; RAL, XI/115/9A, July 9, 1856.

125 Flandreau, *L'or du monde*, pp. 200–11.

126 Green, "Precious heritage," pp. 280ff.

127 RAL, XI/109/73/2, Mr Mathison, Royal Mint, to NMR, Nov. 24, 1849; RAL, XI/109/73/3, Nat, Paris, to his brothers, London, Dec. 27; RAL, T6/284, NMR to Capt. H. D. Harness, Deputy Master of the Royal Mint, Jan. 26, 1852; AN, 132 AQ 5902, James, Gastein, to Salomon and his children, Paris, June 10; AN, 132 AQ 5428/1M32, Master of the Royal Mint to deRF, Oct. 22; RAL, T6/285, NMR to Hankey, Dec. 10. Cf. Davis, *English Rothschilds*, p. 140; Clapham, *Bank of England*, vol. II, p. 279; Kirke Rose, *Metallurgy of gold*, p. 375; Green, *New world of gold*, pp. 11, 110; White, *Silver*, p. 97; Letcher, *Gold mines*, p. 441. The years 1852–3 also saw the appearance of two new brokers, Samuel Montagu & Co. and Pixley & Haggard (later Pixley & Abell), and another new refinery established by Henry Lewis Raphael.

128 Matthew (ed.), *Gladstone diaries*, vol. VI, p. 162.

129 Flandreau, *L'or du monde*, pp. 212ff. Flandreau has gone so far as to say that "bimetallism was the Rothschilds' system": *ibid.*, pp. 193ff.

130 AN, 132 AQ 5432/1M36, NMR to deRF, July 18, 1853.

131 AN, 132 AQ 5431/1M35, Itzel, London, to James, Paris, June 9, 1853; CPHDCM, 637/1/122/40, Salomon, Vienna, to Anselm, Frankfurt, July 11.

132 Conacher, *Aberdeen coalition*, p. 189.

133 Hübner, *Neuf ans*, pp. 203, 320. Cf. Corti, *Reign*, pp. 355f.

134 Darmstadter, *Bismarck*, p. 141; Pflanze, *Bismarck*, vol. II, p. 81.

135 Trevelyan, *Life of Bright*, p. 234.

136 RAL, XI/109/74, James, Paris, to his nephews, London, Jan. 15, 1850; RAL, RFamC/1/177, Hannah, Frankfurt, to Lionel, London, Jan. 24. The deal was brokered by the St Petersburg banker Baron Ludwig von Stieglitz.

137 Cobden, still fulminating on behalf of the Hungarians, denounced it as an "unholy and infamous transaction"; in fact, like so many loans in this period, the funds raised were earmarked for railway construction: Ziegler, *Sixth great power*, p. 171.

138 It is nevertheless true that Barings continued to pay interest on the earlier Russian bonds; the idea of prohibiting this did not occur to the British Foreign Secretary Clarendon, though he was aware that it was going on. Indeed, Russian bonds continued to be traded in London throughout the war: *ibid.*, p. 173.

139 RA, G45/6, Palmerston, Piccadilly, to Queen Victoria, Feb. 22, 1856. The terms of these loans were rather complex. The terms for the 1855 loan were: for every £100 in cash subscribed, £100 in 3 per cent consols at par, with an additional annuity of 14s 6d terminable in 30 years (implying an effective interest rate of 3.725 per cent); the first 1856 loan: for every £100 in cash, £111 2s 2d in 3 per cents (i.e. 3.33 per cent, compared with Lionel's offer of £112 5s or 3.37 per cent); and the second 1856 loan: for £100 in cash, £107 10s 7d in 3 per cents (i.e. 3.23 per cent, compared with Lionel's offer of £108 or 3.24 per cent). The average yield on consols in February 1856 was 3.29 per cent and in May 3.21, leaving a difference of 0.04 and 0.02 per cent respectively. Cf. *The Times*, May 15, 1856, p. 4; May 20, p. 11; Buxton, *Finance*, vol. I, pp. 147ff.; Hargreaves, *National debt*, pp. 168ff.; Davis, *English Rothschilds*, pp. 100f., 138–9; Kynaston, *Cazenove*, p. 46.

140 The national debt at this time was around 5,012 million francs. The conversion affected around 3,740 million of this, and implied an annual saving of around 19 million francs.

141 AN, 132 AQ A-12–2/7, Agreement between Bineau and deRF, March 19, 1852; Revised agreement, March 24; Agreement between Bineau and James, Aug. 27; AN, 132 AQ 32 A-12–2/8, Agreement between Bineau and deRF, Feb. 7, 1853. Altogether, the Paris house agreed to buy rentes with a capital value of 25 million francs, charging the government a 0.75 per cent commission. It seems that James

also demanded an extension of one of his railway concessions as a secret condition of the arrangement: RAL, XI/109/80, James, Paris, to his nephews, London [postscript to an undated letter from Nat], *c.* March; RAL, XI/109/81, same to same, April 2.

142   Plessis, *Banque de France*, vol. III, pp. 99–104; Gille, *Maison Rothschild*, vol. II, pp. 57f.

143   Saxe-Coburg-Gotha, *Memoirs*, vol. III, p. 709. I am grateful to Professor Stanley Weintraub for this reference. See also Corti, *Reign*, p. 356. Both Weintraub and Corti cast doubt on the reliability of the source, but there is no question that James was keen to make the loan.

144   Mirès, *À mes juges*, pp. 23–6, 95; Marion, *Histoire financière*, vol. V, p. 364; Dupont-Ferrier, *Marché financier*, pp. 72–4; Gille, *Maison Rothschild*, vol. II, pp. 123–31; Ponteil, *Institutions*, pp. 397f.

145   Corley, *Democratic despot*, p. 164.

146   Corti, *Reign*, pp. 359f.; Gille, *Maison Rothschild*, vol. II, pp. 273–5; Aycard, *Crédit Mobilier*, pp. 135–8; Ayer, *Century of finance*, pp. 44f. Investors were offered 3 per cents at an effective price of 89.46 or 4.5 per cents at 63.23.

147   Gille, *Maison Rothschild*, vol. II, pp. 255f.

148   *Ibid.*, pp. 147–50; Dupont-Ferrier, *Marché financier*, pp. 75–80. Cf. Mirès, *A mes juges*, p. 96.

149   RAL, T6/289, Landau, Constantinople, to NMR, Aug. 30, 1855. The 4 per cent bonds were taken at a price of 102.675, a significantly more generous offer than that made by Palmer, MacKillop & Dent. Cf. Ayer, *Century of finance*, pp. 46f.; Gille, *Maison Rothschild*, vol. II, pp. 290ff., 298ff., 575–80; Cameron, *France and Europe*, pp. 459f.

150   Gille, *Maison Rothschild*, vol. II, pp. 260–65, 297. Interestingly, the Paris house was being encouraged by the French government to establish the proposed bank rather than leave the field clear to "English capital," whereas it was the London house which had the more sceptical view of Turkey's economic prospects.

151   Gille, *Maison Rothschild*, vol. II, pp. 348, 367–9, 606–8. Cf. AN, 132 AQ 5441/1M46, NMR to deRF, Jan. 22, 1856; AN, 132 AQ 5445/1M51, same to same, Jan. 1; Jan. 19; AN, 132 AQ 5902, James, Carlsbad, to his children, Paris, June 24, 1858.

152   Huertas, *Economic growth*, pp. 36–50.

153   Apponyi, *Vingt-cinq ans*, vol. IV, pp. 329f.

154   Corti, *Reign*, pp. 345f., 359.

155   *Ibid.*, pp. 347–9. Cf. Gille, *Maison Rothschild*, vol. II, p. 145.

156   AN, 132 AQ 3/1, Loan agreement between Austrian government and NMR, May 24, 1852. £2.25 million of the loan was issued in London at 90, the rest in Frankfurt and Paris. Cf. Ayer, *Century of finance*, pp. 42f.; Corti, *Reign*, pp. 346f.; Gille, *Maison Rothschild*, vol. II, pp. 66–8. The London house charged 1.5 per cent commission, a further 0.5 per cent brokerage and 0.2 per cent on the interest payments due to bondholders.

157   AN, 132 AQ 5435/1M40, SMR to deRF, Feb. 11, 1854; AN, 132 AQ 5435/1M33, NMR to deRF, Feb. 24. Cf. Gille, *Maison Rothschild*, vol. II, pp. 145–7; Macartney, *Habsburg Empire*, p. 484; Jenks, *Francis Joseph*, p. 48.

158   RAL, XI/109/79, James, Paris, to his nephews, London [postscript to a letter from Nat], Sept. 25, 1851.

159   Corti, *Reign*, pp. 319–27; Darmstadter, *Bismarck*, p. 119.

160   Corti, *Reign*, p. 329. Thun was replaced soon after and the Frankfurt protest shelved. Bismarck attributed this Austrian volte-face to "the efforts of the Rothschilds": "That there are occasions when other but purely business considerations are a determining factor on the attitude of the House of Rothschild in financial operations seems to me to be indicated by the success with which Austria has secured the financial services of the House, since I am convinced that, apart from the financial profit to be gained by such transactions, the influence which the Imperial Government was able to bring to bear upon the Jewish problem at Frankfurt profoundly affected the House of Rothschild": *ibid.*, pp. 331f., 334.

161   Ford (ed.), *Correspondence of William I and Bismarck*, vol. II, p. 25.

162   Corti, *Reign*, pp. 317–20, 330f. (The allusion is to Horace, *Odes*, 3.3.)

163   *Ibid.*, pp. 331ff.

164   *Ibid.*, pp. 336–40. The Rothschilds offered to take 15 million thalers in 4.5 per cent at 90, implying a yield of 5 per cent, compared with the Prussian minimum of 93 (4.8 per cent). Cf. Gille, *Maison Rothschild*, vol. II, pp. 142–4, 281–6.

165   Corti, *Reign*, pp. 341–3. Mayer Carl, he reported, "does not go to big functions, and when he does wear orders, prefers to wear the Greek Order of the Redeemer, or the Spanish Order of Isabella the Catholic.

On the occasion of the official reception which I myself gave . . . to celebrate the marriage of H.R.H. Prince Frederick William, which he would have had to attend in uniform, he excused himself on the grounds of ill-health, it being painful to him to wear the Red Eagle decoration for non-Christians, as he would have had to do on that occasion. I draw a similar inference from the fact that whenever he comes to dine with me, he merely wears the Ribbon of the Order of the Red Eagle in his buttonhole." On James's order of 1861, see Stern, *Gold and iron*, p. 115. James urged Bleichröder to keep the award out of the Berlin press, for fear of arousing hostile comment.

166 Gille, *Maison Rothschild*, vol. II, pp. 59–64, 131–3, 347–8, 394, 437–9, 539–42. The principal operations of the period were the somewhat unsuccessful 1853 conversion; the 30 million franc loan of 1854, which was shared between the Banque Nationale, the Rothschilds and the Société Générale; and the 15 million franc loan of 1862, handled by the same trio.

167 Loans to the Duchy totalled 19.4 million gulden between 1849 and 1861: Berghoeffer, *Meyer Amschel*, pp. 206–28.

168 Carl had demanded that Jews be allowed to live where they please in the Papal states and that all special taxes and separate forms of procedure in the courts be abolished. In January, Pius IX gave James a written assurance through the Papal nuncio in Paris that these things would be done. However, when Carl visited Rome four months later, he found little sign of improvement; and the Roman Jews formally complained to James the following year. Another appeal on behalf of the Roman Jews was made by Anselm in 1857. Rather as with the Jews of Damascus and later the Christians of Jerusalem, the Jews of Rome became a political "football" between the great powers, in this case Austria and France. The Rothschilds seem to have played one off against the other rather successfully, though without achieving much for their co-religionists.

169 Corti, *Reign*, pp. 295–300, 366; Gille, *Maison Rothschild*, vol. II, pp. 72ff.; Scott, *Roman question*, pp. 80–82. The bonds were issued at prices of 77.5 to 78, and the Rothschilds retained a 3 per cent commission.

170 Gille, *Maison Rothschild*, vol. II, pp.134–6, 351–3; Cameron, "Papal Finance," pp. 132–5; Cameron, *France and Europe*, p. 432f.

171 See Mirès, *A mes juges*, pp. 97–100. According to this less than objective acccount, James first refused the business, then sought—successfully—to spoil it for Mirès. The author may well, of course, have been seeking a scapegoat for his own failure. Cf. Cameron, *France and Europe*, pp. 131f.; Gille, *Maison Rothschild*, vol. II, pp. 287–9.

172 RAL, XI/109/74, James, Paris, to his nephews, London, Feb. 5, 1850; RAL, XI/109/75, same to same, April 19; April 26; RAL, XI/109/77, same, Turin, to same, Oct. 2; same, Paris, to same, Oct. 10; Oct. 21. For Cavour's view, Cavour, *Nouvelles lettres*, pp. 395, 397ff. Cf. Cameron, *France and Europe*, pp. 435–52; Corti, *Reign*, pp. 301–4; Gille, *Maison Rothschild*, vol. II, pp. 81–3.

173 Cavour, *Nouvelles lettres*, pp. 407f.; Corti, *Reign*, pp. 304ff.; Gille, *Maison Rothschild*, vol. II, pp. 85–7. (Emphasis in original.)

174 Cavour, *Politique*, pp. 1f.; Corti, *Reign*, pp. 305ff.; Whyte, *Life and letters of Cavour*, pp. 77–9; Mack Smith, *Cavour*, pp. 54f.

175 Cavour, *Politique*, pp. 6f., 11; Kynaston, *City*, vol. I, pp. 173f.

176 RAL, XI/109/78, James, Paris, to his nephews, London, June 9, 1851; same to same, June 10; [postscript to a letter from Nat], June 24. Cf. Cavour, *Nouvelles lettres*, p. 425.

177 RAL, XI/109/79, James, Paris, to his nephews, London, July 2, 1851; same to same, July 3; July 4; [postscript to a letter from Nat], July 30.

178 Cavour, *Nouvelles lettres*, p. 425.

179 CPHDCM, 637/1/131–11, Bilan deRF, Dec. 31, 1851; Cavour, *Politique*, pp. 1f.

180 RAL, XI/109/78, James, Paris, to his nephews, London, May 3, 1851.

181 RAL, XI/109/80, James, Paris, to his nephews, London, Jan. 15, 1852; Cavour, *Nouvelles lettres*, p. 433; Corti, *Reign*, pp. 308f.

182 Cavour, *Nouvelles lettres*, pp. 449–54; Corti, *Reign*, pp. 310ff.; Gille, *Maison Rothschild*, vol. II, pp. 137–41.

183 Cavour, *Nouvelles lettres*, pp. 464, 473, 487, 494f. See also pp. 505, 513 for subsequent Rothschild loans in 1854–5.

184 Gille, *Maison Rothschild*, vol. II, pp. 226f.

185 Powell, *Money market*, pp. 366f.

186   Plessis, *Banque de France*, vol. I, pp. 141, 156; vol. II, pp. 13.
187   *Ibid.*, vol. I, pp. 257, 261; vol. II, pp. 61, 67, 81; vol. III, pp. 149–54; Cameron, *France and Europe*, pp. 108–10.
188   Plessis, *Banque de France*, vol. III, pp. 47, 166f.; Ramon, *Banque de France*, p. 260; Gille, *Maison Rothschild*, vol. II, pp. 278–80. Cf. Bouvier, *Banque*, pp. 84f.
189   Plessis, *Banque de France*, vol. III, pp. 175–80; Kindleberger, *Financial history*, pp. 109f.
190   Flandreau, *L'or du monde*, pp. 179–89.
191   Plessis, *Banque de France*, vol. I, p. 134; vol. II, p. 286; vol. III, pp. 194–7, 240; Braudel and Labrousse, *Histoire économique*, vol. III, pp. 400–405, 421–4.
192   Bergeron, *Rothschild*, pp. 91ff.; Cameron, *France and Europe*, p. 166; Gille, *Maison Rothschild*, vol. II, pp.107, 185–92; Plessis, *Banque de France*, vol. III, p. 279. De Rothschild Frères was by far the biggest shareholder (with 25 per cent of the capital), compared with Bartholony's 0.05 per cent.
193   James proposed to establish a new "Comptoir impérial des travaux publics," but he was at pains to stress that, unlike the Crédit Mobilier, it would not "interfere directly in any operation or enterpise on its own account." In other words, what he had in mind was more like a deposit bank, lending to companies against all kinds of securities in the way that the Banque de France did not.
194   Ribeill, *Révolution ferroviaire*, p. 119.
195   Gille, *Maison Rothschild*, vol. II, pp. 200–215.
196   Cameron, *France and Europe*, pp. 213–17; Gille, *Maison Rothschild*, vol. II, pp. 173–6, 205, 307ff.; Girard, *Travaux publics*, p. 183; Blanchard, *Second Empire*, p. 67; Bouvier; *Rothschild*, pp. 149f.
197   Gille, *Maison Rothschild*, vol. II, pp. 342ff., 370–79 (and for the 1860s, pp. 504ff.); Plessis, *Banque de France*, vol. III, p. 282; Girard, *Travaux publics*, pp. 194f.
198   Gille, *Maison Rothschild*, vol. II, pp. 163–6, 252–60, 506ff.
199   Cameron, *France and Europe*, pp. 157–66, 228–41.
200   Gille, *Maison Rothschild*, vol. II, pp. 243–51; Cameron, *France and Europe*, pp. 284–91.
201   *Ibid.*, pp. 166–8, 248–63; Cameron, "Crédit Mobilier," pp. 469–74; Tortella, "Spain 1829–1874," pp. 106f.; Gille, *Maison Rothschild*, vol. II, pp. 228ff., 310–14. The authorised capital of the Pereire bank was 60 million francs, that of the Rothschild bank 80; but in the latter case no more than 24 million francs was actually paid in, and this was later reduced. The Pereires, by contrast, had paid in the maximum capital by 1862, and sought to invest not only in railways but also in the Madrid gasworks and various mines. Significantly, the Rothschild bank was wound up in 1868—after the Pereire threat had disappeared.
202   Gille, *Maison Rothschild*, vol. II, pp. 224ff., 327, 363–6; Cameron, *France and Europe*, pp. 169f., 228–41, 284–91; Clough, *Economic history of modern Italy*, pp. 21f.; Mack Smith, *Cavour*, p. 97.
203   Between 1855 and 1859, the Austrian government raised 118 million gulden by selling off the state-owned sections of the Habsburg railway network, though that figure excludes subsequent payments by the companies which bought the lines: Brandt, "Public finances," p. 99. This should be compared with a total gross budget deficit in the same period of 576 million gulden.
204   The company also acquired a line on the left bank of the Danube to Szeged, via Budapest, as well as various mining and metallurgical interests: Grunwald, "Europe's railways," pp. 181ff.
205   Corti, *Reign*, pp. 356–62; Cameron, *France and Europe*, pp. 153–7, 221–4; Gille, *Maison Rothschild*, vol. II, pp. 231–40, 314–17; Wirth, *History of banking*, pp. 126–7; Jacquemyns, *Langrand-Dumonceau*, vol. II, pp. 33–45. See also März, "Austrian Crédit Mobilier," pp. 178f.; Cameron, "Crédit Mobilier," pp. 467f.; Tapie, *Rise and fall*, pp. 291f.; Macartney, *House*, p. 142; Gerschenkron, *Economic backwardness*, p. 13; Good, *Economic rise*, p. 84.
206   Bouvier, *Rothschild*, pp. 166f.; Gille, *Maison Rothschild*, vol. II, pp. 119f.
207   Corti, *Reign*, p. 364; Gille, *Maison Rothschild*, vol. II, pp. 314–22; Macartney, *Habsburg Empire*, pp. 485f.; Grunwald, "Europe's railways," pp. 182f.; Berend and Ranki, *Economic development*, p. 71f.; Jacquemyns, *Langrand-Dumonceau*, vol. II, pp. 33–45.
208   Grunwald, "Europe's railways," pp. 177f.; Gille, *Maison Rothschild*, vol. II, p. 327.
209   HSM, 3. Best. 16 Rep XV K.5 Nr 1, Bd I, A. M. Neville [SMR], Vienna, to the Interior Minister, Kassel, Oct. 9, 1852; HSM, 3. Best. 16 Rep XV K.5 Nr 1, Bd II, Nr 227f, MAR to Kurfürst of Hesse-Kassel, March 6, 1857.
210   Gille, *Maison Rothschild*, vol. II, pp. 319–22.
211   *Ibid.*, pp. 332–42, 370–79; Cameron, *France and Europe*, pp. 224–8, 241–6; Cameron, "Crédit Mobilier," pp. 468–9; Grunwald, "Europe's railways," pp. 182; Berend and Ranki, *Economic develop-*

ment, pp. 71f. The merger was a relatively profitable one for the Pereires, who were able to exchange the half-finished Franz Joseph line for shares in the new Rothschild company worth 96 million francs.

212 *The Times*, May 29, 1858, p. 10; June 1, p. 10; June 8, p. 10; AN, 132 AQ 5902, James, Carlsbad, to his sons and nephew, Paris, July 17; CPHDCM, 637/1/318, Verwaltungsrat der Credit-Anstalt, Vienna, to Anselm, Feb. 11, 1859. According to one account (Wilson, *Rothschild*, p. 190), his resignation was related to the 1859 war between Austria and Piedmont: however, it preceded this by some months.

213 For an ambitious attempt to divide the French corporate world into four groups by analysing the membership of the boards of some 300 firms in 1863 (around 2,000 individuals, of whom 121 sat on the boards of two or more companies), see Locke, "Corporate businessmen," pp. 261–70. In addition to the Rothschild group, Locke identifies a Pereire group, a [Denys] Benoist d'Azy–[François] Bartholony group and an [Armand] Donon–[Félix] Aubry group. Members of the Rothschild group identified by Locke include bastions of the *haute banque* such as Michel Pillet-Will and Henri Hottinguer. Cf. Plessis, *Banque de France*, vol. II, pp. 373f. Between them the Pereires as a family accumulated more board seats than the Rothschilds, but many of these were on minor companies: Dupont-Ferrier, *Marché financier*, pp. 88f.; Plessis, *Banque de France*, vol. I, p. 80; vol. II, pp. 184–7.

214 Goldschmidt, *Erinnerungen*, p. 98; Cameron, *France and Europe*, p. 276; Gille, *Maison Rothschild*, vol. II, pp. 103–4, 327–32, 575ff.; Ziegler, *Sixth great power*, pp. 175f.

215 AN, 132 AQ 5902, James, Gastein, to his sons, Paris, July 29, 1858.

THREE *Nationalism and the Multinational (1859–1863)*

1 Steele, *Palmerston*, pp. 91ff.

2 Hübner, *Neuf ans*, vol. II, p. 87. Three hand grenades were thrown at their carriage as they arrived at the opera, killing eight bystanders, but not the intended targets.

3 *Ibid.*, p. 235; Corti, *Reign*, pp. 371f.

4 Hübner, *Neuf ans*, vol. II, pp. 248–51; Blumberg, *Accident*, p. 54.

5 Hübner, *Neuf ans*, vol. II, p. 267; Corti, *Reign*, p. 373.

6 Hübner, *Neuf ans*, vol. II, pp. 271, 297.

7 *Ibid.*, vol. II, p. 314.

8 Castellane, *Journal*, vol. V, p. 240.

9 Woodward, "Economic factors," p. 92; Case, *Opinion*, p. 56.

10 Monypenny and Buckle, *Disraeli*, vol. IV, p. 225.

11 As note 1. See also p. 100 for evidence of Lionel's role as a mediator between Palmerston and the Tories over the question of electoral reform.

12 See e.g. Kehr, "Biographische Skizzen," p. 292. Kehr also argued that the period witnessed "the victory of the modern [system of] state and war financing through bank consortiums and national subscriptions over the old principle of advances of money by a large private banking house."

13 Stern, *Gold and iron*, p. 73.

14 Brandt, "Public finances," *passim*.

15 Schremmer, "Public finance," pp. 456ff.

16 Cottrell, "Anglo-Austrian Bank," pp. 128ff.; Macartney, *Habsburg Empire*, p. 533.

17 RAL, RFamC/3/30, Natty, Mentmore, to his parents, London, Jan. 18, 1863.

18 Braudel and Labrousse, *Histoire économique*, vol. III, pp. 384–9, 421–4, 431–41; Bouvier, *Rothschild*, pp. 176ff.

19 Bergeron, *Rothschild*, p. 91ff.

20 Bouvier, *Crédit Lyonnais*, pp. 287, 576.

21 Braudel and Labrousse, *Histoire économique*, vol. III, pp. 397–400. Between 1860 and 1866, the Crédit Mobilier accounted for around 28 per cent of the total deposits of the six biggest deposit institutions.

22 RAL, XI/109/85, Alphonse, Paris, to his cousins, London, Aug. 7, 1863. As Alphonse put it sardonically, "s'il y a trop d'un Mob., que serait ce s'il y en avait deux? D'autant plus que ce qui fait la farce du Mob., c'est l'appui que le Kaiser donne à Pereire et la création d'un nouveu Mob. ne lui retirerait pas le crédit dont il jouit en haut lieu."

23 Berend and Ranki, *Economic development*, pp. 61f.

24 Gille, *Maison Rothschild*, vol. II, pp. 385f.; Jacquemyns, *Langrand-Dumonceau*, vol. III, pp. 363f.

25 See esp. *Ibid.* vol. II, pp. 140–43, 245; vol. III, p. 102; vol. IV, p. 82. For Alexandre Ullmann's and Jules Balasy's *Mémoire secret sur la puissance financière Catholique* (1863), see vol. III, pp. 468–72.

26   Gille, *Maison Rothschild*, vol. II, pp. 346f. Gille estimates that the French house took 50 million francs of rentes.

27   Huertas, *Economic growth*, p. 42; Macartney, *Habsburg Empire*, pp. 485f.; Ayer, *Century of finance*, pp. 48f.; Gille, *Maison Rothschild*, vol. II, p. 360. The Frankfurt house took £1 million of the loan and the Austrian National Bank £1.5 million. The 5 per cent bonds were issued at 80 in London—a disastrous investment for those who bought them.

28   AN, 132 AQ 5902, James, Carlsbad, to his sons, Paris, June 21, 1858; James to his sons and Nat, undated, June 1858; James to his sons, July 4; same to same, July 8. Cf. Gille, *Maison Rothschild*, vol. II, pp. 353ff.; Cameron, *France and Europe*, pp. 435ff. The Piedmontese currency had been reformed shortly before this; the lira was equivalent to the franc.

29   Gille, *Maison Rothschild*, vol. II, pp. 355–60; Mack Smith, *Cavour*, p. 140; Cameron, *France and Europe*, pp. 445f.; Blumberg, *Accident*, pp. 67, 184n.

30   AN, 132 AQ 5453/1M59, NMR to deRF, April 9, 1859; same to same, April 26; April 27.

31   Corti, *Reign*, pp. 377f.; Macartney, *Habsburg Empire*, p. 492.

32   AN, 132 AQ 5453/1M59, NMR to deRF, April 30, 1859.

33   RAL, RFamC/21, Charlotte, London, to Leopold, undated, 1860.

34   Corti, *Reign*, pp. 382–5; Mack Smith, *Victor Emmanuel*, p. 171.

35   RAL, RFamC/21, Charlotte, London, to Leopold, Cambridge, April 3, 1864; same to same, April 10; April 12; April 14; April 15.

36   Gille, *Maison Rothschild*, vol. II, pp. 509–22; Cameron, *France and Europe*, pp. 284–91.

37   Corti, *Reign*, p. 379.

38   CPHDCM, 637/1/122/26–7, James, Paris, to Anselm, Vienna, March 28, 1860. Cf. Corti, *Reign*, pp. 381f.; Huertas, *Economic growth*, pp. 43f.; Gille, *Maison Rothschild*, vol. II, pp. 408f.; Jacquemyns, *Langrand-Dumonceau*, vol. II, p. 55.

39   AN, 132 AQ 5902, James to his children, Aug. 8, 1860; RAL, T6/35d, Landau, Turin, to NMR, Aug. 9. Cf. Gille, *Maison Rothschild*, vol. II, pp. 399–403.

40   Cameron, "Papal finance," pp. 136–8.

41   RAL, RFamC/4/56, Lionel, Paris, to Charlotte, London, April 4, 1861; RAL, RFamC/4/57, same to same, April 5.

42   Holmes, *Triumph of the Holy See*, p. 148.

43   Jacquemyns, *Langrand-Dumonceau*, vol. III, pp. 468–95, 509–41. Roman bonds which had stood at 96.6 on the Paris bourse in 1853 had fallen to 62.2 by 1867. Cf. Felisini, *Finanze pontificie*, p. 239.

44   AN, 132 AQ 5902, James, Nice, to Alphonse, Gustave and Nat, Dec. 17, 1861; same to same, Dec. 18; Dec. 25; Dec. 28; Dec. 31; Jan. 11, 1862; Jan. 16. Cf. Gille, *Maison Rothschild*, vol. II, p. 403.

45   AN, 132 AQ 5902, James to Gustave, Aug. 21, 1865.

46   AN, 132 AQ 5902, James, Nice, to his children, Paris, Feb. 1, 1862; same to same, Feb. 2; AN, 132 AQ 5902, James, Wildbad, to Alphonse, Gustave and Nat, July 22; RAL, XI/109/85, James, Paris, to his nephews, London, March 26, 1863. As late as December 1865, he was still confident that it would return to 70: RAL, XI/109/87, James to his nephews, Dec. 14, 1865.

47   Cecco, *Money and empire*, pp. 44f.; Torido, *Economic history of liberal Italy*, p. 80.

48   RAL, RFamC/21, Charlotte, Paris, to Lionel, Natty and Alfred, Sept. 26, 1864.

49   RAL, XI/109/88/2, Alphonse, Paris, to his cousins, London, March 18, 1866; same to same, March 21.

50   AN, 132 AQ 5902, James, Folkstone, to his sons, Paris, Sept. 14, 1862; RAL, XI/10/88/2, Alphonse, Paris, to his cousins, London, Jan. 19, 1866. Cf. Gille, *Maison Rothschild*, vol. II, pp. 423ff.

51   RAL, XI/109/85, Alphonse, Paris, to his cousins, London, undated, *c.* March 1863; Alphonse, Turin, to his parents, Paris, *c.* March; same to same, March 2; March 6; James, Paris, to his nephews, London, March 9; same to same, March 10; March 11 (two letters); March 12; March 19; April 1. Cf. Gille, *Maison Rothschild*, vol. II, pp. 402ff.; Cameron, *France and Europe*, pp. 435–52. The total loan announced by the government was for 700 million francs, of which 500 million were to be issued immediately. The Paris and London houses contracted to buy 285,720,000 francs of 5 per cents at a price of 71 with a 1 per cent commission, and to underwrite a further 214,300,000 francs. The London house issued just 75 million francs, as the market for Italian bonds was less firm than in Paris: RAL, XI/109/86/1, Lionel to Anthony and Mayer, undated, 1864; Ayer, *Century of finance*, pp. 50f.

52   RAL, XI/109/85, James, Paris, to his nephews, London, June 17, 1863; RAL, XI/109/85, Alphonse, Paris, to his cousins, London, July 31; same to same, Nov. 29; AN, 132 AQ 5902, James, Wildbad, to Alphonse and Gustave, June 22, 1864; RAL, XI/109/86/1, Nat, Paris, to his brothers, London, Aug. 8;

AN, 132 AQ 5902, James, Vienna, to his children and nephew, Aug. 14; RAL, XI/109/86/1, Alphonse to his cousins, Aug. 16; Nat to his brothers, Aug. 23; James, Paris, to Lionel, Aug. 24; Alphonse to his cousins, Aug. 24; same to same, Aug. 25; AN, 132 AQ 5902, James to Alphonse, undated, *c.* Sept. 7; RAL, RFamC/21, Charlotte, Paris, to Lionel, Natty and Alfred, London, Sept. 16; RAL, XI/109/86/1, Nat to his brothers, Sept. 16; same to same, Sept. 18; RAL, XI/109/86, James to his nephews, Sept. 22; RAL, XI/109/86/1, Alphonse to his cousins, Sept. 22; Nat to his brothers, Sept. 22; Alphonse to his cousins, Sept. 22; same to same, Sept. 30. Gille, *Maison Rothschild*, vol. II, pp. 428–39.

53 AN, 132 AQ 5902, James, Wildbad, to his sons, Aug. 5, 1862 (two letters); same to same, Aug. 6; Aug. 7; Sept. 1; Sept. 4; Sept. 7; Sept. 14 (two letters); RAL, XI/109/85, James, Paris, to his nephews, London, June 8, 1863; RAL, XI/109/85, Alphonse, Paris, to his cousins, London, Aug. 7; James to his nephews, Oct. 12; RAL, XI/109/86/1, Nat, Paris, to his brothers, London, June 27, 1864; AN, 132 AQ 5902, James to Alphonse, June 28; RAL, XI/109/86, James to his nephews, June 30; same to same, Sept. 21; Nat to his brothers, Sept. 21; James to his nephews, Sept. 22; RAL XI/109/86/1, Nat to his brothers, Sept. 26; RAL, XI/109/86, James to his nephews, Sept. 27; same to same, Sept. 28; Jan. 4, 1865; RAL, XI/109/86/3, Alphonse to his cousins, Jan. 28; RAL, XI/109/86, James to his nephews, Feb. 2; same to same, March 15; March 16; RAL, XI/109/87/1, Alphonse to his cousins, Sept. 12; same to same, Oct. 15; RAL, XI/109/88/2, Jan. 15, 1866. Cf. Gille, *Maison Rothschild*, vol. II, pp. 509–22; Cameron, *France and Europe*, pp. 435–52; Bouvier, *Crédit Lyonnais*, pp. 532–46.

54 Gille, *Maison Rothschild*, vol. II, pp. 523ff.

55 RAL, XI/109/86, James, Paris, to his nephews, London, Dec. 16, 1864.

56 AN, 132 AQ 5903/437, James, Nice, to his sons, Paris, Feb. 7, 1867.

57 RAL, XI/109/92/1, Alphonse, Paris, to his cousins, London, Dec. 23, 1867.

58 RAL, XI/109/94/1, Alphonse, Paris, to his cousins, London, March 5, 1868.

59 RAL, XI/109/88/2, Alphonse, Paris, to his cousins, London, June 2, 1866; RAL, XI/109/90/1a, same to same, March 27, 1867; AN, 132 AQ 5903/458, James, Homburg, to Alphonse, Paris, July 11. Cf. Gille, *Maison Rothschild*, vol. II, pp. 528–35.

60 AN, 132 AQ 5902, James, Nice, to his children, Paris, Dec. 13, 1861; James to Nat and his sons, Jan. 16, 1862; AN, 132 AQ 32/A-12–2/11, Contract between deRF and French Minister of Finance, June 13.

61 RAL, XI/10/86/1, Alphonse, Paris, to his cousins, London, March 29, 1864; RAL, XI/109/86, James to his nephews, June 30; RAL, XI/109/86/1, Nat to his brothers, Aug. 23; Alphonse to his cousins, Aug. 23; AN, 132 AQ 5902, James, Dieppe, to Alphonse, Sept. 2; RAL, XI/109/86/1, Alphonse to his cousins, Sept. 6; Nat to his brothers, Sept. 6; same to same, Sept. 7; RAL, XI/109/86/3, Jan. 23, 1865; RAL, XI/109/86, James to his nephews, April 6; AN, 132 AQ 5902, James, Ostend, to his children, Paris, Aug. 4; same to same, Aug. 11; Aug. 13. Cf. Gille, *Maison Rothschild*, vol. II, pp. 453–8.

62 RAL, XI/109/88, James, Paris, to his nephews, London, June 15, 1866; RAL, XI/109/89/1, Alphonse to his cousins, Aug. 29; same to same, Sept. 1; Nov. 1; Nov. 5; RAL, XI/109/89, James to his nephews, Nov. 5. Cf. Cameron, "Crédit Mobilier," p. 474; Bouvier, *Crédit Lyonnais*, p. 614.

63 RAL, XI/109/89, James, Paris, to his nephews, London, Dec. 13, 1866; RAL, XI/109/93/1, Alphonse, Paris, to his cousins, London, Jan. 18, 1867; AN, 132 AQ 5903/406, James, Nice, to his children, Jan. 21; AN, 132 AQ 5903/426, same to same, Feb. 2; Feb. 11. Cf. Bouvier, *Crédit Lyonnais*, pp. 609–16; Gille, *Maison Rothschild*, vol. II, pp. 473–84.

64 RAL, XI/109/90/1a, Alphonse, Paris, to his cousins, London, Jan. 28, 1867; AN, 132 AQ 5480/1M86, NMR to deRF, Feb. 18; RAL, XI/109/91/2, Natty, Great Malvern, to his parents, London, Sept. 11; same to same, Sept. 12; Sept. 29; RAL, XI/10/92/1, Nat, Paris, to his brothers, London, undated, *c.* Nov. 1867; RAL, XI/109/92/1, Alphonse, Paris, to his cousins, London, Dec. 19; same to same, Dec. 23.

65 RAL, XI/109/90/1a, Alphonse to his cousins, Feb. 19, 1867; same to same, Feb. 24; March 12; RAL, XI/109/90/1, April 1; April 28; May 2; May 10; June 2; June 3; June 16; June 18; June 19; June 20; June 22; June 24; June 26; July 2; July 3; July 4 (two letters); July 11; July 12; July 25; July 28; July 30; Aug. 2; Aug. 5; Aug. 7; Aug. 9; Aug. 12. See also AN, 132 AQ 5903/457, James, Homburg, to Alphonse, Paris, July 10; /456, July 11; /458, July 11; /464, July 17; AN, 132 AQ 5481/1M87, NMR to deRF, July 26.

66 RAL, XI/109/91/2, Anthony, Paris, to his brothers, London, Sept. 29, 1867.

67 RAL, XI/109/91/2, Alphonse, Paris, to his cousins, London, Sept. 9, 1867; same to same, Sept. 11; Sept. 18; Sept. 21; Sept. 23; Sept. 24; Sept. 25; Sept. 26; Sept. 27.

68   RAL, XI/109/91/2, Alphonse, Paris, to his cousins, London, Oct. 6, 1867. See also same to same, Oct. 9; Oct. 13; Nov. 5; Nov. 6; Nov. 7; Nov. 18; Nov. 24; Nov. 29; Dec. 2; Dec. 6; Dec. 7.

69   RAL, XI/109/93/1, Alphonse, Paris, to his cousins, London, Jan. 28, 1868; same to same, Feb. 1; Feb. 19; Feb. 26; Feb. 27; March 8; March 12; April 20; RAL, XI/109/94/1, April 22; May 6; May 8; May 11; May 14; May 16; May 25 (two letters).

70   RAL, XI/109/96/1, Alphonse, Paris, to his cousins, London, Oct. 6, 1868.

71   RAL, RFamC/4/58, Lionel, Paris, to Charlotte, London, April 7, 1861.

72   Corti, *Reign*, p. 380. As the son of the Rothschilds' old friend, he was a welcome replacement for Hübner.

73   RAL, XI/109/85, Mayer Carl, Frankfurt, to his cousins, London, March 7, 1860.

74   Corti, *Reign*, p. 381.

75   *The Times*, Oct. 10, 1861; Plessis, *Banque de France*, vol. III, pp. 222–37, 242–50; Braudel and Labrousse, *Histoire économique*, vol. III, pp. 421–4; Ramon, *Banque de France*, pp. 284–9; Gille, *Maison Rothschild*, vol. II, pp. 387–92; Cottrell, "London, Paris and silver," pp. 138ff.; Morgan, *Central banking*, p. 176.

76   Gille, *Maison Rothschild*, vol. II, pp. 421ff.

77   Mérimée, *Correspondance générale*, 2e série, vol. X, p. 226.

78   Braudel and Labrousse, *Histoire économique*, vol. III, pp. 441–6; Girard, *Travaux publics*, pp. 279–81.

79   RAL, XI/109/86/1, Alphonse, Paris, to his cousins, London, Oct. 19, 1864.

80   Gille, *Maison Rothschild*, vol. II, pp. 610–14.

81   Plessis, *Banque de France*, vol. III, p. 274; Bouvier, *Banque*, pp. 89–91; Braudel and Labrousse, *Histoire économique*, vol. III, p. 423. As Plessis shows, Alphonse was one of the three most active regents during the 1860s: Plessis, *Banque de France*, vol. II, pp. 288f.

82   Bouvier, *Rothschild*, p. 160; Plessis, *Second Empire*, p. 82.

83   RAL, XI/109/85, James, London, to his children, June 30, 1862 or 1863. Cf. Aycard, *Crédit Mobilier*, pp. 451–3. See also RAL, XI/109/85, Alphonse, Paris, to his cousins, London, Aug. 19, 1863.

84   Corley, *Democratic despot*, p. 243.

85   Plessis, *Banque de France*, vol. III, pp. 22f., 290ff.

86   RAL, RFamC/4/181, Lionel, Paris, to Leopold, London, Nov. 14, 1861.

87   AN, 132 AQ 5902, James, Nice, to his children, Dec. 25, 1861; same to same, Jan. 6, 1862; Jan. 8; Jan. 11; Jan. 16; Jan. 18; Jan. 19; Jan. 20; Jan. 30; Jan. 31; Feb. 2; Feb. 3.

88   AN, 132 AQ 32 A-12–2/11, Contract between Fould and deRF, Jan. 24, 1862; AN, 132 AQ 32 A-12–2/10, Contract, Feb. 4; AN, 132 AQ 32 A-12–2/11, Contract, Feb. 14; AN, 132 AQ 32 A-12–2/10, Contract, May 8; AN, 132 AQ 32 A-12–1/12, Contract, Feb. 19, 1863; AN, 132 AQ 32/A-12–2/12, Contract, Feb. 19. See also RAL, XI/109/85, James, Paris, to his nephews, London, March 3, 1862 (two letters); same to same, March 22. Cf. Corti, *Reign*, pp. 389ff.; Gille, *Maison Rothschild*, vol. II, pp. 387–92; Plessis, *Banque de France*, vol. III, pp. 290–92.

89   Colling, *Roman*, pp. 79–82; Girard, *Travaux publics*, pp. 269–74; Brogan, *French nation*, pp. 125–30; Bergeron, *Rothschild*, pp. 91ff.; Plessis, *Banque de France*, vol. II, pp. 242, 244; Plessis, *Second Empire*, p. 80; Stern, *Gold and iron*, p. 172n.

90   *The Times*, Dec. 19, 1862, p. 12. Cf. Corti, *Reign*, pp. 391–2; Weinstock, *Rossini*, pp. 321f.

91   RAL, RFamC/3/26, Natty, Paris, to his parents, London, Dec. 17, 1862.

92   Merimée, *Correspondance générale*, 2e série, vol. XI, p. 286.

93   Goncourt, *Journal*, vol. I, p. 1196.

94   Also apparently present was the recently dismissed Foreign Minister Thouvenel, who managed to secure a place in the imperial train as president of the board of the Est line.

95   Goncourt, *Journal*, vol. I, p. 1217.

96   RAL, XI/109/85, Alphonse, Paris, to his cousins, London, July 9, 1863.

97   Mérimée, *Correspondance générale*, 2e série, vol. XI, p. 538.

98   RAL, XI/109/86/1, Alphonse, Paris, to his cousins, London, Oct. 19, 1864.

99   RAL, RFamC/21, Charlotte, London, to Leo, Cambridge, Nov. 10, 1864; same to same, Nov. 16.

100 RAL, RFamC/21, Charlotte, London, to Leo, Cambridge, Nov. 10, 1865. Cf. Corti, *Reign*, p. 395; Plessis, *Banque de France*, vol. II, p. 242.

101 RAL, XI/109/91/2, Anthony, Paris, to his brothers, undated, 1867.

102 RAL, RFamC/21, Charlotte, Paris, to Lionel, Natty and Alfred, Sept. 17, 1864; same to same, Sept. 20; Charlotte to Leo, Sept. 19; same to same, Nov. 16; Sept. 6, 1866; Aug. 3, 1867.

103 RAL, RFamC/21, Charlotte, London, to Leo, Cambridge, Oct. 17, 1866; same to same, Oct. 26.

104 Goncourt, *Journal*, vol. I, p. 1143.

105 *Ibid.*, vol. I, p. 1255.

106 Feydeau, *Mémoires*, p. 213.

107 Goncourt, *Journal*, vol. I, pp. 586f. For similar allusions to the role of the Rothschilds in this period, see *ibid.*, pp. 630f., 723, 735.

108 *Ibid.*, vol. I, p. 1217.

109 Feydeau, *Mémoires*, pp. 143–8.

110 Goncourt, *Journal*, vol. I, p. 1033.

111 RAL, RFamC/3/95, Natty, Paris, to Charlotte, Alfred and Leopold, London, undated, *c.* 1863; RAL, RFamC/21, Charlotte to Leo, Cambridge, April 28, 1864: "B. D. says that the Baron is a great man, and the great Baroness a greatly prejudiced lady—immensely conservative, viz. illiberal in her prejudices . . . Mr. Pereire, the Emperor and the English are her favorite aversions. She calls us maniacs, and heaps all the coals of her eloquence upon our press because it declares that the French are not fit for liberty."

112 RAL, XI/109/85, James, Paris, to his nephews, London, June 16, 1862; AN, 132 AQ 5902, James, London, to his sons and Nat, Paris, June 26.

113 RAL, XI/109/91/2, Mayer, Wildbad, to his brothers and nephews, undated, *c.* July 1867; AN, 132 AQ 5903, James, Wildbad, to Alphonse, Paris, July 19; RAL, XI/109/91/1, Alphonse, Paris, to his cousins, London, July 22; same to same, July 28.

114 AN, 132 AQ 5902, James to his children, Aug. 5, 1862; RAL, XI/109/85, James, Paris, to his nephews, London, Oct. 27.

115 RAL, XI/109/85, Alphonse, Paris, to his cousins, London, July 17, 1863; RAL, RFamC/4/228, Lionel, London, to Leo, Cambridge, Oct. 19; RAL, XI/109/85, James, Paris, to his nephews, London, Oct. 24; same to same, Oct. 31; Nov. 9.

116 RAL, XI/109/85, James, Paris, to his nephews, London, Oct. 31, 1863.

117 RAL, XI/109/86, James, Paris, to his nephews, London, April 6, 1865.

118 RAL, XI/109/88, James, Paris, to his nephews, London, March 18, 1866.

119 RAL, XI/109/88, James, Paris, to his nephews, London, March 19, 1866. See also RAL, XI/109/88/2, Alphonse, Paris, to his cousins, London, April 1; James to his nephews, April 4.

120 RAL, RFamC/21, Charlotte, London, to Leo, Cambridge, Feb. 5, 1864; same to same, Aug. 16, 1866. The earlier letter would seem to suggest that Lionel was chairbound for much of the last fifteen years of his life, a fact which makes the success of the London house in this period—when his brothers deferred entirely to his leadership—all the more remarkable; see also April 28, 1865.

121 RAL, RFamC/4/61, Lionel, London, to Charlotte, Grasmere, July 30, 1861; RAL, RFamC/4/156, Lionel, London, to Leo, Evelina and Leonora, Aug. 26. See also RAL, RFamC/3/29, Natty, New Court, to his parents, Jan. 16, 1863; RAL, RFamC/3/30, same to same, Jan. 18; RAL, RFamC/2/5, Disraeli to Charlotte, Aug. 21; RAL, RFamC/2/56, same to same, Oct. 21; RAL, RFamC/2/59, undated, *c.* 1863; RAL, RFamC/4/250, Lionel to Leo, Nov. 30; RAL, RFamC/21, Charlotte to Leo, Sept. 23, 1865; same to same, Nov. 4.

122 RAL, RFamC/21, Charlotte, London, to Leo, Cambridge, Nov. 8, 1865; same to same, Nov. 24; RAL, RFamC/4/319, Lionel, New Court, to Leo, Cambridge, Jan. 29, 1866.

123 RAL, RFamC/21, Charlotte, London, to Leo, Cambridge, April 27, 1866; same to same, April 30. See also RAL, RFamC/21, Charlotte to Leo, June 1; same to same, June 5.

124 RAL, RFamC/3/13, Natty, Cambridge, to his parents, Feb. 12, 1860; RAL RFamC/3/57, same to same, undated, *c.* 1860; RAL, RFamC/3/82, undated, *c.* 1860; RAL, RFamC/3/80, undated, *c.* 1860; RAL, RFamC/3/90, undated, *c.* 1860; RAL, RFamC/3/116, undated, *c.* 1861; RAL RFamC/3/126, undated, *c.* 1861; RAL, XI/130A/4, undated, *c.* 1861.

125 RAL, RFamC/21, Charlotte, London, to Leo, Cambridge, Feb. 2, 1866; same to same, Feb. 3; March 14; April 21; June 1; July 27; July 30; July 31; Aug. 9. See also RAL, XI/109/91/2, Mayer, Newmarket, to Lionel, London, undated, 1867.

126 RAL, RFamC/21, Charlotte, London, to Leo, Cambridge, Jan. 28, 1867; same to same, Feb. 4; Feb. 8; Feb. 12; May 27; RAL, RFamC/4/77, Lionel, London, to Charlotte, Paris, July 7; RAL, RFamC/4/78, same to same, July 9; RAL, RFamC/4/79, July 10; RAL, RFamC/4/82, July 13; RAL, RFamC/4/83, July 15; July 18.

127 RAL, XI/109/88/3, Anselm, Vienna, to Ferdinand, London, March 27, 1866.

128 RAL, XI/109/89/1, Alphonse, Paris, to his cousins, London, July 7, 1866.

129 Katz, *Belmont*, pp. 66f., 82f.

130 *Ibid.*, pp. 96–9.

131 *Ibid.*, pp. 144–8; Glanz, "Rothschild legend," pp. 15f., 20f. The *New York Evening Post* even alleged that Belmont was an illegitimate Rothschild, which prompted Belmont to sue for libel.

132 They are repeated by Corti, *Reign*, p. 387.

133 Diamond (ed.), *Casual view*, esp. pp. 34, 36, 66, 70f., 90. Cf. Gille, *Maison Rothschild*, vol. II, pp. 580–89.

134 RAL, T6/346, Chieves & Osborne to NMR, May 6, 1861; RAL, T6/341, same to same, May 16; RAL, T6/343, July 19; RAL, T6/387, Feb. 5, 1864.

135 RAL, XI/109/85, Lionel, London, to Leo, Cambridge, Oct. 21, 1863.

136 AN, 132 AQ 131/VG3, NMR to deRF, Dec. 5, 1861; AN, 132 AQ 5902, James, London, to his sons and Nat, June 25, 1862; RAL, XI/109/85, James, Paris, to his nephews, London, June 29; RAL, XI/109/85, Alphonse, Paris, to his cousins, London, Aug. 19, 1863. Cf. Kynaston, *City*, vol. I, p. 216.

137 Glanz, "Rothschild legend," pp. 21f.

138 Roberts, *Schröders*, pp. 66f. It was a sound enough judgement; the issuing houses were able to keep the bonds above par only by massive intervention in the market.

139 AN, 132 AQ 5902, James, Wildbad, to Alphonse, Paris, July 5, 1864; same to same, July 18; RAL, XI/109/86/1, Nat, Paris, to his brothers, London, undated, *c.* Aug. Disagreements over American politics may account for the friction between Belmont and members of the London family when he visited them in 1865: RAL, RFamC/21, Charlotte, London, to Leo, Cambridge, Feb. 8, 1865; same to same, Feb. 21; March 13; March 24.

140 Glanz, "Rothschild legend," pp. 17, 20f.

141 AN, 132 AQ 5902, James, Caen, to his children, Paris, Aug. 13, 1865. There was another abortive attempt to bring Belmont to heel in 1866, but, as James and Alphonse fatalistically pointed out, he had become irreplaceable: RAL, XI/109/89/1, Alphonse, Paris, to his cousins, Aug. 22, 1866; RAL, XI/109/89, James to his nephews, Aug. 24; RAL, XI/109/89/1, Alphonse to his cousins. Aug. 28; RAL, XI/109/89, James to his nephews, Oct. 20; same to same, Oct. 26; Nov. 6; Nov. 28; AN, 132 AQ 5903/406, James, Nice, to his children, Paris, Jan. 21, 1867. Cf. Ziegler, *Sixth great power*, pp. 211f.; Carosso, *Investment Banking*, pp. 10, 12, 18.

142 AN, 132 AQ 5902, James, Homburg, to his children, Paris, Aug. 18, 1865; same to same, Aug. 9, 1866; AN, 132 AQ 5903/426, same, Nice, to same, Feb. 2, 1867. Cf. Gille, *Maison Rothschild*, vol. II, pp. 580–89.

143 RAL, T10/85, Alphonse, Paris, to his cousins, London, Jan. 31, 1868.

144 RAL, XI/109/99/1, Alphonse, Paris, to his cousins, London, Aug. 14, 1869; RAL, XI/109/100/1, Natty, London, to his cousins, Paris, Dec. 15.

145 Carosso, *Investment banking*, pp. 24f.; Chernow, *House of Morgan*, p. 36. Lionel was wise: three years later, Cooke & Co. went bust with debts to the Northern Pacific of $5 million.

146 AN, 132 AQ 5481/1M87, NMR to deRF, June 7, 1867. Cf. Katz, *Belmont*, p. 165; Glanz, "Rothschild legend," p. 15.

147 RAL, XI/109/99/1, Alphonse, Paris, to his cousins, London, Aug. 18, 1869; RAL, XI/109/102, same to same, June 6, 1870; June 7; Mayer Carl, Frankfurt to his cousins and nephews, London, July 16; RAL, XI/109/103/1, Mayer Carl, Frankfurt, to his cousins, London, Oct. 17; RAL, XI/109/104, same to same, March 23, 1871; RAL, XI/109/105, April 2; April 5; April 6; AN, 132 AQ 5706/2M52, Mayer Carl to his cousins, France, April 14; RAL XI/109/105, Mayer Carl to his cousins and nephews, London, April 21; same to same, April 26; May 13; AN, 132 AQ 5494/1M100, NMR to deRF, undated, *c.* Oct.; RAL, XI/109/107/1, Mayer Carl to his cousins and nephews, London, Jan. 11, 1872.

148 RAL, XI/109/99/1, Alphonse, Paris, to his cousins, London, Aug. 12, 1869; same to same, Aug. 19; Sept. 20; RAL, XI/109/101/1, Jan. 5, 1870. Cf. Carosso, *Morgans*, pp. 182f.; Ziegler, *Sixth great power*, p. 216; Glanz, "Rothschild legend," p. 22.

149 Katz, *Belmont*, pp. 177, 188, 222, 238; Glanz, "Rothschild legend," p. 7.

150 Corti, *Reign*, p. 387.

151 AN, 132 AQ 5459/1M65, Davidson, Mexico, to NMR, Jan. 28, 1861; same to same, Feb. 28; AN, 132 AQ 5460/1M66, March 28; May 28; May 31; AN, 132 AQ 5461/1M67, June 29.

152 AN, 132 AQ 5463/1M69, Davidson, Mexico, to NMR, Feb. 27, 1862.

153 AN, 132 AQ 5468/1M74, NMR to deRF, Aug. 4, 1863; AN, 132 AQ 5469/1M75, same to same, Oct. 22; Dec. 17; AN, 132 AQ 5474/1M80, NMR to deRF, March 2, 1865.

154   Corti, *Reign*, pp. 273–5. According to Corti it was worth 20 million francs in 1866.

155   RAL, XI/109/85, Alphonse, Paris, to his cousins, London, undated, 1863.

156   AN, 132 AQ 5902, James, Ostend, to his children and Nat, Aug. 13, 1863; RAL, XI/109/85, James, Paris, to his nephews, London, Jan. 31, 1864; RAL, XI/109/86, same to same, Dec. 27; RAL, XI/109/86/3, Alphonse to his cousins, Jan. 28, 1865; RAL, XI/109/86, James to his nephews, March 16. See also RAL, XI/109/86/1, Nat, Paris, to his brothers, London, June 15, 1865; RAL, XI/109/90/1a, same to same, undated, *c.* March 1867.

157   RAL, XI/109/85, James, Paris, to his nephews, London, Oct. 12, 1863; Alphonse, Paris, to his cousins, London, Nov. 11; same to same, Nov. 29; Dec. 1; RAL, XI/109/86/1, March 7, 1864; March 10; March 15. Cf. Gille, *Maison Rothschild*, vol. II, pp. 413–17.

158   RAL, XI/109/86/1, Alphonse, Paris, to his cousins, London, March 27, 1864; undated, *c.* June; RAL, XI/109/94/1, undated, *c.* June; AN, 132 AQ 5902, James, Ischl, to his sons, Aug. 5; RAL, XI/109/86, James to his nephews, undated, Nov.; same to same, March 7, 1865; March 9; March 15; March 20; March 21; March 22; March 29; March 30; April 3.

159   AN, 132 AQ 5475/1M81, NMR to deRF, May 3, 1865; same to same, Aug. 17; RAL, XI/109/87/1, Lionel, Wiesbaden, to Natty, London, Aug. 19; AN, 132 AQ 5902, James, Homburg, to Gustave, Paris, Aug. 21; RAL, XI/109/87, James, Paris, to his nephews, London, Nov. 22; same to same, Nov. 25; RAL XI/109/87/1, Nat, Paris, to his brothers, London, Nov. 25; RAL, XI/109/87/1, Alphonse, Paris, to his cousins, Nov. 30; RAL, XI/109/87, same to same, Dec. 14; Dec. 18; Dec. 20; Dec. 26; RAL, XI/109/88, Jan. 15, 1866; Jan. 21; RAL, T9/186, Davidson, Mexico, to NMR, Feb. 27; RAL, T9/187, same to same, April 28; RAL, XI/109/88/2, Alphonse to his cousins, June 11. These were presumably the subject of Alphonse's unhappy interview with the Empress Charlotte that August: RAL, RFamC/21, Charlotte, London, to Leo, Cambridge, Aug. 24.

160   RAL, XI/109/85, James, Paris, to his nephews, London, June 8, 1863.

161   RAL, XI/109/91/1, Alphonse, Paris, to his cousins, London, July 3, 1867.

FOUR   *Blood and Silver (1863–1867)*

1   RAL, XI/109/87, James, Paris, to his nephews, London, Sept. 25, 1865. Almost certainly an allusion to Bismarck's celebrated comment on Austria's role in the Schleswig–Holstein crisis of 1864: "Il travaille pour le roi de Prusse."

2   Bismarck, *Gesammelte Werke*, vol. XIV, p. 546.

3   Stern, *Gold and iron*, pp. 17f., 96ff.; Pflanze, *Bismarck*, vol. II, p. 71.

4   Stern, *Gold and iron*, p. 22. See also pp. 27–31.

5   *Ibid.*, p. 114. Mayer Carl had his eye on a Grand Cross with a broad ribbon, but the Prussian King William I continued to regard this as too high an honour for a Jew: "Baron von Rothschild," he minuted, "has developed a bad attack of tape-worm at the approach of the investiture ceremony. I can't provide a remedy for this, but I could cure *Kreuzschmerzen* [literally "cross-ache," a pun on the German expression for lumbago]": Corti, *Reign*, pp. 430f.; Ford (ed.), *Correspondence of William I and Bismarck*, vol. I, p. 160.

6   Bleichröder's average profits between 1867 and 1869 were just under 60,000 thalers (£8,770), compared with an equivalent figure for the London house of £220,000 (annual average 1860–69).

7   Corti, *Reign*, pp. 410–15.

8   RAL, XI/109/88, James, Paris, to his nephews, London, March 26, 1866.

9   RAL, XI/109/88/3, Anselm, Vienna, to James, March 28, 1866.

10   RAL, XI/109/88, James, Paris, to his nephews, London, April 27, 1866.

11   RAL, RFamC/21, Charlotte, London, to Leo, Cambridge, Sept. 3, 1866.

12   RAL, RFamC/21, Charlotte to Leo, Oct. 7, 1868.

13   RAL, T13/101/12, 13/2/65/175, Alphonse, Paris, to his cousins, London, March 19, 1885; RAL, T13/101/12, 13/2/113/177, same to same, May 15, 1885.

14   RAL, T15/35, Alphonse, Paris, to his cousins, London, March 18, 1890.

15   He rued the occasion he disregarded Amschel's investment advice: Corti, *Reign*, pp. 343f.

16   Gall, *Bismarck*, vol. I, p. 282.

17   High-powered money increased by 30 per cent between 1857 and 1867, primarily as a result of government deficits and the suspension of convertibility.

18   Calculated from various figures in Schremmer, "Public finance," Brandt, "Public finances"; Good, *Habsburg Empire*.

19 Taylor, *Struggle*, p. 156.

20 Calculated from figures in *Jahrbuch für die Statistik des Preussischen Staates* (1869), pp. 442f., 544f.

21 Stern, *Gold and iron*, pp. 20–47.

22 RAL, XI/109/85, James, Paris, to his nephews, London, March 28, 1862; same to same, April 7 (two letters); April 12; April 13; Alphonse, Paris, to his cousins, London, undated, *c.* April; same to same, May 12; AN, 132 AQ 5463/1M69, NMR to deRF, May 16; same to same, May 20; May 21; June 10; July 16; AN, 132 AQ 5902, James, Wildbad, to his sons, Paris, July 16; same to same, July 25; July 27; Sept. 1; RAL, XI/109/85, James to his nephews, Oct. 27. Cf. Gille, *Maison Rothschild*, vol. II, pp. 404–8.

23 So damaging was the Alvensleben convention to Bismarck that Bleichröder arranged a special code with which he would notify the Paris Rothschilds of his resignation: Stern, *Gold and iron*, p. 30.

24 Monypenny and Buckle, *Disraeli*, vol. IV, p. 339; Froude, *Beaconsfield*, p. 185; Corti, *Reign*, p. 393; Renouvin, *Relations*, vol. V, p. 269.

25 RAL, XI/109/85, James, Paris, to his nephews, London, March 8, 1863; same to same, March 9; March 10; March 11; March 12; March 18; March 19; June 6; June 8; June 17; AN, 132 AQ, James, Wildbad, to his children and Nat, Paris, July 11; same to same, July 18; July 19; July 24; July 27; Aug. 2. See also RAL, XI/109/85, Alphonse, Paris, to his cousins, London, Aug. 19; James to his children, Sept. 8; James, Paris, to his nephews, London, Nov. 5; same to same, Nov. 10; Nov. 12; Nov. 25.

26 RAL, RFamC/4/225, Lionel, London, to Leo, Cambridge, Oct. 14, 1863. The crisis in Poland had sparked a major debate within the British Jewish community, in which Lionel emerged as a leading opponent of intervention on the Poles' behalf: Pollins, *Economic history of the Jews*, p. 113; Cesarani, *Jewish Chronicle*, p. 41. See also *The Times, History of The Times*, vol. II, p. 333.

27 RAL, XI/109/85, James, Paris, to his nephews, London, Nov. 1, 1863; same to same, Nov. 9; Nov. 23; RAL, XI/109/86/1, Lionel to Anthony, undated, 1864; RAL, XI/10/86/1, Alphonse, Paris, to his cousins, London, March 29, 1864. Cf. Gille, *Maison Rothschild*, vol. II, p. 407.

28 RAL, XI/109/87/1, Nat, Paris, to his brothers, London, undated, 1865; RAL, XI/109/97/1, same to same, Feb. 24, 1867.

29 RAL, RFamC/21, Charlotte, London, to Leo, Cambridge, April 18, 1864. See also RAL, XI/109/89/1, Alphonse, Paris, to his cousins, London, Nov. 19, 1866.

30 Ziegler, *Sixth great power*, p. 175; Kynaston, *City*, vol. I, p. 219.

31 RAL, XI/109/86/1, Alphonse, Paris, to his cousins, London, Aug. 29, 1864; same to same, Oct. 10; RAL, XI/109/86, James, Paris, to his nephews, London, Nov. 22; same to same, Feb. 5, 1865; March 23; AN, 132 AQ 5770/3M37, Anselm, Vienna, to James and his cousins, Paris, April 18; RAL, XI/109/86, James to his nephews, June 15; RAL, XI/109/89/1, Alphonse, Paris, to his cousins, London, Sept. 5, 1866.

32 RAL, XI/109/90, James, Paris, to his nephews, London, Feb. 22, 1867; RAL, XI/109/90/1a, Alphonse, Paris, to his cousins, London, March 22; same to same, March 24; RAL, XI/109/90/1, June 3; June 8; June 11; James to his nephews, June 11; Alphonse to his cousins, June 15; AN, 132 AQ 5903/463, James to Alphonse, July 17, 1867; RAL, XI/109/91/1, Alphonse to his cousins, July 23.

33 Macartney, *Habsburg Empire*, p. 516; Pamlenyi, *History of Hungary*, p. 305. See also Macartney, *House*, p. 156.

34 AN, 132 AQ 5902, James, London, to Alphonse, July 11, 1860; AN, 132 AQ 571/3M38, 39, SMR to deRF, Oct. 29; AN, 132 AQ 5902, James, Nice, to his sons and Nat, Paris, Dec. 15, 1861; same to same, Dec. 17; Dec. 25; AN, 132 AQ 5462/1M68, NMR to deRF, Jan. 24, 1862; NMR to Nat, Jan. 24; AN, 132 AQ 5902, James to his children, Jan. 27; AN, 132 AQ 5462/1M68, NMR to deRF, Feb. 14; same to same, Feb. 25.

35 RAL, XI/109/85, James, Paris, to his nephews, London, April 13, 1862; CPHDCM, 637/1/38/1, MAR to deRF, May 1; CPHDCM, 637/1/38/6, SMR to deRF and MAR, June 2; CPHDCM, 637/1/38/12, same to same, June 5; CPHDCM, 637/1/38/18–28, June 6–June 10; CPHDCM, 637/1/38/59, MAR to SMR, June 8; CPHDCM, 637/1/38/71, same to same, June 10 Cf. Gille, *Maison Rothschild*, vol. II, pp. 408f.

36 RAL, XI/109/85, Alphonse, Paris, to his cousins, London, July 22, 1863; RAL, XI/109/85, James, Paris, to his nephews, London, Oct. 19; same to same, Oct. 25; Alphonse to his cousins, Nov. 29; AN, 132 AQ 5902, James to Alphonse, Gustave and Salomon, Dec. 6; RAL, XI/109/87, James to his nephews, Jan. 1, 1864; AN, 132 AQ 5902, James, Wildbad, to Alphonse and Gustave, June 22; RAL, XI/109/86, James to his nephews, June 30; AN, 132 AQ 5902, James, Ischl, to his sons, Aug. 5; RAL,

XI/109/86, James to his nephews, Sept. 16; RAL, XI/109/87/1, Nat, Paris, to his brothers, London, undated, 1864. Cf. Cameron, *France and Europe*, pp. 415f.; Cottrell, "Anglo-Austrian Bank," pp. 131–5; Gille, *Maison Rothschild*, vol. II, pp. 439–49; Jacquemyns, *Langrand-Dumonceau*, vol. II, p. 65; Fulford, *Glyn's*, p. 160.

37   AN, 132 AQ 5902, James, Wildbad, to his sons, July 9, 1862; same to same, July 22; Sept. 5; RAL, XI/109/85, James, Paris, to his nephews, London, June 8, 1863.

38   RAL, RFamC/21, Charlotte, London, to Leo, Cambridge, Feb. 4, 1864; same to same, Feb. 10; Feb. 23; March 10; March 12; Aug. 8. For sceptical Parisian comments on the gap between British bark and bite, see RAL, XI/109/86/1, Nat, Paris, to his brothers, London, June 29; RAL, RFamC/21, Charlotte, Paris, to Lionel, Natty and Alfred, London, Sept. 18; RAL, RFamC/4/71, Lionel to Charlotte, Sept. 20.

39   RAL, XI/109/86, James, Wildbad, to Alphonse and Nat, Paris, July 10, 1864; AN, 132 AQ 5902, James to Alphonse, July 12; James, Ischl, to his children, July 30; RAL, XI/109/86/1, Gustave, Paris, to his cousins, London, Aug. 2; Nat, Paris, to his brothers, Aug. 4. Cf. Clark, *Franz Joseph and Bismarck*, p. 85. Characteristically, James also asked Bleichröder "to keep an eye out for old paintings or other antiques because the war against the poor Danes probably has brought many beautiful and interesting pieces on the market": Stern, *Gold and iron*, p. 109.

40   RAL, XI/109/86, James, Paris, to his nephews, London, July 24, 1864.

41   RAL, XI/109/86, James, Paris, to his nephews, London, June 14, 1865; AN, 132 AQ 5902, James, Wildbad, to Alphonse, Paris, June 24, 1865; AN, 132 AQ 5902, James to Nat and Alphonse, July 10; RAL, XI/109/87/1, Nat, Paris, to his brothers, London, undated, 1865.

42   RAL, XI/109/86/3, Nat, Paris, to his brothers, London, Jan. 15, 1865; Anselm, Vienna, to James and his cousins, Paris, Jan. 28; Mayer Carl, Frankfurt, to his cousins and nephews, London, Jan. 29; RAL, XI/109/86, James, Paris, to his nephews and Alphonse, London, Feb. 1; RAL, XI/109/86/3, Mayer Carl to his cousins and nephews, Feb. 5; AN, 132 AQ 5770/3M37, Anselm to deRF, April 7; same to same, May 27. Cf. Gille, *Maison Rothschild*, vol. II, pp. 439–49; Jacquemyns, *Langrand-Dumonceau*, vol. II, p. 352.

43   AN, 132 AQ 5770/3M37, Anselm, Vienna, to deRF, June 9, 1865; same to same, June 19; June 22. Cf. Steefel, "Rothschilds and the Austrian loan," p. 28.

44   CPHDCM, 637/1/25/7, Privatdepesche des Frankfurter Journals, June 26, 1865; CPHDCM, 637/1/24/17, MAR to SMR, June 29; CPHDCM, 637/1/25/38, unidentified German newspaper cutting, July 12; CPHDCM, 637/1/25/15, SMR to MAR, Aug. 1; *Frankfurter Handelszeitung*, Aug. 3.

45   CPHDCM, 637/1/24/22, Additional agreement between Paul Esterházy and MAR and S. G. Sina, June 12, 1863; CPHDCM, 637/1/24/5, Documents detailing loans of 1861, 1862 and 1864, 1865.

46   AN, 132 AQ 5902, James, Nice, to his children, Dec. 18, 1861.

47   Steefel, "Rothschilds and the Austrian loan," p. 27.

48   Stern, *Gold and iron*, pp. 38–65. See also Clark, *Franz Joseph and Bismarck*, p. 212.

49   Stürmer *et al.*, *Striking the balance*, pp. 166ff.

50   Stern, *Gold and iron*, pp. 62–5; Stürmer *et al.*, *Striking the balance*, pp. 168ff. The government also recovered control of a guarantee fund which had been set up for certain minor lines associated with the Cologne–Minden. Payment was to be partly in cash (3 million thalers on October 1, 2.7 million by January 2, 1866) and the rest in new Cologne–Minden shares.

51   Stern, *Gold and iron*, pp. 65ff.

52   AN, 132 AQ 5902, James to his sons, Paris, Aug. 13, 1865.

53   RAL, XI/109/87, James, Paris, to his nephews, London, Sept. 9, 1865. For an account based on the Austrian government records, see Steefel, "Rothschilds and the Austrian loan," pp. 27–39. Cf. Gille, *Maison Rothschild*, vol. II, pp. 439–49.

54   RAL, XI/109/87, James, Paris, to his nephews, London, Sept. 11, 1865; RAL, XI/109/87/1, Alphonse to his cousins, London, Sept. 11; same to same, Sept. 12; Sept. 16; Sept. 17; Sept. 20; James to his nephews, Sept. 17 (two letters); Sept. 19; Sept. 25; Sept. 26.

55   RAL, XI/109/87/1, Alphonse to his cousins, Sept. 16, 1865; RAL, XI/109/87, James, Paris, to his nephews, London, Sept. 19.

56   RAL, XI/109/87, James, Paris, to his nephews, London, Sept. 23, 1865.

57   RAL, XI/109/87/1, Alphonse, Paris, to his cousins, London, Sept. 18, 1865; same to same, Sept. 22; Sept. 26; RAL, XI/109/87, James, Paris, to his nephews, London, Sept. 25; same to same, Sept. 26; Sept. 28; Sept. 29.

58   Steefel, "Rothschilds and the Austrian loan"; Gille, *Maison Rothschild*, vol. II, pp. 443f.

59　RAL, RFamC/21, Charlotte, London, to Leo, Oxford, Oct. 4, 1865.

60　RAL, XI/109/87/1, Alphonse, Paris, to his cousins, London, Sept. 3, 1865.

61　RAL, XI/109/87/1, Alphonse, Paris, to his cousins, London, Sept. 17, 1865.

62　RAL, XI/109/87/1, Alphonse, Paris, to his cousins, London, Sept. 18, 1865.

63　RAL, XI/109/87/1, Nat, Paris, to his brothers, London, four undated letters, Sept. 1865.

64　RAL, XI/109/87/3, Mayer Carl, Frankfurt, to his cousins and nephews, London, undated, *c.* Oct. 1865; RAL, XI/109/87/3, same to same, Oct. 12. Only if the loan were "*excessively* cheap"—he suggested a price of 61—did he advise going ahead.

65　RAL, XI/109/87/1, Alphonse, Paris, to his cousins, London, Sept. 22, 1865. For Ferdinand's reassurances on this score, RAL, XI/109/87/3, Ferdinand, Schillersdorf, to his uncles and cousins, London, Oct. 2, 1865; same to same, Oct. 3; Oct. 13. Cf. Helleiner, "Free trade and frustration," pp. 66f.

66　Stern, *Gold and iron,* p. 60.

67　AN, 132 AQ 5902, James to his children, July 25, 1865.

68　AN, 132 AQ 5902, James, Ostend, to his children, Paris, Aug. 4, 1865; same to same, Aug. 5; Aug. 7. Cf. Stern, *Gold and iron,* p. 34n.

69　AN, 132 AQ 5902, James, Spa, to his children, Paris, Aug. 9, 1865.

70　AN, 132 AQ 5902, James, Baden, to Gustave, Paris, Sept. 3, 1865; RAL, XI/109/87, James, Baden, to his nephews, London, Sept. 3.

71　RAL, XI/109/87, James, Paris, to his nephews, London, Oct. 6, 1865; RAL, XI/109/87/1, Alphonse, Paris, to his cousins, London, Oct. 6; same to same, Oct. 7; James to his nephews, Oct. 12.

72　Steefel, "Rothschilds and the Austrian loan," pp. 32ff.; Clark, *Franz Joseph and Bismarck,* p. 212.

73　Stern, *Gold and iron,* pp. 67ff.

74　Steefel, "Rothschilds and the Austrian loan," pp. 32ff.; Gille, *Maison Rothschild,* vol. II, p. 445.

75　RAL, XI/109/87/1, Alphonse, Paris, to his cousins, London, Oct. 13, 1865; same to same, Oct. 15; RAL, XI/109/87, James, Paris, to his nephews, London, Oct. 14.

76　RAL, RFamC/21, Charlotte, London, to Leo, Cambridge, Oct. 27, 1865.

77　Ral, XI/109/87, James, Paris, to his nephews, London, Oct. 18, 1865 (two letters, English and *Judendeutsch*); same to same, Oct. 20; Alphonse to his cousins, Oct. 20; James to his nephews, Oct. 24; Alphonse to his cousins, Oct. 26; same to same, Oct. 27; RAL, XI/109/87/3, Ferdinand, Schillersdorf, to his uncles and cousins, London, Oct. 27; James to his nephews, Oct. 29.

78　RAL, XI/109/87/1, Alphonse, Paris, to his cousins, London, Oct. 30, 1865; same to same, Nov. 2; RAL, XI/109/87, James, Paris, to his nephews, London, Nov. 2; same to same, Nov. 3; Nov. 6; Nov. 11; Nov. 14 (three letters); Nov. 17; Nov. 20; Nov. 23; RAL, XI/109/87/1, Alphonse to his cousins, Nov. 4; same to same, Nov. 6; Nov. 7; Nov. 16; Nov. 17; Nov. 20; Nov. 25; RAL, XI/109/87/3, Ferdinand, Schillersdorf, to his uncles and cousins, London, Nov. 11; RAL, RFamC/21, Charlotte, London, to Leo, Cambridge, Nov. 1; same to same, Nov. 6; Nov. 8; RAL, XI/109/87/3, Nathaniel, Vienna, to his uncles and cousins, London, Dec. 4. Cf. Steefel, "Rothschilds and the Austrian loan," pp. 37ff.; Macartney, *Habsburg Empire,* p. 544; Pottinger, *Napoleon III and the German crisis,* pp. 41–52; Stürmer *et al., Striking the balance,* p. 170.

79　Steefel, "Rothschilds and the Austrian loan," p. 31.

80　RAL, XI/109/87, James, Paris, to his nephews, London, Nov. 18, 1865; same to same, Dec. 8; Dec. 29; RAL, XI/109/88, Jan. 1, 1866; RAL, XI/109/88/2, Alphonse, Paris, to his cousins, London, Jan. 4; same to same, Jan. 7; James to his nephews, Jan. 10; Jan. 17; Jan. 20; Jan. 22; Jan. 23; Jan. 24; Jan. 25; Jan. 26; Jan. 29; RAL, XI/109/88/2, Alphonse to his cousins, Jan. 15; same to same, Jan. 17; Jan. 19; Jan. 31.

81　RAL, XI/109/88/2, Alphonse, Paris, to his cousins, London, Feb. 8, 1866.

82　RAL, XI/109/88/1, Mayer Carl, Frankfurt, to his cousins and nephews, London, Jan. 16, 1866.

83　RAL, T9/182, Leopold, Cambridge, to his parents, undated, early 1866.

84　RAL, XI/109/88, James, Paris, to his nephews, London, Feb. 7, 1866; same to same, Feb. 12; Feb. 14; Feb. 15.

85　RAL, XI/109/88/2, Alphonse, Paris, to his cousins, London, Feb. 22, 1866; same to same, March 4.

86　RAL, XI/109/88, James, Paris, to his nephews, London, March 14, 1866; RAL, XI/109/88/2, Alphonse, Paris, to his cousins, London, March 15. Cf. Stern, *Gold and iron,* pp. 69–87; Stürmer *et al., Striking the balance,* p. 171; Gille, *Maison Rothschild,* vol. II, pp. 449–51. Goltz wrongly believed that

James had also turned down the Saar mines, but Bismarck insisted this had "not been offered to him": Stern, *Gold and iron*, p. 74.

87   RAL, XI/109/88, James, Paris, to his nephews, London, March 15, 1866.

88   RAL, RFamC/4/318, Lionel, London, to Leo, Cambridge, March 8, 1866.

89   RAL, XI/109/88/2, Alphonse, Paris, to his cousins, London, March 11, 1866.

90   Corti, *Reign*, pp. 397ff.

91   RAL, XI/109/88/1, Anthony, Paris, to his brothers, undated, March, 1866.

92   Corti, *Reign*, p. 398.

93   Stern, *Gold and iron*, p. 73.

94   *Ibid.*, pp. 73f.

95   RAL, XI/109/88, James, Paris, to his nephews, London, March 20, 1866.

96   RAL, RFamC/21, Charlotte, London, to Leo, Cambridge, March 22, 1866.

97   RAL, T9/125, Gustave, Paris, to his cousins, London, March 20, 1866.

98   RAL, T9/145, Mayer Carl to his cousins, London, March 23, 1866.

99   RAL, XI/109/88, James, Paris, to his nephews, London, March 26, 1866. Cf. RAL, XI/109/88/2, Alphonse, Paris, to his cousins, London, April 3.

100   Stern, *Gold and iron*, p. 78.

101   RAL, XI/109/89/1, Alphonse, Paris, to his cousins, London, April 5, 1866; RAL, XI/109/88, James, Paris, to his nephews, London, April 8; same to same, April 22; RAL, XI/109/88/2, Nat, Paris, to his brothers, London, April 22; RAL, T9/133, Nathaniel, Vienna, to James, Paris, April 27.

102   RAL, T40/3, XI/64/0/2/17, Bleichröder, Berlin, to James, Paris, April 27, 1866.

103   RAL, T40/5, XI/64/0/2/30, Bleichröder, Berlin, to Lionel, London, May 5, 1866.

104   Stern, *Gold and iron*, pp. 78f.; Stürmer *et al.*, *Striking the balance*, p. 171.

105   RAL, XI/109/88/2, Alphonse, Paris, to his cousins, London, June 9, 1866.

106   AN, 132 AQ 5902, James, Homburg, to his sons, Aug. 13, 1865; same to same, Aug. 21; RAL, XI/109/87, James, Paris, to his nephews, London, Sept. 21; RAL, XI/109/87/1, Alphonse to his cousins, Sept. 22.

107   RAL, XI/109/87/1, Lionel, Paris, to his brothers and Natty, Sept. 6, 1865.

108   RAL, XI/109/87, James, Paris, to his nephews, London, Sept. 19, 1865.

109   RAL, XI/109/87, James, Paris, to his nephews, London, Dec. 14, 1865; RAL, XI/109/88, same to same, Jan. 6, 1866.

110   RAL, XI/109/88/2, Alphonse, Paris, to his cousins, London, March 21, 1866.

111   RAL, XI/109/88/2, Alphonse, Paris, to his cousins, London, Jan. 15, 1866; RAL, XI/109/88, James, Paris, to his nephews, London, Feb. 1; Feb. 20; RAL, XI/109/89/1, Alphonse to his cousins, March 3; RAL, XI/109/88, James to his nephews, March 14; RAL, XI/109/88/2, Alphonse to his cousins, March 15; same to same, March 18. The terms of the Lombard deal were complex: the government guaranteed a 6.5 per cent return on the bonds of the Italian part of the line, extended the concession to ninety-nine years, and freed it from the levy on foreign bonds until 1880. In return the company agreed to construct new lines worth 9 million francs, to reduce its fares and to undertake the expansion of the port facilities at Trieste and Venice at a cost of 15 million gulden, to be repaid over twelve years. Alphonse described the costs of this deal to the company as "almost illusory."

112   RAL, XI/109/88, James, Paris, to his nephews, London, March 19, 1866; RAL, XI/109/88/2, Alphonse, Paris, to his cousins, London, March 21.

113   RAL, XI/109/88/2, Alphonse, Paris, to his cousins, London, March 22, 1866.

114   RAL, XI/109/88/1, Anselm, Vienna, to his uncle, Paris, London, March 24, 1866; same to same, March 25; RAL, XI/109/88/3, Anselm to Ferdinand, London, March 27. Cf. Pottinger, *Napoleon III and the German crisis*, p. 80.

115   RAL, XI/109/88, James, Paris, to his nephews, London, March 27, 1866; same to same, March 29; RAL, T9/135, SMR to deRF, April 9.

116   RAL, XI/109/88/2, Nat, Paris, to his brothers, London, April 6, 1866. Clark, *Franz Joseph and Bismarck*, p. 409; Corti, *Reign*, pp. 397ff.

117   RAL, XI/109/88/2, Alphonse, Paris, to his cousins, London, March 28, 1866.

118   Gille, *Maison Rothschild*, vol. II, pp. 435–8. The Italian treaty did not become public in Paris until July 22. When it did, James and Alphonse were enraged: RAL, XI/109/88/2, Alphonse, Paris, to his cousins, London, April 24, 1866; same to same, April 25; April 27.

119   RAL, XI/109/88, James, Paris, to his nephews, London, April 27, 1866.

120   RAL, XI/109/88, James, Paris, to his nephews, London, April 9, 1866; same to same, April 10; RAL, XI/109/88/1, Mayer Carl, Frankfurt, to his cousins, London, April 10; AN, 132 AQ 5697/2M42, MAR to deRF, April 12.

121   RAL, T40/6, XI/64/0/2/33, Bleichröder, Berlin, to Lionel, London, June 2, 1866.

122   RAL, XI/109/88, James, Paris, to his nephews, London, March 19, 1866; RAL, XI/109/88/2, Alphonse, Paris, to his cousins, London, March 21.

123   RAL, XI/109/88/3, Anselm, Vienna, to his uncle, Paris, March 28, 1866; RAL, XI/109/88, James, Paris, to his nephews, London, April 1; same to same, April 4; RAL, XI/109/88/2, Alphonse, Paris, to his cousins, London, April 1; RAL, XI/109/88/2, Nat, Paris, to his brothers, London, April 4.

124   RAL, RFamC/21, Charlotte, London, to Leo, Cambridge, May 12, 1866.

125   RAL, XI/109/88, James, Paris, to his nephews, London, May 13, 1866; same to same, May 28.

126   RAL, XI/109/88/1, Natty, Paris, to his parents, London, April 8, 1866.

127   RAL, XI/109/88, James, Paris, to his nephews, London, April 11, 1866 (two letters).

128   RAL, XI/109/88/2, Alphonse, Paris, to his cousins, London, April 12. Cf. Corti, *Reign*, pp. 399f.; Case, *Opinion*, p. 198; Pottinger, *Napoleon III and the German crisis*, pp. 123–7.

129   RAL, XI/109/88, James, Paris, to his nephews, London, April 23, 1866; same to same, April 24.

130   RAL, XI/109/88/2, Alphonse, Paris, to his cousins, London, April 25, 1866; same to same, April 26; RAL, XI/109/88, James, Paris, to his nephews, London, April 25; same to same, April 26.

131   RAL, XI/109/88/2, Alphonse, Paris, to his cousins, London, May 7, 1866; same to same, May 11.

132   Mérimée, *Correspondance générale*, 2e série, vol. XIII, pp. 101, 133; Pottinger, *Napoleon III and the German crisis*, p. 125; Girard, *Travaux publics*, p. 361.

133   Corti, *Reign*, p. 401.

134   RAL, XI/109/88/1, Anselm, Vienna, to his uncle and cousins, Paris, April 20, 1866; RAL, XI/109/88, James, Paris, to his nephews, London, April 20.

135   RAL, XI/109/88/2, Alphonse, Paris, to his cousins, London, April 15, 1866; RAL, XI/109/88/1, Anselm, Vienna, to his uncle, Paris, April 19; RAL, XI/109/88, James to his nephews, April 19; same to same, April 20; RAL, XI/109/88/1, Goldschmidt, Vienna, to NMR, April 21. James noted that he had been "applauded like an actress" at the meeting.

136   RAL, XI/109/88, James, Paris, to his nephews, London, May 15, 1866; same to same, May 16; May 17 (two letters); RAL, XI/109/88/2, Alphonse, Paris, to his cousins, London, May 22; same to same, May 24; May 29; June 4; RAL, XI/109/88, James to his nephews, May 24; same to same, May 25; May 30; RAL, XI/109/88/1, Mayer Carl, Frankfurt, to his cousins and nephews, June 1; AN, 132 AQ 5771/3M38,39, SMR to deRF, June 8, 1866; RAL, XI/109/88/1, Mayer Carl, Frankfurt, to his cousins and nephews, June 9; RAL, XI/109/88/2, Alphonse to his cousins, June 9.

137   RAL, XI/109/88/2, Alphonse, Paris, to his cousins, London, May 24, 1866.

138   Wawro, *Austro–Prussian War*, pp. 294f. I am grateful to Dr Brendan Simms for this reference.

139   RAL, T40/4, XI/64/0/2/26, Bleichröder, Berlin, to Lionel, London, May 4, 1866. Cf. Vincent (ed.), *Disraeli, Derby and the Conservative party*, p. 250.

140   RAL, XI/109/88, James, Paris, to his nephews, London, June 13, 1866.

141   RAL, T9/152, Nathaniel, Vienna, to deRF, July 4, 1866.

142   Corti, *Reign*, pp. 402f.

143   According to *The Times*, Aug. 13, 1874, p. 12, the Austrian Minister of State Count Richard Belcredi "put forth the notion of requiring the Jewish congregations to organise several battalions of volunteers at their own expense. Now as the Jews necessarily undertook the obligations of military service in common with other citizens Count Belcredi's plan was neither more nor less than an extraordinary tax levied on the Jews, a disguised renewal of the special Jews' tax." Anselm wrote to him "that he would close his offices, break off all financial negotiations with the Government and leave Austria if the Minister persisted in carrying out a project which would be so injurious to the Jews. His letter had the desired effect." When Betty suggested that money be raised for Austrian soldiers who were Jews, Anselm (according to his son Ferdinand) "answered that the money was [to be] equally divided between all soldiers, quite regardless of creed, and that a distinction would create a bad effect": RAL, T9/147, Ferdinand, Scarborough, to Lionel, London, Aug. 9, 1866.

144   RAL, XI/109/89/2, Anselm, Vienna, to his uncle and cousins, Paris, July 16, 1866; same to same, July 18; July 19; July 20; July 21.

145   RAL, T9/155, Nathaniel, Vienna, to deRF, July 14, 1866.

146   RAL, XI/109/89/1, Ferdinand, Scarborough, to Lionel, London, Aug. 15, 1866; RAL, T9/180, same to same, Aug. 21.

147   RAL, XI/109/89/1, Ferdinand, Schillersdorf, to Lionel, London, Sept. 18, 1866.

148   RAL, XI/109/88/1, Mayer Carl, Frankfurt, to his cousins and nephews, London, May 8, 1866.

149   RAL, XI/109/88/1, Mayer Carl, Frankfurt, to his cousins and nephews, London, June 11, 1866; same to same, June 11. See also RAL, XI/109/88, James, Paris, to his nephews, London, June 15.

150   RAL, T9/157, Mayer Carl, Frankfurt, to his cousins and nephews, London, June 20, 1866; RAL, T9/158, same to same, June 22.

151   RAL, XI/109/89/1, Alphonse, Paris, to his cousins, London, July 8, 1866; RAL, XI/109/89/2, Mayer Carl, Frankfurt, to his cousins and nephews, July 13; same to same, July 14; RAL, T9/160, July 15.

152   RAL, XI/109/89/2, Mayer Carl, Frankfurt, to his cousins and nephews, July 17, 1866.

153   RAL, XI/109/89/1, Nat, Paris, to his brothers, London, July 21, 1866; RAL, RFamC/21, Charlotte, London, to Leo, Cambridge, July 31.

154   RAL, XI/109/88, James, Paris, to his nephews, London, June 25, 1866; same to same, June 28.

155   AN, 13 AQ 5697/2M42, Mayer Carl, Frankfurt, to deRF, June 28, 1866; RAL, XI/109/88, James, Paris, to his nephews, London, June 28. Cf. Stern, *Gold and iron*, p. 87.

156   RAL, XI/109/89, James, Paris, to his nephews, London, July 2, 1866.

157   RAL, T9/185, Bettina, Paris, to her grandparents, July 2, 1866.

158   RAL, XI/109/88/2, Alphonse, Paris, to his cousins, London, April 12, 1866.

159   RAL, XI/109/89/1, Alphonse, Paris, to his cousins, London, July 1, 1866.

160   RAL, XI/109/89/1, Alphonse, Paris, to his cousins, London, July 3, 1866.

161   RAL, XI/109/89/1, Alphonse, Paris, to his cousins, London, July 8, 1866; RAL, XI/109/89, James, Paris, to his nephews, London, July 10.

162   RAL, XI/109/89, James, Paris, to his nephews, London, July 12, 1866; same to same, July 13; July 14; July 16; RAL, RFamC/21 Charlotte, London, to Leo, Cambridge, July 13.

163   RAL, XI/109/89/1, Alphonse, Paris, to his cousins, London, July 16, 1866; RAL, XI/109/89, James, Paris, to his nephews, London, July 24.

164   RAL, XI/109/89/1, Alphonse, Paris, to his cousins, London, Aug. 12, 1866.

165   RAL, RFamC/21, Charlotte, London, to Leo, Cambridge, July 10, 1866.

166   RAL, XI/109/89/1, Alphonse, Paris, to his cousins, London, July 11, 1866; same to same, July 13.

167   RAL, RFamC/21, Charlotte, London, to Leo, Cambridge, July 31, 1866.

168   RAL, RFamC/21, Charlotte, London, to Leo, Cambridge, July 20, 1866.

169   RAL, XI/109/88, James, Paris, to his nephews, London, April 9, 1866. Emphasis added.

170   Stern, *Gold and iron*, pp. 75f.

171   RAL, XI/109/88, James, Paris, to his nephews, London, April 10, 1866.

172   RAL, XI/109/88, James, Paris, to his nephews, London, June 6, 1866.

173   RAL, XI/109/88/2, Alphonse, Paris, to his cousins, London, April 27, 1866.

174   RAL, T9/138, SMR to James, Paris, May 18, 1866.

175   RAL, XI/109/88/1, Mayer Carl, Frankfurt, to his cousins and nephews, June 26, 1866; same to same, June 27; June 29.

176   RAL, XI/109/88/1, Mayer Carl, Frankfurt, to his cousins and nephews, London, April 8, 1866.

177   RAL, XI/109/88/1, Mayer Carl, Frankfurt, to his cousins and nephews, London, May 6, 1866; AN, 132 AQ 5697/2M42, Mayer Carl to deRF, May 26; same to same, June 8; RAL, XI/109/88/1, Mayer Carl to his cousins, June 11.

178   RAL, XI/109/89/2, Mayer Carl, Frankfurt, to his cousins and nephews, London, Feb. 26, 1866; AN, 132 AQ 5697/ 2M42, Mayer Carl to James, Paris, June 17; Mayer Carl to deRF, June 24. Cf. Gille, *Maison Rothschild*, vol. II, pp. 451ff.

179   RAL, XI/109/89, James, Paris, to his nephews, London, Aug. 21, 1866.

180   RAL, XI/109/88/2, Alphonse, Paris, to his cousins, London, June 7, 1866; RAL, XI/109/88, James, Paris, to his nephews, London, June 8; RAL, XI/109/88/2, Alphonse to his cousins, June 17; same to same, June 27; RAL, XI/109/89/1, July 1; July 3.

181   RAL, XI/109/89, James, Paris, to his nephews, London, July 5, 1866; same to same, July 8; RAL, XI/109/89/1, Alphonse, Paris, to his cousins, London, July 7; same to same, July 8; July 16; July 17; RAL, XI/109/89/1, Nat, Paris, to his brothers, London, July 17; same to same, July 18; RAL, XI/109/89, James to his nephews, July 18; same to same, July 19.

182   RAL, XI/109/89/1, Alphonse, Paris, to his cousins, London, July 20, 1866, same to same, July 23; July

24; July 26 (two letters); RAL, XI/109/89, James, Paris, to his nephews, London, July 22; same to same, July 23.

183   RAL, XI/109/89, James, Paris, to his nephews, London, July 30, 1866; RAL, XI/109/89/2, Alphonse, Paris, to his cousins, London, Aug. 2; same to same, Aug. 8; AN, 132 AQ 5902, James, Deauville, to Alphonse, Paris, Aug. 8; RAL, XI/109/89/2, Anselm, Vienna, to Betty, Aug. 9; RAL, XI/109/89, James to his nephews, Aug. 12; RAL, XI/109/89/2, Anselm to Landau, Florence, Aug. 13; RAL, XI/109/89/1, Alphonse, Paris, to his cousins, London, Sept. 4; RAL, XI/109/89/1, Nat, Paris, to his brothers, London, Sept. 5; RAL, T9/179, Nat, Paris, to his brothers, London, Sept. 7; RAL, XI/109/89/1, Alphonse to his cousins, Sept. 11; RAL, XI/109/89/1, same to same, Sept. 13; Sept. 14; Sept. 17; RAL, XI/109/89/1, Ferdinand, Schillersdorf, to Lionel, London, Sept. 23; RAL, XI/109/88/2, Nat, Paris, to his brothers, London, Sept. 24; RAL, XI/109/89, James, Paris, to his nephews, London, Sept. 25; RAL, XI/109/89/1, Alphonse to his cousins, Oct. 6; same to same, Oct. 7; Oct. 11; Oct. 13; Oct. 16; Oct. 23; RAL, XI/109/89, James to his nephews, Nov. 7; RAL, XI/109/89/1, Alphonse to his nephews, Nov. 21; same to same, Nov. 28; James to his nephews, Nov. 29. It was especially galling that Stern and the Crédit Foncier offered to advance 100 million lire which the Rothschilds' Lombard line was due to pay the government over four years. See also AN, 132 AQ 5772/3M41, Anselm, Vienna, to James and Alphonse, Paris, Oct. 16, 1867.

184   Stern, *Gold and iron*, pp. 87–95; Sheehan, *German history*, p. 909.

185   RAL, XI/109/88, James, Paris, to his nephews, London, June 28, 1866.

186   Corti, *Reign*, pp. 403ff.

187   RAL, XI/109/89/1, Alphonse, Paris, to his cousins, London, Oct. 25, 1866; AN, 132 AQ 5698/2M43, Mayer Carl, Frankfurt, to deRF, Nov. 9; same to same, Nov. 11; Dec. 13; AN, 132 AQ 5699/2M44, April 28, 1867. Cf. Stern, *Gold and iron*, pp. 109f. Such was the competition that the Rothschild houses had to be content with 4 million gulden.

188   RAL, XI/109/89/2, Anselm, Vienna, to his uncle and cousins, Paris, Aug. 2, 1866; same to same, Aug. 3; AN, 132 AQ 5771/3M38,39, Goldschmidt, Vienna, to deRF, Aug. 28; Goldschmidt to James, Aug. 29; Goldschmidt to deRF, Sept. 6; RAL, XI/109/89/2, Mayer Carl, Frankfurt, to his cousins and nephews, Sept. 9; same to same, Sept. 16; RAL, T9/180, Gustave, Paris, to his cousins, London, Sept. 18; AN, 132 AQ 5771/3M38,39, Goldschmidt to deRF, Oct. 28; RAL, XI/109/89/1, Alphonse to his cousins, Oct. 29; RAL, XI/109/89, James to his nephews, Oct. 31; RAL, XI/109/89/2, Anselm to James and his cousins, Nov. 27.

189   RAL, XI/109/89/2, Mayer Carl, Frankfurt, to his cousins and nephews, London, Aug. 8, 1866; AN, 132 AQ 5698/2M43, Mayer Carl, Hirschberg, to his uncle and cousins, Paris, Aug. 23; RAL, XI/109/89/2, Mayer Carl, Stuttgart, to his cousins and nephews, Sept. 1; RAL, XI/109/89/1, Alphonse, Paris, to his cousins, London, Sept. 2; RAL, XI/109/89/2, Mayer Carl, Frankfurt, to his cousins and nephews, Sept. 6; same to same, Sept. 7; Sept. 12; Sept. 13; AN, 132 AQ 5698/2M43, Wilhelm Carl, Frankfurt, to his uncle and mother, Paris, Sept. 17; RAL, XI/109/90/1, Mayer Carl to his cousins and nephews, May 10, 1867; same to same, May 14; RAL, XI/109/90/2, May 17; May 26; May 30. Cf. Gille, *Maison Rothschild*, vol. II, pp. 451–3; Kitchen, *Political economy*, pp. 117f.

190   RAL, XI/109/91/2, Mayer Carl, Berlin, to Lionel, Sept. 20, 1867.

191   RAL, RFamC/21, Charlotte, London, to Leo, Cambridge, Sept. 3, 1866.

192   RAL, RFamC/21, Charlotte, London, to Leo, Cambridge, Dec. 1, 1866.

193   RAL, T9/186, Adolph, Geneva, to Lionel, London, July 9, 1866.

194   Schwemer, *Geschichte*, vol. III/2, pp. 339, 344, 352, 383, 386, 393ff. Manteuffel contemptuously likened Mayer Carl to the Merchant of Venice.

195   RAL, XI/109/89/1, Alphonse, Paris, to his cousins, London, July 23, 1866; same to same, July 24; July 26 (two letters); July 29; RAL, T9/156, Nathaniel, Vienna, to deRF, July 24.

196   RAL, RFamC/21, Charlotte, London, to Leo, Cambridge, July 26, 1866.

197   Schwemer, *Geschichte*, vol. III/2, pp. 373f.

198   RAL, XI/109/89/2, Anselm, Vienna, to his uncle and cousins, July 26, 1866. For Bismarck's reply see RAL, XI/109/89/2, *Bismarck*, Nikolsburg, to Anselm, July 28.

199   RAL, XI/109/89/2, Mayer Carl, Frankfurt, to his cousins and nephews, London, July 22, 1866; RAL, T9/164, MAR to NMR, July 23; RAL, XI/109/89/2, Mayer Carl to his cousins and nephews, July 31; same to same, Aug. 1; Aug. 12; RAL, RFamC/21, Charlotte, London, to Leo, Cambridge, Aug. 4, 1866; same to same, Aug. 11. Cf. Stern, *Gold and iron*, p. 91.

200 RAL, RFamC/21, Charlotte, London, to Leo, Cambridge, Aug. 20, 1866; same to same, Aug. 21; RAL, T9/204, Bleichröder to Lionel, London, Aug. 22.

201 RAL, RFamC/21, Charlotte, London, to Leo, Cambridge, Aug. 27, 1866; same to same, Dec. 1; RAL, RFamC/3/42, Natty, Frankfurt, to Lionel and Charlotte, Feb. 3, 1867. Cf. Heuberger, *Rothschilds*, pp. 180ff.

202 RAL, RFamC/3/45, Natty, London, to his cousins, Paris, April 16, 1867; Schwemer, *Geschichte*, vol. III/2, p. 451.

203 RAL, XI/109/89/1, Alphonse, Paris, to his cousins, London, Aug. 14, 1866.

204 AN, 132 AQ 5968/2M43, Mayer Carl, Frankfurt, to deRF, Aug. 16, 1866; RAL, XI/109/89/1, Alphonse, Paris, to his cousins, London, Aug. 20.

205 Böhme, *Foundation of the German Empire*, p. 176; Pflanze, *Bismarck*, vol. II, p. 16; Kitchen, *Political economy*, p. 118.

FIVE *Bonds and Iron (1867–1870)*

1 AN, 132 AQ 5903/422, James, Nice, to his children, Paris, Feb. 1, 1867.

2 AN, 132 AQ 5903/426, James, Nice, to his children, Feb. 2, 1867.

3 RAL, T10/128, Ferdinand, Paris, to Lionel, London, April 15, 1868.

4 RAL, T10/77, James, Paris, to his nephews, London, Oct. 1, 1868; RAL, T10/76, same to same, Oct. 4.

5 RAL, XI/109/96/1, Edmond, Paris, to his cousins, London, Oct. 31, 1868.

6 RAL, XI/109/96/1, Alphonse, Paris, to his cousins, London, Nov. 2, 1868; same to same, Nov. 3; Nov. 9.

7 RAL, XI/109/96/1, Alphonse, Paris, to his cousins, London, Nov. 17, 1868.

8 RAL, XI/109/96/1, Leo, Paris, to his parents, London, Nov. 19, 1868.

9 RAL, XI/109/96/1, Natty, Paris, to his parents, London, Nov. 19, 1868.

10 *The Times*, Nov. 19, 1868. Cf. Muhlstein, *Baron James*, pp. 213f.

11 Corti, *Reign*, p. 408; Stern, *Gold and iron*, p. 109; Rosenbaum and Sherman, *M. M. Warburg & Co.*, p. 65. According to the authors, "the expenses for his coach to the cemetery were debited to the Warburg current account."

12 RAL, XI/109/96/1, Alfred, Paris, to his parents, London, Nov. 19, 1868.

13 *The Times*, Nov. 23, 1868, p. 7. Cf. Bouvier, *Rothschild*, pp. 141f.; Dupont-Ferrier, *Marché financier*, pp. 75ff.

14 The lack of detailed accounts for the period 1852–79 makes it difficult to be sure when the Paris house made its dramatic leap forward ahead of the other houses in terms of capital. We do know that in the five years to 1868 the Paris house made profits in excess of £4 million, an annual average of £800,000: RAL, T10/166, Leo, Paris, to his uncle [Anthony] and Natty, London, Aug. 20, 1869. This was very nearly double the average figure for the entire period 1852–79, suggesting that much if not all the credit for the growth of de Rothschild Frères should go to James.

15 *The Times*, Dec. 19, 1868.

16 RAL, [formerly CPHDCM], OC 222, James's will, June 16, 1864. Altogether, James left Betty lump sums and annuities worth around 16 million francs, the house at 19 rue Laffitte and its contents, the house at 7 rue Rossini and its contents, as well as use of the houses at Boulogne and Ferrières. Ownership of Ferrières James wished to pass to his eldest son Alphonse and to carry on through the male line according to the rule of primogeniture. This was at odds with French law (which favoured partible inheritance), but James explicitly requested his descendants to put his wishes first! In addition, Alphonse was given 100,000 francs a year for the upkeep of the Ferrières. However, most of the other real estate (Boulogne, 21, 23 and 25 rue Laffitte, 2 rue Rossini, 2 and 4 rue St Florentin, 267 rue St Honoré, the three houses in the rue Mondovi and the Lafite estate) was divided equally between his three sons, with the remainder going to Charlotte and Hélène. On attaining his majority, Edmond was to receive various sums amounting to around 3 million francs. The rest of James's fortune, including his share in the bank, was divided between Alphonse, Gustave and Edmond (*c.* 26 per cent each) and Charlotte and Hélène (11 per cent each). Various codicils distributed further sums to his children (400,000 francs), their spouses (300,000) and Salomon James's widow Adèle (100,000).

17 Muhlstein, *Baron James*, p. 211.

18 Mérimée, *Correspondance générale*, 2e série, vol. XIII, p. 343.

19 RAL, [formerly CPHDCM], OC 222, James's will, June 16, 1864.

20 Braudel and Labrousse, *Histoire économique*, vol. III, pp. 441–6.

21 RAL, XI/109/89/1, Alphonse, Paris, to his cousins, London, Nov. 19, 1866. Cf. Palmade, *Capitalism*, pp. 139–48.

22 Girard, *Travaux publics*, pp. 367f.; Bouvier, *Rothschild*, p. 162.

23 RAL, XI/109/90/1a, Alphonse, Paris, to his cousins, London, March 4, 1867; same to same, March 25.

24 RAL, XI/109/91/2, Alphonse, Paris, to his cousins, London, Sept. 9, 1867; same to same, Sept. 10; Sept. 11; Sept. 18; Plessis, *Banque de France*, vol. III, pp. 300f.; Braudel and Labrousse, *Histoire économique*, vol. III, p. 446.

25 Gille, *Maison Rothschild*, vol. II, pp. 113, 117.

26 AN, 132 AQ 5902, James, Nice, to his children, Jan. 24, 1867 [wrongly dated 1866].

27 Girard, *Travaux publics*, pp. 367f.

28 RAL, T10/130, Adolph, Paris, to Lionel, May 10, 1868. Cf. Prevost-Marcilhacy, *Rothschild*, pp. 83f.

29 Roqueplan, *Baron James*, p. 4. Cf. Chirac, *Haute Banque*, p. 225.

30 Girard, *Travaux publics*, pp. 279–81.

31 Marion, *Histoire financière*, vol. V, pp. 343–8.

32 Cobban, *Modern France*, vol. II, pp. 192f.

33 See e.g. RAL, XI/109/89, James, Paris, to his nephews, London, Nov. 12, 1866; RAL, XI/109/89, same to same, Nov. 24; RAL, XI/109/99/1, Alphonse, Paris, to his cousins, London, Aug. 28, 1869; same to same, Sept.1; Sept. 6; Sept. 7; Sept. 11; Sept. 13.

34 Einaudi, "Money and politics," esp. pp. 126ff.

35 RAL, XI/109/93/1, Alphonse, Paris, to his cousins, London, Jan. 23, 1868. Cf. Corley, *Democratic Despot*, p. 292.

36 RAL, T10/94, Nat, Paris, to his brothers, London, Aug. 17, 1868; RAL, T10/85, Alphonse, Paris, to his cousins, London, Sept. 5.

37 Vincent (ed.), *Disraeli, Derby and the Conservative party*, p. 279. See also pp. 311, 319.

38 AN, 132 AQ 5902, James, Nice, to his children, Paris, Jan. 20, 1867 [wrongly dated 1866]; same to same, Jan. 23; AN, 132 AQ 5903/419, same to same, Jan. 30.

39 AN, 132 AQ 5903/422, James, Nice, to his children, Paris, Feb. 1, 1867.

40 RAL, XI/109/90/1a, Alphonse, Paris, to his cousins, London, Jan. 23, 1867. See also RAL, XI/109/91/1, same to same, July 3; Oct. 8.

41 RAL, RFamC/21, Charlotte, London, to Leo, Cambridge, Dec. 29, 1866.

42 RAL, XI/109/92/1, Alphonse, Paris, to his cousins, London, Dec. 18, 1867.

43 RAL, XI/109/91/1, Alphonse, Paris, to his cousins, London, July 22, 1867; same to same, July 28; Aug. 4; Aug. 5.

44 RAL, T10/40, Mayer, Paris, to his brothers, London, undated, Aug. 1867.

45 RAL, XI/109/91/2, Mayer, Wildbad, to his brothers and nephews, London, undated, summer 1867; AN, 132 AQ 5903, James, Wildbad, to Alphonse, July 19; same to same, Aug. 2; RAL, T10/6, Aug. 6.

46 Plessis, *Second Empire*, p. 121. Gustave and Say had become friends at college: RAL, T16/140, Gustave, Paris, to his cousins, London, April 22, 1896.

47 Loménie, *Dynasties*, vol. I, p. 212; Bouvier, *Rothschild*, pp. 182–4.

48 Gille, *Maison Rothschild*, vol. II, pp. 392f.; Pinkney, *Paris*, pp. 196f.

49 RAL, XI/109/97/1, Alphonse, Paris, to his cousins, London, March 3, 1869.

50 Pinkney, *Paris*, pp. 204f.; Bouvier, *Rothschild*, pp. 184–7; Gille, *Maison Rothschild*, vol. II, pp. 461f.

51 RAL, XI/109/98/1, Alphonse, Paris, to his cousins, London, May 18, 1869; RAL, T10/158, Gustave, Paris, to his cousins, London, May 25; RAL, XI/109/98/1, Nat, Paris, to his brothers, London, June 13; same to same, June 17; RAL, XI/109/100/1, Nov. 25.

52 RAL, XI/109/99/1, Alphonse, Gastein, to Lionel, London, July 14, 1869; Alphonse, Paris, to his cousins, London, Aug. 28; same to same, Oct. 13; Oct. 18; Oct. 19; Oct. 21; Oct. 26; RAL, XI/109/100/1, Nov. 25.

53 RAL, XI/109/99/1, Nat, Paris, to his brothers, London, July 6, 1869; same to same, July 18.

54 RAL, XI/109/100/1, Alphonse, Paris, to his cousins, London, Dec. 27, 1869; RAL, XI/109/101/1, same to same, Jan. 4, 1870; Jan. 6.

55 Vincent (ed.), *Derby diaries, 1869–78*, p. 46.

56 RAL, XI/109/101/1, Alphonse, Paris, to his cousins, London, Jan. 12, 1870; same to same, Jan. 13; Jan. 20; Feb. 7; Feb. 9; Feb. 12; Feb. 23; March 20; March 24; April 2.

57   RAL, XI/109/102, Alphonse, Paris, to his cousins, London, April 4, 1870 (two letters); same to same, April 5; April 6; April 9; April 13; April 14; April 25; May 1; May 5; May 6; May 7.

58   RAL, XI/109/102, Alphonse, Paris, to his cousins, London, May 10, 1870 (two letters); same to same, June 2.

59   RAL, RFamC/21, Charlotte, London, to Leo, Cambridge, Aug. 30, 1866.

60   RAL, T10/120, Gustave, Paris, to his cousins, London, undated, *c.* Nov. 1868.

61   RAL, XI/109/89/1, Alphonse, Paris, to his cousins, London, Oct. 20, 1866; RAL, XI/109/92/1, same to same, Nov. 24.

62   RAL, XI/109/89, James, Paris, to his nephews, London, Dec. 8, 1866.

63   RAL, XI/109/90/1a, Alphonse, Paris, to his cousins, London, Jan. 17, 1867; same to same, Feb. 15; RAL, XI/109/92/1, Dec. 19; RAL, XI/109/93/1, Jan. 2, 1868; Jan. 9; Jan. 15.

64   RAL, XI/109/90/1a, Alphonse, Paris, to his cousins, London, Jan. 11, 1867. For other illustrations of his over-optimism about French military preparedness, see RAL, XI/109/90/1, same to same, April 18; RAL, XI/109/92/1, Dec. 18; RAL, XI/109/94/1, May 8; May 14.

65   RAL, RFamC/21, Charlotte, London, to Leo, Cambridge, Feb. 21, 1867.

66   AN, 132 AQ 5903, James to Alphonse, July 26, 1867. The military weaknesses exposed by the Luxembourg crisis changed James's view on the need for rearmament somewhat: RAL, XI/109/91, James, Paris, to his nephews, London, Nov. 28.

67   RAL, XI/109/93/1, Alphonse, Paris, to his cousins, London, Jan. 15, 1868; RAL, T10/83, same to same, Jan. 24; RAL, XI/109/93/1, Jan. 27; Jan. 30; RAL, XI/109/94/1, undated, *c.* April 22; April 29; May 25. It was a sign of the widening gulf between the government and the Rothschilds that the loan was underwritten by the Société Générale: RAL, XI/109/95/1, James, Paris, to his nephews, London, Aug. 5; RAL, XI/109/95/1, Alphonse to his cousins, Sept. 10.

68   RAL, T10/89, Alphonse, Paris, to his cousins, London, April 10, 1868; RAL, XI/109/94/1, same to same, April 17.

69   RAL, XI/109/94/2, Mayer Carl, Berlin, to his cousins and nephews, London, April 17, 1868; same to same, April 20; April 21.

70   RAL, XI/109/100/1, Alphonse, Paris, to his cousins, London, Dec. 13, 1869.

71   RAL, XI/109/101/1, Alphonse, Paris, to his cousins, London, Jan. 10. 1870; same to same, Feb. 18; March 2; March 5; March 8.

72   Kindleberger, *Financial history*, p. 222.

73   Corti, *Reign*, pp. 406f.; Lyons, *Internationalism*, p. 111.

74   See in general Enaudi, "Money and politics."

75   RAL, XI/109/90/1a, Alphonse, Paris, to his cousins, London, March 7, 1867; same to same, March 16; RAL, T10/11, Nat, Paris, to his brothers, London, undated, June.

76   RAL, RFamC/21, Charlotte, London, to Leo, Cambridge, Aug. 16, 1866.

77   RAL, RFamC/2/6, Disraeli to Charlotte, Jan. 2, 1867. Cf. Vincent (ed.), *Disraeli, Derby and the Conservative party*, pp. 319, 332.

78   RAL, T10/17, Alphonse, Paris, to his cousins, London, Jan. 16, 1867; RAL, XI/109/90/1a, same to same, March 11; March 14; March 25; March 26; March 29; March 31; April 1; April 2; April 3; RAL, XI/109/90/1, Mayer Carl, Frankfurt, to his cousins and nephews, London, April 1; RAL, XI/109/91, James, Paris, to his nephews, London, April 2; same to same, April 3; April 4; April 6; RAL, XI/109/90/1, Alphonse to his cousins, April 5 (two letters); same to same, April 7; April 8; April 9; April 10 (two letters); April 12; April 14; April 15; April 17; April 18; RAL, XI/109/91, James to his nephews, April 16; same to same, April 17; April 18; RAL, RFamC/3/44, Natty, Frankfurt, to his parents, April 16; same to same, April 19; RAL, RFamC/3/45, April 16; RAL, T10/52, Bleichröder, Berlin, to deRF, April 19; RAL, XI/109/90/1, James to his nephews, April 19; Alphonse to his cousins, April 20; same to same, April 21; April 28 (two letters); April 30; May 1; May 6; May 7; James to his nephews, April 23; same to same, April 24; April 25; May 1; May 2; May 7; May 8; RAL, T10/54, Bleichröder to deRF, May 9; RAL, XI/109/90/2, Alphonse to his cousins, June10; RAL, T10/29, same to same, June 12; RAL, T10/3, James to his nephews, July 22. Cf. Corti, *Reign*, pp. 406f.; Davis, *English Rothschilds*, pp. 145f.

79   RAL, XI/109/91/2, Anthony, Paris, to his brothers, Aug. 31, 1867.

80   RA, J82/158, Lionel, New Court, to Foreign Office [extract], Sept. 3, 1867.

81   Monypenny and Buckle, *Disraeli*, vol. IV, p. 470; Davis, *English Rothschilds*, p. 146; Kynaston, *City*, vol. I, p. 251.

82 RA, J82/157, Lord Stanley, Foreign Office, to Victoria, Sept. 9, 1867.

83 Davis, *English Rothschilds*, p. 104.

84 RAL, XI/109/94/1, Alfred, Paris, to his parents, April 20, 1868.

85 Corti, *Reign*, p. 394. Cf. on Rothschild relations with Leopold II, Dosne, *Mémoires*, vol. II, pp. 294f.

86 RAL, XI/109/92/1, Alphonse, Paris, to his cousins, London, Oct. 30, 1867. Cf. Gille, *Maison Rothschild*, vol. II, pp. 425–8, 462–6. See also pp. 539–42.

87 RAL, T10/144, Gustave, Paris, to his cousins, London, Feb. 15, 1869.

88 RAL, XI/109/95/1, Alphonse, Paris, to his cousins, London, Sept. 27, 1868; same to same, Sept. 29; RAL, XI/109/96/1, Oct. 24; Oct. 27; Nov. 2; Nov. 7; Nov. 9; Nov. 21; Nov. 25; Nov. 29; Dec. 9; James, Paris, to his nephews, London, Oct. 31; Anselm, Schillersdorf, to deRF, Nov. 29. Cf. Gille, *Maison Rothschild*, vol. II, pp. 473–84; Bouvier, *Rothschild*, pp. 182–4, 218–21; *idem, Crédit Lyonnais*, pp. 609–16.

89 RAL, XI/109/99/1, Alphonse, Paris, to his cousins, London, Sept. 16, 1869; same to same, Sept. 17.

90 RAL, XI/109/96/1, Alphonse, Paris, to his cousins, London, Dec. 13, 1868; RAL, XI/109/97/1, same to same, Jan. 13, 1869; Jan. 21; RAL, XI/109/97/1, Nat, Paris, to his brothers, London, Jan. 24; Alphonse to his cousins, Jan. 25; same to same, March 1; March 10; RAL, T10/152, March 14; RAL, XI/109/98/1, April 1; Nat to his brothers, April 1; Alphonse to his cousins, April 8. Cf. Gille, *Maison Rothschild*, vol. II, pp. 480–84, 528–35: the Zaragoza company's debt to the Rothschild banks now totalled 42.7 million francs.

91 RAL, XI/109/98/1, Alphonse, Paris, to his cousins, London, April 11, 1869; same to same, April 13.

92 RAL, XI/109/99/1, Alphonse, Paris, to his cousins, London, Sept. 21, 1869; same to same, Sept. 23; Sept. 27; Sept. 28; RAL, XI/109/100/1, Oct. 4; Oct. 12; Oct. 13; Oct. 14; Oct. 15; Oct. 19; Oct. 21; Oct. 22; Mayer Carl, Frankfurt, to his cousins and nephews, London, Oct. 23; same to same, Nov. 18; Dec. 11. Cf. Gille, *Maison Rothschild*, vol. II, p. 482.

93 RAL, XI/109/100/1, Alphonse, Paris, to his cousins, London, Nov. 22, 1869; RAL, XI/109/101/1, same to same, Jan. 12, 1870; Jan. 13; Jan. 20; Leo, Paris, to his parents, London, Feb. 23; Alphonse to his cousins, March 15; same to same, March 18; March 20; March 23; March 24; RAL, XI/109/102, April 1; April 9; April 13; April 22; Mayer Carl, Frankfurt, to his cousins and nephews, London, April 28; Alphonse to his cousins, May 3; same to same, June 2. The London and Paris houses jointly advanced £1.7 million to the Spanish government, which was to be repaid over twenty years. This debt was then converted into 5 per cent bonds with a nominal value of £2,318,000: Gille, *Maison Rothschild*, vol. II, pp. 483f. As Lionel was heard to observe in January 1870, "whatever might be the condition of the Spanish government as regards money matters it could always raise funds . . . in England. This is certainly not the result of the peculiar honesty of Spanish administration, but of a vague tradition of the ancient wealth of Spain . . .": Vincent (ed.), *Derby diaries, 1869–78*, p. 46.

94 RAL, XI/109/106, Alphonse, Paris, to his cousins, London, July 7, 1871; same to same, Sept. 1; RAL, RFam/C/4/357, Lionel, London, to Leo, Innsbruck, Sept. 7; RAL, RFamC/4/358, same to same, Sept. 8. The syndicate included Fould, Pillet-Will, Crédit Lyonnais, the Banque Franco-égyptienne, Oppenheim, the Société Générale and the Banque Impériale Ottomane—one of the heterogeneous combinations so characteristic of the period after 1870.

95 RAL, XI/109/108/1, Alphonse to his cousins, April 22, 1872; RAL, XI/109/109/1, Natty, Birnam, to his parents, London, Aug. 21; RAL, XI/109/109/1, Alphonse, Paris, to his cousins, London, Aug. 31; same to same, Sept. 23. Cf. Bouvier, *Rothschild*, pp. 218–21; *idem, Crédit Lyonnais*, pp. 628–35 (see also p. 651 for the loan of 1876).

96 Calculated from figures in Martin, *Rothschild*, pp. 285f., 413; Mitchell, *European historical statistics*, p. 789; Carreras, *Industrializacion Espanola*, pp. 185–7.

97 RAL, XI/109/107/1, Alphonse, Paris, to his cousins, London, Nov. 29, 1871; RAL, XI/109/108/1, same to same, April 6, 1872; April 24; RAL, T11/43, Weisweiller, Madrid, to Lionel, London, Nov. 17, 1873; RAL, T11/63, Weisweiller to NMR, July 5, 1874.

98 Martin, *Rothschild*, pp. 258f., 308–10, 389, 491–4.

99 RAL, XI/109/109/1, Natty, Birnam, to his parents, London, Aug. 20, 1872; Alphonse, Paris, to his cousins, London, Sept. 19; RAL, T10/410, same to same, Nov. 30; RAL, T11/6, undated, *c.* Feb. 1873. The possibility had been raised before: see *The Times*, May 17, 1870, p. 10.

100 RAL, T11/79, Alphonse, Paris, to his cousins, London, Dec. 31, 1874.

101   Cameron, *France and Europe*, pp. 263–73; Carr, *Spain*, p. 266n.

102   AN, 132 AQ/322/A-4-1/4 Espagne, deRF agreement with comte de Girgenti; Sept. 10?, 1868; AN, 132 AQ/322/A-4-1/1 Espagne, Separation agreement between Isabella at Francis of Assisi, May 9, 1874; AN, 132 AQ/322/A-4-1/2 Espagne, Isabella to deRF, Sept. 9, 1881; AN, 132 AQ/322/Succession (Alphonse XII), Moreno to Bauer, April 13, 1901; AN, 132 AQ/322/Succession Alphonse-François d'Assise, Bauer to deRF, June 6, 1904.

103   RAL, T10/104, Gustave, Paris, to his cousins, London, Oct. 5, 1868; RAL, T10/105, same to same, Oct. 20; RAL, XI/109/96/1, Mayer to his brothers, Oct. 21; RAL, XI/109/97/1, Alphonse, Paris, to his cousins, London, Jan. 13, 1869.

104   RAL, XI/109/96/1, Alphonse, Paris, to his cousins, London, Oct. 10, 1868. Erroneously, Alphonse described Amadeo as "of all the candidates, the most dangerous."

105   RAL, XI/190/97/1, Nat, Paris, to his brothers, London, Feb. 7, 1869.

106   Figures from Mitchell, *European historical statistics*, pp. 407, 698; Mack Smith, *Italy*, pp. 85ff.

107   Ciocca and Ulizzi, "I tassi di cambio," pp. 354f.

108   See e.g. RAL, XI/109/92/1, Alphonse, Paris, to his cousins, London, Jan. 22, 1867; RAL, XI/109/90/1a, same to same, Jan. 25; RAL, XI/109/90/1a, March 23; RAL, XI/109/90/1, May 31; RAL, XI/109/91/1, July 3; RAL, XI/109/100/1, Dec. 9, 1869.

109   AN, 132 AQ 5902, James, Nice, to his children, Paris, Jan. 1, 1867; same to same, Jan. 9; Jan. 16; RAL, XI/109/90/1a, Alphonse, Paris, to his cousins, London, Jan. 11; AN 132 AQ 5903/396, James to his children, Jan. 17; AN, 132 Q 5903/399, same to same, Jan. 18; AN, 132 AQ 5903/400, Jan. 20. Cf. Jacquemyns, *Langrand-Dumonceau*, vol. IV, pp. 152f.

110   RAL, XI/109/93/1, Alphonse, Paris, to his cousins, London, Jan. 18, 1867; RAL, T10/81, James, Nice, to his children, Paris, Jan. 21; RAL, XI/109/90/1a, Alphonse to his cousins, Jan. 28.

111   AN, 132 AQ 5903, James, Nice, to his children, Paris, Jan. 30, 1867; AN, 132 AQ 5903/426, same to same, Feb. 2; AN, 132 AQ 5903/429, Feb. 3; AN, 132 AQ 5903/431, Feb. 4; RAL, XI/109/90/1a, Alphonse, Paris, to his cousins, London, Feb. 5; AN, 132 AQ 5903/433, James, Nice, to Landau, Feb. 6; AN, 132 AQ 5903/443, James to his children, Feb. 11; RAL, XI/109/90/1a, Alphonse to his cousins, Feb. 23; RAL, XI/109/97/1, Nat, Paris, to his brothers, London, Feb. 24; RAL, XI/109/90/1a, Alphonse to his cousins, March 12; same to same, March 31; RAL, XI/109/90/1, undated, *c.* April 14; April 28. Cf. Gille, *Maison Rothschild*, vol. II, pp. 466–72; Jacquemyns, *Langrand-Dumonceau*, vol. IV, pp. 179–91; Bouvier, *Crédit Lyonnais*, pp. 532–46.

112   RAL, XI/109/90/1a, Nat, Paris, to his brothers, London, undated, *c.* March 1867 (several letters); RAL, XI/109/93/1, James, Paris, to his nephews, London, Feb. 14; RAL, XI/109/90/1a, Alphonse, Paris, to his cousins, London, Feb. 27; RAL, XI/109/90/1, same to same, undated, *c.* April (several letters); RAL, RFamC/3/47, Natty, Genoa, to his parents, London, May 4; RAL, XI/109/90/1, Alphonse to his cousins, May 7; same to same, May 8; May 9; May 10; May 11; May 14; RAL, XI/109/91, James to his nephews, May 14.

113   AN, 132 AQ 5902, James, Ostend, to his children, Paris, July 30, 1865.

114   RAL, XI/109/91, James, Paris, to his nephews, London, May 15, 1867; same to same, May 16; May 17; May 22. Cf. RAL, XI/109/90/1, Alphonse, Paris, to his cousins, London, May 15; same to same, May 17; May 19. Cf. Bouvier, *Rothschild*, pp. 221ff.

115   RAL, XI/109/90/1, Alphonse, Paris, to his cousins, London, May 19, 1867; same to same, May 20.

116   RAL, XI/109/91/2, Mayer, Wildbad, to his brothers, London, undated, *c.* July 1867; RAL, XI/109/91/1, Alphonse, Paris, to his cousins, London, July 7; AN, 132 AQ 5903, James, Homburg, to Alphonse, undated, *c.* July; AN, 132 AQ 5903/459, same to same, July 13; RAL, XI/109/91/1, Alphonse to his cousins, July 15; same to same, July 17; July 19; July 20; July 22; undated, *c.* July 23; July 25; Aug. 2; Aug. 4; Aug. 12; Aug. 15; AN, 132 AQ 5903, James to Alphonse, July 17; RAL, XI/109/91/2, Ferdinand, St Moritz, to Lionel, London, July 26.

117   RAL, T10/39, Nat, Paris, to his brothers, London, undated, *c.* Aug. 1867; RAL, XI/109/92/1, Alphonse, Paris, to his cousins, London, Sept. 23; RAL, T10/4, James, Paris, to his nephews, London, undated, *c.* Sept.; RAL, XI/109/91/2, Nat to his brothers, undated, *c.* Sept.; RAL, XI/109/92/1, Alphonse to his cousins, Oct. 2; same to same, Oct. 4; Oct. 5; Oct. 6; Oct. 10; Oct. 21; Oct. 27; Oct. 29 (two letters); Oct. 30; Oct. 31; Nov. 2; Nov. 4; Nov. 5; Nov. 6; Nov. 24; Dec. 2; Dec. 6; Dec. 7; Dec. 14; Dec. 16; Dec. 23; RAL, XI/109/93/1, Jan. 2, 1868.

118   RAL, RFamC/3/41, Natty, Paris, to his parents, London, May 16, 1867. Interestingly, the London

house tendered for a contract to supply rifles to the Italian government in the aftermath of the Roman crisis: AN, 132 AQ 5483/1M89, NMR to deRF, Jan. 13, 1868.

119   RAL, XI/109/96/1, Alphonse, Paris, to his cousins, London, Oct. 14, 1868; same to same, Oct. 22; Oct. 27; Dec. 28; Dec. 29; RAL, XI/109/97/1, Jan. 7; Feb. 1.

120   RAL, XI/109/93/1, Alphonse to his cousins, Feb. 1, 1868. Cf. Alphonse to his cousins, Jan. 14; same to same, Jan. 15; Jan. 17; Jan. 22; Jan. 23; James, Paris, to his nephews, London, Jan. 29; Alphonse to his cousins, Feb. 3; same to same, Feb. 11; Feb. 14.

121   RAL, XI/109/97/1, Nat, Paris, to his brothers, London, Feb. 7, 1869. James's death considerably enhanced Nat's influence in Paris; he became the senior figure to whom Alphonse, unaccustomed to taking decisions for himself, turned for counsel.

122   RAL, XI/109/97/1, Alphonse, Paris, to his cousins, London, Feb. 12, 1869; same to same, Feb. 20.

123   RAL, XI/109/93/1, Alphonse, Paris, to his cousins, London, Jan. 14, 1868; same to same, Feb. 4; Feb. 6; Feb. 7; Feb. 13; Feb. 14; Feb. 19; Feb. 23; March 2; March 8.

124   RAL, XI/109/97/1, Mayer Carl, Frankfurt, to his cousins and nephews, London, Feb. 5, 1869; same to same, Feb. 11; Feb. 20; April 6; April 8.

125   Clough, *Economic history*, p. 52n.; Bouvier, *Rothschild*, pp. 221f.

126   AN, 132 AQ 5520/1M126, NMR to deRF, May 20, 1881.

127   RAL, XI/109/90/1, Alphonse, Paris, to his cousins, London, May 22, 1867; same to same, May 25; May 27; RAL, XI/109/91, James, Paris, to his nephews, London, May 28; RAL, XI/109/90/1, Alphonse to his cousins, June 4; same to same, June 5; June 14; June 16. See also RAL, XI/109/99/1, Sept. 18, 1869. Cf. Gille, *Maison Rothschild*, vol. II, pp. 469f.; Bouvier, *Crédit Lyonnais*, p. 542.

128   Cameron, *France and Europe*, pp. 300f.

129   RAL, RFamC/3/47, Natty, Genoa, to his parents, London, May 4, 1867; RAL, XI/109/97/1, Nat, Paris, to his brothers, London, Jan. 24, 1869; RAL, XI/109/99/1, Anthony, Vienna, to his brothers, undated, summer 1869; same, Venice, to same, Sept. 19; Sept. 20; RAL, XI/109/100/1, same, Turin, to same, Oct. 12.

130   RAL, XI/109/96/1, Alphonse, Paris, to his cousins, London, Oct. 10, 1869; same to same, Nov. 9. Cf. Gille, *Maison Rothschild*, vol. II, pp. 519f.

131   Gille, *Maison Rothschild*, vol. II, p. 520.

132   Ayer, *Century of finance*, pp. 50, 54.

133   AN, 132 AQ 5500/1M106, NMR to deRF, Jan. 23, 1874; same to same, Jan. 30; Feb. 3; Feb. 13; Feb. 17; March 3; March 10; March 27; April 14; April 17; April 24; April 28; AN, 132 AQ 5501/1M107, May 1; May 5; May 12; May 19; June 1; July 3; July 7; July 10; July 14; July 17; July 21; July 24; July 31; Aug. 7; Aug. 14; Aug. 28; AN, 132 AQ 5502/1M108, Sept. 4; Sept. 11; Sept. 22; Oct. 2; Oct. 6; Oct. 9; Oct. 13; Oct. 16; Oct. 20; Oct. 23; Oct. 27; Nov. 3; Nov. 13; Nov. 27; Dec. 29.

134   RAL, XI/109/89, James, Paris, to his nephews, London, Nov. 5, 1866; RAL, XI/109/89/1, Alphonse, Paris, to his cousins, London, Nov. 6; same to same, Nov. 9; Nov. 20; Nov. 21; Nov. 27; RAL, XI/109/89, James to his nephews, Dec. 10; AN, 132 AQ 5902, James, Nice, to his children, Jan. 1, 1867; AN, 132 AQ 5903, same to same, Jan. 12; RAL, XI/109/92/1, Alphonse to his cousins, Nov. 16; same to same, Dec. 6; RAL, XI/109/93/1, Jan. 20, 1868; Jan. 22; Jan. 23; Feb. 3; RAL, XI/109/94/2, Mayer Carl, Berlin, to his cousins and nephews, London, April 10; RAL, XI/109/94/1, Alphonse to his cousins, April 11; AN, 132 AQ 5701/2M46, Mayer Carl to deRF, April 27; RAL, XI/109/94/1, deRF to NMR, May 11; AN, 132 AQ 5701/2M46, Mayer Carl to deRF, Aug. 11; RAL, XI/109/101/1, Alphonse to his cousins, Jan. 4, 1870; RAL, XI/109/102, same to same, April 13; April 19; RAL, XI/109/102/1, Salbert, Vienna, to Lionel, April 30; RAL, XI/109/102, Alphonse to his cousins, May 4; RAL, XI/109/102, Lionel, London, to his cousins and nephews, Paris, May 9; RAL, XI/109/104, Alphonse to his cousins, March 5, 1871; RAL, XI/109/105, Mayer Carl, Frankfurt, to his cousins and nephews, London, April 19; same to same, April 21; Salbert, Vienna, to Lionel, London, April 23; Anselm to Alphonse, May 12; RAL, XI/109/106/3, Anselm, Homburg, to Lionel, Aug. 7; RAL, XI/109/107/1, Alphonse to his cousins, Feb. 21, 1871; same to same, Feb. 23; RAL, T10/408, Nov. 2.

135   AN, 132 AQ 5903/396, James, Nice, to his children, Paris, Jan. 17, 1867; AN, 132 AQ 5903/422, same to same, Feb. 1; AN, 132 AQ 5903/443, Feb. 11; AN, 132 AQ 5903, James, Inverness, to his children, undated, summer 1868; RAL, XI/109/95/1, Alphonse, Paris, to his cousins, London, Sept. 19.

136   RAL, XI/109/94/1, Alphonse, Paris, to his cousins, London, April 29, 1868; RAL, XI/109/102, same to same, June 6; June 17; June 20; June 30; July 4; July 31; Aug. 1. An exemption from the new tax, which would have cost the company around 4 million lire a year, could be bought only by giving the government an advance payment of 22 million lire. Cf. Gille, *Maison Rothschild*, vol. II, pp. 520ff.

137   RAL, XI/109/93/1, Alphonse, Paris, to his cousins, London, Feb. 16, 1868; same to same, Feb. 21; Feb. 26; James, Paris, to Anselm, Feb. 28; Alphonse to his cousins, March 1; same to same, March 5; March 8; March 12; RAL, XI/109/94/2, Anselm to deRF, April 25; RAL, XI/109/94/1, Alphonse to his cousins, May 16.

138   AN, 132 AQ 5705/2M50&51, Mayer Carl to deRF, June 1, 1870; same to same, June 6.

139   RAL, XI/109/103/1, Salbert, Vienna, to Lionel, London, Nov. 1, 1870; same to same, Jan. 14; AN, 132 AQ 32/1D2(16), Anselm to deRF, Jan. 7, 1871.

140   Cameron, *France and Europe*, p. 301; Bouvier, *Rothschild*, pp. 221ff.

141   Bodleian Library, Queen Victoria Papers 5–7 0340, Lionel, New Court to Disraeli, Sept. 3, 1867.

142   On the diplomatic ramifications, see RAL, XI/109/91, James, Paris, to his nephews, London, March 7, 1867; RAL, XI/109/90/1a, Alphonse, Paris, to his cousins, March 16; RAL, T10/16, C. de B. [Alexandre de Saint-Chéron] to deRF, July 25; RAL, XI/109/92/1, Alphonse to his cousins, London, Nov. 6.

143   RAL, XI/109/96/1, Anselm, Vienna, to Lionel, London, Dec. 10, 1868; same to same, Dec. 16; Anselm to Alphonse, Paris, Dec. 17; RAL, XI/109/96/1, Alphonse to his cousins, Dec. 22; RAL, XI/109/97/1, Salbert, Vienna, to his cousins, Jan. 14, 1869; Anselm to deRF, Jan. 16.

144   RAL, XI/109/89, James, Paris, to his nephews, London, Nov. 29, 1866; AN, 132 AQ 5903/398, James, Nice, to his children, Paris, Jan. 19, 1867. Cf. RAL, XI/109/91/2, Mayer, Paris, to his brothers, London, undated, 1867. The London house also took a bullish view of Austrian securities at this point: RAL, RFamC/3/42, Natty, Frankfurt, to his parents, London, Feb. 3.

145   RAL, XI/109/91/2, Mayer, Wildbad, to his brothers, London, undated, summer 1867 (two letters); same, Frankfurt, to same, July 20; RAL, XI/109/91/2, Alphonse, Paris, to his cousins, London, Sept. 3.

146   RAL, XI/109/91/2, Mayer Carl, Frankfurt, to James, Paris, undated, *c.* Sept. 1867; Mayer Carl to James and his cousins, Sept. 3; Mayer Carl, Berlin, to James, Sept. 14; same to same, Sept. 18; Mayer Carl, Berlin, to Lionel, Sept. 19; same to same, Sept. 23.

147   RAL, XI/109/91/2, Natty, Great Malvern, to his parents, London, Sept. 22, 1867.

148   RAL, XI/109/92/1, Anselm, Vienna, to James and his cousins, Nov. 8, 1867; RAL, XI/109/92/1, Alphonse, Paris, to his cousins, London, Nov. 11; same to same, Nov. 25; RAL, XI/109/93/1, Feb. 1, 1868; Feb. 5; March 1; March 3.

149   RAL, XI/109/93/1, Alphonse, Paris, to his cousins, London, March 4, 1868; same to same, March 8; March 26 (two letters); RAL, XI/109/94/1, Alphonse to his cousins, April 22; same to same, May 31; RAL, XI/109/95/2, Natty, Frankfurt, to his parents, London, Aug. 2. Whenever a government imposed a tax on securities—and it happened increasingly often after 1866—the Rothschilds were outraged, predicting collapsing bond prices if not national bankruptcy. Yet, as Alphonse himself on occasion admitted, the effect of such taxes, if they served to reduce a government's budget deficit, could actually be to strengthen bond prices. This paradox perplexed "practical men" like Alphonse and Natty, so they generally ignored it and continued to denounce such taxes.

150   RAL, XI/109/92/1, Anselm, Vienna, to James and Alphonse, Paris, Oct. 3, 1867; same to same, Nov. 4; RAL, XI/109/95/2, Anselm to James, Sept. 2, 1868; RAL, XI/109/96/2, Mayer Carl, Frankfurt, to his cousins and nephews, London, Dec. 12. Cf. Macartney, *House*, p. 208.

151   RAL, XI/109/90/1a, Alphonse, Paris, to his cousins, London, Feb. 13, 1867; same to same, Feb. 15; AN, 132 AQ 5903/447, James, Nice, to his children, Feb. 15; RAL, XI/109/90/1a, Alphonse to his cousins, Feb. 19; same to same, Feb. 24.

152   Berend and Ranki, *Economic development*, pp. 64, 101; Michel, *Banques et banquiers*, p. 225. On the Creditanstalt's capital reduction after 1867, Wirth, *History of banking*, pp. 126f.

153   RAL, XI/109/94/2, Anselm, Vienna, to NMR, April 16, 1868; CPHDCM, 637/1/38/10, SMR to MAR, June 3; RAL, XI/109/97/1, Anselm, Vienna, to Lionel, March 20, 1869; RAL, XI/109/108/2, Anselm and Salbert to Lionel, March 11, 1872; same to same, April 24; May 30. For Beust's vain efforts to secure James's approval of this measure, see Corti, *Reign*, p. 407; Gille, *Maison Rothschild*, vol. II, pp. 484–7.

154   RAL, XI/109/101/2, Anselm, Vienna, to Lionel, London, Feb. 25, 1870; Salbert to Lionel, Feb. 28.

155   RAL, XI/109/107/1, Mayer Carl, Frankfurt, to his cousins and nephews, London, Oct. 16, 1871; same
       to same, Nov. 5; Dec. 14; Dec. 17; Dec. 18; Dec. 30; Dec. 31; Jan. 10, 1872. For details of Hungarian
       bond issues, see Ayer, *Century of finance*, pp. 56ff.

156   RAL, XI/109/102/1, Salbert, Vienna, to Lionel, London, April 13, 1870; RAL, XI/109/107/1, same to
       same, Oct. 2, 1871; Oct. 12; Oct. 16; Oct. 21; Oct. 25; Nov. 3; Nov. 7. Cf. RAL, XI/109/107/1,
       Anselm, Vienna, to Lionel, Nov. 8, 1871; RAL, XI/109/107/1, Anselm to Ferdinand, Nov. 27.

157   RAL, XI/109/92/1, Alphonse, Paris, to his cousins, London, Dec. 11, 1867.

158   RAL, XI/109/106/3, Mayer Carl, Frankfurt, to his cousins and nephews, London, July 22, 1871; RAL,
       XI/109/107/1, Alphonse, Paris, to his cousins, London, March 14, 1872.

159   AN, 132 AQ 5772/3M41, Anselm, Vienna, to James, Paris, Nov. 13, 1867.

160   RAL, XI/109/98/1, Ferdinand, Wiesbaden, to Lionel and Charlotte, April 15, 1869.

161   RAL, XI/109/99/1, Anthony, Vienna, to his brothers, undated, *c.* Sept. 1869; same to same, Sept. 6;
       Sept. 10. He was right: Huertas, *Economic growth*, p. 44.

162   RAL, XI/109/102/1, Anselm, Vienna, to Lionel, London, April 14, 1870.

163   RAL, XI/109/97/1, Anselm, Vienna, to deRF, Jan. 5, 1869 (two letters); same to same, Jan. 12; Jan. 16;
       RAL, XI/109/98/2, Salbert, Vienna, to deRF, May 19; same to same, Feb. 20.

164   RAL, XI/109/99/1, Alphonse, Gastein, to Lionel, London, July 14, 1869; RAL, XI/109/99/1, Nat,
       Paris, to his brothers, London, July 18; RAL, XI/109/99/1, Alphonse, Paris, to his cousins, London,
       Aug. 4; same to same, Aug. 5; Aug. 6; Aug. 11; Aug. 12; Alfred, Paris, to his parents, Aug. 13; RAL,
       XI/109/100/1, Alphonse to his cousins, Aug. 21; same to same, Sept. 11; Oct. 4; Oct. 11; Oct. 16; Oct.
       27; RAL, XI/109/101/2, Anselm to NMR, Jan. 17, 1870; Albert to NMR, Jan. 25. Cf. Gille, *Maison
       Rothschild*, vol. II, pp. 500, 525–8; Bouvier, *Union Générale*, pp. 73–80; Grunwald, "Europe's railways,"
       pp. 203f.

165   RAL, XI/109/102, Alphonse, Paris, to his cousins, London, June 20, 1870; RAL, XI/109/107/1, same
       to same, Jan. 24, 1872; Feb. 14.

166   RAL, XI/109/108/2, Anselm, Vienna, to Ferdinand, London, March 9, 1872.

167   RAL, XI/109/91, James, Paris, to his nephews, London, May 27, 1867.

168   RAL, RFamC/21, Charlotte, London, to Leo, Cambridge, May 29, 1867; RAL, RFamC/4/79, Lionel,
       London, to Charlotte, Paris, July 10. Cf. Vincent (ed.), *Disraeli, Derby and the Conservative party*, p.
       310.

169   Stern, *Gold and iron*, p. 355. The Hohenzollern-Sigmaringens were the senior but Catholic branch of
       the Hohenzollern family, and hence related to the Prussian royal family.

170   RAL, XI/109/91/2, Ferdinand, St Moritz, to Lionel, July 20, 1867.

171   RAL, XI/109/93/1, Mayer Carl, Berlin, to his cousins and nephews, London, March 30, 1868.

172   RAL, XI/109/94/2, Mayer Carl, Berlin, to his cousins and nephews, London, April 1, 1868.

173   Stern, *Gold and iron*, p. 356.

174   RAL, XI/109/94/2, Mayer Carl, Berlin, to his cousins and nephews, London, April 8, 1868.

175   RAL, XI/109/100/1, Alphonse, Paris, to his cousins, London, Oct. 14, 1869. See also Gille, *Maison
       Rothschild*, vol. II, pp. 596–7.

176   RAL, XI/109/107/1, Mayer Carl, Berlin, to his cousins and nephews, London, March 16, 1872; RAL,
       XI/109/108/1, Anselm, Vienna, to his cousins, London, April 4; RAL, XI/4/37, Gustave, Paris, to
       Lionel, London, July 3, 1876; RAL, XI/4/37, Samson Tauber, Rabbi of Vaslui near Jassy, to Chief
       Rabbi Adler, London, Jan. 4, 1867; same to same, Jan. 18; Adler to Lionel, Jan. 15; illegible signature,
       Jassy, to Lionel, Jan. 18; Frankl, Secretary of the Alliance Universelle in Vienna, to Goldschmidt,
       Vienna, Jan. 28; Salbert, Vienna, to Lionel, Jan. 29; Adler to Lionel, Feb. 16; same to same, Feb. 26;
       RAL, T13/85, Alphonse, Paris, to his cousins, London, May 25, 1881; AN, 10 132 AQ 132, Discon-
       togesellschaft to Kornfeld (Hungarian Credit Bank), Aug. 21, 1900.

177   RAL, RFamC/3/42, Natty, Frankfurt, to Lionel and Charlotte, London, Feb. 3, 1867.

178   RAL, RFamC/21, Charlotte, London, to Leo, Cambridge, Feb. 3, 1867.

179   RAL, RFamC/21, Charlotte, London, to Leo, Cambridge, Feb. 15, 1867; same to same, Feb. 16. Cf.
       The Times, Feb. 21, 1867, p. 7, quoting "a mercantile letter from Frankfort": "This choice was not influ-
       enced by party feeling. Baron Rothschild can do a deal of good for our commercial interests, and par-
       ticularly by insisting on the maintenance of the florin currency, which is essential to our commerce with
       the South . . . There has rarely been such general enthusiasm for a candidate, and all was done without
       any previous understanding, and even without a regular committee."

180   RAL, T10/13, Nat, Paris, to his brothers, London, undated, summer 1867; RAL, XI/109/90/1, Alphonse, Paris, to his cousins, London, undated, summer 1867.

181   RAL, T10/49, Alphonse, Paris, to his cousins, London, Nov. 29, 1867. Cf. Pulzer, *Jews and German state*, p. 74.

182   RAL, XI/109/106/3, undated, unsigned note to NMR, 1871; Corti, *Reign*, pp. 430f.

183   RAL, XI/109/94/2, Mayer Carl, Berlin, to his cousins and nephews, London, April 30, 1868. See also RAL, XI/109/101/2, same to same, March 30, 1870.

184   RAL, XI/109/97/1, Mayer Carl, Berlin, to his cousins and nephews, London, March 14, 1869.

185   RAL, XI/109/101/2, Mayer Carl, Berlin, to his cousins and nephews, London, March 7, 1870; same to same, March 8; April 1.

186   RAL, XI/109/94/2, Mayer Carl, Berlin, to his cousins and nephews, London, April 4, 1868; same to same, April 15; April 22.

187   Monypenny and Buckle, *Disraeli*, vol. V, p. 85.

188   RAL, XI/109/94/2, Mayer Carl, Berlin, to his cousins and nephews, London, April 23, 1868. A similar letter was sent to the Paris house: Mayer Carl to deRF, April 23.

189   Monypenny and Buckle, *Disraeli*, vol. V, p. 85.

190   RAL, XI/109/94/2, Mayer Carl, Berlin, to his cousins and nephews, London, April 25, 1868. See also same to same, April 26; April 27; May 1.

191   Vincent, *Disraeli, Derby and the Conservative party*, p. 332.

192   RAL, XI/109/97/1, Mayer Carl, Berlin, to his cousins and nephews, London, March 15, 1869; same to same, March 19.

193   AN, 132 AQ 5705/2M50&51, Mayer Carl to deRF, June 1, 1870.

194   RAL, XI/109/102, Mayer Carl, Frankfurt, to his cousins and nephews, London, July 3, 1870.

195   Gall, *White revolutionary*, vol. I, p. 343.

196   Stern, *Gold and iron*, pp. 121–6.

197   RAL, XI/109/96/1, Alphonse, Paris, to his cousins, London, Oct. 10, 1868; RAL, XI/109/96/2, Mayer Carl, Frankfurt, to his cousins and nephews, London, Oct. 17.

198   AN, 132 AQ 5701/2M46, Mayer Carl, Berlin, to deRF, Jan. 6, 1867; same to same, Jan. 8; Jan. 9; Jan. 13; RAL, XI/109/90/1a, Alphonse, Paris, to his cousins, London, Feb. 24.

199   Gille, *Maison Rothschild*, vol. II, pp. 496–8.

200   AN, 132 AQ 5701/2M46, Mayer Carl, Berlin, to deRF, May 24, 1868; RAL, XI/109/95/2, Mayer Carl, Frankfurt, to his cousins and nephews, London, July 15; AN, 132 AQ 5903, James, Dieppe, to Gustave, Paris, July 22.

201   AN, 13 AQ 5702/2M47, Mayer Carl, Berlin, to deRF, Nov. 10, 1868; same to same, Nov. 15; RAL, XI/109/96/2, Mayer Carl, Frankfurt, to his cousins and nephews, London, Nov. 23; same to same, Dec. 5; AN, 132 AQ 5703/2M48, Mayer Carl, Frankfurt, to deRF, May 8, 1869; RAL, XI/109/98/1, Mayer Carl to his cousins and nephews, London, May 8; same to same, May 10; AN, 132 AQ 5703/2M48, Mayer Carl to deRF, May 12. Cf. Gille, *Maison Rothschild*, vol. II, pp. 496–8.

202   RAL, XI/109/100/2, Mayer Carl, Frankfurt, to his cousins and nephews, London, Dec. 25, 1869.

203   RAL, XI/109/101/2, Mayer Carl, Berlin, to his cousins and nephews, London, March 3, 1870; same to same, March 21.

204   *Jahrbuch für die Statistik des Preussischen Staates* (1869), pp. 372–443, 466–545.

205   Schremmer, "Public finance," p. 454.

206   RAL, XI/109/94/2, Mayer Carl, Berlin, to his cousins and nephews, London, May 9, 1868.

207   RAL, XI/109/96/1, Mayer Carl, Frankfurt, to his cousins and nephews, London, Oct. 2, 1868; same to same, Oct. 9.

208   RAL, XI/109/98/1, Mayer Carl, Berlin, to his cousins and nephews, London, April 6, 1869.

209   RAL, XI/109/98/1, Mayer Carl, Berlin, to his cousins and nephews, London, May 10, 1869; same to same, May 23; May 25; May 27; May 31; June 3; June 5; June 10. Emphasis added.

210   RAL, XI/109/98/1, Mayer Carl, Berlin, to his cousins and nephews, London, June 10, 1869; same to same, June 14; June 15; June 16; June 21; RAL, XI/109/99/1, July 24; July 28; RAL, T10/182, same, Lucerne, to same, Aug. 10; same, Frankfurt, to same, Aug. 21; RAL, XI/109/100/1, Oct. 9; Oct. 11; Oct. 31. After lengthy negotiations, Mayer Carl had secured a 12 million thaler share of this operation. Cf. Stern, *Gold and iron*, p. 111. Undaunted, Hansemann revived the scheme by floating the bonds exclusively outside Germany, but the Paris Rothschilds declined to participate, to Mayer Carl's annoy-

ance: RAL, XI/109/101/1, Mayer Carl, Frankfurt, to his cousins and nephews, London, Jan. 28, 1870; same to same, Jan. 29; Feb. 9; Feb. 10; RAL, XI/109/101/1, Alphonse, Paris, to his cousins, London, Feb. 21; Mayer Carl to his cousins and nephews, Feb. 24; same to same, Feb. 26; March 4. Cf. Gille, *Maison Rothschild*, vol. II, pp. 496ff.

211   RAL, XI/109/101/1, Mayer Carl, Berlin, to his cousins and nephews, London, Feb. 18, 1870; RAL, XI/109/101/2, same to same, March 31; April 6; May 5.

212   RAL, XI/109/101/2, Mayer Carl, Berlin, to his cousins and nephews, London, March 2, 1870.

213   RAL, XI/109/100/1, Mayer Carl, Frankfurt, to his cousins and nephews, London, Nov. 9, 1869; RAL, XI/109/100/2, same to same, Dec. 25; RAL, XI/109/101/1, Jan. 1, 1870; RAL, XI/109/101/2, March 20; May 1; RAL, XI/109/102, July 2; July 3; July 5.

214   AN, 132 AQ 5704/2M49, Mayer Carl, Frankfurt, to deRF, July 4, 1869; RAL, XI/109/101/1, Mayer Carl, Frankfurt, to his cousins and nephews, London, Feb. 3, 1870; same to same, Feb. 13; Feb. 18; Feb. 21; Feb. 23; Feb. 24; March 1; March 6; March 7; March 8; March 11; March 12; March 19; March 20; March 25; April 4; Alphonse, Paris, to his cousins, London, March 20; March 24; June 7. Cf. Pflanze, *Bismarck*, vol. II, pp. 88f.; Stürmer *et al.*, *Striking the balance*, pp. 174f. According to Mayer Carl, he and Hansemann "first applied for the concession in 1867"; Oppenheim became involved only "after all the work has been done by Mr Hansemann and myself."

215   RAL, XI/109/102, Mayer Carl, Frankfurt, to his cousins and nephews, London, June 25, 1870; same to same, June 29; Gustave, Paris, to his cousins, London, June 30; same to same, July 1; Mayer Carl to his cousins and nephews, July 6. Cf. Stern, *Gold and iron*, p. 127.

216   RAL, XI/109/96/2, Mayer Carl, Frankfurt, to his cousins and nephews, London, Nov. 15, 1868.

217   RAL, XI/109/99/1, Mayer Carl, Frankfurt, to his cousins and nephews, London, July 24, 1869.

218   RAL, XI/109/101/2, Mayer Carl, Berlin, to his cousins and nephews, London, March 3, 1870; same to same, March 4; March 29.

219   RAL, XI/109/102, Mayer Carl, Frankfurt, to his cousins and nephews, London, April 26, 1870; same to same, June 29; July 24.

220   RAL, XI/109/103/1, Mayer Carl, Frankfurt, to his cousins and nephews, London, Oct. 10, 1870; same to same, Oct. 23; Dec. 1; RAL, XI/109/104, March 7, 1871.

221   AN, 132 AQ 5699/2M44, Mayer Carl, Frankfurt, to deRF, April 28, 1867; RAL, XI/109/90/1, Mayer Carl, Frankfurt, to his cousins and nephews, London, May 10; same to same, May 14; RAL, XI/109/90/2, May 17; May 26; May 30; RAL, XI/109/96/2, Oct. 17, 1868; Nov. 20; RAL, XI/109/97/1, Jan. 11, 1869 [wrongly dated 1868]; Jan. 13; Jan. 19 [wrongly dated 1868]; RAL, XI/109/101/2, March 14, 1870; March 17; RAL, XI/109/102, April 13; April 16; April 18; April 20; April 22; April 26.

222   AN, 132 AQ 5700/2M45, MAR to deRF, Aug. 27, 1867; RAL, XI/109/91/2; Mayer Carl, Frankfurt, to his cousins and nephews, London, Sept. 3; Sept. 4; Sept. 8; AN, 132 AQ 5700/2M45, Mayer Carl to James and his cousins, Sept. 12; RAL, XI/109/91/2, Mayer Carl to his cousins and nephews, Sept. 16; RAL, XI/109/94/2, same to same, May 5, 1868; RAL, XI/109/101/1, Jan. 19, 1870; Jan. 28; Feb. 2.

223   RAL, XI/109/96/2, Mayer Carl, Frankfurt, to his cousins and nephews, London, Dec. 12, 1868; RAL, XI/109/100/1, same to same, Nov. 13, 1869; RAL, XI/109/100/2, Dec. 11; Dec. 16; RAL, XI/109/101/1, Feb. 8, 1870; RAL, XI/109/102, June 25.

224   RAL, XI/109/100/1, Mayer Carl, Frankfurt, to his cousins and nephews, London, Nov. 14, 1869; same to same, Nov. 22; RAL, XI/109/100/2, Dec. 21.

225   RAL, XI/109/94/2, Mayer Carl, Berlin, to his cousins and nephews, London, April 6, 1868; RAL, XI/109/96/2, same, Berlin, to same, Oct. 14; AN, 132 AQ 5702/2M47, Mayer Carl to deRF, Oct. 14; RAL, XI/109/98/1, Mayer Carl to his cousins and nephews, April 26, 1869; same to same, May 5; RAL, XI/109/98/1, June 5; RAL, XI/109/101/1, Jan. 15, 1870; RAL, XI/109/101/2, Feb. 28; RAL, XI/109/102/1, March 27; RAL, XI/109/103/1, Dec. 11.

226   RAL, XI/109/94/2, Mayer Carl, Berlin, to his cousins and nephews, London, April 16, 1868.

227   RAL, XI/109/100/2, Mayer Carl, Frankfurt, to his cousins and nephews, London, Dec. 4, 1869; same to same, Dec. 17; RAL, XI/109/101/2, March 5, 1870; RAL, XI/109/102, April 2; April 7; April 10.

228   AN, 132 AQ 5703/2M48, Mayer Carl, Berlin, to deRF, May 16, 1869; RAL, XI/109/102, Mayer Carl, Berlin, to his cousins and nephews, London, May 2, 1870; same to same, May 3; May 8.

229   RAL, XI/109/92/1, Alphonse, Paris, to his cousins, London, Nov. 7, 1867; same to same, Nov. 12; Nov. 21.

230   RAL, XI/109/95/1, James, Paris, to Lionel, London, Aug. 26, 1868; RAL, XI/109/95/2, Natty, Paris, to

his parents, London, Sept. 4; RAL, XI/109/95/1, Alphonse, Paris, to his cousins, London, Sept. 19; same to same, Sept. 22; RAL, XI/109/96/1, Oct. 12; Oct. 14; RAL, XI/109/96/2, Mayer Carl, Frankfurt, to his cousins and nephews, London, Oct. 21. Cf. Gille, *Maison Rothschild*, vol. II, pp. 491, 539–42. The Russian government kept a large deposit at the Paris house until April 1869: RAL, XI/109/98/1, Mayer Carl, Frankfurt, to his cousins and nephews, London, April 25, 1869.

231 RAL, XI/109/96/2, MAR to deRF, Nov. 8, 1868.

232 RAL, XI/109/97/1, Mayer Carl, Frankfurt, to his cousins and nephews, London, Feb. 6, 1869.

233 AN, 132 AQ 5703/2M48, Mayer Carl to deRF, Feb. 7, 1869. See also RAL, XI/109/97/1, Nat, Paris, to his brothers, London, Feb. 7; Alphonse, Paris, to his cousins, London, Feb. 9; Mayer Carl to his cousins, Feb. 10; Alphonse to his cousins, Feb. 24; same to same, March 1; Anselm, Vienna, to Gustave, Paris, March 6; RAL, XI/109/98/1, Mayer Carl, Berlin, to his cousins and nephews, London, April 9.

234 RAL, XI/109/99/1, Alphonse, Paris, to his cousins, London, Aug. 6, 1869; RAL, XI/109/100/1, Nat, Paris, to his brothers, London, Oct. 8; Mayer Carl, Frankfurt, to his cousins and nephews, London, Oct. 10; Alphonse to his cousins, Oct. 11; same to same, Nov. 13. Cf. Gille, *Maison Rothschild*, vol. II, pp. 494f.

235 RAL, XI/109/106/3, Mayer Carl to his cousins and nephews, London, Aug. 16, 1871.

236 RAL, XI/109/108/2, Anselm, Vienna, to his nephews, Paris, March 22, 1872; RAL, XI/109/107/1, Alphonse, Paris, to his cousins, London, March 27.

237 RAL, XI/109/92/1, Mayer Carl, Berlin, to Lionel, London, Oct. 11, 1867; RAL, XI/109/93/1, Alphonse, Paris, to his cousins, London, Jan. 3, 1868; same to same, Jan. 8; Jan. 20. Cf. Gille, *Maison Rothschild*, vol. II, p. 487; Stern, *Gold and iron*, p. 342.

238 RAL, XI/109/93/1, James, Paris, to his nephews, London, Feb. 21, 1868; RAL, XI/109/94/2, Mayer Carl, Berlin, to his cousins and nephews, London, May 6; same to same, May 13; June 7; June 10; RAL, XI/109/95/2, Natty, Frankfurt, to his parents, London, Aug. 2; RAL, XI/109/96/2, Mayer Carl, Frankfurt, to his cousins and nephews, London, Nov. 6; MAR to deRF, Nov. 8; Mayer Carl to his cousins and nephews, Dec. 15; same to same, Dec. 16. See also RAL, XI/109/105, April 16, 1871; April 18.

239 RAL, XI/109/92/1, Mayer Carl, Berlin, to Lionel, London, Oct. 11, 1867; RAL, XI/109/94/1, Alphonse, Paris, to his cousins, London, May 25, 1868; RAL, XI/109/94/2, Mayer Carl, Berlin, to his cousins and nephews, London, May 27; same to same, June 22; RAL, XI/109/95/2, July 13; RAL, XI/109/95/2, Natty, Paris, to his parents, London, Sept. 5; AN, 132 AQ 5702/2M47, Mayer Carl to deRF, Oct. 6.

240 RAL, XI/109/98/1, Mayer Carl, Berlin, to his cousins and nephews, London, May 10, 1869. See also RAL, XI/109/100/1, same, Frankfurt, to same, Oct. 21; RAL, XI/109/101/2, same, Berlin, to same, March 8, 1870; March 10; March 13; March 14; RAL, XI/109/103/1, Nov. 27; RAL, XI/109/105, April 20, 1871; AN, 132 AQ 32, Bleichröder, Berlin, to Alphonse, May 4; RAL, XI/109/105, Mayer Carl to his cousins and nephews, May 26; RAL, XI/109/106/3, same to same, July 24; RAL, XI/109/107/1, same to same, Oct. 23; Nov. 1; Jan. 10, 1872; March 13.

241 RAL, XI/109/98/1, Mayer Carl, Berlin, to his cousins and nephews, London, April 9, 1869; same to same, April 10.

242 RAL, XI/109/100/2, Mayer Carl, Frankfurt, to his cousins and nephews, London, Dec. 3, 1869; RAL, XI/109/100/1, Alphonse, Paris, to his cousins, London, Dec. 12; RAL, XI/109/101/1, Mayer Carl to Natty, Jan. 13, 1870; same to his cousins and nephews, Jan. 16; Jan. 27; Alphonse to his cousins, Jan. 28; same to same, Feb. 1; RAL, XI/109/101/2, Anselm, Vienna, to Anthony, London, Jan. 28; RAL, XI/109/101/1, Alphonse to his cousins, Feb. 3; same to same, Feb. 7; AN, 132 AQ 5489/1M95, NMR to deRF, Feb. 3.

243 RAL, XI/109/101/1, Mayer Carl, Frankfurt, to his cousins and nephews, London, Feb. 1, 1870; same to same, Feb. 5.

244 RAL, XI/109/104, Mayer Carl, Frankfurt, to his cousins and nephews, London, March 7, 1871; same to same, March 10; March 12; March 14; March 24; RAL, XI/109/107/1, Dec. 20; March 28, 1872; RAL, XI/109/108/1, April 1 (two letters); April 6; April 8; April 12; RAL, XI/109/108/1, Anselm, Vienna, to Lionel, London, April 18; AN, 13 AQ 5500/1M106, NMR to deRF, Feb. 20, 1874; same to same, March 20. Cf. Davis, *English Rothschilds*, p. 156; Gille, *Maison Rothschild*, vol. II, p. 496; Rosenbaum and Sherman, *M. M. Warburg & Co.*, p. 66; Bouvier, *Crédit Lyonnais*, pp. 586–8.

245 AN, 132 AQ 5705/2M50&51, Mayer Carl, Frankfurt, to deRF, Feb. 9, 1870; RAL, XI/109/101/1, Alphonse, Paris, to his cousins, London, Feb. 10; Mayer Carl, Frankfurt, to his cousins and nephews, London, Feb. 12; same to same, Feb. 13; Feb. 18; Alphonse to his cousins, Feb. 22; same to same, Feb.

28; RAL, XI/109/101/2, Mayer Carl, Berlin, to his cousins and nephews, London, March 23; RAL, XI/109/102, same to same, June 28; RAL, XI/109/103/1, Nov. 1; RAL, XI/109/105, Anselm, Cologne, to Lionel, London, April 21, 1871.

246 RAL, XI/109/107/1, Mayer Carl, Berlin, to his cousins and nephews, London, March 9, 1872. See also RAL, XI/109/108/1, same to same, May 14.

247 RAL, XI/109/103/1, Mayer Carl, Berlin, to his cousins and nephews, London, Nov. 7, 1870; Salbert, Vienna, to Lionel, London, Nov. 16; same to same, Nov. 17; Anselm, Vienna, to Lionel, London, Nov. 18.

248 RAL, T11/53, Alphonse, Paris, to his cousins, London, Feb. 16, 1874; RAL, T11/62, Edmond, Paris, to his cousins, London, Feb. 18.

SIX   *Reich, Republic, Rentes (1870–1873)*

1 RAL, XI/109/102, Mayer Carl, Frankfurt, to his cousins and nephews, London, Sept. 1, 1870.
2 RAL, XI/109/102, Alphonse, Paris, to his cousins, London, Aug. 22, 1870.
3 Goldschmidt, *Erinnerungen*, p. 87.
4 Paret, *Art as history*, pp. 174f. Civilians are wholly absent in the later 1885 version.
5 Stern, *Gold and iron*, p. 127.
6 RAL, T10/251, Mayer Carl, Berlin, to his cousins and nephews, London, April 5, 1870.
7 RAL, XI/109/102, Alphonse, Paris, to his cousins, London, May 5, 1870.
8 RAL, XI/109/102, Mayer Carl, Frankfurt, to his cousins and nephews, London, July 2, 1870.
9 RAL, XI/109/102, Mayer Carl, Frankfurt, to his cousins and nephews, London, July 7, 1870; same to same, July 8.
10 Kynaston, *City*, vol. I, p. 255.
11 Carr, *Wars of German unification*, pp. 183–203.
12 RAL, XI/109/102, Gustave, Paris, to his cousins, London, July 4, 1870; same to same, July 5.
13 RAL, XI/109/102, Gustave, Paris, to his cousins, London, July 6, 1870. It is worth asking whom Gustave referred to when he used the pronoun "on." The answer would seem to be that this was not just bourse gossip but a Rothschild version of "sources close to the government," if not the government itself.
14 RAL, XI/109/102, Gustave, Paris, to his cousins, London, July 6, 1870.
15 RAL, XI/109/102, Gustave, Paris, to his cousins, London, July 11, 1870.
16 RAL, XI/109/102, Mayer Carl, Frankfurt, to his cousins and nephews, London, July 14, 1870.
17 Morley, *Gladstone*, vol. II, p. 325; Corti, *Reign*, pp. 410–15. Cf. Matthew (ed.), *Gladstone diaries*, vol. VII, pp. 100f. It cannot be entirely coincidental that three days later Lionel sent Gladstone two tickets for the Derby via Granville: Ramm (ed.), *Gladstone–Granville correspondence, 1868–1876*, vol. I, p. 101.
18 RAL, XI/109/102, Gustave, Paris, to his cousins, London, July 7, 1870.
19 The London Rothschilds also intimated to the Prussian ambassador Bernstorff that war would be "inevitable" if Leopold accepted: Lord, *Origins of the War of 1870*, p. 135. By the 11th, Gustave was writing to Bleichröder "as if the war between France and Prussia had already broken out": Stern, *Gold and iron*, p. 128.
20 RAL, XI/109/102, Gustave, Paris, to his cousins, London, July 11, 1870. Emphasis added.
21 Morley, *Gladstone*, vol. II, p. 328; Ramm (ed.), *Gladstone–Granville correspondence, 1868–1876*, vol. I, p. 109.
22 RAL, XI/109/102, Gustave, Paris, to his cousins, London, July 12, 1870.
23 RAL, XI/109/102, Mayer Carl, Frankfurt, to his cousins and nephews, London, July 12, 1870.
24 RAL, XI/109/102, Gustave, Paris, to his cousins, London, July 14, 1870.
25 RAL, XI/109/102, Gustave, Paris, to his cousins, London, July 14, 1870.
26 RAL, XI/109/102, Mayer Carl, Frankfurt, to his cousins and nephews, London, July 15, 1870; same to same, July 18; July 20; RAL, T10/260, July 22; RAL, XI/109/102, July 23. Cf. Stürmer *et al.*, *Striking the balance*, pp. 176f.
27 Compare RAL, T10/236, Gustave, Paris, to his cousins, London, Aug. 5, 1870, with RAL, T46/24, M. M. Warburg & Co. to NMR, Aug. 5; RAL, XI/109/102, Mayer Carl, Frankfurt, to his cousins and nephews, London, Aug. 5; Alphonse, Paris, to his cousins, London, Aug. 6; same to same, Aug. 9; RAL, T46/25, M. M. Warburg & Co. to NMR, Aug. 9.
28 Matthew, *Gladstone, 1809–1874*, p. 185. Lionel told Disraeli that "the cabinet had been completely

taken by surprise: none of them knew anything of foreign affairs except Granville: and Gladstone really believed Cobden's theory that men were growing to civilised for war": Vincent (ed.), *Derby diaries, 1869–78*, p. 66.

29   RAL, XI/109/102, Gustave to his cousins, Sept. 3, 1870; RAL, XI/4/29, deRF to NMR, March 30, 1871; Stern, *Gold and iron*, p. 134; Wilson, *Rothschild*, pp. 206f.

30   RAL, XI/109/102, Gustave, Paris, to his cousins, London, July 17, 1870; RAL, XI/109/102, Alphonse, Paris, to his cousins, London, July 20; same to same, July 21; July 25; Gustave to his brothers, July 25; Alphonse to his cousins, Aug. 1; same to same, Aug. 2; Aug. 12; Nathan James to his uncles and cousins, Aug. 19; Alphonse to his cousins, Aug. 21; same to same, Aug. 22; Sept. 12.

31   Landes, "Spoilers foiled," p. 86; Kynaston, *City*, vol. I, p. 256. Morgan issued the 6 per cent bonds at 85, terms which were regarded by the French as excessively harsh.

32   RAL, XI/109/102, Mayer Carl, Frankfurt, to his cousins and nephews, London, July 24, 1870; RAL, XI/109/103/1, same to same, Oct. 9; Oct. 10; Oct. 12; RAL, T10/275, Oct. 19; RAL, XI/109/103/1, Nov. 4.

33   RAL, XI/109/103/1, Mayer Carl, Berlin, to his cousins and nephews, London, Nov. 23, 1870. Cf. Stern, *Gold and iron*, p. 131; Stürmer *et al.*, *Striking the balance*, p. 177.

34   RAL, XI/109/103/1, Mayer Carl, Berlin, to his cousins and nephews, London, Nov. 25, 1870; same to same, Nov. 26; Nov. 27; Nov. 29; Dec. 1; Dec. 4; Dec. 5; Dec. 6; Dec. 8; Dec. 9; RAL, XI/109/101/1, Jan. 8, 1871 [wrongly dated 1870].

35   RAL, XI/109/102, Gustave, Paris, to his cousins, London, July 19, 1870; Alphonse, Paris, to his cousins, London, July 20; same to same, July 23. Cf. Davis, *English Rothschilds*, p. 142.

36   RAL, XI/109/102, Alphonse, Paris, to his cousins, London, July 25, 1870; same to same, July 27; July 28; Aug. 1; Aug. 24. Cf. Davis, *English Rothschilds*, pp. 147–9. It is worth noting, on the other hand, that Gustave had himself mentioned the possibility of French designs on Belgium less than two weeks before.

37   Matthew, *Gladstone, 1809–1874*, p. 181.

38   RA, I66/70, Ponsonby to the Queen, Oct. 16, 1870.

39   "[Disraeli] gives me the Rothschild view of the war: his friends fear it will be long . . . they think the Prussians well armed and well prepared; and that neither is a decisive result to be expected for the present, nor can either party acquiesce in a defeat which is not decisive": Vincent (ed.), *Derby diaries, 1869–78*, p. 66 (July 19, 1870).

40   RAL, XI/109/102, Mayer Carl, Frankfurt, to his cousins and nephews, London, Aug. 4, 1870; RAL, T10/267, same to same, Aug. 9. Cf. Stürmer *et al*, *Striking the balance*, p. 176.

41   RAL, XI/109/102, Mayer Carl, Frankfurt, to his cousins and nephews, London, Aug. 7, 1870 (two letters); same to same, Aug. 14.

42   RAL, XI/109/102, Mayer Carl, Frankfurt, to his cousins and nephews, London, Aug. 27, 1870.

43   RAL, XI/109/102, Mayer Carl, Frankfurt, to his cousins and nephews, London, Sept. 1, 1870; same to same, Sept. 3; Sept. 7; Sept. 17; RAL, XI/109/103/1, Oct. 9; Oct. 10; Oct. 11; Oct. 12; Oct. 29.

44   RAL, XI/109/103/1, Mayer Carl, Berlin, to his cousins and nephews, London, Nov. 23, 1870.

45   RAL, XI/109/103/1, Mayer Carl, Berlin, to his cousins and nephews, London, Nov. 30, 1870.

46   RAL, T10/266, Mayer Carl, Frankfurt, to his cousins and nephews, London, undated, Aug. 1870; RAL, T10/277, same to same, Oct. 24.

47   RAL, T10/286, Bleichröder, Berlin, to Lionel, London, Dec. 11, 1870; RAL, T10/285, Mayer Carl, Frankfurt, to his cousins and nephews, London, Dec. 28.

48   Bundesarchiv Potsdam, Alphonse to Bismarck, July 17, 1870.

49   RAL, XI/109/102, Alphonse, Paris, to his cousins, London, Aug. 21, 1870; same to same, Aug. 24.

50   RAL, XI/109/102, Gustave, Paris, to his cousins, London, July 17, 1870; Alphonse, Paris, to his cousins, London, July 23.

51   RAL, XI/109/102/1, Ferdinand, Paris, to Lionel, Paris, Aug. 6, 1870; same to same, Aug. 6.

52   RAL, XI/109/102, Alphonse, Paris, to his cousins, London, July 31, 1870.

53   RAL, T10/239, Gustave, Paris, to his cousins, London, Sept. 14, 1870; RAL, XI/109/102, Alphonse, Paris, to his cousins, London, undated, *c.* Sept. 14; RAL, XI/109/103/1, Arthur, Brussels, to his uncles, Dec. 7.

54   Merimée, *Correspondance générale*, 2e série, vol. XV, p. 147. According to the anecdote, he had to be shown how to polish his shoes and make soup by his *valet de chambre*.

55   RAL, T10/273, Anselm, Paris, to NMR, July 17, 1870.

56 RAL, XI/109/102, Alphonse, Paris, to his cousins, London, July 20, 1870.

57 RAL, XI/109/102, Alphonse, Paris, to his cousins, London, July 27, 1870; same to same, July 28; Alphonse and Gustave, Paris, to their cousins, London, July 28. Cf. Ramon, *Banque de France*, pp. 316f.

58 RAL, XI/109/102, Alphonse, Paris, to his cousins, London, Aug. 4, 1870.

59 RAL, XI/109/102, Alphonse, Paris, to his cousins, London, Aug. 11, 1870; same to same, Aug. 16.

60 RAL, XI/109/102, Alphonse, Paris, to his cousins, London, Aug. 3, 1870.

61 RAL, XI/109/102, Alphonse, Paris, to his cousins, London, Aug. 6, 1870; same to same, Aug. 8.

62 RAL, XI/109/102, James Edouard, Paris, to Natty, London, Aug. 11, 1870.

63 RAL, T41/209, Lambert, Brussels, to NMR, Sept. 30, 1870.

64 Stern, *Gold and iron*, p. 135.

65 RAL, XI/109/102, Gustave, Paris, to his cousins, London, July 19, 1870; Alphonse, Paris, to his cousins, London, July 25.

66 RAL, XI/109/102, Alphonse, Paris, to his cousins, London, Aug. 1, 1870.

67 RAL, XI/109/102, Alphonse, Paris, to his cousins, London, Aug. 3, 1870; same to same, Aug. 6.

68 RAL, XI/109/102, Alphonse, Paris, to his cousins, London, Aug. 9, 1870; same to same, Aug. 10; Aug. 11; Aug. 12.

69 RAL, XI/109/102, Alphonse, Paris, to his cousins, London, Aug. 13, 1870.

70 RAL, XI/109/102, Alphonse, Paris, to his cousins, London, Sept. 4, 1870.

71 RAL, XI/109/102, Alphonse, Paris, to his cousins, London, Sept. 12, 1870.

72 Corti, *Reign*, p. 424.

73 RAL, T10/240, Gustave, Paris, to his cousins, London [postscript by Alphonse], Aug. 30, 1870.

74 Stern, *Gold and iron*, p. 137.

75 RAL, T10/306, F. Bergman, Ferrières, to Leonora, Jan. 1, 1871.

76 Stern, *Gold and iron*, pp. 137f.

77 Bismarck, *Gesammelte Werke*, vol. XIV/2, p. 793.

78 Corti, *Reign*, pp. 416–18.

79 Bismarck, *Gesammelte Werke*, vol. XIV/2, p. 794.

80 *The Times*, Oct. 29, 1870, p. 6; Stern, *Gold and iron*, p. 137.

81 Stern, *Gold and iron*, p. 141n. See also pp. 146f.

82 RAL, T10/306, Bergman, Ferrières, to Leonora, Jan. 1, 1871.

83 RAL, T10/338, Gustave, Paris, to his cousins, London, July 21, 1871; RAL, RFamC/21, Charlotte, London, to Leo, Brussels, Aug. 29.

84 RAL, XI/109/106/1, Anthony, Paris, to his brothers, London, Sept. 1, 1871.

85 RAL, T10/337, Alphonse, Paris, to his cousins, London, March 28, 1871.

86 RAL, XI/109/102, Alphonse, Paris, to his cousins, London, Aug. 8, 1870.

87 RAL, XI/109/102, Alphonse, Paris, to his cousins, London, Aug. 13, 1870. Cf. RAL, XI/109/102, Gustave, Paris, to his cousins, London, undated, between Aug. 7 and Aug. 14.

88 RAL, XI/109/102, Alphonse, Paris, to his cousins, London, Sept. 4, 1870. See also Gustave, Paris, to his cousins, London, Sept. 3; Alphonse to his cousins, undated, *c.* Sept. 5; same to same, Sept. 5.

89 RAL, XI/109/102, Alphonse, Paris, to his cousins, London, Sept. 6, 1870; same to same, Sept. 7.

90 Corti, *Reign*, p. 421.

91 RAL, XI/109/102, Alphonse, Paris, to his cousins, London, Sept. 11, 1870.

92 RAL, XI/109/102, Mayer Carl, Frankfurt, to his cousins and nephews, London, Aug. 15, 1870; same to same, Aug. 20; Aug. 21.

93 RAL, XI/109/102, Mayer Carl, Frankfurt, to his cousins and nephews, London, Aug. 26, 1870.

94 RAL, XI/109/102, Mayer Carl, Frankfurt, to his cousins and nephews, London, Sept. 8, 1870.

95 RAL, XI/109/102, Alphonse, Paris, to his cousins, London, Sept. 6, 1870.

96 RAL, XI/109/102, Alphonse, Paris, to his cousins, London, Sept. 12, 1870; Sept. 14; Sept. 16; Sept. 17.

97 Matthew, *Gladstone, 1809–1874*, p. 185.

98 Ramm (ed.), *Gladstone–Granville correspondence, 1868–1876*, vol. I, pp. 126, 134.

99 It was a sign of Gladstone's growing wariness towards the Rothschilds that in March 1871 he declined to provide them with "inside information" about the international conference then being held in London to discuss this old question: Matthew (ed.), *Gladstone diaries*, vol. VII, pp. 457, 460; Ramm (ed.), *Gladstone–Granville correspondence, 1868–1876*, vol. I, p. 226.

100   RAL, XI/109/102, Alphonse, Paris, to his cousins, London, Sept. 6, 1870.

101   RAL, XI/109/102, Gustave, Paris, to his cousins, London, Sept. 17, 1870; RAL, T10/226, Alphonse, Paris, to his cousins, London, Sept. 18; RAL, XI/109/102, same to same, Sept. 21.

102   Bismarck, *Gesammelte Werke*, vol. XIV/2, p. 793. Cf. Howard, *Franco–Prussian War*, pp. 231f.; Stern, *Gold and iron*, p. 149.

103   RAL, XI/109/102/1, Mayer Carl, Frankfurt, to his cousins and nephews, London, Sept. 30, 1870; RAL, T10/289, deRF to NMR, Nov. 16; RAL, XI/109/103/1, Mayer Carl to his cousins and nephews, Nov. 19; RAL, T10/290, deRF to NMR, Nov. 23; RAL, T10/293, Mayer to Lionel, undated, Dec. Other correspondence, such as Bleichröder's to the Paris house, accumulated in London after September 1 and was not received until February: Stern, *Gold and iron*, p. 135. For the circular newsletters sent to (among others) the London Rothschilds by "C. de B." (an obscure Bourbon legitimist named Alexandre de Saint-Chéron), see Henrey, *Letters*; Bury, "Identity," pp. 538ff.

104   RAL, T10/291, Alphonse, Paris, to his cousins, London, Dec. 10, 1870.

105   RAL, XI/109/104, Alphonse, Paris, to his cousins, London, Feb. 3, 1871.

106   Stern, *Gold and iron*, p. 148.

107   The reparations imposed on France in 1815 had been 700 million francs, in the region of 7 per cent of gross national product. The figure of 5,000 million demanded by Germany in 1871 represented around 19 per cent of GNP: see Schremmer, "Public finance," p. 398.

108   Using net national product figures in Hobson, "Wary Titan," p. 505.

109   For one of the few published attempts, see Kindleberger, *Financial history*, pp. 247ff.

110   RAL, XI/109/103/1, Anselm, Vienna, to Lionel, London, Nov. 11, 1870; same to same, Nov. 18. Cf. Stern, *Gold and iron*, p. 142. Keudell noted to Bleichröder, "As a rule we would prefer to use native [meaning Prussian] firms."

111   Stern, *Gold and iron*, pp. 148ff.; Landes, "Spoilers foiled," pp. 76f.

112   RAL, XI/109/104, Mayer Carl, Frankfurt, to his cousins and nephews, London, Jan. 7, 1871.

113   At this stage, communications were so poor that it was impossible to involve the Frankfurt and Vienna houses—that at least was Alphonse's excuse for not doing so: RAL, XI/109/104, Anselm, Vienna, to deRF, Feb. 7, 1871; Alphonse, Paris, to his cousins, London, Feb.11; Mayer Carl, Frankfurt, to his cousins and nephews, London, Feb. 12; same to same, Feb. 14.

114   RAL, XI/109/104, Alphonse, Paris, to his cousins, London, Feb. 6, 1871; same to same, Feb. 9; Feb. 11; Feb. 12; Feb. 13. Unlike the later payments, this was not an especially profitable transaction for the banks; Alphonse felt compelled by the circumstances to charge a low commission of just 0.5 per cent and grumbled that he was only acting under duress.

115   Stern, *Gold and iron*, p. 148; Landes, "Spoilers foiled," p. 84.

116   Bouvier, *Crédit Lyonnais*, p. 40.

117   RAL, XI/109/104, Alphonse, Paris, to his cousins, London, Feb. 4, 1871. Cf. Kindleberger, *Financial history*, pp. 239–43; Bouvier, *Rothschild*, pp. 184–7; Bouvier, *Crédit Lyonnais*, p. 433; Landes, "Spoilers foiled," p. 84.

118   RAL, T10/369, Lionel Davidson, Paris, to Lionel, London, Feb. 16, 1871; Stern, *Gold and iron*, pp. 151ff. See also Landes, "Spoilers foiled," pp. 70f. on the German bankers' conflicting estimates.

119   RAL, XI/109/104, Gustave, Paris, to his cousins, London, Feb. 22, 1871; same to same, Feb. 24; Alphonse, Paris, to his cousins, London, Feb. 24.

120   RAL, XI/109/104, Alphonse, Paris, to his cousins, London, Feb. 26, 1871. Alphonse's numerous grammatical errors and missing accents in this important letter testify to the intensity of the strain he was under.

121   Corti, *Reign*, p. 419; Stern, *Gold and iron*, p. 154.

122   The interest amounted in the end to 301 million francs, slightly less than the value of the railways (325 million), so the final total paid was in fact 4,976 million: Kindleberger, *Financial history*, p. 241 (though he quotes a higher figure of 4,993 on p. 247).

123   RAL, XI/109/104, Alphonse, Paris, to his cousins, London, Feb. 12, 1871.

124   RAL, XI/109/104, Gustave and Alphonse, Paris, to their cousins, London, March 1, 1871; same to same, March 8; March 13.

125   Bismarck himself had proposed "the phased withdrawal from the occupied territory in proportion to the sums paid."

126   The Prussians agreed to accept gold, silver, banknotes from the central, banks of England, Prussia, Holland and Belgium, cheques on the same banks and immediately payable first-class bills of exchange on

London, Amsterdam, Berlin or Brussels. In May it was also agreed to accept a further 125 million in French banknotes. From the outset Bismarck and the German bankers opposed the idea of accepting French rentes.

127   RAL, XI/109/104, Alphonse, Paris, to his cousins, London, March 1, 1871; same to same, March 2; March 5; March 8; March 13; March 14; March 15; March 17.

128   At Alphonse's initiative, and with an eye to "public opinion," the Banque had reduced the interest it charged the government from 6 per cent to 3 per cent: Ramon, *Banque de France*, pp. 333f.; Bouvier, *Rothschild*, p. 187.

129   There was never any serious discussion of other possibilities such as amortisable bonds or a lottery loan; rentes were what investors in London and Paris expected from a French government: Landes, "Spoilers foiled," p. 81.

130   The National Assembly initially met at Bordeaux but moved to Versailles on March 20.

131   See Tombs, *War against Paris*.

132   RAL, XI/109/104, Alphonse, Paris, to his cousins, London, March 18, 1871; Gustave to his cousins, undated, *c.* March 20; same to same, March 21; Gustave and Alphonse to their cousins, March 24; March 26; Gustave, Versailles, to his cousins, March 28; same to same, *c.* March 30.

133   RAL, XI/109/105, Alphonse, Paris, to his cousins, London, April 2, 1871. He took the opportunity to go to London for further financial discussions.

134   RAL, XI/109/105, Alphonse, Paris, to his cousins, London, May 25, 1871; same to same, May 29.

135   RAL, T10/331, Alfred, Paris, to his parents, June 23, 1871.

136   RAL, XI/109/106/1, Ferdinand, Dieppe, to Lionel, Aug. 9, 1871.

137   RAL, XI/109/105, Alphonse, Paris, to his cousins, London, April 8, 1871.

138   RAL, XI/109/104, Gustave, Versailles, to his cousins, London, March 28, 1871.

139   RAL, XI/109/105, Alphonse, Paris, to his cousins, London, April 5, 1871; same to same, April 8.

140   RAL, XI/109/104, Alphonse, Paris, to his cousins, London, Feb. 14, 1871; same to same, Feb. 15; March 14; RAL, XI/109/105, same, Versailles, to same, April 2; Gustave, Versailles, to his cousins, April 14; Alphonse to his cousins, June 1.

141   RAL, XI/109/107/1, Alphonse, Paris, to his cousins, London, Jan. 4, 1872.

142   RAL, XI/109/109/1, Alfred, Paris, to his parents, London, Sept. 30, 1872.

143   RAL, XI/109/107/1, Alphonse, Paris, to his cousins, London, Oct. 21, 1871; RAL, XI/109/104, same to same, Jan. 3, 1872 [wrongly dated 1871]. See also RAL, XI/109/106, Aug. 25; RAL, XI/109/107/1, Nov. 15.

144   RAL, XI/109/105, Alphonse, Paris, to his cousins, London, June 5, 1871. See also same to same, June 8; RAL, XI/109/107/1, Dec. 11; Jan. 22, 1872; Feb. 20; RAL, T10/385, March 14. The main obstacle to this was the existence of an alternative monarchist party around the Bourbon claimant, the duc de Chambord. To draw another Weimar parallel, Alphonse was, on balance, a "Vernunftsrepublikaner"; he spoke disparagingly of crypto-monarchists he had to deal with on the Seine et Marne council.

145   RAL, XI/109/105, Alphonse, Paris, to his cousins, London, June 7, 1871.

146   Bouvier, *Rothschild*, pp. 201–3; Chapman, *Third Republic*, p. 38. In fact, Thiers fell in May 1873, two months before the last instalment of the indemnity was paid.

147   RAL, XI/109/105, Gustave, [Versailles?], to his cousins, London, May 10, 1871; Mayer Carl, Frankfurt, to his cousins and nephews, London, May 10; Gustave to his cousins, May 11; same to same, May 15; RAL, T46/29, M. M. Warburg & Co., Hamburg to NMR, May 31; AN, 132 AQ 32/Bleichröder, Bleichröder, Berlin, to Alphonse, Paris, June 11; same to same, June 12; June 14; RAL, XI/109/105, Leo, London, to his cousins, Paris [draft], June 12; Alphonse to his cousins, June 12.

148   Landes, "Spoilers foiled," pp. 87f.

149   Bouvier, *Crédit Lyonnais*, pp. 403f.

150   RAL, XI/109/105, Alphonse, Paris, to his cousins, London, June 7, 1871. This raises the possibility that he never intended to allow Bleichröder or Hansemann into the underwriting syndicate and that the negotiations described by Landes were a sham. That would certainly explain the numerous garbled telegrams. Alternatively, the Berlin bankers wanted their rentes at too low a price: Landes, "Spoilers foiled," pp. 90, 96, 99f.

151   Bouvier, *Crédit Lyonnais*, pp. 404f.

152   RAL, XI/109/105, Alphonse, Paris, to his cousins, London, June 1, 1871; same to same, June 2; June 6; June 7; June 9; June 12; June 14; June 18; undated, *c.* June 20; June 21; Edmond to his cousins, June

21; Alphonse to his cousins, June 22; same to same, June 23; June 24; AN, 132 AQ 32/1D2 (16), NMR to deRF, June 24 (two telegrams).

153 AN, 132 AQ 33/A-12–3/4, Pouyer-Quartier to Alphonse, July 27, 1871. Cf. Landes, "Spoilers foiled," pp. 82, 88f., 104f.

154 *Ibid.*, p. 102.

155 RAL, XI/109/105, Alphonse, Paris, to his cousins, London, June 21, 1871; RAL, XI/109/106, same to same, July 7.

156 AN, 132 AQ 33/A-12–3/4, Contract between deRF and joint-stock banks, June 26, 1871; Contract between deRF and private banks, June 26. The underwriting syndicate in London was simply a duopoly of Rothschild and Baring and I have assumed that they shared the total of 325 million francs equally; in Paris, the underwriting shares were distributed as follows: de Rothschild Frères 248 million; *haute banque* (twelve houses, including Fould, Mallet Frères, Hottinguer and Pillet-Will) 362 million; Société Générale 60 million; other joint-stock banks 65 million. The Société Générale was given preferential treatment because of the French Rothschilds' common railway interests with Talabot: Bouvier, *Crédit Lyonnais*, pp. 405f.; Mayeur, *Troisième République*, p. 23.

157 This should be regarded as an upper limit; it seems unlikely that the Rothschilds acted in quite this optimal way. Cf. the lower estimates in Bouvier, *Rothschild*, p. 191 and Palmade, *Capitalism*, p. 127. By way of comparison, the Crédit Lyonnais made only 5.7 million francs from the 1871 operation.

158 RAL, XI/109/105, Alphonse, Paris, to his cousins, London, June 25, 1871; same to same, June 26; June 27. This is the only pre-1914 allusion by a Rothschild I have come across to the possibility of holding a governmental office, something they always avoided.

159 RAL, XI/109/105, Alphonse, Paris, to his cousins, London, June 28, 1871; same to same, June 29; RAL, XI/109/106, July 20. The target of 2.6 billion francs had been more or less met by the end of June 26 from subscriptions in Paris alone.

160 Bouvier, *Crédit Lyonnais*, pp. 407ff. The signatories included the Banque de Paris, the Crédit Foncier and the Crédit Lyonnais.

161 Landes, "Spoilers foiled," pp. 100ff. Cf. Stern, *Gold and iron*, pp. 320ff.

162 His vain efforts can be followed in AN, 132 AQ 32/1D2, deRF [via S. Lambert, Brussels] to Bleichröder, Berlin, June 21, 1871; AN, 132 AQ 32/Bleichröder, Bleichröder to Lehmann, June 21; same to same, June 22; AN, 132 AQ 32/1D2 (16), Bleichröder, Berlin [via Lambert, Brussels], to Nathan James, Boulogne, June 22; Bleichröder to deRF, June 23; same to same, June 24; M. M. Warburg, Hamburg, to deRF, June 26; AN, 132 AQ 32/Bleichröder, Bleichröder to deRF, June 26; same to same, June 29.

163 AN, 132 AQ 32/1D2(16), Anselm, Carlsbad, to deRF, June 24, 1871; AN, 132 AQ 32/1D2 (16), SMR to deRF, June 27.

164 RAL, XI/109/105, Mayer Carl, Frankfurt, to his cousins and nephews, London, June 26, 1871; AN, 132 AQ 32/1D2(16), Mayer Carl to his cousins, Paris, June 28; AN, 132 AQ 5706/2M52, same to same, Nov. 17. He wisely sold half at the peak of the *hausse* in November.

165 RAL, XI/109/105, Alphonse, Paris, to his cousins, London, June 28, 1871.

166 RAL, XI/109/106, Alphonse, Paris, to his cousins, London, July 2, 1871; same to same, July 5; July 6; RAL, T10/333, July 9; RAL, XI/109/106, July 12; July 13; Aug. 21; Aug. 23; Aug. 24; Aug. 25. Cf. Kindleberger, *Financial history*, p. 247.

167 The desire to minimise the influx of bills on London reflected fears of pressure on the thaler. It is worth noting that Mayer Carl failed to persuade the Seehandlung to entrust the London house with the remittance of money from London to Berlin: RAL, XI/109/107/1, Mayer Carl, Berlin, to his cousins and nephews, London, Dec. 1, 1871; same to same, Dec. 17; Dec. 20; Dec. 31.

168 AN, 132 AQ 32/Bleichröder, Bleichröder, Berlin, to deRF, June 28, 1871; same to same, undated, *c.* July 1; July 2; Aug. 24; Aug. 28; Aug. 31; Sept. 8; Sept. 23; Sept. 29; Oct. 17; Oct. 23; Nov. [1?]; Nov. 11.

169 RAL, XI/109/107/1, Alphonse, Paris, to his cousins, London, Oct. 6, 1871.

170 RAL, T10/339, Nathan James, Paris, to Lionel, London, undated, 1871; RAL, XI/109/106, Alphonse, Paris, to his cousins, London, Aug. 17; RAL, XI/109/107/1, same to same, Dec. 19; Dec. 21; Dec. 28; Dec. 30; Jan. 13, 1872; Jan. 22; Jan. 23; Jan. 24; March 5; March 7; RAL, XI/109/108/1, April 2; April 9; May 4.

171 RAL, XI/109/106, Alphonse, Paris, to his cousins, London, July 7, 1871; same to same, Sept. 2; Sept.

4; Sept. 5; Sept. 6; Sept. 11; Sept. 17; Sept. 19; Sept. 20; Sept. 21; Sept. 22; Sept. 23; Sept. 28; RAL, XI/109/107/1, Oct. 5; Oct. 14; Oct. 16; Oct. 17; Oct. 21; Oct. 30; Nov. 2; Nov. 15; Nov. 16; Nov. 24; Nov. 27; Nov. 30; Dec. 2; Dec. 8; Dec. 12; Dec. 27; Jan. 10, 1872; Jan. 12.

172   In January 1872 the Banque de Paris merged with the Amsterdam-based Banque de Crédit et de Dépôts des Pays Bas to form the Banque de Paris et des Pays-Bas, usually known as "Paribas" for short: Bussière, *Paribas*, pp. 25ff.

173   RAL, XI/109/107/1, Mayer Carl, Berlin, to his cousins and nephews, London, Dec. 19, 1871; same to same, Jan. 21, 1872; RAL, XI/109/107/1, Alphonse, Paris, to his cousins, London, Jan. 2; same to same, Feb. 26; Feb. 27.

174   AN, 132 AQ 32/1D2 (16), Bleichröder, Berlin, to deRF, Nov. 15, 1871; AN, 132 AQ 32/Bleichröder, same to same, Dec. 27; Jan. 10, 1872; Jan. 28; Feb. 3; Feb. 15; Feb. 20; Feb. 23; March 2; March 24; April 20; May 25; June 20; June 24. Cf. Stern, *Gold and iron*, pp. 324f.

175   RAL, XI/109/108/1, Alphonse, Paris, to his cousins, London, May 22, 1872.

176   RAL, XI/109/107/1, Alphonse, Paris, to his cousins, London, Jan. 31, 1872; same to same, Feb. 1; Feb. 3; Feb. 5; Feb. 6; Feb. 7; Feb. 13; Feb. 26; Feb. 27; March 8; March 18; March 22; RAL, XI/109/108/1, April 11; May 2; May 7; May 11; May 14; undated, *c.* May 19; May 20; May 29; May 30; June 7; June 15.

177   RAL, XI/109/109/1, Alphonse, Paris, to his cousins, London, undated, *c.* July 1, 1872; Gustave to his cousins, undated, *c.* July 3; Alphonse to his cousins, July 6; same to same, July 8; July 9.

178   RAL, XI/109/109/1, Alphonse, Paris, to his cousins, London, July 10, 1872; same to same, July 11; July 12; July 13; July 16; July 17.

179   RAL, XI/109/109/1, Alphonse, Paris, to his cousins, London, July 18, 1872; same to same, July 19; Natty, Paris, to his parents, undated, *c.* July 19.

180   RAL, XI/109/109/1, Alphonse, Paris, to his cousins, London, July 23, 1872; same to same, July 24; July 25; July 26; AN, 132 AQ 33/A-12–3/4, Contract between deRF, NMR and Barings, July 26; Contract between Goulard, Minister of Finance, deRF, NMR, Barings, representatives of German banks, Daru, Germain and Goubert (as representatives of the French "credit establishments") and others, July 26; Contract signed by eleven private Paris banks, July 27; Alphonse to his cousins, July 27. Cf. Bouvier, *Crédit Lyonnais*, pp. 411–18.

181   RAL, XI/109/107/1, Mayer Carl, Berlin, to his cousins and nephews, London, March 11, 1872. Cf. Kindleberger, *Financial history*, p. 247.

182   AN, 132 AQ 32/Bleichröder, Bleichröder, Berlin, to deRF, July 30, 1872. Cf. Stern, *Gold and iron*, p. 326. Bleichröder was convinced that Hansemann was conspiring against him with Harry von Arnim, the Prussian ambassador in Paris. Bismarck certainly disliked Arnim (as did the Rothschilds) and used Bleichröder to communicate indirectly with Thiers via the French ambassador in Berlin, Gontaut-Biron; but the financial significance of this was minimal. Cf. Corti, *Reign*, p. 440.

183   RAL, XI/109/108/1, Mayer Carl, Bad Kissingen, to Natty, London, June 23, 1872; same to same, June 25; Mayer Carl, Frankfurt, to his cousins, Paris, June 29; RAL, XI/109/109/1, Mayer Carl to Natty, July 7; same to same, July 19; July 21; July 22; July 23; RAL, T10/354, Mayer Carl to Alfred, July 24; RAL, T10/355, Mayer Carl to Natty, July 29; RAL, XI/109/109/1, same to same, July 31; Aug. 1.

184   Cf. the lower estimates in Bouvier, *Rothschild*, pp. 192–8.

185   RAL, XI/109/109/1, Alphonse, Paris, to his cousins, London, July 29, 1872; same to same, July 31.

186   AN, 132 AQ 32/Bleichröder, Bleichröder, Berlin, to deRF, Sept. 12, 1872; RAL, XI/109/109/1, Alphonse, Paris, to his cousins, London, Sept. 14; same to same, Sept. 26; Sept. 28; Sept. 30.

187   AN, 132 AQ 32/Bleichröder, Bleichröder to deRF, Oct. 30, 1872; same to same, Nov. 3; Nov. 4; Nov. 5; Nov. 15; Nov. 19. The rejection of Hamburg bills reflected the pressure within Berlin to put Germany on to a new gold currency; the Hamburg "marc banco" was silver-based. On the role of the Hamburg bank M. M. Warburg & Co. in supplying bills to the Paris house see Rosenbaum and Sherman, *M. M. Warburg & Co.*, p. 75.

188   RAL, T10/411, Alphonse, Paris, to his cousins, London, Dec. 18, 1872.

189   RAL, T11/10, Alphonse, Paris, to his cousins, London, May 28, 1873; RAL, T11/14, same to same, Aug. 13; RAL, T11/16, Sept. 3.

190   RAL, XI/109/104, Mayer Carl, Frankfurt, to his cousins and nephews, London, Jan. 16, 1871.

191   RAL, XI/109/107/1, Mayer Carl, Frankfurt, to his cousins and nephews, London, Oct. 25, 1871.

192   RAL, XI/109/107/1, Mayer Carl, Frankfurt, to his cousins and nephews, London, Nov. 11, 1871.

193 RAL, XI/109/108/1, Mayer Carl, Frankfurt, to his cousins and nephews, London, May 10, 1872.

194 RAL, XI/109/104, Mayer Carl, Munich, to his cousins and nephews, London, Jan. 12, 1871; same, Frankfurt, to same, Jan. 16; Jan. 19; Jan. 21; Jan. 31.

195 RAL, XI/109/107/1, Mayer Carl, Frankfurt, to his cousins and nephews, London, Oct. 29, 1871; RAL, XI/109/107/1, same, to same, Feb. 7; Feb. 14; Feb. 20.

196 RAL, XI/109/107/1, Mayer Carl, Berlin, to his cousins and nephews, London, Dec. 17, 1871; same, Frankfurt, to same, Jan. 21, 1872; March 19.

197 RAL, XI/109/104, Mayer Carl, Frankfurt, to his cousins and nephews, London, Feb. 7, 1871; same to same, Feb. 21; RAL, XI/109/107/1, Oct. 22.

198 RAL, XI/109/108/1, Mayer Carl, Frankfurt, to his cousins and nephews, London, April 11; same to same, May 28, 1872; June 5; June 7; June 25.

199 Goldschmidt, *Erinnerungen*, pp. 89f.; Corti, *Reign*, p. 434.

200 RAL, XI/109/107/1, Mayer Carl, Berlin, to his cousins and nephews, London, March 4, 1872; same to same, March 14.

201 Kindleberger, *Financial history*, pp. 248f.

202 Borchardt, "Währung," pp. 3–17.

203 RAL, T41/243, Lambert, Brussels, to NMR, May 5, 1875.

204 RAL, RFamC/21, Charlotte to Leo, May 11, 1875; same to same, May 14.

SEVEN *"The Caucasian Royal Family"*

1 Kynaston, *City*, vol. II, p. 314.

2 RAL, XI/109/87/1, Alphonse, Paris, to his cousins, London, July 22, 1865.

3 A fourth son, Anselm Alexander, had died in 1854 at the age of eighteen; scarcely anything is known about him.

4 RAL, XI/109/101/1, John Carl [Nat's servant], Paris, to Lionel, London, Jan. 5, 1870; same to same, Feb. 19; Leo, Paris, to his parents, Feb. 20; RAL, RFamC/21, Charlotte, London, to Natty, Alfred and Leo, Paris, Feb. 20; RAL, XI/109/101/1, Natty to his parents, Feb. 21; RAL, XI/109/101/2, Albert, Vienna, to Lionel, Feb. 22; Anselm, Vienna, to Lionel, Feb. 22.

5 Disraeli remembered him fondly as "a thoro[ugh]ly good hearted fellow, the most genial being I ever knew, the most kind-hearted, and the most generous": Monypenny and Buckle, *Disraeli*, vol. V, p. 430.

6 *The Times*, June 4, 1879, pp. 9f. (emphasis added). Delane, who had retired in 1877, also died in 1879, though it is possible that he wrote Lionel's obituary while still working: as today, obituaries were often written well in advance of an eminent figure's death.

7 Monypenny and Buckle, *Disraeli*, vol. VI, p. 434.

8 RAL, RFamFP/20, Lionel's draft will, Nov. 1866 (which seems to omit his share in the business); *The Times*, June 27, 1879, p. 12.

9 Kynaston, *City*, vol. I, p. 316. Bleichröder's son Hans noted sourly that "few people genuinely mourned because Lionel did not know how to make himself liked and did next to nothing for the poor": Stern, *Gold and iron*, p. 479. This is not borne out by the obituary in the *Middlesex County Times*, June 7, 1879: I am grateful to Lionel de Rothschild for this reference.

10 Brock and Brock (eds), *Asquith letters to Venetia Stanley*, p. 484.

11 RAL, XI/109/99/1, Anthony, Schillersdorf, to his brothers, London, undated, *c*. Sept. 1869.

12 See e.g. RAL, XI/109/91/2, Mayer, Paris, to his brothers and Natty, London, undated, *c*. Aug. 1867: "Anselm admires a Russian Countess, accompanies her to the theatres & even orders dresses for her at the shops"; and RAL, T10/38, Alphonse, Paris, to his cousins, London, Aug. 19; RAL, T11/27, Anselm, Vienna, to Ferdinand, London, undated, 1873 (recalling an affair with Lady Ellenborough, "who after various marriages dissolved and she always the guilty party, finally married in Damascus an Arab chieftain with whom she lived during 15 years steadily in most peaceful wedlock"). So much for Goldschmidt's claim that Anselm was a misogynist.

13 RAL, XI/109/95/2, Ferdinand, Schillersdorf, to his cousins, London, Aug. 23, 1868.

14 Goldschmidt, *Erinnerungen*, pp. 70ff., 92f.; Prevost-Marcilhacy, *Rothschild*, pp. 144, 153f. See also RAL, RFamC/21, Charlotte, London, to Leo, Lucerne, July 19, 1864; same, July 22; July 30.

15 RAL, T11/63, Alphonse, Paris, to his cousins, London, July 27, 1874; RAL, RFamC/21, Charlotte to Leonora and Leo, Trouville, July 28; same to same, July 30; July 31.

16 *The Times*, Aug. 13, 1874, p. 12; Aug. 15, p. 9.

17 Corti, *Reign*, p. 432.

18 *The Times*, June 7, 1879. Carriages were also sent by the Duke of Wellington, Disraeli (now the Earl of Beaconsfield), the Duke of Manchester, the Duke of St Albans and the Duchess of Somerset, to say nothing of numerous ambassadors.

19 To speak of "generations" presents problems because of the extent to which the Rothschild generations overlapped: in the period 1827 to 1884 when the fourth generation was born, six members of the third were also born and ten members of the fifth. I am grateful to Lionel de Rothschild for his assistance on this and related points.

20 Goncourt, *Journal*, vol. I, p. 586.

21 RAL, RFamC/2, Disraeli to Leopold, Dec. 11, 1880.

22 For comments on this subject, see RAL, RFamC/21, Charlotte, Paris, to Lionel, Natty and Alfred, London, Sept. 16, 1864 (two letters); same to same, Sept. 17; Sept. 18; Sept. 21; Sept. 25; Charlotte to Leo, Cambridge, Sept. 17; same to same, Sept. 25; Oct. 22, 1865; Oct. 24; Nov. 9. These premature male deaths were somewhat "counterbalanced" by the premature deaths of six Rothschild women: Clementine in 1865 (aged twenty); Evelina in 1866 (aged twenty-seven); Georgine in 1869 (seventeen); Hannah in 1878 (thirty-nine); Bettina in 1892 (thirty-four); and Bertha in 1896 (twenty-six).

23 Davis, *English Rothschilds*, pp. 63, 111; RAL, RFamPD/1–2, Charlotte's Commonplace Book, April 1855. She continued to comment adversely on his shyness even when he was in his twenties: RAL, RFamC/21, Charlotte, London, to Leo, Cambridge, Feb. 4, 1867. See also Rothschild, *Dear Lord Rothschild*, p. 25.

24 History was his strong suit. Disraeli once remarked: "If I want to know a date in history, I ask Natty": Corti, *Reign*, p. 450.

25 Honours in the "Little Go" required knowledge of one of the Gospels in Greek, prescribed Latin and Greek texts, William Paley's anti-Deist *Evidences of Christianity*, the first three books of Euclid and arithmetic as well as the fourth and sixth books of Euclid, elementary algebra and mechanics: Davis, *English Rothschilds*, pp. 107f.

26 RAL, RFamC/21, Charlotte, Paris, to Leo, Cambridge, Feb. 2, 1867.

27 RAL, RFamC/3/57, Natty, Cambridge, to his parents, London, undated, 1860; RAL, RFamC/3/82, same to same, undated, 1860; RAL, RFamC/3/90, undated, 1860; RAL, RFamC/3/129, undated, 1860; RAL, RFamC/3/30, Jan. 18, 1863. Cf. Davis, *English Rothschilds*, pp. 102, 107–14.

28 RAL, RFamC/21, Charlotte, London, to Leo, London, May 14, 1875; same to same, May 15. Two years later he served as a member of the Royal Commission on the London Stock Exchange: see *Minutes of Evidence . . . Royal Commission on the London Stock Exchange*, pp. B9–3A3.

29 Cassis, *City bankers*, p. 102.

30 RAL, RFamC/21, Charlotte, London, to Leo, Cambridge, Nov. 9, 1864; same to same, Sept. 20, 1865; Sept. 5, 1866; Sept. 29; Oct. 23.

31 RAL, RFamC/21, Charlotte, London, to Leo, Cambridge, Nov. 21, 1866.

32 Davis, *English Rothschilds*, pp. 108, 115.

33 RAL, RFamC/21, Charlotte, London, to Leo, Cambridge, Jan. 23, 1867; same to same, Jan. 26; Feb. 2.

34 RAL, T10/127, Nat, Paris, to his brothers, London, undated, 1868. Cf. Cassis, *City bankers*, pp. 34f., 87; Black, *Social politics*, p. 9; Allfrey, *Jewish court*, p. 33. It has been claimed that Alfred was obliged to decline re-election in 1890 after taking the illicit liberty of looking at the account of someone from whom the National Gallery was considering buying a painting; the difference between what the seller was asking and what he had originally paid he considered "out of all proportion to convention and decency." His interest supposedly stemmed from his role as trustee of the National Gallery. However, the Bank of England archives do not corroborate this. In fact, Alfred seems to have retired because of ill health despite an attempt by the Governor to persuade him to stay on: Bank of England, G2/47 423 1908/8, Lidderdale, Bank of England, to Alfred de Rothschild, Feb. 3, 1890; G2/47 423 1908/8, Alfred, New Court, to Lidderdale, Bank of England, Feb. 4; Bank of England, G16/4 Historical Index, Feb. 4.

35 RAL, RFamC/21, Charlotte, London, to Leo and Leonora, Aug. 14, 1874.

36 RAL, RFamC/21, Charlotte, London, to Leo, Cambridge, Feb. 2, 1864; same to same, March 9; May 30; Charlotte, Paris, to Lionel, Natty and Alfred, London, Sept. 25; Charlotte to Leo, Oct. 1; same, Brighton, to same, Oct. 4; Oct. 12; Oct. 25; Nov. 9; Nov. 28; April 20, 1865; Sept. 20; Feb. 17, 1866; Feb. 19; Feb. 23.

37 Davis, *English Rothschilds*, p. 116.

38 RAL, RFamC/21, Charlotte, London, to Leo, Cambridge, July 20, 1866. See also same to same, Nov. 22; May 23, 1867; May 28; June 5; July 30.

39 RAL, RFamC/21, Charlotte, London, to Leo, Cambridge, Nov. 15; same to same, Nov. 21 (two letters). Though Flower later marrried a Rothschild, he appears to have been a homosexual and the intimacy of his friendship with Leo evidently perturbed Charlotte.

40 Black, *Social politics*, p. 9. Leo was elected to the Jockey Club in 1891 and was one of the founders of a motoring club which later became the Royal Automobile Association.

41 RAL, RFamC/21, Charlotte, London, to Leo, Cambridge, Sept. 17, 1864; same to same, Feb. 20, 1865; Nov. 9; Nov. 30; Jan. 29, 1866; Dec. 23. After practising law for a short time, he joined the firm, beginning by taking over his father's post on the Nord board: RAL, XI/109/100/1, Alphonse, Paris, to his cousins, London, Dec. 10, 1869.

42 For an assessment of his contribution to bibliography, see Damascène and Fatout, *Baron James*, pp. vii–xiv. Cf. Goncourt, *Journal*, vol. IV, p. 767. Nat's younger son Arthur was another obsessive collector in the same generation: see Rothschild, *Dear Lord Rothschild*, pp. 110, 332f.

43 RAL, RFamC/21, Charlotte, London, to Leo, Cambridge, Nov. 3, 1866.

44 Dasent, *Piccadilly*, pp. 141ff., 292; Roth, *Magnificent Rothschilds*, pp. 179ff.

45 Kynaston, *City*, vol. I, p. 389.

46 *The Times*, Oct. 1, 1902, p. 10.

47 Roth, *Magnificent Rothschilds*, p. 182. The model was a gift to Leo from his wife Marie in 1912.

48 Goldschmidt, *Erinnerungen*, pp. 70ff., 90, 105; Corti, *Reign*, p. 435.

49 RAL, T10/404, Ferdinand, Ostende, to Lionel, London, Aug. 14, 1872.

50 RAL, RFamC/21, Charlotte, London, to Leo, Cambridge, Feb. 27, 1864; same to same, Feb. 1, 1866.

51 RAL, T11/76, Anthony, Homburg, to Lionel, London, undated, Aug. 1874; RAL, T11/70, Alphonse, Paris, to his cousins, London, Aug. 1; RAL, RFamC/21, Charlotte, London, to Leo and Leonora, Trouville, Aug. 3; same to same, Aug. 13. Cf. Corti, *Reign*, pp. 435f.; Michel, *Banques et banquiers*, pp. 106f. The Frankfurt Grüneburg estate went to his unmarried daughter Alice.

52 Feydeau, *Mémoires*, pp. 143–8.

53 Goncourt, *Journal*, vol. I, pp. 1033, 1082.

54 Briggs, *Victorian things*, p. 349.

55 Bouvier, *Rothschild*, p. 239.

56 Goncourt, *Journal*, vol. II, p. 255.

57 *Ibid.*, vol. I, p. 1082.

58 AN, 132 AQ 5902, James, Edinburgh, to Alphonse and Gustave, Paris, Aug. 14, 1861.

59 Plessis, *Banque de France*, vol. I, pp. 198, 219. This explains the relatively small sum he left in his will: just 1,200,000 francs (£48,000).

60 Goncourt, *Journal*, vol. II, p. 48.

61 RAL, RFamC/21, Charlotte, London, to Leo, Cambridge, May 17, 1864; same to same, May 18; May 19; May 22; May 23; same, Paris, to same, Sept. 16; Charlotte to Lionel, Natty and Alfred, Sept. 25. To judge by her descriptions of his parents' intense grief, Salomon was something of a favourite. Natty and Alfred "found the whole deeply afflicted family awfully calm, with the exception of poor Uncle James, who burst into tears when he saw the travellers, and sobbed convulsively; it was quite dreadful to hear him.—Addy's intense sorrow is quite alarming, she is so fearfully quiet, and utterly unable to shed a single tear—she speaks—never a word of herself—only of her husband's qualities; she thinks he was too good to live . . . Aunt Betty thought he might be in a trance, and would not hear of the last mournful ceremony taking place . . . ."

62 RAL, RFamC/21, Charlotte, Paris, to Leo, Cambridge, Sept. 17, 1864; Charlotte to Lionel, Natty and Alfred, Sept. 20.

63 RAL, T10/351, Mayer Carl, Frankfurt, to his cousins and nephews, London, May 10, 1872.

64 Its extent is usually said to have been 15,000 acres in this period, but a figure of 30,000 seems more likely: Kynaston, *City*, vol. I, p. 387; Davis, *English Rothschilds*, pp. 94f.; Rothschild, Garton and Rothschild, *Rothschild gardens*, p. 131. In fact, Ferdinand had initially tried to persuade his father to buy him an estate in Northamptonshire, but Anselm dismissed the idea, making the very Rothschildian point that the yield of English agricultural land was 1.5 per cent lower than that of Austrian: RAL, T10/404, Ferdinand, Ostend, to Lionel, London, Aug. 14, 1872; RAL, T10/413, Anselm, Schillersdorf, to Ferdi-

nand, London, Aug. 20. It was only with after his father's death that he was able to buy Waddesdon (for £220,000 from the 7th Duke of Marlborough): RAL, T11/76, Anthony, Homburg, to Lionel, London, undated, Aug. 1874; Cannadine, *Aspects*, p. 11.

65   Rothschild, *Dear Lord Rothschild*, pp. 4ff.; Davis, *English Rothschilds*, pp. 174, 226. Lionel paid £230,000 for Tring in 1872, near the peak of rural property prices.

66   Rothschild, Garton and Rothschild, *Rothschild gardens*, pp. 72–82; Rothschild, *Gilt-edged life*, p. 12.

67   Prevost-Marcilhacy, *Rothschild*, pp. 161ff., 181f., 198ff., 336, 341f. Cf. Timberlake, "Hastoe near Tring," pp. 1ff. for the recollections of a Tring tenant's son.

68   The others were: Charlotte (Nat's widow)'s medieval abbey des Vaux-de-Cernay at Auffargis, restored for her by Félix Langlais; Gustave's château de Laversine at Saint-Maximin (Seine-et-Oise), designed by Alfred-Philibert Aldrophe after 1882; James Edouard's château des Fontaines (Oise), again by Langlais (1878–92); his widow Thérèse's maison Normande built there by Girard in 1892; as well as a new sea-side villa at Cannes (for Betty): Prevost-Marcilhacy, *Rothschild*, pp. 152, 175, 178ff., 182, 202, 204, 206, 211, 296, 314, 327ff., 354. Mention should also be made of château de Vallvère à Mortefontaine (Oise), built by Aldrophe for the duc and duchesse de Gramont (Mayer Carl's daughter Margaretha) in 1890.

69   Goldschmidt, *Erinnerungen*, pp. 70ff., 105; Prevost-Marcilhacy, *Rothschild*, pp. 161, 173, 183f., 354f.

70   Rothschild, Garton and Rothschild, *Rothschild gardens*, pp. 152ff.

71   Prevost-Marcilhacy, "Rothschild architecture," pp. 245ff.; idem, *Rothschild*, pp. 205f., 218, 305.

72   Leo's at 5 Hamilton Place, designed by William Rogers of William Cubitt & Co. in the French style; Alfred's at 1 Seamore Place, purchased from the courtier Christopher Sykes; Ferdinand's at 143 Piccadilly; Edmond's at 41 rue du Faubourg-Saint-Honoré, reconstructed by Langlais after 1878; baronne Salomon James's at 11 rue Berryer, designed by Léon Ohnet in 1872–8; Nathaniel's Vienna "hôtel" at 14–16 Theresianumgasse; and Albert's at 24–26 Heugasse (later Prinz Eugen-Strasse), the latter built by Gabriel-Hippolyte Destailleur in 1876: Prevost-Marcilhacy, *Rothschild*, pp. 152ff., 156f., 177f., 194f., 218, 225, 228, 350ff., 355ff.

73   Bartetzko, "Fairy tales and castles," pp. 237f. The architect Franz von Hoven took a number of liberties with the original house, moving it back several feet, replacing the old slate front with more picturesque oak timbers and effectively merging what had originally been two very narrow houses, though the interiors were more faithful to the early part of the century. Bartetzko suggests a conscious effort to imitate the Goethe house in Grosser Hirschgraben, which had been renovated in 1863 and had become Frankfurt's main tourist attraction. In 1890 Von Hoven was also asked to alter and extend the Bockenheimer Landstrasse house, once Amschel's.

74   Reitlinger, *Economics of taste*, vol. I, pp. 176, 178, 180; vol. II, p. 119. Cf. RA, L20/1, Charlotte, Gunnersbury, to Lady Ely, Feb. 9, 1882.

75   Reitlinger, *Economics of taste*, vol. II, pp. 5, 12, 45f., 113, 116, 237.

76   *Ibid.*, pp. 3, 138.

77   *Ibid.*, vol. I, pp. 193, 197.

78   Hall, "English Rothschilds as collectors," pp. 274–8.

79   Prevost-Marcilhacy, *Rothschild*, pp. 230, 233.

80   Prevost-Marcilhacy, Les Rothschild, pp. 161ff., 181f., 198ff.; Hall, "English Rothschilds as collectors," pp. 278–84; Davis, *English Rothschilds*, p. 221; *The Times*, April 4, 1885.

81   See in general Escott, "Story of Halton House"; Adam, *Beechwoods and bayonets*, esp. pp. 19–105.

82   Wilson, *Rothschild*, pp. 256–60.

83   Allfrey, *Jewish court*, p. 36. See also p. 201.

84   Vincent (ed.), *Crawford papers*, p. 600.

85   Rothschild, Garton and Rothschild, *Rothschild gardens*, pp. 20, 24, 32–47. See also Rothschild, *Rothschilds at Waddesdon Manor*; Schwartz, *Waddesdon*.

86   Prevost-Marcilhacy, *Rothschild*, pp. 164ff., 173, 185ff., 196f., 223; Reitlinger, *Economics of taste*, vol. I, pp. 185ff., 189. For a detailed catalogue of the collection, much of which passed into the hands of Edmond's son Jimmy see Blunt (ed.), *James A. de Rothschild collection*; Sutton *et al.*, *Waddesdon Manor*.

87   Allfrey, *Jewish court*, p. 36.

88   Vincent (ed.), *Crawford papers*, p. 49. For a different version of the tea story, see Heuberger, *Rothschilds*, p. 111: "When the curtains were drawn, a powdered footman entered the room, followed by an underling with a tea trolley, and would query politely: 'Tea, coffee or a fresh peach, Sir?'—'Tea, please.'—

'China, Indian or Ceylon, Sir?'—'China, if you please.'—'With lemon, milk or cream, Sir?'—'Milk, please.'—'Jersey, Hereford or Shorthorn, Sir?'"

89   Barnbougle Castle, Rosebery Papers, Ferdinand to Rosebery, undated, *c.* Sept. 1878: "[M]y heart is so full that I must pour out some of its contents into your hearing.—Ill as I have been during the whole of my stay with you I assure you to have never felt more happy. I have so often told you that I am devoted to and fond of you that I will not repeat these expressions from fear of annoying and wearying you; but you will allow me to add, that since I have lived under your roof I have learnt to estimate your character more highly still than I did and that I am more devoted to and fonder of you than I ever was . . . Pray don't, as you threatened, withhold your trust from me in the future.—I assure you I am worthy of it.— I have had very few friends in my life, hardly any true ones, and it would grieve me beyond anything if I thought that when we meet there was no longer the free exchange of thought and feeling between us which has existed and on which I pride myself.—I am a lonely, suffering and occasionally a very miserable individual despite the gilded and marble rooms in which I live.—There is but one thing in the world, that I care for; and that is the sympathy and the confidence of the few persons whom I love. Believe me that I am neither low nor morbid nor even sentimental at this moment . . ." See also same to same, Feb. 17, 1881: "You know I love you more than any man in the world"; Nov. 7, 1882: "I wish Parliament, the Cabinet and Politics at the bottom of the sea, as they have estranged you from me"; May 7, 1884: "That I am 'yours' entirely you are aware of and if I am occasionally 'peculiar' put it down to my nervous system and not to any other cause"; also Nov. 13, 1888.

90   Allfrey, *Jewish court*, pp. 189f.

91   Fritsche, *Bilder*, pp. 233–41; Prevost-Marcilhacy, *Rothschild*, pp. 158, 194, 350f.

92   Of course, the business of gardening was done by small armies of servants: Nathaniel employed enough at Hohe Warte to start one of Austria's first football clubs; Haldane joked that Ferdinand employed 208 at Waddesdon—almost certainly an exaggeration: Vincent (ed.), *Crawford papers*, p. 49. In fact fifty gardeners were employed at Waddesdon and at Ascott, though there were a hundred at Grasse: Rothschild, Garton and Rothschild, *Rothschild gardens.*

93   Goldschmidt, *Erinnerungen*, p. 105.

94   Cf. Tait, *Waddesdon bequest.* The bequest was valued at £400,000.

95   Davis, *English Rothschilds*, p. 222; Prevost-Marcilhacy, *Rothschild*, p. 148. See also pp. 239f. on donations to museums by Edmond and Adolph.

96   Wilde, *Works*, pp. 219–23.

97   Rosenbaum and Sherman, *M. M. Warburg & Co.*, p. 93; Farrer, *Warburgs*, pp. 44f.; Chernow, *Warburgs*, pp. 38f. Interestingly, this was the first time an outsider had been allowed to work in such a capacity; a similar request from the Bleichröders had been turned down: RAL, T15/65, Arthur, Paris, to Natty, April 24, 1891; RAL, T46/33, Moritz Warburg to Natty, Jan. 5, 1898.

98   Palin, *Rothschild relish*, p. 63.

99   Kynaston, *City*, vol. I, p. 354.

100 Davis, *English Rothschilds*, p. 204.

101 Ziegler, *Sixth great power*, p. 285.

102 Kynaston, *City*, vol. II, pp. 271f.

103 *Ibid.*, vol. I, pp. 354f., 410f.

104 Cassis, *City bankers*, p. 141n.

105 Kynaston, *City*, vol. II, p. 171.

106 *Ibid.*, vol. II, pp. 271f., 563.

107 Bouvier, *Rothschild*, pp. 176ff., 198.

108 Palmade, *Capitalism*, pp. 181f., 211.

109 Pose, *Monnaie*, p. 244; Plessis, *Banque de France*, vol. II, pp. 109–13.

110 RAL, XI/109/98/1, Mayer Carl, Berlin, to his cousins and nephews, London, April 8, 1869; RAL, XI/109/101/2, same to same, March 6, 1870; March 25; May 11.

111 RAL, XI/130A/0, Natty, London, to his cousins, Paris, May 7, 1906.

112 RAL, T15/60, Alphonse, Paris, to his cousins, London, Jan. 15, 1891.

113 RAL, XI/130A/0, Natty, London, to his cousins, Paris, April 4, 1906.

114 CPHDCM, 637/1/38/59, MAR to SMR, June 8, 1862.

115 RAL, XI/109/85, Alphonse, Paris, to his cousins, London, March 1, 1863.

116 RAL, XI/109/86, James, Paris, to his nephews, London, April 3, 1865.

117 See e.g. AN, 13 AQ 5697/2M42, Mayer Carl, Frankfurt, to deRF, June 28, 1866; RAL, XI/109/89/1, Alphonse, Paris, to his cousins, London, Aug. 28; RAL, XI/109/91/2, Mayer Carl, Berlin, to his cousins and nephews, London, Sept. 16, 1867; RAL, T110/119, Gustave, Paris, to his cousins, London, Nov. 17, 1868; RAL, XI/109/96/1, Alphonse to his cousins, Nov. 17; RAL, XI/109/100/1, same to same, Dec. 11, 1869; RAL, XI/109/101/1, Feb. 21, 1870; RAL, XI/109/103/1, Mayer Carl, Berlin, to his cousins and nephews, London, Nov. 27; RAL, T12/6, Alphonse to his cousins, May 19, 1875; RAL, T13/101/6, same to same, June 5, 1879; RAL, T16/121, Jan. 2, 1896.

118 Barth, *Hochfinanz*, p. 16.

119 RAL, XI/109/85, James, Paris, to his nephews, London, April 27, 1863; RAL, XI/109/85, Alphonse, Paris, to his cousins, London, Aug. 11; AN, 132 AQ 5902, James, London, to his sons, Paris, Sept. 7; RAL, RFamC/4/215, Lionel, Paris, to Natty and Leo, London, Sept. 8; RAL, XI/109/85, Alphonse, Paris, to his cousins, London, Sept. 9; RAL, RFamFD/3, 9, Quittance, Sept. 22; AN, 132 AQ 3/1, Bordereau et Règlement des Droits et Reprises de M. le Baron Adolphe de Rothschild, Sept. 22; same, Sept. 20. Cf. Gille, *Maison Rothschild*, vol. II, pp. 568–72, 575–80; Born, *International banking*, pp. 53ff.

120 AN, 132 AQ 5902, James to Alphonse, undated, *c.* June 1864; James, Wildbad, to Alphonse and Gustave, June 22; James to Adolphe, June 22; RAL, XI/109/86, James to his nephews, London, July 24; AN, 132 AQ 5902, James, Nuremberg, to Alphonse, Paris, July 26.

121 RAL, XI/109/87/1, Lionel, Wiesbaden, to his brothers and Natty, London, Aug. 20, 1865; AN, 132 AQ 5902, James, Homburg, to Gustave, Aug. 21; same to same, Sept. 3.

122 RAL, XI/109/91/2, Nat, Paris, to his brothers, London, July 11, 1867.

123 AN, 132 AQ 3/Projets 1863, Reinganum, Frankfurt, to Anselm, Vienna, Sept. 8, 1863.

124 RAL, XI/109/88/2, Alphonse, Paris, to his cousins, London, Feb. 22, 1866.

125 RAL, XI/109/90/1a, Alphonse, Paris, to his cousins, London, March 16, 1867.

126 AN, 132 AQ 5772/3M41, Anselm, Vienna, to James, Paris, Nov. 13, 1867.

127 RAL, XI/109/92/1, Alphonse, Paris, to his cousins, London, Dec. 11, 1867; RAL, XI/109/93/1, same to same, undated, 1868.

128 RAL, XI/109/101/2, Mayer Carl, Berlin, to his cousins and nephews, London, March 17, 1870.

129 RAL, T10/142, Nat, Paris, to his brothers, London, Feb. 20, 1868.

130 RAL, RFamC/21, Charlotte, Paris, to Lionel, Natty and Alfred, London, Sept. 21, 1864.

131 RAL, XI/109/91/2, Alfred, Paris, to his parents, London, Sept. 26, 1867.

132 RAL, XI/109/106/1, Ferdinand, Dieppe, to Lionel, London, Aug. 9, 1871; RAL, XI/109/109/1, same, Paris, to same, Sept. 1, 1872. For similar comments see RAL, XI/109/108/1, Mayer Carl, Kissingen, to Natty, London, June 21, 1872; RAL, T11/26, Anthony, Vienna, to his brothers, London, undated, 1873. And see also RAL, T12/4, Alphonse to his cousins, April 6, 1875.

133 See e.g. RAL, XI/109/92/1, Nat, Paris, to his brothers, London, undated, Nov. 1867; RAL, XI/109/95/2, Natty, Paris, to his parents, London, Sept. 4, 1868; RAL, XI/109/96/1, Mayer Carl, Frankfurt, to his cousins and nephews, London, Oct. 10; RAL, XI/109/96/2, same to same, Oct. 21.

134 RAL, XI/109/99/1, Leo, Paris, to his uncle and Natty, London, Aug. 30, 1869.

135 Since the mid-1860s, the system of shared accounts had more or less broken down, so that balance sheets were being drawn up two years late, if at all: RAL, XI/109/87, James, Paris, to his nephews, London, June 6, 1865. See also AN, 132 AQ 5902, James, Spa, to his children, Paris, Aug. 9; RAL, XI/109/89/1, Alphonse, Paris, to his cousins, London, Aug. 6, 1866. A major fraud at the Paris office in 1870 exposed the deficiencies in the accounting system there: RAL, XI/109/102, Alphonse, Paris, to his cousins, London, April 8, 1870; RAL, XI/109/102, Mayer Carl, Gotha, to his cousins and nephews, London, April 10. For later accounting problems see RAL, XI/109/107/1, Alphonse to his cousins, Jan. 16, 1872; and a case of embezzlement by a clerk in Frankfurt, RAL, T16/07, same to same, April 21, 1892.

136 RAL, XI/109/100/1, Mayer Carl, Frankfurt, to his cousins and nephews, London, Nov. 13, 1869; RAL, XI/109/101/1, same to same, Jan. 25, 1870.

137 RAL, XI/109/107/1, Mayer Carl, Berlin, to his cousins and nephews, London, Nov. 29, 1871; same to same, Feb. 6, 1872 (emphasis in original).

138 RAL, XI/109/107/1, Alphonse, Paris, to his cousins, London, Dec. 17, 1871; same to same, Jan. 14, 1872.

139 RAL, T13/101/10, Alphonse, Paris, to his cousins, London, Oct. 12, 1882.

140 Corti, *Reign*, pp. 429f.

141 RAL, XI/109/98/1, Alphonse, Paris, to Lionel, London, May 21, 1869; RAL, XI/109/99/1, same,

Salzburg, to same, July 1; RAL, XI/109/99/1, Alfred, Paris, to his parents, London, Aug. 13; same to same, Aug. 15.

142 RAL, XI/109/101/1, Natty, Paris, to his parents, London, Feb. 21, 1870; RAL, XI/109/104, Alphonse, Paris, to Lionel, London, Jan. 12, 1871. See also RAL, T10/397, Alphonse to his cousins, undated, *c.* Dec. 1872.

143 Davis, *English Rothschilds*, p. 227.

144 RAL, XI/109/99/1, Mayer Carl, Frankfurt, to his cousins and nephews, London, July 28, 1869.

145 RAL, T10/406, Alphonse, Paris, to his cousins, London, Oct. 11, 1872.

146 RAL, XI/109/109/1, Alphonse, Paris, to his cousins, London, Sept. 9, 1872; RAL, T10/414, Albert, Vienna, to Lionel, London, Oct. 15. Cf. Davis, *English Rothschilds*, pp. 150f.

147 AN, 132 AQ 3, Gesamtbilanz, July 27, 1874; AN, 132 AQ 3/1, Règlement de la question Amschel, undated, 1874. Cf. RAL, T12/5, Alphonse, Paris, to his cousins, London, May 3, 1875.

148 AN, 132 AQ 2, 2, Partnership act, Sept. 1, 1879.

149 AN, 132 AQ 2, Partnership act no. 2, Oct. 1882; Partnership act no. 2, bis, Oct. 24.

150 AN, 132 AQ 3/Inventaires, Balance sheets of NMR, deRF, MAR, Oct. 16, 1886; AN, 132 AQ 2, Partnership act, June 28, 1887; Partnership act, Oct. 20; Partnership act, April 2, 1888; Partnership act Jan. 1898; Partnership act, Nov. 1899.

151 AN, 132 AQ 2, Partnership act, Dec. 16, 1901; Partnership act, Oct. 31, 1904; Partnership act, July 25, 1905; Partnership act, Oct. 17. These withdrawals make it very hard to assess the actual profitability of the partnership in these years; certainly a bald statement of the capital account would understate total earnings.

152 RAL, RFamFD, 3, B/1, Articles of partnership between Natty, Alfred and Leo, July 15, 1909. Cf. Davis, *English Rothschilds*, p. 193.

153 RAL, T11/78, Alphonse, Paris, to Lionel, London, Dec. 10, 1874.

154 Ferdinand had no objection to entrusting his share entirely to Albert "provided only that I don't suffer any diminution of income": CPHDCM, 637/1/318, Ferdinand, London, to Nathaniel, Vienna, Oct. 28, 1887.

155 AN, 132 AQ 3/1, Partnership act, June 14, 1875. This clause was deleted in the 1879 act: AN, 132 AQ 2, Partnership act no. 1, Sept. 1879.

156 RAL, RFamFD/3, 1, Agreement between Natty, Alfred and Leo, June 10, 1879.

157 Heilbrunn, "Haus Rothschild," p. 39.

158 AN, 132 AQ 2, Partnership act, Dec. 18, 1899; AN, 132 AQ 3, Note sur l'association, Dec. 18.

159 Vincent (ed.), *Crawford papers*, p. 498.

160 RAL, XI/130A/0, Leo, London, to his cousins, Paris, Dec. 21, 1906; RAL, XI/130A/1, Natty to his cousins June 28, 1907; RAL, XI/130A/2, same to same, May 12, 1908.

161 Roqueplan, *Baron James*, pp. 6ff. Emphasis added.

162 For complaints on this subject, see RAL, XI/109/85, James, Paris, to his nephews, London, April 13, 1862; CPHDCM, 637/1/38/63, MAR to SMR, June 9; AN, 132 AQ 5902, James, London, to his children and nephew, Sept. 1; RAL, XI/109/85, James, Paris, to his nephews, London, Oct. 29; RAL, XI/109/85, James to his nephews, Nov. 1, 1863; RAL, XI/109/85, Alphonse, Paris, to his cousins, London, Nov. 29; AN, 132 AQ 5902, fragment of a letter from James to Alphonse, undated, 1865; RAL, XI/109/89, James to his nephews, Nov. 29, 1866; AN, 132 AQ 5903/447, James, Nice, to his children, Feb. 15, 1867; RAL, XI/109/90/1a, Alphonse to his cousins, Feb. 15; same to same, Feb. 19.

163 RAL, XI/109/102, Alphonse, Paris, to his cousins, London, April 9, 1870; RAL, XI/109/102/1, Anselm, Vienna, to Lionel, London, April 14. See also RAL, XI/109/102, Mayer Carl, Frankfurt, to his cousins and nephews, London, July 2; RAL, XI/109/104, same to same, Jan. 7, 1871; RAL, XI/109/106, Alphonse to his cousins, Sept. 5; RAL, XI/109/106/3, Mayer Carl to his cousins and nephews, Sept. 18; RAL, XI/109/107/1, Alphonse to his cousins, Feb. 6, 1872; same to same, Feb. 21; Feb. 23; March 14; March 27; RAL, XI/109/108/2, Anselm, Vienna, to his nephews, London, March 22; RAL, XI/109/109/1, Alphonse to his cousins, July 10; same to same, July 12; RAL, T10/356, Mayer Carl to his cousins, Dec. 23.

164 RAL, XI/109/102/1, Albert, Vienna, to Lionel, London, April 30, 1870; RAL, XI/109/103/1, Mayer Carl, Frankfurt, to his cousins and nephews, London, Nov. 2; RAL, XI/109/108/2, Anselm, Vienna, to Ferdinand, London, March 9, 1872.

165 See e.g. RAL, T13/101/12, Alphonse, Paris, to his cousins, London, Jan. 16, 1885; RAL, T13/203, same to same, Dec. 10; RAL, T15/01, Jan. 22, 1889.

166   RAL, XI/109/104, Alphonse, Paris, to his cousins, London, March 2, 1871; RAL, XI/109/104, Mayer
      Carl, Berlin, to his cousins and nephews, London, March 7; same to same, March 26; March 30; April
      12.

167   RAL, XI/109/109/1, Natty, Birnam, to his parents, London, Aug. 20, 1872.

168   RAL, T11/29, Mayer Carl, Frankfurt, to his cousins and nephews, London, Jan. 13, 1873.

169   Hansert, "Dynastic power," pp. 175f.

170   RAL, T15/47, Alphonse, Paris, to his cousins, London, Dec. 1, 1890. See also the accounts for 1899
      and 1901, AN, 132 AQ 4/Bilanz MAR 1901 ff. 44–6.

171   AN, 132 AQ 4, Natty, London, to Alphonse, Paris, May 22, 1901; J. Nauheim to Natty, May 30;
      Nauheim liquidation report, Nov. 19, 1901.

172   Corti, *Reign*, p. 432; Mosse, *Jews in the German economy*, pp. 179, 181, 211. On total capital of 359
      million marks, the Frankfurt Rothschilds had a total income of just 12 million marks, implying a rate
      of return of just 3.3 per cent. Max and his sons did not try their hands at banking until after the First
      World War.

173   Heuberger, "Family history," pp. 15ff. The house in the Neue Mainzer Strasse was sold, the house on
      the Untermainkai became a library, and the house in the Zeil became an old people's home.

174   Fourteen if we include the marriage in 1910 between Edmond's daughter Miriam and Albert von Gold-
      schmidt-Rothschild, son of Wilhelm Carl's daughter Minna and Max Goldschmidt.

175   Corti, *Reign*, p. 395; Davis, *English Rothschilds*, pp. 124–7.

176   RAL, RFamC/21, Charlotte, London, to Leo, Cambridge, Feb. 3, 1865.

177   RAL, RFamC/21, Charlotte, London, to Leo, Cambridge, March 1, 1865; same to same, April 26.

178   Possibly because of complications arising from a railway accident.

179   RAL, RFamC/21, Charlotte to Lady Ely, Dec. 10, 1866; Charlotte, London, to Leo, Cambridge, Dec.
      17; same to same, Dec. 18.

180   Spencer-Silver, *Pugin's builder*, pp. 180f. Inscribed on the wall of the mausoleum in Hebrew and Eng-
      lish were the following lines:

          She opened her lips with wisdom
          And in her speech was the law of kindness
          My darling wife.
          If I ascend up into heaven
          Thou art there
          If I lie down in the grave
          Behold I find thee
          Even where thy hand leads me
          And thy right hand supports me.

      He also donated money to the tuberculosis hospital in Brompton Road and St George's Hospital at
      Hyde Park Corner.

181   RAL, RFamC/21, Charlotte, London, to Leo, Cambridge, Nov. 22, 1866; same to same, Jan. 28, 1867.

182   RAL, RFamC/21, Charlotte, London, to Leo, Cambridge, Sept. 26, 1866; same to same, Oct. 11; Feb.
      1, 1867. Cf. Rothschild, *Dear Lord Rothschild*, p. 10; Davis, *English Rothschilds*, pp. 127f.

183   RAL, XI/109/109/1, Ferdinand, Paris, to Lionel, London, Sept. 1, 1872.

184   RAL, RFamC/21, Charlotte, London, to Leo, May 13, 1875.

185   RAL, RFamC/21, Charlotte, London, to Leo, Cambridge, March 14, 1865. Cf. Corti, *Reign*, pp. 435f.

186   RAL, RFamC/21, Charlotte, London, to Leo, Stockport, July 21, 1874.

187   Lord Hardwicke had a distinguished naval career and served as Postmaster-General in Lord Aberdeen's
      Cabinet in 1852 and Lord Privy Seal under Palmerston in 1858. His son was equerry to the Duke of
      Edinburgh: Allfrey, *Jewish court*, p. 31.

188   Corti, *Reign*, p. 444; Palmade, *Capitalism*, pp. 214f.

189   Endelman, *Radical assimilation*, p. 224; Finestein, *Jewish society*, pp. 198f.

190   Endelman, *Radical assimilation*, p. 91. As Endelman points out, this was not unique: the daughters of
      Henry Bischoffsheim also married Christians without converting.

191   Davis, *English Rothschilds*, p. 162; Endelman, *Radical assimilation*, pp. 89f.

192   Vincent (ed.), *Derby diaries, 1869–78*, p. 119.

193   See e.g. Barnbougle Castle, Rosebery Papers, Natty, London, to Rosebery, Dalmeny, Oct. 22, 1889.

194 Rothschild, *Dear Lord Rothschild*, p. 321; Allfrey, *Jewish court*, p. 29.

195 Rothschild, *Whims*, pp. 213ff.; Lottman, *Rothschilds*, p. 182. Cf. Goncourt, *Journal*, vol. IV, pp. 493, 958.

196 Rothschild, *Whims*, pp. 254ff.

197 RAL, RFamC/21, Charlotte, London, to Leo, Cambridge, March 6. 1864; same to same, April 5; Sept. 4; Oct. 1; Oct. 31; Nov. 3; April 26, 1865; March 5, 1866; April 26; June 7. But see also May 4, 1865; Sept. 7, 1869; Sept. 23: A Bischoffsheim, a Cohen or a Morpurgo was considered suitable, but not a Sichel or a Davidson. The latter family's reputation was badly damaged by the suicide of one of its members, which was evidently occasioned by his own bankruptcy: RAL, RFamC/21, Charlotte to Leo, Nov. 9, 1865; same to same, Nov. 11.

198 RAL, RFamC/21, Charlotte, London, to Leo, Cambridge, March 16, 1865; same to same, March 26; March 28; March 29; April 1; May 4; Sept. 13; Sept. 25; Nov. 15.

199 RAL, RFamC/21, Charlotte, London, to Leo, Cambridge, Sept. 26, 1866.

200 RAL, RFamC/21, Charlotte, London, to Leo, Cambridge, Nov. 19, 1866.

201 Wilson, *Rothschild*, pp. 222ff.

202 Surtees, *Coutts Lindsay*, pp. 92ff., 102–31; Davis, *English Rothschilds*, pp. 162ff.; Rothschild, *Dear Lord Rothschild*, p. 15; Wilson, *Rothschild*, pp. 264ff. Cf. RAL, RFamC/21, Charlotte, London, to Leo, Cambridge, July 8, 1864; same to same, Dec. 1, 1865. Flower was MP for Brecon after 1880. He died of diabetes in 1907.

203 Allfrey, *Jewish court*, p. 35.

204 RAL, T13/33, Mayer Carl, Frankfurt, to his cousins and nephews, London, Jan. 9, 1878; RA, B54/43, Disraeli, 10 Downing Street, to Queen Victoria, undated, *c.* Jan. 1878.

205 Davis, *English Rothschilds*, pp. 164f.; James, *Rosebery*, pp. 79ff.

206 Vincent (ed.), *Crawford papers*, p. 600.

207 John Sholto Douglas, the 9th Marquess of Queensberry, is best known as the father of Lord Alfred Douglas, the lover of Oscar Wilde. A "homophobe" *avant la lettre* and quite mad, Queensberry was convinced that Rosebery was drawing his eldest son Lord Drumlanrig (then Rosebery's private secretary) into the homosexual milieu. In August 1893 he sought to confront Rosebery with a horsewhip at Bad Homburg, though he was dissuaded by the effectual combination of the police and the Prince of Wales. When Drumlanrig shot himself in October 1894, Queensberry was convinced he had committed suicide to avoid blackmail over his relations with Rosebery, whom he denounced as a "Snob Queer" and "that cur and Jew friend *Liar* Rosebery." When Wilde took Queensberry to court for libel, a letter from Queensberry was read out in court which referred to Rosebery (and Gladstone); this made it more or less inevitable that Wilde would be prosecuted for homosexuality after the Queensberry trial, lest the government appear to be protecting him. According to one account, Rosebery considered trying to help Wilde, but was told by Balfour: "If you do, you will lose the election." The first trial of Wilde failed to reach a verdict; there would not have been a second, the Solicitor General Sir Frank Lockwood confided, "but for the abominable rumours against Rosebery": Ellmann, *Wilde*, pp. 381, 402, 423f., 434, 437, 524.

208 Davis, *English Rothschilds*, pp. 166–8.

209 Barnbougle Castle, Rosebery Paper, Diary, Feb. 9, 1877; March 12; March 16; May 1; May 3; May 25; June 20; Jan. 3, 1878; March 20; April 16.

210 Another unpleasant fantasist, Billing claimed that Rosebery's son, along with Evelyn Achille de Rothschild, had encouraged his campaign against the supposed 47,000 "perverts" in the British establishment and, grotesquely, that both men had in fact been killed to silence them: Hoare, *Wilde's last stand*, pp. 107, 119, 164–7, 184.

211 Davis, *English Rothschilds*, p. 169.

212 See esp. Ward, *Sir George Tressady*, pp. 87ff. The weakness of this identification lies in the absence of any allusion to religion.

213 Barnbougle Castle, Rosebery Papers, Diary, Nov. 18, 1890. Cf. Davis, *English Rothschilds*, p. 169; Rothschild, *Dear Lord Rothschild*, pp. 15ff.

214 Crewe, *Rosebery*, vol. II, p. 369.

215 For examples of this, *ibid.*, pp. 376, 378, 557, 558, 636, 653, 655; Rothschild, *Dear Lord Rothschild*, p. 16.

216 Endelman, *Radical assimilation*, p. 91; Davis, *English Rothschilds*, p. 167; Kynaston, *City*, vol. I, p. 387.

217 Davis, *English Rothschilds*, p. 173.

218   It is worth noting in this connection another possible symptom of decadence: Alfred was one of three male members of his generation who did not marry.

219   Rothschild, *Dear Lord Rothschild*, p. 11. It was this money which helped finance Lord Carnarvon's fateful 1922 expedition with Howard Carter to find the tomb of Tutankhamun: Wilson, *Rothschild*, pp. 343f.

220   Barnbougle Castle, Rosebery Papers, Ferdinand to Rosebery, Oct. 23, 1870; Crewe, *Rosebery*, vol. II, pp. 55, 115; Davis, *English Rothschilds*, pp. 90f.; Weintraub, *Disraeli*, p. 611. The first of their children was christened Sybil, presumably in allusion to Disraeli's heroine.

221   Cassis, *City bankers*, pp. 204f.

222   McCagg, *History*, p. 149; *idem, Nobles and geniuses*, p. 124.

223   *The Times*, Dec. 27, 1887, p. 3. Cf. Morton, *Rothschilds*, pp. 184–9; Corti, *Reign*, pp. 437–8.

224   The Empress Elizabeth paid a visit to Ferdinand and Alice at Waddesdon in 1876, riding and dining with them: RAL, RFamC/21, Charlotte, London, to Leo, Paris, March 18, 1876; same to same, March 21. Ferdinand also held a ball in honour of Crown Prince Rudolf when he visited London two years later.

225   May, *Habsburg monarchy*, p. 180; Allfrey, *Jewish court*, p. 66.

226   RAL, T15/04, Alphonse, Paris, to his cousins, London, Feb. 6, 1889. Cf. Allfrey, *Jewish court*, p. 68; Wilson, *Rothschild*, pp. 275f.

227   Mayer, *Persistence*, p. 142.

228   RAL, XI/109/107/1, Mayer Carl, Berlin, to his cousins and nephews, London, March 2, 1872; same to same, March 8; March 18. Interestingly, Mayer Carl suspected Bleichröder of intending to convert to Christianity.

229   RAL, XI/109/107/1, Mayer Carl, Berlin, to his cousins and nephews, London, Dec. 17, 1871; same to same, Dec. 19; Feb. 3, 1872; March 8; RAL, XI/109/108/1, May 2. See also RAL, T10/132, Mayer Carl, Berlin, to his cousins and nephews, London, May 24, 1868; RAL, T12/20, Mayer Carl to Lionel, July 2, 1875.

230   Leo Baeck Institute, New York, Sally Bodenheimer Collection, AR 7169, 47, draft letter of condolence to Empress Friedrich, undated, 1888; Cf. Heuberger, *Rothschilds*, p. 187.

231   Mosse, *Jews in the German Economy*, p. 179n. According to the French ambassador George Louis in 1908, William II invited the Rothschilds to re-establish a house in Germany; this seems to have been a figment of the ambassador's imagination: Corti, *Reign*, pp. 432f.

232   RA, Queen Victoria's Journal, April 10, 1856.

233   RAL, RFamC/21, Charlotte, London, to Leo, Cambridge, May 9, 1864; same to same, May 30.

234   RAL, RFamC/21, Charlotte, London, to Leo, Cambridge, May 25, 1864; same to same, May 17, 1866.

235   These ranged from large balls to routine levees and private games of whist: RAL, RFamC/21, Charlotte, London, to Leo, Cambridge, June 1, 1864; same to same, June 8; Feb. 26, 1865; March 25; May 16; May 19; May 23; June 9; March 3, 1866; March 16; May 23; July 12; June 3, 1867. See also Wilson, *Rothschild*, pp. 221f.

236   For example, Lionel gave a dinner in May 1865 attended by "the Duke of Cambridge and Colonel Macdonald, Prince and Princess Edward of Saxe-Weimar, the Duke and Duchess of Manchester, the Duchess of Newcastle, Lord and Lady Proby, Lord Hartington, Lord Sefton [and] Lord Hamilton": RAL, RFamC/21, Charlotte, London, to Leo, Cambridge, May 19, 1865. To Charlotte's anger, the Duchess of Manchester did not reciprocate: same to same, July 12, 1866.

237   RAL, RFamC/4/92, Lionel, London, to Charlotte, Paris, March 6, 1868; RAL, RFamC/3/50, Natty, London, to Charlotte, March 6; RAL, T10/86, Alphonse, Paris, to his cousins, London, April 5. See also RAL, T10/132, Mayer Carl, Berlin, to his cousins and nephews, London, May 24. Cf. Davis, *English Rothschilds*, pp. 121f.

238   RA, Add. A12/13, Maj. Gen. Hon. A. E. Hardinge, Marlborough Club, to Col. Henry Frederick Ponsonby, June 5, 1871; Monypenny and Buckle, *Disraeli*, vol. VI, p. 98.

239   Allfrey, *Jewish court*, pp. 35, 53.

240   Hence the lines in Iolanthe: "The shares are a penny and ever so many are taken by Rothschild and Baring; And just as a few are allotted to you, you awake with a shudder despairing": Rothschild, "Musical associations," pp. 294f.

241   RA, Z458/39, Ferdinand, 143 Piccadilly, to Sir Arthur Bigge, July 21, 1898; *The Times*, July 20, 1898. Their friendship was close enough for the Prince to attend Ferdinand's funeral: RA, Add. A4/91 Prince of Wales to Vicky, Dowager Empress of Germany, Dec. 26.

242 RAL, RFamC/21, Charlotte, London, to Leo, Cambridge, Nov. 26, 1866; same to same, Nov. 30; May 21, 1867; May 28; July 4; RAL, T10/8, Natty to his brothers, undated, *c.* May; RAL, XI/109/91, James, Paris, to his nephews, London, May 9.

243 RAL, T10/385, Alphonse, Paris, to his cousins, London, March 14, 1872; RAL, T10/395, same to same, May 11; RAL, T14/40, Oct. 22, 1888. See also Allfrey, *Jewish court*, pp. 41ff. According to Allfrey, it was Margaretha's husband the duc de Gramont who introduced the Prince to Giulia Beneni ("La Barucci"), "the greatest whore in the world." The Prince's yacht *Aline* was also reputedly named after Gustave's daughter (the wife of Sir Edward Sassoon).

244 RAL, T16/55, Gustave, Paris, to his cousins, London, March 19, 1894.

245 RAL, XI/130A/0, Natty, London, to his cousins, Paris, July 9, 1906; RAL, XI/130A/1, same to same, March 4, 1907; May 7.

246 Cassis, *City bankers*, p. 257.

247 RAL, RFamC/3/11, Natty, Cambridge, to his parents, London, undated, 1861; RAL, RFamC/21, Charlotte, London, to Leo, Cambridge, Aug. 1, 1866. Cf. Pollins, *Economic history of the Jews*, pp. 167ff.; Davis, *English Rothschilds*, pp. 113ff.; Allfrey, *Jewish court*, pp. 27ff.

248 RAL, RFamC/21, Charlotte, London, to Leo, undated, *c.* May 1866; same to same, Cambridge, May 1.

249 RAL, RFamC/21, Charlotte, London, to Leo, Cambridge, June 1, 1866.

250 RAL, RFamC/21, Charlotte, London, to Leo, Cambridge, Jan. 26, 1867; same to same, Jan. 28.

251 RAL, RFamC/21, Charlotte, London, to Leo, Cambridge, Oct. 1, 1866; Charlotte, London, to Leo and Leonora, June 29, 1867; same to same, Aug. 8; Aug. 14.

252 Fulford (ed.), *Darling Child*, p. 147. I owe this reference to Professor Stanley Weintraub. When Anthony died, the Queen wrote to her son: "You will be very sorry for poor Sir Anthony Rothschild who was so very kind and loyal and so fond of you and a good man": Davis, *English Rothschilds*, p. 162.

253 Allfrey, *Jewish court*, pp. 191f. After Edward's accession, Sir Ernest Cassel seems to have played a more important role in the royal finances.

254 RAL, RFamC/21, Charlotte, London, to Leo and Leonora, Trouville, July 28, 1874; same to same, July 31. Cf. Kynaston, *City*, vol. I, pp. 326f.

255 RAL, XI/130A/1, Leo, London, to his cousins, Paris, June 26, 1907.

256 RAL, RFamC/3/129, Natty, Cambridge, to his parents, London, undated, 1861.

257 Kynaston, *City*, vol. I, p. 387.

258 RAL, RFamC/21, Charlotte, London, to Leo, Cambridge, Nov. 3, 1866.

259 RAL, RFamC/21, Charlotte, London, to Leo, Cambridge, Oct. 29, 1864.

260 RAL, RFamC/21, Charlotte, London, to Leo, Cambridge, Dec. 13, 1864.

261 RAL, RFamC/21, Charlotte, London, to Leo, Baden, Sept. 4, 1871.

262 RAL, RFamC/3/8, Natty, Cambridge, to his parents, London, undated, Dec. 1861; RAL, RFamC/3/9, same to same, Dec. 16.

263 RAL, RFamC/21, Charlotte, London, to Leo, Cambridge, March 16, 1866; same to same, April 25.

264 RAL, RFamC/21, Charlotte, London, to Leo, Cambridge, June 3, 1867.

265 RAL, RFamC/21, Charlotte, London, to Leo, Cambridge, May 19, 1865.

266 RAL, RFamC/21, Charlotte, London, to Leo, Paris, March 21, 1876.

267 RAL, RFamC/3/34, Natty, Mentmore, to his parents, London, Jan. 25, 1863.

268 RAL, RFamC/21, Charlotte, London, to Leo, Cambridge, May 6, 1864.

269 Allfrey, *Jewish court*, p. 31.

270 Lant, *Insubstantial Pageant*, p. 135.

271 RA, Add. A12/13, Maj. Gen. Hon. A. E. Hardinge, Marlborough Club, to Col. Henry Frederick Ponsonby, June 5, 1871.

272 RAL, RFamC/21, Charlotte, London, to Leo, Cambridge, March 8, 1865.

273 RAL, RFamC/21, Charlotte, London, to Leo, Cambridge, Oct. 29, 1864; same to same, Feb. 8, 1865; Feb. 14; March 4; March 11. For Lady Ely's condolences on Evelina's death see Charlotte, Gunnersbury, to Lady Ely, Dec. 10, 1866.

274 RAL, RFamC/21, Charlotte, London, to Leo and Leonora, Dieppe, Aug. 5, 1867.

275 RAL, RFamC/4/93, Lionel, London, to Charlotte, Paris, March 9, 1868.

276 RA, R51/8, Lord Granville to Queen Victoria, Aug. 23, 1869. Cf. RA, R51/4, Gladstone to Queen Victoria, Aug. 11; RA, R51/19, same to same, Oct. 28.

277 RA, R51/5, Maj. Gen. Sir T[homas] M[yddleton] Biddulph to Queen Victoria, Aug. 15, 1869; RA,

R51/10, same to same, Aug. 24. Biddulph was master of the Queen's household from 1851 and keeper of the privy purse from 1867. He had to withdraw his initial advice that a Jewish peer would be unable to take his seat in the Lords.

278   RA, R51/6, Queen Victoria, Balmoral, to Granville, Aug. 22, 1869; RA, R51/11, same to same, Aug. 24.

279   RA R51/19, Gladstone to Queen Victoria, Oct. 28, 1869.

280   Ramm (ed.), *Gladstone–Granville correspondence, 1868–1876*, vol. I, pp. 47–52, 59, 67, 70. Cf. Gille, *Maison Rothschild*, vol. II, pp. 599f.; Kynaston, *City*, vol. I, pp. 251f.

281   Endelman, *Radical assimilation*, p. 101.

282   Revealingly, she described Natty as "a handsome man, of about 38 or 40, with a fine type of Jewish countenance" when she met him for the first time (in his capacity as one of Disraeli's executors): RA, Queen Victoria's Journal, May 4, 1881.

283   RA, Queen Victoria's Journal, Oct. 31, 1869.

284   RA R51/21, Queen Victoria to Gladstone, Nov. 1, 1869.

285   Kynaston, *City*, vol. I, pp. 215f. Alexander Baring had been created Baron Ashburton in 1835, Samuel Loyd (of the London and Westminster Bank) had been created Baron Overstone in 1850 and George Glyn had subsequently been created Baron Wolverton.

286   Quinn, *Patronage and piety*, pp. 22, 27; Smith, *House of Lords*, pp. 52, 124.

287   Ramm (ed.), *Gladstone–Granville correspondence, 1868–1876*, vol. II, p. 403. See also p. 289.

288   *Ibid.*, p. 401.

289   BL, Add MS Gladstone 44491 f. 189, Natty to Gladstone, June 25, 1885. Cf. Davis, *English Rothschilds*, pp. 196f.

290   In fact the Queen continued to resist, but when Gladstone resubmitted his original list unaltered, she tacitly acquiesced: RA, C36/126, Gladstone to Queen Victoria, June 15, 1885; RA, Add. A/12/1154, Queen Victoria to Sir Henry Ponsonby, June 17.

291   Corti, *Reign*, pp. 450f.

292   Ziegler, *Sixth great power*, p. 187.

293   Cassis, *City bankers*, pp. 260f.

294   Checkland, *Industrial society*, p. 289.

295   Pollins, *Economic history of the Jews*, p. 168; Allfrey, *Jewish Court*, p. 188.

296   Matthew (ed.), *Gladstone diaries*, vol. XI, p. 361. Cf. Kynaston, *City*, vol. I, pp. 382, 387.

297   RAL, T13/184, Alphonse, Paris, to his cousins, London, June 25, 1885; RAL, T13/185, same to same, June 26; RAL, T13/186, June 27. The Lord Lieutenancy of Buckinghamshire followed in 1889: Hatfield House, 3M, Natty to Salisbury, May 7, 1889.

298   Buckle (ed.), *Letters of Queen Victoria*, vol. III, pp. 123, 183; Lant, *Insubstantial pageant*, p. 135; Davis, *English Rothschilds*, p. 169.

299   RA, Queen Victoria's Journal, May 14, 1890; RA, L11/25d, Anonymous account of the Queen's visit to Waddeson, May 14; RA, L11/25e, Ferdinand, Waddesdon, to Sir Henry Ponsonby, May 16; RAL, T15/36, Alphonse, Paris, to his cousins, London, May 14. Between 1881 and 1898, other royal visitors included the Prince of Wales, who visited every summer except 1882, 1887, 1888, 1894 and 1898; Vicky, Crown Princess of Germany, (1887) and Prince Henry of Battenberg (1890): Brassey, "Visitors to Waddesdon Manor."

300   See RA, F40/108, Prince of Wales to Queen Victoria [telegram], Dec. 18, 1898; RA, Add. A4/88, Prince of Wales to Vicky, Dowager Empress of Germany, Dec. 18; RA, Add. A15/6246, Duke of Connaught to Queen Victoria, Dec. 18; RA, Add. A17/932 Prince of Wales to Princess Louise, Dec. 20. Cf. Lee (ed.), *Empress Frederick*, pp. 144, 246, 279, 291.

301   RA, Queen Victoria's Journal, March 26, 1891; March 28; March 31; April 8; April 14; April 17; April 22. According to family legend she was told to get off a newly planted flower-bed: Corti, *Reign*, pp. 450f.; Morton, *Rothschilds*, pp. 188f.; Allfrey, *Jewish court*, pp. 185f.; Heuberger, *Rothschilds*, p. 106. However, the Queen's journal merely records that "Miss de Rothschild . . . most kindly purposely had the road widened to enable my donkey chair to go along it."

302   Dairnvaell, *Histoire édifiante*, pp. 8f.

303   RAL, T16/25, Alfred, Brussels, to his brothers, London, Dec. 5, 1892. In 1835 Thomas Raikes had recorded a similar conversation, though this was probably an apocryphal story: "When Rothschild was at Vienna, and contracted for the last Austrian loan, the Emperor sent for him to express his satisfaction at the manner in which the bargain had been concluded. The Israelite replied: 'Je peux assurer votre

Majesté que la maison de Rothschild sera toujours enchantée de faire tout ce qui pourra être agréable à la maison d'Autriche'": Raikes, *Journal*, vol. II, pp. 221ff. For an interesting American comparison of the Rothschilds and royalty, see Phillips, "Empire of Rothschild," pp. 501ff.

EIGHT   *Jewish Questions*

1   Herzl, "Dem [Rothschild] Familienrat," in *Tagebücher*, vol. I, pp. 187f.
2   See e.g. RAL, RFamC/21, Charlotte, Paris, to Leo, Cambridge, Oct. 1, 1864; same, London, to same, Oct. 26. For a different view, see Muhlstein, *Baron James*, p. 118.
3   Allfrey, *Jewish court*, p. 73; Heuberger, *Rothschilds*, pp. 190ff.
4   Mosse, *Jews in the German Economy*, p. 179n.; Heilbrunn, "Haus Rothschild," p. 39. Interestingly, he did this only after Minna's death.
5   According to Edouard's daughter Jacqueline, the Halphen girls' mother had hoped they would not marry Jews: Piatigorsky, *Jump*, pp. 5ff. Background on the Anspach and Halphen families is provided in Capdebièle, "Female Rothschilds."
6   Heuberger, *Rothschilds*, p. 96; Jackson, *Sassoons*, pp. 54, 71, 85; Cassis, *City bankers*, p. 208; Black, *Social politics*, p. 9; Allfrey, *Jewish court*, p. 53.
7   Jackson, *Sassoons*, pp. 81f.; Allfrey, *Jewish court*, p. 56. Albert later became the Unionist MP for Hythe, the seat previously held by Mayer.
8   Gustave's daughter Zoé married Baron Léon Lambert of the Belgian agency in 1882 and a year later her cousin Béatrice married Maurice Ephrussi, who was involved in the French Rothschilds' oil business in Russia. In 1892, Gustave's daughter Bertha Juliette married Baron Emmanuel Leonino; and in 1913 Edmond's son James Armand (usually known as "Jimmy") married Dorothy Pinto.
9   Bermant, *Cousinhood, passim*.
10 RAL, RFamC/4/160, Lionel, Paris, to Leo, London, Oct. 21, 1861; RAL, RFamC/21, Charlotte, Paris, to Leo, Gunnersbury, Nov. 4; same to same, Nov. 6.
11 RAL, RFamC/21, Charlotte, London, to Leo, Cambridge, Sept. 26, 1864.
12 RAL, RFamC/21, Charlotte, London, to Leo, Cambridge, Feb. 4, 1867.
13 RAL, RFamC/3/11, Natty, Cambridge, to his parents, London, undated, 1861.
14 RAL, XI/109/99/1, Leo, Vienna, to his parents, London, Sept. 16, 1869.
15 *The Times*, June 11, 1877.
16 Alderman, *British Jewry*, p. 216.
17 *Ibid.*, pp. 211f.; Newman, *United Synagogue*, p. 49. Lionel Louis Cohen, Chairman of the organisation's Executive Committee, was in practice the more important figure.
18 Lipman, *Social service*, p. 41.
19 Black, *Social politics*, pp. 48f. On the Jews' Free School and the Rothschilds in this period, see Black, *JFS*, pp. 56, 58.
20 Lipman, *Social service*, pp. 267f.
21 Cesarini, *Jewish Chronicle*, p. 105.
22 Heuberger, *Rothschilds*, p. 122; Prevost-Marcelhacy, *Rothschild*, pp. 145–7, 249f.
23 Cf. Wistrich, *Jews of Vienna*, p. 165; McCagg, *Vienna and Budapest*, p. 251.
24 Gartner, *Jewish immigrant*, p. 202.
25 *Ibid.*, p. 203.
26 Black, *Social politics*, pp. 10, 53.
27 Alderman, *British Jewry*, pp. 161ff.
28 Newman, *United Synagogue*, pp. 91f.; Alderman, *British Jewry*, pp. 161ff.
29 Anglo-Jewish Archives, Southampton, Natty to Lord Swaythling, Feb. 1, 1912. Cf. Alderman, *Federation of Synagogues*, p. 51. For an account which emphasises Natty's tendency to ride roughshod over other members of the United Synagogue, see Newman, *United Synagogue*, pp. 100f.
30 Mace, "From Frankfurt Jew," p. 191.
31 Zimmermann, *Marr*, p. 124f.
32 Germanicus, *Frankfurter Juden*, esp. pp. 17f. The argument is taken further in *idem, Die Rothschild-Gruppe*, published the following year.
33 Pulzer, *Rise of political anti-Semitism*, p. 106n.; Evans, *Proletarians*, p. 169.
34 Scherb, *Geschichte*, esp. pp. 145f.
35 Sombart, *Juden*, pp. 115ff.
36 Bauer, *Bismarck und Rothschild*, pp. 21 ff.

37   Anon., *Untergang Oesterreichs*; Anon., *Ruin des Mittelstandes*.

38   Pulzer, *Rise of political anti-Semitism*, p. 138.

39   Wistrich, *Jews of Vienna*, p. 214; Pulzer, *Rise of political anti-Semitism*, p. 147; Macartney, *Habsburg Empire*, p. 672. Cf. Jenks, *Iron Ring*.

40   Wistrich, *Jews of Vienna*, p. 179. See also May, *Habsburg monarchy*, p. 178. Schönerer's father had been a railway engineer employed by the Rothschilds.

41   Wistrich, *Socialism*, pp. 217, 250, 253, 259, 273, 284, 318; Wistrich, *Jews of Vienna*, pp. 233, 333.

42   Rozenblit, *Jews of Vienna*, p. 69.

43   Sigurd, "Contexts and nuances," p. 101.

44   Bouvier, *Union Générale*, pp. 147–54, 172–8. See in general Poliakov, *Antisemitismus*, vol. VII, pp. 52, 54.

45   Zola, *L'Argent*, pp. 21f., 91f., 202.

46   Here Zola draws heavily on Feydeau's descriptions of the offices in the rue Laffitte: see esp. *ibid.*, pp. 90–95.

47   *Ibid.*, p. 182.

48   Charnacé, *Baron Vampire*, pp. 26f., 66f.

49   Bontoux, *Union Générale*, esp. p. 139.

50   Drumont, *France juive*, vol. I, p. 22; vol. II, p. 268.

51   *Ibid.*, vol. I, esp. pp. 327f., 335, 344, 348, 352, 354f., 363ff., 401, 462f., 508; vol. II, pp. 322–6. Most of the passages on the Rothschilds were later republished in Drumont, *Barons juifs*, pp. 15–65.

52   Drumont, *France juive*, vol. II, pp. 98, 106f. Though see also *idem*, *Testament*, p. 337.

53   *Ibid.*, pp. 14f., 29ff., 91f., 102f.

54   Not all these charges went unchallenged. For example, Drumont was sued for alleging that a parliamentary deputy had taken bribes from Rothschild to pass a piece of legislation convenient to Banque de France: Lindemann, *Jew accused*, p. 85.

55   Drumont, *Testament*, pp. 132ff., 137f., 312.

56   Drumont, *Juifs contre la France*, p. 38. See also Hémont, *Juifs et Bazaine*, p. 39.

57   Drumont, *Testament*, p. 131.

58   Chirac, *Rois de la République*, pp. 127–54.

59   Chirac, *L'agiotage*, esp. pp. 36, 45, 50, 52f., 56, 62, 64ff., 68f., 72, 80ff., 88, 100ff., 106.

60   Père Peinard, *Rothschild*, in Fuchs, *Juden in der Karikatur*, p. 186.

61   Drumont, *France juive*, vol. II, pp. 93, 95f., 108–18, 119–22, 179f.

62   Drumont, *Testament*, pp. 34, 42, 219f.

63   Chirac, *Rois de la République*, pp. 128f.

64   Goncourt, *Journal*, vol. III, pp. 87, 285, 293, 326, 387, 406, 410, 575f., 733, 746, 1108, 1150; vol. IV, pp. 219f, 235, 493.

65   *Ibid.*, vol. II, p. 981; vol. III, pp. 460, 562, 733, 745, 887, 982f., 1150, 1171, 1178; vol. IV, p. 58.

66   RAL, T16/72, Alphonse, Paris, to his cousins, London, Nov. 2, 1894; RAL, T16/78, same to same, Dec. 14; RAL, T16/79, Dec. 24; RAL, T16/155, Sept. 14, 1896; RAL, T16/164, Nov. 19.

67   Monsignor Montagnini, quoted in Bouvier, *Rothschild*, pp. 203f.

68   See esp. Proust, *Recherche*, vol. III/2, p. 189.

69   *Ibid.*, p. 263.

70   *Ibid.*, vol. IV, pp. 67f.

71   *Ibid.*, vol. V, pp. 32f.

72   *Ibid.*, vol. V, p. 35.

73   Wistrich, *Redemption*, p. 135.

74   Vincent (ed.), *Crawford papers*, p. 62.

75   Cassis, *City bankers*, p. 220.

76   Paucker, "Image," p. 317.

77   Reeves, *Rothschilds*, p. 86.

78   Davis, *English Rothschilds*, p. 228.

79   Rubinstein, *History of the Jews*, pp. 111ff.

80   Hobson, *Imperialism*, pp. 56ff. See chapter 25 below.

81   Hofstadter, *Age of reform*, pp. 75ff. Cf. Harvey, *Coin's financial school*.

82   Rothschild, *Dear Lord Rothschild*, p. 224; Endelman, *Radical assimilation*, pp. 98f.

83   *The Times*, Aug. 26, 1895, p. 7.

84   Kynaston, *City*, vol. II, pp. 545f.; Wilson, *Rothschild*, p. 321.

85   RAL, T15/32, Alphonse, Paris, to his cousins, London, Jan. 24, 1890; *The Times*, April 2, 1900, p. 6; *The Times*, April 3, 1900, pp. 5f. Edouard fought his duel, which was typically French in that neither party was killed. Robert's challenge was not accepted because his antagonist, the comte de Lubersac, was declared too young to fight by his seconds.

86   Stern, *Gold and iron*, p. 521. See also p. 506.

87   Lipman, *History of the Jews*, p. 73. The figure is for all Jewish emigration in the period 1881–1914. On average 5,000 arrived every year in Britain between 1881 and 1905, though the majority did not stay, continuing on to the New World, principally the United States.

88   Bodleian Library, dep. Hughenden 141/3 f. 146, Natty to Disraeli, Nov. 22, 1880 (enclosing f. 150, Bleichröder to NMR). Cf. Stern, *Gold and iron*, pp. 520, 525; Davis, *English Rothschilds*, pp. 227, 234.

89   Lipman, *Social service*, pp. 267f.; Rothschild, *Dear Lord Rothschild*, p. 20.

90   Heuberger, *Rothschilds*, pp. 124, 191ff.; Mosse, *Jews in the German economy*, p. 319.

91   Morton, *Rothschilds*, pp. 184f.

92   Prevost-Marcilhacy, *Rothschild*, pp. 142–5, 245f.; Rothschild, Garton and Rothschild, *Rothschild gardens*, p. 158.

93   Prevost-Marcilhacy, *Rothschild*, p. 145.

94   Mosse, *Jews in the German economy*, p. 189. It is striking that the Rothschilds specified in their foundation's charter that "no condition regarding the religious denomination of any nominee for a professorship shall be attached to any of the Chairs, and in accordance with that, religious or confessional status shall not in any instance be grounds for exclusion in filling a Chair or a position in the research institution": Pulzer, *Jews and the German state*, p. 113. This was as prescient as it was—ultimately—ineffective.

95   Bergeron, *Rothschild*, pp. 128–30.

96   Rothschild, *Dear Lord Rothschild*, pp. 19ff.; Rothschild, Garton and Rothschild, *Rothschild gardens*, p. 156.

97   Prevost-Marcilhacy, *Rothschild*, p. 243.

98   Dumont, *Logement social*, pp. 31–57, 79–93.

99   Prevost-Marcilhacy, *Rothschild*, pp. 143f. The école consistoriale israélite at 60 rue des Feuillantines (1879) and the école israélite Edmond de Rothschild, 37 avenue de Ségur (1880).

100 *Ibid.*, p. 144.

101 Heuberger, *Rothschilds*, pp. 124, 191ff.

102 RAL, RFamC/21, Charlotte, London, to Leo, Cambridge, March 23, 1876. Cf. Hyamson, *Jews' College*, p. 82.

103 RAL, XI/130A/2, Leo, London, to his cousins, Paris, April 9, 1848. Cf. Davis, *English Rothschilds*, pp. 236f.

104 Black, *Social politics*, pp. 143ff.

105 *Ibid.*, p. 240.

106 Lipman, *Social service*, p. 252.

107 Black, *Social politics*, pp. 143ff. See also Anglo-Jewish Archives, Southampton, AJ 136, Leo to Mrs Mocatta, Feb. 20, 1900 (inviting the West Central Working Lads' Club to visit Gunnersbury).

108 *The Times*, June 3, 1891, p. 9.

109 Wohl, *Eternal slum*, pp. 144, 169.

110 White, *Rothschild buildings*, pp. 1–30. See also Lipman, *History of the Jews*, p. 48; Davis, *English Rothschilds*, p. 234.

111 Black, *Social politics*, p. 225.

112 Lipman, *Social service*, p. 248; Marks, *Model mothers*, pp. 110f.

113 Rothschild, *Dear Lord Rothschild*, p. 19.

114 100,000 francs to be invested to provide dowries for daughters of officials of the Chemin de Fer du Nord; 60,000 francs for the poor of Ferrières, Pontcarre and Lagny; 1,000 francs a year for public works in the same localities (implying a capital sum of around 25,000 francs); 250,000 francs to the Jewish hospital in the rue Picpus; and 200,000 francs to the Jewish Charities Commission.

115 Feldman, *Englishmen and Jews*, p. 220; Gartner, *Jewish immigrant*, p. 125. Cf. Pollins, *Economic history of the Jews*, p. 157; Davis, *English Rothschilds*, pp. 236f.

116 White, *Rothschild buildings*, p. 72.

117 See Morris, "Voluntary action." I am grateful to Susannah Morris for her assistance on this point.

118 Gartner, *Jewish immigrant*, pp. 54f.

119   Warnke-Dakers, "Lord Rothschild and his poor brethren," pp. 121ff.

120   Alderman, *British Jewry*, p. 136; Garrard, *English and immigration*, pp. 119f.; Finestein, *Jewish Society*, p. 222; Warnke-Dakers, "Lord Rothschild and his poor brethren," p. 125.

121   Garrard, *English and immigration*, pp. 39f.

122   Warnke-Dakers, "Lord Rothschild and his poor brethren," pp. 121ff.

123   *Ibid.*, p. 124.

124   Davis, *English Rothschilds*, p. 233. Selig Brodetsky went on to become Professor of Applied Mathematics at Leeds University. I am grateful to Aubrey Newman for this information.

125   *The Times*, Jan. 23, 1905, p. 6.

126   In May 1904 he led a delegation from the Jewish Board of Deputies to lobby the Home Secretary: Warnke-Dakers, "Lord Rothschild and his poor brethren," pp. 121ff.

127   Thompson, *Socialists, Liberals and Labour*, p. 30n.

128   Churchill, *Churchill*, vol. II, p. 82.

129   Alderman, *British Jewry*, p. 136; Lipman, *History of the Jews*, pp. 74f.; Black, *Social politics*, p. 308; Feldman, *Englishmen and Jews*, p. 358; Garrard, *English and immigration*, p. 131; Lipman, *History of the Jews*, p. 73.

130   Lindemann, *Jew accused*, p. 169.

131   Iliowzi, *"In the Pale,"* pp. 255–308.

132   RAL, XI/109/91, Glickstein, London Jewish Board of Guardians, to unidentified recipient, Aug. 13, 1867; RAL, XI/109/94/3, The Secretary of the "East End Emigration and Relief Fund," London to Alfred, May 12, 1868.

133   White, *Rothschild buildings*, p. 16.

134   Rothschild, *Dear Lord Rothschild*, p. 19n.

135   RAL, T15/82, Maurice de Hirsch, Austria, to Natty, London, Sept. 3, 1891. Cf. Sokolow, *History of Zionism*, vol. I, pp. 253f.; Black, *Social politics*, p. 48; Allfrey, *Jewish court*, pp. 115, 120f.

136   Rhodes House, Rhodes MSS Afr. S. 228 C3a f. 184, Grey to Rhodes, July 31, 1891.

137   Black, *Social politics*, p. 253.

138   Warnke-Dakers, "Lord Rothschild and his poor brethren," p. 124.

139   Iliowzi, *"In the Pale,"* p. 260.

140   RAL, T14/49, Dr. Schwarz, Jerusalem, to Leo, London, April 21, 1886.

141   Mayorek, "Between East and West," pp. 130f.

142   Schama, *Two Rothschilds*. See also Sokolow, *History of Zionism*, vol. I, pp. 232f., Heuberger, *Rothschilds*, pp. 159ff.; Wistrich, *Jews of Vienna*, pp. 77, 438; Friedman, *Germany*, pp. 38, 43; Gower, *Years of endeavour*, pp. 178f.

143   Bergeron, *Rothschild*, p. 126.

144   Heuberger, *Rothschilds*, pp. 159ff.; Sokolow, *History of Zionism*, vol. II, p. 10.

145   Mayorek, "Between East and West," p. 144n.

146   Lipman, *History of the Jews*, p. 120; Cohen, *English Zionists*, p. 9.

147   Lipman, *History of the Jews*, pp. 123, 125; Cohen, *English Zionists*, p. 101.

148   RAL, T15/73, Edmond, Paris, to his cousins, London, Sept. 22, 1891.

149   The following is based largely on Herzl, *Tagebücher*, vols I–III. Cf. Schorske, *Fin-de-siecle Vienna*, pp. 167f.; Heuberger, *Rothschilds*, p. 165.

150   Herzl, *Tagebücher*, vol. I, pp. 28, 42ff., 50, 79, 83, 90, 103, 110.

151   *Ibid.*, pp. 120–25, 144–210. The "family council" was a typical figment of Herzl's imagination: in many ways he exaggerated the Rothschilds' power in much the same way as Drumont and the other anti-Semites: see esp. pp. 186f. The Address was subsequently published as *Der Judenstaat*.

152   Cf. Hüttl, *Ludwig II*, p. 376. I am grateful to Tim Blanning for this reference.

153   Herzl, *Tagebücher*, vol. I, pp. 219, 266, 271f., 288, 307, 331, 375, 398, 423, 456f., 466ff., 472, 478, 482, 499, 504–7. Cf. Wistrich, *Jews of Vienna*, pp. 62, 85, 450f.

154   Herzl, *Tagebücher*, vol. I, pp. 511, 518, 526f., 541; vol. II, pp. 26ff., 48ff., 59, 67ff., 80, 83, 110, 198f., 206f., 243f., 358; vol. III, pp. 60f., 181. For Edmond's version see RAL, T45/1, Edmond, Paris, to his cousins, London, Oct. 11, 1898.

155   Herzl, *Tagebücher*, vol. II, pp. 476, 550, 576ff.; vol. III, pp. 197f., 202, 208, 215ff. Cf. Cohen, *English Zionists*, pp. 54, 61, 81, 89.

156   Lipman, *History of the Jews*, pp. 123, 125; Cohen, *English Zionists*, p. 101.

157 Herzl, *Tagebücher*, vol. III, pp. 219f., 228ff., 232, 236f., 276, 280ff., 292, 299–307, 324ff., 332–4, 348f., 373, 376ff., 404, 408, 410f., 415–19, 440–46, 454f., 481ff., 507f., 574–9.

NINE   *"On the Side of Imperialism" (1874–1885)*

1   Hobson, *Imperialism*, pp. 56ff., chapter entitled "Economic parasites of imperialism."

2   Braudel and Labrousse, *Histoire économique*, vol. III, pp. 431ff.

3   Whales, *Joint Stock Banking*, pp. 231, 340–54.

4   Cottrell, "Domestic commercial banks," pp. 48f.

5   Gall *et al.*, *Deutsche Bank*, p. 129.

6   Chapman, *Merchant banking*, p. 209.

7   RAL, RFamFD/13A/1; 13B/1; 13C/1; 13D/1; 13D/2; 13/E; Ziegler, *Sixth great power*, pp. 372–8; Roberts, *Schroders*, pp. 527–35.

8   Rubinstein, "British millionaires," pp. 210–14. On bankers, Cassis, *City*, pp. 143f.; *idem*, *City bankers*, p. 198.

9   Carosso, *Morgans*, pp. 276, 643f.

10   Cassis, *City bankers*, p. 41n. The organisation of the Morgan group was indeed somewhat similar to that of the Rothschilds: it was a partnership between three houses, one in New York, one in Philadelphia and one in Paris. After J. P. Morgan's reorganisation in 1895 these were called: J. P. Morgan, Drexel & Co. and Morgan, Harjes. The London house (J. S. Morgan until 1910 when it became Morgan Grenfell) was always run separately.

11   Brockhaus, *Real-Enzyklopädie* (1827), pp. 431–4.

12   There is some reason to doubt them. In 1906 Leo told his Paris cousins: "We ourselves discounted £28,000,000 of bills this year, of which £12,000,000 have been for your account." That figure would have made Rothschilds by far the biggest bill-broker in the London market: RAL, XI/130A/0, Leo, London, to his cousins, Paris, Dec. 21, 1906.

13   Morgan and Thomas, *Stock Exchange*, pp. 88f.

14   *Financial Times*, May 6, 1997, p. 18: gross direct plus portfolio investment in the period 1990–95 was just under 12 per cent of GDP.

15   Pollard, "Capital exports," pp. 491f.

16   See Cain, *Economic foundations*, pp. 43ff.

17   Edelstein, *Overseas investment*, pp. 24ff., 48, 313ff.

18   Davis and Huttenback, *Mammon*, pp. 81–117; Pollard, "Capital exports," p. 507; O'Brien, "Costs and benefits," p. 179.

19   Davis and Huttenback, *Mammon*, p. 107.

20   *Ibid.*, p. 28.

21   Michie, *London and New York Stock Exchanges*, p. 114; Ayer, *Century of finance*, pp. 14–81. This total includes a small number (nine) of substantial loans—totalling £526 million—which were issued jointly with other non-Rothschild banks, mainly Barings but also J. S. Morgan and, in one instance, Schröders. Cf. Pollins, *Economic history of the Jews*, p. 112; Jenks, *Migration of British capital*, pp. 421–4; Morgan and Thomas, *Stock Exchange*, pp. 88, 94f.; Kynaston, *City*, vol. I, pp. 350f.; Ziegler, *Sixth great power*, p. 196.

22   Kynaston, *City*, vol. II, pp. 271f.

23   *Ibid.*, vol. I, pp. 405ff., 410; Ziegler, *Sixth great power*, pp. 198ff.

24   RAL, XI/109/108/1, Alphonse, Paris, to his cousins, London, May 19, 1872; RAL, T16/57, same to same, April 9, 1894. See also on the profits made by Belmont from the New York Interborough Rapid Transit, Hood, *722 Miles*, pp. 122ff.

25   RAL, XI/130A/0, Natty, London, to his cousins, Paris, Nov. 5, 1906. See also RAL, RFamC/21, Charlotte, London, to Leo, Cambridge, July 9, 1866; RAL, XI/109/108/1, Alphonse, Paris, to his cousins, London, May 28, 1872; RAL, T12/1, same to same, Jan. 12, 1875; AN, 132 AQ 5520/1M126, NMR to deRF, June 25, 1880.

26   Kynaston, *City*, vol. I, pp. 407, 410.

27   RAL, T15/69, Edmond, Paris, to Natty, London, Sept. 9, 1891; RAL, T15/70, Alphonse, Paris, to his cousins, London, Sept. 16; RAL, T16/11, same to same, June 14, 1892.

28   Chapman, *Merchant banking*, esp. pp. 17–45, 172.

29   RAL, XI/130A/0, Natty, London, to his cousins, Paris, May 31, 1906; same to same, Nov. 21; Nov. 29.

30 See esp. Wolf, "Rothschildiana," pp. 287–308.

31 The title of Khedive was purchased from the Sultan by Ismail in 1867 in return for an increase in the Egyptian tribute to Constantinople from around £337,000 to £682,000.

32 Details and figures in Shaw, "Ottoman expenditures," pp. 374ff.; Issawi, *Economic history of the Middle East*, pp. 94–106; Hershlas, *Introduction*, pp. 53–66; Owen, *Middle East*, p. 106.

33 Details and figures in Crouchley, *Economic development*, pp. 274–8; Issawi, *Economic history of the Middle East*, pp. 439–45; Hershlas, *Introduction*, pp. 99–122.

34 Calculated from figures in Mitchell, *British historical statistics*, pp. 396–9, 402f.

35 Landes, *Bankers and pashas*, pp. 169, 176, 209–12, 302; Grunwald, "Europe's railways," pp. 202f.

36 RAL, RFamC/21, Charlotte, London, to Leo, Cambridge, June 6, 1867; same to same, Boulogne, July 21; July 22; July 24.

37 According to the concessions granted in 1854 and 1856, the Khedive Said was given preference shares in Lesseps's Compagnie Universelle du Canal Maritime de Suez, the interest on which accounted for 15 per cent of its net profits. The Khedive also bought 96,517 ordinary shares in the first subscription, just under a quarter of the total, for which he paid £3.56 million (largely in 10 per cent treasury bills); and his nephew Ismail took up a further 85,606 shares on becoming Khedive in 1863 (though some of the total of 182,123 shares must subsequently have been sold, as only 176,602 were available for sale in 1875). On all these shares, the Khedive was supposedly entitled to a minimum 5 per cent dividend. In return, the Company was given a strip of land rather wider than was needed for the canal itself, exemption from tax and (under a secret annexe to the second concession) free forced labour for the completion of the canal. Moreover, as a result of legal action taken by the Company against the Khedive, he had to pay it a further £3.36 million; to raise the money, he had to mortgage his share coupons for twenty-five years. By 1875 the Egyptian Treasury had paid £16 million for the construction of the canal and had borrowed £35.4 million at rates ranging from 12 to 27 per cent: Wolf, "Rothschildiana," pp. 289f., 299; Rothschild, *"You have it, Madam,"* pp. 10f., 54f.

38 AN, 132 AQ/324/Suez, Lesseps to James, June 23, 1854.

39 RAL, T51/3, 000/43/1, E. Landau, Alexandria, to H. Landau, Turin, undated, 1864; RAL, XI/109/86/1, Alphonse, Paris, to his cousins, London, July 14; RAL, XI/109/86, Nat, Paris, to his brothers, London, July 14; RAL, XI/109/56, James, Wildbad, to his sons, Paris, July 17; AN, 132 AQ 5902, same to same, July 18; RAL, XI/109/86/1, Nat to his brothers, Aug. 8; Alphonse to his cousins, Aug. 9; same to same, Aug. 22; Aug. 23; Aug. 24; Aug. 30; AN, 132 AQ 5902, James, Wildbad, to Nat and Alphonse, Paris, July 10, 1865; RAL, XI/109/86, same to same, July 17; RAL, XI/109/87, James to his nephews, Aug. 23; RAL, XI/109/87/1, Alphonse to his cousins, Sept. 19; RAL, T6/394, E. Landau to NMR, Nov. 29. On Landau, see RAL, XI/109/100/1, Anthony, Turin, to his brothers, London, Oct. 12, 1869.

40 RAL, XI/109/90/1, Alphonse to his cousins, April 14, 1867; RAL, RFamC/21, Charlotte, London, to Leo, Cambridge, June 5; RAL, RFamC/4/79, Lionel, London, to Charlotte, Paris, July 10; RAL, RFamC/4/80, same to same, July 11; RAL, RFamC/4/82, July 13; RAL, RFamC/4/83, July 15.

41 RAL, T10/174, Alphonse, Paris, to his cousins, London, Nov. 23, 1869; RAL, T10/175, same to same, Nov. 28; RAL, T10/185, March 5, 1870; RAL, XI/109/109/1, Gustave, Paris, to his cousins, London, Aug. 2, 1872; RAL, T41/231, Lambert, Brussels, to NMR, July 30, 1873.

42 RAL, XI/109/99/1, Alphonse, Paris, to his cousins, London, Aug. 4, 1869; RAL, XI/109/108/2, Anselm, Vienna, to Ferdinand, London, March 9, 1872.

43 RAL, T11/47, Landau, Turin, to Lionel, London, March 5, 1874; RAL, T11/55, Alphonse, Paris, to his cousins, London, undated, *c.* April; RAL, T11/57, same to same, May 9.

44 Kent (ed.), *Great powers*, p. 56.

45 Weintraub, *Disraeli*, p. 541.

46 Rothschild, *"You have it, Madam,"* p. 17.

47 RAL, T11/59, Gustave, Paris, to his cousins, London, May 5, 1874; RAL, T11/60, same to same, May 6; RAL, T11/61, May 7.

48 Wolf, "Rothschildiana," pp. 287–301.

49 It was originally intended that only half the coupons due on external debts would be redeemed in cash, the remainder to be paid in bonds carrying 5 per cent interest that would mature five years later; within three months even this was abandoned: Hershlas, *Introduction*, p. 63; Issawi, *Economic history of the Middle East*, p. 101.

50 Sokolow, *History of Zionism*, vol. II, pp. 246f.; Corti, *Reign*, pp. 446f. The Paris Rothschilds do not

seem to have relayed this information until November 23: RAL, T12/15, Alphonse, Paris, to his cousins, London, Nov. 23, 1875.

51 Rothschild, *"You have it, Madam,"* pp. 15ff.; Davis, *Disraeli*, pp. 190f.

52 Buxton, *Finance*, vol. II, p. 351.

53 Powell, *Money market*, p. 522.

54 Monypenny and Buckle, *Disraeli*, vol. V, pp. 446ff.; Blake, *Disraeli*, pp. 583f.

55 RA, O12/127, Disraeli, Whitehall Gardens, to the Prince of Wales, Dec. 11, 1875.

56 RAL, T51/8, *The Times* Money-Market and City Intelligence, Alexandria, to Bank of Egypt, London, Nov. 26, 1875.

57 Rothschild, *"You have it, Madam,"* p. 19.

58 *Ibid.*, pp. 29f. The figure was slightly less than £4 million because the Khedive's shareholding turned out to be slightly smaller than stated in the contract (176,602 instead of 177,642). This constituted a 44 per cent shareholding; the remaining 56 per cent were largely in French hands.

59 Bank of England, C40/492 1652/1, NMR to the Chief Cashier, March 31, 1876.

60 RAL, T51/17, 000/43/46, W. H. Smith, Treasury Chambers, to the Barons Rothschild, Feb. 2, 1876; Rothschild, *"You have it, Madam,"* p. 44; Buxton, *Finance*, vol. II, p. 237n. Cf. Hargreaves, *National debt*, p. 205; Davis, *English Rothschilds*, pp. 151ff.; Johnson (ed.), *Diary of Gathorne Hardy*, p. 262.

61 Rothschild, *"You have it, Madam,"* pp. 15f.

62 RAL, RFamC/2, Disraeli, 2 Whitehall Gardens, to the Queen, Nov. 24, 1875.

63 Monypenny and Buckle, *Disraeli*, vol. V, pp. 449f. Cf. Murray, *Disraeli*, p. 223; Maurois, *Disraeli*, p. 263f.; Clarke, *Disraeli*, pp. 234f.

64 RA, O12/127, Disraeli, Whitehall Gardens, to the Prince of Wales, Dec. 11, 1875. This seems unlikely. It is true that no correspondence exists to indicate that Alphonse knew of the transaction before it became public on November 25: RAL, T12/16, Alphonse, Paris, to his cousins, London, undated, *c.* Nov. 26; Rothschild, *"You have it, Madam,"* p. 27. But Lionel could not have raised the money without the assistance of the Paris house. The possibility cannot be ruled out that there was telegraphic communication, the records of which have not survived.

65 Whibley, *Lord John Manners*, pp. 178f.

66 RAL, T40/10, Bleichröder, Berlin, to Lionel, London, Dec. 1, 1875.

67 Matthew, *Gladstone, 1875–1898*, p. 14; Jackson, *Hartington*, p. 71; Rothschild, *"You have it, Madam,"* p. 37.

68 Ramm (ed.), *Gladstone–Granville correspondence, 1868–1876*, vol. II, p. 474.

69 Winter, *Lowe*, pp. 306f.; Briggs, *Victorian people*, p. 260; Blake, *Disraeli*, p. 584.

70 Rothschild, *"You have it, Madam,"* p. 19.

71 Swartz, *Politics of British foreign policy*, p. 202.

72 RA, O12/127, Disraeli, Whitehall Gardens, to the Prince of Wales, Dec. 11, 1875; Rothschild, *"You have it, Madam,"* p. 22.

73 *The Times*, Feb. 29, 1876, p. 6. In this respect, Lionel's election defeat was fortunate.

74 Wolf, "Rothschildiana," pp. 307f.

75 Kynaston, *City*, vol. I, pp. 336f.

76 RAL, T51/9 000/43/4, Alphonse, Paris, to his cousins, London, Nov. 29, 1875; RAL, T12/24, same to same, Dec. 1.

77 RAL, T51/7, Gustave, Paris, to his cousins, London, Dec. 31, 1875; RAL, T12/44, Alphonse, Paris, to his cousins, London, Jan. 15, 1876.

78 Park (ed.), *British Prime Ministers*, pp. 237ff.

79 RAL, T12/21, Mayer Carl, Frankfurt, to Natty, London, Dec. 7, 1875.

80 Kynaston, *City*, vol. I, p. 335.

81 Rothschild, *"You have it, Madam,"* pp. 23ff.; Monypenny and Buckle, *Disraeli*, vol. V, p. 448.

82 Woodward, "Economic factors," pp. 111f.

83 Rothschild, *"You have it, Madam,"* pp. 46, 49. In strictly financial terms, that was the moment to sell. However, it was not until 1979 that the government sold the shares, by which time they had fallen in value to £22 million, in real terms rather less than their original purchase price.

84 Blake, *Disraeli*, p. 586. Nor could the French complain that they had been wholly excluded from the profits of Egyptian insolvency: the Crédit Foncier did acquire the Khedive's rights to 15 per cent of the Canal's revenues for 22 million francs in 1880.

85 RAL, T12/114, Alphonse, Paris, to *Bismarck*, Berlin, July 7, 1876.

86   RAL, T12/27, T51/10, 000/43/27, Austro-Egyptian Bank circular, December 1875.

87   RAL, T12/59, Elliot to Parkinson, Feb. 1, 1876; RAL, T12/50, Alphonse, Paris, to his cousins, London, March 4; RAL, T12/53, Wilson to Lionel, March 8; RAL, T12/60, Alphonse to his cousins, March 8; RAL, T12/61, same to same, March 10; RAL, T12/62, March 13; RAL, T51/16, 000/43/61, Stanton, Cairo, to Foreign Office, London, March 20. Cf. Davis, *English Rothschilds*, pp. 157f.

88   RAL, T12/33, Lionel, London, to Leo, Cambridge, undated, *c.* Feb. 1876; RAL, RFamC/4/374, same to same, Paris, undated, *c.* March; RAL, RFamC/4/443, *c.* March; RAL, RFamC/4/444, undated, *c.* March. Cf. RAL, T12/32, Austro-Egyptian Bank circular, Feb. 5.

89   RAL, T51/13, 000/43/59, Lionel, London, to Leo, Paris, March 17, 1876; RAL, T12/68, Alphonse, Paris, to his cousins, London, May 1; RAL, T12/73, same to same, Sept. 11.

90   RAL, T12/45, Alphonse, Paris, to his cousins, London, Jan. 20, 1876; RAL, T12/48, same to same, Feb. 23.

91   RAL, T12/58, Alfred, Paris, to his parents, London, March 20, 1876; RAL, T51/14, 000/43/66, Lionel, London, to Leo and Laurie, Paris, March 25.

92   RAL, T12/67, Alphonse, Paris, to his cousins, London, March 29, 1876; RAL, T12/63, same to same, April 16; RAL, T12/69, Rivers Wilson, Cairo, to Lionel, London, May 21.

93   Hershlas, *Introduction*, vol. II, pp. 103f. There were four foreign representatives, one apiece for Britain, France, Italy and Austria.

94   Crouchley, *Economic development*, p. 276.

95   Hershlas, *Introduction*, vol. II, pp. 104f.

96   RAL, T13/101/6,7–1/151/19, Alphonse, Paris, to his cousins, London, June 22, 1878; RAL, T13/101/6,7–1/226/25, same to same, Sept. 24; RAL, T13/101/6,7–1/230/26, Sept. 29. See *The Times*, Nov. 13, 1878, p. 10; Dec. 20, p. 3; Dec. 25, p. 8; Jan. 18, 1879, p. 7; March 17, p. 6.

97   *The Times*, Nov. 13, 1878, p. 5.

98   Bodleian Library, dep. Hughenden 141/3 f. 31, Lionel to Disraeli, May 26, 1876.

99   Blake, *Disraeli*, pp. 589f.

100 Bodleian Library, dep. Hughenden 141/3 f. 33, Lionel to Disraeli, Sept. 8, 1876; f.35, same to same, Sept. 16; f.41, Oct. 12.

101 RAL, T12/91, Mayer Carl, Frankfurt, to Natty, London, Oct. 23, 1876; RAL, T13/34, same to same, Feb. 10, 1878; RAL, T12/115, Alphonse, Paris, to his cousins, London, undated, 1877; RAL, T12/124, same to same, Oct. 19; RAL, T12/134, Dec. 19; RAL, 101/6,7–1/1, Jan. 2, 1878; RAL, 101/6,7–1/2, Jan. 3; RAL, 101/6,7–10/3, Jan. 4; RAL, 101/6,7–1/4, Jan. 5; RAL, 101/6,7–1/9, Jan. 10; RAL, 101/6,7–1/11, Jan. 14; RAL, 101/6,7–1/16, Jan. 19; RAL, 101/6,7–1/17, Jan. 21; RAL, 101/6,7–1/19, Jan. 24; RAL, 101/6,7–1/26, Jan. 31; RAL, 101/6,7–1/27, Feb. 1; RAL, 101/6,7–1/28, Feb. 2; RAL, 101/6,7–1/30, Feb. 5; RAL, 101/6,7–1/31, Feb. 6; RAL, 101/6,7–1/33, Feb. 8; RAL, 101/6,7–1/35, Feb. 11; RAL, 101/6,7–1/36, Feb. 12; RAL, 101/6,7–1/37, Feb. 13.

102 Powell, *Money market*, p. 515.

103 Girault, *Emprunts russes*, pp. 86f., 140; Bouvier, *Crédit Lyonnais*, pp. 586ff., 748–55. It is possible that the French house took a share in this loan; however, Alphonse's letters make it clear that he supported Disraeli's policy.

104 RA, B52/25, Disraeli, Osborne, to Queen Victoria, Aug. 17, 1877. In fact, Lionel had intimated to Disraeli that he would not give Russia financial assistance as early as October the year before: Bodleian Library, dep. Hughenden 141/3 f. 39, Lionel to Disraeli, Oct. 11, 1876.

105 RAL, T12/14, Alphonse, Paris, to his cousins, London, Aug. 30, 1875; RAL, T12/74, same to same, Sept. 30, 1876; RAL, T12/122, Edmond, Paris, to his cousins, London, Aug. 16, 1877.

106 RAL, T12/75, Alphonse, Paris, to his cousins, London, Oct. 3, 1876.

107 Vincent (ed.), *Derby diaries, 1869–78*, p. 333.

108 Bodleian Library, dep. Hughenden 141/3 f. 37, Lionel to Disraeli, Sept. 19, 1876.

109 Corti, *Reign*, pp. 449f.; Alderman, *Jewish community*, pp. 38f.; idem, *British Jewry*, p. 99; Weintraub, *Disraeli*, p. 572.

110 Stern, *Gold and iron*, pp. 338, 373f.

111 Bodleian Library, dep. Hughenden 141/3 f. 43, Lionel to Disraeli, March 31, 1877. Cf. Davis, *English Rothschilds*, p. 155; Corti, *Reign*, pp. 448f.

112 "Turkish as I have always been, I am astonished at the Turkish feeling everywhere": Bodleian Library, dep. Hughenden 141/3 f.110, Natty to Montagu Corry, Aug. 31, 1877.

113 RA, B52/25, Disraeli, Osborne, to Queen Victoria, Aug. 17, 1877. See also Bodleian Library, dep. Hugenden 141/3 f. 114, Natty to Corry, Sept. 4; f. 7, Alfred to Disraeli, Sept. 13.

114 Vincent (ed.), *Derby diaries, 1869–78*, p. 473.

115 Ramm (ed.), *Gladstone–Granville correspondence, 1868–1876*, vol. II, p. 490; Matthew, *Gladstone, 1876–1898*, p. 18.

116 Ramm (ed.), *Gladstone–Granville correspondence, 1876–1886*, vol. I, pp. 64f.

117 Vincent (ed.), *Later Derby diaries*, p. 131.

118 For Bleichröder's communications of Bismarck's views (e.g., on the acceptability to Germany of the British acquisition of Cyprus), see RAL, T40/14, Bleichröder to Lionel, London, Jan. 4, 1878; RAL, T40/15, same to same, Feb. 28; RAL, T40/11, July 6; RAL, T40/12, July 10.

119 Bodleian Library, dep. Hughenden 141/3 f. 47, Lionel to Disraeli, March 15, 1878; RAL, RFamC/21, Charlotte, Piccadilly, to Disraeli, July 18. See also RAL, RFamC/2/33, Disraeli to Charlotte, Jan. 13, 1879.

120 Kynaston, *City*, vol. I, p. 338; Davis, *English Rothschilds*, p. 176.

121 Bodleian Library, dep. Hughenden 141/3 f. 200, Rivers Wilson, Paris, to NMR, April 8, 1879.

122 Bodleian Library, dep. Hughenden 141/3 f. 196, Barington to Disraeli, April 10, 1879. Cf. Davis, *English Rothschilds*, pp. 181–5.

123 Bodleian Library, dep. Hughenden 141/3 f. 202, deRF to Disraeli, June 5, 1879.

124 Bodleian Library, dep. Hugenden 141/3 f. 120, Natty to Disraeli, Aug. 21, 1879; f. 122, same, Tring, to same, Aug. 30; f. 128, Oct. 25; f. 130, Dec. 1; f. 132, Dec. 8; f. 134, Dec. 8; f. 136, Dec. 9; *The Times*, Nov. 21, 1879, p. 5; Nov. 26, p. 5; Dec. 13, p. 5; Dec. 23, p. 3.

125 Hershlas, *Introduction*, p. 63.

126 Bodleian Library, dep. Hughenden 141/3 f. 144, Natty to Disraeli, Oct. 7, 1880.

127 Davis, *English Rothschilds*, pp. 186f.

128 Ramm (ed.), *Gladstone–Granville correspondence, 1876–1886*, vol. I, p. 194.

129 Davis, *English Rothschilds*, pp. 186f.

130 The total debt was reduced from 237 million to 142 million Turkish pounds and the annual charges from 15 to just 3 million—i.e. from 6 per cent to just 2 per cent of the capital sum. This was a generous if realistic settlement.

131 Barth, *Hochfinanz*, p. 74.

132 RAL, T14/32, Alphonse, Paris, to his cousins, London, Aug. 6, 1888.

133 Hershlas, *Introduction*, p. 64; Issawi, *Economic history of the Middle East*, pp. 102ff.

134 Stern, *Gold and iron*, p. 311n.

135 *Ibid.*, p. 341.

136 Hershlas, *Introduction*, p. 65; Issawi, *Economic history of the Middle East*, pp. 102ff. By 1914, Germans held 22 per cent of the Ottoman public debt, compared with figures of 63 per cent for France and 15 per cent for Britain. See also Barth, *Hochfinanz*, p. 117.

137 Bouvier, *Union Générale*, pp. 73–86. See also Allfrey, *Jewish court*, pp. 76–89; Grunwald, "Europe's railways," pp. 203f.

138 Bouvier, *Union Générale*, pp. 7–19, 44–50, 58–70, 87–98; *idem, Crédit Lyonnais*, pp. 13–20; Corti, *Reign*, pp. 435f.

139 Bouvier, *Union Générale*, pp. 52–8.

140 *Ibid.*, pp. 21–6, 31–44; *idem, Rothschilds*, pp. 223–7.

141 Braudel and Labrousse, *Histoire économique*, vol. III, p. 449; Bouvier, *Union Générale*, pp. 44–50, 110ff.

142 Bouvier, *Union Générale*, pp. 129–36, 167.

143 Ebstein, *Crise*, pp. 5f.; Bouvier, *Union Générale*, pp. 136–47; Braudel and Labrousse, *Histoire économique*, vol. III, pp. 450f.

144 Bouvier, *Union Générale*, pp. 162ff., 204ff.; Priouret, *Caisse des Dépôts*, p. 168.

145 BL, Add. MS 43912 f. 4, Natty to Dilke, Jan. 25, 1882, enclosing a letter from Alphonse, Paris, to his cousins, London, Jan. 25.

146 RAL, T13/101/10, Alphonse, Paris, to his cousins, London, Feb. 6, 1882.

147 BL, Add. MS 43912 f. 11, Natty to Dilke, Feb. 16, 1882.

148 Ramm (ed.), *Gladstone–Granville correspondence, 1876–1886*, vol. I, p. 348.

149 RAL, T13/101/10,11–1/73/99, Alphonse, Paris, to his cousins, London, March 30, 1882; RAL, T13/101/10,11–1/76/100, same to same, April 3; RAL, T13/101/10,11–1/90/101, April 20; RAL,

T13/101/10,11–1/142/105, June 22; RAL, T13/101/10,11–1/143/106, June 23; RAL, T13/101/10,11–1/145/107, June 26.

150   RAL, T13/101/10,11–1/161/109, Alphonse, Paris, to his cousins, London, July 15, 1882; RAL, T13/101/10,11–1/166/110, same to same, July 21; RAL, T13/101/10,11–1/168/111, July 24; RAL, T13/101/10,11–1/211/113, Sept. 13; RAL, T13/101/10,11–1/212/114, Sept. 16.

151   Matthew, *Gladstone, 1875–1898*, p. 137.

152   Ramm (ed.), *Gladstone–Granville correspondence, 1876–1886*, vol. I, p. 417.

153   Matthew, *Gladstone, 1875–1898*, pp. 137–42.

154   RAL, T13/101/10,11–1/224/116, Gustave, Paris, to his cousins, London, Oct. 2, 1882; RAL, T13/101/10,11–1/227/118, Alphonse, Paris, to his cousins, London, Oct. 5; RAL, T13/101/10,11–1/252/120, same to same, Nov. 10; RAL, T13/101/10,11–2/50/124, March 3, 1883; RAL, T13/101/10,11–2/125/128, June 4; RAL, T13/101/10,11–2/164/131, July 20; RAL, T13/101/10,11–2/16/132, July 24; RAL, T13/101/10,11–2/273/138, Gustave to his cousins, Dec. 5. Cf. Ramm (ed.), *Gladstone–Granville correspondence, 1876–1886*, vol. I, p. 440; vol. II, p. 69.

155   RAL, T13/101/10,11–2/115/126, Alphonse, Paris, to his cousins, London, May 23, 1883.

156   Baring had been a member of the board of the Caisse since 1877 and served as one of the Anglo-French Comptrollers in 1879. After a brief tour of duty in India, he had returned to Egypt in 1881 to become consul-general. With the abolition of dual control in 1883, financial power effectively was transferred to him as British Agent, a post he retained until 1907: Hershlas, *Introduction*, p. 112.

157   Childers, *Life of Childers*, pp. 208f.; Ziegler, *Sixth great power*, p. 195.

158   Matthew (ed.), *Gladstone diaries*, vol. XI, pp. 184, 236, 287, 297, 299–305. Cf. Swartz, *Politics of British foreign policy*, p. 152.

159   Davis, *English Rothschilds*, p. 206.

160   BL, Add. MS 44787 f. 204, Natty to Hamilton, Nov. 26, 1884; Ramm (ed.), *Gladstone–Granville correspondence, 1876–1886*, vol. II, p. 241.

161   Davis, *English Rothschilds*, pp. 191f.

162   Dugdale (ed.), *German diplomatic documents*, vol. I, p. 139.

163   Crewe, *Rosebery*, vol. II, pp. 212f.

164   Rothschild, *Dear Lord Rothschild*, p. 30.

165   RAL, T13/101/12,13–1/2/14, Gustave, Paris, to his cousins, London, Jan. 3, 1884; RAL, T13/101/12,13–1/23/144, same to same, Jan. 28; Ramm (ed.), *Gladstone–Granville correspondence, 1876–1886*, vol. II, p. 136.

166   Barnbougle Castle, Rosebery Papers, Rosebery Diary, Feb. 8, 1885.

167   Barnbougle Castle, Rosebery Papers, Natty to Rosebery, Feb. 11, 1885. Cf. Davis, *English Rothschilds*, p. 199.

168   RAL, T13/101/12,13–2/29/167, Gustave, Paris, to his cousins, London, Feb. 6, 1885; RAL, T13/180, Alphonse, Paris, to his cousins, London, June 6. The surviving balance sheets indicate substantial holdings of Egyptian paper, e.g. £144,348 of Suez Canal shares in 1886: AN, 132 A Q 3, Inventarium des englischen Hauses, Oct. 16, 1886.

169   RAL, T13/101/12,13–2/36, Alphonse, Paris, to his cousins, London, Feb. 13, 1885; RAL, T13/189, Edmond to his cousins, July 14; RAL, T13/190, same to same, July 21; RAL, T13/191, July 22; RAL, T13/192, Alphonse to his cousins, July 23; RAL, T13/193, same to same, July 24. Cf. Clapham, *Bank of England*, vol. II, p. 316; Swartz, *Politics of British foreign policy*, pp. 152ff.; Stern, *Gold and iron*, p. 422; Kynaston, *City*, vol. II, pp. 352f.

170   Details in Issawi, *Economic history of the Middle East*, pp. 439–45; Hershlas, *Introduction*, pp. 113–22.

171   RAL, T15/18, Vincent, Cairo, to Natty, London, Feb. 25, 1889; RAL, T15/79, Palmer, Cairo, to Natty, Feb. 9, 1891; RAL, T15/77, Milner to Natty, April 29.

172   Calculated from Crouchley, *Economic development*, pp. 274ff.

173   RAL, T15/78, Milner, Cairo, to Natty, London, July 20, 1891; BL, MS Milner dep. 27 ff. 72–3, Natty to Milner, July 31. See also AN, 132 AQ/324/Suez, Suez Canal Co. to deRF, Dec. 1, 1894; same to same, April 7, 1898.

174   RAL, XI/130A/1, Natty, London, to his cousins, Paris, May 8, 1907; RAL, XI/130A/2, same to same, May 6, 1908; RAL, XI/130A/4, April 25, 1910.

175   Hatfield House, 3M, Herbert von Bismarck, Berlin, to Natty, London, Sept. 15, 1885; Natty to Salisbury, Sept. 19.

176   Spinner, *Goschen*, pp. 158f.

177 Matthew, *Gladstone, 1875–1898*, pp. 14n., 135f., 375f. Matthew's figures are not quite consistent.

178 Taylor, *Struggle*, p. 288.

TEN *Party Politics*

1 RAL, T12/57,25/03/1876, Lionel, London, to Leo and Laurie, March 25, 1876.

2 Disraeli was created Earl of Beaconsfield in 1876, but he will continue to be referred to as "Disraeli" to avoid confusion.

3 Barnbougle Castle, Rosebery Papers, Ferdinand, Chislehurst, to Rosebery, July 29, 1880.

4 RAL, RFamC/21, Charlotte, London, to Leo, Cambridge, Nov. 19, 1866; RAL, XI/109/95/2, Mayer to his brothers and nephews, Oct. 16, 1868; RAL, XI/109/96/1, same to same, Oct. 21; RAL, XI/109/95/2, Oct. 28. See also RAL. RFamC/3/29, Natty to Lionel and Charlotte, Jan. 16, 1863; RAL RFamC/3/30, same to same, Jan. 18.

5 Corti, *Reign*, pp. 406f.

6 Davis, *English Rothschilds*, pp. 103f., 119f.

7 Ramm (ed.), *Gladstone–Granville correspondence, 1868–1876*, vol. I, p. 12.

8 Matthew (ed.), *Gladstone diaries*, vol. VII, p. 36; BL, Add. MS Gladstone 44428 f. 121, Charlotte, Piccadilly, to Gladstone, Sept. 28, 1870.

9 Matthew (ed.), *Gladstone diaries*, vol. VII, p. 52; vol. VIII, p. 357; vol. IX, p. 45.

10 RAL, T12/57, Lionel, London, to Leo and Laurie, March 25, 1876; Ramm (ed.), *Gladstone–Granville correspondence, 1876–1886*, vol. I, p. 75.

11 BL, Add. MS 44443 f. 62, Charlotte, Piccadilly, to Gladstone, March 6, 1874; 44446 f. 306, same to same, March 9, 1875; 44450 f. 301, July 27, 1876; 44451 f. 40, Aug. 11; 44452 f. 74, Aug. 21. Cf. Matthew (ed.), *Gladstone diaries*, vol. IX, p. 18.

12 BL, Add. MS 44485 f. 304, Natty to Gladstone, March 19, 1884. Cf. Weintraub, *Disraeli*, p. 611.

13 BL, Add. MS 44787 f. 204, Natty to Hamilton, Nov. 26, 1884; 44505 f. 133, Emma to Gladstone, Nov. 19, 1888; 44789 f. 3, same to same, March 5, 1889; 44512 f. 111, Feb. 18, 1891; f. 118, Feb. 20; 44517 f. 244, Walter to Gladstone, Sept. 11, 1893; Matthew (ed.), *Gladstone Diaries*, vol. XI, pp. 331, 488; vol. XII, p. 368.

14 BL, Add. MS 44504 f. 204, Gladstone, Hawarden, to Emma, London, Aug. 21, 1888; f. 225, Emma to Gladstone, Aug. 25; f. 284, same to same, Sept. 26; 44505 f. 70, Gladstone to Emma, Oct. 27; f. 85, Emma to Gladstone, Nov. 3; 44490 f. 164, same to same, April 30, 1889; 44490 f. 197, May 6; 44509 f. 21, Jan. 6, 1890; 44511 f. 204, Nov. 28; Dec. 3; 44512 f. 145, March 2.

15 Barnbougle Castle, Rosebery Papers, Leo, New Court, to Hannah [Rosebery], April 3, 1888; BL, Add. MS 44798 f. 121, Ferdinand to Gladstone, Feb. 24, 1893; Matthew (ed.), *Gladstone diaries*, vol. XI, p. 378; vol. XII, pp. 22, 109, 114, 279; vol. XIII, p. 295.

16 Wilson, *Rothschild*, pp. 309f.

17 Davis, *English Rothschilds*, p. 226.

18 BL, Add. MS, 44523 f. 295, Emma, Tring, to Gladstone, Hawarden, Sept. 20, 1896. Emma requested that Gladstone send her, by way of "remembrance," "a little chip when you remove a branch from one of your beautiful trees."

19 Most of the documents detailing Disraeli's financial dealings with the Rothschilds were apparently destroyed when he died, so it may be that they assisted him in more ways than this account suggests: see Wintraub, *Disraeli*, pp. 431f.

20 Blake, *Disraeli*, pp. 424, 754. Cf. RAL, T13/92, Mayer Carl, Frankfurt, to his cousins, London, April 22, 1881: "I suppose that your late friend Lord Beaconsfield left a great name and a very small fortune."

21 RAL, RFamC/21, Charlotte, London, to Leo, Cambridge, Jan. 29, 1866. See also same to same, Paris, Nov. 5, 1867.

22 RAL, RFamC/4/78, Lionel, London, to Charlotte, Paris, July 9, 1867; RAL, RFamC/4/79, same to same, July 10; RAL, RFamC/4/82, July 13; RAL, RFamC/4/83, July 15; RAL, RFamC/4/85, July 18.

23 RAL, RFamC/21, Charlotte, London, to Laurie and Leo, Dieppe, Aug. 5, 1867; same to same, Aug. 8; Aug. 9.

24 RAL, XI/109/92/1, Mayer, Wildbad, to his brothers, London, undated, Sept. 1867; RAL, RFamC/3/48, Natty, London, to Charlotte, Feb. 28, 1868.

25 RAL, RFamC/2/10, Mary Anne Disraeli to Lionel and Charlotte, Feb. 25, 1868; RAL, XI/109/93/1, Alphonse, Paris, to his cousins, London, Feb. 25, 1867.

26 RAL, RFamC/4/88, Lionel, London, to Charlotte, Paris, Feb. 29, 1868; RAL, RFam/C/4/340, Lionel
    to Charlotte and Leo, March 2; RAL, RFamC/4/90, Lionel to Charlotte, March 4; RAL, RFamC/4/92,
    March 6; RAL, RFamC/4/93, March 9.

27 Bodleian Library, dep. Hughenden 141/3 f. 206, Lionel to Disraeli, March 22, 1869.

28 Blake, *Disraeli*, pp. 517ff.; Cohen, *Lady de Rothschild*, pp. 30f. Ten years later, it was a signed copy of
    Lothair which Natty's wife Emma requested as "a precious souvenir": Bodleian Library, dep. Hughen-
    den 141/3 f. 170, Emma to Disraeli, April 26, 1880; f. 168, same to same, May 21.

29 Bodleian Library, dep. Hughenden 141/3 f. 90, Charlotte, Piccadilly, to Disraeli, May 19, 1870; f. 92,
    same to same, July 12; f. 94, Aug. 12; f. 210, Constance to Disraeli, July 19; f. 98 Charlotte to Disraeli,
    Jan. 30, 1873.

30 Bodleian Library, dep. Hughenden 141/3 f. 102, Charlotte, Gunnersbury, to Disraeli, Hughenden,
    Sept. 11, 1873.

31 Monypenny and Buckle, *Disraeli*, vol. V, pp. 234, 399.

32 Weintraub, *Disraeli*, pp. 610ff.

33 Bodleian Library, dep. Hughenden 141/3 f. 65, Alfred and Leo, June 3, 1879; f. 162, Natty to Disraeli,
    June 7.

34 Swartz, *Politics of British foreign policy*, p. 40; Alderman, *British Jewry*, p. 99.

35 Jenkins, *Gladstone, Whiggery and the Liberal party*, p. 71.

36 Parry, *Democracy and religion*, pp. 226f.; Alderman, *Jewish community*, p. 226.

37 Jenkins, *Gladstone, Whiggery and the Liberal party*, pp. 295ff, 301ff..

38 Bodleian Library, dep. Hughenden 141/3 f. 160, Natty, Turf Club, to Montagu Corry, undated, *c.*
    1878.

39 Bodleian Library, dep. Hughenden 141/3 f. 118, Natty to Corry, March 22, 1879. See also f. 126, same
    to same, Oct. 22; f. 138, Dec. 17.

40 Bodleian Library, dep. Hughenden 141/3 f. 136, Natty to Disraeli, Dec. 9, 1879; f. 140, same to same,
    Dec. 30. Cf. Davis, *English Rothschilds*, pp. 158f., 178.

41 Barnbougle Castle, Rosebery Papers, Ferdinand, Chislehurst, to Rosebery, July 29, 1880.

42 Bodleian Library, dep. Hughenden 141/3 f. 146, Natty to Disraeli, Nov. 22, 1880; f. 152, same to
    same, Nov. 29; f. 154, Dec. 15; f. 152, Dec. 21.

43 Bodleian Library, dep. Hughenden 141/3 f. 152, Natty to Disraeli, Nov. 29, 1880.

44 Monypenny and Buckle, *Disraeli*, vol. V, p. 599; Blake, *Disraeli*, pp. 723, 736f., 743, 746; Clarke, *Dis-
    raeli*, pp. 287, 296; Davis, *English Rothschilds*, pp. 178f.

45 BL, Add. MS Gladstone 44469 ff. 122 and 123, Natty to Gladstone, April 20, 1881; Ramm (ed.),
    Gladstone–Granville correspondence, 1876–1886, vol. I, pp. 261, 266; Blake, *Disraeli*, pp. 751ff. Glad-
    stone himself did not attend the funeral.

46 RAL, T13/81, Alphonse, Paris, to his cousins, London, April 19, 1881.

47 Davis, *English Rothschilds*, pp. 103f., 119f.

48 RAL, XI/109/96/1, Anthony, Paris, to his brothers, London, Oct. 1, 1868. Cf. Southgate, *Passing of the
    Whigs*, p. 335.

49 Cesarini, *Jewish Chronicle*, p. 39. That there was a "Jewish vote" which could be to some degree influ-
    enced by the Board of Deputies or the Chronicle is clear: see e.g. RAL, T10/373, Moses Montefiore to
    Lionel, Aug. 3, 1871.

50 *The Times*, June 4, 1879, p. 10; Dasent, *Piccadily*, p. 291; Corti, *Reign*, pp. 449f. See also RAL,
    RFamC/4/377, Lionel, London, to Leo, undated, 1874. It was revealing that Lionel (vainly) appealed
    for a return to the Liberal unity of the 1840s: Parry, *Democracy and religion*, p. 392.

51 Ramm (ed.), *Gladstone–Granville correspondence, 1876–1886*, vol. I, pp. 8, 10; Swartz, *Politics of British
    foreign policy*, p. 40. Lionel was meanwhile keeping Disraeli informed about the campaign: Bodleian
    Library, dep. Hughenden 141/3 f. 31, Lionel de Rothschild to Disraeli, May 26, 1876.

52 Ramm (ed.), *Gladstone–Granville correspondence, 1876–1886*, vol. I, pp. 113f. See also Vincent (ed.),
    Derby diaries, 1869–78, p. 333.

53 RAL, T13/62, Gustave, Paris, to his cousins, London, April 1, 1880.

54 RAL, T13/204, Gustave, Paris, to his cousins, London, Dec. 19, 1885.

55 BL Add MS 43913 ff. 89–90, Ferdinand, Paris, to Dilke, London, Jan. 14, 1885.

56 Davis, *English Rothschilds*, p. 195.

57 *Ibid.*, pp. 197f.

58 *The Times*, March 23, 1884, p. 4; April 16, 1890, p. 8; March 18, 1891, p. 6.

59   Brassey, "Visitors to Waddesdon Manor." Other regular visitors included Henry Calcraft (twenty visits), Permanent Secretary to the Board of Trade, the banker Horace Farquhar, the Austrian diplomat Albert Mensdorff and the Russian ambassador Baron de Staal.

60   BL, Add. MS 43913 ff. 89–90, Ferdinand, Paris, to Dilke, London, Jan. 14, 1885. Harcourt's Ground Game Act had given tenants equal rights with landowners to kill ground game and was much resented by dedicated hunters like the Rothschilds.

61   Davis, *English Rothschilds*, p. 199.

62   RAL, RFamC/21, Charlotte, Gunnersbury, to Leo, Sept. 15, 1865.

63   RAL, XI/109/96/1, Ferdinand, Killarney, to Lionel and Charlotte, Oct. 19, 1868.

64   RAL, RFamC/21, Charlotte, London, to Leo, Cambridge, Oct. 24, 1865.

65   Davis, *English Rothschilds*, pp. 207f.

66   Southgate, *Passing of the Whigs*, pp. 370f.; Jenkins, *Gladstone, Whiggery and the Liberal party*, pp. 300ff.

67   Davis, *English Rothschilds*, pp. 194f.

68   James, *Churchill*, pp. 225ff.

69   Foster, *Churchill*, p. 241.

70   James, *Churchill*, p. 228.

71   Churchill College, Cambridge, Randolph Churchill Papers Add. 9248/1350, Alfred to Churchill, Jan. 30, 1886. Cf. Davis, *English Rothschilds*, pp. 207f.

72   Harcourt Williams (ed.), *Salisbury–Balfour correspondence*, pp. 133f.; Dugdale, *Balfour*, vol. I, p. 97.

73   Kynaston, *City*, vol. I, p. 371; Ziegler, *Sixth great power*, p. 188.

74   Alderman, *British Jewry*, p. 99; Southgate, *Passing of the Whigs*, p. 420.

75   RAL, T14/05, Alphonse, Paris, to his cousins, London, April 9, 1886.

76   Churchill College, Cambridge, Randolph Churchill Papers Add. 9248/1489, Natty to Churchill, May 4, 1886; 9248/1510, same to same, May 23.

77   Dugdale, *Balfour*, vol. I, p. 103; Egremont, *Balfour*, p. 76.

78   Churchill College, Cambridge, Randolph Churchill Papers Add. 9248/1534, Natty to Churchill, June 17, 1886.

79   Blewett, *Peers, parties and people*, pp. 14f. Cf. Churchill College, Cambridge, Randolph Churchill Papers Add. 9248/1537a, Natty to Churchill, June 10, 1886; 9248/1534, same to same, June 17; Birmingham University, Chamberlain Papers, JC 8/5/3/48, Natty to Chamberlain, June 22; JC 5/76/43, Chamberlain to Natty, June 22.

80   Barnbougle Castle, Rosebery Papers, Natty, Tring, to Rosebery, India, Dec. 6, 1886.

81   Birmingham University, Chamberlain Papers, JC 5/76/44, Chamberlain to Natty, Dec. 20, 1886; James, *Churchill*, p. 285; Hurst, *Chamberlain and Liberal reunion*, p. 105.

82   Churchill College, Cambridge, Randolph Churchill Papers Add. 9248/2401, Natty to Churchill, Feb. 18, 1887; 9248/2416, same to same, March 19.

83   Davis, *English Rothschilds*, p. 205.

84   Churchill College, Cambridge, Randolph Churchill Papers Add. 9248/2423, Natty to Churchill, March 25, 1887. See also 9248/2641, same to same, Aug. 24.

85   Barnbougle Castle, Rosebery Papers, Natty to Rosebery, Feb. 18, [1887]: "[T]he cause of the Union seems more assured than ever although Joe is of opinion that the liberal party will be reunited . . . If so what was the use of Gladstone making a fuss last year[?]."

86   Bahlman (ed.), *Hamilton diary*, pp. 64f., 89.

87   Churchill College, Cambridge, Randolph Churchill Papers Add. 9248/3155, Natty to Churchill, April 1, 1889; 9248/3156, same to same, undated, April. See also Birmingham University, Chamberlain Papers, JC 6/5/5/1, Natty to Chamberlain, Dec. 19.

88   Vincent (ed.), *Later Derby diaries*, p. 87.

89   Kynaston, *City*, vol. I, p. 373.

90   RAL, T16/03, Alphonse, Paris, to his cousins, London, March 8, 1892; RAL, T16/38, same to same, Sept. 9, 1893. Cf. Brooks, *Destruction of Lord Rosebery*, p. 186.

91   RAL, RFamC/21, Charlotte, London, to Leo, Cambridge, Oct. 24, 1865; same to same, Oct. 26.

92   The lines were the Bengal Central; the Rohilkund–Kumaon; the Bengal and NorthWest; and the Bengal–Nagpur.

93   Foster, *Churchill*, p. 194n.

94   Kynaston, *City*, vol. I, p. 378.

95   Foster, *Churchill*, pp. 195, 210f.

96   Kynaston, *City*, vol. I, p. 410; Turrell and van Helten, "Rothschilds, the Exploration Company and mining finance," p. 191.

97   Foster, *Churchill*, p. 277; Davis, *English Rothschilds*, p. 205.

98   Foster, *Churchill*, p. 331; Kynaston, *City*, vol. I, p. 374; Rothschild, *Dear Lord Rothschild*, p. 29.

99   Foster, *Churchill*, pp. 349, 394f.

100   *Ibid.*, pp. 289–303.

101   Davis, *English Rothschilds*, pp. 204f.

102   Vincent (ed.), *Later Derby diaries*, p. 128.

103   Foster, *Churchill*, p. 349.

104   *Ibid.*, pp. 313, 375. See Churchill College, Cambridge, Randolph Churchill Papers Add. 9248/2440, Natty to Churchill, April 1, 1887; 9248/2718, same to same, Nov. 1; 9248/2962, Sept. 1; 9248/3231, April 1, 1889; 9248/3316, Nov. 8; 9248/4016, Oct. 16, 1892; 9248/4055, Jan. 15, 1893; 9248/4525, Emma to Churchill, June 25, 1895.

105   Churchill, *Churchill*, vol. I, pp. 206, 285, 330, 342, 443. The younger Churchill visited Tring in 1893, in 1896, when he met the Asquiths and Balfour, and again in 1899 (a similar cast). See Rose, "Churchill and Zionism," pp. 148f.

106   Barnbougle Castle, Rosebery Papers, Ferdinand to Rosebery, Sept. 6, 1878.

107   Barnbougle Castle, Rosebery Papers, Ferdinand, Piccadilly, to Rosebery, Nov. 2, 1878.

108   Barnbougle Castle, Rosebery Papers, Natty to Rosebery, undated, *c.* Feb. 1880.

109   Crewe, *Rosebery*, vol. II, p. 212.

110   Barnbougle Castle, Rosebery Papers, Rosebery Diary, Feb. 13, 1885; Feb. 15; Feb. 20; Feb. 23. By June Natty was addressing his letters to "Dear Archie," rather than "Dear Archibald" or "Dear Rosebery."

111   Barnbougle Castle, Rosebery Papers, Natty to Rosebery, Aug. 18, 1885; Alfred to Rosebery, Sept. 3.

112   Davis, *English Rothschilds*, pp. 210f.

113   Bahlman (ed.), *Hamilton Diary*, p. 64; Kynaston, *City*, vol. II, p. 373.

114   Barnbougle Castle, Rosebery Papers, Alfred, New Court, to Rosebery, April 2, 1886.

115   Barnbougle Castle, Rosebery Papers, Natty, Bentley Priory, Gt Stanmore, Middlesex, to Rosebery, Dec. 25, 1888.

116   RAL, T16/10, Alphonse, Paris, to his cousins, London, May 4, 1892.

117   Dugdale (ed.), *German diplomatic documents*, vol. II, p. 163.

118   RAL, T16/53, Alphonse, Paris, to his cousins, London, March 2, 1894.

119   Bank of England, G4/117 2061/1 f. 21, Court of Directors Minutes, April 26, 1894; ff. 7–8, Court of Directors Minutes, May 3; David Powell, Governor, to Alfred , April 27; Alfred to Governor, April 27; Rosebery to Chief Cashier, April 30. It is impossible to establish the details of this extraordinary affair because "papers in the case were put away in the drawer of the Secretary's cupboard": Bank of England, G16/4, Historical Index.

120   Barnbougle Castle, Rosebery Papers, Natty, Tring, to Rosebery, Naples, Feb. 27, 1897. Cf. on Harcourt's increases in direct taxation RAL, T16/66, Alphonse, Paris, to his cousins, London, July 10, 1894; RAL, T16/69, same to same, Aug. 28.

121   Martel, *Imperial diplomacy*.

122   Davis, *English Rothschilds*, pp. 210f. Emphasis added.

123   See e.g. RAL, T11/51, Alphonse, Paris, to his cousins, London, Jan. 28, 1874.

124   RAL, T11/12, Alphonse, Paris, to his cousins, London, June 27, 1873; RAL, T11/13, same to same, Aug. 9; RAL, T11/17, Oct. 3; RAL, T11/18, Oct. 16; RAL, T11/56, March 23, 1874; RAL, T11/79, Dec. 31. See also RAL, T11/74, Ferdinand, Paris, to his uncle and cousins, London, undated, 1874.

125   RAL, T11/8, Alphonse, Paris, to his cousins, London, May 26, 1873; RAL, T11/9, same to same, May 27; RAL, T13/101/6, Jan. 30, 1879.

126   RAL, T12/126, Alphonse, Paris, to his cousins, London, Nov. 5, 1877; RAL, T12/128, same to same, Nov. 8; RAL, T12/128, Nov. 9; RAL, T12/130, Nov. 26; RAL, 101/6,7–1/6, Jan. 7, 1878.

127   Loménie, *Dynasties*, vol. II, p. 26; Bouvier, *Rothschild*, pp. 198ff.; Mayeur, *Troisième République*, p. 120.

128   AN, 132 AQ 33/A-12–3/5, Contract between Finance Ministry and deRF, March 16, 1881; AN, 132 AQ 33/A-12–3/6, Ministry of Finance to deRF, May 23. As Bouvier notes, the Rothschilds now shared the spoils of government bond issues with an elite of joint-stock banks: the Crédit Lyonnais, the Société Générale, the Comptoir d'Escompte and Paribas.

129   RAL, XI/109/104, Gustave, Paris, to his cousins, undated, *c.* May 1871; RAL, XI/109/106, Alphonse,

Paris, to his cousins, London, Sept. 4; RAL, XI/109/107/1, same to same, Dec. 16; Dec. 21; Jan. 4, 1872; Jan. 15; Jan. 17.

130   RAL, T11/17, Alphonse, Paris, to his cousins, London, Oct. 3, 1873; RAL, T12/82, same to same, Nov. 15; RAL, 101/6,7–1/2, Alphonse, Paris, to his cousins, London, Jan. 3, 1878; RAL, 101/6,7–1/14, Jan. 16.

131   RAL, T13/101/6, Alphonse, Paris, to his cousins, London, March 21, 1878.

132   Bouvier, *Rothschild*, pp. 201ff.; Loménie, *Dynasties*, vol. II, p. 52; Chapman, *Third Republic*, p. 214.

133   Bouvier, *Union Générale*, pp. 159ff.

134   Corti, *Reign*, pp. 440f.; Bouvier, *Rothschild*, pp. 199f.

135   RAL, T15/53, General Boulanger, Jersey, to Natty, April 14, 1890; RAL, T15/54, same to same, April 22. Cf. Loménie, *Dynasties*, vol. II, p. 208; Bouvier, *Rothschild*, pp. 204ff.

136   RAL, T16/14, Edmond, Paris, to his cousins, London, July 19, 1892; RAL, T16/16, Alphonse to his cousins, Sept. 3; RAL, T16/51, same to same, Feb. 19, 1894; RAL, T16/135, Feb. 25, 1896.

137   RAL, T16/10, Alphonse, Paris, to his cousins, London, May 4, 1892; RAL, T15/02, same to same, May 5.

138   RAL, T16/22, Alphonse, Paris, to his cousins, London, Nov. 16, 1892.

139   Palmade, *Capitalism*, pp. 216f.; Bouvier, *Rothschild*, pp. 233–9.

ELEVEN   *The Risks and Returns of Empire (1885–1902)*

1   Rotberg, *Rhodes*, pp. 234f.

2   Bahlman (ed.), *Hamilton diary*, pp. 89ff.; Kynaston, *City*, vol. I, pp. 411ff.

3   RAL, T15/58, Churchill to Alfred, Nov. 17, 1890.

4   RAL, T14/39, Alphonse, Paris, to his cousins, London, Oct. 12, 1888.

5   RAL, T14/41, Gustave, Paris, to his cousins, London, Oct. 24, 1888.

6   RAL, T15/14, Gustave, Paris, to his cousins, London, Aug, 29, 1889.

7   RAL, T15/29, Alphonse, Paris, to his cousins, London, Jan. 8, 1890; RAL, T15/30, same to same, Jan. 16; RAL, T15/62, Jan. 31.

8   Kynaston, *City*, vol. I, p. 426.

9   Spinner, *Goschen*, p. 146; Kynaston, *City*, vol. I, p. 426.

10   Cecco, *Money and empire*, p. 89.

11   Kynaston, *City*, vol. I, pp. 427f.

12   Fulford, *Glyn's*, p. 210.

13   Clapham, *Bank of England*, vol. II, pp. 326f.

14   Kynaston, *City*, vol. I, pp. 410f. Revelstoke had in fact been a guest at Tring in February 1890: "It is rather amusing to see the heads of the two great rival financial Houses together," noted Edward Hamilton. "They take stock of each other with jealous eyes, the jealousy being somewhat ill-disguised."

15   Ziegler, *Sixth great power*, p. 245.

16   RAL, T15/42, Alphonse, Paris, to his cousins, London, Nov. 12, 1890.

17   Davis, *English Rothschilds*, p. 230.

18   Clapham, *Bank of England*, vol. II, pp. 335f.

19   *Ibid.*, pp. 328f.; Spinner, *Goschen*, pp. 147f.

20   Ziegler, *Sixth great power*, pp. 246f.; Kynaston, *City*, vol. I, p. 431.

21   RAL, T15/42, Alphonse, Paris, to his cousins, London, Nov. 12, 1890.

22   As usual, the Rothschilds charged a fee and costs amounting to £6,000, though in fact the money does not even seem to have crossed the Channel: Clapham, *Bank of England*, vol. II, p. 337; Sayers, *Bank of England operations*, p. 103n.

23   Bank of England, G23/68 2881/1 ff. 297–8, Lidderdale, Bank of England, to Governor of Banque de France, Paris, Nov. 12, 1890. Cf. Morgan, *Central Banking*, p. 206.

24   AN, 132 AQ 122/A-10–3/3, Lidderdale to NMR, Nov. 12, 1890; RAL, T15/43, Alphonse, Paris, to his cousins, London, Nov. 13. A further £1.5 million was borrowed from St Petersburg.

25   Spinner, *Goschen*, p. 148.

26   Chandler, *Four centuries*, p. 331.

27   Clapham, *Bank of England*, vol. II, pp. 334f.

28   Cecco, *Money and empire*, p. 93.

29   Fulford, *Glyn's*, p. 211; Kynaston, *City*, vol. I, p. 433.

30 RAL, T15/44, Alphonse, Paris, to his cousins, London, Nov. 15, 1890. The *Economist* took a similar view.

31 RAL, T15/23, Ernesto Tornquist & Co., Buenos Aires, to NMR, Nov. 20, 1890.

32 The other members were Walter Burns of J. S. Morgan, Everard Hambro, Charles Goschen of the Bank of England, Herbert Gibbs; George Drabble of the Bank of London and the River Plate. There was also a French representative (Cahen d'Anvers) and a German (Hansemann): Bank of England, G15/260 3662/1 f. 2, The Rothschild Committee, first meeting, Nov. 27, 1890. The committee met regularly until December 1897.

33 AN, 132 AQ 122/A-10–3/3, NMR to Lidderdale, Dec. 3, 1890.

34 *The Times*, April 19, 1893.

35 Ziegler, *Sixth great power*, pp. 258ff.; Cain and Hopkins, *Imperialism*, vol. I, pp. 157, 295.

36 RAL, T15/51, Alphonse, Paris, to his cousins, London, Dec. 29, 1890.

37 Ziegler, *Sixth great power*, p. 263f.

38 Kynaston, *City*, vol. II, p. 372.

39 Bodleian Library, Harcourt MSS dep.120 f. 66, Natty to Harcourt, Jan. 23, 1893; dep.120 f. 68, Harcourt to Natty, Jan. 24; dep.120 f. 73, Herbert Wagg to Natty, Jan. 27; dep.120 f. 71, Natty to Harcourt, Jan. 28; dep.120 f. 74, Harcourt to Natty, Jan. 29. See also dep.124 f. 89, Alfred to Harcourt, April 11, 1895.

40 Ziegler, *Sixth great power*, p. 272.

41 RAL, T14/04, Alphonse, Paris, to his cousins, London, Feb. 25, 1886; Ayer, *Century of finance*, pp. 14–81.

42 Levy, "Brazilian public debt," pp. 218f.; Fritsch, *External constraints*, pp. 1ff. Cf. Joslin, *Century of banking*, pp. 152f.

43 RAL, T15/17, Alphonse, Paris, to his cousins, London, Dec. 19, 1889. Cf. Kynaston, *City*, vol. I, p. 410.

44 AN, 132 AQ 3, Inventarium, Oct. 16, 1886.

45 RAL, T16/47, Alphonse, Paris, to his cousins, London, Jan. 16, 1894.

46 Calculated from figures in Levy, "Brazilian public debt," pp. 232–54.

47 AN, 132 AQ 5586/1M184, Ministry of Finance, Rio, to NMR, Jan. 4, 1910.

48 *The Times*, June 20, 1898. See also AN, 132 AQ 5563/1M164bis, NMR to deRF, July 4, 1898. Cf. Levy, "Brazilian public debt," pp. 224f.; Joslin, *Century of banking*, p. 157.

49 For the challenge from Deutsche Bank in Chile after 1906, see RAL, XI/130A/0, Natty, London, to his cousins, Paris, Feb. 12, 1906; same to same, March 5; March 16; March 19; March 21; March 29; March 30. Cf. Barth, *Hochfinanz*, p. 92; Ziegler, *Sixth great power*, p. 303; Kynaston, *City* vol. II, pp. 419f.

50 RAL, XI/130A/0, Natty, London, to his cousins, Paris, March 27, 1906; Alfred to his cousins, April 8; RAL, XI/130A/1, Natty to his cousins, Jan. 28, 1907; Leo to his cousins, Jan. 31; Natty to his cousins, Feb. 11; same to same, Feb. 20; March 26.

51 RAL, XI/130A/0, Natty, London, to his cousins, Paris, Nov. 22, 1906; same to same, Nov. 23; Nov. 26.

52 Cf. Roberts, *Schroders*, pp. 140ff.; Fritsch, *External constraints*, pp. 14ff.; Kynaston, *City*, vol. II, pp. 483f.

53 RAL, XI/130A/1, Natty, London, to his cousins, Paris, April 3, 1907; same to same, May 29; July 5; Oct. 1; Oct. 3. See also RAL, XI/130A/2, May 28, 1908.

54 Roberts, *Schroders*, p. 142.

55 Joslin, *Century of banking*, pp. 158f.

56 Kynaston, *City*, vol. II, p. 572. On the difficulties of the 1908 loan, see RAL, XI/130A/2, Natty, London, to his cousins, Paris, July 20, 1908; same to same, July 21; July 22; July 23.

57 AN, 132 AQ 5593/1M191, NMR to deRF, June 10, 1914; RAL, XI/130A/8, Natty, London, to his cousins, Paris, July 17; same to same, July 22; July 27. Cf. Fritsch, *External constraints*, pp. 30ff. on Charles Rothschild's visit to Rio.

58 The French Rothschilds were consistent critics of the Panama scheme: RAL, T13/72, Gustave, Paris, to his cousins, London, Nov. 23, 1880; RAL, T13/74, same to same, Dec. 22; RAL, T14/06, Alphonse to his cousins, May 18, 1886; RAL, T14/07, same to same, May 18; RAL, T14/10, July 9; RAL, T14/12, July 30; RAL, T14/21, Feb. 22, 1888; RAL, T14/23, Edmond to his cousins, March 12; RAL, T14/24, Gustave to his cousins, March 13; RAL, T14/28, Alphonse to his cousins, June 3; RAL, T14/43, same

to same, Nov. 27; RAL, T14/44, Dec. 1; RAL, T14/45, Dec. 15; RAL, T15/02, Jan. 24, 1889; RAL, T15/10, July 10.

59   Hatfield House, 3M, Schomberg McDonnell to Salisbury, Oct. 21, 1895. Cf. Davis, *English Rothschilds*, pp. 219f.

60   Ziegler, *Sixth great power*, pp. 305f.

61   RAL, XI/130A/2, Natty, London, to his cousins, Paris, May 28, 1908.

62   It has recently been suggested that the Rothschilds' interest in the bullion business had waned by the 1870s because of a lack of commitment on the part of Anthony: Kynaston, *City*, vol. I, p. 314. However, it is worth noting that as late as 1875 a nominal fine of £5 (plus £1 8s costs) was imposed on him for allowing excessive smoke emissions from the refinery—hardly a sign of inactivity: *The Times*, July 27, 1875.

63   Carosso, *Morgans*, pp. 182f.

64   Russell, *International monetary conferences*, pp. 178ff. See also Kynaston, *City*, vol. I, p. 312; Davis, *English Rothschilds*, p. 156; Kynaston, *Cazenove*, p. 73.

65   Ellis, *Heir of adventure*, pp. 108f.; Carosso, *Morgans*, pp. 196f. Pierpont Morgan was resentful of the Rothschilds' *de haut en bas* manner: "[H]aving anything to do with Rothschilds & Belmont in this matter is extremely unpalatable to us and I would give almost anything if they were out. The whole treatment of Rothschilds to all the party, from Father downwards[,] is such, as to my mind, no one should stand": Chernow, *House of Morgan*, p. 40. Natty never called on Walter Burns, the resident senior partner at J. S. Morgan; Burns always came to New Court.

66   Ziegler, *Sixth great power*, p. 216. Between 1865 and 1890, £121 million worth of US railway stocks were issued through London merchant banks, of which Rothschilds were responsible for just £800,000. It was not until 1908–9 that New Court undertook major issues totalling £6 million for the Pennsylvania Railway and the Grand Trunk Pacific line. For Belmont's complaint at lack of Rothschild enterprise in the US, see Kynaston, *City*, vol. I, p. 314.

67   RAL, T16/90, Alphonse, Paris, to his cousins, London, Jan. 29, 1895; RAL, T16/91, same to same, Feb. 5; RAL, T16/92, Feb. 9; RAL, T16/93, Feb. 20; RAL, T16/94, Feb. 22. Cf. Carosso, *Morgans*, pp. 312ff., 328ff.; Chernow, *House of Morgan*, pp. 76f.

68   Eichengreen and Flandreau, "Geography," table 2.

69   Bramsen and Wain, *Hambros*, pp. 310–15; Bouvier, *Rothschild*, pp. 221–3; Kynaston, City, vol. I, pp. 350f. Cf. Seton-Watson, *Italy from liberalism to fascism*, p. 64; Torido, *Economic history of liberal Italy*, p. 80; Deutsche Bank (ed.), *Studies*, pp. 686ff.; Mack Smith, *Italy*, p. 151.

70   Eichengreen and Flandreau, "Geography," p. 11.

71   Bodleian Library, Harcourt MSS dep. 166 f. 70, "Remarks by Mr Rothschild," Nov. 9, 1886.

72   Bodleian Library, Harcourt MSS dep. 166 f. 59, Natty to Harcourt, Aug. 31. 1892; dep. 166 f. 61, Harcourt to Natty, Sept. 1; RAL, T16/20, Alphonse, Paris, to his cousins, London, Oct. 6; Davis, *English Rothschilds*, pp. 222ff.; Kynaston, *City*, vol. I, p. 391; vol. II, pp. 56, 71–5. Cf. Matthew (ed.), *Gladstone diaries*, vol. XIII, p. 74.

73   Bodleian Library, Harcourt MSS dep. 166 f. 68, Alfred to Harcourt, Sept. 2, 1892; dep. 166 f. 66, Natty to Harcourt, Sept. 2; dep. 166 f. 72, Harcourt to Alfred, undated *c.* Sept. 3; dep. 166 f. 87, Alfred to Harcourt, Oct. 5.

74   Bodleian Library, Harcourt MSS dep. 166 f. 233, Harcourt to Leo, Nov. 24, 1892; dep. 167 f. 5, Alfred to Harcourt, Dec. 5; dep. 167 f. 7, Harcourt to Alfred, Dec. 6; dep. 167 f. 26, Harcourt to Natty, Dec. 7; dep. 167 f. 41, Alfred to Harcourt, Dec. 7; dep. 167 f. 55, Harcourt to Alfred, Dec. 8; dep. 167 f. 102, same to same, Dec. 15; dep. 167 f. 124, Alfred to Harcourt, Dec. 17; dep. 168 f. 76, same to same, Feb. 2, 1893; dep. 168 f. 82, Harcourt to Alfred, Feb. 2. Cf. Russell, *International monetary conferences*, pp. 384–97. The other British delegates at Brussels were Sir Charles Rivers-Wilson, Comptroller General of the Public Debt Office, Sir Charles Fremantle, Deputy Master of the Mint and the bimetallist Sir William Houldsworth. The Rothschild plan was in many ways more practicable than the two other plans presented to the conference by Adolf Soetbeer and Moritz Levy.

75   Bodleian Library, Harcourt MSS dep. 167 f. 100, Harcourt memorandum, Dec. 14, 1892.

76   Hatfield House, 3M, McDonnell to Salisbury, July 27, 1897; same to same, Sept. 11. Cf. Cassis, *City bankers*, pp. 292f.; Kynaston, *City*, vol. II, pp. 116f., 164f. The proposal to raise the legal-tender ceiling had also been put forward by Alfred at Brussels.

77   RAL, T16/93, Alphonse, Paris, to his cousins, London, Feb. 20, 1895.

78   Enaudi, "Money and politics," pp. 115, 120f.; Flandreau, *Or du monde,* pp. 222, 225, 233n.
79   Flandreau, "Emergence," pp. 24ff.
80   *Ibid.,* pp. 1–23.
81   RAL, T13/76, Alphonse, Paris, to his cousins, London, Jan. 25, 1881; RAL, T13/79, same to same, April 7; RAL, T13/80, April 8. See also RAL, T15/29, Jan. 9, 1890; RAL, T15/30, Jan. 16; RAL, T15/62, Jan. 3; RAL, T15/41, Nov. 8; RAL, T15/48, Dec. 2; RAL, T15/75, Nov. 27, 1891; RAL, T15/76, Dec. 11; RAL, T15/09, April 23, 1892; RAL, T16/16, Sept. 3; RAL, T16/37, Sept. 7, 1893. See also Witte, *Memoirs,* p. 60.
82   Calculated from figures in Martin, *Rothschild,* pp. 395, 421. This was around 2.5 per cent of total Rothschild profits; as a percentage of the total Spanish budget, the revenue received by the government was a little less than 1 per cent.
83   What follows is based on Turrell and van Helten, "Rothschilds, the Exploration Company and mining finance," pp. 181–205.
84   *Ibid.,* p. 193.
85   AN, 132 A Q 3, Inventarium, Oct. 16, 1886.
86   Kubicek, *Economic imperialism,* pp. 93f., 112.
87   *Ibid.,* pp. 54, 64, 68, 71, 77. Rothschilds also took shares in Wernher, Beit's African Ventures Syndicate in 1903.
88   Turrell and van Helten, "Rothschilds, the Exploration Company and mining finance," p. 192.
89   AN, 132 AQ 5554/1M157, Natty, London, to his cousins, Paris, Jan. 10, 1894. See also Kubicek, *Economic imperialism,* pp. 180, 185.
90   In 1887 South Africa had accounted for 0.8 per cent of world gold production; by 1892 the figure was 15 per cent and by 1898 25 per cent: Green, *New world of gold,* p. 18.
91   RAL, T43/5, Carl Meyer, Johannesburg, to NMR, March 26, 1892; RAL, T43/35, same to same, March 26.
92   See for example Chapman, "Rhodes and the City of London," p. 663; Kynaston, *City,* vol. II, pp. 82f.
93   RAL, T43/8, Alphonse, Paris, to his cousins, London, Dec. 29, 1888. For a joking reference to the need for a new precious metal if gold discoveries continued see RAL, T16/27, Gustave to his cousins, Feb. 17, 1893.
94   RAL, T16/21, Alphonse, Paris, to his cousins, London, Oct. 27, 1892; RAL, T16/24, same to same, Nov. 21.
95   Bouvier, *Rothschild,* pp. 204ff. Cf. Harvey, *Rio Tinto,* p. 70.
96   *Ibid.,* pp. 75, 188. By 1905, their stake amounted to 39 per cent. See also Carr, *Spain,* pp. 265, 391.
97   The price of "Tintos" begins to feature in the Rothschild correspondence regularly in the 1880s and by the early 1900s appears almost every week: see RAL, T13/78, Alphonse, Paris, to his cousins, London, Feb. 7, 1881; RAL, XI/130A/0, Natty to his cousins, Feb. 14, 1906; same to same, March 2; March 16; March 23; March 27; March 28; April 11; April 17; RAL, XI/130A/1, May 31; Oct. 3.
98   Harvey, *Rio Tinto,* p. 107.
99   *Ibid.,* p. 74. The price was raised still higher—to above £79—by a similar agreement in 1899.
100 Turrell and van Helten, "Rothschilds, the Exploration Company and mining finance," p. 195.
101 Loménie, *Dynasties,* vol. III, p. 80.
102 Turrell and van Helten, "Rothschilds, the Exploration Company and mining finance," p. 191.
103 Bodleian Library, Harcourt MSS dep.120 f. 48, Ochs Brothers, Hatton Garden, to Natty, Jan. 9, 1893.
104 McKay, "House of Rothschild (Paris)," pp. 76ff.
105 Heuberger, *Rothschilds,* p. 146. Cf. AN, 132 AQ 5526/1M132, NMR to deRF, Dec. 28, 1882; RAL, XI/130A/0, Natty, London, to his cousins, Paris, March 27, 1906; same to same, April 9.
106 McKay, "House of Rothschild (Paris)," pp. 78ff.
107 Michel, *Banques et banquiers,* p. 186.
108 Mackay, "Baku oil," p. 617.
109 McKay, "House of Rothschild (Paris)," pp. 80ff. See also Heuberger, *Rothschilds,* pp. 143f.
110 Cameron, *France and Europe,* pp. 96f.
111 RAL, T16/44, Alphonse, Paris, to his cousins, London, Nov. 29, 1893. Cf. Girault, *Emprunts russes,* pp. 86f., 254, 272–7.
112 Girault, *Emprunts russes,* p. 590; Yergin, *Prize,* pp. 60–72, 122f., 132f. Cf. Gerretson, *History of the Royal Dutch,* vol. II, pp. 238, 245, 250; vol. IV, pp. 132ff.

113   RAL, XI/4/47, Gansl, Kimberley, to NMR, Aug. 30, 1882; same to same, Sept. 21; Nov. 16. Cf. Chapman, "Rhodes and the City of London," pp. 651ff.

114   For the murky pre-history of De Beers, see Turrell, "Rhodes, De Beers and monopoly," pp. 313ff.

115   *Ibid.*, pp. 326–34; Turrell and van Helten, "Rothschilds, the Exploration Company and mining finance," pp. 187ff. Cf. the romanticised version of events in Flint, *Rhodes*, pp. 86ff.

116   Turrell, "Rhodes, De Beers and monopoly," p. 330; Rotberg, *Founder*, pp. 203f. Cf. RAL, T43/9, Edmond, Paris, to his cousins, London, Aug. 6, 1887; RAL, T43/10, Gustave to his cousins, Aug. 26; RAL, T43/11, Oct. 5; RAL, T43/2, Carl Meyer, Paris, to NMR, Oct. 5; RAL, T43/16, same to same, undated, *c.* Oct. 5; RAL, T43/12, Alphonse to his cousins, Oct. 6.

117   Cf. RAL, T43/9, Edmond, Paris, to his cousins, London, Aug. 6, 1887; RAL, T43/10, Gustave to his cousins, Aug. 26; RAL, T43/11, same to same, Oct. 5; RAL, T43/2, Carl Meyer, Paris, to NMR, Oct. 5; RAL, T43/16, same to same, undated, *c.* Oct. 5; RAL, T43/12, Alphonse to his cousins, Oct. 6. Cf. Newbury, "Technology, capital and consolidation," p. 30.

118   Turrell, "Rhodes, De Beers and monopoly," pp. 331f. For a rather different version of these convoluted negotiations, see Rotberg, *Founder*, pp. 204–8.

119   RAL, T43/15, de Crano, Kimberley, to NMR, Nov. 8, 1887. This seems to predate the decision to start buying Central shares described by Rotberg (*Founder*, p. 206).

120   Newbury, *Diamond Ring*, p. 90.

121   RAL, T14/17, Alphonse, Paris, to his cousins, London, Jan. 14, 1888; RAL, T43/14, same to same, Jan. 17; Rhodes House, Rhodes MSS Afr. t.14 f. 313, Rhodes to Natty, Jan. 20; RAL, T43/3, Alfred to Natty, Feb. 2; RAL, T43/6, Alphonse to his cousins, Feb. 13.

122   RAL, T43/19, De Beers to NMR, March 19, 1888; RAL, T43/21, same to same, April 16.

123   RAL, T43/23, Natty, London, to Barnato, Kimberley, March 12, 1888; RAL, T43/24, Barnato to Natty, May 14; RAL, T43/25, same to same [telegram], May 14. Cf. Turrell, "Rhodes, De Beers and monopoly," pp. 332ff.; Newbury, "Technology, capital and consolidation," p. 33; Chapman, "Rhodes and the City of London," p. 656. The other life governors were to be Rhodes, Alfred Beit, F. S. P. Stow and Baring Gould, though the last was ultimately excluded at the insistence of either Barnato or Rhodes. After much negotiation, it was agreed that the governors should receive 25 per cent of all annual profits in excess of £1.44 million, a right they enjoyed until 1901: Newbury, *Diamond Ring*, p. 94; Rotberg, *Founder*, pp. 207–10.

124   RAL, T43/28, Rhodes, Kimberley, to Natty, London, Aug. 20, 1888; Rhodes House, Rhodes MSS Afr t.14 f. 317, same to same, Oct. 29; RAL, T43/27, Paul Dreyfus, Kimberley, to NMR, Nov. 19.

125   Newbury, "Technology, capital and consolidation," pp. 33ff.; Rotberg, *Founder*, p. 211.

126   Rhodes House, Rhodes MSS Afr. t.14 f. 304, Rhodes, London, to Natty, April 18, 1890. Details in Newbury, *Diamond Ring*, pp. 95f.

127   Newbury, *Diamond Ring*, p. 93.

128   Rotberg, *Founder*, p. 211; Kynaston, *City*, vol. II, p. 397.

129   Newbury, *Diamond Ring*, p. 96.

130   Rhodes House, Rhodes MSS Afr. t.14 f. 192, Rhodes to Beit, July 2, 1890.

131   Newbury, "Capital accumulation," pp. 36f., 45.

132   RAL, T43/7, Gustave, Paris, to his cousins, London, June 5, 1888.

133   Newbury, "Technology, capital and consolidation," p. 36.

134   Newbury, *Diamond Ring*, p. 130.

135   Rhodes House, Rhodes MSS Afr. S. 228 C27 f. 9 (23), Natty to Rhodes, July 7, 1891. Cf. Newbury, "Capital accumulation," p. 32; Chapman, "Rhodes and the City of London," pp. 654f.; Newbury, *Diamond Ring*, pp. 144f.

136   Rotberg, *Founder*, p. 499.

137   Newbury, *Diamond Ring*, pp. 136f.; Newbury, "Capital accumulation," p. 35; Rotberg, *Founder*, pp. 490ff., 499, 644.

138   Rhodes House, Rhodes MSS Afr. t.14 f. 313, Rhodes to Natty, Jan. 20, 1888.

139   Rhodes House, Rhodes MSS Afr t.14 f. 317, Rhodes, Kimberley, to Natty, London, Oct. 29, 1888.

140   Rhodes House, Rhodes MSS Afr. t.1 f.23, Rhodes Will, June 27, 1888.

141   Rotberg, *Rhodes*, pp. 234f. Cf. Davis, *English Rothschilds*, pp. 212ff.; Flint, *Rhodes*, pp. 92, 216.

142   Flint, *Rhodes*, p. 111; Galbraith, *Crown and charter*, pp. 84f.

143   Of the £1 million capital, Natty provided £10,000: Rotberg, *Founder*, p. 286. Cf. Rhodes House, Rhodes MSS Afr. S. 228 C9 f. 48, Natty to Rhodes, Jan. 23, 1899.

144   Rhodes House, Rhodes MSS Afr. S. 228 C3b f. 201a, Natty, London, to Rhodes, Cape Town, Jan. 15, 1892.

145   Foster, *Churchill*, pp. 372f. Cf. RAL, T15/84, Churchill to Natty, March 22, 1891; Rhodes House, Rhodes MSS Afr. S. 228 C3b f. 201a, Natty to Rhodes, Cape Town, Jan. 15, 1892. See also Rhodes House, Rhodes MSS Afr. S. 228 C25 f. 1, Merriman, London, to Rhodes, Feb. 5, accusing Churchill of having told the Portuguese government that Rhodes's British South Africa Company was close to bankruptcy. Cf. Rotberg, *Founder*, p. 422.

146   Kynaston, *City*, vol. II, p. 81.

147   RAL, T16/39, Arthur, Paris, to his cousins, London, Oct. 20, 1893; RAL, T16/42, Alphonse to his cousins, Nov. 4; RAL, T16/43, Gustave to his cousins, Nov. 11.

148   Flint, *Rhodes*, p. 170.

149   Rhodes House, Rhodes MSS Afr. S. 228 C3a f. 58, Grey to Maguire, Oct. 24, 1890; RAL, XI/38/244, Randolph Churchill to Natty, May 17, 1891; Rhodes House, Rhodes MSS Afr. t.14 f. 325, Rhodes to Natty, June 6. Cf. Galbraith, *Crown and charter*, pp. 184ff.

150   Rhodes House, Rhodes MSS Afr. S. 228 C3a f. 172a, Maguire to Rhodes, June 12, 1891; S. 228 C3b f. 201c, John Xavier Merriman, London, to Rhodes, Jan. 22, 1892; S. 228 C25 f. 1, same to same, Feb. 5.

151   Rhodes House, Rhodes MSS Afr. S. 228 C3b f. 201a, Natty, London, to Rhodes, Cape Town, Jan. 15, 1892.

152   Rhodes House, Rhodes MSS Afr. S. 228 C25 f. 2, Maguire to Rhodes, Feb. 10, 1893; S. 228 C25 f. 4, Sir Charles Mills to Rhodes, April 20; S. 228 C25 f. 5, same to same, April 20; S. 228 C25 f. 6, April 21; S. 228 C25 f. 8 (4), Natty to Rhodes, April 21; S. 228 C25 f. 9, Mills to Rhodes, April 24; S. 228 C25 f. 10, same to same, May 9; S. 228 C25 f. 11, May 11; S. 228 C25 f. 12, Rhodes to Mills, May 12; S. 228 C25 f. 13, Mills to Rhodes, May 15.

153   RAL, T16/40, Rhodes to Natty, May 16, 1893.

154   For further discussions on the Delagoa Bay question, see Rhodes House, Rhodes MSS Afr. S. 228 C25 f. 17, Maguire to Rhodes, Aug. 26, 1893; S. 228 C25 f. 23, Sir Henry Loch to Rhodes, April 26, 1894; S. 228 C25 f. 24, Natty to Rhodes, May 4; S. 228 C25 f. 27, Loch to Rhodes, May 11; S. 228 C25 f. 26, same to same, May 11; S. 228 C25 f. 24, Rhodes to Natty, May 12; S. 228 C25 f. 29, Rhodes to Loch, May 15; S. 228 C25 f. 28, Natty to Rhodes, May 15; S. 228 C25 f. 31, Rhodes to Loch, June 22; S.228 C2a f. 90, Mills to Rhodes, Nov. 13; S. 228 C16 f. 39, Natty to Rhodes, Feb. 22, 1895; S. 228 C16 f. 39, same to same, Feb. 26. See also Birmingham University, Chamberlain Papers, JC 3/2D/16, Alfred to Chamberlain, July 1, 1896; JC 3/2D/16, Chamberlain to Alfred, July 1; JC 3/2D/21, Alfred to Chamberlain, July 3; JC 3/2D/17, Natty to Chamberlain, July 5; JC 3/2D/18, Alfred to Chamberlain, July 24; JC 3/2D/19, Chamberlain to Alfred, July 28; JC 3/2D/20, Alfred to Chamberlain, July 29; JC 3/2D/23, same to same, Nov. 2.

155   Davis, *English Rothschilds*, pp. 212–14.

156   Rotberg, *Founder*, p. 316. See also pp. 416, 663, 678. In later versions of Rhodes's will, this idea was transformed into the more realistic scheme for Oxford scholarships to encourage (in Natty's words) "Colonials and even Americans to study on the banks of the Isis and to learn, as Rhodes did there, to love his country and to make it prosperous." Any remaining interest on his fortune was to be used by the Trustees "in the interest of, for the development of the Anglo-Saxon race." In this final version Natty had in fact been replaced as a Trustee.

157   Rhodes House, Rhodes MSS Afr. t.14 f. 325, Rhodes, Cape Town, to Natty, London, June 6, 1891; S. 228 C3a f. 172a, Maguire to Rhodes, June 12; S. 228 C27 f. 9 (23), Natty to Rhodes, July 7.

158   Rhodes House, Rhodes MSS Afr. S. 228 C3b f. 201a, Natty, London, to Rhodes, Cape Town, Jan. 15, 1892; S. 288 C3b f. 201b, Farquhar, London, to Rhodes, Jan. 20. Cf. Rotberg, *Founder*, pp. 497f.

159   Rhodes House, Rhodes MSS Afr. S. 228 C9 f. 36, Natty to Rhodes, July 12, 1892. Alphonse agreed: RAL, T16/21, Alphonse, Paris, to his cousins, London, Oct. 27; RAL, T16/132, same to same, Feb. 6, 1896.

160   See e.g., Rhodes House, Rhodes MSS Afr. S. 228 C7a f. 96, Natty to Rhodes, May 17, 1893; S. 228 C7b f. 197, same to same, Dec. 17, 1898. Cf. Rotberg, *Founder*, pp. 491f.

161   Rhodes House, Rhodes MSS Afr. S. 228 C7b f. 210, Natty to Rhodes, April 19, 1899; S. 228 C7b f. 210, Rhodes to Natty, April 21; S. 228 C7b f. 210, Natty to Rhodes, April 22 [several letters]. Cf. Chapman, "Rhodes and the City of London," pp. 653, 656, 658; Newbury, "Capital accumulation," pp. 38f.

162 Rhodes House, Rhodes MSS Afr. S. 228 C9 f. 45, NMR to Rhodes, July 10, 1895; S. 228 C9 f. 45, same to same, Aug. 22. Cf. Newbury, "Capital accumulation," p. 39.

163 Rhodes House, Rhodes MSS Afr. S. 228 C3a f. 184, Grey to Rhodes, July 31, 1891. Cf. Chapman, "Rhodes and the City of London," p. 665n.

164 RAL, T43/35, Carl Meyer, Johannesburg, to NMR, March 26, 1892; Rhodes House, Rhodes MSS Afr. S. 228 C9 f. 33, Natty to Rhodes, May 9.

165 Hatfield House, 3M, Natty to Salisbury, June 9, 1892; Salisbury to Natty, June 10. Cf. RAL, T16/12, Alphonse, Paris, to his cousins, London, July 1.

166 Rhodes House, Rhodes MSS Afr. S. 228 C9 f. 36, Natty, London, to Rhodes, July 12, 1892.

167 Chapman, "Rhodes and the City of London," pp. 659f. Cf. Kynaston, *City*, vol. II, pp. 63f.; Davis, *English Rothschilds*, pp. 215f.

168 The Uitlanders' main grievance was that in 1890 the Transvaal government had effectively disfranchised them by extending the residence qualification necessary for the right to vote in elections to the First Volksraad and the Presidency: O'Brien, *Milner*, pp. 128f.

169 RAL, T16/110, Gustave, Paris, to his cousins, London, Dec. 26, 1895; RAL, T16/121, Alphonse to his cousins, Jan. 2, 1896; Hatfield House, 3M, Natty to Salisbury, Jan. 6; RAL, T16/128, Alphonse to his cousins, Jan. 23. Cf. Davis, *English Rothschilds*, pp. 216f.; Marsh, *Chamberlain*, pp. 378–86.

170 Birmingham University, Chamberlain Papers, JC 5/6/18, Brett to Chamberlain, undated, *c.* March 1896; JC 5/6/19, Natty to Kruger, undated, *c.* March; JC 3/2D/21, Alfred to Chamberlain, July 3.

171 Barth, *Hochfinanz*, p. 196. The loan was subsequently issued in Germany.

172 Birmingham University, Chamberlain Papers, JC 7/2/2C/8, Alfred to Kruger, June 12, 1899; JC 7/2/2C/3, Alfred to Chamberlain, June 12.

173 Fraser, *Chamberlain*, p. 185.

174 Hatfield House, 3M, Natty to McDonnell, July 18, 1899.

175 Kynaston, *City*, vol. II, p. 193.

176 Rotberg, *Founder*, p. 619.

177 Hatfield House, 3M, Lewis, London, to Marks, Pretoria, Sept. 25, 1899. Emphasis added: the phrase "without conditions" was inserted at the request of Devonshire. Cf. Jackson, *Hartington*, pp. 300f.

178 Hatfield House, 3M, Lewis and Marks, Pretoria, to Lewis, London, Sept. 26, 1899; McDonnell to Salisbury, Sept. 27; McDonnell to Natty, Sept. 29.

179 Hatfield House, 3M, McDonnell to Salisbury, July 20, 1899; Natty to McDonnell, July 24. Cf. Davis, *English Rothschilds*, pp. 217f.

180 Hatfield House, 3M, Natty to McDonnell, Oct. 18, 1899.

181 Allfrey, *Jewish court*, pp. 179f.

182 BL, MSS Milner dep 214 f. 286, Natty to Milner, Southampton, May 24, 1901; dep 186 f. 132, same to same, Jan. 1, 1902.

183 Rhodes House, Rhodes MSS Afr. S. 228 C7b f. 267, Natty to Rhodes, Nov. 2, 1900.

184 RA Add. A/15/78686, Duke of Connaught to the Duchess of Connaught, July 18, 1902. The Duke (the King's brother) declined his invitation "to meet a Boer Gen[era]l."

185 Rhodes House, Rhodes MSS Afr. S. 228 C27 f. 10 (136), Natty to Rhodes, July 5, 1901. For Rhodes's "panicky" demands that Kimberley be relieved, see Rotberg, *Founder*, p. 627.

186 Rothschild, *Dear Lord Rothschild*, p. 82.

187 Kynaston, *City*, vol. II, pp. 206–11. See also Cassis, *City*, p. 176; Ziegler, *Sixth great power*, p. 291; Chapman, "Rhodes and the City of London," pp. 660f.; Allfrey, *Jewish court*, pp. 181f.

188 Burk, *Morgan Grenfell*, pp. 120–23.

189 Kynaston, *City*, vol. II, pp. 222–5.

190 Burk, *Morgan Grenfell*, pp. 121f.; Kynaston, *City*, vol. II, pp. 234f.

191 Kynaston, *City*, vol. II, pp. 267f.; Allfrey, *Jewish court*, p. 196.

192 Rhodes House, Rhodes MSS Afr. S. 228 C7b f. 240, Natty to Rhodes, March 9, 1900.

193 Rhodes House, Rhodes MSS Afr. S. 228 C7b f. 267, Natty to Rhodes, Nov. 2, 1900.

194 Rhodes House, Rhodes MSS Afr. S. 228 C7b f. 314, Rhodes to Natty, Aug. 17, 1901; S. 228 C7b f. 313, Natty to Rhodes, Aug. 20.

195 Rotberg, *Founder*, p. 644. Cf. RAL, XI/130A/0, Natty, London, to his cousins, Paris, March 14, 1906.

196 RAL, XI/130A/0, Natty, London, to his cousins, Paris, Feb. 20, 1906; same to same, Feb. 22; Feb. 23;

March 5; March 30; Dec. 13. For the crisis in Natal in 1906, which Natty blamed on Churchill and Asquith, see RAL, XI/130A/0, Natty to his cousins, March 30; same to same, April 3; June 15.

197   RAL, XI/130A/0, Natty, London, to his cousins, Paris, Dec. 18, 1906; RAL, XI/130A/1, same to same, April 8, 1907; July 15; July 17; July 18; July 22; July 23; July 24; July 25; Aug. 30; Sept. 2; Sept. 11; Dec. 13; Dec. 17; RAL, XI/130A/4, Feb. 1, 1910. Cf. Chilvers, *De Beers*, pp. 157ff.

198   Kynaston, *City*, vol. II, p. 220.

TWELVE   *Finances and Alliances (1885–1906)*

1   Hatfield House, 3M, McDonnell to Salisbury, Jan. 2, 1899.
2   RAL, XI/130A/1, Natty, London, to his cousins, Paris, May 8, 1907.
3   Kennedy, *Anglo-German antagonism*, p. 304.
4   Allfrey, *Jewish Court*, p. 221.
5   Kennedy, *Anglo-German antagonism*, pp. 47f.
6   Churchill College, Cambridge, Randolph Churchill Papers Add. 9248/1842, Natty to Churchill, Sept. 25, 1886; Add. 9248/1844, same to same, Sept. 27. Cf. Swartz, *Politics of British foreign policy*, pp. 152ff.
7   Stengers, "King Leopold," pp. 147f. See also RAL, T14/01, Alphonse, Paris, to his cousins, London, Jan. 9, 1886.
8   Davis, *English Rothschilds*, pp. 199f.
9   Kynaston, *City*, vol. I, p. 382.
10 Foster, *Churchill*, p. 198.
11 Barnbougle Castle, Rosebery Papers, Alfred, New Court, to Rosebery, April 2, 1886.
12 RAL, T14/34, Alphonse, Paris, to his cousins, London, Aug. 23, 1888; RAL, T14/33, Edmond to his cousins, Aug. 18; RAL, T14/35, Alphonse to his cousins, Sept. 8. Note also the Goncourts' comment: "[D]ans cette ancienne cité [Samarcande] . . . on ignore qui'il y a en Europe un pays qui s'appelle la France, on ignore qu'il y a un homme politique du nom de Bismarck, on sait seulement qu'il existe dans cette Europe un particulier immensément riche, qui s'appelle Rothschild": Goncourt, *Journal*, vol. III, p. 746.
13 Barnbougle Castle, Rosebery Papers, Natty to Rosebery, Sept. 15, 1885. See also RAL, T13/198, Alphonse, Paris, to his cousins, London, Oct. 27; RAL, T13/207, Mayer Carl, Frankfurt, to Leo, Nov. 3; RAL, T13/199, Alphonse to his cousins, Nov. 12; Barnbougle Castle, Rosebery Papers, Natty to Rosebery, Nov. 12.
14 Churchill College, Cambridge, Randolph Churchill Papers Add. 9248/1842, Natty to Churchill, Sept. 25, 1886. See also Davis, *English Rothschilds*, p. 206, for similar remarks to Rosebery.
15 Churchill College, Cambridge, Randolph Churchill Papers Add. 9248/1844, Natty to Churchill, Sept. 27, 1886; Add. 9248/1883, same to same, Oct. 6; Add. 9248/1907, Oct. 19. Cf. Foster, *Churchill*, pp. 284–9.
16 Harcourt Williams (ed.), *Salisbury–Balfour correspondence*, pp. 158f. See also p. 173.
17 Barnbougle Castle, Rosebery Papers, Natty to Rosebery, Nov. 23, 1886; same to same, Dec. 16; Feb. 18, [1887?]. Davis, *English Rothschilds*, pp. 206ff.
18 RAL, T13/101/10, Alphonse, Paris, to his cousins, London, May 26, 1883; RAL, T13/188, same to same, July 6, 1885.
19 Dugdale (ed.), *German diplomatic documents*, vol. I, p. 284.
20 RAL, T16/32, Alphonse, Paris, to his cousins, London, July 17, 1893; RAL, T16/32, same to same, July 19.
21 Taylor, *Struggle*, p. 342. Cf. RAL, T16/15, Arthur, Paris, to his cousins, London, Aug. 16, 1892; RAL, T16/54, Alphonse, Paris, to his cousins, London, March 5, 1894.
22 NLS, Rosebery MS 10135 ff. 35–9, Alfred, New Court, to Rosebery [relaying report from Julius Blum of the Creditanstalt], Jan. 9, 1894; NLS, Rosebery MS 10102 f. 149, same to same [enclosing telegram from Cairo], Feb. 19; f. 167, Natty to Rosebery, Feb. 21 [enclosing telegram from Cairo].
23 RAL, T16/63, Alphonse, Paris, to his cousins, London, June 8, 1894.
24 Hatfield House, 3M, McDonnell to Salisbury, March 6, 1896.
25 And by late 1897 McDonnell was negotiating with Natty about the possibility of Rothschild financial support for Sudanese railways: Hatfield House, 3M, McDonnell to Salisbury, Dec. 4, 1897.
26 Hatfield House, 3M, Natty, North Berwick, to McDonnell, London, Sept. 13, 1898; McDonnell to Salisbury, Nov. 2.

27 Bouvier, *Rothschild*, p. 231.

28 From a low of 3 roubles to the pound in 1874, the rouble appreciated to 4.67 in 1887, then fell back to 3.57 in 1890. It was initially stabilised at a rate of 3.88, then revalued to 9.45 in 1897.

29 RAL, T13/83, Alphonse, Paris, to his cousins, London, May 16, 1881; RAL, T13/91, same to same, Dec. 21. Cf. Russo-Jewish Committee, *Russian Atrocities*.

30 *Rich and Fisher (eds)*, Holstein papers, vol. III, p. 107; Kennan, *Franco-Russian relations*, pp. 162ff.

31 Bouvier, *Crédit Lyonnais*, pp. 766ff.; Kennan, *Franco-Russian relations*, p. 228.

32 RAL, T13/101/10, Gustave, Paris, to his cousins, London, Oct. 2, 1882.

33 Cyon, *Histoire de l'entente*, pp. 235–8. Cf. Kennan, *Franco-Russian relations*, pp. 292f.; Stern, *Gold and iron*, p. 443.

34 Cyon, *Histoire de l'entente*, pp. 239f.; Kennan, *Franco-Russian relations*, pp. 296ff.

35 Cyon, *Histoire de l'entente*, pp. 275, 283, 297f.; Kennan, *Franco-Russian relations*, p. 339.

36 Cyon, *Histoire de l'entente*, p. 354. See also pp. 318, 334.

37 Kennan, *Franco-Russian relations*, pp. 338ff.

38 Cyon, *Histoire de l'entente*, pp. 301–5.

39 *Ibid.*, p. 340; Girault, *Emprunts russes*, pp. 146–50, 314–20.

40 Girault, *Emprunts russes*, pp. 159–62; Kennan, *Franco-Russian relations*, pp. 382f.; Stern, *Gold and iron*, pp. 446f. Cf. Kynaston, *City*, vol. I, p. 312.

41 RAL, T13/101/10, Gustave, Paris, to his cousins, London, Jan. 17, 1882.

42 RAL, T13/101/10, Gustave, Paris, to his cousins, London, Oct. 2, 1882.

43 RAL, T14/25, Gustave, Paris, to his cousins, London, March 13, 1888.

44 RAL, T14/18, Alphonse, Paris, to his cousins, London, Feb. 7, 1888.

45 Kennan, *Franco-Russian relations*, pp. 387–90; Poidevin, *Relations économiques*, pp. 46–50. Cf. Davis, *English Rothschilds*, pp. 230–32.

46 Girault, *Emprunts russes*, pp. 171–84.

47 Kennan, *Franco-Russian relations*, pp. 401–3; Stern, *Gold and iron*, pp. 446f.; Poidevin, *Finances et relations internationales*, p. 64; Poidevin, *Relations économiques*, pp. 21f.

48 Girault, *Emprunts russes*, pp. 218f.; Poidevin, *Relations économiques*, pp. 46–50.

49 *The Times*, May 9, 1891, p. 7; May 12, p. 5; May 18, p. 5; Nov. 23, p. 5.

50 Taylor, *Struggle*, pp. 333f.: "The French gave the final push [towards entente with Russia] when they got the Paris House of Rothschild to refuse to float a new Russian loan, ostensibly because of Russian ill treatment of Jews. The Russians were threatened with a disastrous harvest; they had to have the French money on any terms. They yielded towards the Jews; what was more important, they yielded in foreign policy." Cf. Michon, *Alliance Franco-Russe*, p. 25; Mayeur, *Troisième République*, p. 223; Corti, *Reign*, pp. 442f.

51 Renouvin, *Relations*, vol. VI, pp. 119f.

52 Davis, *English Rothschilds*, pp. 229f.

53 Cf. Stern, *Gold and iron*, p. 481.

54 Barnbougle Castle, Rosebery Papers, Leo to Rosebery, May 9, 1891; Natty to Rosebery, Oct. 20. Leo added revealingly that "it would have been better if he had refused at once—[but] the finance minister fortunately is a good practical man of business & will do nothing to spite the R[othschild]s as people imagined." Cf. Heilbrunn, "Haus Rothschild," p. 35, for Natty's comments to the American ambassador Andrew Dickson White. In addition to rebutting the Russian government's charges against the Jews, "He incidentally referred to the money power of Europe as against Russia."

55 RAL, T15/67, Edmond, Paris, to Natty, London, Aug. 21, 1891; RAL, T15/73, same to same, Sept. 22.

56 RAL, T16/08, Alphonse, Paris, to his cousins, London, April 22, 1892. See also RAL, T16/19, Gustave to his cousins, Sept. 28.

57 Girault, *Emprunts russes*, pp. 223, 230.

58 *Ibid.*, pp. 188–93; Kennan, *Fateful alliance*, pp. 77f.

59 Girault, *Emprunts russes*, p. 205.

60 *Ibid.*, p. 299.

61 Corti, *Reign*, pp. 443f.; Girault, *Emprunts russes*, pp. 235f.

62 RAL, T16/17, Alphonse, Paris, to his cousins, London, Sept. 12, 1892.

63 Poidevin, *Relations économiques*, pp. 46–50.

64 RAL, T16/155, Gustave, Paris, to his cousins, London, Sept. 14, 1896. Cf. Girault, *Emprunts russes*, pp. 314–20.

65   RAL, T16/152, Alphonse, Paris, to his cousins, London, July 27, 1896. Cf. Girault, *Emprunts russes*, pp. 73f.

66   Ramm, *Morier*, pp. 322–9. The Gunzbergs were a Jewish family who had made their fortune in the vodka business and then diversified into banking and mining. However, see Witte, *Memoirs*, p. 60, which suggests that Alphonse was opposed to Russia going on to gold.

67   AN, 132 AQ 5555/1M158, NMR to deRF, Dec. 21, 1894 (two letters); same to same, Dec. 24; RAL, T16/116, Natty, London, to his cousins, Paris, Jan. 30, 1896.

68   Lipman, *History of the Jews*, pp. 74f.

69   Alphonse also cited the Tsar's enthusiasm for the occult as a cause for concern: Witte, *Memoirs*, p. 198.

70   Hatfield House, 3M, McDonnell to Salisbury, Aug. 16, 1898; Girault, *Emprunts russes*, pp. 330–34.

71   Poidevin, *Relations économiques*, pp. 46–50; Girault, *Emprunts russes*, p. 73.

72   Hatfield House, 3M, McDonnell to Salisbury, Dec. 31, 1898; same to same, Jan. 3, 1899.

73   Hatfield House, 3M, McDonnell to Salisbury, Jan. 6, 1899; same to same, Jan. 13.

74   Rich and Fisher (eds), *Holstein papers*, vol. IV, pp. 46f.

75   *Ibid.*, p. 147; Girault, *Emprunts russes*, pp. 114, 340ff.

76   Rich and Fisher (eds), *Holstein papers*, vol. IV, p. 224.

77   Deutsche Bank (ed.), *Studies*, pp. 693f.

78   Poidevin, *Finances et relations internationales*, p. 88; Seton-Watson, *Italy from fascism to liberalism*, p. 143.

79   Seton-Watson, *Italy from fascism to liberalism*, pp. 148f.; Corti, *Reign*, p. 442; Poidevin, *Relations économiques*, pp. 52f.; Askew, *Europe and Italy's acquisition*, p. 18n.; Nichols, *Germany*, p. 121.

80   Poidevin, *Relations économiques*, pp. 21f., 52f.

81   Hatfield House, 3M, McDonnell to Salisbury, Nov. 6, 1897.

82   Ferguson, "Kaiser's European Union," *passim*.

83   Kynaston, *City*, vol. I, p. 351.

84   RAL, T13/101/12, Alphonse, Paris, to his cousins, London, March 19, 1885; RAL, T14/09, same to same, June 29, 1886.

85   Deutsche Bank (ed.), *Studies*, p. 31; Stern, *Gold and iron*, p. 428.

86   RAL, T14/09, Alphonse, Paris, to his cousins, London, June 29, 1886.

87   Kynaston, *City*, vol. I, p. 380.

88   RAL, T14/13, Alphonse, Paris, to his cousins, London, Aug. 5, 1886. Cf. Deutsche Bank (ed.), *Studies*, p. 31; Barth, *Hochfinanz*, pp. 39f.

89   RAL, T14/19, Alphonse, Paris, to his cousins, London, Feb. 9, 1888; RAL, T14/20, same to same, Feb. 10; RAL, T14/22, March 5.

90   RAL, T14/26, Gustave, Paris, to his cousins, London, March 20, 1888. See also RAL, T14/30, Alphonse, Paris, to his cousins, London, June 25. Alphonse was equally suspicious of the Kaiser's short-lived aspiration to woo the working classes: RAL, T15/33, Alphonse to his cousins, Feb. 7, 1890.

91   RAL, T14/29, Alphonse, Paris, to his cousins, London, June 14, 1888.

92   RAL, T15/35, Alphonse, Paris, to his cousins, London, March 18, 1890; Stern, *Gold and iron*, p. 453.

93   Stern, *Gold and iron*, pp. 480, 540.

94   RAL, T15/71, Arthur, Paris, to his cousins, London, Sept. 17, 1891.

95   Stern, *Gold and iron*, p. 250; Rich and Fisher (eds), *Holstein papers*, vol. III, p. 515.

96   Barth, *Hochfinanz*, pp. 142ff.; Kynaston, *City*, vol. II, pp. 125ff.

97   RAL, T16/98, Alphonse, Paris, to his cousins, London, June 14, 1895.

98   Poidevin, *Relations économiques*, pp. 77–9. See also pp. 82f. for the involvement of some German bankers, including Max Warburg.

99   Thane, "Cassel," pp. 83f.; Kynaston, *City*, vol. II, pp. 126f. On the enigmatic Cassel, see also Allfrey, *Jewish court*, pp. 137–55.

100 Hatfield House, 3M, McDonnell to Salisbury, March 6, 1896; same to same, Jan. 3, 1898. This second letter contradicts Edward Hamilton's malicious claim that "the Rothschilds have not been consulted": Bahlman (ed.), *Hamilton diary*, p. 349. Cf. Barth, *Hochfinanz*, pp. 149f., 158; Allfrey, *Jewish Court*, pp. 156ff.

101 Hatfield House, 3M, Natty to McDonnell, Feb. 23, 1898; McDonnell to Salisbury, Feb. 23.

102 In November 1897 the Germans seized Kiao-Chow, the main port of the Shantung province, a move partly influenced by Salisbury's refusal to give of them control of Samoa as they had requested in 1894; the Russian demand for a "lease" of Port Arthur in March 1898 prompted a British naval response.

103 Barth, *Hochfinanz*, pp. 160f.

104 Dugdale, *Balfour*, vol. I, p. 258; Rich and Fisher (eds), *Holstein papers*, vol. IV, p. 65n.; Jay, *Chamberlain*, pp. 218f. Chamberlain favoured an alliance of powers against Russia, foreseeing the piecemeal partition of China if Britain continued to act alone as over Wei-hai-wei.

105 Barth, *Hochfinanz*, p. 163.

106 Hatfield House, 3M, McDonnell to Salisbury, Jan. 6, 1899.

107 Barth, *Hochfinanz*, pp. 166f.

108 Rich and Fisher (eds), *Holstein papers*, vol. IV, p. 197.

109 Barth, *Hochfinanz*, pp. 280f. See also Gooch and Temperley (eds), *British documents on the origins of the War*, vol. II, p. 72.

110 Barth, *Hochfinanz*, p. 288.

111 Dugdale, *Balfour*, vol. I, pp. 258f. Cf. *The Times, History*, vol. III, p. 816.

112 Dugdale, *Balfour*, vol. I, p. 258f.

113 Rich and Fisher (eds), *Holstein papers*, vol. IV pp. 46f., 147, 164; Dugdale (ed.), *German diplomatic documents*, vol. III, p. 59.

114 Rich and Fisher (eds), *Holstein papers*, vol. IV, p. 260.

115 Jay, *Chamberlain*, p. 219.

116 The argument is presented more fully in Ferguson, "Public finance" and *idem*, "The Kaiser's European Union."

117 Gooch and Temperley (eds), *British documents on the origins of the War*, vol. I, pp. 44–8; Egremont, *Balfour*, p. 139; Steiner, *Foreign Office*, pp. 38f.

118 Hatfield House, 3M, McDonnell to Salisbury, Jan. 13, 1899. Cf. Rich and Fisher (eds), *Holstein papers*, vol. IV, p. 71.

119 Hatfield House, 3M, McDonnell to Salisbury, April 4, 1899; Birmingham University, Chamberlain Papers, JC 7/2/2C/4, Alfred to Chamberlain, Oct. 17; JC 7/2/2C/5, Schwabach to NMR, Oct. 18; JC 7/2/2C/6, Alfred to Chamberlain, Oct. 19; JC 7/2/2C/7, same to same, Oct. 27. Cf. Brandenburg, *From Bismarck to the World War*, p. 125; Rich and Fisher (eds) *Holstein papers*, vol. IV, pp. 46f.

120 RAL, T14/38, Gustave, Paris, to his cousins, London, Oct. 11, 1888.

121 Hatfield House, 3M, McDonnell to Salisbury, Dec. 2, 1896; same to same, March 30, 1897.

122 Hatfield House, 3M, NMR to Witte, Aug. 18, 1887; McDonnell to Salisbury, Aug. 20; same to same, Aug. 21; Natty to McDonnell, Aug. 24; McDonnell to Salisbury, Aug. 26.

123 Hatfield House, 3M, Natty to McDonnell, Sept. 3, 1897; McDonnell to Salisbury, Sept. 3.

124 Barth, *Hochfinanz*, p. 134; Allfrey, *Jewish court*, pp. 220f.

125 Gooch and Temperley (eds), *British documents on the origins of the War*, vol. II, pp. 178f.

126 Allfrey, *Jewish court*, pp. 222f.; Steiner, *Foreign Office*, pp. 186f.; Ziegler, *Sixth great power*, pp. 316f.

127 Kynaston, *City*, vol. II, pp. 566–71.

128 Barth, *Hochfinanz*, p. 240; Kynaston, *City*, vol. II, p. 514.

129 RAL, XI/130A/0, Natty, London, to his cousins, Paris, May 10, 1906.

130 RAL, XI/130A/1, Natty, London, to his cousins, Paris, Sept. 20, 1907; same to same, Oct. 1.

131 RAL, XI/130A/2, Natty, London, to his cousins, Paris, Nov. 11, 1908; RAL, XI/130A/4, same to same, April 26, 1911. Cf. Barth, *Hochfinanz*, p. 258.

132 RAL, T16/122, Alphonse, Paris, to his cousins, London, Jan. 4, 1896; RAL, T16/131, same to same, Feb. 4; RAL, T16/139, Gustave, Paris, to his cousins, London, March 16; RAL, T16/143, same to same, May 2; RAL, T16/146, May 12; RAL, T16/147, Alphonse to his cousins, June 22.

133 Birmingham University, Chamberlain Papers, JC 7/2/2C/1, Alfred to Chamberlain, April 8, 1897; JC 7/2/2C/2, Chamberlain to Alfred, April 8.

134 Hatfield House, 3M, Natty to McDonnell, July 18, 1899; McDonnell to Salisbury, July 20.

135 Dugdale (ed.), *German diplomatic documents*, vol. III, p. 101.

136 Corti, *Reign*, pp. 454ff.; Morton, *Rothschilds*, pp. 204f.; Wilson, *Rothschild*, pp. 330f.

137 *The Times, History*, vol. III, pp. 318, 365ff. However, there was no substance to the suspicion that Natty tried to push Moberly Bell out of Printing House Square during the financial reorganisation of *The Times* in which he had a hand in 1907–8: *ibid.*, pp. 510–17, 556, 838. In Schwabach's view Natty was "by no means particularly pro-German" and "would not dream of allowing German influence on the paper."

138 RAL, T46/43, M. M. Warburg & Co. to NMR, May 7, 1903; RAL, T46/44, same to same, May 13. Warburg applied for £1 million but had to be content with £26,000—still a substantial sum.

139   See e.g. BL, MSS Asquith 19, ff. 180–82, Hamilton to Asquith, Jan. 22, 1907: "[T]he state cannot raise
       an indefinite amount of money. We all thought so during the Boer War, but we now know that we have
       damaged our credit very materially by the amount we borrowed during that war."
140   Spinner, *Goschen*, pp. 208f.
141   Rich and Fisher (eds), *Holstein papers*, vol, IV, pp. 257, 260.
142   Corti, *Reign*, pp. 459f.; Rich and Fisher (eds), *Holstein papers*, vol. IV, p. 275.
143   Hatfield House, 3M, McDonnell to Salisbury, Jan. 2, 1899.
144   Hatfield House, 3M, Alfred to Salisbury, Jan. 16, 1899; same to same, Jan. 17. He was also awarded the
       Grand Cross of the Order of Francis Joseph of Austria.
145   Hatfield House, 3M, McDonnell to Salisbury, July 20, 1899.
146   Hatfield House, 3M, McDonnell to Salisbury, Oct. 5, 1899.
147   Dugdale (ed.), *German diplomatic documents*, vol. III, p. 50.
148   Rich and Fisher (eds), *Holstein papers*, vol. IV, p. 257.
149   *Ibid.*, pp. 173f.
150   Brandenburg, *From Bismarck to the World War*, pp. 171f.
151   Thane, "Cassel," pp. 86ff., 89ff.
152   Guillen, "Entente," pp. 349ff.
153   Ziegler, *Sixth great power*, pp. 311f.; Rothschild, *Gilt-edged life*, p. 190.
154   Kynaston, *City*, vol. II, p. 350.
155   Dugdale (ed.), *German diplomatic documents*, vol. III, p. 175. Cf. Chernow, *Warburgs*, p. 100.
156   *The Times*, Nov. 9, 1905, p. 6.
157   Rothschild, *Dear Lord Rothschild*, p. 33.
158   Corti, *Reign*, pp. 459f.
159   Girault, *Emprunts russes*, pp. 118, 402. As usual in the Third Republic, there was a political dimension
       to this financial problem: Paul Cambon claimed that Rouvier had speculated on a rise in Russian bonds
       on the basis of Delcassé's assurances that there would be no war. Delcassé called Rouvier a man "who
       would sell France for a speculation on the stock exchange": Taylor, *Struggle*, p. 428n.
160   Ziegler, *Sixth great power*, p. 312.
161   BL, Add. MS Gladstone 46064 f. 170, Walter to Herbert Gladstone, March 18, 1904.
162   Corti, *Reign*, p. 460.
163   RAL, XI/130A/0, Natty, London, to his cousins, Paris, Jan. 25, 1906; same to same, Jan. 29; Jan. 30;
       Feb. 5; Feb. 12; Feb. 14; Feb. 16; March 6; March 9; March 23; April 8; May 8; RAL, XI/130A/1, Jan.
       8, 1907; Jan. 9; Jan. 10; Jan. 14; Leo to his cousins, Feb. 4; same to same, Feb. 6; Natty to his cousins,
       Feb. 11; same to same, Feb. 12; Feb. 18; Feb. 20; March 1; April 16. Cf. Kynaston, *City*, vol. II, p. 412.
       The London share of the loan was issued jointly by the Hong Kong & Shanghai, Parr's and the Japan-
       ese Yokohama Specie Bank.
164   RAL, XI/130A/1, Natty, London, to his cousins, Paris, Feb. 25, 1907.
165   RAL, XI/130A/0, Natty, London, to his cousins, Paris, May 7, 1906.
166   RAL, XI/130A/1, Natty, London, to his cousins, Paris, May 7, 1907.
167   RAL, XI/130A/1, Natty, London, to his cousins, Paris, May 7, 1907; same to same, May 8.
168   Dugdale (ed.), *German diplomatic documents*, vol. III, p. 213.
169   RAL, XI/130A/0, Natty, London, to his cousins, Paris, Jan. 3, 1906; same to same, Jan. 4.
170   RAL, XI/130A/0, Natty, London, to his cousins, Paris, Jan. 24, 1906; same to same, Jan. 29; Feb. 2;
       Feb. 5; Feb. 8; Feb. 9; Feb. 12; Feb. 14; Feb. 15; Feb. 16; Feb. 19; Feb. 20; Feb. 21; Feb. 22.
171   RAL, XI/130A/0, Natty, London, to his cousins, Paris, Feb. 22, 1906. See also same to same, Feb. 23;
       Feb. 26; Feb. 27; March 2.
172   Gooch and Temperley (eds), *British documents on the origins of the War*, vol. III, p. 280.
173   RAL, XI/130A/0, Natty, London, to his cousins, Paris, March 5, 1906; same to same, March 6; March
       9; March 16.
174   RAL, XI/130A/0, Natty, London, to his cousins, Paris, March 20, 1906; same to same, March 21;
       March 23; March 28.
175   Taylor, *Struggle*, p. 434.
176   Poidevin, *Finances et relations internationales*, p. 93; Poidevin, *Relations économiques*, pp. 300f.;
       Deutsche Bank (ed.), *Studies*, p. 709.
177   RAL, XI/130A/0, Natty, London, to his cousins, Paris, Nov. 5, 1906; same to same, Nov. 12; Bodleian

Library, Asquith MSS 10, f. 212, Hamilton to Asquith, Dec. 24, RAL, XI/130A/0, Natty to his cousins, Dec. 26; same to same, Dec. 31; RAL, XI/130A/1, Jan. 3, 1907; Jan. 4; Jan. 7; Jan. 8; Jan. 9; Jan.15; March 11.

178 RAL, XI/130A/1, Natty, London, to his cousins, Paris, Jan. 4, 1907.

179 AN, 132 AQ 122/B-24–1/2, NMR to deRF, Nov. 9, 1906; RAL, XI/130A/0, Natty, London, to his cousins, Paris, Nov. 9; Nov. 16; Nov. 20; Nov. 21; Nov. 22; Nov. 23; AN, 132 AQ 122/B-24–1/2, NMR to deRF, Nov. 19; deRF to Gouverneur, Banque de France, Nov. 19; AN, 132 AQ 5579/1M177, NMR to deRF, Nov. 20; same to same, Nov. 21; Nov. 22; Nov. 23; Nov. 28; Nov. 30; Dec. 4.

180 RAL, XI/130A/0, Natty, London, to his cousins, Paris, Nov. 30, 1906.

181 RAL, XI/130A/0, Natty, London, to his cousins, Dec. 17, 1906; same to same, Dec. 19; Dec. 20; Leo to his cousins, Dec. 21; Natty to his cousins, Dec. 24; AN, 132 AQ 122/B-24–1/2, deRF to NMR, Dec. 19; NMR to deRF, Dec. 20; deRF to NMR, Dec. 20; NMR to deRF, Dec. 21; AN, 132 AQ 5579/1M177, NMR to deRF, Dec. 31; RAL, XI/130A/1, Natty to his cousins, Jan. 3, 1907; AN, 132 AQ 122/B-24–1/2, Jimmy to Gouverneur, Banque de France, Jan. 5; AN, 132 AQ 5580/1M178, NMR to deRF, Jan. 23; AN, 132 AQ 122 B-24–1/2, Natty to his cousins, Paris, Feb. 21; AN, 132 AQ 5580/1M178, NMR to deRF, Feb. 25; same to same, Feb. 27; March 1; March 4; March 11; March 17; April 8.

182 RAL, XI/130A/1, Natty, London, to his cousins, Paris, Nov. 1, 1907.

183 RAL, XI/130A/1, Natty, London, to his cousins, Paris, March 23, 1907; same to same, March 25. See also March 14.

184 AN, 132 AQ 5580/1M178, NMR to deRF, April 12, 1907; RAL, XI/130A/1, Natty, London, to his cousins, Paris, May 8; same to same, May 27; June 20; July 5.

185 RAL, XI/130A/1, Natty, London, to his cousins, Paris, Aug. 14, 1907; same to same, Aug. 19; Aug. 20.

186 RAL, XI/130A/1, Natty, London, to his cousins, Paris, Oct. 29, 1907; same to same, Oct. 30.

187 RAL, XI/130A/1, Natty, London, to his cousins, Paris, Nov. 1, 1907; same to same, Nov. 4; Nov. 5; Nov. 6; Nov. 7; Nov. 8; Nov. 11; Nov. 15; AN, 132 AQ 122/B-24–1/3, NMR to deRF, Nov. 4; same to same, Nov. 5; deRF to NMR, Dec. 6; deRF to Gouverneur, Banque de France, Dec. 6. Cf. Kynaston, *City*, vol. II, pp. 444ff.

188 RAL, XI/130A/1, Natty, London, to his cousins, Paris, Nov. 11, 1907; same to same, Nov. 12; Nov. 13. Cf. Kynaston, *City*, vol. II, pp. 445f. It should be remembered that at this stage the Federal Reserve System did not yet exist.

189 AN, 132 AQ 122/B-1–24/3, Governor of Bank of England to Natty, Nov. 21, 1907. See also RAL, XI/130A/1, Natty, London, to his cousins, Paris, Nov. 27.

190 RAL, XI/130A/2, Natty, London, to his cousins, Paris, Jan. 13, 1908; Leo to his cousins, Jan. 14; Natty to his cousins, Jan. 15; same to same, Jan. 16.

191 RAL, XI/130A/2, Natty, London, to his cousins, Paris, July 10, 1908; same to same, Oct. 7; AN, 132 AQ 122/B-24–1/4, NMR to deRF, July 15.

192 AN, 132 AQ 5585/1M183, NMR to deRF, Nov. 12, 1909; RAL, XI/130A/3, Natty, London, to his cousins, Paris, Nov. 15.

193 RAL, XI/130A/1, Natty, London, to his cousins, Paris, Nov. 19, 1907.

194 RAL, XI/130A/4, Natty, London, to his cousins, Paris, May 5, 1910.

195 Ferguson, "Kaiser's European Union," pp. 261–70.

196 RAL, XI/130A/2, Natty, London, to his cousins, Paris, June 1, 1908.

197 RAL, XI/130A/1, Natty, London, to his cousins, Paris, April 19, 1907.

198 RAL, XI/130A/0, Natty, London, to his cousins, Paris, April 5, 1906.

199 RAL, XI/130A/1, Natty, London, to his cousins, Paris, Jan. 3, 1907. See also same to same, March 13; March 18.

200 RAL, XI/130A/1, Natty, London, to his cousins, Paris, April 17, 1907; same to same, April 18; April 19; April 30.

201 RAL, XI/130A/1, Natty, London, to his cousins, Paris, Jan. 28, 1907.

202 RAL, XI/130A/1, Natty, London, to his cousins, Paris, Dec. 10, 1907; Alfred to his cousins, Dec. 11; Leo to his cousins, Dec. 20.

203 RAL, XI/130A/2, Natty, London, to his cousins, Paris, April 2, 1908; RAL, XI/130A/3, same to same, Jan. 7, 1909.

204 See e.g. Dugdale (ed.), *German diplomatic documents*, vol. III, p. 407.

205   Poidevin, *Relations économiques*, pp. 635, 655–9.

206   Michon, *Alliance Franco-Russe*, p. 132.

207   RAL, XI/130A/0, Natty, London, to his cousins, Paris, Jan. 3, 1906.

208   RAL, XI/130A/0, Natty, London, to his cousins, Paris, Jan. 5, 1906; Girault, *Emprunts russes*, p. 434.

209   RAL, XI/130A/0, Natty, London, to his cousins, Paris, Jan. 23, 1906.

210   RAL, XI/130A/0, Natty, London, to his cousins, Paris, Feb. 14, 1906.

211   RAL, XI/130A/0, Natty, London, to his cousins, Paris, March 5, 1906.

212   RAL, XI/130A/0, Natty, London, to his cousins, Paris, Feb. 14, 1906; same to same, Feb. 15; Feb. 16; Feb. 23; March 2; March 16.

213   RAL, XI/130A/0, Natty, London, to his cousins, Paris, Feb. 6, 1906.

214   RAL, XI/130A/0, Natty, London, to his cousins, Paris, March 14, 1906. Cf. Ziegler, *Sixth great power*, pp. 312ff.; Kynaston, *City*, vol. II, pp. 419ff.

215   RAL, XI/130A/0, Natty, London, to his cousins, Paris, April 5, 1906. Cf. Ziegler, *Sixth great power*, p. 314. "Naturally," Natty reported in a revealing postscript, "I have given the most categorical denial & I have done all in my power to prevent the Jewish writers in the International Press from attacking Russian Finance."

216   RAL, XI/130A/0, Natty, London, to his cousins, Paris, March 19, 1906; same to same, March 21; April 2; April 4; Alfred to his cousins, April 8; Natty to his cousins, April 9; Alfred to his cousins, April 11.

217   RAL, XI/130A/0, Natty, London, to his cousins, Paris, April 17, 1906; same to same, April 18; April 19; April 20; April 23; April 24; April 26; May 9.

218   Ziegler, *Sixth great power*, pp. 424f.

219   RAL, XI/130A/0, Natty, London, to his cousins, Paris, June 18, 1906; same to same, June 19.

220   RAL, XI/130A/0, Natty, London, to his cousins, Paris, May 23, 1906.

221   RAL, XI/130A/0, Natty, London, to his cousins, Paris, June 18, 1906; same to same, June 19; June 20; June 21; June 22.

222   RAL, XI/130A/1, Natty, London, to his cousins, Paris, Feb. 8, 1907; Leo to his cousins, April 22; Natty to his cousins, April 24; same to same, June 6.

223   RAL, XI/130A/1, Natty, London, to his cousins, Paris, Sept. 2, 1907; same to same, Sept. 26. Cf. Davis, *English Rothschilds*, pp. 229f.

224   RAL, XI/130A/1, Natty, London, to his cousins, Paris, Oct. 7, 1907. Cf. *Daily News*, Oct. 10; Allfrey, *Jewish court*, pp. 216f.

225   RA, W53/98, Natty, Alfred and Leo to the King, June 3, 1908; RAL, XI/130A/1, Natty, London, to his cousins, Paris, June 3, 1908. Cf. Rothschild, *Dear Lord Rothschild*, pp. 34f.; Lipman, *History of the Jews*, pp. 74f.; Davis, *English Rothschilds*, p. 232.

226   RA, W53/105, Charles Hardinge, H.M. Yacht *Victoria & Albert* to Natty, June 13, 1908. Stolypin replied vaguely that he was "contemplat[ing] legislation for the amelioration of the lot of the Jews in Russia."

227   RAL, XI/130A/1, Natty, London, to his cousins, Paris, June 15, 1908. See also RA, W53/106, Hardinge to Knollys, June 16, 1908.

228   RAL, XI/130A/1, Natty, London, to his cousins, Paris, June 15, 1908; same to same, June 16.

229   Rothschild, *Dear Lord Rothschild*, p. 36.

230   Bridge, *Great Britain and Austria–Hungary*, p. 98.

231   On the problems of financing the Austrian dreadnought programme, see May, *Habsburg Monarchy*, p. 452; Gebhard, *Austria's dreadnought squadron*, p. 257.

232   Rich and Fisher (eds), *Holstein papers*, vol. III, pp. 302f.

233   Michel, *Banques et banquiers*, pp. 121–53.

234   Poidevin, *Relations économiques*, pp. 550–53; Komlos, *Habsburg monarchy*, p. 194.

235   May, *Habsburg monarchy*, pp. 221f.; Poidevin, *Finances et relations internationales*, p. 97.

236   Michel, *Banques et banquiers*, pp. 121–35.

237   RAL, XI/130A/0, Natty, London, to his cousins, Paris, April 9, 1906.

238   RAL, XI/130A/1, Leo, London, to his cousins, Paris, Feb. 4, 1907; RAL, XI/130A/2, Alfred to his cousins, Feb. 21, 1908; Natty to his cousins, May 12.

239   Bridge, *Great Britain and Austria–Hungary*, p. 31.

240   For fragmentary evidence of the Rothschilds' involvement with Alexander Obrenovic, the King of Serbia, who was murdered in 1903, see CPHDCM, 637/1/35/6–8, Alexander of Serbia, Belgrade, to

SMR, March 18, 1893; CPHDCM, 637/1/35/2, Milan [his father], Paris, to SMR, March 22; CPHDCM, 637/1/35/3, Milan to Albert, March 22; CPHDCM, 637/1/35/17, Alexander to SMR, July 4; CPHDCM, 637/1/35/22, Milan to SMR, July 16.

THIRTEEN   *The Military–Financial Complex (1906–1914)*

1   RAL, XI/130A/0, Natty, London, to his cousins, Paris, June 7, 1906.
2   *The Times*, June 25, 1909.
3   Hobson, *Imperialism*, p. 57.
4   Steed, *Thirty years*, vol. II, pp. 8f.
5   *Nation*, April 10, 1915.
6   Rothschild, *Dear Lord Rothschild*, pp. 80f.
7   *The Times*, Oct. 17, 1902. See also RAL, XI/130A/1, Leo, London, to his cousins, Paris, Dec. 6, 1907; RAL, XI/130A/2, same to same, Jan. 10, 1908; Jan. 14.
8   Rothschild, *Dear Lord Rothschild*, pp. 82f.
9   RAL, XI/130A/2, Natty, London, to his cousins, Paris, Nov. 10, 1908; RAL, XI/130A/3, Alfred to his cousins, Paris, April 1, 1909. Cf. Kynaston, *City*, vol. II, pp. 492f.
10   See for reports to Natty of the Maxim gun trials, RAL, T43/4, W. Brodrich Cloete, Washington, to Natty, London, Feb. 29, 1888. Natty also kept Lord Salisbury informed about foreign purchases of Maxim guns, which he regarded as a sign of bellicose intent.
11   Allfrey, *Man of arms*, pp. 41, 46, 51, 63, 69; Thane, "Financiers and the British state," pp. 83, 88. Kynaston, *City*, vol. I, pp. 400, 403; Davis, *English Rothschilds*, pp. 219f.; Allfrey, *Jewish court*, pp. 160f.
12   RAL, T14/53, Charles Beresford, Admiralty, to Natty, Jan. 12, 1888.
13   RAL, XI/130A/1, Natty, London, to his cousins, Paris, Nov. 28, 1907.
14   Michel, *Banques et banquiers*, pp. 56, 136f., 165, 168, 192; Wistrich, *Jews of Vienna*, p. 166; Heuberger, *Rothschilds*, pp. 132ff.; Mayer, *Persistence*, pp. 58f.; McCagg, *Jewish nobles*, p. 188.
15   *The Times*, March 18, 1909, p. 19.
16   Cf. *The Times*, April 1, 1909; *Outlook*, April 3. The latter periodical inferred that Natty envisaged increased borrowing—"a loan such as the City of London would take up in a few hours"—rather than taxation.
17   RAL, XI/130A/3, Natty, London, to his cousins, Paris, May 6, 1909.
18   Ferguson, "Public finance," *passim*; Hobson, "Wary Titan," *passim*.
19   RAL, XI/130A/1, Natty, London, to his cousins, Paris, Jan. 28, 1907.
20   Rothschild, *Dear Lord Rothschild*, p. 38.
21   *Ibid.*, pp. 26, 32, 322.
22   Allfrey, *Jewish court*, p. 216. Salisbury made Natty a Privy Councillor shortly before retiring as Prime Minister: Hatfield House, 3M, Natty to Salisbury, June 20, 1902.
23   On Rosebery in this period, see RAL, XI/130A/1, Natty, London, to his cousins, Paris, March 27, 1907; same to same, Aug. 14; RAL, XI/130A/2, March 13, 1908.
24   Robert Offley Ashburton Crewe-Milnes, Earl and later Marquess of Crewe, was Lord President of the Council from 1906 until 1908, Colonial Secretary until 1910 and then Secretary of State for India until 1915: *DNB*.
25   RAL, XI/130A/0, Natty, London, to his cousins, Paris, June 21, 1906. See also same to same, July 6; Ziegler, *Sixth great power*, p. 278.
26   Jay, *Chamberlain*, p. 251; Perkin, *Rise of professional society*, pp. 162f.; Mackay, *Balfour*, p. 88. Natty seemed to regard the creation of new private pension funds on an *ad hoc* basis as the only way to proceed: for his involvement in the Royal National Pension Fund for Nurses, see Maggs, *Century of change*, esp. pp. 21f.
27   RAL, T13/195, Alphonse, Paris, to his cousins, London, July 31, 1885; RAL, T15/38, same to same, Sept. 18, 1890; RAL, T15/39, Oct. 16; RAL, T15/40, Nov. 6; RAL, T16/154, Aug. 28, 1896; RAL, T16/160, Nov. 10.
28   Cassis, *City bankers*, p. 304; Kynaston, *City*, vol. I, p. 373; vol. II, p. 376.
29   Bahlman (ed.), *Hamilton diary*, pp. 442f.
30   Amery, *Chamberlain*, vol. VI, pp. 467f.
31   Cassis, *City bankers*, pp. 304ff.; Kynaston, *City*, vol. II, p. 379.
32   Kynaston, *City*, vol. II, pp. 382ff.

33 Bahlman (ed.), *Hamilton diary*, p. 455.

34 RAL, XI/130A/0, Natty, London, to his cousins, Paris, Jan. 9, 1906; same to same, Jan. 10.

35 RAL, XI/130A/0, Leo, London, to his cousins, Paris, Jan. 12, 1906; Natty to his cousins, Jan. 15; Jan. 16.

36 RAL, XI/130A/0, Leo, London, to his cousins, Paris, Jan. 26, 1906; Natty to his cousins, Jan. 29. Cf. Amery, *Chamberlain*, vol. VI, pp. 863, 867.

37 Kynaston, *City*, vol. II, pp. 414f.

38 RAL, XI/130A/0, Natty, London, to his cousins, Paris, Jan. 17, 1906; same to same, Jan. 24; Jan. 25.

39 RAL, XI/130A/0, Natty, London, to his cousins, Paris, Feb. 5, 1906; Leo, London, to his cousins, Paris, Feb. 7; Natty to his cousins, Feb. 8; same to same, Feb. 20; Feb. 21.

40 RAL, XI/130A/4, Natty, London, to his cousins, Paris, Jan. 13, 1910.

41 RAL, XI/130A/0, Natty, London, to his cousins, Paris, Feb. 21, 1906; same to same, Feb. 26; Feb. 23; March 5; March 21.

42 RAL, XI/130A/0, Natty, London, to his cousins, Paris, March 5, 1906; same to same, March 19; March 28; April 9; April 19; April 23; May 15.

43 RAL, XI/130A/0, Natty, London, to his cousins, Paris, April 3, 1906.

44 RAL, XI/130A/0, Natty, London, to his cousins, Paris, Feb. 19, 1906.

45 RAL, XI/130A/0, Natty, London, to his cousins, Paris, Nov. 2, 1906; same to same, Nov. 5; RAL, XI/130A/1, Leo to his cousins, Feb. 6, 1907; Natty to his cousins, Feb. 28; same to same, March 4; RAL, XI/130A/2, Jan. 20, 1908; Leo to his cousins, Feb. 14; Natty to his cousins, Feb. 17; Alfred to his cousins, Feb. 22; Natty to his cousins, March 25; same to same, Nov. 3.

46 RAL, XI/130A/0, Natty, London, to his cousins, Paris, Jan. 9, 1906; same to same, Jan. 10.

47 RAL, XI/130A/0, Natty, London, to his cousins, Paris, Jan. 22, 1906; same to same, Feb. 1; Feb. 19.

48 RAL, XI/130A/0, Natty, London, to his cousins, Paris, April 2, 1906; same to same, April 3.

49 RAL, XI/130A/0, Natty, London, to his cousins, Paris, May 2, 1906; same to same, May 5.

50 RAL, XI/130A/0, Natty, London, to his cousins, Paris, May 22, 1906; RAL, XI/130A/1, same to same, Jan. 22, 1907. See also Leo to his cousins, Jan. 30; Natty to his cousins, March 20.

51 RAL, XI/130A/1, Natty, London, to his cousins, Paris, May 24, 1906; same to same, June 14; June 22; June 29; July 2; July 3; Oct. 2; Oct. 3. See also Dec. 17.

52 RAL, XI/130A/1, Natty, London, to his cousins, Paris, March 14, 1907; same to same, April 12; June 17; June 18; July 22; July 31; Aug. 12; Aug. 15; Aug. 16; Sept. 26; Sept. 30; Nov. 26.

53 RAL, XI/130A/1, Natty, London, to his cousins, Paris, Feb. 19, 1907; same to same, April 2.

54 *Daily News*, Oct. 9, 1907. Cf. RAL, XI/130A/1, Natty, London, to his cousins, Paris, Oct. 10; same to same, Oct. 11.

55 RAL, XI/130A/2, Natty, London, to his cousins, Paris, March 4, 1908; Alfred to his cousins, March 18; Natty to his cousins, March 23; same to same, March 25. It was, he wrote, "a measure which threatened all kinds of property & might have inflicted severe harm in banking and financial circles, & if the principle embodied in this measure had once been conceded everything & everybody might be expropriated for the so-called benefit of the State & without any compensation." See also Leo to his cousins, April 9; Natty to his cousins, Oct. 21; same to same, Nov. 3; Nov. 24; Dec. 3.

56 RAL, XI/130A/3, Natty, London, to his cousins, Paris, Jan. 19, 1909; Alfred to his cousins, Feb. 17.

57 RAL, XI/130A/3, Natty, London, to his cousins, Paris, April 20, 1909; same to same, April 30; May 3.

58 RAL, XI/130A/3, Natty, London, to his cousins, Paris, May 10, 1909; Alfred to his cousins, May 13; Natty to his cousins, May 18; same to same, June 8; Leo to his cousins, June 22. Cf. *The Times*, May 20; June 5; June 9; June 12; June 18. The meeting was certainly not a purely Conservative affair: Schuster and Avebury were both present and also signed the earlier petition, but their criticisms of the budget were very different from Natty's and Schuster declined to join the Budget Protest League set up to continue the campaign: see Murray, *People's Budget*, p. 178; Kynaston, *City*, vol. II, pp. 494ff.; Lipman, "City," pp. 18ff.

59 *Parliamentary debates (official report): House of Lords*, 9 Edward VII, vol. IV, pp. 1153ff., Nov. 29, 1909.

60 RAL, XI/130A/4, Natty, London, to his cousins, Paris, Feb. 3, 1910.

61 RAL, XI/130A/0, Natty, London, to his cousins, Paris, May 2, 1906; same to same, May 15.

62 RAL, XI/130A/0, Natty, London, to his cousins, Paris, Jan. 9, 1906; same to same, Jan. 10.

63 RAL, XI/130A/1, Leo, London, to his cousins, Paris, Feb. 4, 1907; same to same, Feb. 6.

64 RAL, XI/130A/1, Natty, London, to his cousins, Paris, May 8, 1907; same to same, June 27.

65 RAL, XI/130A/2, Natty, London, to his cousins, Paris, Nov. 24, 1908; same to same, Dec. 3.

66 Grigg, *People's champion*, p. 200; RAL, XI/130A/3, Leo, London, to his cousins, Paris, June 22, 1907; Natty to his cousins, Aug. 25; AN, 132 AQ 5585/1M183, NMR to deRF, Sept. 10; RAL, XI/130A/3, Natty to his brothers, Oct. 4.

67 *The Times*, Nov. 23, 1909.

68 RAL, XI/130A/0, Natty, London, to his cousins, Paris, June 29, 1906; same to same, July 9; Oct. 2.

69 Lipman, "City," appendix VI.

70 RAL, XI/130A/1, Natty, London, to his cousins, Paris, March 12, 1907; same to same, May 29. Cf. Cassis, *City bankers*, p. 287.

71 RAL, XI/130A/1, Natty, London, to his cousins, Paris, April 19, 1907; Leo to his cousins, April 22; Natty to his cousins, April 24; same to same, May 6; May 13; May 21.

72 RAL, XI/130A/1, Natty, London, to his cousins, Paris, June 7, 1907; same to same, June 25; June 27; July 3. For a detailed explanation of the fall in the price of consols covering both economic and political factors, see July 31.

73 RAL, XI/130A/2, Natty, London, to his cousins, Paris, Jan. 17, 1908; same to same, Jan. 29; Feb. 28; March 3.

74 RAL, XI/130A/2, Leo, London, to his cousins, Paris, Feb. 14, 1908; Natty to his cousins, April 9; same to same, April 29; May 5; June 2; July 3; July 17; July 24; RAL, XI/130A/3, Feb. 16, 1909; March 5; March 10. Cf. Lipman, "City," pp. 45ff.

75 BL, MSS Asquith 99, ff. 156–7, Natty to Lloyd George, March 7, 1909 [printed for circulation to Cabinet]; *The Times*, Sept. 10; Sept. 20. Details in Murray, *People's Budget*, p. 158; Lipman, "City," pp. 32–45.

76 RAL, XI/130A/3, Natty, London, to his cousins, Paris, April 30, 1909; same to same, May 3; May 10; May 12; Alfred to his cousins, May 13; Natty to his cousins, May 14; same to same, July 23.

77 RAL, XI/130A/3, Natty, London, to his cousins, Paris, Dec. 1, 1909; RAL, XI/130A/4, same to same, Jan. 6, 1910. Cf. *Economist*, Dec. 4, 1909.

78 RAL, XI/130A/3, Natty, London, to his cousins, Paris, Aug. 30, 1909.

79 RAL, XI/130A/0, Natty, London, to his cousins, Paris, Nov. 5, 1906. See also RAL, XI/130A/3, same to same, Feb. 15, 1909.

80 RAL, XI/130A/0, Natty, London, to his cousins, Paris, Dec. 5, 1906; same to same, Dec. 10; Dec. 11; Dec. 12; Dec. 13.

81 RAL, XI/130A/1, Natty, London, to his cousins, Paris, Feb. 12, 1907; same to same, March 21.

82 RAL, XI/130A/1, Natty, London, to his cousins, Paris, April 2, 1907; same to same, April 12.

83 RAL, XI/130A/1, Natty, London, to his cousins, Paris, April 15, 1907; same to same, April 17; RAL, XI/130A/3, March 5, 1909; Oct. 5.

84 RAL, XI/130A/1, Leo, London, to his cousins, Paris, April 22, 1907. Cf. *Parliamentary debates (official report): House of Lords*, 9 Edward VII, vol. IV, pp. 1153f.

85 For details of the campaign RAL, XI/130A/3, Natty, London, to his cousins, Paris, July 6, 1909; same to same, July 8; July 9; Oct. 6; Nov. 15; Nov. 19; Dec. 8; Dec. 12; Dec. 13; Dec. 14; Dec. 16; Leo to his cousins, Dec. 17; same to same, Jan. 29; RAL, XI/130A/4, Natty to his cousins, Jan. 3; Alfred to his cousins, Jan. 4; Natty to his cousins, Jan. 6; same to same, Jan. 7; Jan. 11; Jan. 13; Alfred to his cousins, Jan. 14; Natty to his cousins, Jan. 18; same to same, Jan 19; Jan. 29.

86 RAL, XI/130A/4, Natty, London, to his cousins, Paris, Jan. 5, 1910.

87 RAL, XI/130A/1, Natty, London, to his cousins, Paris, Feb. 14, 1907.

88 RAL, XI/130A/2, Leo, London, to his cousins, Paris, Jan. 10, 1908. As Leo commented, "It certainly wants a great deal of tact to steer clear of Scylla and Charybdis, i.e. to work for Haldane on Friday and to speak publicly against his policy on Tuesday."

89 RAL, XI/130A/2, Leo, London, to his cousins, Paris, Feb. 7, 1908; same to same, Feb. 14; Natty to his cousins, Nov. 10; RAL, XI/130A/3, same to same, Feb. 9.

90 *The Times*, March 18, 1909; Kynaston, *City*, vol. II, pp. 492f.

91 *The Times*, June 25, 1909. Cf. Grigg, *People's champion*, pp. 197f.; Jenkins, *Balfour's poodle*, p. 87. The speech was addressed to a lunch given by the Land and Housing Reform Joint Committee.

92 RAL, XI/130A/3, Natty, London, to his cousins, Paris, June 25, 1909.

93 HoL, Lloyd George Papers C/33/2/19, cutting from *The Times*, Dec. 18, 1909.

94 Alderman, *British Jewry*, pp. 192f.; *idem, Jewish community*, pp. 83f.

95 *The Times*, December 29, 1909. Cf. RAL, XI/130A/3, Leo, London, to his cousins, Paris, Dec. 29. Cf. Vincent (ed.), *Crawford papers*, p. 136.

96   HoL, Lloyd George Papers C/34/1/8, cutting from *Western Daily Mercury*, Jan. 10, 1910: "Lord Roth-schild . . . knowing that this is a Free Trade country with a good deal of money to spare, gathers his money together and loans it to foreigners. And very properly! In a speech in the House of Lords not so long ago, he quoted his father as saying that there was nothing more fruitful for the trade of a country than the fact that it was able to advance money to foreign lands. I don't know why he quoted his father, unless he wanted to prove that wisdom is not always hereditary (laughter)." Cf. RAL, XI/130A/4, Natty, London, to his cousins, Paris, Jan. 11; same to same, Jan. 13. The two continued to quarrel publicly for many months. In 1913 Natty attacked Lloyd George's use of funds from the National Insurance scheme for building houses as "jerry building speculation": Rothschild, *Dear Lord Rothschild*, pp. 43f.

97   RAL, XI/130A/8, Natty, London, to his cousins, Paris, July 6, 1914.

98   RAL, XI/130A/8, Natty, London, to his cousins, Paris, July 10, 1914.

99   RAL, XI/130A/3, Natty, London, to his cousins, Paris, Aug. 30, 1909; RAL, XI/130A/4, same to same, Jan. 11, 1910.

100 RAL, XI/130A/4, Natty, London, to his cousins, Paris, Jan. 24, 1910.

101 Rowland, *Last Liberal governments*, p. 298.

102 RAL, XI/130A/4, Natty, London, to his cousins, Paris, Feb. 21, 1910; same to same, Feb. 23; Feb. 25; March 3; March 21; March 24; April 7.

103 Davis, *English Rothschilds*, pp. 240f.

104 Shannon, *Balfour and Ireland*, p. 194.

105 Davis, *English Rothschilds*, pp. 242f.

106 RAL, XI/130A/8, Natty, London, to his cousins, Paris, July 2, 1914; same to same, July 6; July 7; July 14; July 17.

107 Rothschild, *Dear Lord Rothschild*, p. 37.

108 HoL, Bonar Law Papers 12/2/48, Natty to Bonar Law, Jan. 2, 1911; 25/2/55, Lionel to Bonar Law, Feb. 26.

109 HoL, Bonar Law Papers 26/3/39, Steel-Maitland to Bonar Law, May 26, 1912. Cf. Blewett, *Peers, parties and people*, p. 461. For details see Ramsden (ed.), *Real old Tory politics*, pp. 25, 38; Vincent (ed.), *Crawford papers*, p. 286. Sassoon was nevertheless adopted as the Conservative and Unionist candidate and won the seat.

110 Kynaston, *City*, vol. II, pp. 542f.

111 Halévy, *Rule of democracy*, p. 666n.

112 Barth, *Hochfinanz*, p. 448.

113 Kynaston, *City*, vol. II, pp. 432f., 578f., 586ff.

114 RAL, XI/130A/8, Natty, London, to his cousins, Paris, March 16, 1914.

115 Rosenbaum and Sherman, *M. M. Warburg & Co.*, p. 111.

116 RAL, XI/130A/8, Natty, London, to his cousins, Paris, June 29, 1914. Cf. Cassis, *City bankers*, p. 309.

117 RAL, XI/130A/8, Natty, London, to his cousins, Paris, July 6, 1914.

118 RAL, XI/130A/8, Natty, London, to his cousins, Paris, July 14, 1914.

119 RAL, XI/130A/8, Natty, London, to his cousins, Paris, July 22, 1914.

120 RAL, XI/130A/8, Natty, London, to his cousins, Paris, July 23, 1914.

121 RAL, XI/130A/8, Natty, London, to his cousins, Paris, July 24, 1914.

122 RAL, XI/130A/8, Natty, London, to his cousins, Paris, July 27, 1914.

123 RAL, XI/130A/8, Natty, London, to his cousins, Paris, July 28, 1914; same to same, July 29.

124 RAL, XI/130A/8, Natty, London, to his cousins, Paris, July 30, 1914.

125 RAL, XI/130A/8, Natty, London, to his cousins, Paris, July 31, 1914.

126 RAL, XI/130A/8, Natty, London, to his cousins, Paris, July 27, 1914.

127 Brock and Brock (eds), *Asquith Letters to Venetia Stanley*, p. 131. RAL, XI/130A/8, Natty, London, to his cousins, Paris, July 28, 1914 (two letters); same to same, July 29.

128 Brock and Brock (eds), *Asquith letters to Venetia Stanley*, p. 131.

129 RAL, XI/130A/8, Natty, London, to his cousins, Paris, July 30, 1914.

130 RAL, XI/130A/8, Natty, London, to his cousins, Paris, July 31, 1914.

131 RAL, XI/130A/8, Natty, London, to his cousins, Paris, Aug. 4, 1914.

132 Rothschild, *Whims*, p. 36f.

133 Steed, *Thirty years*, vol. II, pp. 8f.; *The Times, History*, vol. IV, p. 208.

134 Barth, *Hochfinanz*, p. 455; Pulzer, *Jews and German state*, p. 201.

135   Joll, *Origins*, p. 30.
136   RAL, XI/130A/8, Natty, London, to his cousins, Paris, Aug. 4, 1914.
137   RAL, XI/130A/8, Natty, London, to his cousins, Paris, Aug. 14, 1914; same to same, Sept. 15.
138   AN, 132 AQ 5594/1M192, Alfred, London, to his cousins, Paris, Aug. 3, 1914.
139   Cohen, *Lady de Rothschild*, pp. 304f.
140   *Ibid.*, pp. 303f.
141   Lloyd George, *War memoirs*, vol. I, pp. 115f. Cf. Allfrey, *Jewish court*, p. 271.
142   Rothschild, *Dear Lord Rothschild*, p. 45; Kynaston, *City*, vol. II, p. 609.
143   Rothschild, *Dear Lord Rothschild*, p. 45.
144   Haldane, *Autobiography*, pp. 162f.
145   Wake, *Kleinwort Benson*, pp. 138–42, 207f.
146   Cecco, *Money and empire*, p. 160. Cf. RAL, XI/130A/8, Natty, London, to his cousins, Paris, Aug. 5, 1914.
147   *Ibid.*, pp. 161–7.
148   HoL, Lloyd George Papers C/11/2/2, Alfred and Leo to Lloyd George, Aug. 13, 1914. Cf. RAL, XI/130A/8, Natty, London, to his cousins, Paris, Aug. 14.
149   Bank of England G15/59 2481/3 f. 37, Memorandum by Lord Rothschild for the Chancellor of the Exchequer, Aug. 27, 1914; Lloyd George Papers C/11/2/6, Natty to Lloyd George, Aug. 31; RAL, XI/130A/8, Natty, London, to Edouard, Paris, Sept. 25.
150   Cecco, *Money and empire*, p. 164.
151   AN, 132 AQ 5594/1M192, Alfred to deRF, Aug. 8, 1914; NMR to deRF, Aug. 21; same to same, Aug. 28; RAL, XI/130A/8, Natty, London, to his cousins, Paris, Aug. 15.
152   See e.g. HoL, Lloyd George Papers C/4/14/20, Francis Bertie to Grey, Jan. 18, 1915.
153   AN, 132 AQ 34, NMR to deRF, Sept. 17, 1914; deRF to NMR, Sept. 18; NMR to deRF, Sept. 22; deRF to NMR, Sept. 23; NMR to deRF, Oct. 1; AN, 132 AQ 5594/1M192, NMR to deRF, Dec. 4.
154   Lottman, *Return*, pp. 157ff.
155   RAL, XI/130A/8, Natty, London, to his cousins, Paris, Aug. 4, 1914.
156   *Ibid.*, p. 160.

FOURTEEN   *Deluges (1915–1945)*

1   Cohen, *Lady de Rothschild*, pp. 312f.
2   *Western Morning News*, April 1, 1915.
3   *Financier and Bullionist*, April 1, 1915. See also *Daily Telegraph*, April 1.
4   For accounts of the funeral see *Daily Mirror*, April 3, 1915; *Reynolds*, April 4.
5   Dugdale, *Balfour*, p. 135.
6   Hertz, *Memorial sermon*, p. 10.
7   *New Witness*, April 8, 1915.
8   *Daily News and Leader*, April 1, 1915.
9   *Nation*, April 10, 1915.
10   RAL, RFamFD/7A, Charles de Rothschild, Memorandum, 1915.
11   Bagehot, *Lombard Street*, pp. 132ff.
12   Cassis, *City bankers*, p. 41n.
13   RAL, RFamC/21, Charlotte, London, to Leonora and Leo, Paris, Aug. 7, 1874; same to same, Aug. 11; Charlotte to Leo, July 28, 1875; same to same, March 24, 1876.
14   Rothschild, *Dear Lord Rothschild*, pp. 54ff.
15   *Ibid.*, pp. 104f.
16   *Ibid.*, pp. 230f., 254; Vincent (ed.), *Crawford papers*, p. 105. Rumour had it that his debts were in excess of £750,000. Thereafter, Walter was effectively pensioned off with an allowance to finance his researches and the Tring museum: *ibid.*, p. 222.
17   Rothschild, *Dear Lord Rothschild*, pp. 92f., 220ff. The author identifies the blackmailer only as a "peeress." On Walter's other amorous entanglements, see pp. 68, 104, 216–23.
18   *Ibid.*, p. 108.
19   BL, Add. MS 46064 f. 27, Walter to Herbert Gladstone, March 17, 1904; f. 170, same to same, March 18. Cf. Rothschild, *Dear Lord Rothschild*, pp. 226f.

20   Though it should be noted that like his brother he did dismally at Cambridge, obtaining a Third in finals: theirs was a talent unsuited to established academic institutions.

21   Rothschild, Garton and Rothschild, *Rothschild Gardens*, pp. 82–107. When he came across the property he was delighted to discover that his father already owned it.

22   I am grateful to Miriam Rothschild for details of her father's life.

23   Rothschild, Garton and Rothschild, *Rothschild gardens*, pp. 48–71; *The Times*, Sept. 3, 1903; Sept. 7, 1905. See also Harper, *Mr Lionel*.

24   Prevost-Marcilhacy, *Rothschild*, pp. 267–70; Souhami, *Bakst*. They were not completed until 1922 and are now at Waddesdon.

25   Rothschild, *Crosières autour de mes souvenirs, passim*; Rothschild, *Milady Vine*, pp. 5ff.

26   Rothschild, *Whims*, pp. 31f., 149.

27   On the elegant manoir Sans-Souci which he had built for himself near Chantilly, see Prevost-Marcilhacy, *Rothschild*, pp. 251–4.

28   Michel, *Banques et banquières*, pp. 121–35.

29   Morton, *Rothschilds*, pp. 215–17.

30   Wilson, *Rothschild*, p. 338.

31   Crewe, *Rosebery*, vol. II, pp. 649f. He was killed on the same day that Evelyn died of his wounds in hospital.

32   Cohen, *Lady de Rothschild*, pp. 307f.

33   *Ibid.*, pp. 312f. According to Cohen, "Her immaculate butler, Lester, used to open the door and proclaim, as though he were announcing a visitor: 'The Zeppelins, my Lady.'"

34   Cohen, *Lady de Rothschild*, pp. 304, 307.

35   *Ibid.*, p. 313.

36   *Ibid.*, p. 314.

37   HoL, Lloyd George Papers D/11/3/6, Printed pamphlet about the Volunteer Munitions Brigade, 1915; D/16/9/6, Marquess of Crewe to Lloyd George, Dec. 9.

38   HoL, Lloyd George Papers D/20/1/58, Alfred to Lloyd George, July 30, 1915; D/20/1/58A, Lloyd George to Charles, Aug. 2; D/20/1/69, Charles to Lloyd George, Aug. 3.

39   HoL, Lloyd George Papers F/72/16/3, Alfred to Lloyd George, Feb. 28, 1917.

40   Cohen, *Lady de Rothschild*, p. 311.

41   See e.g. HoL, Lloyd George Papers D/20/1/51, Alfred to Lloyd George, July 21, 1915.

42   Jenkins, *Asquith*, p. 462.

43   Palin, *Rothschild relish*, pp. 94f.

44   Peyrefitte, *Juifs*, p. 379; Lefebvre, "Rothschild," p. 16.

45   Walter served on committees of the Jewish Board of Guardians and the Jewish Peace Society; Lionel succeeded Leo as treasurer of the Board of Deputies; and the presidency of the United Synagogue remained in Rothschild hands until 1942. Cf. Rothschild, *Dear Lord Rothschild*; Alderman, *British Jewry*, pp. 211f.; Lipman, *Social service*, p. 257.

46   Black, *Social politics*, pp. 240f.

47   Levene, *War, Jews and the new Europe*, p. 30.

48   Lipman, *History of the Jews*, p. 144.

49   Levene, *War, Jews and the new Europe*, pp. 60f.

50   Kadish, *Bolsheviks and British Jews*, p. 60.

51   Born, *International banking*, p. 57.

52   Cohen, *Lady de Rothschild*, pp. 323f.

53   *Ibid.*, p. 325.

54   Rothschild, *Dear Lord Rothschild*, p. 234; Alter, "German-speaking Jews," p. 210.

55   Leo Baeck Institute, New York, Sally Bodenheimer Collection, AR 7169, 46, 47, letters from Hannah Mathilde, April 12, 1921; March 7, 1923; Feb. 27, 1924.

56   Wilson, *Rothschild*, pp. 339f. Cf. Mayorek, "Between East and West," pp. 139ff.

57   Rothschild, *Dear Lord Rothschild*, pp. 241f.; Lipman, *History of the Jews*, pp. 127f.

58   HoL, Lloyd George Papers F/45/2/4, C. P. Scott to Lloyd George, Feb. 5, 1917. See also F/3/2/28, R. G[raham] to Lord Hardinge, July 23.

59   Cohen, *Lady de Rothschild*, p. 315.

60   Black, *Social politics*, pp. 368f.

61   RAL, RFam AD/1/4, Leo to Lucien Wolf, Oct. 18, 1916. I am grateful to Lionel de Rothschild for this
     reference.
62   Finestein, *Jewish society*, p. 196.
63   Mackay, *Balfour*, p. 315.
64   Egremont, *Balfour*, pp. 294ff.; O'Brien, *Milner*, pp. 288, 325.
65   Dugdale, *Balfour*, p. 233.
66   Rothschild, *Dear Lord Rothschild*, pp. 235–69, 300f.; Sokolow, *History of Zionism*, vol. II, pp. 44–113;
     Weizmann, *Trial and error*, pp. 144–262; Litvinoff, *Essential Chaim Weizmann*, pp. 191ff.
67   Wilson, *Rothschild*, p. 342.
68   Lipman, *History of the Jews*, p. 132.
69   Black, *Social politics*, p. 380.
70   Anglo-Jewish Archives, Southampton University, AJ 232/1, Waley-Cohen, Stern and Swaythling to
     Lionel, May 5, 1919; AJ 232/2, Lionel to Waley-Cohen, Stern and Swaythling, May 7. Lionel was
     enthusiastic and funds were raised, though the scheme was never realised.
71   Black, *Social politics*, p. 384; Mayorek, "Between East and West," p. 141.
72   Black, *Social politics*, p. 381.
73   Mackay, *Balfour*, p. 317.
74   Egremont, *Balfour*, p. 295.
75   HoL, Lloyd George Papers F/3/4/8, A. J. B[alfour] to Curzon, Jan. 20, 1919.
76   For Jimmy's defence of Samuel, see HoL, Samuel Papers A 155 (viii) 127, Jimmy to Lady Samuel, Feb.
     3, 1922.
77   HoL, Lloyd George Papers F/92/16/2, Jimmy to Lloyd George, March 18, 1919. See also G/31/1/60,
     Jimmy to Lloyd George, Nov. 30, 1926.
78   HoL, Bonar Law Papers 115/5/102, Jimmy to Bonar Law, Oct. 22, 1922.
79   Mayorek, "Between East and West," p. 142. Cf. Heuberger, *Rothschilds*, pp. 159ff. He and his wife
     asked to be buried in Palestine after their deaths (in 1934 and 1935 respectively), though this did not
     happen until 1954. The PICA's assets were donated to the state of Israel after Jimmy's death in 1957.
80   HoL, Lloyd George Papers F/3/4/8, Alfred Mond to Lloyd George, Oct. 13, 1919. Cf. Mayorek,
     "Between East and West," pp. 140f.
81   RAL, RFamFD/13/E; Ziegler, *Sixth great power*, pp. 372–8; Roberts, *Schroders*, pp. 527–35.
82   Palin, *Rothschild relish*, pp. 1ff.
83   *Ibid.*, p. 63.
84   Rothschild, *Gilt-edged life*, pp. 82ff.
85   *Ibid.*, pp. 68, 78f.
86   *Ibid.*, p. 25.
87   Rothschild, *Dear Lord Rothschild*, p. 287.
88   Rothschild, *Whims*, pp. 57ff.
89   Ziegler, *Sixth great power*, p. 351.
90   Dayer, *Finance and empire*, p. 123.
91   Deutsche Bank (ed.), *Studies*, p. 501.
92   Ziegler, *Sixth great power*, pp. 352ff.
93   Rosenbaum and Sherman, *M. M. Warburg & Co.*, p. 136.
94   Rothschild, *Gilt-edged life*, pp. 123ff.
95   Wiskemann, *Czechs and Germans*, p. 115.
96   März, *Creditanstalt*, pp. 542f.
97   *Ibid.*, p. 130.
98   Lottman, *Return*, p. 191.
99   By contrast, Rothschild links to North America were few: the French house raised money for the Com-
     pagnie du Nord with a $15 million bond issue in New York, and returned the compliment by invest-
     ing—unwisely, as it proved—in the New York City Interborough Rapid Transit.
100 Fritsch, *External constraints*, p. 45. On the agreement reached in October 1914 to reschedule the Brazil-
     ian debt by partial suspension of interest and amortisation payments see *ibid.*, pp. 35ff.
101 Details in chapter 27.
102 Fritsch, *External constraints*, p. 90.
103 *Ibid.*, p. 91.

104 *Ibid.*, p. 117.

105 *Ibid.*, p. 155; Cain and Hopkins, *Crisis and deconstruction*, pp. 162ff.; Dayer, *Finance and empire*, pp. 161ff.

106 Turrell and van Helten, "Rothschilds, the Exploration Company and mining finance," pp. 197f., 201. By 1928 it was operating in twenty-two different countries with a host of different interests in metallurgy and chemicals.

107 Harvey, *Rio Tinto*, pp. 171, 217ff., 231.

108 Newbury, *Diamond Ring*, pp. 211, 259, 308.

109 Kynaston, *Cazenove*, pp. 113, 148.

110 Sir William Leese at Freshfield, Leese & Munns played a vital role in negotiations with Hungary, while Geoffrey Vickers played an analogous part with respect to Brazil: Palin, *Rothschild relish*, p. 104.

111 Green, *New world of gold*, pp. 113ff.; Green, "Precious heritage," pp. 455f.

112 After an initial period when the bidding was done by telephone, it was decided to hold a formal meeting in the Rothschild office. Represented were the four bullion brokers—Mocatta & Goldsmid, Pixley & Abell, Sharps & Wilkins and Samuel Montagu—and the other major refiner Johnson Matthey. Quaintly, all the bidders were given a small Union Jack flag which they could raise when they needed to telephone their head offices. When a flag went up, the bidding was suspended until it was lowered again.

113 Pringle, *Banking in Britain*, p. 66; Balogh, *Studies in financial organization*, pp. 213f., 218f. The South African mines entrusted their agency to the South African Reserve Bank in 1926 and in 1932 the Bank of England took over the role of principal seller, though N. M. Rothschild continued to act as the Bank's agent: Green, "Precious heritage," pp. 460, 497.

114 Green, "Precious heritage," pp. 460–64.

115 *Daily Telegraph*, 28 Aug., 1937.

116 Lottman, *Return*, p. 167.

117 Moreau, *Souvenirs*, for a hostile account.

118 Ziegler, *Sixth great power*, p. 351.

119 Lottman, *Return*, p. 164.

120 *Ibid.*, pp. 175ff.

121 Fritsch, *External constraints*, pp. 157f.

122 Palin, *Rothschild relish*, pp. 113f.

123 Dennett, *Slaughter and May*, pp. 49, 187.

124 See Eichengreen, *Golden fetters*, pp. 264–70.

125 Lottman, *Return*, p. 372. Interest on the loan was charged at 4 per cent until the end of 1933 and 5 per cent thereafter; the money itself was from the French Rothschilds' private fortunes: Edmond put up 70 million francs, Edouard 35 million, Robert 15 million, Henri 10 million, his son James 3 million and Philippe also 3 million.

126 *Ibid.*, p. 192.

127 *Ibid.*, p. 193.

128 Stiefel, "Reconstruction of Credit-Anstalt," pp. 414ff.

129 Born, *International banking*, p. 275.

130 Kopper, "Rothschild family," pp. 322f.

131 Palin, *Rothschild relish*, p. 106.

132 *Ibid.*, pp. 106ff.

133 See Lefebvre, "Rothschild," p. 17.

134 Rothschild, *Whims*, pp. 38ff.; Piatigorsky, *Jump*, pp. 5ff. See also Rothschild, *Milady Vine*, pp. 4ff.

135 Rothschild, *Gilt-edged life*, pp. 5ff.

136 Rothschild, *Milady Vine*, pp. 10–117. After dabbling in cinema, Philippe eventually devoted his energies to developing the vineyards on his father's estate at Mouton. It was he who introduced the practice of château-bottling after the war.

137 Rothschild, *Gilt-edged life*, p. 21.

138 Nicolson (ed.), *Vita and Harold*, p. 301.

139 Rothschild, Garton and Rothschild, *Rothschild gardens*, pp. 148ff. The offer was refused.

140 I am grateful to Miriam Rothschild for this information.

141 33 rue du Faubourg St Honoré was acquired by the Cercle de l'Union Interalliée in 1920; two years

later the house in the rue Berryer was given to the state; and the villa Ephrussi on the Riviera was left to the Académie des Beaux Arts in 1934: Prevost-Marcilhacy, *Rothschild*, p. 242.

142 Alter, "German-speaking Jews," p. 210.

143 Rubinstein, *History of the Jews*, p. 231.

144 Palin, *Rothschild relish*, pp. 118ff.

145 Cohen, *Mangeclous*, esp. pp. 59ff., 124.

146 Roth, *Magnificent Rothschilds*, p. 284. Anthony's daughters Annie and Constance died in 1926 and 1931; Natty's widow Emma in 1935; and Leo's widow Marie in 1937.

147 Rothschild, *Meditations*, p. 17.

148 Bower, *Perfect English spy*, pp. 47f., 63. According to Bower, he went so far as to stuff a bundle of Ultra documents through the Soviet embassy's letter-box.

149 Costello and Tsarev, *Illusions*, p. 222.

150 The fact that the government explicitly denied that Victor Rothschild was the "fifth man" in 1986 did not prevent an entire book being written in 1994 insisting—on the basis of wholly circumstantial evidence—that he was: Perry, *Fifth Man*. To some extent, Victor's dabbling in the Byzantine internal politics of MI5—in particular, his relationship with Peter Wright—was to blame for encouraging this notion. As Victor discovered while at the CPRS, Wright firmly believed that the former director-general of MI5, Roger Hollis, had been a Soviet agent. (Victor also knew of Wright's involvement in the MI5 attempt to smear Harold Wilson and other Labour politicians as communists after 1974.) When speculation began about his own role following the exposure of his friend Anthony Blunt in 1979, Victor rashly turned to Wright, now living in embittered retirement in Australia. In the belief that the allegations against Hollis would distract attention from himself, Victor encouraged Wright to collaborate with Chapman Pincher on the book *Their trade is treachery* (1981). This backfired badly when, five years later, Wright decided to publish his own book *Spycatcher* in defiance of the British government. The ensuing trial brought Victor more unwelcome publicity. In a final effort to clear his name, Victor wrote to a letter to the *Daily Telegraph* in which he demanded public exoneration from the head of MI5. Mrs Thatcher's response, though formally sufficient, was frosty in its tone—reflecting her reluctance to comment on intelligence matters: "I am informed that we have no evidence that he was ever a Soviet agent."

151 See Rothschild, *Window, passim*, and Rothschild, *Gilt-edged life*, pp. 45ff.

152 Lottman, *Return*, p. 197.

153 Lefebvre, "Rothschild," pp. 17f.; Rothschild, *Whims*, pp. 62ff.

154 The phrase derived from the fact that only the 200 largest shareholders in the Banque de France could vote at its General Assembly.

155 Lottman, *Return*, pp. 202ff.

156 *Ibid.*, p. 204.

157 *Ibid.*, p. 195.

158 Kopper, "Rothschild family," pp. 321ff.

159 Heuberger, *Rothschilds*, pp. 191ff. They were the Clementine Interdenominational Girls' Hospital at Bornheimer Landwehr; the Baron Carl von Rothschild public library; the Anselm Salomon von Rothschild Foundation for the Arts and the Old People's Home for Jewish Gentlewomen named after Wilhelm Carl and Mathilde.

160 Rothschild, *Dear Lord Rothschild*, plate 39c.

161 Kopper, "Rothschild family," pp. 321ff. The Grüneburg house was destroyed by bombs in 1944, but the house at Königstein survived.

162 Ziegler, *Edward VIII*, p. 343.

163 This was a complex operation for two reason: first, the other major shareholders, the Gutmanns, had to be bought out; second, the transfer had to be made indirectly via Swiss and Dutch institutions to avoid possible confiscation by the British government in the event of a future war.

164 Nicholas, *Rape*, p. 39.

165 Kopper, "Rothschild family," pp. 326ff.

166 Morton, *Rothschilds*, pp. 220–28. Cf. Lang, *Karl Wolff*, pp. 89f.

167 Kopper, "Rothschild Family," pp. 326ff.; Overy, "Göring's Multi-national Empire," pp. 271ff. See also Heimann-Jelinek, "'Aryanization' of Rothschild assets," pp. 351–64.

168 Nicholas, *Rape*, pp. 41ff.

169   Rubinstein, *History of the Jews*, p. 334; Rothschild, *Gilt-edged life*, pp. 85ff. Anthony became appeal chairman in 1939 as well as being chairman of the Emigration Planning Committee for Refugees. He, Lionel and Jimmy were also on the appeal committee of the Council for German Jewry set up in 1936.

170   Chernow, *Warburgs*, pp. 389, 436.

171   Victor had experienced at first hand the English version of anti-Semitism: at Harrow he remembered being called a "dirty little Jew," and in 1934 (when he was twenty-four) he had been refused membership of a "road house" and country club in Barnet on religious grounds: Rubinstein, *History of the Jews*, pp. 291f.

172   *Daily Telegraph*, Oct. 26, 1938.

173   *Ibid.*, Dec. 10, 1938.

174   *Ibid.*, March 20, 1939.

175   *Ibid.*, Aug. 1, 1946.

176   Lottman, *Return*, p. 209. The second sentence did not appear in the official minutes, but was reported in the press.

177   Costello and Tsarev, *Illusions*, pp. 235, 239ff.

178   Lottman, *Return*, p. 211.

179   Heuberger, *Rothschilds*, p. 157.

180   Rothschild, *Whims*, pp. 84–145.

181   Rothschild, *Milady Vine*, pp. 118ff.

182   For example, Edouard was incensed when, following the recovery of Algeria in 1942, the Free French General Giraud failed to restore the Crémieux legislation granting citizenship to the Algerian Jews.

183   Nicholas, *Rape*, p. 308.

184   Lottman, *Return*, p. 240.

185   *Ibid.*, pp. 219ff., 241ff., 246–9. Cf. Prevost-Marcilhacy, *Rothschild*, p. 152.

186   Nicholas, *Rape*, pp. 127ff. The proceeds supposedly went to French war orphans.

187   Lottman, *Return*, p. 259.

188   Nicholas, *Rape*, p. 345.

189   *Ibid.*, pp. 315ff.

190   Rothschild, *Gilt-edged life*, pp. 90ff.

191   RAL, P. C. Hoyland, "New Court Great War 1939–1945. Attack by the German Luftwaffe on the City of London on the night of Saturday 10th May, 1941."

192   Rothschild, Garton and Rothschild, *Rothschild gardens*, pp. 67ff., 92ff.

193   *Ibid.*, p. 94.

194   Rothschild, *Dear Lord Rothschild*, p. 323.

195   Rothschild, *Milady Vine*, p. 142.

196   Rothschild, *Gilt-edged life*, pp. 121f.

EPILOGUE

1   Plumb, *Vintage Memories*, p. 6f. I am grateful to Sir John Plumb for this reference.

2   Jimmy had been one of those who donated £5,000 towards the purchase of the cash-strapped Churchill's house at Chartwell in 1946 to allow the Premier to go on living there: Gilbert, "*Never despair*," p. 256.

3   I have followed Roberts, *Schroders*, in dropping the umlaut (as in Schröder) after 1939, though it fell into disuse gradually between 1930 and 1957.

4   Construction on the Churchill Falls did not begin until 1966; but in 1974, just three years after the plant had been opened, a new government in Newfoundland decided on nationalisation, paying Brinco $160 million in compensation (compared with total construction costs of $1 billion): Rothschild, *Gilt-edged life*, pp. 144ff., 184ff.

5   Anthony gave Palace House at Newmarket to the Jockey Club in 1944 and Ascott to the National Trust in 1950; Jimmy left Waddesdon to the National Trust in 1957; Mentmore and its contents were sold in 1977 and Tring is now a school run by the Arts Education Trust. In France, the villa Rothschild in Cannes passed out of family hands, as did the house at Boulogne, the châteaux des Fontaines, de la Muette and de Laversine, and the houses in the rue Saint-Florentin and the rue du Faubourg-Saint-Honoré. Cf. Prevost-Marcilhacy, *Rothschild*, esp. pp. 282f., 306–32.

6   Siegmund Warburg had proposed such a merger to Edmund as early as 1955: Rothschild, *Gilt-edged life*, p. 183.

7   Other examples from this period included the former chairman of the Electricity Council Sir Francis Tombs, who became a non-executive director in 1980, and the former Under-Secretary for Trade Iain Sproat, who joined N. M. Rothschild as a consultant after losing his seat in the 1983 election.

8   N. M. Rothschild paid $9.2 million for a 9.9 per cent shareholding in Smith Brothers and $7 million for a 51 per cent stake in what became Smith New Court—in all, an investment of around £10 million. Big Bang ended the strict separation of banks, brokers (who dealt with the public) and jobbers (who executed transactions on the stock exchange).

9   Lawson, *View from No. Eleven*, pp. 757ff.

10 Clients included Sir James Goldsmith, the Reichmann brothers' Olympia & York and the Hanson Trust—not to mention Robert Maxwell, whose campaign to acquire an American publishing house Pirie backed, earning fees worth $17 million in the process: Bower, *Maxwell*, pp. 20, 94, 98f. When Maxwell died in 1991, leaving a legacy of peculation and towering debt, it was N. M. Rothschild which was called in to investigate his books and arrange the sale of his heirs' 54 per cent stake in Mirror Group Newspapers.

11 It had at least symbolic significance that many of the French family's most treasured houses, including Ferrières, were disposed of in this period. The house in the rue du Monceau was destroyed; 23 avenue de Marigny was sold to the state in 1975; Ferrières was given to the Sorbonne in 1975; Sans-Souci, Gouvieux, was sold in 1977 and is now a hotel, as is the abbaye des Vaux-de-Cernay; the château d'Armain-villiers was sold in the 1980s to the King of Morocco.

12 The others are Schröders, Flemings and Lazards.

13 CPHDCM, 637/1/7/53–69, Vollständige Abschrift des Societäts-Vertrags . . . Übereinkunft, July 30, 1836.

APPENDICES

1   Flandreau, "Emergence," pp. 1–23.

2   Armstrong and Jones, *Business documents*, pp. 137–53.

PRINCIPAL ARCHIVES, LIBRARIES AND MANUSCRIPT COLLECTIONS USED

Anglo-Jewish Archives, University of Southampton
Archives Nationales, Paris
Bank of England, London
Bayerisches Hauptstaatsarchiv
Birmingham University Library
Bodleian Library, Oxford
British Library, London
Cambridge University Library
Centre for the Preservation of Historical
    Documentary Collections, Moscow
Geheimes Staatsarchiv Preussischer Kulturbesitz,
    Berlin-Dahlem
Hessisches Staatsarchiv, Marburg
House of Lords Record Office
Institut für Stadtgeschichte, Frankfurt

Jüdisches Museum, Frankfurt
Leo Baeck Institute, New York
London School of Economics Library
Mecklenburgisches Landeshauptsarchiv Schwerin
National Library of Scotland
Rhodes House, Oxford
Rosebery Papers, Dalmeny House and Barnbougle
    Castle, Edinburgh
Rothschild Archive, London
Royal Archives, Windsor Castle
Salisbury Papers, Hatfield House
The Times Archive, London
Thüringisches Hauptstaatsarchiv, Weimar
University College, London
Warburg Institute, London

SECONDARY SOURCES

Achterberg, Erich, *Frankfurter Bankherren* (Frankfurt am Main, 1956)

Acton, Harold, *The Bourbons of Naples* (London, 1956)

Adam, Andrew E., *Beechwoods and bayonets: The book of Halton* (Buckingham, 1983)

Adler, Hermann, "*Remember the Poor*": *A Sermon preached in memory of the late Baroness Lionel de Rothschild at the Central Synagogue, March 22, 1884* (London, 1884)

Agulhon, Maurice, *The Republican experiment, 1848–52* (Cambridge, 1983)

Albert, Harold A., *Queen Victoria's sister: The life and letters of Princess Feodora* (London, 1967)

Alderman, Geoffrey, *The Jewish community in British politics* (Oxford, 1982)

———, *The Federation of Synagogues, 1887–1987* (London, 1987)

———, *Modern British Jewry* (Oxford, 1992)

Alice, Countess of Athlone, *For my grandchildren: Some reminiscences of Her Royal Highness Princess Alice* (London, 1966)

Allfrey, Anthony, *Man of arms: The life and legend of Sir Basil Zaharoff* (London, 1989)

———, *Edward VII and his Jewish court* (London, 1991)

Alter, Peter, "German-speaking Jews as patrons of the arts and sciences in Edwardian England ," in Werner E. Mosse and Julius Carlebach (eds), *Second chance: Two centuries of German-speaking Jews in the United Kingdom* (Tübingen, 1991), pp. 209–19

Amery, Leopold, *Joseph Chamberlain and the Tariff Reform campaign: The life of Joseph Chamberlain*, vols V and VI (London, 1969)

Andrew, Christopher, *Théophile Delcassé and the making of the Entente Cordiale* (London, 1968)

Anon. [? Heinrich Doering], *Die Familie Rothschild und die Fugger: Lebensgeschichte der Gründer und der vorzuglichsten Glieder dieser Häusern* (Liepzig, 1837)

————, *The Hebrew Talisman* (London, 1840)

———— [David M. Evans], *The City or, the physiology of London business: with sketches on 'change, and at the coffee houses* (London, 1845)

————, *Jugement rendu contre Rothschild et contre Georges Dairnvaell, auteur de l'histoire de Rothschild 1er, par la Tribunal de la saine raison, accompagné d'un jugement sur l'accident de Fampoux* (Paris, 1846)

————, *Rothschild: Ein Urtheilspruch vom menchlichen Standpunkt aus* (Herisau, 1846)

———— [F. A. Steinmann], *Das Haus Rothschild: Seine Geschichte und seine Geschäft. Aufschlüsse und Enthüllungen zur Geschichte des Jahrhunderts, insbesondere des Staatsfinanz-und Börsewesens* (Prague/Leipzig, 1857)

————, *M. Mirès et M. de Rothschild* (Paris, 1861)

———— [Charlotte de Rothschild], *Addresses to young children, originally delivered in the Girls' Free School, Bell Lane* (London, 1861, 2nd edn, 1864)

————, *Gewaltsachen: Eine Auswahl der besten jüdischen Anekdoten, illustriert von Wilhelm Scholz* (Berlin, 1866)

————, *Der Ruin des Mittelstandes* (n.p. [Vienna?], n.d. [1891?])

————, [Constance Battersea], *Light on the way* (London, 1900)

————, *Histoire d'une famille regnante: Les Rothschild, par un petit porteur de fonds russes, série I* (Paris, 1925)

————, *Le pillage par les allemandes des oeuvres d'art et des bibliothèques appartenant à des Juifs an France* (Paris, 1947)

Apostol, P. N., M. V. Bernatzky and A. M. Michelson, *Russian public finances during the war* (New Haven, 1928)

Apponyi, comte Rudolf, *Vingt-cinq ans à Paris (1826–50)*, 4 vols (Paris, 1914)

Aris, Stephen, *The Jews in business* (London, 1970)

Armstrong, John, and Stephanie Jones, *Business documents: Their origins, sources and use in historical research* (London/New York, 1987)

Arnaud, E. Baron de Vitrolles, *Mémoires et réflections politiques: Mémoires de Vitrolles*, 3 vols (Paris, 1951)

Arnsberg, Paul, *Die Geschichte der Frankfurter Juden seit der Französischen Revolution*, 3 vols (Frankfurt, 1983)

Aronson, Theo, *Victoria and Disraeli* (London, 1977)

Artz, Frederick B., *France under the Bourbon Restoration, 1814–30* (Cambridge, Mass., 1931)

Askew, William C., *Europe and Italy's acquisition of Libya, 1911–12* (Durham, North Carolina, 1942)

Aspey, Melanie, "Mrs Rothschild," in Victor Gray (ed.), *The life and times of N. M. Rothschild 1777–1836* (London, 1998), pp. 58–67

Aspinall, A. (ed.), *The letters of King George IV, 1812–30*, 3 vols (Cambridge, 1938)

———— (ed.), *Politics and the press, c.* 1780–1850 (London, 1949)

Atkins, H. G., *Heine* (London, 1929)

Aycard, M., *Histoire du Crédit Mobilier, 1852–67* (Bruxelles/Leipzig/Livorno, 1867)

Ayer, J., *A century of finance, 1804 to 1904: The London house of Rothschild* (London, 1904)

Backhaus, Fritz (ed.), *"Und groß war bei der Tochter Jehudas Jammer und Klage . . ." Die Ermordung der Frankfurter Juden im Jahre 1241* (Frankfurt am Main, 1991)

————, " '. . . da dergleichen Geschäfte eigentlich durch große Konkurrenz gewinnen': Meyer Amschel Rothschild in Kassel," in Stadtsparkasse Kassel, "*. . . da dergleichen Geschäfte eigentlich durch große Konkurrenz gewinnen*" (Kassel, 1994), pp. 9–61

————, "Die Rothschilds und das Geld: Bilder und Legenden," in Johannes Heil and Bernd Wacker (eds), *Shylock? Zinsverbot und Geldverleih in jüdischer und christlicher Tradition* (Munich, 1997), pp. 147–70

————, "The last of the court Jews—Mayer Amschel Rothschild and his sons," in Vivian B. Mann and Richard I. Cohen (eds), *From court Jews to the Rothschilds: Art, patronage, and power, 1600–1800* (New York, 1997), pp. 79–95

————, "The Jewish ghetto in Frankfurt," in Victor Gray (ed.), *The Life and times of N. M. Rothschild 1777–1836* (London, 1998), pp. 22–33

———— and Heike Drummer, *Museum Judengasse: Katalog der Dauerausstellung* (Frankfurt am Main, 1992)

Bagehot, Walter, *Lombard Street: A description of the money market* (London, 1873)

Bahlman, Dudley W. R. (ed.), *The diary of Sir Edward Walter Hamilton, 1885–1906* (Hull, 1993)

Bairoch, Paul, "Europe's gross national product: 1800–1975," *Journal of European Economic History* (1976), pp. 273–340

Baker, Kenneth, *The turbulent years: My life in politics* (London, 1993)

Balderston, Theo, "War finance and inflation in Britain and Germany, 1914–1918," *Economic History Review* (1989), pp. 222–44

Balfour, Lady Frances, *The life of George, 4th Earl of Aberdeen*, vol. I (Paris, 1922)

Balla, I., *The romance of the Rothschilds* (London, 1913)

Balogh, Thomas, *Studies in financial organization*, National Institute of Economic and Social Research, Economic & Social Studies, vol. VI (Cambridge, 1947)

Balzac, Honoré de, *Lettres à l'étrangère, 1845–1846*, vol. III (Paris, 1933)

———, *Correspondance*, 5 vols, ed. Roger Pierrot (Paris, 1962)

———, *La comédie humaine*, vol. III: *Etudes de moeurs: Scènes de la vie privée. Le père Goriot* (Paris, 1976)

———, *La comédie humaine*, vol. VI: *Etudes de moeurs: Scènes de la vie parisienne: La maison Nucingen* (Paris, 1977)

———, *La comédie humaine*, vol. VI: *Un homme d'affaires* (Paris, 1914)

———, *La comédie humaine*, vol. VI: *Etude de moeurs: Scènes de la vie parisienne. César Birotteau* (Paris, 1976)

———, *La comédie humaine*, vol. VI: *Etudes de moeurs: Scènes de la vie parisienne. Splendeurs et misères des courtisanes* (Paris, 1977)

———, *La comédie humaine*, vol. VII: *Etudes de moeurs: Scènes de la vie parisienne (suite). La cousine Bette* (Paris, 1977)

Banquier [pseud.], *Que nous veut-on avec ce Rothschild Ier, roi des juifs et dieu de la finance?* (Bruxelles, 1846)

Barany, George, *Stephen Széchenyi and the awakening of Hungarian nationalism* (Princeton, 1968)

Barea, Ilse, *Vienna* (London, 1966)

Barnett, R. D., "A diary that survived: Damascus 1840," in Sonia and Vivian D. Lipman (eds), *The century of Moses Montefiore* (Oxford, 1985), pp. 149–70

Baron, Joseph L. (ed.), *A treasury of Jewish quotations* (London, 1965)

Bartetzko, Dieter, "Fairy tales and castles: On Rothschild family buildings in Frankfurt on Main," in Heuberger (ed.), *Essays*, pp. 221–44

Barth, Boris, *Die deutsche Hochfinanz und die Imperialismen: Banken und Außenpolitik vor 1914* (Stuttgart, 1995)

Barthélemy, *Le peuple Juif: A M. le Baron de Rothschild* (Paris, 1847)

Barthélemy, J., "La Banque, auxiliaire de l'Etat: I," *L'Information* (Dec. 13, 1932)

Battenberg, Friedrich, *Das europäische Zeitalter der Juden*, 2 vols (Darmstadt, 1990)

Battersea, Constance (ed.), *Lady de Rothschild: Extracts from the notebooks with a preface by her daughter* (London, 1912)

———, *Waifs and strays* (London, 1921)

———, *Reminiscences* (London, 1922)

Bauer, Hans-Peter, *Merchant banks*, Bankwirtschaftliche Forschungen, 57 (Bern/Stuttgart, 1979)

Bauer, Max, *Bismarck und Rothschild* (Dresden, 1891)

Bäuerle, Adolf, *Wien vor zwanzig Jahren: oder Baron Rothschild und die Tischlerstochter* (Pest/Wien/Leipzig, 1855)

Baumier, Jean, *Les grandes affaires françaises* (Paris, 1967)

———, *Ces banquiers qui nous gouvernent* (Paris, 1983)

Beales, Derek, *From Castlereagh to Gladstone, 1815–1885* (London, 1969)

Beck, Karl, *Lieder vom armen Mann, mit einem Vorwort an das Haus Rothschild* (Leipzig, 1846)

Beer, Adolf, *Die Finanzen Österreichs im IX. Jahrhundert* (Vienna, 1873, repr. 1877)

Bender [Johann Heinrich], *Ueber den Verkehr mit Staatspapieren in seinen Hauptrichtungen . . . Als Beylageheft zum Archiv für die Civilist[ische] Praxis*, vol. VIII (Heidelberg, 1825)

Benson, A. C. and R. Esher (eds), *The letters of Queen Victoria: A selection from Her Majesty's correspondence between the years 1837 and 1861*, 3 vols (London, 1908)

Berend, Ivan T. and Györgi Ranki, *Economic development in East-Central Europe in the 19th and 20th centuries* (New York/London, 1974)

Bergeron, Louis, *Banquiers, négociants et manufacturiers parisiens du Directoire à l'Empire* (Paris, 1978)

———, *Les Rothschild et les autres: La gloire des banquiers* (Paris, 1991)

———, "The myth of the banker in France in the 19th and 20th centuries," in Heuberger (ed.), *Essays*, pp. 297–306

Berghoeffer, C. W., *Meyer Amschel Rothschild: Der Gründer des Rothschildscher Bankhauses* (Frankfurt am Main, 1924)

Bermant, Chaim, *The Cousinhood: The Anglo-Jewish gentry* (London, 1971)

Bertaut, Jules, *La bourse anécdotique et pittoresque* (Paris, 1933)

Bertier de Sauvigny, Guillaume André de, *Metternich and his times* (London, 1962)

———, *Metternich et la France après le congrès de Vienne* (Paris, 1968)

————, *Nouvelle histoire de Paris: La Restauration, 1815–1830* (Paris, 1977)

Bethmann, Johann Philipp Freiherr von, " 'Er kannte keine größere Wonne als Wohltun': Mayer Amschel Rothschild," in Hans Sarkowicz (ed.), *Die großen Frankfurter* (Frankfurt am Main/Leipzig, 1994)

Billig, Joseph, *Le Commissariat Général aux Questions Juives (1941–1944)*, vol. I (Paris, 1960)

Bismarck, Otto von, *Die Gesammelten Werke*, vol. XIV, 1 and 2: *Briefe 1822–1898* (Berlin, 1933)

Black, David, *The King of Fifth Avenue: The fortunes of August Belmont* (New York, 1981)

Black, Eugene C., *The social politics of Anglo-Jewry, 1880–1920* (Oxford, 1988)

Black, Gerry, *JFS: A history of the Jews' Free School, London, since 1732* (London, 1997)

Blake, Robert, *Disraeli* (London, 1966)

———— and Wm Roger Louis (eds), *Churchill* (Oxford, 1993)

Blakiston, Georgina, *Lord William Russell and his wife, 1815–1846* (London, 1972)

Blanchard, Marcel, *Le Second Empire* (Paris, 1950)

————, "The railway policy of the Second Empire," in F. Crouzet, W. H. Chaloner and W. M. Stern (eds), *Essays in European economic history* (London, 1969), pp. 98–112

Blewett, Neal, *The peers, the parties and the people: The general elections of 1910* (London, 1972)

Blount, Edward, *Memoirs of Sir Edward Blount KCB (1815–1902)* (London, 1902)

Blum, Jerome, "Transportation and industry in Austria, 1815–48," *Journal of Modern History* (1943), pp. 24–38

Blumberg, A., *A carefully planned accident* (London, 1990)

Blunt, Anthony (ed.), *The James A. de Rothschild collection at Waddesdon Manor*, 11 vols (Fribourg, Switzerland, 1967–)

Bocher, Charles, *Mémoires de Charles Bocher, 1816–1907: Précédés par des souvenirs de famille, 1760–1816* (Paris, 1907)

Boehme, H., *The foundation of the German Empire* (Oxford, 1971)

Boime, Albert, "Entrepreneurial patronage in nineteenth century France," in Edward C. Carter, Robert Forster and Joseph N. Moody (eds), *Enterprise and entrepreneurs in nineteenth and twentieth century France* (Baltimore/London, 1976), pp. 137–209

Bontoux, E., *L'Union Générale: Sa vie, sa mort, son programme* (Paris, 1888)

Borchardt, Knut "Währung und Wirtschaft in Deutschland," in Deutsche Bundesbank (ed.), *Währung und Wirtschaft in Deutschland, 1876–1975* (Frankfurt am Main, 1976), pp. 1–53

Born, Karl Erich, *International banking in the nineteenth and twentieth centuries* (Leamington Spa, 1983)

Börne, Ludwig, *Mittheilungen aus dem Gebiete der Länder-und Völkerkunde, zweiter Theil* (Offenbach, 1833)

Bosworth, R. J. B., "Italy and the end of the Ottoman Empire," in Kent, Marian (ed.), *The great powers and the end of the Ottoman Empire* (London, 1984), pp. 52–75

Bourne, Kenneth, *Palmerston: The early years, 1784–1841* (London, 1982)

Bouvier, Jean, *Les Rothschild* (Paris, 1960)

————, *Le krach de l'Union Générale (1878–1885)* (Paris, 1960)

————, *Le Crédit Lyonnais de 1863 à 1882* (Paris, 1961)

————, *Un siècle de banque française* (Paris, 1973)

Bower, Tom, *Maxwell: The final verdict* (London, 1995)

————, *The perfect English spy: Sir Dick White and the secret war, 1935–90* (London, 1995)

Bowie, Karen, "The Rothschilds, the railways and the urban form of 19th century Paris," in Heuberger (ed.), *Essays*, pp. 87–98

Bradford, Sarah, *Disraeli* (London, 1982)

Bramsen, Bo and Kathleen Wain, *The Hambros, 1779–1979* (London, 1979)

Brandenburg, Erich, *From Bismarck to the World War: A history of German foreign policy* (Oxford, 1933)

Brandt, Harm-Heinrich, "Public finances of neo-absolutism in Austria in the 1850s: Integration and modernisation," in Peter-Christian Witt (ed.), *Wealth and taxation in Central Europe* (Leamington Spa/Hamburg/New York, 1987), pp. 81–109

Brassey, Maria, "Visitors to Waddesdon Manor, 1881–1898," unpublished MS, RAL (n.d.)

Braudel, Fernand and Ernest Labrousse, *Histoire économique et sociale de la France*, vol. III: *L'avènement de l'ère industrielle, 1789–1880* (Paris, 1976)

Brewer, John, *The sinews of power: War, money and the English state, 1688–1783* (London, 1989)

Brewitz, Walther, *Die Familie Rothschild* (Stuttgart, 1939)

Bridge, F. R., *Great Britain and Austria–Hungary, 1906–14: A diplomatic history* (London, 1972)

Briggs, Asa, *The age of improvement, 1783–1867* (London/New York, 1959)

————, *Victorian things* (London, 1988)

————, *Victorian people* (Chicago, 1995)

Bright, John (ed.), *Speeches on questions of public policy, by Richard Cobden MP*, ed. James E. Thorold Rogers (London, 1880)

Brock, Michael, *The Great Reform Act* (London, 1973)

———— and Eleanor Brock (eds), *H. H. Asquith, letters to Venetia Stanley* (Oxford, 1982)

Brockhaus, F. A., *Allgemeine deutsche Real-Enzyklopädie für die gebildeten Stände: Conversations Lexikon*, 7th edn, vol. IX (Leipzig, 1827)

————, *Allgemeine deutsche Real-Enzyklopädie für die gebildeten Stände: Conversations Lexikon*, 8th edn, vol. IX (Leipzig, 1836)

————, *Allgemeine deutsche Real-Enzyklopädie für die gebildeten Stände: Conversations Lexikon*, 9th edn, vol. XII (Leipzig, 1847)

————, *Allgemeine deutsche Real-Enzyklopädie für die gebildeten Stände: Conversations Lexikon*, 11th edn, vol. XII (Leipzig, 1867)

Brogan, D. W., *The French nation from Napoleon to Pétain, 1814–1940* (London, 1957)

Brooks, David (ed.), *The destruction of Lord Rosebery: From the diary of Sir Edward Hamilton, 1894–1895* (London, 1986)

Browne, Cohen Goodman, *Baron Rothschild of Frankfurt and the Rabbi* (London, 1912)

Browne, Lewis Allen, *The House of Rothschild* (London, 1934)

Buckle, George Earle (ed.), *The letters of Queen Victoria*, vol. III, 3rd Ser. (London, 1932)

Buckman, Peter, *The Rothschild conversion* (London, 1979)

Buderus von Carlshausen, Lothar, "Carl Friedrich Buderus: Das Leben eines kurhessischen Beamten in schwerer Zeit," *Monatsschrift für Landes-und Volkskunde, Kunst und Literatur Hessens* (1931), pp. 33–103

Buist, Marten G., *At spes non fracta: Hope and Co., 1770–1815* (The Hague, 1974)

Bullen, Roger, *Palmerston, Guizot and the collapse of the Entente Cordiale* (London, 1974)

———— and Felicity Strong (eds), Palmerston, vol. I: *Private correspondence with Sir George Villiers* (London, 1985)

Burk, Kathleen, *The first privatisation: The politicians, the City and the denationalisation of steel* (London, 1988)

————, *Morgan Grenfell, 1838–1988: The biography of a merchant bank* (Oxford, 1989)

Bury, J. P. T., "The identity of 'C. de B.,'" *French Historical Studies* (1964), pp. 538–41

Bussche, Albrecht von dem, *Heinrich Alexander von Arnim: Liberalismus, Polenfrage und deutsche Einheit. Das 19. Jahrhundert im Spiegel einer Biographie des preußischen Staatsmannes* (Osnabrück, 1986)

Bussiere, Eric, *Paribas, Europe and the world, 1872–1992* (Antwerp, 1992)

Butler, J. R. M., *The passing of the Great Reform Bill* (London, 1914)

Buxton, Charles (ed.), *Memoirs of Sir Thomas Fowell Buxton*, 3rd edn (London, 1849)

Buxton, Sydney Charles, *Finance and politics: an historical study, 1783–1885* (London, 1888)

Byron, Lord, *The complete poetical works*, vol. V: *Don Juan*, ed. Jerome J. McGann (Oxford, 1986)

Cabanis, Jose, *Charles X: Roi ultra* (Paris, 1972)

Cadoux, Gaston, *Les finances de la ville de Paris de 1798 à 1900* (Paris/Nancy, 1900)

Cain, P. J., *Economic foundations of British expansion overseas, 1815–1914* (London, 1980)

———— and A. G. Hopkins, *British imperialism: Innovation and expansion, 1688–1914* (London, 1993)

———— and ————, *British imperialism: Crisis and deconstruction, 1914–1990* (London, 1993)

Cameron, Rondo, "The Crédit Mobilier and the economic development of Europe," *Journal of Political Economy* (1953), pp. 461–89

————, "French financiers and Italian unity: The Cavourian decade," *American History Review* (1957), pp. 552–69

————, "Papal finance and the temporal power, 1815–71," *Church History* (1957), pp. 132–42

————, *France and the economic development of Europe, 1800–1914* (Princeton, 1961)

———— (ed.), *Banking in the early stages of industrialization* (New York/Oxford, 1967)

————, "France 1800–1870," in idem (ed.), *Banking in the early stages of industrialization* (New York/Oxford, 1967), pp. 100–128

————, "Belgium 1800–1875," in idem (ed.), *Banking in the early stages of industrialization* (New York/London/Toronto, 1967), pp. 129–50

Canfield, C., *Outrageous fortunes: The story of the Medici, the Rothschilds and J. P. Morgan* (New York, 1981)

Cannadine, David, *Aspects of aristocracy: Grandeur and decline in modern Britain* (New Haven/London, 1994)

Capdebièle, François, "Female Rothschilds and their issue," unpublished MS, RAL (n.d.)

Capefigue, M., *Histoire des grandes opérations financières, banques, bourses, emprunts, compagnies industrielles etc.*, 4 vols (Paris, 1855)

Carden, Godref L., *The machine tool trade in Austria–Hungary* (Washington, 1909)

Cardoso, Eliana A. and Rudiger Dornbusch, "Brazilian debt crises: Past and present," in Barry Eichengreen and Peter H. Lindert (eds), *The international debt crisis in historical perspective* (Cambridge, Mass./London, 1989), pp. 106–39

Carlisle, Robert B., "Les chemins de fer, les Rothschild et les saint-simoniens," *Economies et Sociétés, Cahiers de l'ISEA* (1971), pp. 647–76

Caron, François, *An economic history of modern France* (London, 1979)

————, "France," in Patrick O'Brien (ed.), *Railways and the economic development of Western Europe* (London/Basingstoke, 1983), pp. 28–48

Carosso, Vincent P., *Investment banking in America* (Cambridge, Mass., 1970)

————, *The Morgans: Private international bankers, 1854–1913* (Cambridge, Mass., 1987)

Carr, Raymond, *Spain, 1808–1939* (Oxford, 1966)

Carr, William, *The wars of German unification* (Harlow, 1991)

Carreras, A., *Industrializacion Espanola: Estudios de historia cuantitiva* (Florence, 1995)

Case, Lynn M., *French opinion on war and diplomacy during the Second Empire* (Philadelphia, 1954)

Cassis, Youssef, "Management and strategy in the English joint stock banks, 1890–1914," *Business History* (1985), pp. 301–15

————, "Bankers in English society in the late nineteenth century," *Economic History Review* (1985), pp. 210–29

————, *La City de Londres, 1870–1914* (Paris, 1987)

———— (ed.), *Finance and financiers in European history, 1880–1960* (Cambridge, 1992)

————, *English City bankers, 1890–1914* (Cambridge/New York, 1994)

———— and P. L. Cottrell, "Financial history," *Financial History Review* (1994), pp. 5–22

Castellane, Maréchal de, *Journal du Maréchal Castellane, 1804–1862* (Paris, 1895)

Castex, Pierre-Georges, "L'univers de la comédie humaine," in Balzac, Honoré de, *La comédie humaine* (Paris, 1976), pp. ix–lxxvi

Caussidière, Marc, *Mémoires de Caussidière, ex-prefet de police et représentant du peuple* (Paris, 1849)

Cavour, Count Camille Benso di, *La politique du Comte Camille de Cavour de 1852 à 1861: Lettres inédites avec notes* (Turin, 1885)

————, *Nouvelles lettres inédites* (Turin, 1889)

Cecco, M. de, *Money and empire: The international gold standard, 1890–1914* (Oxford, 1973)

Cecil, Algernon, *Metternich, 1773–1859: A study of his period and personality* (London, 1933)

Cesarani, David, *The Jewish Chronicle and Anglo-Jewry, 1841–1991* (Cambridge, 1994)

Chamberlain, Muriel E., *Lord Aberdeen: A political biography* (London, 1983)

Chandler, George, *Four centuries of banking* (London, 1964)

Chapman, Guy, *The Third Republic of France* (London, 1962)

Chapman, Stanley, "The international houses: The continental contribution to British economic development, 1800–1860," *Journal of European Economic History* (1977), pp. 5–48

————, *The foundation of the English Rothschilds: N. M. Rothschild as a textile merchant, 1799–1811* (London, 1977)

————, "The establishment of the Rothschilds as bankers," *Transactions of the Jewish Historical Society of England* (1982–6), pp. 177–93

————, *The rise of merchant banking* (London, 1984)

————, "British-based investment groups before 1914," *Economic History Review* (1985), pp. 230–51

————, "Rhodes and the City of London: Another view of imperialism," *Historical Journal* (1985), pp. 647–66

————, "The establishment of the Rothschilds as bankers in London," in Heuberger (ed.), *Essays*, pp. 71–86

Charnacé, Guy de, *Le Baron Vampire* (Paris, 1885)

Chastenet, Jacques, *Une époque de contestation: La monarchie bourgeoise, 1830–48* (Paris, 1976)

Chateaubriand, François René, vicomte de, *Correspondance générale de Chateaubriand*, 5 vols (Paris, 1913)

————, *Mémoires d'outre-tombe*, 2 vols (Paris, 1958)

Checkland, S. G., *The rise of industrial society in England, 1815–1885* (London, 1964)

Chekhov, Anton, "Rothschild's fiddle," in Ronald Wilks (ed.), *The fiancée and other stories* (Harmondsworth, 1986), pp. 52–61

Chernow, Ron, *The House of Morgan* (London/Sydney/New York/Tokyo/Toronto, 1990)

————, *The Warburgs* (London, 1993)

Childers, Spencer, *The life and correspondence of the Rt. Hon. Hugh C. E. Childers*, vol. II (London, 1901)

Chilvers, Hedley A., *The story of De Beers* (London, 1939)

Chirac, Auguste, *La Haute Banque et les révolutions* (Paris, 1876)

———, *Les rois de la République: Histoire des juiveries* (Paris, 1883)

———, *L'agiotage de 1870 à 1884* (Paris, 1887)

Christophe, Robert, *Le duc de Morny, "Empereur" des français sous Napoléon III* (Paris, 1951)

Christopher, John B., "The desiccation of the bourgeois spirit," in Edward Mead Earle (ed.), *Modern France: Problems of the Third and Fourth Republics* (Princeton, 1951), pp. 44–61

Churchill, Randolph S., *Winston S. Churchill*, vol. I (Boston, 1966)

———, *Winston S. Churchill*, vol. II (London, 1967)

Ciocca, Pierluigi and Ulizzi Adalberto, "I tassi di cambio nominali e 'reali' dell'Italia dall'unità nazionale al sistema monetario europeo (1861–1979)," *Ricerche per la Storia della Banca d'Italia*, vol. I (Rome, 1990), pp. 341–68

Clapham, J. H., *The economic development of France and Germany, 1815–1914* (Cambridge, 1921)

———, *The Bank of England: A history*, 2 vols (Cambridge, 1944)

Clark, Chester W., *Franz Joseph and Bismarck before 1866* (Cambridge, Mass., 1934)

Clarke, Edward, *Benjamin Disraeli* (London, 1926)

Clerc, Christine, *Fondations Rothschild: 130 ans de solidarité* (Paris, 1982)

Clough, S. B., *France: A history of national economics* (New York, 1939)

———, *An economic history of modern Italy* (New York, 1964)

Cobban, Alfred, *A history of modern France*, vol. II: *1799–1871* (Harmondsworth, 1961)

———, *A history of modern France*, vol. III: *1871–1962* (Harmondsworth, 1965)

Cohen, Albert, *Mangeclous* (Paris, 1938, 2nd edn 1965)

Cohen, Lucy, *Lady de Rothschild and her daughters, 1821–1931* (London, 1935)

Cohen, S. J., *Musterhaftes Leben des verewigten Herrn Bankiers Meyer Amschel Rothschild, Mitglied des Großherzoglich-Frankfurtischer Wahlkollegiums* (Frankfurt am Main, 1813)

Cohen, Stuart A., *English Zionists and British Jews: The communal politics of Anglo-Jewry, 1895–1920* (Princeton, 1982)

Colby, Reginald, "The Waterloo Dispatch," in Drew Middleton (ed.), *The battle of Waterloo* (Westport, Connecticut, 1977), pp. 87–99

Collett-White, Ann and James, *Gunnersbury Park and the Rothschilds* (Hounslow, 1993)

Colling, Alfred, *Le roman de la finance* (Monaco, 1945)

Collins, Michael, "The banking crisis of 1878," *Economic History Review* (1989), pp. 504–27

Conacher, J. B., *The Aberdeen coalition, 1852–1855* (Cambridge, 1968)

———, *The Peelites and the party system, 1846–1852* (Newton Abbot, 1972)

Contador, Claudio R., and Claudio L. Haddad, "Produto real, moeda e preços: A experiênca Brasileira no periodo 1861–1970," *Revista Brasileira de Estatistica* (1975)

Cope, S. R., *Walter Boyd: A merchant banker in the Age of Napoleon* (Gloucester, 1983)

Coppa, Frank, *Cardinal Giacomo Antonelli and Papal politics in European affairs* (New York, 1990)

Corley, T. A. B., *Democratic despot: A life of Napoleon III* (London, 1961)

Corti, Count Egon, *The rise of the House of Rothschild* (London, 1928)

———, *The reign of the House of Rothschild* (London, 1928)

Costello, John and Oleg Tsarev, *Deadly illusions: The KGB secrets the British government doesn't want you to read* (London, 1993)

Coston, Henry, *Les financiers qui mènent le monde* (Paris, 1955)

———, *La Haute Banque et les trusts* (Paris, 1958)

Cottrell, P. L., "London financiers and Austria, 1863–75: The Anglo-Austrian Bank," *Business History* (1969), pp. 107–19

———, "Anglo-French financial co-operation, 1850–80," *Journal of European Economic History* (1974), pp. 54–86

———, "London, Paris and silver, 1848–1867," in Anthony Slaven and Derek H. Aldcroft (eds), *Business, banking and urban history: Essays in honour of S. G. Checkland* (Edinburgh, 1982), pp. 102–11.

———, "The business man and financier," in Sonia and Vivian D. Lipman (eds), *The century of Moses Montefiore* (Oxford, 1985), pp. 23–44

———, "The domestic commercial banks and the City of London, 1870–1939," in Youssef Cassis (ed.), *Finance and financiers in European history, 1880–1960* (Cambridge, 1992), pp. 39–62

Coudray, H. du, *Metternich* (London, 1935)

Courtney, Cathy and Paul Thomson, *City lives: The changing voices of British finance* (London, 1996)

Cowles, Virginia, *The Rothschilds: A family of fortune* (London, 1973)

Cox, E. M. and Charles Whibley (eds), *Letters of the King of Hanover to Viscount Strangford G.C.B.* (London, 1925)

Crewe, Marquess of, *Lord Rosebery*, 2 vols (London, 1931)

Crouchley, A. E., *The economic development of modern Egypt* (London, 1938)

Crouzet, François, "Wars, blockade and economic change in Europe, 1792–1815," *Journal of Economic History* (1964), pp. 567–88

Cyon, Elie de, *Histoire de l'entente franco-russe* (Paris, 1895)

Dairnvaell, Georges ["Satan" (pseud.)], *Histoire édifiante et curieuse de Rothschild Ier, roi des Juifs* (Paris, 1846)

———, *Guerre aux fripons: Chronique secrète de la Bourse et des chemins de fer* (Paris, 1846)

Damascène, Morgand and Charles Fatout, *Le Baron James de Rothschild, 1844–1881* (Paris, 1881)

Darmstadter, F., *Bismarck and the creation of the Second Reich* (New York, 1965)

Darmstädter, Paul, *Das Grossherzogtum Frankfurt: Ein Kulturbild aus der Rheinbundszeit* (Frankfurt am Main, 1901)

Dasent, Arthur Irwin, *Piccadilly in three centuries, with some account of Berkeley Square and the Haymarket* (London, 1920)

Davenport-Hines, R. P. T, *Capital, entrepreneurs and profits* (London, 1990)

Davis, Lance E. and R. A. Huttenback, *Mammon and the pursuit of empire: The political economy of British imperialism, 1860–1912* (Cambridge, 1986)

Davis, Richard, *Disraeli* (London, 1976)

———, "The Rothschilds and English Society," unpublished paper given to the Seeley Society, Christ's College, Cambridge, RAL (1981)

———, *The English Rothschilds* (London, 1983)

Dawson, Frank Griffith, *The first Latin American debt crisis* (London, 1990)

Dayer, Roberta Albert, *Finance and empire: Sir Charles Addis, 1861–1945* (Basingstoke, 1988)

Deak, Istvan, *The lawful revolution: Louis Kossuth and the Hungarians, 1848–9* (New York, 1979)

Demachy, J. (ed.), *Les Rothschild, une famille des financiers juifs au XIXe siècle* (Paris, 1896)

Dennett, Laurie, *Slaughter and May: A century in the City* (Cambridge, 1989)

Deschamps, Henry-Thierry, *La Belgique devant la France de Juillet: L'opinion et l'attitude françaises de 1839 à 1848* (Paris, 1956)

Deutsche Bank (ed.), *Studies on economic and monetary problems and on banking history* (Mainz, 1988)

Diamond, S. (ed.), *A casual view of America: The home letters of Salomon de Rothschild, 1859–1861* (London, 1962)

Diaper, S., "Merchant banking in the inter-war period: The case of Kleinwort, Sons & Co.," *Business History* (1986), pp. 55–76

Dickson, P. G. M., *The financial revolution in England: A study in the development of public credit, 1688–1756* (London, 1967)

Dietz, Alexander, *Frankfurter Handelsgeschichte*, vol. IV (Frankfurt, 1925)

———, *The Jewish community of Frankfurt: A genealogical study* (Camelford, 1988)

Dines, Michael, *The Jewish jokebook* (London, 1986)

Disraeli, Benjamin, *Novels and tales by the Earl of Beaconsfield, with portrait and sketch of his life*, vol. VI: *Coningsby or The New Generation* (London, 1881)

———, *Novels and tales by the Earl of Beaconsfield, with portrait and sketch of his life*, vol. IX: *Tancred or the New Crusade* (London, 1881)

———, *Novels and tales of the Earl of Beaconsfield, with portrait and sketch of his life*, vol. XI: *Endymion* (London, 1881)

Doering, Heinrich, *Das Haus Rothschild: Eine historische–biographische Skizze* (Jena, 1842)

———, *Des Handelshauses Rothschild: Ursprung, Wachstum und Schicksale* (Leipzig, 1851)

Dosne, Mme, *Mémoires de Madame Dosne, l'égérie de M. Thiers*, 2 vols (Paris, 1928)

Draper, Hal (ed.), *The complete poems of Heinrich Heine* (Oxford, 1982)

Droz, Jacques, *Les révolutions allemandes de 1848* (Paris, 1957)

———, *Europe between two revolutions, 1815–48* (New York, 1967)

Druck, David, *Baron Edmond de Rothschild: The story of a practical idealist* (New York, 1928)

Drumont, Edouard, *La France juive: Essai d'histoire contemporaine, 2 vols* (Paris, 1885)

———, *Gambetta et sa Cour: Barons juifs* (Paris, 1892)

———, *Le testament d'un antisémite* (Paris, 1894)

———, *Les juifs contre la France* (Paris, 1899)

Dugdale, Blanche E. C., *Arthur James Balfour, 1st Earl of Balfour, 1906–1930*, 2 vols (London, 1936)

Dugdale, E. T. S. (ed.), *German diplomatic documents, 1871–1914*, 4 vols (London, 1928)

Dumont, Marie-Jeanne, *Le logement social à Paris, 1850–1930: Les habitations à Bon Marché* (Paris, 1991)

Dunham, Arthur Louis, *The Industrial Revolution in France, 1815–48* (New York, 1955)

Dupeux, Georges, *French society, 1789–1970* (London, 1976)

Dupont-Ferrier, Pierre, *Le marché financier de Paris sous le Second Empire* (Paris, 1925)

Duveau, Georges, *1848: The making of a revolution* (London, 1967)

Ebstein, Georges, *Etude sur la crise financière de 1882* (Paris, 1882)

Edelstein, M., *Overseas investment in the age of high imperialism* (London, 1982)

Egremont, Max, *Balfour* (London, 1980)

Ehrenberg, Richard, *Große Vermögen*, vol. I: *Die Fugger, Rothschild, Krupp* (3rd edn, Jena, 1925)

Ehrman, John, *The Younger Pitt*, vol. III: *The consuming struggle* (London, 1996)

Eichendorff, Joseph von, *Werke in einem Band* (Munich, 1955)

———, *Deutsche Lustspiele vom Barock bis zur Gegenwart: Das Incognito*, ed. Helmut von Arntzen and Karl Pestalozzi (Berlin, 1968)

Eichengreen, Barry, *Golden fetters: The gold standard and the great depression, 1919–1939* (New York/Oxford, 1992)

———, Marc Flandreau, "The geography of the gold standard," *International Macroeconomics*, 1050 (October 1994)

Einzig, Paul, *The history of foreign exchange* (London/New York, 1962)

Eliot, George, *Daniel Deronda* (Oxford, 1984)

Elliot, A. R. D., *Life of Lord Goschen*, 2 vols (London, 1911)

Ellis, Aytoun, *Heir of adventure: The story of Brown, Shipley & Co. merchant bankers, 1801–1960* (London, 1960)

Ellmann, Richard, *Oscar Wilde* (Harmondsworth, 1988)

Elon, Amos, *Founder: Meyer Amschel Rothschild and his time* (London, 1996)

Elston, D. R., *Israel: The making of a nation* (London, 1963)

Emden, Paul H., "The brothers Goldsmid and the financing of the Napoleonic Wars," *Transactions of the Jewish Historical Society of England* (1935–39), pp. 225–46

———, *Money powers of Europe in the nineteenth and twentieth centuries* (New York, 1938)

———, *Jews of Britain: A series of biographies* (London, 1944)

Einaudi, Luca, "Money and politics: European Monetary Union and the international gold standard (1865–1873)," unpublished PhD thesis (Cambridge University, forthcoming)

Endelman, Todd M., *The Jews of Georgian England, 1714–1830: Tradition and change in a liberal society* (Philadelphia, 1979)

———, *Radical assimilation in English Jewish history, 1656–1945* (Bloomington/Indianapolis, 1990)

Erb, Rainer, "The 'Damascus Affair' 1840: The role of the Rothschilds in mobilising public opinion," in Heuberger (ed.), *Essays*, pp. 99–112

Ernouf, le Baron A. A., *Paulin Talabot: Sa vie et son oeuvre, 1799–1885* (Paris, 1886)

Escott, Beryl E., "The Story of Halton House," unpublished MS, RAL (1984)

Evans, Richard J., *Proletarians and politics: Socialism, protest and the working class in Germany before the First World War* (London, 1990)

Farrer, David, *The Warburgs* (London, 1974)

Fase, Martin M. G., Gerald D. Feldman and Manfred Pohl (eds), *How to write the history of a bank* (Aldershot, 1995)

Faucher, Léon, *Notes et correspondance*, 2 vols (Paris, 1867)

Feaveryear, Sir Albert, *The pound sterling: A history of English money* (Oxford, 1963)

Feis, Herbert, *Europe, the world's banker, 1870–1914* (New York, 1930)

Feldman, David, *Englishmen and Jews: Social relations and political culture, 1840–1914* (New Haven/London, 1994)

Felisini, Daniela, *Le finanze pontificie e i Rothschild, 1830–1870*, Collona di ricerche in Storia Economica (IUN) (Naples, 1990)

Ferguson, Niall, "Public finance and national security: The domestic origins of the First World War revisited," *Past & Present* (1994), pp. 141–68

———, "The Kaiser's European Union: What if Britain had stood aside in August 1914?," in *idem* (ed.), *Virtual history: Alternatives and counterfactuals* (London, 1997), pp. 228–80

Fernández-Armesto, Felipe, *Millennium: A history of the last thousand years* (London, 1995)

Feydeau, Ernest Aymé, *Mémoires d'un coulissier* (Paris, 1873)

Fieldhouse, D. K., *Economics and empire, 1830–1914* (London, 1973)

Finestein, Israel, *Jewish society in Victorian England: Collected essays* (London, 1993)

Fischer, W., J. Krengel and J. Wietog (eds), *Sozialgeschichtliches Arbeitsbuch: Materialien zur Statistik des Deutschen Bundes 1815–1870* (Munich, 1982)

Flandreau, Marc, *L'or du monde: La France et la stabilité du système monétaire international, 1848–1873* (Paris, 1995)

———, "An essay on the emergence of the international gold standard, 1870–80," *International Macroeconomics*, 1210 (1995)

Flint, John, *Cecil Rhodes* (London, 1976)

Fontana, J., *La revolucion liberal* (Madrid, 1977)

Ford, J. A. (ed.), *The correspondence of William I and Bismarck*, 2 vols (London, 1903)

Forrest, D. M, *A hundred years of Ceylon tea* (London, 1967)

Forstmann, Wilfried, *Simon Moritz Bethmann, 1768–1826: Bankier, Diplomat und politischer Beobachter*, Studien zur Frankfurter Geschichte, ed. Frankfurter Verein für Geschichte und Landeskunde (Frankfurt am Main, 1973)

———, "Frankfurt am Main—Ein europäisches Finanzzentrum. Aspekte zu Banken-und Bankpolitik in Frankfurt am Main im 18. und 19. Jahrhundert," in Johannes Heil and Bernd Wacker (eds), *Shylock? Zinsverbot und Geldverleih in jüdischer und christlicher Tradition* (Munich, 1997), pp. 101–12

Foster, R. F., *Lord Randolph Churchill* (Oxford, 1981)

Fournier-Verneuil, M., *Paris: Tableau moral et philosophique* (Paris, 1826)

Fraenkl, Josef, "Herzl and the Rothschild family," *Herzl Family Yearbook* (1960), pp. 217–36

———, "The Chief Rabbi and the visionary," in *idem* (ed.), *The Jews of Austria: Essays on their life, history and destruction* (London, 1967), pp. 11–129

Frankel, Jonathan, "A historiographical oversight: The Austrian consul-general and the Damascus blood libel (with the Laurin–Rothschild correspondence, 1840)," unpublished MS, RAL (n.d.)

idem, The Damascus affair: "Ritual murder," politics and the Jews in 1840 (Cambridge, 1997)

Fraser, Peter, *Joseph Chamberlain: Radicalism and empire, 1868–1914* (London, 1966)

Freimann, Aron, *Stammtafeln der Freiherrlichen Familie von Rothschild* (Frankfurt am Main, 1906)

——— and I. Kracauer, *Frankfort: Jewish community series* (Philadelphia, 1929)

Friedman, I., *Germany, Turkey and Zionism, 1897–1918* (Oxford, 1977)

Friedman, Régine Mihal, "The Rothschilds: One family—two films," in Heuberger (ed.), *Essays*, pp. 333–50

Fritsch, Wilson, *External constraints on economic policy in Brazil, 1889–1930* (Basingstoke, 1988)

Fritsche, Victor von, *Bilder aus dem österreichischen Hof-und Gesellschaftsleben* (Vienna, 1914)

Froude, J. A., *Lord Beaconsfield* (London, 1890)

Fuchs, Edouard, *Die Juden in der Karikatur: Ein Beitrag zur Kulturgeschichte* (Berlin, 1985)

Fulda, Bernhard, "The Prussian loan in London 1818: Politics and finance in the late stages of the Prussian Reform period," unpublished BA thesis (Oxford University, 1998)

Fulford, Roger, *Glyn's, 1753–1953* (London, 1953)

——— (ed.), *Darling Child: Private correspondence of Queen Victoria and the German Crown Princess, 1871–1878* (London, 1976)

Galbraith, J. A., *Crown and charter* (London, 1974)

Gall, Lothar, *Bismarck, the white revolutionary*, vol. I: *1815–71* (London, 1986)

———, Gerald D. Feldman, Harold James, Carl-Ludwig Holtfrerich and Hans E. Büschgen, *The Deutsche Bank, 1870–1995* (London, 1995)

Garrard, John A., *The English and immigration, 1880–1910* (London/New York/Toronto, 1971)

Gartner, Lloyd P., *The Jewish immigrant in England, 1870–1914* (London, 1973)

Gash, Norman, *Mr Secretary Peel* (London, 1961)

Gatrell, Peter, *Government, industry and rearmament in Russia, 1900–1914: The last argument of Tsarism* (Cambridge, 1994)

Gay, Ruth, *The Jews of Germany* (New Haven/London, 1992)

Gebhard, Louis A. Jnr, "Austria's dreadnought squadron and the naval outlay of 1911," *Austrian History Yearbook* (1968–9), pp. 245–58

Gentz, Friedrich von, *Briefe von Friedrich von Gentz an Pilat: Ein Beitrag zur Geschichte Deutschlands im XIX. Jahrhundert*, 2 vols, ed. Karl von Mendelssohn Bartholdy (Leipzig, 1868)

———, *Tagebücher von 1829–1831* (Vienna, 1920)

Gerber, J., "The Damascus blood libel: Jewish perceptions and responses," in *Proceedings of the Eighth World Congress of Jewish Studies: Division B* (Jerusalem, 1982), pp. 105–10

Gerloff, Wilhelm, "Der Staatshaushalt und das Finanzsystem Deutschlands, 1820–1927," in *idem* (ed.), *Handbuch der Finanzwissenschaft*, vol. III (Tübingen, 1929), pp. 4–69

Germanicus, *Die Frankfurter Juden und die Aussaugung des Volkswohlstandes: Eine Anklage wider die Agiotage und wider den Wucher* (Leipzig, 1880)

Germanicus, *Die Rothschild-Gruppe und der "monumentale" Conversions-Schwindel von 1881* (Leipzig, 1881)

Gerretson, F. C., *History of the Royal Dutch*, 4 vols (Leiden, 1953–7)

Gerschenkron, Alexander, *Economic backwardness in historical perspective* (Cambridge, Mass., 1962)

Gilam, Abraham, *The emancipation of the Jews in England, 1830–1869* (New York, 1982)

Gilbert, B. B., *David Lloyd George: A political life*, vol. I: The architect of change, 1863–1912 (Columbus, 1987)

———, *David Lloyd George. A political life*, vol. II: *Organizer of victory, 1912–1916* (London, 1992)

Gilbert, Felix, *Bankiers, Kunstler und Gelehrte* (Tübingen, 1975)

Gilbert, Martin, "*Never Despair": Winston S. Churchill*, vol. VIII: *1945–1965* (London, 1990)

Gille, Bertrand, *La banque et le crédit en France de 1815 à 1848* (Vendôme, 1959)

——— (ed.), *Lettres adressées à la Maison Rothschild de Paris par son représentant à Bruxelles* (Louvain/Paris, 1961)

———, *Histoire de la Maison Rothschild*, vol. I: *Des origines à 1848* (Geneva, 1965)

———, *Histoire de la Maison Rothschild*, vol. II: *1848–70* (Geneva, 1967)

Gillett Brothers Discount Co. Ltd, *The bill on London or, The finance of trade by bills of exchange* (London, 1964)

Girard, Louis, *La politique des travaux publics du Second Empire* (Paris, 1952)

Girault, René, *Emprunts russes et investissements français en Russie* (Paris, 1973)

Giuffrida, Romualda, *I Rothschildi e la finanza pubblica in Sicilia (1849–1955)* (Caltanessitta/Rome, 1968)

Glanz, Rudolf, "The Rothschild legend in America," *Jewish Social Studies* (1957), pp. 3–28

Glyn, Mills & Co., *Glyn, Mills & Co.* (London, 1933)

Goethe, Johann Wolfgang von, *Dichtung und Wahrheit, Werke, Kommentare und Register*, Hamburger Ausgabe in 14 Bänden, vol. IX: *Autobiographische Schriften I* (Munich, 1981)

Goldschmidt, Hermann von, *Einige Erinnerungen aus längst vergangenen Tagen* (Vienna, 1917)

Goncourt, Edmond and Jules de, *Journal: Mémoires de la vie littéraire*, 2 vols (Paris, 1956)

Gooch, G. P., and Harold Temperley (eds), *British documents on the origins of the War, 1898–1914*, 9 vols (London, 1926–27)

Good, David F., *The economic rise of the Habsburg Empire, 1750–1914* (Berkeley/Los Angeles, 1984)

Gower, Sir George Leveson, *Years of endeavour, 1886–1907* (London, 1942)

Gray, Denis, *Spencer Perceval: The Evangelical prime minister, 1762–1812* (Manchester, 1963)

Gray, Victor (ed.), *The Life and times of N. M. Rothschild 1777–1836* (London, 1998)

Green, Edwin, *Debtors to their profession: A history of the Institute of Bankers, 1879–1979* (London, 1979)

Green, Timothy, "Precious heritage: The three hundred years of Mocatta & Goldschmid," unpublished MS, RAL (n.d.)

———, *The new world of gold* (London, 1981)

Greenfield, Kent Roberts, *Economics and liberalism in the Risorgimento: A study of nationalism in Lombardy, 1814–48* (Baltimore, 1934)

Greville, Charles C. F., *The Greville memoirs: A journal of King George IV and King William IV*, vol. I, ed. Henry Reeve (London, 1875)

———, *The Greville memoirs (second part): A journal of the reign of Queen Victoria from 1837 to 1852*, vol. II, ed. Henry Reeve (London, 1885)

Grigg, John, *Lloyd George: The people's champion, 1902–1911* (London, 1978)

———, *Lloyd George: From peace to war, 1912–1916* (London, 1985)

Grunwald, Kurt, "Europe's railways and Jewish enterprise: German Jews as pioneers of railway promotion," *Leo Baeck Institute Year Book* (1967), pp. 163–209

Guedalla, Philip, *Palmerston* (London, 1926)

Guillen, Pierre, "The Entente of 1904 as a colonial settlement," in Prosser Gifford and Wm Roger Louis (eds), *France and Britain in Africa: Imperial rivalry and colonial rule* (New Haven/London, 1971), pp. 333–69

Guizot, François and Princess Dorothea Lieven, *Lettres de François Guizot et de la Princesse de Lieven*, 3 vols (Paris, 1963)

Gunn, J. A. W., John Matthews, Donald M. Schurman and M. G. Wiebe (eds), *Benjamin Disraeli: Letters*, vols I and II (Toronto, 1982)

Gutzkow, Karl, *Öffentliche Charaktere: Erster Theil* (Hamburg, 1835)

Haldane, Richard Burdon, *An autobiography* (London, 1929)

Halévy, Elie, *The rule of democracy* (London, 1952)

Hall, Michael, "The English Rothschilds as collectors," in Heuberger (ed.), *Essays*, pp. 265–86

———, "Nathan Rothschild as an owner of paintings," in Victor Gray (ed.), *The Life and times of N. M. Rothschild 1777–1836* (London, 1998), pp. 68–78

Hambros Bank Ltd, *Hambros Bank Ltd., 1839–1939* (London, 1939)

Hammond, Bray, *Banks and politics from the Revolution to the Civil War* (Princeton, 1957)

Hamon, Augustin and X.Y.Z., *Les maitres de la France* (Paris, 1936)

Handelskammer zu Frankfurt, *Geschichte der Handelskammer zu Frankfurt, 1707–1908* (Frankfurt, 1908)

Hansard, T. C. (ed.), *The parliamentary debates: forming a continuation of the work entitled "The parliamentary history of England from the earliest period to the year 1803." New Series; commencing with the accession of George IV*, vol. XVIII (January 29–April 22, 1828) (London, 1828)

Hansen, B. and K. Tourk, "The profitability of the Suez Canal as a private enterprise, 1859–1956," *Journal of Economic History* (1978), pp. 938–58

Hansert, Andreas, "The dynastic power of the Rothschilds: A sociological assessment," in Heuberger (ed.), *Essays*, pp. 165–78

Harcourt Williams, Robin (ed.), *Salisbury–Balfour correspondence: Letters exchanged between the 3rd Marquess of Salisbury and his nephew Arthur James Balfour, 1869–1892* ([Ware], 1988)

Hardach, Gerd, *The First World War, 1914–1918* (Harmondsworth, 1987)

Hardwick, Molly, *Mrs Dizzy: The life of Mary Anne Disraeli, Viscountess Beaconsfield* (London, 1972)

Hargreaves, Eric Lyde, *The national debt* (London, 1930)

Harman, A., *Metternich* (London, 1932)

Harper, Martin, *Mr Lionel: An Edwardian episode* (London, 1970)

Harvey, C. E., *The Rio Tinto Company: An economic history of a leading international mining concern* (London, 1981)

Harvey, William H., *Coin's financial school*, ed. Richard Hofstadter (Cambridge, Mass., 1963)

Hawke, G. and J. Higgins, "Britain," in Patrick O'Brien (ed.), *Railways and the economic development of Western Europe* (London/Basingstoke, 1983), pp. 170–202

Hawtrey, Sir Ralph George, *A century of bank rate* (2nd edn, London, 1962)

Healey, Edna, *Coutts & Co., 1692–1992: The portrait of a private bank* (London, 1992)

Heckscher, Eli F., *The continental system: An economic interpretation* (Oxford, 1922)

Hedley, Arthur, *Selected correspondence of Fryderyk Chopin* (London, 1962)

Heffer, Simon, *Moral desperado: A life of Thomas Carlyle* (London, 1995)

Heilbrunn, Rudolf M., "Das Haus Rothschild: Wahrheit und Dichtung," Vortrag gehalten am 6. März 1963 im Frankfurter Verein für Geschichte und Landeskunde (1963)

———, "Die wirtschaftliche und politische Bedeutung des Hauses Rothschild," Vortrag gehalten vor dem Lions Club Frankfurt-Goethestadt (1965)

———, "Der Anfang des Hauses Rothschild: Wahrheit und Dichtung," *Jahrbuch des Instituts für deutsche Geschichte* (1973), pp. 209–38

Heimann-Jelinek, Felicitas, "The 'Aryanisation' of Rothschild assets in Vienna and the problem of restitution," in Heuberger (ed.), *Essays*, pp. 351–64

Heine, Heinrich, *Sämtliche Schriften*, vols. II–VI (Munich, 1971)

Helleiner, Karl F., *Free trade and frustration: Anglo-Austrian negotiations, 1860–1870* (Toronto, 1963)

———, *The imperial loans: A study in financial and diplomatic history* (Oxford, 1965)

Hémont, L'Abbé, *Les juifs et Bazaine* (Paris, 1899)

Henderson, W. O., *The Zollverein* (London, 1939)

Henrey, R., *A century between* (London/Toronto, 1937)

——— (ed.), *Letters from Paris: Written by C. de B., a political informant, to the head of the London house of Rothschild, 1870–1875* (London, 1942)

Henriques, Robert, *Bearsted: A biography of Marcus Samuel, 1st Viscount Bearsted and founder of "Shell" Transport and Trading Company* (New York, 1960)

Henriques, U. R. Q., "The Jewish emancipation controversy in nineteenth century Britain," *Past & Present* (1968), pp. 113–43

Herding, Klaus, "Die Rothschilds in der Karikatur," in Cilly Kugelmann and Fritz Backhaus (eds), *Jüdische Figuren in Film und Karikatur. Die Rothschilds und Joseph Süß Oppenheimer* (Sigmaringen, 1996), pp. 13–64

Herries, Edward, *Memoirs of the public life of the Rt Hon. John Charles Herries* (London, 1880)

Hershlas, Z. Y., *Introduction to the modern economic history of the Middle East* (Leiden, 1964)

Hertz, J. H., *The Rt. Hon. Lord Rothschild: Memorial sermon* (London, 1915)

Herzen, Alexander, *My past and thoughts: The memoirs of Alexander Herzen*, 4 vols (London, 1968)

———, *Letters from France and Italy, 1847–1851* (Pittsburgh, 1995)

Herzl, Theodor, *Tagebücher, 1895–1904*, 3 vols (Berlin, 1922)

Heseltine, William, *A family scene during the panic at the Stock Exchange in May 1835* (2nd edn, Canterbury, 1848)

Hessen, Rainer von, " 'You did not recommend a fool to me'—Elector William II of Hesse and Meyer Amschel Rothschild," in Heuberger (ed.), *Essays*, pp. 21–36

———, *Wir Wilhelm von Gottes Gnaden: Die Lebenserinnerungen Kurfürst Wilhelms I. von Hessen 1743–1821* (Frankfurt/New York, 1996)

Heuberger, Georg, *The Rothschilds: A European family*, Catalogue of the exhibition "The Rothschilds—A European Family" in the Jewish Museum of the City of Frankfurt am Main, October 11, 1994–February 27, 1995 (Sigmaringen, 1994)

——— (ed.), *The Rothschilds: Essays on the history of a European family* (Sigmaringen, 1994)

———, "The Rothschilds: Family history in the museum context," in *idem* (ed.), *Essays*, pp. 15–20

Heuberger, Rachel and Helga Krohn, *Hinaus aus dem Ghetto . . . Juden in Frankfurt am Main, 1800–1950* (Frankfurt am Main, 1988)

Heyn, Udo, "Private banking and industrialization: The case of Frankfurt am Main, 1825–1875," unpublished DPhil thesis (University of Wisconsin, 1969)

Hidy, R. W., *The House of Baring in American trade and finance: English merchant bankers at work, 1763–1861*, Harvard Studies in Business History, XIV (Cambridge, Mass., 1949)

Hilton, Boyd, *Corn, cash and commerce: The economic policies of Tory governments, 1815–1830* (Oxford, 1977)

Hoare, Philip, *Wilde's last stand: Decadence, conspiracy and the First World War* (London, 1997)

Hoare's Bank, *Hoare's Bank: A record, 1672–1955. The story of a private bank* (London, 1955)

Hobson, J. A., *Imperialism: A study* (London, 1988 [1st edn 1902])

Hobson, J. M., "The military-extraction gap and the wary Titan: The fiscal sociology of British defence policy, 1870–1913," *Journal of European Economic History* (1993), pp. 461–506

Hoffmann, W. G., F. Grumbach and H. Hesse, *Das Wachstum der deutschen Wirtschaft seit der Mitte des 19. Jahrhunderts* (Berlin, 1965)

Höffner, Corinna, "Frankfurter Privatsammlungen: Stifter und Bestände—Eigenart und Umfang," unpublished Staatsexamen für das Lehramt an Haupt-und Realschulen thesis (J. W. Goethe-Universität Frankfurt, 1992)

Hofstadter, Richard, *The age of reform from Bryan to F.D.R.* (London, 1962)

Holmes, A. R. and Edwin Green, *Midland: 150 years of banking business* (London, 1986)

Holmes, Derek, *The triumph of the Holy See* (London, 1972)

Homer, Sidney, *A history of interest rates* (2nd edn, New Brunswick, 1977)

Hood, Clifton, *722 Miles: The building of the subways and how they transformed New York* (Baltimore/London, 1993)

Howard, Michael, *The Franco–Prussian War* (London, 1961)

Howe, Irving and Ruth R. Wisse (eds), *The best of Shalom Aleichem* (Washington, DC, 1979)

Huber, Heinrich, "Fürstprimas Karl von Dalberg und das Haus Rothschild: Ein Beitrag zur Geschichte der Judenemanzipation in Frankfurt a.M.," *Weltkampf* (1943), pp. 19–27

———, "Bayern und das Haus Rothschild: Eine geschichtliche Betrachtung," *Allgemeine Zeitung der Juden in Deutschland* (March 15, 1957)

Hübner, comte de, *Neuf ans de souvenirs d'un ambassadeur d'Autriche à Paris sous le Second Empire, 1851–59*, 2 vols (Paris, 1904)

Huertas, Thomas, *Economic growth and economic policy in a multi-national setting: The Habsburg Monarchy, 1841–1865* (New York, 1977)

Hugelmann de Vegny Saint-Salmon, M. Gabriel, *A Rothschild: L'inauguration du chemin de fer du Nord* (Paris, 1846)

Hunt, Herbert J., *Balzac's Comedie Humaine* (London, 1964)

Hurst, Michael, *Joseph Chamberlain and Liberal reunion* (London, 1967)

Hüttl, Ludwig, *Ludwig II. König von Bayern: Eine Biographie* (Munich, 1986)

Hyamson, Albert M., *David Salomons* (London, 1939)

———, *Jews College London, 1855–1955* (London, 1955)

Icke, David, . . . *And the truth shall set you free* (Ryde, Isle of Wight, 1995)

Iliowzi, Henry, *"In the Pale": Stories and legends of the Russian Jews* (Philadelphia, 1897)

Imlah, Albert H., *Economic elements in the Pax Britannica* (Cambridge, Mass., 1958)

Ingrao, C., *The Hessian mercenary state* (Cambridge, 1987)

Israel, Jonathan I., *European Jewry in the Age of Mercantilism, 1550–1750* (Oxford, 1985)

Issawi, C., *Economic history of the Middle East, 1800–1914* (Chicago, 1966)

Jäckel, Eberhard and Axel Kuhn (eds), *Hitler: Sämtliche Aufzeichnungen, 1905–1924* (Stuttgart, 1980)

Jackson, Patrick, *The last of the Whigs: A political biography of Lord Hartington, later 8th Duke of Devonshire (1833–1908)* (Rutherford, New Jersey/London, 1994)

Jackson, Stanley, *The Sassoons: Portrait of a dynasty* (London, 1968)

Jacobson, Jacob, "Die Auflösung des Rothschildarchivs in Frankfurt a.M.," *Zeitschrift für die Geschichte der Juden in Deutschland* (1931), p. 279

Jacquemyns, G., *Langrand-Dumonceau: Promoteur d'une puissance financière catholique*, 5 vols (Brussels, 1960)

Jahrbuch für die Statistik des Preussischen Staates, ed. Königliches Statistisches Bureau (Berlin, 1869)

James, Robert Rhodes, *Lord Randolph Churchill* (London, 1959)

———, *Rosebery* (London, 1963)

Janik, A. and S. Toulin, *Wittgenstein's Vienna* (London, 1973)

Jardin, André and André-Jean Tudesq, *Restoration and reaction, 1815–1848* (Cambridge, 1983)

Jay, Richard, *Joseph Chamberlain: A political study* (Oxford, 1981)

Jenkins, Roy, *Mr Balfour's Poodle: An account of the struggle between the House of Lords and the government of Mr Asquith* (London, 1968)

———, *Asquith* (London, 1986)

Jenkins, T. A., *Gladstone, Whiggery and the Liberal Party, 1874–1886* (Oxford, 1988)

Jenks, Leland Hamilton, *The migration of British capital to 1875* (New York/London, 1927)

Jenks, William A., *Francis Joseph and the Italians* (Charlottesville, 1978)

———, *Austria under the Iron Ring* (Charlottesville, 1965)

Jennings, Louis J. (ed.), *Correspondence and diaries of John Wilson Croker, Secretary to the Admiralty 1809–1830*, vol. III (London, 1884)

Jewish Theological Seminary of America, *The Jew as Other: A century of English caricature, 1730–1830* (New York, 1995)

Johnson, Christopher H., "The revolution of 1830 in French economic history," in John Merriman (ed.), *1830 in France* (New York/London , 1975), pp. 139–89

Johnson, Nancy E. (ed.), *The diary of Gathorne Hardy, later Lord Cranbrook, 1866–1892: Political selections* (Oxford, 1981)

Johnston, Thomas, *The financiers and the nation* (London, 1934)

Joll, James, *The origins of the First World War* (London, 1992)

Jones, Steve, *In the blood: God, genes and destiny* (London, 1996)

Joslin, David, *A century of banking in Latin America* (Oxford, 1963)

Jullian, Philippe, *Les styles* (Paris, 1961)

Jurk, Michael, "The other Rothschilds: Frankfurt private bankers in the 18th and 19th centuries," in Heuberger (ed.), *Essays*, pp. 37–50

Kadish, Sharman, *Bolsheviks and British Jews: The Anglo-Jewish community, Britain and the Russian Revolution* (London, 1992)

Kaplan, Marion A., *The making of the Jewish middle class: Women, family and identity in imperial Germany* (Oxford, 1991)

Kapp, Freidrich, *Der Soldatenhandel deutscher Fürsten nach Amerika, 1775–1783* (Berlin, 1884)

Kapralik, C. I., *Reclaiming the Nazi loot* (London, 1962)

Katz, David, *Philosemitism and the readmission of the Jews to England* (Oxford, 1982)

Katz, David S., *The Jews in the history of England, 1485–1850* (Oxford, 1994)

Katz, Irving, *August Belmont: A political biography* (New York, 1968)

Katz, Jacob, *Tradition and crisis: Jewish society and the end of the Middle Ages* (New York, 1961)

———, *Jews and Freemasons in Europe, 1723–1939* (Cambridge, Mass., 1970)

———, *Out of the ghetto: The social background of Jewish emancipation, 1770–1870* (New York, 1978)

Katzenstein, Peter J., *Disjoined partners: Austria and Germany since 1815* (Berkeley/Los Angeles, 1976)

Kehr, Eckart, "Zur Genesis der preußischen Bürokratie und des Rechtsstaats," in Hans-Ulrich Wehler (ed.), *Der Primat der Innenpolitik. Gesammelte Aufsätze zur preußisch-deutschen Sozialgeschichte im 19. und 20. Jahrhundert* (Berlin, 1970), pp. 31–52

———, "Biographische Skizzen: Fugger; Carnot und Scharnhorst; Rothschild," in Wehler (ed.), *Primat der Innenpolitik*, pp. 284–92

Kemp, Tom, *Economic forces in French history* (London, 1971)

Kennan, George F., *The decline of Bismarck's European order: Franco-Russian relations, 1875–1890* (Princeton, 1979)

———, *The fateful alliance: France, Russia and the coming of the First World War* (Manchester, 1984)

Kennedy, Paul M., *The rise of Anglo-German antagonism, 1860–1914* (London, 1982)

Kent, Marian (ed.), *The great powers and the end of the Ottoman Empire* (London, 1984)

Kessler, David, "The Rothschilds and Disraeli in Buckinghamshire," *Transactions of the Jewish Historical Society of England* (1982–86), pp. 231–52

Kindleberger, Charles P., *Economic growth in France and Britain, 1851–1950* (Cambridge, Mass., 1964)

———, *A financial history of Western Europe* (London, 1984)

Kipping, E., *Die Truppen von Hessen-Kassel im amerikanischen Unabhängigkeitskrieg 1776–1783* (Darmstadt, 1965)

Kirke Rose, T., *The metallurgy of gold* (London, 1896)

Kissinger, Henry, *Diplomacy* (London, 1994)

Kitchen, Martin, *The political economy of Germany, 1815–1914* (London, 1978)

Klein, Ernst, "Preußens 30–Million-Anleihe in London vom 31. März 1818," *Zeitschrift für Geschichtwissenschaft*, (1956), pp.

Knapp, Vincent J., *Europe in the era of social transformation: 1700 to the present* (Englewood Cliffs, New Jersey, 1976)

Knight, G. A., "Das Rothschildsche Banken-und Wirtschaftsarchiv in London: Empfängerüberlieferung in Überblick," *Bankhistorisches Archiv* (1979), pp. 61–6

———, "The Rothschild–Bleichröder axis in action: An Anglo-German co-operative, 1877–1878," *Leo Baeck Year Book* (1983), pp. 43–57

Koch, Gertrud, "Tabuen oder Falken—die Rothschild-Filme im Vergleich," in Cilly Kugelmann and Fritz Backhaus (eds), *Jüdische Figuren in Film und Karikatur: Die Rothschilds und Joseph Süß Oppenheimer* (Sigmaringen, 1996), pp. 65–95

Koch, Rainer, *Grundlagen bürgerlicher Herrschaft: Verfassungs-und sozialgeschichtliche Studien zur bürgerlichen Gesellschaft in Frankfurt am Main (1612–1866)*, Frankfurter Historische Abhandlungen, 27 (Wiesbaden, 1983)

Kolb, Louis, "The Vienna Jewish Museum," in Josef Fraenkl (ed.), *The Jews of Austria: Essays on their life, history and destruction* (London, 1967), pp. 147–59

Komlos, John, *The Habsburg Monarchy as a customs union: Economic development in Austria–Hungary in the nineteenth century* (Princeton, 1983)

Kopper, Christopher, "The Rothschild family during the Third Reich," in Heuberger (ed.), *Essays*, pp. 321–32

Kracauer, Isidor, "Die Geschichte der Judengasse in Frankfurt am Main," in *Festschrift zur Jahrhundertfeier der Realschule der israelitischen Gemeinde (Philanthropin) zu Frankfurt am Main 1804–1904* (Frankfurt am Main, 1904), pp. 303–464

———, *Geschichte der Juden in Frankfurt am Main (1150–1824)*, 2 vols (Frankfurt, 1925, 1927)

Kriegel, Abraham D. (ed.), *The Holland House diaries, 1831–40: Diary of Henry Richard Vassall Fox, 3rd Lord Holland* (London, 1977)

Kriegk, Georg Ludwig, *Geschichte von Frankfurt am Main* (Frankfurt am Main, 1871)

Kropat, Wolf Arno, *Frankfurt zwischen Provinzialismus und Nationalismus: Die Eingliederung der "Freien Stadt" in den preußischen Staat (1866–1871)* (Frankfurt am Main, 1971)

———, "Die Emanzipation der Juden in Kurhessen und in Nassau im 19. Jahrhundert," in Christiane Heinemann (ed.), *Neunhundert Jahre Geschichte der Juden in Hessen: Beiträge zum politischen, wirtschaftlichen und kulturellen Leben* (Wiesbaden, 1983), pp. 325–50

Kübeck von Kübow, Carl Friedrich, *Tagebücher des Kübeck von Kübow* (Vienna, 1909)

———, *Aus dem Nachlaß des Freiherrn Carl Friedrich Kübeck von Kübow: Tagebücher, Briefe, Aktenstücke 1841–55*, Veröffentlichungen der Kommission für neuere Geschichte Österreichs, 45 (Graz/Cologne, 1960)

Kubicek, R.V., *Economic imperialism in theory and practice: The case of South African gold mining, 1886–1914* (Durham, 1979)

Kynaston, David, *Cazenove and Co.: A history* (London, 1991)

———, *The City of London, vol. I: A world of its own, 1815–90* (London, 1994)

———, *The City of London, vol. II: Golden years, 1890–1914* (London, 1996)

———, "The City of London in Nathan Rothschild's time," in Victor Gray (ed.), *The Life and times of N. M. Rothschild 1777–1836* (London, 1998), pp. 42–9

Laffitte, Jacques, *Mémoires de Laffitte* (Paris, 1932)

Laffut, "Belgium," Patrick O'Brien (ed.), *Railways and the economic development of Western Europe* (London/Basingstoke, 1983), pp. 203–26.

Lancaster, Osbert, *From here of all places* (London, 1959)

Landes, David S., *Bankers and pashas: International finance and economic imperialism in Egypt* (London, 1958)

———, "The old bank and the new: The financial revolution of the nineteenth century," in F. Crouzet, W. H. Chaloner and W. M. Stern (eds), *Essays in European economic history, 1789–1914* (London, 1969), pp. 112–27

———, "The spoilers foiled: The exclusion of Prussian finance from the French Liberation Loan of 1871," in Charles P. Kindleberger and Guido di Tella (eds), *Economics in the long view: Essays in honour of W. W. Rostow* (London/Basingstoke, 1982), pp. 67–110

Landmann, Salcia, *Der jüdische Witz: Soziologie und Sammlung* (Olten/Freiburg im Breisgau, 1963)

Lane, Barbara Miller and Leila J. Rupp (eds), *Nazi ideology before 1933: A documentation* (Manchester, 1978)

Lang, Jochen von, *Der Adjutant. Karl Wolff: Der Mann zwischen Hitler und Himmler* (Berlin, 1985)

Lant, Jeffrey L., *Insubstantial pageant: Ceremony and confusion at Queen Victoria's court* (New York, 1980)

Launay, vicomte de [Gay, Delphine, later Mme de Girardin], *Lettres parisiennes*, 3 vols (Paris, 1856)

Lawson, Nigel, *The view from No. 11: Memoirs of a Tory radical* (London, 1992)

Lears, Rufus, *Filled with laughter: A fiesta of Jewish humor* (New York, 1961)

Lee, A. G. (ed.), *The Empress Frederick writes to Sophie her daughter, Crown Princess and later Queen of the Hellenes, 1889–1901* (London, 1955)

Lee, Samuel J., *Moses of the New World: The work of Baron de Hirsch* (New York/South Brunswick/London, 1970)

Lefebvre, René, "Les Rothschild," *Crapouillot* (n.d. [1951?]), pp. 6–20

Lefèvre, André, *Sous le Second Empire: Chemins de fer et politique* (Paris, 1951)

Lenarz, Michael, *Der alte jüdische Friedhof zu Frankfurt am Main* (Frankfurt am Main, 1996)

Letcher, Owen, *The gold mines of Southern Africa* (London, 1936)

Levene, Mark, *War, Jews and the new Europe: The diplomacy of Lucien Wolf, 1914–1919* (Oxford, 1992)

Levy, Maria Barbara, "The Brazilian public debt: domestic and foreign," in Reinhard Liehr (ed.), *La dueda pùblican en América en perspectiva historica* (Frankfurt am Main, 1995), pp. 209–54

Lévy-Leboyer, Maurice, "Capital investment and economic growth in France, 1820–1930," in Peter Mathias and M. M. Postan (eds), *The Cambridge economic history of Europe, vol. VII: The industrial economies: Capital, labour and enteprise, part I* (Cambridge, 1978), pp. 231–395

Lewnsohn, Solomon, *Die treue Anhänglichkeit zu Jerusalem und die Liebe zu Zion* (n.p., 1858)

Liberles, Robert, *Religious conflict in social context: The resurgence of Orthodox Judaism in Frankfurt am Main, 1838–1877* (Westwood, Conn., 1985)

———, "The world of Dietz's *Stammbuch*: Frankfurt Jewry, 1349–1870," in Alexander Dietz (ed.), *The Jewish community of Frankfurt: A genealogical study* (Camelford, 1988), pp. i–xxxi

———, "The Aristocrat and the synagogue: the Rothschilds and Judaism," in Heuberger (ed.), *Essays*, pp. 195–204

Lieven, Princess Dorothea, *The private letters of Princess Lieven to Prince Metternich, 1820–1826* (London, 1948)

Lindemann, Albert S., *The Jew accused: Three anti-Semitic affairs (Dreyfus, Beilis, Frank), 1894–1915* (Cambridge, 1991)

Lipman, Edward, "The City and the 'People's Budget,'" unpublished MS (1995).

Lipman, Sonia, "The making of a Victorian gentleman," in Sonia and Vivian D. Lipman (eds), *The century of Moses Montefiore* (Oxford, 1985), pp. 3–22

Lipman, Vivian D., *A century of social service, 1859–1959: The Jewish Board of Guardians* (London, 1959)

———, *A history of the Jews in Britain since 1858* (Leicester, 1990)

List, Friedrich, *Grundlinien einer politischen Ökonomie und andere Beiträge der amerikanischen Zeit, 1825–1832, Friedrich List, Schriften/Reden/Briefe, vol. II*, im Auftrag der Friedrich List-Gesellschaft e.V., ed. Erwin von Beckerath, Karl Goeser, Friedrich Lenz, William Notz, Edgar Salin, Artur Sommer (Berlin, 1931)

Litvinoff, Barnet (ed.), *The essential Chaim Weizmann: The man, the statesman, the scientist* (London, 1982)

Lloyd George, David, *War memoirs of David Lloyd George*, 2 vols (London, 1933)

Locke, Robert R., "A method for identifying French corporate businessmen (the Second Empire)," *French Historical Studies*, 10, 2 (1977), pp. 261–93

Loewe, Louis (ed.), *Diaries of Sir Moses and Lady Montefiore*, 2 vols (Oxford, 1983)

Loménie, E. Beau de, *Les responsabilités des dynasties bourgeoises*, 5 vols (Paris, 1954)

Longford, E., *Wellington: The years of the sword* (London, 1969)

———, *Wellington: Pillar of state* (London, 1972)

——— (ed.), *Darling Loosy* (London, 1991)

Lord, Robert H., *The origins of the War of 1870* (Cambridge, Mass., 1924)

Losch, Philipp, *Geschichte des Kurfürstentums Hessen, 1803 bis 1866* (Marburg, 1922)

———, *Kurfürst Wilhelm I, Landgraf von Hessen* (Marburg, 1923)

Lottman, Herbert R., *Return of the Rothschilds* (London/New York, 1995)

Luna, Frederick A. de, *The French Republic under Cavaignac* (Princeton, 1969)

Lyons, F. S. L., *Internationalism in Europe 1815–1914* (Leyden, 1936)

Macartney, C. A., *The Habsburg Empire, 1790–1918* (London, 1969)

———, *The House of Austria* (Edinburgh, 1978)

McCagg, William O., Jr, *Jewish nobles and geniuses in modern Hungary* (New York, 1972)

———, "Vienna and Budapest around 1900: The problem of Jewish influence," in György Ránki and Attila Pok (eds), *Hungary and European civilisation* (Budapest, 1989), pp. 241–64

———, "The Jewish position in interwar Central Europe: A structural study of Jewry at Vienna, Budapest and Prague," in Victor Karady and Yehuda Don (eds), *A social and economic history of Central European Jewry* (New Brunswick, New Jersey, 1989), pp. 47–81

———, *A history of the Habsburg Jews* (Bloomington, Indiana, 1989)

Mace, Simone, "The archives of the London Merchant Bank of N. M. Rothschild & Sons," *Business Archives* (1992), pp. 1–14

———, "From Frankfurt Jew to Lord Rothschild: The ascent of the English Rothschilds to the nobility," in Heuberger (ed.), *Essays*, pp. 179–94

McGrath, William J., *Dionysian art and populist politics in Austria* (New Haven, 1974)

Mack Smith, Denis, *Italy: A modern history* (Ann Arbor, Michigan, 1959)

———, *Victor Emmanuel, Cavour and the Risorgimento* (Oxford, 1971)

———, *Cavour* (London, 1985)

———, *Mazzini* (New Haven, 1994)

McKay, John, "Baku oil and Transcaucasian pipelines, 1883–1891: A study in Tsarist economic policy," *Slavic Review* (1984), pp. 604–23

———, "The House of Rothschild (Paris) as a multinational industrial enterprise, 1875–1914," in A. Teichova, M. Lévy-Leboyer and H. Nussbaum (eds), *Multinational enterprise in historical perspective* (Cambridge, 1986), pp. 74–86

Mackay, Ruddock F., *Balfour: Intellectual statesman* (Oxford, 1985)

Mackenzie, Compton, *Realms of silver* (London, 1954)

Maggs, Christopher, *A century of change: The story of the Royal National Pension Fund for Nurses* (London, 1987)

Magnus, Lady Katie, *Jewish portraits* (London, 1897)

Malchow, Howard Le Roy, *Gentleman capitalists: The social and political world of the Victorian businessman* (London, 1991)

Malia, Martin, *Alexander Herzen and the birth of Russian socialism* (Cambridge, 1961)

Mann, Golo, *Secretary of Europe: The life of Friedrich von Gentz, enemy of Napoleon* (New Haven, 1946)

Marcus, Joseph, *Social and political history of the Jews in Poland* (Amsterdam, 1983)

Margoliouth, Rev. Moses, *The history of the Jews of Great Britain*, 3 vols (London, 1851)

Marion, Marcel, *Histoire financière de la France depuis 1715*, vol. V: *1819–1875* (Paris, 1928)

Marks, Lara V., *Model mothers: Jewish mothers and maternity provision in East London, 1870–1939* (Oxford, 1994)

Marsh, Peter T. *Joseph Chamberlain: Entrepreneur in politics* (New Haven/London, 1994)

Martel, Gordon, *Imperial diplomacy: Rosebery and the failure of foreign policy* (Kingston, Ontario/London, 1986)

Martin, V. M., *Los Rothschild y las Minas de Almadén* (Madrid, 1980)

Marx, Julius, *Die wirtschaftliche Ursachen der Revolution von 1848 in Österreich* (Graz/Cologne, 1965)

Marx, Karl, "On the Jewish question," in *idem* and Friedrich Engels (eds), *Collected works*, vol. III: *1843–1844* (London, 1975), pp. 146–74

März, Eduard, *Österreichische Bankpolitik in der Zeit der großen Wende 1913–1923: Am Beispiel der Creditanstalt für Handel und Gewerbe* (Munich, 1981)

———, "The Austrian Crédit Mobilier in a time of transition," in John Komlos (ed.), *Economic development in the Habsburg monarchy in the nineteenth century: Essays* (New York, 1983), pp. 117–36

Matthew, H. C. G. (ed.), *The Gladstone diaries with Cabinet minutes and prime ministerial correspondence*, 14 vols (Oxford, 1968–94)

———, "Disraeli, Gladstone and the politics of mid-Victorian budgets," *Historical Journal* (1979), pp. 615–643

———, *Gladstone, 1809–1874* (Oxford, 1986)

———, *Gladstone, 1875–1898* (Oxford, 1995)

Maurois, André, *Disraeli* (London, 1927)

May, Arthur J., *The Habsburg monarchy* (Cambridge, Mass., 1951)

Mayer, Arno J., *The persistence of the old regime* (New York, 1971)

Mayeur, Jean-Marie, *Les débuts de la Troisième République, 1871–98* (Paris, 1973)

Mayorek, Yoram, "Between East and West: Edmond de Rothschild and Palestine," in Heuberger (ed.), *Essays*, pp. 129–46

Melville, Lewis, *The life and letters of William Cobbett in England and America, based upon hitherto unpublished family papers*, 2 vols (London/New York/Toronto, n.d.)

Mende, Fritz, *Heinrich Heine: Chronik seines Lebens u. Werkes* (Berlin, 1970)

Merimée, Prosper, *Correspondance générale*, 6 vols (Paris, 1945)

———, *Correspondance générale*, 2e série, 9 vols (Paris, 1953–61)

Metternich, R. (ed.), *Aus Metternichs nachgelassenen Papieren*, 8 vols (Vienna, 1880–84)

Meyer, Michael, *Response to modernity: The Reform movement in Judaism* (New York, 1988)

Mezerey, Jean de, "Les origines de la famille Rothschild," *La Revue* (1901), pp. 186–91

Michel, Bernard, *Banques et banquiers en Autriche au début de XXe siècle* (Paris, 1976)

Michie, R. C., *The London and New York Stock Exchanges, 1850–1914* (London, 1987)

Michon, Georges, *L'alliance Franco-Russe, 1891–1917* (Paris, 1927)

Milward, A. and S. B. Saul, *The development of the economies of continental Europe, 1850–1914* (London, 1977)

Minchton, Walter, "Patterns of demand, 1750–1914," in C. M. Cipolla (ed.), *The Fontana economic history of Europe: The Industrial Revolution* (Glasgow, 1973), pp. 77–186

Mirès, Jules Isaac, *A mes juges: Ma vie et mes affaires* (Paris, 1861)

Mitchell, B. R., *European historical statistics, 1750–1975* (London, 1975)

———, *Abstract of British historical statistics* (Cambridge, 1976)

Modder, Frank Montagu, *The Jew in the literature of England to the end of the nineteenth century* (New York/Philadelphia, 1939)

Monypenny, W. F. and G. E. Buckle, *The life of Benjamin Disraeli, Earl of Beaconsfield*, 6 vols (London, 1910–20)

Moreau, Emile, *Souvenirs d'un gouverneur de la Banque de France (1926–1928)* (Paris, 1954)

Morgan, E. Victor, *The theory and practice of central banking, 1797–1913* (Cambridge, 1943)

——— and W. A. Thomas, *The Stock Exchange* (London, 1962)

Morgan Grenfell & Co. Ltd, *George Peabody & Co., J. S. Morgan & Co., Morgan Grenfell & Co., Morgan Grenfell & Co. Ltd* (Oxford, 1958)

Morley, John, *The life of William Ewart Gladstone*, vols II and III (London, 1903)

Morris, Susannah, "Voluntary action and the housing of the working classes in London, 1840–1914," unpublished DPhil thesis (Oxford University, forthcoming)

Morton, Frederick, *The Rothschilds: A family portrait* (London, 1961)

Moss, David J., *Thomas Attwood: The biography of a Radical* (Montreal/London, 1990)

Mosse, Werner, *Jews in the German economy: The German-Jewish economic elite, 1820–1935* (Oxford, 1987)

Mount, Ferdinand, *Umbrella* (London, 1995)

Muhlstein, Anka, *Baron James: The rise of the French Rothschilds* (London, 1983)

Murray, B. K., *The People's Budget, 1909/10: Lloyd George and liberal politics* (Oxford, 1980)

Murray, D. L., *Disraeli* (London, 1927)

Nash, W. G., *The Rio Tinto mine* (London, 1904)

Neal, Larry, *The rise of financial capitalism: International capital markets in the age of reason* (Cambridge, 1990)

Nesselrode, comte Charles de, *Lettres et papiers du Chancelier comte de Nesselrode, 1760–1850*, 11 vols (Paris, 1904–11)

Newbury, Colin, "Out of the pit: the capital accumulation of Cecil Rhodes," *Journal of Imperial and Commonwealth History* (1981), pp. 25–49

——, "Technology, capital and consolidation: the performance of De Beers Mining Company Limited, 1880–1889," *Business History* (1987), pp. 1–42

——, *The Diamond Ring: Business, politics and precious stones in South Africa, 1867–1947* (Oxford, 1989)

Newman, Aubrey, *The United Synagogue, 1870–1970* (London, 1976)

Nicholas, Lynn, *The rape of Europa: The fate of Europe's treasures in the Third Reich and the Second World War* (London, 1994)

Nicolle, André, *Comment la France a payé après Waterloo* (Paris, 1929)

Nicholls, David, "Fractions of capital: The aristocracy, the City and industry in the development of modern British capitalism," *Social History* (1988), pp. 71–83

Nichols, Irby C., Jnr, "Britain and the Austrian war debt, 1821–3," *The Historian* (1958), pp. 328–46

——, *The European pentarchy and the Congress of Vienna* (The Hague, 1971)

Nichols, J. Alden, *Germany after Bismarck: The Caprivi era, 1890–1984* (Cambridge, Mass., 1958)

Nicolson, Harold, *The Congress of Vienna: A study in allied unity, 1812–1822* (London, 1946)

Nicolson, Nigel, (ed.), *Vita and Harold: The letters of Vita Sackville-West and Harold Nicolson* (London, 1992)

Niecks, Frederick, *Frederick Chopin as a man and musician* (London, 1890)

Nipperdey, Thomas, *Germany from Napoleon to Bismarck, 1800–1866* (Dublin, 1996)

Obenaus, Herbert, "Finanzkrise und Verfassungsgebung. Zu den sozialen Bedingungen des frühen deutschen Konstitutionalismus," in Gerhard A. Ritter (ed.), *Gesellschaft, Parlament und Regierung: Zur Geschichte des Parlamentarismus in Deutschland* (Düsseldorf, 1974), pp. 57–75

O'Brien, P. K. (ed.), *Railways and the economic development of Western Europe* (London/Basingstoke, 1983)

——, "The costs and benefits of British imperialism, 1846–1914," *Past & Present* (1988), pp. 163–200

——, "Power with profit: The state and the economy, 1688–1815," Inaugural lecture, University of London (1991)

O'Brien, Terence H., *Milner: Viscount Milner of St. James's and Cape Town, 1854–1925* (London, 1979)

Offer, Avner, *Property and politics, 1870–1914: Landownership, law, ideology and urban development in England* (Cambridge, 1981)

Oppenheim, Moritz, *Erinnerungen*, ed. Alfred Oppenheim (Frankfurt am Main, 1924)

Osborne, Richard, *Rossini* (London, 1986)

Otazu, Alfonso de, *Los Rothschild y sus Socias en Espana, 1820–1850* (Madrid, 1987)

Ouvrard, Gabriel-Julien, *Mémoires sur sa vie et ses diverses operations financières*, 3 vols (Paris, 1825)

Overy, Richard, "Göring's 'multi-national' empire," in A. Teichova and P. L. Cottrell (eds), *International business and Central Europe, 1919–1939* (Leicester, 1984), pp. 269–98

Owen, R., *The Middle East and the world economy, 1800–1914* (London, 1981)

Oxaal, Ivor, "The Jews of the young Hitler's Vienna," in *idem*, M. Pollack and G. Botz (eds), *The Jews, antisemitism and culture in Vienna* (New York/London, 1987), pp. 11–38

Palin, Ronald, *Rothschild relish* (London, 1970)

Palmade, Guy P., *French capitalism in the nineteenth century* (Newton Abbot, 1972)

Palmer, Alan, *Metternich: Councillor of Europe* (London, 1972)

——, *The chancelleries of Europe* (London, 1983)

Pamlenyi, E. (ed.), *A history of Hungary* (London, 1975)

Paret, Peter, *Art as history: Episodes in the culture and politics of nineteenth century Germany* (Princeton, 1988)

Parfitt, T., " 'The Year of the Pride of Israel': Montefiore and the Damascus blood libel of 1840," in Sonia and Vivian D. Lipman (eds), *The century of Moses Montefiore* (Oxford, 1985), pp. 131–48

Park, Joseph H., *British Prime Ministers of the nineteenth century, policies and speeches* (New York, 1950)

Parry, J. P., *Democracy and religion: Gladstone and the Liberal Party, 1867–1875* (Cambridge, 1986)

Partridge, Monica, *Alexander Herzen, 1812–1870* (Paris, 1984)

Paucker, Pauline, "The image of the German Jew in English fiction," in Werner E. Mosse and Julius Carlebach (eds), *Second Chance: Two centuries of German-speaking Jews in the United Kingdom* (Tübingen, 1991), pp. 315–33

Payard, Maurice, *Le financier G.-J. Ouvrard, 1770–1846* (Rheims, 1958)

Perkin, Harold, *The rise of professional society: England since 1880* (London, 1989)

Peron, Jean, *Les Rothschild* (Paris, 1942)

Perry, Roland, *The Fifth Man* (London, 1994)

Persigny, duc de, *Mémoires du duc de Persigny* (Paris, 1896)

Peter, Roland, "Geburt einer Geldmacht: 250 Jahre Rothschild," *Damals: Das aktuelle Geschichtsmagazin* (1993), pp. 56–9

Petit, Henri-Robert, *Rothschild: Roi d'Israël et les Américains* (Paris, 1941)

Peyrefitte, Roger, *Les juifs* (Paris, 1965)

Pflanze, Otto, *Bismarck and the development of Germany*, vol. I: *The period of unification, 1815–71* (Princeton, 1990)

———, *Bismarck and the development of Germany*, vol. II: *The period of consolidation, 1871–1880* (Princeton, 1990)

Phiebig, Albert J., *The descendants of Mayer Amschel Rothschild* (n.p., 1948[?])

Phillips, David Graham, "The empire of Rothschild," *Cosmopolitan* (1905), pp. 501–15

Piatigorsky, Jacqueline, *Jump in the waves: A memoir* (New York, 1988)

Picciotto, J., *Sketches of Anglo-Jewish history* (London, 1875)

Pinkney, David H., *Napoleon III and the rebuilding of Paris* (Princeton, 1958)

Pinney, Thomas (ed.), *The letters of Thomas Babington Macaulay*, 6 vols (Cambridge, 1974–81)

Platel, Baron Félix, *Les hommes de mon temps* (Paris, 1878)

Platt, D. C. M., *Finance, trade and politics in British foreign policy, 1815–1914* (London, 1968)

———, *Foreign finance in continental Europe and the United States, 1815–1870: Quantities, origins, functions and distribution* (London, 1984)

Plender, John and Paul Wallace, *The Square Mile: A guide to the new City of London* (London, 1985)

Plenge, Johann, *Gründung und Geschichte des Crédit Mobilier* (Darmstadt, 1976)

Plessis, Alain, *La Banque de France*, vol. I: *La Banque de France et ses deux cents actionnaires sous le Second Empire* (Geneva, 1982)

———, *La Banque de France*, vol. II: *Régents et gouverneurs de la Banque de France sous le Second Empire* (Geneva, 1985)

———, *La Banque de France*, vol. III: *La politique de la Banque de France de 1851 à 1870* (Geneva, 1985)

———, *The rise and fall of the Second Empire, 1852–71* (Cambridge, 1985)

Plumb, Sir John, *Vintage Memories* (Cambridge, 1988)

Plutarch, *Plutarchi chaeronensis apophthegmata Regium et Imperatorum, eiusdem Apophthegmata Laconica, Raphaële Regio interprete* (Paris, 1530)

Pohl, Manfred, *Einführung in die deutsche Bankengeschichte* (Frankfurt, 1976)

———, "From court agent to state financier—the rise of the Rothschilds," in Heuberger (ed.), *Essays*, pp. 51–70

Poidevin, Raymond, *Les relations économiques et financières entre la France et l'Allemagne de 1898 à 1914* (Paris, 1969)

———, *Finances et relations internationales, 1887–1914* (Paris, 1970)

Poliakov, Léon, *Jewish bankers and the Holy See* (London, 1977)

———, *Geschichte des Antisemitismus*, 8 vols (Frankfurt am Main, 1989)

Polisensky, Josef V., *Aristocrats and the crowd in the revolutionary year 1848* (Albany, New York, 1980)

Pollard, Sidney, *European economic development, 1815–70* (London, 1974)

———, *Peaceful conquest: The industrialization of Europe, 1760–1970* (Oxford, 1981)

———, "Capital exports, 1870–1914: Harmful or beneficial?," *Economic History Review* (1985), pp. 489–514

Pollins, Harold, *Economic history of the Jews in England* (East Brunswick, New Jersey, 1982)

Ponteil, Félix, *Les institutions de la France de 1814 à 1870* (Paris, 1966)

Ponting, Clive, *Churchill* (London, 1994)

Pool, Bernard (ed.), *The Croker papers, 1808–1857* (London, 1967)

Pope-Hennessy, John (ed.), *Baron Ferdinand de Rothschild's livre d'or* (Cambridge, 1957)

Porter, Andrew, *Victorian shipping, business and imperial policy: Donald Currie, the Castle Line and Southern Africa*, Royal Historical Society Studies in History, 49 (Woodbridge/New York, 1986)

Pose, Alfred, *La monnaie et ses institutions: Histoire, théorie et technique*, 2 vols (Vendôme, 1942)

Pottinger, E. Ann, *Napoleon III and the German crisis, 1865–1866*, Harvard Historical Studies, LXXV (Cambridge, Mass., 1966)

Powell, Ellis T., *The evolution of the money market, 1385–1915* (London, 1966)

Prawer, S. S., *Heine the tragic satirist: A study of the later poetry, 1827–1856* (Cambridge, 1961)

———, *Heine's Jewish comedy: A study of his portraits of Jews and Judaism* (Oxford, 1983)

———, *Israel at Vanity Fair* (Leiden/New York/Copenhagen/Cologne, 1992)

Preissler, Dietmar, *Frühantisemitismus in der Freien Stadt Frankfurt und im Großherzogtum Hessen (1810 bis 1860)* (Heidelberg, 1989)

Prevost-Marcilhacy, Pauline, *Les Rothschild: Bâtisseurs et mécènes* (Paris, 1995)

———, "Rothschild architecture in England, France, Germany, Austria and Italy," in Heuberger (ed.), *Essays*, pp. 245–64

Pringle, Robin, *A guide to banking in Britain* (London, 1975)

Priouret, Roger, *La Caisse des Dépôts: Cent cinquante ans d'histoire financière* (Paris, 1966)

Proust, Marcel, *A la recherche du temps perdu*, vol. II: *A l'ombre des jeunes filles en fleurs* (Paris, 1988)

———, *A la recherche du temps perdu*, vol. III: *Le côté de Guermantes 1* (Paris, 1988)

———, *A la recherche du temps perdu*, vol. III: *Le côté de Guermantes 2* (Paris, 1988)

———, *A la recherche du temps perdu*, vol. V: *La prisonnière* (Paris, 1989)

———, *A la recherche du temps perdu*, vol. IV: *Sodomme et Gomorrhe* (Paris, 1989)

Pückler [-Muskau], Hermann Fürst von, *A tour in England, Ireland and France in the years 1826, 1827 and 1829, with remarks on the manners and customs of the inhabitants, and anecdotes of distinguished characters. In a series of letters by a German prince*, trans. Sarah Taylor Austin (Philadelphia, 1833)

———, *Briefe eines Verstorbenen: Vollständige Ausgabe*, ed. Heinz Ohff (Kupfergraben, 1986)

———, *Pückler's Progress: The adventures of Prince Pückler-Muskau in England, Wales and Ireland as told in letters to his former wife, 1826–9* (London, 1987)

Puder, H., *Das Haus Rothschild: Die internationalen verwandtschaftlichen Beziehungen der judischen Hochfinanz* (Leipzig, 1933)

Pulzer, Peter, *The rise of political anti-Semitism in Germany and Austria* (London, 1964)

———, *The Jews and the German state: The political history of a minority, 1848–1933* (Oxford, 1992)

Quinn, Dermot, *Patronage and piety: The politics of English Roman Catholicism, 1850–1900* (Basingstoke, 1993)

Raikes, Thomas, *A portion of the journal kept by Thomas Raikes, Esq. from 1831 to 1847: Comprising reminiscences of social and political life in London and Paris during that period*, 4 vols. (London, 1856)

Ramm, Agatha (ed.), *The political correspondence of Mr. Gladstone and Lord Granville, 1868–1876*, Camden 3rd Ser., LXXXI and LXXXII (London, 1952)

——— (ed.), *The political correspondence of Mr. Gladstone and Lord Granville, 1876–1886*, 2 vols (Oxford, 1962)

———, *Sir Robert Morier: Envoy and ambassador in the age of imperialism, 1876–1893* (Oxford, 1973)

Ramon, Gabriel, *Histoire de la Banque de France* (Paris, 1929)

Ramsden, John (ed.), *Real old Tory politics: The political diaries of Sir Robert Sanders, Lord Bayford, 1910–35* (London, 1984)

Ratcliffe, Barrie M., "The origin of the Paris–Saint-Germain railway," *Journal of Transport History* (1972), pp. 197–219

———, "Railway imperialism: The example of the Pereires' Paris–Saint-Germain Company, 1835–1846," *Business History* (1976), pp. 66–84

Rath, R. John, *The Viennese revolutions of 1848* (Austin, 1957)

Ravage, M[arcus] E[li], *Five men of Frankfort: The story of the Rothschilds* (London/Bombay/Sydney, 1929)

Ray, Cyril, *Lafite: The story of Château Lafite-Rothschild* (London, 1978)

———, *Mouton-Rothschild: The wine, the family, the museum* (London, 1980)

Read, Donald, *The power of news: The history of Reuters, 1849–1989* (Oxford, 1992)

Reader, W. J., *A house in the City: A study of the City and of the Stock Exchange based on the records of Foster and Braithwaite, 1825–1975* (London, 1979)

Reeves, John, *The Rothschilds: The financial rulers of nations* (London, 1887)

Reid, Stuart J., *Lord John Russell* (London, 1895)

Reinerman, Alan J., *Austria and the Papacy in the Age of Metternich*, vol. II: *Revolution and reaction, 1830–38* (Washington, DC, 1989)

Reinharz, Jehuda and W. Schatzberg, *The Jewish response to German culture* (Boston, 1986)

Reitlinger, Gerald, *The economics of taste*, vol. I: *The rise and fall of picture prices, 1760–1960* (London, 1961)

———, *The economics of taste*, vol. II: *The rise and fall of objets d'art prices since 1750* (London, 1963)

Rémond, René, *The right wing in France* (Philadelphia, 1966)

Remusat, Charles de, *Mémoires de ma vie*, 4 vols (Paris, 1959–67)

Renouvin, Pierre, *Histoire des relations internationales*, vol. V: *1815–1871* (Paris, 1954)

———, *Histoire des relations internationales*, vol. VI: *1871–1914* (Paris, 1955)

Ribeill, Georges, *La révolution ferroviaire: La formation des compagnies de chemins de fer en France (1823–1870)* (Paris, 1993)

Rich, N. and M. H. Fisher (eds), *The Holstein papers: The memoirs, diaries and corrrespondence of Friedrich von Holstein, 1837–1909*, vol. I: *Memoirs and political observations* (Cambridge, 1955)

―――― and ―――― (eds), *The Holstein Papers: The memoirs, diaries and correspondence of Friedrich von Holstein, 1837–1909*, vol. III: *Correspondence, 1861–96* (Cambridge, 1961)

―――― and ―――― (eds), *The Holstein papers: The memoirs, diaries and corrrespondence of Friedrich von Holstein, 1837–1909*, vol. IV: *Correspondence, 1897–1909* (Cambridge, 1961)

Richman, Jacob, *Laughs from Jewish lore* (New York, 1926)

Richter, Werner, *Bismarck* (London, 1964)

Ridley, Jane, *The young Disraeli* (London, 1995)

Ridley, Jasper, *Lord Palmerston* (London, 1972)

Riker, T. W., *The making of Roumania: A study of an international problem 1856–1866* (London, 1931)

Riley, James C., *International government finance and the Amsterdam capital market, 1740–1815* (Cambridge, 1980)

Rintoul, M. C., *Dictionary of real people and places in fiction* (London/New York, 1993)

Robb, Graham M., *Balzac: A biography* (London, 1994)

Robert, S. Paul [Raben, L. F.], *La verité sur la maison Rothschild* (Paris, 1846)

Roberts, Richard, *Schroders: merchants and bankers* (Basingstoke, 1992)

Rohr, Donald G., *The origins of social liberalism in Germany* (Chicago, 1963)

Roqueplan, Nestor, *Le Baron James de Rothschild* (Paris, 1868)

Rose, Norman, "Churchill and Zionism," in Robert Blake and Wm. Roger Louis (eds), *Churchill: A major new assessment of his life in peace and war* (Oxford, 1993), pp. 147–66

Rose, Paul Lawrence, *Revolutionary anti-Semitism in Germany from Kant to Wagner* (Princeton, 1990)

Rosenbaum, E. and A. J. Sherman, *M. M. Warburg and Co, 1798–1938: Merchant bankers of Hamburg* (London, 1979)

Rosenberg, Alfred, *Der Mythus des 20. Jahrhunderts: Eine Wertung der seelisch-geistigen Gestaltenkämpfe unserer Zeit* (Munich, 1935)

Rosenberg, Edgar, *From Shylock to Svengali: Jewish stereotypes in English fiction* (Stanford, 1960)

Rößler, Carl, *Die fünf Frankfurter: Lustspiel in drei Akten* (Berlin, 1923)

Rössler, Hellmuth, *Graf Johann Philipp Stadion: Napoleons deutscher Gegenspieler*, vol. II: *1809 bis 1824* (Vienna/Munich, 1966)

Rotberg, Robert I., *The Founder: Cecil Rhodes and the pursuit of power* (New York/Oxford, 1988)

Roth, Cecil, *The magnificent Rothschilds* (London, 1939)

――――, *A history of the Jews in England* (Oxford, 1949)

――――, *The Great Synagogue London, 1690–1940* (London, 1950)

Rothschild, A. Freiherr von, *Offenes Sendschreiben. Von A. Frhr. v[on] Rothschild in Wien an Hofprediger Stöcker in Berlin. Übers. in's Hebräische von A. Rudoll* (Pressburg, 1880)

Rothschild, Alain de, *Le Juif dans la cité* (Paris, 1982)

Rothschild, Arthur de, *Histoire de la poste aux lettres: Depuis ses origines les plus anciennes jusqu'à nos jours* (Paris, 1873)

Rothschild, Charlotte de [Baroness Lionel], *Prayers and meditations: For daily use in the House of Israelites* (London, 1876)

Rothschild, Charlotte de, "A brief history of the Rothschild family and their musical associations," *Family Connections* (compact disk), (1994), pp. 3–7

――――, "The musical associations of the Rothschild family," in Heuberger (ed.), *Essays*, pp. 287–96

Rothschild, C[onstance] and A[nnie] de, *The history and literature of the Israelites, according to the Old Testament and the Apocrypha*, 2 vols (London, 1870)

Rothschild, Edmund de, *Window on the world* (London, 1949)

――――, *A gilt-edged life: Memoir* (London, 1998)

Rothschild, Guy de, *The whims of fortune* (London, 1985)

――――, *Mon ombre siamoise* (Paris, 1993)

Rothschild, Henri de, *Croisières autour de mes souvenirs* (Paris, 1932)

――――, *Tour du monde* (Paris, 1936)

Rothschild, Lord [Victor], *Meditations of a broomstick* (London, 1977)

――――, *"You have it, Madam": The purchase, in 1875, of Suez Canal shares by Disraeli and Baron Lionel de Rothschild* (London, 1980)

――――, *The shadow of a great man* (London, 1982)

――――, *Random variables* (London, 1984)

Rothschild, Miriam, "Nathaniel Charles Rothschild, 1877–1923," MS (1979)

———, *Dear Lord Rothschild: Birds, butterflies and history* (London, 1983)

———, "The Rothschilds and the original EEC—family reflections I: The men," in Heuberger (ed.), *Essays*, pp. 147–54

———, "The silent members of the first EEC—family reflections II: The women," in Heuberger (ed.), *Essays*, pp. 155–64

———, Kate Garton and Lionel de Rothschild, *The Rothschild gardens* (London, 1996)

Rothschild, Mrs James de, *The Rothschilds at Waddesdon Manor* (London, 1979)

Rothschild, Nadine de, *La Baronne rentre à cinq heures* (Paris, 1984)

Rothschild, Philippe de, *Milady Vine: The autobiography of Philippe de Rothschild* (London, 1984)

Rousseau, Jean-Claude, "La mésaventure Rothschild: Fevrier 1848 à Suresnes," *Bulletin de la Société Historique de Suresnes* (1972)

Rowland, Peter, *The last Liberal governments: The promised land, 1905–1910* (London, 1968)

Rozenblit, Marsha L., *The Jews of Vienna, 1867–1914: Assimilation and identity* (Albany, New York, 1983)

Rubens, Alfred, "The Rothschilds in caricature," *Transactions of the Jewish Historical Society* (1968–69), pp. 76–87

———, *Anglo-Jewish Portraits* (London, 1935)

Rubin, Abba, *Images in transition: The English Jew in English literature, 1660–1830* (Westport, Conn./London)

Rubinstein, W. D., "British millionaires, 1809–1989," *Bulletin of the Institute of Historical Research* (1974), pp. 203–23

———, *A history of the Jews in the English-speaking world: Great Britain* (Basingstoke, 1996)

Rudolph, Richard R., "Austria, 1800–1914," in Rondo Cameron (ed.), *Banking and economic development: Some lessons of history* (New York/London/Toronto, 1972), pp. 26–57.

Rumney, J., "Anglo Jewry as seen through foreign eyes," *Transactions of the Jewish Historical Society of England* (1932–5), pp. 323–40

Rurüp, Reinhard, "Emanzipation—Anmerkungen zur Begriffsgeschichte," in *idem, Emanzipation und Antisemitismus: Studien zur "Judenfrage" der bürgerlichen Gesellschaft* (Göttingen, 1975), pp. 159–66

———, "The tortuous and thorny path to legal equality: 'Jew Laws' and emancipatory legislation in Germany from the late 18th century," *Leo Baeck Institute Year Book* (1986), pp. 3–33

Russell, Henry Benajah, *International monetary conferences: their purposes, character, and results; with a study of the conditions of currency and finance in Europe and America during intervening periods and in their relations to international action* (New York/London, 1898).

Russo-Jewish Committee, *Russian atrocities, 1881: Supplementary statement issued . . . in confirmation of* The Times *narrative* (London, 1882)

Sabouret, Anne, *MM. Lazard Frères et Cie.* (Paris, 1987)

Salbstein, M. C. N., *The emancipation of the Jews in Britain: The question of the admission of Jews to Parliament, 1828–1860* (Rutherford, New Jersey, 1982)

Sammons, Jeffrey L., *Heinrich Heine: A modern biography* (Manchester, 1979)

Samson, Jim, *The music of Chopin* (London, 1985)

———, *Chopin* (Oxford, 1996)

Sauer, J., *Finanzgeschäfte des Landgrafen von Hesse-Kassel: Ein Beitrag zur Geschichte des Kurhessischen Haus und Staatschatzen und zur Entwicklungsgeschichte des Hauses Rothschild* (Fulda, 1930)

Saxe-Coburg-Gotha, Duke of, *Memoirs of Ernest II Duke of Saxe-Coburg-Gotha*, 4 vols (London, 1888)

Sayers, Richard Sidney, *Bank of England operations, 1890–1914* (London, 1936)

———, "The development of central banking after Bagehot," *Economic History Review* (1951), pp. 109–16

———, *Central banking after Bagehot* (Oxford, 1957)

———, *Modern banking* (7th edn, Oxford, 1967)

———, *The Bank of England, 1891–1944*, 3 vols (Cambridge, 1976)

Schachar, Isaiah, *The Judensau: A medieval anti-Jewish motif and its history* (London, 1974)

Schama, Simon, *Two Rothschilds and the state of Israel* (London, 1978)

Schembs, Hans-Otto, " 'For the care of the sick, the good of the community, the embellishment of their home town': The charitable Rothschild foundations in Frankfurt am Main," in Heuberger (ed.), *Essays*, pp. 205–20

Scherb, Friedrich Edlen von, *Geschichte des Hauses Rothschild* (Berlin, 1893)

Schimpf, Dorothea, *Emanzipation und Bildungswesen der Juden im Kurfürstentum Hessen 1807–1866: Jüdische Identität zwischen Selbstbehauptung und Assimilationsdruck*, Schriften der Kommission für die Geschichte der Juden in Hessen, 13 (Wiesbaden, 1994)

Schischa, A., "The Saga of 1855: A study in depth," in Sonia and Vivian D. Lipman (eds), *The century of Moses Montefiore* (Oxford, 1985), pp. 269–346

Schnee, Heinrich, *Die Hoffinanz und der moderne Staat*, 3 vols (Berlin, 1953)

———, *Rothschild: Geschichte einer Finanzdynastie* (Göttingen/Berlin/Frankfurt, 1961)

Schneider, Georg, *Die Schlüsselliteratur* (Stuttgart, 1951)

Schnerb, Robert, *Rouher et le Second Empire* (Paris, 1949)

Schnur, Harry S., *Jewish humour* (London, 1945)

Schooling, Sir William, *Alliance Assurance, 1824–1924* (London, 1924)

Schorske, Carl, *Fin-de-siècle Vienna: Politics and culture* (London, 1979)

Schremmer, D. E., "Taxation and public finance: Britain, France and Germany," in Peter Mathias and Sidney Pollard (eds), *The Cambridge economic history of Europe*, vol. VIII: *The industrial economies: The development of economic and social policies* (Cambridge, 1989), pp. 315–494

———, *Steuern und Staatsfinanzen während der Industrialisierung Europas: England, Frankreich, Preußen und das deutsche Reich 1800 bis 1914* (Berlin, 1994)

Schroeder, Paul W., *Metternich's diplomacy at its zenith, 1820–2* (Austin, 1962)

Schwemer, Richard, *Geschichte der Freien Stadt Frankfurt a.M.* (1814–1866), 3 vols (Frankfurt am Main, 1910–18)

Scott, Ivan, *The Roman question and the powers, 1848–1865* (The Hague, 1969)

Serre, comte Pierre François Hercule de, *Correspondance du comte de Serre 1796–1824, annotée et publiée par son fils*, 6 vols (Paris, 1876)

Seton-Watson, Christopher, *Italy from liberalism to fascism* (London, 1967)

Seton-Watson, Hugh, *The Russian Empire, 1801–1917* (Oxford, 1967)

Shannon, Catherine B., *Arthur J. Balfour and Ireland, 1874–1922* (Washington, DC, 1988)

Shaw, S. J., "Ottoman expenditures and budgets in the late nineteenth and twentieth centuries," *International Journal of Middle East Studies* (1978), pp. 373–8

Sheehan, James J., *German history, 1770–1866* (Oxford, 1989)

Sherwig, John M., *Guineas and gunpowder: British foreign aid in the wars with France, 1793–1815* (Cambridge, Mass., 1969)

Sievers, Leo, *Juden in Deutschland* (Hamburg, 1977)

Sigurd, Paul Scheichl, "Contexts and nuances of anti-Jewish language," in Ivor Oxaal, M. Pollac and G. Botz (eds), *The Jews, anti-Semitism and culture in Vienna* (London and New York, 1987), pp. 89–110

Sington, Derrick and Arthur Weidenfeld, *The Goebbels experiment: A study of the Nazi propaganda machine* (London, 1942)

Sked, Alan, *The survival of the Habsburg Monarchy* (London/New York, 1979)

———, *The decline and fall of the Habsburg Empire, 1815–1918* (London/New York, 1989)

Skolnik, Esther Simon, *Leading ladies: A study of eight late Victorian and Edwardian political wives* (New York/London, 1987)

Slinn, Judy, *A history of Freshfields* (London, 1984)

Smith, E. A., *The House of Lords in British politics and society, 1815–1911* (London, 1992)

Smith, Philip, *Brinco: The story of Churchill Falls* (Toronto, 1975)

Sokolow, Nahum, *History of Zionism, 1600–1918*, 2 vols (London/New York, 1919)

Sombart, Werner, *Die Juden und das Wirtschaftsleben* (Leipzig, 1911)

Somervell, D. C., *Disraeli and Gladstone* (London, 1925)

Sorkin, David, *The transformation of German Jewry, 1780–1840* (New York, 1987)

Sotheby Parke Bernet & Co., *Mentmore sale catalogues*, 5 vols (London, 1977)

Souhami, Diana, *Bakst: The Rothschild panels of The Sleeping Beauty* (London, 1992)

Southgate, D., *The passing of the Whigs, 1832–1886* (London, 1962)

Spalding, Henry D., *Encyclopaedia of Jewish humour* (London/New York, 1972)

Spalding, William F., *Tate's modern cambist, centenary edition: A manual of the world's monetary systems, the foreign exchanges &c.* (28th edn, London, 1929)

Sparr, Thomas, "The Rothschilds in literature," in Heuberger (ed.), *Essays*, pp. 307–20

Speitkamp, Winfried, "Restauration als Transformation: Untersuchungen zur kurhessischen Verfassungsgeschichte, 1813–1830," in Uwe Schultz (ed.), *Die Geschichte Hessens* (Stuttgart, 1983), pp. 160–70

Spencer-Silver, Patricia, *Pugin's builder: the life and work of George Myers* (Hull, 1993)

Spiegelberg, Richard, *The City: Power without accountability* (London, 1973)

Spiel, Hilde, *Fanny von Arnstein* (Oxford, 1991)

Spinner, Thomas J., Jr, *George Joachim Goschen: The transformation of a Victorian Liberal* (Cambridge, 1973)

Srbik, Heinrich Ritter von, *Metternich: Der Staatsman und der Mensch*, 3 vols (Munich, 1925–54)

Stapleton, Augustus Granville, *George Canning and his times* (London, 1859)

Stapleton, Edward J. (ed.), *Some official correspondence of George Canning*, 2 vols (London, 1887)

Steed, Henry Wickham, *Through thirty years, 1892–1922*, 2 vols (London, 1924)

Steefel, Lawrence D., "The Rothschilds and the Austrian loan of 1865," *Journal of Modern History* (1936), pp. 27–40

Steele, E. D., *Palmerston and Liberalism, 1855–65* (Cambridge, 1991)

Steiner, Zara S., *The Foreign Office and foreign policy, 1898–1914* (Cambridge, 1969)

Stendhal [Henri Beyle], *A life of Rossini* (London, 1956)

———, *Lucien Leuwen* (Paris, 1973)

Stengers, Jean, "King Leopold and Anglo-French rivalry, 1882–1884," in Prosser Gifford and Wm Roger Louis (eds), *France and Britain in Africa: Imperial rivalry and colonial rule* (New Haven/London, 1971), pp. 121–66

Stephen, Leslie and Sidney Lee (eds), *Compact edition of the dictionary of national biography*, 2 vols (Oxford, 1975)

Stern, Fritz, *Gold and iron: Bismarck, Bleichröder and the building of the German Empire* (Harmondsworth, 1987)

Stern, Selma, *The court Jew: A contribution to the history of the period of absolutism in Central Europe* (Philadelphia, 1950)

Stiefel, D., "The reconstruction of Credit-Anstalt" in Herbert Matis (ed.), *The economic development of Austria since 1870* (Aldershot, 1994), pp. 511–28

Stürmer, Michael, Gabriele Teichmann and Wilhelm Treue, *Striking the balance: Sal. Oppenheim jr & Cie: A family and a bank* (London, 1994)

Stüve, Gustav (ed.), *Briefwechsel zwischen Stüve und Detmold in den Jahren 1848 bis 1850*, Quellen und Darstellungen zur Geschichte Niedersachsens ed. Historischen Verein für Niedersachsen, XIII (Hanover/Leipzig, 1903)

Supple, Barry, *The Royal Exchange Assurance: A history of British insurance, 1720–1970* (Cambridge, 1970)

Surtees, Virginia, *Coutts Lindsay, 1824–1913* (Norwich, 1993)

Sutton, Denys *et al.*, *Waddesdon Manor: Aspects of the collection* (London, 1977)

Swartz, Helen M. and Marvin (eds), *Disraeli's reminiscences* (London, 1975)

Swartz, Marvin, *The politics of British foreign policy in the era of Disraeli and Gladstone* (London, 1985)

Sweet, Paul R., *Friedrich von Gentz* (Westport, Conn., 1970)

Tait, Hugh, *The Waddesdon bequest: The legacy of Baron Ferdinand Rothschild to the British Museum* (London, 1981)

Talleyrand, Prince de, *Memoirs of the Prince de Talleyrand*, ed. the duc de Broglie (London, 1891)

Tapie, Victor L., *The rise and fall of the Hapsburg Monarchy* (London, 1971)

Taylor, A. J. P., *The Habsburg Monarchy, 1815–1918* (London, 1948)

———, *The struggle for mastery in Europe, 1848–1918* (Oxford, 1954)

Teichova, Alice and P. L. Cottrell (eds), *International business and Central Europe, 1918–1939* (Leicester, 1983)

Thackeray, William Makepeace, *The history of Pendennis* (London, 1904)

———, "The book of snobs," in George Saintsbury (ed.), *The Oxford Thackeray, vol. IX* (London/New York/Toronto, 1908), pp. 257–493

———, *The letters and private papers of William Makepeace Thackeray*, 4 vols, ed. Gordon N. Ray (London, 1945)

Thane, Pat, "Financiers and the British state: The case of Sir Ernest Cassel," *Business History* (1986), pp. 35–61

Thatcher, Margaret, *The Downing Street years* (London, 1993)

The Times, *The history of The Times*, vol. II: *The tradition established, 1841–1884* (London, 1939)

———, *The history of The Times*, vol. III: *The twentieth century test, 1884–1912* (London, 1947)

———, *The history of The Times*, vol. IV: *The 150th anniversary and beyond, 1912–1948* (London, 1952)

Thielen, Peter Gerrit, *Karl August von Hardenberg, 1750–1822* (Cologne/Berlin, 1967)

Thompson, Neville, *Wellington after Waterloo* (London, 1986)

Thompson, Paul, *Socialists, Liberals and Labour: The struggle for London, 1885–1914* (London, 1967)

Tilly, Richard, *Financial institutions and industrialisation in the Rhineland, 1815–70* (Madison, Wis., 1966)

Tilney Bassett, A. (ed.), *Gladstone to his wife* (London, 1936)

Timberlake, R. R., "Hastoe near Tring: Recollections of life on the Rothschild Estate in the time of the first Baron Rothschild," *Hertfordshire's Past* (1995), pp. 11–21

Tombs, Robert, *The war against Paris, 1871* (Cambridge, 1981)

Torido, Gianni, *An economic history of liberal Italy, 1850–1918* (London, 1990)

Tortella, Gabriel, "Spain 1829–1874," in Rondo Cameron (ed.), *Banking and economic development: Some lessons of history* (New York/London/Toronto, 1972), pp. 91–121.

Toussenel, Alphonse, *Les juifs, rois de l'époque: Histoire de la féodalité financière* (Paris, 1847)

Trebilcock, Clive, *The industrialisation of the continental powers, 1780–1914* (London, 1981)

Trentmann, Frank, "New sources on an old family: The Rothschild papers at the Special Archive, Moscow—and a letter from Metternich," *Financial History Review* (1995), pp. 73–9

Treskow, A. von, *Nathan Meyer Rothschild. Biographische Skizze (Nebst seinem Testament). Nach englischen Quellen* (Quidlinburg/Leipzig, 1837)

Trevelyan, G. M., *The life of John Bright* (London, 1913)

Trollope, Mrs Frances, *Vienna and the Austrians*, vol. II (London, 1838)

Turrell, Robert Vicat, "Rhodes, De Beers and monopoly," *Journal of Imperial and Commonwealth History* (1982), pp. 311–43

———, " 'Finance . . . the Governor of the imperial engine': Hobson and the case of Rothschild and Rhodes," *Journal of Southern African Studies* (1987), pp. 417–32

——— and Jean-Jacques van Helten, "The Rothschilds, the Exploration Company and mining finance," *Business History* (1986), pp. 181–205

Tyson, Geoffrey, *100 years of banking in Asia and Africa, 1863–1963* (London, 1963)

Ude-Meier, Klaus and Valentin Senger, *Die jüdischen Friedhöfe in Frankfurt* (Frankfurt am Main, 1985)

Valentin, Veit, *1848: Chapters of German history* (London, 1965)

Verity, William, "The rise of the Rothschilds," *History Today* (1968), pp. 225–33

Viel-Castel, comte Horace Salviac de, *Mémoires du comte Horace de Viel-Castel sur la règne de Napoleon III*, 6 vols (Paris, 1883)

Villèle, Jean Baptiste de, *Mémoires et corréspondance du comte de Villèle*, 5 vols (Paris, 1888–90)

Vincent, John (ed.), *Disraeli, Derby and the Conservative party: Journals and memoirs of Edward Henry, Lord Stanley, 1849–1869* (Hassocks, 1978)

——— (ed.), *The later Derby diaries: Home rule, Liberal Unionism and aristocratic life in late Victorian England* (Bristol, 1981)

——— (ed.), *The Crawford papers: The journals of David Lindsay, 27th Earl of Crawford and 10th Earl of Balcarres, 1871–1940, during the years 1892–1940* (Manchester, 1984)

——— (ed.), *A selection from the diaries of Edward Henry Stanley, 15th earl of Derby (1826–93), between September 1869 and March 1878*, Camden 5th Ser., vol. IV (London, 1994)

Vogel, Walter (ed.), *Briefe Johann Carl Bertram Stüves*, vol. II: *1848–1872*, Veröffentlichungen der Niedersächsischen Archivverwaltung, XI (Göttingen, 1960)

Völker, H. (ed.), *Die Stadt Goethes: Frankfurt am Main im 18. Jahrhundert* (Frankfurt, 1932)

Vuilleumier, Marc, Michel Aucouturier, Sven Stelling-Michaud and Michel Cadot, *Autour d'Alexandre Herzen: Révolutionaires et exilés du XIXe siècle* (Geneve, 1973)

Wake, Jehanne, *Kleinwort Benson: The history of two families in banking* (Oxford, 1997)

Waller, Bruce, *Bismarck at the crossroads, 1878–80: The reorientation of German foreign policy after the Congress of Berlin* (London, 1974)

Walpole, Spencer, *The life of Lord John Russell* (London, 1889)

Ward, Mrs Humphrey [Mary Augusta], *Marcella* (London, 1894)

———, *Sir George Tressady* (London, 1909)

Warnke-Dakers, Kerstin, "Lord Rothschild and his poor brethren—East European Jews in London, 1880–1906," in Heuberger (ed.), *Essays*, pp. 113–28

Wasson, Ellis Archer, *Whig renaissance: Lord Althorp and the Whig Party, 1782–1845* (London, 1987)

Watson, J. Steven, *The reign of George III, 1760–1815* (Oxford, 1960)

Wawro, Geoffrey, *The Austro-Prussian War: Austria's war with Prussia and Italy in 1866* (Cambridge, 1996)

Weber, Max, *The Protestant ethic and the spirit of capitalism*, transl. Talcott Parsons (London, 1991)

Webster, Sir Charles, *The foreign policy of Palmerston*, 2 vols (London, 1951)

Weil[l], Alexandre, "L'état des Juifs en Europe," *La revue indépendante*, vol. XVI (1844), pp. 481–518

———, "Rotschild et les finances de l'Europe," *La revue indépendante*, vol. XVII (1844), pp. 424–9

Weinberg, David H., *Les juifs à Paris de 1933 à 1939* (Paris, 1974)

Weinstock, Herbert, *Rossini: A biography* (London, 1968)

Weintraub, Stanley, *Disraeli: A biography* (London, 1993)

———, *Albert: Uncrowned king* (London, 1997)

Weizmann, Chaim, *Trial and error: The autobiography of Chaim Weizmann* (New York, 1949)

Welch, David, *Propaganda and the German cinema, 1933–1945* (Oxford, 1983)

Wemyss Reid, T., *Life of the Rt. Hon. W. E. Forster* (London, 1888)

Werner, Moritz, "Eine vergessene Tat des Barons Amschel: Dokumente Rothschildschen Geimeinsinns aus dem Frankfurter Stadtarchiv," *Frankfurter Israelitisches Gemeindeblatt* (1934)

Whale, P. Barrett, *Joint stock banking in Germany: A study of the German Creditbanks before and after the War* (London, 1930)

Whibley, Charles, *Lord John Manners and his friends*, vol. II (London, 1925)

White, Benjamin, *Silver: Its history and romance* (London, 1917)

White, Jerry, *Rothschild buildings: Life in an East End tenement block, 1887–1920* (London, 1980)

Whyte, A. J. (ed.), *The life and letters of Cavour, 1849–61* (Oxford, 1930)

Wiebe, M. G., J. B. Conacher and John Matthews (eds), *Benjamin Disraeli: Letters*, vol. III: *1838–1841* (Toronto, 1987)

———, *Benjamin Disraeli: Letters*, vol. IV: *1842–1847* (Toronto, 1989)

———, *Benjamin Disraeli: Letters*, vol. V: *1848–1851* (Toronto, 1992)

Wilde, Oscar, *The works of Oscar Wilde*, ed. with an introduction by G. F. Maine (London/Glasgow, 1952)

Williams, Bill, *The making of Manchester Jewry, 1740–1875* (Manchester, 1976)

———, "Nathan Rothschild in Manchester," in Victor Gray (ed.), *The Life and times of N. M. Rothschild 1777–1836* (London, 1998), pp. 34–41

Williamson, Edwin, *The Penguin history of Latin America* (London, 1992)

Wilson, Derek, *Rothschild: A story of wealth and power* (London, 1988)

Wilson, J. S. G., *French banking structure and credit policy* (London, 1957)

Winter, James, *Robert Lowe* (Toronto, 1976)

Winton, J. R., *Lloyd's Bank, 1918–1969* (Oxford, 1982)

Wippermann, Wolfgang, *Das Leben in Frankfurt zur NS-Zeit: Darstellung, Dokumente und didaktische Hinweise* (Frankfurt am Main, 1986)

Wirth, Max, *A history of banking in all the leading nations*, vol. IV (New York, 1896)

Wiskemann, Elizabeth, *Czechs and Germans: A study of the struggle in the historic provinces of Bohemia and Moravia* (Oxford, 1938)

Wistrich, Robert S., *Socialism and the Jews: The dilemmas of assimilation in Germany and Austria–Hungary* (Rutherford, New Jersey, 1982)

———, *The Jews of Vienna in the age of Franz Joseph* (Oxford, 1989)

———, *Between redemption and perdition: Modern antisemitism and Jewish identity* (London/New York, 1990)

Witte, S. I., *Memoirs of Count Witte* (London, 1921)

Wohl, Anthony S., *The eternal slum: Housing and social policy in Victorian London* (London, 1977)

Wolf, Lucien, "Rothschildiana," in *idem, Essays in Jewish History*, ed. Cecil Roth (London, 1934), pp. 261–308

Wolf, Siegbert, *Liberalismus in Frankfurt am Main: Vom Ende der Freien Stadt bis zum Ersten Weltkrieg*, Studien zur Frankfurter Geschichte, 23 (Frankfurt am Main, 1987)

Wolff, Otto, *Ouvrard: Speculator of genius, 1770–1846* (London, 1932, 2nd edn 1962)

Woodward, E. L., "Economic factors making for peace or war," in *idem, War and peace in Europe 1815–1870 and other essays* (London, 1931), pp. 70–113

Wulf, Joseph, *Literatur und Dichtung im Dritten Reich* (Frankfurt am Main/Berlin, 1989)

Yellen, Sherman, Jerry Bock and Sheldon Harnick, "The Rothschilds: A musical legend," unpublished MS, RAL (1969)

Yergin, Daniel, *The prize: The epic quest for oil, money and power* (2nd edn, London, 1993)

Yogev, Gedaliah, *Diamonds and coral: Anglo-Dutch Jews and eighteenth century trade* (Leicester, 1978)

Yonge, Charles Dilke, *Life and administration of Robert Banks, 2nd Earl of Liverpool* (London, 1868)

Zetland, Marquis of (ed.), *The letters of Disraeli to Lady Bradford and Lady Chesterfield*, vol. I: *1873 to 1875* (London, 1929)

Ziegler, Philip, *The sixth great power: Barings, 1762–1929* (London, 1988)

———, *King Edward VIII: The official biography* (London, 1990)

Zielenziger, Kurt, *Juden in der deutschen Wirtschaft* (Berlin, 1930)

Zimmerman, Judith E., *Midpassage: Alexander Herzen and European revolution* (Pittsburgh, 1989)

Zimmermann, Moshe, *Wilhelm Marr: The patriarch of anti-Semitism* (New York/Oxford, 1986)

Zola, Emile, *Les Rougon Macquart*, vol. V: *Histoire naturelle et sociale d'une famille sous le second Empire: L'Argent* (Paris, 1967)